PEARSON

ALWAYS LEARNING

Jan D. Weir • Fran Smyth

Critical Concepts of Canadian Business Law

Sixth Edition

ISBN 10: 1-269-97041-0
ISBN 13: 978-1-269-97041-9

Contents

Part 4 Forms of Business Organizations

Foreword

I am pleased to contribute a foreword to *Critical Concepts of Canadian Business Law* written by my former partner Jan Weir.

The work is designed to enable students pursuing a business-related education to acquire general knowledge of business law. The importance of this objective for future business readers cannot be overstated. The book contains the most comprehensive survey of the law relating to business, accompanied by a number of hypothetical fact situations that serve as teaching aids. In my opinion, it will make a substantial contribution to the knowledge of business law among students at the college and university level.

I congratulate the author for the efforts exerted in bringing this fine work to publication.

The late Honourable Justice John Sopinka of the Supreme Court of Canada

Preface

Why This Book

The seed motivation for writing this book started with the writer's first meetings with clients and the realization that a new lawyer could argue the latest issues in the Supreme Court of Canada, but could not answer the simple questions the clients brought.

The writer kept track of these problems and resolved to one day write a book that was not a précis of law school courses, which are topics intriguing to the legal academic mind, but of the issues that most frequently impacted on business clients, mundane though they may be. The guide to content became not only personal experience, but the items that recurred on continuing education programs, as these were selected by practicing lawyers for other lawyers.

Writers of self help series books innovated a very different approach based on a way that people were beginning to more efficiently absorb information. The paragraph text was no longer the most effective way. In fact, it was boring to most students who had adapted to the more modular structured presentation that was reflected in the popular 'Dummy' series books.

The approach of using small "bits" of information has proved the most appealing to students and increased in appeal perhaps because of its use on the Internet. It is a process of information absorption very different from that most instructors are used to. However, if the instructors will take the time to use a chapter of this book with the students and get a comparative feedback with similar topics in other texts, they may find the students prefer, and benefit from, this model of instruction over the traditional text book.

The story approach, emphasized in this book, underlies all topics. Each legal topic is presented with several illustrations formulated to reveal its inherent drama. For when the graduates are at their office desks they will not likely remember avoiding the limitations of privity principles but they will remember the story of the misplaced comma that cost a business a million dollars—and the necessity for a lawyer's careful drafting advice for a contract involving significant amounts of money; the patrons of a game park who were attached by Bengal tigers—and the risk of running an inherently dangerous business; or the little girl who went down her backyard pool slide becoming an instant paraplegic on her second use—and the responsibility of a business for warning of possible dangerous use of products.

Only The Essentials

The word "critical" was chosen to reflect the objective of selecting from among the many issues most frequently confronted by businesses, only the most crucial, without all the mind-dulling details. Space is therefore devoted to teaching that one topic through several illustrations in different forms. Every major topic is expressed in at least four and sometimes more formats. For example, the topic of misrepresentation in Chapter 7: Defects in Contracts and Remedies:

a) There is a short narrative introduction of the topic.
b) The Critical Concepts summarize the essential points of a misrepresentation in bulleted format.
c) The Critical Concepts are followed by the brief of an actual case illustrating the principle.
d) Then follows a question or two, "Business Law Applied", which questions are simple illustrations in question format. The answers are in the Critical Concepts and designed to help the student understand these concepts.
e) At the end of the chapter, "In Summation" the topic is again restated in bulleted format. While similar to the Critical Concepts it is restated in different terminology and it may give students a different insight.
f) There are more complicated questions at the end of the chapter—"Closing Questions".
g) On the Website there are review exercises again done effectively in the bulleted format but this time not only restating the issue but leaving the critical term blank.

Interactive Approach

Instructors are often told that student attention span is somewhere between ten and twenty minutes. Some change must be introduced at about that time so that the students can hold their attention. The above structure permits the instructors to do this.

The modules are short enough so that the instructor can use this text in the classroom. There is, in effect, a suggested lesson plan for every major topic. Although each instructor has their preferred method of presenting a topic, they can give a short introduction of the topic in under ten minutes and then ask the students to read a part of the text, for example the reported case brief or the "Business Law Applied" questions. These are short enough and simple enough in language so that the average student can easily comprehend them in the class situation without prior preparation. The modules permit the opportunity for the instructor to use any of them in the classroom, thus varying his/her presentation and permitting a more interactive method of teaching.

Narrative And Case Method

The presentation of an issue is a balance of both narrative and case study methods. The premise is that it not important for students to learn to analyze cases or even to extract legal principles from several pages of text explanation. It is more important for them to be able to clearly see the principle of law so the briefs and critical concepts are made as simple as possible. However, when taken over a number of topics the concepts are challenging for most students.

Risk management has always been a topic that pervades all sections of the book. Sometimes it is identified by the "Business Alert" feature, but more often it is included simply as a question: What could have been done to prevent the result in the situation presented?

Law As Students Will Confront It

One particular concern about teaching contract law is the fact that standard terms in business contracts often modify or completely reverse the common law principles. Business people will see actual contracts frequently in dealings. Therefore, at the end of the contract chapters actual examples of contracts are given. Some of the questions refer to these contracts so that the students will not only have a general idea of how the legal issues actually apply to these contracts; but will understand that it is important for them to seek legal advice before signing major contracts as they may be giving away important rights. Most business people understand how to negotiate for price but they do not understand the consequences of many of the other terms.

Standard form contracts are good outlines of the issues that will most frequently arise in business deals and also a review of contract law principles.

The Danger of a Little Knowledge

By the end of the first year of practice all lawyers realize that they have completely wasted all law school tuition fees. Every client knows the law without going to law school. Clients do not ask for an opinion, they tell you the law. There is always a danger that in teaching students a little knowledge of the law, they will believe they can be their own lawyer. It is hoped that through the examples shown and the emphasis on the unforeseeable and often unexpected happenings in business deals, combined with the knowledge that terms in contracts can completely reverse common law statements of the law, students will learn caution and use their knowledge only to identify legal issues and seek advice where there is any significant consequence involved.

Student Centred

The use of the book so far has suggested that students will read it independently, they will enjoy the examples, and find them informative and of practical value to improve their job skills.

ESL Sensitive

From experience in developing curriculum and teaching ESL, the language used in the text has been selected to make the concepts more comprehensible to those students who have learned English as their second language.

Jan Weir

Taking Advantage of the Unique Features

1. **Critical Concepts** attempt to answer the perennial favourite question of students: "What do I really need to know?" Often the lists are summaries of preceding material, but sometimes they include succinct new points that require no further explanation.

> ### ■ *Critical Concepts of* Assault and Battery
>
> - Assault is threatening another with violence, with the ability to carry out the threat causing fear in the victim.
> - Battery is the least touching of another without consent and with the intention to cause harm.
> - Self-defence is a complete defence to assault and battery.

2. **Business Alert!** points out common and/or especially damaging legal pitfalls that may be encountered in business. The items illustrate the consequences of failing to apply certain legal concepts to business dealings, or discuss how to avoid those consequences.

> **Business Alert!** Deposits Be careful in giving any deposits. The business receiving them may not be able to refund them. It is a common complaint by purchasers of franchises that they have given large deposits in the order of $100,000 for initiation payments, but the franchise company has gone bankrupt. If giving a large deposit, have a credit check done on the company. Credit bureaus such as Dunn & Bradstreet will do credit checks for members of the public. Also, make certain the deposit is acknowledged to be held "in trust" for your purpose so it can't be used in the business generally. If the deposit is held in trust and the business goes bankrupt, it cannot be used to pay off other creditors and will be returned in full. Try to get a personal guarantee of the return of the deposit from the owner of the company. If that individual won't give a personal guarantee, be cautious!

3. Though this text attempts to use plain language whenever possible, sometimes the use of specialized terminology is unavoidable. When that occurs, **Legalese** provides an explanation of the term to help students understand it in context.

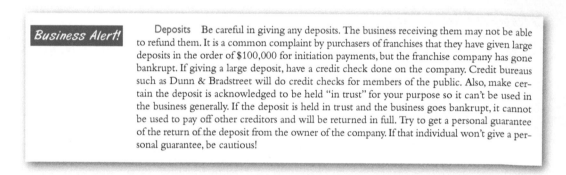

> Consideration **Consideration** derives from the same word as the term *consider*, which means to mentally weigh the merits of an issue, or in other words to take it seriously. The paying of something of value indicates that you have considered the matter and are agreeing to be bound.   **Legalese**

4. It is always useful to illustrate a point through a real incident that had to be resolved in the judicial arena. **Case summaries** cut through the legalese and highlight the main point. Cases were selected both to highlight the business context and to illustrate particular legal concepts.

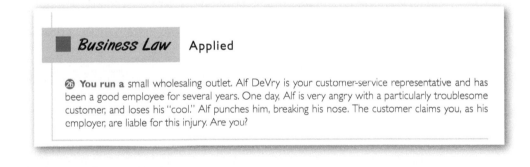

Khosla v. Korea Exchange Bank of Canada, [2008] CanLII 56011 (ON S.C.)

Satwant Khosla was a solicitor who acted for clients who purchased a house. The house was sold using a fraudulent power of attorney. The fraudster was a tenant in the house.

The purchasers borrowed the purchase price of $492,000.00 and had it paid into Khosla's bank account in trust for themselves. Khosla drew a cheque in the name of the true owner of the house. Hence the true owner was the payee named on the cheque.

One month before closing the fraudster, using authentic identification taken from the owner, opened a bank account in the owner's name at the Korea Exchange Bank of Canada ("Korea Bank"). The fraudster deposited the cheque from the payment of the purchase price of the house in that bank account and shortly thereafter withdrew the funds and disappeared.

Khosla's insurer, a title insurance company, paid the purchasers their money, then using its right under the insurance policy [subrogation right] sued the Korea Bank using Khosla's name, for conversion of the cheque.

The Court's Decision

The Court held that there was well settled law that conversion was a strict liability defence. That meant that neither innocence on the bank's part, nor negligence by Khosla was a defence if the elements for conversion were established.

Conversion is wrongful interference with the property of another in a manner inconsistent with the owner's right to possession. The damage amount regarding cheques is the face amount of the cheque. Khosla, as drawer of the cheque, had the right to possession.

A bank commits conversion by collecting, i.e. obtaining the money from the drawer's [Khosla's] bank and then paying it to a person who is not the payee named on the cheque. Here the bank did not pay the funds to the true owner of the property, who was the payee on the cheque, but to a fraudster.

The bank was liable to pay Khosla the full amount of the face amount of the cheque plus interest.

5. Business Law—Applied questions follow each subject unit and are designed to discover whether the students "get it" before moving on. The questions are not meant to provide detailed review or analysis; often, they are effectively simple illustrations in question format.

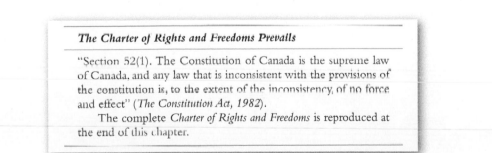

■ *Business Law* Applied

㉖ **You run a** small wholesaling outlet. Alf DeVry is your customer-service representative and has been a good employee for several years. One day, Alf is very angry with a particularly troublesome customer, and loses his "cool." Alf punches him, breaking his nose. The customer claims you, as his employer, are liable for this injury. Are you?

6. Where we have felt that quoting actual legislation would help students' understanding, **excerpts from legislation** have been included. Often, however, relevant statutes have been summarized in plain language.

The Charter of Rights and Freedoms Prevails

"Section 52(1). The Constitution of Canada is the supreme law of Canada, and any law that is inconsistent with the provisions of the constitution is, to the extent of the inconsistency, of no force and effect" (*The Constitution Act, 1982*).

The complete *Charter of Rights and Freedoms* is reproduced at the end of this chapter.

7. **In Summation** provides an executive summary of all major principles. Law schools are currently using the overview approach with apparent success, relying on bulleted summaries of areas of law. This method is employed at the end of each chapter.

In Summation

Defects in a Contract

- A contract is based on the assumption that each party has freely given consent to perform the promises contained in it. If this is not the case, there are five main areas of concern the courts will consider in deciding whether to allow a claim by one party that consent was not freely given.

Misrepresentation

- This is a statement, made by one party at the time of contracting, which is designed to persuade the other party to enter into the agreement, but which does not appear in the final contract. The

8. **Closing Questions** provide an in-depth review and analysis of the chapter. They vary in degree of difficulty but generally provide a good self-test to determine whether students truly understand and can apply the chapter content.

Closing Questions

2. Dewey, Cheatem and Howe is an accounting firm which is considering using an application service provider (ASP) to do its on-line billings and to store its back-up data from all computers.
   a) What business risks is the firm facing if it uses the services of the ASP as contemplated?
   b) What terms in the ASP's service contract would likely cover that risk and with what result?
   c) How could the firm protect itself with the legal or business solutions respecting this contract? Which is likely to be the more effective, the legal or the business solutions?

3. In the case of *Trigg v. MI Movers International Transportation* the exemption clause in the contract was not enforceable against Mr. Trigg because he had not read the clause. In the case of *Fraser Jewelers (1982) Ltd. v. Dominion Electric Protection Co.*, the president of Fraser Jewelers also claimed he had not read the exemption clause, but it was enforced against him. Are these cases reconcilable. If so, how?

9. Appendices at the back of certain chapters include sample **contracts** that the students can refer to and analyze, which will help them put the legal issues raised into a real-world context.

Appendix
6

Used Car Bill of Sale

	DAY	MONTH	YEAR

PURCHASER'S INFORMATION

PURCHASER'S NAME: FIRST   MIDDLE INITIAL   LAST

PURCHASER'S ADDRESS

CITY/TOWN   PROVINCE   POSTAL CODE

HOME TELEPHONE NO.   BUSINESS TELEPHONE NO.

DRIVER'S LICENCE NO.   EXPIRY DATE

TERMS OF SETTLEMENT

SELLING PRICE	
ADMINISTRATION FEE	
TRADE-IN ALLOWANCE (IF ANY)	
NET DIFFERENCE (ADD LINES 1 AND 2 AND DEDUCT LINE 3)	
P.S.T. ON NET DIFFERENCE	
LICENCE FEE	
GASOLINE	
PAYOUT LIEN ON TRADE-IN	
G.S.T. PAYABLE ON TRADE-IN	
BALANCE DUE	
DEPOSIT: ❑ CHEQUE ❑ CASH ❑ CREDIT CARD	
PAYABLE ON DELIVERY (CERTIFIED FUNDS ONLY)	
INSURANCE: ❑ LIFE ❑ ACCIDENT ❑ LOSS OF INC.	
P.S.T. ON INSURANCE	
LIEN REGISTRATION FEE	
BALANCE FINANCED SUBJECT TO APPROVAL	
NET AMOUNT TO BE FINANCED	
COST OF BORROWING %	
TOTAL BALANCE DUE $	

CAR INFORMATION

YEAR   MAKE   MODEL   COLOUR   STOCK#

SERIAL OR V.I.N. #

DISTANCE TRAVELLED   ❑ KMS   PURCHASER'S   IF MANUFACTURER'S WARRANTY
                     ❑ MILES INITIALS   APPLICABLE, TIME IS MEASURED FROM:

THIS CAR WILL BE DELIVERED WITH
A SAFETY STANDARDS CERTIFICATE ❑ YES   ❑ NO
                               CERTIFICATE NUMBER

DEALER GUARANTEE

IS THERE A DEALER GUARANTEE ON THIS CAR? ❑ YES ❑ NO
IF YES, COMPLETE THIS SECTION.

_____ DAYS OR _____ KM
                (WHICHEVER COMES FIRST)

DESCRIPTION _____

TERMS OF THE CONTRACT

1. **PURCHASER'S OFFER:** By signing this form I have made an offer to purchase the car described above ("the car"). I understand that this offer becomes a binding contract between the dealer and me when it is accepted by the signature of an authorized official of the dealer.

2. **CAR SOLD "AS IS":** I agree that if the appropriate space below is initialed by me, the car is sold "As Is" and is not represented as being in a road worthy condition, mechanically sound or maintained at any guaranteed level of quality. The car may not be fit for use as a means of transport and may require substantial repairs at my expense.

   _____   If this space is not initialled by me, this clause
   Purchaser's Initials   does not form part of this agreement.

3. **ACKNOWLEDGEMENT OF TERMS:** I acknowledge having read all terms of the contract, including those on the reverse. I understand that they form part of this agreement. I also agree that no verbal promises have been made to me by the dealer or its employees. The dealer and I agree that the written terms contained in this contract make up the entire agreement between us.

SIGNATURES:

Purchaser's _____

Co-Signer (if any) _____

TERMS ON BACK FORM PART OF THIS CONTRACT

VENDOR'S ACCEPTANCE

DATE REGISTRATION No.   NAME OF OFFICIAL (PLEASE PRINT)

ACCEPTOR'S REGISTRATION No.   TITLE

DATE   SIGNATURE

The text is modularized to provide maximum in-class interaction with the material. Any of the features outlined above can be used in a variety of ways to stimulate in-class discussion. For example, "Business Law—What's Your Opinion?" could be used for in-class review, while "Closing Questions" could form the basis for mock trials.

Any response from instructors is welcome and it is hoped that this edition will spur debate on and reform of the approach and content of business law courses. Our business law courses need constant pruning and revising to keep pace with the fast-changing pace of business practice and business law.

Supplements

Instructor's Manual: This manual contains additional teaching ideas—including background information, case summaries, news articles that illustrate how legal concepts work in the real world, and photocopy masters of cases, charts, and assignments—as well as suggested answers for "Business Law—What's Your Opinion?" and "Closing Questions."

Test Item File: This testbank includes multiple-choice, true/false, and short-essay questions for each chapter. It is available in printed and electronic formats.

Pearson Education Canada TestGen: This computerized version of the Test Item File allows instructors to edit existing questions, add new questions, and generate custom tests.

Companion Web Site: The Companion Web Site for *Critical Concepts of Canadian Business Law*, Third Edition, offers student resources such as practice questions, key terms, weblinks to related sites, answers to Business Law: Applied questions, and streaming CBC videos with cases. Visit the site at www.pearsoned.ca/weir.

How This Book Is Different

The genius underlying the effectiveness of the common law is that it is based on real situations. Judges have a concrete case in front of them and devise an abstract principle from that situation. That principle may be adjusted or modified, but again only based on actual cases, and usually in very small increments. The approach used in this book is similar and based on the assumption that students will be able to understand what is at issue better if they have concrete situations presented at the earliest occasion. This is in contrast to the usual approach of giving a series of explanations of the abstract principles of law and related corollary rules.

In this text, while a short explanation of the abstract issue is first presented, students are quickly given example after example of the application of the issue.

That time honored teaching belief in the effectiveness of repetition captured in the phrase "the 3 tellems"—tell them what you are going to tell them, tell them, and tell them what you told them—is amply applied. A single issue is repeated under a different face a number of times.

The basic principles of business law that a business-person needs to know do not change significantly. The students do not need leading edge cases on esoteric principles. However, there are new cases that better illustrate a principle or that will catch and hold a student's interest. These have been selected for this new edition. It is hoped with these cases that reflect the drama of the law, students will catch some of the passion for this discipline that has attracted the instructors.

Acknowledgments

Probably no book is a result of a single effort and this one is no exception. The ideas contributed by many people have influenced the revisions small and large. The authors and publisher would also like to thank the reviewers whose feedback on the previous edition provided some valuable suggestions for the new edition:

To those who have not undertaken the excruciating task of writing a textbook, the important contributions to the refinement of the finished product by the publisher's professional staff would be unrecognized. So special recognition has to be given to Gilaine Waterbury, acquisition editor for taking the time to discover the unique approach of the book, to Vanessa Karmazyn, Michele Cronin, and Jill Haber Atkins, who creatively found better ways to make the form better reveal the distinct functions of the features of the text.

Special acknowledgment must be given to Prof. Murray Horowitz whose insights in explaining complex concepts continue to influence every edition of this book. Special acknowledgement goes to John King for his valuable contributions to the development of the power points and website material for this text.

Many practicing lawyers have also made suggestions of tips and topics that they frequently encounter but which are usually not covered in texts. My colleagues at the Law Chambers, Toronto, have been especially generous in donating their time to review sections for practical advice.

Photograph of Osgoode Hall by Binnie Chee reproduced with permission of Pinto Wray James LLP.

We would like to acknowledge the contribution by Mark Tjan for his cover design for this text.

Table of Cases

Table of Statutes

Fundamental Rights

Why Study Business Law?

By studying business law you will learn the legal rules that govern businesses, but you will also learn valuable business practices. For in studying business law you will learn the unexpected. Many of the situations that you will read about are not easily foreseeable and often took at least one business by surprise. As you would when studying history, you will learn the mistakes that others have made so that hopefully you will not repeat them.

The study of law is the study of business in crisis. The reported cases are a result of a fight between at least two businesses which could not agree or reach a compromise solution, and which had to spend a great amount of time and expense fighting over legal and factual issues. A judge had to decide between the two conflicting positions. There was only one winner.

Using this text you will study primarily by the case method, the method used in law schools; however, there will also be narrative explanations of the principles. There are summaries of actually reported cases for each major topic. The questions, which follow the cases and which are at the end of the chapters, are most often based on practical situations from the authors' files or from reported cases. Thus, although some situations may seem bizarre, they actually did happen.

This course is practical and meant to help you to improve your business skill. The topics that have been selected are those that most frequently occur in modern business situations. What you will be reading actually happened to a business. Large businesses know the importance of considering legal consequences, and not only have in-house legal departments but additionally retain large law firms to advise them regularly. Small businesses often do not realize the importance of legal risk or don't have the financial resources to have lawyers on staff. This book is written from the perspective of the small-business entrepreneur who does not have easy access to lawyers (and who may regard a lawyer's services as the ultimate grudge purchase). This person typically knows, for example, how to negotiate a contract regarding price but is often unaware of how other terms in most contracts, especially standard form contracts, shift risks. This is particularly true of the ever-present disclaimer clause. You will learn to understand these terms in real agreements and the need to have them reviewed by a lawyer if there is a significant transaction involved.

Businesses are becoming increasingly sophisticated in using law suits to harm competitors. Thus, it is important for you to know how to protect your business from attacks by other businesses, such as stealing key employees or trade secrets. There are an increasing number of laws that give consumers rights. At various times in establishing a new business, you will be signing contracts, bank guarantees, and partnership agreements, incorporating companies, and carrying out other such activities. By studying business law you will understand the legal responsibilities and the pitfalls respecting these various situations.

A goal of this text is to make you more informed business people who can recognize important legal issues that you will encounter in your business activities, so that you will know when to seek legal advice. It is often much more cost effective to obtain legal advice at an early stage, than to avoid lawyers and make legal decisions on your own. This may create major legal problems that result in large legal costs at a later date that could have been avoided with early legal consultation. In the case of *Lyons v. Multari* (see Chapter 5) two orthodontists decided to write up their own legal agreement when they went into business together, rather than hire a lawyer. A few years later a major disagreement arose when one left to practice elsewhere. This case went to the trial court; the Ontario Court of Appeal and Lyons even tried to have the case heard by the Supreme Court of Canada, though it refused to hear the appeal. The legal fees were in the hundreds of thousands of dollars, and it could have been easily resolved for a very small amount if they had obtained legal advice when they first created their business agreement.

An experienced lawyer will charge approximately $250-$900 per hour and the legal costs for a case that results in a three day civil trial are now estimated at more than $60,000. More complicated cases result in much longer trials and enormous legal fees. Many of Canada's top judges have complained that one of the major problems facing the legal system today is that it has become so expensive; it is only accessible to wealthy Canadians who can afford the high legal costs. Justice in the civil court system should not be exclusive to only wealthy citizens and large corporations.

You are at this point a consumer protected by a large number of consumer-protection laws that ensure fairness in most transactions. However, when you leave your present institution and enter into transactions as a businessperson, you will have few of these protections. The law of business is designed to promote competition, that is, the survival of the fittest.

Bill Gates is a good example of someone who used business law effectively to establish his Microsoft Empire. He knew that he should negotiate a term in a contract with IBM so that Microsoft kept the rights to the DOS system, which was the first foundation of the Microsoft Empire. He successfully fought a patent battle with Apple Computer to get the rights to use the mouse-graphic interface, which became the basis for Windows. Some criticize business law as being cutthroat, and however extreme that description and however undesirable, that is likely the best way to understand it. If you do not have a general knowledge of business law, you may find yourself in the same situation as some of the people in the cases that you are going to read.

Thus, one answer to the question, "Why should we bother to study business law?," may be: business self-defence.

Analyzing Court Decisions

Law is developed by decisions on actual cases. Lawyers must analyze cases such as the above to abstract more-general principles to attempt to predict how the law will apply to new situations where there is no similar decided case. In some questions, you will be shown this process of analysis at its most simplified level. This may assist you in understanding that many times a lawyer does not have a precise precedent and has to give an opinion based on his or her best estimate of how the principles developed to that point in time will be applied to your case.

In reading a reported case in this text it may be helpful to make a **brief**, which is a summary of a case (for use at trial) including evidence and law, or a summary of a court decision such as those used in this text. Use the following outline:

- the facts
- the legal principle to be applied, stated in one sentence
- the arguments for both sides
- the application of the legal principle (the result)

The Constitution of Canada

The Formation of Confederation

Prior to the formation of the country of Canada, the collection of British colonies, that would eventually form this country (including Quebec now under British control), faced a number of problems including: deterioration in relations with the United States and the possibility of loss of land to that foreign power and the increasing unwillingness of Britain to come to the defence of its colonies along with other factors. The solution, aided by the building of the railways and the possibility of a trans-continental railway, was unification on an east-west direction by way of confederation.

The Division of Powers Under the Constitution

In 1867, the four colonies of British North America—Upper Canada (now Ontario), Lower Canada (now Quebec), Nova Scotia, and New Brunswick—decided to form a new country, to be called Canada. The colonies had to decide which powers they would keep for themselves and which should be handed over to the new central, or federal, government. The *British North America (BNA) Act*, passed by the British Parliament in 1867, outlined the division of powers. Matters of common interest across Canada, such as the Post Office, were given to the federal government. One matter of particular interest to business is the regulation of trade and commerce, which includes advertising. Matters of a local provincial nature, such as city hospitals, were given to the provinces.

For the most part, sections 91 and 92 of the *BNA Act* divide legislative powers between the federal and provincial governments, and list specific areas of power. The federal government also has the power to make laws for the peace, order, and good government of Canada (this is colloquially known as the POGG clause of the constitution) in relation to all matters except those given exclusively to the provincial governments by section 92. This phrasing is intended to give the federal government authority over matters not specifically mentioned in section 92 as being of national concern.

Matters specifically set out in section 91 include:

- unemployment insurance (section 91(2A))
- postal service (section 91(5))
- regulation of trade and commerce (section 91(2))
- incorporation of banks and issuing of paper money (section 91(15))
- criminal law (section 91(27))

Section 92(16) gives the provinces exclusive jurisdiction over "all matters of a merely local or private nature in the province." This is a very wide clause, capable of embracing a large range of topics.

The *BNA Act* was drafted in 1867, and was intended to cover all areas of government. But who, at that time, when milk was delivered to the door in horse-drawn carts, could have anticipated computers and the Internet, or the importance of environmental pollution issues? The constitution today must be interpreted, and responsibility for such issues assigned to either provincial or federal government.

One guiding principle in deciding who is in charge is, obviously, whether the matter is of national concern, crossing provincial boundaries, or if it is purely local. In pollution control, for example, it is the federal government that regulates pollution caused by shipping, since that activity seldom takes place only within one province. The provinces, however, also have water pollution legislation to protect local lakes and rivers.

■ *Critical Concepts of* The Scheme for Division of Powers in the Constitution

- Specific matters to federal government
- Specific matters to provincial governments
- Matters not listed in either of above to the federal government under POGG, or to provincial governments under s. 92(16)

Legalese   **Ultra Vires**   When a matter is outside a government's designated power, that matter is said to be **ultra vires**. The term is derived from the Latin *ultra*, meaning beyond, and *vires*, meaning power.

Bringing the Constitution Home

During the 1960s and 1970s, the provincial and federal governments were anxious to make several changes to the *British North America Act*. Specifically they wished to change the act:

- to allow amendment to it without having to go before the British Parliament
- to agree to a new division of the law-making powers among the federal and provincial governments
- to add a guaranteed set of rights and freedoms

Accordingly, in 1982, the *BNA Act*—the Constitution—was patriated, or brought home to Canada. The power to make changes to it now rests with the governments of Canada. The *Charter of Rights and Freedoms* was incorporated into the Constitution at that time. However, no agreement was reached on a new division of powers among federal and provincial governments—the issue of division of powers continues to be a perplexing political concern.

The name of the *British North America Act* was officially changed to the *Constitution Act*, and the new Canadian Constitution was called the *Constitution Act, 1982*.

Legalese   **Civil Rights**   Section 92.13 of the Constitution mentions **civil rights**. Because of more recent civil rights movements, there is now some confusion about the use of this term. *Civil rights* is a very general term that is derived from the same Latin root as the word *citizen* (*civitas*). It refers to the rights of citizens and includes areas of law such as contracts, *torts*, and so on. In order to distinguish between the more modern, but narrow, use of the term, Canadian legal writers refer to laws that deal with *discrimination* as human rights, or civil liberties, legislation.

■ *Business Law*   Applied

(**Note to students:** In answering the "Business Law—Applied" questions, you should justify every answer by referring to a principle of law. You will find that these are often contained in the critical concepts or in sections of statutes.

Other principles may be contained in the text or in the reported cases. In any event, your answer should refer specifically to the principle of law and indicate also where it is found in the textbook. In other words, you must give the authority for your answer.)

❶ **You are a** policy advisor in the Attorney General's department. You are asked to give your opinion as to which level of government, federal or provincial, has the power to make laws relating to the following topics. Examine sections 91 and 92 of the Constitution provided by your instructor, and identify the specific section and item number that enables you to provide your opinion.

a) bankruptcy
b) the solemnization of marriage in the province
c) murder
d) a railway that runs only between two cities within one province
e) the protection of inventions

Businesses Use Division of Powers

Governments, both federal and provincial, often pass laws to regulate business activities. Because of the division of powers in the Constitution, business can challenge a law as being *ultra vires* that level of government.

Example: A city is created by the provincial legislature and so can have no more powers than a province under the Constitution. The City of Toronto passed a Bylaw prohibiting restaurants from serving shark fin soup. A group of businessmen successfully had the Bylaw set aside on the basis that it was *ultra vires* provincial power. Sharks do not naturally occur in Ontario freshwater. (Eng v. Toronto (City), 2012 ONSC 6818 (CanLII))

Local Land Use

In *Maple Ridge v. Meyer* 2000 BCSC 902, Linda Meyer went topless at a community swimming pool which upset some local residents. The Maple Ridge Council passed a park by-law making it an offence for women over age 8 to go topless in local parks with a maximum fine of up to $2,000 and 6 months imprisonment. The B.C. court ruled the law invalid as the "pith and substance" of the by-law was criminal law, which is within the exclusive power of the federal government. Though Maple Ridge had argued the law was valid under provincial and local jurisdiction over property and civil rights, this argument was rejected by the court and the law was struck down.

In 2009, the Supreme Court decided two similar cases that dealt with disputes over the location and operation of small local airports. There was an obvious conflict between the federal government's power to regulate aviation in Canada as opposed to provincial and local powers to regulate civil and property rights. In both cases the court ruled that the local laws were invalid as they were primarily dealing with the regulation of aviation and that fell exclusively within the power of the federal government.

Quebec (Attorney General) v. Canadian Owners and Pilots Association, 2010 SCC 39, [2010] 2 S.C.R.536 and Quebec (Attorney General) v. Lacombe, 2010 SCC 38, [2010] 2 S.C.R.453

Two similar separate cases heard by the Supreme Court of Canada in 2009 both dealt with the right of small private airports (aerodromes) to operate in Quebec. Under the Federal Aeronautics Act, the two aerodromes had been legally operating, when the provincial and municipal governments tried to have them shut down for violating local land use by-laws. The local governments asserted that they had the right to regulate business activities and zoning in their towns and for those reasons they had the right to prohibit the aerodromes. The owners of the aerodromes argued that aviation falls under s. 91 of The Constitution Act and the exclusive jurisdiction of the federal government, so the provincial and local governments had no right to restrict their operations. They asserted that for safety reasons airports and aerodromes could not be separated from Canada's network of landing facilities and made subject to the laws of various local authorities. The Quebec government contended that their powers under s. 92 entitled them to pass laws regarding local land use, and that should include airfields, so therefore it had the power to enforce local laws that prohibited these aerodromes.

The Court's Decision

The Supreme Court in both cases upheld the right of the aerodromes to continue to operate. The court confirmed that the federal government has exclusive jurisdiction over aviation in Canada, including the location and operation of airports of any size. It ruled that the real object of the local by-laws was in essence to regulate the location of aerodromes in their regions and that was beyond provincial powers. Quebec and local governments could not use their s. 92 powers to regulate aviation land uses and prevent the operation of aerodromes, as that is a matter solely within the control of the federal government. The Canadian Owners and Pilots Association (COPA) had intervened in both cases on behalf of the thousands of aerodrome owners across Canada and they were relieved by these decisions of the Supreme Court. This had been a contentious issue for decades in Canada as municipal and provincial governments had frequently attempted to restrict local aviation activities across the country.

Securities Regulations

A more significant case dealing with the division of powers involved the regulation of the securities industry (stocks and bonds) in Canada. This important sector of the financial industry has always been regulated by provincial and territorial governments. Each one sets up its own separate rules and regulations which causes considerable problems. In the following reference the federal government asked the Supreme Court if it could pass a law to set up one national securities regulator for the whole country. The Supreme Court recognized the need for one national securities law that would apply consistently across the country, but it ruled the federal government had no authority to pass this law. The court upheld the provincial right to regulate this area of the economy under its s. 92 powers, even though it acknowledged a federal law in this area would be more desirable.

Reference Re Securities Act [2011] 3 S.C.R.837, 2011 SCC 66

Securities (stocks and bonds) are a key area in Canada's financial sector. Each province and territory has established its own rules and regulations for securities under the civil and property rights powers granted in s. 92 of The Constitution. This has created significant problems for both corporations and investors. Corporations are upset about the duplication, added expenses, inconvenience and inconsistencies encountered when having to deal with so many different regulatory agencies across the country. Investors assert this complex provincial structure has led to weak regulation of the industry and poor investor protection. Many believe this complex mixture of laws has contributed significantly

to Canada's reputation as a haven for stock fraud schemes and other white-collar crimes. Since the 1930s the federal government has recognized the need for one law to regulate the entire securities industry in Canada. Finally in 2010 the federal government developed a draft national law, The Securities Act, which if passed would have replaced all the existing provincial and territorial securities laws and given the federal government exclusive power over this industry. The federal government posed a reference question to the Supreme Court of Canada asking if it could legally enact this proposed federal Securities Act.

The Court's Decision

The Supreme Court ruled that since the proposed law focussed on the operational aspects of securities transactions and regulations, it fell within the s. 92(13) provincial powers over property and civil rights and their right to regulate local matters and industries within their boundaries. The federal powers in s. 91(2) over trade and commerce could not be used to deny the provinces their well-established rights in this financial sector. Though the Supreme Court recognized that for the stability and integrity of our financial markets and to ensure investor confidence, there is a need for one national securities regulator, it concluded that this law was not the way it could be achieved. The court stressed that negotiations with the provinces and territories and their agreement to relinquish their authority in this area would be necessary to achieve a new national law. Unfortunately many believe it is highly unlikely that all of the provinces and territories will ever willingly agree to transfer their powers over this lucrative sector of the economy to the federal government. Even though it would lead to more efficient, stable and reputable capital markets for Canadian businesses and investors, the constitutional division of powers may regrettably prevent this from becoming a reality.

Canadian Securities Administrators. In the absence of any relinquishment of provincial powers, the provincial securities regulators have formed The Canadian Securities Administrators (CSA), an umbrella organization of Canada's provincial and territorial securities regulators whose objective is to improve, coordinate and harmonize regulation of the Canadian capital markets. While it is an informal association, it has developed a "passport" system so that approval by one provincial regulator will be accepted as approval by others. All provinces except Ontario accept this passport.

The Canadian Charter of Rights and Freedoms

The Supremacy Clause

The *Canadian Charter of Rights and Freedoms* is a piece of legislation that sets out the fundamental rights of all Canadians. When the Constitution was patriated, the *Canadian Charter of Rights and Freedoms* was enacted. It was made an integral part of the Constitution, so that the Charter would be difficult to change. An act such as the *Bill of Rights*, or the *Canadian Human Rights Act*, can be amended by a majority of the Canadian Parliament. However, the Constitution can only be altered according to a complex formula that involves agreement among the federal and provincial governments. Two attempts to amend the Constitution—the Meech Lake Accord and the Charlottetown Accord—failed, demonstrating how difficult it is to amend a provision of the Constitution.

The *Charter of Rights and Freedoms* changed the concept of the supremacy of Parliament. Before, the government in power could make any laws that it wanted, the only qualification being that the division-of-powers section of the Constitution entitled Parliament to pass that particular legislation.

When the Charter came into being, a new qualification was put on laws—they must also be in accordance with the principles of the Charter. Those principles take precedence over any of the laws enacted by the federal or provincial governments. Hence, the Charter, with some limitations, is superior to the acts of Parliament and the provincial legislatures.

Companies have successfully used the Charter to attack the legislation that affects their businesses. In one of the first successful Charter cases, Southam Publishing Inc.,[1] which owned many of the newspapers and magazines across Canada, challenged a section of the *Combines Investigation Act* (now the *Competition Act*) which permitted search warrants to be issued without the usual protections that apply to the issuance of police search warrants. That section was struck, or declared invalid, and so also was a search warrant that had been issued against Southam.

The tobacco companies had federal legislation that banned all commercial advertising of tobacco products successfully struck on the basis that the act was an unjustified infringement of freedom of expression.[2]

1. *Hunter v. Southam*, [1984] 2 S.C.R. 145.

2. *R.J.R. MacDonald v. Canada (Attorney General)*, [1995] 3 S.C.R. 199.

The Charter of Rights and Freedoms Prevails

"Section 52(1). The Constitution of Canada is the supreme law of Canada, and any law that is inconsistent with the provisions of the constitution is, to the extent of the inconsistency, of no force and effect" (*The Constitution Act, 1982*).

The complete *Charter of Rights and Freedoms* is reproduced at the end of this chapter.

■ *Critical Concepts of* The Constitution and the Charter of Rights and Freedoms

- The Constitution outlines which government (federal or provincial) can make which law
- The Charter determines whether the law conforms to certain protected rights
- The Charter, as part of the Constitution, prevails over all other laws
- The Charter only applies to the actions of the government or a government agency

The Charter Does Not Always Apply

The purpose of the Charter is to protect the rights of people, businesses and organizations from violations by the government. The Charter applies only to the actions of the government (federal, provincial and municipal) but this can include the actions of government agencies such as the CBC, RCMP, colleges and universities, schools and hospitals, when they are acting in a government capacity. Private disputes with these agencies however, such as employee complaints, may result in the application of laws other than the Charter. Most Charter cases are concerned primarily with the validity of a law that a government has created and whether the law violates the rights guaranteed in the Charter. If a person's rights are violated by a private citizen or company, such as discrimination by an employer or a landlord, the Charter does not apply, but a Human Rights code could be the appropriate legislation to deal with their complaint.

■ *Business Law* Applied

❷ **You are a** policy analyst in the Attorney General's office in Ottawa. The following matters have been referred to you for your comments as to whether the Charter applies.

a) A section of the criminal code which makes abortion illegal
b) The firing of an employee by the Bay
c) The refusal by the British Columbia Pulp and Paper Company Limited to hire a Sikh because he wears a turban
d) A provision of the *Nova Scotia Liquor Control Act* that prohibits lap dancing in licensed taverns

Protected Charter Rights

The Charter guarantees many important rights for individuals, businesses and organizations. There are 34 sections in the Charter, (the entire Charter is included in the appendix at the end of this chapter), but some of the most important sections and relevant Charter cases in relation to business law are discussed below.

Section 1 Reasonable Limits

1. The Canadian Charter of Rights and Freedoms guarantees the rights and freedoms set out in it subject only to such reasonable limits prescribed by law as can be demonstrably justified in a free and democratic society.

This section is often referred to as the reasonable limits clause because this section recognizes that the rights in the Charter are not absolute and are in certain circumstances it may be justified to override these rights. Tobacco companies have repeatedly argued that their section 2 rights to free speech are violated by laws that restrict their rights to advertise their products. In 1995 the Supreme Court recognized that restrictions on advertising are a violation of companies' free speech rights. However in their decision in *RJR-MacDonald Inc. v. Canada (A.G.)* [2007] 2 S.C.R. 610, the court ruled that given the proven serious health consequences of smoking, it is justified under section 1 to override their free speech rights and significantly limit tobacco companies abilities to advertise these dangerous and deadly products. Restrictions on where tobacco products can be advertised, large warnings on cigarette packages and limits on in-store displays are all considered legal infringements of tobacco companies' free speech rights given the overwhelming evidence on the harmful effects from these products. In *Irwin Toy v. Quebec*, [1989] 2 S.C.R. 927, the Supreme Court of Canada ruled that a Quebec law that prohibited commercial advertising directed at persons under 13 years of age was valid despite infringing on companies' free expression rights. The court justified the law under s. 1 as it was considered the minimal restraint on free expression consistent with the important goal of protecting children against manipulation through advertising. The toy company could still advertise its products by directing its promotions towards adult consumers, not children.

Section 2 Fundamental Freedoms

2. Everyone has the following fundamental freedoms:
   a) freedom of conscience and religion;
   b) freedom of thought, belief, opinion and expression, including freedom of the press and other media of communication;
   c) freedom of peaceful assembly; and
   d) freedom of association

Freedom of Religion

The first appeal the Supreme Court of Canada heard involving the Charter of Rights was the *R. v. Big M Drug Mart* [1985]1 S.C.R. 295, often referred to as the Sunday shopping law case. The 1906 federal Lord's Day Act prohibited most commercial activities on Sundays as it was considered the Sabbath and a day of rest in the Christian faith. Stores that opened on Sundays were fined. The Jewish owner of Big M Drug Mart argued that this law imposed a mandatory Christian religious observation on non-Christians and therefore was a violation of s. 2 freedom of religion provision. The Supreme Court agreed and the law was struck down, which had a dramatic impact on the Sunday activities of businesses and families across Canada. Almost complete Sunday shopping activities are the norm in most of Canada as a result of this case. Though protection of religious differences was the key in this famous decision, given the hectic pace of life for many Canadians, people of various faiths have frequently lamented the loss of a weekly day of rest which resulted from this ruling.

Freedom of Speech

While companies have used the freedom of expression section to try to protect their right to advertise as shown in the tobacco advertising challenges, individuals have also used it for similar purposes. In *Rocket v. Royal College of Dental Surgeons*, [1990] 1 S.C.R. 232 two dentists challenged an Ontario law that greatly restricted the content of advertisements that dentists could use to advertise their dental practices. The court ruled the law did violate their freedom of expression and though certain standards should exist when advertising professional services, this law was too extreme in its restrictions, so it was declared invalid. Similar laws regulating the right of lawyers to advertise their services were also changed as a result of this section of the Charter and consumers can now more easily compare professional services.

The freedom of expression provision has also been used to permit companies to erect billboard advertising despite opposition by municipalities that claim it infringes on the visual and aesthetic character of their neighbourhoods. The Supreme Court recognized the right of companies to set up billboards, but did allow municipalities to impose restrictions on the size of the billboards by using section 1. It considered the size limits to be a justified minimal infringement on the companies rights.(*Vann Niagara Ltd. v. Oakville (Town)*, [2003] 3 S.C.R.158,2003 SCC 65.)

A Montreal strip club however was not so successful when trying to use this section of the Charter. A Montreal noise by-law restricted any noise produced by sound equipment that could be heard outside of a building. The club had a loudspeaker near its entrance and the music and announcer could be heard outside on the street. When the city fined the club under the by-law, the strip club complained that the by-law violated its freedom of expression rights. The court upheld the by-law and the fine as it ruled that the by-law was justified to restrict noise pollution and only minimally impacted the club's right to freedom of expression. (Montreal (City) v. 2957-1366 Quebec Inc., 2005SCC 62 (CanLII).

The Canadian Federation of Students successfully had the Vancouver Transit Authority policy restricting political advertising on the outside of its buses struck down. The students wanted to place advertising, which among other statement, said "Tuition Fees – ROCK THE VOTE.COM." The bus line refused to run the ad, but the court said that the Transit Authority's policy had violated the Charter and it must display the students' ad. (*Canadian Federation of Students v. Greater Vancouver Transit Authority*, 2006 BCCA 529 (CanLII).

Human rights laws that protect people from hateful discriminatory statements can come in conflict with freedom of expression rights. The debate is between hate speech versus free speech. In *Saskatchewan Human Rights Commission v. Whatcott* 2013 SCC 11, the Supreme Court had to deal with these conflicting issues. Bill Whatcott ,a religious anti-gay activist, distributed flyers with very strong anti-gay comments on them. The Saskatchewan Human Rights Commission ruled the flyers violated the Saskatchewan Human Rights Code as the wording promoted hatred against people due to their sexual orientation. Whatcott challenged this law claiming it violated his freedom of speech right. The Supreme Court went over each specific flyer and ruled that all the flyers contained offensive language, but only the ones that promoted hatred of homosexuals and caused a "reasonable apprehension of harm" were illegal. The court recognized that the Saskatchewan law did violate the section 2 Charter protection for freedom of speech, but ruled it was a justified infringement. Whatcott insists he will continue to express his religious opposition to homosexuality and assert his freedom of speech rights.

The debate continues as to whether Human Rights tribunals should be regulating free speech in Canada. In 2013 several months after the Whatcott decision, the hate crime provision in the Canadian Human Rights Code that made hate speech communicated on the telephone or the internet illegal was removed. This leaves the Criminal Code as the law to regulate hate speech on the internet and over the telephone. Some fear the police have little desire to become involved in these issues so the internet may become a greater source for hate propaganda. Free speech advocates are pleased that freedom of speech should be decided in criminal courts not by human rights tribunals. Provincial human rights laws can still deal with hate speech communicated in other ways though, so this debate on freedom of expression and hate speech will continue.

The rights of freedom of speech and expression protect the opinions of those with whom you disagree. This value has been no better expressed than as: I may disagree with everything you say, but I will defend your right to say it with my life. (Attributed to Voltaire, probably wrongly).

The absolute necessity for freedom of speech for a successful society can be seen in examples not only historically, but in the present day. Currently, there was a Western belief that if democracy was established in place of repressive regimes, those countries would be at peace. However from experience, political commentators now suggest that democracy cannot work unless the society has developed an appreciation of the values of freedom of speech.

■ *Business Law*   Applied

❸ **Again, in** your position as policy analyst for the federal Attorney General, decide if any of the following situations relate to a right protected by the Charter. Make reference to a specific section of the Charter in your answer.

   a) A provincial legislature passes a law stating:

   "No person shall bear arms of any type for any purpose within the limits of any city in this province."

   b) The federal government passes this law:

   "No person on being arrested need be informed that he/she has a right to consult a lawyer."

   c) A city passes this by-law:

   "Smoking shall be prohibited in any restaurant in this city."

   d) The federal government, in a time of peace, passes this law:

   "The present government shall continue in power for 10 more years."

SLAPP Lawsuits

In Canada the right to hold and express contrary opinions in politics and religion has been securely established. The new issue is the right of citizens to criticize businesses for reasons of public interest, which may include health, safety, ethics and the like. Groups protesting a business may cause it loss of profits. People are protesting development projects as harmful to the environment; wind farms as dangers to health; the use of dolphins in Marine Park shows as cruel to animals; using bull hooks on elephants in circuses and so on. The allegations on the signs and chants of the protesters may be defamatory and opinions incapable of proof.

For example, protest groups at a Marine Park may say the owner is guilty of animal abuse. That statement is defamatory. Under the law of libel, the protesters would have the onus of proving the truth of the statement. That would require very extensive expert evidence in a lengthy trial. In the end it may only be a matter of opinion. So the protesters could be, under the present law, prohibited from expressing that opinion publicly and might be liable for damages.

Example: Don Staniford, an environmental activist, posted pictures on his website of mock cigarette packages with warnings such as: Salmon farming kills like cigarette smoke. He also used extreme language the court characterized as crude, clumsy and foolish. The Court of Appeal awarded damages for defamation against Staniford of $75,000 and costs of the trial and the appeal. (*Mainstream Canada v Staniford*, 2012 BCSC 1433)

It is now contended that some businesses have responded to these protest groups by commencing meritless legal actions against the organizers solely to squash protests, knowing the citizen cannot afford the hundred thousand dollars in legal fees to defend against this kind of lawsuit. These actions are alleged to be either totally without merit, or of minimum merit, and being used as an excuse (i.e. strategically) to silence criticism. They are called Strategic Lawsuits Against Public Participation ("SLAPP").

Provincial governments have been discussing giving protest groups a special protection against these lawsuits. Only Quebec has enacted anti-SLAPP legislation permitting the protesters to bring an early motion to have a judge review an action started by a business to see if there is real merit to it or if it is primarily an attempt to deny freedom of speech. If the judge decides the lawsuit is brought to squash protesting, then it will be dismissed. The critical issue is whether the harm to the business is sufficiently serious that it would outweigh the public interest in protecting that expression.

The anti-SLAPP legislation with its test of "public interest" may have wide implications. For example, if a newspaper ran an article alleging that the mayor of a city used crack cocaine and the mayor sued, the newspaper might have protection under anti-SLAPP legislation.

Anti-SLAPP legislation applies to public interest issues but not to private issues. A man picketed in front of a Canadian Tire Store with a sandwich board claiming Canadian Tire cheated him. The court granted Canadian Tire an order prohibiting the man from picketing using those types of allegations. That behavior would not likely be protected by anti-SLAPP legislation. (*Canadian Tire Corp. v. Desmond*, 1972 CanLII 380 (ON SC))

Freedom of Association — Rights to Collective Bargaining

Employees and labour unions have fought to have their rights protected under the freedom of association provision in section 2. (d) of the Charter with mixed results. In *Health Services and Support – Facilities Subsector Bargaining Association v. B.C.* [2007] S.C.R. 27, the Supreme Court ruled that employees do have a limited right to collective bargaining under the freedom of association section. When the B.C. government passed legislation that took away several key contract provisions a health care union had negotiated and also limited future bargaining rights, including the right to prevent the contracting out of work, the top court ruled this law violated the workers s. 2(d) Charter rights. This decision met with much approval by labour groups and was seen as a major change from previous supreme court rulings.

But a few years later in *Ontario (Attorney General) v. Fraser*, 2011 SCC 20, the Supreme Court narrowed the rights of employees to bargain collectively. At issue in this case was an Ontario law that prohibited farm workers from joining unions, though it did allow them to form employee associations. By denying them the right to unionize, the farm workers were denied the rights provided under the Labour Relations Act, including the right to strike, so their negotiating powers were significantly reduced. The Supreme Court ruled the Ontario law was valid though as it did provide the right to form associations and this fulfilled their freedom of association right under the Charter. It made it clear though that there was no Charter right to belong to a union. This decision has caused considerable discussion and uncertainly as to how much protection the freedom of association provision grants to workers and unions in Canada.

Courts have recognized the right of unions to picket is protected under the s. 2 (b) freedom of expression provision. Even secondary picketing at locations of parties not directly involved in the labour dispute can be legal. In *R.W.D.S.U., Local 558 v. Pepsi-Cola Canada Beverages*

Ontario (Attorney General) v. Fraser, 2011 SCC 20

About 300 farm workers, employed at a mushroom farm owned by Rol-Land Farms near Windsor, complained about the terrible work conditions they endured. They claimed it was dark, moldy, bug infested and they were forced to work grueling hours. They were referred to by numbers not names and told to only speak English. Management threatened that if they joined a union, they would be fired. Ontario had passed the Agricultural Employees Protection Act (AEPA) in 2002 which allowed farm workers the right to form employee associations, but denied them the right to join a union. Family farm owners had argued that planting and harvesting times are so short and time sensitive, that if farm workers were unionized and therefore had the ability to strike or take other job action, it could jeopardize their farming operations. Because of the unsatisfactory conditions, the workers at Rol-Land voted to join a union and with support from several unions, challenged the Ontario law which prohibited their membership. They claimed that the AEPA, by denying farm workers the right to unionize, violated their section 2. (d) right to freedom of association. They argued that since farmers in all other provinces except Alberta have the right to unionize and collective bargaining, it was not a justified infringement and the Ontario law should be struck down as it violated their Charter rights.

The Court's Decision

In a decision that upset the labour movement and they view as a step backward from the B. C. Health Services case, the Supreme Court ruled the Ontario law was valid. The court decided that since the AEPA did allow farm workers to form an employee association, that was enough to fulfil the section 2. (d) Charter right for freedom of association. The court stated that there is protection for meaningful good faith group bargaining with employers under section 2. (d) of the Charter, but it does not guarantee any specific form the collective bargaining must take or the specific right to union participation or any particular model of labour relations or dispute resolution mechanism. The court ruled that the Ontario law was valid since the workers are given the right to form employee associations and negotiate with their employers and this fulfils the freedom of association requirement. It would not use the Charter to guarantee collective bargaining rights such those given to unions under the Labour Relations Act. The farm workers were allowed to form associations, (though they had little negotiating power without the right to strike) so the ban on union membership was therefore legal. The right to join a union is not a specific protected Charter right. Many labour supporters saw this Supreme Court decision as unfair and a denial of full legal rights to some of Canada's most vulnerable workers. After this case, it is now uncertain how far the Supreme Court will extend the freedom of association section of the Charter to protect collective bargaining rights for workers.

(West) Ltd., [2002] 1 S.C.R. 156, 2002 SCC 8 striking Pepsi workers were legally allowed to strike at the retail outlets that sold Pepsi products, though picketing at the homes of Pepsi managers was considered illegal.

Section 7 Life, Liberty and Security of the Person

7. *Everyone has the right to life, liberty and security of the person and the right not to be deprived thereof except in accordance with the principles of fundamental justice.*

Canadians and the medical profession have been significantly impacted by this section in several famous cases. In *Rodriguez v. British Columbia (Attorney General)* [1993] 3 S.C.R.519, Susan Rodriguez requested the right to have a doctor assisted suicide as she was suffering from ALS, a terminal illness. Under the Criminal Code it is illegal for anyone to assist another to commit suicide punishable by up to 14 years in jail. Rodriguez argued that denying her the right to have a doctor help her end her life denied her s. 7 right to security to the person, the right to have control over her body. The Supreme Court ruled that the Criminal Code's prohibition on assisted suicide does violate Section 7. But the court ruled this law is justified under s. 1 to protect the sanctity of life and prevent abuses that could occur if it became legal to assist a suicide. This important medical and moral issue has been debated again and the Supreme Court may have to reconsider this issue a second time given that in 2012 a B.C. trial court judge ruled that the prohibition on assisted suicide does violate section 7 of the Charter. The case will probably go on to the Supreme Court of Canada for further consideration. This issue of euthanasia (mercy killing) remains a controversial topic especially given Canada's aging population and the high cost of health care in Canada.

Another medical and ethical issue where the Charter applies involves the right to an abortion. Under the Criminal Code to obtain a legal abortion women had to obtain the permission from a panel of 4 doctors within a hospital. In *R. v. Morgentaler* [1988] 1 S.C.R. 30, the Supreme Court ruled this law was a violation of section 7, the woman's right to security of the person interpreted to mean the right to have control over her body. This law was clearly government interference with a woman's rights over her body. Forcing a woman, by threat of criminal punishment, to carry a fetus to term unless she meets certain criteria unrelated to her own priorities and feelings was a profound interference with her legal rights to control her own body. As a result, the abortion law section of the Criminal Code was struck down by the Supreme Court and it has never been rewritten. There is no abortion law in Canada now and if a woman can find a doctor willing to perform the procedure, it is legal at any stage of the pregnancy. This has caused pro-life groups to actively object, especially to late term abortions. No new law was ever written and the federal government appears unwilling to reopen discussions on this topic.

Assisted suicide and abortion are two of the most controversial issues involving medical, ethical and moral issues that the Supreme Court has ruled upon. People who are opposed to judicial activism believe that it should be the government that is elected by the people that should make these important decisions, not 9 appointed judges. The federal government has however chosen to defer to the court's decision on these key issues.

Section 8 Unreasonable Search or Seizure

s. 8 Everyone has the right to be secure against unreasonable search or seizure.

Though most of the cases heard under this section of the Charter relate to people searched by police officers during criminal investigations, it can have relevance in business situations as well. In the investigation of illegal business activities the right to search for relevant evidence has triggered the application of this section as seen in the RBC v. Welton [2008] 89 O.R. (3d) 532. In this case the investigation of a suspected bank fraud involved the release of confidential information which was permitted under a federal law. It was argued that the federal law that allowed the release of the private information created an illegal search and seizure and violated section 8. The court ruled it was a violation of section 8 but it was a justified infringement when the information was used by banks to try and prevent fraud.

In a Vancouver case, the police received information that an unknown person was planning to throw a pie in the Prime Minister's face at a ceremony in the city. The police arrested Alan Ward, strip-searched him at the station, but released him four and a half hours later for lack of evidence. Ward was not charged. He sued the city for damages for breach of his Section 8 Charter rights against unreasonable search and seizure. The court ruled in Ward's favour and also agreed that a breach of Charter rights would give the person a right to damages and confirmed an award of $5,000 to Ward. (Vancouver (City) v. Ward, 2010 SCC 27, [2010])

There is a saying that one person's garbage is another's treasure. Businesses regularly dispose of paper documents and copies of documents and information stored electronically on hard drives at desktop computers, laptops, blackberries and other similar devices. It is said that a garbage bag may be accurately described as a bag of information whose contents, viewed in its entirety, paint a fairly accurate and complete picture of a business's activities.

It is known that competitors sometimes hire private investigators to search the garbage of other businesses. In the case *Meditrust Health Care Inc. v. Shopper's Drug Mart* 2002 CanLII 4710 (ON C.A.) a private investigator from Meditrust allegedly found evidence that a vice president of Shopper's Drug Mart had sent out false letters disparaging Meditrust products.

Can police do the same if they are investigating possible criminal charges against a business? Can the target business raise the defence under Section 8 of the Charter that the search and seizure is unreasonable because the business has an expectation of privacy in garbage. In *R. v. Patrick* [2009] SCC 17 the Supreme Court had to rule on the admissibility of evidence when the police who were investigating a possible illegal drug lab, took bags of garbage from open garbage cans the accused had placed at the edge of his property for collection. The court ruled that the accused had effectively abandoned his interest and control over the garbage so the police actions were a legal search and the section 8 rights of the accused were not violated.

Businesses frequently dispose of not only paper documents but electronic versions of documents.

Business Alert!

Given the court's ruling that the information and garbage is not subject to an expectation of privacy, businesses are well advised to consider not only policies regarding the shredding of paper documents but the complete elimination of data on copies of any electronic storage devices that they are disposing of. It is now well understood that deleting is not erasing. Data recovery specialists can often reconstruct much of the data from any type of hard drive or other storage device. The hard drives have to be erased by special software or removed and destroyed.

Section 15 Equality Rights

s. 15. (1) Every individual is equal before and under the law and has the right to equal protection and equal benefit of the law without discrimination and, in particular, without discrimination based on race, national or ethnic origin, colour, religion, sex, age or mental or physical disability.

(2) Subsection (1) does not preclude any law, program or activity that has as its object the amelioration of conditions of disadvantaged individuals or groups including those that are disadvantaged because of race, national or ethnic origin, colour, religion, sex age or mental or physical disability.

Section 15. (1) is probably the most well-known section of the Charter as it grants individuals protection from discrimination. Though section 15 lists many of the protected grounds for discrimination such as nationality, race, sex, age and disability, the courts have been asked to determine if there are other areas not specifically mentioned in the Charter that can be included in this protection against discrimination. One of the most famous cases heard under this section is *Vriend v. Alberta* [1998] 1 S.C.R. 493. This was the first Supreme Court case to rule that a person's sexual orientation is also entitled to Charter protection and discrimination against homosexuals is prohibited under the law. Though this case dealt with a man wrongfully being fired because he was gay, the case impacted many other areas where homosexuals had not received equal protection or benefits under the law. As a result many other laws had to be changed to end discrimination based on sexual orientation such as laws regulating pension benefits and the right to claim financial support under family law if a same-sex couple split up.

A key remaining issue that still existed after the Vriend decision was whether it would be legal for homosexuals to marry in Canada. This issue involves freedom of religion as well as freedom from discrimination. In 2003 the federal government drafted a bill to allow same-sex marriage, but before it was passed the government asked the Supreme Court in a reference question whether this law was valid. (*Reference re Same-Sex Marriage* [2004]3 S.C.R. 698, 2004 SCC 79) The government asked the top court to rule on whether Parliament had the authority to pass this law and if Charter section 2. (a), freedom of religion, would protect religious officials from being forced to perform same-sex marriages that were contrary to their religious beliefs. There was much debate in the country on this important moral and religious question. Many were opposed to allowing same-sex marriage as they claimed it violated their freedom of religion. Some of the world's major religions view homosexuality as a sin and their officials refuse to perform marriage ceremonies for same-sex couples. Not surprisingly though, the Supreme Court removed this last major discrimination against homosexuals. The court ruled same–sex marriage was legal in Canada. Under section 2. (a) freedom of religion, no religious official will ever be forced to marry a same-sex couple if it offends their religious beliefs. However the government will perform legal civil marriage ceremonies for same-sex couples or any religious organizations that want to perform these ceremonies can also do so. This decision achieves a balance between two key Charter rights, freedom of religion and freedom from discrimination.

Vriend v. Alberta
[1998] 1 S.C.R. 493 (S.C.C.)

Delwin Vriend was a lab instructor in a private Christian college in Edmonton Alberta. He had received positive performance evaluations, salary increases and was promoted to a full time position. After being questioned by the college president, Vriend disclosed that he was homosexual. Soon after, the president requested Vriend's resignation claiming Vriend violated the college's position on homosexuality. Vriend refused to quit, so the college fired him. Vriend applied to be reinstated but this was rejected, so he then turned to the Alberta Human Rights Commission for help. He wanted to lay a complaint of discrimination based on his homosexuality against the college. The Alberta Human Rights Commission advised him that under the relevant law, the Alberta Individual's Rights Protection Act (IRPA), no protection existed for discrimination based on sexual orientation. Believing that the Alberta law was unfair, Vriend and others who joined his cause, then challenged the law in an Alberta trial court. The trial judge found that the omission in the IRPA of protection against discrimination on the basis of sexual orientation was a violation of s. 15 of the Charter and she ordered that the words "sexual orientation" be added to the IRPA. The Alberta government upset with that ruling appealed the decision to the Alberta Court of Appeal. The appeal court ruled that the trial judge did not have the right to alter the Alberta law elected officials had written and she had no authority to add those words (sexual orientation) to the IRPA

protections. Vriend then appealed that decision to the Supreme Court of Canada.

The Court's Decision

The Supreme Court ruled that the Alberta IRPA was under-inclusive and by not extending protection to homosexuals from discrimination, the government had effectively stated all persons were equal in Alberta, except gays and lesbians. By not extending IRPA protection to homosexuals it was sending a message that it is permissible and perhaps even acceptable to discriminate against individuals based on their sexual orientation. The Supreme Court ruled the IRPA was therefore in violation of s. 15 of the Charter and agreed with the trial court that the amendment to the IRPA to include protection against discrimination based on sexual orientation was the necessary legal change to provide the equality rights the Charter had envisioned. This was a landmark case and set the precedent that discrimination based on sexual orientation would not be tolerated in Canada. It resulted in many laws and policies being changed across the country to extend this protection against discrimination to gays and lesbians. Opponents of this case claim that unelected judges should not rewrite laws that elected officials have passed, but Vriend stands as a landmark case on discrimination and the power of the judiciary.

The rights of the disabled were adjudicated in the *Jodhan v. Canada (Attorney General)* 2010 FC 1197. Donna Jodhan claimed that the federal government had violated s. 15(1) as it had failed to provide adequate internet services for those blind and visually impaired on numerous government websites. She asserted that she was entitled to equal benefit of government services and several government websites were not properly accessible for visually disabled persons. She said it was degrading and violated her privacy rights to have to use personal assistants to access government employment websites and the census website. She claimed 47 government departments and agencies had never fully funded nor implemented its own mandate for accessibility. Since the government had made no arguments that it was not technically feasible, nor would it have caused undue financial hardship, the court ruled in Ms. Jodhan's favour and the federal government had to pay $150,000 in legal costs to Ms. Jodhan.

Section 15 (2) is often referred to as the affirmative action provision. This section can permit government programs that do actually discriminate against certain groups, if the purpose of the program is to improve the conditions of another group that had been previously disadvantaged due to their race, nationality, religion, sex, age or disability.

In *R.v. Kapp* 2008 SCC 41 the Federal Aboriginal Fisheries Strategy, which granted special fishing rights to 3 aboriginal bands in B.C., was challenged by non-aboriginals who were excluded from the program. Among other benefits, the federal strategy granted 3 native bands the right to exclusively fish in the Fraser River for a 24 hour period. The non-native residents complained that this program was discrimination under s. 15 (1) since they could not participate in the program due to their ethnic backgrounds. The Supreme Court of Canada recognized that this federal program was definitely discriminatory and did violate s. 15 (1), however under s. 15(2) it was legal. The purpose of the program was to promote financial self-sufficiency for the native groups who had been previously disadvantaged in terms of income, education and other factors, so the program contributed to the promotion of their equality and was protected by the Charter.

■ *Business Law*   Applied

❹ **After Wikileaks revealed** confidential U.S. military information, Amazon.com inc. stopped Wikileaks from using Amazon's services. If that happened in Canada, could Wikileaks challenge Amazon's refusal to supply its service under the Charter?

Specific Charter Exemptions

There are exceptions to every rule. The protected rights in the Charter are subject to certain exemptions set out in the various sections. Discrimination, for example, is permitted if it helps a disadvantaged group. Affirmative action programs are one of the specific exemptions under section 15(2).

Section 33 The Notwithstanding Clause

Section 33 of the Charter permits governments to enact laws that can violate rights and freedoms under sections 2 or 7-15 of the Charter, so long as they expressly state that the law is being passed under section 33. This section is called the notwithstanding, or override, clause. It is from the clause's use of the term *notwithstanding* that the shorthand reference is derived. A law passed under section 33 expires automatically after five years. This allows for review of legislation that encroaches on Charter rights.

When the charter was being approved, it was felt that the Quebec government would not agree unless the notwithstanding clause was incorporated. Then-Prime Minister Trudeau stated that he agreed to the incorporation of section 33 "with dread." While most governments have been reluctant to make use of the notwithstanding clause, the Quebec government has done so in a series of laws to restrict the use of the English language in the province of Quebec.

In *Ford v. Quebec (A.G.)* [1988] 2 S.C.R. 712, the Supreme Court ruled that Quebec's Bill 101, which said commercial signs in Quebec had to be in French only, did violate the Charter, but the Quebec government used S. 33 to override the Charter and enforce this discriminatory language law. The Alberta government also used section 33 to override the equality rights in section 15 when it passed its provincial Marriage Act in 2000 to restrict marriage in Alberta exclusively to heterosexual couples. The law automatically expired in 2005 after 5 years as section 33 requires, and Alberta has not re-enacted this law. Other than these two significant cases, there have been no other effective applications of section 33.

Business Law   Applied

❺ **The Quebec government** in 2013 considered passing a new law, the Quebec Charter of Values, which would ban the wearing of obvious religious symbols in public places by government employees. For example, clothing such as turbans by Sikhs, hijabs and niqabs by Muslims, large crucifixes by Christians and kippas by Jews could not be worn by government workers such as doctors, nurses or teachers.

   a) Would this Quebec law violate the Charter of Rights and Freedoms? If so what sections?

   b) If it violates the Charter, could it be justified under section 1?

   c) If the Supreme Court rules the law is illegal, is there anything Quebec could do to still implement the law?

Human Rights Legislation

Not every action which discriminates, or infringes on, what we view as our basic rights is a matter for the *Charter of Rights and Freedoms*. The Charter applies to the actions of governments in making or administering laws.

The actions of individuals, corporations, and governments (when acting like a private person, as opposed to making or administering laws) are governed by human rights legislation. Human rights legislation is aimed at acts of discrimination in three main areas:

- employment
- housing
- provision of goods and services

Say, for example, a business refuses to hire a person because that individual is a member of a minority group. Human rights legislation would apply because the situation:

- is an act of discrimination
- involves a business (viewed as an individual by the law, whether a corporation or not)
- is in the area of employment

Critical Concepts of Application of Fundamental Rights Legislation

- Constitution—states which government (federal or provincial) can make which laws.
- *Charter of Rights and Freedoms*—tells whether the laws passed by all governments, federal and provincial, comply with certain specified principles.
- *Human Rights Acts*—deal with discrimination by persons in employment, housing, and provision of goods and services.

Knowing Which Legislation Applies

The federal and provincial governments, as well as those of the Northwest Territories and Yukon, have all enacted human rights legislation. Most of these statutes have very similar names—the *Human Rights Act* of the province. The practical way to find out whether the federal act or the act of your province applies to a particular situation is to call any of the human rights commission offices listed in the telephone directory. They will be able to advise you, as they are set up to deal with the public without the intervention of lawyers.

The technical answer to deciding the appropriate legislation is found in the division of powers in the Constitution. The *Canadian Human Rights Act* applies strictly to matters in section 91 of the Constitution, which covers the specifically named areas as well as government agencies and private businesses whose activities cross provincial borders. The Canadian National Railway and Air Canada, for example, must comply with the federal legislation. The Bay, on the other hand, has branches throughout Canada, but it is not part of the firm's business to cross provincial boundaries, and therefore it is subject to the human rights act of the province where each branch is located.

Discrimination

In law, **discrimination** is the act of treating someone differently on grounds that are prohibited by human rights legislation. A person can discriminate in ways that are not prohibited under the act. For example, a landlord could refuse a tenant because of the tenant's inability to pay. An employer can refuse to hire someone because of poor references.

> **discrimination**
> the act of treating someone differently on grounds that are prohibited by human rights legislation.

Employers are prohibited from discriminating not only in hiring, but also in advertising for job applicants, as well as in the job-interviewing process.

Discrimination includes actions such as harassment, as well as what has been called systemic discrimination, constructive discrimination, or adverse-effect discrimination. These are all different names for the same thing.

Prohibited Grounds for Discrimination

Section 3 of the *Canadian Human Rights Act* sets out the grounds for discrimination. Sex is specifically stated to include pregnancy. Section 25 extends the meaning of disability to include drug and alcohol dependency.

The grounds for charging discrimination vary among the federal and provincial acts for the different areas, such as for employment, accommodation, and provision of goods and services. In addition, the courts, by interpreting the statute, have declared that, as well as with the Charter, they can add certain grounds by analogy—for example, sexual orientation does not appear in section 3, but according to a decision of the courts, that ground should be considered part of it. Some provincial acts have been amended to include sexual orientation. In other provinces, the provincial human rights commissions consider that sexual orientation is included.

Section 3, Canadian Human Rights Act

3 (1) For all purposes of this Act the prohibited grounds are: race, national or ethnic origin, colour, religion, age, sex, sexual orientation, marital status, family status, disability and conviction for which a pardon has been granted.

3 (2) Where the ground of discrimination is pregnancy or childbirth, the discrimination shall be deemed to be on the ground of sex.

■ *Critical Concepts of* Prohibited Grounds

- The federal *Human Rights Act* lists the usual prohibited grounds for discrimination, such as sex, religion, country of origin, and so on. The act defines sex to include pregnancy or childbirth, and defines disability to include drug and alcohol addiction.
- Because of a court ruling, sexual orientation was added by amendment.
- The Canadian Human Rights Commission has stated that it interprets disability to include AIDS.

In the case *Ont. Human Rights Comm. and O'Malley (Vincent) v. Simpsons-Sears*, [1985] 2 SCR 536, Theresa O'Malley worked at Sears as a full time retail sales clerk. Several years after she began working there she changed her religion to become a Seventh-Day Adventist. As a result, she needed Friday evenings and Saturdays off for religious observations. Sears agreed to let her have this time off, even though it was their busiest time for sales, but Sears cut her from full time status to part time because of this request. The woman complained to the Ontario Human Rights Commission that by reducing her to a part time employee, Sears had discriminated against her due to her religion. The Supreme Court agreed with her and ruled Sears had to give her back her full time employment status and allow her to take off the days for her religion and to reimburse her for her lost wages when she had been reduced to part time hours. The company had to accommodate her religious beliefs and the court ruled it did not impose an undue hardship on the company to continue to employ her on a full time basis while allowing her this time off for valid religious reasons.

Zurich Insurance Company v. Ontario (Human Rights Commission), [1992] 2 S.C.R. 321

Michael Bates challenged Zurich Insurance Company's policy of charging higher rates for males under 25 than for females and married men. The insurance company conceded that the classification system for its premiums discriminated on the basis of sex, age, and martial status, but that the discrimination was reasonable and *bona fide* within the meaning of section 21 of the *Ontario Human Right Code*, which stated that the right to contract without discrimination is not infringed:

> ...where a contract of automobile...insurance...differentiates or makes a distinction, exclusion or preference on reasonable and *bona fide* grounds because of age, sex or marital status...

The court found that the insurance company operated its system in good faith, which met the test of *bona fide*. The issue of reasonableness was difficult in a human rights business context. The underlying philosophy of human rights legislation is that an individual has a right to be dealt with on his or her own merits and not on the basis of group categorization. This right must be balanced with the needs of a business to operate the business safely, efficiently, and economically.

A practice is reasonable if it is based on sound insurance practice and there is no practical alternative. The higher premium for under-25 male drivers was based on statistical evidence compiled in Ontario since 1920 which showed that this group had the highest number of claims, the highest loss per vehicle, and the highest average claim cost of all categories.

This was a reasonable basis for its discrimination and the under-25 male-driver premium policy was upheld.

Example: In *Shinozaki v. Hotlomi Spa*, 2013 HRTO 1027 (CanLII) a massage therapist had been working at a spa, but 1 month after she was hired she became pregnant and informed the spa's owner/ manager. The owner was upset about the pregnancy and repeatedly made negative comments about women working when they were pregnant. As the pregnancy proceeded, the owner repeatedly called the therapist fat and made it obvious she did not want a pregnant therapist working at the spa. The therapist's hours were continually cut and eventually she was terminated because of her pregnancy. The therapist complained to the Ontario Human Rights Commission that the employer had discriminated against her due to her sex and the pregnancy and the tribunal agreed. The spa was ordered to pay her $20,000 as monetary compensation for injury to her dignity, feelings, and self-respect, as well as infringement of her inherent right to be free from discrimination on the basis of sex. It also ordered the spa to pay back wages of approximately $4,000.

Example: In *Chauhan v. Norkam Seniors Housing Cooperative Association*, 2004 BCHRT 262 an Indian woman who cooked strong-smelling curries was told that she would be evicted from her condominium if she did not stop preparing these foods. The strong odors were considered a nuisance by tenants living above her. The woman claimed that her ethnicity included the foods she ate and the threat to evict her due to the odors from her cooking constituted discrimination based on her nationality. The B.C. Human Rights Tribunal agreed and ruled she has the right to prepare her ethnic foods without threat of eviction. It ordered the association to pay her $2,500 for injury to her dignity, feelings and self-respect plus her legal expenses.

Example: Not all cases of differential treatment are a violation of equality rights. In *Maclean v. The Barking Frog*, 2013 HRTO 630 (CanLII) a male who was charged a $20 cover charge at a club when women were asked to only pay $10, claimed he had been discriminated against and it perpetuated a belief that men are less worthy than women. The Ontario Human Rights Tribunal stated that to prove discrimination you have to show that the action creates a disadvantage by perpetuating prejudice and stereotypes. The Tribunal stated that the history of gender discrimination in Canada shows that men have been favoured over women and there is no stereotype they are less worthy. The lower charge for women on ladies nights was not done to exclude men, but to increase bar profits by encouraging more men to show up because more females came. His discrimination complaint was rejected.

In *Demars v. Brampton Youth Hockey Association*, 2011 HRTO 2032 (CanLII) two girls and their mother were awarded a total of $18,000 for discrimination based on sex, because the hockey association had not provided adequate change room arrangements for the girls who were playing on boys hockey teams.

In some cases critics have wondered if human rights tribunals have gone too far in their protection against discrimination. In *Ismail v. B.C. Human Rights Tribunal*, 2013 BCSC 1079 (CanLII), the right to protection from discrimination was pitted against the right of a performer's freedom of expression. Guy Earle, a stand-up comedian was ordered to pay $15,000 and Zesty's, the comedy club where he performed, an additional $7,500, to a lesbian who claimed she suffered discrimination based on her sex and sexual orientation when the comedian directed vicious insults and vulgar lesbian jokes at her during his performance. The woman had exchanged some insults with the comedian, but the rude anti-lesbian comments were so offensive, she claimed it was discriminatory conduct causing her post traumatic stress. Earle maintained that in comedy clubs offensive, irreverent and inappropriate language is the norm. He argued his right to freedom of expression allows for this type of artistic or comedic expression. But the B.C. Supreme Court ruled comedy clubs are not immune from human rights legislation. It ruled that his jokes and comments were discriminatory and not justified by his right to free speech. This case has also received considerable discussion and made some question how far this legislation should extend and the type of complaints that can succeed in Canadian Human Rights tribunals.

In *Gibson v. Ridgeview Restaurant Limited, 2013 HRTO 1163 (CanLII)* a sports bar, Gator Ted's, told a customer, Steve Gibson, that he could not smoke his medicinal marijuana at the entrance to the restaurant as customers had complained. Gibson asserted that he had a disability (a back injury) so that gave him the right to take his medication wherever he wanted, so he continued to smoke marijuana within several feet of the bar entrance. Gator Ted's then barred Gibson from the restaurant. Gibson complained to the Ontario Human Rights Tribunal that the bar had discriminated against him based on his disability. This case took 8 years before it was finally resolved and the Ontario Human Rights Tribunal ruled that Gibson did not have a disability-related right to smoke medicinal marijuana right in front of the restaurant. He could smoke elsewhere and the bar had the right to prevent him from smoking at its entrance. Though this questionable complaint did not succeed, it shows other problems in some cases. The owner of Gator Ted's, estimated it cost him about $80,000 in legal fees to fight this unreasonable complaint and it almost put him into bankruptcy. This case received considerable publicity and many observers feel that it illustrates some people are using human rights legislation to try to win money based on frivolous claims. In Ontario the legal fees of the person who lay the complaint are covered by the government. Gator Ted's had to pay its own legal costs.

Some journalists feel that Human Rights legislation is being misused to limit their right to free speech. In *Elmasry and Habib v. Roger's Publishing and MacQueen* (No. 4), 2008 BCHRT 378 (CanLII), the Canadian Islamic Congress laid complaints of discrimination against

Maclean's magazine and a writer for articles that it felt were discriminatory and promoted hatred against Muslims. The author and the magazine claimed their freedom of speech rights allowed them to express their controversial opinions and they should not be censored by human rights complaints. The human rights tribunal dismissed the case by ruling the statements in question did not rise to the level of hatred and contempt that would constitute hatred under the code. But the debate continues over what power human rights tribunals should have over political commentary and free speech in Canada.

Business Alert!

Job Interviewing   The Law Society of Upper Canada circulated the following as examples of questions that, in light of human rights legislation, are inappropriate to ask in an interview.

- How old are you?
- How will your seniority negatively affect the office operations?
- Are you what is referred to as a "mature student"?
- What is your religion? Are you devout?
- Are you married? Do you have a girlfriend?
- Would your wife be happy living in Ottawa? Are you a "family man"?
- Do you plan to have children?
- Do you plan to get pregnant, and if so, when?
- Are you using birth control?
- How many children do you have? What are your daycare arrangements? How will you cope?
- Where were you born? What is your ancestry? How many years have you been resident in Canada?
- What clubs do you belong to?

Once the applicant has been given a job, questions necessary for employment records, such as age and marital status, can be asked.

Some questions that are related to a *bona fide occupational requirement* (discussed in the material which follows) can be asked at the interview stage.

■ *Business Law* Applied

❻ **Jan Nada has** been a cocktail waitress at the Hot House for two years. The Hot House is a very trendy downtown bar, designed to appeal to sophisticates. The waitresses are obviously chosen because of their looks, and the uniforms are very close fitting. Nada becomes pregnant and, at four months, this is obvious. Her boss fires her.

a) Does Nada have any grounds for a complaint under the *Human Rights Act*? Assume that the applicable provincial legislation is the same as the federal *Human Rights Act*. For now, ignore any defences of the employer.

❼ **You work in** the human resources department and your company has devised a new job-application form. Some of the questions on it are:

- What is your age?
- What is your marital status?
- Where is your country of origin?
- Do you have a criminal record?
- Do you ever use non-prescription, recreational drugs?
- What is your previous work experience?

a) Write a memo to your boss advising on whether human rights legislation allows the company to ask these questions. Refer to the relevant section(s) in your memo.

Systemic Discrimination

The act recognizes that a seemingly neutral policy may in fact result in discrimination. For example, a policy by a police force requiring a certain minimum height and weight for police officers could exclude minority groups whose racial characteristics include a lighter weight and a smaller frame. The same issue has been raised in relation to women and fire departments. The police and fire departments have argued that height and weight are *bona fide* requirements for the job. The question of systemic discrimination is one of intention. Can an individual be said to have discriminated if that person did not intend to do so? The courts have answered this question in the affirmative in interpreting both the *Canadian Human Rights Act* and the provincial legislation. **Systemic discrimination** is discrimination that is the consequence of a policy, whether the effect of discrimination was intended or not; for example, a policy that a police officer be 6-feet tall would discriminate on gender and race.

systemic discrimination
discrimination that is the consequence of a policy, whether the effect of discrimination was intended or not

Business Law   Applied

❽ **Action travail des** femmes (ATF) is a public-interest pressure group originally funded by the federal government, but now incorporated and financed independently. The group alleged that the Canadian National Railway Company (CN) refused to hire women in certain unskilled, blue-collar positions, and was therefore guilty of discriminatory hiring and promotion practices contrary to the *Canadian Human Rights Act*. This was not a complaint by, or on behalf of, any one individual, but was on behalf of women workers in general in the local area.

The lobby group claimed that the percentage of women in the CN workforce was far below the percentage of women available in the general workforce in the area. Therefore, CN's policy of hiring had an adverse effect on working women. Here are the statistics for 1981:

	Percent of Total Labour Force	Percent of CN Workforce
Women workers	40.7	6.11

a) Could the ATF complaint be successful based on the statistical evidence alone?
b) Would the lobby group have to show actual incidents of discrimination by CN against particular women?
c) What is this type of discrimination called?
d) What are the advantages and disadvantages of the use of this type of discrimination in being able to prove discrimination?

Harassment

Harassment on any of the prohibited grounds is also forbidden, and is considered a type of discrimination. Sexual harassment in particular has become a focal point of human rights legislation in recent years. Harassment is any unwanted physical or verbal conduct that offends or humiliates the individual at whom it is directed. It can take many forms, such as:

- threats, intimidation, or verbal abuse
- unwelcome remarks or jokes about subjects such as race, religion, disability, or age
- displaying sexist, racist, or other offensive pictures or posters
- sexually suggestive remarks or gestures
- unnecessary physical contact, such as touching, patting, pinching, or punching
- physical assault, including sexual assault

Harassment can consist of a single incident or several incidents over a period of time, and will be considered to have taken place if a reasonable person ought to have known that the behaviour was unwelcome. Threatening, intimidating, or discriminating against someone who has either filed a complaint, or who is providing evidence or assistance in complaint proceedings, is a summary conviction offence under the federal *Human Rights Act*.

Flirtation/Harassment

Sexual harassment is a major concern in the workplace. The restrictions on sexual harassment are relatively new, and the law is still developing. Normal social behaviour—flirtation—and harassment may well overlap. The difficulty is deciding when the behaviour is part of what is socially acceptable and when it passes beyond.

Human rights legislation recognizes that flirtation is not abnormal, and that it should not be prohibited for people of equal status in their employment situations. However, if a person has supervisory authority over the other person, there is zero tolerance of sexual approach. The employee may feel that his or her job is at risk if there is a refusal.

Evidence of sexual harassment may be difficult to prove because the incident often takes place in private. The case becomes the word of the complainant against the word of the person allegedly harassing. Harassment is also a difficult question because people ordinarily speak of sex in euphemistic or suggestive terms rather than in direct language. The harassment may not be explicit, but suggestive. Even one incident is sufficient to be considered harassment.

Business Alert!

Employer's Responsibilities   Employers are jointly responsible with the offending employee for any harassment that occurs in the workplace. Under all human rights acts, it is the employer's duty to be proactive in preventing harassment. Employers must:

- make it clear that harassment will not be tolerated
- establish a no-harassment policy
- make sure every employee understands the policy and procedures for dealing with harassment
- inform supervisors and managers of their responsibility to provide a harassment-free work environment
- investigate and correct harassment problems as soon as they come to light, even if a formal complaint has not been received

In the Robichaud case below, the Supreme Court made it clear that even if the employer did not know or approve of an employee's harassment, and even had policies to prevent it, under Human Rights legislation, the employer will be held strictly liable for the damages to the victim of this behaviour. In a civil court action the employer may have a due diligence defence, but not in a human rights tribunal.

Robichaud v. Canada (Treasury Board), [1987] 2 SCR 84

In 1979, Bonnie Robichaud, a mother of 5 with a disabled husband, was working as a cleaner on a Canadian military base. She had applied to be the lead cleaner and was working in this position on a probationary basis. Her supervisor, Dennis Brennan, threatened her demanding she perform various sex acts on him, including oral sex, or else he would discipline her and deny her the permanent promotion. Afraid for her job and her family's financial security, Robichaud performed the sex acts. But once she was off probation, she laid a complaint against Brennan and the Department of National Defence for sexual harassment, discrimination and intimidation. After laying

the complaint she was disciplined, demoted and faced social and physical isolation from her coworkers. She suffered depression and severe emotional stress due to the forced sexual activities and the job sanctions imposed after her complaint was filed. She contended that the employer, the Department of National Defence (DND), was strictly liable for the actions of its supervisor. DND argued that the government never knew or approved of Brennan's behaviour, and it had established policies to try to prevent harassment, so it should not be held liable for his inappropriate actions.

The Court's Decision

The Supreme Court ruled that the main concern of the Canadian Human Rights Act was to remove discrimination and its focus was on the effects of discrimination rather than on its causes. The law aims at redressing socially undesirable conditions and coming up with the appropriate remedies to create a healthy work environment. Since a company acts through its employees, in discrimination cases under this law the employer will be held strictly liable for its employees' actions, even if the employee was violating the employer's express rules and policies. It is the employer that is the one who can provide the remedies appropriate in these cases. If an employee acts in defiance of their company policy, which is usually the situation in these cases, the company is still responsible to provide the remedies allowed under the Act. If not then this law would have little impact on reducing discrimination in the workplace. Some of the remedies allowed under the Act such as job reinstatement and back pay can only be done by the employer, so that also justifies imposing liability on the employer for the discriminatory actions of its employees. Bonnie Robichaud had clearly been the victim of extreme sexual harassment in the workplace and this case established the principle that the employer is liable for the illegal actions of employees regardless of policies that had been set to try and prevent such behaviour.

Disability—An Employer's Responsibility to Accommodate

Since an employer must not discriminate because of disability, there is a duty on employers to take a positive step to avoid discrimination. For example, a religious employee should not be forced to work on a religious holiday if other employees can do so. An employer must provide a business environment in which a person with a disability can function.

Creating a workplace that is, for example, fully wheelchair accessible can involve some expense, and businesses sometimes raise the concern of the cost per employee. If the business can prove undue hardship, it will be exempt from this requirement.

In general, the duty to provide an environment that avoids discrimination because of disability involves a combination of factors, including:

- accessible premises (entrances, washrooms, elevators)
- adaptive technology (Braille printers, or speech synthesizers)
- support services (a person to read to a visually impaired employee)
- job restructuring to shift responsibilities around where necessary
- modified work hours, to adapt to the schedules of those requiring medical treatment such as dialysis

Example: In *Commission scolaire régionale de Chambly v. Bergevin*, [1994] 2 SCR 525, the Supreme Court ruled that a school board which required its Jewish teachers to either work on their holy day or to take an unpaid day off was discrimination. The court ruled that the board must allow the teachers the religious days off with full pay. It would not cause the school board undue economic hardship to make these payments, and it would achieve equality in the workplace.

Example: In *Eldridge v. British Columbia (Attorney General)*, [1997] 3 SCR 624, a deaf woman argued that the refusal of the B.C. health care system to pay for sign language interpretation for deaf patients in B.C. health care facilities was discriminatory. She argued it limited the ability of these patients to communicate with the medical staff and increased the possibility of misdiagnosis and ineffective treatment. The Supreme Court agreed and ruled that deaf people were entitled to the sign language accommodation and it was not an undue economic hardship for the B.C. health care system.

Example: In *Canadian National Railway v. Seeley*, 2013 FC 117 (CanLII) the Federal Court ruled the railway had discriminated against a female freight train conductor on the basis of family status, when it did not adequately accommodate her child care needs. The woman was working in Jasper, Alberta when CN asked her to work in Vancouver to cover a worker shortage. Even though her contract stated she could be relocated, she asked to be exempt on compassionate grounds. She and her husband both worked very irregular hours and went out of town with their work and they had 2 small children. She knew she would have considerable difficulty getting adequate day care arrangements. When she did not report to Vancouver, she was fired. The Canadian Human Rights Tribunal ruled CN had not made meaningful inquiries to investigate accommodation options and had not shown it would cause the railway undue hardship. She was awarded $35,000 in damages due to discrimination based on her family status and reinstated in her job in Jasper. In a similar case of *Canada (Attorney General) v. Johnstone*, 2014 FCA 110 (CanLII), Canada Border Services Agency was found to have discriminated based on family status when it would not accommodate the child care demands of a woman working irregular shifts in customs at the Toronto Airport. When she was cut to part time hours she filed a complaint of discrimination and was re-instated into her full time position with back pay.

Undue Hardship

How far does the duty on employers to accommodate their employees extend? Courts have ruled a company must accommodate up to the point of undue hardship? Does this impose an unreasonable financial cost on employers or is it fair given the need to protect workers from discrimination? This is a question frequently at issue in the courts.

In the Hydro–Quebec case below the Supreme Court ruled that after providing various accommodations for over 6 years, the employer had done enough to try and accommodate the illnesses of their worker. Termination of the worker at that point was ruled to be legal.

Hydro-Québec v. Syndicat des employé-e-s de techniques professionnelles et de bureau d'Hydro-Québec, section locale 2000 (SCFP-FTQ), 2008 SCC 43

An employee of Hydro-Quebec had a variety of physical and mental problems, so much so that she had missed 960 days of work between January 3, 1994 and July 19, 2001. She suffered from depression, tendinitis and bursitis, had several surgical procedures, and took medication for various physical and mental conditions. Her main problem was that she had a mixed personality disorder which resulted in poor coping skills and as a result, her relationships with supervisors and co workers were difficult. Over the years, the employer adjusted her working conditions in light of her limitations: such as assigning her new lighter duties, creating new work stations and giving her a gradual return to work following her bouts with depression. On July 19, 2001, after she had been absent from work since February 8, 2001, Hydro-Quebec finally terminated her employment. Her doctor had stated that she must stop working for an indefinite period and a psychiatric assessment determined that she would no longer be able to work on a regular and continuous basis without continuing absences.

The woman complained that Hydro-Quebec had discriminated against her due to her disabilities and it had not made proper accommodations for her. She claimed that there would be no undue hardship if the company had continued to employ her and make accommodations for her condition. Hydro-Quebec claimed that it had met its duties under the Human Rights Code and since she could not return to work in the reasonable future it had the right to end her employment.

The Court's Decision

The arbitrator initially ruled that Hydro-Quebec had the right to terminate the worker because, despite many accommodations given in the past, for the reasonably foreseeable future she would be unable to work. The Court of Appeal however ruled in her favour stating that the employer had not proven it was "impossible" to accommodate her medical condition. The Supreme Court agreed however with the original judgment. It redefined the test for undue hardship. It ruled that the company does not have to prove it is impossible to accommodate the worker's disability. It need only show that if the characteristics of an illness are such that the proper operation of the business is hampered excessively, or if the ill employee remains unable to work for the reasonably foreseeable future, despite accommodations, the employer will have satisfied the test and the worker can be terminated. The employer's duty to accommodate ends where the employee is no longer able to fulfill the basic obligations of the job for the foreseeable future. Given all that Hydro-Quebec had done over the years to accommodate this employee and the low prospects of her returning soon, the court ruled the company finally had the right to terminate her employment.

But in the *Lane v. ADGA Group Consultants Inc.*, 2007 HRTO 34 (CanLII) case, the court ruled that the company had rushed to judgment when firing an employee with bipolar disorder and had not done enough to accommodate his disability. Lane had lied about his mental health problems so he could get the job. But after 8 days it was very obvious by his erratic behaviour he could not handle the stress of the jobs at this firm, so he was fired. But the court ruled the company had not proven it had tried to accommodate his disability up to the point of undue hardship. The tribunal said ADGA had not made a substantial effort to accommodate him, so it was ordered to pay Lane over $80,000 in damages. Many people have questioned whether it is fair that workers can lie about their disabilities to get the job and whether the requirement then to accommodate the worker up to the point of undue hardship is an unreasonably high expensive standard to impose on employers.

Lane v. ADGA Group Consultants Inc., 2007 HRTO 34 (CanLII)

Paul Lane, 43, was hired as a quality assurance analyst by ADGA Group Consultants Inc. The company was an information technology design and engineering company that had many contracts with the Department of Defence (DND). Lane was to be part of a team developing and testing artillery software to be used by the armed forces. It was challenging, stressful work and strict deadlines had to be met. Lane had previously been diagnosed with bipolar disorder and had received treatment. He had been fired from a previous job after a manic episode caused him to miss 5 weeks of work. When Lane joined ADGA he lied and said he had no medical disabilities and had never missed any significant time away from work in previous jobs. He was hired on a 3 month probationary contract that stated ADGA could terminate him at any time for any reason in this period. Several days after he started work he informed his supervisor he was bipolar and to watch out for any abnormal behaviour he may exhibit. He alerted her that he may have to take time off as work as stress may trigger a manic episode. The supervisor contacted the human rights commission and read material about bipolar disorder. In the first week, Lane did almost no work, was excessively socializing with co-workers, sent overly-familiar inappropriate emails to co-workers and exhibited behaviour that indicated a manic episode may soon occur. On the 8th day of his employment his paranoia increased and he complained a co-worker was making death threats against him and he imagined a bomb had gone off in the building. ADGA's operations have significant security dimensions and reliability and quality are essential to its success, so his supervisor was very concerned about Lane's actions. The senior managers discussed Lane's situation on the 8th day and concluded he could not handle the stress of the jobs at this firm, and since there were no other suitable positions for him at ADGA, he was fired. Lane later filed a complaint at the Ontario Human Rights Tribunal claiming he had been discriminated against based on his mental illness and ADGA had not met its duty under the law to accommodate his disability.

The Court's Decision

The judge recognized that Paul Lane suffered from bipolar disorder and did not properly perform his duties when he was at ADGA. The fact Lane had lied about his condition to get the job was not considered relevant to the discrimination complaint, the court believed it was almost necessary to avoid discriminatory stereotyping at the hiring stage. The contractual provision that ADGA could legally terminate within the first 3 months for any reason was also deemed not to be a deciding factor. The court focused on the Human Rights Code obligation not to discriminate and the duty on the employer to try to accommodate a disability up to the point of undue hardship on the firm. The court ruled that the company had not properly assessed Lane's medical condition and had not met the procedural obligations imposed by the duty to accommodate. The judge felt the company jumped to a quick conclusion he had to be fired and had not obtained all relevant information about his medical condition, prognosis for recovery, job capabilities and ability to do alternate work. ADGA had not established that accommodating his disability would cause the firm undue hardship. After Lane was fired he suffered a major depressive episode and was unable to work for an extended time. The court held the company liable for $35,000 in general damages, $10,000 in damages for mental anguish plus $34,278 for 32 weeks of lost wages. Many employers looking at this case are concerned that it imposes an unfair financial burden on companies and makes it very difficult to terminate an employee who lies about a significant disability when they are hired and proves incapable of performing the work they were hired to do.

Exemptions

Bona Fide *Occupational Requirement*

There are several exceptions set out in the *Human Rights Act* that permit discrimination under very restricted circumstances. The one most frequently applied in the business situation is known as a *bona fide* **occupational requirement (BFOR)**, which is a genuine requirement

bona fide **occupational requirement (BFOR)**

a genuine requirement for a job, such as, for example, the need to wear a hard hat when working on a construction site; a BFOR is a defence that excuses discrimination on a prohibited ground when it is done in good faith and for a legitimate business reason

for a job, such as, for example, the need to wear a hard hat when working on a construction site. A BFOR is a defence that excuses discrimination on a prohibited ground when it is done in good faith and for a legitimate business reason.

Rejected BFORs   A BFOR commonly raised by employers as defences to human rights complaints is customer preference. This has almost universally been rejected as a BFOR. For example, it was ruled that a male applicant could not be refused a job as a drapery installer on the basis that a male did not have the requisite care, taste, and delicacy to install drapes. Physical capability has also been rejected. In one case, it was ruled that a woman could not be refused a job on the basis that she was not able to lift heavy truck equipment, and that it was dangerous for a woman to be left alone in an office at night.

In a highly controversial case a Sikh RCMP officer sought to wear a turban as part of his Mountie uniform claiming his right to freedom of religion. The RCMP agreed and decided that Human Rights legislation required it to permit this exception to the normal requirement because wearing the traditional Mountie hat could not be justified as a *bona fide* occupational requirement. A group of retired RCMP officers unsuccessfully challenged this ruling in court.

Efficiency and Safety   An employer may claim that a *bona fide* occupational requirement is necessary because of business profitability or safety to the public. When public safety is involved, a court is more likely to find that a BFOR exemption exists. Many cases heard before various provincial tribunals have dealt with the fact that firefighters must retire at the age of 60, because of public safety. The courts have upheld this mandatory retirement policy for firefighters, but have stated that in other circumstances individual testing should be used if at all possible to determine whether a person is fit for the job.

Is Drug Testing a BFOR?   Previous or existing dependence on alcohol or drugs is specifically defined as a disability by section 25 of the *Canadian Human Rights Act*. Is employment-related drug testing then a violation of this section? Can drug testing be justified as a *bona fide* occupational requirement if it is a violation?

A Health and Welfare Canada survey reported that 85 percent of Canada's labour force drank, and 10 percent considered themselves heavy drinkers. Illicit drug use was reported by 8 percent. Such substances affect the user's motor functions, decision-making capacity, and planning skills, both during use and in the hangover or withdrawal stages.

Studies have shown that alcohol is frequently a contributing factor in accidents in the workplace. Alcohol and drugs also contribute to absenteeism, higher turnover rates, increased sick benefits, more workers' compensation and insurance claims, lower productivity, lower-quality services, theft, and trafficking.

Employers are particularly concerned about substance abuse because of possible accidents:

- on the job, especially those involving other employees
- caused by intoxicated employees—ranging from those involving company-owned motor vehicles, to major disasters such as tankers running aground and spilling oil

Companies are discussing the use of drug testing to try to eliminate some of these problems.

There is some disagreement over the necessity for drug testing, since these tests may also reveal other conditions, such as AIDS or diabetes. Employees are concerned that their privacy is being invaded, or that they might be fired because they have AIDS.

The Toronto-Dominion Bank established a policy of administering drug and alcohol tests randomly to employees who have access to cash and to the confidential financial information of customers. The program was found to be too wide ranging, and the TD Bank and human rights groups are conferring on establishing a policy that meets the needs of the bank without unnecessary violations of employee rights. It is anticipated that there will be many challenges to such testing programs; the development of guidelines for when such programs are in violation of human rights legislation will be one of the tasks facing human rights tribunals in the future.

In an early case, *Bhinder V. Canadian National Railway Company*, [1985] 2 S.C.R. 561, the Supreme Court set the standard for a BFOR. Bhinder had worked for 4 years as a maintenance electrician in the CN coach yard, when the company changed the rules and required all employees in this area to wear a construction helmet. Bhinder was a Sikh and wore a turban as required by his religion. When he refused to wear a hard hat, he was fired. Bhinder then filed a discrimination complaint against the railway. The court ruled that CN had discriminated against Bhinder due to his religion, but the company had established that it was a bona fide occupational requirement and requiring a construction helmet was justified for the safety of the workers. Bhinder's complaint was therefore dismissed.

Meiorin (Public Service Employee Commission). V. B.C. Govn. And Service Employees Union [1999] 3 S.C.R. 3

Tawney Meiorin was a woman already working as a B.C. forest fire fighter, when the B. C. government passed new rules that fire fighters had to pass a series of fitness tests to qualify for the job. Meiorin, who had performed her job well for three years, passed all of the fitness tests but one. She was required to run 2.5 km. in 11 minutes, but after 4 attempts her best time was 11 minutes 49.4 seconds. Since she could not pass this test, she was fired. The B.C. government argued the fitness test was a legitimate BFOR instituted for safety reasons so it had the right to terminate Ms. Meiorin. She filed a discrimination complaint arguing that the test was unfair to females and did not take into account their different aerobic capacities and the test was not a legitimate occupational requirement and constituted discrimination against her due to her sex.

The Court's Decision

The court ruled that to qualify as a valid BFOR a three part test should be applied: 1) the employer must establish that the employers adopted the standard for a purpose rationally connected to the performance of the job. 2) that the employer adopted the standard in an honest and good faith belief that it was necessary to

the fulfillment of the job and 3) that the standard was reasonably necessary and that it is impossible to accommodate the complainant without imposing undue hardship on the employer. The court ruled that the government had implemented the fitness test for safety reasons, but it was based on research that was incomplete and impressionistic and did not take into account the physical differences between men and women. Though the government had met the first two criteria set by the court, it did not fulfill the third requirement. The government had failed to show that this particular aerobic test was necessary to identify which people would be able to perform the tasks of a forest fire fighter safely and efficiently. It also had not proven that it would suffer undue hardship if a different standard was used that took into account the different aerobic capacities of women. The government had not even investigated the use of other tests that could accommodate women's' physical differences. Ms. Meiorin had safely and competently performed her job for 3 years before the fitness testing was instituted. The court felt the government fitness test was discriminatory against women and it had not met the test to qualify it as a legal bona fide occupational requirement. Meiorin was reinstated in her fire fighting job and awarded damages for lost pay and benefits.

■ *Business Law* Applied

❾ Star Caterers Inc. has obtained a new contract to supply food to a college cafeteria. The company wants to have all employees undergo a test for AIDS. Morris Brown, an employee, knows he is HIV-positive, and does not want Star to discover this.

   a) Does Brown have any grounds under human rights legislation for challenging the mandatory AIDS testing?

   b) Does Star Caterers Inc. have any defence?

Affirmative Action and Other Special Programs

Like the Charter, human rights legislation makes exceptions for affirmative action and other special programs. This is done in an effort to relieve the effect of discrimination on minority groups.

It is felt that many people will not complain because of the fear of pressure and consequences. The cost of processing individual complaints is high, and delays before tribunals, and courts, if there is an appeal, are lengthy. Prevention is felt to be a far more effective and efficient remedy. It also has the advantage of not singling out individuals as complainants.

Remedies

The federal and provincial human rights acts all have similar provisions allowing for several remedies upon finding of a violation. The main remedies allow the tribunal to order a person found at fault:

- to stop a discriminating practice
- to adopt a special program and plan to cure the problem
- to pay a money award as compensation to the complainant
- to reinstate a complainant into employment

The term *person* includes a business or corporation. The question in the *Action Travail v. CN* case above was whether a tribunal had the power to make the company adopt an employment equity program. The tribunal ordered CN to hire one woman in four as new employees until the level of female workers reached 13 percent of the company's total workforce—the national average for women working in equivalent jobs.

In Summation

The essential concepts you see here are the basics of this chapter. They are the thread only—you must add the beads to form the necklace. Try using this list as a test. If there's a particular point that you don't recall, review that section of the chapter.

The Constitution

- The ability to make laws is divided between the federal and provincial governments according to specific matters. Residual powers are given to the federal government for matters not specifically listed.

- *The Constitution Act, 1982*, incorporated the *British North America Act* and the *Charter of Rights and Freedoms*, and qualifies the laws that the federal or provincial governments may enact. An amending formula requiring extraordinary measures to change any element of the constitution was also included.

Charter of Rights and Freedoms

- One aspect of the Charter focuses on controlling the government's power to make law. Here neither the federal nor any provincial government can make a law that violates the rights that are listed in the Charter. There are five concepts discussed in the text relating to the Charter:
  a) Application. The Charter applies to governments when making laws, while human rights legislation applies to acts of government and individuals respecting certain prohibited behaviour, particularly discrimination and harassment.

b) Protected Rights. Only some rights are protected. For example, the right to freedom of the press is specifically mentioned, but the right to bear arms, which is part of the United States Constitution, is not set out as a Charter right.

c) Reasonable Limitations. Even if the right is protected, a law can be passed in violation of this protected right if it is reasonable to limit the right. A law limiting advertising is a violation of the freedom of expression of a business, but in the case of advertising directed at children under age 13, it may be reasonable to limit the right of freedom of expression because of the societal interest in protecting children from manipulation through advertising.

d) Specific Charter Exemptions. There are specific exemptions listed in the Charter for areas where laws can be passed even though they are in violation of protected rights. The most common example is affirmative action programs. These programs discriminate in favour of minority groups. While discrimination is generally prohibited, it is permitted in a law that benefits a disadvantaged group.

e) Legislative Exemptions. The controversial "notwithstanding clause" permits a government to pass a law which states that the law is valid in spite of the Charter.

Human Rights Legislation

- Human rights legislation ensures individuals are not discriminated against by the actions of other individuals, corporations, and governments.

- The federal and provincial governments have passed laws dealing with human rights. The law applicable, federal or provincial, to any given situation, basically reflects the division set up in sections 91 and 92 of the Constitution.

- The *Canadian Human Rights Act* lists a number of grounds on which discrimination is not permitted, such as religion, country of origin, and disability. Harassment stemming from any of these grounds will also be considered a type of discrimination. The act also recognizes that systemic discrimination may occur through the enforcement of policies by various organizations.

- There are very few exemptions from the prohibited grounds for discrimination, and only when there are very real occupational reasons behind the action or decision.

- Human rights commissions or councils have been established at the provincial and federal levels with definite procedures for handling investigations, decision making, and the determination of remedies for human rights violations.

Closing Questions

1. A city council considers designating areas that permit prostitution. Its argument is that the city has control over uses of city areas through zoning by-laws. For example, an area can be zoned as residential-only, or the city can permit uses such as slaughterhouses or garbage dumps.
   a) Do you think a city zoning by-law to regulate prostitution is within the provincial power?

2. A provincial government enacted a statute entitled the *Wages Act*. This act provides that if a business goes bankrupt, then the workers' claim for unpaid wages for the six months prior to bankruptcy will take precedence over all other claims against the company. The right to sue for wages is a matter of contract law, and hence is considered within the category of civil rights.
   a) Is the above legislation within the powers of the provincial government?
   b) What are possible categories in federal and provincial jurisdictions?
   c) Is this a matter that affects employment contract, or priority in bankruptcy?

3. In your position as policy analyst for the federal Attorney General's office, determine whether the *Charter of Rights and Freedoms*, the *Canadian Human Rights Act*, or provincial human rights legislation applies to each of the following situations.

   a) A provincial law requires international students to pay $5,000 to the provincial government before they can attend colleges or universities in that province.

   b) An employee in the Ministry of Labour in Manitoba believes that she was fired because she wore a burka to work.

   c) A federal law requires all federal employees to record their fingerprints with the government when they apply for a job.

   d) A lesbian working for Canadian Tire quits because her boss constantly made rude remarks about her sexual orientation.

4. A federal government agency employed electricians in groups of ten on a short-term contract basis. There were seven such groups working on a particular project. In each, only one electrician was black; the others were members of other minority groups or were white.

   The project was entering a new phase, and the project manager ordered the foreman of each group not to renew the contract of one person per group. In each case, the individual let go was the member of the group who was black.

   The black electricians complained to the human rights commission. They said that while they were employed there was no incidence of racism, but claimed that the mass layoff was discrimination against them because of race.

   a) Could the black electricians prove their case without evidence of discriminatory acts by their employer?

5. KidTalk Inc. manufactures a line of cellphones for the pre-teen market. They are the hit toy of the year largely because of the very effective advertising campaign directed at the pre-teen market. Parents are upset. The Manitoba government passes a law that prohibits KidTalk from advertising on daytime television, in order to restrict the company's campaign aimed at children. KidTalk wants to challenge the legislation:

   a) What grounds could it use to attack the legislation?

   b) Based on the cases that you have studied so far, would one of them support either of the parties' position?

   c) Because of the effectiveness of the legislation, KidTalk has to downsize. Employees who are fired claim they are primarily from one minority group. Do they have any remedy against KidTalk?

6. Jake Simms has worked for a printing company as a technician for 20 years and is now 68 years old. He was recently fired as the company said he could not keep up with the technical changes involved in printing now that it is all done by computers. Jake admits that he finds some of the computer requirements difficult but he still thinks he can perform valuable services for the company and the real reason they fired him is because they think he is too old. He can't afford to retire and wants to fight this termination.

   a) Are there any relevant laws that Jake could use to fight this termination?

   b) Are there any defenses that the company could use to justify the termination?

   c) What do you think will be the outcome of this case?

Appendix

1A

The Constitution Act, 1867, Sections 91 and 92

VI. Distribution of Legislative Powers

Powers of the Parliament
Legislative Authority of Parliament of Canada

91. It shall be lawful for the Queen, by and with the Advice and Consent of the Senate and House of Commons, to make Laws for the Peace, Order, and good Government of Canada, in relation to all Matters not coming within the Classes of Subjects by this Act assigned exclusively to the Legislatures of the Provinces; and for greater Certainty, but not so as to restrict the Generality of the foregoing Terms of this Section, it is hereby declared that (notwithstanding anything in this Act) the exclusive Legislative Authority of the Parliament of Canada extends to all Matters coming within the Classes of Subjects next hereinafter enumerated; that is to say,

1. Repealed. (44)
1A. The Public Debt and Property. (45)
2. The Regulation of Trade and Commerce.
2A. Unemployment insurance. (46)
3. The raising of Money by any Mode or System of Taxation.
4. The borrowing of Money on the Public Credit.
5. Postal Service.
6. The Census and Statistics.
7. Militia, Military and Naval Service, and Defence.
8. The fixing of and providing for the Salaries and Allowances of Civil and other Officers of the Government of Canada.
9. Beacons, Buoys, Lighthouses, and Sable Island.
10. Navigation and Shipping.
11. Quarantine and the Establishment and Maintenance of Marine Hospitals.
12. Sea Coast and Inland Fisheries.
13. Ferries between a Province and any British or Foreign Country or between Two Provinces.
14. Currency and Coinage.
15. Banking, Incorporation of Banks, and the Issue of Paper Money.
16. Savings Bank.
17. Weights and Measures.
18. Bills of Exchange and Promissory Notes.
19. Interest.

20. Legal Tender.

21. Bankruptcy and Insolvency.

22. Patents of Invention and Discovery.

23. Copyrights.

24. Indians, and Lands reserved for the Indians.

25. Naturalization and Aliens.

26. Marriage and Divorce.

27. The Criminal Law, except the Constitution of Courts of Criminal Jurisdiction, but including the Procedure in Criminal Matters.

28. The Establishment, Maintenance, and Management of Penitentiaries.

29. Such Classes of Subjects as are expressly excepted in the Enumeration of the Classes of Subjects by this Act assigned exclusively to the Legislatures of the Provinces.

And any Matter coming within any of the Classes of Subjects enumerated in this Section shall not be deemed to come within the Class of Matters of a local or private Nature comprised in the Enumeration of the Classes of Subjects by this Act assigned exclusively to the Legislatures of the Provinces. (47)

Exclusive Powers of Provincial Legislatures
Subjects of Exclusive Provincial Legislation

92. In each Province the Legislature may exclusively make Laws in relation to Matters coming within the Classes of Subjects next hereinafter enumerated; that is to say,

1. Repealed (48).

2. Direct Taxation within the Province in order to the raising of a Revenue for Provincial Purposes.

3. The borrowing of Money on the sole Credit of the Province.

4. The Establishment and Tenure of Provincial Offices and the Appointment and Payment of Provincial Officers.

5. The Management and Sale of the Public Lands belonging to the Province and of the Timber and Wood thereon.

6. The Establishment, Maintenance, and Management of Public and Reformatory Prisons in and for the Province.

7. The Establishment, Maintenance, and Management of Hospitals, Asylums, Charities, and Eleemosynary Institutions in and for the Province, other than Marine Hospitals.

8. Municipal Institutions in the Province.

9. Shop, Saloon, Tavern, Auctioneer, and other Licences in order to the raising of a Revenue for Provincial, Local, or Municipal Purposes.

10. Local Works and Undertakings other than such as are of the following Classes:
    (a) Lines of Steam or other Ships, Railways, Canals, Telegraphs, and other Works and Undertakings connecting the Province with any other or others of the Provinces, or extending beyond the Limits of the Province:
    (b) Lines of Steam Ships between the Province and any British or Foreign Country:
    (c) Such Works as, although wholly situate within the Province, are before or after their Execution declared by the Parliament of Canada to be for the general Advantage of Canada or for the Advantage of Two or more of the Provinces.

11. The Incorporation of Companies with Provincial Objects.

12. The Solemnization of Marriage in the Province.

13. Property and Civil Rights in the Province

14. The Administration of Justice in the Province, including the Constitution, Maintenance, and Organization of Provincial Courts, both of Civil and of Criminal Jurisdiction, and including Procedure in Civil Matters in those Courts.

15. The Imposition of Punishment by Fine, Penalty, or Imprisonment for enforcing any Law of the Province made in relation to any Matter coming within any of the Classes of Subjects enumerated in this Section.

16. Generally all Matters of a merely local or private Nature in the Province.

Canadian Charter of Rights and Freedoms

Schedule B, Constitution Act, 1982 (79)

Whereas Canada is founded upon principles that recognize the supremacy of God and the rule of law:

Rights and freedoms in Canada

1. The *Canadian Charter of Rights and Freedoms* guarantees the rights and freedoms set out in it subject only to such reasonable limits prescribed by law as can be demonstrably justified in a free and democratic society.

Fundamental freedoms

2. Everyone has the following fundamental freedoms:
    a) freedom of conscience and religion;
    b) freedom of thought, belief, opinion and expression, including freedom of the press and other media of communication;
    c) freedom of peaceful assembly; and
    d) freedom of association.

Democratic rights of citizens

3. Every citizen of Canada has the right to vote in an election of members of the House of Commons or of a legislative assembly and to be qualified for membership therein.

Maximum duration of legislative bodies

4. (1) No House of Commons and no legislative assembly shall continue for longer than five years from the date fixed for the return of the writs of a general election of its members.

Continuation in special circumstances

(2) In time of real or apprehended war, invasion or insurrection, a House of Commons may be continued by Parliament and a legislative assembly may be continued by the legislature beyond five years if such continuation is not opposed by the votes of more than one-third of the members of the House of Commons or the legislative assembly, as the case may be.

Annual sitting of legislative bodies

5. There shall be a sitting of Parliament and of each legislature at least once every twelve months.

Mobility of citizens

6. (1) Every citizen of Canada has the right to enter, remain in and leave Canada.

Rights to move and gain livelihood

(2) Every citizen of Canada and every person who has the status of a permanent resident of Canada has the right
    a) to move to and take up residence in any province; and
    b) to pursue the gaining of a livelihood in any province.

(3) The rights specified in subsection (2) are subject to

Limitation

a) any laws or practices of general application in force in a province other than those that discriminate among persons primarily on the basis of province of present or previous residence; and
    b) any laws providing for reasonable residency requirements as a qualification for the receipt of publicly provided social services.

Affirmative action programs

(4) Subsections (2) and (3) do not preclude any law, program or activity that has as its object the amelioration in a province of conditions of individuals in that province who are socially or economically disadvantaged if the rate of employment in that province is below the rate of employment in Canada.

7. Everyone has the right to life, liberty and security of the person and the right not to be deprived thereof except in accordance with the principles of fundamental justice.

Life, liberty and security of person

8. Everyone has the right to be secure against unreasonable search or seizure.

Search or seizure

9. Everyone has the right not to be arbitrarily detained or imprisoned.

Detention or imprisonment

10. Everyone has the right on arrest or detention

Arrest or detention

   a) to be informed promptly of the reasons therefor;
   b) to retain and instruct counsel without delay and to be informed of that right; and
   c) to have the validity of the detention determined by way of *habeas corpus* and to be released if the detention is not lawful.

11. Any person charged with an offence has the right

Proceedings in criminal and penal matters

   a) to be informed without unreasonable delay of the specific offence;
   b) to be tried within a reasonable time;
   c) not to be compelled to be a witness in proceedings against that person in respect of the offence;
   d) to be presumed innocent until proven guilty according to law in a fair and public hearing by an independent and impartial tribunal;
   e) not to be denied reasonable bail without just cause;
   f) except in the case of an offence under military law tried before a military tribunal, to the benefit of trial by jury where the maximum punishment for the offence is imprisonment for five years or a more severe punishment;
   g) not to be found guilty on account of any act or omission unless, at the time of the act or omission, it constituted an offence under Canadian or international law or was criminal according to the general principles of law recognized by the community of nations;
   h) if finally acquitted of the offence, not to be tried for it again and, if finally found guilty and punished for the offence, not to be tried or punished for it again; and
   i) if found guilty of the offence and if the punishment for the offence has been varied between the time of commission and the time of sentencing, to the benefit of the lesser punishment.

12. Everyone has the right not to be subjected to any cruel and unusual treatment or punishment.

Treatment or punishment

13. A witness who testifies in any proceedings has the right not to have any incriminating evidence so given used to incriminate that witness in any other proceedings, except in a prosecution for perjury or for the giving of contradictory evidence.

Self-crimination

14. A party or witness in any proceedings who does not understand or speak the language in which the proceedings are conducted or who is deaf has the right to the assistance of an interpreter.

Interpreter

15. (1) Every individual is equal before and under the law and has the right to the equal protection and equal benefit of the law without discrimination and, in particular, without discrimination based on race, national or ethnic origin, colour, religion, sex, age or mental or physical disability.

Equality before and under law and equal protection and benefit of law

   (2) Subsection (1) does not preclude any law, program or activity that has as its object the amelioration of conditions of disadvantaged individuals or groups including those that are disadvantaged because of race, national or ethnic origin, colour, religion, sex, age or mental or physical disability.

Affirmative action programs

16. (1) English and French are the official languages of Canada and have equality of status and equal rights and privileges as to their use in all institutions of the Parliament and government of Canada.

Official languages of Canada

   (2) English and French are the official languages of New Brunswick and have equality of status and equal rights and privileges as to their use in all institutions of the legislature and government of New Brunswick.

Official languages of New Brunswick

   (3) Nothing in this Charter limits the authority of Parliament or a legislature to advance the equality of status or use of English and French.

Advancement of status and use

English and French linguistic communities in New Brunswick

16.1.(1) The English linguistic community and the French linguistic community in New Brunswick have equality of status and equal rights and privileges, including the right to distinct educational institutions and such distinct cultural institutions as are necessary for the preservation and promotion of those communities.

Role of the legislature and government of New Brunswick

(2) The role of the legislature and government of New Brunswick to preserve and promote the status, rights and privileges referred to in subsection (1) is affirmed.

Proceedings of Parliament

17. (1) Everyone has the right to use English or French in any debates and other proceedings of Parliament.

Proceedings of New Brunswick legislature

(2) Everyone has the right to use English or French in any debates and other proceedings of the legislature of New Brunswick.

Parliamentary statutes and records

18. (1) The statutes, records and journals of Parliament shall be printed and published in English and French and both language versions are equally authoritative.

New Brunswick statutes and records

(2) The statutes, records and journals of the legislature of New Brunswick shall be printed and published in English and French and both language versions are equally authoritative.

Proceedings in courts established by Parliament

19. (1) Either English or French may be used by any person in, or in any pleading in or process issuing from, any court established by Parliament.

Proceedings in New Brunswick courts

(2) Either English or French may be used by any person in, or in any pleading in or process issuing from, any court of New Brunswick.

Communications by public with federal institutions

20. (1) Any member of the public in Canada has the right to communicate with, and to receive available services from, any head or central office of an institution of the Parliament or government of Canada in English or French, and has the same right with respect to any other office of any such institution where
    a) there is a significant demand for communications with and services from that office in such language; or
    b) due to the nature of the office, it is reasonable that communications with and services from that office be available in both English and French.

Communications by public with New Brunswick institutions

(2) Any member of the public in New Brunswick has the right to communicate with, and to receive available services from, any office of an institution of the legislature or government of New Brunswick in English or French.

Continuation of existing constitutional provisions

21. Nothing in sections 16 to 20 abrogates or derogates from any right, privilege or obligation with respect to the English and French languages, or either of them, that exists or is continued by virtue of any other provision of the Constitution of Canada.

Rights and privileges preserved

22. Nothing in sections 16 to 20 abrogates or derogates from any legal or customary right or privilege acquired or enjoyed either before or after the coming into force of this Charter with respect to any language that is not English or French.

Language of instruction

23. (1) Citizens of Canada
    a) whose first language learned and still understood is that of the English or French linguistic minority population of the province in which they reside, or
    b) who have received their primary school instruction in Canada in English or French and reside in a province where the language in which they received that instruction is the language of the English or French linguistic minority population of the province, have the right to have their children receive primary and secondary school instruction in that language in that province.

Continuity of language instruction

(2) Citizens of Canada of whom any child has received or is receiving primary or secondary school instruction in English or French in Canada, have the right to have all their children receive primary and secondary school instruction in the same language.

(3) The right of citizens of Canada under subsections (1) and (2) to have their children receive primary and secondary school instruction in the language of the English or French linguistic minority population of a province

    a) applies wherever in the province the number of children of citizens who have such a right is sufficient to warrant the provision to them out of public funds of minority language instruction; and

    b) includes, where the number of those children so warrants, the right to have them receive that instruction in minority language educational facilities provided out of public funds.

Application where numbers warrant

24. (1) Anyone whose rights or freedoms, as guaranteed by this Charter, have been infringed or denied may apply to a court of competent jurisdiction to obtain such remedy as the court considers appropriate and just in the circumstances.

Enforcement of guaranteed rights and freedoms

  (2) Where, in proceedings under subsection (1), a court concludes that evidence was obtained in a manner that infringed or denied any rights or freedoms guaranteed by this Charter, the evidence shall be excluded if it is established that, having regard to all the circumstances, the admission of it in the proceedings would bring the administration of justice into disrepute.

Exclusion of evidence bringing administration of justice into disrepute

25. The guarantee in this Charter of certain rights and freedoms shall not be construed so as to abrogate or derogate from any aboriginal, treaty or other rights or freedoms that pertain to the aboriginal peoples of Canada including

    a) any rights or freedoms that have been recognized by the Royal Proclamation of October 7, 1763; and

    b) any rights or freedoms that now exist by way of land claims agreements or may be so acquired.

Aboriginal rights and freedoms not affected by Charter

26. The guarantee in this Charter of certain rights and freedoms shall not be construed as denying the existence of any other rights or freedoms that exist in Canada.

Other rights and freedoms not affected by Charter

27. This Charter shall be interpreted in a manner consistent with the preservation and enhancement of the multicultural heritage of Canadians.

Multicultural heritage

28. Notwithstanding anything in this Charter, the rights and freedoms referred to in it are guaranteed equally to male and female persons.

Rights guaranteed equally to both sexes

29. Nothing in this Charter abrogates or derogates from any rights or privileges guaranteed by or under the Constitution of Canada in respect of denominational, separate or dissentient schools. (93)

Rights respecting certain schools preserved

30. A reference in this Charter to a Province or to the legislative assembly or legislature of a province shall be deemed to include a reference to the Yukon Territory and the Northwest Territories, or to the appropriate legislative authority thereof, as the case may be.

Application to territories and territorial authorities

31. Nothing in this Charter extends the legislative powers of any body or authority.

Legislative powers not extended

32. (1) This Charter applies

    a) to the Parliament and government of Canada in respect of all matters within the authority of Parliament including all matters relating to the Yukon Territory and Northwest Territories; and

    b) to the legislature and government of each province in respect of all matters within the authority of the legislature of each province.

Application of Charter

  (2) Notwithstanding subsection (1), section 15 shall not have effect until three years after this section comes into force.

Exception

Exception where express declaration

33. (1) Parliament or the legislature of a province may expressly declare in an Act of Parliament or of the legislature, as the case may be, that the Act or a provision thereof shall operate notwithstanding a provision included in section 2 or sections 7 to 15 of this Charter.

Operation of exception

(2) An Act or a provision of an Act in respect of which a declaration made under this section is in effect shall have such operation as it would have but for the provision of this Charter referred to in the declaration.

Five year limitation

Five year limitation

(3) A declaration made under subsection (1) shall cease to have effect five years after it comes into force or on such earlier date as may be specified in the declaration.

Re-enactment

(4) Parliament or the legislature of a province may re-enact a declaration made under subsection (1).

Five year limitation

(5) Subsection (3) applies in respect of a re-enactment made under subsection (4).

Citation

34. This Part may be cited as the *Canadian Charter of Rights and Freedoms*.

Legal Research

A website that contains all Canadian federal and provincial statutes and many court decisions is: http://www.canlii.org. CanLII is a non-profit organization managed by the Federation of Law Societies of Canada.

The citations for many of the case briefs in the text are given with CanLII citations. However, most other cases referred to in the text can also be found by searching the case name on this website.

Here is what the first Search page looks like. You can fill in the case name or statute in Box no. 2. However, one tip: the search program often does not recognize the "v." in case names. So it is more efficient to put in one or both of the parties names, not the complete citation. For example to find the decision of: *RBC v. Welton* (2008), 89 O.R. (3d) 532; enter the names "RBC Welton".

Statute names can be entered here or you can click on the federal or provincial name on the left hand menu and be brought to a section dedicated to that jurisdiction.

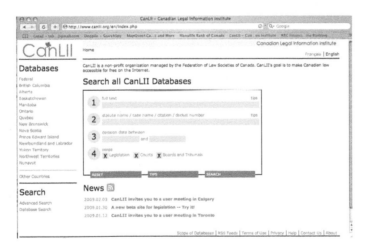

The Canadian Court System

Law and the Legal System

We all encounter laws and the legal system at some time or other in our lives—whether we are buying or selling a house, looking after the estate of a deceased loved one, or getting stopped for speeding on the way to work. When you enter the world of business, encounters with laws and the legal system are likely to be even more frequent. How much time off must you give your employees? Should you incorporate? Can you sue your supplier for delivering goods which were not of the quality you expected? Do you have to pay for injuries suffered by a customer who fell in your store?

There are many ways to define "law." However, laws can be broadly viewed as rules of conduct that are enforced by government-sanctioned agencies (such as the courts or the police). The laws that are set out for individuals and business to follow—or, if not, to face the legal consequences—may be categorized in a variety of ways:

- **private or civil law**—a set of laws that attempt to resolve disputes between individuals (or businesses). For example, if a contract is broken because the wrong goods were delivered, or a person is injured by an unsafe product, these disputes would be governed by civil law. Many contract law and tort law cases fall under civil law.
- **criminal or regulatory law**—a set of laws that attempt to resolve disputes between society generally and certain individuals (or businesses). The results of running afoul of these laws are tickets, fines and or jail time. For example if a company publishes false and misleading advertising it can be fined under The Competition Act. Accountants who assist a client in a tax fraud could be fined and or jailed under the Criminal Code. These laws are created for the best interests of society as a whole.
- **constitutional law**—a set of laws that attempt to resolve disputes between individuals and governments, or between governments and governments, when governments are acting in their capacities as lawmakers. For example, if you are charged under a piece of legislation requiring all bike riders under age 25 to wear helmets, you may try to have the legislation overruled, by claiming that the government that enacted it did not follow the rules of the Constitution (perhaps by discriminating against you on the basis of age).

■ **administrative law**—encompasses a wide variety of government tribunals or boards or commissions that are set up under provincial or federal laws to deal with disputes in specific areas. They are very necessary adjudicators as we do not have the money or resources to handle all of these cases in the regular court system. Often these boards are less formal and sometimes faster and less costly for the parties involved, though not always. For example some of the most well-known administrative tribunals include: the B.C. Human Rights Tribunal, the Immigration Board, the Tax Review Board, the Ontario Landlord Tenant Board and the Ontario Securities Commission. They deal only with complaints in their specific area. Some even have their own second level appeal boards. It can be possible to appeal the decision of an administrative tribunal into the normal civil court system and eventually even proceed up the appeal process to the Supreme Court of Canada, though this rarely occurs. A very large number of legal decisions are made by these administrative tribunals and are necessary for the functioning of society and the legal system.

It is important to note that the goals of each of these types of law are different. Civil law attempts to obtain compensation for the wronged party; criminal or regulatory law attempts to extract punishment (for example, a fine or jail time) from the offending party; and Constitutional or administrative law nullifies certain actions of government if certain rules are not followed. The terminology used is also different—civil law speaks of suing and liability, and the parties involved are called the plaintiff and defendant; criminal or regulatory law speaks of charges or offences, and of guilty or not guilty, and the parties involved are the prosecutor and the accused. Finally, the processes are different. Civil matters are heard in one court, criminal in another, and Constitutional matters are often heard as a separate part of civil or criminal trials.

Note that one incident could lead to an encounter with both the criminal law process and the civil law process. For instance, if you are speeding to make a delivery and run over someone who is crossing the street, that injured person may sue you *and* you may well face charges under the *Highway Traffic Act* of your province. You may have to pay damages to the injured party as well as pay a fine.

Why is all this important? You need to realize that certain actions that you take in the business world may have a variety of consequences. It's important to weigh the possible consequences of your conduct in the business world. You may need to get a lawyer's advice before you take certain action. You may face a civil suit from someone you have allegedly wronged, and you may face criminal charges relating to the same incident. It is possible to get two different results for the same incident in the two different courts. In the criminal trial the accused may be found not guilty because a higher standard of proof is required in criminal law. The crown attorney has to prove **beyond reasonable doubt** that the accused committed the crime. This is a high difficult standard to meet and good defence lawyers can often create reasonable doubt in the mind of the judge or jury. But in civil court the plaintiff has a lower easier burden of proof to meet. They only have to prove **on the balance of probabilities** that the defendant did it. If there is a 51% or more likelihood the defendant committed the act then they can be found liable in a civil trial, even though in a criminal trial with that much doubt they would be found not guilty. For example in a famous U.S. case, the former football star O.J. Simpson was found not guilty in criminal court of the double murder of his ex-wife and a man who was at her home. But in a civil trial almost 2 years later, the families of the two murder victims sued Simpson for the tort of wrongful death. In the civil trial he was found liable for their deaths and ordered to pay them $8.5 million. He never went to jail for their murders, as only the criminal trial could have ordered that punishment, but the civil court held him responsible for the deaths and awarded financial compensation to the victims' families.

criminal law burden of proof
beyond reasonable doubt

civil law burden of proof
on the balance of probabilities

COMPARISON OF CRIMINAL AND CIVIL LAW	
Criminal Law	**Civil Law**
Purpose	
To punish the wrong doer (jail / fines) and to deter others from committing similar crimes	Compensate the victim
Terms	
Accused (wrongdoer), accused is charged with an offence	Defendant (wrongdoer) is sued
Complainant (injured party)	Plaintiff—(the injured party) sues the defendant
Accused is either guilty or not guilty	Defendant is liable or not liable
Lawyers	
The accused selects and pays their own lawyer	Each side selects and pays their own lawyer
Victim does not hire a lawyer, a <u>crown attorney</u> (government lawyer) will prosecute the accused	
Jury	
12 people on the jury, all 12 must agree, if they cannot all agree it is a mistrial	It varies by province—some do not allow juries—in Ontario a 6 person jury and 5 of 6 must agree
Timing	
s.11(b) of the Charter, requires the trial to occur in a "reasonable" time. About 12–14 months for smaller offences, longer if more complicated case	No right to a trial in a reasonable time, often wait 3-5 years for a court date for a large civil trial in a large Canadian city
Burden (Standard) of Proof	
Higher, harder standard of proof, hard to get a conviction, as the crown must prove **BEYOND REASONABLE DOUBT** the accused did it	Easier, lower standard, the plaintiff's lawyer has to prove **ON THE BALANCE OF PROBABILITIES** that the defendant did it

The Common Law System

Judge-Made Law

Judges frequently met and discussed similar cases, and tried to discover those principles that extended generally to all of England and were common to all the people. It is from this that the term common law arose. One such principle was that the eldest son was to be the sole heir to his ancestors. Another was that a transfer of land had to be in writing under seal, or it was ineffective.

It has been said that the unique feature of English culture is not the development of the parliamentary system, for that may be found in many parts of the world, but the survival of a common law system. Many countries today, most of which are former members of the British Empire, including the United States and Canada (except Quebec), use the common law system.

Courts of Equity

This concentration on the strict application of laws—known as the black-letter-law approach—became rigid and was viewed as unfair. So the monarch started his own court to apply fairness, or equity. Now two systems were in place, each with its own court—the common law and equity.

For example, if Joseph Levitt defaulted on his mortgage payment to Susan Scott, in common law court, Susan Scott could take Joseph Levitt's house immediately and sell it. But in a court of equity, Joseph Levitt was given an automatic extension of six months to pay the mortgage.

The courts of equity devised remedies to soften the harsh results of some of the common-law principles. The two courts were merged in 1873, so Canadian courts can apply both common law and equitable law. Where there is a conflict between the two, the laws of equity prevail.

However, it is important to understand that in the Court of Equity, the Judges did not apply their own view of fairness; rather the Courts developed laws that were intended to incorporate principles of fairness. It is a mistake, that even young lawyers make, to believe that a party can go to court and simply say to the judge in spite of the law do what is fair. Judges must apply the law whether the source is equity or common law, and not their own believe of what is fair in a situation.

Binding Precedent

Precedent is the principle in the common law system which requires judges to follow a decision made in a higher court in the same jurisdiction. Once a common principle is declared, it is to be applied in similar circumstances by all judges of equal or lower rank. This principle is called *stare decisis*.

The decisions of individual judges are written down. Certain of these decisions are selected and collected in volumes resembling large sets of encyclopedias. Cases are referred to by a special citation, which tells in which book the case is located. For example, the landmark case in tort law cited as *Donoghue v. Stevenson [1932], A.C. 532* means that the case can be found on page 532 of the 1932 edition of the report on all appeal cases. It is from these law reports that lawyers and judges learn what the law is on a given point.

Legal Research

Today many written decisions are available on-line. The on-line databases contain search features. You can see an example at **www.lexum.com**: if you want to find a case on punitive damages, you search for that term. You can also go to **www.canlii.org** as it also is a very useful source for finding past cases.

The intent of the common law was to eliminate as far as possible the discretion of the individual judge—the law, not a judge's personal belief of what is fair and good, should govern. The outcome of a case should not depend on which judge hears it.

Stare decisis   *Stare decisis*: when a court has once laid down a principle of law as applicable to a certain set of facts, it will adhere to that principle, and apply it to all future cases where facts are substantially the same.

When courts decide a case on specific facts, a general principle from that case can be applied to other similar cases. For example in 1932 in the *Donoghue v. Stevenson* case, a woman drank from a dark bottle of ginger beer that had a dead snail in it. The principles developed in that case set the guiding principles for manufacturers' liability cases ever since. It also established the concept that every person or business has a legal duty to take reasonable care for others who you should reasonably foresee will be affected by your actions.

statutes

summarized or codified short-code formats of common law, comprising acts or legislation passed by Parliament

Government-Made Law

Common law was created by judges. But as the principles became settled, they were sometimes gathered together as **statutes**, summarized or codified short-code formats of common law, comprising acts or legislation passed by Parliament. The *Partnership Act* is an example of a set of principles developed by judges, then put into a statute form that has remained mostly unchanged since.

In some cases, the principle of *stare decisis* meant judges could not alter laws to reflect changing social conditions. Thus, new laws, or modifications to existing laws, had to be introduced by government. Sometimes government has set up special groups to study and advise on new statutes. The *Competition Act* is an example of such a statute—it contains laws concerning abusive monopolistic power and unfair trade practices, such as misleading advertising. These are modern problems, and their solution requires input from many sources, such as economists and businesses. A judge sitting alone on a case would not have access to such resources, and so could not develop principles of law that took into account the complexities of the modern business environment.

In statutory law, if you do not like a law, a way to change it is to elect a new government that promises to pass different legislation. In Ontario in 1995, the Conservative party promised if elected, it would introduce a new law that would allow companies to hire replacement workers when unionized workers were on strike. They were elected and very soon after this new law was passed. The NDP has tried to get the law changed since then, but since it has not been in power the law still stands. Unfortunately politicians also do not always make the changes to laws they promised when they were running for office. A law to significantly change the GST was promised by the federal Liberal party when it was campaigning in the 1993 election. The Liberals won, but the hated GST/HST still very much remains.

The Civil Law (Quebec) System

The legal system in Quebec is different from that in the rest of Canada, and follows a civil-code system rather than a common law approach. Under the civil code, derived from the Greco-Roman approach and later the Napoleonic code, the law is established by government in a written code. The Canadian Criminal Code is another example of a code system that is not made by judges, but is passed by Parliament. A judge cannot create a new criminal offence—only governments can.

If you are doing business in the province of Quebec, be aware that the laws may be quite different from those in the rest of Canada.

Rule of Law

The Rule of Law if stated in modern speech would be: "Law rules!" which means that law is supreme. No one—president, king or prime minister—is above the law. Even a President of the United States, Richard Nixon, was forced to resign in 1974 to avoid impeachment proceedings because he knew that members of his political party were spying on the headquarters of the opposition party.

While the principle of the Rule of Law ensures everyone, even leaders, must obey the law, there is little check on the justice of the law in this concept. Apart from the control that voters may have in a democracy over the fairness of laws, the Charter of Rights and Freedoms was enacted to guarantee that laws could not be passed that violated the principles set out in it. To safeguard this protection the Charter was made part of the Constitution and made supreme.

The role of the courts has been traditionally considered as also subject to the Rule of Law in that their function is limited to deciding whether laws are valid under the Constitution: either under the division of powers sections or the Charter. However, courts cannot force the government to make laws. Only if the government makes a law can the court rule on it. This limitation was in issue in the case of Omar Khadr outlined below.

Canada (Prime Minister) v. Khadr, 2010 SCC3

Omar Khadr is a Canadian citizen who was raised by a radical Islamic family. At the age of fourteen he was brought by his father to Afghanistan to train with Al Qaeda. In 2002, at age 16, the boy allegedly threw a grenade that killed a U.S. medic during a firefight. He was captured and the U.S. government held him prisoner at the Guantanamo Bay military prison in Cuba and eventually charged him with war crimes. The military subjected the boy to interrogation procedures, including sleep deprivation, that violated his Canadian Charter of Rights protections. Canadian government representatives questioned the boy during the time these objectionable procedures were employed and made the transcripts available to the U.S. military. Thus even though Khadr was in U.S. custody and charged with violating U.S. laws, the Supreme Court of Canada held it had jurisdiction to rule on the situation and apply Canadian laws. Khadr's lawyer argued that his Charter rights had been violated. The interrogation of a youth detained without counsel, to elicit statements about serious criminal charges knowing that the youth had been subjected to sleep deprivation

and sharing those statements with U.S. prosecutors he claimed offended the most basic Canadian standards about the treatment of detained youth suspects and our Charter.

The Court's Decision

The Supreme Court agreed that Khadr's Charter rights of fundamental justice had been violated, but it could not do more than make this a declaration. It could not order the federal government to take any action such as seek repatriation of Mr. Khadr from Guantanamo Bay to Canada. Despite this ruling by the Supreme Court, the federal government did not request the U.S. return Khadr to Canada. In 2010 Khadr pleaded guilty to 5 war crimes and was sentenced to 40 years in jail, but a plea bargain reduced it to 8 years. In 2012 he was transferred to Canada to continue to serve his out his jail term. Khadr also has started a civil law suit suing the Canadian government seeking $10 million for the illegal interrogation and for sharing the information it obtained with U.S. officials.

The Canadian Court System

The court system in Canada today has its roots in the history of England, developing over centuries and altering radically with each age. It is currently in a state of change as citizens wonder whether it is the best system for a society entering the 21st century. Litigants are experimenting with other private procedures, such as mediation or arbitration, to resolve disputes, replacing or supplementing the traditional court process. Such procedures are known as **ADR (alternative dispute resolution)**, which is discussed at the end of this chapter.

ADR (alternative dispute resolution)

private procedures, such as mediation or arbitration, to resolve disputes, replacing or supplementing the traditional court process

The Court Structure

There are basically two types of courts in Canada—trial and appeal. There are also three tiers to the court system in Canada. The first tier is the trial court (the court of first instance), the second tier is the provincial court of appeal, and the third tier is the Supreme Court of Canada. The first tier is the only level that does actual trials. The second and third tiers do not conduct trials and are primarily for appeals. Only appeal-court decisions are binding in the sense of creating *stare decisis*. Each province has its own court of appeal, and the final court of appeal is the Supreme Court of Canada, in Ottawa. There are many different names for the various courts in all the provinces, but basically they divide into the two functions. Some higher trial-division courts function as appeal courts for lower trial-division courts.

The trial-level court is the one with which most of us are familiar from television and movies. There, a judge presides, either with or without a jury, and hears witnesses, who are examined and cross-examined by lawyers.

There are different names for trial courts in each province. They are generally divided into two levels; the Provincial (inferior) courts and the Superior court. The Provincial courts would usually conduct trials for small claims court cases (e.g. claims under about $25,000, the amount varies among the provinces though), minor criminal offences, youth court (ages 12–17), provincial offences and traffic violations, and family law matters (except divorce). The Superior trial courts hear major criminal cases, civil cases above the small claims court limit, divorce, surrogate/ probate court cases (dealing with the financial matters of deceased people) and bankruptcy courts. The Superior court in some provinces can act as a Divisional Court and hear appeals on some decisions from provincial courts and various provincial administrative tribunals. Some provinces have also established very specialized trial courts such as; domestic violence courts, drug treatment courts, mental health courts and unified family courts to deal in a more effective way with these specific legal problems.

The appeal court normally hears appeals based on the transcripts of the trial. Because it does not actually see the witnesses, and cannot therefore judge their credibility, appeal courts are reluctant to change findings of fact made by a trial judge or jury. Appeals are usually based on matters of law.

A common basis for an appeal on law is that no appeal-court decision on that point exists in the province, or that there are conflicting decisions. Since Canada is a confederation—a union of separate states—each province is still a separate jurisdiction; therefore a decision of, say, the Ontario Court of Appeal is not binding on any level of court in, for example, the Manitoba court system. Only a Supreme Court of Canada decision is binding throughout Canada.

If the same type of case, involving a new point of law, is heard on the same day by a trial judge in Ontario and one in Manitoba, it is possible that each court will give a different decision. That decision might be appealed to the court of appeal in each province—which also may result in conflicting decisions. The matter would go on to the Supreme Court of Canada, and there the principle that will apply in all of Canada is decided.

Every party to a lawsuit has a right to appeal to the provincial Court of Appeal from a judgment after trial. However, a further appeal to the Supreme Court of Canada is only granted with leave [permission] from that court. The Supreme Court of Canada only gives leave if the case involves a matter of national interest, which normally means it will add to the development of the law. For example, if a new piece of legislation is enacted such as privacy laws, then cases involving issues under that new legislation would likely get permission. This court only gives leave to develop new law.

The Supreme Court of Canada usually gets over 700 applications for appeals annually, but it will only hear about 80–90 appeals per year. There are only 9 judges on the Supreme Court of Canada and when they hear an appeal there are either 5, 7 or 9 judges hearing the appeal.

Appeal courts do not conduct trials, only trial courts can do that. Most appeals, almost 90% lose, as the appeal court agrees with the lower decision and the appeal is dismissed. It is often humorously referred to as the Court of No Appeal. This is a good statistic though as it shows that our lower courts are performing well and not making many errors. There are barriers to success on appeal. Even at the provincial level, there is a test called 'standard of review'. The trial judge sees live witnesses, but the Court of Appeal sees only a transcript of the witnesses' testimony. Therefore the trial judge is in a better position to evaluate credibility, that is whether the witness is truthful. So the appellate court gives respect, called judicial **deference**, to the trial judge's finding of fact. It is very rare that an appellate court overturns a trial judge's finding of fact. To succeed, the appeal usually has to be on a point of law.

deference
to defer to, that is give respect to, another's opinion

However in the approximately 10% of appeals that succeed, the appeal court can take various actions. It can vary the original judgment such as increasing or decreasing the damages awarded or the jail time given. An appeal court can also reverse the trial judgment, such as overturn a criminal conviction. The appeal court can even send a case back down to the trial level and order an entirely new trial if it decides that a significant error was made at the original trial. But the appeal court does not conduct a new trial itself.

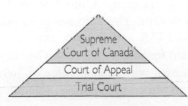

The Role of the Lawyer

solicitors

lawyers who deal with commercial and other legal matters that do not involve going to court

barristers

lawyers who represent clients in court

Lawyers in Canada are technically called barristers and solicitors. **Solicitors** are lawyers who deal with commercial and other legal matters that do not involve going to court. **Barristers** are lawyers who represent clients in court. In England, where the profession developed, these were two separate functions, and remain so today. In pioneer times in early Canada, there were not enough professionals to allow for specialization, and so each lawyer was qualified both as a barrister and a solicitor.

Lawyers originally in Britain were very wealthy members of the ruling class and they would represent the uneducated peasants for free, as their *noblesse oblige*, the obligation of the nobility. As economic circumstances evolved and a middle class grew, they began to charge for their services. Today in Canada there are over 90,000 lawyers (2.8 per 1,000 people) and they charge anywhere from $75 to over $1,000 per hour for their services. A lawyer with 10 years' experience would normally charge about $300 per hour. If a low income person requires a lawyer and cannot pay for one, in some situations they will qualify for government funded Legal Aid which will allow them to hire a lawyer. There are many types of cases where people are not entitled to Legal Aid or they make more than the qualifying income level so won't qualify for Legal Aid, but they still can't afford a lawyer. This can create many difficulties when someone goes to court without a lawyer and it is a growing problem in Canada of people representing themselves in court. It is estimated that in Ontario and B.C. now about 60 per cent of people who appear in family court have no lawyer and end up representing themselves. This creates significant problems and shows how the legal system is becoming inaccessible for the average Canadian person due to the high price of legal services.

Juries

There is a difference between civil and criminal juries. The right to a jury in most serious criminal offences applies everywhere in Canada, but civil juries have been abolished in about half of the provinces. In Ontario civil jury trials still exist and a jury is composed of 6 people. Five of the six jurors must agree to reach a decision. A plaintiff or a defendant can request a jury trial, but a judge can refuse to have a jury try the case if they think the evidence is too technical or difficult for an average person to understand, such as in some complex commercial trials or medical malpractice cases. In B.C. if a party requests a civil jury trial they have to pay significant fees to have a jury and this has significantly reduced the number of jury trials in that province.

Juries decide issues of fact, not law. The judge instructs the jury in the law they must apply to the facts that the jury determines. For example, a homeowner is sued by a pedestrian for not clearing the snow from the sidewalk in front of the house. The evidence is that the snowfall occurred overnight, and ended by 7:00 a.m. The pedestrian slipped at 4:00 p.m. the same day. The judge would instruct the jury that, by law, they must decide how soon after such a snowfall a reasonable homeowner would have cleared the sidewalk.

American jury awards have become notorious. They are so much larger than those in other countries that many European nations, as well as Australia, have passed specific laws, informally called blocking statutes, to prevent the enforcement of U.S. jury awards in their countries. Canadian juries typically do not give large awards. In fact, in many cases, it is the defending insurance-company lawyer who chooses the jury because of the Canadian jury's reluctance to find liability or make large awards. Also, Canadian courts of appeal will set aside lower jury awards which they consider unjustified—U.S. courts of appeal will not generally do this.

The large awards given by juries in the United States have made an impact on how Canadians view the civil court system. The population in general does not realize the vast difference between Canadian and U.S. jury awards, and decries what is seen as outrageous amounts of money being awarded for minor suffering. One of the most controversial cases in the early 1990s was that of a woman who spilled coffee on herself and was awarded US $3.5 million against McDonald's. This award was reduced on appeal to $800,000. Such cases are not representative of Canadian jury findings of liability or awards, and make the task of Canadian lawyers in advising clients regarding potential court claims more difficult. Some people, influenced by the American jury decisions, feel that if they are injured, someone automatically has to pay, and pay a large amount, no matter how trivial the injury.

Juries are more frequently used in the US because American state judges are elected. American trial lawyers do not trust their competence or independence. All Canadian judges are appointed after consultation with the legal profession, and are more trusted by Canadian civil trial lawyers than their American elected counterparts.

The Stages in a Lawsuit (Higher-Level Courts)

Jurisdiction

Before you can sue another party you must determine what court has **jurisdiction**, the legal right to hear the civil case. The plaintiff has the choice and they can sue where the event occurred or where the defendant lives. The court in that location(s) is allowed to try the case. Under certain circumstances either side may ask the trial to be moved to a different jurisdiction, but there must be a compelling reason to do so.

jurisdiction
the court which has the legal right to hear the civil case

Limitation Periods

The right to sue does not last forever. A plaintiff must sue within a certain time after the event happened that gave rise to the right to sue, technically called a **cause of action**. Action is the name used in litigation for a lawsuit. The plaintiff in a civil action must be sure to start the legal proceedings within a specific time limit referred to as the **limitation period**. These limitation periods vary greatly across Canada from a matter of days to up to 20 years. It depends very much on the type of claim that is being made, who is being sued, what court has jurisdiction and if there are any relevant laws establishing a specific limitation period.

cause of action
the right to sue
limitation period
time limit on a right to sue

Several provinces have moved to have a 2 year limitation period for all civil claims. This means the plaintiff must start the legal proceedings within two years from the day on which the plaintiff discovered or should have discovered the damages or cause of action. If you do not start the court action within the appropriate limitation period, it will be too late and you will be prohibited from pursuing your claim. It is very important to contact a lawyer to find out how much time you have to start your claim so that you do not miss the limitation date. For the purposes of the book we will assume a two year limitation period.

For example, a business supplies a shipment of mobile phones to a retailer who agrees to pay $10,000 for them on July 1, 2013 but does not. The plaintiff supplier would have until June 30, 2015 (2 years later) to start a lawsuit. One day past that and the right to sue would be barred because of the expiry of the limitation period.

A fundamental issue: when does the period begin to run? It starts when the plaintiff knew, or should have known, all the elements that would give rise to the cause of action. Thus, it is not only when the breach of a legal obligation happened, but when the plaintiff knew of a right to sue because of the event.

For example, a business purchases a piece of vacant land for future development by relying on an expert report that there are no environmental issues. The report is made on June 1, 2013. In normal circumstances, the limitation period would begin to run from that date. However, the land is not developed for 10 years, until June 1, 2023. On that day a contractor discovers underground pools of toxic waste: the expert was negligent. Since the toxic pools were not discoverable until the contractor started digging, the limitation period runs from that date even though it is 10 years after the report was done.

Acknowledgment of a Debt

Most provinces have an extension provision. If the debt is acknowledged after the time that the cause of action arose and before the expiry of the limitation time, that acknowledgment will start the limitation period running from that date. So in the example above involving the sale of the mobile phones, if the purchaser had acknowledged that debt, say, one day before the expiry of the limitation period, the period would start to run from that date:

- Default in payment—July 1, 2013
- Normal expiry of limitation—June 30, 2015
- Acknowledgment—June 30, 2015
- New limitation period expires—June 29, 2017

In one case a business noted an amount owing to a supplier in its financial statements. The supplier sued after the default in payment (which was after the basic limitation period), but within the limitation time after the note in the financial statement. The court held that the note in the financial statement was an acknowledgment of debt and the limitation period began again from that date. The lawsuit was not barred. (*Freeway Properties Inc v Genco Resources Ltd*, 2012 BCCA 258

Ultimate Limitation Period

Beyond the basic discoverable time limit, there is an ultimate period of fifteen years. Even if the matter is not discoverable until after that time, the lawsuit is still barred. So in the example above, if the owner did not discover the toxic waste pools and hence the negligence of the expert until June 2, 2028, its lawsuit would be barred.

Critical Concepts

- A limitation period on the right to sue begins to run when a person knew, or should have known of, the cause of action
- There is a basic limitation period, which is usually 2 years
- The basic limitation period can be extended if a person acknowledges a debt within the limitation period
- There is an ultimate limitation period of fifteen years.

■ *Business Law* Applied

❶ **Faruk Vahman lent** Miller Enterprises $10,000. Miller agreed to repay it on June 1, 2014. Miller could not pay on that day and wrote on August 1, 2014 saying it had a cash flow problem and asked for an extension of time. Vahman did nothing then to enforce payment, but put the letter in a file and forgot about it.

On June 2, 2016 he came across the file and noted that the loan was never repaid. Vahman wants to sue.

a) What is the basic limitation period here?
b) When did it expire?
c) Is there any ground for extending the basic limitation period?

Even if it is the government who is taking legal action, the limitation periods apply to them as well. The Markevich case clearly illustrate this as the federal and provincial governments lost out on $1.26 billion in unpaid taxes as Revenue Canada failed to take a large number of taxpayers to court within the limitation period. Revenue Canada pursued tax offenders much faster after this decision and the government also passed a law to extend the limitation period for unpaid taxes.

Markevich v. Canada, 2003 SCC 9

Joe Markevich, a B.C. stock promoter, was informed in 1986 by the Ministry of National Revenue that he owed unpaid federal and provincial taxes totalling $234,136 for the years 1980 to 1985. Markevich did not challenge the assessment, but he didn't pay any of the amount owing. Revenue Canada wrote off the debt internally since Markevich had not paid. From 1987 until 1998 Revenue Canada made no effort to collect the debt, and in fact annual notices sent to him during this period, did not even refer to this large unpaid tax debt still owing. Finally in 1998, 12 years later, Revenue Canada notified Markevich that the unpaid tax debt with accrued interest had grown to $770,583 and it was going to take legal action to obtain this money. Markevich however argued that a 6 year limitation period applied in this case to both the federal and provincial taxes owed. He argued that since Revenue Canada had made no legal efforts to collect this debt for 12 years, the limitation period had passed, so he no longer had to pay this debt. Revenue Canada vigorously rejected this argument claiming that those statutes did not apply to it and an unpaid tax bill was enforceable at any time, like a final judgment given by a court.

The Court's Decision

The Supreme Court ruled that the 6 year limitation periods set in the relevant federal law and B.C. law applied to Revenue Canada. It had clearly not taken any action to enforce the debt within the 6 year limit, it had waited 12 years, so it could no longer collect the unpaid taxes from Markevich. Limitation periods are established so that cases will proceed in a reasonable time and the government cannot sleep on its rights. If it makes no effort to collect unpaid taxes for an extended period, after a certain point a taxpayer may reasonably expect that they will not have to pay and conduct their lives accordingly. This case set an important precedent and applied to over 70,000 Canadians who had back taxes owing under similar time frames. As a result the federal and provincial governments were unable to collect $1.26 billion dollars in unpaid taxes because Revenue Canada had waited for more than 6 years to enforce these debts. Since this case, the law has been changed extending the limitation period for unpaid tax debts to 10 years.

Pleadings

A lawsuit involves several different stages. It is commenced by a document issued under the seal of the court. In some provinces this document is called a writ of summons, and in others it is called a statement of claim. There is a charge for issuing one of these with the courts, which can be substantial (it varies by province, but is in the range of $150 to $250). After the initial document is issued by the courts, it has to be served on the party who will be the defendant in the lawsuit. Then the other party will file a document called the statement of defence, giving his answer to the allegations set out in the statement of claim. The statement of defence is filed with the courts, and then served on the plaintiff (the person who started the lawsuit). The statements of claim and defence are referred to as the pleadings—they are very brief outlines of each party's case, the law that they claim applies and the monetary damages and/or other remedies they want, plus interest plus legal costs. The defendant must file their statement of defence within a specified time period, often one month. If you are served with a statement of claim do not ignore it. If a statement of defence is not filed within the appropriate time, the plaintiff can ask the court to rule in their favour and make a default judgment against the defendant, even though the defendant has never presented their side of the case.

Plaintiff   The word **plaintiff** derives from an old French word, *plaint*, which means accuse or charge. *Complaint* derives from the same word. The plaintiff is the person who starts the lawsuit.

Legalese

Discovery of Documents

While the pleadings set out the basic claim and defence, particularly in business litigation, documentary evidence can be key to assessing the case. The next stage of a lawsuit is an exchange of documents by both sides of the case. Each side provides a list of the relevant documents it has, usually sworn in the form of an affidavit. Each side can then examine the documents in possession of the other side—unless one side is using special legal rules to claim that the opposing side is not entitled to look at a particular document. If there are a lot of documents in the case, they are scanned and entered into a computer database for easy review and management.

E-mail and files on a computer are considered documents and must be revealed in each party's affidavit of documents.

Affidavit   An **affidavit** is a document sworn under oath, used as evidence in a judicial proceeding. Instead of physically getting up in a court and swearing to tell the truth, a person swears to tell the truth in the written document. Affidavit derives from *affiance* (Old French) which means to promise or swear.

Examination for Discovery

After receiving the opposite party's documents, the next step is usually the examination for discovery. This is a process in which each side gets to ask the other any relevant questions pertaining to the case. Though the proceeding does not take place in a courtroom and no judge is present, the person giving the testimony is sworn in, and there is a court reporter present, taking down the evidence word for word. A transcript is produced from the court reporter's work, so that the lawyers can review and use it in the proceedings.

Examinations for discovery are a very useful part of the court process. Sometimes a lawyer can get the other side to make an admission useful to his or her case. As well, the person testifying is committed to certain answers on paper, and cannot change the story at trial without his or her credibility coming into question. Discovery can also be used to encourage settlement. Once the whole story comes out, the sides are better able to assess their chances for success. Settlement before a trial may well be the desirable course of action.

Pretrial Conference

If no settlement is forthcoming, there may be an opportunity for an assessment by an independent third party—usually in the form of a pretrial conference or a case conference. In this process, the parties meet with a judge or senior trial **counsel** (a lawyer, usually a barrister or a mediator), who discusses the case and gives an opinion on who has the stronger one. Cases often settle at this stage, after both sides hear the view of one of these experienced legal professionals. The success of these meetings has caused some provinces to move them up earlier in the course of the lawsuit.

counsel
a lawyer, usually a barrister

Settlement

At any stage of a lawsuit the parties can negotiate an out of court settlement. It is estimated that almost 90 percent of cases never go to trial, as the parties have settled. It is usually faster, cheaper as it saves on the legal fees of a trial, and there is no uncertainty as to the result, as the parties have negotiated an outcome that is acceptable to all concerned. If a settlement is reached the plaintiff is usually required to sign a **release** that releases the defendant from any further legal action regarding this case. Often in the release is a **confidentiality clause**, a gag clause, which prohibits the plaintiff from revealing any details of the settlement. Many businesses want to avoid publicity or setting a precedent in the amount of awards so they insist upon the confidentiality clause. Parties must be very careful not to breach this confidentiality clause because if the other party finds out it may result in having to pay back some or even all of the settlement money that you received. People or their relatives who have put Facebook postings or written indicating they got "something," have been held liable for breach of this term and had to pay back money, even though no specific dollar amount was mentioned. (see the Jan Wong case in Chapter 13)

release
document that releases defendant from any further legal action in this case

confidentiality clause
prohibits parties from disclosing the terms of a settlement with others

The Trial Process

After all this, if the parties still cannot agree on a settlement, a trial will be conducted. The trial itself is based on a combat model, and is purely adversarial. That means each party's lawyer tries to win and there is no compromise. At the end, there is a winner and a loser. An ancient Arab felt the full force of this process, for there is an old Arab curse that says: "May you be involved in a lawsuit in which you know you are right!"

In a civil trial the plaintiff and the defendant make opening arguments to the court briefly outlining the case they plan to present. Then the plaintiff begins to present their case and call their witnesses. A witness is asked questions by the plaintiff's lawyer in a process called an examination in chief. The defendant can then cross-examine that witness immediately after. Given that trials are often not held until 3–5 years after the critical event occurred, good cross examination may reveal weaknesses in the perception or memory of a witness. This questioning process continues on for every witness for the plaintiff's case. The defendant then calls its witnesses and the questioning proceeds in the same manner. Once all the witnesses have been called each side presents its closing arguments.

The trial process can be viewed as containing two sections: first, fact finding; and then, application of law to those facts. What the parties claim in their pleadings are considered allegations. They are not facts until a judge so decides based on the evidence that the parties present to establish those facts.

The fact finding process is governed by the law of evidence. From experience gained over centuries of hearing disputes, judges developed rules to assist in dealing with the fact finding process. The laws of evidence perform a critical sort function. They exclude some evidence judges have found to be so unreliable and hence potentially misleading, that it should not even be admitted into the fact finding stage of the trial.

One of the most well known of these rules is the Hearsay Exclusion rule. Witnesses can only testify to what they know from direct personal knowledge not from what others have told them. For simplification hearsay can be thought of as a repetition by a witness of what someone else said (or wrote). The person who originally said the statement is not in the courtroom.

Example: Hearsay: during a pedestrian knockdown traffic accident trial, the defendant driver, who is accused of running a red light, says: "I have proof the light was green. My friend John was standing on the corner and he told me he saw for certain the light was green." But John is not called as a witness. The repetition of what John has allegedly said is hearsay.

Hearsay is not rejected because it is untrue. In the example above John may very well have said that. It is rejected because of its form. The courts have heard so many people claim to repeat what others say, but when that person is called as a witness, that person often has quite a different version of the statement.

So the judges decided that they could not rely on hearsay statements, but decided to exclude them and require that the person who made the statement be called. Again referring to the example above, if John were called he might not confirm that he was even on the street corner, or that he recalls the light. Under cross-examination it might be disclosed that he actually needs to wear glasses and wasn't wearing them at the time, his view was blocked because a large truck was in the intersection as well and many other possibilities.

Business Records

Proof of fact by business records is commonly necessary in business litigation. These records are often hearsay and would require that the employees who made them would have to be called. This could be a serious problem because the employees may be out of the country, sick or even dead. Perhaps a large number of employees would be involved and given the modern use of the internet, many may be living in a large number of countries. So a business records exception to the Hearsay Rule was developed.

Example: Business Record Exception. A business that manufactures cell phones has to prove loss of profits as part of its claim. It has records on its computers of all of its sales for the past five years. These records are made by any number of the twenty staff in its accounting department some of whom are in Toronto, Canada and some of whom are in New Delhi,

India, some have left the employment. All input was by data entry from invoices. The litigation started 2 years ago.

Under business records exception to the hearsay rule, if the business can prove that the records were made in its ordinary course of business, and that seems probable in the above example, then the records are admissible without having to call each of the staff who actually made the entry.

That business has to give notice in advance of the trial and permit the opposite party to inspect the records if demanded.

What is the guarantee of truth of business records? Businesses will usually keep accurate records for their own purposes. In the above example the records go back five years three of which were before the litigation became known. In addition, the ability of the opposite party to inspect is a further guarantee of the truth.

The Standard of Proof

Who wins? If the plaintiff can meet the civil "standard of proof," he or she will win. Standard of proof refers to how strong a case the plaintiff must have to win. In a civil case, it is a "balance of probabilities"—in other words, "more likely than not," or a 51 percent probability. In a criminal trial the standard of proof (usually on the Crown) is considerably higher—beyond a reasonable doubt—and so the Crown has to have a very strong case to convict someone under the criminal law.

The Impact of Electronic Documents on Litigation

Computers have affected the use of evidence in litigation. Relevant e-mail and other electronic data stored on computer hard drives are documents which must be disclosed. Sometimes lawyers obtain a court order to have the opposite party's hard drive inspected by a computer technician to see if all documents have been produced and to recover any deleted documents and earlier drafts.

Documents that are "deleted" are not completely erased from a hard drive. Usually only the first letter of the file is turned to a symbol such as an asterisk so that when the original file name is entered, there is no match and the file will not be found. However, the file remains until all "bits," which are randomly scattered over the hard drive, have been overwritten. A data-recovery expert can often recover much of the content of deleted files.

Even technically sophisticated people get caught by this. Bill Gates was confronted with recovered deleted e-mail comments that were damaging to his company's case in an antitrust suit brought by the U.S. government against Microsoft.

There has been some suggestion that judges may tend to give more weight to e-mail messages over their paper counterparts on the belief that e-mail reflects the true thoughts of the author. Written letters are often edited by other parties but that rarely happens to e-mails.

"Throw down your E-mail address!"

Business Alert!   Destruction of Business Documents   The near universal use of computers and the ease of printing on paper and of copying and storing documents electronically has caused new concerns in business litigation. Often the news media reports cases of business documents surfacing in high profile inquiries and litigation to the embarrassment of the author.

It is now crucial for a business to determine a document retention/destruction policy in advance of any litigation to avoid charges that the business has destroyed the documents to eliminate harmful evidence. In general, three principles are recommended to determine a document retention policy:

(i) records should be destroyed as a class rather than selectively,

(ii) records pertaining to known litigation should not be destroyed, and

(iii) confidential records should be destroyed in a way that preserves their confidentiality.

During a trial it may come out that one or both of the parties have been involved in tax fraud to either avoid income tax or payment of GST or PST. Judges have noted this in their decisions and instructed the Registrar of the court to send the decision to the relevant government departments.

Business Alert!

Social Networking Sites

Another relatively new development in litigation is the use of information posted on social networking sites. Pages from those sites, if they contain relevant information must be disclosed.

For example, if a plaintiff is involved in a motor vehicle accident and claims disability and loss of enjoyment of life, pictures on his Facebook page showing him drinking and dancing at a party would be relevant. Note that the entire Facebook contents may have to be produced as it would be reasonable to conclude that there would likely be relevant photographs. The fact that a site is private does not alter the disclosure obligation.

Employers, who have been sued for wrongful dismissal, have successfully used employees' postings on Facebook and similar sites against former employees in lawsuits.

Judgment

At the end of the trial, the judge pronounces a conclusion in the form of a judgment. Sometimes he or she does this immediately after the end of the trial, sometimes months afterward (depending on the complexity of the case). If a party is unhappy with the outcome, there is a possibility of appeal to a higher court, and ultimately perhaps to the Supreme Court of Canada.

Remedies

The court judgment will then set out any remedies that are appropriate for the case. In most civil cases the most common and important remedy is money, referred to as monetary damages. Damages are meant to compensate the injured party for the losses they have suffered. There are various categories for monetary damages:

Types of Monetary Damages:

a) **Pecuniary Damages** – this is money awarded to the victim to compensate for financial losses such as lost wages, medical costs and repair costs. This can include provable economic losses up until the actual trial as well as estimates of future losses such as future lost wages and future care costs. There is no maximum limit on these damages and the award can be in the millions if the injured party had a high paying job and cannot work or if there are very high medical costs for a long period of time.

b) **Non-pecuniary Damages** – this is money awarded for non-financial losses such as pain and suffering, loss of enjoyment of life and a shortened life expectancy. In 1978 the Supreme Court of Canada set a maximum limit on these types of damages at $100,000 and this amount has only increased with inflation. Today a person suffering a catastrophic

Stages of a Law Suit

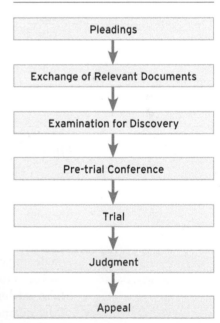

injury, the most they could receive for non-pecuniary damages would be approximately $375,000. Many people have questioned whether this amount is too low. In the United States there is no limit on the damages for pain and suffering and often millions are award under this category of compensation. In Canada they may get millions under pecuniary damages, but not or non-pecuniary damages.

c) **Aggravated Damages** – Aggravated damages are awarded because of the malicious nature of the defendant's conduct. They are designed to compensate the plaintiff specifically for the additional harm caused to the plaintiff's feelings by reprehensible or outrageous conduct on the part of the defendant. This is money awarded for mental anguish, mental distress, humiliation or emotional upset. There must be medical proof of this claim, and though there is no maximum limit set on this type of damages, in Canada an award of $50,000 would be considered quite large. The amount awarded is included in the total for non-pecuniary damages, so this amount is combined with any other award for general damages for pain and suffering and together they cannot exceed the maximum cap allowed. These damages are sometimes awarded in an employment law case where an employer has wrongfully fired a worker in a cruel and embarrassing manner causing significant psychological impact.

d) **Punitive Damages** – Punitive (or exemplary) damages are extra money awarded to punish intentionally bad behaviour. If the court finds that the defendant's behaviour is malicious, deliberate, high-handed and beyond the ordinary standards of decent behaviour, these damages may be awarded. There is no maximum limit on punitive damages in Canada, but $1 million is considered to be at the upper limit in many cases. In *Whitten v. Pilot Insurance* 2002 SCC 18 (See chapter 15) an insurance company was ordered to pay a client $1 million in punitive damages when it falsely accused them of setting their own house on fire. The highest ever awarded in punitive damages in Canada in a corporate case is just under $5 million. In the U.S. the highest award for punitive damages was $145 billion made against tobacco companies for intentionally selling cigarettes that they knew were dangerous deadly products.

e) **Nominal Damages** – A nominal (or small) amount is awarded when the plaintiff suffered no real economic losses or injury but a legal right was violated. The court will order the defendant to pay a nominal amount such as $1–1,000 to acknowledge their legal claim. Given the high cost of legal fees, there are not many cases involving claims for nominal damages.

Non-monetary Remedies

Though in the great majority of civil cases the plaintiff is seeking money as their main remedy there are some important non-monetary remedies that the court can also award. These include:

a) **Injunction** – An injunction is a stop order from the court. For example a court can order a defendant to: stop trespassing, stop polluting or stop soliciting former clients. This can be a very powerful and important remedy in certain cases

b) **An order of Specific Performance** – in certain contract law cases a court can order the defendant to perform the exact contract. This remedy however is generally limited to contracts that are for the sale of something rare and unique such as the sale of a rare antique car or a unique piece of real estate. If a seller refused to complete the deal in one of these sales, the buyer could ask the court for an order of specific performance so that the contract would be completed. If the contract was for the sale of a 2012 used Ford F150 truck though, the court would not issue an order of specific performance as that truck as it is not rare or unique. The plaintiff would have to buy a replacement truck and sue for any difference in price.

c) **An Accounting of Profits** – in certain cases the defendant is ordered to pay the plaintiff any profits that they have wrongfully earned (e.g. such as profits from the sales of illegal copies of DVDs)

d) **Deliver Up Order** – the court may order the defendant to deliver to the plaintiff certain illegal items that the defendant has in its possession (e.g. such as illegal copies of DVDs still in the defendant's possession).

e) **Anton Piller Order** – the court may issue an Anton Piller order which allows a search of the defendant's property and the seizure of evidence such as illegal goods (e.g. this could be requested when a creator wants to raid the warehouse where they know illegal copies are being made of their products)

Louis Vuitton Malletier S.A. v. 486353 B.C. Ltd., 2008 BCSC 799

The famous French designer, Louis Vuitton aggressively pursues companies around the world that make or sell illegal copies of their expensive products such as: purses, wallets, luggage and scarves. They have conducted over 13,000 legal actions around the world, made over 6,000 raids and have had over 950 arrests of people who make and sell illegal copies of their products. In B.C. in 2004 they suspected two companies and 4 people, who operated several stores in the Greater Vancouver area, were selling fake Louis Vuitton products. Louis Vuitton got an Anton Piller order to search their premises and discovered hundreds of illegal items. The court also issued an injunction to stop them from continuing to sell any more of these illegal copies. The owners ignored the court order and continued to sell the fakes in 2006. Louis Vuitton threatened legal action again, but to avoid going to court, the offenders agreed to stop their activities. However they continued to import and sell the fake Louis Vuitton products until 2008 when they were caught again and finally went to trial.

The Court's Decision

The Court ruled that this was a repeated intentional violation of Canada's laws on passing off, copyright and trademark and the defendants had violated the court's injunction order to seize and desist this behaviour. The court awarded damages of over $980,000 including an award of $300,000 in punitive damages because the behaviour of the defendants was a deliberate and inexcusable repeat violation of the plaintiff's legal rights. Court costs of about $50,000 were also awarded against the defendants. At the time this was the highest award given for counterfeit products in Canada. In 2011 Louis Vuitton and Burberry were awarded a total of $2.5 million in damages in a similar B.C. case involving the sale of illegal copies of their products. These large awards may help to establish protection for copyrights and trademarks in Canada.

Legal Costs

Both parties in a civil law suit will ask for their legal costs when filing their initial pleadings. The losing party usually will be required to pay part, but not all of the legal costs of the successful side. The amount they have to pay is determined by a pre-set scale set by the province and this does not usually cover the full legal costs. Costs can be awarded on a "party and party" cost basis or sometimes a higher "solicitor and client" cost basis, but this results in usually only about 50–65% of the actual costs of the successful party being paid by the losing party. So even if you successfully sue someone, you still must pay close to one third to one half of your own legal expenses. This often discourages people from taking legal action.

Enforcing the Judgment

Obtaining a judgment does not mean that you will get paid. There is no magic in a judgment. If the debtor does not have any assets, the individual cannot be made to pay. Also, the courts do not automatically enforce a judgment: the successful party must do so. There are several ways to enforce a judgment. If:

- you do not know whether the debtor has assets, or where they might be located, you can ask to have the individual brought in front of the court to reveal assets by a process known as an examination of a debtor, or a **judgment debtor examination**
- someone else owes money to the debtor, such as an employer or a bank, you can ask the court to seize this money from the third party directly by a process known as **garnishment**

debtor examination
debtor reveals under oath what assets they own

garnishment
court order that allows another to get money from a debtor's bank account or part of their wages

- the debtor owns personal property, such as a car or boat, you can ask the court for a **writ of seizure and sale** which is a court order to have specific property seized by a court official (often a sheriff) and sold at a government auction. Not all the personal possessions of the defendant can be seized, as there are limits on personal goods that the defendant is allowed to keep and cannot be taken.
- the debtor owns real estate, the court will seize and sell this property

While debtor's prison has been abolished, if a debtor is served with an appointment by the court to attend on a debtor's examination, but refuses to do so, that is contempt of court. For repeated violations, the court may issue a warrant for arrest, and have the debtor detained in jail. Usually, the debtor is released after one night. However, it is a very effective remedy.

The Small Claims Court

The procedure of a small claims court is very similar to that of a higher court (described above), but it is more streamlined. The small claims court is basically a do-it-yourself court, designed to be used without the need for a lawyer. Small claims court clerks are trained to help people conduct their own litigation.

The small claims court offices are usually listed under the provincial ministry of the Attorney General, and they supply free pamphlets on how they function. It is easy to sue in the small claims court, and therefore they are of great use to a business in collecting unpaid accounts, bad cheques, and the like.

If you feel uncomfortable conducting an action by yourself, you can retain a lawyer, a law student, or a paralegal to assist you.

Which Small Claims Court?

There are many small claims courts within a province, and even within any particular city. You must file your claim in the office closest to:

- where the problem occurred—for example, where the contract was made, or
- where the defendant lives, or carries on business

It is often advisable to choose the court closest to where the defendant lives or carries on business, for any judgment obtained will have to be enforced through that court. If you file your claim in a different court, then you will be required to take the extra step of registering the judgment in the court closest to the defendant anyway.

Monetary Limits

Small claims court can deal, literally, only with small claims. The monetary limit varies with each province, and changes from time to time. In Quebec the small claims courts will only hear claims up to $7,000 but claims of up to $25,000 will be heard in small claims courts in B.C., Alberta, Newfoundland, Nova Scotia and Ontario. In Alberta they are considering raising this limit to $50,000 to help relieve the backlog of cases in the higher courts and to make access to justice affordable for more people. If your claim exceeds your provincial limit, you can waive (give up the right) to the excess amount over the small claims limit and then proceed to small claims court. . For example if a person wants to sue a company in Ontario for $29,000 they could waive $4,000 of their claim and sue for $25,000 in small claims court. People will often do this because after you pay lawyer's fees and endure the long wait for a higher court, it is more cost effective to reduce your claim to the maximum amount allowed in small claims court, represent yourself in a small claims court trial and get a quicker decision.

How to Start a Small Claims Court Action

An action is started by having the court issue a claim. Formal documents in a court action are called pleadings. The main ones are a statement of claim and a statement of defence.

You can obtain a form for a claim free from any small claims court office. It merely asks you to fill in background data, such as your own name and address, and the defendant's name and address, and to give a very short statement of the reasons for your claim.

You should attach any documents, such as an NSF cheque, purchase orders, or invoices, to support your claim.

Interest and Costs

You can claim interest on the sum owed if interest is part of the contract. For example, if someone purchased goods from a business whose purchase order said that interest at 2 percent per month (26.82 percent per annum) would be charged on the unpaid balance after 30 days, then interest at that stated amount could be included in the claim. Even if interest is not agreed upon, the courts will allow interest at a rate established by the Rules of Court. This rate is roughly equivalent to the current prime rate.

Fast Judgments

Many small claims court actions are not defended. If that is the case, the clerk of the small claims court may sign a judgment for you in the office. If the claim is of some complexity, the clerk may refer the matter to an uncontested hearing before a judge. In any event, the time taken to obtain such a judgment is much faster than if the matter is defended.

The Defendant's Options

There are several possible responses to a claim. The defendant:

- may feel that none, or only a part, of the money is owing, and must then file a defence;
- may have a claim—a counterclaim—against the plaintiff;
- may be responsible to the plaintiff, but may in turn have a claim against another party for some or all of the amount owed to the plaintiff. This is called a third-party claim.

■ *Business Law*   Applied

❷ **Ukani Enterprises Inc.** wants to sue Moez Amyn because he has not paid for supplies delivered to him. Amyn owes $32,000, and the limit of the small claims court in Ukani's province is $25,000. After Ukani consults a lawyer and is quoted a fee of $8,000, the firm realizes that it would be better to proceed in small claims court. Ukani Enterprises drafts a claim for $32,000, but the clerk at the court refuses to accept it, saying it is over the limit.

a) Is there any way Ukani could proceed in the small claims court? If so, how?

Trial

If the claim is defended, it will have to go to trial. Small claims court judges are used to dealing with people prosecuting their own claims, and they will assist. All you have to do is tell your story as briefly and concisely as possible, and show the judge all documents related to the claim. Make certain the defendant has copies of all documents well in advance of the trial.

Getting the Money

To enforce a small claims judgment it is the same method as other civil judgments. If the defendant will not pay, you may need to have a debtor's examination and then once you have determined their assets, request garnishment orders and/or seizure and sale orders from the court so that you can actually get the money awarded in the judgment.

Business Law Applied

❸ **Natasha Pushkov has** a judgment against Al's Carpentry Shop for $2,000 because of poor-quality work. Al refuses to pay. Pushkov believes Al is doing current work, and probably has money in a bank account. She has no idea at which bank that account is located.

a) How can Pushkov find out where Al's bank account is?
b) If Al fails to appear, what can be done to him?

Business Alert!

Collecting Accounts   In collecting accounts, the race is to the swift. A business must have a system in place for identifying overdue accounts, and taking immediate action.

- Have customers agree in their purchase orders to pay all accounts within 30 days, or to pay interest on any overdue amount. The interest must be stated at an annual rate, e.g., 2 percent per month (26.82 percent per annum).
- Set up a collection procedure—preferably a phone call—that operates routinely whenever accounts are not promptly paid.
- Follow up with a demand letter insisting that if the account is not paid by a certain date, then collection proceedings will be started.
- If these actions are unsuccessful, consider going to small claims court, or hiring a collection agency or lawyer, to sue on the outstanding debt.

The Class Action Law Suit

The difficulty of an ordinary citizen's bringing a court action against a huge multinational corporation was dramatized in the public eye by the thalidomide cases in the 1970s. An ordinary family with a baby severely deformed by a prescription drug not only faced the emotional trauma of the situation, but they would also have to meet significant additional medically related expenses. Then they would face bringing a lawsuit against a large drug company that could hire the best team of lawyers and medical experts, and that could afford to spend millions of dollars in defence of the case. The plaintiff family would have to pay for a lawyer, medical witnesses, and various court costs that could easily exceed $100,000 or more. A typical family could not afford such litigation.

The solution to righting the balance of power between ordinary persons and giant corporations was the development of the class action. Although the concept had existed earlier, the right to bring such an action was severely restricted. A class action is an action brought by one or more individuals on behalf of all persons who were injured by similar acts by the same defendant. Thus, the word class is used in the sense of a group with similar characteristics.

In a class action, plaintiffs can pool their funds and start one action rather than many separate actions. In situations such as the thalidomide case, one parent would be able to sue on behalf of all parents and affected children. This also means that the defendant corporation is facing a large damage award. It also means that many of the expensive issues common to all cases, such as the manufacturer's negligence, would be determined once and for all.

The three major goals of permitted class actions are:

- increased access to the courts
- economy in the conduct of the trial
- deterrence of actual or potential wrongdoers

Certification

In order to be able to bring a class action, the plaintiff who claims to represent the class must first obtain court approval. This is known as certification of the class action. There are two hurdles to be overcome in obtaining certification:

- representation—the person seeking to be certified must be truly representative of all the people on whose behalf the action is brought.
- economy—the action must not be frivolous; it must have common issues so that some economy is achieved. If a person who has a claim does not wish to participate in the class action, that person can opt out and conduct a separate individual lawsuit. If a class action fails to be certified by the court, people can still sue individually.

The court can refuse certification for a class if it thinks that each individual plaintiff's case is different enough that it should be tried separately, not as a class. In *Dennis v. Ontario Lottery and Gaming Corporation*, 2013 ONCA 501 (CanLII) the Ontario Court of Appeal refused to certify a class action brought on behalf of approximately 10,000 people who had severe gambling problems and wanted to sue the Ontario Lottery and Gaming Corporation. They had designated themselves for self-exclusion from casinos, but OLG encouraged them to gamble even though it knew of their designations. The group was seeking $3.5 billion in damages. The court ruled that this was not an appropriate group for class certification. Several people had already filed claims that had been settled out of court for on average $167,000 per claim. The court felt the facts of each individual case should be tried separately, so certification was denied.

Ramdath v. George Brown College, 2010 ONSC 2019 (CanLII), Ramdath v. George Brown College 2013 ONCA 468 (Can LII)

Approximately 120 students, enrolled in an international business program at a college in Toronto, sought court certification for a class action. The students, two thirds who were from India, China, Turkey, Brazil, Russia and Syria, each paid almost $11,000 in tuition to enroll in an 8 month International Business Post Graduate Certificate program. The college calendar indicated the course would provide them the opportunity to complete 3 industry designations/certifications in addition to the college's certificate. The professional designations were in international trade, customs specialist and international freight forwarding. It turned out the college had no agreement with the industry associations and the students were required to pass other expensive examinations and in some cases take additional courses and training to obtain these designations on their own. The students wanted the right to sue the college in a class action for negligence and breach of contract and to also seek remedies under the unfair practices section of the Ontario Consumer Protection Act. Two students were chosen as the representative plaintiffs for the class. The college claimed that this was not appropriate for a class action as there were individual issues that would need to be adjudicated separately. It also asserted that the class was too broad, and not identifiable and since many claimants were from India and China, an Ontario class action judgment would not be recognized in those jurisdictions.

The Court's Decision

The court did certify this group as a valid class action. The court ruled that there was an identifiable class, the representative plaintiffs could fairly and adequately represent the class and there were significant common issues. The court stated individual damages may vary, but the class action could proceed. This class action did proceed and was successful at both the trial court and the Ontario Court of Appeal. The court ruled that the college was liable for negligent misrepresentation and had violated the Ontario Consumer Protection Act and damages were awarded to the students.

Legal Costs

In Ontario, B.C., and Quebec there are agencies that will provide some funding to assist in class actions. In Quebec, it is possible to obtain money for lawyers' fees and disbursements— expenditures necessary to the lawsuit. In Ontario, only disbursements are funded. These costs, however, can be significant since they include the costs of experts' reports.

There is also the question of whether the plaintiffs in a class action will be liable to pay the defendants' legal costs if the plaintiffs lose. In Canada, courts make an award of costs, and the usual principle is that the loser must pay the winner's costs—this does not mean the winner's entire legal bill, but some part of it, usually a third to a half.

The importance of the "loser pay" rule was seen in Quebec where an unsuccessful class action against Canadian Honda Motors resulted in an award of costs of $675,650 against the plaintiffs. As a result of this decision, the Quebec code of civil procedure was amended to provide that costs ordered against an unsuccessful plaintiff in a class action would be limited to what is in effect the small claims court scale—a small sum. In Ontario, if the funding is approved by the class proceedings committee established by the Law Society of Upper Canada, the fund is then responsible for paying the plaintiff's costs.

Recently a private corporation was set up to fund Canadian class actions in return for a percentage of the winnings. The company would finance the substantial legal and expert costs and would be responsible for any costs awarded to defendants if the class action was successful.

Avoidance of Class Actions

While the right to bring class actions has been expanded by statute, there have been corresponding attempts by businesses to restrict opposite parties rights to bring class actions by inserting terms in standard form agreements requiring disputes to be referred to arbitration and also giving up the party's rights to a class-action.

In a consumer case brought on behalf of plaintiffs alleging that Telus Communications Inc. overcharged by the way it calculated its cell phone rates, the court held both an arbitration clause and a clause giving up rights to a class-action were unenforceable where consumer protection legislation had provisions that guaranteed access to the courts. (*Seidel v. TELUS Communications Inc.*, 2011 SCC 15 (CanLII)).However, these clauses may be enforceable in some other business agreements.

Recent Class Actions

Class actions in Canada started to develop in the 1990's and the range of cases is continually expanding. It is not uncommon now to find class actions involving consumer protection law, government negligence, defective products and manufacturer's liability, shareholder disputes, employment law disputes, franchise law and major environmental accidents. Some of the cases involve claims for very small amounts of money per person while other cases include claims for very large amounts per class member. In some of the cases where the damage awards to each individual class members are very small, it is actually the lawyers who benefit the most from the class actions. Some question whether certification of these class actions should be questioned by the courts when there is little benefit in the class action, except to the law firms who charge large fees. Some of the most well-known recent class actions in Canada are listed below.

- **Residential Schools** – The federal government settled a class action by aboriginal Canadians who as children were forced to leave their native families and attend residential boarding schools often operated by the Catholic and Anglican churches. The children often suffered physical and sexual abuse and were prevented from speaking their native languages. As of May 2013 over 37,000 Aboriginal people had applied for compensation and almost $2 billion had been paid out. Final estimates of damages are estimated at close to $4 billion after all legal fees and expenses are included.

- **Hepatitis C** – Provincial governments, the Red Cross and insurance companies settled class actions where a possible 20,000 people contracted hepatitis C from blood transfusions between 1986- 1990 when a test to detect hepatitis C in blood was available but was not used. Over 14,500 people applied for compensation. Claimants received between $8,453–$408,834 depending on the state of their health. The total cost of settling all the class actions is estimated at $2.7 billion. Lawyers earned $56 million in this case.

- **Nortel Shareholders** – In 2008 about 145,000 Canadians were part of a global class action against Nortel Networks which settled for $2.64 billion. They had sued Nortel due to financial irregularities and financial statements that misrepresented the company's financial position. Unfortunately Nortel declared bankruptcy in 2009 and there are about $25 billion in outstanding claims from a variety of groups such as former employees and pensioners. When Nortel's assets were sold off there was only $9 billion left to satisfy all these claims plus very large legal fees.

- **Lac Megantic Railway Disaster** – In 2013 a parked 74 car railway train carrying crude oil, broke away and rolled down into a small Quebec town. It derailed and exploded and a large fire ensued killing close to 50 people and destroying a large part of the downtown core. A class action lawsuit against the railway is expected to be one of the largest class action cases in Canada given the significant loss of life and economic impact on this town of 6,000 people.

- **Quebec Smokers and Tobacco Companies** – In 2012 a trial began for a class action representing 1.8 million smokers in Quebec who are suing Canada's three largest tobacco companies. It is the biggest class action in Canadian history and damages could be as high as $27 billion. The trial has begun but it is anticipated it will last for several years. Other provinces and countries are closely watching this case. Huge awards have been given out in the U.S. in similar previous cases.

- **Cell Phone System Access Fees** – In 2012 certification was granted for a class action against Canada's largest mobile telecom providers claiming they illegally charged $12 billion in system access fees to every cell phone user in Canada. It is alleged the cell phone companies lied to customers stating the fee was required by federal regulators. This class action is worth potentially $18 billion and could be one of the largest class actions in Canadian history.

- **Maple Leaf Foods** – In 2008 a class action began against Maple Leaf Foods for cold meats it sold across Canada that were contaminated with listeriosis bacteria. There were 22 deaths and over 5,000 people were sick due to the bad meats. The class action settled very quickly for about $27 million with claimants receiving damages ranging from $750 - $225,000 depending on how seriously affected they were.

- **Banks and Unpaid Overtime** – In 2013 the Supreme Court of Canada allowed the certification of two similar class actions. In *Fulawka v. The Bank of Nova Scotia and Fresco v. Canadian Imperial Bank of Commerce*, both actions claim that the banks involved required thousands of employees to frequently work overtime "off the clock" not paying them overtime. They allege this was in violation of their employment contracts and the Canada Labour Code. The claims in these two class actions total about $900 million and similar class actions against other banks may also occur depending on the outcomes of these two cases.

- **Chocolate Companies – Price Fixing** – In 2013 four major chocolate producers agreed to pay $23 million to settle a class action brought against them. It was alleged that Hershey, Cadbury, Nestle and Mars had violated the Competition Act with price fixing and price maintenance for chocolates sold in Canada in 2007. Most individuals will receive $50 in damages unless they have proof they purchased large amounts of chocolate during the relevant time period.

- **Ernst & Young LLP and Sino Forest** – In 2013 a $ 117 million settlement was approved in a class action against Ernst & Young LLP the accounting firm that acted for Sino-Forest. Sino-Forest created a $6 billion stock fraud by falsely claiming it had large timber reserves in China. Investors had claimed that the accounting firm had failed to properly scrutinize the books and holdings of the forest company. A $9.18 billion dollar class action was started against Sino-Forest and its executives, but the company has since become insolvent. This was the largest successful class action claim against an accounting firm in Canada.

■ **Merck – Vioxx Drug** – In 2012 one of the world's largest drug companies agreed to settle a class action lawsuit brought by 1,000 Canadians who used their drug Vioxx for arthritic pain. Vioxx was a best seller since it was introduced in 1999 but several years later it was revealed that many Vioxx users had suffered heart attacks and strokes. The claimants alleged that Merck knew but did not adequately warn people of these serious side effects. Merck agreed to pay between $21.8–$36.8 million to settle this Canadian class action. That amount seems small compared to the $4.85 billion it paid to settle a similar class action in the U.S.

■ **Pfizer – Champix Drug** – A class action was certified in 2013 against Pfizer, a large drug company, for people who had used Champix, a drug to help people stop smoking. People claim Champiz caused significant adverse psychiatric reactions such as depression, anxiety, violent outbursts and suicide. Pfizer has already agreed to pay $273 million to settle a similar class action over this drug in the U.S.

■ **Ticketmaster** – In 2012 a court ordered Ticketmaster to pay an $850,000 settlement in a class action to people in 4 provinces who had bought tickets for concerts and other events on Ticketmaster's TicketsNow resale site. Claimants had argued Ticketmaster had diverted ticket requests to its TicketsNow site which charged a higher price for tickets. The settlement reimbursed people about $36 for each ticket they had purchased through this resale site.

■ **GM Dealers** – In 2009 General Motors was close to bankruptcy so as part of a cost cutting move it notified 240 GM dealers in Canada that they should voluntarily close their dealerships and take a payout, or risk getting nothing if GM went bankrupt. The dealers had hired a large law firm, Cassels Brock, months earlier to represent them in case of a GM bankruptcy. The law firm also represented the federal government in the potential GM bankruptcy. GM gave the dealers 6 days to decide on the payout. Many dealers had been in business for 20–30 years and were running very successful dealerships. The law firm told them to seek independent legal advice, but allegedly told the dealers they didn't have much choice but to accept the GM payout. In 2010 the dealers received certification for a class action law suit against GM claiming violations of franchise and contract law. The dealers also are suing the law firm for conflict of interest. The dealers are claiming damages of $750 million. Cassels Brock in turn has sued 164 other lawyers for the independent advice each gave to individual dealers.

■ **Consumers' Gas Illegal Late Penalties** – In 1994 Gordon Garland began a class action against Consumers' Gas claiming the late payment fees it charged for unpaid gas bills were over the legal interest rate of 60% per annum. He sought $85 million in returned penalty payments plus interest on the money dating back to 1981. The Supreme Court agreed that the charges were an illegal rate and in 2004 a settlement was agreed upon and Consumer's Gas agreed to pay $22 million. Unfortunately this case has a bitter ending though, as Consumer's Gas then applied to the Ontario Energy Board for a rate increase to pay for this class action settlement. The customers who had been unfairly charged the late fee in the first place were then charged again to pay the penalty when the company was caught breaking the law. Lawyers in this case received almost $10 million of the $22 million settlement. Gas bills went up for all their customers to pay for this settlement. Two other similar class actions against Union Gas ($9.22 million settlement) and Toronto Hydro ($18.35 million settlement) for illegal penalty rates had similar impacts on customers' gas bills.

- **Money Mart Pay Day Loans** – in 2003 a class action representing 264,000 borrowers who had taken over 4.5 million small pay day loans from National Money Mart Co. and Dollar Financial Group Inc. over a 10 year period was commenced. They claimed that the lenders had charged illegally high interest rates. The case proceeded to trial in 2009 but in mid trial a settlement was reached. The defendants agreed to pay $ 27.5 million in cash, forgive $56 million in loans and give $30 million in $5 vouchers for future loans. Lawyers then tried to claim the $27.5 million in fees, but the courts cut the legal fees to $14.5 million, so that the borrowers could actually receive some cash (maybe $50 each) from this settlement. Most of the loans had already been written off and most borrowers did not want vouchers as they did not want to have to deal with these lenders again. This case has made many question the usefulness of class actions to the class members when individual damages are small, though the law firms made substantial revenues.

- **Durham Region** – Lost Personal Data- In 2009 a nurse for Durham region lost a USB key laden with unencrypted personal information on 83,524 people who had received flu vaccinations at regional clinics. Fearing identity theft, a class action was launched in against Durham region and a settlement of $500,000 was agreed to in 2012. This amounts to about $6.00 per patient whose files were on the lost USB key.

Jeffery v. London Life Insurance Company, 2011 ONCA 683 (CanLII)

Bill Rudd, former chief actuary and senior vice president of London Life Insurance Co. and James Jeffery, launched a class action against London Life Insurance Co. and Great West Life, claiming that they had improperly transferred $220 million from surplus funds belonging to participating policy holders to the shareholders of Great West Life Assurance Co. to help pay for the purchase of London Life. Great West bought London Life in 1997 for $2.95 billion. Rudd claimed that under the Insurance Act, the surplus funds belonged to the participating policyholders and could not be taken by the corporations for these buy-out purposes. The class action was launched on behalf of 1.8 million London Life policy holders and took almost 14 years before it was finalized.

The Court's Decision

The Ontario Court of Appeal agreed with the trial judge that this was a violation of the Insurance Act and London Life and Great West Life had no authority to take the money from the surplus funds of the participating policy holders. The insurance companies tried to appeal the decision to the Supreme Court of Canada, but leave to appeal was not granted. The trial judge had originally ordered the insurance company to pay $455.7 million, but later that amount was reduced to $284.6 million. Though this does not work out to a large amount of money per policy holder, Rudd believed the suit was worth the time because it may force large companies to respect their stakeholders in the future.

Business Law   Applied

❹ **John King** had gone to the Northern Lakes Hospital for a CT scan of his lungs. He was told by the radiologist Dr. Leonard that everything looked good. John continued to have difficulty breathing and 18 months later went to a different hospital and had another CT scan which showed he had advanced lung cancer. Dr. Leonard had misread his original CT scan and should have diagnosed the cancer when it was at an earlier and more treatable stage. The Northern Lakes Hospital has now gone over all the CT scans Dr. Leonard had conducted over the past 5 years and has realized that there are possibly hundreds of scans that he had misread. Patients are being contacted and many have cancer and other illnesses that he had failed to diagnose at earlier stages.

a) Would each individual patient have to sue Dr. Leonard and the hospital on their own or could they do it together?

b) If they wanted to sue together what steps would they have to take?

c) What are the advantages and disadvantages of the patients suing as a group or on their own?

Apology Act

Several provinces in Canada have enacted an *Apology Act*. The legislation recognizes that some people who have been harmed by a wrong doing are somewhat satisfied by an apology. There is anecdotal evidence of people claiming that if a person had apologized at the beginning, the plaintiff would never have instituted a lawsuit. There is also a belief that an injured party may accept less compensation if there is an apology.

Apology acts have been legislated in other countries and the reports post introduction of this type of legislation have been favourable in that observers believe that plaintiffs have accepted lower compensation if an apology was made at an early stage. In the U.S. this is believed to be particularly effective regarding the medical profession.

Previously lawyers advised their clients never to apologize because it could be an admission of guilt and used against them at a trial. The *Apology Act* specifically states that an apology cannot be used in litigation against the person making it. Businesses may now want to consider having a policy for an early apology if accused of some tort or other harmful act before faced with such a situation.

Alternative Dispute Resolution

Trying to resolve a conflict between parties through the court system can be both expensive and time consuming. The French philosopher, Voltaire, known for his wit, commenting on the cost of litigation quipped that he lost money twice in lawsuits: "once when I lost and once when I won." Additionally, when one party feels like "the loser," he or she can be, understandably, reluctant to provide the compensation that "the winner" was awarded. In recognition of these difficulties, there has been recent encouragement from the courts themselves—as well as among business people—to try another approach to conflict resolution. This alternative approach is called alternative dispute resolution (or ADR), and normally consists of mediation or arbitration.

Mediation

What is mediation, and how is it different from going to court? The difference is one of both philosophy and process.

Mediation attempts to reach a compromise between the parties, while the court system is adversarial. In other words, mediation allows for the parties to compromise, negotiate, and reach a mutually agreeable solution. The parties themselves decide the outcome. In an adversarial system, both sides present and argue their cases in the best possible light—and then a winner and loser are declared by the third party (usually, a judge, though it could be a jury, too). The judge or jury imposes an outcome on the parties.

The adversarial court process is based on a historic combat model from the Court of Champions, so aggression within the boundaries of the rules is rewarded. There is an all-or-nothing consequence: only one will win. This has a strong effect on making parties settle before a trial, because the courts will not, especially in business disputes, give any compromise solution. As well, the loser will pay not only his or her costs, but quite likely a good portion of the winner's as well (though at the discretion of the judge, the loser is usually ordered to pay a portion of the winner's costs). Because of this all-or-nothing nature of a trial, settlements can be literally concluded on the courthouse steps.

From a process point of view, both methods of conflict resolution involve an impartial third party, but their roles are very different. A mediator is involved in the ADR process. This person is someone both parties can trust. He or she acts as a facilitator, assisting the parties in reaching a solution they can both live with. A judge decides who is "right" and prescribes a solution according to legal principles.

When it comes to actually doing mediation, the process is quite different from that of a trial. With mediation, parties to a dispute meet with the mediator in some neutral setting. Discussions are held until a conclusion is reached. A lawyer may or may not be present. In a court proceeding, witnesses and/or the parties themselves are called upon to present their sides of the story, under oath. Lawyers often (though they do not have to) assist the parties to follow the formal rules of courtroom conduct and to present their cases as favourably as possible. They also present legal arguments to the judge about why their client should win, based on the stories the witnesses and the parties have provided. The judge then decides on the winner and the result.

What about the cost of mediation? It depends on how your case was referred to the process. For example, in Alberta, if you start a case in the Civil Division (popularly called "small claims court"), you are likely to be referred to mediation by the court itself, under the Civil Claims Mediation Project. In this case there is no charge for the service. In Ontario, on the other hand, there is mandatory mediation for some civil actions, but the parties must bear the cost of the mediator. Another option is that you and the party with whom you have a dispute may agree to try mediation before embarking on the court process. In such cases, you would have to agree on how to cover the fees charged by the mediator, as well as any costs associated with the location you chose for the meeting. The cost could be significant, since mediators are trained professionals. Nevertheless, mediation may still be preferable to recourse to the courts, given the cost and time involved in that process.

Note that parties can agree to try mediation in the event of a conflict, prior to any conflict actually arising. As part of the terms of a contract, the parties may include a term that mediation is to be attempted before a court action is started, or that the dispute must go to arbitration and not to court.

Mediation is not without its critics. Opponents to mandatory mediation claim it is not suitable for all cases and will just be another level of bureaucracy and expense in the court process. They also suggest that governments are in favour of implementing mediation so they can download the costs of the administration of the justice system onto the parties involved in a dispute, by making them pay for mediators.

Proponents of mediation claim that its non-adversarial process promotes settlement. The parties meet in the same room and tell their sides of the story personally rather than having lawyers present their cases. The parties are encouraged to find some areas of compromise rather than having a judge impose a final resolution on them.

Arbitration

Another alternative to court proceedings for resolving disputes is arbitration. An arbitrator acts in a manner similar to a judge by hearing the cases of both sides and conducting what is in effect a mini-trial (but without many of the procedural requirements of a formal trial).

An arbitration decision is binding and can be enforced just as a Court Judgment. There are federal and provincial arbitration acts that govern the procedure on arbitration. A clause in the contract agreeing to arbitration means that the parties agree to arbitration under the relevant act, and the procedures given in those acts apply in place of court procedures. In the event of a dispute relating to the contract, the parties must use arbitration to settle it. They cannot use a lawsuit unless, of course, both parties agree to cancel the arbitration clause.

Arbitration is often chosen because it is faster than a court proceeding. In some cases it is cheaper, but the parties must pay for the arbitrator and necessary office space. The parties choose a neutral arbitrator. The arbitrator may be an expert in the business area in dispute. When a party wants to avoid a trial in a foreign court that may be hostile, arbitration is a frequently chosen method to avoid that foreign jurisdiction.

Internet ADR

While the same laws apply to *e-commerce* as to traditional business, the Internet has added new problems requiring new solutions. The customer, retailer, and supplier may speak different languages, and may be located in different countries subject to different laws and cultural customs. Thus, when conflicts arise, recourse to traditional methods such as lawsuits may be ineffective and too expensive.

Some businesses are supporting on-line mediation. One such business is eBay. It reports the example of a Canadian customer who bought a software package for $320 from a seller in China. When the customer tried to install it, he could not find workable registration codes. The buyer then followed the SquareTrade link from the eBay website. A mediator based in Texas was assigned to the case. The mediator worked with the parties to overcome the anger, frustration, and language problems, and discussed possible solutions. Eventually, the seller agreed to refund the full price of the software and part of the shipping cost to the customer. The cost of the mediation to the customer was minimal. The major cost was born by eBay because it believes that the SquareTrade service makes eBay a better place to trade.

Business Alert!

ADR Options   Governments have recognized that there are significant cost savings not only to the citizens but to the governments by having many disputes resolved using ombudsmen, mediation and arbitration programs funded by governments. There are a number of such programs for banks and other financial service providers such as insurance companies and mortgage companies. There are also some for resolving disputes regarding car purchases and disputes within the franchise industry.

The availability to participate in the procedures vary within each industry and within each province. However, all have information available through an internet search.

In Summation

Laws and the Legal System

- Laws can be characterized in three main ways: private or civil law (which governs disputes between individuals), criminal or regulatory law (which governs disputes between individuals and society generally), and constitutional law (which governs disputes with governments as lawmakers).
- One incident may invoke more than one legal proceeding, depending on whether more than one of the categories of law are involved.

The Court System

- The Canadian legal system is based on both judge-made law—known as common law—which in turn is based on the principle of *stare decisis*, and on government-made law created through the acts of Parliament or the provincial legislatures.
- Decisions of fact and law are made at the trial-court level, while provincial appeal courts and the Supreme Court of Canada hear only arguments based on issues of law.
- Whether you will require a lawyer depends on the level of court. Small claims court is designed to allow individuals or businesses to handle the presentation and enforcement of their legal case without the involvement of a lawyer.
- Hearsay is the repetition in evidence at a trial of the statement, oral or documentary, by a person who is not called as a witness.

- A class action suit is a way for many plaintiffs, who allege harm by one large corporate defendant, to pool resources in bringing a lawsuit. All plaintiffs join in one lawsuit rather than each bringing his or her own.

- Alternative dispute resolution, either mediation or arbitration, is a method to resolve conflict separate from the court system. Mediation is based on a model of negotiated compromise rather than of adversarial "winners" and "losers." Arbitration is conducted similar to a trial but the formal procedures are relaxed. The parties choose the arbitrator(s).

Closing Questions

1. There is judge-made law and government-made law. If there is a conflict, which governs?

2. Describe the stages of a law suit.

3. What is the difference between a trial court and a court of appeal?

4. What is the standard of proof in a criminal proceeding and in a civil proceeding?

5. a) What are the main pleadings in a civil case?
   b) What is the purpose of each pleading?

6. What is the difference between a barrister, a solicitor, and an attorney?

7. a) Describe mediation and arbitration.
   b) How does each differ from a trial?

8. Match the following:
   1) trial lawyer   a) binding precedent
   2) *stare decisis*   b) mediation
   3) alternate dispute resolution   c) statement of defence
   4) certification   d) barrister
   5) pleading   e) approval

9. Hearsay is a form of evidence relevant to the fact-finding process in a trial. It is sometimes excluded. Is the reason for the exclusion because it is not true? Explain

10. Bill Morgan has a judgment against Rita Roman for $5,000. He learns that Roman owns a 1993 Mustang that has a chattel mortgage on it with a balance owing of $5,000. From looking at newspaper ads, Morgan thinks the car is worth $10,000.
    a) Can Morgan seize the car and have it sold? If so, how?
    b) Will he necessarily recover any money from the sale?

11. Small Claims Court Drafting Exercise
    a) Read the following information, and draft a claim against Sure Finance, Inc. with yourself as plaintiff, using any relevant personal data necessary.

    On July 15, 1997, you applied for a loan for your new business in the amount of $5000 from Sure Finance, Inc. You were told by Sure Finance that it would have no trouble getting you a loan, and were asked for a $500 deposit. Sure Finance said the deposit would be refunded if the loan did not go through, as long as you told the truth on your application form. Sure Finance told you on September 1 that it had found a lender, but that a co-signer was required. You cannot get one. That's why you went to Sure Finance in the first place, rather than to a bank. Sure Finance refuses to repay the deposit.

    b) Draft a defence for Sure Finance.
    [Note: There are filled-in precedents and blank forms in the Appendix to assist with this exercise.]

12. a) Attend at a small claims court and listen to one civil case. Do a report on it containing the following:

- the plaintiff's case
- the defendant's case
- the judge's reasons

b) Find in this text the area of law relevant to the case that you saw. Write a summary of the law. Tell whether you agree with the judge's application of the law or not.

13. Kiani Kapital Inc. lends money to businesses on the security of mortgages on their real estate. It gave one loan relying on an appraisal of the value of the land by Hasty Appraisals Inc., done June1, 2013 that the land was worth $300,000.

The borrower defaulted July 2, 2015. On September 1, 2015 the real estate agent, who listed the property for sale, told Kiani, that the appraiser may have been negligent, and recommended listing the property for $200,000 On December 1, 2015 sells for $200,000. On January 2, 2016 Kiani checked with another appraiser who said the first appraiser was negligent.

In doing questions like this is helpful to do a chronology of relevant dates, such as the one that follows:

Appraisal done—June 1, 2013
Borrower defaults—July 2, 2015
Real estate agent advises of possible negligence—September 1, 2015
Property sells determining there was a loss—December 1, 2015
Expert confirms negligence—January 1, 2016

a) When did the negligence occur?
b) When does the basic Limitation period expire?
c) Is there a ground for extending the basic limitation time? If so, what is it called?
d) What is the last day on which Kiani can sue Hasty Appraisals?

Small Claims Court Claim and Defence

SMALL CLAIMS COURT COMPLAINT FORM (Complete)

WHEN REFERRING TO THIS DOCUMENT PLEASE USE NUMBER IN UPPER RIGHT CORNER

PLAINTIFF

Name NEWCOMP, INC	Claim No.

DEFENDENT(S)

Name ROSE TESSA		
Street No. 62 OXFORD LANE	Address	Apt. No.
Borough/City TORONTO	Postal Code M6S 2Z3	Phone No. 888-8800

DEFENDENT(S)

Name		
Street No.	Address	Apt. No.
Borough/City	Postal Code	Phone No.

To the Defendant

The Plaintiff claims from you $3,039.00. and costs for the reason(s) set out below

IF YOU DO NOT FILE A DEFENCE WITH THE COURT WITHIN TWENTY DAYS AFTER YOU HAVE / RECEIVED THIS CLAIM, JUDGMENT MAY BE ENTERED AGAINST YOU.

TYPE OF CLAIM

Unpaid account	(Contract)	Motor vehicle accident	Promissory note	Lease
Services rendered	N.S.F. cheque	Damage to property	Other _____ (describe)	

Reasons for Claim and Details
(Explain what happened, where and when the amounts of money involved.)

1. The Plaintiff's claim is for $3,039.00 for goods sold and delivered.

2. The Plaintiff states that on or about the 1st day of June, 2014, at the request of the Defendant, it supplied and delivered to the Defendant an IBM computer at a price of $3,000.00 plus H.S.T and provincial sales tax, plus interest at 3% per annum on the unpaid balance. On or about the 1st day of June, 2014, the Plaintiff also delivered its invoice No. A101 in the amount of $3,039.00.

3. The Plaintiff states that despite numerous requests for payment, no payment has been forthcoming.

4. the Plaintiff therefore claims:

    a) the sum of $3,039.00;
    b) pre-judgment interest at the rate of 3% per annum from the 1st day of June, 2014 to the date of payment or judgement, whichever shall first occur;
    c) his costs of this action; and
    d) such further and other relief as to this Honourable Court may seem just.

(Where claim is based on a document, attach a copy for each copy of the claim, of if it is lost or unavailable, explain why it is not attached.)

SMALL CLAIMS COURT DEFENCE FORM (Complete)

Claim No.

PLANTIFF		DEFENDENT(S)	
Name NEWCOMP, INC		Name ROSE TESSA	
Address	Postal Code	Address 62 OXFORD LANE	Postal Code M6S 2Z3
City/Borough	Phone No.	City/Borough TORONTO	Phone No. 888-8800

LAWYER OR AGENT		DEFENDENT(S)	
Name		Name	
Address	Postal Code	Address	Postal Code
City/Borough	Phone No.	City/Borough	Phone No.

☒ I/We dispute the full claim made by the plaintiff.

❑ I/We admit the plaintiff's claim and propose the following terms of payment.

   $ _____ per _____ commencing _____

❑ I/We admit part of the plaintiff's claim amounting to $ _____ and propose the following terms of payments:

   $ _____ per _____ commencing _____

❑ I/We dispute the balance claim.

REASONS FOR DISPUTING THE CLAIM AND DETAILS:

1. On June 1, 2014, the Plaintiff delivered a computer to my office which was not the same model as the one which I had ordered. In addition, the top of this computer was badly scratched.

2. Despite numerous requests, the Plaintiff has refused to remove this computer from my office and has refused to deliver the model which I agreed to buy.

NOTE:

If the defence contains a proposal for terms of payment, the plaintiff is deemed to have accepted th terms unless the plaintiff, in writing to the clerk, dispute the proposal and requests a hearing within 20 days of service of a copy of the defence.

If a hearing is requested, the defendant should still make any payments required under the proposal and provide proof of payment at the hearing.

All payments should be forwarded directly to the plaintiff or the plaintiff's representative at the address shown in the bottom left-hand corner of the claim.

IF THE DEFENDANT FAILS TO MAKE PAYMENT IN ACCORDANCE WITH THE TERMS OF PAYMENT PROPOSED, THE CLERK MAY SIGN JUDGMENT FOR THE UNPAID BALANCE WITHOUT A HEARING.

_____   _____
           Date   Defendant's Signature/Solicitor or Agent's Name

Note

These forms are regularly changed by the government offices. They have to be updated by searching the relevant provincial Small Claims Court websites.

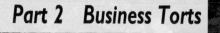

Intentional Torts

The Concept of Civil Wrong

A wrong can give rise to two different types of remedy in law—civil or criminal. Sometimes the two occur together, as can happen in the common motor-vehicle accident, when there may be an action in tort for negligence, as well as criminal charges for careless driving. Consider the case of two motorists who get into an angry argument that quickly progresses from fist shaking to heated verbal insults. One of the drivers deliberately rams the other car, severely injuring that driver. The threatening gestures and intentional collision constitute a civil tort of assault and battery. These same actions might also result in criminal charges of assault causing bodily harm, careless driving, or criminal negligence.

    Tort   The best definition of **tort** is *wrong*. The word is derived from the Latin *torquere*, to twist. To commit a tort is to do something twisted or crooked—to carry out an action that is wrong. It is a civil wrong, not a criminal wrong.

Legalese

Two Major Types of Torts

Torts generally fall into one of two main categories.

- **Intentional torts,** harmful acts that are committed on purpose and for which the law provides a remedy. Common ones are assault, trespass, malicious prosecution, false arrest and false imprisonment, defamation.
- **Unintentional torts,** when someone acts carelessly or without thought, and causes unintentional harm to another person or that individual's property. This is called the tort of negligence. Unlike intentional torts, it is a flexible concept, and is not broken up into smaller categories. A doctor who is careless while operating on a patient and thus causes injury, is guilty of the tort of negligence. Someone who drives without proper care or attention—is careless—is also guilty of negligence. The number of situations to which negligence applies is open ended.

intentional torts
harmful acts that are committed on purpose and for which the law provides a remedy

Vicarious Liability

vicarious liability

the responsibility of an
employer to compensate for
harm caused by employees
in the normal course of their
employment

In many tort actions the plaintiff will sue the person responsible for the conduct as well as their employer. **Vicarious liability** is the responsibility of an employer to compensate for harm caused by their employees in the normal course of their employment. If the employee is at fault in normal job duties, then the employer is responsible. Questions do arise in some cases around what is meant by "within the scope of their employment." The reason for making employers liable, as well as the employee, is that employees often have little or no funds. In addition, employers are the ones who make the profit and, therefore, must bear the loss. Employers can insure for such losses.

Intentional Torts

Control of Shoplifters

Sometimes a set of actions can give rise to a series of breaches of both tort and criminal law. Shoplifting, for example, normally results in a criminal charge being laid against the offender. But, depending on the response of the business to the incident, it can also lead to one or more of the tort actions described in this section.

The intentional torts affecting the rights of business and customer in a shoplifting situation are:

- false arrest and false imprisonment
- malicious prosecution
- trespass to land
- conversion

Citizen's Arrest and False Imprisonment

One of the most common—and legally uncertain—situations in which a business person may face tort liability is in the handling of persons suspected of shoplifting. The situation generally unfolds as follows. Store personnel either suspect, or see, a person shoplifting. The store personnel, who must call the police, can detain the person until the police arrive (or until they conclude that the person did not commit the offence). The detained person, if shown not to have shoplifted, brings an action for false imprisonment. The store defends itself by saying it had the legal authority to detain the person.

The courts jealously guard an individual's right to liberty. Any time you attempt to deal with a suspected shoplifter, there is an element of legal risk involved. From a practical point of view, the following should be noted:

- any person has legal authority to arrest a person found in the act of committing a criminal offense, or a reasonable time after the offense has been committed, if they believe it is not feasible for a police officer to make the arrest
- citizens have no right to search people against their will, but can ask them to permit a search (such as to empty pockets or open a purse)
- if the person objects to a search or to opening purses or parcels, the person should be turned over to the police
- security guards, as persons in authority, when making an arrest, have to warn the person of the right to remain silent and the right to counsel at the point at which they have enough evidence to conclude that the person has committed the offence of shoplifting

What is false imprisonment? There are three requisite elements that must be proven by the plaintiff:

- a deprivation of liberty
- against the will of the person detained
- caused by the defendant

Note that the deprivation of liberty can take several forms:

- physical restraint, in which the shoplifter is actively prevented from leaving the store
- threat of physical restraint, in which no actual touching occurs
- neither physical restraint nor threat of it, but the impression is given that refusing to remain in the store until police arrive will cause the suspect shoplifter embarrassment and public humiliation, or will result in the application of physical restraint

If the plaintiff makes out his or her case on the foregoing elements, it is then up to the defendant store to prove it was justified in detaining the plaintiff (making the citizen's arrest). There is only one way legally to justify such actions, and that is by claiming "legal authority." The onus of proving both these elements is on the defendant store. It will be very difficult to show there was legal authority in the absence of a criminal conviction. Consequently, the store should be cautious in detaining a suspected shoplifter, or else the detained person would likely succeed in an action for false imprisonment. A citizen's arrest for the purpose of investigation only is not permitted. Stores must prove on the balance of probabilities that it was reasonable for them to believe that an individual committed an offence, and they may also be required to show on a balance of probabilities that an offence did in fact occur.

Example: In *Sangha v. Home Depot of Canada Inc.*, 2005 BCPC 300 (CanLII) the plaintiff went to the defendant's store to purchase some brackets and a light bulb. He paid for the brackets and one new bulb. Upon leaving the store he was stopped by a loss prevention officer who thought he had stolen a second bulb. Sangha had brought a used bulb into the store to compare sizes and had it in his pocket. Sangha was taken to a wire fenced security area in the back of the store and held for 45 minutes. His jacket was taken and searched and he was photographed without consent. The court determined he had not stolen anything, so it was a false imprisonment. He was awarded $4,000 in general damages for loss of liberty, injury to feelings, indignity and humiliation.

■ *Critical Concepts of* Citizen's Arrest and False Imprisonment

- Any person (not just police) has a right to arrest, but the circumstances where this is legally justified are fairly limited.
- An arrest may be justified by claiming legal authority, that is:
  a) a crime has in fact been committed by someone
  b) there were reasonable grounds to believe that the detained person committed the offence.
- If a citizen's arrest is not justified, the detained person may succeed in a lawsuit for false imprisonment.
- Security guards have no higher rights of arrest than an ordinary citizen.

Nichols v. Wal-Mart Canada Corp., 2003 CanLII 41235 (ON SC)

Ms. Nichols went with her landlord, Mr. Thorne and his two children to a Wal-Mart store. In the camera department she reached up to a higher shelf and handed a camera to him, but then left him there to go to another department. When they all left the store together, the two adults were stopped by Wal-Mart security and told they had unpaid merchandise. Two security personnel took the adults by the arms and led them to the back of the store to the security office. They were asked to empty their pockets and police were called. Mr. Thorne had two cameras and cologne inside his jacket that had not been paid for. There was also mascara in the cart also not purchased. Thorne pleaded guilty to theft in criminal court and the charges were dropped against Ms. Nichols. The woman then sued Wal-Mart for false imprisonment and malicious prosecution. She claimed she had no knowledge he had taken the items and she sought damages for humiliation and embarrassment and the impact this incident had on her.

The Court's Decision

The court ruled that the store was justified in believing the theft was a joint effort, and so it had reasonable grounds to detain her. Though the court ruled she was unaware of his illegal activities and not responsible for the theft, the store could still use the defence of justification because a theft had occurred.

The store was not liable to her for false imprisonment because a crime had actually been committed by someone and it had reasonable cause to believe she was a participant. There was no malice in holding her, they were merely pursing their legal rights in a theft case, so the claim for malicious prosecution also failed. The case against Wal-Mart was dismissed with costs awarded to the store.

Proper Detention

Stores must be cautious in how they imprison people or they may face civil liability or criminal charges. The cases below illustrate this clearly. The Chen case received much media attention as people were outraged that an honest businessman had been charged criminally when he arrested a thief. Both cases show how stores must use their powers to arrest carefully.

Example: In *Chopra v. T. Eaton Co. Ltd.*, 1999 ABQB 201 (CanLII) a 64 year old customer who had a dispute over a refund, initially shoved a store security guard on his way out of the store. He was quickly put in a headlock and handcuffed, racial slurs were made and he was held for 4 hours by store security before the police came. The court ruled that the customer had been falsely imprisoned and because of the excessive force used by the guard and the unreasonable delay in calling the police, the court awarded him $38,000 in damages.

R. v. Chen et al., 2010 ONCJ 641 (CanLII)

David Chen owned the Lucky Moose Food Mart in Toronto. Anthony Bennett had stolen plants from Chen's store earlier in the day, but one hour later Bennett returned. Chen recognized him and told him to pay for the plants he'd taken, but Bennett refused and ran. Chen and his two employees, then chased him. They caught Bennett and forced him into the back of a van, wrestled with him and tied him up, locked the van and then called the police. Bennett was charged with theft, but the police also charged Chen and his two employees with assault and forcible confinement. This caused much public outrage that the shopkeeper was charged as well.

The police position was that the law states citizens could only make an arrest if they caught the person "in the act" of committing the crime. The police believed that since the theft had taken place an hour earlier, Bennett had not been caught "in the act" so it was not a legal citizen's arrest.

The Court's Decision

Bennett in an earlier trial, pleaded guilty to theft and was sentenced to 30 days in jail. At the Chen trial, the thief admitted that he when he had returned to the store his intent was to steal more plants. With this admission, the judge then ruled that the two trips to the store were really one ongoing crime, so Chen had then caught Bennett "in the act" of committing a crime. This then made it a lawful detention, so Chen was found not guilty of assault and forcible confinement. This case grabbed significant media attention and sympathy for shop keepers who are regularly victimized by thieves. Chen was seen as a hero by many for rightfully defending his property.

As a result of this case, an amendment to the Citizen's Arrest and Self-Defense Act was made in 2013. It is now legal to make a citizen's arrest within a "reasonable amount of time" after a crime was witnessed, it does not have to be done while the crime is actually being committed.

■ *Business Law*   Applied

❶ **Luke Wishart was** shopping at High-Mart Department Store. He went over to the sunglasses department and tried on several pairs. A store security guard, John Picard, saw him look up and down the aisle a number of times, remove the price tag from one particular pair of glasses, and throw the tag under a counter. The tag was large and attached to the bridge of the glasses. Wishart passed several checkout stations and then headed for the door.

Once outside the store, Picard approached him, and asked if he had forgotten to pay for anything. He replied, after a few seconds, "Oh my God, you're right," and handed the sunglasses to Picard, who then escorted Wishart back to the store and called police.

At Wishart's trial for shoplifting, he was acquitted, because the judge believed that he had merely removed the price tag to see better how the sunglasses suited him.

   a) Do you think Wishart will succeed in a lawsuit for false imprisonment?

❷ **Wilfred Wilson was** enjoying some drinks after work at the Roaring Dragon Bar and Grill. He was there for some time and became rather intoxicated. He decided to leave, and so got up and left to walk home. About the time he left, someone went on a rampage in the Roaring Dragon's parking lot, vandalizing several vehicles extensively.

As Wilfred was on his way home, he was jumped from behind by the Dragon bouncer and pinned on the ground until police arrived. It seems that the person who actually damaged the vehicles fit Wilfred's general build, and was wearing jeans and a dark jacket (also like Wilfred).

   a) Will Wilfred be successful in a suit for false imprisonment?

Malicious Prosecution

For an action based on **malicious prosecution** (causing a person to be prosecuted for a crime without an honest belief that the crime had been committed) to succeed, four criteria must be met:

   ■ criminal charges were laid
   ■ those charges were later dismissed or withdrawn

malicious prosecution

causing a person to be prosecuted for a crime without an honest belief that the crime had been committed

- there were no reasonable or probable grounds for bringing the charges
- there was malice or an improper motive for laying the charges

The last two criteria are very difficult to establish. Actions for malicious prosecution succeed only in the most clear and extreme cases. We commonly say that one person lays a charge against another, but technically this is not correct. The person gives information to the police, who then investigate and decide if charges should be laid. At a later stage, a crown attorney will decide if those charges should proceed. However, all the individuals involved in the incident can be the subject of a malicious prosecution action. Most malicious prosecution cases are brought against crown attorneys or the police. It is estimated that 1 in 8 Ontario crown attorneys are sued for malicious prosecution, though in the vast majority of cases the plaintiffs are unsuccessful, as malice is not proven.

Malicious prosecution claims can also be brought against individuals or companies if they caused a person to be charged for a crime they knew the person did not commit.

Example: In *McNeil v. Brewers Retail Inc.*, 2008 ONCA 405 (CanLII) McNeil was fired and charged with theft when video showed him taking money from the till. The employer, however, withheld video that showed he had put the money back. McNeil was convicted of theft and fired. At a labour arbitration later the full video was discovered. McNeil appealed his criminal convictions successfully and then sued the employer for malicious prosecution. He had lost his job, endured public humiliation and suffered significant financial losses. He was awarded a total of $2,078,120 in damages including $500,000 in punitive damages.

Trespass to Land

trespass

the entry onto the property of another without the owner's permission, or some lawful right, to do so

Trespass is defined as the entry onto the land of another without the owner's permission, or some lawful right, to do so. For example, a police officer acting under a search warrant has the lawful right to enter without the owner's permission. As well, trespass, a common law tort, occurs if an individual refuses to leave when ordered to do so by the owner or person in legal possession. Standing outside a particular property and throwing a brick through a window also amounts to trespass. There are provincial statutes making trespass a minor criminal matter that can be dealt with by the courts—usually resulting in a fine.

The law assumes that a business dealing with the public, such as a grocery store, invites the public to enter with a view to making a purchase. This is permission as required in law. However, a business can refuse entry to a person for any reason, as long as human rights legislation is not contravened. No one can be barred because of race, colour, national origin, and so on.

Businesses who deal with the public are sometimes faced with the problem of trying to control troublesome customers. Although businesses have certain rights to protect their interests, they also have responsibilities to the customers and their rights.

Business Alert!

Trespass and the Control of Shoplifting   Criminal law contains many technical defences to charges of shoplifting. Because of this, and the fact that the trial process is slow and time consuming, stores are sometimes reluctant to press charges against an offender. If the accused individual is eventually acquitted, the store might face a civil action for false imprisonment. There is no defence of reasonable grounds if this happens.

While the use of hidden cameras to catch shoplifters "in the act" is fairly common, another solution that appeals to many businesses is to ban the offender from the store, rather than take the matter to court. A business need not give a reason for preventing anyone from entering the premises, as long as the ban does not violate human rights legislation. If the store is located in a mall or plaza, the individual could be barred from entering the entire property.

Under the provincial trespass acts, the individual must be given notice of the ban, and it is usually best to do this in writing. If a larger area is involved, a formal written notice should be prepared in co-operation with the property manager. Some businesses choose to give a six-month ban initially, following this with a permanent ban should a second suspicious incident take place. If the person has been asked to leave and refuses, the business can use **reasonable force** to remove the trespasser.

■ *Critical Concepts of* Trespass to Land

Business premises are private property and no one has the automatic right to enter.

- Businesses that deal with the public by implication give the public permission (licence) to enter to transact business.
- A business can revoke that permission without any reason, subject to human rights legisla tion. This **revocation**—withdrawal of an offer before acceptance, and communicating the withdrawal to the offeree—makes the customer a trespasser.
- A business can use reasonable force to eject a trespasser, but must first ask the trespasser to leave.

revocation

withdrawal of an offer before acceptance, and communicating the withdrawal to the offeree

Trespass to Goods

Trespass to goods or trespass to chattels involves intentional interference that causes damage or interference to another's goods. So if a person means to break another person's windows or scratch their car on purpose, or someone wrongfully seizes someone's goods temporarily, these would be examples of trespass to goods. The court would award damages to compensate for the damages caused by this trespass.

Example: In *Pelletier v. Forbes, 2010 NSSC 309 (CanLII)*, Forbes, who was drunk, wanted to drive his friend's car, but the car owner (Pelletier) refused. Forbes then punched Pelletier in the face breaking his nose and drove off with the car. Soon after Forbes was in an accident and the car was destroyed. Pelletier successfully sued the defendant for trespass to goods and battery. The court ruled there had been a definite trespass to goods, and possibly even conversion, so it awarded him $ 5,500 for the value of the car as well as $15,000 in general damages for the battery.

Conversion

This tort is very similar to theft in criminal law, and involves taking the property of another individual, with intent to exercise control over them. Shoplifting is an example.

Conversion (unauthorized use of the property of another) can be committed in two ways. The property might come into an individual's possession by the permission of the owner, but the recipient then refuses to return it. Alternatively, the property might be obtained by false pretences, such as when a customer pays using a bad cheque. In this instance, the owner would either have the goods returned, or would receive their equivalent dollar value.

conversion

unauthorized use of the goods of another

Where one partner, who was in a dispute with his other partners, took a computer purchased and used by the partnership business, that partner was found guilty of conversion and made to pay damages of $50,000.[1]

Conversion is a strict liability offence meaning that innocence and negligence are not a defence. This tort is often used against a bank that pays on a fraudulent cheque even though the bank had no knowledge of the fraud nor could have discovered the fraud with reasonable diligence as the following case demonstrates.

---

1. *Gu v. Tai Foong International Ltd.*, Ont. Sp. Ct., July 18, 2001.

Khosla v. Korea Exchange Bank of Canada, [2008] CanLII 56011 (ON S.C.)

Satwant Khosla was a solicitor who acted for clients who purchased a house. The house was sold using a fraudulent power of attorney. The fraudster was a tenant in the house.

The purchasers borrowed the purchase price of $492,000.00 and had it paid into Khosla's bank account in trust for themselves. Khosla drew a cheque in the name of the true owner of the house. Hence the true owner was the payee named on the cheque.

One month before closing the fraudster, using authentic identification taken from the owner, opened a bank account in the owner's name at the Korea Exchange Bank of Canada ("Korea Bank"). The fraudster deposited the cheque from the payment of the purchase price of the house in that bank account and shortly thereafter withdrew the funds and disappeared.

Khosla's insurer, a title insurance company, paid the purchasers their money, then using its right under the insurance policy [subrogation right] sued the Korea Bank using Khosla's name, for conversion of the cheque.

The Court's Decision

The Court held that there was well settled law that conversion was a strict liability defence. That meant that neither innocence on the bank's part, nor negligence by Khosla was a defence if the elements for conversion were established.

Conversion is wrongful interference with the property of another in a manner inconsistent with the owner's right to possession. The damage amount regarding cheques is the face amount of the cheque. Khosla, as drawer of the cheque, had the right to possession.

A bank commits conversion by collecting, i.e. obtaining the money from the drawer's [Khosla's] bank and then paying it to a person who is not the payee named on the cheque. Here the bank did not pay the funds to the true owner of the property, who was the payee on the cheque, but to a fraudster.

The bank was liable to pay Khosla the full amount of the face amount of the cheque plus interest.

Nuisance

Like many terms nuisance has a meaning in law that is not necessarily the same as its meaning on the street. The tort of nuisance involves a use by one land owner that substantially and unreasonably interferes with another occupier's ordinary use of the land, but does not include every interfernce.

In day-to-day living because of close contact property owners may often disturb or inconvenience a neighbour. Minimal annoyances do not amount to the tort of nuisance. It is only when the disruptions of the enjoyment of the property are substantial do they become legally unacceptable. Thus the key to understanding when the harm reaches the level that it becomes the tort of nuisance is in the adjectives "substantial and unreasonable". Determining when the interference is substantial and unreasonable is largely a matter of judgment. While there will be some clear areas, there will also be some gray areas where, as it is said, "reasonable people will reasonably disagree".

Unlike many torts it is not the conduct that is the object of the inquiry, but the degree of harm. Individual circumstances will have a significant weight in determining the degree of harm. For example, a rooster crowing every morning at 5:00 a.m. may not be unreasonable in the country but would be in the city. Smoke from an industrial smokestack that blows onto adjoining property causing paint to peel on houses would be a nuisance; however, smoke from a neighbour's occasional Sunday bar-b-q would likely not.

While the tort of trespass involves intrusion on property by a person or an object, nuisance can include intangibles such as smoke or noise. It has been called an early developed common law environmental protection remedy.

The restriction imposed by a nuisance prevent one owner from interfering with the use of the adjoining lands. It is no defence that the offending owner may have been carrying on the business before there was any use of the adjoining land.

The courts have found that temporary construction and demolition would usually not be a nuisance. However, if a cheaper method of construction was used which significantly delayed the construction, there might be a cause of action in nuisance. The courts will look at the nature of the area, the severity and duration of the nuisance, the plaintiff's sensitivity and the importance or utility of the activity.

Example: In *Antrim Truck Centre Ltd. v. Ontario (Transportation)*, 2013 SCC 13, the Supreme Court ruled that a nuisance claim could be successful, even if the interference was for the public good. The Ontario government opened a new section of a highway that eliminated drivers' access to a truck stop diner. The highway expansion was needed, but it virtually destroyed the business at the restaurant. The Supreme Court stressed that for a nuisance claim the interference had to be substantial and unreasonable. When it involved a public project, the benefit to the public had to be balanced against private interests. Individual members of the public should not have to bear a disproportionate share of the costs of obtaining that benefit. The court ruled that the impact of this project on the diner could fall within the definition of a nuisance. The owner of the diner was awarded $393,000 for the loss of his business and decreased market value of his property.

Most nuisance cases involve private disputes, but some cases can be a **public nuisance**. In these situations public property is interfered with, so it is the government that has the legal right to sue for the nuisance. If the action endangers public health, safety, morality, comfort, convenience or welfare it may be considered a public nuisance. Often public nuisance cases deal with environmental problems such as a spill of toxic chemicals into a waterway or a blockage of a highway.

public nuisance
government can sue for nuisance that affects public property

Example: In *Universal Sales, Limited v. Edinburgh Assurance Co. Ltd.*, 2012 FC 418 (CanLII) an oil tanker filled with 4,700 tons of fuel oil sank in the Gulf of St. Lawrence in 1970 while it was being towed. It took 26 years before the oil was removed and the ship was refloated and towed away at a cost of close to $40 million. The court ruled that the ship and its oil had been an ongoing public nuisance and the oil company, towing company and insurance companies involved were liable for the recovery costs.

Example: The City of Toronto wanted to prevent people from scalping tickets (reselling at a higher price) on the streets surrounding the Rogers Centre. So the city used its powers to pass by-laws to prevent a public nuisance, to deal with this problem. The city by-law that made it illegal to resell event tickets on city streets. The court ruled this activity was a public nuisance and the by-law was valid. (*R. v. Koverko*, 2005 ONCJ 420 (CanLII)

If there is legal action for a public nuisance, an individual can also sue for a private nuisance arising at the same time, but only if they can prove that they suffered more harm than the other members of the general public. If for example there was toxic spill on a lake, the government could sue for public nuisance, but an individual cottage owner may not be able to sue. But if there is one commercial resort on the affected lake, it may be able to sue under private nuisance, as it suffered more harm than individual cottagers.

Remedies in a nuisance action are often an injunction to stop the nuisance from continuing, or remedial action to limit the nuisance such as structural changes to reduce loud noises or bad smells, or a golf course layout as in the *Sammut* case, plus damages.

Picketing

Picketing by dissatisfied employees, done peacefully, near a business' property disturbs the business' use of its property but is justified on the basis that the employees have the right to inform the public and is not considered a nuisance in law. However, focused or secondary picketing directed at employees' homes, restaurants where employees eat, or hotels or motels where they stay, is an invasion of privacy which is an integral part of the use of land, especially residential land.

Example: Anti-abortionists picketed the houses of doctors who performed abortions. The Court found that the purpose was not to inform the public but to intimidate the occupants of the houses. The right to residential privacy was an important element of the use of residential land (*AJ of Ontario v. Dielmann et al*, (1995), 20 O.R. 3d 229 (Ont.) G.D.).

Example: Striking workers often get very aggressive when picketing, but their behaviour can be restricted if the courts consider it a nuisance. In *Telus v. T.W.U.*, 2005 BCSC 1236 (CanLII) striking telecommunications workers were picketing the homes of their managers and co-workers as well as local restaurants and hotels where these managers went. The strikers were very aggressive and insulting and used intimidating behaviour. The court issued an injunction against the picketing workers to stop picketing at these locations stating their conduct was both a public and private nuisance.

■ *Critical Concepts of* Nuisance

- Nuisance involves intentional actions on one party's property that substantially and unreasonably interferes with another 's use or enjoyment of their property.
- Not every interference with another's land use will be nuisance; the harm must be substantial and unreasonable.
- It is not the type of conduct by the defendant landowner that establishes nuisance, but the level of harm that the conduct causes.
- Courts can consider the nature, severity and duration of the interference, character of the neighbour, sensitivity of the plaintiff and the utility of the action

Sammut v. Islington Golf Club, Ltd., [2005] 16 C.E.L.R. (3d) 66 (Ont.) S.C.J.

The Islington Golf Club ("IGC") had been operating its golf course since 1923. In 2000 developers obtained approval from the Ontario Municipal Board ("OMB") to build houses on the east side of the golf course.

Golf ball spray is a well-known problem for land use adjoining a golf club. The IGC opposed the granting of building permits before the OMB, but the OMB authorized development with a narrow "no touch" zone between the course and any structures on the new development.

The Sammut's house was built close to the line of the no touch zone. Golf balls from the third tee from the golf course frequently hit the house causing damage. The Sammut's could not use that part of the lawn for fear of being hit.

The Sammuts sued IGC seeking damages and a permanent injunction stopping the use of that part of the golf course by golfers.

The Court's Decision

The court held that the Sammuts had made a case for nuisance. The conduct of IGC, while reasonable on its own property, unreasonably and significantly interfered with the use of adjoining land.

It was not a defence that the golf course came there first. An owner could not effectively make adjoining land unusable by starting harmful conduct next to vacant land.

A court awarded the Sammuts damages for the cost of repairs and for inconvenience and annoyance. It also ordered an injunction prohibiting IGC from using that part of the golf course that might result in golf balls being hit on the Sammuts' property. However, the court delayed the enforcement of the injunction for 2 weeks to allow IGC to implement some solution such as screening, landscaping or repositioning the tee or such.

■ *Business Law* Applied

❸ **Farang Afnam** bought a new long distance transport truck from Honest Al's Trucks. The truck manufactured by a large international corporation, Vareva, Inc. It came with a two year warranty. In the first twelve months it broke down fifteen times always at distances hundreds of miles from home.

Afnam contacted a lawyer who advises that there is no lemon law in his province and a battle in a court of law would be too expensive. Afnam's wife, Nadia, decides to go to the court of public opinion. She:

a) Pickets in front of the dealership and hands out flyers telling of the defects in the truck,
b) Puts up a YouTube video telling of the effect of the breakdowns on her family,
c) Goes to Honest Al's home and paces up and down on the sidewalk holding signs complaining about the quality of the truck.

Honest Al wants an injunction to stop her on the basis of nuisance. Will he be successful?

Assault and Battery

Businesses, especially where liquor is served, have to control their unruly customers and protect their premises. To accomplish this, business people must understand not only the tort of trespass to land, but also assault and battery.

The terms *assault* and *battery* are often used interchangeably to mean a physical attack. However, these terms have distinct meanings in the law of tort. And these terms are used with slightly different meaning in the criminal law. In general, **assault** can be thought of as the threat to do harm to a person, while **battery** is physical contact with a person without consent. The freedom to throw a punch ends at the tip of the other person's nose. For example, if two drivers get into an argument at an intersection and one driver shakes her fist menacingly at the other driver but does not hit him, the first driver has likely committed an assault by the threatening gesture. If the driver does intentionally hit him then he will also be liable for battery.

Battery requires the intention to make physical contact without consent. If someone carelessly but unintentionally knocks over another person and breaks their arm, this is not battery, as they did not intend the physical contact. They would probably be liable for negligence (which will be discussed in the next chapter), but it is not battery.

Though many battery cases involve fights, battery can occur in situations that do not involve anger. Doctors can be liable for battery if they perform medical procedures on patients without the patient's consent. In *Malette v. Schulman* [1990] O.J.No.450 (Ont. C.A.), a patient successfully sued a doctor for battery after he performed a lifesaving blood transfusion knowing she was opposed to it due to her religious beliefs. The court awarded her damages of $20,000. In *Mohsina v. Ornstein*, 2012 ONSC 6678(CanLII), a doctor was liable for $350,000 in damages for performing procedures he felt were necessary, but resulted in an outcome (infertility) the patient had not consented to.

Consent can be a defence to a claim for assault or battery. If the person agreed to the physical contact it is not battery. In sporting activities, athletes consent to a certain level of physical contact and violence when they play a sport. In boxing, hockey or football games for example, athletes cannot sue opponents for every legal hit that occurs, because there is an implied consent to a certain level of contact when they agreed to participate in the sport. If however a player is hurt by an exceptionally vicious or dirty hit, then the player responsible may be sued for assault and battery, since nobody would have consented to that level of violence. Evander Holyfield certainly did not consent to Mike Tyson biting off part of his ear when he agreed to a boxing match with Tyson. Violence in hockey is a much discussed topic and the *Moore v. Bertuzzi* case highlights the violence and dangers of the sport.

Example: In the *Moore v. Bertuzzi* [2012] ONSC 597 (CanLII) case, Todd Bertuzzi, while playing for the Vancouver Canucks, violently attacked Steve Moore of the Colorado Avalanche in a 2004 NHL game. Bertuzzi, angry at a previous hit Moore had made on a teammate in an earlier game, hit Moore from behind in the back of the head and then drove his face into the ice. Moore suffered three broken vertebrae and a serious concussion and was never able to play in the NHL again. He still suffers memory and concentration problems and Moore, a Harvard grad, is unable work at the high level he could have before he was hit. Bertuzzi was charged and pleaded guilty to criminal assault charges and received a one year probation. Moore has also sued Bertuzzi in civil court for battery and is seeking $60 million in damages. The trial has been delayed repeatedly, and if it does not settle out of court, will attract major media attention when it commences.

Even if a person has given their consent, it has to be an **informed consent** to be a valid defence. They must be aware or informed of all the significant risks. If they are not aware of these possible outcomes, then their consent is not an informed one, so it is not a valid consent. In *Halushka v. University of Saskatchewan* [1965] S.J.No. 208 (C.A.), a student accepted $50 to participate in a medical experiment at the university and signed the consent form. He had been told it was a minor procedure they were testing. Unfortunately during the procedure, his heart stopped and he went into a coma for 4 days. He sued the hospital for battery, though

assault
the threat to do harm to a person

battery
physical contact with a person without consent

consent
is a defence to a claim of assault or battery if the person agreed to the physical contact

informed consent
the person must be informed of all significant risks when they consented

it claimed he had consented. He had agreed to the procedure, signed the consent form and been paid to participate. The student was successful at trial though as the court ruled he had not been fully warned of the possible significant risks involved. He had not been able to give an informed consent, so the hospital was liable for battery.

self-defence

a response to an assault or battery with as much force as is reasonable in the circumstances

Self-defence (a response to an assault or battery with as much force as is reasonable in the circumstances) is a complete defence to assault or battery. To establish self-defence, the defendant must prove a genuine fear of injury at the hands of the plaintiff and that the defendant only struck the plaintiff for self-protection. While **provocation** is not a defence, it may lessen the damage award to the plaintiff. Provocation means conduct that would cause a reasonable person to lose self-control, such as irritating, taunting, insulting or angering someone to the point that they can't take it any longer and will react in an uncontrolled or often violent manner.

Spanking Law

The Criminal Code does make an exception for assault permitting teachers and parents to use physical discipline in correcting children or students, provided that the correction is done in the course of providing discipline and the force used is reasonable. The Supreme Court of Canada recently upheld this section under a Charter challenge by children's rights groups. The Supreme Court made it clear that parents should not hit children, it is not good or effective parenting, and child abuse will not be tolerated. However, under the following circumstances, spanking can be considered reasonable and not a violation of criminal or civil law. The guidelines the Supreme Court set down for spanking are : it should only be used on a child between the ages of 2-12, only using an open flat hand, spanking on the butt only, and only a few times and it should not done when the parent is angry or frustrated. Teachers cannot strike children, but can use limited force to restrain students during violent outbursts for safety reasons.

■ Critical Concepts of Assault and Battery

- ■ Assault is threatening another with violence, with the ability to carry out the threat causing fear in the victim.
- ■ Battery is the least touching of another without consent and with the intention to cause harm.
- ■ Self-defence is a complete defence to assault and battery.

Tootoosis v. Doe, 2006 SKQB 75 (CanLII)

Teddy Tootoosis and a friend went to the Vibe Nightclub and drank heavily. A verbal disagreement involving Tootoosis was starting, so his friend went to take him out of the bar. As they were leaving, the bartender jumped over the bar and attacked the pair. Soon fourteen people were hitting and kicking the two friends. The bartender hit the friend over the head with a beer bottle and continued to attack them with the broken bottle. Tootoosis was viciously beaten and then dragged out by bar staff and left unconscious with his pants down at his hips lying on the street outside of the bar. Police arrived and an ambulance came and took both men away. The club owner warned the friend not to press criminal charges or he would say Tootoosis had started the fight. Tootoosis was in intensive care for 5 days with a serious concussion, a broken jaw, broken teeth and multiple cuts and bruises. He sued the nightclub for assault, battery and negligence.

The Court's Decision

The judge ruled that Tootoosis had been the victim of a vicious assault and battery. He said that the nightclub had a responsibility to take reasonable care that an altercation would not occur and that its patrons would not be injured. In this case the club's own employees actually initiated the fight and actively participated in the assault. It is not a defence that the customers were drunk, since the nightclub had contributed to that condition by selling them drinks. The court said the club was vicariously liable for the actions of its employees and their attack on Tootoosis and his friend. The plaintiff was awarded $30,0000 in general damages, $3,190 in special damages and $10,000 in punitive damages.

■ *Business Law* Applied

❹ **Jennifer Mouty was** refused admission to a bar by a bouncer because she did not have ID. She was of the legal drinking age and objected, before going home and returning with appropriate ID. The bouncer was annoyed, and told her he would not admit her anyway. Mouty stated that, as she was over the drinking age, she had a right to enter.

   a) Who was correct?

❺ **John Chaytor was** a fashion buyer employed by a department store, Fashions Inc., of London, New York, and Paris. When he and a colleague visited a store of a competing chain in order to compare prices, an employee at the store recognized Chaytor, accused him of being a spy, and exchanged angry words. The store detectives were summoned and told to "watch these people."

Police were called, and two officers arrived shortly afterwards. They were told by the store manager to arrest Chaytor. The officers did so, then escorted him out of the store. When Chaytor started to go in another direction, the police took him by the arm and said, "You must come with us." Chaytor was taken to the police station, but no charges were laid.

   a) Was Chaytor rightfully on the business premises of the fashion company? If not, what law did he violate?
   b) Did the business have the right to make a citizen's arrest, or merely order him to leave?
   c) Did the words, "You must come with us," spoken by the police, equal imprisonment, as there was no physical restraint?

Invasion of Privacy—Intrusion upon Seclusion

The courts for well over 100 years have been reluctant to create a tort of invasion of privacy. Some statutory laws have provided some protection, but not enough. Four provinces (B.C., Manitoba, Saskatchewan and Newfoundland and Labrador) have passed Privacy Acts, as well there is some protection in Quebec under its Civil Code. But there was no tort that specifically protected privacy. The Federal Privacy Act regulates how the federal government collects, uses and discloses personal information. Statutory laws, such as PIPEDA—Personal Information Protection and Electronic Documents Act, were passed across the country that restrict companies from sharing personal information that it collects on its customers. But many of these statutes have narrow applications and often involve violations of privacy by the government, not by individuals. Plaintiffs have sometimes been able to use other tort claims to protect their privacy, for example if a person's photo was used to promote a product without their permission, they could sue for defamation. But there was no specific tort that specifically provided privacy protection.

However in 2012 in the case of *Jones v. Tsige*, the Ontario Court of Appeal established the new tort of **intrusion upon seclusion**. In establishing this new cause of action, the court cautioned that it should be narrowly applied, and only in cases of deliberate and significant invasions of personal privacy. The court defined the tort and when it would be appropriate and gave an upper range of $20,000 for the damages that could be awarded. Though many believe it was time for this tort to be recognized, they question whether the suggested upper limit of $20,000 for damages is too low, and it will not be enough to deter significant privacy invasions.

intrusion upon seclusion
intentionally intrude upon the seclusion or private affairs of another and it would be highly offensive to a reasonable person

Jones v. Tsige, 2012 ONCA 32 (CanLII)

Winnie Tsige had been dating the ex-husband of Sandra Jones. Both women worked at The Bank of Montreal. Ms. Tsige was having a dispute with him over finances and wanted to see if he was paying child support to his ex-wife. Ms. Tsige then accessed Ms. Jones' personal bank records approximately 174 times over a four-year period to see if the payments had been made. Jones became suspicious, told the bank, and then Ms. Tsige confessed. The bank suspended Ms. Tsige for one week without pay and denied her a bonus for that year. Ms. Jones however sued her for invasion of privacy and sought $90,000 in damages. At the trial court the judge ruled there was no Charter or common law right to dignity or privacy, so her claim was dismissed. She then appealed the decision to the Court of Appeal.

The Court's Decision

The Court of Appeal did an extensive examination of the law in Canada, U.S. U.K., New Zealand and Australia. It concluded that there is a need to protect privacy in Canada. It created a new tort of **intrusion on seclusion** to protect privacy rights but it only applies under strict conditions.

The court stated that three requirements would have to be met to succeed in an action for this new tort. First there defendant's actions must be intentional (which includes recklessness); second the defendant must have invaded, without lawful justification the plaintiff's private affairs or concerns; and third, that a reasonable person would regard the invasion as highly offensive, causing distress, humiliation or anguish. Proof of economic harm is not required.

The court said this new tort is only meant to apply to serious intrusions and gave examples of the types of situations where it could apply; intrusions into one's financial or health records, sexual practices or orientation, employment, diary or private correspondence would qualify as highly offensive. It does not want the courts to be overwhelmed with frivolous cases by overly sensitive people.

The court also established guidelines on the amount of damages that should be awarded for this new tort. It emphasized that damages for invasion of privacy should rarely be higher than $20,000 and even then, only in the most serious cases. In Ms. Jones case, the court awarded her $10,000.

Business Reputation Management

Defamation

defamation

making an untrue statement that causes injury to the reputation of an individual or business, including both libel and slander

Defamation is making an untrue statement that causes injury to the reputation of an individual or business, including both libel and slander. The test of whether harm has been done is the question, "Does it cause others to think less of the person or the business?" The key word to remember is reputation. An insulting comment that injures only pride can be unpleasant and annoying, but it is not defamation. In a very early defamation case, one judge stated, "The best defence to insult is a thick skin."

Eminem wrote a song from his 1999 CD 'Slim Shady LP' which contained lyrics mentioning a neighbourhood acquaintance:

> "I was harassed daily by this fat kid named D'Angelo Bailey,
> He banged my head against a urinal until he broke my nose.
> Soaked my clothes in blood. Grabbed me and killed my throat."

D'Angelo Bailey sued Eminem for $1 million on the basis that the lyrics were untrue and slanderous (*Bailey v. Eminem*, Michigan Trial Court, 2003). Judge Deborah Sarvitto, who appears to have been of the "thick skin" school, decided this case and wrote in her reasons in response:

> "Mr. Bailey complains that this rap is trash
> so he is seeking compensation in the form of cash.
> Bailey thinks he is entitled to some money gain
> because Eminem used his name in vain.
> The lyrics are stories, no one would take them take as fact.
> They are an exaggeration of a childish act.
> It is therefore this Court's ultimate position
> That Eminem is entitled to summary disposition."

In short Judge Sarvitto ruled in favour of Eminem.

Defamation has traditionally been divided into two categories:

- **libel**, defamation in which the harmful statement is written or broadcast
- **slander**, defamation in which the harmful statement is spoken

The right to freedom of expression, and the right to protection of reputation, sometimes conflict. Because of this, there are special rules governing such situations as the media's treatment of public figures. The importance of business reputation is also recognized, and, in fact, is given more protection than personal reputation. The right to sue for defamation arises only if the false statement is communicated to a third party. Comments made between two individuals, and not passed on to others, cannot be regarded as defamation. The requirement of communication is called publication of the defamation. Even a tweet is considered to be communicated and published.

Once the plaintiff has established the three elements of defamation; the statement is made about the plaintiff; it lowers the plaintiff's reputation; and there has been publication, then falsity and damage are presumed and the onus shifts to the defendant to advance a defence to escape liability.

All provinces have either defamation acts or libel and slander acts. In some provinces, the distinction between libel and slander has been abolished, so that all actions for injury to reputation are called actions for defamation.

Sometimes a comment might seem innocent if considered on its own. If another factor, such as knowledge of other information, or of the context in which the remark is made, is added, the innocent phrase can take on a whole new meaning. This is known as **innuendo**, a statement that implies something derogatory about another individual without directly saying it.

Innuendo derives from a Latin word which means to nod, or to indicate by pointing the head. So *innuendo* means to hint at a meaning, rather than to express it directly. In an old British case, *Monson v. Tussaud's Ltd.*, [1894] 1Q.B. 671, Madame Tussaud's Wax Museum was held liable for defamation by innuendo when it placed a very life-like wax replica of a man who had been found not guilty of murder, in its section called Chamber of Horrors, that included replicas of some of Britain's most notorious convicted killers.

Repetition

Repeating a defamatory statement is also defamation. It is no defense to say "I am merely repeating what I was told."

Businesses may repeat statements: newspapers may quote them, libraries may distribute books that contain them and websites might link to them. There are some defenses to repetition of defamation that will be explored later; but in general a business must be very careful not to repeat a defamatory statement.

Think before you Link

A recent number of law suits against service providers of websites such as Yahoo and Wikepedia and operators of websites have brought the question of whether the posting of a hyperlink to a website that contains defamatory comments, without any comment, is publication.

In the U.S. there is statutory authority that says there is none (the Communications Decency Act). Under that Act providers are not liable for what users say. In Canada the law is not clear. One of the concerns is that a newspaper's repetition of a defamatory comment is republication and attracts liability. A simple posting of a hyperlink, not repeating the content, may be distinguishable. If the posting is associated with a comment such as, "read this for the true story," that is more similar to re-publication.

The decision to sue in defamation always involves the consideration that the Court action will attract wide attention and prolong the defamation. For example, the Crookes lawsuit, the brief of which follows, attracted wide attention not only from bloggers, on-line and paper newspapers, but also TV news special feature reports: even the BBC ran one on Crookes.

libel
defamation in which the harmful statement is written or broadcast

slander
defamation in which the harmful statement is spoken

innuendo
a statement that implies something derogatory about another individual without directly saying it

In a more extreme case the Labatt's brewing company sent a cease and desist letter to a Montreal newspaper demanding that it stop showing a picture of an alleged murderer and body parts mailer, Luka Magnotta, holding a bottle of Labatt's beer. The newspaper refused, posted the demand letter on its website and it went viral increasing the bad publicity for Labatt. One commentator quipped: this is an example of bad judgment that should be taught in all business 101 courses.

Crookes v. Wikimedia Foundation Inc., [2007] BC SC 1424 (CanLII)

Wayne Crookes, a former campaign manager of the Green Party of Canada sued a number of persons associated with websites that contained links to websites where alleged defamatory comments about Crookes were posted. One of these actions was against John Newton who operated a website called www.p2p.net which contained commentaries on issues surrounding the Internet as well as other political subjects.

After the first of Crookes' lawsuits against website providers and operators was commenced, Newton published an article on p2p.net with comments on the implications of defamatory actions for those who operate Internet forums. Newton's article included a hyperlink to other sites: www.openpolitics.ca and www.usgovernetics.com. Newton made no comment about the truth of the allegations. Crookes sued Newton in defamation. Newton defended the basis that merely posting a hyperlink was not publication.

The Court's Decision

The Court first found that merely posting a link on a website did not prove that anyone had actually seen the posting, nor had gone to the link and seen the defamatory comment. In particular, it did not prove that anyone who knew the Plaintiff had read the defamatory material because of the posting of this link. That issue would have to be proved by actual evidence.

Secondly, the mere posting of a hyperlink without anything more did not equal publication. Newton had no control over the target website where the alleged defamatory material was published. He did not make any comment on its accuracy nor did he reprint any part of it; therefore, there was no publication.

The Court cautioned, however, that the result might be different if the website host made comments on the accuracies of the statements in the linked article.

Disclosure of Information on Websites

What if you do not know who posted the defamatory material? Courts are ordering Internet service providers to divulge the names of persons who posted defamatory material on their websites. In one highly reported case eBay was ordered to produce information on its Canadian "power sellers" pursuant to sections of *The Income Tax Act*. The Court held that eBay was not foreign-based because it is readily accessible in Canada. Although this latter decision was made under *The Income Tax Act*, it probably reflects the Court's readiness to both assume jurisdiction over foreign located Internet service providers and to require disclosure (*eBay Canada Limited v. Canada (National Revenue)*, 2008 FCA 141 (CanLII)).

■ *Critical Concepts of* Defamation

- Defamation involves a false statement that is harmful to the reputation of a person or business.
- The harm caused can be by innuendo.
- The statement must be published, that is, communicated, to a third party.
- Defamation can be either libel or slander.

Libel

Traditionally, libel was defamation in written form. However, libel also includes harm to an individual's reputation that is caused by the conduct, or actions, of another person. More recently, libel has been expanded by statute to include modern methods of communication, including broadcasting, movies, pictures, film, and computer technology.

Monetary damages are presumed by the court in libel cases.

Slander

Slander is defamation in spoken form. The provincial acts state that a slander suit will not be upheld by the courts without proof of actual monetary loss suffered by the individual or business claiming defamation.

Damages

Damages for defamation contain a unique element. Not only is there compensation for ordinary loss, but money is also given for injured feelings, such as humiliation, and to show that the defamed person is innocent the defamed person or business is innocent and to provide vindication of reputation.

In awarding general damages for defamation, there is no maximum limit. In cases of personal injury in negligence cases, general damages for pain and suffering had a maximum limit set in 1978, which with inflation increases is now about $375,000. The Supreme Court recognized however, that in most defamation cases pecuniary damages for financial losses are not claimed. This is very different from personal injury cases where those losses are often very large if there were major physical injuries. This difference justifies allowing greater general damages in defamation cases.

Defamation cases are also quite rare in Canada and their damage awards are quite low. In *Hill v Church of Scientology of Toronto* [1995] 2 SCR 1130, the court noted that from 1987 to 1995 there were only 51 reported libel judgments in Canada, which in all but one case, the average damage award was less than $30,000. Because of these low amounts, the court stated there is no need to cap general damages in defamation cases. In the Hill case, he was a crown attorney who was awarded a total of $1.6 million in general, aggravated and punitive damages, after the church and its lawyers made false accusations that damaged his integrity and credibility as a lawyer.

Example: In the case of Rick Fennimore v. Skyservices Airlines, a jury awarded a pilot $3 million in damages, the highest amount ever awarded in Canada for defamation. The airline he worked for and its chief pilot falsely accused him publicly of drinking 7 hours before a flight and fired him. As a result of the statements, and others the employer made, he was unable to get a job in the industry. He was forced to abandon his "dream" career and eventually took lower paying work as an IT consultant. The airline filed an appeal of this decision, but the two sides reached a settlement before it was heard. (*Fennimore v. Skyservice Airlines Inc.*, 2009 ONCA 246 (CanLII).

Leenen v. Canadian Broadcasting Corp., 2001 CanLII 4997 (ON CA) and Myers v. Canadian Broadcasting Corp., 2001 CanLII 4874 (ON CA)

Two heart surgeons interviewed by the CBC for its show the 5th Estate sued the broadcaster for defamation. The doctors had been participating in a trial for a heart drug and had willing agreed to discuss the drug trials with the television journalists. When the interview was edited, it created the innuendoes that the doctors were prescribing killer drugs just to receive payoffs from the drug company that had created the medication. It implied the heart specialists had risked their patients' health for their own personal gain and had acted dishonestly and negligently. The doctors were appalled when the show was broadcast and demanded an apology, claiming it was false, biased, misleading and seriously damaged their reputations as medical professionals. The CBC refused to apologize, so the two doctors sued the CBC for libel.

The Court's Decision

The trial court ruled, and the Court of Appeal agreed, that the CBC had presented a false and slanted report that it knew was inaccurate or simply untrue. The court concluded that the CBC never meant to be fair and knew that many of its claims were false or ill founded. It knew that this biased report could have significant negative impact on the professional reputations of the two heart specialists, but chose to present the malicious report anyway.

The defence of the truth failed as many of their statements were clearly not true and the 5th Estate had intentionally presented the facts in a false and misleading way. It was not justified as being in the public interest, in fact it was found to be contrary to the public interest, as it could create a panic among patients taking heart medications.

The court ruled that the television network was liable for libel and set the total damages for the two doctors at almost $2 million. It was the largest award for defamation in Canadian history at the time.

■ *Business Law* Applied

❻ Igor Taras returned to his desk one day after a meeting, to find a file folder with "This guy is crazy" written in large letters, right in the centre of the front cover. The file could be seen by everyone who passed by. Taras discovered that the remark had been written by a fellow employee, Gustaf Hermann.

   a) Is the comment libel or slander?
   b) Could the statement be considered to have been published?
   c) Taras suffered no monetary loss as a result of the statement. Could he sue Hermann in tort?

❼ John Nowark and Peter Youssoff were employed in the same company, and disliked each other intensely. A series of thefts occurred in the office.

On Monday, Youssoff whispered to Nowark, "I know you're the thief."

On Tuesday, Nowark overheard Youssoff say to a fellow employee, "Nowark is a jerk."

On Wednesday, Nowark heard Youssoff comment to their boss, "Nowark is incompetent."

The Monday statement:

   a) Is it libel or slander?
   b) Give two reasons for which Nowark cannot successfully bring an action against Youssoff.

The Tuesday statement:

   c) Is it libel or slander?
   d) Can Nowark successfully bring an action for defamation against Youssoff?

The Wednesday statement:

   e) Can Nowark successfully bring an action against Youssoff?

Defamation on the Internet

How do defamation laws apply to material published over the Internet? Communication over the Internet presents some unique features:

   ■ there is no editor, or intervenor of any sort, filtering potentially defamatory material
   ■ there is the possibility of posting material anonymously
   ■ there is immediate and widespread access to the material (to, potentially, millions of people around the world)

The web gives more people the ability to reach a large audience with ease; but the responsibilities in law are the same. Defamatory statements will bring liability. It is often difficult to determine who is making the statements on the internet as they are often posted on message boards and the writer usually uses a fake name. Many people make outrageous comments and think they can get away with it because it is an online remark and they cannot be traced, though this may be changing.

Example: Brian Burke, the former General Manager of the Toronto Maple Leafs was the target of on line defamatory remarks that falsely stated he'd had an affair with a Toronto sportscaster and had fathered her child. Those statements were lies and caused much upset for the two families involved. Burke then wanted to sue 18 "John Does" who posted these remarks on various message boards using names such as; No Fixed Address, Lavy 16, Tulowd and Naggah. Burke got permission to serve notice of his statement of claim to these people on the message boards where they had posted their comments. Burke convinced the court that it would be impractical and potentially impossible to determine who these people were, so the court allowed service this way. Burke then obtained default judgments against 5 of these anonymous on line commenters when they failed to file a statement of defense. Burke said he pursued this lawsuit to try to stop the growing tide of online libel and the belief people can post lies on the internet without any repercussions. (*Burke v. John Doe*, 2013 BCSC 964 (CanLII) — 2013-05-31

Example: In *Barrick Gold Corp. v. Lopehandia*, 2004 CanLII 12938 (ON CA), the court examined extensively the damages that should be awarded for defamation of a corporation on the internet. It commented that the Internet is "potentially a medium of virtually limitless international defamation." In this case the defendant had posted hundreds of libelous messages over two years on various Internet web sites and bulletin boards read by those interested in the gold industry. He claimed that Barrick had fraudulently acquired mining projects in Chile that belonged to the defendant. He accused Barrick, one of the world's largest gold mining companies, of major criminal activities such as; fraud, murder, tax evasion, involvement in organized crime and crimes against humanity. The court found the comments to be emotional, incoherent, ramblings that were defamatory and published with malice, and hurt Barrick Gold's reputation. The court awarded general damages of $75,000 for damage to their reputation, $50,000 for punitive damages and granted a permanent injunction prohibiting the defendant from posting or publishing any further defamatory remarks against Barrick or its employees.

Example: In a similar case of *Hunter Dickinson Inc. v. Butler*, 2010 BCSC 939 (CanLII), Rob Butler was held liable for a total of $450,000 in damages for comments he posted on Stockhouse. ca an online unregulated forum or bull-board where users argue about stocks. He claimed the mining company and its management company and its chairman and directors were "crooks, liars and thieves" and had committed "outrageous and despicable fraud on their own investors" and had used investors' money "to keep their butts out of jail." It was ruled to be libelous and these large damages were awarded.

Example: In *Newman et al v. Halstead et al*, 2006 BCSC 65 (CanLII) a woman repeatedly over a number of years in chat rooms, on websites and in emails defamed 9 teachers, a trustee and another parent who were involved in her child's school. The vicious personal attacks included may false statements alleging improper conduct, criminal behaviour and sexual misconduct. The 11 plaintiffs sued her but she said she was "judgment proof" and lacked the financial resources to compete with the plaintiffs and she refused to appear at the trial. The court however, went over the many outrageous statements that she had made. It found that they definitely constituted defamation and were shockingly vicious attacks made with malice. The plaintiffs were awarded a total of $676,000 in general and punitive damages and an injunction was also granted to prevent Ms. Halstead from continuing her stream of lies.

Defences

Innocent Dissemination

An individual who is in the business of distribution might well be unaware of the contents of a defamatory publication. Bookstores or libraries, for example, will not be held liable if it can be proven that it was not reasonable for them to know of the contents. Bookstores and libraries do not regularly review the contents of every book, magazine, or newspaper they have. However, a publisher does review the contents and often makes changes to the material submitted. So, a publisher cannot claim the defence of innocent dissemination. The principle underlying Innocent Dissemination may be extended to give protection to website owners who link to another website which contains defamatory statements.

Truth

An action for defamation will succeed only if the statement is untrue. The law presumes that a harmful statement is false, and it is up to the individual who made it to prove that it is true, and not harmful to the plaintiff's reputation. Merely claiming that the statement was repeated is not a defence if the statement is untrue. The defence of truth is called **justification**.

■ *Business Law* Applied

❽ **A library,** looking to expand its collection of Canadian heritage books, ordered several volumes from a publisher's catalogue. One of these, called *Towers of Gold, Basements of Clay*, was about the Canadian banking industry. In it, the author falsely claimed that the vice-president of a large Canadian bank had been associated with stock market fraud.

The book proved extremely popular with library patrons, and was often out on loan. One member of the library happened to be a friend of the banking executive mentioned, and told him what was said in the book. The banker sued the book's author, the publisher, and the library.

a) What defence(s) could each claim, if any?

Absolute Privilege

absolute privilege
complete immunity from liability for defamation, whereby the defamatory statement cannot be the grounds for a lawsuit

In certain situations, an individual can say anything, even if it is outrageous or untrue. During such proceedings as court trials, or legislative and parliamentary sessions, false statements can be made, and there is no possibility of a successful action for defamation. The comment must, however, be made during the actual proceedings. A member of Parliament can make a defamatory statement about a colleague while Parliament is in session, but cannot repeat that statement outside the House of Commons. **Absolute privilege**—complete immunity from liability for defamation, whereby the defamatory statement cannot be the grounds for a lawsuit—ends at the door of wherever the proceedings take place. You may hear one politician say to another in a debate in the House of Commons: I dare you to repeat that comment outside the house. That Member of Parliament is trying to get the other member to repeat the statement in a place where absolute privilege does not apply.

Qualified Privilege

qualified privilege
immunity from liability for defamation when the statement is made in good faith to a person or body which has authority over the person defamed

Qualified privilege is immunity from liability for defamation when the statement is made in good faith to a person or body which has authority over the person defamed. There are occasions when it might be necessary to report an individual to an organization that oversees a particular profession—the law society, or the college of physicians and surgeons, for example. In such situations, the person who makes the complaint does so out of duty, and does not deliberately set out to harm another's reputation. The statement is made without malice, and is not defamatory.

Statements made under these circumstances are privileged, and the individual against whom they are made cannot sue. Even if the allegations are later found to be false, a suit for defamation will not succeed. However, if it can be proved that the complainant was malicious, and made the statement for an improper purpose, an action is possible.

A client might be infuriated with his accountant, for example, because of some exchange of insults, and report her to the accountants' professional society alleging fraud, when in fact he knows there is no basis for doing so. Such a motive is improper and malicious—and the accountant could sue her client for defamation. Knowledge that the allegation is false is enough to establish the element of malice.

Fair Comment

fair comment
a defence to an action for defamation in which the harmful statements were made about public figures

Comments on matters of public concern—normally relating to politics or art—can fall under the umbrella of fair comment. **Fair comment** is a defence to an action for defamation in which the harmful statements were made about public figures. Such statements must offer opinions, rather than claim to be a true fact. If a newspaper columnist writes that a well-known rock star is a thief, that is a statement of fact; if the columnist says that the singer's latest CD is a disaster, that is an opinion—a comment on the artist's work. Media frequently rely on this defence. A comment is considered fair if any person could honestly express that opinion on the proven facts.

WIC Radio Ltd. v. Simpson, 2008 SCC 40 (CanLII)

Rafe Mair was a shock jock radio talk show host in British Columbia. A local school board had approved materials that could be used to teach tolerance of homosexuality in the schools. The defendant, Kari Simpson, was very opposed to this material being included in the curriculum as she believed it was promoting homosexuality. Ms. Simpson was a well-known social activist who was very opposed to the gay lifestyle.

In a radio broadcast editorial Mair compared Simpson's anti-gay attitude to famous bigots and said:

"There is no distinction between condemning the rights of blacks or Jews and condemning the civil rights of homosexuals. Whether she realizes it or not, Kari has by her actions placed herself alongside skinheads and the Ku Klux Klan. I'm not talking the violent aspects of those groups but the philosophical parallels to other examples of intolerance."

Simpson sued alleging the comment was defamatory in that it implied that she was advocating violence against homosexuals. Mair raised the defense of fair comment.

The Court's Decision

The court recited that there were two competing values in the defence of fair comment: one, in favor of protecting freedom of expression and the concern of the media about libel chill—lawsuits that inevitably follow if they report a controversial statement; the other, the need to protect a person's reputation, which may be their most valuable personal asset.

The court said that the defense of fair comment had to be restated in light of Charter values even though this did not involve government legislation. The court gave five tests to establish the defense of fair comment:

a) the comment must be on a matter of public interest;
b) the comment must be based on fact;
c) the comment, though it can include inferences of fact, must be recognizable as comment;
d) *the comment must satisfy the following objective test: could any [person] honestly express that opinion on the proved facts?*
e) even though the comment satisfies the objective test the defence can be defeated if the plaintiff proves that the defendant was actuated by express malice.

A core issue here was whether a reasonable viewer would understand that what was said was a 'comment', that is an opinion, not an attempt to report a fact. It found that a reasonable listener would understand that Mair, a radio personality with controversial opinions on everything, was not a reporter of facts. These personalities are as much entertainer as journalist.

The court concluded that Mair had established all elements of fair comment. Simpson's claim of defamation was dismissed.

Business Law Applied

9 A 12-year-old alleged that he was sexually abused by a popular rock singer. The allegations were later proven to be untrue.

a) Could the singer bring an action against the boy (a minor)?
b) If the boy states his claims in open court, could he later be successfully sued for defamation?
c) If the boy held a news conference, and said he intended to sue the rock star for abuse, would the boy have a defence against the alleged defamatory statement?
d) If a newspaper reported the statements made in court and at the news conference, would it have any defence against a claim of defamation?

Responsible Communication

The Supreme Court of Canada has recently created a new defence of responsible communication regarding matters of public interest. It will be of most use to journalists, publishers and perhaps even bloggers. The defendant must show, as the term suggests, that he or she acted responsibly in reporting on a matter of public interest. Responsibility can be established by showing due diligence in trying to verify the allegation. Recall that a defence of this type is successful even if it turns out that the "facts" are not true.

The Court also recognized a defence of "reportage". A journalist or publisher will not be liable for (quoting) (repeating) defamatory statements if they are clearly reported as quotes and repeated in order to report what was said in a given dispute (*Grant v. Torstar Corp.* 2009 SCC 61).

Injurious Falsehood

injurious falsehood

a false statement about goods or services that is harmful to the reputation of those goods or services

Products and services, too, develop a reputation. Deliberate harm to their reputation is known as injurious falsehood. It can also be known as product defamation or trade slander. To succeed in an action for injurious falsehood the plaintiff must establish that a false statement was made, directly or by implication, that hurts the reputation of their goods or services, was done maliciously with the intent to cause injury, and it caused or will cause economic losses.

Often lawsuits in this area involve an advertisement by the defendant that makes false claims about the plaintiff's product, hoping customers will then buy the defendant's product instead. Courts however often allow much leeway in the language used in advertisements and recognize the competitiveness in a free market, as shown in the Bell Canada v. Rogers case discussed here. Falsely claiming that a company is going bankrupt, is using illegal products or has violated patent or trademark laws can also be the basis for an injurious falsehood claim.

Companies can also use other laws to protect themselves from a false advertisement by a competitor. In *Go Travel Direct.Com Inc. v. Maritime Travel Inc.*, 2009 NSCA 42 (CanLII) a court awarded $216,842 in damages to Maritime Travel for misleading comparative advertising by Go Travel in violation of the Competition Act. Go Travel gave comparative rates with Maritime travel in such a way as to give the incorrect impression that Go's rates were cheaper. The Competition Act provides another possible remedy to deter unfair competition by a competitor in addition to a claim for injurious falsehood.

People who are angry about a bad product can make complaints or protest their bad product, so long as the statements they make are true or fall within qualified privilege. One angry car buyer parked his defective car across from the dealership, painted it yellow, and wrote damaging comments all over the car. The court ruled that this was legal because the statements on the car were true. People may also be able to use qualified privilege as a defence if their comments are not malicious and they are trying to warn the public of bad products.

Bell Canada v. Rogers Communications Inc. et al., 2010 ONSC 2788 (CanLII)

Bell Canada requested the court issue an interlocutory injunction to prevent Rogers from continuing to run an ad campaign that claimed Rogers' television, internet or wireless services were more reliable than Bell's services and that Rogers was more reliable in bad weather conditions. Bell claimed that the ads were a violation of the Competition Act and the Trade-Marks Act and Roger's was liable for injurious falsehood.

The ads showed a man sitting frustrated in front of a "frozen" computer screen, then sitting in front of a television set with a scrambled picture and then showed him standing on his balcony in the rain adjusting his satellite dish. The man then says "First my Internet now my satellite TV won't work in this weather." The next shot is of his neighbour, who is a Rogers' customer, easily surfing the net with a clear television picture on in the room. Then a voice

and caption say "Whether it's Internet, TV or wireless, Rogers is Canada's Reliable Network."

Rogers said the claim was without merit and an injunction was inappropriate since the ad was not false or misleading and it had only used that ad campaign for 6 weeks and would not be using it again. Rogers also claims that it has not specifically mentioned Bell in the ads and Bell had not suffered any harm. Rogers claimed the legal action was merely an attempt by Bell to limit Roger's ability to compete and restrict its free speech rights.

The Court's Decision

The court did a three stage analysis of the Bell's claim. First the court had to decide if there was a serious issue to be tried. It believed that Bell had been the target of the Rogers ad campaign and the factual accuracy of the commercial was a serious issue the court could consider. The second stage of analysis questioned whether Bell had or would suffer harm. The court stated Bell had not submitted any proof that it had suffered any harm from these ads and considered Bell's claims of financial loss to be an over-reaction. The court was not satisfied that Bell did or will suffer irreparable harm from the ads. Stage three of the analysis was a balance of convenience test. The court had to weigh who would suffer the greater harm if the injunction was granted or rejected. Would the harm Bell might suffer be worse than denying Rogers the right to make commercial comparisons of its services and exercise its freedom of speech rights? The court felt the balance was in Rogers favour.

The court recognized that these two companies were both aggressive advertisers and had repeatedly taken each other to court over previous advertisements. The court indicated Bell had not shown any proof of actual harm done to it and Rogers had a right to commercial freedom of speech. This right should not be constrained unless it had been abusing that right, and Bell had not proven abuse. It noted that consumers also could benefit from the two companies comparing their services to each other. The court had no interest in "micro-managing" an advertising battle between two major competitors and it had "little doubt Bell can through its own advertising, counter the effects which it says Rogers has caused." For these reasons the interlocutory injunction was denied.

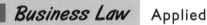

Business Law Applied

⑩ Angela McGowan had continual trouble with her new car, which required substantial repairs every few months. The manufacturer honoured its warranty and made the necessary repairs, but refused to take the vehicle back and refund McGowan's money.

After two years of frustration, McGowan painted the car bright yellow, and fixed a large plastic lemon on the roof. She then had "purchased at Fred's Car Dealer" painted in large letters on the side of the vehicle, and for the next few weeks parked it outside that dealership as often as she could.

The manufacturer and the dealer decided to ask for help from the courts.

   a) Did McGowan commit a tort? If so, which one?
   b) Are there any defences she could use if taken to court by the dealer and/or the manufacturer?

⑪ Shelly McLachlin bought some software form Macro Hard Inc. She had a lot of trouble with the software but Macro Hard Inc. would not refund her money.

McLachlin created a website called macrohardsucks.com. She posted a page describing her problems with the software and the company's refusal to be of any assistance. She also asked other people to post stories about their experience with the software and dealings with the company.

Assume that Macro Hard Inc. sues McLachlin for injurious falsehood for making statements posted on the website damaging its business's product.

   a) Will Macro Hard Inc. be successful against her respecting her personal complaint or does McLachlin have some defences? If so, what are they?
   b) Will McLachlin be responsible for the comments posted by other people on her website?

Deceit

The tort of deceit is often called civil fraud. It is often dealt with in contract law under fraudulent misrepresentation as well. It is essentially a lie that causes economic losses. Deceit involves the defendant making a false statement which it knows was untrue or partially untrue and intentionally misleads the plaintiff and actually causes them to suffer losses. Situations where companies have intentionally lied about the value of property or projected profits from a business or franchise are examples of instances when the court has ruled deceit has occurred. Often in these cases, punitive as well as pecuniary damages are awarded. In the XY Inc. case below a licensee using cattle sperm technology lied to decrease the royalty payments it owed and was found liable for the tort of deceit.

Intentional Business Torts

Competition is encouraged, so businesses are at liberty to attempt to drive a competitor from the market by legal means. There are some limitations on the right to compete; some business practices are considered to be unfair or anti-competitive. The Competition Act deals with many of these anti-competitive behaviours and can result in criminal penalties as well as damages. These will be discussed in a later chapter.

There are also several intentional business torts that may result from these situations when the defendant intended to hurt the plaintiff's business and actually did. Proof of actual damages is often required to be successful in these tort claims. Some of the more common intentional business torts include:

- Passing off
- Inducing breach of contract
- Misuse of confidential information and inducing breach of confidential information
- Intentional interference with economic relations
- Conspiracy

Passing Off

This is the business form of plagiarism—taking someone else's work and calling it your own. In everyday language, these products are called "knock-offs," or imitations. Examples of *passing off* include:

- fake Rolex watches
- a garage displaying a sign indicating it is recommended by an automobile association, when it is not
- a singer's name on a CD, when in fact the recording is made by an imitator
- a product displaying the "Good Housekeeping Seal of Approval," when it is not in fact approved

In general, people can use their own name as a business name. The exception to this is when that name has become associated with a particular business or product, and its use elsewhere in the same industry would deceive the public. Two obvious examples are the name McDonald's in the fast food business, or Campbell's in connection with soups or other prepared canned foods. If the business is unrelated, the exception does not apply. Anyone could open up a clothing store called McDonald's Fashions, or Campbell's Creations.

To succeed in a passing off action, the plaintiff must meet three requirements. First there must be goodwill or a reputation attached to the plaintiff's product such as its name, mark or a distinguishing feature. Secondly there is a misrepresentation by the defendant that will confuse the public into thinking that the defendant's product is the plaintiff's product or authorized by the plaintiff. The third requirement is that the plaintiff must show it has suffered or will suffer damage to their business or goodwill.

If these requirements are met, the plaintiff can succeed for passing off. The court will often award many monetary and non-monetary remedies in a passing off action. Compensatory and punitive damages are often awarded as well as an injunction, an Anton Piller order, a deliver up order and an accounting of profits.

Example: Passing off was the issue in the *Dentec Safety Specialists Inc. v. Degil Safety Products Inc.*, 2012 ONSC 4721 (CanLII) case. Two feuding brothers each operated competing companies that sold industrial safety equipment. Claudio Dente's company, Dente Safety Specialists Inc., had registered its internet domain name in 2004 as **dentesafety.com**. In 2009 Martino Dente who owned Degil Safety Products Inc., registered the domain name **dentesafety.ca** and when users went to that site, it automatically redirected people to his company's website degilsafety.com.

Claudio sued Martino for passing off. The court ruled the 3 elements of passing off were established, the names for the website were almost identical, it could confuse the public and could cause damage to the plaintiff's business. Damages of $10,000 were awarded.

■ *Critical Concepts of* Passing Off

The plaintiff must prove three elements to establish passing off:

- The appearance of the product is well-enough known to indicate the source of the product.
- The defendant's adoption of the similar appearance of its product is likely to cause confusion in the public.
- There are damages to the plaintiff as a result.

Kirkbi AG v. Ritvik Holdings Inc., 2005 SCC 65, [2005] 3 SCR 302

The plaintiff held the patents for LEGO construction sets, a distinctive children's' toy recognized around the world. The colour plastic small building bricks are well-known internationally. Kirkbi had registered a patent for LEGO but it had expired in Canada in 1988. The defendant Ritvik Holdings, also a toy manufacturer, began producing and selling Mega Blocks, plastic bricks that were interchangeable with LEGO bricks after the patent had expired. The plaintiff tried to claim that the upper surface of the LEGO bricks with raised studs distributed in a regular geometric pattern was an unregistered trademark and it sought a declaration that it had been infringed by Ritvik under the Trade-marks Act as well as the common law doctrine of passing off. It was seeking damages and a permanent injunction preventing Ritvik from selling its plastic toy bricks that were so similar to LEGO unless it attached a disclaimer that indicated their products were not LEGO.

The Court's Decision

The Supreme Court of Canada upheld the appeal court's decision that it was not a valid trademark or passing off claim. The plaintiff could not use the purely functional features of the product as a successful basis for a trademark or a passing off claim. The purpose of these laws is to protect the distinctiveness of the product, its name, symbol or guise, not the techniques and processes that are used to create the product. The court also noted that the company had been given an exclusive monopoly right when it had first registered its trademark but that protection had expired. It was now trying to extend that right using this new trademark and passing off claim based on functionality, but the court would not allow this. When the trademark expired, an open, freely competitive market was allowed. The exact process and techniques were now common to the trade and could not be exclusive to LEGO. The plaintiff's appeal was dismissed.

Inducing Breach of Contract

Inducing breach of contract most often occurs when a company persuades another company or person that it knows has a contract with a third party, to break that contract with the third party and they do break the contract causing harm to the third party.

inducing breach of contract
intentionally causing one party to breach their contract with another

Example: One of the most famous examples of this tort involved U.S. oil companies. In 1984 Getty Oil had orally agreed to sell about 1 billion barrels of oil to Pennzoil for $3.4 billion. Texaco then offered Getty $3.87 billion if it would break its contract with Pennzoil and sell the oil to Texaco. Getty knew it would be liable to Pennzoil for breach of contract and Texaco was liable for the tort of inducing breach of contract, but when Texaco agreed to pay all the damages the court would award against them both, Getty sold the oil to Texaco. Texaco had estimated the damages would be about $1 billion, but unfortunately it had not anticipated that the Texas jury that heard the case would set excessive punitive damages. The total award to Pennzoil was a shocking $11 billion. They eventually settled the case for $3 billion, but it still caused major financial problems for Texaco which sought bankruptcy protection. Canadians suffered as a result of this case too as Texaco Canada, one of the few gas retailers in this country, was sold to Imperial Oil for $1 billion to help pay for this damage award.

Misuse of Confidential Information and Inducing Breach of Confidential Information

A company's confidential information such as client lists, plans and designs or trade secrets are some of its most important assets and it does not want that information to become available to competitors. Employees, agents or people doing business with the company often sign contracts that include terms that specifically prohibit them from taking, selling or in any way using this private information outside of the company. This issue is discussed further in the chapter on Employment Law. If a person takes or uses this confidential information outside of the business without permission, they can be liable for **breach or misuse of confidential information**.

If a third party, for example a new employer, encourages someone to take this confidential information then they can also be liable for the separate tort of **inducing breach of confidential information**.

Example: When a General Motors executive, Jose Lopez, left to join Volkswagen in 1993, GM claimed Lopez took over 2 million pages of confidential GM documents with top secret plans, designs, factory blueprints and purchasing strategies to VW. GM claimed that this information destroyed the competitive advantage it had over Volkswagen in Europe. GM sued Lopez and VW for $5 billion alleging breach of confidential information by Lopez and inducing breach of confidential information by VW. They settled the case out of court when VW agreed to pay $100 million and purchase $1 billion in GM parts from 1997-2004. Lopez was convicted of criminal offences in Germany and fined $280,000 and he refused to return to the U.S. to face criminal charges there.

Even if it is not specifically stated in a contract, the court can rule that the important and private nature of the material imposes a duty on them to keep it confidential. If someone violates this obligation they can be liable for misuse of confidential information.

XY, LLC v. Zhu, 2013 BCCA 352 (CanLII)

XY Inc. developed specialized sperm sorting technology that allowed cattle breeders to sort sperm based on chromosomes into female (X) and male (Y) groups. This lead to very efficient breeding in both dairy and beef cattle and revolutionized the industry. Sex specific semen and embryos for in vitro fertilization were then possible. This complex technology had been developed after years of research. XY signed a licensing agreement to allow Jing Jing Genetics to use this technology in Canada and in China, but the agreement allowed XY to maintain strict control over this confidential information. Jing Jing was to pay XY royalties based on its use of the product and process.

XY however discovered that Jing Jing was falsely reporting its use of the technology to avoid paying proper royalties and it was also violating the confidentiality clauses in the licensing agreement and trying to challenge its patents in China and encouraging others to cut out XY from its royalty rights. XY sued Jing Jing and three of its key employees for breach of contract, breach of confidentiality, deceit and conspiracy and sought damages and a permanent injunction.

The Court's Decision

The court ruled that Jing Jing was liable for the tort of **deceit** as it had clearly under reported its usage of the technology and intentionally lied in its reports to avoid paying XY the required royalty amounts. It was also liable for **breach of confidentiality** as it had taken XY's information to try to set up its own operations in China and exclude XY. The court ruled that Jing Jing and the employees were liable for **conspiracy** as they had intentionally created a scheme that would under report their usage of XY processes so that they would pay XY much less in royalties than required under the licensing agreement.

The court granted XY a permanent injunction against Jing Jing prohibiting it from using XY's technology and set the damages including unpaid royalties at $8,500,000.

Example: In *Lac Minerals Ltd. v. International Corona Resources Ltd.*, [1989] 2 S.C.R. 574, a junior mining company made some preliminary explorations and suspected it had discovered large gold deposits on land owned by an elderly lady in northern Ontario. Knowing it might not have the resources to develop such a large find, it approached Lac Minerals, a large mining company. Corona shared its geological information with Lac in contemplation of a joint venture or similar business arrangement between them. Lac however proceeded to purchase the land from the elderly lady and claim the site exclusively for itself. Lac cut Corona out completely. The property turned out to contain one of the world's largest gold deposits worth close to $1 billion. Corona sued claiming Lac was liable for misuse of confidential information. The court agreed that the information Corona had shared was not known to the public, so it was confidential. Under the circumstances, when Corona shared this information with Lac, it created an obligation of confidence and Lac was liable for breach of confidence. By purchasing the land for its own exclusive use, Lac had clearly misused the confidential information for its own benefit. The court ruled the appropriate remedy was to force Lac, which had been operating the mine for almost 9 years, to turn over the entire mining operation to Corona along with all the money it had made, minus the costs Lac had incurred developing the site.

Intentional Interference with Economic Relations

This tort of unlawful interference with economic relations has three requirements: 1) that the defendant intended to injure the plaintiff 2) the defendant did interfere with the plaintiff's economic interests by illegal or unlawful means 3) and it caused the plaintiff actual economic losses.

Example: In *67122 Ontario Ltd. v. Sagaz Investments Ltd.*, [1998] 40 O.R. (3d) 329 a bribery scheme designed to destroy a competitor was uncovered. Robert Sommers was the head of Canadian Tire's automotive division. Canadian Tire bought its seat covers from the plaintiff corporation. Stewart Lawson of Aim Inc. offered to pay Sommers 2 per cent of all purchases by Canadian Tire of seat covers from Aim Inc. Somers agreed and Canadian Tire stopped purchasing from the plaintiff. The bribes were paid to a corporation controlled by Sommers called Sagaz Investments Ltd. Canadian Tire learned of this kickback scheme and fired Sommers but continue to deal with Aim Inc. The plaintiff corporation sued Aim and Sommers for intentional interference with economic relations. They intentionally interfered with the plaintiff's business by unlawful means (bribes) and caused significant losses. The court awarded damages of $2 million for loss of business plus $50,000 in punitive damages.

Alleslev-Krofchak v. Valcom Limited, 2010 ONCA 557 (CanLII)

Leona Alleslev-Krofchak was a leader in managing the change to performance-based contracts for the maintenance of military air fleets. She was needed by Valcom to provide consulting services to fulfil a contract that Valcom had been awarded by the Department of National Defense. She was also a part shareholder of Temagami Outfitting Company. Her consulting contract was structured so that Valcom contracted with ARINC, a large U.S. company and one of Valcom's rivals, which then subcontracted with Temagami to provide Ms. A-K's services.

Later Valcom became dissatisfied and wanted Ms. A-K out and one of Valcom's own employees to take her position. Valcom requested that ARINC remove A-K from the project but it refused. Two of Valcom's employees then wrote emails to ARINC with false statements claiming Ms. A-K had lied, lacked integrity, was untrustworthy and lacked the management skills for the job. Valcom finally locked Ms. A-K out of the project knowing it would force ARINC to breach its contract with Temagami and end A-K's services. Ms. A-K could no longer work on this project and since this case, she never worked in this field again. Ms. Alleslev-Krofchak sued Valcom and its two employees for defamation and intentional interference with economic relations and Temagami also sued the three defendants for intentional interference with economic relations and inducing a breach of contract.

The Court's Decision

The court ruled that Valcom and its two employees were liable for defamation as the statements in the emails about Ms. Alleslev-Krofchak's were lies that damaged her reputation. They were also liable for intentional interference with economic relations to both Ms. A-K and Temagami. The three requirements for that tort had been established: the defendants intended to cause injury to her and Temagami, they did use unlawful means (defamation, conspiracy and breach of contract) and it did cause economic losses. They were also liable for inducing breach of contract as they knew when they locked out Ms. A-K from the project it would force ARINC to breach its contract with Temagami. Ms. A-K was awarded $200,000 in general damages and $129,000 for economic losses. Temagami was awarded $373,552 for economic losses as well.

■ *Business Law* Applied

⑫ **Volkswagen Canada Ltd.** gave an exclusive franchise for an area in Halifax to Hillcrest Motors Ltd., which was owned by John Spicer and Stephen Gaetz. Because Volkswagen promised delivery of its new Rabbit in November 1994, but only made delivery in 1995, Hillcrest was not successful.

Volkswagen became concerned about Hillcrest and told Hillcrest's bank not to honour any cheques from Hillcrest unless they were also signed by a Volkswagen representative named Baldwin. The bank did return several cheques because of these directions from Volkswagen.

a) Were there any unlawful acts done by Volkswagen?
b) Does Hillcrest have any rights against Volkswagen respecting its instructions to the bank?

In Summation

Torts

- A tort is a civil remedy for the wrongful harm done by one person to another. The harm will either be done intentionally or unintentionally.

Intentional Torts

false arrest

causing a person to be arrested without reasonable cause

false imprisonment

unlawfully restraining or confining another person

occupier

any person with a legal right to occupy premises

trespasser

one who enters without consent or lawful right on the lands of another, or who, having entered lawfully, refuses to leave when ordered to do so by the owner

- **False arrest** is causing a person to be arrested without reasonable cause. **False imprisonment** is unlawfully restraining or confining another person.

- Citizen's arrest. If a person is sued for false imprisonment as a result of a citizen's arrest, the citizen can establish the defence of legal authority if:
  a) the citizen had reasonable grounds to believe the other person was committing a criminal offence, and
  b) the other person actually committed a criminal offence

- Malicious prosecution. If a person gives information to the police so that another is prosecuted but the charge is dismissed, and if that person acted out of malice and did not have proper grounds for the charge, the tort of malicious prosecution has been made out.

- Trespass. A business's premises is private property. The **occupier**—any person with a legal right to occupy premises—can prevent anyone from entering or can make someone leave upon being given notice. If the person does not leave on being given notice, that person is a trespasser, and reasonable force can be used to remove the individual. A **trespasser** is one who enters without consent or lawful right on the lands of another, or who, having entered lawfully, refuses to leave when ordered to do so by the owner.

- Trespass to Goods. Trespass to goods or trespass to chattels involves intentional interference that causes damage or interference to another's goods.

- Conversion. This is keeping or taking property of another without consent and resembles theft in criminal law.

- Nuisance. Nuisance is the intentional unreasonable interference with another's use or enjoyment of their property.

- Assault. An assault in tort law is akin to a threat of violence. The actual touching without consent with intent to do harm is a battery.

- Intrusion upon Seclusion. This is the tort for invasion of privacy and occurs if one intentionally intrudes on the seclusion or private affairs or concerns of another and the intrusion would be highly offensive to a reasonable person.

- Defamation. Untrue statements, made to a third person about an individual's or business's reputation, and that cause harm to that individual or business, are the basis for defamation.

- There are a number of defences for defamation: innocent dissemination, truth, absolute and qualified privilege, fair comment and public interest responsible communication defence.

- Injurious falsehood. Slander about a business's product is called injurious falsehood. In addition to truth, the defence of qualified privilege applies.

- Deceit. Deceit is a lie that is made to defraud another and actually does cause damages.

- Intentional Business Torts. There are a number of torts under this heading. These are largely unfair business practices by which one business intends to harm another. These include: passing off, inducing breach of contract, misuse of confidential information and inducing breach of confidential information, intentional interference with economic relations.

Closing Questions

Intentional Torts

1. a) What tort is shoplifting?
   b) Some businesses are suing parents for their children's shoplifting. Are parents liable for their children's torts?
   c) Are children liable for their own torts? Does the *Young Offenders Act* protect them?
   d) If a business does not want to lay criminal charges, what other solutions in law are available for the control of shoplifting?

2. Do you think that the courts are correct in limiting a shopkeeper's right to arrest without legal liability? Should there be special rules for businesses that are vulnerable to loss by shoplifting?

3. Anne Dinnert had been general manager of Tough Attitudes, a dress manufacturer, for 10 years. She quit that job and started her own clothing plant on the other side of the city. Her former boss sent letters to Dinnert's customers saying that she had breached her employment agreement and was under criminal investigation. None of this was true.
   a) Does Dinnert have any remedy in tort law against her former employer regarding these letters? If so, what is it?

4. It was the week before Christmas, and all through the mall it was extremely busy. Frank and Marsha DeValeriote were in the mall parking lot searching for a place to park. They noticed a car leaving in the next aisle, so Frank DeValeriote jumped out of their vehicle and ran over to "stand guard" while his wife drove around to park.

   Before Mrs. DeValeriote could reach the spot, Bruno Greyson drove up and honked at Frank DeValeriote to move so that he could park. Frank DeValeriote explained that his wife was on her way, and refused to move. Greyson decided to force the issue, and two or three times moved his car quickly towards DeValeriote, stopping just short of contact. At this point DeValeriote, who had not moved, shouted some obscene words at Greyson who, infuriated, drove forward until his car touched the other man. Greyson kept moving gently forward. DeValeriote slipped, breaking an arm in the fall. Mrs. DeValeriote had driven up as this was happening, and was so upset that she dropped a fresh cup of coffee in her lap, causing third-degree burns.
   a) What is the nature of the tort or torts which have occurred in this normally quiet shopping-mall parking lot at this joyous time of year?
   b) Is provocation available as a defence for Greyson? If not, why not?

5. A young woman applied for a job. Her potential employer asked one of her previous employers for a reference, and was told that there was suspicion the young woman had been stealing during her time with the company. The woman did not get the job for which she had applied, and later

learned about the statement made by her former boss. In fact, the real thief had been caught a few weeks after the young woman had left the company.

a) Can she sue her former employer for defamation?

b) Does that employer have any defences?

6. A man is charged with armed robbery and confesses. In order to get out of the confession he falsely alleges that the police beat him while he was held in custody, and shows bruises to prove his claim. The bruises happened as a result of a fight a few hours before he was arrested. An investigation of the alleged police brutality is held, and the officers involved are charged. At the trial of the police officers, the truth is learned, and they are acquitted.

a) Do the police officers have a remedy against the man for making this allegation?

7. Sun Yat was scheduled to write his final chartered-accountancy exam on Friday at 11:00 a.m. On his way to the exam, he stopped at an office-supply store to pick up some extra pencils and a battery for his calculator. In a hurry, Sun Yat anxiously searched the shelves for the items he wanted, and he was watched by the store manager, who considered the young man's actions suspicious. Suddenly realizing that he was running out of time to make it to his exam, Sun Yat very quickly left the store without buying anything, and began to run through the mall.

The store manager ran after Sun Yat and stopped him at the mall exit. Quietly, the manager asked Sun Yat to return to the store with him or he would shout so loudly that every security guard in the mall would be there within seconds. Protesting, Sun Yat attempted to get by the manager, who then grabbed him by the arm and called a security guard to help escort Sun Yat back to the store, where he was detained until the police arrived. A search of Sun Yat's briefcase revealed that he had not taken anything from the store, and the store manager promptly apologized.

Sun Yat was 30 minutes late for the start of the exam and was not permitted to write it. As a result, he did not receive his chartered-accountancy certificate, which he had been fairly certain of obtaining, and is now required to repeat the course—which is only offered every other year. Consequently, Sun Yat lost a job opportunity that had been offered conditional upon him passing the exam and receiving his certificate. The job would have paid him $40,000 a year to start.

a) What remedy, if any, does Sun Yat have?

b) Does the store manager have any defence if Sun Yat decided to take him to court?

8. Marion Elliot decided to take a year off work and travel around the world. She terminated her apartment lease, put her furniture in storage, and left a very valuable oil painting she owned in the care of a friend of hers, Ilya Shostakovitch. The friend hung the painting in her living room, and during the year, received many compliments on how good it looked. Shostakovitch came to think of the painting as her own. When Elliot returned and asked for the painting back, Shostakovitch refused, saying, "Possession is nine-tenths of the law. I am very possessive."

a) What remedy in law does Elliot have against Shostakovitch?

9. To promote the opening of his new fast-food location, James Kirk stood on the sidewalk at lunchtime, handing out flyers and telling people about the quality of the food available from his outlet. In the course of his statements to passersby, he made the comment that, "In my opinion the cook next door wouldn't know his hand from a spatula, and further, he uses leftovers in the hamburgers." The chef/owner of the restaurant next door happened to be standing near James at the time this comment was made, and the two ended up in a heated argument. The final words were, "You can't say that about me or the food I serve! I'll see you in court."

a) What is the nature of the statements Kirk has made?

b) Will the outraged chef be successful in a court action, or is there a defence available to Kirk?

10. a) What is the reason that, in law, a person cannot sue another for slander without proof of actual monetary loss, but a business can sue someone for damage to the reputation of the business or its product without proof of actual loss to the business?

b) The traditional test for the division of defamation into libel or slander has been whether it was written or spoken. What new tests might be proposed to deal with such categorizations on the Internet?

11. **Internet Research.** You are asked to do a report for this class on the Crookes v. Wikimedia case. If you repeat any of the alleged defamatory comments in your report, are you liable in defamation? Is the mere fact that you are repeating comments a defence? Review all the defences discussed in the text. Do you have any defence?

12. An internet search engine, such as Google, contains results showing websites that a person claims are libelous. If the statements are in fact libelous, will Google be found responsible? Give arguments pro and con and your opinion as to which is the more likely to succeed determining the law on this point. Cite any principle of law or case law to support your positions.

13. The principles underlying the rules of law established in historically different situations are adapted to develop new rules required by advances in technology.
    a) Use the facts in the case of Crookes v Wikimedia Foundation Inc. discuss the defences to defamation to develop a new rule that protects freedom of speech on the Internet but also protects personal reputations against defamation.
    b) Give an example of a wording for a link on a website that would not be defamatory, and one that would be.

14. Walter, a real estate agent, knew of a 200 acre tract of land beside a housing development that everyone thought could not be serviced with municipal water and electricity. Walter discovered a way to service it, by connecting with the services in the next municipality. Walter then approached John, a major real estate developer, and after John promised to keep the information secret, Walter told John how this land could be serviced. They agreed to purchase the land together and split the profits with Walter receiving 30% and John 70%. John, then on his own, purchased the 200 acres through his own company and completely excluded Walter from the development.
    a) What legal action could Walter take?
    b) What defenses could John use and what should the final decision be in this case?

15. Kevin worked as a cable installer for cable company C in the Windsor area for 15 years. Kevin then left to work in the U.S., but several years later returned to Windsor. Kevin was hired by company M a cable industry contractor that did work for cable company C. When company C discovered that Kevin was working for company M, C told M to fire Kevin as it did not want Kevin working on any of their equipment. Company M didn't want to lose business with Company C so Kevin was fired. Kevin was unable to get any work in the cable industry in the Windsor area, so he had to find a new career.
    a) Can Kevin sue one or both of the companies, if so on what basis?
    b) How should damages be calculated in this case?

16. A beer company acquired the exclusive right to provide food and beverages at a rock concert. The beer company then sold the exclusive right to sell water at the concert to Ron. Ron then sold those exclusive rights to Steve for $100,000. On the day of the concert the beer company allowed several other companies to sell water at the event. Ron, who had access to Steve's water sold much of it but did not give the proceeds to Steve. The city told the beer company that it had to give away 650,000 bottles of water free for public health concerns in the heat wave. Steve, who had been told he would sell between 1 to 1.5 million bottles of water ended up only selling 250,000. Steve contacted his lawyer over this event.
    a) What possible causes of action does Steve have in this case?
    b) What should the court decided and what remedies would be appropriate?

Negligence

Negligence

The Concept of Negligence

In everyday language, negligence is another word for carelessness. In law, however, the term has a specific technical meaning. Negligence as a tort requires all the elements discussed in the following section.

An automobile accident is probably the most common instance of the tort of negligence. One car driver seldom intends to injure another. But when that individual's attention wanders for a moment and the vehicle fails to stop at a stop sign, slamming into another car, the driver has committed the tort of negligence.

Not every careless act that causes injury is the tort of negligence. There are a number of questions that help decide whether a particular act of carelessness is, in fact, legal negligence. These include:

- Was there a duty to look out for the injured person?
- What was the standard of care that should have been used?
- Was damage caused by a failure to meet that standard of care?
- Was there a reasonably close causal connection between the conduct and the injury, were the damages reasonably foreseeable (proximate cause)?

The answer to all four questions is "yes" in the automobile accident described above, because:

- The first car driver owed a duty to look out for to the other driver
- The standard of care was to stop at all stop signs
- The failure to meet the standard of care caused the injury
- Compensable damage (to the car) and perhaps injury to the other driver resulted

■ *Critical Concepts of* Negligence

To establish negligence, the courts will ask four questions:

- Was it reasonably foreseeable that the plaintiff would be injured by the defendant's act? (duty owed)
- Did the defendant fail to do what a reasonable person would have done in the circumstances to prevent or avoid injury? (breach of duty)
- Did the failure to act reasonably (carefully) cause the plaintiff's injury? (**causation:** one of the elements of negligence, relating to whether the action produced the damage or injury)
- Did the plaintiff suffer damage or injury as a result, the general nature which was reasonably foreseeable by the defendant (damages)?

causation

one of the elements of negligence, relating to whether the action produced the damage or injury

1) To Whom Is a Duty Owed?

In the early development of the law of negligence, the courts accepted that a duty was not owed to everyone, but only to those who it was reasonable to foresee could be injured as a result of a negligent act. In recent times, this limitation has been worn away, and the scope of duty is very wide, especially for businesses that deal with the public. A reasonable person is always thinking of the safety of others first. There are very few reported cases today where a business has avoided liability because it does not owe a duty to the person injured. The case, *Donoghue v. Stevenson* below, significantly expanded the scope of duty in the business context.

Donoghue v. Stevenson, [1932] A.C. 562 (House of Lords)

Mrs. MacAllister, *née* Donoghue, and a friend went to a restaurant. The friend paid for the meal. One of the items supplied was ginger beer, served in a dark-coloured bottle. When Donoghue finished the bottle, she found the decomposed remains of a snail at the bottom. Donoghue became very ill from drinking the toxic substance.

In looking to sue someone who would be responsible, Donoghue found several problems with the law as it then existed. She did not buy the ginger beer herself, and so could not sue the restaurant owner in contract. The restaurant would not be found negligent, as the bottle was opaque and it was impossible for the snail to be seen, so the restaurant owner was not in breach of what a reasonable person would have done in the circumstances. It was the manufacturer who probably breached the standard of care.

Donoghue therefore sued the manufacturer of the ginger beer in tort, claiming that the company had owed a duty to her as a person who might consume the drink.

The Court's Decision

The case was eventually heard by the House of Lords in England, that country's highest court. There, the decision was that the soft-drink manufacturer had indeed failed to observe a reasonable standard of care, and also had owed a duty towards Donoghue. Lord Atkin, one of the judges, produced what has become the classic statement of the definition of the scope of duty:

> The rule that you are to love your neighbour becomes in law, you must not injure your neighbour; and the lawyer's question, "Who is my neighbour?" receives a restricted reply. You must take reasonable care to avoid acts or omissions which you can reasonably foresee would be likely to injure your neighbour. Who, then, in law, is my neighbour? The answer seems to be persons who are so closely and directly affected by any act, that I ought to have them in contemplation as being so affected when I am directing my mind to the acts or omissions that are called in question.

The test for the scope of duty has become that we owe a duty to anyone we can reasonably anticipate might be harmed by our conduct.

The Expanding Scope of Duty

As the courts' acceptance of the extent of duty broadens, public awareness of what is possible under negligence laws has resulted in new types of claims, many of which are currently in process. Rape victims have sued police forces for not warning of known rapists in their area.[1]

---

1. The case went to trial. The plaintiff was awarded $250,000 against the Metropolitan Toronto Police Commission. See *Jane Doe v. Metropolitan Toronto Commissioners of Police* (1998), 39 O.R. (3d) 487.

A son whose father was convicted of hiring a killer to murder his wife has sued the father for psychological trauma after seeing the mother murdered in front of him. Victims of injuries caused by persons ordered deported because of violent criminal records, but allowed to remain in Canada, have sued immigration officials.

Some cases have resulted in findings that people owe a duty to others with whom they had no direct dealings. Psychiatrists, for example, have been found liable to the families of victims killed by patients whose murderous tendencies were known to the doctor, but who did not warn the authorities of the danger. Doctors in general practice have been held liable to victims of traffic accidents caused by patients with epilepsy when the physicians did not report that disability to the driver-licensing authority. All provincial highway-traffic acts require doctors to report patients who are physically incapable of driving.

In *Ingles v. Tutkaluk Construction Ltd.*, 2000 SCC 12, the Court found that municipal building inspectors owed a duty of care to a homeowner and an owner-builder respectively who incurred repair costs as a result of the inspectors' failure to take reasonable care to ensure that construction on their houses was properly carried out. In *Hill v. Hamilton-Wentworth Regional Police Services Board*, 2007 SCC 41, the Court held that the police owed a duty of care to a suspect of crime who, as a result of their negligent investigation, was wrongfully convicted and imprisoned. In *Adams v. Borrell 2008 NBCA 62 (CanLII)*, the Court held that Agriculture Canada owed a duty of care to commercial potato farmers who suffered economic loss as a result of its faulty investigation of the source of a potato virus. In *Just v. B.C.* [1989]2 SCR 1228, the Court held that government inspectors of rock slopes adjacent to a public highway owed a duty of care to a driver who was injured by a falling rock.

■ *Business Law*   Applied

❶ Easson Seel was returning home around 2:00 a.m., and took a shortcut through the lot belonging to Acupress Inc., a tool-and-die firm. An old wooden shed, badly dilapidated and abandoned for years, stood on one corner of the property. Seel knew the structure was there.

Seel failed to stamp out a cigarette that he dropped as he passed the old shed. The cigarette ignited some dry grass, and the fire quickly spread to the shed. Unknown to Seel, a security guard, Michael Kuz, was asleep in the shed, after having drunk too much before he came on duty that night. The shed was totally destroyed by the flames, and Kuz was killed. Kuz's wife and children brought an action against Seel for the wrongful death of their husband and father.

   a) Did Seel owe a duty to Kuz? What is the test the courts will apply to determine the existence of a duty?

   b) If he does owe such a duty, is the type of injury foreseeable?

❷ A car hit a metal post on a strip of gravel that divided two highway lanes. The post was bent over. A taxicab driver, illegally driving on the gravel strip in order to pass another vehicle, was killed when the post came up through the floorboards of his car and impaled him. His wife and children sued the driver whose car had damaged the metal post.

   a) Did the first driver owe a duty to the taxicab driver?

   b) Did he owe a duty to the taxicab driver's wife and children?

Beyond the Scope of Duty

While the scope of duty has expanded such that a humourist has said: the test should be understood as foreseeable by the reasonable psychic, there are limits to what is reasonably foreseeable.

Example: A group of villagers from Ecuador sued the TSX for listing a mining corporation, Copper Mesa, which had raised money on the TSX to develop a large-scale open pit mine near their village. In addition to environmental damage, the villagers alleged that security forces hired by Copper Mesa harassed and intimidated them including making death threats. They claimed that the TSX owed a duty to them not to let a business raise money on its stock exchange when it could reasonably foresee harm to them. The court disagreed and said the harm to the villagers was not reasonably foreseeable and hence the TSX owed no duty to the plaintiff's. (Piedra v. Copper Mesa Mining Corporation, 2011 ONCA 191 (CanLII))

Example: The Plaintiff, a player on a soccer team in the Ontario Soccer League was made a paraplegic from injuries suffered in a game. He sue the Bank of Montréal that had sponsored the team claiming that as members of the team were a target market for the advertising, the bank had a duty to team members who might be injured. However, the court rejected this wide scope of duty saying the relationship was not close enough (proximate) to establish a duty to someone who purchases advertising and the activity associated with it. The Plaintiff's claim was dismissed. (*Boudreau v. Bank of Montreal*, 2012 ONSC 3965)

Expanding Duties and Negligence

The decision in *Donoghue v. Stevenson* opened a very wide scope of duty on all persons for negligence acts, but liability for the negligent use of words, which include advice, opinions and the like both verbal and written, was not at that time actionable. Then, in another landmark case in the law of negligence, the Courts held a bank employee liable to the customer of a second bank for negligently advising that a business's credit was good (*Hedley, Byrne & Co. Ltd. v. Heller & Partners Ltd.*, [1964] AC 465). However since the bank had a disclaimer clause the court ruled that it was not liable for statements made to the customer. The liability for opinions and advice is discussed in more detail under the topic 'Business Advisor's Liability'.

The courts were concerned that imposing any responsibility for negligence on advice or information may make certain functions financially unviable. One profession noted was that of auditors of a corporation whose shares were traded publicly. The auditors could be held liable to investors around the world who relied on the company's financial statements to make investment decisions. That would be an unlimited liability to an unlimited class of persons. In order to restrict the scope of this new duty, the Courts formulated a separate test originally called the "Special Relationship" test. Now there were two tests for negligence: one for conduct—reasonable foreseeability; and one for words—special relationship.

Reconciliation of the Two Tests

The two types of negligence: one for words/advice (*Hedley, Berne v. Heller*) and for conduct (*Donoghue v. Stevenson*), had at this point two different tests to establish negligence. The Courts harmonized these two tests by developing a single but two stage analysis usually referred to as the "Anns" test after the British case by the name *Anns v. Merton London Borough Council*, [1978] A.C. 728 (H.L.). The two stages are:

1. Is there a sufficiently close relationship between the parties to justify the imposition of a duty (proximity) and, if so,
2. Are there any residual policy considerations to negate or limit the scope of that duty, the class of persons to whom it is owed, or the damages to which breach may give rise?

In the above two stages, there are policy factors in each stage. These policy factors permit the court to limit or deny liability even though a logical application of a previously established precedent would appear to require a finding of liability. The stage one policy factors are relative to the individuals involved; in stage two they are relative to the interest of society generally.

Example: In *Cooper v. Hobart* 2001, SCC 79 the Supreme Court refused to impose a duty of care on the Registrar of Mortgage Brokers for the province of B.C. to individual investors. About 3,000 people had been defrauded of about $182 million by Eron Mortgage Corp. They claimed that the Registrar of Mortgage Brokers should have suspended the company or made its concerns public as soon as it was aware of the illegal conduct, rather than waiting 13 months to suspend it. Investors claim that earlier public announcements could have prevented many losses. The Supreme Court ruled the Registrar owed a duty of care to the public as a whole, but not to individual investors, so the Registrar, and therefore the province of B.C., could not be held responsible for these losses. The court also commented that to impose this duty on the Registrar would effectively create an insurance scheme for an unlimited number of investors that could have enormous financial consequences for the taxpayers of B.C. For obvious policy reasons, this was not a situation the Supreme Court would allow. Similarly, in an action against the Investment Dealers Association (IDA) by investors when a brokerage firm acted illegally, the court ruled that the IDA did not owe a duty to individual investors nor would it serve as an insurance fund for investment losses. *(Morgis v. Thomson Kernaghan & Co., 2003 CanLII 5999 (ON CA)*

Example: A 13 year old boy was hired to do part time work at a cottage for $8.00 per hour. The cottage owner told him not to use any power equipment unless supervised by an adult. When the boy could not get the gas lawn mower to work, he lit a match in the dark boat house to see, but it ignited the gas vapours. A fire broke out causing $285,000 in damages. The cottage owner was insured, but the insurance company then tried to sue the boy for negligence for this loss. The court ruled that under the Anns test the cottage owner had not contemplated the boy would be held liable for any losses he caused, and from a policy perspective, the court did not want to impose liability on an employee. Employers bear the cost of employees' negligence and they buy insurance as a cost of doing business. It would place an unfair burden on employees if they were held liable, especially in this case with a young boy working for menial wages.(*Douglas v. Kinger*, 2008 ONCA 452 (CanLII) leave to appeal to S.C.C. denied)

When there has been an outbreak of certain diseases, some people who became infected and their families tried to sue the government for not adequately protecting them from the outbreak. The courts however would not extend the duty of care that far. In *Eliopoulos Estate v. Ontario (Minister of Health and Long-Term Care)*, 2006 CanLII 37121 (ON CA) the family of a man who died from West Nile Virus tried unsuccessfully to sue the Ontario government for negligence for the way it dealt with the virus. In *Williams v. Ontario* 2009 ONCA 378 (CanLII) similar issues arose when people tried to form a class action and sue the government for the SARS outbreak in Toronto. The two types of policy considerations in these cases are also discussed in the Abarqez case below.

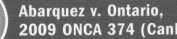

Abarquez v. Ontario, 2009 ONCA 374 (CanLII)

In 2003 Toronto suffered an outbreak of SARS (Severe Acute Respiratory Syndrome) a viral respiratory disease that the medical community knew little about. SARS was easily spread and hospitals and the government were initially not sure how to effectively contain the disease. Over a 4 month period, 251 people became infected with SARS and of these, 44 people died.

In the Abarquez case, 53 front line nurses who claim they suffered serious injuries to their health due to SARS, as well as 95 of their family members, sued the Ontario government for negligence. They claimed that as health care workers they were particularly vulnerable to the risks posed by SARS and that they had no choice but to follow the Directives issued by Ontario to the hospitals. They argued that relationship created a duty of care and was a basis for their negligence claim.

They argued that the government mismanaged the SARS crisis and many of the Directives given were inadequate or inappropriate or failed to properly contain the spread of the disease. If the court ruled the government owed the nurses and their families a duty of care, then their claims of negligence would have to be considered by the court. But the first hurdle was; did the government owe the nurses a duty of care?

The Court's Decision

The court ruled that nurses' claim in the SARS case was similar to the class action claim by patients who had contracted SARS. In both cases the court refused to impose a private law duty of care on the government in this health crisis. The protection of the health of the general public was the main concern of the Chief Medical Officer of Health when he issued Directives. He had to balance many competing interests and factors while trying to achieve a position that best satisfied the public interest. "The very nature of a duty by a public authority to the public at large is ordinarily inconsistent with the imposition of a private law duty of care to any individual or group of individuals."

While recognizing the brave and caring dedication of the nurses in this crisis, the court stated that to impose a private law duty of care upon Ontario to safeguard the health of nurses would put it in conflict with its duty to the general public and would impact health care policy priorities.

The Court ruled that imposing on the government a private law duty of care to individuals to prevent the spread of the virus would not be allowed. It would create an unreasonable and undesirable burden on Ontario and interfere with public health decision-making. For these policy reasons, it would not recognize that the government owed a private law duty of care to individuals affected by the outbreak of a disease.

2) The Standard of Care

reasonable person test

a test or standard based on what a reasonable person would have done in similar circumstances

The Reasonable Person Test The **reasonable person test** is a test or standard based on what a reasonable person would have done in similar circumstances. Once it is established that a duty is owed to the person injured, the next issue is to decide the degree, or standard, of care that is owed. In order to decide the standard of care an individual should follow in a particular situation, the courts ask what a reasonable person would have done. This is used to determine the standards to be applied to, for example, a car driver, a skier, and the owner of a business.

Legalese

Reasonable The word **reasonable** is used often in a legal context, usually along with other words—reasonable foreseeability; reasonable person. *Reasonable* is used, and not *average*. Hence, the reasonable person is more than an average person. The reasonable person is a careful or prudent individual. Reasonable foreseeability is more than just average foreseeability, and implies that some thought has been given to the consequences of an action.

Reasonable also means a finding of fact, not of law. Where civil juries are available, it is a question to be decided by the jury, not the judge. The judge will instruct the jury on the law to be applied. For example, in a slip and fall case where a customer is suing a business for not clearing snow from its parking lot one day after the last snowfall, the judge will tell the jury, "The law is—you must decide what the reasonable business person would have done in the circumstances." The jury decides the question of reasonableness, or fact. Did the business act reasonably (with care) in the circumstances of that case?

Business Law Applied

❸ **A gas station** on a local highway had an open cesspool at the back. A family stopped for gas, and the parents went into the gas station building to buy some refreshments. Their 6-year-old son got out of the car, and wandered round to the rear of the gas station, where he fell into the cesspool. The child swallowed some of the liquid, and became seriously ill. The boy and his parents sued the owner of the gas station.

  a) What test would the court apply to determine if the gas station owed a duty to the child?
  b) What test would the court apply to determine the standard of care owed to the boy?
  c) What should a reasonable gas station owner have done in the circumstances?

❹ **A water main** burst during a severe cold spell, flooding a nearby residence. The pipe had been installed 25 years previously, at a level that was then thought deep enough to prevent freezing under normal winter conditions.

The homeowner claimed that the pipe should have been buried deeper, and sued the water company. The water company claimed that the pipe was deep enough for normal conditions, and locating it any deeper would have meant considerable additional expense.

a) Did the water company act as a reasonable contractor?

b) Freak cold spells happen every so often, and the homeowner brought evidence of one that had occurred 50 years before. Should the water company, knowing of this, have buried the pipe deeper "just in case"?

The duty of care can extend to many individuals or companies in a complex case. The court must then examine if each defendant is owed a duty of care and then what is the reasonable standard of care required of each involved in the situation. The Fullowka v. Pinkerton's case below illustrates this clearly. The murder of nine miners during a bitter lockout/strike at a gold mine resulted in the criminal conviction of the murderer, but also a civil law suit for negligence against the government and the companies and unions involved in the bitter dispute.

Fullowka v. Pinkerton's of Canada Ltd., 2010 SCC 5

In May 1992 a strike occurred at the Giant Mine owned by Royal Oak Mines in Yellowknife, North West Territories (NWT). The gold mine decided to bring in replacement workers (something that had not been done in a miners' strike in Canada in 45 years) and then soon after violence began. In June riots broke out causing property damage and injuries to security guards and workers and 30 people were arrested. Some workers were fired for these activities including Roger Warren. In late June explosives were stolen from the mine and graffiti indicated that "scab" (replacement) workers could be hurt. In late July and in early September explosions occurred at the mine damaging the mine's ventilation shaft and other areas of the property. On September 18th nine men (3 replacement workers and 6 union members who had chosen to cross the picket line and work) were riding in a mining vehicle 230 metres below the surface when a bomb exploded killing all nine men. It was one of the worst mass murders in Canadian history.

After 13 months of investigations Roger Warren pleaded guilty to nine counts of second degree murder. The families of the victims (8 widows and 23 children) and Mr. O'Neil who was the person who first arrived at the murder scene then sued; Royal Oak Mines, Pinkerton's Security (which provided security at the mine during the strike), and the NWT government which regulated the mining industry, for negligence for failing to prevent the murders. They also sued the national CASAW union and the Local union involved for negligence for failing to control Roger Warren and for inciting his violent behaviour. They claimed that the negligence of each defendant contributed to the murders of the miners.

The trial judge ruled that they had owed the victims a duty of care and did not meet a reasonable standard of care. The trial court awarded $10.7 million in damages and apportioned the liability for the deaths as follows: Roger Warren 26%, Royal Oak Mine 23%, National CASAW Union 22%, Pinkerton's Security 15%, NWT Government 9%, 2 other workers involved in the violence and the local union leader a total of 5%.

The decision was appealed to the Court of Appeal which overturned the trial decision. The plaintiffs then appealed to the Supreme Court of Canada.

The Court's Decision

The Supreme Court agreed with the trial judge that Pinkerton's Security did owe a duty of care to the miners, but it agreed with the Court of Appeal that the defendants had not proven that the security company failed to meet a reasonable standard of care. The Supreme Court ruled that the NWT government also owed a duty of care as it regulated mine safety, but it had fulfilled this duty when it had asked for a legal opinion about closing the mine due to the violence. It had been wrongly advised that due to criminal and labour laws it could not shut the mine, but by considering this course of action, the government had met a reasonable standard of care.

The court ruled that the national CAW union was not liable for the actions of a local union and the local union was not vicariously liable for the actions of its own union members. Royal Oak Mines had settled with the plaintiffs during the appeal so the Supreme Court did not comment on its liability. The plaintiffs therefore were unsuccessful in their appeal.

In 1999 Royal Oak Mines declared bankruptcy and closed the mine. The government was then left with a $500 million cleanup bill for the toxic mine site it left behind. Roger Warren was sentenced to life in prison with no eligibility for parole until 2015.

Higher Standards

The courts impose higher standards on businesses that deal with the public where safety is an issue. The greater the risk, the higher the standard of care. Businesses in the food-service industry, for example, must be certain that every possible safety measure is taken.

Higher standards of skill are placed on persons who claim a higher level of skill or expertise. A surgeon is held to the standard of the reasonable surgeon, not to the standard of any careful member of the public.

Paxton v. Ramji, 2008 ONCA 697 (CanLII) Leave to appeal to the S.C. C. was denied 2009

Debbie Paxton was a married mother of 3 children and she suffered from severe acne. Dr. Ramji prescribed her Accutane, a strong acne drug that can cause serious birth deformities in babies if their mothers take the drug during their pregnancy. Dr. Ramji discussed the serious side effects of Accutane with Ms. Paxton. She informed the doctor that her husband had had a vasectomy 4 ½ years before and it had been successful. Dr. Ramji, knowing of the vasectomy and that Mr. Paxton was her only sexual partner, prescribed Accutane to Ms. Paxton.

Unfortunately the vasectomy failed shortly after Ms. Paxton started taking Accutane and she became pregnant. When she was told she was pregnant and the risks to the baby, she chose to continue the pregnancy and not to abort. The daughter, Jaime Paxton, was born with severe birth defects including; brain damage, facial deformities, deformed ears and hearing difficulties and frequent seizures.

The parents and the siblings made a claim under the Ontario Family Law Act for compensation for the loss of care, guidance and companionship. The parents then began a lawsuit on behalf of their disabled daughter and sued the doctor for negligence. They claim that the doctor owed a duty of care to the unborn child and by prescribing Accutane to the mother while still in child bearing years, the doctor had breached his duty of care to the child she was carrying.

The Court's Decision

The trial court ruled that the doctor did owe a duty of care to the unborn child, but he had met a reasonable standard of care. Relying on a vasectomy that had been successful for 4 ½ years as

the way to ensure the mother did not get pregnant while taking Accutane, met the standard for reasonable care by the doctor, so the negligence claim by the child failed. The Court of Appeal agreed that the doctor was not liable for negligence, but for different a reason.

The Court of Appeal ruled that the doctor did not owe a duty of care to the unborn child. His duty of care was owed only to the mother and he did not owe a duty to the fetus. Imposing a duty to the unborn child as well as to the mother could place the doctor in a position of conflicting duties. "Because the woman and her fetus are one, both physically and legally, it is the woman whom the doctor advises and who makes the treatment decisions affecting herself and her future child. The doctor's direct relationship and duty are to the female patient."

The court also noted that recognizing a duty to the unborn child would have other implications in law. The legal and medical systems recognize that a woman has a right to choose to abort a fetus. Imposing a duty on a doctor to the unborn child would interfere with the woman's right to an abortion. Until a child is born alive, a doctor must act in the mother's best interests.

The court acknowledged that deciding a doctor cannot be liable in negligence to an unborn child because the doctor owes no duty of care to the future child, significantly limits the compensation that the child will be able to receive. Damages for lifetime care costs, loss of income and pain and suffering could be very large amounts, but since no duty exists, these moneys will not be awarded. The parents can receive some compensation, but much less than the amount the child would receive if she could sue successfully. The judges commented that this is a serious issue that the government should address with possible legislative changes.

Note: An exception does exist when a pregnant woman is in a car accident. If her child is born alive and it can be proven that as a fetus the child suffered injuries in the car accident, the child can then sue the third party driver who caused the accident. (*Duval v. Seguin*, 1972 CanLII 371 (ONSC)). If however it was the mother who drove negligently, the child cannot sue its own mother. The court refused to impose this duty of care on a mother as it would place an unfair burden on pregnant women and unreasonably intrude on her rights. (*Dobson (litigation guardian) v. Dobson* 1999 2 S.C.R. 753) The court stated the government could pass legislation to allow the child to claim against the mother's car insurance company to achieve compensation for the child, but common law will not impose an unfair duty on expectant mothers.

3) Causation

but for test

but for this negligent act, the damages would not have occurred

To succeed in negligence the plaintiff must prove that the defendant actually caused the plaintiff's damages. If the plaintiff cannot establish the defendant caused their injuries then the negligence claim must fail. The test for causation is called the **"but for"** test. The plaintiff must show on the balance of probabilities that "but for' the defendant's negligence, the plaintiff's injury would not have occurred. The plaintiff must show that it was the defendant's negligent act that was necessary to create the injury or damages that occurred. They must prove that there would not have been any injury without the defendant's negligent act or failure to act.

The "but for" test is a factual test and requires a common sense approach, not necessarily a scientific approach. There can be difficulties with this test though when there is more than one possible cause for the plaintiff's injuries. The plaintiff may not be able to prove which one of multiple defendants actually caused their damages. If the court thinks it is impossible to say which particular defendant caused the injury, it can use a different test, the **"material contribution" test.** This test imposes liability not because the defendant's act actually caused the injury, but because their actions contributed to the risk that an injury would occur. This test would only be used when the "but for" test has not established causation, but principles of fairness and justice would allow for another test so liability can be determined. The Supreme Court has not used the material contribution to risk test yet in any cases so far.

material contribution test
did the defendant's act cause the risk of harm

Example: In *Resurfice Corp. v. Hanke*, 2007 SCC 7 the Supreme Court ruled that the "but for" test is what should be used when determining causation in a negligence case, even if there is more than one party who possibly caused the injury. Ralph Hanke was filling an ice resurfacing machine at an Edmonton rink. The gas tank and the water tank were next to each other and he put the water hose into the gas tank by mistake. This caused vaporized gas to form and it was ignited by overhead heaters. Fire broke out and Hanke suffered serious burns. Henke sued the manufacturer and distributor of the ice machine for negligent design. He claimed that the similarity and location of the two tanks caused confusion and resulted in his injuries. The trial court ruled Henke had not been confused and using the "but for" test, the manufacturer did not cause the injuries. The Appeal Court ruled that the "but for" test should not have been used because there were two possible causes of the injury, so instead the material contribution test should have been applied. This allows the court to compare the blameworthiness of both parties. But the Supreme Court reversed the Court of Appeal's decision and said that even if there are multiple defendants the "but for" test is the standard that must be used. The plaintiff must apply that test to each defendant and show "but for" their negligence the injury would not have occurred. The trial judge had used that test and found that the manufacturer was not liable for negligence, so the Supreme Court restored that original decision. The court stressed that the material contribution test is only applied in very special restricted circumstances. It is only used when it is impossible to use the "but for" test to prove negligence and the defendant's injuries fall within the risk created by the defendant's breach of a duty of care it owed to the plaintiff.

Circumstantial Evidence and Causation

In some cases there is very strong circumstantial evidence that infers the defendant was negligent, such as a sponge left in a patient's stomach after an operation or a decomposed insect in a beer bottle. The judge must weigh the circumstantial evidence and any direct evidence, and then decide if the plaintiff on the balance of probabilities has established a *prima facie* (on the face of it) case of negligence. If so, the plaintiff can succeed in their claim, unless the defendant can present evidence disproving this logical inference of negligence.

Sometimes however, the circumstantial evidence is not very strong and does not create a *prima facie* case of negligence. If the defendant can introduce other reasonable explanations for the injuries that do not involve negligence by them, the plaintiff can lose the case. For example in *Fontaine v. B.C.* [1998] 1 S.C.R. 424, the Supreme Court considered the case where two men were found dead in a truck that had gone off the side of a winding mountain road on the night of a heavy rain storm. The family of the dead passenger claimed that the driver must have been negligent for the truck to have gone off the road. The defendant's position was that there are several other possible explanations for why the truck crashed that do not involve driver negligence. The court stated that when road and weather conditions are very bad, accidents can occur and the driver was not negligent. The court ruled in this case that the defence's explanations were reasonable and realistically there were other possible causes of the accident that could be accepted other than driver negligence. There was no other direct evidence of what occurred that night to tip the scales in favour of the plaintiff's explanation. Therefore the plaintiff, on the balance of probabilities, had not established that the defendant was negligent, so their claim failed.

Example: In *Michel v. John Doe and Insurance Corporation of B.C.*, 2009 BCCA 225 the court considered a case where a woman was walking down a B.C. highway when a rock flew off a logging truck that drove past her. The rock hit her between the eyes and she suffered a major permanent brain injury. Witnesses saw it happen but didn't get the name of the logging company. She put in a claim to the Insurance Corporation for B.C. for negligence under its no-fault plan. She claimed that if the truck driver had inspected his load properly before leaving, he would have discovered the rock and removed it. The Insurance Corporation argued that even with a proper inspection the rock could have easily been hidden among the logs and become loose only after the truck started down the highway. The court ruled that on the balance of probabilities the plaintiff had not shown that the logging company was negligent. It was just as likely that a careful inspection would have not discovered the rock. Given that there was no other evidence available, the plaintiff had not established on the balance of probabilities that the logging company was negligent, so despite her serious injuries, her claim failed.

Causation and Manufacturers' Negligence

The issue of causation has become a significant factor in class action lawsuits against manufacturers for negligence. There has been concern that in jury trials in the U.S. the jury is often biased against "big rich" companies in favour of the "little guy." This can result in juries finding that the manufacturer did cause the injuries to the consumer, even though this causal link is based on very weak or questionable scientific evidence. The fear has been expressed that "junk" science can make it difficult for a large business in the United States to obtain a fair jury trial if sued by consumers.

For example in the 1980s women in the U.S. who had received silicone breast implants complained that the implants had leaked and caused various serious health problems. Jury trials accepted the medical evidence of the experts who testified for the women and multi-million dollar awards were given. Class actions formed involving over 200,000 women and Dow Corning, a major manufacturer, plus other companies who made these implants, eventually agreed to settle the class actions in 1998 for about $4 billion. Some companies filed for bankruptcy protection. Several years later, independent medical experts concluded there was no causal connection between the implants and the women's' health problems.

Many Canadian provinces have abolished the civil jury system. In those provinces where it still exists, complex cases are often taken from juries and tried by judges sitting alone.

Business Law   Applied

⑤ **John Linden had** his driver's licence suspended for one year because of careless driving. During the suspension he drove anyway. One day an oncoming car driven by Mary Kwan crossed over the road because Kwan was momentarily distracted. Her car hit Linden's car, causing $10,000 damage to each car.

    a) On learning of Linden's suspension, Kwan wants to sue Linden. Will she be successful? Answer the following questions to justify your conclusion.
       i) Did Linden owe a duty to Kwan?
       ii) Did Linden breach the relevant standard of care?
       iii) Did Linden's breach, if any, cause the accident?

b) Linden wants to sue Kwan. Will he be successful? Answer the following questions to justify your conclusion.

  i)   Did Kwan owe a duty to Linden?
  ii)   Did Kwan breach the standard of care?
  iii) Did Kwan's breach, if any, cause the accident?

c) If Linden was found not to be negligent, would Linden be subject to any other penalty?

d) What if a bee had flown into the open window of Kwan's car, stinging her and causing her to lose control of the car so that she crossed over the centre lane and crashed into Linden's car? Would Kwan be responsible for the damage to Linden's car? Which element, if any, of negligence is missing?

Damages

Damages in tort law are usually are usually awarded on the basis that an injured person should be put back in the position that he or she was in before the accident and as if the accident had not happened. They are called compensatory damages because they are to compensate or make up to the plaintiff for the loss. As discussed in Chapter 2 various types of monetary damages can be awarded such as; pecuniary damages for financial losses, non-pecuniary damages (general damages) for pain and suffering, loss of enjoyment of life and shorter life expectancy, aggravated damages for emotional anguish and distress and punitive damages to punish intentionally bad behaviour by the defendant.

4) Remoteness of Damages—Drawing the Line

Courts will only hold a defendant liable for damages that are reasonably foreseeable. If the court believes that the damages are too remote, and would not have been reasonably foreseen, then even though the defendant caused the damages, they will not be held liable for those unforeseen losses. Sometimes there is a chain of events, one event leading to the next, each with its own consequences. The possible unlimited chain of effects has been dramatized in the theoretical "butterfly effect" by mathematicians. Is the person responsible for the first incident responsible for all the following events? The courts have decided that an individual will not have unlimited liability to an unlimited number of people. Some damages will be found too **remote**. A line will be drawn, but this test may end up being determined on social-policy grounds.

Consider the following example: Helen Orestion drove into a self-service gas station, and got out of her car while still smoking a cigarette. William Klippert was pumping gas into his car at the time. The fumes from this action ignited because of the cigarette, and the explosion caused the following events:

- Klippert's car blew up.
- Klippert was severely burned.
- The gas station caught fire and eventually exploded.
- The gas station was closed for two months, with the resulting loss of profits.
- Klippert's wife was watching from her home, which had a view of the gas station. She knew that her husband was stopping there for gas, and fainted when she saw the gas station explode. She had an unusual calcium deficiency causing thin bones, and she fractured her skull as a result of the fall.
- Tai Sun, a neighbour, saw Mrs. Klippert faint, and tried to revive her. In the panic, Sun fell off the porch, breaking her hip.
- An employee dragged Klippert to safety, but was severely burned on the hands in doing so.
- Glenda Carthy had her car in the gas station for servicing. It was damaged in the explosion, and she had to rent a car for two weeks while she had the damaged car repaired.

- The employees at the gas station lost two month's wages.
- The gas company that supplied gas lost the profits from sales to the gas station.

reasonably foreseeable
a defendant is only liable for damages that are reasonably foreseeable

It is difficult to predict where the courts will draw the line. In the case described here they would not award damages to all of the parties who suffered loss. Instead, they would use a test such as the **reasonable foreseeability, or proximate cause test**. Which incident(s) in the long list of events described do you think was (were) reasonably foreseeable? Did any of the events surprise you as not being reasonably foreseeable?

Judges admit that foreseeability is in the eye of the beholder. This means that decisions on this issue will vary because of the individual values of the judge making the decision. Judges are applying value choices, not logic, when drawing the line. At some point they feel "enough is enough." When that feeling will arrive is hard to predict.

Fortunately, most cases fit into common recurring situations or patterns, or deal with rather closely connected events so that remoteness is not an issue. There may be a tendency to make businesses responsible for a larger scope of damages in order to force them to take greater care and to insure for these losses. Thus, businesses are forced to spread the cost of the loss over the their products or services. The loss does not fall on any one individual.[2]

Business Law Applied

6   A 14-year-old boy was careless when he started his father's snowmobile. The machine ran wild, and collided with a defective gas pipe, which projected above the ground. Gas escaped, leaking into a nearby school, where it exploded. The school board sued the gas company and the boy for the cost of repairing the school.

a) What test would the court use to determine whether the boy should be responsible for the damages to the school, and with what result?
b) Would the gas company be liable to the school?

7   A ship's captain had too much to drink at lunch, and let the vessel run into a bridge that carried traffic over the river. The bridge had to be closed to all traffic, and a doctor on the way to treat a patient suffering from a heart attack was delayed about one hour. The heart-attack victim died. If the doctor had not been delayed, it is very likely that the patient would have survived. The patient's wife and children want to sue the shipowner for their loss.

a) Did the actions of the shipowner cause the death of the patient?
b) Is causation sufficient to make the shipowner liable to the wife and children? What test would the court apply, and with what result?

Psychiatric Injury

One of the situations in which the reasonable foresight test has been applied to limit the responsibility for negligence relates to claim for psychiatric injury that occurs alone and not as a result of physical injury. This term includes all forms of mental illness. The Courts were very reluctant to give any award of damages for this type of injury and continue to be cautious in granting relief in this area.

Example: A woman witnessed an accident in which a runaway car killed her husband and several of her children. She was awarded damages for nervous shock. However, the Courts have put limits on responsibility for this type of injury relative to hypersensitive individuals as the next case shows.

2. Allen M. Linden, *Canadian Tort Law*, p. 343.

Mustapha v. Culligan of Canada, [2006] 2 SCR 114

In placing a bottle of Culligan Water on a dispenser in their home, Mr. and Mrs. Mustapha saw a dead fly and part of a dead fly in the bottle. Nobody drank from the container.

Mrs. Mustapha immediately vomited, had stomach pains and cramps. Mr. Mustapha felt nauseous but did not vomit but felt stomach pains. Mr. Mustapha remained obsessed with the incident. He could not get the image of the dead fly in the water out of his mind. He continually worried about the health of his family who he believed had been compromised and his trust in Culligan had been betrayed.

The Mustaphas sued for damages claiming psychiatric injury.

The Trial Judge rejected the claim of Mrs. Mustapha finding that it did not rise to the level of recognized psychiatric injury. However, he found Mr. Mustapha's reaction amounted to a psychiatric illness as a result of the incident and awarded damages to him of about $337,000.00. Culligan appealed.

The Supreme Court's Decision

The main issue on appeal was whether the test for foreseeability of damages for negligence (remoteness) that causes psychiatric illness is possible or probable.

The Court stated that the test is: was it reasonably foreseeable that a person of ordinary robustness and fortitude would likely suffer psychiatric injury from seeing the flies in the water bottle.

The Court accepted that Mr. Mustapha did in fact have the symptoms that he claimed, but they were not foreseeable on the above test. A person of reasonable robustness would not have had these reactions. The Court of Appeal overturned the Trial Judge's award and dismissed Mr. Mustapha's claim.

The Supreme Court heard Mr. Mustapha's appeal and it agreed with the Court of Appeal's decision. It accepted the trial court's ruling that Mr. Mustapha had suffered a serious psychological reaction to seeing the flies; however these damages were too remote. It was not a reasonably foreseeable injury, as a normal person would not have this type of reaction, so therefore Culligan was not liable for negligence. Mustapha was also ordered to pay Culligan's legal costs.

Example: TD Auto Finance Services sent a tape containing the personal information of its customers by courier. The tape was lost in transit, and customers were informed of this. Anna Mazzonna, one of the customers, alleged that this had caused her and others anxiety and fear about possible identity theft, as well as potential inconvenience in obtaining credit and having to monitor for fraud.

The court refused to certify the proposed class action for the simple reason there is no cause of action for the stress caused by being informed of a possible risk of misuse of personal information. The judge relied in part on the *Mustapha case.* (*Mazzonna v. Daimlerchrysler Financial Services Canada Inc.*, 2012 QCCS 958.)

Thin Skull Plaintiffs

Reasonable foreseeability eliminates the unexpected, if not bizarre, consequences of some acts. However, some consequences that might not be reasonably foreseen regularly result in relief from the courts. While no general principle exists, there are certain recurring situations that, although unforeseeable, are protected by court awards. Two of the most common are those in which people have a pre-existing medical condition—called the thin skull plaintiff rule—and those in which rescuers are injured in the course of their actions. The **thin skull plaintiff rule** is the principle that a defendant is liable for the full extent of a plaintiff's loss even where a prior weakness makes the harm more serious than it otherwise might have been. The nature of the personal injury is foreseeable, but not the extent. Both of these exceptions are illustrated in the exploding-gas-station example above.

A variation of the thin skull plaintiff rule is called the **crumbling skull plaintiff rule** (the principle that a defendant may be responsible for increasing a pre-existing weakness). For example, a person has a medical condition that will eventually result in a complete deterioration of the spine. That person is injured in a car accident and his spine is damaged. Will that person be able to establish that the accident caused injury to his spine? The courts have said

thin skull plaintiff rule
the principle that a defendant is liable for the full extent of a plaintiff's loss even where a prior weakness makes the harm more serious than it otherwise might have been

crumbling skull plaintiff rule
the principle that a defendant may be responsible for increasing a pre-existing weakness

yes. Where there are two causes to the injury, some weight will be given to each, but the plaintiff can still recover for the extent that the accident increased the pre-existing injury.[3]

Physical vs Psychiatric Injuries

From the discussions above it can be seen that there is a difference between the responsibility for injury for unusual physical injury (thin skull plaintiff) and injury that is purely psychiatric in nature and which is not as a result of physical injury. For psychiatric injury claims the foresight test is strictly applied; however, for claims relating to physical injuries, an exception is made so that even unforeseen physical conditions attract liability and negligence.

Business Law Applied

8 Luisa Mammolita held a yard sale in front of her house. As she moved a table, it collapsed, and a jagged piece cut a visitor, Ambrozine Taylor, on the leg.

Taylor was treated in the emergency ward of the local hospital. The metal that had cut her was rusty, and the doctor gave her a tetanus shot. Unknown to Taylor, she suffered from a rare allergy to tetanus, and her whole leg became paralyzed for life.

a) Was the paralysis reasonably foreseeable by Luisa Mammolita?
b) What test would the court apply, and what would be the result?

Defences

A defendant can defeat a plaintiff's claim by showing that the plaintiff has failed to prove one of the elements of negligence outlined above. Additionally, there are two specific defences to a claim in negligence; contributory negligence or voluntary assumption of risk.

Contributory Negligence

contributory negligence
negligence by an injured party that helps to cause or increase (contribute) to his or her own loss or injury

Contributory negligence is negligence by an injured party that helps to cause or increase (contribute) to his or her own loss or injury. The standard of care required of a plaintiff is no different than that demanded of a defendant. In other words, one must act as a reasonable person for one's own safety as well as for the protection of others. The amount of the award will be apportioned according to the degree the incident was the plaintiff's fault. A common instance of contributory negligence is not wearing a seat belt. Contributory negligence is often a factor in auto accidents that happen at an intersection. Consider the following example.

Leonard Bruno was driving a little too fast and failed to see a stop sign until the last moment. He braked, but skidded into the intersection. Stacy Lavery was driving with the right of way, but was adjusting her radio and did not see Bruno until it was too late. She stepped on her brakes, but collided with Bruno. Both drivers were injured.

Bruno would likely be found at fault for causing the accident by running the stop sign. However, it is possible that Lavery would have been able to avoid, or at least reduce, the injury to both drivers had she braked faster. Because her inattention contributed to the severity of their injuries, Lavery's claim would be reduced by the percentage her carelessness contributed to the accident.

---

3. *Athey v. Leonati*, [1996] 3 S.C.R. 458.

Assuming that the court found that the value of Lavery's injuries was $100,000, and that her negligence was 25 percent to blame for the accident, her final award would be reduced accordingly, to $75,000. The Kahlon case below illustrates how important it is for a patient to follow up on diagnostic tests, even if the doctors fail to. In this case the young man suffered catastrophic injuries due to a hospital's negligence, but the court ruled there was contributory negligence by the patient as well. He was held 30% responsible for his own injuries and as a result the damages he received were reduced by over $2 million.

■ *Critical Concepts of* Contributory Negligence

- In the case of negligence, both parties may be at fault.
- The fact that the plaintiff was also careless will not be a complete bar to the plaintiff's claim.
- The award of damages to the plaintiff will be reduced in proportion to the plaintiff's own carelessness.

Kahlon v. Vancouver Coastal Health Authority, 2009 BCSC 922 (CanLII)

In 1998 Shawn Kahlon was a 31 year old athletic high school teacher who was about to get married. He felt back pain and went to see his doctor. The doctor thought it was a muscular back sprain and told him to exercise and seek massage therapy. The pain continued to increase and his doctor then suspected a minor disc problem. He sent him to a sports medicine specialist in September, 1999 who ordered a CT scan of his back. The radiologist at the Vancouver hospital who looked at the CT scan noticed an abnormality and indicated on the scan that Kahlon should be brought back in for a further more detailed scan.

The hospital called Kahlon to tell him to come in for a further scan but he did not attend. Unfortunately his scan then was misfiled. Normally if a patient does not return for the recall, the original scan is sent to the doctor to deal with the situation. He is notified the patient did not come back for the follow-up and the doctor at least makes a final report on the original scan. Kahlon's original scan was not forwarded to the doctor and was filed in the hospital library where completed files were sent. The sports medicine doctor had told him to book another appointment after the CT scan, but he had not. Kahlon had been seen by a radiologist, a sports medicine specialist, and his family physician, but not one of them followed up on his original CT scan.

Finally a year later, in September 2000 Kahlon returned to his family doctor complaining of increased back and leg pain. The doctor ordered x-rays and then sent him to a rheumatologist. Finally that doctor requested the CT scan and it was then discovered that it had been misfiled. Once they saw the CT scan Kahlon was scheduled to have a MRI, but he became very ill. It turned out that he had TB spinal meningitis. His condition was so severe at this point he suffered severe brain damage and a stroke. As a result he is completely incapacitated and needs 24 hour care. He cannot walk or talk and is fed through a tube. If the TB spinal meningitis had been diagnosed in September 1999 or within several months

thereafter, he could have been completely cured with no long term effects. As a result, Kahlon sued the doctors and the hospital for negligence. The defendants argued he was responsible for his own injuries or at least partially responsible.

The Court's Decision

The court ruled that the hospital was to blame for misfiling his original CT scan. The hospital had a system of reporting and following up on CT scans that were marked for patient recall and it had not followed its own procedures. It had fallen below the reasonable standard of care expected of a hospital. The court ruled the doctors were not negligent. The court believed that they had met a reasonable standard of care, and it was the hospital and Kahlon who had been negligent.

The court ruled that the doctor/patient relationship is a two way street with duties running in both directions. The patient has a duty to participate fully and honestly in their own care. Kahlon had been negligent in not going in for the second CT scan when the hospital had called and not doing a follow-up visit with the sports medicine specialist as he had been advised. The court felt that due to his own contributory negligence he was 30% responsible for his own injuries.

Given his catastrophic injuries, he received the maximum of $324,500 in non-pecuniary general damages for pain and suffering and loss of enjoyment of life and shorter life expectancy. He also received about $1.7 million in lost wages and very large future care costs which the court determined would continue for 17 years (his remaining life expectancy was estimated to be to age 59). His damage award was about $7.2 million. Since the court found there was 30% contributory negligence on his part, that reduced the hospital's liability to about $5 million. His wife and parents who had cared for him received damage awards as well.

Voluntary Assumption of Risk

In some situations, the courts would consider that the injured person had consented to the risk of injury. If this happens, it is not possible to bring any action for damages because if the court finds that there is voluntary assumption of risk then the plaintiff is 100 per cent liable for their own injuries. The courts therefore try whenever possible to classify the activity as contributory negligence, so that the plaintiff has at least some chance of receiving some compensation.

The plaintiff must have known and clearly appreciate the nature and character of the risks though for this defence to be used. The assumption of the risk can be actual or implied by their conduct. People who participate in sports are taken to consent to injuries they might suffer in the ordinary course of play. Spectators are assumed to have consented to injuries that result from normal risks of the sport. A baseball fan, for example, accepts the possibility of being struck by a foul ball during a game. But if an unusual event occurs, such as the stadium roof collapses injuring players and spectators, they would not have voluntarily assumed that risk when they came to the game, so they could pursue their claims for negligence.

People who ride as passengers in cars as members of drinking binges may be denied any recovery under the voluntary assumption of risk principle if their drunk driver has an accident. Passengers can be found to have consented to the risk if they encouraged or participated in the drinking. Courts do have some discretion in these situations though and may instead choose to label this decision to ride with a drunk driver as contributory negligence rather than voluntary assumption of risk. In *Joe v. Paradis*, 2008 BCCA 57 (CanLII) the court stated that the drunk passenger may have voluntarily accepted the physical risk of riding with a drunk driver but they probably did not consider nor voluntarily accept the legal risks of riding with a drunk, so therefore they have not waived their legal rights. It therefore was not voluntary assumption of risk, but instead it was contributory negligence. This ruling then allowed the injured passenger to recover a percentage of their damages from the drunk driver. Depending on the facts of the case, the passenger's liability for his own injuries from riding with a drunk driver can range usually range from 15–50%.

Waiver and Disclaimer Clauses

waiver

a party gives up their legal rights to sue for any damages they suffer

Often in dangerous sporting activities the company running the activity makes the plaintiff read and sign a contract that includes a **waiver**. The waiver is a form of an exemption clause or a disclaimer of liability. The waiver usually clearly states that the person acknowledges that they are about to participate in a dangerous activity and that they voluntarily agree to assume the risk and responsibility for any injuries that may result, so the company will not be liable for any damages they suffer.

Whether these clauses are effective and allow the company to avoid liability depends on several factors. The clause must clearly be **brought to the attention of the participant** and there can be no misrepresentation by the company or it will be invalid. If the clause is not clearly worded, then it will be interpreted strictly against the company that prepared it and it may be useless. If the court thinks that it is unconscionable or against public policy (community standards of commercial morality) it could be considered invalid as well. The courts rarely come to those conclusions though. There are cases where people have died in skiing, scuba diving and white water rafting activities and the operators avoided liability due to the waivers the participants signed. It is often difficult to predict with certainty whether a waiver or disclaimer will be considered valid by the court. It very much depends on the facts of the case. The following examples illustrate some important cases and the Crocker case shows a divergent decision.

Example: In the case of *Dyck v. Manitoba Snowmobile Association and Wood*, [1985] 1 S.C.R. 589, a 19 year old entered a snowmobile race and signed an entry form with a waiver that stated he could not sue the race organizers and its employees if he was injured. A race official stepped into the middle of the race course during the race and Dyck swerved to miss him. Dyck then crashed and suffer permanent injuries assessed at $90,000. Dyck claimed that the association had not brought the waiver to his attention so the clause should be unenforceable. But the court ruled that Dyck had read and signed the form and it clearly exempted the defendant. So despite the race official's negligence, the waiver was valid and Dyck could not succeed in his lawsuit. This precedent has been applied in many other cases where more serious injuries occurred.

Example: In *Mayer v. Big White Ski Resort Inc.*, 1998 CanLII 5114 (BCCA), a skier who was hit by a snowmobile driven by a ski resort employee was unsuccessful in his claim against the resort. He had signed a form when he purchased a season's pass which included a waiver that exempted the resort from liability for negligence. Mayer said that he had never read the waiver when he got the pass, but the court would not let his failure to read the waiver prevent it from being effective. The waiver was written in big bold black print so the resort had made a reasonable effort to bring it to his attention. He chose not to read it, but that did not prevent the resort from using it to avoid liability.

Example: In *Ochoa v. Canadian Mountain Holidays Inc.*, 1996 CanLII 378 (BCSC), Mr. Ochoa was one of 9 people heli-skiing in B.C. who were swept away by an avalanche and killed. When his family sued the ski company that ran the heli-skiing adventure the court ruled that the waiver expressly covered this type of situation. The company had specifically discussed the risk of avalanches with the skiers, so the disclaimer was valid and the company was not held liable for the skier's death.

Example: In *Loychuk v. Cougar Mountain Adventures Ltd.*, 2012 BCCA 122 (CanLII), two women who collided on a zip line due to the negligence of the zip line guides were unable to sue the company as they had signed a waiver releasing the company from liability for negligence. Both women clearly understood what a waiver was and the terms in the company's waiver were specific and clearly included acts of negligence by their guides.

Waivers Not Effective

In the examples below, the courts ruled that the waivers were not effective. The defendants had not adequately drawn the disclaimer clause to the attention of the plaintiff when they agreed to take part in the activities. Since the injured parties had not been fully aware of the waiver, the defendant could not rely on it to avoid liability.

Example: *Parker v. Ingalls*, 2006 BCSC 942 (CanLII) a man suffered a severe knee injury when injured by his martial arts instructor during a demonstration. The court ruled that the martial arts studio was liable for his injuries and the waiver was unenforceable. It was written in very small print, there was no reference to exemption from acts of negligence and it was not sufficiently brought to the participant's attention. There was no emphasis on its importance and the student had not agreed to release the instructor from negligently hurting him.

Example: In *Crocker v. Sundance Northwest Resorts Ltd.*, [1988] 1 S.C.R. 1186, a ski resort was running a tube race at its Winter Carnival. Three days before the race Crocker paid his $15 entry fee and signed a waiver. The day of the race he arrived at the resort drunk after sharing 40 oz. of rye with his friend for breakfast. Crocker and his friend were in first place after the first run and then continued to drink alcohol during the lunch break. Before the second race, the resort owner and resort manager told Crocker he should not go tubing as he was clearly drunk. But Crocker became belligerent, so they let him go. Part way down the run, Crocker flew out of the tube and landed on his neck and was permanently paralyzed. Crocker then sued the resort for his injuries. The resort said the waiver should apply, he had voluntarily assumed the risk. The trial court ruled he had not read the waiver nor had he accepted the physical or legal consequences of going in the race. Since the resort had not drawn it to his attention properly, the waiver was unenforceable. The court held the resort 75% liable for his injuries and due to contributory negligence, Crocker was 25% responsible for his own injuries. Since Crocker had frequently been unemployed, he was only awarded about $200,000 in damages. The resort appealed and the Ontario Court of Appeal ruled that Crocker knew tubing was a dangerous activity and the waiver was a simple clear form he should have read. He chose to get drunk and ignore the warnings from the resort personnel, so he had voluntarily assumed the risk of injury and the resort was not liable. The Supreme Court however restored the trial judge's decision. It agreed the waiver did not work because the resort should have brought it to Crocker's attention. The resort had not met a reasonable standard of care and should have done more to prevent him from tubing when he was drunk.

Waivers also can be considered in consumer products cases. These situations are often quite different from risky sporting activities. In the risky sports cases the clauses are often clearly printed on the company's simple participation form. But in consumer products cases the waiver or disclaimer is often hidden in the fine print of a long standard form contract. The clause attempts to negate the business's responsibility for losses caused by the products or services, which go against principles developed by the courts or set out in legislation. The consumer does not truly agree to the terms of the exemption clause, and in fact often is not even aware of its existence until there is a problem. The effectiveness of these clauses is often determined by whether the company had clearly brought it to the attention of the consumer and whether the court believes that consumer had knowingly assumed all the risks of injury or losses.

■ *Critical Concepts of* Voluntary Assumption of Risk

- If the plaintiff has consented to the risk of injury, there is no possibility of obtaining any compensation, as the plaintiff is liable for 100% of their own injuries.
- The plaintiff must know and clearly appreciate the nature and character of the risks to be run.
- The plaintiff must have voluntarily incurred the risk.
- The assumption of the risk can be actual or implied by conduct.
- Waiver or disclaimer clauses are often used in high risk sporting activities so that the participant will voluntarily assume the risk of injury they may sustain
- Waivers may not be enforceable though if the company had not bought it to the customers attention and the participant did not understand the legal risks they were assuming
- If a disclaimer is not clearly worded, then it will be interpreted strictly against the party that prepared it, and it may be unenforceable
- If there was misrepresentation by the defendant the waiver may be unenforceable or if the court feels to enforce it would be unconscionable

IN THE BLEACHERS

Isildar v. Rideau Diving Supply, 2008 CanLII 29598 (ONSC)

Ali Isildar was a 28 year hardware designer for Nortel Networks. He had become interested in scuba diving and had decided to obtain his certification. In June, 2003 he undertook a deep water dive, a mandatory component of an Advanced Open Water recreational scuba certification course offered by the defendant Kanata Dive Supply and led by the defendant Sarah Dow, a certified Open Water scuba instructor. The dive took place in the St. Lawrence River and went to a depth of 88 feet.

There were two groups diving at this location on this date. The group Mr. Isildar was in was led by Sarah Dow who had been certified as an instructor for 8 months. This was her first time running an open water certification course and she had little rescue experience. There were 3 other divers in the group in addition to Mr. Isildar. Mr. Isildar had done a total of 3 ½ hours of diving previous to this certification course.

As they descended into their dive they disturbed the silt on the bottom of the river and visibility was soon reduced to almost zero as they got to the bottom. Ms. Dow indicated they should swim over to a clearer location, but due to visibility problems the divers became separated from each other. Mr. Isildar could not find his dive buddy and he came upon another diver from his group and was alarmed. He grabbed at the other diver's breathing regulator and knocked off his mask. That diver swam away to try and locate his partner. Ms. Dow then came across Isildar and realized he was panicking. He grabbed at her regulator and knocked her mask off. She tried to get his weight belt off so he would rise to the surface, but he would not let her. He also refused to use the extra breathing regulator on her air tank. Isildar was thrashing about so much Dow swam away from him and then ascended to the surface to get help from the other instructor and his assistant. When she descended again with the two others they could not find Mr. Isildar and Ms. Dow had to resurface as she was running out of air. The two men then finally found Isildar lying face up without his regulator in his mouth and no signs of life. They brought him to the surface and tried CPR, but he had drowned.

The wife and son of Mr. Isildar sued the company and the instructor for negligence. The defendants claimed that their actions were not negligent and they were also protected from liability as Mr. Isildar had read and signed a waiver/release that exempted them from liability.

The Court's Decision

The judge ruled that the instructor had failed to provide a reasonable standard of care to the students in her certification course. She had not meet industry standards nor followed the proper procedures in the manual. She had not had a reasonable dive plan and should not have conducted the dive in this location. She also did not; "stop, think and act" as the instructor's manual indicates is the appropriate conduct in an emergency situation. She should not have left Mr. Isildar alone and gone to the surface for help when he was in an obvious state of panic. She should have waited until he became unconscious and then taken him to the surface. Her conduct fell below the reasonable standards of a competent diving instructor. The diving company was vicariously liable for Ms. Dow's negligence.

The court ruled that Mr. Isildar was 15% responsible for his own death as he had failed to stay with his dive buddy and he hadn't followed proper safety procedures.

However, the court ruled that since Mr. Isildar had signed a clear Release of Liability and Assumption of Risk Agreement the defendants would not be liable for his death. The release was very clearly worded and specifically included negligence and the risk of panic and drowning. The instructors had specifically gone over the release at the orientation session when they had signed up for the course just days before the dive. Mr. Isildar was intelligent and would have understood it and he knew that scuba diving was a dangerous sport and the risks that it involved. To allow this waiver to work would not be unconscionable nor "divergent from community standards of fairness and morality "and it followed with the recent line of cases. Therefore the release of liability clause was valid and enforceable, so despite their negligence, the defendants were able to avoid liability for the death.

Business Law Applied

9 An 18-year-old spectator at a hockey game was injured when the puck flew over the boards and struck him in the eye. The hockey rink provided glass screens only at either end of the arena, as is customary.

a) Would the young man be successful in claiming damages from the hockey club?

10 A hockey player got into a fight with a member of the opposing team. The fight took place near the boards, and a spectator was injured by one player's stick.

a) Did the spectator have a valid claim for negligence against the player?

⑪ **A golfer was** injured when her partner's club slipped, hitting the first player in the face.

a) Could the golfer claim damages from her playing partner?

⑫ **A skier fell** into a gully that had not been properly marked by the ski lodge. The woman broke both legs, as well as both of her skis, and was in traction for four months.

Occupiers' Liability

occupiers' liability

an occupier of property has to take reasonable care to make their property safe

The occupier of a property, not the owner, has to take reasonable care that the property is safe. The person who has the right to supervise and control the premises—the right to permit or deny entry to other people—is the occupier. Therefore, in rented premises, the tenant is responsible. The reason for this is that some potentially unsafe conditions can happen very quickly, and need immediate attention. If the owner is absent, it is up to the person on the site to take whatever action is needed.

Few laws are simple, and those surrounding occupier's liability are no exception. Various standards of care, required for different types of persons—customers, paying customers, trespassers, and so on—were developed in earlier times, and have served to complicate a complex issue. As a result, several provinces have passed occupier's liability acts to create a uniform standard of care for lawful users. Only Saskatchewan, Newfoundland and Labrador and the three territories have not passed a specific statute on occupiers' liability, so they rely instead on common law principles when cases arise in this area.

The provinces that have passed occupier's liability acts in an effort to simplify this area of law are Alberta, British Columbia, Manitoba, Nova Scotia, Ontario, P.E.I. It is the standard of care required under these provincial statutes that we examine here.

Areas of Responsibility

There are generally four categories of responsibility for the safety of premises:

- physical condition of the property
- safety of customers from attacks by others
- safety of persons injured by drunks after leaving the premises
- safety of people injured as a result of the business of selling alcoholic beverages, and who injure themselves or others on the premises, or after they leave

In the various provincial occupiers' liability statutes the standard of care required of the occupier is similar to the standard developed in negligence law. It is up to the occupier to ensure that the premises are kept reasonably safe for lawful users in all circumstances. If a slippery substance is spilled, for example, it should be cleared up immediately. Similarly, ice and snow must be removed as soon as possible. The test to decide the care required is "what is reasonable in all the circumstances?" The court will look at; what was the reason the person came onto the land, the nature of the premises, what was the potential danger and what was the cost of removing the danger.

The occupier cannot simply put up a notice warning that a danger exists. A large sign saying, for example, "Hole in carpet, watch your step!" is no defence if a customer trips and breaks a leg because of the worn floor covering. If there is a problem, steps must be taken to correct it.

The premises must be maintained in a condition that makes them physically safe for customers. Many retail stores are designed to attract customers' attention to products, displays, and shelf advertising. The floors must be very safe. The occupier is also responsible for making sure that those customers are not likely to be at risk of harm from other users of the premises.

The occupier of land even owes a duty to trespassers. The duty is a lower standard but it requires the occupier to take care so that the trespasser is not wilfully or recklessly harmed. For example you can't set a trap to injure trespassers in Canada. In common law there is a duty of common humanity to warn them of deadly conditions on the land which would be hidden to them, but of which the occupier is aware of. A warning sign at the entrance to the land is often enough in these situations involving a trespasser to avoid liability. Courts will apply a higher duty of care to children who trespass if the occupier knew or should have known they were on the property. A lower standard is often also set in some statutes when people enter onto certain types of land for recreational purposes and are presumed to have voluntarily assumed the risks involved. Some provinces have passed specific laws in relation to some recreational uses of land such as snowmobiling where there are frequent injuries involving trespassers.

Occupiers' Liability—Reasonable Care

The fact a person was injured on another's property does not necessarily mean the occupier is liable. The plaintiff must prove that the occupier had not taken reasonable care and that their actions or inactions actually caused the plaintiff's injuries. Often the person is held partly responsible for their own injuries as well. The examples below illustrate these issues.

Example: In *Zsoldos v. Canadian Pacific Railway Company* 2009 ONCA 55 (CanLII), a 22 year old motorcyclist hit a train at a crossing on a country road at night where there were no advance warning bells or lights or gates stopping motorists from crossing the train tracks. By the time he saw the train it was too late and his motorcycle skidded and he suffered severe injuries, losing both arms and a leg. There was only a sign indicating tracks ahead and to reduce speed to 20 mph. There were also tall corn crops blocking the view of the tracks. The plaintiff had been drinking beer and had not slowed down enough and it was too late to stop when he eventually saw the train. The court examined the duty of care owed by the railroad and the township under the Ontario Occupiers' Liability Act and found that CP had not met a reasonable standard of care. It had not done an inspection of the site at night and if it had, then it would have realized the only warning sign was placed too close to the track to allow a driver to react in time. A better active warning system with flashing lights and possible gates should have been in place. CP and the township were liable for 75% of the plaintiff's injuries and due to contributory negligence the motorcyclist was 25% responsible for his own injuries.

Example: In *Charlie v. Canada Safeway Limited*, 2011 BCCA 202 (CanLII), a woman sued a grocery store after she fell near the floral department and claimed the court should infer there must have been water on the floor when she fell. As she fell she knocked over several displays holding flowers and water so it was impossible to tell if there had been water on the floor before she fell. The store employees testified they had finished cleaning that area just before she fell and the store stressed it had a strict policy of regular cleaning and reporting if there was a spill. The court ruled that the plaintiff had not proven that the store was negligent.

The Occupiers Liability Act does not create a presumption of negligence against the occupier whenever a person is injured on their premises. A plaintiff must still be able to point to some act (or some failure to act) on the part of the occupier which caused the injury before liability can be established.

In a similar case *Fulber v. Browns Social House Ltd.*, 2013 BCSC 1760 (CanLII), a 28 year old woman wearing 4 ½ inch stiletto heels who had consumed 3 glasses of wine fell on the floor in a restaurant as she was returning from a cigarette break outside. She suffered a severe ankle injury requiring three surgeries. There was nothing unusual on the floor at the time she fell. The court ruled that the customer had not proven on the balance of probabilities that the restaurant had been negligent and caused her injury, so her claim did not succeed.

■ *Critical Concepts of* Occupier's Liability

- Premises must be kept reasonably safe for lawful users in all circumstances. A business must do what a careful person would do to make the property safe.
- The occupier, not the owner, is responsible for making the premises reasonably safe under all circumstances.
- The occupier must take action to make the property reasonably safe. It is not sufficient merely to post a warning of the danger.
- A lower standard of care is required for users of recreational property and trespassers.
- Safety includes not only the physical aspects of the property, but danger from other users.

Business Alert!

Occupier's Defence   There are many occupier's liability cases against supermarkets for slip and fall accidents caused by customers falling on an astonishing number of things, from a squashed grape to food sauce. Sometimes the supermarket is held liable and sometimes not. One authority, who reviewed a large number of the cases, suggested that those supermarkets who were successful in defending themselves demonstrated two factors:

a) the store had in place reasonable policies and procedures to deal with preventative safety, and
b) the policies were actually followed that day[4]

Duddle v. Vernon (city of)
2004 BCCA 390 (CanLII)

Justin Duddle was 19 years old when he went to the pier at Kal Beach on the shore of Kalamlaka Lake in Vernon B.C. He dove into the lake and struck his head on the bottom and suffered a spinal fracture that left him a quadriplegic. At the time of the accident, the Vernon Parks and Recreation Department maintained the pier. Duddle sued the city of Vernon under the Occupiers Liability Act of B.C. claiming that the city had not taken reasonable care of the pier and was responsible for his injuries.

The pier was shaped like an "h" and the water depth off the ends of the pier ranged from 4 feet 10 inches to about 9 feet in some places. The distance from the pier to the water ranged from 2–3½ feet depending on the water levels. According to safety standards, it is unsafe to dive if there is a drop from the diving surface to the water of two feet or more into water that is 9 feet deep. Thus at no point on the pier was it safe to dive into the water. Where Mr. Duddle dove the water was quite clear and it was only 4½ feet deep.

There were many signs posted around the beach warning people there was no diving allowed. On the actual pier there were 12 signs or symbols indicating no diving. Security personnel employed by the City did patrol the beach, but their focus was on people drinking alcohol and other violations. Security did not patrol the pier for diving infractions.

Mr. Duddle had been going to Kal Beach six to twelve times per summer since he was eight years old. He admitted that he was aware of the warning signs and knew diving was prohibited and that it could be dangerous as the water was shallow and severe injuries could result.

He sued the city claiming that under the Occupiers Liability Act that the city owed a duty of care to make sure that a person will be reasonably safe in using their premises. The plaintiff claimed that the city could have considered four other actions to make the pier reasonably safe. It could have put up guard rails on the pier, hired life guards to keep watch on the pier and beach, had officers patrol the pier and enforced the no diving rules and post the depth of the water on the side of the pier. He also suggested that the pier could even be torn down due to the dangers it created.

The trial judge quickly dismissed the guard rails as they could actually contribute to more accidents as people may dive from the railings. The city, 30 years earlier had employed life guards, but it became too expensive so they were discontinued. The judge accepted that was a reasonable decision. The judge also ruled out tearing down the pier. Once when the city had considered tearing down the pier, the citizens angrily opposed the idea. She stressed that the general public should not have to suffer to protect a few reckless characters from the consequences of their own bad choices.

4. Allen M. Linden, *Canadian Tort Law*, p. 621.

The judge did however accept the position that the city could have patrolled the pier to enforce the no diving rules and should have posted the water depth on the side of the pier. She concluded that since the city had not taken these actions it had not met a reasonable standard of care. The city was held 25% responsible for Duddle's injuries and due to contributory negligence Duddle was himself 75% responsible.

The city of Vernon appealed this finding of liability on their part.

The Court's Decision

The B.C. Court of Appeal disagreed with the trial judge. It believed the judge had been diverted by Mr. Duddle's submissions and not addressed the proper question that was; Had the city taken reasonable care in all of the circumstances to see that Mr. Duddle was reasonably safe? The city was not required "to do all they could have done" to prevent the accident. The appeal court ruled the trial judge effectively fixed the appellants with a standard of perfection. It ruled her application of that incorrect standard was an error of law.

It also stated that the trial judge failed to address properly the question of causation. Mr. Duddle was required to show on a balance of probabilities that, "but for" the appellants' failure to take reasonable care, he would not have suffered his injury. The trial judge had not used this test and had wrongly based her decision on the assumption that he "might not have been injured" if the water depth was marked and the pier had been patrolled. That is not the standard that is to be used for causation. Mr. Duddle had not met the "but for" test so his claim fails to meet the causation requirements.

The Court of Appeal ruled the city could not be held liable for failing to warn Duddle of dangers that he admitted he was already aware of. He had been to the beach many times growing up and he knew the depth of the water and the risks of diving. Thus, the conclusion that the failures to mark water depths on the pier and to have security personnel warn people not to dive contributed to Mr. Duddle's injury, was clearly wrong. The court held that the city had met a reasonable standard of care, had not caused the injury, and was not liable in this tragic accident.

The Premeditated Slip and Fall Like all laws intended to benefit a particular group of people, occupier's liability laws can be subject to abuse by someone who sees a chance to make easy money. The rise in the number of slip and fall claims has caused some businesses to install video-surveillance systems at the areas these incidents happen most often. In supermarkets, for example, these systems are often found in self-serve meat and fresh-vegetable sections. Cameras have caught individuals tearing off a piece of lettuce, dropping it on the floor, circling around the store, and returning to slip and fall on the lettuce.

Business Alert!

An important part of the system is making sure the videotape of the incident is saved for review and possible evidence at trial. There is normally a two-year limitation period respecting slip and fall claims. Thus the retention time of a tape of a known slip and fall accident should be discussed with a legal advisor.

Stores should place large, simply worded notices and barriers if there is an area being cleaned or repaired. Designate one or more staff to be available for immediate response to changing conditions. Keep good business records of preventative measures such as salting, sanding and snow removal as it will provide evidence that the business too all reasonable precautions. Make certain that your business has insurance as well to cover the risk and costs of defending lawsuits.

Municipal By-laws Regarding Ice and Snow

There are municipal by-laws requiring the occupiers of property to clear ice and snow from public sidewalks adjoining their property within a certain time limit after a snowfall—usually 24 hours. This, however, is a minimum standard, not necessarily the standard of the reasonable person which the court will apply.

The Role of Insurance It is absolutely essential for a business to have insurance for occupier's liability. Members of the public are well informed of their rights, or become so if and when required. Thus, if there is an accident on business premises, it is very likely that there will be a claim. Insurance will not only pay for a claim, but will also pay for the cost of defending

Business Alert!

a lawsuit—a considerable expense in itself. As well, professional adjusters will be involved to help settle the claim. The insurance agent will assist in risk management and inspection of the premises to help the business in loss-prevention practices.

It is also important for property owners and occupiers to have a term in any contract with an independent business doing work on the premises, such as a snow removal company, that it will take out liability insurance, including coverage for the cost of any lawsuits, naming the owner and occupier as co-insureds, and that it will have the insurance company send a copy of the policy directly to the co-insureds.

Safety of Others

People are entitled to assume that they can use business premises without the risk of being attacked by others. This is particularly true of places where alcohol is sold, where there must be adequate staff to control and evict troublesome customers. The following examples describe situations in which liability for failing to control customers was claimed.

Example: One evening, while responding to a woman's screams for help, two campers at a government-run conservation area were severely beaten with a baseball bat by another camper. The assailant, who was well known to the conservation authority as a troublemaker, had memos on file about him relating to earlier incidents. Earlier that same evening, he had threatened one of the conservation staff, a 20-year-old recent college graduate, with a piece of firewood over allegations of theft. Nothing was done at that time by the conservation authority to evict or control this camper, and as a result the conservation authority was held to be in breach of its duty of care (*McGinty v. Cook* (1991), 2 O.R. (3d) 283 (C.A.)).

Example: Walker was drinking at a hotel when he was struck by another patron. The blow was sudden and unprovoked. There was no evidence that the attacker was drunk, or that he was a known troublemaker. Because it was relatively early in the day, no bouncers were on duty. The court held that the tavern was not liable because the attack was sudden and unexpected, and nothing could have been done to prevent it. The absence of bouncers at that time was not negligence because it was so early in the day (*Walker v. Friesen* (1979), 22 A.R. 431).

Example: A man who left an Oktoberfest celebration in downtown Vancouver was struck in the eye by another man who had left the same venue. He was struck by a glass beer mug that the event organizers had given free to each guest. The man suffered a serious eye injury and damages were set at $350,000. The injured man sued the promoter of the event and the owner of the venue claiming that he was owed a duty of care and that by giving patrons free glass beer mugs this type of injury was foreseeable. The Court of Appeal agreed that there was a duty owed, but there was not enough evidence to show that the event organizers had not met a reasonable standard of care nor had caused the plaintiff's injury, so the claim was dismissed. (*Donaldson v. John Doe*, 2009 BCCA 38(CanLII))

■ *Business Law* Applied

⓭ **Peter Giroux developed** a new food product. In order to do some market testing, he arranged with a local supermarket to set up a table inside the store, and give out free samples to customers. One customer dropped some of the food sample on the floor. Giroux was so enthusiastic about the response he was getting that he failed to notice the spill. He had thought about the possibility beforehand though, and decided it was the responsibility of the supermarket to supervise the conditions of the premises.

About five minutes later, another customer walked past, slipped on the piece of food, fell, and broke her leg.

  a) What is the name for the action the injured customer could bring against the relevant business?
  b) Did he take reasonable steps to ensure the safety of the area where his table was set up?
  c) What could the supermarket have done to better protect itself?

⑭ Bob Klee was a regular customer at a club called the Hot House. He was known to be very aggressive when drunk but, being such a regular, Hot House management tolerated his conduct. Occasionally, Klee would become involved in a fight and would be barred for a week. One night, when his favourite hockey team was eliminated from the playoffs, Klee was drinking at the Hot House and got into a fight with a fan of the other team. Klee stabbed his adversary.

  a) Klee has no money, and an action against him would be worthless. Does the victim have anyone else whom he could sue for the injuries? On what basis?
  b) What does the victim have to prove regarding the standard of care?

Special Responsibility for Intoxicated Persons

1) Commercial Host Liability

Businesses operating in areas where they are likely to encounter people who are intoxicated, should take this condition into account. This is particularly true if the business makes money by selling alcohol. There are two broad categories involving business responsibility to intoxicated persons. One is when an intoxicated individual sustains personal injury on the premises; the other is when he leaves the premises, and either suffers personal injury or causes harm to a stranger. The issue then becomes; what is the reasonable standard of care that a commercial host must meet when serving alcohol to customers?

Example: In the early Supreme Court decision in the *Jordan House v. Menow* [1974] SCR 239, the court clearly stated that the commercial host must take reasonable steps to prevent the intoxicated customer from obvious and serious dangers that were reasonably foreseeable. They must take reasonable steps to prevent them from hurting themselves. In this case a regular customer had been thrown out of the bar because he was drunk and he was hit by a car as he walked home down the highway. The court held the driver, the drunken man and the bar equally liable (33.3% each) for Menow's injuries. The court said it would not have taken much to call a taxi or make sure he left with a sober person or offered him a room in this hotel to keep him safe. This case established the reasonable standard of care expected of commercial hosts with respect to drunken customers.

Example: In *Holton v. MacKinnon et al.*, 2005 BCSC 41 (CanLII), three young men in Whistler B.C. drank at two separate bars and then went back to a house to continue drinking. They then drove to a party but their car went off the road and one of the passengers was injured and became a quadriplegic. The court found each of the bars 15% responsible for the injuries, the driver 40% and the drunken passenger who was injured was 30% responsible for his own damages.

Example: In *Hague v. Billings*, 1993 CanLII 8581 (ONCA), two men went on a drinking binge. They drank 50 bottles of beer over a 10 hour period plus a bottle of whiskey and smoked some marijuana. They went into one bar and had a beer but were thrown out as they were drunk. They then went to a second bar and drank 4 beers in 90 minutes. They left the second bar and drove down the wrong side of the highway and hit a car killing the mother and severely injuring the daughter. The court ruled that the first hotel was not liable as it had evicted the drunks, but the second hotel was partly liable for the injuries. The trial court held the drunk driver 50% responsible and the second bar also 50% responsible. On appeal the liability was increased to 85% on the driver and reduced to 15% on the second bar.

McIntyre v. Grigg
2006 CanLII 37326 ONCA

Andrea McIntyre was first year university student at McMaster University in Hamilton Ontario. She was an outgoing athletic young woman on the varsity rugby team and hoped to become a chiropractor. One late night after leaving the McMaster Student Union run pub "The Downstairs John" with some friends, she was hit by a car driven by Andrew Grigg and suffered serious injuries. Andrew Grigg was a member of the Hamilton Tiger Cats professional football team. He had been drinking at several establishments that night and finally at The Downstairs John. He was 2–3 times over the legal limit for alcohol when the accident occurred. He had driven through a stop sign and made a very wide and reckless turn and the car went up onto the sidewalk and hit a light post and Andrea McIntyre. Ms. McIntyre sued both Grigg and the McMaster Student Union for her injuries.

Andrea had suffered a badly broken leg; she had mild brain trauma and other injuries to her legs and back. The accident caused her to suffer depression, a personality change and she attempted suicide twice as a result of the accident.

Mr. Grigg pleaded guilty to careless driving and had to pay a $500 fine. In civil court the trial judge found he was drunk and drove carelessly and caused Andrea's injuries so he was liable for negligence. The court apportioned 70% liability to him. The court also found the McMaster Student Union which owned and operated the pub 30% liable for McIntyre's injuries. The pub had over-served him, or served him when he was intoxicated, or they should have known he was intoxicated, and they had not made any attempt to prevent him from driving drunk. Under the provincial law and common law, the pub was partly liable for McIntyre's injuries. The court set the damages at; general damages of $250,000, aggravated damages $100,000 and punitive damages of $100,000. The two defendants appealed the decision to the Ontario Court of Appeal.

The Court's Decision

This case has become famous as it is the first one to award punitive damages in a case involving a drunk driver. The Appeal Court noted:

"This is a novel case. The parties were unable to produce any Canadian case law in which punitive damages were awarded as a result of injuries sustained in a motor vehicle accident caused by an impaired driver nor were they able to produce any appellate authority that prohibited such damages in this context."

The appellants argued that punitive damages were inappropriate as Andrew Grigg did not act in a high-handed, malicious or oppressive manner, and thus there is no basis upon which the jury could have properly awarded punitive damages. The court however ruled that Grigg had a conscious disregard for the life and safety of others and that drunk driving is a social evil. The $500 criminal fine was not a major deterrent, so awarding punitive damages here fulfils the objectives of retribution, deterrence and denunciation.

But while the appeal court decided that punitive damages were appropriate it reduced the amount to $20,000. The dissenting judge disagreed with this award and felt it could lead to many more people claiming these damages and as a result car insurance rates increasing significantly. Punitive damages are meant to be a deterrent but since most insurance policies cover punitive damages, then the drunk defendants may not be deterred from this behaviour since it is the insurance company that pays not the drunk driver. The rest of society also ends up paying as the insurance rates will surely be increased if these punitive damage awards become commonplace in cases of this kind.

The court also discussed the 30% liability imposed on the McMaster pub and stated that amount of liability was at the high end of the scale, but it was still an acceptable percentage under the circumstances. The award of aggravated damages should have been included in the award for general non-pecuniary damages so that $100,000 was denied.

The real impact of this case will only be determined in the future if courts consistently award punitive damages in similar drunk driving cases. Insurance rates will certainly increase if this occurs.

Liability to Strangers

Businesses that sell liquor to an individual who is already intoxicated may also be liable to strangers who are injured after the person served leaves the premises. This principle is included in all provincial liquor-control acts, which clearly relate to business situations involving the sale of alcohol (commercial host liability).

The bartender and waiter can be liable if they over serve the drunk customer, and the employer is vicariously liable for their actions. The standard of care required is often not that difficult to determine. If the drunken person leaves the establishment with a sober adult, the court has ruled that the business had met a reasonable standard of care.

Example: In *Stewart v. Pettie* [1995] 1SCR 131, two men and their wives went to a dinner theatre and the men drank well over the legal limit for alcohol, but the women were sober. When they went home one of the drunken men drove and the car left the road and hit a light pole and wall. One of the wives did not have her seatbelt on, so she was thrown across the car, hit her head and as a result became a quadriplegic. The other people wore seatbelts and were not injured. The court stated the law is clear that at common law a tavern owner owes a duty to take positive action to protect patrons and others from the dangers of intoxication. But it ruled that the dinner theatre had met a reasonable standard of care. It knew that the men were drunk, but it had assumed that one of the two sober women with them would drive or call a taxi. Even though it was never discussed with the waiter how they were getting home, the commercial host had done enough. There was also no proof that failing to question them or intervene had caused the injury. The court ruled that the driver was 75% liable for the injuries and the passenger's contributory negligence was set at 25%.

2) Business Host Liability

Business Alert!

When a company hosts an event, such as an office Christmas party or company picnic, the issue of business host liability arises. If the company serves alcohol it must take a number of precautions to protect itself from possible legal action if one of their employees becomes intoxicated and leaves and is involved in an accident. The duty of care imposed on the business host is similar to the commercial host, even though they are not selling alcohol for a profit. However the business is often in a position of power over the employee and it is a reasonably foreseeable risk that if someone at their event leaves drunk, an accident could occur.

In one Ontario case a boss had offered an employee a taxi ride or even a hotel room for the night when she had been drinking at the office Christmas party, but she declined the offers. She then attempted to drive home, but had an accident and suffered a significant brain injury. The judge ruled that the company had not done enough and said the boss should have actually taken her keys away and forced her to get in a taxi or go to a hotel to spend the night. This case was declared a mistrial because the judge had dismissed the jury part way through the trial, but the case was never retried. So this judge's ruling is not the new standard of care for business hosts, but the case has made many question how much does a company have to do to avoid liability and to protect its employees. (*Hunt v. Sutton Group Incentive Realty Inc.*, 2001 CanLII 28027) ONSC)

The following list outlines some of the precautions a company should take before it has an event to both prevent an accident and provide a defence to any claim in negligence.

- Do not have a self-serve bar. Rather have a bartender who can monitor consumption.
- Hold the event at or near a hotel and arrange for a discounted rooms.
- Have free taxi voucher available.
- Do not announce "last call."
- Stop serving alcohol one hour before the end of the event.
- Serve food at all times that alcohol is served.
- Send an office e-mail advising of the options available so that people do not have to drink and drive.

3) Social Host Liability

The remaining situation involving alcohol is social host liability, where people are drinking at a private gathering, such as at a friend's party. The common law has not traditionally held social hosts to the same standards of care as commercial or business hosts. Given that there are over 1,000 deaths caused by drunk drivers every year in Canada, it becomes an open question as to whether a person who supplies alcohol at a private gathering could or should be liable to strangers for accidents caused by their intoxicated guests after leaving their party.

Do we have to police our friends? Under what circumstances does the duty of care arise and what standard of care would be required? What would a host have to do to first create a duty to others on the roadways and then what actions must they take to fulfil the standard of care required to then avoid liability? What are the impacts on home insurance rates if social hosts are held liable? These are all important questions not yet clearly answered in the case law.

Childs v. Desormeaux, [2006] 1 S.C.R. 643

This case arises from a tragic car accident in Ottawa in the early hours of January 1, 1999. At 1:30 a.m., after leaving a New Year's Eve party hosted by Dwight Courrier and Julie Zimmerman, Desmond Desormeaux drove his car into oncoming traffic and collided head-on with a car driven by Patricia Hadden. One of the passengers in Ms. Hadden's car was killed and three others seriously injured, including Zoe Childs, who was 18 at the time. Ms. Childs' spine was severed and she was left paralyzed from the waist down. Mr. Desormeaux and the two passengers in his car were also injured. Mr. Desormeaux was a 39 year old alcoholic who had been convicted of impaired driving twice before and that night he had consumed about 7-8 beer at the party. He was legally intoxicated and had no car insurance. Childs sued the party givers claiming they owed a duty of care to prevent their drunken guest from injuring others on the highway. This was the first Canadian case to consider the liability of social hosts.

The party was a BYOB (bring your own booze) party and the defendant Mr. Desormeaux had a few drinks earlier in the evening and brought his own alcohol to the party. The hosts only provided a small amount of champagne for a toast. When Desormeaux was leaving the party the host asked if he was all right to drive and he replied "no problem."

This trial court ruled that there was no positive duty imposed on the social hosts to prevent drunken friends from driving, that duty only exists in special relationships such as the commercial host, but not in social settings. The trial court did decide however that there was such close proximity between the hosts and others on the road that their guest might encounter, that this did impose a duty on them to not turn out a drunk driver onto the roads. Under this duty the court would have allocated 15% of the liability for Child's injuries to the host.

However the trial judge went on to analyze the policy issues in this case. It recognized that to impose liability on social hosts could make it very difficult on people from both a practical and financial perspective. It would require that hosts have to monitor the alcohol consumption of their guests and home owner insurance rates would rise significantly. The court believed that this impact on insurance rates and compensation issues were so important that the government, not the courts, should determine whether social hosts should be liable for accidents their guests cause. For these policy reasons the court ruled the social hosts in this case were not liable.

Childs appealed the decision to the Ontario Court of Appeal and lost, and then the Supreme Court agreed to hear her final appeal.

The Supreme Court's Decision

The Supreme Court found that the fact that someone hosts a party where liquor is served is not sufficient to impose a duty on the party givers to members of the public using roads and highways. It also found that there was no evidence that the party hosts knew that Desormeaux was drunk when he left. The allegation was that the party givers failed to watch how much alcohol their guests were consuming, in particular Desormeaux, and prevent them from driving drunk. The court refused to place that obligation on people who gave parties in private homes. However, it was reasonable to impose this obligation in commercial situations where staff had to keep track of the drinks to bill the customer's and were given special training on monitoring alcohol consumption by customers.

The Supreme Court did however leave the door open somewhat for imposition of this liability on party hosts in a future case if the facts are different. It stated "a social host at a party where alcohol is served is not under a duty of care to members of the public who may be injured by a guest's actions, unless the host's conduct implicates him or her in the creation or exacerbation of the risk." This statement indicates that if the facts had been different perhaps the social host could be held liable. Possibly if the host had provided the alcohol and knew that the guest was very drunk and encouraged this behaviour, the host may be partially liable for damages their guests cause. Unfortunately the Supreme Court did not give more clarification on how a host could "create or exacerbate the risk".

The Supreme Court also failed to discuss whether policy reasons relating to the impact on insurance rates and compensation for injured people may be so significant that it would not be appropriate to impose liability on social hosts.

This case has left the liability of social hosts still an area of some legal uncertainty. Zoe Childs lost in her final appeal to hold the host responsible for her injuries.

In the *Childs v. Desormeaux* case above social host liability was the key issue. The top court, based on the specific facts of the case, refused to impose liability on the party hosts after their friend who left caused a fatal accident. But the court did not rule out social host liability completely. If the facts in another case are different and the hosts "create or exacerbate" the risks of the drunk driver, then the court seemed to indicate social hosts could be held liable.

Courts have held parents liable when under age teens got drunk at a party at their home and were in an accident after they left. The court ruled in *Prevost v. Vetter* 2002 BCCA 202 (CanLII), that the parents had failed to supervise the party properly, so they were partly liable for the serious injuries to a 17 year old male who was driven home by a drunk 18 year old female who crashed her car.

The Insurance Factor

The result in *Childs*, above, may appear unfair, but there are other considerations beyond the issues in a specific action. One is which person is more likely to have insurance, the car driver or the party-giver. As there is a scheme in place to ensure all cars have insurance, by private policies or the uninsured motor vehicle fund, placing liability on the party-giver, who may have no insurance and no assets, might result in many victims having a right but no real remedy.

Another issue is: who are the real parties? Judges realize many decisions in negligence law involve the shifting of liability from one insurance company to another. For example, Childs may have recovered from Desormeaux' insurance company or the uninsured motor vehicle fund and one of them was suing to recover payments made using her name as is permitted by the terms of insurance policies. The party-givers may have had homeowner insurance that covered the type of liability in question here, and that insurance company was defending.

Even though the *Childs* case has stated that there is no duty on a private party giver to monitor drinking so as to prevent someone driving drunk, such a party host is still at risk, at least of a lawsuit, and perhaps a change in attitude, which may be bring a change in the law and put a duty on party givers to ensure no one leaves their party drunk. Also, the question remains: what if, on the balance of probabilities, the evidence establishes the party hosts know the guest is drunk?

Business Alert!

Remember such a duty will be imposed on businesses that host functions that serve liquor. The lesson then is: Consider the risk and consider insuring for it, even for private parties. Don't let your customers, employees or friends drive drunk, it could save lives as well as a lot of money.

■ *Critical Concepts of* Liability for Intoxicated Persons

A business that sells alcohol should take reasonable steps to:
- make the premises safe for individuals who are drunk
- ensure that customers do not become so intoxicated that they suffer personal injury after leaving the premises
- ensure that customers do not become so intoxicated that they cause injury to others after leaving the premises.

■ **Business Law** Applied

⑮ **Sam Umali was** drinking at the Bull and Bear Tavern from 6:00 p.m. until 11:00 p.m. The waiter, realizing that Umali was getting very drunk, asked if he was driving. When Umali said no, the waiter continued to serve him. Umali left and, in his drunken state, fell directly into the path of an oncoming car. He was killed instantly. Umali was survived by his wife and three infant children. The car driver was not negligent.

  a) Did Umali's wife and children have the grounds for an action against the Bull and Bear Tavern for loss of a husband and father?

⑯ **Kathleen Oakley** became very drunk while celebrating at the office Christmas party, held at the Espresso Restaurant and Tavern. When she left, her car would not start, so she flagged down a passing driver and asked for assistance to jump-start it.

Roger Vitali, who was always willing to help someone in distress, stopped and helped her. Oakley said she had cables and would attach them to her vehicle. Because of her drunken state, she attached the positive cable to the negative pole, causing the battery to explode, injuring both her and Vitali.

  a) Did Oakley have grounds for an action against the Espresso Restaurant and Tavern?
  b) Did Vitali have grounds for an action against the Espresso Restaurant and Tavern?

⑰ **Laura King** hosted a 30th birthday party for her husband William and 3 other couples attended. Laura provided a 4 course meal and all the wine that was consumed. Seven of the adults drank red wine and together finished off 3 bottles that night. Rob was the only guest who drank white wine and he alone drank 2 bottles of white. Rob began to get quite loud and was slurring his words when he spoke. He stumbled as he walked through the house to the washroom and he even knocked over a lamp and broke it.

When Rob and his wife Maria were leaving Laura and her husband William said "Maria you better drive home, Rob is in no shape to get behind the wheel." Maria replied "I can't drive Rob's car as it has a manual transmission and I can only drive automatic. Don't worry we'll be fine, we don't have far to go." The guests all then left the party. Four blocks from Laura's home Rob drove through a red light and hit the Centas family and killed the 2 adults and seriously injured their two children.

  a) Who will be held liable for the death and injuries to the Centas family?
  b) What factors will influence the judge in determining liability in this case?
  c) Would punitive damages be awarded?

Products Liability

Modern Business Methods

Product manufacture is one of the most important business activities in modern times. Sometimes, these products can be dangerous and seriously injure consumers. Products liability law has been developed to deal with this type of situation. It is primarily aimed at consumers and personal injuries to them, but it has more recently been extended to give some protection to businesses dealing with other businesses.

The complexity of the modern business process means that there may be many companies involved in a chain-like fashion from point of origin to the consumer.

The Supply Chain of a Modern Automobile Business

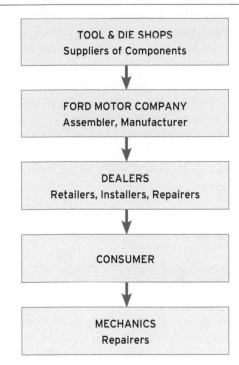

TOOL & DIE SHOPS
Suppliers of Components

↓

FORD MOTOR COMPANY
Assembler, Manufacturer

↓

DEALERS
Retailers, Installers, Repairers

↓

CONSUMER

↓

MECHANICS
Repairers

Who Is Liable?

Each of the people detailed in the supply chain could be held liable as the one who caused an injury to a consumer. Where there are many involved, they may all share equally unless they can specifically prove that they were not responsible for the defect. The lawsuit often becomes a fighting match among the businesses in the supply chain, each trying to prove its own innocence, and usually pointing a finger at the others in the process.

Who Can Sue?

This question is answered by the test of reasonable foreseeability as described in the "snail in the bottle" case, *Donoghue v. Stevenson* (see p. 85). The duty of a product supplier has been defined as being owed to everyone who might reasonably be foreseen as a user or handler of the product. This means that the supplier owes a duty not only to the purchaser, but also to someone who uses a product paid for by another, or even to a bystander injured by, for example, an exploding product. In effect, virtually anyone can sue any member of the manufacturer's supply chain.

Grounds for Suing

There are three bases for bringing an action based on products liability principles:

- defects in the manufacturing process
- negligent design
- duty to warn

Defects in the Manufacturing Process   This includes not only defects in the manufacturing process itself, but also in the testing, packaging, and distribution of goods. The courts are very strict in applying liability for such defects. You will recall the case of *Donoghue v. Stevenson* discussed earlier. A manufacturer was held liable for its bottling process. It failed to properly ensure snails did not crawl into its bottles.

Many manufacturers today are also assemblers, in the sense that some of their component parts are supplied by other companies. The car manufacturers, for example, rely heavily on components from outside sources, and make few themselves.

Manufacturers of products that are made from many parts are liable for any injuries caused by defects in the components supplied to them by other firms. This is partly because the manufacturers create consumer reliance on a brand name—usually through expensive, sophisticated advertising schemes. Another reason is the difficulty for the consumer in trying to identify, then find and sue, all the possible suppliers of components.

The manufacturer can claim against the supplier of the component, so that the supplier must ultimately pay. However, the cost of bringing a claim against the supplier must be borne by the manufacturer. This is a large expense saved by the consumer, especially when the supplier is located in a foreign country.

■ *Critical Concepts of* Products Liability

- A manufacturer is liable to a consumer in tort even though there is no contract between them, if fault can be established.
- A manufacturer is liable for all component parts from outside suppliers included in its product.
- If there are several companies involved in the supply chain, and they cannot prove their innocence (that is, they cannot prove how the incident occurred), they will be held equally liable.

Resch v. Canadian Tire Corporation, 2006 CanLII 11930 (ONSC)

Days before Nathan Resch's 16th birthday he was riding a new CCM Heat mountain bike that his stepfather had bought for him from the local Canadian Tire store in Fort Erie Ontario. As he was riding down a city street the front wheel assembly broke and Nathan was thrown off and he landed face first on the road. He suffered a fractured forehead and lower jaw, disfiguring facial lacerations and the frontal lobe of his brain was seriously injured. His stepfather had taken the bicycle back to Canadian Tire three days earlier as he had seen a recall notice on the bicycle. There had been problems with the front suspension mechanism separating from the frame of these bicycles. The Canadian Tire employee adjusted the bicycle, but did not repair it, as the replacement parts were not in stock, and he then let the stepfather take the bicycle home. Three days later Nathan had the serious accident.

Resch sued the bicycle manufacturer Procycle Group Inc., Canadian Tire Corporation Ltd. (the franchisor and head office) and Mills-Roy Enterprises (the Fort Erie Canadian Tire dealership) that sold the bicycle. They were all sued for negligence and a claim was also made for breach of contract under the Sale of Goods Act. Since Nathan had not bought the bicycle himself, the Sale of Goods Act did not apply though. Resch was seeking pecuniary and non-pecuniary damages as well as punitive damages.

The defendants claimed that Resch was responsible for his own injuries as he did not have a helmet on at the time of the accident and he was riding too fast.

Resch had multiple surgeries and will need up to 10 more operations over the next decade to repair his nose, lip and mouth.

The brain injury has affected his focus on doing tasks and drastically altered his personality. Before the accident he had his own lawn-care and snow removal business and worked part-time at an auto glass replacement firm. After the accident he was unable to hold down any job.

Before the jury trial began the Fort Eric dealership reached a settlement with the plaintiff, but the trial continued against the other defendants.

The Court's Decision

The court ruled that the manufacturer was 55% responsible for the accident, the head office/franchisor Canadian Tire was 35% responsible and the local Canadian Tire dealership 10% responsible for Resch's injuries. The jury did not find any contributory negligence by Nathan Resch. The damage award was set at $3.5 million.

The jury found that the manufacturer was negligent for using unproven forks on the wheel from an unvalidated supplier and for issuing a recall notice that was vague and lacked urgency. Punitive damages of $35,000 were awarded against the manufacturer for inadequately validating the safety of the new component designs in the product.

The jury also awarded punitive damages of $160,000 against Canadian Tire for failing to implement its professed "safety above all policy" and by failing to communicate to its individual store owners the urgency of the safety issue with the front wheels

■ *Business Law*   Applied

⑱ **Pseka Mbele,** a student, ran a refreshment booth at a beach as a summer job. He sold two cans of pop to Phatima Abdi, who gave one to her boyfriend, Arief Rumi. Rumi drank it and, at the last gulp, saw the partly decayed body of a mouse at the bottom of the can. Rumi became ill, spent three weeks in a hospital, and was off work for five weeks.

  a) Does Rumi have an action against Pseka Mbele even though Rumi has no contract with Mbele?
  b) What if Mbele, a student, has no money? Is the action against Mbele advisable?
  c) On what basis in law does Rumi have an action against the manufacturer of the product?

⑲ **Peter Boychuk bought** a used brand-name mountain bike from a retailer, Future Cycle, with no mention of any warranties. The bike was manufactured by Euro Cycle Ltd. When Boychuk rode it out of the showroom, the bike lost a defective front wheel and Boychuk hit a pedestrian, Jean Shabot, injuring him.

  a) Does Boychuk have grounds for an action against the dealer for the cost of repair of the bicycle?
  b) Does Shabot have grounds for an action against the dealer and manufacturer of the bike for personal injury?
  c) Shabot has three potential defendants: Boychuk (owner/rider), Future Cycle (dealer), and Euro Cycle (manufacturer). He does not know who is at fault, and has no money to hire expensive experts to prove his case. What principle in products liability law will help him to prove negligence against any or all of these three possible defendants?
  d) What will the result be if the three defendants cannot determine how the accident occurred? How will liability be shared among them?

High Standard of Care

The courts are very rigorous in imposing a high standard of care on companies whose business it is to make money by supplying products to consumers. This is not only to ensure safety and to protect consumers from harm, but also to make the business bear the responsibility for paying for any injury that it causes in the process of earning profits. The cost of product-caused injuries becomes a cost of doing business.

There is a duty to inspect in the manufacturing process, but the manufacturer can still be liable even if they have adequate inspection procedures. The courts recognize that accidents can still occur and no inspection system if perfect, so if the evidence does not point to any other cause, then negligence can be inferred and the manufacturer held liable.

Example: In *Oland Breweries Limited v. Leblanc*, 1994 CanLII 6464 (NBCA), Paul Leblanc was putting bottles of beer into large tubs of ice at a softball tournament sponsored by Oland Breweries when one of the bottles exploded and cut his hand badly. He sued the manufacturer of the beer for negligence. The court heard testimony that beer bottles do explode during the bottling process at a rate of about 100 to 200 bottles in a 25,000 to 30,000 dozen bottle production. The brewery pointed out that it had a state of the art inspection method for the detection of defective bottles and it inspected all bottles twice before the bottling process is completed and some bottles are discarded in the inspection process.

But the court found that it was impossible to detect all defective bottles by the inspection process and that some defective bottles do actually make it into the hands of the consumers and can explode without any pressure, abuse or interference by the customer. The court found that every case has to consider the facts and if the evidence rules out any other probable cause of injury, then the court can make the permissible inference that the manufacturer was negligent. In this case the court did not believe Leblanc had done anything wrong as he was putting the beer on ice and there was enough space in the tub, so the explosion was not caused by friction with the other beer bottles. The brewer was found liable for negligence and damages were set at $8,000.

More v. Bauer Nike Hockey Inc., 2011 BCCA 419 (CanLII)

Darren More was a 17 year old AAA midget hockey player who suffered a catastrophic head injury at a hockey tournament. More was near the goal when either, as the result of a check or in trying to avoid the check and catching an edge, Darren rotated, fell and slid on his rear end. He hit the boards back first and his then hit his head on the boards. It looked like a routine fall and he skated to the bench. But soon after he began to vomit and EMS was called. He was rushed to hospital with bleeding in the brain (SDH subdural hematoma) and was in a coma for 6 weeks. He is permanently physically and mentally disabled and requires 24 hour care. He sued both the manufacturer of the hockey helmet and the Canadian Standards Association (CSA) which had certified the helmet, for negligence, seeking $10 million in damages. The player argued that the helmet was not designed properly and should have had better impact protection. He also argued that the safety standards were not strict enough and the certification label misled the plaintiff to believe that the helmet would fully protect him from the risk of a serious head injury.

The defendants maintained that the helmet was properly designed and proper warnings had been provided. They argued that the defendant knew of the risks involved in playing hockey and the injury was a rare and unforeseeable event and the defendants did not cause the injury.

The Court's Decision

The trial court ruled that neither the helmet manufacturer nor the CSA was liable for More's injuries. The helmet was state of the art and came with adequate warnings of the dangers of playing hockey. The warning label on the helmet read as follows:

"**WARNING:** Ice hockey is a collision sport which is dangerous. These helmets afford no protection from neck, spinal or certain types of brain injuries including those that may

be caused by rotational forces. Severe head, brain or spinal injuries including paralysis or death may occur despite using this helmet."

Darren's injury was partly due to a rotational force (the brain rotating inside the skull) but no helmet has yet been designed or created that can protect from rotational force injuries to the brain. The court found that the warning was clearly presented to the plaintiff and he still chose to play hockey. He had suffered two previous concussions, so he knew the dangers of the sport and he still decided to play.

The trial court ruled that the CSA did owe More a duty of care, but the CSA had met a reasonable standard of care in its testing and warning on helmets. Darren was injured in 2004 and the helmet he wore even met the stricter 2009 certification standards, that were not yet in place at the time of his accident.

The trial court found that the defendants were not liable because they had met a reasonable standard of care, they were not the proximate cause of his injury, and Darren's injury was not reasonably foreseeable. A SDH injury is extremely rare in hockey.

The court emphasized that the manufacturer is not an insurer, nor is it to be held to a standard of perfection. The manufacturer and the CSA had met a reasonable standard of care and provided proper warnings about the risks, so the defendants were not liable for negligence.

Darren More appealed the trial decision, but was unsuccessful. The Court of Appeal upheld the trial decision. However the Appeal Court noted that it would not have considered imposing a duty of care on the CSA. The appeal court said that the CSA performs a valuable service to the public and if the courts impose a duty of care on this association, it may not financially be able to survive and then the public would lose its valuable services. So for these policy reasons the appeal court did not think a duty of care should be imposed on the safety association.

Negligent Design: Duty to Warn

Negligent design of an object is also a basis for breach of the standard of care required by the law of negligence. A design defect is usually more damaging than a manufacturing process defect. Defects of design in a product likely affect every product. A manufacturing process defect, such as a snail in a bottle, may only affect a single user.

A manufacturer is under a heavy obligation to ensure that a product is designed safely to the current state of the art standards, and to warn if there is danger of any use of the product.

Warnings of any danger must be clearly communicated.

Example: In *Hutton v General Motors of Canada Limited*, 2010 ABQB 606 (CanLII), Jennifer Hutton sued GM for injuries sustained when the side airbags in a Chevrolet Cavalier she was a passenger in accidentally deployed while her boyfriend, Kent Wobst, was driving. GM had issued a recall notice regarding the air bags and Wobst's car had been brought in and recalibrated to reduce the chance that the airbags would go off inappropriately. GM had not redesigned nor replaced the airbags as it claimed that was too expensive. Wobst was driving on a gravel road at less than 30 km/h and when he drove through a puddle with water 3-4 inches deep, the air bags went off. Hutton suffered a broken arm, cuts and abrasions.

The court ruled that just recalibrating the air bags instead of the costlier redesign or replacement was reasonable under the circumstances. GM did not have to totally eliminate the problem. But the court did find GM negligent because once the car was recalibrated, GM failed to give owners adequate notice that the air bag problem could still reoccur. GM owed a continuing duty to warn of the remaining risk the airbags could still deploy at the wrong time after the recalibration was completed. Since that warning was not given, GM was found to be negligent for damages totalling almost $40,000.

One of the most notorious cases in legal lore is that of the U.S. case of an elderly woman who spilled a hot cup of coffee on herself while going through a McDonald's drive-through. She sued McDonald's for failure to warn her that the coffee was hot enough to burn. A jury awarded her $7,000,000.00 at first instance. You might check labels on coffee cups at places where you purchase take-out coffee and see if there is a warning on the label. Do you think it is adequate in that any purchaser would notice it?

Berry's World

PRODUCT LIABILITY MESSAGE

© 1995 by NEA, Inc.

Walford v. Jacuzzi Canada Ltd., [2007] ONCA 729 (CanLII) (leave to appeal denied S.C.C. 2008-04-03)

At the age of 15¾ years Correna Walford went down a used slide her parents had just installed beside their 4 foot deep backyard pool. She went down on her knees, hit her chin on the bottom of the pool breaking her neck, causing her to float to the surface an instant quadriplegic.

She sued, through her parents as litigation guardians, a number of people who had anything to do with supplying the slide to her parents including the private seller; a retailer, Pioneer Pools, who sold parts for the installation; the manufacturer of the pool, and the manufacturer of the slide (Jacuzi Canada Ltd.).

The Walfords had wanted a slide for their backyard pool. Correna's mother was concerned as to the safety for use with a 4 foot shallow pool. New ones were too expensive, so upon seeing an ad in a newspaper for a used one she bought it and then brought the slide to Pioneer Pools, which company she had been dealing with for two years for pool supplies. She asked employees if the slide could be used in a four foot pool safely and they said there would be no problem. Mrs. Walford gave very strict instructions to all the children about the use of the pool and the slide including going down "only feet first".

However, Correna had gone down slides at Canada's Wonderland on her knees and thought that would be fun. On her second use of the slide she did this. When she hit the bottom she went unconscious and floated to the surface, now a quadriplegic.

The Trial Judge dismissed the action against all of the Defendants. Correna appealed only against Pioneer Pools.

The Court of Appeal's Decision

This Court held that there was a sufficiently close relationship between Pioneer Pools and Mrs. Walford because she had relied on its advice for over two previous years including specific advice with respect to the installation of the slide in question.

The Court held that all manufacturers and suppliers are required to warn all those who may reasonably be affected by potentially dangerous products. This includes not only the original purchaser but any users.

The duty to warn of potentially dangerous products applies only to dangers that are not obvious. The danger of going down the slide on a child's knees was not obvious.

The Court held that the only reference for a standard was the U.S. Consumer Product Safety standard regarding back yard swimming pools. Those standards stated that with a pool four feet or less there was a danger of catastrophic injury if the user did not go down feet first.

The Court agreed the damages were $6.25 million but reversed the Trial Judge's decision. It found Pioneer Pools 80% responsible for the injuries, so it was liable for $5 million in damages. Due to contributory negligence, the plaintiff was 20% responsible for her own injuries.

■ *Critical Concepts of* Duty to Warn

- Manufacturers must warn customers about dangerous properties of their product.
- If a product can be produced in a safer way, that must be done.
- Manufacturers cannot use the cheaper way of making their product, and rely on warning customers of the danger.
- Manufacturers must also warn of dangers discovered after the product has been sold and distributed.
- The warning must be reasonably communicated.
- The warning should be printed on the label, clearly noticeable, and must describe the specific danger.

Strict Liability

strict liability

liability imposed when something dangerous escapes from property even though no fault by the owner

In Canada it is often difficult to succeed in a manufacturer's negligence case as the plaintiff must prove on the balance of probabilities that the manufacturer was negligent. This can involve obtaining and analyzing much detailed technical information at great expense. In the United States it is much easier, as almost every state imposes strict liability on manufacturers. If they sell a defective dangerous product and it causes damages, the manufacture will be held strictly liable. In strict liability the injured party does not have to prove fault on the part of the defendant manufacturer.

Strict liability does not exist in manufacturers' liability in Canada. The plaintiff must establish that the manufacturer on the balance of probabilities was negligent, so causation and fault must be established.

Strict liability does exist as a separate intentional tort in Canada in other situations, though it is not frequently used. The traditional test for strict liability required a defendant to have made an unnatural use of his land, brought something onto his land which would probably cause damage if it escaped and then when it did escape, it caused damages to the plaintiff. The original British case that developed these requirements for strict liability involved a man who had a large reservoir of water that escaped and flooded his neighbour's mine and he was held strictly liable. He had done nothing wrong but this large amount of water he had accumulated was considered unusual and inherently dangerous, so he was responsible for the damages it caused when it escaped through no fault of the reservoir owner. (*Rylands v. Fletcher* (1868) L.R. 3H.L. 330). For example, if someone has toxic chemicals, or hazardous waste or a dangerous animal, they may be held strictly liable if it escapes and causes damage, even if it escaped through no fault of the owner. Most courts prefer to look at these situations as negligence rather than impose strict liability. When it comes to defective products causing damages though, Canada has not applied strict liability as courts have in the U.S.

■ *Business Law* Applied

㉑ Mark went to a local store and bought a new ceiling fan made in Canada from New-Lite and had an electrician install the fan. Shortly after installation the fan caught on fire and the fire spread to the rest of the house and did $60,000 in damages. The fan was installed as a unit and the electrician did not open or tamper with the fan's motor in any way. The fire inspector believes that inside the fan the automatic shut-off fuse made in China failed to work to prevent the motor from overheating.

  a) Who can Mark sue and what must he prove to recover his $60,000?
  b) Can any company involved be held strictly liable for the damages caused by the defective fan?

㉑ Chemtar Inc. is a big chemical company and it has large storage tanks at its factory where it stores industrial chemicals. One night vandals broke into Chemtar's factory and smashed the storage tanks and destroyed much of their equipment. Some of the industrial chemicals leaked onto the property of Electo Inc., an electronics factory next door, and destroyed $100,000 worth of their electronic components. Electro is planning to sue Chemtar for these damages, but Chemtar denies any liability. It claims that it had new proper tanks to store the chemicals and a proper alarm system and it was the vandals who caused the damages and Chemtar was in no way responsible.

  a) Can Electro successfully sue Chemtar for negligence?
  b) If Electro fails in a negligence claim, what other tort may Electo claim to find Chemtar responsible for their damages? Would this other claim be successful?

Professional Liability

Sources of Liability

Professional liability in law, which is rapidly expanding, primarily involves three areas:

- contracts
- torts
- agency

Take the example of an elderly client who retains a lawyer to sell her house so that she can move into a retirement home. She will likely be asked to sign a retainer agreement, which outlines what the lawyer will do for her, and details of billing and payment. This is a contract. There is a term implied into that contract that the lawyer will act competently (that is, not negligently).

The lawyer also owes a concurrent duty (a duty existing at the same time as the one in contract) in tort, in particular, under the law of negligence. The lawyer must use the skill of a prudent or careful lawyer. Note that the standard of care required of the lawyer is the same in tort and in contract.

Additionally, the lawyer is her agent and has a fiduciary duty towards her. The client might be quite unfamiliar with current house prices and believe that her house is worth only $100,000, when in fact it is worth $300,000. The lawyer has the ethical obligation, as a person in a position of trust (a fiduciary), not to buy the house for himself at a price below its true value.

Liability in Tort

The differences between liability in tort and liability in contract are fast disappearing. Contractual liability will be covered later; this section will focus on the unique issues that occur in professional liability in negligence.

The same elements are necessary to establish negligence against a professional as to establish negligence generally:

- duty of care
- breach of the standard of reasonable care
- causation
- compensable damages that are reasonably foreseeable

It is the first two elements, scope of the duty of care and breach of the standard of care, which entail additional issues for professional liability. Scope of the duty of care is of real concern—under the law of negligence, professionals may be liable to people whom they have not even met and who have not paid for their services, a type of client justifiably called a "phantom client." In contract law the liability of a professional is generally limited to persons with whom there is direct dealing and to those who pay for their services.

Regulation of Professionals   There are no regulations for the use of many professional names, such as psychotherapist, counsellor, financial planner, financial advisor, or even accountant (although there are restrictions on the use of names such as public accountant, chartered accountant, etc.). Anyone can use these terms without any qualifications or training.

Not only is lack of training a concern, but an unregulated professional has no particular rules that must be followed concerning money that you may hand over. If, for example, a business gives a financial planner $100,000 to invest, the planner might use it to pay expenses and then declare bankruptcy. The business would lose its $100,000. In contrast, if a business gave $100,000 to a lawyer, the lawyer must put the money in a trust account for the business (by virtue of law-society regulations). Even if the lawyer declares bankruptcy, that money does not belong to the lawyer, but is clearly set apart as belonging to the business (and would be returned to the business).

Additionally, you may wish to check whether your professional carries insurance for negligence. Real estate agents, for example, are not required to carry such insurance, although they may do so voluntarily.

Restricted Scope of Duty of Care

In an earlier time, the courts were hesitant to make a professional liable in negligence for giving information or advice that caused financial loss to the phantom client.

Assume a firm of engineers prepares a report for a publicly traded company. The report advises that, contrary to popular belief (which has lowered stock values), the company's land is not environmentally contaminated. A shareholder visits the company's office and picks up a copy of the report. Then this shareholder posts the report on his website. Persons all over the world buy shares in this company, based on what has appeared on the Web. Creditors also relied on this report in advancing credit to the company.

Now, assume the report proves to be false because of the negligence of the engineering firm. Would the engineers be liable to everyone who would suffer loss in this situation?

The courts have said no. In contract, the scope of obligation is severely limited by the doctrine of privity of contract. Historically, in tort, the scope of obligation has been very wide ranging (based on the test of reasonable foreseeability). That test could effectively result in unlimited liability to an unlimited class of plaintiffs in a situation like the one outlined above. Professionals could not get insurance for such broad liability exposure, and could be driven out of practice.

Consequently, if professionals are to be liable to a particular class of plaintiff, they must know that their advice will be given to that person or class of persons who will rely on their advice for a specific purpose or transaction. Actual knowledge of such a potential group or class of plaintiffs will give the professional the opportunity to decline the job if she thinks the exposure is too great, or to take extra precautions (such as an increased fee and/or insurance coverage).

For the above reasons the courts have said that on a policy basis, even though it is reasonably foreseeable that investors would rely on audited financial statements and decided to invest in a public company, the scope of duty would be restricted.

That scope of duty was also restricted in a private corporation in the Hercules Management case below on the grounds that an audit opinion is given so the corporation can make decisions, not so persons can make decisions to invest.

Hercules Managements Ltd. v. Ernst & Young, [1997] 146 D.L.R. (4th) 577 (S.C.C.)

Ernst & Young performed the yearly audit of Hercules Managements. Because of the negligence of Ernst & Young, the Hercules financial statements overstated its income and assets. Shareholders who relied on the audited statements in buying shares of Hercules sued Ernst & Young for their investment losses.

The Court's Decision

It was admitted that the auditors had breached the relevant standard of practice. So the question before the court was, does the company's auditor owe a duty of care to the shareholders?

Because this was a claim for economic loss, the test of reasonable foreseeability as set out in *Donoghue v. Stevenson* should be restricted by the test of a special or proximate relationship. The test for special relationship or proximity is a two-part test. The first part of the test has two questions:

1) Would the defendants have reasonably foreseen that the plaintiffs would rely on the financial statements? and
2) Was reliance by the plaintiffs in the particular circumstances reasonable?

If the above questions are answered yes, the second part of the test requires the court to consider policy reasons for excluding these particular plaintiffs from the scope of duty of the professionals. The court may consider whether there is a possibility of unlimited liability that would be undesirable.

Here, the plaintiffs' case gave yes answers to both questions which are part one of the test. It was reasonable for the auditors to foresee that the plaintiffs, as investors, would rely on the financial statements in making their decision whether to buy shares of Hercules Managements. It was also reasonable for these plaintiffs to rely on the financial statements, since that's what auditors do—it is within their expertise. In addition, these statements were prepared in a business context; they were not a casual statement passed off in a social occasion.

However, the plaintiffs' case could not pass part two of the test. There were policy reasons to limit the scope of an auditors' duty. If this duty was not limited, auditors would have unlimited liability.

The statements must be used only for the purpose or transaction for which they were created. This was to have them placed before the annual general meeting of shareholders. The shareholders, as a group, could then evaluate how the company was being run, assess the performance of the existing officers and directors, and decide if they wanted them to remain in office. The statements were not prepared for shareholders to decide whether to buy more shares in the company, nor for new investors to decide on purchasing shares. (The **annual general meeting (AGM)** is the general meeting of shareholders of a corporation that is required by law to be held each year to transact certain specified business, including election of directors. A **general meeting of shareholders** is a formal meeting of shareholders at which they are able to vote on matters concerning the corporation.) The shareholder's claim for investment loss was dismissed.

Duty to Corporation not Investors

The restriction on the scope of duty for auditors and accountants relates to investors, that is, people who are deciding to make investments in the company either as *future* shareholders or bondholders. The restricted scope of duty does not apply to the corporation that retained them.

Shareholders do not have a personal right to sue for a wrong done to the corporation. An individual could not buy one share in Bell Canada and sue a neighbour who breached a contract with it. This is a trade-off: As a shareholder is not responsible for corporate debts, a shareholder cannot sue on them.

Example: Investor—Joan Singh was given a hot tip by a stockbroker friend. He also sent her the financial statements of Ghansha Gold Inc., a mining company. Relying on the financial statements of the company that reported high income, Singh bought $100,000 of shares in Ghansha Gold. The statements contained an audit opinion on the first page signed by Scrooge and Marley, Chartered Accountants.

It turns out that Scrooge and Marley were negligent in that when they did a count of the bars of gold in Ghansha Gold's safe, they failed to apply the standard practice of sending a random sampling of bars to a geological expert, for as auditors know: all that glitters is not gold. The bars were brass. Singh lost her $100,000. Singh will not be successful in a lawsuit against Scrooge and Marley because it did not owe a duty to her as an investor.

Example: Corporation—The Board recommended developing a new mine that meant entering into contracts with construction companies for $10,000,000. The Board of directors read the financial statements and relied on the report that Ghansha Gold has 1,000,000 gold bars as assets, well more than needed to fund the project, and approved the contract. It turns out, as above, the bars were merely brass. Ghansha Gold could not pay on the construction contract and the contractor got a $10,000,000 judgment against it.

Ghansha Gold can sue the auditors for negligence. Singh, as shareholder, still has no right against the auditors in negligence. Only the corporation has. Theoretically, if the corporation recovers from the auditor, then investors and shareholders, such as Singh have their investment restored to its value.

■ *Critical Concepts of* Professional Liability and the Duty of Care

- Under the law of negligence, professionals owe a duty to persons beyond those with whom they deal directly and to persons who may not pay for their services.
- To establish proximity, the plaintiff(s) must have been foreseeable, the reliance by the plaintiff(s) upon the advice given must have been reasonable, and there must not be any policy reason to restrict liability in these particular circumstances.

annual general meeting (AGM)

the general meeting of shareholders of a corporation that is required by law to be held each year to transact certain specified business, including election of directors

general meeting of shareholders

a formal meeting of shareholders at which they are able to vote on matters concerning the corporation

Professional Standards

In professional and business situations, the reasonable-person test becomes more specific. A surgeon, for example, is measured against what a reasonable surgeon would have done in the same circumstances; a lawyer is judged by how another lawyer might have acted. A rural doctor will be held to rural, not urban, standards. The same is true for all professions and businesses.

To help decide what that particular standard should be, the courts will hear evidence from another qualified person in the same field. An act may have been a mistake or caused an injury, but that is not sufficient to constitute a breach of the standard of care. In non-legal terms, the question would be, did the professional act competently? This does not mean a professional must act perfectly. Not every act which causes injury will breach the standard of care.

In *Cavan v. Wilcox*, [1975] 2 S.C.R. 662 a nurse injected a drug into the patient's bloodstream instead of the muscle and caused him to develop complications resulting in his fingers being amputated on one hand. She was not held liable for negligence though as she had followed the standard medical procedures.

The Supreme Court clarified in *Ter Neuzen v. Korn* [1995] 3 SCR 674, that the conduct of physicians must be judged in the light of the knowledge that out to be reasonably possessed at the time of the alleged negligent act. In that case a woman had contracted HIV when receiving artificial insemination treatments in January 1985, but the possibility of HIV being transmitted this way had not been published in medical journals until later in 1985. The court ruled a jury could not find that the doctor should have known of the HIV risk at the time of her procedure. The court did state that though "conformity with common practice will generally exonerate physicians of any complaint of negligence, there are certain situations where the standard practice itself may be found to be negligent." This will only occur where the standard practice has such obvious risks such that anyone is capable of finding it negligent, without the necessity of diagnostic or clinical expertise.

In *Kripps v. Touche Ross & Co.*, 1997 CanLII 2007 (BC CA), the B.C. Court of Appeal ruled that an accounting firm was liable for negligence even though it had followed GAAP (Generally Accepted Accounting Principles). There were 560 plaintiffs who lost over $10 million when they purchased debentures from Victoria Mortgage Corp. Ltd. (VMCL). The accounting firm of Touche Ross had prepared the financial statement for the prospectus when the debentures were issued. The financial statements indicated the mortgages held were valued at $14.5 million, but did not show that over one quarter of the mortgages were in default for more than 90 days. Of the interest that was listed as earned, over 40% was unpaid. GAAP however at that time did not require disclosure of mortgage arrears. The court ruled however that the accounting firm was liable for negligence as this was material information that should have been disclosed to the plaintiffs. It had been withheld so that debenture sales would not be reduced. Touche knew that a simple application of GAAP would omit material information and lead to financial statements that could not be said to have fairly presented the financial position of VMCL. Given this actual knowledge, Touche fell below the required standard of care when it made its auditor's report, even though it had followed the standard practice of the profession listed in GAAP.

■ *Business Law*   Applied

㉒ **An auditor signed** the financial statements of a small business that was up for sale. In them, he confirmed that the amount of an outstanding bank loan was $10,000. In fact, the loan was for $150,000.

During the auditing process, the accountant had asked the business for a letter from the bank, confirming the loan amount. He received that letter, typed on plain paper without letterhead, signed by the bank manager, stating that the loan was $10,000. Someone purchased the business, relying on the financial statements. When the error was discovered, the new owner sued the auditor for professional negligence.

The auditor defended by saying he really believed the loan amount to be $10,000, and had checked with the bank.

  a) Was the fact that the auditor truly believed the loan amount to be $10,000 relevant to the question of negligence?
  b) What test would the court apply to determine if the accountant met the standard of care required? How might the purchaser establish the required practice?
  c) Even if the purchaser is successful in establishing that the accountant was careless, will she be successful in her action against him?

Exemption Clauses

Professionals are increasingly using exemption clauses as a method of protection against lawsuits. Exemption clauses may be individually worded, and so each one must be read carefully. However, in professional liability, disclaimers are normally aimed at either limiting the professional's scope of responsibility, or exempting the professional from claims for negligence. Such clauses are subject to the same principles as discussed in "Exemption or Disclaimer Clauses" in Chapter 6.

However, that part of the disclaimer which attempts to limit the scope of duty of a professional requires a closer look. Here is an example of a clause used by auditors:

> These financial statements are prepared for the use of Newcom Enterprises
> Limited. They are not to be disclosed to any other person, except with the consent
> in writing, of Bean, Counter & Crunchers.

Note that the attempt to limit the scope of duty in this disclaimer is in accord with the court-developed principles of special or proximate relationship. The auditors are saying that it is reasonable to conclude that only Newcom will utilize the statements—is in a special relationship with them—unless they give permission otherwise. These clauses are therefore very often enforced. One such clause was enforced in the case of *Hedley, Byrne & Co. Ltd. v. Heller & Partners, Ltd* [1964] A.C. 465.

Hedley Byrne was a firm of advertising agents that sought advice from its banker about the creditworthiness of a prospective client, Easipower. That bank then contacted Easipower's bank (Hedley, Byrne & Co.) for the information. Easipower's bank provided the information for free and at the top of the letter was written "without responsibility on the part of this bank" and then it went on to state; Easipower was "good for its ordinary business engagements." So based on this letter, Hedley Byrne did the advertising work. Easipower was however not in good financial shape and was unable to pay the advertising bill of about $50,000. When Hedley Byrne sued Easipower's bank for negligence for their losses, the court ruled that the bank did owe Hedley Byrne a duty of care and it had been negligent. However, since the bank's clause clearly disclaimed any assumption of responsibility for losses, the disclaimer was effective, and the bank was not liable.

Example: In *Wolverine Tube (Canada Inc.) v. Noranda Metal Industries Limited*, 1995 CanLII 785 (ON CA), the court followed the Hedley Byrne principle. Noranda Metal hired ADL to do an environmental audit on its property. ADL stated the property had no environmental problems, but the report had a disclaimer that stated ADL was not responsible to anyone other than Noranda, unless ADL had consented in writing to the other's use of the report. Noranda gave the audit report to Wolverine Tube without ADL's consent and Wolverine relied on the information and purchased the Noranda property. It was soon discovered that the land had some severe environmental problems and Wolverine had to pay to clean up the site. When Wolverine sued ADL for negligence for the false report, the court ruled the disclaimer was effective, so ADL was not liable for Wolverine's clean-up expenses.

This strict application of disclaimer clauses that was established in Hedley Byrne however has not been accepted in all cases recently. Other judges have adopted a "reasonable reliance" approach as outlined in the Hercules Management case. This allows the judge to look at the relationship of the parties in a contextual and policy based approach. The court determines if there was a reasonable reliance that the other side knew of and whether there are any policy reasons to refuse to impose a duty of care on the party that made the negligent statement. They can no long rely exclusively or absolutely on a boilerplate disclaimer to avoid responsibility for false statements in all situations. In the *Micron Construction Ltd.* case below, the B.C. Court of Appeal used this approach and held a bank liable for its false statements to a contractor that a construction project was properly funded when in fact the bank knew it was not. Even though the bank had a disclaimer denying its liability, the court ruled it was a reasonable reliance by the contractor, so the bank was liable for the contractor's losses.

Business Law Applied

㉓ An engineer agreed to design staircases for a business, and told the proprietor he would save a lot of money by using a cheaper covering on them. The business owner agreed. The contract between the business and the engineer contained an exemption clause absolving the engineer of any liability for negligent advice. The cheaper covering was not in accordance with the building-code standards because it was too slippery.

A few months after the new staircases were built, a customer slipped and injured himself. He sued the business and the engineer for the poor covering on the stairs. The business has declared bankruptcy. The engineer claims no liability on the basis of the exemption clause.

a) Does the customer have a contract with the engineer? If not, on what basis could the customer bring an action?

b) Could the engineer rely on the exemption clause?

Micron Construction Ltd. v. Hong Kong Bank of Canada, 2000 BCCA 141 (CanLII)

The case concerns the failure of a major construction project, the Newport City Club, which involved the conversion of an office building in downtown Vancouver into a business, social and recreation club. The action was brought by 11 corporations (including Micron) and individuals who were left unpaid when the entire project was abandoned part way through the construction, due to financial difficulties. Seven months after construction began, the project was shut down. It owed over $3.8 million, including $916,000 to Micron.

The construction manager and the sub-contractors sued the three developers/promoters of the project and the Hong Kong Bank of Canada which was to provide financing to the promoters. The bank had assured the contractors that adequate financing was in place, though the bank knew that the financial commitments by the developers had not been fulfilled.

The main contractor had requested proper assurances from the bank that the project was adequately funded before work began. Initial statements from the bank were not satisfactory but 3 months into the project the Hong Kong Bank issued a letter indicating that the developers had maintained an operating account with the Bank, to which loans in the $20–$50 million range have been authorized, on a secured basis, to finance the renovation. The letter stated that the account was being operated as agreed. But the letter then added, "This bank reference is given at the request of the developer and without any responsibility on the Bank and its signing officers."

This information the bank gave out was false. The developers had not provided the proper security that was required for the large line of credit. Instead of providing $33 million in cash and guarantees as security as they had promised, the three developers had only put up $12 million, which had been used primarily to buy the property. The bank knew the project was significantly underfunded and the developers were not meeting the terms it had set up for the line of credit.

The bank also knew that the contractors were relying on this information to decide whether they should start work. Micron began construction and was paid for the first 2 months, but when it was not paid in September 1994 it became concerned. In November, Micron, along with its own bank, The Royal Bank, called the Hong Kong Bank to question the financial state of the developers. The Hong Kong Bank assured Micron and the Royal Bank over the telephone that there was "ample financing available and no reason for concern." But payment did not come and by January the project was shut down, deeply in debt.

The plaintiffs sued the Hong Kong Bank and its commercial manager Mr. Tam for fraudulent and negligent misrepresentation. The claim of fraudulent misrepresentation failed at the trial court as they could not prove that Mr. Tam of the Hong Kong Bank intentionally gave out the false information. The trial judge also dismissed the claim of negligent misrepresentation because of the disclaimer clause. The judge applied the Hedley Byrne principle, so Micron could not succeed in its claim.

Micron appealed the decision to the B.C. Court of Appeal.

The Court's Decision

The appeal court agreed that there was insufficient evidence to establish a claim for fraudulent misrepresentation; however it did not use the *Hedley Byrne* approach for negligent misrepresentation. Instead the court ruled that the *Hercules Management* case had set a new test for negligent misrepresentation in Canada based on "reasonable reliance."

The bank had a direct financial interest in the contractor's decision and it met the test for "reasonable reliance"; the advice was given in the course of business, by a banking professional, in a business setting, in response to a specific request by Micron. The court ruled that under these circumstances, even with the knowledge of the disclaimer, it was reasonable for the plaintiff to rely on the Bank's assurances and it was reasonably foreseeable to the Bank that Micron would rely on their statements. There was also no other alternative source of information available to Micron to get this financial information. The appeal court preferred to even call it "justified reliance" rather than "reasonable reliance." It ruled that the disclaimer did not negate a duty of care by the Hong Kong bank and grounds for negligent misrepresentation had been established.

The second part of the test in *Hercules* requires the court to determine if there are any policy reasons why liability should not be imposed. In the *Hercules* case that was a key element for not imposing potentially unlimited liability on auditors. However in this case, the court ruled that there were no such policy considerations to prevent the court from holding the bank liable. Micron's appeal was successful and the court remitted the case to the trial court to determine the damages. The Supreme Court refused to hear a further appeal.

Disclaimers   Many professionals, such as lawyers, accountants, engineers, and the like, are prohibited by their professional bodies from using disclaimers that exempt them from negligence. However, many other professions, such as stockbrokers, financial advisors and planners, and real estate agents do not have such restrictions, and often have their clients sign such disclaimers.

Business Alert!

If a disclaimer is presented to you by a professional, consider it very carefully before signing it. If it contains an exemption for negligence, you may want to shop around for another advisor who does not use such a disclaimer.

Incorporation   Many *Business Corporations Act* specifically state that the limitation of liability provisions of the *Corporations Act* do not apply to professionals when they act pursuant to their professional licenses. Professionals do incorporate but this is usually for tax purposes but not to limit personal liability. See, for example, section 3.4(3) of the *Ontario Business Corporations Act*.

What professionals must do to protect themselves then is to purchase professional malpractice insurance that will protect them if they are found liable for negligence. Malpractice insurance rates vary greatly among the professions. It can be just over a thousand dollars annually for many accountants to close tens of thousands of dollars per year for certain medical specialists such as obstetricians/gynecologists. Like most types of insurance, the greater the risk of large damage claims, the higher the insurance premiums.

Accountants' and Auditors' Liability

auditors

outside accountants ("watchdogs" over accountants) who review financial statements for a company according to accepted auditing principles to determine whether the statements are properly done

Accountants prepare a company's financial statements and are often its employees. **Auditors** are outside accountants ("watchdogs" over accountants) who review financial statements for a company according to accepted auditing principles to determine whether the statements are properly done. They give an opinion as to whether the financial statements have been prepared according to standard accounting practices. Auditors could be considered as a watchdogs over the accountants. As noted above, the problem is that auditors are not truly independent because they are paid by the very business whose accounting statements they are reviewing.

Accountants and auditors are caught in a conflict by the very nature of their tasks. Their client is a business that may be in financial difficulty, and therefore wants its financial reports to look good in order to continue in business and be able to raise money. If the professional does not comply with the pressure to bend the rules, the client will go elsewhere, resulting in the loss of a substantial amount of money to the accounting firm. In the case of a large organization such as a bank, this includes not only a large fee but also spin-off work in receivership and bankruptcy trustee work. On the other hand, if the accountants do comply, they will be personally responsible. Where they are part of a larger firm, they may make the entire firm responsible.

The Enron Crisis

The conflict between an auditor's interest in being accurate to the shareholders and investing public with the loss of large fees from the client corporation was the focus of the Enron crisis. Enron was a rising star in the US energy industry. Originally a small energy company in Omaha, Nebraska, in a few short years it grew to become America's fourth-largest company controlling a quarter of U.S. natural gas reserves with substantial international holdings.

However its profitability was maintained by an accounting practice known as: "off balance sheet items". A series of subsidiary companies were formed. Many of Enron's expenses were shown on the books of the subsidiary companies; but they were not reflected in any consolidated financial statements with Enron, thus making it appear that Enron was far more profitable than it really was.

Enron auditors, Arthur Andersen, approved financial statements as being prepared in accordance with accepted accounting standards, but the statements were not. This pressure to approve improper practices is not that rare. A study done in 2002 by *CFO* magazine reported that one in six CFOs said they had been pressured to deviate from accepted accounting practices.

The Enron auditing scandal was not new. Canada had similar situations some years ago. In investigating the causes for the failures of the Canadian Commercial Bank and the Northland Bank, Mr. Justice Esty said of the auditors who acted for the Canadian Commercial Bank:

"It is clear that management did succeed in maintaining an appearance of financial health by its tactics. The financial statements became gold fillings covering cavities in the assets and in the earnings of the bank. By conventional standards of banking and bank accounting, the bank would have been shown as short on assets and earnings."[5]

"As the line of sound and prudential banking went, so did the accounting treatment, until the bank statements and reality no longer coincided. At the end of fiscal year 1984, the auditors had become, and perhaps, unwillingly, a part of the survival tactics of the bank..."[6]

Auditor Immunity

Most of the cases respecting scope of duty of responsibility for economic loss have involved auditors and accountants. The courts have been concerned that if they make auditors and accountants liable to investors/shareholders, no one could prepare or audit financial statements for public companies or even large private ones. No insurance company would give insurance to the professionals for such a large risk.

In the *Hercules Managements* case, the Supreme Court of Canada accepted the above reasoning and effectively gave auditors and accountants immunity from lawsuits for negligence. In the wake of Enron, there has been a call for serious reform of the law in order to restore investor confidence. One suggestion has been to establish an independent board of auditors to monitor the largest of public corporations. These auditors would not be paid directly by the company nor be able to accept other business from it. For discussions on corporate law reform respecting audits and other issues see www.citizenworks.org.

In the U.S. legislation was passed to attempt to make a public corporation's financial statements more reliable especially by increasing the true independence of auditors. It is commonly called Sarbanes-Oxley or for short "SOX". It is referred to by the names of the two U.S. Senators who sponsored the Act.

Major Accounting Negligence Cases in Canada

Though the *Hercules Management* decision greatly limited the ability of shareholders to sue accounting firms, there have been some cases in Canada where major accounting firms have been held liable for negligence or agreed to settle class actions brought against them for negligence. In the Castor Holdings case below of *Wightman c. Widdrington (Succession de)*, the Quebec Court of Appeal upheld the finding of the trial court that the major accounting firm, Coopers & Lybrand (which later merged with Price Waterhouse), was negligent in its auditing of failed real estate investment firm Castor Holdings Ltd. Castor suffered a $1.8 billion financial collapse and Coopers and Lybrand may be liable for over $1 billion. The Supreme Court refused to hear the appeal in 2014. This case was decided under the Québec Civil Code which does not have a test for duty of care as under the common law. The Québec test is simply did the act directly cause the damage.

Example: In *Livent Inc. v Deloitte & Touche LLP*, 2014 ONSC 2176 (CanLII), acting for two creditors, the Receiver of bankrupt Livent Inc. (rather than the shareholders because of the Hercules Management ruling) sued Livent's auditors, Deloitte & Touche. The Receiver claimed the accountants had been negligent in the audit services that they provided, for not detecting the fraud committed by the Livent senior executives. These executives, Garth Drabinsky and Myron Gottlieb, who had founded the entertainment and theatre corporation Livent, were convicted of fraud in 2009 and sent to jail (See Chapter 10). The court ruled that the accounting firm was negligent and was liable for $85 million. This case has been appealed as of the date of this text. Any proceeds will go to the corporate treasury and distributed in priority to secured creditors, then unsecured creditors, likely leaving nothing for the shareholders.

---

5. W. Z. Esty, *Report of the Inquiry into the Collapse of the CCB and Northland Bank* (Ottawa: Ministry of Supply and Services Canada, 1984), p. 52.

6. *Ibid.*, p. 83.

Securities Acts

Because of the scandals regarding auditor practices in Enron, WorldCom and other public corporations, it became apparent that the virtual immunity granted by the common-law restrictions on auditor's duty to investors was being abused by the auditors. Provincial securities acts were amended to give investors the right to sue auditors who certify financial statements used to raise capital. (See, for example, Sections 203 of the Alberta and 130 of the Ontario Securities Acts.)

Example: In 2013 a court approved a $117 million settlement reached by Sino-Forest investors with the accounting firm of Ernst & Young for the auditor's negligence. Sino-Forest was listed on the Toronto Stock Exchange and its market capitalization rose to $6 billion based on statements it had multi-billion dollar forestry reserves in China. But rumors circulated concerning the true value of the company and suspicions it was a stock fraud. Months later Sino-Forest filed for bankruptcy, and investors losses were in excess of $1 billion. Ernst & Young was sued for negligence for not properly reporting the true value of the company's assets.

Example: In 2010 the accounting firm of KPMG LLP settled a lawsuit for negligence with Hollinger Inc. for an undisclosed sum. Shareholders of Nortel Networks Corp. are attempting to sue the firm's auditors Deloitte & Touche, but that case is on hold pending resolution of issues involved in Nortel's bankruptcy. Nortel was once valued at $398 billion in 2000, but by 2009 its shares were worthless.

Wightman c. Widdrington (Succession de), 2013 QCCA 1187 (CanLII), leave to appeal to the Supreme Court of Canada denied January, 2014.

Castor Holdings was a Montreal based privately owned investment banking and finance organization which specialized in real estate investments and was created by Wolfgang Stolzenberg. It raised, borrowed and loaned money for large real estate operations in Canada and the U.S. It presented itself as a spread lender, earning profits based on the difference between its cost of borrowing and the rates it would loan the money out to borrowers. It appeared to be a financial success earning large profits. In reality though it was a Ponzi scheme concocted by a major swindler who lied and stole from investors and went undetected for years. It could not have done it though, unless it had financial statements from one of the Canada's most respected accounting firms, which indicated the company was successful.

Coopers & Lybrand (C&L) were the auditors for Castor Holdings and Elliott Wightman was the partner at C&L in charge of the Castor file. Castor reported significant growth over its 17 year life and its audited financial reports stated its assets in 1990 were $1.87 billion. But it was all a façade, by June of 1992 Castor filed for bankruptcy. Most of Castor's borrowers were real estate development companies that had continually been unable to repay their loans. Castor however would classify the unpaid interest as revenue (rather than bad debts) and using financial statements that falsely indicated Castor was in good financial shape, borrow more money from other lenders to keep afloat. This scheme finally failed leaving almost 100 private and institutional investors claiming losses of over $1 billion.

The investors sued Cooper & Lybrand for negligence, claiming that they had relied on the audited financial statements when making their decisions to invest in Castor. It was not a class action, but the Quebec trial court agreed to hear the test case of Peter Wid-

drington, one of the investors. The decision in that case regarding the issue of negligence of C&L would be binding on other separate claims against the accounting firm.

The entire court proceedings lasted 17 years, the trial alone was 12 years long. Widdrington died before judgment was given and the first judge had to resign due to bad health. Finally, after all the delays C&L could create, the Quebec trial court ruled that the accounting firm was negligent. The financial statements and opinions that Coopers & Lybrand had prepared for Castor were **materially misstated and misleading.** C&L had failed to follow GAAP (generally accepted accounting principles) and GAAS (generally accepted auditing standards) and the judge noted 29 different faults. The audit *"was performed in an automatic manner without professional judgment or serious consideration of anything other than going through the motions of mindlessly filling out forms."*

The judge concluded that if those rules had been followed, anyone reading the accounting documents would have seriously questioned the profitability and solvency of Castor and would have noticed that the loans were non-performing and the borrowers were unable to meet their obligations. Coopers & Lybrand did not give an accurate picture of the true financial position of Castor. C&L was negligent in not discovering and reporting the significant financial difficulties this company was in. The financial statements showing Castor as a profitable company were mere "window dressings" that concealed a company in deep financial distress. Widdrington had relied on the financial statements and "but for" C&L's negligence, he would not have invested in Castor.

As C & L's breach of the auditor's standard of care was the direct (proximate) cause of the investor's loss under the Civil Code, this close causative connection made C & L liable to the investor.

Coopers & Lybrand were found liable for negligence and ordered to pay Widdrington's estate $2.7 million. If the other separate law suits are also successful, C&L will be liable for claims totalling about $1 billion, well in excess of their insurance coverage. Coopers and Lybrand appealed to the Quebec Court of Appeal.

The Court's Decision

The Quebec Court of Appeal upheld the trial court's decision. It stated that "the auditing work was botched" and it was "easy to see why the result was a fiasco." Wightman had lost the independence required of an auditor and he was too involved in Castor's business. He was a director of Castor and actively was promoting the company. His critical judgment of the company was lacking. When his audit team informed him of disturbing irregularities or red flags, he did nothing. On the contrary he issued reports that confirmed the enterprise was flourishing. Audited statements set the market value of the shares at $580 each, when months later the company was bankrupt. The financial statements were the vital for the Ponzi scheme to succeed.

The judge stated "Stolzenberg was the engine of the fraud, but it would not have worked so well without the lubricant provided by Wightman."

Widdrington was an experienced investor and he had used a financial advisor. They proved to the court that they had gone over the financial statements of Castor line by line before investing in this company. His reliance was clearly established. Castor was not a company that traded on the stock market, it was privately owned, with about 100 experienced investors, including institutional investors such as Chrysler Canada's Pension Fund and several European banks.

Wightman as well as Coopers & Lybrand were liable for negligence. The Court of Appeal decision was appealed to the Supreme Court of Canada, but in January 2014 leave to appeal was denied. Other investors are continuing their claims against C&L now that the Widdrington test case decision is final and the liability of C&L is anticipated to be near $1 billion.

Recap: Limiting Liability

You have just reviewed 2 areas of professional liability: one respecting the scope of obligations to clients, and the other respecting the standard of competence to which a professional will be held. There are ways for a professional to somewhat limit this liability by contractual terms.

Example: Limiting Professional Liability: Lee Rowshan (not an accountant), was a former manager with a credit union. He now works for himself as a consultant. George Takach, an investor, asked Rowshan to review the assets of another credit union to give an opinion on the collectability of certain accounts. He is willing to pay Rowshan $10,000 for the review.

Rowshan has two major issues to face considering his overlapping contractual and tort liability. One is the scope of the duty in negligence. Will he be liable only to that investor or to anyone who relies on his report?

Another issue is the amount of his liability for damages for negligence. He may be paid $10,000 but he may be liable for millions of dollars in losses if he makes a mistake that is considered professional negligence.

Business Law Applied

㉔ (a) In the Rowshan / Takach example above, how can Rowshan protect himself?

(b) Would your answer be the same if he was an accountant? Explain?

㉕ **Jean Schure was** the accountant for Newform Industries Inc., and regularly prepared the company's annual financial statements. An unexpected business opportunity arose, for which Newform needed new capital. The company approached a group of venture capitalists, showed its most recent financial statements, and obtained a loan of $1 million to finance the new project.

It was subsequently discovered that, because of Schure's negligence, the financial statements were incorrect. The venture-capital group wants to sue Schure, as it would not have lent the money if the statements had been accurate.

a) Would the venture capital group be successful in suing Schure for negligence based simply on the fact that he was negligent?

b) What type of relationship would the venture-capital group have to establish in order to be successful against Schure? Would they be successful in doing so?

Fiduciary Duty

fiduciary duty

a duty of good faith imposed on a person who stands in a relation of trust to another

The term **fiduciary duty** appears several times in this book—it is one of the most important examples of duty that the courts are imposing in certain types of business transactions. It is a duty of good faith imposed on a person who stands in a relation of trust to another. As it relates to business advisors, fiduciary duty occurs in a situation where the advisor is trusted by a client who is vulnerable, and who is hurt because of reliance on the advice given. The advisor must give up its own self-interest and act solely on behalf of the vulnerable party.

The test is a flexible one, and can be used in a number of situations. It originally was applied to the traditional professions such as lawyers, doctors, or accountants, but today it is also applied to other business advisors such as stockbrokers, real estate agents, and financial advisors.

Fiduciary duty does not mean that the advisor must have additional skill. Rather, it means that there is an obligation of good faith involved in the relationship—fiduciary duty could be thought of as business ethics. In an ordinary business transaction, each party is completely entitled to try to get the best personal deal possible. In a fiduciary relationship, the advisor must always put the client's interests first. Consider the following example.

Example: Steven Ng is known to be looking for a piece of land on which to build a manufacturing plant. Georges Cartier approaches Ng and takes him to see a parcel of vacant land that is ideal for the proposed plant. Cartier agrees to sell the property to Ng for $100,000. What Ng does not know is that Cartier, a speculator, is not the owner of the property, which is currently on the market at $50,000. Cartier buys the property, then resells it to Ng, making a profit of $50,000. There is nothing wrong with this business deal.

If, however, Cartier is Ng's lawyer, he has a fiduciary duty to his client to reveal all the facts of the transaction. If he does not, and Ng finds out afterwards, he can sue Cartier for the secret profit of $50,000.

Some of the most common types of the breaches of fiduciary duty include the following.

Misuse of Confidential Information/Disclosure

This is the use of a client's confidential information for the business advisor's own advantage. For example, a business may ask a real estate agent to search for a piece of property for a new location. During the search, the real estate agent discovers a piece of property at half the market value. The agent realizes it is possible to make a much greater profit by buying the property and reselling it directly to the client.

Conflict of Interest

Conflict of interest arises when the advisor's interests are at odds with those of the client. It can be broken down into a number of categories, including:

- Secret commissions—this amounts to the equivalent of working for two employers. A stockbroker, for example, may charge a client for advice about which stocks to buy. The broker may also be getting paid by that company for selling its shares.
- Secret profit—the business advisor may have an undisclosed interest in the property that is being sold to the client, and thus receive an advantage from the transaction. For example, a stockbroker may recommend purchasing certain shares, and already own shares in the same company. By advising the client to buy the shares, the broker's own shares rise in value.
- Kickbacks—there is no end to the number of ways kickbacks can be made, nor to the number of situations in which they occur. For example, a real estate agent, acting for the buyer of a house, may recommend a certain trust company as having

good mortgage rates. The trust company may be paying a kickback to the real estate agent for this recommendation. The kickback may not always come in the form of a cash payment. The agent might receive some type of preferential interest rate or other benefit, such as the right to list all the houses the trust company repossesses under mortgage power of sale proceedings. While these forms of kickback may be the subject of a fiduciary-duty action, they are very difficult for the client to detect. There are usually few regulations in these professions specific enough to catch the various ways that kickbacks can be made. Taking or receiving kickbacks is a criminal offence (secret commissions) under the Criminal Code.

Example: In *Strother v. 3464920 Canada Inc.* 2007 SCC 24 (CanLII), (see Chapter 9) the Supreme Court held a lawyer and his law firm liable for breach of fiduciary duty. Robert Strother was a tax partner with the law firm Davis LLP when he acted for two competing film companies. He had a personal interest in one of the companies and failed to advise the other of changes in the tax laws that seriously impacted their business. It was clearly a conflict of interest. He owed the company a duty of trust, loyalty and confidence and he had breached that by acting in the best interests of the competitor and for his own personal gain. Strother and the law firm were liable.

Canadian National Railway v. McKercher LLP
2013 SCC 39(CanLII)

Gordon Wallace was a Saskatchewan farmer and the representative plaintiff in a class action brought by 100,000 grain growers seeking $1.75 billion from the Government of Canada, the Wheat Board of Canada, CN Rail and CP Rail. The class claimed that they had been overcharged for grain transportation for over 25 years. He hired a Saskatoon law firm, McKercher LLP, to act for him and the class.

However when McKercher LLP took the retainer to act for the class, it was also representing CN Rail on several other unrelated matters at the same time. The law firm, both before and right after the class Statement of Claim was issued, informed CN that is could no longer be its attorney for service in Saskatchewan. Several weeks later though, McKercher asked CN's permission to continue to act for CN in a real estate deal, but CN refused and withdrew all of its work from the law firm. CN also then went to court asking for an order disqualifying McKercher from representing Wallace and the farmers in the class action.

CN claimed that the law firm owed it a duty of loyalty and it had clearly crossed the court's "bright line rule" that a lawyer or a law firm, may not represent clients with opposing interests at the same time without first obtaining their consent. Since CN was one of the defendants in a $1.75 billion law suit and McKercher had not obtained CN's consent to represent the plaintiffs, it was clearly a conflict of interest and McKercher should not be allowed to represent the class.

The trial judge agreed and ruled McKercher could not represent the class, but the Saskatchewan Court of Appeal ruled that disqualifying the law firm from the class action was too

extreme a remedy. CN then appealed to the Supreme Court of Canada.

The Court's Decision

The Supreme Court ruled that a lawyer's duty of loyalty has three key components: the duty to avoid conflicting interests (and protecting the client's confidential information), a duty of commitment to the client's cause (and to not just drop them as a client to avoid a conflict when a new client comes along) and a duty of candour (to disclose to an existing client any factors relevant to their ability to provide effective representation before accepting a retainer from a new client who has opposing interests).

It confirmed that McKercher's conduct clearly fell within the scope of the "bright line rule." CN and the class have clearly conflicting interests. The law firm had not obtained CN's consent before accepting a retainer from the class. McKercher had terminated its retainer with CN which breached its duty of commitment to CN. Its failure to advise CN it intended to represent the class breached its duty of candor.

However the court did rule that McKercher possessed no relevant confidential information that could be used to prejudice CN in the class action. The court then ordered the case to go back to the trial court to determine if disqualification was the appropriate remedy in this situation. The trial court would have to decide if disqualification was necessary to maintain faith in the administration of justice. The conduct of both CN and McKercher and the ability of the class to find new counsel are the factors that should be taken into consideration when determining the appropriate remedy.

Statutory Liability: Tax Fraud Rules

However, the *Income Tax Act* makes advisors who are involved in the filing of such returns (or assist in the preparation of fraudulent supporting documentation, such as financial statements) liable civilly. If an advisor gives advice that results in a false claim on an income tax return, she may be liable for up to 100 percent of the gross amount of the fraud. So, accountants who give aggressive tax advice should be cautious—if they step over the line from tax avoidance to tax evasion, they may be personally liable.

Additionally, an advisor who provides documents that can be used to support false claims (such as inaccurate financial statements) will be liable for up to 50 percent of the amount of the tax fraud. Accountants are often under pressure from businesses to provide two financial statements, one for the business and one for the government for tax purposes. If accountants acquiesce to such requests, the accountants will now be personally liable in a civil suit, where many of the criminal law protections for the accused are absent.

In 2011–2012 there were 137 convictions in Canada for tax evasion or fraud based on $29.9 million in lost revenues. There were $6.4 million in fines levied and 35 people were given jail sentences totalling 36.17 years.[7]

In Summation

Negligence

- Negligence is not merely carelessness, but is a technical term that requires four elements:
  a) scope of duty: was it reasonably foreseeable that the plaintiff would be injured?
  b) breach of standard of care: what would a reasonable person have done in the circumstances?
  c) causation: did the conduct cause the damage?
  d) was the damage proximate (reasonably foreseeable)?

Defences

- There are two defences to negligence:
  a) contributory negligence: the plaintiff may also have been careless and contributed to his or her loss
  b) voluntary assumption of risk: the plaintiff may have known fully of the risk of injury and consented to it

Damages

- General damages are intended to compensate the plaintiff for loss by putting that individual in the same position as if the incident had not occurred.

- Aggravated damages are to compensate the plaintiff because of high-handed conduct of the defendant that increased the injury to the plaintiff's dignity.

- Punitive damages are not compensation to the plaintiff, but punishment to the defendant for outrageous conduct that requires an additional award for deterrence.

---

7. Canada Revenue Agency, http://www.craarc.gc.ca/nwsrm/cnvctns/yt/menu-eng.html)

High-Risk Activities

- A risk of injury is often associated with participation in a sporting event or game. The standard of care to be applied in determining the liability, if any, of the organizers of the sport depends on a number of factors. These include the danger inherent in the particular activity, whether instructions or qualifications for participation are required, and the level of supervision necessary.
- Disclaimer clauses are frequently used in high risk sporting activities and they can effectively protect the company that ran the risky activity from liability, even if deaths occur, if they had properly pointed out the clause to the participants and they understood and voluntarily accepted the risk of the activity

Occupier's Liability

- The occupier of property or premises is the person who exercises control over it. As the party in control of the premises, the occupier is responsible for the physical condition of the property, and the safety of individuals who enter it.
- If the sale of alcohol is part of the business activity on the premises, the responsibility of the occupier extends beyond the door to ensure the safety of intoxicated customers, as well as individuals who are injured by those customers after they leave the premises.
- Canadian courts have not yet held social hosts liable for damages caused by their drunken guests after they have left the host's home

Products Liability

- The aim of tort law is to compensate for injuries caused to the property or person of an individual or business. The liability of a manufacturer for its products has been extended considerably, creating a relationship in tort law with the ultimate consumers of the product, as well as an accompanying duty not to injure.
- The grounds for a tort action for products liability are varied, and include defects in the manufacturing process, failure to warn of inherent dangers from use of the product, and negligent design.
- Defences, such as voluntary assumption of risk, and contributory negligence, are available to the product's manufacturer in defending against liability for the injuries caused.
- Strict liability where a defendant is held liable though they were not at fault, does not apply to cases of manufacturer's liability in Canada, though it does in most of the U.S.
- Strict liability does exist as a tort in Canada when someone brings something onto their property that is unusual and dangerous and through no fault of theirs escapes and causes damages to someone else

Professional Liability

- The liability of professionals can be based on a breach of contract, a breach of the standard of care required in the law of negligence, or the breach of the duty as an agent (which could include a breach of fiduciary duty).
- A professional may be found liable to a plaintiff even in the absence of a direct contractual relationship between the two.
- Professionals may include exemption clauses in their contracts for service, in an effort to avoid liability.
- A breach of fiduciary duty can be committed by a misuse of confidential information or by acting contrary to the client's interests.

Closing Questions

Professional Liability

1. Gilbert Sullivan graduated from dental school three months ago, and set up his own dental practice. In his second month of business, he failed to clean out a cavity in a patient's tooth properly before placing a filling in it. As a result, the patient required an extensive, expensive root-canal operation, and lost several days from work.
   a) What must the patient prove in order to succeed in a suit against Sullivan for the injuries suffered?
   b) Which standard must Sullivan meet?
      i)   that of a recently qualified dentist?
      ii) that of a reasonable dentist?
      iii) that of the average dentist in that city?

2. Frank's Heating Company was retained to do a heating installation at 21 Flower Street. In writing up the invoice, the salesperson accidentally put down the address as 21 Power Street. Joe Jackson, an employee of Frank's Heating, went to 21 Power Street with all the necessary equipment and supplies. When there was no answer at the door, he left the pipes in front of the garage, along with a note on the door indicating he would return the next day to do the job. Mrs. Hall, the resident at 21 Power Street, arrived home in the dark, and while walking to her garage to open it, tripped over the pipes and broke her leg.
   a) Who should be responsible for Mrs. Hall's injuries?
      i)   Jackson?
      ii) the salesperson?
      iii) Frank's Heating Company?
      iv) Mrs. Hall for not taking more care when she was walking?
   b) What must Mrs. Hall prove in order to win her case in court?

3. Identify the issue of negligence in the following:
   a) Selma had a breast implant and later developed breast cancer.
   b) An auditor approved a financial statement for a corporation. Selma found a copy on a subway car and relying on it, invested in the company and lost all her investment and wants to sue the auditor.
   c) Selma, young in perfect health, had a sudden heart attack without warning while driving; her car ran into a fence demolishing it.
   d) Selma took a prescription drug for a month. Some recent research showed it could cause heart attacks. Selma stopped taking it and never had symptoms. There is a class action and she wants to join.

4. a) Why have the courts placed a duty on businesses that serve liquor at social events but not on private party givers?
   b) In what circumstances might a private party giver be held liable to a victim of an accident caused by a guest at the party who drove drunk?

5. Diane is confined to wheelchair because she was hit by Brittany who was driving drunk after drinking at a party given by Joe. Joe knew she was leaving and driving drunk but said, "Hey she's a big girl. What am I supposed to do, tie her up, call the cops on her?" Joe has never held a job for more than few months, lives in a basement one bedroom rented apartment and has no assets other than $10 in his bank account.

   Diane sues John for letting Brittany drink to the point she was noticeably drunk and likely to drive after the party.
   a) What element of the law of negligence would be relevant?
   b) Would she be successful under the present law?
   c) Would this result be of benefit to her?
   d) What facts might be relevant to developing a fair law on point? What rule would you propose?

6. Branko Dubrovnik had been unable to obtain tickets to a heavy metal rock concert by the group Blow It Out Your Head. He decided to go to the stadium anyway, to see if any last-minute tickets would be available. Because there was no opportunity for a second performance, the stadium manager decided to sell extra tickets, and allow fans into the area that stretched the first 10 feet (3 metres) in front of the speakers, right in front of the stage. Dubrovnik managed to obtain one of these tickets, and when he was told that it was directly in front of the stage and the speakers, he responded, "The louder the better, man. I wanna be taken out of my head."

   For two hours, the young man's ears were subjected to extreme high-volume sound. When he awoke the next morning, he was surprised at how quiet the house was—and then suddenly realized that he had lost his hearing. Over the next several months, his hearing returned, but he had permanently lost 60 percent of the hearing in his right ear, and 30 percent in the left. The young man's hope of becoming a classical flautist appeared to be hopeless now.

   a) If Dubrovnik were to sue the stadium management for his loss of hearing and career opportunity, would either of the defences of contributory negligence or voluntary assumption of risk apply to his action?

7. Lawrence Basset joined the local scuba club to go on a trip to the lovely tropical atoll of Pirogie. Although an experienced scuba diver, Basset had never gone cave diving and thought it would be very interesting to try. The scuba club screened a video of cave diving to the members one evening, showing a full dive, from moment of entry into the water to return aboard the dive boat. Towards the very end of the video there were a few warnings that this type of dive was not for the inexperienced or the faint of heart, but if you persevered, the wonders of the underwater world would dazzle you.

   Next day, Basset asked for a registration form for the dive, and placed his signature at the end of this document—below the clause stating that all divers going into the caves did so at their own risk, and that the club assumed no responsibility for any injuries or difficulties arising from the activity. He was asked if he understood the clause before he signed, and replied, "Oh, sure. I haven't been under water so long that I can't understand plain English."

   On the dive the next day, Basset lost sight of the guide, and became disoriented inside the system of caves, using 15 minutes of the air in his tank as he tried to find his way out. As a result, Basset exited the caves, which were at depths of 100 feet (30 metres), just as he was running out of air. His rapid ascent to the surface brought on a case of the bends, and he was hospitalized for several days. Basset's medical treatment in Perogie was very expensive, and he is now attempting to obtain compensation from the diving club. The club has told him not to hold his breath.

   a) Would the defence of voluntary assumption of risk be successful if Basset were to sue the scuba club for his injuries?

   b) Is the nature of the injuries suffered by Basset covered by the *waiver*?

   c) If the club is found to be negligent in his actions, and Basset had not worn a compass as suggested by the dive master, what would be the argument presented by the scuba club?

Sports and High-Risk Activities

8. Bart enjoyed the outdoors and had often thought about taking part in one of the war games offered by a hunters' organization in his area. At a promotion meeting, it was explained to the attendees that the organization preferred to refer to their exercises as paintball games, and that a capsule with harmless paint is used as a substitute for bullets in order to indicate when someone had been hit in the course of the game.

   Bart decided to sign up for the paintball game to take place the next day. As he paid his money, he was requested to sign an entrance form which included a paragraph absolving the organization from any liability or responsibility for injuries suffered by the participants in the course of the game. The next morning, while preparing the paint pellets, Klaus, a member of the hunters' organization, ran out of the normal paint used and decided to substitute some paint that was on hand for the last 20 pellets. During the game, Bart was directly hit on the side of his nose, next to his eye, by Klaus, who was leading one of the opposing teams.

   Half an hour after the game was over, Bart began to experience tingling in his eye and over the next hour lost vision in it. Analysis indicated that the pellet that had hit Bart was one of the last 20 made, using the substitute paint which was found to contain a substance that was highly toxic. As a result of his injury, Bart has lost the use of his eye. This has interfered with his job as a cartographer, in which he needs the use of both eyes for the stereoscopes used for 3-D interpretation of land forms when drawing maps.

a) Will the waiver act as a full defence for the hunting organization if Bart proceeds to court with this matter?

b) Would voluntary assumption of risk be an alternative answer should the waiver not protect the hunting organization?

c) What is the nature of the court action that Bart would bring, and what would he have to prove to be successful?

9. A school held a regular hockey practice Monday, Wednesday, and Friday, immediately after school hours, at a local arena run by Riverside Arena Inc. The school hockey coach was always in attendance.

Bill Smart high-sticked Angus King, catching him in the throat and causing serious injury to his trachea. The young man required several operations over the course of the next two years. King, aged 15, had signed the school's standard form waiver exempting the school from liability in accidents occurring during hockey games and practices. The doctors noticed that the blade on the stick had an unusually sharp edge and were of the opinion that this sharpness had aggravated the injury. The stick had been manufactured by Bower Equipment Ltd. and sold by Sports Distributors Inc. to Bill Smart.

When King was hit, he fell against the glass barrier at the end of the arena. The glass was loose, fell, shattered, and cut a bystander, Robert Gould. Other arena patrons testified that they noticed the glass had been loose for weeks. Riverside Arena admitted that they had no system for regular inspection.

a) Who are the potential defendants?

b) Give the legal term for each basis of possible liability against each of the potential defendants.

c) Which of the defendants do you believe has breached the expected standard of care? Does it have any defences?

d) What is the effect of the waiver signed by King? Which defendant can rely on it?

e) If you were the risk-management consultant for both Bower Equipment and Riverside Arena, what recommendations would you make to those businesses?

f) Who has the best ability to insure for these kinds of accidents? What effect do you think the ability to insure has on judges when making findings against defendants in this type of action?

10. Before taking a two-day course to learn how to ride and jump horses, Dale Gauley was asked to sign a form that exempted the stables from any responsibility for injury suffered by the rider as a result of the riding lessons or jumping.

By that afternoon, Gauley had a pretty good handle on the jumping and had already gone over two metre-high jumps. While approaching the last jump, someone in the parking lot next to the arena honked a horn and Gauley's horse bolted, heading straight for the arena's six-foot fence. As the horse attempted to jump the fence, Gauley fell off, breaking her collarbone, three ribs, and her right hip. She was in hospital for three months as a result.

When she approached the stables for compensation for her injuries, the owner refused to even discuss it. Waiving the form Gauley had signed, he said, "Try getting over this."

a) Assess, with reasons, the likelihood of Gauley's success should she take this matter to court.

11. Roy Smith was staying at a ski resort. After drinking at the bar for most of the afternoon he decided to enter the inner-tube race which the resort held each evening. At the top of the hill, Smith was asked to sign a standard form agreement which included an exemption clause relieving the resort of any liability for damages suffered by him or any other participant in the inner-tube race. Being very drunk and unable to focus well on the form, Smith asked what the paragraphs said and a resort employee explained it was an exemption clause that relieved the resort from any responsibility if Smith injured himself in the race. Smith nodded his head, and the employee then went on to say, "But don't worry: we haven't lost a contestant yet." Smith signed at the bottom of the form and staggered over to his waiting inner tube. In the course of the race he was thrown from the inner tube and hit another contestant. Both of them were severely injured.

a) Will the exemption clause protect the ski resort from being sued by Smith for his injuries?

b) If the exemption clause does not protect the ski resort from responsibility, will the resort also be responsible for the injuries suffered by the other contestant injured by Smith when he fell out of his inner tube?

Occupier's Liability

12. Ann Rai took her husband's gasoline-soaked clothes to Koziar's Laundromat to wash. The fumes were ignited by electricity in the washing-machine motor and exploded, causing Rai first-degree burns. Koziar rents the store from Cadillac Management Limited. Rae sues Koziar for suffering caused by the burns.
   a) Koziar pleads as his first defence that Rai sued the wrong person because he is not the owner. Would this be a successful defence?
   b) Does Koziar have any successful defences?

13. John Stitt tripped over a paving brick that jutted two inches above the surface of a parking lot, breaking his arm. He sued the plaza owner. The owner says: "If it is big enough to trip over, it is big enough to see."
   a) What is the legal term for the defence that the plaza owner is asserting?
   b) What conduct by the owner might help to defend itself?

Products Liability

14. Yvon Marchand was one of several passengers severely injured when an aircraft experienced a hard landing and collapsed on the runway while still travelling at a high speed. Examination of the plane determined that the cause of the accident had been a bolt in the aileron (the wing flap) which had come loose during the flight, and had jammed the right aileron—making it useless for the landing procedure.

   The aircraft had been manufactured by the Luft Aircraft Company in Canada. That firm had bought the aileron assembly from Nowsky Manufacturing in Yugoslavia. Luft has denied any responsibility, and told Marchand to pursue Nowsky Manufacturing for any injuries she suffered. Nowsky, with no assets in Canada, has sent a reply that, as far as it is aware, the aileron assembly was in perfect condition when it left the manufacturing plant. They suggested that it had been damaged either in shipping or in final assembly at Luft's premises. The aileron assembly had been shipped by Oshiana Transportation Ltd., a company which had been contracted by Luft.
   a) List the potential defendants in an action to be brought by Marchand for her injuries, and explain the principle in products liability law that will help her to prove negligence on the part of the defendant(s).
   b) Assuming the defect was in the original manufacturing of the aileron assembly, and Marchand was successful in her court action, how would the responsibility for her damages be apportioned among the defendant(s)?
   c) Given the cause of the injuries to the passengers on the aircraft, what legal procedure is available to assist them in bringing their cases to court in the most economic and time-efficient manner?

15. Serena Arfred suffered cuts to her mouth as well as digestive-tract injuries as a result of drinking milk from a bottle purchased from Mimo's Variety Store. The milk was found to have small pieces of glass in the bottom of the bottle. It had been bottled by Keewatin Dairies Ltd.

   The bottle had no chips or cracks, and Keewatin prided itself on having state-of-the-art bottling equipment that not only met current provincial standards, but surpassed them. Evidence showed that the bottle had not been tampered with between the time it left the bottling plant and the time it was opened by Serena for use on her corn crunchies. No one could explain how the glass came to be in the milk bottle.
   a) Is Keewatin's ability to show that it exceeds provincial standards in its bottling processes an absolute defence to Serena's court action?

16. Oars Inc. designed and manufactured a rowing machine for use in health clubs. The unique design utilized a wheel, much like that of a bicycle, that rotated on an axle which was propelled by a series of levers and pulleys, which were moved along a rope pulled by the person rowing. A health club member's hand was severely injured when her fingers became caught in the spokes in the wheel and jammed against a pulley. The rowing machine came with an owner's manual, which was located in the manager's office and contained a warning to keep hands away from the revolving wheel when the machine was in operation.

a) List and explain who the defendants in this action would be.

b) Decide which of these grounds would be the basis for bringing an action and explain your choice:

    i)   defects in the manufacturing process

    ii) negligent design

    iii) duty to warn

c) Would it assist the defendant if evidence was available that the club member had filled her water bottle with a measure of four fingers of vodka and some tonic water a half-hour prior to beginning her exercises on the floor of the health club?

17. Alex, a student, created his own summer job by making the rounds of several lakes in a well-known recreational resort area of his province and obtaining contracts to paint docks and boathouses. With contracts in hand, Alex went out to purchase paint that was specifically manufactured for a marine environment. Halfway through the summer, Alex's first customers began to complain that the paint was flaking off in large patches from the buildings and docks he had painted earlier. On inspection, Alex discovered to his horror that the paint seemed not to be binding to the material painted, and eventually it would all flake off.

The unhappy customers threatened him with lawsuits if he did not rectify the situation. Alex was forced to purchase a different type of paint, strip all the docks and buildings previously done, and repaint them. A consequence of this was that he had to forgo the contracts that were to be completed during the second half of the summer.

Alex estimates his loss of profit at $10,000, and his cost of repurchasing paint at $2,500. In investigating the problem further, he discovered that the paint manufacturer, Polypaints Inc., and his supplier were both aware that in particularly humid weather, which this summer had been, the chemicals in this paint which cause it to bind to the material painted were affected.

a) Does Alex have any grounds for bringing an action against Polypaints Inc. and the paint supplier for the loss of his summer contracts and the cost of the replacement paint?

b) Failing grounds for bringing an action based on tort, explain with reasons whether Alex has any grounds in contract law for bringing an action against the paint manufacturer and/or the paint supplier.

18. A car driver braked, but failed to stop, and hit a pedestrian. The driver had had his vehicle's brakes repaired by a mechanic only a day before the accident.

The pedestrian sued the manufacturer of the vehicle and the mechanic. Both said the other was at fault. The pedestrian had no evidence, and no idea what went wrong.

a) At trial, the manufacturer and the mechanic relied on the pedestrian's lack of knowledge, saying he had not proved any breach of standard and therefore his action should be dismissed. Do you agree?

b) The manufacturer claimed that the pedestrian was not a user of the car, did not purchase the car, and was not foreseeable. Therefore the manufacturer owed no duty to the pedestrian. Do you agree?

19. Dilip Singh was the accountant for Lyon Steel Ltd. whose regular bank was the Industrial Bank of York. Singh was responsible for preparing the company's annual financial statements. Unknown to Singh, Lyon wanted to raise money for a new project, and approached the Commercial Credit Bank, which relied on the financial statements prepared by Singh in advancing a loan of $150,000. Industrial Bank, where Lyon had an operating line of credit, increased the line of credit to $60,000 after receiving the financial statements. Because Singh had not checked to determine if several of the premises operated by Lyon were owned or leased, the financial statements were wrong. Lyon showed a profit when, in fact, it was operating at a loss. The company went bankrupt, and both banks want to sue Singh for their losses.

a) Did Singh owe a duty to the Industrial Bank?

b) Did Singh owe a duty to the Commercial Credit Bank?

c) Was it reasonably foreseeable that Lyon Steel might raise money for a specific project? Is that the test to determine whether Singh owed a duty to the Commercial Credit Bank?

d) Did Singh have actual knowledge of either or both of the loans made by the Industrial Bank or the Commercial Credit Bank?

e) Explain whether it would have made a difference if Singh had placed the following words at the end of the financial statements: "These financial statements are prepared for the use of Lyon Steel Ltd. exclusively."

20. Salton Schnee had bought a rundown ski resort and was now drawing up a business plan for its renovation. In trying to decide whether to invest substantial funds in upgrading the ski lifts from T-bars to chair lifts, he sought advice from the local Chamber of Commerce. Jennifer Schnarr, the representative with whom he met at the Chamber of Commerce, told Schnee that the chamber's tourism statistics indicated that, given past winter traffic patterns, the installation of chair lifts would increase the resort's business by at least 40 percent.

Based on this information, Schnee placed an order for $300,000 worth of chair-lift equipment. The equipment was installed over the summer, and the ski season began early in October that year. Schnee's happy anticipation quickly turned to anger when his eagerly awaited financial statement showed an increase in business of only 19 percent, during one of the best ski seasons for the area in the past six years.

a)   Do Schnarr and/or the local Chamber of Commerce have a legal problem?

b)   What would Schnee need to prove to obtain a legal remedy?

21. Andy Senza is a promoter and financial advisor in the film industry. While attending an opening night party for the most recent film on which he did the promotion, Senza had a conversation with Gina West. She is a legal secretary who had attended the screening of the new film, and had been invited to the opening-night party by a friend of hers. Impressed by Senza's knowledge of the film industry, West asked him for information about investment opportunities in the industry. As an example, he told her about a film company named Stellar Productions Inc., which was about to begin production on what he anticipated to be a blockbuster hit for release the next summer. What Senza didn't tell West is that he is a 60 percent shareholder in Stellar Productions.

The next day, West looked up Stellar Productions in the telephone book, and ultimately invested $30,000 in the company's latest project. Because of several technical problems and a leading actor with an attitude, the project eventually fell apart and the investors lost their money. West has since learned that Senza is the majority shareholder of Stellar Productions, and feels that she was manipulated into investing in a failing project.

a)   Advise Gina West, with reasons, whether she has any legal remedy concerning Senza's advice.

At the same opening-night party attended by West, Jorge Jensen, who had invested in the last film promoted by Senza, asked Senza for financial advice on what to do with the profits expected to be generated by the box-office receipts from the current film. Senza suggested Jensen invest his profits in the same project he had described to West earlier in the evening. Jensen has also recently found out that Senza is the majority shareholder of Stellar Productions.

b)   Describe the nature of the duty, if any, owed by Andy Senza to Jorge Jensen.

c)   What legal remedies are available to Jensen in this situation?

22. Salim Nehru was a stockbroker who specialized in managing registered retirement savings plans (RRSPs). Jason Walmsley, a single father in his mid-40s with a 3-year-old daughter, had hired Nehru to advise him and to manage his RRSP investments. Walmsley was inexperienced with the stock market, and explained his personal circumstances to Nehru. He told Nehru that he wished to have no more than 10 percent of his portfolio held in medium-risk shares, and that the rest was to be kept in a form that could easily be sold, in case Walmsley needed quick cash.

Over the course of a year and a half, Nehru made several investment recommendations to Walmsley, who followed his advice. As a result, the value of Walmsley's RRSP portfolio fell from $100,000 to $45,000. When Walmsley realized that he had lost over 50 percent of the value of his RRSP, he investigated the nature of the shares held in it, and discovered to his horror that 80 percent were high-risk or speculative shares. When he confronted Nehru with his discovery, Nehru replied, "We all have good years and bad years—you have to keep an eye on the long term."

"Exactly what I intend to do," replied Walmsley.

a)   What remedy does Walmsley have?

b)   What would be the basis for his legal action in court against Nehru?

23. Several friends got together and decided to start an investment club, which they named the Pub Night Investment Club. The club members would meet on the third Thursday of every month at a local pub to discuss investment strategies. They decided to hire an accountant to advise them on financial matters, and he agreed to provide them with monthly financial statements and a sheet with investment recommendations on the Monday before their club meeting, so that they could make decisions early before too much beer had flowed across the table.

One club member, Georgia Smith, decided to share the newsletter on the Internet with a friend who lived in another city. She was unaware that other people had begun to monitor the newsletter which she sent to her friend. At one of the meetings, Smith mentioned to the accountant that she had sent his newsletter over the Internet to her friend in Riverbridge, and the accountant responded that he was flattered she thought so much of his newsletter that she would pass it on. In one of the newsletters, the accountant made a strong recommendation—without having properly investigated the company—and the investment club lost 90 percent of its funds. Several people—non-members of the investment club—began to telephone the accountant, indicating that they too had lost considerable amounts of money as a result of following his newsletter advice. The total losses came to $125,000.

a) With full reasons, advise the accountant as to the nature and extent of his liability for the negligent advice given by him in the newsletter.

b) Would it make any difference to your answer if Smith, instead of scanning the newsletter into her computer, had retyped it?

24. Jane Lee saw a note on the personal website of an experienced and well-known investor named Wallace Buffer. The note said Laurentian Gold Mines had just discovered a rich deposit of gold at a drill site in northern Saskatchewan, but that the company was keeping the find secret for a few days.

Jane immediately called her discount broker and ordered $10,000 worth of shares in Laurentian. Unfortunately, Buffer's information was merely an unfounded rumour, and Jane lost her money. She now wants to sue Buffer.

a) Is there a contract between Jane and Buffer? If not, in what area of law might Jane find a remedy?

b) What legal principles apply to determine if there is a legal relationship (duty) between Jane and Buffer? Will Jane be successful in her lawsuit?

Making Enforceable Business Agreements

What Is a Contract?

Every business deal may be a contract. So the law of contract is the law of the deal. Contracts can be for large or small matters: buying a business or buying a computer. So we all make contracts on a frequent basis. Even handshake agreements may be contracts.

Because many complicated deals have common or standard terms, standard form contracts are regularly used by both businesses and consumers. Some examples of these standard forms are included in the Appendices at the end of the chapters. In this chapter you will learn not only the theory of contract law, but the practice of making contracts. By the end of the chapters on contract law, you will be able to read and understand most of the significant terms in the standard form contracts that you will encounter as a business person.

Many of these standard terms began as issues raised before trial judges and the judges then developed law on these points. Later the issues became specific terms in written agreements. For example, early in the common law, judges developed rules governing whether there was a time limit on an offer. Now you can see actual terms in standard form contracts on time limits and the usual business practices.

Because of the principle of **freedom of contract**, the parties are free to accept the common law contract rules, vary them or even reject them when they make their own specific contracts. Thus, studying the common law is not sufficient for a modern businessperson. You have to be able to understand a **standard form agreement**, as there are customized terms (fill in the blanks style) which must be completed.

Many start-up and small businesses do not have a budget to retain a lawyer to negotiate and draft contracts for them and free precedents from the Internet are being used more frequently. While businesspeople generally understand the significance of the key terms such as the price, many do not understand the meaning of other important terms. Some of these terms can have serious financial consequences. Though some of these terms may govern situations that rarely occur, if that infrequent event does happen, you need to be sure of your legal rights.

A **contract** is an agreement that is enforceable in a court of law. A contract normally is an exchange of promises between two or more people that will be upheld by a court. But not

contract
an agreement that is enforceable in a court of law

every agreement is a contract. For an agreement to be considered a contract, and thus legally binding, it must contain certain factors:

capacity

the legal capability of entering into an agreement; some individuals, such as minors, and mentally incompetent or intoxicated persons, are not seen in law as having the capacity to enter into a contract

- Contractual capacity. The participants have the **capacity**, that is, the legal capability of entering into an agreement. Some individuals, such as minors, and mentally incompetent or intoxicated persons, are not seen in law as having the capacity to enter into a contract.
- Legality or lawful object. The purpose must be neither criminal nor against the public good.
- Consensus. There must be complete agreement, or consensus, among the participants.
- Intention. The intent must be that legally enforceable obligations will result from the agreement.
- Consideration. All parties must offer a **consideration**, which is the price paid for a promise, something of value promised or paid that is taken to indicate that the person has considered the agreement and consents to be bound by it.

consideration

the price paid for a promise, something of value promised or paid that is taken to indicate that the person has considered the agreement and consents to be bound by it

Working with a Commercial Lawyer

Drafting individual contracts for significant business matters requires cooperation between the business person and the commercial lawyer. The written contract must record the business deal with precision while it protects and advances your business's interest. Thus, the best contracts are a result of cooperation between the commercial lawyer and the business client. For effective communication, the lawyer needs to have some understanding of the business issues, and the business person needs to have some understanding of the legal issues.

In these chapters, provisions that occur in most agreements and are called "boiler plate clauses," such as entire agreement clauses, liquidated damage clauses, are discussed. By reviewing both the legal issues and terms that occur in real agreements, you will be well prepared to discuss the legal-business issues in any specific contract with the commercial lawyer.

We now start a review of the elements which are necessary to make a contract. These elements are significant for, if they are not present, the agreement may not be enforceable.

Written Requirement and Oral Contracts

People commonly think that most contracts have to be in writing to be valid. However, the truth is that very few contracts have to be in writing to be legal. Verbal or oral contracts are completely valid in most situations. The problem however is that even if an oral contract is legal, it usually is not a good idea. If there is no permanent record of the terms the parties agreed to, disputes can develop. It will be "one person's word against another." Each party may have a different memory of what terms were in the contract. It is quite surprising the number of large business deals that were done orally and then end up in major legal battles, when this could have been avoided if they had put the deal in writing originally. As one famous quote goes: "An oral agreement is not worth the paper it is printed on."

A good rule to follow is: If a contract is of any significance, put it in writing. That way there should be no future fights over what terms you actually had agreed to.

The difficulty of proving an oral contract frequently arises when people claim to be part owners of a winning lottery ticket. There are often oral contracts when a group of friends or co-workers agree to pool their money and buy lottery tickets together. The problems arise though when they do get a winning ticket and arguments begin over who should be included as a winner. What if someone was sick or on vacation or not scheduled to work on the day the ticket was bought, but they regularly contributed to the group purchase, should they be included? What if a regular player was short on cash that day and another person agreed to loan them the money? What if someone says they never agreed to these terms? These are the type of problems that arise when there is no written agreement.

Example: In the case of *Miller v. Carley* 2009 CanLII 39065 (ONSC), two drug dealers went into a variety store and Carley purchased a scratch ticket and won $5 million. Miller claimed he had loaned Carley $10 to buy the tickets and they had agreed to split any winnings. Carley denied Miller had given him any money and there was never any agreement to split the winnings. The dispute went to trial and the judge found both men very unreliable and untrustworthy witnesses. But the court ruled that Miller had not established on the balance of probabilities that there was an oral contract, so Carley did not have to share the $5 million. But in the *Chamberland* case below the trial judge accepted the plaintiff's testimony regarding an oral agreement and included him in the office lottery pool.

Chamberland v. Provincial, [2008] CanLII 67399 (ON S.C.)

A group of five employees at the Waste Management Department of the City of Sudbury won a lottery of $13 million on July 9, 2005. As with many such groups, the parties participated in a pool for a number of years by contributing a sum such as $5. While there was a core of regular contributors, some joined for certain periods or certain draws only.

All agreements regarding participation were oral. It was agreed that all would contribute equally and all would share equally.

The Plaintiff had been a regular member but when transferred to another division for about a year, he did not participate. Shortly before the win, he returned to the same division as the other defendants.

The Plaintiff testified that on the morning of July 8, 2005 he drove the organizer of the pool, Mr. Provincial, to work and asked if he could "spot" (lend) the Plaintiff the $5 to participate in the pool and Provincial agreed. Provincial denied this conversation.

The Court's Decision

On a review of the evidence the Court found that the conversation had taken place and that the Plaintiff had proved a contract to share equally in the proceeds.

The Ontario Lottery and Gaming Corp. (OLG), which runs major lotteries for the province, has a sample office lottery pool agreement posted on its website. OLG encourages people to download and use this contract for office pools to help avoid the costly legal battles that frequently occur when groups win. Millions of dollars are often at stake, so a written agreement is advisable.

Statutory Requirements for Written Agreements

Various statutory laws do impose a requirement for written contracts in certain situations. The *Statute of Frauds* is a law brought over from Britain that still applies in some provinces and requires certain contracts to be in writing to be enforceable. Other laws in areas such as consumer protection, bills of exchange, sale of goods and family law also require that some contracts must be written to be legal. The entire contract does not have to be in writing, just the major terms. If the contracts are not written they are not void, the court will just not enforce the contract. But there are even some exceptions, if there has been part performance of certain contracts, the contract can still be enforceable even though the written requirement was not met.

Since there are a variety of different statutes that have the written requirement and these vary among the provinces, it is not possible to include them all in this text. Therefore the following is a list of some of the most important contracts that many provinces require to be in writing to be enforceable. You should check specific laws in your province if you have any questions, or to be safe, just put it in writing anyway. Some contracts that some provinces require to be in writing to be enforceable include:

- Contracts involving an interest in land such the sale or mortgage of real estate or leases for longer than 3 years
- A guarantee by a third party to pay the debt of another party
- A marriage or cohabitation agreement
- Some insurance contracts and financial contracts involving credit, loans and interest payments
- Some contracts specifically included in consumer protection legislation such as: time share condominium agreements, direct or door to door sales contracts and personal development service agreements(such as fitness club memberships, dance lessons, martial arts lessons)

Since e-commerce is an important and expanding area of our economy, paper documents are drastically declining in usage. Laws have been adapted to e-contracts and as a result digital documents and electronic signatures are considered legal in most situations. Provinces require companies that sell goods on line to provide the purchaser with a digital copy of the contract. Like any contract, purchasers should read the terms on line before they agree to any contract. Clauses such as return policy, taxes, currency rates, shipping charges, applicable laws can be very important and online customers need to read these carefully.

■ *Business Law*   Applied

❶ John hired Sarah to be his housekeeper and promised her verbally that because of all her hard work for him, when he died he would leave her his house. He also promised her that he would leave her his valuable coin collection upon his death for all she had done for him. John frequently told his neighbours what a wonderful housekeeper Sarah was and how the house and his valuable coin collection would be hers when he died.

Several years later though, when John died, he left no will. His only relative was his brother Max who under the law that applied when a person dies with no will, Max claimed all of John's assets including the house and the coin collection.

   a) Is John's oral promise to leave Sarah the house enforceable?
   b) Is John's oral promise to leave Sarah the coin collection enforceable?

Capacity

The law recognizes that some individuals need special protection when making contracts. Young people under the age of majority—minors—are considered to lack full judgment in business affairs, and therefore there are particular rules to safeguard their interests. People who are mentally incompetent, and individuals who are intoxicated, are also given specific protection at law.

Minors

In the Middle Ages, when a man reached 21 years of age, he was considered strong enough to bear armour and fight for his country. Since he was able to do so he was given full status to conduct his own affairs—he was legally an adult.

In modern times, many countries, including Canada, have lowered the age at which young people bear full responsibility for their own affairs. In Canadian provinces, the

age of majority—the age at which a person is recognized as an adult according to the law of his or her province—is not always the same as the age at which a young person is permitted to get married, drive, or drink alcohol. The age of majority is 18 years of age in Alberta, Manitoba, Ontario, Prince Edward Island, Quebec and Saskatchewan. In all other provinces and territories the age for adulthood is 19.

In general courts are unlikely to enforce a contract against a minor. Parents of a minor are not liable unless they had previously authorized or co-signed the contract. It also does not matter if the minor appeared to be over the age of majority and the other party to the contract honestly believes that the young person is an adult. This is true even if the minor has deliberately lied or misled the adult. If a minor ratifies the contract (accepts it and acts upon it) once they reach the age of majority, such as making further payments on the contract, then the contract becomes binding and the former minor cannot get out of the deal.

If a contract is cancelled by the court, the minor is entitled to have any money paid refunded, but must return the goods purchased. If the goods have become damaged or are reduced in value, the minor is responsible for that amount.

In any dispute over a contract, the courts try to balance the interests of both the adult and the minor. If, for example, the contract is for goods that the young person has purchased, the seller might receive financial compensation for taking back a "used" item. A minor who buys a car for $5,000 and drives it for three months could expect to pay rental for its use over that time if the contract is cancelled.

Example: In *Cininni c. Lavoie* 2010 QCCQ 2432 (CanLII) a 17 year old paid $950 for a 16 year old car with 302,000 km. that broke down right after he bought it. Two days later he had to have it towed and the mechanic said it was not worth fixing. His father tried to negotiate a settlement with the seller, but when that failed, the minor sold it for scrap for $50. The seller complained that the car was worth more if it had been sold for parts. The minor then sued the seller for $1,100 (the purchase price and the cost of the tow). The court ruled that the price charged was excessive in view of the age of the minor, the circumstances and the advantage he gained from the contract. Since the car had been scrapped, restitution was not possible, but a reduction in the price was the appropriate remedy, so the court ordered the seller to reimburse the minor for $600. The minor therefore did not get all his money back, he still was out of pocket $500.

Repudiation   When parties cancel a contract before it is fully performed, as the minors are doing in the examples in this section, they are repudiating (rejecting) the contract. **Repudiation** is an indication by a party that he or she will not go through with the agreement as promised. It is also called **anticipatory breach.**

Business Law   Applied

❷ **Sabrina Costa,** aged 17, was given $500 by her grandparents to help pay for her future education. On her way to the bank to deposit the cash, she passed an electronics store that had a large sign in the window.

SPECIAL! ONE DAY ONLY! CD PLAYERS regular price $1,000 TODAY'S PRICE $500 (all taxes included) Buy yours now!

Costa did buy hers, telling the salesperson as she handed over her money, "I'm 19 today and this is my birthday present from my grandparents." Later that day, when the CD player was delivered to her house, she was not at home. Her mother refused to accept the delivery and, when her daughter returned, told the young woman to go back to the store and ask for her money to be refunded.

a) Did the business have to return the money?

Sidebar definitions:

age of majority
the age at which a person is recognized as an adult according to the law of his or her province

minor
a person who has not attained the age of majority according to their provincial law and therefore is not legally an adult

Legalese

repudiation (anticipatory breach)
an indication by a party that he or she will not go through with the agreement as promised

Minors' Contracts for Necessities

Contracts that involve matters necessary for the young person's survival can be enforced by the courts. Necessities are those goods and services that are needed every day—food, clothing, shelter, education, medical care, job training, and apprenticeship programs.

In deciding whether an item or service is a necessity, the court considers the minor's need for the goods or services, as well as the young person's position, or station, in life. Family and financial background are looked at, and what is seen as a necessity for one individual might not be considered so for another. A full-time student, for example, would likely have no need of a formal business suit; a trainee accountant, on the other hand, could not attend the office every day without one. A minor only has to pay a reasonable price for the necessities and the court will reduce the price if it is not fair.

Minors must fulfill any contracts they make for necessities. If this were not the law, then no one would be willing to supply them with those necessities. Loans to minors are not recoverable unless they are used for necessities. The Canada Student Loan Act specifically provides that minors are responsible for repaying loans granted under that program.

Employment contracts and apprenticeship contracts can be considered as necessities, but only if they are for the minor's benefit.

Example: In *Toronto Marlboro Major Junior "A" Hockey Club et al. v. Tonelli et al.*, 1979 CanLII 1969 (ON CA), John Tonelli, a 17 year old hockey player, signed a contract to play for the Toronto Marlies. The contract was for 3 years, but the Marlies alone could extend, assign or terminate it at any time. It also stated if Tonelli left the team and played in an alternate league (the WHA) he would have to pay the Marlies 20% of his new salary. Tonelli switched to a WHA team at a 3 year salary of $320,000, so the Marlies sued him for breach of contract and $64,000 in damages. The court ruled that Tonelli was a minor when he made the deal and though employment contracts can be necessities and be enforceable, this contract benefitted the team not the minor, so it was unenforceable and Tonelli was not liable for breach of contract.

Parents' Consent   Businesses may have parents involved in paying for their children's purchases. However, the parents must consent to each purchase.

Apple agreed to refund U.S. customers at least $32.5million after a settlement with the US Federal Trade Commission (FTC). The FTC's complaint alleged that Apple failed to inform parents that by entering a password, they were approving not only a single in-app purchase, but also 15 minutes of additional time for unlimited purchases of apps and games their children could make without further consent. One woman said her daughter had spent $2,600 without consent. (*Wall Street Journal*, January 15, 2014)

■ *Critical Concepts of* Contracts with Minors

- A minor is a person under the age of majority which is age 18 or 19 depending on what province or territory they live in
- Contracts made by minors are not usually enforced, and parents are not liable for contracts their minor children made unless they agreed to be
- If a contract made by a minor is not enforced by the court, the minor is entitled to some or all of the money paid to be refunded
- Contracts made by minors for necessities; such as food, clothing, shelter and employment may be enforceable in some circumstances, though the minor only has to pay a fair price
- Loans to minors for necessities are enforceable as well as loans made under the Canada Students Loan Act

Royal Bank of Canada v. Holobroff
1998 ABQB 288 (CanLII)

When Colin Holobroff was 17 years old, he obtained a bank card from the Royal Bank and signed the cardholder agreement the bank had prepared. It stated he must keep his PIN number confidential and the card was only for his personal use.

Holobroff soon after sold the bank card to another student for $500 and that student then used it to defraud the bank of $4,931. The Bank then sued Holobroff for the money in both tort and contract law. Holobroff claimed that since he was a minor at the time he signed the banking agreement the contract was not enforceable, nor could he be held liable under tort law. The trial court ruled that Holobroff had not breached the contract with the bank, and the bank could not sue in tort law to try and avoid the rules on a minor's lack of capacity in contract law. The trial judge found Holobroff was only liable for the $500 that the student had paid him for the bank card, not the full bank losses. The bank appealed the decision.

The Court's Decision

The Alberta Queen's Bench ruled that the minor was well aware of the fraudulent intentions of the student who purchased his bank card from him. He had also clearly breached the contract when he gave out his card and PIN to the other student. The bank could pursue an independent tort claim as well as a contract law claim against the minor. The court then held Holobroff liable for the tort of conspiracy to commit fraud and ordered him to compensate the bank for the full losses it claimed.

■ *Business Law*   Applied

❸ **Afshan Dahl,** aged 16, found a part-time job as a receptionist in an office. She needed some new clothes for work, and bought two outfits from a local clothing store. On the way home, she saw something she liked better and went back to the first store to return what she had just purchased. The store refused to let her return the clothes, or to refund her money.

   a) Was Dahl able to get out of the contract because she was a minor at law?
   b) Afshan loaned $100 to her friend 17 year old friend Erik, so Erik could bet on a hockey game. Erik lost the bet and then he told Afshan he couldn't repay her. Can Afshan legally make Erik repay her the money?

Mentally Incompetent and Intoxicated Persons

Contract laws give special protection to individuals who suffer from mental impairment at the time of entering into an agreement. The impairment may be due to a variety of causes, including:

- physical disease (for example, stroke or brain tumours)
- mental illness (for example, senile dementia)
- drug use (including both legal and illegal use)
- alcohol use

In order for the incapacitated person to avoid liability on the contract, the other party must have known (or reasonably should have known) of the incapacity. The court will consider circumstances surrounding the transaction, such as the price paid for the goods or services, in assessing what the other party knew (or should have known). Contracts that these incapacitated people make for the necessaries of life are enforceable, but the courts will ensure that they only pay a fair price.

If an individual wishes to avoid liability based on incapacity, he or she must do so promptly upon return to a capable mental state. In cases where individuals suffer from permanent mental impairment, another party may promptly challenge the agreement on their behalf.

Example: One of the most famous claims for mental incompetency was made by Tim Horton's widow, Dolores Horton. She sold the doughnut franchise in December of 1975 for $1,000,000.

In 1995 she claimed she could not remember anything about the deal because she had been a drug addict at the time and had, in effect, performed a chemical lobotomy on herself. Now she was clear of the addiction and wanted her interest in the doughnut chain back, which interest was worth about $350,000,000 in 1995.

Unfortunately for Mrs. Horton, the trial judge did not believe that she was unable to understand what she was doing at the time; she lost.

Critical Concepts of Mental Incompetence or Intoxication

Contract laws give special protection to individuals who are impaired by drunkenness, or who are mentally incompetent. A contract made by such a person can be voided by the courts, as long as the following rules apply.

- The contract is not one for necessities.
- The impairment was sufficiently serious that the individual was unable to understand the nature and consequence of what was going on.
- The other party had actual knowledge, or was put on notice (termed constructive notice), of the impairment at the time the contract was entered into.
- The incapacitated person must cancel the agreement promptly after the return to mental competence or sobriety.

Business Law Applied

❹ **Ritchie Brothers**, a large firm of industrial auctioneers, specialized in the sale of heavy equipment such as earth movers and road graders. Ron Barr, owner of a construction company, attended an auction and purchased $1 million worth of earth-moving equipment, giving a $250,000 cheque as a deposit. The cheque was drawn on a bank in another city, and Barr was a new customer, so Ritchie Brothers asked that his bank manager confirm the cheque would be honoured. Barr called the bank manager, and then handed the phone to the Ritchie representative, who confirmed the money was on deposit.

The cheque bounced. Ritchie was still in possession of the equipment, and resold it for $50,000, yielding a loss of $200,000. Ritchie Brothers sued Barr for that amount.

Barr claimed that the day before the auction he had been visiting his daughter in Vancouver. He had returned to his hotel room in the evening, where he took medication for a heart condition, and drank two beers. Barr said he remembered nothing after that until he woke up in his own home two days later. During the 48-hour blank period Barr attended the Ritchie Brothers auction, but claimed all he knew of the events of the two days was what other people had since told him.

The Ritchie Brothers' representative said that he was aware of the law of capacity, and therefore had spoken directly to Barr at the auction to make certain that he was competent. The auctioneer had seen no indication of any impairment.

a) Did Barr have to pay?
b) If Barr had been a minor, would the result have been the same?

Legality

illegal contracts

contracts which cannot be enforced because they are contrary to legislation or public policy

Courts will not enforce illegal contracts. **Illegal contracts**—contracts which cannot be enforced because they are contrary to legislation or public policy—fall into either of two situations:

- The agreement involves breaking a civil or criminal statute. This is known as statutory illegality.
- The agreement is against public policy and violates the public interest or the common sense of morality in society.

Statutory Illegality

Within statutory illegality there are also two categories. The first is those acts that are criminal or considered morally wrong. If a hit man successfully carries out his contract and his employer refuses to pay, he could not sue in court. The second category is those acts that are wrong only because a statute makes them wrong. For example, a statute may prohibit the sale of electrical machinery unless it is CSA (Canadian Standards Association) approved. Also, electricians may be prohibited from carrying on business without a provincial licence.

In the second category of illegal acts, those that are wrong only because they are prohibited by statutes, the contract may still be enforced if there was no intention to violate the relevant statute and there is compliance with the statute before performance of the contract is completed. If an agreement was made to sell a machine that at the time had not been CSA approved, this contract would be unenforceable as illegal. However, if before delivery the machine was certified, the contract would be enforced, as the seller had no intention to violate the statute and had complied before completion of the contract.

Examples of statutory illegal contracts are:

- Agreements by a worker with an employer not to make a claim for workers compensation
- Agreements to lend money to a person who intends to use it to gamble
- Agreement to arbitrate family law matters according to religious law
- Agreements to act as a surrogate mother, supply sperm to a sperm bank or conduct business regarding these two activities (Section 6, The Assisted Human Reproduction Act, S. C. 2004 c. 2).

The Assisted Human Reproduction Act prohibits only the enforcement of the agreement but not the making of one. So a woman could agree to act as a surrogate mother, but if it is for a fee, she could not sue to collect the sum. Likewise the "donor" parents could not sue either to recover any money paid or force the surrogate mother to deliver over the baby.

■ *Critical Concepts of* Statutory Illegality

- Statutory illegality can arise from two different situations: those that are criminal, and those that are wrong only because they are prohibited by civil statutes or regulations.
- Those contracts that are illegal only because they are prohibited by statute may be enforced if there was no intention to violate the statute.
- The court may find that there was no intention to violate the statute if at the time of the performance the illegality was cured.

Illegal Interest Rate

Under the Criminal Code section 374 (1), it is illegal in Canada to charge an interest rate greater than 60% per annum. Frequently lenders charge clients in excess of this amount. Courts usually then consider the contract to be void because of this illegal rate of interest. In the case below, Transport North American Express Inc. however, the Supreme Court ruled that the contract is not necessarily void. The court can look at the entire circumstances of the deal and then decided what was appropriate. The court could rule that the entire contract was void due to the illegal clause or it could do a "**notional severance**" and remove the illegal clause and enforce the rest of the contract if it was unobjectionable and even set a new interest rate the court deemed appropriate under the circumstances. This case has caused considerable discussion as traditionally if a clause violated a law it was "**blue penciled" or struck down**. Many question whether this new approach, as it allows a judge to re-write a key term of a contract.

Transport North American Express Inc. v. New Solutions Financial Corp., 2004 SCC 7 (CanLII)

New Solutions Financial Corp. entered into a credit agreement with Transport North American Express (TNAE) and advanced it $500,000. In addition to various other fees and charges, the agreement provided for interest to be paid at the rate of 4% per month, calculated daily and payable in monthly arrears. These various payments together exceeded the maximum legal interest rate of 60% allowed in s. 347 of the Criminal Code. When TNAE was unable to make its payments, it applied to the court for a declaration that the agreement contained an illegal rate of interest and should not be enforced.

The trial court ruled that the interest rate was illegal, but the entire agreement is not void. Rather than just severing the illegal interest rate clause totally from the agreement, the judge applied "notional severance" and reduced the interest rate to the legal maximum of 60%. TNAE appealed to the Ontario Court of Appeal which rejected the use of notional severance and applied the "blue pencil" technique which only allows to the court to strike out the illegal interest rate clause (run a blue pencil through it). This left the rest of the agreement in place and the remaining terms then provided for an effective interest rate of 30.8%. This decision was appealed to the Supreme Court.

The Supreme Court's Decision

The Supreme Court reversed the appeal court ruling and adopted the trial court's application of notional severance. The court stated the traditional rule that an entire contract is completely void when there is a clause that violates a statue may not be applicable when it is the interest rate section 367 of the Criminal Code that is the concern. The court also decided that the blue pencil rule may also not be appropriate in some situations as it could allow a borrower to receive an interest free loan if the interest rate section is just "blue penciled" (ruled out).

The court indicated it could examine the context of the contract and provide specific remedies appropriate to that situation. Judicial discretion and a spectrum of remedies are available. If it was a situation of a "loan shark" taking advantage of a borrower, the court could void the entire contract from the outset. But that was not the situation in this case as both parties were experienced in commercial lending. In other situations the court could exercise the "maximum level of remedial flexibility" to tailor its remedy to the contractual context.

The court indicated that the following 4 factors should be considered when deciding to apply notional severance: whether the public policy of s. 347 would be subverted, whether the parties entered into the agreement for an illegal purpose or with an evil intention, the relative bargaining position of the parties and the potential for the debtor to enjoy a windfall.

Given these considerations in this case, since there was no illegal intent and equal bargaining power, the court ruled that it was appropriate to apply notional severance and allow a 60% effective interest rate, as it more closely aligns with the intention of the parties when the contract was made.

This case got considerable attention and the dissenting judge's view that courts should not be rewriting contracts under the label of notional severance was supported by many. The blue pencil test of striking down offending clauses was well established and consistent with the parties' intentions. But this new approach of notional severance can create uncertainty in contract law as it allows judges to rewrite key provisions of contracts. Whether it will be expanded into areas other than illegal interest rate terms will be interesting to observe.

In international business transactions a foreign company will sometimes ask a Canadian company to issue a phony invoice to assist the foreign business in avoiding its country's exchange-control laws. This makes the contract illegal. Any illegal act in performance of the contract affects the entire contract. If the Canadian company finds that it must sue on the contract, it may be left without a remedy because of this illegal act.

Pay Day Loan Rates

Pay day loans are another area of concern when it comes to illegal interest rates. The typical payday loan in Canada is for $300 to be repaid within 2weeks. They are provided by small non-traditional lenders and have increased in popularity in Canada since the 1990s. It is a $2 billion industry in Canada and it is estimated about 3% of Canadians have used pay day loans one time or more and 750,000 of these loans are made annually in this country.[1]

Names such as Money Mart, CashOne, Money Provider and Wonga are well known pay day lenders. Though these payday companies offer a convenient service, they also charge extremely large fees, which are effectively really interest rates, for their services and their "real"

---

1. Theresa Tedesco Financial Post Feb. 27, 2012 Pay Day Loan Companies in the Government Crosshairs, http://business. financialpost.com/2013/02/27/payday-loan-companies-in-government-crosshairs/

interest rates are well above the criminal rate. When people complained about these high rates, provincial governments agreed to regulate the industry within their province, but pay day lenders then became exempt from s. 367 (1) of the Criminal Code in provinces where laws were passed regulating this industry.

The problem is that the caps that the provinces have set on pay day loan interest rates are shockingly high. For example in 2009 Ontario limited the cost of borrowing to $21 per $100 borrowed in a 2 week period. But that works out to an annual rate of 546%, and since the Criminal Code does not apply, it is legal. This rate is about 15 times greater than what credit card companies charge. It was also higher than the rate the leading pay day loan company already was charging its customers. When Ontario passed the law, it was heralded as an important consumer protection law, when in reality it just legalizes criminal lending practices. Class actions against these lenders have been of little use, as they are slow, expensive, and in one case the plaintiffs were given vouchers as compensation, which they could use if they took out more pay day loans.

The people who use pay day loans are often among the most financially vulnerable people in the country, and governments have legalized these obscene interest rates, so these desperate consumers continue to be exploited. In the U.S. there are 15 states which have put interest caps on small loans to protect consumers which effectively results in a ban on pay day loans in those states. Hopefully Canadian governments eventually come to a similar realization in this country.[2]

Business Law   Applied

❹ The relevant provincial act states that a builder must be registered with the provincial Home Warranty Plan office before being able to sell a new home. A builder entered into an agreement of purchase and sale for a house yet to be built. The agreement was to close in eight months. In the sixth month, in compliance with the statute, the builder registered with the plan office. When the time came for closing two months later, the purchaser refused to close on the basis that the agreement was illegal because it violated the *Home Warranties Act*.

   a) Was the agreement illegal at the time that it was made?
   b) Was it enforceable at the time of closing?

❺ Susan Jones agreed to be a surrogate mother for Carol and John Brown by artificial insemination using John's sperm for the sum of $50,000; 20,000 paid at the time of the insemination and 30,000 on delivery of the baby.

However, just before the child was born, Carol became pregnant so the couple did not want the child and refused to pay the further $30,000.

   a) Jones wants to sue the couple for the balance owing and the cost of raising the child. Do the Browns have a defense?
   b) Could the 3 parties be charged with a criminal offense for violation of a statute?

❻ Peter Green agreed to loan Janice Payne $50,000 at an interest rate of 58% compounded weekly plus other fees and charges. After a month, Janice was unable to make the interest payments on the loan but now wonders if there is any way she could get out of the contract.

   a) Would the court enforce the lending agreement? Explain why or why not.
   b) What actions could the court take and what will it most likely do in this situation?
   c) If Janice had borrowed $500 from a payday loan company with similar interest rates as the loan from Peter, would there be a different result?

2. Theresa Tedesco Financial Post Feb. 27, 2012 Pay Day Loan Companies in the Government Crosshairs, http://business. financialpost.com/2013/02/27/payday-loan-companies-in-government-crosshairs/

Common Law Illegality

Agreements in Restraint of Trade

There are a number of situations in which the Courts will not enforce a contract as being against public policy, which means against the good of the community generally.

One of the most common situations in business subject to the public policy consideration are agreements that restrict a person's ability to earn a living, which are called agreements "in restraint of trade". The word "trade" was more generally used historically to mean carrying on business or earning a livelihood.

These clauses are usually found in two situations: sale of a business and employment contracts.

Sale of a Business.   A seller agrees not to enter into a similar competing business within a certain distance for a specific time. For example, Idries Shah, who has been running a small food store and who is very popular in the neighbourhood, agrees to sell his business to Farhani Khan. Khan may want a clause in the agreement that Shaw not open up a competing business within a five mile radius for five years. This clause is called a non-competition clause.

Employment Agreements.   An employer may hire an employee who is a super salesman and give him access to confidential lists of his customers scattered throughout not only Canada but other parts of the world. The employer may seek restrictions on the employees right to compete in a similar business after leaving his present employment such as not being able to solicit (approach) customers of his present employers for six months after leaving. This is called a non-solicitation clause.

In reviewing these clauses the Courts start from a premise that such agreements are unenforceable as contrary to public policy because it is in the public interest that everyone be able to earn a living and not need to claim welfare. The clauses will be enforced if the clauses can be considered reasonable. The test for reasonableness examines whether the clause is necessary to protect the business and if the restrictions on time, area and subject matter are no greater than what is needed to protect the business. If it is an employee that is being restrained, the worker must possess some special skill, or have knowledge of trade secrets or special techniques, or represent major potential competition to the employer or the clause will not be considered reasonable.

Although the principle of reasonableness of the restraint (restriction) is the same for both sale of business contracts and employment contracts, it is applied more leniently in the sale of business contracts. The Courts will be more likely to find such terms enforceable in these agreements because there is equality of bargaining power and the seller is getting paid for goodwill (goodwill explained below).

In contrast the Courts are more sympathetic to employees and so more likely to strike down such clauses in employment contracts if they are too wide of scope and not necessary to protect the former employer.

goodwill

the value of the good name, reputation, and connection of a business

Goodwill—the value of the good name, reputation, and connection of a business—can't really be measured in dollars and cents. But when a business is sold, its goodwill is often considered one of its assets, and the selling price includes a sum for it, because when you buy a business, you are also acquiring its location, name, credit rating, reputation, and, most important, its customers—which all add up to that business's goodwill.

Since you have paid for the goodwill of the business you've bought, it might cause your operation a great deal of harm if the seller opened up a new, competing, firm close by. For this reason, a buyer often includes a contract clause that says the seller agrees not to open a competing business anywhere in the same city, or within a reasonable distance of it, for a certain number of years.

But it is in the public interest to make sure that all members of society have the chance to work and thus provide for their own support. If those selling a business agree to severe restrictions on their own ability to work, they could be forced to claim welfare, thus adding to the financial burden on society. Because an employee is seen as being at a disadvantage when negotiating a contract, the courts will, in general, be more likely to strike down restrictive clauses in employment agreements than they would in agreements for the sale of a business.

In any dispute over unreasonable restraint of trade, the courts attempt to balance the two interests—those of the parties to the contract, and those of the public. The following cases illustrate the factors considered in these two different situations.

■ *Critical Concepts of* Restraint of Trade

The following principles apply to terms that restrain an individual's right to earn a living, in both sale-of-business and employment contracts:

- In general, any contract clause that limits a person's right to earn a living is presumed to be against public policy, and therefore unenforceable.

- This presumption can be overturned if the restraint clause can be proved to be reasonable. To be considered reasonable it must:

  a) be necessary to protect the business

  b) contain restrictions on time, area, and subject matter that are no greater than are needed to protect the business

  c) not be against the interests of the public.

- The person to be restrained must possess some special skill, or knowledge of trade secrets or special techniques. Alternatively, the individual must represent major potential competition to the business sold or to the employment the individual has left.

Payette v. Guay
2013 SCC 45 (CanLII)

Payette was the largest crane rental company in Quebec and in October of 2004 it purchased another crane rental business from Guay for $26 million. As part of the purchase agreement there was a non-competition clause that restricted Guay from participating in the crane rental industry in Quebec for 5 years and there was also a non-solicitation clause that stated Guay could not solicit any of Payette's customers nor encourage any of Payette's employees to join Guay at a different crane company for a period of 5 years.

When Payette purchased Guay's business it stipulated Guay was to work for Payette for 6 months to help in the transition. After this 6 month period Guay continued to work for Payette for over 1 years. Finally Payette terminated Guay and 7 months later Guay went to work for another Quebec crane rental company, Mammoet Crane. Within days, 7 other employees of Payette joined Guay at Mammoet. Payette went to court to enforce the agreement and get an injunction to stop Guay from working at Mammoet.

The trial court looked at the 3 parts to the reasonableness test for non-competition clauses; the time, place and type of restriction. It ruled that 5 years was a reasonable time restriction for the sale of a business, but the geographic scope of the non-competition clause was unlawful. It was too broad as it applied to all of Quebec and Guay's business had only operated in the Montreal area. For that reason the court ruled the clause was unenforceable. The trial judge also ruled that the non-solicitation clause was also unlawful so the court denied Payette the injunction.

Payette appealed the decision and the Quebec Court of Appeal overturned the trial decision and ruled that both clauses were reasonable and lawful. The restriction on the entire province of Quebec was reasonable given the mobility of crane equipment. The two sides were business people and had carefully negotiated the contract when Guay sold the business and the terms were reasonable and should be enforced. Guay could not work in the crane industry in Quebec until 5 years after he had left Payette. Guay appealed the decision to the Supreme Court.

The Supreme Court's Decision

The Supreme Court agreed with the Court of Appeal. It ruled that the two clauses were reasonable and lawful. It recognized that in employment law cases the courts scrutinize non-competition clauses very carefully because of the unequal bargaining power that exists between and employer and an employee. But in this case it was a commercial transaction involving the sale of a business and the employment law issue must be seen in that context. Restrictive covenants must be interpreted in a manner consistent with the intention of the parties and their right to freedom to contract. There was no unequal bargaining problem in this contract and no public policy concerns for restraint of trade, so the clauses the two parties had agreed to were lawful and enforceable.

In the *Mason* case below, it involved an ordinary employee challenging a restrictive covenant that had both a non-competition clause and a non-solicitation clause and it shows the different attitude of the Supreme Court in this situation where there was unequal bargaining power between an employer and an employee an excessive restriction imposed in the employment contract.

Mason v. Chem-Trend Limited Partnership
2011 ONCA 344 (CanLII)

Thomas Mason was a technical sales representative for Chem-Trend, a world-wide chemical company for 17 years, when he was fired. In his employment contract there was a restrictive covenant that imposed a one-year prohibition on engaging in any business activity in competition with the company or soliciting business from any business entity which was a customer of Chem-Trend any time during the 17 years Mason had worked there. Another separate clause stated that he could not divulge any confidential information or trade secrets of the company. Mason challenged the restrictive covenant claiming it was excessive and too restrictive and therefore unenforceable. The trial judge looked at the company's interests, the time limit, the geographic area and the subject matter and ruled the restrictive covenant was legal. Mason appealed to the Ontario Court of Appeal.

The Court's Decision

The Ontario Court of Appeal ruled that the non-competition clause was excessive and too restrictive and declared it unreasonable and unenforceable. The separate clause that protected the company's trade secrets and confidential information adequately protected Chem-Trend, so the restrictive covenant was excessive.

The prohibition on Mason dealing with any customers or competitors of Chem-Trend over the past 17 years world-wide was unreasonable. Mason wouldn't even know who many of these companies were. Mason was part of the technical sales force for a large company, but he only operated in a limited sales territory. He was prohibited not just from soliciting former customers, but from dealing with any of their world-wide customers or competitors in any way. This was clearly excessive. Mason was not the president or a key executive, where there might be more justification for a broader prohibition on competition commented the court. He was just an ordinary employee and this broad restriction was unreasonable and unenforceable.

Lyons v. Multari,
[2000] 50 O.R. (3d) 126 (Ont. C.A.) (leave to appeal to S.C.C. denied)

Multari, a recent graduate, went to work as an oral surgeon with Lyons, an established oral surgeon with a five-year practice. They signed a short handwritten employment contract less than a page long, which contained a non-competition clause by which Multari would not operate a competing oral surgeon practice within five miles of Dr. Lyons's office for three years after leaving his employment.

As oral surgeons, they got all patients by referrals from regular dentists. Multari worked for Lyons for 17 months, gave six months' notice, and went to work for a competitor over five miles away. About a year later Multari moved to another office 3.7 miles from Lyons's office, which location was in breach of the non-competition clause.

Lyons sued Multari for loss of business.

The Court's Decision

The court found that Multari had breached the non-competition clause. The question became: was this non-competition clause enforceable? Did the space and time limits go too far and restrict competition generally?

The court observed that in the context of employment contracts, non-competition clauses were drastic weapons compared to non-solicitation clauses.

The court ruled that a non-competition clause should be enforced only in exceptional cases. This was not an exceptional case because Multari had worked only a short time for Dr. Lyons and Lyons was always the main contact with the referring dentists. Lyons did not need this level of protection, and the clause was declared unenforceable.

In employment law cases involving restrictive covenants, the courts will not rewrite the unenforceable clause to create a reasonable restriction on an employee. If the court thinks the clause is invalid it will be struck down. This is unlike the *Transport North American Express* case where the court used "notional severance" to change the illegal interest rate to make the agreement enforceable. The court will not rewrite clauses in employment law cases that it rules are unlawful, so far that remedy appears to be restricted to the illegal interest rate cases.

If the court rules that a non-competition clause is unlawful, then the "blue pencil" rule is used and the clause is eliminated. The case of *Lyons v. Multari* below clearly illustrates this as well. It is important that employers draft reasonable clauses initially or they can end up with no protection at all. Courts will not redraft the clause for them.

Business Alert!

Read the Agreement   In a case very similar to *Lyons v. Multari*, a partner at the major accounting firm of Ernst & Young left to go to a rival firm, Arthur Andersen. The Ernst & Young partnership agreement contained a non-competition clause preventing any partner from practicing public accounting within a 50-mile radius of his former office for one year after leaving Ernst & Young.

The court held this clause was unenforceable as being unreasonable. However, the partnership agreement also contained a clause requiring the partner to give one year's notice. The partner did not give any notice and was made to pay damages based on that one-year period in the amount of $250,000.[3]

This case illustrates the importance of not only knowing the relevant common law principles but also closely reading the terms of any relevant agreement.

Effect of Evolving Case Law

Cases such as *Lyons v. Multari* often signal a change in the law and perhaps also in judges' attitudes against wide non-competition clauses in employment agreements. Lawyers watch such cases carefully to see if standard clauses in relevant contracts should be revised.

While employers often try to get the widest terms in an employment contract, lawyers realize that this strategy can backfire as the *Lyons v. Multari* case shows. If an employer wants to make sure that an employee cannot harm the employer when the employee leaves, in light of the evolving case law, it may be better to have an employee sign a clause agreeing, for example, not to work for the employer's three major competitors for a reasonable period of time in place of the traditional clause that restricts area and time. This clause focuses on where the most harm can be done. It is more likely that such a clause will stand up under the court's review in light of cases such as *Lyons v. Multari*.

■ *Business Law* Applied

❼ **In the *Payette v. Guay* case and in the *Lyons v. Multari* case:**

  i) what is the subject matter of the agreements;   iii) what is the geographic limitation.
  ii) what is the time provision;

❽ **Frank and Joanna** Demp were the principal shareholders of Fieldstream Arms Co., a small firearms-manufacturing company. The Fieldstream products were only sold in British Columbia.

Frank, a very popular ex-professional football player, was considered a super-salesman. It was mainly through his selling abilities that the firm had grown so successfully over the years. Joanna was the company accountant and business manager.

Fieldstream was sold. A clause in the sale agreement stated that both of the Demps agreed not to carry on or work in any similar business in the province of British Columbia for the next five years.

One year later, Joanna was appointed comptroller of a firm called Target Rifles Inc.; Frank became sales manager of the same company. Target operated out of Vancouver, British Columbia.

  a) Was the restraint clause in the sale agreement necessary to protect Fieldstream Arms?
  b) Did it meet the three tests for reasonableness?
  c) Did Frank represent a potential competitive danger to Fieldstream Arms? Did Joanna? Were there different considerations for each one?
  d) Was the agreement enforceable against either or both of the Demps?

---

3. *Ernst & Young v. Stewart, Lawyers Weekly*, April 25, 1997.

The Standard Non Competition Term

See paragraph 4 in the Agreement for Purchase and Sale of a Business in a Leased Premises in Appendix 5. It is entitled "Non-Competition". There are blanks left as every situation may call for different limits to comply with the common law requirements that restrictions put on the ability to earn income must be reasonable in the circumstances. In the example given the limit is 5 km for 3 years. This is a common term and thought to be in compliance with the law of illegality for most small businesses.

Consensus

Before any contract is finalized, there must be general agreement, or consensus, between the parties involved. There can be several stages in the process before consensus is reached:

- bargaining or negotiating
- **offer** (a promise made by one party that contains all necessary terms so that the other party need only say "I accept" and a contract is formed)
- counter-offer (this stage does not always take place)
- acceptance

offer
a promise made by one party that contains all necessary terms so that the other party need only say "I accept" and a contract is formed

Bargaining—An Invitation to Treat

invitation to treat
the technical legal term for the invitation to engage in the bargaining process

It is through bargaining, or negotiating, that parties to a contract try to reach an agreement that is to their individual advantage. **Invitation to treat** is the technical legal term for the invitation to engage in the bargaining process. Bargaining also involves the making of offers and counter-offers (discussed later).

The law recognizes the necessity for not interfering with this bargaining process. It is only when a definite offer has been made that some very technical rules come into force. If one party wants to get out of the deal, then these laws must be followed strictly.

If you were seriously considering the purchase of a store, for example, you might write to the owner, saying: "I'll buy your business for the asking price of $100,000. But first I want to speak to my accountants and see if they think it's a good idea." This statement is not an offer; it is part of the bargaining process. Depending on the advice you receive from the accountants, you might want to negotiate for certain terms to be included in the deal. Only when you and the seller have agreed on these terms does the process enter the offer stage.

Merchandise on display in a store usually has the price attached. Is the store making an offer by doing so? In fact, the courts consider that the store is making an invitation to treat, or invitation to buy, rather than an offer. It is the customer who decides to make a definite offer to purchase the goods. This rule is designed to protect the merchant, and is known as the "retail sales exception rule."

The same concept applies to goods in advertisements, catalogues, and price lists. Advertising has become so important that it is the subject of special additional rules under the *Competition Act*.

No Duty to Negotiate in Good Faith

There is no duty imposed upon people negotiating to act in good faith. Rather, each party is permitted to try to get the best deal possible for itself. The conduct of business is based on the competition model, and the courts try to preserve competition in business deals. Even when parties agree to negotiate in good faith, courts have said that such a term is not enforceable because it is uncertain.

However, even in competition there are some restrictions, and so there are rules governing the negotiating process. A party cannot, for example, make a false representation, or take advantage of an obvious mistake, or use undue pressure or influence. The principles which apply to the negotiating process are covered in Chapter 7 ("Defects in a Contract and Remedies").

■ *Business Law*   Applied

❾ **Fatima DeSouza** was walking along the main street of town, browsing through a sidewalk sale. Outside a bookstore, she saw a bin filled with books, and a large sign above it.

Great bargains!!!!! $1 each

She searched through the books, and found a very old, yellowed copy of *Alice's Adventures in Wonderland*. DeSouza took the book to the cashier. As she was about to pay for it, the owner of the business saw the book, and took it from her hand, saying, "This is an original edition signed by the author. It's worth thousands of dollars. It got into that bin by mistake. I'm sorry. It's not for sale."

DeSouza claimed the bookstore made an offer, and she accepted it, so there was a binding contract.

a) Did the bookstore have to sell her the book?

Offers

Requirement for an Offer

Once the bargaining stage is over, a contract is formed by final acceptance of an offer. "I'll sell you my car for $10,000" is an offer. "It's a deal" is an acceptance. It is only when the process has reached this point that a contract exists, and the court will enforce the agreement. The owner of the car must sell it for $10,000, even if the individual has a change of mind or receives a better offer from someone else. The purchaser must pay the $10,000, despite any change of mind. Even if the buyer learns one hour later that the same car is available elsewhere for $5,000, the first contract is binding.

Completeness

The parties to an agreement might genuinely believe that they have passed the offer/acceptance stage of the process and thus have a firm, legally binding contract. However, the law says that all essential details must be included in an offer. The essential terms in an offer usually include the price, the terms of payment and the subject matter. It is possible that an offer could seem to be complete with all the essential terms, when in fact it also includes a clause saying that some of these are still open to *negotiation*.

The question of what is an essential term in an offer is a difficult legal problem. If you are involved in a business deal involving a significant amount of money, it is advisable to consult a lawyer before entering into the negotiations, or even have the lawyer assist in the negotiating process.

Offer   The law sometimes uses words in a way that is different from their accepted, everyday meaning. The term **offer** is one such word. For example, when a house is put up for sale, we normally say that the house is offered for sale. While this is quite correct in ordinary language, it is not correct in law. Putting the house on the market is an invitation to treat. Similarly, advertisements in media and displays of merchandise for sale have often been found not to be offers as that term is used in law, but rather mere attempts to induce offers. The study of law involves learning how to classify the same thing using both regular terms and legal terms.

Legalese

offeror

the person who makes an offer

offeree

the person who receives the offer

Offeror   The **offeror** is the person who makes an offer. The **offeree** is the person who receives the offer. Iveta Kuz, the offeror, says to Jean Roget, "I'll buy your car for $10,000 today." Roget, the offeree, receives the offer, but need take no further action.

■ *Critical Concepts of* Offer

- An offer must contain all of the terms that will be included in the contract, so that the other party need merely say, "I accept."
- The essential terms necessary for a contract will vary with the circumstances but they normally are: the parties, the price, the terms of payment, and the subject matter.
- If a term indicates that the party making the offer does not intend to be bound, but may want to negotiate further, there is no offer, but an invitation to treat.

UBS Securities Canada, Inc. v. Sands Brothers Canada, Ltd., 2009 ONCA 328 (CanLII)

UBS Securities Canada is the Canadian branch of a global network of securities dealers and brokers. It has a history of investing in stock exchanges around the world. In 2008 it wanted to increase its holdings in Bourse, the company which operated the Montreal Stock Exchange. Bourse was a privately held company so its shares were not listed on a public exchange and no party was allowed to own more than 10% of the shares. UBS assigned Asheef Lalahi, a UBS portfolio manager, the task of acquiring more Bourse shares for UBS.

After research, Lalahi contacted Steven Sands, a successful U.S. entrepreneur, who owned several investment businesses. Lalahi and Sands had several discussions about the sale of Sand's Bourse shares to UBS. Lalahi indicated UBS was willing to purchase 100,000 shares at a price of $50 per share. Initially Sands declined to sell, but on Nov. 21 2006 in a telephone call Sands agreed to the deal so long as it would close on Jan. 3, 2007 and he could have a "material out" clause that would let him out of the deal if a material event occurred that affected the share price before the closing date.

Lalahi contacted his manager who refused the material out clause. Lalahi then contacted Sands later that day with this information and asked if they had a deal. Lalahi testified Sands agreed and told him to draw up the papers. About 20 minutes after the phone call, Lalahi sent Sands an email dated Nov. 21st 2006, to confirm the sale of 100,000 shares @ $50 Canadian with settlement on Jan. 3, 2007.

On Dec. 11 Bourse announced it would be going public in a few months, and soon after Sands contacted Lalahi and they disagree over whether they had a deal. On Dec. 14 UBS sought a court declaration that there was a valid contract and requested an order of specific performance forcing Sands to complete the sale.

At the trial later that month, the judge ruled there had not been a valid contract formed. That decision was successfully appealed and the case was sent back for a new trial. At the second trial the court ruled that there had been a valid oral contract made on the telephone. The essential terms had been agreed upon, the amount, price and the closing date. The trial court then ordered specific performance, requiring Sands to turn over the shares to UBS. Sands then appealed to the Ontario Court of Appeal.

The Court's Decision

The appeal court agreed with the trial judge. A valid contract had been formed over the telephone. It was customary in the securities industry to make oral agreements and without that custom the securities industry could not operate effectively. An objective reasonable bystander would have concluded that a binding agreement had been made on the telephone. The essential terms had been agreed upon quantity, price and date. The email later that day was not an offer to purchase as Sands had contended; it was a written confirmation of the verbal agreement that had been made on the phone 20 minutes earlier. A written agreement was not necessary to create this contract and there had been a valid offer and acceptance done orally. When Sands refused to sell his shares, he had breached the contract.

The order of specific performance was the proper remedy because at the time of the breach UBS could not purchase other shares in Bourse from another shareholder, so mitigation was not possible. The trial judge's ruling was upheld.

Conditional Clauses   Conditional clauses are sometimes inserted into contracts. These clauses can make an agreement incomplete if they are not worded carefully. They may indicate that a party may want to change, add or delete terms and hence still wants to negotiate. The line between acceptable and unacceptable clauses is fine. The clause "subject to such terms as my solicitor may suggest" has been held to void an offer because it suggests the deal is not complete. The lawyer may suggest new terms. However a term such as, "subject to my solicitor's approval within 2 days" has been held acceptable in that the solicitor will either approve or disapprove of all the terms, but not attempt to change any.

The courts do not require that a written contract has to be flawlessly written, the courts must look at the intention of the parties as a determining factor and rule there is a valid contract despite wording and grammatical errors.

Example: In *Hoban Construction Ltd. v. Alexander*, 2012 BCCA 75 (CanLII), a $1.5 million agreement to sell shares in a forestry products company was very poorly drafted and even signed while one party was standing in a gravel pit. The documents were "inelegantly and inartistically drafted and they contained typographical and substantive mistakes." The seller had even agreed to sell preferred shares even though his shares were common shares. The trial judge ruled that the terms were too vague and uncertain and there was no meeting of the minds, so there was no valid contract.

The appeal court however disagreed. It felt the trial judge had been too concerned with form and should have focussed more on the substance of the agreements. The appeal court admitted the agreements were very badly written and missing some non-essential terms, but an **objective reasonable bystander** would have understood that an agreement had been made. Since the essential terms had been included, and looking at how the parties had performed after the papers were signed, it was clear valid contracts had been formed. It is the court's responsibility to evaluate the parties' true intentions as to the substance of the agreement and to ascribe meaning where possible in the language the parties used, and to resolve any inconsistencies or ambiguities with reference to the other relevant evidence. Even though the grammar and wording posed significant problems, a legal contract was still created.

objective reasonable bystander
What would a reasonable person, who had been eavesdropping on the negotiations, have believed the parties must have agreed to without expressing it

Olivieri v. Sherman
2007 ONCA 491 (CanLII)

Nancy Olivieri was a doctor who had conducted research for Apotex, a Canadian drug company, on a proposed drug, deferiprone. It was to be used to treat children suffering from thalassemia, a blood disorder that required many blood transfusions which resulted in the dangerous build-up of iron in the patients. Olivieri became very concerned over the efficacy and safety of the drug and spoke out about it. Apotex was concerned about her negative statements and eventually stopped the trials of this drug. After considerable media attention given to this drug and the negative statements by both sides, law suits were commenced. Olivieri sued Apotex and its owner Barry Sherman seeking $20 million in damages for defamation and they counter-sued her for $10 million for defamation and injurious falsehood.

The parties with their lawyers then went through mediation and settlement negotiations until finally Apotex made a counteroffer to Olivieri that she accepted. It provided Olivieri would not make any comments that would "disparage" Apotex or the drug and any future opinions about the drug would only occur in "scientific" forums. Soon after the settlement was agreed upon, Apotex denied there was any legal agreement. It claimed that the settlement was conditional upon the two sides agreeing to

specific definitions for the words "disparage" and "scientific." Apotex claimed that since these definitions had not been agreed to, there was no consensus, so no contract had been formed. Olivieri claimed that a legally binding settlement agreement had been created. The trial court ruled in favour of Apotex and Olivieri appealed.

The Court's Decision

The Ontario Court of Appeal ruled that the settlement was a legally binding contract. It noted that for a contract to exist the court must first find that the parties had a mutual intention to create a legally binding contract and had reached agreement on all the essential terms of the settlement. It was a written agreement and should be read objectively.

There was nothing in Apotex's counter-offer that suggested it was subject to a future agreement on the definition of specific terms. There are clear meanings of the two terms in question and elaboration was not necessary. This was not a conditional agreement, as the parties had agreed on all the essential terms. The court ruled that the settlement was an enforceable agreement.

Business Law Applied

⑩ **Rychjohn Investments** negotiated a deal to buy out a tenant's lease on the terms evidenced by this receipt:

Received from _Rychjohn Investments Ltd._
five thousand _____ dollars as down-payment on total
of __$125,000__ _____ for purchase of lease from Hunters Bowl Arena as of May 1, 1977, pending drawing up of legal document.

Ken Hunter
Signature

Rychjohn wants to back out of the deal but the tenant wants to enforce it.

a) Was there an offer by Rychjohn Investments, as the term is defined legally?
b) How might the tenant have protected himself against having the receipt declared not to be an offer, and thus losing the deal?
c) How might Rychjohn have protected itself so that the firm could get out of any agreement to purchase the lease?

Termination of Offers: Acts of the Parties

Offers can be terminated [revoked] by acts of the parties or operation of law. Four ways the parties can end an offer are:

- withdrawal
- written terms of expiry
- rejection of the offer
- counteroffer (which creates a new offer on new terms)

Withdrawing an Offer

revoke
an offer is retracted or withdrawn

An offer can be withdrawn (**revoked**) by the person who made it any time before acceptance.

Example: On Monday Lana says to Kim, "You can buy my car for $10,000. You have until 5 PM this coming Friday to accept." Kim says, "Okay, I'll try and raise the money and let you know by Friday." On Thursday Lana gets an offer for $12,000 and calls Kim and tells him the deal is off and that she sold to another guy.

consideration
each party to a contract must receive something of value (consideration)

Even though Lana said she would keep the offer open, she can withdraw at any time because the offer is not yet a contract. A primary reason is the lack of one of the essential elements of a contract called **consideration**, each party must receive something of value.

irrevocable
an offer that cannot be withdrawn

Irrevocable   **Irrevocable** describes an offer which cannot be revoked or withdrawn. Within the work *revoke* you can see the letters *voke*, which come from *vocal*. *Revoke* literally means to call back. When *ir* is put in front of it, it creates a negative meaning cannot call back.

Option

If however the person who made the offer was paid for an **option** to keep the offer open to a specific date, then they cannot legally revoke it. An option is a new and separate contract to keep an offer open for a specified time in return for consideration, such as money. Money paid for an option is not considered part of the purchase price. So if the offer eventually is rejected by the offeree(the person receiving the offer), the option is not refundable. If the offer is eventually accepted, the money paid for the option is not considered part of the purchase price.

For example in the case above, if Kim had paid Lana $100 to keep the offer open to Friday at 5 p.m. then Lana could not withdraw her offer to Kim before that date.

option
a new and separate contract to keep an offer open for a specified time in return for a sum of money

Stock Options

A form of offer that is playing an increasingly significant role in modern business is the stock, or share, option. In the case of a stock option, a potential purchaser pays the owner of the stock an agreed sum of money. In return, the owner guarantees to keep the buyer's option to purchase open for a given length of time. The money paid is for the option only, and is not applied to the purchase price.

Employers sometimes give employees a stock option on the company's shares as an incentive to encourage good work. If the shares increase in value, the employee stands to gain financially. Stock options such as these are part of an employment contract, and no money is paid for them by the employee.

How Do Stock Options Work?   On January 4, Miller says to Gardi, "Your 500 shares in Apple Computers are selling for $10 each on the stock market today. I'll take a 30-day option to buy your shares at that price, paying you $1000 for the option." Gardi agrees, and Miller hands over $1,000. If, at the end of the 30 days, Miller decides to exercise his option and actually buy the shares, he will pay Gardi $5,000. If Miller decides that he does not want to purchase the shares, he does not receive a refund of his $1,000.

What would persuade Miller to buy Gardi's shares? Consider two possible scenarios:

a) One week after Miller pays for the option to purchase, the price of the shares on the stock market rises to $15. If Miller exercises his option and buys the shares, he will make a profit of $5 a share, a total of $2,500.

b) One week after Miller takes the option, the price of the stock falls to $5 a share. Miller obviously does not buy. He has paid $1,000 for the chance that the stock will go up, and has lost that amount. Gardi has made a profit of $1,000 on the arrangement.

■ *Business Law*   Applied

⑪ Rei-mar Investments Ltd. offered to purchase a business from Mrs. R. E. Christie. The offer contained the clause: "This offer is subject to inspection and purchaser's financial arrangements on or before October 12, 2003."

Rei-mar had difficulty finding financing, and asked that the date by which the inspection must be completed be extended to November 23; the firm also requested the *closing date* should be November 30. In return, it agreed to pay $2,500.

The company needed a second extension of both dates, to December 21 and 27, 2003, respectively. Mrs. Christie agreed, but received no more money.

On November 27, Mrs. Christie wrote to inform Rei-mar that she had cancelled the second extension and had sold the property to another buyer for a far better price.

Rei-mar sued Mrs. Christie for breach of contract.

a) Was Mrs. Christie entitled to cancel the agreement?
b) How might Rei-mar have protected its interests?

■ *Critical Concepts of* *Withdrawing an Offer*

- Even though an offer is made, it can be withdrawn, or revoked, at any time before it is actually accepted.
- Even if an offer contains a term that states it will remain open till a certain time and date, it can still be revoked provided that:
  a) the offer is withdrawn before it has been accepted.
  b) the other party is informed that the offer is no longer valid. The information that the offer has been revoked can be communicated directly or indirectly.
- If an option is paid for(a separate contract to keep an offer open to a specified time), the offer cannot be revoked
- Money paid for an option does not count as part of the purchase price if the offer is accepted, nor is it refunded if the offer is rejected

Standard Offer Terms

While the common law gives rules concerning the termination of offers, most standard form contracts contain a specific clause setting out the time the offer expires, which may vary the common law rules. Thus, any agreement has to be read for this clause. See for example clause no. 1 in the Agreement of Purchase and Sale for a Business at the end of this chapter.

The length of time an offer is kept open depends on various considerations. Purchasers often set out a short time frame, such as two days, in the irrevocability clause. The purchaser may be interested in other properties and will not be free to make an offer on those if the offer is left open for a longer time, say a week.

Sellers have similar concerns. If a seller signs back an offer, the seller will usually give only a day or two for acceptance. "Signing back" an offer means altering the offer presented by changing a term, for example, the price, initialing the change(s), and delivering it to the other party. Otherwise, the seller's property is tied up for a long period. A better offer may come in, but the seller cannot accept until the first prospective purchaser declines the offer.

The first paragraph in the sample agreement for the purchase of a business in Appendix 5,is reproduced below:

> "1. Irrevocability. This Offer shall be irrevocable by the Purchaser until 5 PM on the 1st day of July 2014 after which time, if not accepted, this Offer shall be null and void and the deposit shall be returned to the Purchaser in full without interest."

■ *Business Law* Applied

⑫ **At 3:00 p.m.** on Monday, Dodd offered to sell Dickenson some property, and stated that the offer had to be accepted before 9:00 a.m. the following Friday. However, on Wednesday morning Dodd sold the property to someone else. Dickenson found out about this sale, and put an acceptance in Dodd's hands before the deadline arrived.

  a) Was Dodd legally entitled to revoke the offer before the stated date?
  b) Was the fact that the offer was no longer valid communicated to Dickenson?
  c) If Dickenson had paid $1 to Dodd to keep the offer open until Friday 9:00 a.m. how would this change your answer?

Termination of Offers: By Operation of Law

Offers may also be terminated by operation of law in the following circumstances:

1. After reasonable time, if no time is specified in the offer. What is reasonable will depend on the circumstances of each case.

Example: A purchase of stocks listed on the stock market—that time may be a matter of a few moments. In a real estate deal it may be two to three days. In other circumstances it could be a week.

2. If the subject matter is destroyed through no fault of either party
3. Prior to acceptance of the offer, either the offeror or the offeree dies or becomes incompetent, and
4. Prior to the acceptance of the offer, the object of the offer is made illegal by statute, regulation, court decision or other law.

Example: A distributor has agreed to purchase a product from a supplier. Before the shipping of the product, the government passes a regulation prohibiting the sale of products that contain a chemical which this product has.

Counter-Offer

During the course of negotiating an agreement, the parties involved often put several different positions to one another. An individual might offer to sell a car for $20,000, only to have the potential buyer say, "I'll give you $19,000." The $19,000 thus proposed is a **counter-offer**—the rejection of one offer and the proposal of a new one—and the original offer to sell for $20,000 is ended.

counter-offer
the rejection of one offer and the proposal of a new one

The buyer cannot then insist that the vendor sell at the first offer price of $20,000. The vendor is free to walk away from the deal, as its offer is terminated. Of course, the vendor has a choice and may agree to sell at the first offer price, but it does not have not do so.

Sign Back   A counter-offer in real estate transactions is a called a **sign back**. A seller might list a property for $500,000—this is an invitation to treat.[4] A purchaser then submits an offer for $450,000, and the vendor makes a counter-offer—signs back the deal—at $490,000.

Legalese

■ *Critical Concepts of* Counter-Offers

- ■ When an offer is rejected it is put to an end.
- ■ When a counter-offer is made, it ends the previous offer.
- ■ An acceptance that includes any change in terms is a counter-offer.

■ *Business Law* Applied

⑬ **Lee Tran bought** a new office and warehouse building. It was in a new industrial estate, so the landscaping around the area left something to be desired. He decided to have four 20-foot tall maple trees planted on the north side of the property. He received an offer from Salvia Landscaping that it would supply and plant the trees for $800. Tran replied that he was willing to pay $600.

Salvia Landscaping said that, for $600, it would supply four trees, 15 feet in height.

Tran then said that at that price he would like the four 20-foot tall trees. Salvia Landscaping replied that it was not interested.

At this point, Tran decided that he would accept the offer for four trees, 15-feet tall, at a price of $600.

Salvia Landscaping decided that it didn't want to deal with this client and walked away.

  a) Was Tran legally entitled to accept Salvia's offer of $600 for the four 15-foot trees?
  b) Was Salvia Landscaping in a position simply to opt out of the deal?

---

4. The listing is an invitation to treat because some essential terms, such as the closing date, are not usually mentioned in the listing.

Conditional Offers

Often an offer is conditional on specific criteria first being met. For example, in a real estate deal, the offer often depends on the purchaser's finding the property in good condition after inspecting it, and then obtaining adequate financing for the deal. See the Agreement of Purchase and Sale for a Business in Leased Premises in the Appendix at the end of this chapter for similar conditional clauses.

In buying a building such as a house or a store, the physical condition of the property is extremely important. For that reason, a purchaser is unlikely to finalize the agreement until the structure is inspected by a competent building contractor. When a business is sold, profitability is of major concern. Thus, the purchaser will only finalize a sale agreement when the books and records have been inspected and shown to support the profit level claimed by the seller.

If the interests of both parties are affected by the condition, it cannot be waived by one party alone. This type of condition is called a true condition precedent. If, for example, an agreement to purchase land is made subject to the purchaser obtaining a zoning change within 60 days, and the change is not made in time, the purchaser cannot waive the condition and conclude the deal without the consent of the seller. The courts have held that the seller in this type of situation has an interest affected because it has not been able to sell its property to others for 60 days.

When a conditional offer is accepted, a conditional contract is created. All parties must co-operate in attempting to fulfill conditions.

In real estate take the situation where you want to purchase a new building worth $200,000 for your business. You have enough for a down payment of $100,000 and expect to be able to borrow the balance from a bank on a mortgage. If you sign the agreement to purchase the building and later find out that you cannot get an approval for the mortgage loan, you will be in breach of the contract. At the very least, you will lose your deposit. You have assumed the risk that you will be able to get the loan. If you ask the bank for pre-approval, it may refuse because it may want to get its own appraisal to verify that the property you want to buy is worth what you think it is. However, banks do not readily give pre-approvals in business situations.

A common solution for this problem is for a purchaser to put a conditional clause in the agreement. A typical financing clause follows:

> **Subject to Financing.** This agreement is conditional upon the purchaser being able to raise suitable financing for the balance of the purchase price within 30 days of the acceptance of this offer. If the purchaser is unsuccessful in arranging this financing, then this agreement is null and **void** (never formed in law) and the deposit money is to be returned in full forthwith together with interest, if any, upon receipt of written notice by the purchaser.

void

a contract is not just cancelled as of the date of the court decision, but it is treated as if it had never been made

You can refer to the Agreement of Purchase and Sale for a Business in the Appendix to this chapter for a similar clause in Schedule "A".

The risk for the 30-day time period has shifted to the seller. The property is tied up and the seller cannot accept any other offers, even unconditional offers or offers with a higher price, for that period of time. Thus, before accepting a conditional offer, the seller will want to be as certain as possible that the purchaser is serious about wanting the property and has the creditworthiness to obtain the required financing.

Such a conditional offer is also a risk for the real estate agents (if any): if the purchaser is unsuccessful, the agents probably will not get any commission. The seller gets some assistance from the common law in this situation. There is a duty of good faith in carrying out terms of contracts, so the purchaser must take reasonable and honest steps to obtain financing. The purchaser cannot use this clause as an excuse to get out of the deal, just because, for example, the purchaser has found another property that is more appealing.

Marshall v. Bernard Place Corp., [2002] CanLII 24835 (ON.C.A.)

Mr. and Mrs. Marshall agreed to purchase a home from Bernard Place Corporation for $500,000.00 and gave a deposit of $150,000.00. The Agreement contained the following clause:

"This Agreement is conditional upon the Purchasers obtaining a inspection report satisfactory to them in their sole and absolute discretion."

The Plaintiffs obtained a report that identified several deficiencies which could be repaired at a minor cost. The Plaintiffs refused to close and sued for return of the deposit relying on the above clause. The Defendant claimed that as the deficiencies were minor, the Plaintiffs were not acting in good faith.

The Court's Decision

The clauses drafted gave the Plaintiffs the right to make a subjective decision. There was no restriction saying that minor deficiencies would be acceptable. The wording of the clause permitted the Plaintiffs to assess whether the risks, uncertainties and inconvenience associated with the deficiencies were acceptable according to their own subjective circumstances.

The Defendant was ordered to return the deposit.

While the concept of true condition precedent has been much criticized, it is well entrenched in the law. To give the purchaser the right to waive the condition without the consent of the seller, there must be a phrase to that effect in the contract, for example: "This condition is solely for the purchaser's benefit and can be waived by the purchaser unilaterally." Because it is difficult to tell when the court may find that the vendor had an interest affected by a condition precedent, it is the better practice to add such a phrase to all conditional clauses—assuming the vendor will agree!

Business Alert!

■ *Critical Concepts of* Conditional Offers

- An offer can contain a condition which, if not fulfilled, means the contract will not become an enforceable agreement.
- The party who asked for the condition must act in good faith in trying to fulfill it.
- All parties must co-operate in attempting to fulfill conditions.
- Conditions often require the consent of both parties in order to be waived, unless the contract specifies otherwise.

■ *Business Law* Applied

⓮ a) **Does the *Marshall v. Barnard Place Corporation*** decision permit a purchaser to cancel an agreement with such a clause in it because the market price has dropped? What wording in the decision prevents that from happening?
   b) How could a seller protect itself in negotiations respecting a similar conditional clause?

⓯ **Kumar Sharma made** an offer to buy a house. The offer was conditional on his being able to obtain financing. Before the offer expired, he found another house that was more to his liking, and so made no effort to arrange financing for the first property.

On the day the conditional offer expired, Sharma told the seller that he did not have financing and, since the condition was unfulfilled, the agreement was at an end.

   a) Did Sharma make reasonable efforts to fulfill the condition?
   b) Could he rely on the financing condition to escape from the agreement?

Acceptance

When an offer is accepted, a contract is formed. The deal is legally binding, and will be enforced by the courts.

acceptance

an unqualified and unconditional agreement to the terms of the offer

The **acceptance** must be an unqualified and unconditional agreement to the terms of the offer. This unequivocal acceptance requirement is called "the mirror image rule." This metaphor demonstrates the requirement that the acceptance has to reflect the offer exactly as it is made without variation just like a mirror. You cannot say, "I'll accept if my accountant tells me that your records are in order." If you do, you have not in fact accepted the offer in the eyes of the law, and no contract exists.

Silence is not acceptance. Additionally, the person making the offer cannot impose a term such as "if we do not hear from you, we will assume that you have accepted."

While failing to respond will not be acceptance, silence plus use of the goods could be acceptance by conduct. The court may infer from the use of the goods that the party accepted the deal. Assume a seller sends your business some software indicating that the price is $500. If you do nothing, the seller cannot enforce payment. However, if you use the software, that use is acceptance by conduct and you will have to pay for it.

Recently however there has been some lessening of this strict requirement that acceptance has to be unqualified. When a person accepting said "I accept and want a Release in the standard form" the court said that a minor added term did not violate the acceptance. The acceptor could enforce the terms of the offer but without the added term of the release. (*Perri v. Concordian Chesterfield Company Ltd.*, 2004 CanLII 2904 ON CA)

The problem for a businessperson, however, is to determine; what is a minor additional term. To avoid having to litigate that issue, it is still safer staying within the mirror image rule and accept without adding any terms.

If the contract states that acceptance has to be done in a specific manner, then no contract is formed unless this requirement is fulfilled.

Example: In *Hunter v. Baluke*, 1998 CanLII 14719 (ON SC), hockey player Wayne Gretzky put in an offer to purchase a $1.86 million cottage in Muskoka. After receiving the initial offer, both the buyer and seller wanted to make changes. The deal was to close on January 30th, but the sellers wanted to leave their furniture and boats in the boat house until the spring when the ice was gone. Gretzky wanted to have a longer inspection period, but he did agree to allowing the vendors to leave the furniture and boats in the boat house until the spring. Gretzky initialled these changes on the offer but the vendor never did. The agreement specifically stated that the agreement had to be in writing as was also required by the Statute of Frauds.

The vendor then refused to complete the deal and Gretzky sued for breach of contract and requested specific performance to force the sale of the cottage. The court ruled however that the contract stated the acceptance had to be done in writing and the vendors had not initialled the last changes made by Gretzky. Since these were significant changes and there was no written acceptance as required, a legal contract had not been created, so Gretzky was unable to force the sale of the cottage.

The courts can rule that conduct can be the form of acceptance in some situations. In another hockey example, the General Manager of the Quebec Nordiques had asked other NHL teams to "make him an offer" for Eric Lindros, a number one draft choice who had indicated he would not play for the Nordiques. Many teams proposed a deal to the Quebec GM but he gave vague responses to their offers. He repeatedly told teams there would be no final deal until Lindros's parents agreed and the GM gave the successful bidder the secret Lindros phone number so the successful bidder could speak to Eric's parents. Finally a dispute arose when both the Philadelphia Flyers and the New York Rangers contended that the Nordiques had made a deal with them. The dispute was finally resolved in ADR when an arbitrator ruled that the conduct of giving out the telephone number constituted acceptance. Philadelphia had been given the phone number first so Lindros became a Flyer.

Electronic Acceptance

Some businesses' websites permit persons to create contracts simply by clicking on a graphic. Electronic commerce acts have provided that the "click" is a valid acceptance provided that the software permits the customer to correct any errors.[5]

Sometimes a debtor sends a cheque to a creditor for a lesser amount and writes "accepted in full settlement" on the back of the cheque. The creditor can cash the cheque and still claim the full amount of the loan. Cashing the cheque is consistent with simply taking a payment on the loan; it is not unequivocal acceptance of the term written on the back of the cheque (see *Brilliant Silk Manufacturing Co. v. Kaufman*, [1925] S.C.R. 249). The creditor would be well advised to write a letter at the time of cashing the cheque indicating that it has accepted the payment as a part payment.

Business Alert!

■ *Critical Concepts of* Acceptance

- Acceptance must be communicated to the other party and must be unconditional.
- Generally, silence cannot be acceptance.
- Acceptance can be by word—"I'll take it"—or by conduct. Acceptance by conduct might be as simple as using a product rather than returning it immediately.

Negative Option Marketing

In the simplest of terms, negative option marketing means that a firm presents its customers with a product, and says, "You're stuck with this deal unless you notify us you don't want it." Such techniques are illegal in many provinces under censure protection legislation. You can check your provincial government website for the rule in your province.

■ *Business Law* Applied

⑯ Juan Rodriguez, who lived in a province where negative option marketing was legal, signed an agreement with a book club. One term of it read:

Subscriber agrees that the club will send notices of a new book at the beginning of each month. Subscriber must mail rejection by the 15th of the month or subscriber will be deemed to have accepted the book of the month.

a) Was this term enforceable by law?

⑰ A purchaser sends its purchase order to a vendor requesting 50 kilograms of sulphuric acid. On the reverse side of the purchase order, the purchaser says that the vendor is to insure all goods in transit.

The vendor send back its confirmation order form which says (on the back) that the purchaser is to insure all goods in transit.

The purchaser then sends a deposit, the goods are shipped, and the purchaser accepts delivery. Later, it is discovered that the acid strength is weak and unusable because of improper care during shipping.

a) What are the legal terms for the submission of the purchase order, the sending of the confirmation, and the sending of the deposit money?
b) Assume the shipping company has a valid exemption clause absolving it from liability for the damaged acid. Who bears the loss as between the vendor and the purchaser?

---

5. *Electronic Commerce Act*, 2000, S.O. 2000, c. 17; *The Electronic Commerce and Information Act*, C.C.S.M., c. E150.

Acceptance Scams

Acceptance by conduct has been abused in the past by some firms who sent unsolicited credit cards, books, and other items in the mail. The common law rule is that if these items were in fact used by the recipient, then that use is acceptance by conduct. Consumers were liable to pay for the goods even though they didn't ask for them in the first place.

Some provincial governments have enacted legislation to control this type of marketing. The laws vary greatly from province to province, and some have none dealing with this activity. In Ontario, the law is that the recipient can treat items received in this way as gifts, and is not liable to pay for them. In British Columbia, unsolicited credit cards can be used and the recipient will not be charged for the expenditures made on them.

Contact the consumer affairs branch of the provincial government to find out what the laws are in your province.

The Battle of the Forms

Acceptance by conduct as it relates to a business has resulted in what has been called the "battle of the forms."

Form 1: You own a business and, with legal advice, have created a purchase order that outlines specific terms. Using this form you order goods from one of your suppliers.
Form 2: The supplier sends you a sales confirmation, using its standard sales order. The reverse of this form also sets out a list of terms. The goods are then shipped. You accept them, and place them on display in your store.

Each form was created by lawyers; each described specific terms and conditions. Which set of conditions is legally enforceable?

- When you sent the purchase order, you made an offer for the goods described on it
- The supplier sent a sales confirmation, and thus made a counter-offer
- You received the shipment and put the items on the shelves of your store, thereby showing acceptance by conduct of the counter-offer

So, the terms printed on your supplier's sales confirmation order are the terms of the contract; your purchase-order terms are of no effect under law. The last form that is exchanged usually governs.

The Formation of a Contract

There are four steps to the formation of a contract to sell/purchase a business

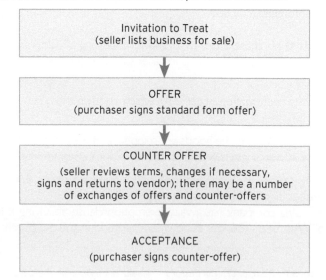

Cooling-Off Periods

When an agreement is accepted, it is binding. There is no general rule that allows a party to change its mind and back out of the deal-without, of course, legal consequences. There is no cooling-off period for any business agreement. There are circumstances under consumer protection legislation that permit a person to cancel the contract. A **cooling-off period** is a specified time after a contract is made during which a buyer may terminate the contract by giving written notice to the seller. One cooling-off period relates to what are called "direct sales" contracts made by door-to-door salespersons. The purchaser has a short time to cancel this agreement. The salesperson must give a written copy of the agreement to the purchaser. This cooling-off period applies to contracts for both goods and services. The notice of cancellation must be given in writing.

Unfortunately, there are many small differences among all the provincial consumer protection acts—such as, how long you have to cancel the contract (it varies from two to 10 days), and from when the time period starts. A call to your local consumer affairs department is necessary to check the details for your particular province. You will find these departments very helpful in dealing with consumer law matters.

There is also a cooling-off period, usually of 10 days, for any purchase of a new condominium or time-share arrangement in Ontario and British Columbia. Consumer protection laws are relevant if the business deals with consumers. However, when a business deals with another business, the general rule that there is no cooling-off period applies. In Ontario there is a 10 day cooling off period for contracts for personal development services such as fitness clubs, dance lessons, martial arts lessons and modelling contracts as well as pre-paid funerals and the direct sales contracts. There is a 2 day cooling off period for pay day loan agreements in Ontario as well. The cooling off period allows you to get out of the contract even if you have paid and used the good or service, but you must notify the company in writing within the cooling off period.

Intention

The parties to an enforceable contract must have intended from the start of the process that legal obligations would result from their agreement.

The test to decide whether the parties intended to be legally bound is from the point of view of the promisee (the person who receives the promise). The courts ask, "Would an objective reasonable person hearing the promise assume that the promisor (the individual making the promise) intended to be bound?"

When the promise is made between family members or friends, the court assumes they do not intend to be legally bound. If these parties can produce evidence of their serious intention though, such as a formal written agreement, then the presumption will be ignored and a legal contract may be established. In commercial situations, courts have the opposite presumption. The court assumes that promises between business people were serious and meant to be enforced as a valid contract. Only if there is sufficient evidence to prove there was no serious intention will the court override the presumption and decide no valid contract was formed, even though the promise was made in a commercial setting.

Another situation where the courts assume there is no serious intention involves broad exaggerated advertising claims by companies. When a company claims its product is the "best or cleanest or most refreshing," or other boastful statements, the court categorizes this as mere advertising "puff" and assumes the company did not intend to be seriously bound by these claims. If a company however makes a more serious statement, such as "we will refund your money if you are not completely satisfied," this would be seen as indicating a serious intention to form a contract. If the customer is not satisfied, they would be entitled to a refund.

The law does recognize what in former times was called a "gentleman's agreement." This meant neither party would sue if the other broke his promise. So, parties can specify that their agreement is not to be enforced in the courts.

cooling-off period
a specified time after a contract is made during which a buyer may terminate the contract by giving written notice to the seller

An example of such an agreement is a letter of comfort. A bank may require a parent company to give a letter of comfort to support a subsidiary company's application for credit. The comfort letter is phrased in terms similar to a guarantee but says it is given as comfort only. It is not enforceable. If the subsidiary defaults on its loan, the bank cannot sue the parent on the letter of comfort. For this reason, these letters are often called "cold comfort."

■ *Critical Concepts of* Intention

- Courts assume that parties to an agreement intend to be bound by it.
- In family and social agreements, the court assumes that the parties do not intend to be legally bound.
- Advertising claims by companies that are just boastful "puff" of their product do not indicate a serious intention to be bound
- Individuals can state in the agreement that they do not intend to be legally bound, and therefore no contract or enforceable agreement has been created.

Letters of Intent—Memorandum of Understanding

It is common business practice to use a letter of intent to set out the intentions of both parties involved in an agreement. This document is not itself a contract, but describes what the individuals are willing to agree about. One of the parties, for example, may have to seek budget-committee approval because the arrangement involves a new project. It is understood that neither side has an intention to create legal relations or a contract at that time, but that negotiations might well lead to that end. Probably, it would be clearer if the document were called a "Letter of Intent Only." Likely because of the misleading meaning of the term "Letter of Intent," the more common practice today is to call it a Memorandum of Understanding (MOU).

NEW DISCOUNT CAR RENTAL
23 Crow Trail Drive
Calgary, Alberta

August 31, 2002

Dear Jim:

Letter of Intent

This letter is an indication by New Discount that it is interested in having you as a franchisee with a location possibly at the Newgate Plaza. The contemplated terms are an initiation fee of $30,000, royalties and advertising contributions of 6% of gross sales, and other terms as set out in our standard franchise agreement.

Please return our confidential questionnaire a.s.a.p. so we can have the usual credit checks, etc. done.

This letter indicates our intent, and is not binding.

Yours truly,

NEW DISCOUNT CAR RENTAL
Per:

Ali Rashid

Ali Rashid
Vice President, Franchising

A letter of intent drafted by a business. It indicates that a contract has not yet been concluded.

Objective Test   The phrase **objective test** is frequently used in law. It means that the court does not try to discover the actual intentions of the person at the time in question, but instead asks what a reasonable person might think in similar circumstances.

The decision the court reaches is a matter of fact, not of law. Where juries are available in civil matters, the decision is left to the jury and not to the judge. To see how this works, take an in-class vote to determine how many people think that a reasonable person would have expected Torres (p. 166) to be legally bound by his promise.

■ *Business Law*   Applied

⑱ **Nicole Cormier and** Valentino Torres were at the local variety store. Each of them bought a lottery ticket, agreeing that if either won, they would split the winnings.

Two days later, Torres discovered he had won $1,000,000. When Cormier asked for her share, Torres said that it was just a friendly arrangement and that he did not intend to be legally bound.

 a) Was Torres legally bound to share his winnings?
 b) Would a reasonable person have believed that Torres intended to be legally bound at the time that he made the agreement?

⑲ **Giovanna Genat was** keen to run her own doughnut shop, and signed a franchise agreement with a large organization. The agreement was eight pages long, and contained the following term:

23. The franchisee [here, Genat] hereby agrees and accepts that the franchisor does not intend to be legally bound by this agreement and the franchisee relinquishes any right to enforce any **covenants** [terms of agreement] contained in this agreement by action, suit, or other means.

covenants
terms of agreement

Another clause in the agreement said that the franchisor would provide advertising support, paid for in part by a monthly percentage of Genat's business profits. After a few months in operation, she thought that the franchisor was not living up to his side of the agreement to provide advertising, and she decided to sue.

 a) According to the law regarding the intention to create legal relations, could the franchisor rely on paragraph 23, above, to prevent Genat from winning a suit against him?

The Fine Print   In the franchise case (above), Genat would likely be bound by the term in the agreement that states the franchisor could not be sued on the intention to create legal relations principle. However, this is not the only principle of law that might apply in such a situation. Often, there are several possible remedies available.

The practical point for you as a business person is to recognize that such clauses do exist in these long printed forms. The agreements therefore should not be signed without the advice of a lawyer.

Consideration

Not all agreements or promises are enforceable, since not all are contracts. To be regarded as a contract that is enforceable by a court, the promise must be supported by consideration, or be given in writing under seal.

Consideration is given in exchange for a promise. The consideration must be given by the promisee to the person who makes the promise (the promisor).

What Is Consideration?

The consideration can be anything of value in the eyes of the law usually money or services, and the amount is not important. One early judge said that if the value given was equal to that of a peppercorn, that would be enough to support a contract. An exchange of mutual promises is adequate consideration. Judges will not let a person out of a contract because that individual has made a bad bargain. However, the aggrieved party may have other remedies, such as misrepresentation, duress and the like, discussed in Chapter 7.

gratuitous promise
a promise for which no consideration is given

A **gratuitous promise** is a promise for which no consideration is given, and is not a contract. Such an agreement will not be enforced by the courts. The requirement of consideration means that courts will more often find promises enforceable in commercial situations than in family or social agreements. For example, if a contractor (the promisor) says, "I'll paint your house," and the owner (the promisee) replies, "I'll pay you $5,000 for the job," the $5,000 is consideration for the promise to paint the house, and the contract is enforceable.

If however the contractor says that he would paint the house for free, there would not be a valid contract as the contractor is not receiving any consideration. The courts also do not inquire into the amount or fairness of the consideration that is given. If the contractor said that he would paint the house for $70, even though it is a job worth $5,000, the court would not change the price to $5,000 or something near its real value. By getting $70 the contractor is receiving "something of value", (even though not very much), so the consideration requirement is met.

■ *Critical Concepts of* Consideration

- Consideration is anything of value given or promised in exchange for the promise sought to be enforced.
- The courts will not inquire into the adequacy of consideration. It need not be fair or equivalent to the value received.

Legalese

Consideration   **Consideration** derives from the same word as the term *consider*, which means to mentally weigh the merits of an issue, or in other words to take it seriously. The paying of something of value indicates that you have considered the matter and are agreeing to be bound.

■ *Business Law* Applied

⑳ **Jana Taddeo tells the Red Cross**, "If I pass my final exams, I'll give $5,000 to the Red Cross." In fact, she passed all her exams with excellent marks—but did not give the money to the Red Cross.

a) Could the Red Cross sue to have the agreement enforced under law?

Past and Future Consideration

past and future consideration
past consideration is not valid consideration, but future consideration is valid

For consideration to be valid the "value" must occur in the present or in the future. Past consideration is not valid consideration because when it was given there was no contract in place. The courts will not allow the parties to take an event from the past that was not part of a contract when it occurred and use it as consideration for a valid contract being made in the present or to be performed in the future.

Example: Ann went on vacation in July and her neighbour Paul said he would water her flowers while she was gone and Paul did. The following December Paul was going on vacation and Ann said that while he was gone she would shovel his snow because he had been kind enough to water her flowers last summer. If Ann does not shovel Paul's snow while he is away, Paul cannot sue Ann for breach of contract. At the time they made an agreement in December, Paul was getting something of value, (his snow shovelled), but Ann was not getting anything of value. She was in the same position as she was before they made the December deal. Past consideration is not valid consideration now. Paul cannot use the watering from the summer as valid consideration now, because when it occurred it was not considered to be part of a contract.

If however Ann promised to shovel Paul's snow in December and in return Paul would cut her grass in the following July, that would be a valid contract. Each party would be getting something of value in the present or in the future. Future consideration is valid consideration, but not past consideration.

Existing Legal Obligations

Additionally, an agreement to continue to perform a contract is not viewed as consideration. This problem has arisen most frequently in the construction industry. For example, an electrical subcontractor may know that a general contractor is desperate to have the electrical system completed so it can get the last payment from the property owner. This subcontractor purposely delays and then demands extra payment to meet the contract deadline. The contractor agrees to pay the extra amount because it will be penalized by the owner if there is a delay.

There is no consideration for this agreement to pay the extra money because the subcontractor was already obligated by its contract to meet the deadline.

Businesses aware of this legal loophole will offer to do slightly more work at minimal cost, which is consideration, or to have the new agreement put under seal. However, this type of agreement may also be attacked on the grounds of economic duress, which is discussed in Chapter 7.

Gilbert Steel Ltd. v. University Construction Ltd., 1976 CanLII 672 (ON CA)

Gilbert Steel agreed to supply steel to University Construction at a price specified in a written contract for a specified project. The price of steel rose after the construction project had started. Representatives of University Construction met with representatives of Gilbert Steel. University Construction orally agreed to a higher price requested by Gilbert Steel. When Gilbert Steel sent its bills, University Construction paid at the old price. Gilbert Steel sued on the oral agreement claiming it either varied the original contract or replaced it as a new one. University Construction never denied it had promised to pay the increased price, it just believed that legally that promise was unenforceable.

The Court's Decision

The Court found that there was no consideration for the oral agreement. Gilbert Steel was already obligated to supply the steel, the only change was an increase in the price, which was agreed to without any consideration [value] given by Gilbert Steel to University Construction, so University Construction did not have to pay the price increase it had agreed to.

■ *Business Law* Applied

21. a) Which party assumed the risk of rising steel prices in the contract to supply in the Gilbert Steel v. University Construction case?
    b) Was there anything that Gilbert Steel could have done to protect itself from rising steel prices?
    c) Draft such a clause.
    d) Do you think the result in the Gilbert Steel case was fair given that steel prices did increase? Could Gilbert Steel have used fairness as a ground to uphold the variation of the contract?
    e) Why do you think University Construction agreed to the oral variation but then paid according to the old agreement?

■ *Critical Concepts of* What Is Not Consideration

- Past consideration is not consideration for later terms in a contract, but future consideration is valid.
- A promise to continue to perform a contract is not consideration.

Agreements Enforceable without Consideration

Agreements under Seal

seal

if a contract has a seal on it then consideration is not an issue

In earlier times even members of the ruling classes were often illiterate; some could not even write their own names, but could indicate that they had agreed to a contract only by placing their seal on the it. The seal was made by dripping red wax on the document. Then the person pressed the **seal**, often a signet ring, into the wax. Even after people could sign their names, the practice of using a seal on a document continued. The seal was taken as an indication that the person intended to be legally bound. In such a case consideration is not needed. The seal is sufficient evidence of intent to be bound.

You can experience the effect of the legal seal. If a document were put in front of you to sign with a red seal on it, would it make you more cautious about signing it?

The use of a wax seal became obsolete; a small red paper seal replaced it. On today's standard form documents, sometimes the seal is simply shown as a black circle. Even this printed seal is considered a legal seal and will make the document enforceable without consideration.

Promissory Estoppel

promissory estoppel

a remedy against a person who made a promise without giving any consideration for it, often used when a creditor waives strict compliance with payment dates and then notifies the debtor in default for not making timely payments

There is another exception to the concept of consideration in addition to documents under seal. It is called promissory estoppel, and is also known as detrimental reliance or the invisible handshake. **Promissory estoppel** is a remedy against a person who made a promise without giving any consideration for it, often used when a creditor waives strict compliance with payment dates and then notifies the debtor in default for not making timely payments. It was created to prevent injustice caused by the strict application of the doctrine of consideration. It can be formed by words or conduct.

■ *Critical Concepts of* Promissory Estoppel

Promissory estoppel has three factors. It is a promise
- which the **maker** (the party who signs and delivers a promissory note) should realize would induce the hearer to rely upon it.
- on which the hearer does actually rely, and
- that reliance is to the hearer's detriment.

The Limits of Promissory Estoppel   Promissory estoppel has certain limits. For example, a creditor may accept a late payment on one occasion. This does not mean that the creditor has created a promissory estoppel and the debtor can pay late again. In a commercial situation, this is considered a mere indulgence on the part of the creditor, and is not assumed to be a promise to waive strict compliance of the contract. Creditors must clearly and unambiguously indicate their intention to waive strict compliance of the contract. While late acceptance on one occasion may not be sufficient, a continuous acceptance of late payments over a period of time may satisfy the conditions for promissory estoppel. If the creditor wishes to resume strict compliance, it would have to give adequate notice to the debtor.

Canada (Attorney General) v, Adamoski
2004 BCCA 625 (CanLII)

David Adamoski had attended the University of British Columbia for 5 years and by the time he had left school his student loan totalled $23,805. He was required to make monthly payments of $326.01 including interest at 10.125% per annum. Adamoski had failed to make complete payments in the first six months, so the Government of Canada turned the debt over to a collection agency to recover the money.

For over 5 years Adamoski made payments that he could, but by then he felt his financial position was bleak, so he decided to make a consumer proposal under the *Bankruptcy and Insolvency Act*. He informed the collection agency of this and said he would continue to make payments if his proposal was rejected.

The proposal was rejected and Adamoski then sent four cheques of $100 each to the collection agency. The cheques were never cashed nor returned. Finally the collection agency called him to tell him to stop sending cheques as the debt no longer existed. He also got a letter from the Canada Student Loans office that showed his student loan account owed no more money. The court found that the collection agency and the government had wrongfully concluded Adamoski had gone bankrupt. Then 2½ years later a different collection agency contacted him saying he owed money on the student loan. Adamoski sent them the government letter stating the debt had been extinguished. Finally 18 months later, the Government of Canada commenced legal action to get the money owed.

Adamoski claimed that he had relied on the statements by the collection agency and the government that the debt had been extinguished, so on the basis of promissory estoppel the govern-

ment could no longer demand payment. The government claimed that Adamoski had not relied on their statements to his detriment and promissory estoppel could not be used to prevent the government from its duty to collect student loan debts. The trial court accepted the promissory estoppel argument and ruled Adamoski did not owe the government any money. The government appealed.

The Court's Decision

The B.C. Court of Appeal ruled that promissory estoppel did apply. It stated the principles the Supreme Court established: *The party relying on the doctrine must establish that the other party has, by words or conduct, made a promise or assurance which was intended to affect their legal relationship and to be acted on. Furthermore, the representee must establish that, in reliance on the representation, he acted on it or in some way changed his position.*

The court ruled Adamoski had relied on the government's statement that the debt was extinguished, as he had not chosen to declare bankruptcy in recent years which he could have done. He had relied and acted on the government's statements. The government's duty to collect student loan debts only requires it to take reasonable steps, which is had done when it hired the initial collection agency. Pursuing a debt that for over 4 years it had insisted was extinguished was not required. Adamoski had ordered his financial affairs and not declared bankruptcy based on the notice his student loan was cancelled, so his detrimental reliance was established. The government was therefore estopped from claiming the balance of the student loan debt.

For an example of a clause relevant to estoppel see paragraph 9 of the Purchase Order in the Appendix to Chapter 8.

Promissory estoppel in Britain does not allow a party to create a new cause of action, it can only be used as a defence, or as a British judge famously said: it can only be used as a "shield not as a sword."[6] Canadian courts have also adopted the British approach that it can only be used as a defence (a shield). In *Adamoski*, promissory estoppel was used as a defence to not have to pay the student loan debt. In the *Gilbert Steel* case previously discussed though, a promissory estoppel argument was not successful as a basis for its claim to get the increased payments the construction company had promised. The court said Gilbert Steel was using promissory estoppel as a sword (the basis of a claim) and not as a shield(a defence), so the steel company failed in its promissory estoppel claim.

Estoppel **Estoppel:** a means to barring or precluding. The word *stop* drives from the same source, *estoper* (Old French), and it can be seen in the term *estoppel*.

Legalese

6. Combe v. Combe, [1951] 1 All E.R. 767 (C.A.)

㉒ **Deluxe French Fries** Ltd. sold frozen french fries and other frozen vegetable products to Maxim Fine Dining, an upscale restaurant. Maxim had been in business for over two years. Deluxe's purchase order required that payment be made on delivery, but Deluxe had never insisted on timely payment during the two years that it had done business with Maxim.

Growing tired of delays in payment, on one delivery Deluxe insisted on immediate payment from Maxim. Maxim's manager did not have a cheque available, because the office was locked, and so Deluxe refused to leave the order. Maxim could not serve any meals that night and sued for the loss of the night's profit and for damage to its reputation.

a) When did the contractual terms require that payment be made?
b) Was there any consideration given by the restaurant to Deluxe for the right to pay late? Why is consideration an important factor?
c) Is there any basis in which Maxim can establish a variation of the contractual term? What elements must be established?
d) What could Deluxe have done, if anything, to legally require payment on delivery on the occasion mentioned in the question?

In Summation

The Contract

■ A contract is an agreement containing certain key factors which, if present, make it enforceable in law. Those factors are:

Written Requirement and Oral Contracts

■ Most contracts do not have to be in writing to be valid, oral contracts are legal, but not advisable as written proof of the terms can prevent future disputes over what had been agreed upon

■ Different statutes do require certain contracts to be in writing to be enforceable, but this varies among the provinces

■ Some of the contracts that some provinces require to be in writing include: interests in land(such as the sale or mortgage on real property), third party guarantees of a debt, marriage or cohabitation agreements, insurance and financial contracts involving credit and interest calculations

■ Consumer protections laws in some provinces require other contracts to be in writing such as direct sales, time share condominiums and personal development contracts such as fitness clubs and dance lessons

Capacity

■ An individual must be able to understand the nature of the business agreement being entered into. In certain instances, the law recognizes that a person may lack this capacity, and will not allow the contract to be enforced against that person. These instances include:
a) Minors. A contract with a person under the age of majority is generally not enforceable, whether the other party to the contract is aware of the minor's age or not. An exception to this rule exists if the contract is for necessities. In this situation, the minor will be responsible for paying a reasonable price for the goods or services received.
b) Mentally incompetent and intoxicated persons. A contract will be unenforceable if the impairment is serious enough to affect an individual's understanding, and the other party was aware

of the incapacity at the time the contract was signed. The condition of being impaired is the key, and not the means by which the impairment has been caused. An exception exists for contracts providing necessities to the impaired person.

Legality

- A contract will be considered illegal and unenforceable if its purpose is contrary to the interest of society (public policy) or the result will break the law (statutory illegality).

- Illegal contracts are divided into two categories: those that are wrong in and of themselves (criminal wrongs), and those that are wrong only because they are prohibited by statute.

- If the contract involves a matter that is only wrong because it is prohibited by statute, the contract may be enforced if the party who violated the statute shows that it had no intention to do so and corrects the violation before the contract is completed.

- Contracts involving restrictions on a person's ability to earn a living often arise on the sale of a business or when an individual is employed, and are considered contrary to public policy. Contracts of this nature may be enforceable provided the restriction is reasonable, based on factors of time, geography, and content.

Consensus

- Consensus means the parties have reached a final agreement and a contract is created. Consensus is arrived at through the bargaining process of negotiation, offer, and unconditional acceptance of the offer. (**Negotiation** is direct communication between the parties to agree on a contract, or efforts to resolve disputes without third-party intervention.)

- Unless a separate contract is made to keep an offer open for a particular period of time, an offer must come to an end at some point. This may occur in one of several ways, including lapse of time, expiry of a time limit, the making of a counter-offer, or the withdrawal of the offer prior to unconditional acceptance occurring.

- In general, a contract is not completed until acceptance is communicated to the person who made the offer.

negotiation
direct communication between the parties to agree on a contract, or efforts to resolve disputes without third-party intervention

Intention

- It is assumed that parties to a contract intended to create an enforceable agreement. Whether the intention was present or not is viewed from the eyes of a reasonable person receiving the offer. It is presumed that in circumstances such as advertisements and family agreements, such intention is lacking.

- Parties can put a term into an agreement indicating that it is not to be enforced as a contract. The courts will then not enforce the agreement.

- For door-to-door sales, there is a cooling-off period, the length of which varies by province. During this time, a contract may be cancelled without legal consequences.

Consideration

- Consideration is anything of value. It is the price for which the promise or act of the other party is bought.

- The courts will not look at the adequacy of consideration and will not let a person out of a contract because of a poor bargain.

- Past consideration and a promise to perform an obligation under a contract are not viewed as consideration for a new term or contract. Future consideration is legal consideration though.

- Consideration will not be required in documents under seal or where promissory estoppel can be established.

- Promissory estoppel occurs when one party to a contract does or says something that it should realize that the other party may rely upon, and upon which that other party does rely, to its detriment.

- Promissory estoppel may occur when a party waives strict compliance with the terms of the contract, such as the terms of payment. But a mere indulgence will be assumed in commercial situations.

Closing Questions

Written Requirement and Oral Contracts

1. Kenneth wanted to borrow $25,000 from the TD Bank to purchase a new car. The TD Bank told Kenneth that it would not lend him the money unless he got someone else to guarantee the loan if Kenneth did not make the payments. Kenneth spoke to his older sister Maggie who called the TD Bank and assured the manager she would pay if Kenneth missed his car loan payments. About 10 months later Kenneth lost his job and stopped making payments on the loan, so the TD Bank contacted Maggie for the loan payments. Maggie does not want to have to make Kenneth's payments but the bank insists she is liable for the money.
   a) Will a court force Maggie to make the car loan payments for Kenneth? Explain your answer.

2. On June 1st Jill agreed to sell her condo to Sam for $200,000 over the telephone. The two sides knew each other well and Sam had been to Jill's condo many times. The deal was to close on July 15th. After the phone call Sam sent her a cheque for $20,000 and said he would give Jill a certified cheque for the balance of $180,000 on the closing date. On July 10th Sam called Jill to tell her he would not be buying her condo. Jill was furious and told Sam that she would be suing him for breach of contract.
   a) Will Jill succeed if she sued Sam for breach of contract? Discuss the legal issues involved.

Capacity

3. Boris Ivanovich, aged 17, was accepted as a student at the Cabbage Town School of Welding. Tuition was $3,000 for the term. Because Ivanovich had limited funds, the school agreed to let him pay $200 at the commencement of the term, with the balance to be paid on completion of the course. At the end of the term, Ivanovich refused to pay the balance of the tuition, and requested the return of his $200 because he was a minor.
   a) Would the Cabbage Town School of Welding be successful if it sued Ivanovich for the balance of the tuition owing?
   b) Would your answer be any different if Ivanovich could produce evidence that two other welding schools in the same city have an average tuition fee of $2,200?
   c) If the manuals and textbooks for the welding course had cost $300, and the same books were used by the other welding schools, would Ivanovich be required to pay that amount over and above the tuition?
   d) If instead of the Cabbage Town School of Welding, Ivanovich had attended the Northern School of Origami (Japanese Paper Folding), would the school be successful in suing for the balance of his tuition?

4. Eighteen-year-old Vadim Maclinsky had spent the early part of the afternoon in a Vancouver park drinking half a bottle of scotch, and watching people in-line skate along the paths. After leaving the park, Maclinsky wandered into a sporting goods store, where he saw a wall display of in-line skates. When a salesperson approached, Maclinsky explained, his speech slurred, that he lived four miles from where he worked, and there was no direct bus connection between his apartment and workplace. He thought the skates would help him get to work faster, probably cutting his travel time in half, and he wouldn't have to pay bus fare anymore.
   The salesperson handed Maclinsky a roll of mints, said, "Do something about your breath," and suggested he try the $900 pair of skates. Maclinsky slumped into a chair, his eyes glazing over, while the salesperson fitted the skates and tied up the laces. The young man staggered to his feet, shakily rolled 10 feet across the floor and into a wall, and then said: "This is gonna be great. I'll take them." He handed over his credit card and the salesperson completed the transaction.
   Next day, Maclinsky was at the store's door when it opened and handed the skates back to the salesperson. He demanded a credit be put on his credit card, saying, "I took law in high school and I didn't have the capacity to make this contract."
   a) On what grounds would Maclinsky argue that he did not have capacity to enter into the contract?
   b) Which of these would you recommend he use? Why?

Legality

5. Assume an unmarried woman signs an agreement to be a "gestation mother" for a married couple that cannot have a child. A gestation mother carries another woman's fertilized egg to birth. The "mother" is implanted with an egg from the wife which has been fertilized by her husband's sperm in a test tube. The married couple agreed to pay the woman $10,000 for the service, and they actually paid the money. After birth the gestation mother does not want to give up the child to the couple. The couple wants the court to order that she do so, or return the $10,000.
   a) What principle of contract law would be applied and with what result?
   b) Do you think matters such as custody of a child should be determined by contract law?
   c) Should gestation-mother contracts be enforceable? What problems might occur? Do you think women in low-income groups or in Third World countries might be exploited?

6. Apprentice Industries has replaced much of their office equipment and have agreed to sell the used equipment to Kurtz Liquidators for $20,000. Kurtz has given a deposit of $5,000. Both parties have agreed that nothing would be put in writing and the deal would be all cash to avoid paying the GST. Apprentice Industries has found a use for its used equipment and now does not want to go through with the deal. It refuses to return the money and Kurtz wants to sue for his deposit.
   a) What legal defences can Apprentice Industries raise?

7. Arc Industries wants to buy a used truck from the Depot of Reliable Repos. It obtains a six-month complete warranty. The sale price is $20,000, but the Depot sales rep says, "Arc can have it for $15,000, if $5,000 is 'under the table' money."
   Arc agrees. One month later, the truck has serious problems and the Depot refuses to honour its warranty. Arc wants to sue. What defences might the Depot raise and with what result?

8. Thelma Eisenstein and Louis Leforge had been arguing for several months over who had the faster car. Feeling absolutely certain of his ability to win, Leforge proposed a race from Saskatoon to Nanaimo, B.C.—the winner to receive ownership of Leforge's vintage 1965 Mustang convertible. Eisenstein agreed, and the race took place.
   Eisenstein won, and asked Leforge to transfer ownership of the Mustang. He reneged on the agreement, believing that Eisenstein could not enforce it, in spite of her threats to take him to court.
   a) Explain the arguments that would be presented by both Eisenstein and Leforge about the enforceability of this contract.
   b) Which argument do you think would be successful?

9. Contracts that are illegal, and those that are against the public good, will not be upheld by the courts. Decide which category each of the following falls into. A contract:
   a) to employ an illegal immigrant
   b) for the sale of a business in which the seller agrees never to enter into a competing business
   c) in which an employee agrees never to work for any competitor of the current employer
   d) in which an employer agrees not to report to the police acts of theft by his employee

10. Sylvia Park owned a very successful retail clothing store, located on a main street in Sydney, Nova Scotia. On selling the business she signed an agreement that contained a term stating she would not become involved in a similar business anywhere in Canada for a period of five years.
   a) Which principles of the law relating to restraint of trade should be applied here?
   b) Is this restrictive clause valid?

11. Rasa Persaud, a professional engineer, was an estimator with Foundation Consulting Engineers in the borough of Alandale. Her job was to predict the cost of certain construction projects, which involved calculating the cost of supplies such as steel and concrete, as well as the cost of labour.
   Her work meant she learned how to complete the estimates, and which were the best sources of supply for various types of materials. Persaud worked exclusively in the firm's offices and had no direct contact with the suppliers or clients. Her employment contract stated that for a period of five years after she left the firm she would not "engage in the professional practice of an engineer either alone or in association with, or as an employee of any persons within Alandale, or two miles thereof."
   Alandale has a mix of industrial parks and residential areas, and is part of the largest metropolitan area in the province. There were two other firms of engineering consultants in the borough, and 100 more in the whole metropolitan area.

Persaud decided to open her own business as a professional engineer, specializing in estimating. Her firm would be based in Alandale. Accordingly, she advised her former employer that she did not view the restrictive clause in her contract as being enforceable. Foundation Consulting Engineers sued Persaud to obtain a court order to stop her from breaking the contract.
   a) Does the law initially presume that the restrictive clause in Persaud's contract is valid?
   b) What factors must the employer prove to have the restrictive term upheld.
   c) What case discussed in the text could Persaud rely on to support her position?

12. In the cases of *Payette v. Guay* and *Lyons v. Multari* different results occurred with non-competition clauses. Explain why the clause was enforceable in the Guay case but not the Multari case?

Consensus

13. What is the "legal term" for the "business term" sign back?

14. Sally Bernstein went into a clothing store where she had never shopped before. Immediately, she saw a dress—exactly what she was looking for—lying on a chair among several other outfits. Another woman, obviously a very fussy but long-time customer whom the assistants knew well, was examining them. When the first customer went into the changing room, Bernstein took the dress she liked to the cashier, and said she wanted to buy it.
   a) Is the store required in law to sell the dress to her?

15. Marilyn Stein's mail carrier delivers a book with a letter enclosed. The letter states that the book is on sale for half its normal price and, if she doesn't want it, she must return it by a certain date or be billed for it.
   a) Does Stein have any obligation, either by common law or statute, to pay for this book?
   b) Do her rights change if she starts to read the book, and then decides she doesn't want it?

16. Which of the following brings an offer to an end? (There may be more than one correct answer.)
   a) the given time period has expired
   b) the offer is revoked
   c) the vendor sells it to another person without you knowing about it

17. Ben Letterman agreed to purchase a building from Robert Zimmer for $200,000, and gave a deposit of $20,000. Letterman also had Zimmer sign an agreement showing a sale price of $250,000, which Letterman would show to his credit union. The credit union would only lend up to 75 percent of the value of the property, and Letterman needed the extra money.
   The agreement was also made subject to Letterman's being able to obtain financing from the credit union in 30 days. It had a clause saying that Letterman could waive this condition.
   Property values have dropped drastically so Letterman wants to get out of the deal and have his deposit back. He does nothing about attempting to arrange financing, and so the condition is not fulfilled. Letterman now wants to sue for the return of his $20,000, as Zimmer refuses to return it.
   a) What various legal defences can Zimmer raise?
   b) Does it matter that Letterman did not actually apply for financing from the credit union and did not give the credit union a copy of the phony agreement?

18. Kris offers to sell his truck to Gina for $10,000 payable in cash in 30 days. Three weeks go by. Kris wakes up that morning and decides he does not want to sell his truck. He has forgotten completely about the offer to Gina. One hour later, Gina calls and says, "I accept your offer".
   a) Does Kris have of any grounds for not selling the truck to Gina?
   b) What could Kris have done to better protect himself and avoid any controversy over the expiry issue?

19. A purchaser of a business wants to have her lawyer review the offer to purchase before she is finally committed. She wants to insert the following clause:

"This Agreement of Purchase and Sale is conditional upon the approval of the Purchaser's' Solicitor, in his absolute discretion, as to the provisions of the Agreement of Purchase and Sale, within two business days after Vendor's acceptance of this Agreement; failing which, this Agreement shall be null and void and the Purchasers' deposit shall be returned without interest and without deduction forthwith."

a) The document that she signs to give to the vendor is headed "Agreement of Purchase and Sale". Does the document represent an agreement? What is it in law despite what it says on the document?

b) What is the name for the type of clause that she is intending to insert?

c) If the lawyer approves the agreement, can the purchaser still enforce it, or will any contract be nullified by the insertion of the clause because of incompleteness?

20. Chris Benoit owns a gym that he agrees to sell to Fit Finley. Benoit agrees to stay on for three years to help with the changeover. Among other clauses, the sales agreement contains the following:

i) Chris Benoit agrees that he will not be involved directly or indirectly in the business of a gym or a similar business that is carried on within five kilometres of the present establishment for five years after leaving the employ of Fit Finley

ii) Benoit agrees not to make any claim against the Workers' Compensation Fund while in the employ of Finley

iii) This agreement is conditional on Fit Finley's obtaining a zoning change to allow the running of a restaurant on part of the gym premises

Finley decides that he wants out of the deal, and so he does not apply for the zoning change.

a) What is the legal term for the first clause?

b) What are the three legal criteria that will be applied to determine whether the first clause is enforceable, and with what result?

c) Is the clause not to claim against the Workers' Compensation Fund enforceable?

d) Can Finley rely on the fact that the condition was not satisfied to get out of the deal?

Intention

21. At Christmas dinner your brother told you that if you could get the second week in March off, he would take you with him to the Bahamas for a holiday. On your return to work in January you made arrangements for that week off and, at the end of January when your holiday time was confirmed, you contacted your brother to get information about the trip. Your brother's response was, "Get real: you took me seriously?"

a) Will you be successful in getting to the Bahamas on your brother's money, and why?

22. Which of the following legal doctrines allows both sides in a business deal to be able to settle all the terms of the agreement without triggering contract law and thus making the deal legally binding?

a) Failure of consideration

b) Lack of capacity

c) Lack of consensus

d) Intention to create legal relations

Consideration

23. Read the limitation of liability clause from Global Village Communication, Inc.'s software licence on p. 169. Assume that one of the terms of the licence agreement states that Global Village Communication, Inc. is not responsible for the failure of the fax software, for any cause.

a) What legal principle is this clause written to avoid? What are the consequences to the supplier if this principle applies?

b) What legal principle is Global Village attempting to use to make the exemption clause effective? Will the clause as drafted avoid the problem that the exemption terms were not shown to the purchaser at the time of the purchase?

c) What types of loss might the failure of fax software cause? What are some of the most extreme cases?

d) Do you think a supplier of software should be permitted to limit or exclude its liability in this way?

24. Is consideration required in a contract under seal?

25. A contract is a legal idea that has been developed mainly for use in commercial situations. The element that makes it more likely that a court will find a contract existing in a commercial rather than a social situation is called:
    a) mutuality of promises
    b) consensus
    c) intention to create legal relations
    d) consideration

26. While walking along the edge of the river, Meredith Drew suddenly heard someone calling out for help. Unravelling a rope she kept for just such occasions, she threw it to Franklin Morris in the water and pulled him to shore. Morris repeatedly thanked Drew for saving him, and then told her to come to his house later and he would give her a reward of $100.

    When Drew appeared at Morris's door that evening, he was feeling much less shaken by the incident. Advising Drew not to walk too close to the riverbank, he said he had no intention of paying a reward and closed the door.
    a) Can Drew successfully sue Morris on his promise to pay her the reward?

27. Sylvan Corporation was in financial trouble and approached one of its major suppliers, Bolts R Us Inc., to see if some arrangement could be made to extend payment for the material Bolts supplied. Bolts was worried that Sylvan would switch to a cheaper plastic material available from its competitors, and so it agreed to extend the payment from its usual 30 days following delivery, to 120 days, in order to assist Sylvan in its refinancing.

    At the end of the year, Bolts R Us presented Sylvan with an invoice for the interest due on the payments that were made after the 30-day period. This was a substantial amount of money, and when Sylvan complained, Bolts replied that it had received no benefit from the extension of the payment dates and, as far as it was concerned, the money was due and payable immediately.
    a) The president of Sylvan Corporation has asked you to write a memo explaining in detail whether Sylvan must pay the money claimed by Bolts R Us Inc.

28. a) Is there consideration in the Agreement for Purchase and Sale for a Business in Leased Premises in the Appendix? If so, what is it?
    b) What is consideration?
    c) How does consideration distinguish between: a promise, an agreement and a contract?
    d) What consideration is the purchaser giving, and what consideration is the seller giving?

Multi Issue

29. On June 1, Maria, aged 17, a child-prodigy entrepreneur, agrees to buy a job-search website business called Big Bucks for Young Turks from Bill, aged 21, for $5,000. The website permits employers to post jobs suitable for entry-level positions for a small advertising fee, which allows job seekers to search for free.

    Bill tells Maria that the basis for success is that many job seekers from other countries find out about jobs and come as illegal immigrants hoping to get landed-immigrant status if they can stay long enough before getting caught.

    Maria gets Bill to agree that he will never again open a job-search or similar business in competition with her. Bill agrees but says, "This is just an agreement between you and me and we agree neither can sue the other; we are honest people and do not want lawyers and courts involved." Maria agrees and gives a deposit of $500. The deal is scheduled to close in 30 days.

The next day, Sally, aged 21, hears of Maria's deal and asks Maria to sell the deal to her for $7,000. Maria is delighted about making $2,000 profit in one day and signs an agreement to give the deal to Sally for $7,000, which Sally pays to Maria immediately.

a) Identify all the legal issues raised in the above question.

b) Can Bill enforce the June 1 agreement against Maria?

c) Can Maria sell her deal to Sally? What is the legal term for the selling of this deal? What steps, if any, must Maria take to make certain that the sale to Sally is proper in law?

30. Find a standard form contract that you, or someone you know, has signed recently. When this part of the text on contracts has been completed, identify three clauses in the agreement that were covered in this part and discuss the legal issues involved.

Appendix 5

Agreement of Purchase and Sale for a Business in Leased Premises

AGREEMENT OF PURCHASE AND SALE
FOR A BUSINESS IN LEASED PREMISES

PURCHASER ___ JOHN CONVISER ___ , agrees to purchase from
(Full legal names of all Purchasers)

VENDOR ___ JENNIFER CARTHY ___
(Full legal names of all Vendors)

all the assets of the business known as ___ URBAN ATTITUDES ___
(including the chattels, fixtures and inventory of the business set out in schedule "A" as are now located upon the premises and inspected and approved by Purchaser)

situated at ___ 345 MAIN STREET ___ (the "Business")
together with the lease of the premises, and the trade name and goodwill of the business (the "Assets").

PURCHASE PRICE: ___ TWO HUNDRED AND FIFTY THOUSAND ___ Dollars (CDN$ ___ 250,000.00 ___)

which total Purchase Price include the amount of $ ___ ONE HUNDRED THOUSAND ___ in respect of inventory of the Business.

DEPOSIT:
Purchaser submits (___ TWENTY-FIVE THOUSAND ___ Dollars (CDN$ ___ 25,000.00 ___)
(Herewith/Upon acceptance)

cash or negotiable cheque payable to ___ FIRST CORPORATION REALTY, INC. ___ to be held in trust pending completion or other termination
of the Agreement and to be credited toward the Purchase Price on completion. Purchaser agrees to pay the balance as follows:

SCHEDULES(S), A ___ attached hereto form(s) part of this Agreement.

1. **IRREVOCABILITY.** This Offer shall be irrevocable by ___ PURCHASER ___ until ___ 5:00 ___ p.m. on the ___ 1ST ___ day of ___ JULY ___ , ___ 2004 ___
(Vendor/Purchaser) (year)
after which time, if not accepted, this Offer shall be null and void and the deposit shall be returned to the Purchaser in full without interest.

2. **COMPLETION DATE:** This agreement shall be completed by no later than 6:00 p.m. on the ___ 1ST ___ day of ___ SEPTEMBER ___ , ___ 2004 ___
(year)
on which date possession of the Business and Assets is to given to Purchaser, title to the Assets shall be conveyed to Purchaser and Purchaser shall pay or satisfy the total Purchase Price.

3. **NOTICES:** Vendor hereby appoints the Listing Broker as Agent for the purpose of giving and receiving notice pursuant to this Agreement. **Only if the Co-operating Broker represents the interests of the Purchaser in this transaction,** the Purchaser hereby appoints the Co-operating Broker as Agent for the purpose of giving and receiving notices pursuant to this Agreement. Any notice relating hereto or provided for herein shall be in writing. This offer, any counter offer, notice of acceptance thereof, or an notice shall be deemed given and received, when hand delivered to the address for service provided in the Acknowledgement below, or where a facsimile number is provided herein, when transmitted electronically to that facsimile number.

FAX No ___ 532-6691 ___ (For delivery of notices to Vendor) FAX ___ 392-7742 ___ (For delivery of notices to Purchaser)

4. **NON-COMPETITION:** Vendor and the undersigned ___ jointly and severally covenant not to carry on or be engaged in or concerned with (either directly or indirectly in any manner whatsoever including without limitation as a principal, agent, partner or shareholder) any business competitive with or similar to the Business as presently carried on, within a radius of ___ 5 ___ miles of the premises for ___ 36 ___ months after completion. The aforesaid covenant shall survive the completion of the transaction provided for herein.

5. **VENDOR REPRESENTS AND WARRANTS** that:
   (a) the Assets are now and shall at the time of completion be owned by Vendor free and clear of all encumbrances, liens or charges and no other person has now or shall at the time of closing have any interest in the assets except
   (b) Vendor is not now and shall not at the time of completion be a non-resident person within the meaning of section 116 of the Income Tax Act (Canada);
   (c) the Business has been carried on in the ordinary course and all financial statements and other information provided to Purchaser are true, accurate and correct in all material respects and have been prepared in accordance with generally accepted accounting principles applied on a consistent basis and Vendor shall, at the time of completion, have no liabilities, contingent or otherwise, except as reflected therein or in the statement to be delivered pursuant to the Bulk Sales Act (none of which shall be inconsistent with past practice or materially adverse);
   (d) no expenditures shall be made out of the ordinary course of business prior to closing and the Business shall be carried on up to the time of completion in the ordinary course and in a commercially reasonable manner with a view to preserving the goodwill of the Business;
   (e) the tangible Assets are now and shall at the time of completion be in good condition, subject only in the case of equipment to reasonable wear and tear;
   (f) Vendor is not in default of any agreements related to the Business and there are no actions, suits or proceedings against or on behalf of the Vendor, pending or threatened, which may affect the Business, and the Vendor is not aware of any existing grounds on which any such action, suit or proceeding might be commenced;
   (g) there is a good, valid and subsisting lease of the premises for a term of ___ 2 ___ years at a monthly rental of $ ___ 2,000.00 ___ expiring on the ___ 1ST ___ day of ___ SEPTEMBER ___ (a copy of which lease is attached hereto);
(year)
   (h) there are not now and shall not at the time of completion be any employees of the Business except the following, all of whom can be dismissed on the minimum applicable statutory notice period without further liability: ___ N/A ___

208

6. **VENDOR COVENANTS:**
   (a) to comply with section 5 of the Retail Sales Tax Act;
   (b) to comply with the Bulk Sale Act;
   (c) to deliver to Purchaser at or before the time of completion the written consent of the lessor to the assignment of the lease of the premises to Purchaser;
   (d) to indemnify and save harmless the Purchaser from and against all liabilities, claims and demands in connection with the purchased business existing or incurred as at the time of completion and not shown on the financial statements provided to the Purchaser or in the statement delivered pursuant to the Bulk Sales Act or expressly agreed to be assumed by the Purchaser in this Agreement.

7. **PURCHASER REPRESENTS AND WARRANTS** that Purchaser is not now and shall not at the time of completion be a non-eligible person within the meaning of the Investment Canada Act.

8. **PURCHASER COVENANT** to pay all applicable retail sales tax and federal sales tax on completion (or furnish appropriate exemption certificates) eligible in respect to this transaction.

9. **THE OBLIGATION OF PURCHASER** to complete this transaction shall be subject to satisfaction of the following conditions (which may be waived in whole or in part by Purchaser without prejudice to any claim for breach of covenant, representation or warranty):
   (a) the representations and warranties of Vendor shall be true at and as of completion as if given at that time;
   (b) Vendor shall have performed all covenants to be performed by Vendor at or prior to the time of completion.

10. **INVENTORY:** Prior to completion, either party may elect by written notice to the other that the inventory shall be physically counted after the close of business on the day prior to completion and valued at Vendor's cost thereof in which case the total Purchase Price shall be increased or decreased to the extent that the valuation so obtained is greater than or less than the amount set for inventory stated above. Failing such an election, neither Vendor or Purchaser may dispute the amount of valuation of inventory.

11. **ADJUSTMENTS:** Any business taxes, insurance, rent, hydro, water, fuel, employee's wages and vacation pay and usual prepaid items being transferred to Purchaser, as applicable, shall be apportioned and allowed to the day of completion, the day of completion itself to be apportioned to the Purchaser.

12. **THE BILL OF SALE** and other transfer documents are to be prepared at Vendor's expense and any security documents are to be prepared at the expense of Purchaser, and each party is to pay the costs of registration of their own documents.

13. **AGENCY:** It is understood that the brokers involved in the transaction represent the parties as set out in the Confirmation of Representation below.

15. **TENDER:** Any tender of documents or money hereunder may be made upon Vendor or Purchaser or their respective lawyers on the day set for completion. Money may be tendered by bank draft or cheque certified by a Chartered Bank, Trust Company, Province of Ontario Savings Office, Credit Union or Caisse Populaire.

16. **AGREEMENT IN WRITING:** This offer when accepted shall constitute a binding agreement of purchase and sale, and time shall in all respects be of the essence of this Agreement. There is no representation, warranty, collateral agreement or condition affecting this Agreement other than as expressed herein. If there is conflict between any provision added to this Agreement (including any Schedule attached hereto) and any provision in the standard pre-set portion hereof, the added provision shall supersede the standard pre-set provision to the extent of such conflict. This Agreement shall be read with all changes of gender or number required by the context. The heirs, executors, administrators, successors and assigns of the undersigned are bound by the terms herein.

DATED at _____ this _____ 30TH _____ day of _____ APRIL, 2004 _____
SIGNED, SEALED AND DELIVERED   IN WITNESS whereof I have hereunto set my hand and seal:
in the presence of:

_____   _____ John _____ (Affix Seal) _____
                                (Purchaser)   (Date)

_____   _____ (Affix Seal) _____
                                (Purchaser)   (Date)

VENDOR accepts the above Offer and agrees with the Agent above named, in consideration for his services in procuring the said Offer, to pay him on the date above fixed for completion, a commission of ___ 6 ___ % of the Total Purchase Price, which commission may be deducted from the deposit. I hereby irrevocably instruct my solicitor to pay direct to the Agent any unpaid balance of commission from the proceeds of the sale.

DATED AT _____ this _____ 1ST _____ day of _____ JULY, 2004 _____
SIGNED, SEALED AND DELIVERED   IN WITNESS where of I have hereunto set my hand and seal:
in the presence

_____   _____ Jeniffer _____ (Affix Seal) _____
                                (Vendor)   (Date)

_____   _____ (Affix Seal) _____
                                (Vendor)   (Date)

(THE UNDERSIGNED _____ in consideration of Purchaser
entering into this Agreement, hereby executes this Agreement for the purpose of paragraph 5.

DATED at _____ this _____ day of _____ 19 _____
SIGNED, SEALED AND DELIVERED   IN WITNESS whereof I have hereunto set my hand and seal:
in the presence of:

_____   _____ (Affix Seal) _____
                                (Vendor)   (Date)

SCHEDULE "A"

1. This offer is conditional upon the Purchaser's approval of the gross weekly sales figure which shall be not less than $4,000.00 upon expiration of the one (1) week inspection period. In this respect, the Vendor agrees to allow the Purchaser to inspect the operation of the business during the normal business hours and assist the Purchaser in familiarizing with the daily operation of the business for the period of one (1) week after the acceptance of this offer, such one week period to be determined by the parties hereto.

2. It is a further condition of this offer that the Purchaser will have the right to continue the use of the business name, "Urban Attitudes" and in that regard, the Vendor shall register the Declaration of Dissolution of the partnership name.

3. All conditions in this offer are for the benefit of the Purchaser only and may be waived at any time or times at the option of the Purchaser.

4. This offer is conditional upon the Purchaser arranging satisfactory financing on or before July 1, 2004; otherwise this offer shall become null and void and the deposit is to be returned to the Purchaser without any deduction or penalty.

6

Important Contract Terms and Contract Interpretation

Contract Law Principles

A major principle of contract law is that the parties have the freedom to contract and the courts will enforce the contract according to the exact terms that the parties chose. Judges do not want to easily let people out of contracts that they have agreed to, nor does the court want to rewrite contracts for the parties involved. This strict enforcement of the exact contract terms reinforces the principles of certainty and predictability that we need in our legal system. We need this so that we can rely on contracts as we conduct our business activities. Image the problems that would occur if people thought that when they made a contract the courts would easily strike it down or freely rewrite parts of the contract. This could not occur. Many strict contract rules and terms have been developed to protect the strict enforceability of contracts and to thereby preserve the necessary certainty and predictability of our legal system.

However, sometimes strictly enforcing the contract the exact way it is written leads to unfairness. Over the years courts have developed ways to interpret contracts that let parties avoid certain contracts or contract terms if strict application would lead to significant problems. In Chapter 5 we saw that the courts will not enforce a contract for an illegal purpose or against a person who lacked the capacity to contract. This chapter examines some important contract terms, some strict contract rules that can apply and factors that influence the courts' interpretation of these terms and rules to achieve fair results. The courts sometimes have to balance the principles of freedom to contract, certainty and predictability against the considerations of fairness and public policy concerns and decide whether it is appropriate to enforce a contract taking all these factors into consideration.

The Age of the Standard Form Contract

Contract law was developed in an age when both the purchaser and the seller usually knew and dealt with each other on a face-to-face basis. The seller often made the product or supplied the service, and all the terms of the sale were specifically negotiated. One hundred years ago, if you wanted to buy a dresser you would have gone directly to a cabinetmaker. There, you might see a model of the exact dresser that you wanted. You would be able to talk to the maker, a skilled craftsman, about the quality, and you would be able to bargain about the price. The contract would be custom made to your purchase.

Today, if you want to purchase a television at an electronics store, you will probably deal with a salesperson who may or may not know much about these units, or about electronics at all. That salesperson will work for a dealer who purchased the unit already boxed from a wholesaler or a distributor. The distributor will have obtained the product from the manufacturer. Even the manufacturer may have obtained components from other suppliers. The price is not negotiable, and you will pay whatever is asked. The terms of the contract are also not negotiable.

Mass-production and mass-marketing techniques have created standardized approaches to all aspects of the business process. Just as the transactions are standardized or similar, and the marketing approach is standardized, so too are the contractual terms. This modern business contract has come to be known as the **standard form contract**: an offer presented in a printed document, the terms of which are the same for all customers, and which becomes a contract when signed (accepted) by the customer.

The standard form contract has proven to be a great advantage to business, and is in harmony with mass-marketing approaches. However, it has also created inequalities for those who are purchasing goods or services according to such an agreement.

Standard form contracts are drawn up by teams of lawyers employed by large business organizations or special interest groups. For example, the standard form agreement for the purchase and sale of a car (see Appendix) is prepared by an automobile dealers' association. New—and used—car dealership associations use forms adapted from a similar precedent. If you are going to be buying or selling a car through a dealership, this is the type of agreement that you will likely be asked to sign. Similarly, the common printed contract for the purchase of a small business (see Appendix to Chapter 5) is not only drawn up by the real estate brokers' associations, but is also often filled out by the real estate agent and not by a lawyer.

In a consumer retail sale the salesperson who presents the agreement may have absolutely no understanding of what the form actually means. The contract is put in front of the purchaser, who is told, "Sign here," and neither the salesperson nor the customer realizes the implications of many of the terms.

In several cases involving car rental contracts courts have refused to uphold standard form contracts when there were onerous clauses or unfair unusual terms that the rental companies had not brought to the attention of the customers. The contracts were quite long, were signed very quickly and the customers never read them. The controversial clauses usually allowed the rental company to deny insurance coverage for situations that the customer would never have anticipated nor agreed to. In one case the contract tried to deny insurance coverage if the driver had consumed "any" alcohol at all. The courts ruled that the companies can only rely on these unfair surprising terms if at the time the contract was formed they took "reasonable measures to bring theses clauses to the attention of the customer". If this was not done, the rental company could not use these terms even though the customer had signed the contract. (see *Tilden Rent-A-Car v. Clendenning* 1978 CanLII 1446 (ONCA) and *Richardson-Watson v. 443496 Ontario Inc.,* 2005 CanLII 6383 (ON SC)).

---

standard form contract

an offer presented in a printed document, the terms of which are the same for all customers, and which becomes a contract when signed (accepted) by the customer

Business Protections   It cannot be overstressed that many of the protections that are developed by both courts and legislatures respecting the abuse of standard form contracts are focused on the consumer. A business person does not necessarily have these protections. As a general rule, it is better to assume that you will be held to any agreement that you sign.

Hidden Clauses

Lengthy standard form agreements full of opaque and archaic legal language have become the standard of business contracts. Sign and initial clauses have evolved through shrink-wrap to web-wrap. Customers often do not understand what they are agreeing to when they click.

To dramatize this, a UK videogame company, GamePlay, put a clause in their online agreement on April 1, 2010 that by clicking on the agreement, the purchasers gave Game-Play the option to purchase their immortal soul. To be fair, the clause continued that if the purchaser clicked on the clause, that clause would be nullified and the purchaser would be sent a coupon worth $5.00. GamePlay reported that only 10% of the purchasers saved their souls that day.

Interpretation of Terms

It is difficult to think of every detail when making a contract. Many terms and meanings are often understood without the need of saying them. For example, if you tell a clerk in your business to buy a box of new file folders because supply is running low, you do not have to tell the clerk all the details. He will know many of them (such as colour, kind, price, and supplier) by customary usage. It may be that the office uses only manila-coloured folders, buys one box of 100 folders at a time, and buys them from Business Supplies R Us. Common sense will tell the clerk whether he should fill your order immediately or as soon as his present task is finished. If he sees a sign advertising a sale at half price at a different store, he knows he has the authority to buy at that store without having to check first. If you specifically mention all these details to the clerk, he would be insulted. And where would the need for such particularity end?

So it is with contracts. There are aspects that are seemingly ambiguous or incomplete, but the courts strain to fill in the gaps to give effect to the contracts either by interpretation or by reading extra terms into a contract even though they may not be expressly included (implication of terms).

The potential for genuine misunderstanding between parties is very real. A host may look out the window and say, "It has stopped raining." A guest may take that to mean that she should leave. A bystander overhearing the comment may conclude that the host was only commenting on the weather and nothing more. Can you tell which interpretation is correct?

The courts always begin contract-interpretation cases by saying that they are trying to find the true intention of the parties. But they don't ask the parties to get into the witness box and testify as to their understanding at the time the contract was made. If they did, of course, each party would likely give an interpretation that would help that individual win. The courts apply an objective test; they try to determine what a reasonable person would have thought the words used in the agreement meant.

The courts do not apply special legal meanings to the words in the contract, but use meanings that business people would give to those words. It may appear that legal terminology is being employed, but the term is likely a business word from a past era. The courts will also look to dictionary definitions to see if standard meanings contained there will solve the problem. As well, a contract often provides definitions of terms within the contract.

Additionally, the courts consider specific meanings used within a particular type of business. For example, in the baking industry it is widely accepted that a dozen means 13 (a baker's dozen). An order by a bake shop from a supplier for a dozen croissants will mean 13 croissants are to be sent, not 12.

Businesses frequently use long standard form contracts. There is a rule of interpretation that applies to this type of contract which gives some relief to the other party. If there is an ambiguity in a term so that it has two or more meanings, that term is construed so as to give any benefit of the doubt to the non-drafting party—or *contra proferentem*, which literally translates as "against the one who offers" (proffers) the contract. But as the one who offers is usually the drafter, the phrase is thought of as meaning "against the one who drafted."

This rule applies only to standard form contracts. It does not apply to contracts that are custom drafted with input from both sides to meet individual situations.

Example: In *Shafron v. KRG Insurance Brokers Western (Inc.)*, [2009] SCC 6 (CanLII), Morley Shafron was an insurance agent with KRG Insurance Brokers. His employment contract contained a clause that restricted his right to work for another insurance company after he left KRG, for a three year period within the "Metropolitan City of Vancouver." Shafron left KRG and the next month started to work for a different insurance company in Richmond, B.C. Richmond is a separate city bordering Vancouver. KRG sue Shafron for breach of contract claiming the term "Metropolitan City of Vancouver" included Richmond. Shafron claimed the term was unclear and ambiguous so it was unenforceable and he could work in Richmond.

The trial court agreed with Shafron and ruled the term was ambiguous and struck it down. The B.C. Court of Appeal disagreed and using notional severance, rewrote the term "Metropolitan City of Vancouver" to include Richmond, Burnaby and lands at UBC. The Supreme Court of Canada however disagreed with the Court of Appeal decision. The Supreme Court found that the term "Metropolitan City of Vancouver" was uncertain and ambiguous. There was no evidence that demonstrated a mutual understanding by the parties of a definition for that term when they made the contract. It was inappropriate for the court to use notional severance to rewrite a non-competition clause in an employment contract in to what the court considered to be a reasonable term. The term was ambiguous, and so it had to be struck down. As a result, Shafron had no restrictions on when or where he could work.

contra proferentum

the court will interpret a term that is uncertain against the party that drafted the contract

TD General Insurance Company v. Baughan, 2013 ONSC 333 (CanLII)

Lynn Baughan was in a car accident in the U.S. Virgin Islands and suffered serious injuries. Her Ontario insurance company denied her coverage and benefits because the policy and the Ontario Insurance Act, R.S.O 1990, only provided coverage in Canada and "The United States of America". Ms. Baughan argued that the U.S. Virgin Islands, which is an incorporated territory of the U.S., was included in the term "The United States of America," but the insurer disagreed.

Ms. Baughan introduced evidence that people born in the U.S. Virgin Islands are American citizens, hold U.S. passports, and can be drafted into the U.S. military. The insurance company said that only the 50 states were included in this term, not the U.S. territories as well. Both sides introduced a large amount of evidence to support their particular definition of what was meant by "The United States of America." There had been no other case in Canada that had dealt with defining this term previously.

The Court's Decision

The court said that neither her insurance policy nor the Ontario insurance law specifically defined this term and there was no "ordinary" accepted definition of this term. The court also noted that one of the main objectives of insurance law is consumer protection, particularly in the field of automobile and home insurance. The court ruled that since there was so much evidence supporting various definitions of this term, the term was obviously ambiguous. The court then decided that since it was ambiguous, it should apply the doctrine of **contra proferentum** and interpret the term against the party that drafted the contract, which was the insurance company. Therefore the court ruled in Ms. Baughan's favour and the U.S. Virgin Islands was considered to be part of the term "The United States of America" and she received insurance coverage under her TD General Insurance policy and under the Ontario Insurance Act.

■ *Critical Concepts of* Interpretation

- The meaning of a term is that which a reasonable person would understand.
- A dictionary meaning may be accepted to establish the commonly understood meaning.
- If a term has a special meaning within a particular trade, expert evidence by a member of that trade will be used to determine that special meaning.
- If one party drafted the document, ambiguities will be construed against that party and in favour of the other party. This applies to standard form contracts, which are usually presented to the other side simply for signature.
- All words will be interpreted in context. So if the word is not clear standing alone, reading other provisions in the contract may clarify the meaning.
- The context of the business and any prior course of dealings may be considered in interpreting the terms.

■ *Business Law* Applied

❶ Franklin had a lump-sum snow-removal contract with Neige Geht Inc. for the parking lot, driveway, and sidewalk areas of the hotel he owned in Prince George. The short written contract was drawn up by both. It required Neige to remove snow from the specified areas "until the end of the winter season." April that year was cooler than usual and there were two unexpected snowfalls at the end of that month. Neige gave an invoice to Franklin for extra snow removal for April. Franklin objects, claiming that winter means until the last snowfall of the year.

a) Is there an ambiguous or uncertain term in the snow-removal contract?
b) Would the court apply the contra proferentem rule?
c) Assume the dictionary definition of winter says: "coldest season of the year, December-February." Assume the astronomical definition is: "from the winter solstice (December 22nd) to the vernal equinox (March 20th)." What argument can you make for the owner and what argument for the contractor to support each party's position?
d) What test would the court apply if asked to interpret the contract between Franklin and Neige?
e) Is that test objective or subjective? Would the judge ask each of the parties what the term meant to them?

Adding Terms

Parol Evidence Rule

A party may claim that there was a term agreed upon that was not written down. However, the **parol evidence rule** may prevent any changes to the written agreement by adding terms that vary or contradict the written document if the written document appears to contain the whole contract. Evidence of any kind, whether oral or written, that contradicts or varies the written term will likely be excluded. If the written terms are clear, the courts will not listen to any new extrinsic (outside) parol evidence that tries to establish a different meaning. This presumption that the written terms prevail is strongest when the parties have produced a document that they have both negotiated and drafted together. If however it was a printed form or standard form contract (especially when it is an exemption clause that is in question) the presumption is much weaker.

> **parol evidence rule**
> extrinsic evidence cannot be used to change clearly written contract terms

One reason for this exclusion is that the courts mistrust oral evidence. When things go wrong, parties are apt to make up a story that varies from the written document. Also, some terms agreed upon in negotiation might have been replaced by later terms. Only the written document represents the final agreement.

There are exceptions to the parol evidence rule and oral evidence can be admissible to prove that there were major problems such as fraud or duress, to rectify a mistake(see chapter 7), to resolve ambiguities or to show that the contract was an incomplete agreement.

There are exceptions to the parol evidence rule. For example, sometimes a contract is **partly oral and partly written**. Additionally it may consist of an exchange of letters or telephone calls. There may even be a situation where the parties actually form two contracts relating to the same transaction—one oral and one written. Only when the court decides that the document contains the entire agreement does the parol evidence rule apply.

collateral contract

a separate independent agreement that one party makes in exchange for the other party entering into the main contract

A way around the parol evidence rule is if a party can establish that there was a **collateral contract** in existence as well. A collateral contract is a separate independent agreement that one party makes in exchange for the other party entering into the main contract. If a party can establish that there were two separate valid contracts, then this is avoids the problems of the parol evidence rule.

It is obvious that commercial lawyers must be very careful in how they negotiate and draft contracts for their clients and written evidence should be kept of every statement relied upon in every agreement.

Example: In *Gallen v. Butterley* 1984 CanLII 752 (BCCA), a grain company made an oral representation to Gallen, a farmer, that their new buckwheat seeds would control weeds and the buckwheat crop would thrive. Gallen signed the purchase contract which contained a clause that stated the grain company gave no warranty as to the productiveness of the seed. Unfortunately Gallen's buckwheat crop was completely destroyed by weeds. The B.C. Court of Appeal held that the oral statement and representations by the grain salesman were admissible. Whether this evidence is included by determining the original contract was incomplete or by ruling this

King v. Operating Engineers Training, 2011 MBCA 80 (CanLII)

The case involves the interpretation of a contract between Robert King and the Operating Engineers Training Institute of Manitoba Inc. (OETIM). King was hired as an instructor for a heavy equipment course being offered by OETIM. The parties disagreed on whether the remuneration referred to in the written contract was to be "net" of income taxes and other deductions or "gross" income.

King did not claim the pay as income (he was paid between $2,000 and $3,500 per week for the 4-6 week courses each year) and then Revenue Canada assessed him with $34,295 owing in back taxes. King sued OETIM for this money claiming that his pay was to be "clear of taxes."

King showed that in a separate written memorandum the director who had hired him had stated that the pay was to be "clear of taxes." King also testified that it was standard in this business to have the pay calculated as net income. He claimed he would never have taken the job unless it was "net" as there were other jobs at the same time paying the equivalent net income.

OETIM claimed that the contract did not specify whether it was gross or net income. OETIM claimed that since it was a clearly written contract, the parol evidence rule applied and extrinsic evidence could not be allowed in to interpret the contract. King asserted that the written contract was not the complete agreement, so the parol evidence rule did not apply and extrinsic evidence can be considered. King claimed the contract was partly written and partly

oral or the separate written memorandum should be included as a collateral contract.

The trial judge found that the language of the written contract was clear, but also found, as a result of considering the evidence of prior oral discussions and written memoranda, that the written contract was not intended to be the complete agreement between the parties. He accepted the plaintiff's position that the evidence of prior discussions and memoranda were admissible to determine the question of whether the pay was to be "gross" or "net." The trial judge ruled the pay was "net income," so OETIM was liable for the $34,295 owing in back taxes. OETIM appealed the decision.

The Court's Decision

The Manitoba Court of Appeal ruled the parol evidence rule may not apply when there is an allegation that the contract is partially written and partially oral or that a collateral contract exists. In such cases, certain extrinsic evidence is admissible to substantiate those claims to aid the court in understanding and interpreting the language and meaning of the written contract. In this case there was significant oral and written evidence that the pay was to be "net" and "clear of taxes" so the trial decision was upheld and OETIM was liable for the income taxes King owed.

oral statement was a collateral contract, the statement should be included in this sales contract. By including the salesman's promise, the farmer then succeeded in his claim against the grain company for the crop losses.

■ *Critical Concepts of* Parol Evidence Rule

- Where evidence is sought to be admitted to contradict a term in a written document, there is a strong presumption that the written terms govern.
- This presumption will be stronger where the parties produce an individually negotiated document than where a printed form is used.
- This presumption will be less strong where the contradiction is between a specific representation and a general exemption clause in a standard form contract.
- Exceptions to the parol evidence rule can occur if there are major problems alleged such as fraud, duress, mistake, major ambiguities or it is an incomplete contract
- A court may rule that the contract was partly written and partly oral and this can avoid the strict parol evidence rule
- If there is a collateral contract, a separate independent contract, this can also be a way around the parol evidence presumption

---

Entire Agreement Clauses

In standard form contracts you will inevitably see a clause that says that the written document contains the whole agreement between the parties and that there are no other obligations by way of representations, warranties, terms, or collateral (side) agreements.

An **entire agreement clause** is a term in a contract in which the parties agree that their contract is complete as written: it seems similar to an exemption clause but it has a completely different purpose. Entire agreement clauses are primarily aimed at any oral statements that are made before a contract is signed. They are an attempt to ensure that the parol evidence rule will be upheld. The classic example of this situation concerns the sales rep who tells a customer that the car was owned only by a little old lady who drove it to church on Sundays. After purchasing the car, the purchaser learns that there were a number of prior owners and none of them were little old ladies or churchgoers. However, the entire agreement clause says that there were no such statements relied upon by the purchaser. See paragraph 3 of the Used Car Bill of Sale (in the Appendix to this chapter) and paragraph 13 of the Purchase Order (in the Appendix to Chapter 8) for examples of entire agreement clauses.

For a complete understanding of the rules respecting entire agreement clauses some knowledge of the law of misrepresentation is also necessary and will be discussed in Chapter 7. Often the court imposes similar requirements on entire agreement clauses in consumer contracts that they place on disclaimer or exemption clauses; that the clause must be brought to the consumer's attention to be enforceable. There are special statutory rules that protect consumers by nullifying the entire agreement clauses in certain consumer retail transactions. However, no such special statutory rules exist to nullify entire agreement clauses for business-to-business transactions. In those situations the entire agreement clause is more likely to be enforced.

entire agreement clause
a term in a contract in which the parties agree that their contract is complete as written

The Enforceability of Entire Agreement Clauses

Sometimes entire agreement clauses are very strictly enforced and sometimes they are ignored. It is hard to find a principle that accurately predicts when entire agreement clauses will be enforced. One commentator suggested that entire agreement clauses are used by judges to avoid having to make a finding against a party's credibility. When a judge really does not believe the additional evidence, the judge relies on the entire agreement clause and says the evidence is excluded. When however, the judge does believe the evidence, the judge finds that the entire agreement clause is ineffective.[1]

In comparing the *Bank of Montreal v. Bal* and the *Corey Developments* cases below, a distinguishing feature may be that *Bal* had very weak evidence to corroborate (back up) his version of events, but in Corey there was a written note by the defendant's lawyer to prove their claim.

Bank of Montreal v. Bal
2012 BCSC 1505 (CanLII)

The Bank of Montreal granted credit to Interline Motor Freight Inc. in Nov. 2010 and as security for this credit, Hardev Bal, an officer and employee of Interline, personally guaranteed payment to the bank of all present and future debts and liabilities of Interline up to the sum of $400,000 plus interest. In a second personal guarantee, Hardev and Sukhraj Bal both guaranteed another $20,000 of Interline debts. Bal claimed that when he considered switching to the Bank of Montreal for Interline lending, he was told by Mr. Sharma, who he believed to be an agent of BMO, that the personal guarantees would only apply for the first 6 months. An email from Sharma's hotmail account, not a BMO account, stated the 6 month limit on the personal guarantees. The Bals signed the personal guarantees but there was no 6 month limit on them. The standard form guarantees clearly stated the written guarantee was the entire agreement and no other representations other than those in the written agreement apply. Bal claims he never read the guarantee and barely discussed it with his lawyer.

About 15 months later, Interline was deeply in debt and the bank demanded from the Bals the $420,000 plus interest that they had guaranteed. The Bals claimed that the guarantee had only been effective for 6 months, so they were not liable for the debt. The bank asserted that the written guarantee was clear and there was no 6 month limit on the guarantees. BMO claimed the parol evidence rule applied so no other extrinsic evidence could be admitted to contradict the terms of the guarantee. BMO relied on

this well established principle that was set in a similar case by the Supreme Court in Hawrish v. Bank of Montreal [1969] S.C.R.515, where a business man claimed the bank told him he would not be liable despite signing a guarantee.

The Court's Decision

The B.C. court followed the precedent established in the Hawrish case and ruled that the parol evidence rule applied. The written terms in the guarantee governed this case and the Bals were liable on the personal guarantees. The court found that the Bals had not introduced any reliable evidence about Mr. Sharma, and the 6 month restriction they suggested was neither clearly defined nor proven. The purpose of an entire agreement clause is to prevent misunderstandings based on discussions prior to the signing of the documents. The exceptions include situations where collateral contracts consistent with the written contract occur or if it can be shown that what is written does not truly represent the contract itself. Neither was the situation in this case.

The point of a formal agreement is to fix the obligations of the parties and to prevent misunderstandings. The defendants cannot successfully assert that the "real" agreement included a term wholly inconsistent with the agreements they signed. The Bals were liable for the $420,000 plus interest.

Corey Developments Inc. v. Eastbridge Developments (Waterloo) Ltd.,
[1997] 34 O.R. (3d) 73 Aff'd (1999) 44 O.R. (3d) 95 (C.A.)

Corey Developments agreed to purchase a parcel of real estate from Eastbridge Developments for $2,015,000. The agreement was conditional upon Eastbridge obtaining permits for water and sewage services for the land. Corey put up a deposit of $201,500, which was not to be held in trust but to be used for development costs of the land. Because the deposit was not to be held in trust, Corey wanted the personal guarantee of well-known

Calgary developer Nader Gerhmazian, who was a principal of Eastbridge, such that the deposit would be returned if the deal was not completed. Nothing was said about the personal guarantee in the agreement of purchase and sale.

The condition was not satisfied and Eastbridge was by then insolvent and so it could not pay back the deposit. Corey claims that he had the personal guarantee of Nader Gerhmazian.

---

1. Paul Perrel, "A Riddle Inside an Enigma: The Entire Agreement Clause," *Advocates' Quarterly* 28 (March 1998), p. 287.

Gerhmazian denied giving it and pleaded the parol evidence rule and the entire agreement clause in defence.

The Court's Decision

The trial judge found that Gerhmazian's assertion that he had not given a personal guarantee was "preposterous" on the evidence. There was documentary evidence that Gerhmazian's lawyer had given a written undertaking to Corey on Gerhmazian's behalf stating that Gerhmazian would give the guarantee, among other evidence.

The legal issue was whether the evidence could be admitted in light of the Supreme Court of Canada's decision in *Hawrish v.*

Bank of Montreal (above). The entire agreement clause stated that there were no additional terms apart from the written terms. The parol evidence rule states that no evidence can be admitted to contradict this term, which says that there are no additional terms.

The court quoted a judge in the *Gallen v. Butterley* case (above), who said that **the "principle in *Hawrish* is not a tool for the unscrupulous to dupe the unwary."** The court applied the restatement of the parol evidence rule as set out *Gallen v. Butterley* to say that **in exceptional circumstances** external evidence may be introduced to vary the written terms of the agreement. Those exceptional circumstances occurred here. Gerhmazian was held liable on the guarantee.

■ *Business Law*   Applied

❷ a) **What was the** key factual issues in the *Corey Developments* case and how was it decided?

b) What was the key legal issues in this case and how was it decided?

c) Why might the combination of the entire agreement clause and the parol evidence rule exclude the evidence that the plaintiff wanted to introduce at the trial?

d) How did the trial judge avoid the rigid application of the principle in *Hawrish v. Bank of Montreal*? Did she strictly follow *stare decisis*?

❸ **Pat Monteiro agreed** to sign a bank guarantee for her husband's business's term loan for $100,000. The clause on the guarantee form said that she was guaranteeing the business's debts to the bank from all sources. The form also contained an entire agreement clause.

Monteiro said she wanted to make it clear that she was responsible only for the term loan. The bank manager told her not to worry; the wording was a mere formality, but he couldn't change the bank's standard form. However, the bank would never enforce the guarantee except for the term loan.

Five years later the husband's business went bankrupt. Fortunately, the term loan had been fully paid off, but his business owed $50,000 to the bank from a mortgage on the store that it owned. The bank now sues Monteiro for the $50,000 based on the wording of the guarantee form that she would guarantee all of the business debts to the bank from all sources.

The bank manager says he cannot remember details about a transaction from five years ago, but he very much doubts he would have said what Monteiro now alleges.

a) Can Monteiro rely on the statements by the bank manager that she would be responsible only for the term loan at trial? What clause in the guarantee is relevant and what rule of evidence?

Implied Terms

The parties will have agreed on certain terms of an agreement. These are called **express terms**: actual stated terms, written or oral. However, at times there are gaps left in the contract, and the parties or the courts must try to determine how those gaps should be filled in. Sometimes statutes provide that certain terms must be included in every contract of a particular kind. For example, statutes such as the sale of goods acts and the partnership acts are a collection of terms that were implied by courts into agreements based on the practices of the businesses of the day. For example, the courts accepted that, by custom, a term should be implied into an agreement to sell products that the seller owned the goods and had the right to sell them. This term and other terms implied by custom were collected together to form the *Sale of Goods Act*. Additional terms may also be added by custom and usage of a particular business, though not expressly implied by a statute.

implied terms

terms that a court or statue add into a contract

The courts will impose **implied terms** which are based on the parties' expectations and which are necessary to give effect to the agreement. For example, when a business engages the service of a lawyer or an accountant, there is usually no express term that the professional will act competently. However, the court will imply such a term on the basis that it is so obvious a term that it was understood to be agreed between the parties. In oral employment contracts there is usually no agreed term that an employee will be given notice for a period of time if fired without a good reason. The courts imply this term into such agreements.

In an early case a tenant leased a house by way of an oral lease agreeing only to a price and the length of the lease. The house was infested with cockroaches. The court implied a term that the house be habitable and free of noxious insects, and set aside the lease.

However, the courts will not necessarily imply a term just because one of the parties wants it. The principle is meant to be used only to repair an obvious oversight.

The test for when a court will imply a term was expressed by a judge of the U.K. Court of Appeal as follows:

> If it is such a term that can be confidently said that if at the time the contract was being negotiated someone had said to the parties, "What will happen in such a case?" they would both have replied, "Of course, so and so will happen; we did not need to say that; it is too clear."[2]

Thus, it can be seen that the court will only add a term that it feels *both* parties would have readily agreed to if it had been suggested to them at the time that they negotiated the contact. Another judge phrased the above test to the effect that if an officious (meddlesome) bystander were to have suggested some provision in the agreement, the parties would have responded, "Oh, of course."[3]

So the test for a court-implied term based on both parties' fair expectation is sometimes called the "officious bystander" test. The purpose of the implication of a term is to give business efficacy to the agreement. Efficacy in this sense means to produce the effect intended.

In *Toronto-Dominion Bank v. Magnolia Tree Holdings Inc.*, 2006 CanLII 5136 (ON CA), the landlord tried to prevent the bank from using its laneway to access parking spaces it had rented to the bank. The court ruled that since the landlord had leased the building and the parking spaces to the bank, there was an implied term that the bank had access to the laneway, which was the only route to access the parking spaces.

Courts have also stated in numerous cases that there is a fundamental implied term in any employment contract that the employer will treat the employee properly with; civility, decency, respect and dignity. This issue will be discussed further in the employment law chapter later.

Duty to Act in Good Faith

One term that is implied into agreements with an increasing frequency in the modern business context is a duty to co-operate in carrying out the contract. This is sometimes expressed as a duty to act in good faith. For example, a bank was a landlord of a large office building. Its tenant was also its bank customer. The tenant/customer successfully sued the bank over the cashing of a fraudulent cheque. When it came time to renew the lease the bank would not co-operate, in retaliation for the tenant's lawsuit. The court held that the bank had a duty to

---

2. *Reigate v. Union Manufacturing Co. (Ramsbottom)*, [1918 1 K.B. 592 per Sutton L.J. p. 605.

3. *Shirlaw v. Southern Foundries Ltd.* (1926), [1939] 2 K.B. 206.

Nickel Developments Ltd. v. Canada Safeway Ltd., 2001 MBCA 79 (Can LII)

Nickel Developments Ltd. owned a shopping centre and leased a supermarket building to Safeway, which was the anchor tenant. There were 12 other smaller stores in the mall. Nickel agreed to a non-competition clause such that during the lease Nickel would not lease to any competing businesses that sold similar supermarket products. The lease was for a 20-year term, providing for renewals every five years according to market rates.

After operating its supermarket for 13 years at that location, Safeway closed down its operation and let the store stand vacant. Safeway continued to renew the lease and pay the rent. Safeway did this because it had a more profitable store a short distance away and did not want a competitor to lease the closed store.

Nickel sued Safeway for breach of contract. Safeway defended saying there was no express term in the lease requiring it to continue to operate a store at that location. It was paying its rent and that was all that was necessary.

The Court's Decision

The court found that Safeway had received benefits from Nickel, particularly the non-competition clause. Safeway was the anchor tenant and a closed supermarket would obviously affect other businesses in that shopping plaza.

Even though there was no actual term requiring continuous operation of the supermarket, the court implied one to give the effect to the arrangement that the parties must have intended. Here the court found that it was reasonable that the parties intended, at the time the contract was made, that Safeway would continue to operate the business. Because Safeway had not done so, it was in default and the lease was terminated.

act in good faith and co-operate in renewal of the lease. It could not use this opportunity to retaliate against the tenant. The tenant was a good tenant by all criteria.

Similarly, the court will often imply duties on sellers to co-operate so that the sale can take place. The seller of an export business was held to have an implied obligation to assist the buyer with the transfer of the export license. There was no express term regarding this transfer. The failure to include such a term was an obvious oversight and it was a term that was necessary to give effect to the sale agreement.

While a duty to act in good faith will be implied in carrying out a contract, recall that such a duty will not be implied in the negotiation process.

■ *Business Law*   Applied

❹ **Haroun Rashid agreed** with Calgary Lumber Ltd. to sell lumber for the lumber mill on commission. After the agreement, the mill raised its prices by 25 percent. Rashid made no sales and blamed the increase in prices. Sales reps for other companies netted about $60,000 in that year, but Rashid sold nothing. Assume Rashid's failure to earn commissions was, in fact, due to the increase in prices by Calgary Lumber.

   a) Was there a term in the agreement between Rashid and Calgary Lumber that it would not raise its prices?
   b) Is there any basis on which Rashid could sue Calgary Lumber? What could he recover?

Limitation and Exemption (Disclaimer) Clauses

Limitation and exemption clauses are terms that regularly appear in contracts. **Limitation clauses** limit the amount of damages that a court can award against a party who breached a contract. For example an airline may have a term that limits its liability to $300 for any lost baggage. **Exemption** (or **disclaimer clauses** as they are often called), try to eliminate any damages that can be awarded against the party that breached the contract. For

limitation and exemption (disclaimer) clauses
clauses in a contract that limit or completely eliminate the damages or other relief that the court would normally award against a party who has breached a contract

example a parking lot may state that "it is not liable for any loss or damage to vehicles however caused."

A reader's initial response to the topic of limitation or exemption clauses is often that the business that uses them is "getting away with something." But these clauses are a necessary party of business and are fair to both sides if both understand the effect of the clause and the risk each is assuming.

Limitation and exemption clauses are regularly used in contracts for daily activities such as; dry cleaners tickets, coat checks in restaurants or theatres, or for lockers rented in gyms. Computer software will typically contain a limitation of liability clause on an early screen in the installation process, and if you click on "continue" you have accepted the terms of the limitation clause.

Limitation and exemption clauses are also often used in major commercial contracts between corporations where damages could run into the millions of dollars if a major problem occurs. In these situations the clauses are fair when there is equal bargaining power and often lawyers for both sides are advising their clients. For example if Chrysler Canada buys engine parts from a supplier and agrees to the supplier's exemption clause, Chrysler could negotiate a lower price for the parts. Both parties will have the risks assessed by lawyers and be well aware of all possible eventualities.

Are Limitation and Exemption Clauses Enforceable?

The issue with these clauses is whether or not they will be enforced by the courts. Normally courts want to uphold the terms of a contract that the parties had agreed upon and to respect their freedom to contract. In consumer situations however courts will take a very narrow and restrictive approach when interpreting and enforcing these clauses. If there is any ambiguity or the clause does not refer to the exact situation in the specific dispute, it will be unenforceable. In consumer cases, it is usually a standard form contract so there is the problem of unequal bargaining power. The contract was written by the lawyers for the company that wants to avoid liability. The consumer often never read the contract, nor saw the limitation clause, and wouldn't have even understood the clause if they had read it due to the complicated legal language used.

So in cases involving individual consumers, the court often takes a restricted interpretation of the clause and can refuse to enforce the clause unless the company that wants to rely on it has "taken reasonable steps to bring it to the attention" of the consumer at the time the contract was made. This might include bold larger print in a contrasting colour, large signs or clear warnings to get the individual's attention. It is similar to the requirements in tort law that companies face when they run high risk sporting activities and want to rely on disclaimers when participants are injured. The courts also will not enforce these clauses if there was misrepresentation by the company's representative that led the individual to believe the exclusion clause did not apply.

Example: In *Trigg v. MI Movers International Transport Services Ltd.* (C.A.), 1991 CanLII 7363 (ON CA), Mr. Trigg shipped two expensive cars from Ontario to Ireland. The shipping agent told him that the company would be liable for damages caused by its negligence, but if it was an Act of God, their liability was limited to 10 cents/lb. Based on this statement, Trigg did not purchase marine insurance. The two cars were badly damaged due to the shipper's negligence and repair costs were $54,082. The shipping contract however limited the liability of the shipping company in ALL situations to 10 cents/lb.- a total of $940 in Trigg's case. The court ruled that the shipping company had not brought the limitation clause to the attention of Trigg at the time the contract was made, he had not read it and he had not agreed to be bound by it, so the term was not part of the contract. The company's agent had misrepresented the insurance coverage and the limitation clause had not been properly brought to Trigg's attention when the contract was formed, so the shipping company could not rely on it. MI was liable for the full repair costs.

Example: In *Solway v. Davis Moving* 2002 CanLII 21736 (ON CA) a couple hired a moving company to transport all their belongings to a new home, but the goods had to remain on the truck for 2 weeks until the new home was renovated. The moving company assured them their goods would be kept in a locked truck on their lot which would be safe and secure. The movers did tell the couple it limited its liability to 60 cents/lb. and advised the couple to get insurance. Mr. Solway did purchase insurance for the goods during the move with $170,200 in coverage. Unfortunately one night the moving company stored the trailer on the street, so snow ploughs could clear their lot, and the trailer was stolen. It was found empty weeks later. The couple were devastated as the goods included very rare and valuable artifacts and antiques as well as many sentimental items. The couple said the real value of the goods was about $750,000. Davis Moving tried to rely on its limitation clause of 60cents/lb. which resulted in liability of about $7,000. The court however ruled that it would be unfair and unreasonable to enforce the limitation clause. The movers should not have left the trailer on the street in an industrial area with no surveillance, so they had seriously breached the contract and it would be unconscionable to let the company limit its liability to $7,000. The court held the moving company liable for the full value of the goods stolen.

When the contract however is between two companies, the courts treat limitation and exemption clauses differently. In commercial situations where it is a business-to-business agreement, the courts assume there is equality in bargaining power and are much more likely to enforce these clauses. The courts expect that businesspeople will have read, or had their lawyers read the contract, so they were aware of the risks and these are the terms they had agreed upon, so these clauses should be enforced. There is no duty on one side to alert the other to the exclusion clause in commercial contracts.

Example: In *Fraser Jewelers (1982) Ltd. v. Dominion Electric Protection Co.*, 1997 CanLII4452 (ON CA), a jewelry store hired ADT to provide a security system for the store. ADT charged an annual service charge of $890 and the contract had a limitation clause that stated ADT limited its liability for any losses or damages the jewelry store may incur to the lesser of one year's service fee or $10,000. One day two thieves robbed the store and tied up two employees and made off with $50,000 in jewelry. While they were tied up, the employees managed to press the hidden holdup alarm button that signalled to ADT there was a robbery in progress. Unfortunately ADT waited 10 minutes to call the police and the thieves had left by the time the police arrived. The trial judge accepted that if ADT had called the police immediately the thieves would have been caught.

Fraser Jewelers sued ADT for its $50,000 in losses, but ADT maintained that it only owed $890 due to the limitation clause. Fraser argued that it would be unconscionable, unfair and unreasonable to apply the limitation clause, as there had been a major fundamental breach by ADT so it should not be allowed to use the clause to reduce its liability. The jewelry store owner admitted that he had not read the contract and ADT had not brought the clause to his attention.

The court ruled that the limitation clause was valid and all ADT owed was $890. There was no duty on ADT to show the clause to the jeweler, they were both business people. The court did not think the limitation clause was unconscionable. It would not strike down the limitation clause, because if it did, it would effectively turn ADT into the jeweler's insurer for the low annual fee of only $890 and that did not make commercial sense. The court ruled that Fraser should have been aware of the terms and purchased insurance to protect itself. The limitation clause was upheld and ADT's liability was limited to $890.

Fundamental Breach

The principle of fundamental breach in contract law was frequently used in relation to exclusion clauses. A fundament breach meant that the breach was so large or enormous, that the innocent party had essentially been denied all the main benefits of the contract. A fundamental breach therefore destroyed the entire contract, including the limitation or exemption clause the defendant wanted to use. The use of the fundamental breach doctrine was applied in the *Plas-Tex v. Dow Chemical* case below, when Dow Chemical had tried to rely on its disclaimer, even though it knew the product it supplied to Plas-Tex was dangerous and defective and risked public safety.

Plas-Tex Canada Limited v. Dow Chemical of Canada
2004 ABCA 309 CanLII

In a case that went on for 28 years, Dow Chemicals tried to rely on an exclusion clause to avoid liability when it had knowingly supplied defective plastic resin to Plas-Tex. Dow knew that Plas-Tex, (and many other companies) would use the resin to make plastic pipes that would distribute natural gas throughout rural Alberta. Dow knew that the resin would deteriorate and cause the pipes to crack and leak, but it never warned Plas-Tex, nor any of its other customers, of the problem.

Some years later, due to the defective resin, the plastic pipes began to degrade with considerable damage to property and risk to human health from the leaks and natural gas explosions. The Alberta government ordered that all gas pipes in the province with the Dow resin had to be replaced. Plas-Tex was forced to undertake a very expensive remedial repair program which Dow refused to help fund. The government and some pipe companies sued Dow in a class action that settled out of court, but Plas-Tex chose not to join the class. Plas-Tex did the expensive repairs, it lost many customers as its reputation was ruined and it was finally forced into bankruptcy.

Plas-Tex sued Dow for breach of contract and negligence. Dow admitted that it knew the resin was "inherently dangerous and intrinsically harmful", but claimed that the exclusion clause stated that Plas-Tex "accepted all liability for loss or damage resulting from the use of the resin." Dow said they were both sophisticated business parties, so there was equality of bargaining power and the court should enforce the exemption clause both sides had freely agreed to.

The Court's Decision

The trial court and the Alberta Court of Appeal both agreed that there was a fundamental breach and it would be unfair and unreasonable to allow Dow to escape liability by enforcing the exemption clause. The importance of preserving the right to freedom to contract cannot override the obvious unfairness that would occur if a company that intentionally sold a defective dangerous product could avoid responsibility by relying on an exemption clause. Dow was liable for both breach of contract and negligence. The damages awarded were almost $3 million including the cost of the resin, the costs of repairing the pipelines and Plas-Tex's lost profits(which were almost $2 million).

New Approach to Exclusion Clauses

The problem with the use of the fundamental breach doctrine is that it caused considerable uncertainty and was not particularly helpful. It became very difficult to predict when a court would characterize a breach as a "fundamental" or "immense" or "colossal" breach.

Because of the inconsistencies that this approach created, the Supreme Court finally stated in the Tercon Contractors case that "it should again attempt to shut the coffin on the jargon associated with fundamental breach" and its application to limitation and exemption clauses. Instead, when determining the enforceability of these clauses, the courts should analyze three issues when making their decision: 1) whether the exclusion clause actually applied to the specific facts of the breach, 2) whether it was unconscionable at the time the contract was formed (i.e. due to unequal bargaining power) and 3) if there are public policy reasons why the clause should not be enforced. In Tercon, the court ruled that the disclaimer did not apply to the specific circumstances in this case, so the defendant, the B.C. government, could not use it to avoid liability.

Tercon Contractors Ltd. v. British Columbia (Transportation and Highways), 2010 SCC 4, [2010] 1 SCR 69

The B.C. government planned to build a new highway. After initial interest had been shown by six companies, the B.C. government asked for final proposals from these six bidders and stated that only these six companies could be considered for the contract. The government contract included an exclusion clause that stated, none of the companies shall have any claim for compensation of any kind as a result of submitting a proposal.

One of the six companies that bid, Brentwood, lacked the expertise, so it formed a joint venture with an ineligible company. The government narrowed it down to two finalists, Tercon and the Brentwood joint venture. The contract was finally awarded to the Brentwood joint venture and Tercon sued the B.C. government for breach of contract. Tercon said the government had awarded the contract to the Brentwood joint venture knowing it included an ineligible company. Tercon claimed its lost profits of over $3 million. The B.C. government admitted it had given the contract to an ineligible company but relied on its exemption clause that stated no bidder shall have any claim for compensation from the bidding process.

The trial court ruled that there had been a fundamental breach by the government and it had clearly broken its own rules and its actions damaged the integrity and transparency of the tendering process. The judge ruled the exemption clause was unfair and unclear and ambiguous and she ruled in favour of Tercon. The case was appealed to the B.C. Court of Appeal and it disagreed with the trial decision. It held that the clause was clear and unambiguous and therefore prevented Tercon from any claims for damages due to the breach of contract. Tercon appealed to the Supreme Court of Canada.

The Supreme Court's Decision

The Supreme Court ruled that the doctrine of fundamental breach was to no longer be used when determining whether exclusion clauses applied as it had caused considerable uncertainty. The court said that the new proper analysis should consider three issues. First the court must decide if the terms of the exclusion clause even apply to the exact circumstances of the specific dispute. If it does apply to these facts, the next issue is whether the clause was unconscionable and thus invalid at the time the contract was made. If there was unequal bargaining power that could establish it was unconscionable from the outset. The third issue then to consider is whether there is a public policy reason that justifies overriding the parties' important right of freedom to contract. The court indicated that obvious situations such as fraud or other criminal behaviour would establish a valid public policy issue that would justify not enforcing an exclusion clause that the parties had knowingly and willingly agreed to.

In a close 5-4 decision, the court ruled the exemption clause did not apply to the specific breach that occurred in this case. They ruled that the clause was ambiguous and only meant to exclude claims involving eligible companies, not claims involving ineligible bidders. The government's conduct violated the integrity of the entire tender/bidding process by awarding the contract to an ineligible company. A vague limitation clause should not be interpreted to favour the government and exempt it from liability in this situation. Tercon was successful and awarded over $3million in lost profits.

The dissenting judges would have upheld the exclusion clause because these were sophisticated business parties familiar with the bidding process and had freely agreed to these contract terms including the exemption clause.

■ *Critical Concepts of* Limitation and Exemption Clauses

- Adequate notice: the exemption clause must be brought to the attention of the person signing the agreement.
- Timing: notice of the clause must be at the time of purchase.
- Misrepresentation: If a salesperson misrepresents the effects of the clause, this could be grounds for making the clause unenforceable.
- Interpretation: The exemption clause will be narrowly and strictly interpreted. If damage occurs in a way not expressly stated in the clause, the clause will be ineffective.
- The fundamental breach doctrine has been replaced with three issues that have to be analyzed to see if an exclusion clause applies: does the clause apply to the specific fact situation, was it unconscionable when the contract was formed, and is there a public policy reason why it should not be enforced.

■ *Business Law* Applied

❺ Review the *Trigg v. MI Movers* and *Solway v. Davis Moving* cases above and then answer the following:

a) What were the critical facts of the cases?
b) What were the legal issues?
c) Who won? Were the disclaimers enforced?

❻ Review the *Fraser Jewellers v. Dominion Electric* case and the *Plas-Tex v. Dow Chemical* cases above and answer the following:

a) What were the critical facts of the cases?
b) What were the legal issues?
c) Who won? Were the disclaimers enforced?

❼ Review the *Tercon Contractors v. B.C.* case and answer the following:

a) What were the critical facts of the case?
b) What was the legal issue?
c) Who won? Was the disclaimer enforced?
d) Has this case cleared up the issues associated with fundamental breach? What problems could still exist?

❽ Kathy Nelson made a New Year's resolution to get fit and lose 10 kilograms by Easter. She joined Curves-R-Us Spa and on January 5, 2000, signed its standard form contract taking out a one-year health-club membership requiring monthly payments of $50. Nelson's resolve cooled by March of that year. She had made payments for January, February, and March and then stopped going and making payments.

At the end of the second year (2001) of the contract term, she started to receive nasty calls from the spa's collection manager claiming she owed almost three years worth of payments. He told her to read the contract. Unlikely as it seemed, she was able to find a copy of her contract and read with horror the second last paragraph on the reverse side that said:

Renewal. This contract is automatically renewed every year for a one-year period unless the customer gives written notice of cancellation 90 days before the anniversary date of the contract and any renewals thereof.

a) If the renewal clause is effective, how much does Nelson owe?
b) Does Nelson have any defence to the claim?
c) Why do you think the spa waited until the end of the second year to contact her? Why didn't it begin collection immediately within 30 days after the first default?
d) Why do you think the cancellation term was set at 90 days before the end of the anniversary date of the contract?

Miscellaneous Clauses

Agreements to Specify Damages

liquidated damages
the amount of damages (in cash, or liquid, form) to be paid should the agreement be breached

penalty clauses
terms specifying an exorbitant amount for breach of contract, intended to force a party to perform

The innocent party in a breach of contract suit might be awarded damages as monetary compensation for the loss suffered. Some contracts contain terms specifying **liquidated damages**, which are the amount of damages (in cash, or liquid, form) to be paid should the agreement be breached. The term in the contract might contain an exact dollar figure, or it could give a formula that sets out how the damages will be calculated.

The courts have developed strict rules surrounding this type of clause because of possible abuse by businesses that hold a superior bargaining position. Such firms have been able to force other companies to accept damages clauses out of proportion to any realistic estimate of loss. In reality these are **penalty clauses**—terms specifying an exorbitant amount for breach of contract, intended to force a party to perform—included to make sure that the contract is met.

The principle the courts have developed to guarantee fairness in damages clauses is: the liquidated damages clause will be enforced only if, at the time the contract is made, the amount is a genuine pre-estimate of the damages that a court would award. If the court rules that a clause is a penalty, then the court will strike down the clause and the innocent party can sue for its actual losses.

Consider this example:

A contractor agrees with a mine owner to dig a shaft by June 1. The mine owner calculates that his loss, if the shaft is not completed on time, will be $10,000 a day.

If the mine owner insists on a clause setting damages at $100,000 per day after June 1, this is not a reasonable pre-estimate of damages, and will be struck down by the court.

If the mine owner sets the damages at $10,000 per day in the contract, this is a reasonable pre-estimate, and will be enforced without proof of actual loss. The mine owner might in fact lose only $1,000 a day. On the other hand, if the real loss was actually $100,000 a day, he would still receive only the $10,000 a day specified in the contract.

See paragraphs 7 and 9 of the Used Car Bill of Sale in the Appendix for examples of clauses that attempt to specify damages.

■ *Critical Concepts of* Liquidated Damages and Penalty Clauses

- Liquidated damages are genuine pre-estimates of the amount the courts would award.
- Penalties are estimates of damages unrelated to the real damages.
- The fact that a term is called liquidated damages in a contract is disregarded by the court. The courts will apply the genuine pre-estimate test to determine whether the estimate is valid.
- If a liquidated damages clause is struck down, the innocent party can still sue for its real loss.

■ *Business Law* Applied

❾ New East Manufacturing Company ordered a quantity of steel from Cansteel Inc. The contract contained a clause that put the manufacturing company's loss estimate at $10 per unit should the supplier fail to deliver. Cansteel did breach the contract. New East Manufacturing discovered that its actual loss was in fact close to $50 per unit, rather than the $10 specified in the agreement.

a) What is the name for this type of clause?
b) What test would the courts apply to decide whether the term was enforceable?
c) Could New East claim the full $50 per unit loss?

Deposits

A deposit is an amount paid at the beginning of the contract as a sign of good faith. It suggests that the purchaser is serious about the agreement, and intends to follow through with it. The amount of a deposit must also be based on a pre-estimate of damages.

The Used Car Bill of Sale specifies in several places what happens to the deposit paid by the purchaser. Should the purchaser fail to complete the agreement, the deposit is forfeited, or lost. Clauses 7 and 10 deal specifically with the purchaser's deposit. While most standard form agreements specifically deal with what happens to a deposit under various possible circumstances, some do not. If this is the case, common law rules apply.

In common law if the person who paid the deposit does not complete the deal, the innocent party who received the deposit can keep the entire deposit, but cannot sue for any other losses. The exception to this is in real estate transactions where they can keep the deposit and sue for any additional losses. The penalty issue does apply to deposits as well. If the court rules that the deposit is excessive and not a genuine pre-estimate of damages, the court can rule it is a penalty and strike it down and then set appropriate damages.

In studying the law of contracts, it is not safe to draw conclusions about the law based on retail business practices. For the sake of good public relations, businesses often waive compliance with the law. Businesses often permit customers to take back a deposit or return goods for a refund. In law, the business may not legally be required to do so.

Real Estate Transactions

An example of a deposit and a down payment in the same transaction can be seen in the normal real estate deal.

A real estate deal is normally completed in two stages. First, an offer is presented on a standard form, along with a deposit. When the offer is accepted, it becomes the agreement for purchase and sale. The second stage may not happen till several weeks or months later, when the final amount is paid and the purchaser receives the deed (or is registered on *title* as owner)—the deal is closed. A house sale might involve amounts such as:

Deposit	$10,000
Down payment	$40,000
Mortgage to seller	$150,000
TOTAL	$200,000

Deposits   Be careful in giving any deposits. The business receiving them may not be able to refund them. It is a common complaint by purchasers of franchises that they have given large deposits in the order of $100,000 for initiation payments, but the franchise company has gone bankrupt. If giving a large deposit, have a credit check done on the company. Credit bureaus such as Dunn & Bradstreet will do credit checks for members of the public. Also, make certain the deposit is acknowledged to be held "in trust" for your purpose so it can't be used in the business generally. If the deposit is held in trust and the business goes bankrupt, it cannot be used to pay off other creditors and will be returned in full. Try to get a personal guarantee of the return of the deposit from the owner of the company. If that individual won't give a personal guarantee, be cautious!

Down Payments

The court will determine if the payment in advance is a deposit or a down payment (also called a pre-payment) by examining the circumstances surrounding the making of the agreement, and what the parties said at the time. A **down payment** is a sum of money paid by the buyer as an initial part of the purchase price, and not completely forfeited if the contract is breached. If a contract specifies that a payment in advance was in fact a deposit, this will be of some influence on the court.

The key difference between a deposit and a down payment is that if the agreement is breached, the holder can deduct any actual loss from the down payment, but must refund the balance. With a deposit, the holder can keep the entire amount no matter what the actual loss is.

■ *Critical Concepts of* Deposits and Down Payments

- A deposit is forfeited if the deal is not completed by the fault or choice of the depositor.
- The loss of the deposit can be attacked as a penalty if that deposit was larger than a genuine pre-estimate of damages.
- The innocent party who holds the deposit must accept it as the complete payment, or remedy, for damages, and cannot sue for more, even if damages actually are greater.

- There is an exception for real estate transactions. The innocent deposit holder can retain the deposit and sue for any additional actual loss.
- It is common practice for retailers to refund deposits, but this is business practice, not law.
- If it is a down payment the innocent holder can deduct any actual losses from the down payment and then refunds the balance, if any, to the other party. If the down payment does not cover the full loss, the innocent holder keeps the full down payment and can sue for the additional amount owing

■ *Business Law* Applied

⑩ **Silverio Ranieri paid** a deposit of $1,000 while the landlord of a retail store had a written lease prepared. The next day, as he was on his way to sign the lease, Ranieri saw a location that he liked better, and rented it. He returned to the first landlord and asked for his deposit back. The retail store was located in a busy area, and it was likely that the landlord could re-let it easily without suffering any actual loss.

a) Did the landlord have to return the deposit to Ranieri?
b) If Ranieri had paid first and last months' rent on the first unit, would the landlord have to return that amount?

⑪ Thomas agreed to purchase a car from Sophia for $9,000 and gave her a $1,000 deposit when they made the contract. Before he was to complete the deal, Thomas changed his mind and told Sophia he would not buy the car and he wanted his $1,000 back. Sophia was angry, and refused to return the $1,000 deposit. Sophia was able to sell the same car to Peter for $8,500 several days later.

a) Can Thomas get any money back from Sophia since she has resold the car?
b) If Thomas had paid her a $1,000 down payment, would this change your answer?
c) If Sophia had only been able to resell the car for $7,500, would this change your answer on the $1,000 deposit Thomas had paid? Would it change your answer if the $1,000 had been a down payment?

Interest Charges

The rate of interest to be charged is a significant factor in the decision to give or accept credit in business. Interest costs, and the way they are calculated, can add considerably to the principal involved. There are both federal and provincial statutes governing the charging of interest. Violation of these provisions could mean that you would not be permitted to charge interest at all, or could do so only at a much lower rate.

The Criminal Code prohibits interest rates above 60 percent per annum. This provision is commonly referred to as the "loansharking" section. All sums payable for the granting of credit are to be included as part of the interest calculation. So, sums called bonuses or finder's fees may be included in the calculation of the effective interest rate.[4]

Pay Day loans, as discussed in Chapter 5, are exempt from the Criminal Code criminal rate of interest in provinces where laws have been passed to regulate this industry. Unfortunately the provincial laws have made it legal for these loans to effectively charge more than 500% interest.

Interest must be stated at the time the contract is made and not added in as a term later on. Interest must be stated as an annual rate. Often companies will state for example a monthly rate, such as 2 per cent per month. It is legal to state a monthly or daily rate, but only so long as the full annual rate is included as well. If there is no annual rate given then *The Interest Act* R.S.C. 1985, states that the maximum rate that can be charged is 5 per cent per year.

---

4. Canadian Criminal Code, s. 347.

■ *Critical Concepts of* Interest

- The right to charge interest is a matter of contract, and must be included as a term at the time the agreement is made. It cannot be added by one party later.
- Interest must be expressed in an annual form, such as 24 percent per annum. If it is put in any other way, the *Interest Act* states that only 5 percent per annum can be charged. It can be put as a daily or monthly charge as long as the per-annum rate is also stated.
- In consumer contracts, in addition to the annual interest rates, all costs associated with the credit—such as administration costs, fees, bonuses, insurance, and the like—must be disclosed.

■ *Business Law* Applied

🔟 **Sookraj Deva needed** some extensive dental work. It was to cost $2,000, and he arranged with his dentist to make monthly payments on the total amount.

The work was performed and the dentist sent his bill. Printed at the foot of the invoice was: "2% per month on the unpaid balance."

Deva complained to the dentist that there had been no agreement to pay interest, and that the rate was too high anyway.

a) Does he have any grounds to challenge the interest charges?

Business Alert!

Credit Card Interest Charges   Consumer groups frequently warn that credit card interest rates are unnecessarily high. A user, unaware of the effect of interest charges, can easily become caught in an inescapable trap of spiralling debt.

Most bank credit cards charge interest at about three times the prime rate. Retail credit cards are even higher. It is good business sense to pay any credit card balance in full every month. If this is not possible, and a purchase is absolutely necessary for the business, a bank loan can usually be negotiated on a short-term basis, at less than half the credit card interest rates.

Stating Interest Charges

This excerpt from a Bell Canada statement of account shows the correct way to indicate interest charges:

> **Late Payment Charge Increase**
>
> Due to an increase in the prime interest rate, effective June 26, 2002, Bell Canada increased the amount it charges on overdue accounts to 1.25 percent per month or 16.07 percent per year.

Cancellation Charges

Some businesses attempt to claim an administrative charge at the time of cancellation. Amounts claimed will vary. Amounts of $100 to $200 are common, but some businesses claim much larger sums. There are two common legal issues involving cancellation charges:

- They may not be part of the contract, but are added on at the time of cancellation. These are not enforceable for lack of consideration. One party cannot add a term without the consent of the other party.
- They may be made a term of the contract, but the courts could regard them as a penalty clause, and therefore declare them unenforceable (see p. 133).
- To be enforceable, a cancellation fee must be a genuine pre-estimate of the damages that a court would award. If the amount is excessive, the clause will not be enforced.

Business Law   Applied

⑱ Accucomp Computers Inc. had a fire-insurance policy on its premises. The company found a new insurance broker, who offered a much lower rate, and as a result Accucomp wrote to its current broker to cancel the existing policy. The broker replied that there would be a $100 cancellation fee. Accucomp does not want to pay this.

a) What two rules about cancellation fees might help Accucomp avoid having to pay?
b) What facts would make the cancellation charge enforceable or not?
c) If the broker can establish that the administrative costs involved in cancelling the policy were $100, would this affect the situation?

Forum Selection Clauses

Venue refers to place: a venue clause determines in which place a trial over a contract dispute will take place. Since the growth of international trade and especially since NAFTA (the North American Free Trade Agreement), Canadian businesses are increasingly making contracts with foreign-based companies. For example, an English wholesaler purchases bananas from a Columbian farmer. The English whole-seller resells these bananas to an American distributor and directs the Columbian farmer to ship directly to the U.S. using a ship registered in Liberia. The American distributor has by this time resold the bananas to a Canadian business located in Ontario. The ship sinks in international waters. There is a serious problem determining which country or province has jurisdiction and which law applies Thus, businesses are cautioned to have governing law and venue clauses in any contract. See paragraph 10 of the Purchase Order in the Appendix to Chapter 8 for a governing law and venue clause.

The importance of this issue was dramatized by the case of Canadian funeral franchise company Loewen Group Inc. A Mississippi franchisee sued Loewen in a dispute over a franchise agreement. The matter was heard before a Mississippi jury. The plaintiff's counsel made a point of the defendant's being a foreign company. He referred to foreign companies' taking advantage of simple Mississippi folk and even mentioned the sneak attack on Pearl Harbor by foreigners.

In a case that most observers felt was of doubtful merit, the jury awarded punitive damages of $500 million against Loewen. It appealed, but the Mississippi Appellate Court was of no help. That court ordered Loewen to post a bond for the full $500 million or the appeal would be dismissed. Loewen could not raise that amount of money and was forced to settle with the plaintiff by paying him about $200 million. The lawyer for the successful plaintiffs received $69 million in legal fees.

Canadian companies can avoid foreign courts, especially American jury trials, by insisting on a venue clause that names a province in Canada where the company carries on business as the place of trial.

Alternatively, if the foreign company will not agree to a Canadian jurisdiction there can be an arbitration clause so the matter can be heard before an international arbitration tribunal.

Online Agreements

Online agreements typically use forum selection clauses as users may live in any part of the world. Here is an example of Facebook's forum selection clause.

"You will resolve any claim, cause of action or dispute ("claim") you have with us arising out of or relating to this Statement or Facebook in a state or federal court located in Santa Clara County. The laws of the State of California will govern this Statement, as well as any claim that might arise between you and us, without regard to conflict of law provisions. You agree to submit to the personal jurisdiction of the courts located in Santa Clara County, California for the purpose of litigating all such claims."

Z.I. Pompey Industrie v. ECU-Line N.V.
2003 SCC 27 CanLII

A U.S. company purchased a photo processor and four sub-assemblies from Z.I. Pompey in France for resale to its customer in Seattle, Washington. ECU-Line agreed to provide the transportation for the shipment which was to go from France to Antwerp, Belgium where it was then placed on a ship to Montreal and then was to travel by rail to Seattle, Washington. The transportation contract (the Bill of Lading) was a C.I.F. contract that meant the seller (Z.I. Pompey) bore the risk of any damages to the cargo until it was delivered to the buyer and the contract clearly stated that:

> this bill of Lading is governed by the law of Belgium, and any claim or dispute arising hereunder or in connection herewith shall be determined by the courts in Antwerp and no other Courts.

When the goods arrived in Seattle they were damaged and the seller, Z.I. Pompey, sued the transportation company ECU-Line for $60,761 in damages in Federal Court in Canada as it alleged the damage occurred while in transit in Canada. It claimed that because the case would involve Canadian and American witnesses, the case should be heard in Canada. It argued that since the Belgian court would conduct the proceedings in Flemish, it would pose considerable language problems for the witnesses. ECU-Line denied liability and claimed that the contract clearly stated that the dispute could only be heard in the courts in Antwerp, Belgium and a Canadian court had no right to decide the case.

The Canadian Federal Court of Appeal ruled that the plaintiffs had met the "strong cause" test and established good reasons why this case should be heard in Canada. The shipping company appealed this decision to the Supreme Court of Canada.

The Court's Decision

The Supreme Court reviewed the well-established "strong cause" test that applies when considering whether a venue clause should not be enforced. The court emphasized that in the context of international commerce, order and fairness must be preserved. The "strong cause" test rightly imposes the burden on the plaintiff to satisfy the court that there are very good reasons it should not be bound by the forum selection clause. They must show that it is unreasonable or unjust in the circumstances to apply the contract term. It is essential that the courts give full weight to the desirability of holding contracting parties to their agreements. If parties are using this clause for improper motives or to gain an unfair procedural advantage, then a strong cause will be established and a different venue can be set.

In this case however a "strong cause" was not established. There was no improper motive or advantage by insisting on Belgium. Even though the companies were more familiar with the Canadian system and there would be some language difficulties in Belgium, those were not good enough reasons to override the terms the two parties had agreed upon. A judgment in Belgium would be enforceable in North America with little difficulty and strong enough arguments had not been made to justify transferring the case to Canada. The Supreme Court ruled a court in Antwerp should resolve this dispute.

Business Alert!   There are often "governing law" clauses in international agreements. Such a clause may say, for example, that any disputes are to be governed by the laws of Alberta. This is not protection from a foreign court. A Florida court, for example, would still hear the trial but apply Alberta law. Experts from Alberta would be called to testify as to the relevant Alberta law.

Example: In Dell Computer Corp. v. Union des consommateurs, 2007 SCC 34, Dell computers mistakenly advertised on its website two computers for sale priced at $89 and $118. The actual prices of the computers were $379 and $549. When Dell realized the error it immediately blocked the site and posted corrected prices. All Dell's online sales contracts clearly stated that any disputes will be determined by mandatory arbitration conducted by the National Arbitration Forum (NAF). NAF is an online arbitration forum based in the U.S. Mr. Dumoulin found a way into the blocked Dell site and was one of the 354 people in Quebec who had ordered a total of 509 computers from Dell at these erroneous low prices that weekend. Dell refused to sell the computers at the incorrect low price. Dumoulin and a consumers' group then attempted to form a class action to sue Dell in a Quebec court for breach of contract. Dell insisted that only the NAF had the right to hear this dispute as was clearly stated in the contract. Dumoulin claimed that the clause referring to the NAF resolution should not be enforceable as it had not been adequately brought to their attention. The clause was not in the body of the main contract but was in a hyperlink in the terms and conditions.

But the Supreme Court made it very clear that the clause had been adequately brought to the consumers' attention. The hyperlink was mentioned on every page in the terms and conditions and it was no different than if a paper contract had been provided. This dispute could not be tried in the Quebec court, only the NAF arbitration forum could decide this case.

Privity of Contract

Privity of contract is the principle in law that since a contract is created by two or more people exchanging promises, it is generally only those individuals who are direct parties to the agreement who are subject to its obligations and entitled to its benefits.

Exceptions to this general rule exist for certain situations. An example is a contract for life insurance. Referred to as an insurance policy, such a contract is entered into by the insurance company and the **insured** (the one who buys insurance coverage). However, if the insured individual dies in circumstances that require a payment to be made under the terms of the policy, it is an outside party—the **beneficiary**—who is the person who enforces the contract against the insurance company and receives the benefits.

Privity   **Privity** comes from the Latin word *privatus*, which means private. Thus, privity refers to a private arrangement. Only those who are part of a contract have rights connected with it; outsiders have none. Privity is the legal expression of the "one on one" concept.

Legalese

Limitations of Privity

The concept of privity developed at a time when supplier and purchaser dealt directly with each other. (If you wanted a dresser, you went to the cabinetmaker and made the deal directly with him.) Today there is often a chain of businesses between the manufacturers and end-users.

The retailer is usually the last link in the chain and deals directly with the end-user. The contract for sale is between the retailer and the end-user. By the doctrine of privity, the end-user can sue the retailer only for any loss because of a defect in the product.

However, it is the manufacturer who is responsible for quality control, length of warranties, and the like. The retailers are little more than a conduit for the product. The customer, however, has no contract with the manufacturer, and so cannot sue it in contract.

This inadequacy in the law has been the subject of much discussion but little action. To date, only Saskatchewan (*Consumer Product Warranties Act, R.S.S. 1978, c. C-30*) and New Brunswick (*Consumer Product Warranty and Liability Act, S.N.B. 1978, c. C-181*) have passed legislation that gives consumers (but not businesses) a direct right to sue manufacturers for loss caused by defective products.

The Supreme Court did however rule in a trilogy of cases[5] in 2013 that indirect third party purchasers could sue a manufacturer in a class action for violating the price fixing provisions of the Competition Act. Companies who had supplied their products to other companies in the distribution chain had been involved in illegal price fixing schemes. The higher costs were then eventually passed on to the consumers as the final price of the goods was increased. These practices went on in cases involving products as diverse as electronics and soft drinks. The court ruled that even though the consumers did not have a direct contract with the manufacturers who were guilty of the illegal price fixing, they could still sue them in a class action for the higher prices they had been forced to pay when the increased costs were passed on to them. This decision may cost manufacturers millions in class action settlements. The court hoped this right of consumers to sue would act as a deterrent to this illegal price fixing behaviour.[5]

priority of contract
the principle in law that since a contract is created by two or more people exchanging promises, it is generally only those individuals who are direct parties to the agreement who are subject to its obligations and entitled to its benefits

insured
the one who buys insurance coverage

beneficiary
the person who enforces the contract against the insurance company and receives the benefits

---

5. *Pro Sys Consultants Ltd. v. Microsoft Corporation*, 2013 SCC 57 (CanLII), *Sun Rype Products Ltd. v. Archer Daniels Midland Company*, 2013 SCC 58 (CanLII), *Infineon Technologies AG v. Option consommateurs*, 2013 SCC 59 (CanLII)

Avoiding the Limitations on Privity

Generally, a party who is not a party to a contract cannot take legal action on it. Nevertheless, there are exceptions to this general rule, though they are not wide ranging. For example, if a transaction is based on an agency relationship (which will be discussed in the Employment Law chapter later) or the contract has been assigned, a person who was not part of the original agreement may be able to enforce it through the legal process.

Assignment

Contractual rights can be assigned. Assigning means transferring the contractual rights to another person who then stands in the place of the original party and can enforce the contract in the same way. **Assignments** frequently occur in business. For example, when a business applies for a bank loan, it will often be asked to assign its accounts receivable as security for the loan. **Accounts receivable (book debts)** are amounts owed to a person which can be sold, usually at a discount, or pledged as security for a loan. Accounts receivable are contracts. Assume a furniture store has sold some items on credit to a customer who agrees to pay in monthly installments for a year. The agreement to purchase and pay over the year is a contract.

The furniture store often sells off the contract to a finance company at a discount (often 30-50%), so it can get money right now. This is called **factoring** its accounts receivable. The furniture company (the **assignor**) has transferred or assigned its right to collect the money to the finance company (the **assignee**). The consumer now is in a contractual relationship with the finance company, whether they wanted to be or not.

Statutory Assignment

If the customer does not pay the finance company, the finance company can sue the customer directly without involving the furniture company, so long as the assignment qualifies as a **statutory assignment**. The requirements for a statutory assignment are: the assignment must be for the entire amount in the contract and be a complete transfer with no restrictions, it was done in writing and signed by the assignor (the furniture company) and written notice was given to the customer. If these requirements are met then it qualifies as a statutory assignment and then if the customer does not pay the finance company, it can sue the customer directly without having to join the furniture company in the lawsuit.

The customer cannot assign its duty to pay over to a third party. Benefits can be assigned, but obligations or duties (such as a duty to pay a debt) cannot be assigned. If the customer wanted to transfer its duty to pay to a third party, that would require a novation (a new contract) and it could only be done if the finance company consented to the **novation**.

Equitable Assignment

If there is a defect in any of the procedures required for a statutory assignment, it will likely still be valid as an equitable assignment. An **equitable assignment** is an assignment, other than a statutory assignment, which does not require that the assignment be absolute, unconditional, in writing, or that notice, written or oral, be given by the assignor. However, in this case the assignor retains an interest in the contract and must be part of any settlement and a party to any litigation. This can create extra problems and significant expense if the assignor (the creditor) leaves the country (as in the above question), dies, or refuses to co-operate.

accounts receivable (book debts)
amounts owed to a person which can be sold, usually at a discount, or pledged as security for a loan

assignor
the party that assigns its rights under a contract to a third party

assignee
the third party to whom rights under a contract have been assigned

statutory assignment
an assignment that complies with statutory provisions enabling the assignee to sue the debtor without joining the assignor to the action

equitable assignment
an assignment, other than a statutory assignment, which does not require that the assignment be absolute, unconditional, in writing, or that notice, written or oral, be given by the assignor

Business Law   Applied

⑫ **Nelson Markelj sold** his car to Helen Zawada for $10,000, to be paid in monthly installments of $1,000. When only the first payment had been made, Markelj decided that he wanted to travel around the world. He assigned the balance of the payment in writing to Norman Richler. Markelj phoned Zawada and told her of the assignment; he then got on a plane to Papua New Guinea. Zawada refuses to pay, and Richler wants to sue.

   a) Identify the transactions and the parties. What is the contract and who are the parties to it? What is the assignment and who are the parties to it?

   b) Can Richler alone enforce the assignment against Zawada?

Competing Claimants

A dishonest creditor may assign (that is, sell) the debt twice or more to separate purchasers. The assignment that governs will be the one of which the debtor received notice first. The other assignment(s) will be completely ineffective.

   For example, On May 1, Lara buys a stove from Ace Furniture Inc. and agrees to pay $100 a month for 24 months. On May 3, Ace assigns Lara's contract to ABC Finance Co., but does not notify Lara of this assignment until May 20th. On May 5, Ace wrongfully also assigns Lara's contract to the XYZ Finance Co. and Lara receives notice of this assignment that same day. Lara obviously will not pay both companies, she must make her payments to the XYZ Finance Co., even though ABC was first given the assignment. The company that first gave Lara notice of their assignment, XYZ, gets the payments. All ABC can do is commence legal proceedings against Ace for its illegal actions.

Debtor's Defences

The **assignee** (the XYZ Finance Co. in the above example) cannot acquire a better interest in the contract than the person who gave the assignment. In law this is called taking the assignment "subject to the equities." Equities here means the rights of the original parties. This applies to both statutory and equitable assignments.

   Assume in the example above that the stove Lara bought needed $150 in repairs 3 weeks after she bought it, which are Ace Furniture's responsibility. That $150 could be deducted from the amount that Lara owes XYZ Finance Co.

assignee
the third party to whom rights under a contract have been assigned

Critical Concepts of   Assignments

- The assignment must be complete and unconditional (that is, absolute)—except in Manitoba and Saskatchewan; see *Law of Property Act*, R.S.M., s. 31, and *Choses in Action Act*, R.S.S., s. 2.
- The assignment must be in writing.
- Notice of the assignment must be given in writing to the debtor and must be signed by the person making the assignment (again, except in Manitoba and Saskatchewan).
- Even if the assignment does not comply with statutory procedures, it will still likely be valid as an equitable assignment, but the original party to the contract must be a co-plaintiff, or a defendant if he or she refuses to co-operate in any lawsuit.
- Only benefits can be assigned, obligations or duties (such as to pay a debt) cannot be transferred to a third party, this requires a novation and the other party's consent
- When the same contract is assigned several times, the first date on which the debtor received valid notice of the assignment determines which assignment is enforceable.
- The debtor can set up any defences against the person who makes the assignments that could be asserted against the assignor (the creditor).

In Summation

Standard Form Contracts

- Standard form contracts are essential in the business world, however problems of unequal bargaining power occur when a corporation tries to impose unfair terms on an unwary consumer

Interpretation

- The courts do not apply legal meanings but interpret contract terms according to what a reasonable person would think the terms meant.
- The parol evidence rule prevents parties from testifying as to their understanding of the terms.
- In making an interpretation, the courts will consider various factors including:
  a) dictionary meanings
  b) custom and usage in the trade
  c) prior dealings
  d) the context in which the contract was made
- If one party drafts a standard form contract, any ambiguities will be interpreted against the drafter (*contra proferentem*).

Attempts by Parties to Add Terms

- Even though a long, printed contract is signed, a party may claim there were additional terms not written down.
- An aspect of the parol evidence rule raises a presumption that where a document appears to contain the entire agreement, there are no other terms, verbal or written.
- There are many exceptions to this application of the parol evidence rule, such as when a series of documents as an exchange of letters constitutes the contract. Then no single document appears to contain the entire agreement.
- Other exceptions to the parol evidence rule may occur if the court rules that there is a collateral contract or that the contract is partly written and partly oral

Entire Agreement Clauses

- An entire agreement clause states that all terms are contained in the agreement in writing and that there are no other terms, verbal or written.

Implied Terms

- Some terms of a contract may be statutorily implied. These are terms which must be included in a contract because legislation requires that they be.
- When it is necessary to add a term to give effect to an agreement, the court will imply one only when it concludes that both parties would have readily agreed to it at the time the contract was made.
- A term that is being implied with greater frequency today is the duty to act in good faith in carrying out obligations undertaken in the contract.

Limitation and Exemption (Disclaimer) Clauses

- Limitation clauses attempt to partially limit the liability of a business and exemption or disclaimer clauses attempt to completely exclude the liability that would normally flow from the breach of a contract
- The courts have developed several principles that control the abuse of exemption clauses, such as interpretation *contra proferentem* and ineffectiveness in the case of misrepresentation or inadequate

notice. Inadequate notice has been the most successful ground for avoiding the effects of exemption clauses.

■ Courts are less likely to enforce exemption clauses in retail consumer transactions, but more likely to enforce them in business-to-business transactions.

Agreement to Specify Damages

■ A term in a contract can set out how the damages are to be quantified, such as $1,000 per day until construction is complete.

■ If the amount is not a reasonable estimate of the damage that a court would award (a liquidated damages clause), it will be viewed as a penalty and not enforced.

Deposits and Down Payments

■ A deposit is a sum of money given at the time a contract is entered into as a sign of good faith that the person who gave the deposit will go through with the deal.

■ A deposit is not refundable if the contract is not completed through the fault of the person giving the deposit.

■ A down payment is a part payment on the contract and usually is made when the deal is closed.

■ Businesses may elect to refund deposits as a gesture of good will, even though they are not legally obligated to do so.

■ A down payment can be refunded but only if money remains after the innocent party deducts their losses

Miscellaneous Clauses

■ A cancellation clause must be included at the time the contract is made. A cancellation charge cannot be added by one party.

■ Interest charges must state the annual rate and be included as part of the contract. Effective annual rates over 60 percent are prohibited by the Criminal Code.

■ A venue clause states in which jurisdiction (that is, country, province) a trial over a contract dispute will take place.

■ An arbitration clause determines that disputes over the contract will not be heard in court but before a private arbitrator chosen by the parties.

Privity

■ Generally, only those individuals who have been involved in the creation of the contract can receive the benefits and be subject to the obligations which have been agreed to by them.

■ The limitations of the doctrine of privity may be avoided in some situations where agency, tort, or collateral warranty apply.

■ Assignment of contractual rights to another party will also avoid the doctrine of privity.

Assignment

■ The privity of contract rule restricts enforcement of contractual rights to those parties who entered into the original contract.

■ An exception to the privity of contract rule permits contractual rights to be transferred (assigned), allowing the party receiving the rights (the assignee) to enforce the terms of the original contract.

■ Statutory assignment requires the assignment of rights under a contract to be unconditional and in writing, with written notice of the assignment being given to the debtor.

■ Where the statutory assignment requirements are not met, the assignment may still be a valid equitable assignment.

■ If a debtor received two or more notices of assignment, the debtor need honour only the first one received.

■ The assignments are "subject to the equities" between the original parties.

Closing Questions

Interpretation

1. a) What is the name of the rule that prohibits parties generally from testifying as to their interpretation of what a term in a contract means? What justification is given for this rule?
   b) If a term in a contract is ambiguous, what types of evidence would a court admit to assist in resolving the ambiguity?
   c) What is the name of the rule of construction (interpretation) that applies especially to standard form contracts respecting ambiguity, and what is its effect?

2. Protagoras was a sophist in Greece during the 5th century B.C. A sophist was someone who used his skill at logic and reasoning for practical purposes. The lawyers of the day sought him out as a teacher. He put the following question to his lawyer students.

   "A student asked a law teacher to teach him for a fee. The professor refused to take the money, saying, 'You can pay me after you win your first case.' The student readily agreed. After a short time went by, the law professor approached the student and said, 'You owe me your fee.' The student replied, 'But I haven't won my first case yet!' Said the professor, 'Pay or I'll sue.' "Who wins?"

Parol Evidence Rule

3. John Conrad was negotiating with Marney Lansky for the sale of Conrad's house, for which he asked $300,000. Lansky counter-offered $280,000, but said, "Okay to $300,000 if you throw in that grand piano."

   They signed a standard form agreement of purchase and sale of a house at the sale price of $300,000. No mention was made of the piano in the contract, in order to avoid paying HST. Lansky moved in to find out that Conrad had moved out with the piano. She now wants to sue for it. What two principles of law will assist Conrad in defending any lawsuit brought by Lansky?

4. a) What does *parol* mean in the parol evidence rule?
   b) What are the two situations to which it applies?

5. One application of the parol evidence rule prevents parties from giving evidence to add or vary terms to an agreement that appears to be the entire agreement between the parties. Why does the strength of this presumption differ between an individually negotiated agreement and a standard form agreement?

Exemption Clauses

6. What is the purpose of:
   a) an entire agreement clause?
   b) an exemption clause?
   c) Discuss when will the courts choose not to enforce these two types of clauses?

7. Dewey, Cheatem and Howe is an accounting firm which is considering using an application service provider (ASP) to do its on-line billings and to store its back-up data from all computers.
   a) What business risks is the firm facing if it uses the services of the ASP as contemplated?
   b) What terms in the ASP's service contract would likely cover that risk and with what result?
   c) How could the firm protect itself with the legal or business solutions respecting this contract? Which is likely to be the more effective, the legal or the business solutions?

8. In the case of *Trigg v. MI Movers International Transportation* the exemption clause in the contract was not enforceable against Mr. Trigg because he had not read the clause. In the case of *Fraser*

Jewelers (1982) Ltd. v. Dominion Electric Protection Co., the president of Fraser Jewelers also claimed he had not read the exemption clause, but it was enforced against him. Are these cases reconcilable. If so, how?

9. Identify some of the situations where you have seen a disclaimer, limited liability, or exemption clause. Where they are contained in written documents, bring them to class and study the language that is used.

10. You have designed a complete small-business accounting software package that can be operated on a computer the size of a calculator, and you want to market it.
    a) What possible claims might purchasers make against you?
    b) Draft in your own words (that is, ignore legal terminology) an exemption clause that would reduce the risks associated with such possible claims. Compare your clause with clauses found in agreements that came with a calculator, personal organizer, or accounting software that you may have purchased.

11. When asked to sign a contract in which the exemption clause had been pointed out, Ralph replied: "Sure, no problem. They're not worth the paper they're written on anyway."
    a) Discuss whether his attitude towards exemption clauses is an accurate one.
    b) What further information would you require in order to determine whether Ralph's assessment of this clause is accurate or not?

12. Vesna Yevtoshenko purchased a colour printer for her computer, which she used in her business of making advertising flyers for retail stores. The printer was advertised as being able to print five pages per minute, with clear colour separation, and laser-quality letters.

    In the course of the first month of using the new printer, Yevtoshenko found that it printed at a rate of two pages per minute, and the colours were constantly bleeding into each other, making the flyers appear messy and unprofessional. The store that sold the printer to her attempted to correct the problems three times. After the third visit, they advised Yevtoshenko there was nothing more they could do unless she wanted to use this machine as a trade-in for a much more expensive piece of equipment.

    At this point, Yevtoshenko had lost three contracts totalling $5,000, and her business reputation was suffering as a result of her being unable to meet her contract deadlines. When she pointed this out to the store, it replied that the contract contained an exemption clause protecting the store from any damages suffered by a purchaser of the printer, and the store had done all it needed to do in assisting her with correcting the problems.
    a) Yevtoshenko has come to you for advice on her situation. Outline the issues involved and advise whether she has the right to return the printer to the vendor and demand a refund of her money, as well as the damages suffered by her from the loss of the printing contracts.
    b) If Yevtoshenko bought the printer for personal use and experienced the same problem, what legislation would apply to the sale?
    c) Yevtoshenko bought the printer for personal use and experienced the same problem. She used the machine to print her résumé, and a letter applying for a job as a computer technician, at an annual salary of $40,000. She didn't get the job, and heard later that it had been given to another, less-qualified, applicant, because the firm thought the poor quality print of Yevtoshenko's résumé meant she did not have the necessary skills. Does Yevtoshenko have any remedy?

13. Joan Spetz took her white satin wedding dress, trimmed with beads and sequins, to a dry cleaner for cleaning. When the clerk gave her a receipt to sign, Spetz asked why she had to do so. The reply was that the form exempted the dry cleaner from liability for damages to the beads and sequins on the dress. In fact the clause read: "The company is not liable for any damage, however caused."

    When Spetz picked up the dress after it was cleaned, she discovered a large stain on the satin. The beads and sequins were not damaged at all.
    a) If sued for the replacement cost of the dress, could the dry cleaner rely on the exemption clause?
    b) If the receipt form had contained an entire agreement clause, would the result be the same?

Deposits, Down Payments, and Damages

14. Lalka Industries buys a delivery truck for $100,000 from Gibraltar Manufacturing on credit and gives a $25,000 deposit on signing, then a down payment of $5,000 on delivery. Lalka Industries cannot complete the purchase. Gibraltar Manufacturing repossesses it and sells to another customer for $90,000 for a loss of $10,000.
    a) Can Lalka Industries recover any money from Gibraltar Manufacturing?
    b) If your answer to a) is yes, how much?
       i) $5,000
       ii) $10,000
       iii) $20,000
       iv) $25,000
       v) $30,000

Venue

15. Gibraltar Services sold personal accounting software over the Internet. When Gibraltar sends the software by courier to the purchaser, the package contains a licence agreement that has an exemption clause limiting Gibraltar's responsibility for damages, however caused, to $1,000. It also has a clause saying that the law of British Columbia governs any disputes with respect to the contract.

    One unit was bought by a California customer. There was an error in his bank account resulting in a $10,000 loss to the customer. The software did not detect this error, and the 30-day limitation period contained at the bottom of the customer's bank statement expired, so the customer has no recourse against the bank.

    The customer sues Gibraltar in California for the $10,000 and punitive damages of $1,000,000, and requests a jury trial.
    a) Which law applies, B.C. or California?
    b) Can Gibraltar Services successfully require that the lawsuit be held in British Columbia? If the lawsuit takes place in California, how can that court apply the law of B.C.?
    c) Will the exemption clause be effective?
    d) What could Gibraltar have done with its contractual terms to better protect itself?

Interest

16. Joseph Pereira has opened his own retail home-computing store and sells computers, giving customers two years to pay at 5 percent interest. He gives the customers a one-page bill of sale that says only, "Computers sold at $2,000 at 5 percent interest to be paid in equal installments over two years." In fact, the computer's normal sale price is $1,700 and the balance of the price consists of administration charges and fire and theft insurance.
    a) Has Pereira complied with all the laws regarding charging interest?
    b) What should Pereira have done?

Privity and Assignment

17. A business purchases a recycling machine from a retail environmental-products store. The machine cleans oil so that it can be reused. The retailer purchases the item from a distributor, who in turn purchased the item from an importer, who obtained the item from a Mexican manufacturer.

    The machine completely exploded in the third month of use, because of a defect in design. The explosion seriously injured a workman.

    The business wants to claim a refund of the purchase price, and for business loss because of the shutdown of the plant for one week resulting from the explosion. The workman wants to sue for his injuries (assume that any workers' compensation legislation does not bar this type of lawsuit).

    The retailer is insolvent and has no money to pay a judgment.
    a) Identify all of the contracts in the above scenario, and the parties to each. What lawsuits will have to be started to involve the manufacturer? What problems does the doctrine of privity of contract create in this type of situation?
    b) Are there different considerations for the business and its employee?

c) Would your answer to the above be different if the purchase was made in New Brunswick or Saskatchewan?

d) What changes would you suggest for the simplification of the law respecting the doctrine of privity?

18. Which of the following statements is correct? (More than one may be correct.)
   a) The assignor is the party transferring the contractual rights.
   b) If a creditor assigns a debt twice, the debtor has to pay only the party who received the first assignment.
   c) If a creditor assigns a debt twice, the debtor has to pay the party who first gave notice to the debtor.
   d) A person taking an assignment takes it subject to the equities between the original parties.

19. In this question, all events take place in the same year:
   a) On July 1 a creditor gave written assignment of a debt to a first assignee.
   b) On July 2 this creditor gives a written assignment of the same debt to a second assignee.
   c) On July 3 the second assignee delivers notice of the assignment to the debtor.
   d) On July 4 the first assignee delivers notice to the debtor.

   The creditor, the first assignee, and the second assignee all demand payment from the debtor. Which of the following statements are true?
   a) The debtor must pay half of the amount to the first assignee and half to the second assignee
   b) The debtor need only pay the first assignee as that assignment was made first
   c) The debtor need only pay the second assignee because that assignee gave notice of the debt first
   d) The debtor need not pay either of the assignees because the debtor did not consent to the assignment

20. Joe Creditor sold a computer to Amy Jones on a two-year lease. Creditor assigned the lease in writing to Factor Finance Company. Creditor telephones Amy and tells her to start making payments to Factor Finance. Amy objects, saying that she did not consent to paying Factor. Anyway, the computer needs $200 in repairs. Factor says repair cost is a matter between her and Joe Creditor, as he sold her the computer.
   a) Is the assignment by Creditor to Factor Finance a valid statutory assignment? If not, is it a valid assignment in law?
   b) Does Amy have the right to set off the costs of the repair against the lease payments? If so, what is the name of the legal principle that permits her to do so?

Multi Issue

21. Review the Used Car Bill of Sale in the Appendix to answer the following questions.
   a) Identify the following clauses in that agreement:
      i)   any entire agreement clause(s)
      ii) any disclaimer clause(s)
   b) Review clause number 7. What are the consequences if the purchaser refuses to take delivery? Could this clause be attacked as a penalty clause? What is the legal test for a penalty clause?
   c) Review clause number 9. What are the consequences if a purchaser defaults in payment? Could this clause be attacked as a penalty clause? Again, describe the legal test and the consequences in your opinion.

22. a) Why do you think the courts give little weight to the parties' versions of what a term means in a contract when the meaning of that term is disputed in a court proceeding?
   b) Why do you think the courts will not impose a duty to act in good faith in negotiations but will imply that duty on parties when carrying out a contract?
   c) What is the difference in meaning of an express term and an implied term of a contract?
   d) What type of evidence is excluded by the parol evidence rule when the court is interpreting a contract?

23. John Lindner is the vice-president for marketing of a company that wants to launch a new product. Lindner wants to be certain of several things:

a) that the sales representatives do not make any promises that will result in liability to the company;

b) that the product guarantee is only three months;

c) that any product guarantee is limited to replacement cost and not for any financial loss or business downtime;

d) as he will probably be selling on credit, that if any payment is missed, he has the full range of legal remedies available;

e) as he will be dealing with people overseas, that the disputes will be settled according to his own provincial laws and any trial will take place in his own area;

f) that if he accepts a late payment, he can still insist on strict compliance with future payments.

Identify and name each of the clauses from standard form agreements contained in this text that would satisfy Lindner's concerns.

24. Do a search to find websites that give examples of standard form contracts for businesses that a business can download and use. Download one of the contracts that you think would be useful in a business and bring it to class for discussion. Identify the clauses that relate to issues that have been discussed in the text so far.

25. Review the Business Sales Agreement in the Appendix to Chapter 5 and find the following clauses, all of which have been discussed in the text so far:

1. consideration
2. deposit in trust clause
3. irrevocability
4. non-competition
5. condition on financing
6. acceptance

Used Car Bill of Sale

DAY	MONTH	YEAR

PURCHASER'S INFORMATION

PURCHASER'S NAME: FIRST   MIDDLE INITIAL   LAST

PURCHASER'S ADDRESS

CITY/TOWN   PROVINCE   POSTAL CODE

HOME TELEPHONE NO.   BUSINESS TELEPHONE NO.

DRIVER'S LICENCE NO.   EXPIRY DATE

CAR INFORMATION

YEAR   MAKE   MODEL   COLOUR   STOCK#

SERIAL OR V.I.N. #

DISTANCE TRAVELLED   ❑ KMS   PURCHASER'S   IF MANUFACTURER'S WARRANTY
                ❑ MILES   INITIALS   APPLICABLE; TIME IS MEASURED FROM:

THIS CAR WILL BE DELIVERED WITH
A SAFETY STANDARDS CERTIFICATE   ❑ YES _____   ❑ NO
                                 CERTIFICATE NUMBER

TERMS OF SETTLEMENT

SELLING PRICE	
ADMINISTRATION FEE	
TRADE-IN ALLOWANCE (IF ANY)	
NET DIFFERENCE (ADD LINES 1 AND 2 AND DEDUCT LINE 3)	
P.S.T. ON NET DIFFERENCE	
LICENCE FEE	
GASOLINE	
PAYOUT LIEN ON TRADE-IN	
G.S.T. PAYABLE ON TRADE-IN	
BALANCE DUE	
DEPOSIT: ❑ CHEQUE ❑ CASH ❑ CREDIT CARD	
PAYABLE ON DELIVERY (CERTIFIED FUNDS ONLY)	
INSURANCE: ❑ LIFE ❑ ACCIDENT ❑ LOSS OF INC.	
P.S.T. ON INSURANCE	
LIEN REGISTRATION FEE	
BALANCE FINANCED SUBJECT TO APPROVAL	
NET AMOUNT TO BE FINANCED	
COST OF BORROWING %	
TOTAL BALANCE DUE $	

DEALER GUARANTEE

IS THERE A DEALER GUARANTEE ON THIS CAR?   ❑ YES   ❑ NO
IF YES, COMPLETE THIS SECTION.

_____ DAYS OR _____ KM
                   (WHICHEVER COMES FIRST)

DESCRIPTION _____

TERMS OF THE CONTRACT

1. **PURCHASER'S OFFER:** By signing this form I have made an offer to purchase the car described above ("the car"). I understand that this offer becomes a binding contract between the dealer and me when it is accepted by the signature of an authorized official of the dealer.

2. **CAR SOLD "AS IS":** I agree that if the appropriate space below is initialed by me, the car is sold "As Is" and is not represented as being in a road worthy condition, mechanically sound or maintained at any guaranteed level of quality. The car may not be fit for use as a means of transport and may require substantial repairs at my expense.

   _____   If this space is not initialled by me, this clause
   Purchaser's Initials   does not form part of this agreement.

3. **ACKNOWLEDGEMENT OF TERMS:** I acknowledge having read all terms of the contract, including those on the reverse. I understand that they form part of this agreement. I also agree that no verbal promises have been made to me by the dealer or its employees. The dealer and I agree that the written terms contained in this contract make up the entire agreement between us.

SIGNATURES:

Purchaser's: _____

Co-Signer (if any) _____

TERMS ON BACK FORM PART OF THIS CONTRACT

VENDOR'S ACCEPTANCE

DATE REGISTRATION No.   NAME OF OFFICIAL (PLEASE PRINT)

ACCEPTOR'S REGISTRATION No.   TITLE

DATE   SIGNATURE

Used Car Bill of Sale (continued)

4. **WARRANTIES:** I understand that there are no warranties or representations given by the dealer regarding the car or affecting my rights or those of the dealer, other than those contained in this agreement or set out in any applicable legislation or manufacturer's warranty.

5. **TRANSFER OF OWNERSHIP:** Legal ownership of the car shall not pass to me until the entire purchase price has been paid in full. I agree that until that time, I shall:

   (a) maintain insurance on the car with the dealer as the named beneficiary in the event of a loss;
   (b) not sell or transfer the car to anyone else;
   (c) not allow any lien or other interest to be taken in or against the car;
   (d) not allow the car to be used in the commission of any illegal act; and
   (e) reimburse the dealer for any costs the dealer may incur due to may failure to comply with any of (a), (b), (c), or (d) above.

6. **CREDIT DISCLOSURE:** I authorize the dealer to obtain credit information on me from any credit reporting agency or any credit grantor and to disclose credit information on me to any credit reporting agency or to any credit grantor with whom I have financial relations.

7. **ACCEPTANCE OF DELIVERY:** If I refuse to take delivery of the car when it is made available to me, or on the delivery date specified in this agreement, the dealer shall notify me, by registered mail, sent to my last address known to the dealer, that the car is available for delivery. If I fail to take delivery of the car within seven (7) days of signed receipt of this notice, or if the notice is returned to the dealer unclaimed, the dealer may resell the car with no further notice to me.

   When the dealer resells the car, I agree to pay the dealer the difference between the agreed upon purchase price and the amount obtained on the resale ... as well as any expenses incurred by the dealer in reselling the car. Any deposit or car traded-in may be kept by the dealer to apply against any loss suffered by the dealer. If the loss is greater than the total of the amount paid as a deposit and the value of the trade-in, I agree to pay the difference to the dealer.

   The dealer agrees to provide me with a detailed accounting of the resale and a list of expenses incurred. These expenses may include, but may not be limited to, advertising, insurance, daily interest, etc. The dealer shall maintain the right to use any legal means available to collect any sum owing by me under this agreement.

8. **SECURITY INTEREST:** If the entire amount owing by me is not paid at the time I take delivery of the car, or if any car traded in by me contains an encumbrance of any sort, so that I cannot pass clear title to the dealer, I grant the dealer a security interest in the car being sold to me up to the amount owing, and understand that the dealer may register this interest under the Personal Property Security Act.

9. **DEFAULT IN PAYMENT:** If I miss any payment due under this agreement, then the entire purchase price shall immediately become due and payable. The dealer, or anyone assigned by the dealer, shall then have the right to repossess the car without notice to me.

   On seven (7) days notice to me by registered mail, sent to my last address known to the dealer, the dealer may resell the car by private sale or public auction. The dealer shall have the right to make whatever repairs are deemed necessary to put the car in adequate condition for resale.

   I agree to pay the dealer the difference between the balance of the purchase price still owing by me and the amount obtained on resale ... as well as any expenses incurred by the dealer in repossessing and reselling the car.

10. **CANCELLATION OF AGREEMENT:** This agreement may not be cancelled by me. If by mutual consent, the dealer and I agree to cancel the contract, the dealer shall return any deposit or cars traded-in as part payment of the purchase price. Should any cars traded-in by me be sold prior to the mutual cancellation of this agreement, the dealer agrees to pay me the amount of the trade-in allowance shown on the front of this agreement.

Contract Defects and Breach of Contract

Defects

None of us would agree to a contract without being aware of all it contained—unless we were mistaken as to its nature, deliberately misled by the other party, or forced into the agreement. If any of these situations did occur, it would cancel consent—the intention to create legal relations—and could be seen as a legal reason for getting out of a contract. Some may call these grounds loopholes in a contract.

The laws governing when a contract can be set aside are very restricted, and differ greatly between consumer and business transactions. There are consumer protection laws that do not apply to deals between businesses. Courts have traditionally been very reluctant to set aside agreements, and it is not easy to get out of a business contract once it has been made. Courts will not help a business get out of a bad deal if it was fairly negotiated.

The reasons that a court would consider are:

- **Misrepresentation.** During the bargaining process, one party states a material fact that is untrue, and the other party relies on this fact when entering into the contract.
- **Mistake.** The parties make an error in the agreement. However, a legal mistake is a very limited ground for relief.
- **Duress.** Actual, or threatened, violence, or unreasonable coercion is used to force agreement. Duress can also include threats of economic harm to another party.
- **Undue influence.** An individual, such as a lawyer or accountant, who holds a position of trust because of specialized knowledge, takes advantage of the other party. It is the misuse of influence and the domination of one party over the mind of another to such a degree as to deprive the latter of the will to make an independent decision.
- **Unconscionable.** A contract is considered an unconscionable transaction when there is an overwhelming imbalance of bargaining power due to the victim's desperation, ignorance, or disability and the stronger party knowingly took advantage of the weaker party's vulnerability and a grossly unfair and improvident agreement was made that offends the standards of commercial morality.
- **Non est factum.** One party is misled as to the type of document being signed. *Non est factum* ("it is not my doing") is a plea that a person didn't know what he or she was signing. It applies when a contract is made in a language they do not understand or it is in writing and they cannot read.

Misrepresentation

What Is a Representation?

misrepresentation

a false statement about a material fact that induced another to enter into a contract

Misrepresentation is one of those words that is used differently in law than in ordinary use. A representation, as the term is technically used in law, usually refers to statements made before the contract is formed. In law, misrepresentation is a false statement about a material or major fact that induced the other party into the contract. The false statement must be made during the bargaining process. For example, a salesman tells a customer that the car dealership will provide a courtesy car related to any repair work necessary during the warranty period. The customer then signs the standard form Used Car Bill of Sale (as found in the Appendix to Chapter 6). Nothing is written into the agreement about the courtesy car. That matter is not then a term of the agreement. The purchaser may not have thought to have it included because she has the salesman's assurance and her mind was satisfied on the point. In addition, she is more concerned about price, warranty period, and such.

When she comes for her first repair under the warranty she asks for her courtesy car. The service manager looks puzzled and asks where she got that idea. He pulls out the contract and shows her that there is nothing in it about a courtesy car. She tells her story. Of course, the sales rep has moved on and is not present to confirm it.

In this example the statement regarding the courtesy car is called a representation. If it is false, it is a misrepresentation. If it had been part of the contract, it would have been a term of the type that is called a warranty.

Usually, the law says we must live up to our agreements or face the legal consequences. Therefore, you had better know what you are getting into when you enter into a contract—"let the buyer beware!" However, the courts have developed special rules to give relief to innocent parties who have relied on misrepresentations in entering into a contract.

Of course, it is easy to make up a misrepresentation after the fact, so the courts are reluctant to ignore the written document. The person asserting the representation may have some difficulty in proving that it was made. The evidence may simply be one person's word against another. It will be difficult to predict which version the court will believe. That is why it is advisable to have every promise in writing.

Representations are usually restricted to statements of fact. However, if the maker is an expert, then opinions can be the basis for a representation. For example, one person may tell a purchaser that there will be no difficulty in getting a zoning change respecting the property. This statement is a matter of opinion and not of fact and the purchaser cannot hold the seller liable for it based on misrepresentation. However, if the maker is an expert in the field, such as a lawyer, the maker may be held responsible.

Types of Misrepresentation

There are three types of misrepresentation:

- innocent—one party to a contract makes a statement without being aware that it is incorrect or untrue
- negligent—facts are misstated because of carelessness
- fraudulent—one party deliberately misleads the other

■ *Critical Concepts of* Misrepresentation

- A misrepresentation is a statement of fact made during the bargaining process that is untrue.
- It concerns a material fact that was sufficiently important to persuade an individual to enter into a contract.

- It is not made a final term of the contract.
- An expert may be liable for statements of opinion.

The factors that the court considers for establishing negligent misrepresentation were established in the case discussed in the following example.

Example: In *Queen v. Cognos* [1993] 1 SCR 87, Douglas Queen was an accountant with a secure, well-paying job in Calgary. Cognos Inc., a large software company, offered him a job in Ottawa to work on a new software accounting project that it was undertaking. Queen quit his job in Calgary and moved his family to Ottawa to work on the project. After five months on the job funding for the project ceased. He continued to work at several fill-in positions at Cognos and was finally terminated 18 months after joining Cognos. Queen sued Cognos for negligent misrepresentation. The Supreme Court set out five criteria that had to be met to succeed in a claim for negligent misrepresentation:

1. There must be a duty of care based on a special relationship between the two parties
2. The representation in question must be untrue, inaccurate or misleading
3. The maker must have acted negligently in making the representation
4. The listener must have relied, in a reasonable manner, on the negligent statement
5. The listener suffered damages from relying on the statement

In this case the Supreme Court ruled that the 5 part test had been met. Even though Cognos believed the project would proceed, it was negligent in telling Queen that it was definite. They should have disclosed it still needed further approvals. The court awarded Cognos damages of $67,224 plus interest.

Business Law Applied

❶ Lesley and Philip Sand are thinking of purchasing a house. They see one they particularly like, and arrange to view it. The current owner, Arthur Keye, shows them around the house, stating, "I've owned this house for 20 years, and it's completely sound. There are no problems." In fact, as the Sands later discover, the house is infested with termites.

There are three possible explanations of Keye's making the statement he did:

i) Over the past few months he has noticed some droppings of sawdust in his basement. No one has been sawing wood, and so there is no reason for the sawdust to be there. However, he hasn't bothered to find out the cause of the sawdust.
ii) He does not know that there are termites in the building.
iii) He's seen the termites, but tells the Sands the house is problem-free since he's desperate to sell it so that he can move to Florida.

a) Decide which of the three types of misrepresentation would apply to each of the above situations.

❷ Relying on Esso's estimate that he would sell 800,000 litres of gasoline annually, John Mardon signed the lease for a filling station.

However, Esso's company accountant had made a mathematical error, and this estimate was totally wrong. In fact, annual sales at this particular station were approximately 240,000 litres. The lease agreement that Mardon signed made no mention of the projected annual sales.

a) If Esso claims as a defence the fact that the statement about annual sales was not in fact part of the contract, is that valid?
b) The gasoline company did not intentionally mislead Mardon. It was simply a mistake. Is that a valid defence for Esso if he were to sue Esso?

Ault v. Canada (Attorney General)
2011 ONCA 147 (CanLII)

The federal government's Treasury Board Secretariat (TBS) set up a Reciprocal Transfer Agreement (RTA) whereby federal public service employees who left their jobs could transfer their pension contributions to private pension plans if they went to work for one of the 300 approved companies. Loba Limited initially was one of the approved companies. Loba set up a scheme whereby individuals would quit their government jobs and work for Loba until their pension monies from the federal government were transferred and then they would quit Loba and withdraw their pension monies in cash. The advantages were that the transfer value on their contributions was higher (sometimes twice the value plus interest calculated at a very high rate) plus the cash withdrawal option. Loba would receive a 10% commission for processing the transfer. The 9 plaintiffs in this case, based on this information, quit their federal government jobs and took jobs as consultants with Loba Limited. (There were 120 other people who had similar problems with pension transfers as well.)

What the plaintiffs did not know, but TBS and Loba knew, was that the Canada Revenue Agency was concerned about these RTAs and in particular the legitimacy of the Loba plan. The CRA informed TBS and Loba that it might disallow the Loba plan and told them to convey this information to employees who were thinking of leaving their government jobs. Neither the government nor Loba passed along this information, so the employees were led to believe it was a legitimate opportunity. These 9 plaintiffs quit their federal government jobs, though luckily their pension monies had not yet been transferred to the Loba pension plan, when the CRA disallowed the Loba pension plan.

The plaintiffs sued the Attorney-General and Loba for negligent misrepresentation and breach of fiduciary duty. They claimed that they had relied on the statements given by the TBS and Loba that Loba was an approved pension plan. They were not told but should have been informed of the concerns of the Canada Revenue Agency. If they had been told of these concerns they would never had quit their jobs. They relied on these statements and suffered significant financial losses as a result. They claimed for loss of income and benefits that occurred as a result of quitting their government jobs.

The trial judge ruled that the federal government as both the employer and pension plan administrator and Loba and (Mr. Parent the principal of Loba) were liable for negligent misrepresentation. They knew that the plaintiffs would rely on their information and they had to their detriment. The defendants had withheld important information about serious concerns with the Loba pension plan transfer but did not communicate this information to the employees. The government and Mr. Parent had both breached their fiduciary duty. The damages were in excess of $3 million and the government was held 80% responsible and Loba and Mr. Parent together 20%. The federal government appealed.

The Court's Decision

The Ontario Court of Appeal agreed with the trial judge's finding of negligent misrepresentation. The court agreed that had the employees known of the concerns that the Canada Revenue Agency had about the Loba plan, they would never had quit their jobs. Misleading these people into thinking this was an approved routine transfer of pension funds was a misrepresentation. They owed the plaintiffs a duty, they knew they would rely on their statements and they did and as a result suffered significant losses. The Court of Appeal also ruled that both the government and the Loba group breached their fiduciary duties as well. The court however allocated the liability differently and held the federal government 60% responsible and Loba and Mr. Parent together 40% liable.

Silence

caveat emptor

let the buyer beware

In most contracts, the seller does not have any legal duty to disclose facts that might affect the buyer's decision to purchase. This rule in the sale of products is expressed in the phrase *caveat emptor*, let the buyer beware. A more modern translation of the Latin is "let the buyer be well informed." If I buy a car from Shady Sam's Used Cars, and discover that it gets terrible gas mileage, that is my problem. Sam does not have to tell me that the car is a "gas guzzler," even though he may be well aware of that fact.

There are exceptions to the usual right not to disclose any information harmful to your interests:

■ If there is a special position of trust between the parties, or where the contract is based on good faith, creating a fiduciary duty (see Chapter 4). One of the limited types of contracts where there is a requirement of complete disclosure is an insurance contract. The applicant must reveal any circumstances that might affect the insurance company's decision to grant a policy of insurance or the amount of the premium. The insurance company also has a duty of good faith to the customer. If it fails to pay a claim without a valid reason, it will have to pay damages for breach of this duty in what is called a bad faith action.

Example: In *Schoff v. Royal Insurance Company of Canada*, 2004 ABCA 180 (CanLII), Nancy Goyan obtained car insurance from Royal Insurance and told them she had no previous accidents, was the only licensed driver in her home and she had 3 cars. The truth was that she had previous accidents and had 4 sons at home all who all had their drivers licenses (3 who were under age 25) and she owned 5 cars. Her son Charles caused an accident driving one of the cars Royal insured for his mother. He injured the Schoffs and their damages were set at $496,486. The Alberta Court of Appeal ruled that there was fraudulent misrepresentation by Mrs. Goyan. Royal was still liable for $200,000 under the Alberta insurance law, but nothing more. Luckily the Schoff's had taken extra coverage on their insurance in case of injury by an underinsured driver.

- If there is a statutory requirement of disclosure. For example, if you solicit investment funds through the sale of franchises or shares, legislation requires disclosure of certain relevant information.

Example: In Kerr v. Danier Leather Inc., 2007 SCC 44, [2007] 3 SCR 331,a class action was launched against Danier Leather for misrepresentation in its prospectus when it did its IPO (initial public offering). The class claimed that Danier had not met the disclosure requirements for a prospectus as set out in the Ontario Securities Act. After Danier had filed its prospectus, forecasts for its fourth quarter sales were significantly lowered, but that information was not disclosed before the prospectus was issued. The Supreme Court ruled in Danier's favour, stating that at the revised sales forecasts were not a material change and when the prospectus was filed the statements were true. The class had to pay a large share of Danier's very large legal costs.

- In the sale of land there is an obligation to reveal defects that are latent, which means: hidden, in the sense that they would not be revealed by an ordinary inspection and of which the owner is either aware or is in reckless disregard of evidence that would point to such defects.

Example: In *Krawchuk v. Scherbak*, 2011 ONCA 352 (CanLII), a woman bought a house for $110,000 and the vendor had disclosed some minor problems on a SPIS (seller's property information sheet), but not serious structural or plumbing problems. After she moved in she discovered major structural defects and plumbing defects and it cost $110,742 to repair the house. The Ontario Court of Appeal held the vendor 50% liable for these costs and the real estate agent and her brokerage were also 50% responsible. Ms. Krawchuk had purchased title insurance and was also able to recover $105,742 under that policy as well. The double recovery was allowed as the defendants were not allowed to benefit from the purchaser's wise decision to purchase title insurance.

- If you elect to give information (assuming there is no position of trust, or statutory obligation to disclose), it must be complete and accurate. The law recognizes that a half-truth is the most dangerous of lies. For example, a landlord told a prospective purchaser that the premises were currently rented to a reliable tenant. The landlord did not reveal that the tenant had given notice to terminate the tenancy. This was held to be a misrepresentation.

Note: In the Krawchuk case above the court found the vendor had given half-truths as well as complete lies when it found them liable for misrepresentation.

- If a party makes a statement believing it to be true at the time but later discovers facts that make it untrue, that individual must tell the other side of the change. For example, a company charged an employee with stealing money from it. Some friends of the employee offered to replace the money. The company later learned that the employee had not stolen the money, but it accepted the repayment from the friends. The company was held to have had an obligation to reveal the true state of affairs and therefore had to return the money.

Putting a positive spin on damaging information has become a well-honed skill of the modern business person. However, this practice may come into sharp conflict with the laws regarding accuracy in making a statement. For instance, when a business is in financial difficulty, the rule requiring accurate and complete information in statements may cause difficulties for the officers of that company in dealing with its bank.

Critical Concepts of Accuracy in Statements

- While there is no general duty to reveal harmful information to the opposite party, there is such a duty where there is a relationship of trust between the parties, an implied duty of good faith, a statutory obligation to disclose, or a latent defect known to the party
- If any statement is made, it must be full and complete.
- If any statement is true when made but later proves to be untrue, the change must be revealed to the other party.

N.B.D. Bank (Canada) v. Dofasco Inc., [1997] 34 B.L.R. (2d) 209 (Ont. Gen. Div.)

The National Bank of Detroit agreed to give a rotating line of credit to Algoma Steel. As part of that financing arrangement, the bank required detailed timely financial information from Algoma before each advance. The time came for a $4,000,000 advance. The bank asked for the agreed financial information from two of Algoma's officers and directors. Algoma had just settled a difficult strike. The chief financial officer of Algoma told its board of directors at a meeting that in addition to the problems caused by the strike, the price of world steel had fallen so that the Algoma plant could not produce steel at a competitive price. The company was insolvent.

When speaking to the bank, both Algoma officers, who had been at the board meeting, told the bank that Algoma was in difficulties because of the costs in delays of start-up after the strike. They said nothing of the opinion of the Algoma CFO. One of the officers forgot to send a part of the Algoma financial information requested by the bank. The bank did not notice that this information was missing.

The bank advanced the $4,000,000 and when Algoma went bankrupt, the bank sued the two officers personally for fraudulent and negligent misrepresentation.

The Court's Decision

The court found that silence is normally not a basis for misrepresentation; however, if something is said, it must be complete. Cleverly selecting words that might be literally true by themselves can be a misrepresentation. The maker of a statement must make certain that the listener is not misled. The statement that Algoma was experiencing difficulty because of the strike was true, but it was only part of the story. The failure to provide some of the financial statements was also held to be deliberate. If the bank had seen these statements, it would have made further inquiries before advancing the money.

The trial judge noted that Algoma's officers were "in a box." However, he said that the officers "had a duty of care to give highly relevant information made relevant by the circumstances of the case."

The officers were found personally liable to the bank on the basis of negligent misrepresentation.

Business Alert!   Caveat Emptor   Sellers are rarely obligated to disclose defects in an article being purchased. You must undertake your own research, and calculate the possible risks before entering into any business deal. The courts will not set aside a transaction simply because one side had more—or better—information than the other.

For major purchases, it's always best to have the item inspected by a professional:

- houses and other buildings—a contractor or certified inspector should inspect the condition of the structure
- businesses—an accountant should verify the profitability of the business
- vehicles—a mechanic should inspect for mechanical soundness
- property in commercial areas—the purchaser should inspect for possible contaminated land

Business Law Applied

❸ **Christopher Clause owned** a motel located at the midway point of a highway connecting two large cities—an excellent situation for an overnight stop when travelling between the two. Clause discovered that the government planned to construct a superhighway north of the old road. When it was completed, most traffic would bypass his motel.

Clause immediately put the motel up for sale, and it was bought by Karl Gustaffson at fair market value. One month after taking over the business, Gustaffson learned about the proposed new highway. He sued Clause to have their contract set aside.

a) Does Gustaffson have a valid claim in court?
b) Were the facts misrepresented by Clause before the sale agreement was signed?
c) Did Clause have a duty to reveal the plans of the highway to the purchaser?
d) What, if anything, could the purchaser have done to protect himself?

Oz Optics Limited v. Timbercon, Inc., 2011 ONCA 714 (CanLII)

Oz Optics and Timbercon are both involved in the fibre-optics industry. In 2003 Timbercon approached Oz to design and manufacture an automated attenuator which Timbercon intended to supply to Lockheed Martin (LM) for use in the construction of jet fighter planes. Attenuators adjust the amount of light passing through a fibre-optic component. Timbercon told Oz that it would be the sole supplier of the attenuators and there would be no competitor.

Seven months later, Timbercon contacted DiCon Fibreoptics Inc. with the view of DiCon becoming the supplier of automated attenuators for the Lockheed Martin contract. Timbercon told DiCon it should prepare a bid for the LM contract. Oz continued to prepare its bid assuming it was the only supplier. When Timbercon submitted its bids to LM it included the bids of the attenuator supplier as well. When DiCon prepared its proposal, Timbercon told DiCon its bid was much higher than the Oz price, so DiCon lowered its price. When Timbercon submitted its proposals to Lockheed Martin it then marked up the unit price of the Oz price by 72% but only marked up the DiCon price by 42%. Not surprisingly, Lockheed Martin selected the bid that used DiCon as the supplier.

When Oz found out that DiCon had been competing on the contract with the backing of Timbercon, Oz sued Timbercon for negligent misrepresentation and breach of a duty of good faith.

The trial judge ruled that Timbercon's statements were "mostly accurate" so there had been no negligent misrepresentation. There was also no duty to act in good faith in commercial bargaining so Timbercon was not liable. Oz Optics appealed the decision.

The Court's Decision

The Ontario Court of Appeal ruled that the statements by Timbercon that Oz was the sole supplier and that there would be no competitors, was negligent misrepresentation. Applying the test established in the Queen v. Cognos case, the companies were in a special relationship, Timbercon knew that Oz would rely on these statements, the reliance was reasonable and Oz suffered damages as a result. If Oz had known that it was not the only competitor it could have adjusted its price and other terms in its proposal. The appeal court would not rule that Timbercon had breached a duty of good faith, commenting that it is such an uncertain area of law, and many cases have accepted that there is no such duty in commercial bargaining. Since it found that Timbercon's statements as to the number of attenuators needed was wrong, and that Oz was the sole supplier was false, Timbercon was liable for negligent misrepresentation. The case was sent back to a new trial judge to determine the damages.

Unjustified Claims of Fraud

Fraudulent misrepresentation is based on the action of *deceit* in tort. The tests the courts use to establish whether fraud has taken place are very strict.

Emotions can run high in civil actions, and one party may be absolutely certain that the other was fraudulent. The wronged person tends to see fraud where a more dispassionate observer might not. Because of the level of feelings that can be generated, the individual being sued might well feel unjustly accused and refuse to settle the matter out of court. In an effort to ensure that only valid fraud cases are heard, the courts usually award substantial costs against an individual who unsuccessfully alleges fraud, even if that party eventually wins the court action on other points. The amount of money involved can be a large percentage of any final court award, and is a serious deterrent to allegations of fraud without strong supporting evidence.

Example: In *887574 Ontario Inc. v. Pizza Pizza Ltd.*, 1995 CanLII 7417 (ON SC), a group of Pizza Pizza franchise owners sued the parent company for using incorrect accounting methods that inflated the amount of such items as royalties that were due to the parent company. The franchise owners also alleged fraudulent accounting practices by the parent company.

The judge who arbitrated the matter awarded $2.7 million to the store owners because of the incorrect accounting practices, but found that they had not proved their allegation of fraud. As a result, they were ordered to pay $500,000 in costs to the mother company as compensation for the legal fees it had incurred in defending the fraud issue.

Tort and Contract

Unfortunately, the law respecting misrepresentation is complicated because innocent misrepresentation developed under the law of contract, but both negligent and fraudulent misrepresentation developed under and remain part of the law of tort. **Negligent misrepresentation** (an incorrect statement made without due care for its accuracy) derives from the tort of negligent misstatement (*Hedly, Byrne & Co. Ltd. v. Heller*, [1964] A.C. 64) It was first called negligent misrepresentation in the case *Esso Petroleum Co. v. Mardon* [1976] 2 O.E.R. 5 (C.A.). **Fraudulent misrepresentation** (an incorrect statement made knowingly with the intention of causing injury to another) derives from the tort of **deceit** established in the landmark case of *Derry v. Peek* (1889), 14 Pa.P.P. 337.

These two torts occur in a contractual context and so are often, incorrectly from a technical point of view, considered part of the law of contract. Curiously, then, a large part of the law regarding the negotiation stage of a contract is governed by the law of tort.

negligent misrepresentation

a careless but not intentionally inaccurate statement about a material fact that induced a contract

fraudulent misrepresentation

an incorrect statement made knowingly with the intention of causing injury to another

Remedies for Misrepresentation

The court's approach to awarding damages varies by the type of misrepresentation. There are two possible remedies a court can give for misrepresentations: rescission or damages.

Rescission means the cancelling of the contract, with both parties put back into their original positions. One party must give back the money; the other must return the goods.

Damages are monetary compensation in a lawsuit for the loss suffered by the aggrieved party. The early courts did not want to award damages against a party who made an innocent misrepresentation, but in effect said to the aggrieved party, you have a choice to go through with the contract or to get out of it. In other words, you can take it or leave it!

For example, in the private sale of a car a seller honestly believes it to be a 1999 Mustang and sells it for $15,000. On reading the car manual the purchaser discovers it is a 1998 car worth $2,000 less. The purchaser can either keep the car or return it and get his money back.

rescission

the cancelling of the contract, with both parties put back into their original positions

damages

monetary compensation in a lawsuit for the loss suffered by the aggrieved party

He cannot keep the car and sue for the $2,000. There has been some flexibility to this remedy particularly in small claims court, but the traditional response has been no damages for innocent misrepresentation.

In negligent misrepresentation rescission can be allowed under contract law and damages can be awarded under tort law.

Because fraud is so serious, the innocent party is permitted to choose rescission or to claim damages, and sometimes is permitted both.

Bars to Rescission

The purpose of rescission is to return the parties to their original positions. When a contract is rescinded the goods or property are returned and the money is refunded. The person who is returning the property can be compensated for any expenses that were incurred. In innocent misrepresentation damages are not awarded in addition to the rescission because both parties were innocent, (though in some small claims cases judges have been known to ignore this and have also awarded incidental damages). If there was negligent or fraudulent misrepresentation, rescission and damages are both possible.

Rescission may be denied in situations where it is impossible to return the property, for example it has been destroyed or damaged, or it has been sold to an innocent third party who was unaware of the misrepresentation. Rescission can also be denied if there was a delay in claiming this remedy. The court may see this delay as a sign the party was not acting in good faith and seeking to get out of the contract on a technicality. It is always safe to claim rescission immediately upon discovering the grounds for it.

Rescission **Rescission** is derived from Latin. *Re*, used in this context, means back, as in return; *scission* comes from the Latin verb *scindere*, to cut, (*scissors* comes from the same word). Thus, when a contract is rescinded, it is "cut back," so that it never existed.

Legalese

■ *Critical Concepts of* Remedies for Misrepresentation

- Not all remedies can be given for all types of misrepresentation.
- Innocent—rescission, only
- Negligent—rescission and/or damages
- Fraudulent—rescission and/or damages

Stolen Cars   One of the most frequent misrepresentations concerns the sale of stolen cars. One pattern for stolen car sales is for the car to be stolen in one province, brought to another province, and registered there. This is easy to do. In many provinces there are no checks by the government ownership-permit office on the accuracy of the information given on the transfer registration.

Even where there are checks, these may not be effective. Chop shops buy wrecked cars to obtain valid V.I.N. (vehicle identification numbers) and then have one stolen to match for year, model, and such. The stolen car gets the wreck's V.I.N. and this one will not show up on police stolen-car lists!

So beware of buying cars advertised for sale online or in newspapers, especially if you are getting a fantastic deal on a very popular model. Consumer protection laws will give no value against a sophisticated criminal who will likely be difficult to find. Be sure to get a certified cheque and two or three pieces of photo identification including a driver's license, when selling a car privately.

■ *Business Law* Applied

❹ **Angelo Bolatta advertised** his Mustang car for sale at a price of $16,500. A man who introduced himself as Roland Berry called on Bolatta one evening, tried the car, and said he liked it. In the course of general conversation, the prospective purchaser represented himself as being connected with professional hockey. Roland Berry was well known as a coach at the time.

The purchaser wrote a cheque for $16,500, signing it "Roland Berry." Bolatta asked for identification, and was shown a pass to the local stadium. This carried a photograph of the purchaser, along with an official-looking stamp. Bolatta registered the change of ownership, and allowed Berry to take the car. Two days after Bolatta deposited the cheque, his bank advised him that it had been forged, and that the credit in his account was cancelled.

A few days later, Muriel Gibson, who had advertised for a car of this type, received a visit from a man who said his name was Angelo Bolatta. He showed her a motor-vehicle permit bearing Bolatta's name and address. The car was exactly what Gibson wanted, and she bought it for $14,800. Within the next three or four days, Gibson discovered that the usual driver's manual was missing from the glove compartment, and telephoned Bolatta to ask for further information about the car. The whole story was then revealed in an excited conversation.

Her telephone call proved a fateful one for Gibson, because Bolatta brought an action against her for return of the car.

a) What were the two contracts involved, and who were the parties to each?
b) What type of misrepresentation was made by Berry to Bolatta and Gibson?
c) What steps did Bolatta take to protect his interests? Were they what any reasonable person would have done under the same circumstances?
d) How else might Bolatta have safeguarded his interests?
e) How did Gibson attempt to protect her money? Were the steps she took reasonable?
f) What else might Gibson have done?
g) Which particular remedies for misrepresentation were available to Bolatta?
h) Which principle would the court apply to decide the case? What would be the result?

Entire Agreement and Exclusion Clauses

It will be useful to recall entire agreement and exclusion clauses now that you have seen concrete examples of misrepresentations. The parol evidence rule does not exclude misrepresentations, that is, statements made before the contract was formed. However entire agreement and exemption clauses often try to limit or exclude liability for any misrepresentations at all. As we saw in the previous chapter, it is often difficult to accurately predict whether these clauses will be effective, but courts tend not enforce these clauses when there is misrepresentation, especially fraudulent misrepresentation.

Example: In *1018429 Ontario Inc. v. Fea Investments Ltd.*, 1999 CanLII 1741 (ON CA), Fea sold an apartment building to the plaintiff and in the contract it stated that there was no legal action pending by any tenants and the list of tenancies and rents charge were true and accurate and in accordance with rent review legislation. The contract also stated that the purchaser shall have no remedy with respect to any breach of warranty or any misrepresentation other than rescission. The truth was that the seller knew that many of the tenants had been charged rents that were above the legal limit and they were pursuing legal action. When the purchaser discovered this, he sued the seller for fraudulent misrepresentation and sought damages. The seller denied there was fraudulent misrepresentation and asserted that even if there was, rescission was the only remedy available as stated in the contract. The trial court and the Court of Appeal ruled that fraudulent misrepresentation had occurred and the clause limiting the remedy to rescission was not effective. They cited other decisions where the court held that once fraudulent misrepresentation has been established, the disclaimer would not be effective. In this case the purchaser was not limited to rescission, the court awarded the purchaser $150,000 in damages.

Terms, Representations and Opinions

A representation is a statement made before the contract is made, while a term is part of the contract. Misrepresentation requires that it was a fact that was relied upon, statements that are opinions or forecasts are often not considered to be facts or representations or terms of the contract and cannot be the basis for a claim in misrepresentation. The legal test for finding that a statement is a term or representation is; would the maker have intended to guarantee the statement when it was made. In the case below, the franchisor would not have guaranteed specific future profits. Their statements were their opinions and forecasts at the time the contract was made.

Example: In *Healy v. Canadian Tire Corporation, Limited*, 2012 ONSC 77 (CanLII), an owner of a Canadian Tire store sued the franchisor for negligent misrepresentation because the profit projections he was given did not materialize and after 6 years running the store he was on the verge of bankruptcy. The court held that a profit forecast by its very nature is only an estimate or projection about a matter in the future. Negligent misrepresentation cannot be based on a future forecast; it must be based on a statement of existing fact. Though the franchisor was liable under the provincial franchise law for a breach of duty of good faith and liable for $250,000; that was significantly less than the $1,600,000 the judge would have awarded in damages if the claim for negligent misrepresentation had been successful.

Special Consumer Rules

Most provinces have enacted special rules to control misrepresentation in consumer transactions. The various acts, usually called unfair trade acts or business practices acts, differ in detail. In dealing with misrepresentation, however, each is similar. Each, in effect, makes the representation govern over the written contractual provisions. Any entire agreement clause is nullified. Damages and even criminal sanctions can apply.

False advertising is one of the most common types of misrepresentation and will be discussed in Chapter 8 along with other areas of consumer protection. Always remember that promises by companies that sound too good to be true, probably are. Promises that you should be very wary of include:

- you will become a top model if you just pay for photos to be taken
- you can earn $10,000 a month without leaving home, or $25/hour no experience needed
- loans at low rates for those with bad credit ratings
- someone in Nigeria wants to get $20 million out of that country and will pay if you help them
- you just won an all-expenses paid vacation if you just pay a promotion fee

If you are considering becoming involved with these scams, you probably should not. Check out these companies on the websites for the Better Business Bureau and the RCMP crime prevention site first before you give them any money. In almost all cases, these companies will take your money and give you little or nothing in return and it is best to avoid them entirely.

Business Law Applied

❺ **Bertram bought an** air conditioner in August during Aircontrol Inc.'s end-of-season sale. Concerned that he would not be using it until the next season, Bertram asked Patricia, the salesperson, if the unit would be covered for any problems that might occur during the next year. Patricia responded the unit would be covered up to the next September.

All went well until July of the next year, when the unit developed a strong vibration noise. Aircontrol examined the air conditioner and told Bertram it would cost $400 to make the necessary repairs. When Bertram complained, the store referred to the sales contract, which said there was a six-month warranty. The sales contract also contained a clause saying that the sales contract represented the entire agreement and that there were no other promises made.

  a) What is the name in law for the statement made by the salesperson that the unit would be under warranty until next September?
  b) Does the entire agreement clause in the sales contract deal with the statement made by the sales rep? If so, how?
  c) Does Bertram have any remedy to insist that the warranty period extends until September of the relevant year?
  d) If Bertram had bought this air conditioner for his business, would he be able to rely on the same legal principle?
  e) What must business persons do to protect themselves in this type of situation?

Mistake

A mistake is an erroneous belief or a misunderstanding about an essential term in the contract. The legal concepts surrounding mistake are complex, and are not dealt with in great detail here. There are certain cases in which the courts will give relief because of mistake, but these are few and far between. Instead, the courts tend to preserve business deals, on the basis that businesses need to be able to rely on their transactions, rather than having them reopened later. Mistakes that could have been avoided by due care will not usually result in relief from the court.

Common and Mutual Mistake

If both parties to the contract make the same mistake then it is a common mistake. If both parties are mistaken, but about different things, then it is a mutual mistake.

If there is convincing evidence that both parties made an agreement and the mistake was made when putting that agreement into written form, such as a typing or clerical error, the court may **rectify** (alter) the written agreement to conform to the parties' real agreement. **Rectification** will only occur if the court thinks that it was such a large obvious error, that an objective bystander would have recognized that a mistake had been made when the contract was formed and it prevents one party from being unjustly enriched.

For example: Ilya agreed to sell his house to Kim for $398,000. When the contract was typed up the price was listed as $39,800 but neither party noticed the typing error. On the closing date Kim looked at the contract and gave Ilya a cheque for $39,800. Ilya could claim that this was a major obvious clerical error and an objective bystander looking at it would realize a mistake had been made. Ilya could apply to the court and get a rectification order to correct the mistake and set the price at $398,000. Note however if the typing error had listed the price at $378,000 instead of $398,000 Ilya would probably not get a rectification order. Even though it is an error of $20,000, it is not an obvious error, as someone objectively looking at the price of $378,000 would not recognize that a mistake had been made. In the *Ron Engineering* case below a mistake of $750,000 was not rectified but in *McLean* a $115,000 mistake was rectified.

rectification

a court can alter (rectify) an essential term if there is an obvious error to make it conform to their true intentions

Example: In *R. v. Ron Engineering & Construction* [1981] 1 SCR 111, an engineering firm submitted a bid on a government contract of $2,748,000 along with a $150,000 deposit. The firm realized within an hour after the bidding had closed that due to a calculation error its bid should have been $750,000 higher. The engineering firm claimed that it had made a mistake and so its bid should not be considered and its deposit should be refunded. The court ruled that the mistake was not so large as to indicate that there had been an obvious miscalculation. The bidding process clearly stated the deposits were non-refundable. The court also wanted to protect the integrity of the tendering process and prevent future contractors from claiming a mistake to try to avoid contracts they had underbid on. The court ruled the government was entitled to keep the $150,000 deposit.

McLean v. McLean
2013 ONCA 788 (CanLII)

Helen and Wilmur Mclean agreed to sell their dairy farm to their son Melville and his wife Maureen McLean at fair market value. The real property (the land, farm house, barns and other buildings) was valued at $337,444, of which the farm house was $115,000. When the personal property (such as livestock, milk quota, equipment and furnishings) was included, the fair market value of the entire operation was $733,255. The parents agreed to take back a mortgage for the full value of just the real property. When the agreement, the land transfer and the mortgage documents were typed up, the value of the real property was incorrectly listed as $222,444 instead of $337,444. The value of the farm house had most likely been left out of the calculations, a mistake of $115,000. The documents were signed and registered at the government land titles office with this lower value. The parents eventually realized this mistake and asked the court to rectify the agreement, transfer and mortgage documents by changing the price for the real property to $337,444.

Maureen argued that she thought the fair market value of the entire purchase was only $625,000, so there was no mistake and the documents should not rectified. The trial judge ruled that the parents had not established a common intention about the value of the farm and there was no common mistake, so rectification was denied. The parents appealed.

The Court's Decision

The Ontario Court of Appeal noted that rectification is designed to ensure that one party is not unjustly enriched at the expense of another. It ruled that the parties had both agreed the value of the real property was $337,444. There was a common intention and it was a common mistake when the documents were typed up with an incorrect price for the real property.

Given all the evidence, on the balance of probabilities, a reasonable objective observer would believe the parties intended the real property to sell for $337,444. The families had used an inexperienced lawyer who had acted for both sides and had made multiple drafting errors. The court believed the value of the farm house, which was $115,000, had been mistakenly left out of the calculations and that was why the price was $115,000 lower than they had agreed upon.

The documents as originally drafted did not reflect the true intention of the parties. To allow the son and his wife to purchase the farm at the lower price would unjustly enrich them. The court ordered all the documents to be rectified so that the sale price for the real property would be changed to $337,444.

Other examples of a common mistake that could change a contract would be where the parties both thought the subject matter of the contract was in existence when the deal was made, but in fact it had been destroyed or stolen, so then the contract would be void because of the shared mistake. For example, John agreed to sell his boat to Inga for $25,000 on May 10, and they arranged to go to the marina on May 15th to transfer the boat to Inga. When they got to the marina on May 15th they discovered the boat had been destroyed. The marina owner told them a severe storm had occurred on May 3rd and many boats had been destroyed including John's. John and Inga had both been mistaken that the boat was good shape at the time the contract was made, when in fact it had been destroyed a week earlier. Their contract is therefore void due to the common mistake.

But when both parties make a mistake about the true value of the goods, the contract is enforceable. For example: Raj sells a painting he found in his attic to Maria at his garage sale for $50. Maria then goes home to get her car so she can transport the painting. In the meantime an art dealer tells Raj the painting is really worth $20,000. This was a common mistake by both Raj and Maria about the true value of the painting when he sold it to her. The contract is valid though and Maria is entitled to the painting for the $50 she paid.

The following case illustrates a mutual mistake that resulted in the court ruling there was no consensus, so no contract had been formed.

Example: In *Ron Ghitter Property Consultants Ltd. v. Beaver Lumber Company Limited*, 2003 ABCA 221 (CanLII), Beaver Lumber had a lease with Baxter Estates that included a rental sharing agreement (RSA) whereby Beaver would pay Baxter 45% of the net profits it made from subletting any part of the property. Beaver later entered into an agreement to assign the lease to Ghitter Properties for $1.55 million, but Ghitter was not aware of the RSA. Beaver believed Ghitter knew of the RSA and Beaver had not concealed it. Just before the deal was to close, Ghitter learned of the RSA and refused to close the deal. The trial court and the Alberta Court of Appeal both agreed that the contract was void due to a mutual mistake. There had been no consensus between the two parties. When they had made the agreement, both sides were mistaken on what was included in the deal. It was not a breach of contract, there had been a mutual mistake about a fundamental term so no valid contract had been formed.

Unilateral Mistake

When only one party is mistaken, it is called a unilateral mistake. The courts are very reluctant to give any relief when it is just one party who was mistaken. The courts want to uphold the terms of the contract and the principle of caveat emptor (buyer beware) and enforce the contract. The court will not usually let a party out of a contract because they did not read the contract carefully or had misunderstood a term because they had not done their due diligence, especially if it is a business-to-business contract. There usually has to be unjust enrichment and almost fraudulent behaviour by the defendant for relief to be granted when a unilateral mistake is made.

Example: In *Lee v. 1435375 Ontario Ltd.*, 2013 ONCA 516, the defendant was selling a dry cleaning business he had been running for 5 years. Neither the buyer nor the seller realized that the zoning laws had recently changed and the dry cleaning business was no longer an allowed conforming use in that location. There was a possibility the city would allow the business to continue, but legal permission would have to be obtained. When the buyer discovered the zoning issue just after the purchase, he sued the vendor. The trial judge ruled there was no misrepresentation by the vendor, as zoning had never been discussed. The judge found it was a common mistake and it would be unjust to enforce the contract due to the zoning uncertainty. The judge rescinded the contract and the purchase money was to be returned. The Court of Appeal however reversed the decision. It considered it to be a unilateral mistake by the purchaser since he had not asked the vendor if the business conformed with the zoning. There was no misrepresentation or wrong doing by the seller, and the city might still allow the dry cleaning business to continue in this location. The purchaser should have done its due diligence and should bear the consequences of its own mistake. The contract was valid and the sale was not rescinded.

It is possible in the case of a unilateral mistake for the court to grant rectification or damages, but it is usually only done when the aggrieved party can prove that the opposite party clearly knew of the mistake and was taking advantage of it as in the Sylvan Lake case below.

Example: In *Performance Industries Ltd. v. Sylvan Lake Golf & Tennis Club Ltd.*, 2002 SCC 19, O'Connor and Bell agreed orally that they would form a joint venture to develop housing units around the 18th hole of a golf course. The land for the development was agreed to be 100 yards wide along the 18th fairway, but instead it was typed up as 100 feet wide. O'Connor knew of this error when Bell signed the agreement, but told him the written contract contained the same terms as their oral agreement. Later when Bell discovered this mistake he wanted it rectified. It would not be possible to build two rows of houses if was only 100 feet wide, so the project would not be financially worthwhile. O'Connor insisted that the contract should be enforced as it was written. Bell produced convincing evidence to the court of their oral agreement and that O'Connor knew of Bell's unilateral mistake and was using it to get out of the deal. The trial judge described O'Connor's behaviour as almost fraudulent and stated it would be unjust and unconscionable to let O'Connor take advantage of Bell's unilateral mistake. Though it was too late to rescind the contract as other construction had occurred on the lands, the court ruled it was a unilateral mistake and Bell was entitled to his lost profits of $620,000. Bell had been award an additional $200,000 in punitive damages by the trial judge, but the Supreme Court denied the punitive damages. It considered the compensatory damages for lost profits were large enough to act as a deterrent to this type of behaviour.

A business person must understand that relief for unilateral mistake is rare. Careful proofreading is important. Even a misplaced comma can lead to an opposite party gaining a benefit as the *AGM Campbell* case, next, (which has been called the million dollar comma case), demonstrates.

AMJ Campbell Inc. v. Kord Products Inc., [2003] CanLII 5840 (ON S.C.)

AMJ Transportation Inc. ("AMJ"), a transportation company, sold its subsidiary, Kord Products Limited, which made transportation containers, to ITML Inc. ("ITML") for $13,688,000.00 subject to adjustments depending on evaluation of the inventory.

One of the items for evaluation was "average selling price" which was defined in a non-binding letter of intent as "net of taxes, freight rebates and discounts". At the Purchaser's lawyer's request the phrase was changed to "net of taxes, freight, rebates and discounts".

The change was highlighted in the track changes feature during the exchange of drafts of the final agreement.

The difference in interpretation was that under the first reading only freight rebates (estimated at ten percent of the freight charges) would be deducted. Under the second version, all payments for freight charges plus freight rebates would be deducted. This was a difference, including interest, of about $1 million.

AMJ sued for rectification of the contract based on mistake.

The Court's Decision

The Court found there was no ambiguity in the final version of the phrase.

Only AMJ was mistaken as to the effect of the phrase. ITML was not mistaken, so the mistake was unilateral (one-sided).

While relief of rectification could be granted for unilateral mistakes if certain conditions were met, the Court was influenced by the fact that by highlighting the track changes, AMJ's attention was drawn to the change. The Purchaser did not and could not reasonably be taken to know that AMJ was mistaken. The Purchaser relied on the final version in agreeing to the deal and had acted completely ethically.

AMJ's action for rectification was dismissed.

■ *Critical Concepts of* Mistake

- A mistake is an erroneous belief or misunderstanding by one or more of the parties about an essential contract term
- A common mistake occurs when both parties make the same mistake and a mutual mistake is when they both make mistakes, but about different things
- A unilateral mistake occurs when only one party makes a mistake and relief is only granted if it is proved that the defendant was taking advantage of the other party
- A court can rectify a mistake if it was an obvious clerical error and would cause unjust enrichment unless rectification occurs
- The courts want to enforce contracts as they are written and do not want to change the written agreement unless there was no consensus or unjust enrichment due to the mistake

Business Alert!

E & OE   Businesses often include the notation **E & OE (errors and omissions excepted)** at the bottom of invoices and statements. This is an attempt to say that the transaction can be set aside if it later proves to contain a mistake. It has no effect in law.

■ *Business Law* Applied

❻ **Stephen's Travel Agency** sent a firm quote to a corporate client of $7,500 for a package deal. The client accepted the quote and paid.

One week later, the agency discovered that it had forgotten to include one item for $10,500. Stephen's informed the client of the error, and requested payment. The client refused, claiming it had not known of the mistake, and had paid in good faith.

a) On what legal remedy could Stephen's rely?
b) What would the travel agency have to prove in order to be successful in its attempt to secure payment?
c) Would the size of the error be sufficient to establish that the client must have been aware of it?
d) What circumstances might indicate whether the client knew of the mistake?
e) If the invoice had contained the notation E & OE, could the travel agency rely on this fact?

Duress

duress

actual or threatened violence or unreasonable coercion used to force an agreement

Entering into a contract "under duress" has a fairly limited meaning in law. Duress is not succumbing to a high-pressure sales pitch, nor is it renting a truck at a high rate because there is one rental company in town. Duress is an overt threat inducing someone to enter into a contract.

Actual or threatened violence cannot be used to force an individual to enter into a contract. Duress might also be in the form of blackmail, or the threat of criminal prosecution. Someone who has been forced to consent to a contract can have that agreement set aside by the courts. The threat of force means there is no true consent, so the contract is voidable.

Thankfully there are very few reported cases of the classic type of duress. In *Byle v. Byle* 1990 CanLII 313 (BCCA), a son threatened to "blow off his brother's head" unless the elderly father transferred property to him. The father made the land transfer to the son who had made the threats, but later the court ruled the contract was void due to duress.

Economic Duress

One form of duress is economic duress. Sometimes, one business is aware of another company's financial difficulties, and uses unfair methods to obtain better terms in a contract. To succeed in a claim for economic duress you must establish that you had no other practical alternatives so you had to agree to the demands of the other party, but you had agreed only under protest and later had tried to avoid the contract. The NAV Canada case below illustrates a case of economic duress where this situation occurred.

NAV Canada v. Greater Fredericton Airport Authority Inc., 2008 NBCA 28 (CanLII)

The Greater Fredericton Airport Authority (GFAA) entered into a contract with Nav Canada to improve the airport facilities in Fredericton. As part of a $6 million runway extension GFAA requested that Nav relocate an existing instrument landing system to the runway that was being extended. Nav said it made more economic sense to replace that older system with new distance measure equipment (DME), which would cost an additional $223,000.

GFAA's position was that Nav should pay for this new DME. Nav disagreed and in a letter said it would not include the cost of this new equipment in their budget for that year. GFAA realized this would effectively hold up the completion of the extended runway for at least another year. GFAA had already spent $6 million and knew that unless it agreed to pay for the new equipment, Nav would cause a major delay. GFAA felt it had no other option, and Nav had a government monopoly over airport development, so it wrote to Nav indicating it would pay for the DME but "under protest." On the basis of that letter Nav completed the work, incurred the expense of purchasing the DME, but GFAA then refused to pay for this new equipment.

The dispute was referred to arbitration. The arbitrator said Nav had no right to claim the costs of the DME from GFAA under the original agreement, but he ruled that the letter was a second valid agreement and GFAA had agreed to pay for the equipment, so it must. The decision was appealed to the New Brunswick trial court which reversed the decision and then it was appealed to the New Brunswick Court of Appeal.

The Court's Decision

The Appeal court ruled that there was only one legal agreement and the letter had not established a second contract, merely a variation on the original contract. Under the original contract, it was clearly Nav's duty to pay for the equipment. The court said that it was time for Canadian courts to allow an incremental change on the strict doctrine of consideration. The court ruled that it is possible to enforce a change to a contract even without consideration, so long as the change was not obtained by economic duress. The court believed that the realities of modern business are such that the strict consideration rules should be changed to allow for contractual changes that have a practical benefit even if there is no consideration.

However in this case, the question was whether GFAA had only consented to the variation "under pressure" due to economic duress. A claim for economic duress requires that the party that is being pressured *"had no other practical alternative but to agree to the demands of the other party and had protested the terms of the agreement when it was formed and had later tried to avoid the contract."*

In this case the court ruled that GFAA had no other alternative but to agree to Nav's demand and the "under protest" letter indicated this. The court ruled that there had been economic duress so GFAA's consent to paying for the equipment was vitiated (cancelled), so GFAA did not have to pay for the equipment, it was Nav's responsibility. The court's comments on changes to the consideration doctrine have caused significant discussion as well.

Business Law Applied

❼ **Direct to the** Net Inc. became a great success in only four years after start-up and it decided to go public. About one week before making the announcement of its initial public offering (IPO), it was served with a statement of claim by a former shareholder who alleged the company had used his ideas without paying for them four years ago.

The Directors of Direct to the Net Inc. believe that there is no merit in the claim and feel that they are being blackmailed, but do not want to report a lawsuit of this type on the corporation's disclosure material for the public offering. They agree to pay one million dollars to settle the claim.

   a) Is there any ground in law by which the corporation can have the settlement set aside by a court after the IPO? If so, what is the name for this course of action?
   b) What business considerations are relevant to the decision to sue and the timing of any lawsuit to set aside the settlement?

Undue Influence

Undue influence is that type of influence which prevents a party to a contract from exercising independent judgment or decision making in signing a contract. The doctrine of undue influence was not created to save people from the consequences of their actions, but to save them from being victimized by others. It is of two types, actual and presumed, and it occurs in two types of situations: firstly, where there is no special relationship between the parties, and secondly, where there is a special relationship.

Actual

One example of actual undue influence was a case in which a person claimed to be a medium giving a message from a dead relative that large amounts of money should be paid to the medium to conduct a ritual to save the deceased from suffering in the next world. In another case, a bank manager threatened to lay criminal prosecutions against a son who forged his father's name on a promissory note, unless the father signed a personal guarantee of the son's loan which was then in default. This threat of criminal prosecution against the son was considered actual undue influence by a person (the bank manager) not in a special relationship with the aggrieved party (the father). Thus actual undue influence appears to require an element of express coercion.

Actual undue influence is often an abuse of bargaining power and akin to duress. In the two examples above there was no special relationship and the aggrieved party must prove the undue influence.

Presumed

Sometimes, trust or confidence exists between certain individuals in traditional relationships such as lawyer-client, accountant-client, doctor-patient, and the like. The person who is in the position of trust cannot use that influence to gain a personal advantage at the expense of the other party. This rule is akin to fiduciary duty and abuse of trust. A fiduciary relationship is one in which a weaker or more vulnerable person places trust and confidence in a stronger or more skilled person (see a more complete definition of agency in Chapter 6). In such a relationship undue influence is presumed. That means it does not have to be actually proved. There does not have to be any express coercion or threat. Instead, the presumption would have to be **rebutted** or proven to be false to avoid liability.

There is a second type of special relationship that is not a traditional one but is open-ended. Thus, it is based on the particular facts of a case; one person may in fact give trust and confidence to another and this trust is abused. Because this type of relationship is based on the facts of a case, it is called a *de facto* special relationship. A common example is marriage. A married woman today is, generally, not presumed to be under the influence of her husband. However, in a traditional marriage, if the wife does leave financial matters to her husband and has no business experience, these facts may well support a finding that there was a special relationship, which in turn raises a presumption of undue influence.

Presumption   A **presumption** in law is something assumed to be true without the necessity of proving it to be so. For example, if a lawyer buys a house from a client, and a client wants to set aside the transaction claiming the price was too low, the court will presume that the lawyer used undue influence, that is, took advantage of the trust that the client put in the lawyer.

The lawyer has the right to rebut (disprove) the presumption. Usually this is done by showing that a fair price was paid, and that the lawyer had therefore not taken advantage of the weaker party.

◼ *Critical Concepts of* Undue Influence

- Undue influence means that some unfair advantages have been taken of a weaker person by a stronger person.
- Actual undue influence requires some overt act, and it compares to duress.
- Presumed undue influence arises from a special relationship which is similar to a fiduciary relationship.
- Special relationships can be traditional ones (such as lawyer-client) or ones formed on the individual facts of the case.

Guaranteeing Debts

There is a line of cases that permitted a spouse, usually a wife, in what was called a traditional marriage, to avoid the enforcement of a bank guarantee that she had signed for her husband's business loan on the ground of undue influence. The theory in those cases was that the bank should have known that the wife was in the type of marriage in which she had no experience outside the home, was dominated by her husband and emotionally could not exercise any independent consent.

There do not appear to have been any successful cases in recent times on this basis. That may be because of the changing role of women in society. However the line of cases is relevant because it gave rise to the practice of insisting on Independent Legal Advice (ILA) for any person, not only a spouse, signing or co-signing a guarantee of debt. The lawyer giving the advice must be independent, which means chosen by and paid for by the guarantor.

Example: In *Lewis v. Central Credit Union Limited*, 2012 PECA 9 (CanLII), 77 year old Ella Lewis co-signed a mortgage on property she and her son owned an interest in, so that her son Orville, could get a loan to start a new carrot farming operation. She had signed previous lending agreements over the years and always had received independent legal advice, but not this time. When Orville's carrot crop failed the credit union wanted to sell the property secured by the mortgage, but Ella asserted the mortgage was unenforceable due to undue influence. She claimed that if she had known how deeply in debt Orville was at the time of the mortgage she would have never agreed to it.

◼ *Business Law* Applied

❽ **Mary Row was** a school teacher married for 15 years to James Row, who was a lawyer. Mrs. Row left all decisions on financial matters to her husband and did not even have a credit card in her own name.

Mr. Row wanted to invest in hi-tech stocks and arranged for a bank loan. The bank insisted on a guarantee from Mrs. Row. Since Mr. Row was a lawyer, the bank did not require that she have I.L.A.

The stock investments were a complete loss, the husband became depressed, could not practice law, and eventually went bankrupt. The bank sued Mrs. Row on the guarantee.

a) What facts must Mrs. Row establish to raise a presumption of undue influence? Will she likely be successful in doing so?

b) Was the bank on constructive notice of any special relationship in these circumstances?

c) What possible defence can a bank raise? Will it be successful?

d) If you believe the result would be different in this case than in the *Courtney* case above, why do you believe so?

Bank of Montreal v. Courtney, 2005 NSCA 153 (CanLII)

Holly Courtney signed three promissory notes over a period of several years to enable her husband to borrow $900,000 from the Bank of Montreal so he could purchase shares in IT companies for investment purposes. On all three occasions she never received any independent legal advice when she signed the loan agreements. When the companies he invested in failed, he was unable to make the loan payments, so the bank took legal action against Holly to collect the money. She claimed that the promissory notes were unenforceable as she had been unduly influenced by her husband.

She claimed that since it was a husband-wife relationship and the loans were not for her benefit there was a presumption of undue influence. She said since the bank had not recommended that she obtain independent legal advice, the lending agreements were void. She asserted that he had pressured her into signing the notes and there had been many heated arguments over the deals and she had signed the document to save the marriage.

The bank claimed that Ms. Courtney was well educated and had worked in executive secretary positions for 15 years and was familiar with financial documents. She had never expressed any concerns or given any indication to the bank when she signed the notes that she was being pressured by her husband. The trial court ruled that independent legal advice (ILA) may have been prudent, but it is not mandatory in all husband–wife loan agreements. Since she gave no indication that she misunderstood the contracts or that it was against her free will to sign the documents, the bank was under no obligation to make sure she obtained independent legal advice. The bank also asserted that she would have benefitted from the loans if the husband's investments had been successful.

The trial judge agreed with the bank and ruled Ms. Courtney was liable for the loans. She appealed the decision.

The Court's Decision

The Nova Scotia Court of Appeal agreed with the trial judge's ruling. It stressed that the absence of independent legal advice does not automatically mean there was undue influence. The issue of when ILA is necessary is based on two issues; did they understand the contract and were they free to make their own decision.

In this case the court believed she had the intellect and ability to understand the loans and she had freely and voluntarily entered into these agreements. She had never complained at the time the agreements were signed, nor had she called the bank later to express any concerns. The court stated that ILA would have made no difference in these transactions as she already knew what she was signing. There was no evidence for the bank to presume that she was being unfairly pressured by her husband. The contracts also did not disadvantage her, as she would have benefitted if her husband's investments had been successful.

Therefore the claim of undue influence had not been proven and the loan agreements were enforceable.

The PEI Court of Appeal ruled that this was a case of presumed undue influence given the parent–child relationship and that this contract was disadvantageous to Ella. The credit union had to rebut this presumption by ensuring Ella had independent legal advice or present evidence she fully understood and freely agreed to the contract. Since that was not done, there was no proof that she had given her free and informed consent so the mortgage contract was unenforceable.

The *Courtney* case above illustrates though how even if it is a special relationship, and there was no independent legal advice given, the presumption of undue influence can be rebutted if there is sufficient evidence the dependent person understood and freely agreed to be bound by the contract.

Unconscionable Transactions

unconscionable transaction

a grossly unfair and improvident agreement that so offends community standards of commercial morality it should not be enforced

The doctrine of unconscionability provides courts with another basis to change or rescind a contract in certain circumstances. Unconscionability is based on the belief that some contracts, when seen as a whole, "vary so much from community standards of commercial morality" that they should not be enforced. For a contract to be considered unconscionable there must be two factors present: 1) significant inequality in bargaining power due to the needs, inabilities or distress of the weaker party and 2) as a result they were taken advantage of by the stronger party and a substantially unfair contract was formed. The contract must be a grossly unfair and improvident (hasty and careless) transaction that shocks the conscience of the court.

The relief of unconscionability is often misunderstood and it should not be seen as a synonym for unfairness. A court does not set aside a contract just because it is unfair. The opposite is true. In a business bargaining situation, contract law protects competition and each party is entitled to get the best deal for themselves that they can.

But in some situations, when one side is so much stronger and takes advantage of the other knowing they are in a vulnerable situation, often due to financial difficulties, age or mental impairment, if the deal that is struck is clearly unconscionable, the courts can refuse to enforce the contract.

Example: In one of the first cases to consider unconscionability, a 79-year-old woman, with only a small pension that barely met her living expenses, was convinced by two men, who were not relatives, to take out a mortgage loan against her house. The money was then used to pay off the men's car loan. The men promised to pay her back, which, not surprisingly, they did not. In these extreme circumstances the court would not enforce the mortgage loan on behalf of the financing company saying that the circumstances were so shockingly unfair as to be unconscionable. (*Morrison v. Coast Finance Ltd.* (1965), 55 DLR (2d) 710)

Cases often involve insurance companies offering small amounts for a quick settlement of an insurance claim. The client who is injured is often desperate and has little or no understanding of how serious their injury is, and even less knowledge of the appropriate settlement amount. If the court thinks the amount the injured client accepted in the settlement is so grossly unfair it is unconscionable, a higher amount can be awarded.

Example: In *Burkardt v. Gawdun* 2003 SKQB 100 (CanLII), a 20 year old woman was injured in a car accident and 7 months later had a second car accident. The insurance adjustor advised Ms. Burkardt that she needed to settle the first claim before they could deal with the second accident claim, though this was not true. Ms. Burkardt had suffered a back injury in the first accident and the insurance company knew that the full extent of her injuries had not yet been determined. The client had little understanding of business or insurance contracts, so she agreed and accepted a payment of $4,500 and signed a release. Her back problems continued to increase which led to back surgery several years later. Ms. Burkardt then asked the court to set aside the original settlement agreement as an unconscionable transaction. The court ruled that there had been unequal bargaining power, the settlement was substantially unfair and the insurance company had taken advantage of the young client. The original settlement was rescinded as it was an unconscionable transaction, and the court awarded $53,000 in damages.

Fairly frequently in divorce cases one party will claim that the equal division of family assets or the amount of equalization payments ordered is unconscionable. In family law the courts have set the threshold high and it must be proven that it would "shock the conscience of the court" to qualify as an unconscionable transaction.

Example: In *Sera v. Sera* 2009 ONCA 105 (CanLII) the court considered it unconscionable to have a husband pay his wife $4.129 million based on the value of the family business, when soon after the valuation date was set, his business almost collapsed due to the impact of free trade. The court recalculated his payment and set it at $900,000.

Unconscionability is sometimes raised when people are challenging a will or gifts that have been made, but it can also arise in a variety of different contract situations such as in the Birch case.

Example: In *Birch v. Union of Taxation Employees, Local 700300* 2008 ONCA 809 (CanLII), a union was found to have imposed an unconscionable contract term on its own union members. The union tried to force workers who crossed the picket line to work during the strike, to pay a fine equal to one day's gross pay for each day they worked during the strike, plus they were suspended from union membership for one year for each day worked as well. The court ruled this was a penalty and unconscionable and the workers did not have to pay the fines.

The *Lydian Properties* case below is a clear example of an unconscionable transaction where a company took advantage of a desperate person.

Lydian Properties v. Chambers
2009 ABCA 21 (CanLII)

Lydian Properties is a real estate investment company. As part of its business, it monitors courthouse foreclosure records so it can offer its services to people who are about to lose their homes because they are behind in their mortgage payments. Donna Chambers found herself in such circumstances. She was in debt, pregnant with her fifth child, on a reduced income because she was on maternity leave, and had recently been divorced when, in the fall of 2005, she fell into arrears on her home mortgage.

Foreclosure proceedings were commenced. She had been unable to arrange re-financing, was confused, anxious to retain ownership of her home, and felt pressure to act quickly. She got brochures sent to her by Lydian that promised "several ways to get money to you quickly to pay off arrears and other expenses so you can carry on with your life" and "honest, lasting solutions to help you out of foreclosure."

Chambers contacted Lydian and soon after signed a number of documents, the result of which was that title to her home was transferred to Lydian, and she became its tenant. The equity in her home became a deposit for an option for her to reacquire the home within a year's time at a specified repurchase price ($20,000 higher), provided she made every rental payment on time.

The transaction closed on February 15, 2006 and Chambers immediately fell into arrears. Lydian responded quickly; on March 1, 2006, it served her a Notice of Eviction. On May 16, 2006, Lydian applied for an order terminating her tenancy, granting Lydian possession of the home and judgment for the unpaid rent. The initial court decision ruled in Lydian's favour.

But Chambers then went to court and the judge declared the transaction should be set aside because it was unconscionable. Lydian appealed this decision to the Alberta Court of Appeal.

The Court's Decision

The Court of Appeal reviewed what needed to be established before a court could rule a contract was unconscionable. Four criteria had to be met:

1. It was a grossly unfair and improvident transaction
2. The victim lacked independent legal advice
3. There was an overwhelming imbalance in bargaining power caused by the victim's ignorance of business, illiteracy, ignorance of the language of the bargain or similar disability
4. The other party knowingly took advantage of this vulnerability.

The Appeal Court found that when the entire contract, including the lease and the option, was considered, the transaction was neither fair nor reasonable. It found Chambers would have to pay Lydian $20,000 more than Lydian had purchased the home for. Failure to meet even a single monthly payment resulted in default and she lost all her rights to the property. The court concluded the ultimate effect of the transaction was to transfer the property to Lydian, pay it an inflated rent, and give Chambers the right to buy the property back for an additional $20,000 beyond the approximately $17,000 equity she had in the home.

The contract was grossly unfair and improvident (hasty and careless), Chambers had not obtained legal advice prior to signing the documents, that there was an overwhelming imbalance in the parties' bargaining positions, and that Lydian knowingly took advantage of Chambers in her desperate situation.

The Court of Appeal agreed with the judge's decision that the contract was an unconscionable transaction and therefore it was rescinded. Lydian's appeal failed.

Consumer Protection

Many provinces have enacted sections in their Consumer Protection Legislation giving relief on the basis of unconscionability. These laws will likely be applied to favour the consumer. The legislation lists some factors that the court can look at to determine whether the transaction was unconscionable such as:

- The consumer was not reasonably able to protect his or her interests because of some infirmity, inability to understand the language or similar factors
- The price grossly exceeds the market price for the goods or services
- There was no reasonable probability of payment by the consumer

■ *Critical Concepts of* Unconscionable Transactions

- An unconscionable transaction is one that varies significantly from the community standards for commercial morality
- Courts do not just set aside every contract because it is unfair

- To be an unconscionable transaction there has to be an overwhelming imbalance of bargaining power due to the victim's desperation, ignorance, or disability
- The stronger party knowingly took advantage of the weaker party's vulnerability and a grossly unfair and improvident agreement was made that shocks the conscience of the court

Non Est Factum

The defence of *non est factum* is not usually available to business people. It was developed in a much earlier time, when a large percentage of the population was illiterate. Sometimes, a document was put in front of a person who could neither read nor write, and a signature—an X was sufficient—requested. The individual might be told that the document was a simple letter, when in fact it was really a guarantee of a debt, or a deed to the ownership of land. To have such an agreement set aside by the courts, the illiterate party could plead there was no intention of signing that type of document, and that it was understood to be something entirely different. For example, an elderly widow is told that she is signing a mortgage renewal, but she is actually signing over the deed to her house. A mortgage renewal is a different type of document from a deed to a house. This is the basis of the plea *non est factum*. It does not apply if only some of the terms are different from what the assignor thought (for example, a different price).

non est factum
(it is not my act) a plea that a person didn't know what they had agreed to

In modern times, it is reserved for people the court feels need protection, but who do not technically fit into the legal category of those who lack capacity. Most reported cases have involved very elderly persons who are clearly taken advantage of by unscrupulous relatives or financial institutions. It has also recently been applied to set aside spousal guarantees.

Example: In *Trans Canada Credit v. Judson*, 2002 PESCTD 57 (CanLII), James Judson signed what he thought was a credit reference for his daughter's boyfriend. He actually had signed a promissory note making him liable for the boyfriend's debt with Trans Canada Credit. Judson had very little education, his ability to read was extremely limited and he needed two hearing aids though could only afford one. He did sign the promissory note, but he thought it was for an entirely different purpose. The court recognized that contracts are not rescinded merely because someone was careless. However in this case the court believed that the document lacked the precision and clarity one would expect of a promissory note and it was signed very quickly and Judson had no independent legal advice. What he signed was radically different from what he believed he was signing so the promissory note was void due to non est factum.

■ *Business Law*   Applied

❾ **Inga was** an 80 year old Swedish woman who spoke and read almost no English. Her son Sven came to her with some documents to sign. Sven told Inga that it was an application for a loan and she just had to sign as a reference for him so that he could get the loan. Inga asked Sven if this would risk any of her money and he assured her it wouldn't. The documents that she signed however included a $200,000 mortgage on her house.

Sven got the loan from the bank, but when he was unable to make payments on the loan, the bank contacted Inga and told her it planned to sell her house to get the money Sven owed. Inga was very upset and said this couldn't happen as she had never agreed to any of this.

a) Discuss the defences Inga can use to try to prevent the bank from selling her house and what she must establish to be successful.
b) Discuss the claim that the bank will make and what it must establish to be successful.

Discharge and Remedies

Discharge of Contract

discharge of contract

occurs when all the parties have done exactly what they were required to do under the terms of the agreement: the promises have been completed and the parties have no further obligations to each other

All things must come to an end—including a contract. At some point, the contract must be discharged, and the promises made by the parties brought to an end. Usually, **discharge of contract** occurs when all the parties have done exactly what they were required to do under the terms of the agreement: the promises have been completed and the parties have no further obligations to each other.

For example, a manufacturer agrees to supply a fleet of delivery vans by September 11 of a given year. It does not supply the vans until December 1 of that year. This is a breach of contract. If the person suffered damages because of the delay, the manufacturer will likely have to pay the purchaser for the loss.

Frustration

frustration

an outside event that makes the performance of the contract impossible, and excuses a party from performance

Sometimes circumstances, not created by the parties, have made it impossible, or virtually impossible, for one of the parties to do what was promised, the contractual performance is considered to be frustrated. All the parties are discharged from their obligations under the contract. The circumstances that give rise to frustration occur after the contract has been made. **Frustration** is an outside event that makes the performance of the contract impossible, and excuses a party from performance. The grounds that are necessary to establish frustration are narrow. They must be considered as unforeseeable. Examples of frustration would include situations where goods sold were stolen or destroyed after the contract was made but before the delivery date, or in a personal service contract, the person was injured or became ill and could not perform on the date set in the contract.

If an event that forms the basis of the contract does not occur because of a frustrating event, then dependent contracts may also be considered frustrated. For example if a performer agrees to sing at a concert hall but then is injured and cannot perform, that contract is frustrated. If the concert hall had signed a contract with a security firm to provide security guards for that performance, that contract too may be considered frustrated as well. It is not impossible for the security guards to come, but there would be no need, since there was no longer going to be any concert on that date.

Sometimes actions by the government can cause a contract to be frustrated. If the laws change and prohibit an activity, such as rezoning or new licensing requirements, that may give rise to frustration. A contract is not considered to be frustrated just because it becomes more expensive to perform. It is also not frustrated if it becomes merely inconvenient to perform, it has to be a permanent complete frustrating event that totally affects the nature, purpose and consequences of the contract. A contract is also not frustrated if it is self-induced frustration, such as one person intentionally causing the frustrating event to occur.

In employment law if an employee is ill or injured and cannot work, the contract can be considered frustrated and may allow the employer to consider the contract terminated. The employee cannot then sue for wrongful dismissal. Human rights legislation however does require the employer to make accommodations for workers who are disabled due to illness or injury, so that may provide them with some protection and delay or deny the company's right to claim frustration for many years.

There is a distinction between mistake and frustration. Frustration only occurs when the unexpected event occurs after the contract is made. If the unexpected event occurs before the contract was made and the parties were unaware of it, then the contract is void due to mistake not frustration. For example if John agrees to sell his boat to Lara on May 15th and he will deliver it to her on May 20th, but neither one realized it had been destroyed in a storm on May 10th, this contract is void due to mistake. If the boat is destroyed on May 16th it is void due to frustration.

Force Majeure Clause

Many contracts, especially international agreements, contain a *force majeure* clause, which widens the scope of grounds for not performing a contract because of radically changed circumstances. The following is a common *force majeure* clause:

> St. Anne warrants and represents that its requirements under this contract shall be approximately 15,000 tonnes a year, and further warrants that in any one year its requirements for Secondary Fibre shall not be less than 10,000 tonnes, unless as a result of an **act of God** (the violence of nature), the Queen's or public enemies, war, the authority of the law, labour unrest, or strikes, the destruction of or damages to production facilities, or the non-availability of markets for pulp or corrugating medium.

act of God
the violence of nature

If there is a force majeure clause in a contract then the parties have anticipated that an unexpected event may occur and often have allocated who shall bear the risk, so the contract cannot be considered frustrated.

When frustration does occur it is sometimes difficult to determine who shall bear the losses that result. Common law dictated that if a deposit had been paid it would be returned if there had been no benefit provided. If some benefit had been given then they would get none of the deposit back. The all or nothing rule with deposits caused problems; however this has been overcome in almost every province as specific statutes have been passed to deal with frustrated contracts. These laws now allow a court to apportion the deposit money or losses based on what costs were incurred and the benefits that were received.

KBK No. 138 Ventures Ltd. v. Canada Safeway Limited, 2000 BCCA 295 (CanLII)

Safeway entered into a contract to sell property to KBK for a mixed commercial and residential condominium project. At the time the contract was made the property was zoned to allow a maximum floor space ratio (FSR) of 3.2. KBK had spoken with an official from the City of Vancouver regarding the zoning and the size of developments that would be allowed. On October 28, 1996 the contract was made and it specified that the purchase price would be the greater of $8.8 million or $38 multiplied by the FSR permitted by the City on the closing date. KBK paid a $150,000 deposit on that date.

One month later and before the closing date, the Director of Planning for the City of Vancouver applied to rezone the property allowing a FSR of only 0.3, or only 20% of the floor space originally allowed. Neither Safeway nor KBK had contemplated this event. When the proposed rezoning was approved soon after, KBK informed Safeway that it considered the contract frustrated and demanded the return of its deposit. Safeway denied there was frustration and refused to return the deposit. Safeway then sold the property to another buyer for $5.4 million.

KBK argued that the test for frustration was whether an intervening event that the parties had not contemplated had resulted in a "radically different" contract than the parties had agreed to. It claimed that the rezoning had produced that radically different result. Safeway claimed that the contract was for the sale and purchase of land and that had still been possible after the rezon-

ing, so the contract was not frustrated and it was entitled to keep the deposit.

The trial court ruled it was a frustrated contract and KBK was entitled to the return of the deposit money. Safeway appealed to the B.C. Court of Appeal.

The Court's Decision

The Appeal Court reviewed the three conditions that had to be satisfied for the doctrine of frustration to apply. These are: 1) What, having regard to all the circumstances, was the foundation of the contract? 2) Was the performance of the contract prevented? 3) Was the event that prevented the performance of the contract in the contemplation of the parties when the contract was made?

The court then ruled that all three conditions had been met. The contract was not just a sale of land, it was the sale of land for the development of a mixed commercial residential property with a square footage of about 231,800 square foot. The rezoning struck at the root of the agreement and reduced the size of the development to 30,230 square feet. This was not a mere inconvenience, it transformed the contract into something totally different from what the parties intended. Therefore the contract was frustrated and KBK would have its $150,000 deposit returned.

Business Law Applied

⑩ **Gina hired Sunray Ltd.** to build a sunroom on the back of her home. Sunray agreed to drill footings for the sunroom 10 feet deep to support the structure. The total cost of the project was $25,000 including custom made windows. Gina paid a $3,000 deposit when she signed the contract. Sunray ordered the custom made windows for the sunroom at a cost of $10,000 which Sunray paid for and were delivered before construction began.

Once Sunray began drilling, it discovered that the property was located over an underground stream and neither side knew of it. When it drilled down 4 feet, it hit water. It was not possible to install the 10 deep footings for the sunroom. Sunray said it would not be safe to build the sunroom on this home.

   a) Is Sunray liable for breach of contract? What defense can it use?
   b) Can Gina get her deposit back?
   c) Who should bear the cost of the custom made windows?

Breach of Contract

A breach of contract occurs when a party does not perform the contract as precisely promised. They may have not performed it properly, or completely or they may have refused to do anything at all. They may have broken a small term in the contract or it may be one or more of the key requirements.

Major and Minor Breach

major breach

a major term of the contract is not met entitling the aggrieved party to cancel or continue the contract and seek remedies

minor breach

a minor term of the contract is not met entitling the aggrieved party to damages only

There are two types of breach of contract; a **major breach** (a breach of condition) and a **minor breach** (a breach of warranty). If it is a major breach the innocent party is substantially deprived of the main benefit of the contract. If it is a minor breach then the innocent party did receive the main benefit of the contract, but not all of what was promised. If it is not clear, the court can determine whether it is a major or minor term, (a condition or a warranty), it is not necessarily what the contract calls it. Sometimes it depends on the circumstances whether breaching a term results in a major or minor breach. For example time may be a major term in some contracts and being on time is crucial to the contract performance. In other contracts time is not a major concern so it would be a minor term. Normally time is not a major term unless the contract states otherwise.

The rights and remedies of the innocent party are different depending on whether it is a major or a minor breach. If a major breach occurs the innocent party has two choices. They can choose to discharge or end the contract and seek remedies, (usually damages), or they can choose to continue the contract and treat it as a minor breach and also seek remedies. It is the choice of the innocent party, not the party that breached the contract. If a minor breach occurs the innocent party cannot discharge or get out of the contract, but they can seek remedies (usually damages) for any losses that they suffered.

For example, a college orders 1,000 new computers from Data Inc. to be installed in a new computer lab and they are to be delivered on August 1st. If on August 1st Data delivers only 600 computers that would be a major breach. The college could reject the computers and sue for any increased costs it has when it purchases 1,000 computers from another supplier. The college instead though could choose to accept the 600 computers and sue for any increased costs it incurs obtaining 400 more. If however Data delivered 980 computers on August 1st this would be a minor breach and the college would have to accept the computers, but could sue for any increased costs it incurs getting the other 20 computers.

anticipatory breach

one party in advance of the completion date indicates it will not perform the contract

Sometimes one party will tell, or by its actions indicate, to the other party in advance of the completion date that it will not perform the contract. This is an **anticipatory breach** and the innocent party has two options. It can treat the contract as breached and seek relief immediately and not have to wait until the completion date to sue. The innocent party can however instead reject the anticipatory breach, continue to perform their part of the contract and then claim full damages on the completion date if the other side has not performed. The innocent party must be able prove they can perform their part of the contract on the completion date or they too could be liable.

Remedies

The most common remedy given for breach of contract is the award of monetary damages. There are other non-monetary remedies that the court can also award in certain circumstances as well.

Monetary Damages

Principles of Awarding Damages

When awarding damages in contract law, the court operates on the principle that it should try to *place the injured party in the same position as if the contract was completed properly*. This is a different perspective than what is used in tort law. In torts, the court tries to place the injured party in the same position as if the tort had not occurred.

One principle that applies in both contracts and in torts, is that the party at fault is only liable for damages that are **reasonably foreseeable**. The court must "draw the line" at how far the liability extends. In contract law these losses would include losses that you would anticipate in the normal course of business. The defendant can be liable for other unexpected losses that arise in special circumstances, but only if they had been told of this risk at the time the contract was made and chose to assume the liability.

reasonably foreseeable
what could be expected within reason; probable not merely possible

Example: This principle was clearly established in the often quoted old British case of *Hadley v. Baxendale* [1854] 9 All E.R. Rep. 461. In that case a crankshaft from a machine was sent for a repair, but the shipper who took the part did not know that the entire factory would be shut down until the part was repaired and returned. The factory had anticipated a shutdown of only a few days, but due to the shipper's delays, it took one month before it was returned. The factory then tried to claim for one month's lost profits. The shipper however successfully argued that it had no knowledge the entire operations were dependent on this part, and since it had not been told, it was only liable for the usual damages that could be expected from this breach.

The law does not assume that a loss has been incurred simply because a contract has been breached. The plaintiff must prove that it has suffered a loss directly as a result of the breach. They must be able to *"put a dollar value on the loss."* The expectation principle tries to place the injured party in the same position as if the contract was completed properly. If for example Mitch agreed to sell his car to Anna for $5,000 but then refuses to sell, Mitch's liability will depend on how much Anna has to pay when she buys a car similar to the one Mitch was selling. If she has to pay $6,000, then Mitch owes her $1,000 to put her in the same position as if the contract was completed properly. If she is able to buy a similar car for $5,000 or less she has not suffered a loss so there would be little point in suing Mitch.

Another principle that applies when a breach of contract occurs is the duty of **mitigation** on the innocent party. The plaintiff has an obligation to mitigate their losses and take reasonable steps to keep their losses to a minimum. They cannot just sit back and let their losses mount up. If you fail to do so, the court may take this into account when awarding damages and reduce the amount accordingly. If for example Mitch agrees to sell his car to Anna for $5,000, but Anna decides not to go through with the deal, Mitch cannot simply sue Anna for $5,000. He has to take reasonable steps to resell the car. If he can only resell the car for $4,000, then Anna is liable for $1,000. If he resells it for $5,000 or more then he has fully mitigated

mitigation
duty on the aggrieved party to take reasonable steps to lessen their losses

his losses. As we saw in chapter 5, the rules for deposits, down payments and cancellation fees often also apply in these situations. In employment law, a worker who is wrongfully fired can sue for lost income, but they must try to find alternative employment once they have been terminated. If they are able to get a new job this income may reduce the damages they will be awarded. Failure to look for a new job can also result in a reduction of their damages for wrongful dismissal.

■ *Business Law* Applied

① **Paul Xuereb knew** a collector who wanted a 1957 T-Bird and was willing to pay a premium if it was delivered on or before June 1. In late May, Xuereb found a suitable vehicle in Danny Samutt's garage. This type of car was currently selling on the open market for about $25,000. Xuereb agreed to pay Samutt $20,000, and pick up the vehicle on June 1.

The day after he had made his agreement with Samutt, Xuereb visited the collector and arranged to resell the car to him at a price of $40,000, guaranteeing delivery on June 1. However, when Xuereb went to collect the vehicle, Samutt had changed his mind and decided not to sell. Xuereb would certainly be able to find a similar car elsewhere, for about $25,000, but not by the June 1 deadline. The collector bought from another source.

Xuereb sued Samutt for breach of contract.

  a) Which test would the court apply to decide what type of loss, if any, Xuereb can recover from Samutt?
  b) If Samutt was liable for damages, would he have to pay $5,000 or $20,000?

■ *Critical Concepts of* Quantifying the Loss

- A claim for damages for breach of contract must be proven.
- The party at fault is only liable for damages that are reasonably foreseeable.
- Under the expectation interest principle, damages should place the victim in the same position as if the contract had been fulfilled.
- Business losses are for loss of profit, and normal expenses incurred to earn that profit must be deducted from the gross income.
- The victim must take reasonable steps to reduce the loss. This is called mitigation.

Types of Monetary Damages

There are different types of monetary damages that can be awarded and they were described in detail in Chapter 2. These include:

Pecuniary Damages—are awarded for financial losses. They can be classified as Special Damages if they are provable losses up until the trial date, and General Damages which are based on estimates of future losses. The court will give expectation damages in an amount based on the expected results if the contract had not been breached. Sometimes potential profits may be speculative and difficult to determine. The court will then allow a party to claim expenses that were incurred when they relied on the contract, rather than the profit anticipated, but not both.

Non-pecuniary Damages—are awarded for non-financial losses such as pain and suffering, loss of enjoyment of life and shorter life expectancy. These damages are not often awarded in breach of contract cases as there was no personal injury involved.

Aggravated Damages—are awarded for mental anguish, distress or emotional upset and again they are not usually awarded for breach of contract. In some employment law wrongful dismissal cases they may be given or to a person who went on a vacation that was very bad and very different from what the brochure had promised. These damages require medical evidence.

Punitive (or exemplary) Damages—are money awarded to punish intentionally bad behaviour and are rarely given. There must first be a separate actionable wrong and the punitive award is only given if the damage award already given is not sufficient to deter such conduct. They are considered exemplary, as in setting an example, to others that this behaviour will not be tolerated by the courts. The Whitten v. Pilot Insurance case below illustrates when punitive damages can be awarded.

Nominal Damages—are a small or nominal amount of money awarded when no real losses occurred.

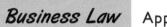

Business Law Applied

⑫ **A theatre retained** a heating contractor to repair its heating system. The contractor agreed to do so, but the work was negligent, and the system broke down one night, leaving the building without heat. The water pipes froze and had to be replaced. The theatre had to cancel a one-night contract, losing the profits related to that event.

The theatre's average gross sales for one evening are $50,000. Its average expenses for one evening are $40,000. The cost of replacing the pipes was $8,000.

    a) What damages would the court award to the theatre in an action against the heating contractor?

⑬ **Keanu Carlton was** the vice-president of International Marketing Company, Ltd. He was let go because of the company's downsizing policy. His lawyer advised him that the company would have to pay him the equivalent of one year's salary as monetary damages because the firing was not for a justifiable reason in law.

Carlton learned of another job opportunity that he could apply for immediately upon his termination, but he decided to wait one year before taking on new employment. He then sued International Marketing for one year's salary.

    a) Would he be successful?
    b) What defence could the company raise? What is it technically called?
    c) What would Carlton have to do to be able to claim the one-year salary equivalent?

⑭ **An employee sued** an employer for wrongful dismissal. The employer claimed that he found marijuana in the employee's desk and reported this to the police. The police investigated and concluded that the employer planted the substance. The police charged the employer with obstruction of justice. The employer pleaded guilty and was fined $20,000.

The employee wins the wrongful dismissal action and is awarded one year's salary plus benefits. Then the employee asks for punitive damages of $100,000.

    a) What must the employee establish to be entitled to an award of punitive damages? Will he be able to meet the test?
    b) What defence can the employer assert to the claim for punitive damages? What case law that you have studied could it rely upon for its position? What if the employer had been given a conditional discharge by the criminal court, or fined $100,000? Would either of these circumstances have an effect on the employer's defence to the claim for punitive damages?

Whitten v. Pilot Insurance Company, [2002] S.C.R. 1

Mrs. Whitten had insured her house for fire. She discovered a fire in the house just after midnight in January. She, her husband, and their two daughters fled from the house wearing only night-clothes into the −18 degree Celsius weather. Mr. Whitten gave his slippers to one of the daughters to go for help, and suffered severe frostbite to his feet. The fire totally destroyed their home and all contents.

The insurance company made a $5,000 expense payment and paid a few months rental, and then cut the Whittens off completely from any payments. The insurance company took the position that the Whittens set fire to their own house, even though the local fire chief and the company's own expert said that was unlikely. At trial a jury awarded $1 million in punitive damages against the insurance company for bad faith. The court of appeal reduced that to $100,000. Mrs. Whitten appealed to the Supreme Court of Canada and asked that the trial award be reinstated.

The Court's Decision

The insurance company's conduct was exceptionally reprehensible. It was intended to force the insured to make an unfair settlement. Insurance contracts are purchased for peace of mind. The more devastating the loss, the more the insured will be at the financial mercy of the insurer and the more difficult it will be for the insured to challenge a wrongful refusal to pay.

The obligation of good faith means that the insured's peace of mind should have been the company's objective and her vulnerability should not have been exploited by a negotiating strategy.

An award of punitive damages in contract cases are rare. Here, in addition to the contractual obligations to pay the claim, the insurance company was under a distinct and separate obligation to deal with its policyholders in good faith. This distinct obligation could support a claim for damages for bad faith.

The jury intended to send a powerful message criticizing the company's behaviour. While the amount was much higher than any previous award in this country, it was, in these circumstances, within rational limits. The trial judgment of $1 million was restored.

Quantum Meruit

quantum meruit

"as much as is merited," the amount a person deserves to be paid for goods or services provided to another person requesting them, even if some of the elements of a contract are missing

In some situations the "guilty" party might benefit from breaking the contract. Consider the example of a construction contract that is to be paid in stages according to the progress of the work:

completion of basement	$10,000
completion of first floor	$10,000
completion of roof	$10,000

The owner of the new building might breach the contract when the basement has been excavated, but the concrete has not yet been poured, so the first payment is not due. If the contractor has other work available and cannot claim loss of profit for the balance of the contract, the court will award damages for the benefit of the work done—the value of excavating the basement.

Quantum meruit is based on the principle called restitution. The courts restore a benefit given to the defendant by the plaintiff. The plaintiff relies on the defendant's promise (in the above example, this is the promise to pay for work done) and the plaintiff gives value (does the work). So the defendant is considered to be unjustly enriched—he got something for nothing. The courts make the defendant pay the value of the benefit. **Quantum meruit**, "as much as is merited," is the amount a person deserves to be paid for goods or services provided to another person requesting them, even if some of the elements of a contract are missing.

Other Remedies

The courts have developed other remedies for breach of contract in situations where damages are not appropriate. Originally, these remedies were developed by the courts of equity. But as the court of law and court of equity have merged, all courts can apply these remedies.

Specific Performance

Sometimes, the court will order a **specific performance**: an order requiring the defendant to undertake a specified task, usually to complete a transaction. This is normally done only if the item is unique. If, for example, a plaintiff arranges to purchase three adjacent pieces of land to build a manufacturing plant, but the vendor of the middle lot refuses to close the deal, damages are of little value to the plaintiff. In these circumstances, the court will make an order forcing the vendor of the middle lot to convey the land. A specific performance order is not given in personal-service contracts.

specific performance
an order requiring the defendant to undertake a specified task, usually to complete a transaction

Injunction

The court can issue an **injunction**, an order instructing one party to stop a particular process or action. A landlord, for example, might wish to force a tenant out because someone else has offered to pay a much higher rent. The current tenant is a furniture distributor, whose loading dock is at the rear of the building and can be accessed only by a lane at one side of the property. The landlord begins to leave his own vehicles blocking the access lane for long periods, thus disrupting the tenant's business. The tenant can obtain an injunction ordering the landlord to stop parking his vehicles in the lane.

injunction
an order instructing one party to stop a particular process or action

Example: Three employees of Whitmar Publishing left its employ and set up a competing business using a LinkedIn site that contain Whitmar's confidential customer contact information to solicit customers away from Whitmar to the new company. The site had been set up in the name of one of the employees, but paid for by Whitmar and was set up for the purpose of promoting its business. The court found that the site was Whitmar's property and ordered an injunction restraining the former employees from using that information. *Whitmar Publications Limited v. Gamage and Others*, [2013] EWHC 1881 (Ch)

Interlocutory (Temporary) Injunction

Sometimes the plaintiff needs immediate relief and cannot wait two or three years for the matter to come to trial. In this case, the plaintiff can sue for an **interlocutory injunction**, a temporary injunction which lasts only until trial.

interlocutory injunction
a temporary injunction which lasts only until trial

Mareva Injunction

If the court believes that the defendants might move their assets from the jurisdiction before the case comes to trial, and thus avoid paying a court judgment, it can order them not to do so. If, for example, the defendant is a foreign-based shipowner whose only asset is a ship currently anchored in Vancouver harbour, the court will make an order restraining removal of the vessel.

The court must be satisfied that the plaintiff has a reasonable case, and that the defendant has no other assets within the jurisdiction to satisfy the judgment. As a practical matter, the defendant will be allowed to post a bond, or letter of credit—a written promise by one person's bank to pay another person when specified conditions are met—for the value of the plaintiff's claim, and then remove the ship.

Technology Issues re Injunctions

The Internet can pose challenges when injunctions are issued. The wording of the injunction and how search engines operate may nullify the effectiveness of the injunction. In one case two companies that were in competition making basketball court flooring agreed to an injunction that prevented the defendant from using the term "SPORT COURT" in any advertising including the Internet. The defendant then purchased the words "court" and "basketball court" from Google so when people were searching these terms, Google listed the defendant's company in priority to the plaintiff. The plaintiff brought a motion for contempt of court (which can result in criminal penalties such as fines or imprisonment), for violating the injunction. The court ruled there was no violation though as the injunction had not specifically prohibited the terms "court" or 'basketball court." (*Rhino Sports Inc. v. Sport Court Inc.*, 2007 WL 1302745 (D Ariz. May 2, 2007).

Civil Search Warrant, or Anton Piller Order

Anton Piller order

an order that the defendant must permit its premises to be searched without informing the defendant, made without notice to the defendant if giving notice would defeat the plaintiff's ability to obtain the remedy

In certain cases the court will issue an **Anton Piller order**, which is an order that the defendant must permit its premises to be searched without informing the defendant, made without notice to the defendant if giving notice would defeat the plaintiff's ability to obtain the remedy. For example, if an employee who has signed a confidentiality agreement leaves the job, secretly taking confidential information, the employer can obtain an Anton Piller order to search the employee's home, car, garage, and so on, to locate these documents.

Rectification

rectification

a court order which corrects a written document to reflect accurately the contract made by the parties

A **rectification** is a court order which corrects a written document to reflect accurately the contract made by the parties. It is most often done when the aggrieved party can prove the terms of an oral agreement, and that there was a mistake made when putting the oral agreement into written form. For example, two parties agree that one will purchase from the other part of a vacant lot having a measurement of 1,000 ft × 1,000 ft, but the written document, because of a typo, describes the lot as 100 ft × 100 ft. One party misses the typo and signs the written document with the mistake.

Accounting

A court can order that one party must produce its private books and records, and then permit an expert chosen by the other party to examine these and prepare a report. For example, two people might set up a small business together, with one taking all responsibility for the bookkeeping. After a while, the other party begins to suspect that the profits are not being divided as they should, but cannot gain access to the books. The remedy is then to sue for an accounting.

Business Alert!

The problem posed by the Sport Court case is how to get a wording that protects the trade name/brand name given the unique, often unexpected results of Internet search engines. A business can get a trademark for a unique name such as "Sport Court" but it can never get a trademark, that is an exclusive right, to own general terms such as: court or basketball court. Can it get the protection by a more comprehensive wording of a court injunction? That remains to be seen.

In Summation

Defects in a Contract

- A contract is based on the assumption that each party has freely given consent to perform the promises contained in it. If this is not the case, there are five main areas of concern the courts will consider in deciding whether to allow a claim by one party that consent was not freely given.

Misrepresentation

- This is a statement, made by one party at the time of contracting, which is designed to persuade the other party to enter into the agreement, but which does not appear in the final contract. The misrepresentation may have been innocent, negligent, or fraudulent in nature. Each type of misrepresentation will result in a particular remedy or choice of remedy for the party who cannot be considered to have freely consented to the agreement because of the misrepresentation that was made.

- Most provinces have passed special consumer protection legislation to guard consumers against misrepresentations or unfair business practices, and there are standard form contracts that contain clauses stating that no representation has been made other than those contained in the contract.

Mistake

- A remedy is sometimes available for the parties where a contract has been based on a mistake. The courts will attempt to determine if the mistake was made by one or both parties, and whether the mistake related to an important element that the parties relied on in creating the contract. This is a complex area of law and not easily proven.

Duress

- Consent obtained through force, whether by threatened violence, blackmail, or economic duress, will result in the contract being treated as though it never existed.

Undue Influence

- Undue influence may be actual or presumed.
- Where there is a special relationship, there is a presumption of undue influence.
- Special relationships may be traditional ones such as lawyer-client, or also relationships of trust based on the facts of the particular situation.
- Where there is a presumption of undue influence, the alleged wrongdoer must prove that undue influence was not used.

Unconscionable Transactions

- A court will set aside a contract as an unconscionable transaction when there is an overwhelming imbalance of bargaining power due to the victim's desperation, ignorance, or disability and the stronger party knowingly took advantage of the weaker party's vulnerability and a grossly unfair and improvident agreement was made that shocks the conscience of the court.

Non Est Factum

- This defence to non-performance by one of the parties to a contract is based on that party not having understood the true nature of the document that was signed. Not normally used by a business person, it usually involves an individual who, through some infirmity, was not able to understand the nature of the document.

Frustration

- A contract is considered to be frustrated and therefore void when an outside event beyond the control of the parties makes it impossible to perform the contract.

Ending a Contract

- The obligations or promises undertaken by the parties to the contract might be brought to an end in one of several ways, the most preferable usually being performance.
- A breach may be a major (breach of a condition) or a minor breach (a breach of a warranty).
- If a major breach occurs the innocent party has two options, it can end the contract and seek remedies or continue the contract and treat it as a minor breach and seek remedies. If it is a minor breach the contract continues and the innocent party can seek remedies.

Remedies

- A contract is breached if a party does not perform according to its terms. A number of remedies arise from such a breach, their purpose being to compensate or assist the non-breaching party.

Damages

- Damages are an award of money that the court has ordered the breaching party to pay as compensation to the non-breaching party for the loss of the bargain represented by the contract. Damages are intended to place the non-breaching party in the same position as if the breach had not occurred, by awarding monetary compensation for any reasonably foreseeable loss caused by the breach.
- What would be reasonably foreseeable as a loss arising from a breach will depend on what was in the minds of the parties at the time of contracting. Certainly those losses, including loss of profit, that would occur in the normal course of business could be anticipated, as well as any losses arising from special circumstances that were brought to the attention of the breaching party at the time the contract was made.
- The courts will consider several factors in calculating the damages to be awarded, including whether the non-breaching party has mitigated its damages by taking whatever reasonable steps are necessary to minimize the losses experienced from the breach.
- Punitive damages are not easily awarded. There must be a separate actionable wrong and the other damages must not be sufficient to deter the wrongful conduct.

Other Types of Damages

- Monetary damages may be awarded for reasons other than putting the party in the position as if the contract had not been breached. These awards will be based on such considerations as pain and suffering (mental suffering) or expenses incurred.

Other Remedies

- In cases where damages are not sufficient to meet the needs of the non-breaching party, various other remedies may be brought into play. Usually these remedies involve a court order requiring the breaching party to complete, or refrain from, some action.
- Various types of injunctions are available to stop the breaching party from pursuing a particular course of action that has caused, or will cause, harm. The injunction may be temporary or permanent in nature.
- The courts may order the breaching party to proceed with the contract and specifically perform the promises made in the agreement.
- Remedial orders allowing a party to obtain information or evidence through a search of the breaching party's property (Anton Piller order), or granting access to financial records for an accounting of profits, are a few of the orders available to the court to assist in situations where a contract has been breached.
- The remedy of *quantum meruit* is available if the parties have not included a means to determine the value to be exchanged under the contract, and ensures that a reasonable price will be paid for the work done.

Closing Questions

Misrepresentation

1. Grouse Nest Resorts Ltd. arranged to borrow $1,250,000 from the First National Mortgage Company to build on two pieces of vacant land. The hotel company gave the mortgage on each of the properties as security for the loan.

    Under the terms of the building loan agreement, the mortgage company was to advance the money in instalments, over several months. The standard form mortgage document contained a clause stating that the mortgage company could refuse to make any further advances for whatever reason it chose. The president of Grouse Nest Resorts complained to the mortgage manager of First National that the clause could place Grouse Nest into bankruptcy if a loan instalment should be refused. The mortgage manager replied, "Don't worry, that clause is only used to prevent borrowers from taking off to Las Vegas." He reassured the president of the hotel company that if the development proceeded, the money would be advanced. On the strength of this representation Grouse Nest signed the mortgage. The first instalment was paid on time, but the mortgage manager was overruled by his superiors and no other advances were made.
    a) Could Grouse Nest Resorts Ltd. rely on the oral representations made by the mortgage manager in order to enforce the loan agreement?

2. Computer Aces Inc. sells a computer system to A.J.M. Leasing Ltd., whose business is financing car purchases by taking the leases as security. The sales representative tells A.J.M. that accounting software for the leasing business worth $10,000 will be supplied with the computer. When the officer from A.J.M. notes that nothing is said in the purchase order about the software, the sales rep explains that the software is in development and will not be ready for three months.

    A.J.M. buys the computers. Three months later when it asks for the software, a new sales rep, who has replaced the previous one, says he does not know anything about this.
    a) Is there an express term regarding the accounting software in the contract?
    b) Will the courts imply a term into the contract saying Computer Aces must supply the software?
    c) What would the results be if this were a consumer purchase? What is the reason for the difference in the laws governing consumer and business transactions?

3. Examine the entire agreement clause in the Agreement of Purchase and Sale for a Business in the Appendix to Chapter 5.
    a) What do the terms *representation* and *warranty* mean? Why are they included in this clause?
    b) Give an example from your own experience, or that of a relative or friend, where an oral statement has been made in the purchase of something and the statement was not written down as part of the contract, and that statement turned out to be false.
    c) Bring a copy of a contract that you or someone you know has signed recently, and note the clauses in it that you have studied in this course.

4. a) In the case of Ault v. Canada, what was the basis of the misrepresentation and what did the plaintiffs have to prove to succeed?
    b) Why did the court find there was a fiduciary duty owed by all of the defendants?
    c) Do you think the allocation of the damages was appropriate? Why?

5. Robert Goddard and Norm Chomsky were friends and worked together as accountants in the same company. Chomsky found what he thought was a great bargain—one acre of vacant land on the edge of the city, selling for $50,000. Chomsky told Goddard, "I can't believe this deal. This property is worth $200,000. We can sell it within three months, and make a ton of money." Goddard agrees to put up $25,000 and the property is purchased. After months of trying to resell it, it becomes clear that the property is of little value because of its bad location, downwind from a mushroom farm. Eventually, the men sell the property for $25,000. Goddard wants to sue Chomsky for his loss of $12,500.
    a) Is Chomsky's statement about the value of the land, or its prospects for resale, a misrepresentation?
    b) Could it be a collateral warranty, or a term of the contract?

6. a)   You sell your car to a stranger. He gives you a cheque that he knows is bad. By the time you find out the cheque has bounced, he has sold the car to a third-party. The third-party paid a fair price and didn't know that the seller was a fraudster. Can you recover the car from the third-party?

   b)   Would it have made any difference to your answer if the car had been stolen from you and you were suing to recover it? Explain.

7. a)   What is the difference between a representation and a term of a contract?

   b)   Although there is generally no duty to give information to an opposing party in negotiating the contract, there are some situations where there is an obligation to reveal information even if it is harmful to yourself. Identify 2 of those situations.

   c)   What does caveat emptor mean?

   d)   A salesman sells a car to Mary for personal use. He tells her it was only driven by a little old lady, mostly to church. A month after buying the car, a friend recognizes it as having belonged to a teenager who used it for drag racing. The Bill of Sale for the car contains an entire agreement clause. Mary sues to get her money back. Can she get the salesman's representation about ownership into evidence at trial?

8. Mary Cunningham was considering buying an antique lamp from Jay Scott, an antiques wholesaler. Cunningham, an antique retailer, said, "This must be a Victorian lamp." Scott did not reply, and Cunningham bought the lamp. Some time later she discovered it had in fact been manufactured in the 1960s.

   a)   Is there a misrepresentation?

   b)   Are there any circumstances where Cunningham could rely on misrepresentation?

9. Maurice Bullen, a mover, is considering buying a van for his business. The salesperson tells him that the model he is interested in will not be a "gas guzzler," and that given the current cost of gas to travel 1,500 kilometres should cost no more than $50. Bullen decides that he wants this model and signs a sales agreement that contains the words:

> This agreement constitutes the entire agreement. No representations or warranties other than those in written form constitute the agreement.

Bullen did not see this clause because the print was small and it appeared on the back of the document. In his first week of using the van, Bullen drove 1,000 kilometres, and spent $60 on gas. Checking his receipts, he determined that the price of gas had not increased since his discussions with the salesperson, but that a recent federal budget would put gas up five cents a litre in three weeks' time.

Bullen is no longer a happy customer.

   a)   Can Bullen get a court to set aside his contract? Why or why not?

   b)   If the term regarding gas consumption was in a brochure, would this change your opinion?

10. During construction of an office building, Jackson Silvermann signed an agreement to rent premises on the main floor for use as a restaurant. He expected the building to be 100 percent occupied within five months of his restaurant opening. For various reasons, businesses were slow to rent in this location and six months after his restaurant opened the building was only 30 percent rented.

Silvermann wants out of his lease. The landlord admits he knew there would be difficulties in renting this location but claims he never discussed this element with Silvermann when they signed the restaurant lease, and that he knew nothing of the restaurateur's expectations.

   a)   On what legal remedy will Silvermann rely?

   b)   Will Silvermann's claim be successful? Why or why not?

   c)   On what legal principle will the landlord rely?

11. Jorge Mendocino was an independent contractor who made his living by purchasing vacant parcels of land, building residential houses on them, and reselling the houses at a profit. One day while driving through a heavily populated area of Toronto, he saw a piece of vacant land for sale that would be perfect for two Victorian townhouses. He immediately telephoned the agent and put in an offer on the property. The offer was accepted and four months later the transaction was completed.

Mendocino proceeded to build the two houses and to landscape the properties before selling them. He was known in the trade for the excellent landscaping of the properties he sold. However, whatever plant material he put in—grass, trees, shrubs, flowers—all would wither and die within a week of planting. One day, Mendocino was talking to a neighbour at the building site, who said she too experienced similar problems with her plants on that side of her property ever since the gas station that used to be there had been taken down two years ago. Mendocino then had the soil tested and discovered the ground was so toxic that nothing would grow, and he probably would not be able to sell the houses. Angry, Mendocino confronted the vendor and demanded his money back as well as damages for the loss of profit from the sale of the houses. The vendor suggested Mendocino go hoe a row of beans.

a) Explain whether Mendocino will be successful in having the court set aside the contract and award him damages.

b) From the sample Offer to Purchase provided by your instructor, identify the clauses that the vendor would rely on for his defence and explain fully if they would be an answer to Mendocino's court action.

Mistake, Duress, Undue Influence, Non Est Factum

12. John Smith has listed his house for sale. Roop and Mira Sharma have submitted an offer to purchase. Smith is told that the couple has 3 young children. Smith's neighbour has just been released from serving 3 years in jail for possession of child pornography.

    Does Smith have a legal obligation to tell the prospective purchasers of his neighbour's criminal record?

13. Eddie Giordano was in the middle of a recession. His business was down, and he needed help. Giordano went to his accountant, who told him he could lend him $20,000 but only if he signed over a 25 percent interest in his business.

    a) Is there a problem of duress or undue influence?

    b) If there is a problem, how should Giordano and his accountant plan for the transaction?

14. Bill Simco was 84 and almost blind. He had two children who, being greedy, wanted his money *now*. They produced what they called a letter of thanks to the grandchildren for taking care of him during his recent illness and told him to sign it. Simco instead signed a promissory note for $50,000.

    a) Is this a case of undue influence or unconscionable *non est factum* or neither?

    b) If there is a problem, what is the solution for Simco?

15. Tara Olsen responded to a newspaper advertisement that read "10-foot fibreglass Sunfish for sale, $400 firm." She telephoned Ben Bartollini, the owner, and told him that she had just finished a sailing course and wanted to buy her own boat. She arranged to meet him the next day with the cash. Olsen arrived at Bartollini's house, handed over the $400 and opened the garage to discover a 10-foot fibreglass Sunfish canoe. When she tried to get her money back Bartollini refused.

    a) On what legal basis might Olsen argue her position and what difficulties might she encounter?

    b) If successful, what would be her remedy?

16. For several years, Geraldine Kikuta had managed Drew Mair's art store. During that time Mair had slowly withdrawn from the business side of the store to pursue his personal interest of creating unique sculptures from discarded junk. Mair had come to rely on Kikuta exclusively to handle the business affairs of the store and to act as his personal *agent* for the sale of his artistic creations. As a result of Kikuta's promotion of his work, Mair was now a well-known name in the contemporary art world.

    One day, Kikuta presented Mair with an ultimatum—either he sold her 60 percent of the store for $10,000 or she would not be back to work the next morning and she would advise the art world that she could no longer in good conscience act as agent for Drew.

    Mair was at a loss. He had become so totally dependent on Kikuta to run the store that he had no idea as to the state of the financial books, business orders, or even where the office coffee machine was located. And, if Kikuta were suddenly to stop acting as his agent in the circumstances she suggested, his reputation and sales would probably drop to nothing. He signed the contract, and accepted the cheque Kikuta just happened to have with her.

    a) Can Mair use duress as a reason to avoid this contract? If so, what is the nature of the duress?

    b) Would Mair be able to raise undue influence as a means of avoiding the contract?

17. You are the manager of a branch of a major bank. Giancarlo and Gina Romero, successful entre-preneurs, have come to meet with you to arrange the financing for the purchase of their latest business venture. You have indicated that before the bank advances funds it requires a guarantee for the loan. The couple shows you the deed to a cottage property registered in the name of Gina Romero. She offers to sign the guarantee today so that they can obtain the funds immediately.
    a) What concerns about this situation, if any, come flooding into your mind?
    b) If you see a problem in this transaction, what steps would you take to avoid it?

18. Gordon Thompson had worked as an engineer with Foundation Consultants Ltd. for ten years. Without any warning, he was called into a supervisor's office to be told that the company was downsizing, and that day would be his last on the job. Thompson was offered three months' salary ($15,000) if he would sign a form releasing the company from any other financial obligation to him. The release exempted the employer from any court action over the firing. The cheque was already made out—it was handed to him along with the release form.

    Thompson had not expected to be fired. Last year he had bought a house, and now had a large mortgage. He also obtained a loan to renovate the house, and his wife had just taken six months' maternity leave without pay. Thompson was worried about surviving financially while looking for employment, so he took the $15,000 and signed the release.

    It took Thompson over a year to find another job. During this time, he sought legal advice. His lawyer told him that the employer would have been liable for one year's salary, approximately $60,000, had Thompson not settled the matter but instead had taken the employer to court. Thompson wants to sue and have the release set aside.
    a) What is the technical name for the grounds Thompson could plead to have the agreement set aside?
    b) Could he plead undue influence? There is a relationship between him and the employer, but is it a special relationship as used in the law of undue influence?
    c) Will he be successful in having the release set aside?

19. The Bank of Credit and Commerce tried to enforce a loan guarantee against Christine Macdaid, who was married to William Macdaid, a farmer. The bank's lending officer visited the farm while the husband was on a business trip, and demanded that Mrs. Macdaid guarantee a loan made for a barn that was currently under construction.

    The bank's officer stated: "These papers have to be signed or the work on the barn will be shut down."

    The woman signed the papers because she did not want the construction to stop, since the barn was needed for the farm operation.

    The loan went into default, and the bank sued Christine Macdaid personally.
    a) Did Christine Macdaid have any grounds in law to attack the guarantee? If so, what are they?
       The bank argued that the statement made by the lending officer was "ordinary business pressure."
    b) Was this an ordinary business transaction?
    c) Who do you think would succeed and why?

20. Tom agreed on April 10th to sell his antique car to Cheryl for $25,000 and she gave him a $5,000 deposit. He kept the car stored in a barn up at a friend's farm. They agreed to meet up at the farm on April 15th to complete the deal. When they arrived at the farm they were surprised to discover that the barn had collapsed and the car was destroyed. The owner of the farm apologized for not telling Tom sooner, but the storm had just happened on April 13th and he had been very busy since then.
    a) Can Cheryl sue Tom for breach of contract? Explain.
    b) Can Tom keep the $5,000 deposit? Explain.
    c) If the storm that destroyed the car had happened on April 9th how would this affect your answers to part (a) and (b)? Explain.

21. Jason Barber was a Canadian teen pop rock sensation. He had toured the world and made millions selling his music and doing concerts. Jason was booked to do 2 concerts in Los Angeles for Star Concerts Inc. on October 9th and 10th. When Jason went to cross the border from Canada on his way to L.A. on October 8th the U.S. border guards refused him entry because he had recently been charged with drug possession and assault in Canada. Jason was furious and contacted his lawyer,

but the lawyer told him it could take a few days before this was sorted out. Jason had to contact Star Concerts Inc. and cancel the two concerts.

a)   Could Star Concerts Inc. successfully sue Jason for breach of contract? What defense will Jason use?

b)   If Jason had been injured in a car accident and unable to perform, would the result be the same? Discuss.

22.   Kerr Shipping Company sent a cable through the RCA telegraph service. The cable was to the captain of one of the Kerr vessels, at that time in the Philippines, instructing him to pick up and deliver certain freight to New York.

The message cost $26.78, and was sent in code so that competitors could not learn of Kerr's plans. Because of an error by RCA, the cable never reached its intended destination.

Kerr sued RCA for $500,000, the loss of profits that would have been made from the shipment.

a)   Would the action be successful?

b)   What steps might Kerr Shipping have taken to safeguard its interests in these circumstances?

23.   Direct to the Net Inc. became a great success in only four years after start-up and it decided to go public. About one week before making the announcement of its initial public offering (IPO), it was served with a statement of claim by a former shareholder who alleged the company had used his ideas without paying for them four years ago.

The directors of Direct to the Net Inc. believe that there is no merit in the claim and feel that they are being blackmailed, but believe they cannot report a lawsuit of this type on the corporation's disclosure material for the public offering. They agree to pay one million dollars to settle the claim.

a)   Is there any ground in law by which the corporation can have the settlement set aside by a court? If so, what is the name for this cause of action?

b)   What business considerations are relevant to the decision to sue and the timing of any lawsuit to set aside the settlement?

Remedies

24.   June Colwood had an e-mail account with Canada On-line (COL). She did not pay her last instalment. Instead of shutting down her mailbox, COL left it open and let e-mails accumulate. Colwood asked for these e-mails but COL refused to release them until she paid. There was no term in the contract dealing with the consequences of non-payment.

One of the e-mails which Colwood did not receive was a response to a job application telling her that she successfully got a job at a salary of $50,000 per annum, but that she had to reply in 24 hours. Because COL did not release her e-mail, she did not learn of the acceptance until a week after the deadline. Because she missed the deadline, the job was given to someone else.

Colwood wants to sue COL for one year's pay for the loss of the job.

a)   If there is no express term covering the retention of e-mails, is there any basis on which Colwood can sue?

b)   What defences respecting damages would COL raise and with what result?

25.   Scientific Feed Diets Inc. sells Cattle Feed "Super Grow" to a rancher. Unfortunately, it is laced with strychnine, because of the carelessness of Scientific Feed Diets Inc. The rancher is a health-diet nut and reads that Cattle Feed contains all the needed nutrients for humans. He decides to experiment with the diet for thirty days, but after the first mouthful of the poisoned cattle feed, he becomes violently sick and cannot work for six months.

He wants to sue Scientific Feed Diets Inc. for damages for breach of contract.

a)   What principle of contract damage law would Scientific Feed Diet raise in its defence and with what result?

26.   Shelina Memarbashi paid an art gallery $50,000 for what she believed was an unknown work by Picasso. However, her judgment was wrong. A few weeks later, an art-critic friend saw the painting and told her that it was created by a minor student of Picasso, and as a result was worth only $10,000. The friend had been present at another auction where the art gallery had bought the piece for about $2,000.

a)   Could Memarbashi successfully sue the art gallery for a refund of the $40,000 excess payment?

27. Ping Lok had a contract to paint the Allensons' house for $5,000. The money was to be paid upon completion of the job. Ping Lok stripped all the paint from the exterior walls, and prepared them for painting. He had completed one wall when the Allensons changed their minds and decided to put up aluminum siding.

Because the job had not been completed, the Allensons refused to pay Ping Lok any money under the contract.

Ping Lok's remedy is:
i)   specific performance
ii)   interlocutory injunction
iii) mareva injunction
iv)   *quantum meruit*
v)   rectification

a)   Explain the nature of the remedy available to Ping Lok, and the approximate dollar amount he might expect to receive as a result of his court action against the Allensons.

28. Theo Stakis had a contract to purchase a thoroughbred racing horse named You Betcha from Brad Taylor, the breeder. The contract was to be completed following the Kentucky Derby, in which the horse was entered to race.

When You Betcha won the Kentucky Derby, Brad Taylor refused to sell the horse to Stakis. Stakis had intended to use You Betcha for breeding, and anticipated huge profits as a result of the breeding program.

a)   What remedy would you suggest Stakis pursue?

29. Roland Clelland negotiated a contract to provide leather bracelets to Bracelets R You, a high-fashion store. The store would pay Clelland $2 for every bracelet he delivered on June 15, in time for the summer bracelet parade in the shopping mall.

On January 31, Clelland arranged with Max Weill to have 3,000 strips of leather delivered to Clelland's house on April 30, at a cost of 25 cents a strip. Clelland intended to use these strips of leather to make his artistic bracelets by June 15. At their meeting, Clelland told Weill all about his deal with the store. He added that, if the contract with Bracelets R You worked out, another chain of fashion stores was prepared to place a three-year order with Clelland, who anticipated an income of $40,000 a year from that contract.

Clelland left Weill's warehouse with assurances the leather would be delivered on time. On April 17, Weill phoned Clelland and said he would not be able to deliver the leather strips after all, but he was sure that Clelland could make other arrangements.

If Clelland does not have the leather by April 30, he will lose the contract with Bracelets R You and all profits he would have made.

a)   Advise Clelland as to his remedies and obligations and make a recommendation on what action he should take.

30. Aly Hamada agreed over the telephone to purchase Judie Home's electric treadmill for $1,500 at the end of the month. She then sent a contract to Home, which Home promptly signed and sent back.

At the end of the month Hamada presented Home with a cheque for $1,000 and asked for the treadmill. When Home checked the contract, she found a mistake had been made in typing and the purchase price was shown as $1,000.

Home's remedy is:
i)   rescission
ii)   accounting
iii) rectification

a)   Explain the nature of the remedy that Home will obtain based on your choice of remedy.

31. A retailer ordered 10 television sets, at a cost of $5,000, from a supplier. Normally, these particular appliances would all be sold in one month, for gross sales of $10,000, and a profit after expenses of $3,000. However, the supplier failed to deliver.

The retailer sued for breach of contract.

a)   How much would the court award in damages for breach of contract?
b)   If the retailer had been able to obtain the televisions from another supplier at the same price, but chose instead to sue the usual supplier, what damages would the court award?

32. A supplier delivered defective sugar to a brewery. As a result, one entire month's production of beer was contaminated and had to be destroyed. Rumours spread throughout the hospitality industry that the brewery was supplying defective beer, and its long-term sales were affected.

The brewery sued the sugar supplier for damages for loss of profit (sales minus expenses) of $100,000, as well as $2 million for damage to its reputation. The sugar company claimed that it should be liable only for $50,000, the replacement cost of the destroyed beer.
a) Could the sugar supplier reasonably have foreseen that delivering defective sugar would result in the loss of one month's profit for the brewery? Was the damage to the brewery's reputation reasonably foreseeable?
b) Should the damages be limited to the replacement cost of the beer?

33. An equipment dealership buys 10 harvesters from General Machines Ltd. for inventory of the dealership. As the harvesters have a design defect that costs $1,000 per unit to repair, it has to repair the five units sold. Word spreads so it cannot sell the remaining five units on which it would have earned a profit of $2,000 per unit. Also, future business will be lost because its reputation will be damaged.
a) What losses are recoverable from General Machines Ltd.?
b) What are the terms in the law of damages for the various types of damages suffered by the dealership?

34. Read the Limitation and Remedies clause from a Masu Inc. software license agreement which is reproduced below.

> Masu Inc. shall have no liability for any indirect or speculative damages (including, without limiting the foregoing, consequential, incidental, and special damages) arising from the use of or inability to use this product, whether arising out of an action in contract or tort, including, but not limited to, negligence, or under any warranty or condition, irrespective of whether Masu Inc. had advance notice of the possibility of any such damages, or such damages are foreseeable, including, but not limited to, loss of use, business interruption, and loss of profits. Notwithstanding the foregoing, Masu Inc.'s total liability for all claims under this agreement, whether in respect of a single occurrence or series of occurrences, shall not exceed the price paid by you for the product. These limitations on potential liabilities were an essential element in setting the product price. Masu Inc. neither assumes nor authorizes anyone to assume for it any other liabilities.

a) Select all the terms in this clause that you have studied in this book. Identify the related topics in the text (by page number), review them, and then discuss the significance of each term.
b) What types of damage claims might business customers make against Masu Inc. resulting from failure of its software?
c) Why does the limitation clause contain the sentence "These limitations on potential liabilities were an essential element in setting the product price"?

35. In the law of damages, it is said that a loss due to a subcontract, that is, a resale to a third party at a higher price, is too remote since it is not the normal result of a failure to deliver goods.
a) What does the above mean?
b) What case mentioned in the text established this principle?
c) What can be done to make a vendor liable for loss of profits on a subcontract?

36. The plaintiff agreed to purchase a used hydraulic blade for the front of his tractor from the defendant for $1,000. At the time the plaintiff had a contract to do work at a gravel pit. The hydraulic pump was defective and the defendant tried unsuccessfully to repair it. Because of the delays in repairing the pump, the gravel pit owner cancelled the plaintiff's contract.
a) What damages could the plaintiff claim?
b) What would the plaintiff have to prove to make the defendant responsible for loss of profit respecting the work at the gravel pit?

37. Joe's Tavern learns of a new beer glass that contains a microchip which signals the bartender when the glass is nearly empty, permitting the bartender to direct a waiter to that table. It orders 100,000 units of the item from a manufacturer at $10 per glass. The manufacturer completes and ships half of the order and is paid in full to that point. Suddenly the market price for these products drops to $5. Joe's Tavern tells the manufacturer that it wants to cancel the contract. The manufacturer advises Joe's Tavern that the manufacturer intends to complete the contract by making the parts, shipping them, and billing in full.

a) Is Joe's Tavern's cancellation a breach of contract?

b) What damages, if any, would the manufacturer be able to claim and why? Would the manufacturer be able to get punitive damages against Joe's Tavern based on the fact that it intentionally breached the contract?

c) Do you think the legal principle achieves an economic result?

Multi Issue

38. a) Identify the clauses which affect or determine how damages will be calculated in the:

    i) Used Car Bill of Sale (Chapter 6)

    ii) Purchase Order (Chapter 8)

    iii) Courier Bill of Lading (Appendix in this chapter)

b) The Courier Bill of Lading contains a clause limiting its liability to $2 per pound (or $4.41 per kilogram). Is this provision consistent with the principle respecting remoteness of damages set out in *Hadley v. Baxendale*? (**Remoteness of damages** is the principle of whether the damages are too far removed from the original negligent act.)

c) The car purchase agreement sets out the formula for calculating damages if a customer fails to accept delivery. What principles of law determine if such a clause will be enforced and with what result?

remoteness of damages

the principle of whether the damages are too far removed from the original negligent act

Courier Bill of Lading

CANADA FAST
....

WE WANT TO BE YOUR COURIER

MONTH	DAY	
		20

CONFIRMATION No.

BILLING COPY
1116999

FROM	CHARGE TO	TO

ADDRESS		ADDRESS

CITY	POSTAL CODE	CITY	POSTAL CODE

SHIPPER'S SIGNATURE	PIECES	PHONE NUMBER	PLEASE PRINT SIGNATURE	RECEIVED IN GOOD ORDER

10   SHIPMENT/DETAILS/EXPED.

ACCOUNT No.

NO. OF PIECES	WEIGHT	**LB**
	SUBJECT TO CORR.	**KG**

DECLARED VALUE (FOR INSURANCE PURPOSES)
$ SEE TERMS

LIMITATION OF LIABILITY IMPORTANT. PLEASE READ

THE AMOUNT OF ANY LOSS OR DAMAGE FOR WHICH THE CARRIER MAY BE LIABLE, SHALL NOT EXCEED $2.00 PER POUND (OR $4.41 PER KILOGRAM) COMPUTED ON THE TOTAL WEIGHT OF THE SHIPMENT UNLESS A HIGHER VALUE IS DECLARED ON THE FACE OF THE BILL OF LADING BY THE CONSIGNOR (SENDER).

N.B. NOTE CAREFULLY CONDITIONS BELOW HEREOF INCLUDING LIMITATIONS AND EXCLUSIONS OF CARRIER'S LIABILITY, WHICH ARE HEREBY ACCEPTED.

TERM 1 RECEIPT & FREIGHT

Received at the point of origin on the date specified, from the consignor mentioned herein, the property herein described; in apparent good order, except as noted (contents and conditions of contents of package unknown) marked, consigned and destined as indicated herein, which the carrier agrees to carry and to deliver to the consignee at the said destination, if on its own authorized route or otherwise to cause to be carried by another carrier on the route to said destination, subject to the rates and classification in effect on the date of shipment.

It is mutually agreed, as to each carrier of all or any of the goods over all or any portion of the route to destination, and as to each party of any time interested in all or any of the goods, that every service to be performed hereunder shall be subject to all the conditions not prohibited by law, whether printed or written, including conditions on back hereof, which are hereby agreed by the consignor and accepted for himself and his assigns.

TERM 2 NOTICE OF CLAIM

No carrier is liable for loss, damage or delay to any goods carried, under the Bill of Lading unless notice thereof setting out particulars of the origin, destination and date of shipment of the goods and the estimated amount claimed in respect of such loss, damage or delay is given in writing to the originating carrier or the delivering carrier within sixty (60) days after the delivery of the goods, or, in case of failure to make delivery, within nine (9) months from the date of shipment.

The final statement of the claim must be filed within nine (9) months from the date of shipment together with a copy of the paid freight bill.

TERM 3 NO SPECIAL AGREEMENT

The parties agree that notwithstanding any disclosure of nature or value of the goods, the amount of any loss or damage, including consequential, incidental or indirect damages, loss of earnings or profits, resulting from the loss of or damage to the goods and/or misdelivery, failure to deliver or delay in delivery of the goods, shall not exceed the maximum liability of the carrier aforesaid.

TERM 4 PAYMENT GUARANTEE

The shipper agrees to pay the carrier all shipping charges in the event the receiver, on a collect shipment or the third party on a third party billing shipment, refuses to pay the carrier.

TERM 5 GOVERNING LAW

The contract for the carriage of goods listed in the bill of lading shall be deemed to include and be subject to the terms and conditions prescribed by law of the jurisdiction where the goods originate which if Newfoundland, Nova Scotia, New Brunswick, Prince Edward Island, Saskatchewan and British Columbia, the regulations made pursuant to the Motor Carrier Act of each Province; Quebec, the bill of lading form and terms and conditions approved by the Quebec Transport Commission; Ontario, the Truck Transportation Act and Regulations thereto; Manitoba, The Highway Traffic Act and Regulations thereto; Alberta, The Motor Transport Act and Regulations thereto.

TERM 6 ENTIRE AGREEMENT

This bill of lading constitutes the entire contract between the carrier and the shipper, and no agent, servant, or representative of the carrier has authority to alter, modify or waive any provision of this contract.

Special Business Contracts and Consumer Protection

Bailment

In personal-property law, there is a distinction between ownership and possession. When you deliver something to someone, you do not necessarily give ownership; you may wish to give only possession. This is the essential concept of **bailment**—transfer of possession of personal property without transfer of ownership. When you hand over your TV set to the repairman for a week, you give the right to possession, but you do not transfer ownership. The repairman is merely the custodian of the TV set for a specific purpose for a limited time. Whenever a person gives possession of an object to another but does not transfer ownership, the legal term for the transaction is "bailment." Bailment can occur in a number of situations:

bailment
transfer of possession of personal property without transfer of ownership

- repair—leaving a car or television with a repair person
- storage—leaving furniture in a warehouse or storage unit
- leasing—renting a car or a fax machine
- couriers—giving a letter or parcel for delivery
- freight—shipping a parcel with a trucking company

Bailment   **Bailment** derives from the French word *baille*, meaning custody. Releasing someone on criminal bail is giving custody of the accused to the person who signs the bail. That person must keep track of the accused and make certain he or she appears for trial, or lose the money put up for bail. *Bail* also occurs in the word *bailiff*. A bailiff seizes goods or takes them into custody to be sold for payment of judgments. The person who owns the goods and gives up possession is called the *bailor*. In this book, such a person will be called the *owner*. The person who receives temporary possession of the goods is termed the *bailee* in law, but will be called the *custodian* in this chapter.

Legalese

Bailment As a Business

Bailment may or may not be for payment. For example, leaving your car parked at a friend's house for a couple of weeks while you are away on vacation is an example of a bailment without payment. This kind of bailment is known as a gratuitous bailment. This chapter deals only with bailment in a business situation, which is normally contractual bailment. It is technically referred to as bailment for hire or reward.

What Is a Bailment?

A bailment consists of three elements:

- Delivery of an item. This is where possession of the object changes hands, but the ownership of the item has not changed. As well, delivery generally requires that the custodian have some awareness that he or she now has possession of the item—or could have possession of the item (such as a coat rack in a reception area, with a sign saying "please leave coats here"). It is often easy to tell whether delivery of an item has occurred, but occasionally it can be more difficult. This is particularly the case if the item is very large (making physical delivery difficult), or if the custodian does not actually know he or she has an item in his or her care.
- Delivery for some purpose. There can be a variety of reasons for which items may be given to another party in a bailment situation. Some of these are noted in the introduction to this section.
- Delivery with the intention that the item be returned, or delivered to a specific party at some later time. This is consistent with the essential concept of bailment, which is that possession changes hands without the intention that ownership should change hands.

■ *Business Law*   Applied

❶ **Ken Kristov's car** broke down one evening on the way home from work. He had been working late, and his favourite car repair shop, Jasper's Fixit and Repair, was closed. Ken had the tow truck driver drop his car in Jasper's fenced parking lot, and Ken dropped his car keys in Jasper's mail slot.

a) Has there been a bailment of Ken's car?

Custodian Responsibilities

Certain concepts affect every commercial bailment relationship:

- The custodian has no ownership right, only a temporary right to possession
- The custodian has a duty to care for the object with the skill of a reasonable and careful person in that particular business
- If the goods are damaged, the burden is on the custodian to show that he or she was not negligent

The following example illustrates the extent of the duty of care for a custodian in the business of operating a warehouse or storage facility. A thief broke into a warehouse facility and stole some of the goods stored inside. The thief got in by breaking a glass pane in one of the warehouse's doors. It was found that the warehouse operator should have realized how easy it would be for a thief to break and enter, and was therefore liable to the owner of the goods. The courts impose a very high standard on these custodians who are in the business of bailment. They say, in effect, if you are going to make money by having possession of goods, you must take every precaution to safeguard those goods.

However, if a computer was left with a friend for a few weeks and a thief broke in by smashing a glass pane in the residential house door, the homeowner would likely not be held negligent for having a glass pane in his door. The extent of the duty of care in this situation is lower, because of the "business" of the custodian.

While the courts put a high duty of care on the custodian, the custodian is not liable for damage to the goods from all causes. A custodian is not an insurer of the goods. There is no requirement at law that the custodian even carry insurance on the goods. So if your goods are damaged by a natural disaster, such as a flood or lightning, the custodian would not be responsible for that damage, unless the custodian had specifically assumed such responsibility by the terms of the bailment contract.

Insurance   Many insurance companies will not cover loss relating to goods put in storage, especially in the small, self-serve-style storage units. Before putting goods in storage, make certain the storage company carries insurance for all risks. If not, check with your own insurance company before signing a contract. If you sign a contract for storage that recites that you are to take out insurance yourself, ascertain that you are, indeed, able to get that insurance.

Business Alert!

Use of Exemption Clauses in Contracts of Bailment

Those businesses which routinely become custodians of items often attempt to limit their liability for loss or damage to those goods through the use of exemption clauses. Exemption clauses, which read something like the following, are regularly found on dry-cleaning claim checks, on signs hung in coat checks, and the like:

> Not responsible for loss or damage, however caused, including by any negligence on
> the part of the company's employees.

As noted in Chapter 6, the courts are generally reluctant to enforce these clauses against consumers, but may be more inclined to do so in business-to-business transactions.

Notice of the exemption clause is key to whether it will be enforced by the courts in bailment situations. If the owner has actual notice of the exemption clause, it has a greater likelihood of being effective. However, if the owner did not actually know about the exemption clause, its enforceability becomes more questionable. If the custodian can successfully argue that she took reasonable measures to draw the clause to the owner's attention, the clause may yet prove effective. For example, a large sign at eye level, well lit and easy to read, may provide the owner adequate "notice" of the exemption.

As well, in order to be effective, the clause must exclude or limit liability for the precise way in which the loss or damage occurred. If a sign posted in a coast check says "Not responsible for lost articles," and a leather jacket was damaged by knife slashing, the clause would not be effective.

Fundamental breach may also apply to nullify the exemption clause. Recall that fundamental breach is a total failure to do what was promised. For example, in a courier contract, delay in delivery would not be a fundamental breach but mere negligence; failure to deliver the item at all may well be a fundamental breach.

If there is a fundamental breach, the exemption clause will not apply unless the court finds that it was reasonable to have the exemption clause in spite of the fundamental breach.

Hogarth v. Archibald Moving & Storage Ltd., [1991] 57 B.C.L.R. (2d) 319 (C.A.)

The defendant, Archibald Moving & Storage Ltd., was in the business of operating a warehouse and storage facility. The plaintiff stored goods in the defendant's warehouse. A fire, which was found to be accidental, destroyed the warehouse, including the plaintiff's goods. Investigations revealed that the building had no smoke detectors, sprinkler system, fire doors, or fire alarms. Also, there were no security personnel to monitor the facilities.

Under the by-laws for the city of Vancouver (where the warehouse was located) and the provincial fire code, the defendant was not required to have sprinkler systems, fire alarms, or detection systems. An expert witness for the plaintiff stated that a sprinkler system would have either contained or extinguished the fire.

The Court's Decision

The court found that a bailment for reward (payment) existed between the plaintiff and the defendant. In the circumstances, the defendant was found to be negligent in failing to provide appropriate fire-detection methods. The court pointed out that, in a bailment relationship, the burden is on the custodian to show there was no negligence on its part, and the defendant, in failing to provide fire-detection methods, had not done that.

The court found the defendant liable to the plaintiff for the loss of the goods.

Example: In *Ferguson v. Birchmount Boarding Kennels Ltd.*, 2006 CanLII 2049 (ON SCDC), a boarding kennel was liable when a dog it was boarding for a couple escaped and was never found. The court ruled that the onus is on the kennel to prove that the loss occurred without any neglect, default or misconduct on their part. The dog had probably squeezed out between the boards of the fence and the kennel did not prove that this could have happened without their neglect. It was liable for $1,110 for the value of the dog and an additional $1,417 for the owners' pain and suffering.

Example: In *Reyes v. D & R Car Co.*, 2003 CanLII 28331 (ON SCSM), a car repair shop was test driving a van it was about to repair, but a few blocks from the shop, it caught on fire and was destroyed. The court ruled that the bailee (the repairer) must exercise due care for the safety of the article entrusted to them by taking such care of the goods as a prudent person would of their own possessions. The repair shop had an onus to show that the loss occurred without any neglect on their part, and it had not satisfied that requirement. The court held the repair shop liable for the value of the van.

Example: In *Foord v. United Air Lines Inc.*, 2006 ABPC 103 (CanLII) a man took his valuable bicycle on a flight packed in a very sturdy special bicycle packaging container. When he arrived at his destination the bicycle frame was badly damaged. He sued the airline for all the damages, but the airline relied on its limitation clause to limit the amount it owed. The court ruled that the limitation clause was never brought to the passenger's attention and the damage must have resulted from a reckless act or omission by the airline. The airline was fully liable for the total damages of $4,032.

Business Law Applied

❷ **Quan Li has** just bought a Store-It-Ur-Self franchise. He rents out a unit to his first customer, John Gould. Gould stores some house furniture in it while he is building a new house. The sewer backs up and floods the unit, ruining Gould's furniture. There is no written contract, only an oral agreement to pay $100 in storage fees.

Li had heard that there were special traps that could be put in sewers. Because only a very few storage businesses had them, Li did not have them installed.

Gould wants Li to pay for the damage. Li claims he did nothing wrong and is not responsible.

a) Who has to bear the loss, Li or Gould?

■ *Critical Concepts of* Bailment

- Bailment involves a change of possession of items, but not a change of ownership.
- There must be a delivery of an item in order for a bailment to arise.
- A custodian of an item must use the care and skill of a reasonable and careful person in his particular business when looking after goods in his possession.
- Businesses attempt to limit their liability for goods they hold as custodian through the use of exemption clauses. These may or may not be effective, depending on whether the owner was aware of them at the time the contract of bailment was entered into, and how comprehensively the clause is drafted.

Courier and Transportation Companies

When a customer gives a package to a courier for delivery, this is a bailment. The courier has possession of the package, but it does not own it. On taking the package the courier normally has the customer sign a document called a **bill of lading**, which is a receipt signed by a carrier or transportation company acknowledging that certain goods have been given to it for shipment. It is one type of contract, and so both bailment and contract laws apply to a bill of lading.

bill of lading
a receipt signed by a carrier or transportation company acknowledging that certain goods have been given to it for shipment

Bill of Lading **Bill** simply means *document*. For example, an account from a doctor may be called a doctor's bill. **Lading** comes from an Old English word meaning load. It is a receipt for goods loaded on board and is sometimes called a waybill. The word *way* is used in the ordinary of sense of *on the way*, again meaning loaded on board.

Concerns of customers regarding couriers and transportation companies usually centre on damage to (or loss of) goods, theft, and delay. The terms for couriers' bills of lading are determined by federal and provincial statutes that govern transportation companies. These terms are normally written on the reverse side of the bill of lading. Usually one of these clauses is an exemption clause that limits a courier's responsibility to a very small amount unless the customer declares a higher value. A sample Courier Bill of Lading is provided in the Appendix to Chapter 7.

Because this limitation clause is implied by statute, one of the defenses to an exemption clause, inadequate notice, does not apply. A customer cannot claim that it did not have notice of the term in order to avoid a statutory exemption clause.[1] This rule applies to all statutorily implied exemption clauses of which the one in courier bills of lading is an example.[2] Also, as the term is drafted by the government legislature, the rule that exemption clauses are to be interpreted against the interests of the drafter (*contra proferentem*) does not apply.

Some transportation statutes require that the bill of lading must be signed, and in the past if it was not signed, some cases found that the carrier could not use the limitation of liability clause. However recent cases have ruled that in a commercial context, where all the parties had acknowledged the contract and they were all well aware of the terms and had made their business decisions based on this, the inability to produce a signed document will not defeat the validity of the contract and the carrier can rely on the limitation clause. A "form over substance" argument based on no signature will not be successful, as the two cases below involving train derailments clearly illustrate.

One note of warning must be stated. There were early cases making couriers liable for delay. However, in these cases the courier companies' staff were explicitly told by the customer that the document contained a tender and verbally warranted that the tender would be delivered on time. Courier companies have learned from such cases. They will now usually not accept tenders at all. Additionally, they carefully instruct their staff not to make any verbal warranties and merely to tell the customers to read the bill of lading.

---

1. *Cornwall Gravel Co. v. Purolator Courier Ltd.* (1978), 18 O.R. (21)551 Aff'd [1980] 2 S.C.R. 118.

2. *B.G. Linton Construction Ltd. v. C.N.R. Co.*, [1975] 2 S.C.R. 678; and Rui M. Fernandes, *Transportation Law*, vol. 2 (Scarborough, Ont.: Carswell, 1991), pp. 35–37.

Canadian Pacific Railway Company v. Boutique Jacob Inc., 2008 FCA 85 (CanLII)

Boutique Jacob hired a freight forwarding company to arrange shipment of an order of women's clothing it had purchased from a Hong Kong supplier. A Chinese carrier was to take the goods by ship from Hong Kong to Vancouver and then CP Rail was to take them from Vancouver to their Montreal warehouse. The CPR train however derailed in Sudbury, Ontario and the clothing Jacob had purchased for $35,000 was destroyed. When Jacob sued CPR for its losses, CPR relied on the limitation clause in the bill of lading that it had with the Chinese carrier that limited its liability to $2 per kilo, which came to $1,432.

The trial court ruled that Jacob was the shipper, not the Chinese carrier, and since there was no written contract between Boutique Jacob and CPR, it could not rely on the limitation clause. It found that the Chinese carrier did not fit the technical definition of "shipper" under the *Canada Transportation Act*, S.C. 1996, c. 10

(Act) and since the bill of lading was not signed as the Act required, the limitation clause could not be used.

CPR appealed this decision to the Federal Court of Appeal.

The Court's Decision

The Federal Court of Appeal focused on what the parties had understood and agreed to and took a much more practical and commercial interpretation of the contract and the statute. It ruled that the Chinese carrier was the "shipper" under the Act, not Jacob. The argument that the Act requires the bill of lading to be signed was simply dismissed as "without merit, as neither party to the confidential rate contract disputed the validity of their agreement." CPR was allowed to limit its liability to $1,432.

Example: The *CPR v. Boutique Jacob* case was also followed in *Mitsubishi Heavy Industries Ltd. v. Canadian National Railway Company*, 2012 BCSC 1415 (CanLII). In this case a CN train derailed and aviation parts worth $1.6 million were destroyed. Again the court rejected a technical argument that the limitation clause does not apply because the bill of lading was not signed. The court stated it would be a completely unfair and arbitrary result to hold that a simple failure to produce a written document with signatures should deny the effect of the limitation clause which both parties had knowingly negotiated in good faith. The written requirement was intended to prevent oral agreements and ensure that all parties had written notification of limitation clauses. In this case there was no doubt that all parties were aware of this term. The limitation clause was effective and limited CN's liability to $50,000.

■ *Critical Concepts of* Defences to Statutory Exemption Clause

- Inadequate notice is not a defence to an exemption clause in a courier's bill of lading, as the clause is implied by statute.
- If the bill of lading is not both completed *and* signed by the customer, the exemption clause is not enforceable.

Business Alert!

subrogation

the right of an insurer who has paid a claim to "step into the shoes" of the insured and sue the person responsible for the loss Out of caution, some businesses send critical documents by several modes to ensure delivery.

Transportation Protection   The law regarding the responsibility of transportation companies and couriers is complex, and so it is difficult to predict with accuracy whether such a company will be responsible for loss in the carriage process. It is far better to have a term with your insurance company that covers loss because of carriage than to have to make a claim against the transportation or courier company. The insurance company then will have to decide whether it will pursue the claim in a subrogation action against the carrier. A **subrogation** is the right of an insurer who has paid a claim to "step into the shoes" of the insured and sue the person responsible for the loss.

■ *Business Law* Applied

❸ Wicked Knits was a sweater manufacturer operating outside of Calgary. It wanted to ship its new line of sweaters to an annual trade show in Vancouver for distributors in western Canada, which was held every year from August 1 to August 3.

Cannex Couriers ran extensive ads saying "Guaranteed overnight delivery or it's free." Wicked Knits sent its shipment by Cannex on July 26, telling the driver that the shipment must arrive before August 1. Wicked Knits signed a bill of lading which contained a term on the reverse saying that Cannex's liability, even for negligence, was limited to three times the cost of the freight charges. This term is set by the provincial statute governing courier and transportation companies.

Because a Cannex employee mistakenly sent the shipment to Montreal, the goods did not arrive until August 3. Wicked Knits claimed that it had lost its opportunity to do business in western Canada for one year and claimed $100,000.

     a) Was the Cannex employee negligent?

     b) Does the exemption clause cover negligence?

     c) Does the advertisement "Guaranteed overnight delivery or it's free" increase Cannex's liability for loss? What does the ad say Cannex will offer as specified damages if it breaches its guarantee?

     d) Is the exemption clause effective, or will Wicked Knits succeed in its claim for loss of business?

Innkeepers

Hotel and motel businesses were singled out for special restrictions by the courts. An **innkeeper** (a person who maintains a business offering lodging to the public) was made responsible for damage to items left in his or her care, whether because of negligence or not. All provincial governments have enacted innkeepers acts to diminish the harshness of these rules. Under the *Innkeepers Act*, if a business providing accommodation posts a notice on the back of the room door, the liability of the innkeeper will be limited to the amount under the act. Various provinces have different amounts, and amounts can vary from time to time, but a limit of $50 to $100 is not unusual. Innkeepers must also provide a safe for guests' valuables. If the guest deposits valuables in the safe, the innkeeper is strictly liable for them and must have insurance to cover their loss.

innkeeper
a person who maintains a business offering lodging to the public

Custodian's Remedies

What options are available to the custodian who does work on an item, but then does not receive payment? The businesses of bailment are based on contracts, so the custodian has the usual contractual remedies (such as suing for any amount owed). However, many different acts, such as the *Repairman's* (or *Garagemen's*) *Lien Act*, the *Transportation of Goods Act*, the *Warehouseman's Act*, and the *Public Vehicles Act*, working together with common law and standard form contracts, also apply and give the custodian the right to a **lien** for unpaid work and the sale of the item if the lien is not paid. The owner must be given written notice of the sale and the opportunity to pay the amounts owing and get the item back.

     If the item is sold after seizure, the proceeds of the sale are applied first to the cost of the sale, and then to the custodian's fee; the balance, if any, is paid to the owner. If there is a shortfall, the custodian can sue the owner for that amount.

lien right
right of a bailee to keep and sell the owner's goods if not paid

Seizure is always subject to the qualification that it can be done without a court order only if there is no breach of the peace. For example, a car owner pays by cheque for the repair of his car and takes his car home. But the cheque bounces. Assuming the garage has the right to a non-possessory lien, the garage can send a bailiff to seize the car if the car is sitting in the owner's driveway. If it is in a locked garage, the bailiff cannot break the lock to seize the car.

If the owner disputes the amount or the quality of the work, the owner can apply to the court and post security in the form of a bond or letter of credit for the amount of the custodian's claim. The court will order the release of the item pending resolution of the dispute between the owner and the custodian. The court application, however, may cost a significant amount of money and may not be cost effective, because most disputes over personal property involve less money than the court costs. Therefore, the right to retain possession of the goods gives the custodian a significant bargaining advantage.

■ *Critical Concepts of* Custodian's Lien

- The custodian has a right to retain the object until paid.
- The costs of the services performed regarding the object are a lien on the object. Such a lien is called a possessory lien.
- If there is a term in the contract, or in applicable legislation, the right to a lien may survive even after the object is taken back by the owner. Such a lien is called a non-possessory lien.
- If payment is not made, the custodian can sell the item after giving notice to the owner and after a period of time, usually about ten days. The owner receives what funds are left after payment of costs and the amount owing to the custodian.

Dean Capital Corp. v. Geneen Automobiles Ltd., 2005 CanLII 19826 (ON SC)

Ernest Anderson was the President and a Director of Golden Gate Capital Corp. and he had the corporation lease a car, a 2000 Bentley, for him to drive. He took the car to Geneen Automobiles to have repairs and other work done on the car.

He was not satisfied with some of the work and did not pay for it. Geneen sent Anderson a bill for $11,670.23 and when Anderson was out of the country his wife arranged for a cheque to be drawn on the company's bank account for the full amount. The auto shop delivered the repaired Bentley to Anderson's home and then picked up the cheque from the company.

Before the cheque was deposited, Anderson found out about the payment and stopped payment on the cheque. The auto shop then registered a non-possessory lien on the car. Anderson sent a cheque for $1,597.23 and later began a court action to have the lien de-registered as an invalid claim. He wanted the lien removed so that he could sell the Bentley. Anderson claimed that the auto shop had no right to a non-possessory lien as it had no signed acknowledgement of the debt, and the cheque had been given after the car had been returned.

Geneen maintained that it had the right to the non-possessory lien.

The Court's Decision

The court emphasized the right of a repairer to be paid for their labour. It found that the wife and the corporation had acted as agents for Anderson. The fact that a cheque had been written for the full amount was acknowledgement of the debt and it did not matter than the car had been delivered, as a courtesy, before the cheque was given.

Anderson did not "come before the court with clean hands." The car was delivered in good faith on the strength of the promise it would be paid. It was entitled to believe that Anderson would act in good faith as well. Its lien claim should not be denied because of Anderson's fraud.

To allow Anderson to defeat the repairer's lien right because Anderson tricked him with the dishonoured cheque would violate the intention of the Repair and Storage Liens Act. It ruled that the first cheque was acknowledgement of the debt and it was a valid non-possessory lien so the court would not discharge it.

■ *Business Law*   Applied

❹ **Barbara Shuster takes** her car into a garage to have her transmission fixed and signs a standard work order to this effect. When she picks up the car, she listens to it and feels that the transmission has not been repaired correctly. She says she wants to get another mechanic's opinion on whether the repair work is adequate. The garage refuses to release the car until payment is made. Shuster is outraged; she refuses to pay and leaves. A few days later, she is served with a notice saying that the mechanic will sell the car in 10 days if she does not pay the bill in full.

    a) Does the mechanic have the right to hold the vehicle until payment is made even when the customer questions the quality of the work?

    b) Can the owner recover the car without paying the mechanic?

    c) If the owner does nothing after the notice of intent to sell, can the mechanic actually sell the car? What will be done with the proceeds of the sale?

Restrictions on Motor Vehicle Repair

The most common complaints to all provincial ministries that deal with consumer affairs concern the repair of motor vehicles. By virtue of the possessory and non-possessory lien rights, car-repair garages have powerful bargaining and enforcement tools. In Ontario, for example, this is offset by new consumer protection legislation that requires the repairer to comply strictly with a number of procedures, or the repair is free. This legislation applies to all vehicle repairs, even business vehicles. The definition of vehicle is wide and includes many types of construction equipment. The legislation is a very direct attempt to control abuse by garages.

Buying and Selling Products

There are a variety of legal rules that govern liability for sale transactions in addition to those of general contract law. The rules are different, depending on whether one is dealing with **real property** (land, buildings, and fixtures; land and anything attached to it), and personal property. **Personal property** is anything that is not real property and it can be divided into two types: a) **tangible** person property which includes hard assets such as equipment, vehicles and furniture and b) **intangible** personal property which can include legal rights such as loans or debts and also **intellectual property** in the form of ideas and creative works some of which can be protected with copyrights, trademarks and patents.

real property
land, buildings, and fixtures; land and anything attached to it

personal property
all property that is not real property

intellectual property
personal property in the form of ideas and creative work, created by the intellect

Buying and Selling Goods

Much of modern business centres on buying and selling goods, so that it is not surprising that there are special laws aimed at goods. Every time a retailer purchases from a supplier and resells the item to a customer, specific rules of contract govern the transaction. Different rules apply to buying and selling between businesses than to transactions that take place between businesses and consumers. This distinction is important for the small-business retailer who buys according to business laws, but sells under consumer protection laws that tend to make the retailer primarily liable. Whether the retailer has a realistic right to recover liability from the supplier depends on the terms of the arrangement. If the supplier is located in a foreign country that does not have consumer protection laws, or the supplier goes out of business, the retailer may be left solely responsible.

How Did the Laws Originate?

Laws relating to land developed during the Middle Ages, when business as we know it today was almost non-existent. With the onset of the industrial age, the sale of goods became the centre of economic activity and so laws governing the practices involved were developed. These laws were collected (codified) and set out in an English statute, the *Sale of Goods Act*. This act has been adopted by all Canadian provinces in essentially the same form, but with different section numbers.

After World War II, other changes took place in society that culminated in an explosion of new consumer protection laws, particularly in the 1960s and 1970s. These laws included provisions making businesses liable for the quality and safety of the goods that they market. In addition, they restricted the ability of businesses to use written contracts as a way of avoiding liability with consumers.

Therefore, in addition to terms agreed to in a contract of sale, a seller's legal liability for the quality, safety, and usefulness of personal property which is sold can be governed by one or more of the following set of legal rules:

- *Sale of Goods Act*
- consumer protection legislation
- products liability in tort

The Sale of Goods Act

All provinces and territories have legislation which holds the seller of goods responsible for minimum guarantees concerning the quality of the goods they sell. This legislation is often known as the *Sale of Goods Act*. It also sets out rules concerning when items sold actually belong to the purchaser and no longer the seller, and rules concerning what action buyer and seller can take if terms of the sale contract are not fulfilled by the other party.

In buying and selling, people often forget to specify some terms of the contract, and may even forget vital items. So, the courts developed special rules for the sale of goods that would apply if the parties forgot some essential terms. For example, in buying an item, if the parties forgot to specify the price, that omission would be fatal and there would be no enforceable contract. However, the *Sale of Goods Act* provides that if the price is not agreed upon, then the price will be a reasonable price.

The *Sale of Goods Act* provides, in effect, a type of standard form contract for the sale of goods where parties omit certain terms. The act is drafted so that the terms are implied only if the parties do not specify them. If the parties agree to specific terms, those, and not the *Sale of Goods Act* terms, are legally enforceable.

The first important thing to notice, however, is that this act applies only to "sales" of "goods."

What Are Goods?

The first step in considering whether the *Sale of Goods Act* applies to any given business transaction is to determine whether that transaction is actually a "sale of goods." If it is not, then the rules in the act will not apply.

A sale can be described as an exchange of goods for money. This is to be distinguished from:

- a **lease**, which is a contractual arrangement where the owner of property (the landlord) allows another person (the tenant) to have possession and use of the property for a certain period in return for the payment of rent. Note, however, that British

lease
a contractual arrangement where the owner of property (the landlord) allows another person (the tenant) to have possession and use of the property for a certain period in return for the payment of rent

Columbia has extended its legislation so that the implied conditions discussed below apply to leases as well as to contracts of sale.
■ barter or trade, which is an exchange of goods or services for other goods or services.

Goods are items such as televisions, clothes, cars, and so on. These are to be distinguished from:

■ services
■ real property, such as a house
■ work and materials

goods

are items such as televisions, clothes, and cars

Historically, goods were treated differently under contract law from other subjects such as services or land. Different considerations relate to goods as distinct from services. For example, if someone sells you a car, you want to know that that person is the legal owner and therefore has the authority to sell the vehicle. Such a question does not arise in the sale of services.

More recently, however, it has been thought that there are many similarities between goods and services, and that they should be treated the same. Nowadays, legislation, particularly consumer protection acts, often specifically includes both goods and services—the goods and services tax GST or HST are examples. However, separate contract rules did evolve for goods alone and this distinction must be remembered in reading the *Sale of Goods Act* principles that are discussed in this chapter.

ter Neuzen v. Korn, [1995] 3 S.C.R. 674

Mrs. ter Neuzen could not have a child and went to Dr. Korn for artificial insemination many times between 1981 and 1985. She was later diagnosed as HIV-positive, the probable cause being the artificial insemination. She sued the doctor both for negligence and for breach of the condition of merchantability under the *Sale of Goods Act*.

The Court's Decision

The court found that the doctor was primarily rendering a service, and not supplying a good, and therefore the *Sale of Goods Act* did not apply in this situation. The tort of negligence was a possible grounds of liability, but the doctor was found not liable, given that there was no test to detect HIV prior to January 1985.

Business Law Applied

❺ Louise Yang was a dog breeder who bought a shipment of champion stock sperm from Nick Shep, who was a well-known breeder in the area. Louise had her female dogs inseminated, but none of the dogs had pups. It was subsequently discovered that the sperm was infected with a virus that rendered it infertile.

a) Is Louise's situation covered by the *Sale of Goods Act?*

❻ Car-lease arrangements are becoming a very popular means of acquiring new vehicles. This is an arrangement whereby you acquire possession and use of the vehicle for a period of time (usually two years), and then either return the car, or purchase it for a predetermined price.

a) Does the *Sale of Goods Act* cover this type of acquisition?

The Requirement of Writing

Except in Ontario and British Columbia, where legislation differs, the *Sale of Goods Act* provides that a contract for the sale of goods (over $40-50, depending on the province) is not enforceable unless one of three conditions is met:

- it is in writing, or
- the buyer has received and accepted the goods, or a portion of them, or
- the buyer gave something in partial payment for the goods when the contract was formed

The courts have been flexible on what will be sufficient to satisfy a statutory requirement of writing. (See Chapter 5 for more on the requirement of writing in contract law.)

Conditions and Warranties

The *Sale of Goods Act* implies certain terms into every contract of sale. In other words, the act automatically makes certain terms a part of every contract of sale.

The terms in a contract are not all of equal importance. The law recognizes this, and divides those terms into two categories:

- conditions
- warranties

conditions

major, essential terms which, if breached, give the innocent party the right to terminate the contract and claim damages

warranties

minor terms which, if breached, permit only a claim for damages but not the refusal to complete the contract

Conditions are major, essential terms which, if breached, give the innocent party the right to terminate the contract and claim damages, while **warranties** are minor terms which, if breached, permit only a claim for damages but not the refusal to complete the contract. If the conditions in a contract are broken, the courts will usually set aside the agreement, as its purpose has become pointless. The buyer can reject the goods. If, for example, you order a dark-blue Chevrolet sedan and the dealer delivers a bright-pink Chevrolet convertible, the conditions of your agreement have been violated and you would be legally entitled to refuse the car. You would be permitted to choose to cancel (repudiate) the contract and obtain a refund of any money paid, such as a deposit.

If the warranties in a contract are broken, the courts will consider a claim for loss caused by the breach, but will not cancel the agreement. If the car delivered to you was a dark-blue

© 1994 Farcus Cartoons/Distributed by Universal Press Syndicate   WAISGLASS/COULTHART

Chevrolet sedan, but the turn signals were not working, you could not refuse the car and cancel the deal. You could, however, claim the cost of repairing the turn signals. You would have to perform the contract by paying for the car and seeking a reduction in price by claiming for the cost of repair.

The parties can agree when a contract term is a condition, so that if it is violated, the innocent party can cancel the agreement if it wishes. If the parties to a contract have not specified which terms are in fact conditions, the courts will decide the issue. A contractual term will be found to be a condition if the breach deprived the innocent party of substantially the whole benefit of the contract.

■ *Critical Concepts of* Conditions and Warranties

- The court will decide whether a term is a condition or a warranty.
- The *Sale of Goods Act* specifies certain terms to be conditions or warranties when the agreement involves selling goods.
- The parties to the agreement can specify terms to be conditions or warranties. Such an agreement supersedes the court-made principles and the *Sale of Goods Act*.
- If there is a breach of a condition, the agreement can be cancelled.
- If there is a breach of a warranty, the victim can claim damages only.

Implied Terms

Some of the most important sections in the Sale of Goods Act are the implied conditions and warranties that this law inserts into contracts of sale, even though the contract did not have these terms. These implied terms give purchasers some level of protection from disreputable conduct by sellers. Since many of these are implied conditions, not warranties, if they are breached it entitles the buyer to cancel the contract. There are four major implied terms in most of the provincial sale of goods laws, and they relate to the owners right to sell, and the quality, fitness and description of the goods sold.

1) Implied Term—Right to Sell the Goods   In regular business transactions, we generally assume that a person selling us goods has the right to do so. However, if this is not so, it can lead to harsh consequences for the innocent purchaser. The *Sale of Goods Act* tries to protect an innocent third-party purchaser by implying a term that the seller has the right to sell the goods into the sale contract.

Consider a situation where stolen property has made its way through several parties:

Ned's car → stolen by "X" → ends up at 123 Car Sales Ltd. → bought by Albert → sold to Pauline

After the car was stolen, no one had the right to sell it. The true owner, from whom the car was stolen, can have it repossessed from Pauline, because in law you cannot give what you haven't got. So the thief gave possession of the car (which he had), but not ownership (which he did not). He only gave an improperly issued permit to own a vehicle. (While this form is generally accepted as proof of ownership, it is merely a permit and the government does not guarantee ownership).

Each "innocent" person in the chain has a remedy against the person from whom they bought the car. This is because the *Sale of Goods Act* implies (adds in) a condition that the seller has the right to sell the goods, even if nothing was specifically said about having this right when the deal was made. Unfortunately, the last "innocent" person in the chain, in this case 123 Car Sales, will likely be unable to seek recourse (unless they can find "X" and he has money to pay). The Ontario law also has an implied term that the goods the person is selling are free from any unpaid charges or claims such as loans, liens or mortgages by a third party, such as a bank.

1) Implied Term—Right to Sell Goods and Goods Clear of Claims

---

Sale of Goods Act, R.S.O. 1990, c.S.1, s.13

In a contract of sale, unless the circumstances of the contract are such as to show a different intention, there is,

(a) an implied condition on the part of the seller that in the case of a sale the seller has a right to sell the goods, and that in the case of an agreement to sell the seller will have a right to sell the goods at the time when the property is to pass;

(b) an implied warranty that the buyer will have and enjoy quiet possession of the goods; and

(c) an implied warranty that the goods will be free from any charge or encumbrance in favour of any third party, not declared or known to the buyer before or at the time when the contract is made.

---

2) Implied Term—Goods Match Description   There is also an implied term that goods sold by description will correspond to that description. For example, if you agree to purchase "one dozen aluminum snow shovels" from a catalogue, you will not receive one dozen plastic snow shovels.

A sale by description has generally been held to be any sale where you set out in descriptive terms the goods to be subject of the contract. This is in contrast to a sale by sample, or situation where one points out goods on display and orders some of whatever is presented.

It should be noted that sales of motor vehicles, including used motor vehicles, are viewed as sales by description. The justification for this is that vehicle sales are either new or used. This is no doubt stretching the interpretation of the word *description*. However, it is done by the courts to give consumers the benefit of the *Sale of Goods Act* implied terms when purchasing cars.

It is usually easy to determine whether the goods delivered conform to the description in the contract of sale. However, this issue can be more difficult if the non-compliance with the description relates to quality.

Condition of Correspondence to Description

Sale of Goods Act, R.S.O., 1990, c. S.1, s.14

Where there is a contract for the sale of goods by description, there is an implied condition that the goods shall correspond with the description and if the sale by samples as well as by description, it is not sufficient that the bulk of the goods corresponds with the sample if the goods do not also correspond with the description.

The Condition Concerning Correspondence to Sample   When a seller provides samples of goods for inspection prior to purchase, the act provides that:

- the goods provided will correspond to the sample in quality, and
- the buyer will be able to compare the goods provided with the sample, and
- the goods provided will be free of any unapparent defect making them unsaleable without a discount (unmerchantable)

■ *Business Law* Applied

❼ Raj Gamba ran a retail greenhouse. In the fall, he visited Nori Nedlov's plant and tree farm, to place an order for delivery the following season. He spent a lot of time examining Nori's stock. The stock looked terrific and healthy, so Raj placed a large order for delivery to his greenhouse in the spring. When the delivery date finally arrived, Raj happened to be tied up with a big client. He took a quick glance at the items, and thought they looked fine. After a few weeks in the greenhouse however, he noticed some growth problems, and some disease damage, which could only have occurred before being shipped.

a) Is Raj's order a sale by sample or a sale by description?
b) If it is a sale by description, which of the implied terms have arguably been breached?
c) If it is a sale by sample, which of the implied terms have arguably been breached?

3) Implied Term—Goods are Merchantable The sale of goods acts require that the goods sold must be merchantable Merchantability means that the product is both saleable and useable for its normal purpose. Is the product of such a quality that a customer would pay the asking price without seeking a deduction? In other words, the product cannot have any defects, and must be able to be used as it should be. A lawn mower must cut grass; a refrigerator must be able to preserve food.

LOADSTAT PRODUCTS LIMITED WARRANTY

Warranty

Model No. ☒☒☐☐☐☐
Serial No. ☒☐☐☐☐☐☐☐☐
Date Purchased ☐☐☐☐☐☐
D D M M Y Y

We warrant that if your LOADSTAT product proves to be defective in material or workmanship under normal use, we will provide, without charge, the parts and labor necessary to remedy any such defect for the applicable warranty periods set forth below:

WARRANTY PERIOD

PRODUCT	LABOUR	PARTS	
· Colour TV	3 Years	3 Years	5 Years (Picture Tube)
· Video Cassette Recorder/Player	1 Year	1 Year	
· Camcorder	1 Year	1 Year	
· Cassette Deck with Stereo Radio	1 Year	1 Year	
· Stereo Amplifier	1 Year	1 Year	
· AM/FM Stereo Tuner	1 Year	1 Year	
· Turn Tables	1 Year	1 Year	
· Speakers	1 Year	1 Year	
· Compact Disk Player	1 Year	1 Year	
· Compact Stereo System	1 Year	1 Year	
· Television/Video Cassette Recorder	1 Year	1 Year	5 Years (Picture Tube)
· Microwave Oven	2 Years	2 Years	5 Years (Magnetron)

These warranty periods commence on the date of purchase by the original retail consumer only in Canada

THE DURATION OF ANY IMPLIED WARRANTY, OR MERCHANTABILITY, FITNESS FOR A PARTICULAR PURPOSE, OR OTHERWISE, ON THIS PRODUCT SHALL BE LIMITED TO THE DURATION OF THE APPLICABLE EXPRESS WARRANTY SET FORTH ABOVE. IN NO EVENT SHALL WE BE LIABLE FOR ANY LOSS, INCONVENIENCE OR DAMAGE WHETHER DIRECT, INCIDENTAL, CONSEQUENTIAL OR OTHERWISE RESULTING FROM BREACH OF ANY EXPRESS OR IMPLIED WARRANTY, OF MERCHANTABILITY, FITNESS FOR A PARTICULAR PURPOSE, OR OTHERWISE, WITH RESPECT TO THIS PRODUCT, EXCEPT AS SET FORTH HEREIN. SOME PROVINCES DO NOT ALLOW LIMITATIONS ON HOW LONG AN IMPLIED WARRANTY LASTS AND SOME PROVINCES DO NOT ALLOW THE EXCLUSION OR LIMITATION OF INCIDENTAL OR CONSEQUENTIAL DAMAGES, SO THE ABOVE LIMITATIONS OR EXCLUSION MAY NOT APPLY TO YOU.

During the applicable warranty period when we will provide, without charge, parts and labor necessary to remedy defects in your product all warranty inspections and repairs must be performed by Loadstat Authorized Service Center. During the applicable warranty period when we will provide, without charge, only the parts necessary to remedy defects in your product, all warranty inspections must be performed and parts obtained at a Loadstat Authorized Service Center.

THE WARRANTY IS NOT VALID UNLESS.
(1) Warranty registration card is completed and mailed within 7 days from the date of purchase.
(2) To obtain service under this warranty, you must present and send your product together with the retail seller's original bill of sale, your charge of credit receipt, or other satisfactory proof of the date of the original retail purchase of the product to any of Loadstat Service Center.
(3) Please check with your dealer for the closest authorized service center. Also, you may obtain the name and address of the nearest Authorized Loadstat Service center by calling Toll Free 1-800-555-5555. Please do not discuss service problems with operators. They can only direct you to one of Authorized Loadstat Service Centers.

SHIPPING: To obtain repairs under the terms of this warranty, please send the unit, freight prepaid, enclosing a copy of the bill of sale.

Any postage, insurance and shipping costs incurred in presenting or sending your product for service are your responsibility.

THIS WARRANTY DOES NOT COVER DAMAGE WHICH OCCURS IN TRANSIT, OR RESULTS FROM ALTERATION, ACCIDENT, MISUSE OR ABUSE, NOR DOES IT COVER SET INSTALLATION, ADJUSTMENT OF CUSTOMER CONTROLS OR RECEPTION PROBLEMS RESULTING FROM INADEQUATE PICKUP BY THE ANTENNA. DAMAGE WHILE IN THE POSSESSION OF THE CONSUMER NOT RESULTING FROM A DEFECT IN MATERIAL OR WORKMANSHIP AND DAMAGE CAUSED BY ACCIDENT TO, TAMPERING WITH OR OPENING THE PRODUCT OR BY OTHER THAN NORMAL USE OR DEFECTS OR DAMAGE RESULTING FRO REPAIRS PERFORMED OTHER THAN BY A LOADSTAT AUTHORIZED SERVICE CENTER ARE NOT COVERED BY THIS WARRANTY.

This warranty gives you specific legal rights, and you may also have other rights which vary from province.

LOADSTAT CANADA LTD.
5555 ACORN AVENUE
TORONTO, ONTARIO
CANADA
M5W 1E8

Although called a condition under the act, this term is usually called a warranty or a guarantee in everyday speech. It has been said that a warranty is an indication of a manufacturer's faith in its product. Note that the Goldstar Products Limited Warranty refers only to warranties and not to conditions. Such clauses are construed *contra proferentem* (against the party who wrote it (the seller)). The quality, or merchantability, warranty applies only to goods sold by description—as most consumer purchases are. Any retail purchase of items in a package or container is a sale by description. There is really no opportunity to inspect the product and determine its quality. For example, a bottle will be labelled "shampoo" and be identified with a brand name. The word *shampoo* is a description of the product. So the bottle must contain usable shampoo. If a shirt label says "100% cotton," the shirt must be cotton and not polyester—the use of the word *cotton* is a description of the goods.

Historically, the laws surrounding the sale of goods dealt only with quality, and remedies for repair or replacement. Regulations governing the safety of goods developed under the law of torts. Recent judgments, however, have applied the *Sale of Goods Act* in such a way that it includes safety, and have awarded damages for personal injury.

The significance of this change in the law is that all businesses in the supply chain will be liable for defects that injure, without regard to whether the businesses was at fault—that is, negligent. The concepts of negligence and product liability are reviewed in depth in Chapter 4.

Condition of Merchantability

Although the section numbers differ among most provincial *Sale of Goods Acts*, they are all very similar. The warranty of merchantability also applies to the sale of used goods, but the requirement of merchantability is that of a used product, not a new one.

The Sale of Goods Act, R.S.O. 1990, c. S1, s.15 (2)

---

s.15 (2). Where goods are bought by description from a seller who deals in goods of that description (whether the seller is the manufacturer or not), there is an implied condition that the goods will be of merchantable quality, but if the buyer has examined the goods, there is no implied condition as regards defects that such examination ought to have revealed.

Legalese

Condition   Implied terms regarding merchantability or quality are called **conditions** in sale of goods acts.

The word *condition* is technically used to describe the term of a contract that allows the innocent parties to cancel an agreement, return the goods, and get their money back (see p. 273). Its use developed historically and, although confusing today, it is so entrenched in the law that there is little hope of it being changed to reflect modern usage.

Business Law Applied

❽ **FabFoods Ltd. ran** a small grocery chain. It purchased a large order of jam from a distributor's catalogue by filling in an order form and sending a payment in advance to take advantage of an offered discount. When the jam arrived, the labels were completely discoloured. FabFoods contacted the distributor, requesting a refund of its money in return for sending the goods back.

The distributor refused, saying that the discoloration was not that firm's fault, but the fault of the manufacturer. The distributor pointed out that there was nothing in the purchase order about any guarantee of the quality or the appearance of the labels, and that FabFoods must take up the problem with the manufacturer. In addition, FabFoods purchased the product at a considerable discount, and should not therefore expect first-rate merchandise.

a) Since there was no agreed term regarding quality in the contract between FabFoods and the distributor, is there any law that would put such a term into the purchase order?

b) Does the fact that the jam was sold at a discount affect any right to a warranty of merchantability?

c) Does FabFoods have a contract with the manufacturer?

❾ **Don Mackenzie bought** a bottle of tropical fruit punch from Pal Paik's variety store by taking the bottle to the cash register and paying $1. After drinking the bottle, Mackenzie became very sick and was hospitalized for several weeks. When he recovered, Mackenzie sued Paik for compensation. Paik claimed that she only put the bottle on a shelf, and the state of its contents was not her fault. She suggested Mackenzie should sue the supplier.

a) Did Mackenzie have any possible remedy against the variety-store owner? If so, what is the basis for this claim in law?

b) Was the fact that Pal Paik's Variety did not bottle the drink a valid defence?

c) Would Paik have any remedy against the supplier? What if the supplier is from Taiwan and refuses to compensate Paik's Variety? What practical problems does Paik face?

4) Implied Term—Goods Fit for Special Use   The *Sale of Goods Act* also provides an implied condition that goods will be suitable or fit for a particular purpose if that purpose is made known to the seller and it is in the seller's line of business to supply such goods. Imagine, for example, that a paint contractor has a project to paint a refinished church that has used a new drywall, made in part with recycled newspaper. The contractor advises his supplier of the new drywall, and asks for a paint that will cover it. The supplier recommends a certain paint, but when the contractor applies it, it streaks. The *Sale of Goods Act* puts an implied term of fitness for this special use in the contract for the sale of the paint. An **implied term of fitness** is a term implied into the contract that the goods are of a type that is suitable for any special purpose for which they are bought. The supplier, who is in the business of selling paint, knows that the contractor is relying on the supplier's skill and judgment in supplying goods that are fit for the purpose. This implied condition is called fitness for use or purpose.

implied term of fitness
a term implied into the contract that the goods are of a type that is suitable for any special purpose for which they are bought

As well, the *Sale of Goods Act* stipulates that the purchase cannot be made by trademark, which means brand name. However, in line with modern commercial practice, that requirement has been interpreted so as not to have as much effect. It will not be a defence for a retailer to claim that an article is sold by a brand name in order to escape liability in a fitness for use situation.

The Sale of Goods Act, R.S.O. 1990, c. S1, s15

s.15 (1) Where the buyer, expressly or by implication, makes known to the seller the particular purpose for which the goods are required so as to show that the buyer relies on the seller's skill or judgment, and the goods are of a description that it is in the course of the seller's business to supply (whether he is the manufacturer or not) there is an implied condition that the goods will be reasonably fit for such purpose, but in the case of a contract of a specified article under its patent or other trade name, there is no implied condition as to its fitness for any particular purpose.

Muskoka Fuels v. Hassan Steel Fabricators Limited, 2011 ONCA 355 (CanLII)

Muskoka Fuels purchased a 2,000 litre fuel storage tank from Hassan Steel. The tanks had a single wall 2.5mm thick with an exterior coating and a bare metal interior. The expected life of a tank of this kind was at least ten years of service. The tank was approved by the provincial body that certified tanks.

Muskoka Fuels took delivery of the tank but did not put it into service until 22 months later. Less than five months after they started to use it, diesel fuel leaked out through a small hole at the bottom of the tank. The fuel leak caused damages totalling $71,589.

How the hole got in the tank was not certain. When the defendant wanted to examine it and take steel samples it was told the plaintiff's expert had examined the tank and then disposed of it. The trial judge believed the hole in the tank was due to a "microbally induced internal corrosion process" of unknown explanation. She also ruled out causes that might be blamed on Muskoka Fuels. She found the tank did not fail due to improper maintenance, had not been damaged during or after installation, had been properly installed and had been used only as intended.

Muskoka Fuels sued Hassan Steel for negligence and under the Ontario *Sale of Goods Act* s. 15 (1) for breach of the implied warranty that the good was fit for the specific purpose. The seller had told Muskoka Fuel that the tank would hold diesel fuel for 10 years. There had been concern in the industry that some tanks could leak due to internal corrosion, but Hassan Steel had not investigated this further.

The trial judge ruled that Hassan Steel had not met a reasonable standard of care and was negligent and that the leak was due to improper coating on the inside of the tank. She also ruled that s. 15(1) of the *Sale of Goods Act* had been breached since the supplier had warranted that the tank was fit for storing fuel oil and it clearly was not.

The steel company appealed the decision.

The Court's Decision

The Court of Appeal also held Hassan Steel liable for the damages from the fuel leak, but due to the hole in the tank, not because of improper coating on the tank. The Appeal Court however used s. 15(2) of the *Sale of Goods Act* as the basis of their decision, not s. 15 (1) as the trial judge had. It ruled that the supplier had breached the implied condition that the tank was of merchantable quality. The seller could not examine the interior of the tank, so the implied condition of merchantability applied. It was supposed to hold diesel fuel for 10 years and it clearly did not, so the steel company had violated the implied condition of merchantability in s. 15 (2) and was therefore liable.

Business Law   Applied

⑩ Lars Larsson, a farmer, designed an apparatus for lifting bales of hay from his truck to the second storey of his barn. He purchased a large quantity of strong metal clothesline wire from the local hardware store for use in the lift. After a few weeks of use, the line snapped. Larsson returned to the hardware store and demanded a refund for the cost of the clothesline wire. The hardware store refused.

a) Was there an implied term of fitness for use in the agreement for the use of these goods?

⑪ Elsa Petherham needed a packaging machine for the assembly line of her plant. From a manufacturer, she purchased a repossessed machine that was designed to use 1.3-mm-thick plastic. Petherham used that thickness as well as thinner plastic in her plant, and the salesman said that there would be no problem—the machine could use anything thinner, but not thicker.

On installation, Petherham found that the machine would not use the thinner plastic. Half of the packaging to be done in her operation required the thinner size. She complained to the manufacturer, who replied that they had offered no guarantees, merely an honest opinion. There was nothing in the contract guaranteeing that the machine would work with thinner plastic. The manufacturer pointed out that it was a repossessed, used machine, and suggested that if Petherham had wanted a guarantee, the manufacturer would have sold a new machine at three times the price.

a) Given that the written purchase order contained no terms regarding fitness for use, did the contract for sale contain such a term?

Exemption Clauses

The *Sale of Goods Act* implies certain terms in contracts for the sale of goods if the parties forget to include them. However, the act also permits parties to agree that those implied terms are excluded. So, in a sale, a warranty of quality that would be implied by the *Sale of Goods Act* could be excluded by an exemption clause. For example, if a company buys a machine for its plant without any mention of warranties, the *Sale of Goods Act* implies certain warranties in the purchase contract. However, if the contract contained a term stating that all warranties implied by law were excluded, then the *Sale of Goods Act* warranties would not apply.

The Sale of Goods Act, R.S.O. 1990, c. S.1, s.53

Where any right, duty or liability under a contract of sale by implication of law, it may be negated or varied by express agreement or by the course of dealing between the parties, or by usage, if the usage is such as to bind both parties to the contract.

Hunter Engineering v. Syncrude, [1989] 1 S.C.R. 426

In early 1975, Syncrude ordered some mining gearboxes from Hunter Engineering. These were to be used to drive conveyor belts at Syncrude's tar-sands project in northern Alberta, and had been specially designed and built for Syncrude, based on specifications it had provided. The contract with Hunter contained a clause limiting its liability for the equipment to 24 months from the date of delivery or 12 months from the date of start-up (whichever came first), but said nothing further concerning liability.

Subsequently, Syncrude entered into a contract for similar equipment with Allis Chalmers Canada Ltd. However, the contract with Allis Chalmers contained a clause excluding any warranties (including the implied *Sale of Goods Act* warranties) other than those found in the agreement.

The gearboxes from both Hunter and Allis Chalmers developed cracks and were unable to do the job required of them. The issue for the court's consideration was whether the *Sale of Goods Act* condition of fitness for a particular purpose applied to either or both of these contracts.

The Court's Decision

The *Sale of Goods Act* conditions applied to the contract with Hunter, but did not apply to the contract with Allis Chalmers. The former had not expressly excluded the *Sale of Goods Act* provisions, while the latter had.

Exemption Clauses   The *Hunter v. Syncrude* case proves that exemption clauses can be effective in business transactions. Failure to clearly state that statutory conditions (that is, contractual terms implied into a contract by virtue of legislation) are not applicable to a given transaction can lead to expensive consequences in the event of product defects.

Rov v 2G Robotics Inc., 2013 CanLII 57484 (ON SCSM)

The plaintiff purchased an underwater scanner from 2G Robotics for $38,850. It paid $13,657 and took delivery, but refused to pay the balance of the contract price due to the alleged failure of the scanner to perform as required.

Rov sued to have its money returned on the basis of two allegations: (1) breach of the implied warranty of reasonable fit-

ness for the purpose under s. 15(1) of the Sale of Goods Act, and alternatively (2) for fundamental breach of the contract.

2G Robotics argued that the implied conditions imposed by the Sale of Goods Act had clearly been excluded in section 9 of the contract so a claim based on this statute was prohibited under the terms of the contract.

In the contract section 9 stated;

EXCEPT AS EXPRESSLY SET OUT IN THESE TERMS AND CONDITIONS, 2G DISCLAIMS ANY FURTHER CONDITIONS, REPRESENTATIONS OR WARRANTIES, WHETHER WRITTEN OR ORAL, EXPRESS OR IMPLIED, INCLUDING BUT NOT LIMITED TO THE CONDITIONS, REPRESENTATIONS AND WARRANTIES OF MERCHANTABILITY, MERCHANTABLE QUALITY, FITNESS FOR A PARTICULAR PURPOSE AND THOSE ARISING FROM STATUTE.

The limitations, exclusions and disclaimers set out in this Section 9 shall apply irrespective of the nature of the cause of action, demand or claim, including but not limited to, breach of contract, tort (including negligence) or any other legal theory and shall survive termination of these terms and conditions, a fundamental breach or breaches and/or failure of the essential purpose of these terms and conditions or any remedy contained herein. The allocations of liability in this Section 9 represent the agreed and bargained for understanding of the parties and 2G's.

2G also claimed that this section clearly excluded the right to sue for fundamental breach as well. 2G also argued that there had never been a fundamental breach. The plaintiff had not told 2G where the scanner was specifically to be used. Rov had taken the scanner to Latvia in an area where the water was full of silt and was very murky, so the scanner naturally would not pro-duce as clear images as when it is used in clear waters, but it had still functioned.

The Court's Decision

The judge ruled that section 9 of the contract clearly prevented Rov from making a claim for a breach of an implied warranty of reasonable fitness for the purpose under the Sale of Goods Act. The judge also noted that even if section 9 was not in the contract, a claim for breach of reasonable fitness under s. 15 (1) of the Act would have failed. Rov had never told 2G of the specific cloudy water conditions that the scanner would be used in. There are other regions of Latvia where the water is much clearer and the scanner would have produced better images. It did not breach a term of reasonable fitness.

The court also ruled that the exclusion clause prevented a claim based on fundamental breach. The court noted that these were two commercial parties and Rov had been told that water quality affects the image quality. The judge found nothing unconscionable or unfair or unreasonable in this context so the exclusion clauses were enforceable.

The judge did not think a fundamental breach had occurred. The scanner had worked and problems were due primarily because of the murky water that Rov had been working in.

Luckily Rov had insurance that had paid the balance owing to 2G Robotics, and the court dismissed Rov's claim against the defendant.

■ *Critical Concepts of* Implied Conditions

The *Sale of Goods Act* provides that certain terms are included in every contract of sale, unless the parties agree otherwise:

- guarantees (called conditions) that the seller has the right to sell the goods
- guarantees (called conditions) that the goods will be fit for general use (merchantability) and for a special purpose made known at the time of sale (fitness for use)
- guarantees (called conditions) that if goods are purchased by description, the goods delivered will correspond to that description
- guarantees (called conditions) that if goods are purchased by sample, their quality will correspond to that of the sample and will not have any latent defect making them of unsaleable general quality

■ *Business Law* Applied

⑫ **Anand Singh bought** a used car "as is" and did not inspect it. The next week the car developed serious problems, and Singh wanted to return it and get his money back.

 a) Does the warranty of quality or merchantability under the *Sale of Goods Act* apply to the contract for the sale of the car?
 b) If not, what steps could Singh have taken to protect his interests?

⑬ **Adolph Gostonyi bought** a used computer from a classmate. Gostonyi knew very little about computers, and visited a branch of a major retailer—High-Comp Inc.—to purchase disks for his new system. Gostonyi had heard about a new disk, with the brand name Digico, that was reputedly of better quality than other disks on the market.

Gostonyi explained to a salesperson that he was a computer novice, had just bought a used machine that had originally been supplied by High-Comp, and wondered whether the Digico disks would be suitable for his computer. The salesperson replied that the disks were the best on the market and would indeed work. In addition, the disks were currently on sale at $5 less than their usual price. Gostonyi bought a box of 10 disks.

When he got home and tried them on his computer, they would not work. A friend advised him that these were high-density disks, and that Gostonyi's computer could read only double-density disks. Gostonyi returned to the store and complained. The store manager stated that Gostonyi had specifically asked for Digico disks and the box was clearly marked in large letters "high-density." So, said the manager, the young man knew what he was buying, and the store was not responsible.

  a) Is there any provision in the *Sale of Goods Act* that would assist Gostonyi?
  b) What are the facts necessary to bring a situation within this section of the *Sale of Goods Act*?

⑩ **Julie Vanderhoof bought** a used car from Ed McMotors Ltd. A sign on the car described it as a six-cylinder Mustang. There was a clause in the sale contract stating that "all conditions, warranties, and liabilities implied by statute, common-law or otherwise, are hereby excluded."

A few weeks after the car was delivered, Vanderhoof discovered that it had only four cylinders.

  a) Does the exclusion clause that excludes all statutory warranties prevent Vanderhoof from obtaining her remedy in court?
  b) Does the fact that the car is a used vehicle mean that the *Sale of Goods Act* does not apply?

Rules Concerning the Transfer of Ownership

The *Sale of Goods Act* also sets out rules concerning when purchasers of goods become the actual owners of those goods. They are often referred to as rules concerning the transfer of **title**—a legal concept roughly equivalent to ownership.

title
a legal concept roughly equivalent to ownership

   In law, the owner of an item usually has the risk of loss. If an item is damaged or destroyed, it is the owner who has to pay for the repair or suffer the complete loss. For example, if you buy a television set, take it home yourself, and drop it when unloading your car, you must pay for the repair.

   There are a number of rules under the *Sale of Goods Act* that determine when a person becomes an owner. As was the case with the conditions discussed above, these rules are implied into every contract of sale, unless the parties agree otherwise. As many of these were developed from the practice of merchants of a much earlier age and are contrary to the expectations of today's business person, businesses normally prefer to use purchase orders. An example Purchase Order is given in the Appendix to this chapter. The terms of the standard purchase orders usually displace the antiquated rules under the act.

   The usual standard contractual terms used in purchase orders are called **Incoterms** and they are used internationally, (such as FOB and CIF). Depending on which incoterms are used in a contract, the duty to insure and the risk of loss or damage to goods that are shipped is allocated to the seller or the purchaser at a specific time in the process.

   If the contract does not state when the legal title passes from the seller to the buyer, the *Sale of Goods Act* will. Under The *Act*, normally once a contract is made the legal title passes to the buyer, even if the money is not yet paid. But if the goods need to put into a deliverable state, such as; need to be created, completed, altered, repaired, or separated from a larger group, under the *Act* the legal title would not pass until the additional action is completed and the buyer is told the goods are ready. If goods are taken on approval the title does not pass unless the buyer agrees or the time period passes and the buyer still has the goods. If no time is set, a reasonable time will apply.

Critical Concepts of Remedies

- The usual legal rule is that "risk follows title," or, whoever owns the goods assumes the risk of loss or damage.
- The *Sale of Goods Act* sets out rules governing when ownership changes hands.
- The *Sale of Goods Act* rules concerning when ownership changes can be altered by agreement between the parties.

Redfern Resources Ltd. (Re), 2012 BCCA 189 (CanLII)

Redfern was a wholly-owned subsidiary of Redcorp, a Vancouver-based mining and exploration company. Redfern was trying to developing a potential zinc, copper, lead, silver and gold mining site in Tulsequah, in north-west B.C. Redfern agreed to purchase mining equipment from Sandvik, a high tech engineering group based in Sweden.

Redfern signed a contract to buy 15 pieces of equipment valued at close to $13 million to be delivered in stages. The first two units to be sent were the Drill and the Loader. The purchase order was lengthy. It included an entire agreement clause, a delivery clause, an inspection and rejection clause and a clause that allowed Redfern, but not Sandvik, the right to terminate the contract under certain circumstances.

On Jan. 5, 2009 the Drill and Loader arrived by ship at the AML (Alaska Marine Lines) terminal in Juneau, Alaska and all parties agreed that according to the FOB terms of the Purchase Agreement, at that point legal title passed from Sandvik to Redfern. Due to the weather the equipment could only be delivered to the mine site between June and October. The two pieces of equipment never left the AML storage yards.

On Feb. 12 Sandvik issued invoices for a total of $2,109,054 for the 2 machines. On Feb. 23 Redfern notified Sandvik that it would have to cancel the entire contract as it was having difficulty getting permits due to environmental concerns and native opposition to the mine. Redfern notified AML to ship the equipment back to its office in Finland, but AML required Redfern's permission to do this. On March 4 an executive at Redfern told AML to ship the goods back to Sandvik, but hours later on the same day, Redcorp and Redfern went into bankruptcy protection and none of its assets could be disposed of. Sandvik later issued an invoice for an additional $3,058,547, the 25% cancellation fee for the rest of the contract.

The issue then became who owned the Drill and Loader. The receiver brought in to deal with the bankruptcy and the assets of Redcorp and Redfern agreed to let Sandvik re-sell the equipment. The court then had to decide who was the owner of this equipment and thus entitled to the sale proceeds.

The receiver argued that the legal title belonged to Redfern. Sandvik claimed that Redfern had not inspected the equipment so it had not yet been obligated to pay for the equipment so the title passed back to Sandvik.

The Court's Decision

The Court ruled that the title had passed to Redfern. Once the goods had been delivered to Redfern's agent (AML) the goods had been "satisfactorily provided" as required under the Purchase Order. The failure to inspect the equipment did not affect the passing of title or cause the title to revert back to Sandvik. Until the goods are inspected the title remained with the buyer. It would only pass back if the goods had been inspected and found not to be satisfactory, which did not occur. Therefore the sale proceeds had to be given to the receiver for distribution to creditors, this money did not belong to Sandvik.

Remedies

If a seller or purchaser breaks one or more of the terms contained in the contract of sale, the usual remedies for breach of contract are available—that is, suing for damages or attempting to back out of a deal without legal liability (rescission). Remember that you can always sue for damages, but whether you can avoid the contract without legal liability will depend on the seriousness of the term breached.

In addition, the *Sale of Goods Act* adds some additional remedies, chiefly for the benefit of an unpaid seller. What makes many of these particularly useful is that they can be implemented on short notice, without recourse to the formal court process.

- suing the purchaser for the purchase price of the goods (which can be different from suing for damages)
- retaining any deposit made

- holding the goods until payment is made (in the absence of credit arrangements being in place, or if the buyer is insolvent)
- stopping delivery of goods that are in transit to the buyer if the seller can prove the buyer has become insolvent (unable to pay debts as they become due), but if they are not insolvent, the seller is liable for losses caused by the stoppage
- exercising the right of resale, if either of these last two measures is utilized

Of course, the buyer also has remedies for a breach of contract under the *Sale of Goods Act*. The buyer may sue for damages for non-delivery, sue for damages for breach of warranty or condition, reject the goods for breach of condition, or sue for specific performance. Note that this last option is one that would be used fairly infrequently. The courts generally do not make people specifically live up to the terms of a contract, since money damages are generally adequate compensation. However, if the goods to be delivered have some unique quality, specific performance may be an option.

Retail Sales

Consumer Protection Legislation

As the face of society has changed, so too has the nature of consumer sales. The business situation of the 1990s is very different from what it was when the *Sale of Goods Act* was first enacted in 1893.

The Manufacturer's Role   When the *Sale of Goods Act* rules were developed, the customer often dealt directly with the person who made the item. Today's seller is often a retailer who, thanks to prepackaged goods, is little more than a conduit for the manufacturer. Yet, the *Sale of Goods Act* rules place responsibility on the seller, not on the manufacturer. This is also true in common law rules of contract, under which only parties to the deal are liable on the agreement.

Standard Form Contracts   The use of printed form contracts and mass-marketing techniques means that there is little or no negotiating over the terms of a contract. If terms are printed on the back of a sales invoice, the purchaser might be unfamiliar with the language, and unable to assess the risks involved in agreeing to them. The purchaser might not even be aware of unusual terms that are completely at odds with how the deal was perceived.

Prepackaged Goods: Complex Technology   Both packaging and the complexity of certain high-tech goods mean that purchasers can no longer inspect many items for themselves, but must accept the quality of the goods as described.

Advertising   The power of advertising to influence purchasers is undisputed. That advertising can be misleading and deceptive has been equally demonstrated.

International Trade   Manufacturers are often not located in the same province or country as the consumer. Consumer protection laws may be much more lenient in the manufacturer's place of business. It is also very costly to try to bring a lawsuit in a foreign country.

The Legislation

In the 1960s and 1970s, federal and provincial governments enacted a number of consumer protection laws. These laws are update frequently so they should be checked regularly. Fortunately, most governments have websites with summaries of the current legislation and information material along with help lines. However, there are differences among the various provincial acts.

What is a Consumer Transaction?

Consumer protection acts govern only transactions for personal use but not for business use. The transactions protected include purchase of goods, services and leases.

Example: Asha buys a clock for her home. That is for personal use and consumer protection acts govern the transaction. She buys the identical model clock for her business; that is not a transaction covered by consumer protection acts.

In this section we look mainly at laws that add warranties regarding quality and performance to consumer transactions and prevent exclusion of these warranties by the use of exemption clauses. Because the number of consumer protection laws is so vast, and is increasing, a summary of major issues and rules is contained at the end of this section. Consumer protection laws are also set out in various chapters as they relate to the relevant subject matter.

Manufacturer's Warranties   Virtually every new consumer item sold in Canada today comes with some sort of product warranty. The Loadstat Warranty (p. 276) is typical of these, containing provisions that:

- give very specific warranties about product quality and the length of that warranty
- limit the repair or replacement obligations
- give specific remedy or complaint procedures
- limit the extent of the manufacturer's liability in the event of defect or loss

Preservation of Sale of Goods Act Implied Conditions and Warranties   Most consumers believe that the express warranty card or brochure that is included with their new purchase outlines the supplier's entire obligation. Few are aware that most consumer products sold in Canada today also come with certain non-excludable statutorily implied warranties of fitness and merchantability. The warranties of fitness and merchantability are a result of the *Sale of Goods Act* discussed previously in this section. The fact that they are non-excludable in consumer transactions comes from consumer protection legislation.

These acts typically provide that the implied conditions and warranties of the *Sale of Goods Act* cannot be waived in the case of a sale to a consumer. In other words, in the case of a sale to a consumer, the parties are prohibited from agreeing that the implied conditions and warranties will not apply. The following is a typical section from such an act.

Consumer Protection Act, 2002, S.O. 2002, c. 30, Sch. A

Quality of services

9. (1) The supplier is deemed to warrant that the services supplied under a consumer agreement are of a reasonably acceptable quality. 2002, c. 30, Sched. A, s. 9 (1).

Quality of goods

(2) The implied conditions and warranties applying to the sale of goods by virtue of the *Sale of Goods Act* are deemed to apply with necessary modifications to goods that are leased or traded or otherwise supplied under a consumer agreement. 2002, c. 30, Sched. A, s. 9 (2).

Same

(3) Any term or acknowledgement, whether part of the consumer agreement or not, that purports to negate or vary any implied condition or warranty under the *Sale of Goods Act* or any deemed condition or warranty under this Act is void. 2002, c. 30, Sched. A, s. 9 (3).

■ *Critical Concepts of* Consumer Protection Legislation

- Legislation prohibits parties to a consumer sale from agreeing that the implied conditions of the *Sale of Goods Act* will not apply. In other words, those conditions cannot be waived by the parties.
- Legislation varies from province to province, and may imply terms in addition to those in the *Sale of Goods Act*, as well as extend liability for the products beyond the immediate parties to the contract.

■ *Business Law* Applied

⑮ **Lisa Desoto had** a swimming pool installed in her back yard. The pool came with a warranty card that guaranteed materials and workmanship on the pool itself for two years, excluding the filtration system. There was also a clause stating that there were no other warranties or conditions, expressed or implied by common law statute or otherwise.

The filtration system broke down the first day and had to be completely replaced. Desoto claimed the replacement cost of the filtration system from the pool manufacturer. The manufacturer pointed to the warranty card and said that the filtration system was not included in the warranty.

a) Was this a consumer sale?

b) Was there an express guarantee? Was there a limitation in the express warranty with respect to the filtration system? Was it effective?

c) What law would imply a warranty (condition) of quality to the filtration system?

⑯ **Alfredo Vincenzo bought** a stain remover, sold under the brand name Stain Out, from a retail store. He tried to remove a stain from a suit coat, and the stain remover discoloured the garment. The instruction sheet inside the box contained the following statement printed in small letters at the bottom:

Not responsible for any loss or damage or injury however caused by the use of Stain Out. Vincenzo demanded a refund of the cost of the stain remover and the replacement cost of his coat.

a) Were there any expressed warranties in the contract of sale of the stain remover? Were there any implied conditions?

b) Was there a breach of any implied conditions?

c) Was the exclusion clause effective?

d) If the retailer refuses to pay Vincenzo and says it is the manufacturer's fault, as the retailer received the stain remover in a package and did nothing to it, does Vincenzo have any remedy against the retailer?

e) What if the manufacturer's place of business is Mexico City and the manufacturer refuses to pay? What practical problems does the retailer face in recapturing money paid to the customer from the manufacturer?

f) If the sales-confirmation order of the manufacturer contains a limitation of warranty clause similar to the one on the instruction clause, can the retailer claim successfully against the manufacturer? What are the practical and legal problems that the retailer faces in trying to bring an action against the foreign manufacturer?

Motor Vehicle Sales

Remember that almost all car salespeople are paid a commission based on profit—the more the dealership makes on a car, the more the salesperson gets paid. Since a "good" deal for a buyer is a "bad" deal for the salesperson, a number of tricks are often used to help sell more cars for higher profits. The most common tricks used by salespeople (and their managers) are described in this chapter; make sure you understand how they work before you start negotiating.

Often if the purchaser is trading in a car when purchasing a new one, the dealer may offer a higher value for the trade-in, making the buyer think they are getting a good deal. Often however the dealer inflates other charges such as dealer prep, transportation, extended warranty, rust proofing and processing fees, and the buyer has not made the great deal they think they have.

If the purchaser indicates that they want a new car so long as the monthly payments do not exceed a certain amount, the dealer can extend the length of the payments by a year or more and add on extra charges to make extra profits, but the naïve buyer is unaware of the extra money they end up paying.

Consumer Protection: Issues and Laws

Consumer protection legislation varies among the provinces. There are a significant number of rights and responsibilities for consumers and businesses in each province. There are so many different areas of protection, only some of the key protections that are provided in Ontario are briefly outlined below. The law applies to "consumers" who are individuals acting for personal, family or household purposes, not for a business. The law applies to goods and services and also to purchases and leases.

Clear and Comprehensible Contracts and Cancellation Rights

All required information in contracts must be clear, comprehensible and prominent. If contracts are missing required information, you have the right to cancel the contract, usually within 1 year.

When you cancel a contract under the CPA (preferably in writing), the business has 15 days to return your money. The business is entitled to any goods the consumer received under the agreement, and may be entitled to some money for goods or services actually used.

If you receive goods that you never requested, you have no obligation to pay for them. You can use them or throw them out. The exception is if the goods were addressed to someone else and delivered by mistake. If you receive an unsolicited credit card you are responsible though if you use it. Negative billing options are also banned, so you cannot be billed for goods or services that you had not requested but the company provided, just because you had not declined the goods or service.

Written Estimates

A consumer is not required to pay more than 10 percent above the written estimate provided by a supplier or a repairer. If a supplier or repairer charges an amount that is 10 percent more than the estimate, the consumer may require the supplier or repairer to provide the goods or services for the estimated amount. They can only exceed the 10 percent limit unless you have agreed to an increase and signed a change to the contract.

Full Disclosure of Credit Terms and Explanation of Costs

Anyone providing goods or services on credit must give the consumer a written statement showing details of the credit terms, including the annual percentage rate. As provided under the federal *Interest Act* if no annual interest rate is stated the maximum rate that can be charged is 5 per cent per annum. (R.S., 1985, c. I-15, s. 4; 2001, c. 4, s. 91.)

All charges in a contract must be what they say they are. For example, a business may not add a $20 surcharge for a "tax" that is not really for tax.

Future Performance Agreements and Late Deliveries

When some part of the contract occurs in the future (e.g. delivery, performance of services, payment in full), written contracts are required if the goods or services are worth more than $50. The contract must contain complete details of the transaction and full disclosure of any credit terms. If delivery of a good doesn't arrive within 30 days of the promised date, you can cancel the contract by sending a cancellation letter, so long as you have proof of the delivery date. But you lose the right to cancel the agreement if you accept delivery after the 30 days.

Cooling Off Period

Because certain industries have a reputation of high pressure sales tactics that often caused people to enter into contracts they did not want, a cooling off period was given for certain types of contracts. A 10 day cooling off period applies to; Direct Sales Agreements (door-to-door sales), Time Share Agreements (such as 1 week ownership of a vacation condo), Personal Development Agreements (such as fitness club memberships, martial arts lessons, modelling contracts, dance lessons) Credit Repair Agreements and Loan Broker Agreements. It is a 20 day cooling off period for door-to-door water heater rentals and sales, because of the constant complaints the government receives over these aggressive sales teams. There is a 2 day cooling off period for a pay day loan contract. You must notify the seller in writing within the cooling off period that you want to terminate and have proof you sent the notification so use a courier, registered mail or fax and send an email as well.

A 10 day cooling off period exists for the purchase of a brand new condominium under *The Condominium Act* but not for a brand new house and not for a re-sale condominium or house.

Protection From Unfair Business Practices

Consumers are provided protection from unfair business practices such as false, misleading or deceptive representations. This includes false advertising, any false statement such as representing that used goods are new, exaggerating the quality of goods or services, or suggesting that a repair is needed when it is not. Protection is also given against unconscionable representations that are grossly unfair or took advantage of a person who had been subject to high pressure sales tactics or was lacking the capacity to understand fully what they had bargained for. Restrictions are also placed on collection agencies and the frequency of calls they can make, who they can contact and the type of language they can use when attempting to collect unpaid debts.

Penalties

Under the Ontario Consumer Protection Act 2002, the penalties can be up to two years less a day in jail, fines of up to $50,000 for an individual and up to $250,000 for a corporation.

The Competition Act

Many of our business laws are based on the economic principle that competition among businesses is good for consumers for the simple reason that it compels producers to offer better deals—lower prices, better quality, new products, and more choice. However, there are a number of business practices believed to reduce competition. The purpose of the Competition Act (hereinafter in this section—the Act) is to maintain and encourage competition in Canada. Its goals include ensuring that small and medium-sized enterprises have an equitable opportunity to participate in the Canadian economy and that consumers are provided with competitive prices and product choices. The Act benefits consumers in preserving competition by controlling practices that undermine it. As one judge put it, "The Act represents the will of the people of Canada that the old maxim caveat emptor, let the purchaser beware, yield somewhat to the more enlightened view, caveat venditor—let the seller beware." (Matheson J., *R. v. Colgate-Palmolive Ltd.*, 1969 CanLII 447 (ON SC))

Major changes were made to the Act in 2009, as in the past there was considerable criticism that the law was ineffective and it was difficult to obtain convictions due to the wording and requirements in the earlier legislation. These issues were taken into consideration when the 2009 revisions were made.

There are many anti-competitive practices set out in the Act. They are divided into three categories: Criminal Matters, Civil Reviewable Matters and Dual Track Matters. The individual practices that are included in each category are included in each category are set out in the Chart below.

Criminal Matters are absolutely banned as the term suggests. There are only a few exclusive criminal offences. Conspiracy is a key criminal offence. It can include a variety of practices aimed at eliminating competition such as cartels where rival producers, who should be competing, instead agree to fix prices and/or allocate customers or control the supply of a product. Through this conspiracy they agree to increase the prices purchasers eventually pay. Bid-rigging and misleading advertising and promotions are also included in the criminal section.

The criminal matters are prosecuted as any crime in the regular courts and must be proved beyond a reasonable doubt. Criminal penalties can include fines of up to $25 million and imprisonment for up to 14 years and "**prohibition orders**" i.e., court orders to stop or modify conduct.

prohibition orders
court orders to stop or modify conduct

Example: In the past major world wide price fixing conspiracies have involved many products used by consumers. In the 1990's major pharmaceutical companies fixed the world prices charged for various vitamins for a 10 year period resulting in world-wide fines of over $1 billion. In 2013 four Chinese drug manufacturers that produced about 80% of the world's vitamin C were convicted in the U.S. for price fixing and fined $162 million. Settlements are still being negotiated on a more than 5 year conspiracy that artificially fixed and inflated world prices for LCD screens for televisions, computers and other electronic products by major electronics manufacturers such as AU Optronics, Toshiba, LG, Samsung Hitachi and Sharp. Prosecutors claimed that the executives met over 60 times to set prices and their sales totalled over $72 billion. The conspiracy is alleged to have cost consumers billions in inflated priced for electronics products with LCD screens. In the U.S. 13 executives have received jail sentences and corporate fines are in excess of $1.3 billion. Civil class action lawsuits have also been formed.

Immunity Program   The Competition Bureau employs several tools to encourage informants to come forward with incriminating evidence in criminal matters. To encourage insiders to give evidence of offenses; the Bureau has created an Immunity/Leniency program. The Bureau will recommend immunity or favourable prosecution and sentencing treatment for parties who come forward with evidence of offences by a business in which they are involved. The program is also based on 'first come first served'. The first to provide evidence likely gets immunity. Those who come later may have to bargain for leniency. There is also whistleblower protection for parties, not involved in an offense, but who report possible violations of the Act. The whistleblower's name is not revealed, and if known, cannot be subject to any retaliatory measures by the employer.

Example: In 2013 a class action civil lawsuit was settled for $23.3 million against four leading chocolate manufacturers for illegally conspiring to fix and increase the price of chocolate products in Canada. The defendants; Cadbury, Mars, Nestle and Hershey, all agreed to pay millions for the settlement. After a 6 year investigation the Competition Bureau laid criminal charges of conspiracy against three of the companies and three executives over this chocolate price fixing scheme. Cadbury was granted immunity from prosecution for coming forward with the information. Hershey pleaded guilty to the criminal charges and paid a fine of $4 million. The others charged pleaded not guilty and as yet those cases have not been resolved. The individuals can face fines of up to $10 million and/or up to 5 years in jail. Increased penalties of $25 million and up to 14 years in jail came in after these offences occurred.

Civil Reviewable Matters may or may not affect competition. Practices under this category include: false and misleading advertising, bait and switch, mergers and abuse of dominant position. Under the category of abuse of dominance practices such as price maintenance, refusal to deal, tied selling and exclusive dealing are included. The reviewable offenses can be brought before the Competition Tribunal, the Federal Court or a provincial court. These charges are proved on the lower civil standard of balance of probabilities. The 2009 amendments moved some offenses from the criminal to the reviewable category in order to more easily obtain findings of a violation.

Penalties can include court orders to stop conduct, orders to resume supply of a product, an **administrative monetary penalty (AMP)**, which is essentially a civil fine, of up to $10 million and restitution orders to compensate consumers that have purchased a product.

Dual Track Matters may be pursued as either criminal or civil (Reviewable). The term 'dual' refers to the fact that certain conduct can fall under either the criminal or civil sections. For example, there is no exact term, misleading advertising, but that type of conduct could be charged under the criminal part—section 53: *False or Misleading Representations*; or the civil part, section 74.01: *Misrepresentations to the Public*. Similarly, certain anticompetitive agreements could be considered under the criminal Conspiracy (cartel) provision, section 45, or the Civil Agreement provision, section 90.1.

The Director of Competition decides which track to use. The director usually chooses the civil track because it is easier to get a finding of violation of the Act. However if the conduct is particularly offensive, or is a repetition of conduct subject to a prohibition order, the Director may choose to proceed by the more serious procedure.

Civil Reviewable Matters
breaches of the Act proved at the civil not criminal standard of proof.

AMP
an administrative monetary penalty and it is essentially a civil fine

Dual Track Matters
conduct that falls under two overlapping sections of the Act

Competition Act Categories and Practices

Criminal Matters	Conspiracy (such as Price Fixing and Market or Supply Allocation), Bid-rigging, Misleading Advertising
Dual Track Matters	Competitor Agreements, Misleading Advertising, Deceptive Telemarketing
Civil Matters	Misleading Advertising, Abuse of Dominant Position, Price Maintenance, Refusal to Deal, Tied Selling, Exclusive Dealing, Mergers

There are provisions for advance Advisory Opinions on whether a practice violates the Act. However, the opinion must be obtained before the practice is started.

Business Alert!

Enforcement   There are four bodies that are relevant to enforcement of the Act. It may be helpful to compare the process to the ordinary criminal prosecution. It is the Competition Bureau that does the investigation, it is the Competition Tribunal or the courts which hear and decide the cases.

- **The Competition Bureau** headed by The Commissioner of Competition, investigates, in like manner to the police, to determine if an offense has likely occurred. The Commissioner prosecutes the reviewable matters.
- **The Attorney General of Canada's office** provides lawyers to prosecute the criminal charges similar to the role of the Crown Attorney.
- **The Competition Tribunal**, which hears Reviewable Practice charges in the same manner as a court.
- **The Courts**, which hear the Prohibited Practices (criminal), and other matters relevant to the Act.

Any person can provide information of alleged violations of the Act to the Commissioner. Many of the successful prosecutions come from businesses against their competitors. These complainants have a good understanding of the relevant business practices, and gather evidence to support the allegations, which makes the Bureau's task easier.

Private parties can start lawsuits in civil court to recover actual losses caused by a violation of criminal matters, or an order of a Court or Tribunal, but this statutory right of action for damages is only in these circumstances (Section 36). Some of these lawsuits are class actions based on criminal convictions rather than lawsuits that attempt to prove violations of the Act (s.36).

Additionally, the Act permits private parties to apply for leave to make an application to the Competition Tribunal for remedial orders under civil reviewable practices in sections 75 (refusal to deal), 76 (price maintenance) and 77 (tied selling, exclusive dealing and market restriction) of the Act. Remedial orders are usually prohibition (cease and desist) orders. There is no right to sue for damages under the Act for civil reviewable practices, so private parties would have to make a claim in civil law for a common law tort, such as civil conspiracy or intentional interference with economic interests, to obtain damages for their losses from these practices.

Example: Ultimate purchasers got certification it a civil class action based on alleged violations of Criminal Matters under the Act in Conspiracy and Misleading Representations, and Torts such as, Intentional Interference with Economic Interests. The unlawful conduct alleged was that Microsoft overcharged on certain of its Intel compatible software. The conspiracy alleged was between Microsoft parent and its subsidiaries. The major issue was whether consumers, who are indirect purchasers, have a right against the manufacturers under the Act. Recall that consumers could not do so under many provincial Sale of Goods Acts (Arora v. Whirlpool Canada LP, 2013 ONCA 657 (CanLII)). In a trilogy of cases decided by the Supreme Court together in 2013, the court said that direct and indirect purchasers (consumers) could bring a civil action together under the Competition Act for conspiracy. (*Pro-Sys Consultants Ltd. v. Microsoft Corporation*, 2013 SCC 57 (CanLII))

While there are a number of convictions under the criminal offences section of the Act as well as prohibition orders under reviewable practices, they are rarely reported in newspapers. The matters often involve well-known retailers. Commentators believe the lack of publicity is due to the fact that these businesses purchase significant amount of advertising from the newspapers. Newspapers do not want to offend the businesses and so do not carry these stories.

Criminal Matters

Conspiracy

In an often-repeated quote of Karl Marx, he said: Whenever two businessmen gather together, there is a conspiracy against the public. Conspiracy is aimed at the various ways prices may be kept above true market prices by agreements among competitors. Conspiracies are, by their secret nature, very difficult to detect and prove. Identical prices are not enough to prove an offence. Thus, informants, protected by the immunity program, comprise an important source of evidence.

It is unlawful for competitors to conspire, agree or arrange to:

- Fix, maintain, increase or control prices (including discounts, rebates, allowances, concessions or other advantages);
- Allocate sales, territories, customers or markets; or
- Fix or control the production or supply of a product.

The penalty for conspiracy is imprisonment for up to 14 years and/or a fine of up to $25 million. Many convictions are obtained through guilty pleas.

Example: Domfoam International Inc. and Valle Foam Industries (1995) Inc. manufacture polyurethane foam, which is used in a variety of products such as cushions, upholstered furniture office chairs, carpet underlay, mattresses and pillows. According to a bulletin on the Bureau's website, it began investigating this cartel in February 2010 after being approached by a company through the Bureau's Immunity Program. Another competitor cooperated with the investigation by way of the Bureau's Leniency Program.

The Bureau obtained wiretap authorizations and executed search warrants in coordination with its international partners. Bureau officers searched five sites, seized thousands of documents and interviewed numerous witnesses.

Domfoam International Inc. and Valle Foam Industries (1995) Inc. pleaded guilty to conspiracy under the *Competition Act* and were fined a total of $12.5 million for participating in a price-fixing cartel for polyurethane foam.

Example: The Bureau investigated air cargo surcharges among several major airlines resulting in eight criminal convictions and fines of over $24 million. Cathay Pacific, Cargolux, Air France, KLM, Martinair, Qantas, British Airways, and Korean Air pleaded guilty to fixing one or more air cargo surcharges on certain routes from Canada.

Example: Panasonic conspired with Embraco North America Inc. and other competitors to fix the price of refrigeration compressors sold in Canada, and elsewhere, from January 2005 to December 2005.

Panasonic sold refrigeration compressors to W.C. Wood Corporation from its manufacturing base in Japan. Prior to negotiating their annual supply contract, Panasonic and Embraco exchanged information on their refrigeration compressor prices, production capacities and other market intelligence, and agreed to increase the price for refrigeration compressors sold to W.C. Wood Corporation in Canada.

Panasonic pleaded guilty and was fined $1.5 million. (All information from the Competition bureau website).

Exceptions: Where Conspiracy is Allowed   Agreements to restrain competition are permitted in two types of situations: First, when the agreement is necessary for a main agreement such as a time limited non-competition agreement by the owner of the business on the sale of the business. While this type of agreement does restrict the owner's ability to compete, this result is considered minimal when balanced with the need to have such agreements to permit the sale of goodwill of businesses; the other type of agreement is one required by government legislation such as marketing boards.

Bid-rigging

Bid-rigging typically involves competitors agreeing to artificially increase the prices of goods and/or services offered in bids to potential customers. It occurs when two or more persons agree that, in response to a call for bids or tenders, one or more of them will:

- submit a bid arrived at by agreement
- not submit a bid
- withdraw a bid

The penalty for bid-rigging is imprisonment for up to 14 years and/or a fine at the discretion of the court, which is usually in the millions of dollars.

Example: In the 1990s three of Canada's largest flour companies were convicted of bid-rigging contracts to supply flour to the federal government for use in foreign aid programs. Ottawa's most exclusive hotels were also convicted of bid-rigging when setting prices they charged the federal government for rooms.

Example: The Ontario Superior Court of Justice fined Japanese automotive parts maker Yazaki $30 million—the largest ever ordered by a Canadian court for a bid-rigging offence to date. The evidence showed that Yazaki secretly conspired with other Japanese motor vehicle components manufacturers to submit bids or tenders in response to requests for quotations to supply Honda of Canada Manufacturing Inc. (Honda) and Toyota Motor Manufacturing Canada Inc. (Toyota) with motor vehicle components. (Competition Bureau Announcement, April 18, 2013)

Misleading Advertising

Misleading advertising is a dual track offence and can be pursued under the criminal matters or the civil reviewable matters sections of the Act. There are more cases heard by the Competition Tribunal for misleading or deceptive advertising than any offence in the Act.

The General Impression of the Ad   Both the criminal section of the Act (s. 52) and the civil section (s.74.01(1)*(a)*,) state that it is an offence for a person to make a representation to the public that is false or misleading in a material respect. There are more cases pursued under this section than any other in the Act. 'Material' means any statement that might influence a customer to make a purchase. The term 'representation' is used the same way as in contract law: it includes statements made verbally or in writing to induce someone to buy a product or service. This section is phrased widely enough to catch almost all forms of advertising, even by a tweet. A statement to a single person who is a member of the public, such as in a telemarketing call, is sufficient. It is not necessary to demonstrate that any person was in fact deceived or misled. The representation is made to the public in Canada even if it was in fact made outside of Canada but viewed in Canada on the internet.

A statement may be open to interpretation. The Act states that the interpretation for the purpose of the Act is not the literal interpretation by a close and careful reading, but the general impression given to a hurried purchaser, or what a credulous and inexperienced consumer would believe.

Any person who contravenes section 52 is guilty of an offence and liable to a fine of up to $200,000 and/or imprisonment up to one year on summary conviction, or to fines in the discretion of the court and/or imprisonment up to 14 years upon indictment.

If a court determines that a person has engaged in conduct contrary to section 74.01(1*(a)*, it may order the person not to engage in such conduct, to publish a corrective notice, to pay an AMP (an administrative monetary penalty) and/or to pay restitution to purchasers. When the court orders the payment of AMP's, on first occurrence, individuals are subject to penalties of up to $750,000 and corporations, to penalties of up to $10 Million. For subsequent orders, the penalties increase to a maximum of $1 Million in the case of an individual and $15 Million in the case of a corporation.

Critical Concepts: Misleading Advertising

- Any representation made to the public to sell a product or service that is false or misleading in any respect constitutes a violation of the Act under both criminal and civil reviewable matters
- The statement need be made to only one member of the public

- No one need actually be deceived. A violation is committed merely if the representation is made.
- The test in deciding whether an advertisement is misleading is: what would the credulous and inexperienced consumer believe from this advertisement?

Many Ways to Mislead by Impression   Advertising can be misleading in many ways. The Bureau's website gives a list of examples all of which have been used by businesses and pursued under the Act to a conviction or consent order. Here are a few.

- An advertisement may represent or suggest that purchasers will save over normal prices. For example, "Selling Gold Jewelry Wholesale to the Public" implies that the items will be sold at wholesale and not retail price. This must be true in order to the advertiser to say so. Similarly, a business name such as, "ABC Manufacturing Co. Ltd.", implies a wholesale price. Where the company is only a retailer, it is misleading.
- Words such as "only" or similar claims of the exclusivity or superiority of a supplier should not be used if the result is to deceive or mislead such as "The only full-time swimming pool company in the area".
- It should not be represented that a specific event, like bankruptcy, end of lease, etc., is causing the supplier to sell off a company's existing stock unless such a representation is true: "Giant Bankruptcy Sale. All our stock must go!" where only part of the stock is from that company and other stock has been brought in from another business.
- When an item is said to be free with the purchase of another product, the free component must be free of all other costs. A snowmobile dealer advertised "Free Florida Vacation with Purchase of a Snowmobile." The free vacation paid only for accommodation, and did not include either transportation or meals. The dealer was convicted under the Competition Act.

Recall that misrepresentations are also offences under provincial consumer protection acts, and so a business that employs misleading advertising could violate two acts and be exposed to prosecution by a federal or provincial authority. Torts such as Intentional Interference with Economic Interests may also apply.

Richard v. Time Inc., 2012 SCC 8 (CanLII), [2012]

Time magazine mailed a letter in English to Jean Marc Richard in Quebec entitled "Official Sweepstake Notification". The letter said in large bold type **"OUR SWEEPSTAKES RESULTS ARE NOW FINAL: MR. JEAN MARC RICHARD HAS WON A CASH PRIZE OF $833,337.00!"** and repeated that in various ways several times. It also stated that the winner would have to return the winning entry in time. There was a self-addressed envelope and a coupon for subscribing to Time Magazine. (The letter is reprinted in the Appendix to the Supreme Court of Canada decision.)

In small print on the return envelope it was explained that a winner had been preselected by a computer. If that winner did not respond, the names of all those who responded would be put on a list for a draw for the price and that the odds of winning were 1:120 million.

Richard responded in a timely way to the notification of his prize and also purchased a subscription to the magazine.

Richard received his magazine but not his cheque for $833,337. On complaining to Time Magazine, he was told that the letter was an invitation to participate in the lottery. Richard pointed out that the document said he was a winner, but Time refused to pay.

Richard sued Time Magazine based on breach of contract for the amount of the prize and violations of the Consumer Protection Act of Québec.

The Trial Court found that the contents of the letter were not an offer and so no contract was formed by sending in the notice to claim the prize. However, the representation was misleading advertising under the Consumer Protection Act of Québec. The qualification that it was an invitation to participate was "buried in a sea of text". The Court awarded $1,000 compensatory damage on a moral basis and $1,250,000 punitive damages to Richard against Time Magazine.

Time appealed and the Quebec Court of Appeal completely reversed the Trial Court's finding and award. It found that Richard, being a sophisticated businessman, who conducted an international business in English and French, could not have been truly misled by the advertisement. The Appeal Court decision was appealed.

The Supreme Court's Decision

The Supreme Court of Canada restored the Trial Court's finding of misleading advertising. The correct test to apply under Québec law was whether a credulous and inexperienced person would be misled. This was an objective test because the intent of the statute is to protect the public not any individual person. Thus Richard's personal level of sophistication was irrelevant to a finding of misleading.

However, applying that same reasoning to the sanctions for a violation, Richard was not entitled to benefit personally. The only consideration was deterrence of this practice. The court felt that a punitive award of $15,000 was sufficient in the circumstance to deter misleading advertising.

The following three examples illustrate that the Competition Bureau is serious about enforcing the provision on misleading advertising. Large AMPs were paid in the following cases and even a jail sentence in one case.

Example: The largest AMP ever agreed to, the maximum allowed $10 million, was paid by Bell Canada plus $100,000 for the Bureau's legal costs. In 2011 Bell agreed to settle with the Competition Bureau for allegations it had false or misleading ads between December 2007 and June 2011 for the prices for its services such as; home phones, internet, satellite television and wireless services. The Bureau had alleged that Bell's ads created "the general impression" that consumers need only pay the advertised prices plus taxes, government fees and optional fees. Bell had used its disclaimer in "fine print" to "hide" additional mandatory fees which made the actual price paid by customers higher, sometimes 15% greater. The Bureau asserted that the general impression conveyed by an ad as well as its literal meaning would be considered in these cases. The perspective of the average consumer is taken into account. Disclaimers can be used but they must be clear, conspicuous and noticeable and likely to be read by the intended audience, not buried in the ad so nobody would normally notice it. (Competition Bureau website June 28, 2011. http://www.competitionbureau.gc.ca/eic/site/cb-bc.nsf/eng/03388.html)

Example: Yellow Pages Marketing B.V. which operated internet directory websites and were in no way related to the well-known Yellow Pages Group, designed websites displaying features similar to the Yellow Pages Business Directories including the use of the words "Yellow Page".

Yellow Pages Marketing B.V. began sending unsolicited faxes to Canadians which contained the Yellow Pages Group's "walking fingers" logo and the words "Yellow Page". The faxes also contained, in fine print, a statement that by returning the faxes, the recipient would be bound by a new two-year contract.

A number of complaints were filed by Canadians. Most of the complainants believed that they were updating their listing not subscribing to a different service unrelated to the Yellow Pages Group and did not understand the fine print.

After a contested hearing, the court found that the faxes were misleading and the fine print did not prevent the false impression that the customers were dealing with the well-known Yellow Pages Group. Yellow Pages B.V. and related corporations were fined $8 million jointly and its two directing minds were fined $500,000 each. (*The Commissioner of Competition v Yellow Page Marketing BV*, 2012 ONSC 927)

Example: In July 2009 Bernard Fromstein, the founder and former president of DataCom Marketing Inc. pled guilty to five criminal charges of deceptive telemarketing operation. He was sentenced to two years in jail for his involvement in a fraudulent telemarketing scheme that generated about $158 million over a 10 year period. DataCom would call businesses and imply that the business had already purchased a listing in the DataCom business directory and it was just updating information. DataCom then would send them a directory later and bill them for it. This is one of the few cases where jail sentences have been given to offenders.

Business Alert Internet Scams

Low initial cost means that the Internet is fertile ground for the scam artist. For the cost of a computer, a modem, and a small monthly fee to an Internet access provider, the scam artist can set up shop and begin taking orders from all quarters of the globe. Scammers promote their fraud through spam. Even if they only get a handful of replies from the millions of emails they send out, it is still worth their while. Be wary of replying, even just to "unsubscribe", because that will give a scammer confirmation that they have reached a real email address. Canada's anti-spam law that took effect on July 1, 2014 tries to regulate some of this behaviour (see Chapter 14).

Canadian authorities can only prosecute an offender who is, or who has assets, in Canada. Extradition is not a realistic possibility for most Internet scams.

Business Law Applied

⑰ Alfred Mungovan purchased a new television set and VCR at Excellent Electronics Inc., after seeing a newspaper advertisement that stated: "No payments or interest for 6 months."

At the end of the six months, Mungovan received a statement from Excellent Electronics Inc., which included an amount for interest calculated over that time. Super Electronics claimed that its advertisement was valid because Mungovan did not have to pay the interest until the six-month period was over. Mungovan claimed he thought the advertisement meant that his purchase was interest-free for six months, and that interest would begin to be charged after that time only if he did not pay the outstanding amount in full.

a) What is the representation? What are the possible interpretations?
b) When there are two or more possible interpretations of an advertisement, how will the court decide which interpretation will govern?
c) Whose interpretation will likely be accepted by the court in this case: the business's or the customer's?

⑱ A poster said: "Great Rates" $199 to Europe, some even lower call 1-900-555-5555; $10 per call."

When they phoned the number given, callers received a list of flights, destinations, and rates. They were also advised that for each flight, varying amounts were added on for tax, landing, and airport charges. The final cost of every flight added up to the standard rates obtainable at any travel agency.

a) What was the representation? What impression did it give?
b) What is the test to be used in deciding if the advertisement is misleading to the reader?

Deceptive Marketing Representations

In addition to the interpretation of an ad as it stands alone, the Act specifies certain practices that may deceive the consumer as to the true price:

- Ads that compare prices to imply a bargain, such as "$52.50. Compare at $60. (s.74.01(2), (3))
- Ads that claim superior performance to a competitor's product must be supported by adequate testing: "Fewer dropped calls than any other cell phone network" (s.74.01(1)(b))
- Double ticketing where there are two or more sticker prices on a product. (s.54)
- Bait and Switch selling where customers are lured to a sale but there is an inadequate supply and the seller then encourages you to buy a higher priced substitute (s.74.04)
- Sale above advertised price (s.74.05)

Scanner Pricing. The Double Ticketing section (a criminal offence but included here for clarity), was written long before the use of computers and scanners. The Bureau has a Scanner Price Accuracy Voluntary Code that companies can voluntarily choose to adopt. If a business adopts this policy and a good is scanned at a price higher than the displayed price, the consumer gets the good for free if it is less than $10. If it priced at more than $10 then $10 is reduced from actual the price. This is a voluntary code and companies do not have to adopt this policy. Most major retailers in Canada however have adopted this policy.

Comparing Prices to Imply a Bargain (s.74.01(2), (3))   One of the oldest marketing tricks is to take an item that would sell for, say, $10, mark the price tag at $15, and then mark the price as 'reduced' to $12. This basic deception, along with sophisticated variations, continues to be used by even the largest retailers. The problem is made more complex in relation to "house brands," for which there is no comparative external market. Retailers have been accused, for example, of putting one mattress bearing a house-brand name in stock at $700 for three months, and then announcing a sale of the mattress at $500. At this time several hundred mattresses are ordered and put into stock for the sale period. Can this retailer claim that the mattress's regular price was $700 on the basis of display for only a few months at this price and only one was available for sale? There are tests to determine the regular price.

Determining the Regular Price   Regular price can be established by comparison to the general market in the same area by market research surveys; or it can be the original price at which this particular store has sold the product. The Act contains two tests to determine a product's regular or ordinary price. One test is in relation to prior sales by the business itself, and the other is in relation to the market. A MSRP (Manufacturer's Suggested Retail Price) is not proof of a regular price.

Where the business making the reduced-price claims has sold the item, a reasonable quantity of that item must have been sold at a reasonable volume at that price by the business for a reasonable time. Except for seasonal products, that reasonable time will likely be at least six months.

The reasonableness of the volume may be determined by market data as to the normal sales of such items. Referring again to the mattress example above, if the business usually had about 20 mattresses for each model in stock over the previous few years and had an average of 20 mattresses of the type in question priced at $700 for a six-month period, then that business could establish that its regular price was $700 for this particular mattress for the purposes of the *Competition Act*.

If the business did not sell the item prior to the reduced-price claim, then the comparison would be to the normal market for the regular price. If, for example, all the drugstores in the city sell a similar size of Crest toothpaste for $1, one store cannot advertise the item as "Regular $1.25. Our Price $0.75." Where there is a range of regular prices, any of the prices would qualify as the comparative price.

There are many well-known cases of falsely inflated original selling prices so that sales appear to be a much greater discount than they truly are.

In 2004 the Forzani Group which operates Sports Chek and Sports Mart stores across Canada agreed with the Competition Bureau to pay an AMP of $1.2 million plus $500,000 in the Bureau's legal fees for misleading representations. It had inflated the ordinary selling price of some of its products to make its sale prices appear to be big reductions.

In 1995 Suzy Shier pleaded guilty and paid a fine of $300,000 for having false original prices on the sales tags of their clothes and then indicating the products were on sale for up to 50-70% off. The retailer had never sold the clothes at the original selling price on the tags.

In *Go Travel Direct.Com Inc. v. Maritime Travel Inc.*, 2009 NSCA 42 (CanLII) the court found that some of Go Travel's ads which compared its prices to Maritime Travel were fair, but others however were not based on representative samples and were misleading. Go Travel was liable for $216,000 in damages.

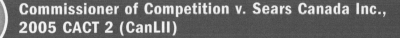

Commissioner of Competition v. Sears Canada Inc., 2005 CACT 2 (CanLII)

The Competition Commissioner alleged that during three sales events in November and December 1999, Sears employed deceptive marketing practices in connection with the stated original selling prices of five brands of all-season tires that it had on sale. The Commissioner alleged this was a violation of subsection 74.01(3) of the Competition Act.

The ads stated "Save 45% Our lowest prices of the year" and the ads compared Sears' regular prices and its sale prices. The Commissioner asserted that the regular prices it listed were inflated because Sears had not sold a substantial volume of these tires at the regular price within a reasonable period of time before making these representations and Sears had not offered these tires in good faith at the regular price for a substantial period of time before making the ads.

The Commissioner introduced evidence that of the 5 brands of tires on sale, Sears had never sold more than 2.9% of those brands at that regular stated price over the previous 12 months. Sears had not met the volume or time period requirements for using this as its regular price.

Sears maintained that subsection 74.01(3) of the Competition Act was a violation of its right to freedom of speech under the *Charter of Rights and Freedoms* and was therefore invalid.

The Court's Decision

The Competition Tribunal agreed that this section of the Competition Act was a violation of Sears' freedom of speech rights under *The Charter*. However using section 1 of *The Charter* this section of the Competition Act was a justified infringement of the retailer's rights.

Sears could not possibly believe that the only regular price quoted in the advertisement was an authentic price offered in good faith. The Tribunal ordered Sears to pay $500,000 and it could not make false ordinary selling price representations with respect to tires for 10 more years. It did not require a corrective notice to be issued as too much time had passed since the sale had occurred (almost 6 years). The Commissioner had wanted the 10 year prohibition to apply to all products Sears sold, not just tires, but it was not successful.

■ *Critical Concepts of* Comparative Pricing (s.74.01(2), (3))

- ■ The comparison price must be a true regular price
- ■ One test for regular price is that the product is actually sold at the comparison price on the market for a substantial time period. This can be established by market survey
- ■ If a business claims that the regular price is one that it has sold as its own house brand, a reasonable amount of the product must have been sold at that price for a reasonable time before the price-reduction claim is put on the sticker

---

■ *Business Law* Applied

⑱ **Smart Drug Mart Inc.** introduced what was to it a new size of a particular product—a 365-ml can of hairspray. The item was displayed in the store with a ticket reading: "Special $1.49."

The company was charged with misleading advertising. The Competition Bureau claimed the market evidence was that all other stores in the area were selling the same new product at prices ranging from 99 cents to $1.49. Nowhere was it sold for more than $1.49. Smart Drug claimed that it based its pricing by multiplying the unit value of smaller bottles of the same product to the increased size. (Simplification: small size 10 oz. at $1.00 = $1/oz.; new size 15 oz. justified at $1.50.)

a) Did Smart Drug Mart Inc. violate the misleading advertising provisions of the Act?
b) The supplier gave an MSRP that was also based on the same formula of multiplying the small size unit value by the volume of the new size. Would that be a defence?

Comparative Tests

Test results used in advertisements must be valid over a comprehensive range of normal conditions of use to justify a claim of superior performance. A representation that affirms a furnace saves energy over other brands supported by a test in southern Ontario would not be sufficient for a national advertising campaign. Also, the test methodology must adhere to scientific standards including, where appropriate, the use of control groups.

Example: Rogers Cable Company formed a subsidiary Chartr Wireless to compete against new entrance WIND Mobile, Mobilicity and others. Chartr launched an advertising campaign claiming "fewer dropped calls then new wireless carriers." Roger's test to support this claim was done in Toronto only but the advertisement was shown in other regions of Canada. The court found the test to be inadequate and fined Rogers an AMP of $500,000. (*Canada (Commissioner of Competition) v. Chatr Wireless Inc.*, 2014 ONSC 1146 (CanLII)

Bait and Switch Selling. Offering a well-known product at a very low price can be very effective at bringing business to a store or website. The product may be a 'loss leader' offered at cost or below cost in the belief that the customers who are drawn by the low price will purchase other items. Some businesses however only have a small quantity of this item on hand. When the item runs out, they tell the customers it was first come first served and encourage them to purchase another higher priced product they have in stock. However the Act requires that when a product is advertised at a bargain price, the business must have a reasonable quantity, if it does not, it is a violation. If however the business can establish that the non-availability of the product was due to circumstances beyond its control, or the quantity obtained was reasonable or the customer was offered a rain check (the right to purchase it later at the sale price), then the company has not violated the Act.

Civil Reviewable Practices

Abuse of Dominant Position

Dominance of a market by a company is not targeted by the Act, as that position may be a result of superior business practices. However, once a business dominates a market, it may resort to anticompetitive practices to keep or improve that supremacy. It is these anticompetitive actions that become offences if they reduce or prevent competition. Some of the practices that can result from abuse of a dominance may include; price maintenance, predatory pricing, exclusive dealing, tied selling, market restrictions and refusal to deal. The Bureau can also review any new practices that may be developed by a dominant company that hinder competition.

Price Maintenance

A manufacturer can suggest a retail price (MSRP). If the retailer is free to sell at another price, the MSRP does not affect the product's price in the marketplace. However, if the manufacturer tells the retailer that it must only sell at that price or the manufacturer will not continue to supply any further product, that would be the offence of price maintenance.

A controversial case involved the rules Visa and MasterCard impose on merchants when customers use premium credit cards and its effect on competition. In the U. S. Visa and MasterCard agreed to settle a similar case by paying $7.25 billion.

The Commissioner of Competition v. Visa Canada Corporation and MasterCard International Incorporated, 2013 CACT 10 (CanLII)

Canadian credit card payments are about $240 billion per year and annual fees paid to the credit card companies are about $5 billion, of which 90% involve Visa and MasterCard cards distributed by Canadian banks. Whenever a customer buys something using a credit card, the merchant must pay a transaction fee, typically a $1.50 to $3.00 per $100. Visa and MasterCard charge merchants higher fees when customers use their premium cards. Premium cards have extra benefits for cardholders such as travel points or cash back allowances.

The two credit card companies prohibit merchants from charging customers extra for using these higher fee cards. Merchants also cannot refuse to accept these premium cards and they cannot encourage customers to use lower cost forms of payment such as cash or debit cards.

These practices alleged the Commissioner of Competition negatively affect competition and penalize purchasers who use cash. Without changes to Visa and MasterCard's rules, merchants will continue to pay excessively high premium card acceptance fees, and these fees will continue to be passed along to consumers in the form of higher prices for goods and services.

Retailers, especially small businesses, want the rules changed. Consumer groups however like the privileges and bonuses these premium cards provide and don't want changes.

The Commissioner of Competition claimed the practices of Visa and MasterCard were a violation of Section 76 and sought an order that would have allowed merchants to refuse, discourage or impose surcharges on the use of premium cards that impose higher fees on sellers.

The Court's Decision

The Competition Tribunal ruled that section 76 of the *Competition Act*, the price maintenance provision, requires a resale and that the Commissioner had not established that Visa and MasterCard customers resell their products. The Tribunal further held that the Commissioner's proposed interpretation of section 76 was not supported by the legislative history of the provision or other decisions.

It stated that the proper solution to the concerns raised by the Commissioner is a regulatory framework, so the government can pass legislation to deal with this situation as has been done in several other countries. The case against Visa and MasterCard was dismissed.

Predatory Pricing   One example of abuse of dominant position can involve predatory pricing. This involves offering a product at a loss—selling it below cost—for a short time in order to drive competition out of the market. The dominant business will offer the product at a price it could not offer in the long run and survive. When the competitor is put out of business, the price goes back up to its usual, higher level. Independent suppliers of gasoline, often called "discounters," frequently complain that if they lower their prices below a certain level, then the nearby gas stations of the major brands lower their prices below cost until the discounter raises its price to an amount acceptable to them. This is a process called "disciplining the discounter." However, there have been no successful prosecutions for such alleged activity. If it could be proved that prices were lowered to force competitors to keep prices high, that would be predatory pricing. Short-term aggressive pricing for real competitive purposes, such as a price war, is not prohibited.

Example: Diazepam is the generic name of a very common tranquilizer, marketed by Hoffman-LaRoche under the brand name Valium. Hoffman- LaRoche (H-L) had 95% of the diazepam sales to hospitals. A competitor wanted to enter the market selling its pill Vival. Hoffman-LaRoche then provided Valium free to hospitals for six months costing the company $2.6 million. Hoffman-LaRoche tried to argue it was a marketing strategy to get patients to use the drug in the hospital so they would request it from their doctor later. The Bureau did not accept this explanation and found that H-L was guilty of predatory pricing in an attempt to drive competition out of the market and it was fined $50,000. (*R. v. Hoffman-LaRoche Ltd.* (Nos. 1 and 2), 1981 CanLII 1690 (ON CA))

Offences Relating to the Distribution of Goods

Companies are usually entitled to choose what customers they will deal with and on what terms, but if a supplier has a monopoly or is in a dominant position, certain behaviours that limit access to products may result in an offence under the Act if it is found that it lessens competition. Reviewable practices in this area include the following:

Exclusive Dealing occurs when a supplier of goods will only sell to a buyer if they purchase exclusively or primarily from them and not purchase other suppliers products.

NutraSweet sold aspartame which accounted for 95% of the artificial sweetener market in Canada. NutraSweet required its purchasers to buy exclusively from them. If their purchasers displayed the NutraSweet trademark on their products they were given discounts of up to 40% off the purchase price. The Tribunal ruled that NutraSweet's was in a dominant position and its conduct did result in substantial lessening of competition. It prohibited NutraSweet from requiring its purchasers to use only their products and it had to stop its financial inducements related to its trademark and advertising allowances. (*Director of Investigation and Research v. The NutraSweet Company* (1990), 32 CPR (3d) 1(Comp.Trib.)

Tied Selling occurs when a supplier ties the supply of one product to the purchase of another product. Microsoft bundles its Windows operating system with its Internet browser and its media player, and this has significantly limited the sales of other software. Microsoft has been challenged in various courts throughout the world and has received fines of over $2 billion for this practice. In the EU Microsoft was ordered to separate the products and share codes that will allow other companies' software access to their systems

In Canada the Canadian Gamers Organization (CGO) laid a complaint of tied selling for the pact between Microsoft (which makes Xbox) and Activision. There was access to extra downloadable content in the Call of Duty game on Xbox that was not available to PS3 users. The Bureau agreed this was tied selling, but when it investigated it found that there was no negative impact on competition so there was no violation of the Act. The sales of PS3 and Xbox were almost identical and people were not purchasing Xbox just to obtain the extra Call of Duty content.

Market Restriction occurs when a supplier restricts who its customers can resell the products to or a restricted geographic area in which they can resell the products

Refusal to Deal occurs when a business refuses to sell goods to a purchaser even though it is willing to meet the terms of other purchasers and this decision has an adverse effect on competition in the market.

Mergers

A separate section of the Act, Part IX, entitled *Notifiable Transactions* requires businesses involved in any proposed large mergers or acquisitions to notify the Bureau. Failure to notify is a criminal offense. The procedure for calculating the value of the transaction is set out on the Bureau website. For example, one factor is combined revenues exceeding $400 million per year. The Bureau may refuse permission to merge or put conditions on its approval.

The Bureau can review proposed mergers and determine if it will substantially lessen or prevent competition. It can also examine potential specific offences of abuse of dominant position, such as price maintenance, that could occur as a result of the merger.

Example: By a proposed $12.4-billion transaction Loblaw, Canada's largest grocery chain, would acquire Shoppers Drug Mart, Canada's largest drugstore chain. The combined retailer would operate approximately 2,738 stores and 1,824 pharmacies across the country.

The Bureau reviewed the proposed transaction and imposed some requirements to protect competition. One regarded price maintenance. Loblaw agreed to exclude sales from Shoppers from an agreement, which Loblaw had with suppliers, that if a competitor advertised a sale price lower than the price Loblaw sold the item, the supplier would compensate Loblaw for the difference (Announcement, Competition Bureau, March 21, 2014).

The Bureau also directed that Shoppers must sell 27 locations to independent operators as part of the approval of the merger.

Privacy

Canada's need for privacy has been dramatized in newscasts of employers opening employee e-mails, Internet service providers withholding e-mails to force payment of accounts, and biometric face scanning at the Super Bowl and at airports.

What if a principal of a company, which has a demand loan with a bank, takes a medical for his insurance company and the medical shows he has developed a serious heart problem? The next day, although his financial statements are favourable and the loan is in good standing, the bank manager calls him at the office and demands an immediate payment of the loan. The bank manager does not have to justify calling the loan because it is a demand loan, and does not tell the business person why. However, the bank and the insurance company share data as marketing partners.

The use of computers and the Internet has made it increasingly easy for businesses to collect a wide range of data about every person in Canada. Some businesses specialize in doing just that. Advertising firms also employ technologies to track users' activities over time through cookies to build profiles used to deliver targeted advertisements. The goal is to deliver relevant and effective advertising to users. These firms can employ a network of computers tracking a user's behaviour across multiple websites to create the profiles such as: Canadian sports enthusiasts who purchase 20 tickets or more to sporting events per year.

These advances in technology permit businesses to collect data with the consumer's knowledge and often without. Businesses frequently use their websites to collect information about customers. Every time a form is filled out, the information is preserved in a database.

"We put all new employees on probation."

Information can also be gathered without the visitor's knowledge. As one example, "cookies" are small computer files placed on the user's hard drive without the user's knowledge or permission (though you can also set your browser to notify you before any cookie is added to your hard drive). They can display advertising such as banner ads personalized for that user's preferences as determined by information collected about that purchaser from many sources, including tracking which website that purchaser visits and with what frequency. This explains why when one user goes to a website, the banner ad displays the latest about upcoming wrestling matches and when another user goes to the same website, the banner ad on that user's computer promotes the latest Harlequin romance novel.

To address these privacy concerns the federal government has enacted the *Personal Information Protection and Electronic Documents Act* (PIPEDA). It was enacted in three phases to allow provinces to enact their own similar legislation, which will displace the federal legislation for matters under provincial jurisdiction. However, if a province has not enacted similar legislation, the federal legislation will govern for that province.

Scope

PIPEDA was drafted to apply to all forms and types of personal information collected, with very limited exceptions, such as a business title, address, phone number, and information that is already public, for example, in a listing in a telephone directory.

Obligations

Two core principles of PIPEDA are knowledge and consent. A consumer must be given full knowledge of the intended use of the information and the opportunity to consent or refuse the disclosure. That consent, however, can be expressed or implied.

Expressed consent is needed for health and financial information; but implied consent will suffice for other information. For example, a business might send a letter to its current customers saying that it would like to provide their names and addresses to another marketing firm after a specified date unless the customer informs the business of an objection.

The disclosure notice must be in clear, simple language so that the consumer can understand the purpose for which the information will be used. A good practice for a website is to have a disclosure notice with a check box or "click through" to obtain the consent of the individual or to permit that person to refuse to have the information used for any named purposes or at all.

There is no "grandfathering," that is, a business cannot use personal information already in its possession without a new consent.

Individuals can withdraw their consents, and so a business will have to keep accurate records that can be updated to delete names of people whose consents are withdrawn.

Example: In *Chitrakar v. Bell TV*, 2013 FC 1103 (CanLII), Bell Canada was found to have violated PIPEDA by doing an unauthorized credit check on a customer who had ordered satellite television service. Bell was very uncooperative in response to Chitrakar's complaint over the credit check, so the court awarded Chitrakar $10,000 in damages plus an additional $10,000 in punitive damages to punish this very profitable company for its intentional violation of his privacy rights.

Example: In *Nammo v. TransUnion of Canada Inc.*, 2010 FC 1284 (CanLII) a credit reporting agency was required to pay $5,000 when it provided wrong information about a customer who had applied for a loan at the Royal Bank. When Nammo was rejected for the loan he inquired and discovered that the credit agency had supplied another person's name, birthdate, social insurance number and address. The court held that the credit agency had not kept as accurate, complete and up-to-date database as was necessary for its business purposes.

Social Networking Sites

Social networking sites have become immensely popular boasting millions of users worldwide. They often have lengthy online membership agreements that contain consents to the use of private information without restriction, perhaps even the resale of it for profit.

Canadian users should be aware that the U.S. does not at the time of the publication of this text have privacy law as does Canada and many European countries. The U.S. has federal and state privacy acts which apply only to government agencies. The regulation of the use of private information is in the control of the individual website operators and depends on both their policy and terms of service.

Users upload a significant amount of confidential personal information including birth dates, phone numbers, race, religion, sexual orientation, daily schedules, etc. While it may be made accessible only to authorized persons, hackers may be able to view it.

The concern is that this information can be used by:

- criminals for identity theft
- employers for background checks
- employers for finding cause for dismissal
- government agencies
- insurance company defendants in law suits for personal injury

The concerns about privacy have been turned into a warning slogan by privacy advocates: Does what happens on Facebook stay on Facebook?

Facebook, for example, warns users that it will collect information about them from other sources. Privacy advocates warn that if you put anything on a networking website you should consider that you are publishing it just as if you published it in a magazine.

To use Facebook again as an example, its licence states:

> "By posting User Content to any part of the Site, you automatically grant, and you represent and warrant that you have the right to grant, to the Company an irrevocable, perpetual, non-exclusive, transferable, fully paid, worldwide license (with the right to sublicense) to use, copy, publicly perform, publicly display, reformat, translate, excerpt (in whole or in part) and distribute such User Content for any purpose on or in connection with the Site or the promotion thereof, to prepare derivative works of, or incorporate into other works, such User Content, and to grant and authorize sublicenses of the foregoing."

Again to take an example from Facebook it warns that privacy is not guaranteed:

> "We cannot and do not guarantee that User Content you post on the Site will not be viewed by unauthorized persons. We are not responsible for circumvention of any privacy settings or security measures contained on the Site."

Use of Facebook information against the interest of the users continues to surface. A court ordered a Plaintiff claiming as a result of injuries in a car accident that he suffered loss of enjoyment of life. He was ordered to disclose his Facebook postings to the defendant. (*Leduc v. Roman*, 2009 CanLII 6838 [ON S.C.])

Anti-Spam Legislation

The federal government passed Canada's Anti-Spam Legislation (CASL) and it came into effect on July 1, 2014. This law will close some loopholes and more clearly include businesses that improperly access a private computer under one of the many exemptions to collect electronic data used in marketing and then uses that for spam (junk email) purposes.

Opt-Out Consent

An opt-out consent is one in which customers must indicate to a business that they do not wish their information to be collected, used, or disclosed by other business. If the customer fails to check that box, the business then infers consent for the proposed use of the information.

The federal Privacy Commissioner has indicated that he has a very low opinion of opt-out consent, which he considers, at best, token observance of privacy protection.

In one finding the commissioner notified Canada Post that it violated the *Privacy Act* by selling new home addresses of Canadians using Canada Post mail-redirection services to business mailers. The commissioner found that Canada Post's opt-out feature did not make it clear that Canada Post was going to sell the information on the change of address card to brokers, mass mailers, or direct marketers. He also found that it would not be reasonable to expect that a person signing a notification of change of address form would be giving consent for the disclosure of personal information to these entities.[3]

Exemptions

The act uses a number of exemptions, most of which will not be of use to businesses. These exemptions include information gathered for academic research, journalism, and the like. However, information collected for debt collection is exempt.

Administrative Obligations

The act imposes a number of administrative obligations on an organization that collects personal information, so as to make that organization responsible for that information. These businesses must:

- retain the personal information only as long as required for the purpose identified at the time of collection
- put security safeguards in place to protect that information from loss, unauthorized use, hacking, etc.
- provide accurate information and allow access and the right to amend incorrect information

Enforcement

The commissioner responsible for PIPEDA will be the Privacy Commissioner under the *Privacy Act* (Canada). Complaints can be made to the commissioner, who has the power to review the organization's information-management practices and assess penalties for breach of the act, including making the businesses' personal-information practices public, and levying fines from $10,000 to $100,000, for which directors, officers, or employees may also be personally liable. The commissioner may also order the business to correct its practices and pay damages to the complainant, including damages for humiliation.

Employee Privacy

The definition of personal information includes data collected by employers regarding employees from all sources: employment applications, health claims, and performance reviews, to name a few.

---

3. Privacy Commissioner Decision, January 14, 2002, *Lawyers Weekly*, June 14, 2002.

Because the equipment belongs to the employers, they can probably monitor e-mail to see if employees are sending personal e-mails at work. Employers will want to have clearly worded policies about personal use of e-mail, or whether a personal use is permitted at all. Employers will need employee consent to review the content of e-mails: they will likely require that consent as a condition of employment.

The employer's interest is that e-mail contains "click stream data" which identifies its source. If the employee e-mail contains defamation, pornography, or an infringement of intellectual-property rights, the employer may be affected.

Breaches of Privacy

Personal data is of great value to marketing and advertising firms. Hackers often target businesses. An alarming occurrence of a data breach occurred in the U.S. with Heartland Payment Systems. This Company processes payments for major credit card companies. Hackers used keyboard loggers and then "sniffers". Sniffers are simple pieces of malwar that collect information as it passes across a network. As of this date there is no legislation requiring businesses to notify customers of breaches of data. There are proposals for legislation. There are voluntary disclosure guides issued by various privacy commissioners in Canada, both federal and provincial, available on their websites.

Consumer Data Collection

There are 2 types of consumer behavior data collection:

- **Contextual Advertising**, which is based on the contents of a single search. If a user searched "sports equipment" on Google, Google could use that subject to send banner ads to the user regarding sports products. This is not considered a violation of PIPEDA.
- **Online Behavioral Advertising**, which involves tracking user interests across websites. This is considered a violation of PIPEDA.

Example: Google published a policy statement affirming that it would not collect or use any information based on health. A user, who searched for a sleep apnea product, was targeted with banner ads relating to health products and complained to the Privacy Commissioner of Canada.

Google claimed it only used Contextual Advertising. However, the investigation revealed Google used Online Behavioral Advertising tracking and included health information contrary to its policy statement. (*Report of Findings*, Office of the Privacy Commissioner of Canada, January 15, 2013).

Problems with the Legislation

The effectiveness of PIPEDA at protecting personal information has frequently been questioned. The law lacks strong enforcement powers, and other than in the Alberta law, there is no mandatory reporting of breaches required. Since reporting a breach could cause an organization bad publicity, many companies just cover up their violations. If organizations were required to disclose their violations, this could strengthen the law. Organizations can also voluntarily share personal information with police authorities without the consent or knowledge of the individual. There is little in the law to hold organizations accountable for their activities in this area. Law reforms have been considered, but as yet have not been passed.

In Summation

Bailment

- Bailment leaves ownership of an item with its owner (the bailor) while possession is passed to another person (the bailee) for various reasons, such as repair or storage.

- Bailment for hire or reward is usually for a business purpose and places a duty on the custodian to care for the object with the skill of a careful and prudent person in that particular business. If damage occurs to the item during the bailment, the onus is on the custodian to prove there was no negligence.

- Exemption clauses are often used by custodians in an attempt to limit liability for loss or damage to the goods they hold. To be effective, these must be drawn to the attention of the owner and expressly cover the way in which loss or damage occurred. These will also not be effective in the case of a fundamental breach of contract.

- Certain businesses involving bailment are subject to terms and exemption clauses imposed by legislation. In such circumstances as a consumer transaction and complicated standard form contracts, the exemption clause may be unenforceable.

- A custodian can retain an item until paid and is entitled to a lien under which the item may be seized and sold. Funds received from the sale may be applied against the outstanding account.

- In some circumstances, provincial statutes have created a right to sell the item upon which work has been done, even if possession has been given up. This is possible if there is a written acknowledgment of debt for services related to the item.

Sale of Goods Act

- The terms of a contract fall within two categories. Conditions are terms essential to the actual performance of the contract, while warranties are terms of a minor nature which, if not met, allow a claim for damages but not cancellation of the contract.

- A contract for the sale of goods contains certain terms that are automatically included, even if the parties do not mention them, because of the operation of the *Sale of Goods Act*.

- The *Sale of Goods Act* details several conditions and warranties that are to be considered present as an implied part of the contract. These include terms concerning fitness for use, merchantable quality, and correspondence of the goods delivered to their description in the contract.

- The *Sale of Goods Act* details when the ownership of goods changes hands, unless the parties agree otherwise. Generally, the owner of goods bears the risk of loss or damage to them.

- There are special protections for an unpaid vendor, which are set out in the *Sale of Goods Act*.

Consumer Protection Legislation

- Consumer protection is a specific area of law aimed at the sale of goods to an individual for personal use. Conditions and warranties are implied as part of the consumer transaction, but exemption clauses attempting to exclude these implied terms are not enforceable under consumer protection legislation.

- Various requirements and protections relate to cancellation rights, written estimates, full disclosure of credit and costs, cooling-off periods and unfair business practices

Competition Act

- There are two agencies created under the Act: the Competition Bureau, which investigates; and the Competition Tribunal, which tries cases.

- Anti-competitive practices can be considered as either criminal matters or civil reviewable matters and some can be dual track matters

- Penalties under the criminal provisions can include fines of up to $25 million and or imprisonment for up to 14 years and court orders such as prohibition orders

- Penalties under the civil reviewable matters are administrative monetary penalties (AMP) which are like a civil fine and can be up to $10 million and also restitution orders to compensate consumers and other court orders

- False or misleading advertising is a common offence and can include deceptive sale prices, misleading contest promotions, bait and switch

- Civil reviewable practices related to abuse of a dominant position can include price maintenance, predatory pricing, exclusive dealing, tied selling, market restriction and refusal to deal

- Mergers are reviewable by the Competition Bureau and it can impose conditions or prevent a merger

Privacy

- Privacy legislation balances the need to protect individual privacy with the desire of businesses to collect personal data.

- Privacy legislation is based on:
  a) informed consent: businesses must clearly indicate how the information will be used, and stick to that use only
  b) consent: businesses must obtain consent to collect, use, or disclose personal data
  c) access: individuals must have access to their personal data and be permitted to correct or withdraw consent
  d) accountability: individuals can complain to the privacy commissioner, who can apply a variety of remedies against an offending business

Closing Questions

Bailment

1. Gobindhar Arbib stored some household furniture with Safe-Store Inc. When Arbib picked up the furniture, some of it had mould and watermarks on it, indicating a flood. The business denies any flood. Arbib wants to sue the storage company, but is concerned that he doesn't have any way to prove how the damage occurred.
   a) Is there any rule in the law of bailment that will assist Arbib?

2. A bailor is:
   a) the possessor of the item bailed
   b) the owner of the item bailed
   c) the cup used to remove water from a boat
   d) the person who seizes goods for payment of judgments

3. A bailment for hire:
   a) involves payment for the services rendered
   b) is a gratuitous bailment
   c) is the opposite of bailment for reward
   d) is the remedy provided by the court when a party does not pay for the services rendered

4. Wanda owned a rare and expensive painting by a well-known artist. It was her pride and joy. When she decided to leave on an extended one-year vacation overseas, Wanda sublet her apartment and arranged to leave her oil painting with her friend Fred, who, because he operated an art galley, would know how to properly take care of it. In return, Fred could enjoy having the painting on his wall for a year.

Several months later, Fred decided to hold an exhibit of oil paintings. Wanda's painting was to be the featured attraction and Fred advertised far and wide. Unfortunately, the exhibit also caught the eye of Skylight Sam, who dropped in one night after the show was closed and took Wanda's painting for his private viewing pleasure.

When Wanda wandered back home and asked Fred for her painting, all he could give her was the picture from the newspaper that had accompanied the report on the theft.

a) Describe the nature of the relationship outlined in this situation and, using legal terms, define the various parties to the relationship.

b) Explain, with reasons, whether this relationship was based on friendship or for value.

c) If Fred has no money, what other source of funds might Wanda look to, assuming she has established the right to recover the value of the painting from Fred?

5. Cathcart Services Limited sent a tender by Purolator Courier Limited. Cathcart clearly indicated on the bill of lading and told the Purolator employee who picked up the package that it was a tender that had to arrive on time. The bill of lading contained the terms limiting liability for loss or damage to $250.

The tender was not delivered. The tender was the lowest one and would have been accepted. If Cathcart had gotten the job it would have made a profit of $37,000. Cathcart wants to sue Purolator for its loss. Purolator says it has lost the records relating to this delivery.

a) Since Purolator cannot find its records regarding the delivery, will Cathcart be able to prove negligence by Purolator? What bailment rule will help?

a) Are there any grounds in contract law that would assist Cathcart in avoiding the limitation of liability to $250,000?

6. Ivan Firchuk put his home-entertainment system in for repair with Electronic Edge Repairs Inc. Electronic Edge did the repair work but, unfortunately, went into bankruptcy. The trustee in bankruptcy claims that the home-entertainment system is an asset of the business and is going to be sold to a liquidation company.

a) What is the legal term for the transaction whereby Firchuk gave the home-entertainment system to Electronic Edge?

b) Does the trustee in bankruptcy have the right to sell the home-entertainment system?

c) Does the trustee in bankruptcy have any rights over the home-entertainment system?

7. Alison Frizelli was attending a business luncheon at Chez Alphred, a trendy downtown restaurant. She pulled up to the entrance and noticed a sign which said "Please allow our parking attendant to assist you." She got out of her car . . .

a) and handed her keys to a well-dressed young man she assumed was the parking attendant. In fact, he had just been forcibly removed from Chez Alphred for disruptive behaviour. The real attendant was off parking another car. The ejected patron took Alison's car for a joyride and crashed into a ravine, causing several thousand dollars in damage.
  i) Can Alison use bailment to recover damages against Chez Alphred?
  ii) Can Alison use any other legal principles to recover damages from Chez Alphred?

b) and handed her keys to the Chez Alphred parking attendant. On the way to the parking garage, the attendant swerved to avoid hitting a young child who ran across the street. He consequently hit a light pole, causing several thousand dollars in damage to Alison's car.
  i) Can Alison use bailment to recover damages against Chez Alphred?

c) and handed her keys to the Chez Alphred parking attendant. As the attendant drove away, she noticed that the bottom of the sign said "We are not responsible for loss or damage to vehicles." While in the parking garage, Alison's car was vandalized by parties unknown, resulting in several thousand dollars in damage.
  i) Can Alison use bailment to recover damages against Chez Alphred?

Sale of Goods Act

8. Calla Lilli wanted to develop a landscape plan for her back yard. She decided to buy a computer program called Green Thumbs Up to help her do this. The promotional material on the box read: "... design the garden of your dreams—everything you need is right in this box!" Unfortunately

for Calla, the program was little more than a listing of plant names. Is the purchase of a computer program a purchase of a "good"?

9. a) Look at clause number 8 in the Used Car Bill of Sale located in the Appendix to Chapter 6. Why does the car dealership want that clause included? What *Sale of Goods Act* rule does it vary?

   b) Look at the Purchase Order reproduced in the Appendix in this chapter.

   i) Review paragraph 3. What is the meaning of the term *FOB*?

   ii) Assume a purchaser is located in Toronto. What is the probable difference in ultimate cost to this purchaser between two products of identical price, both of which are sent FOB port of departure? One supplier is in Taiwan and the other is in Montreal.

10. Meadowview College central supply placed a standing order for Inkblot brand dry-erase whiteboard markers from PaperClips Stationers. Until the year 2004, 1,000 boxes were to be delivered to Meadowview at the start of each term (that is, in September and January of each year). After the first month of use in the classroom, the janitorial staff reported difficulties cleaning the whiteboards and corrosion of whiteboard surfaces where the ink had been left on the boards for more than a day. When contacted about the problem, PaperClips said that whiteboard markers where meant to be erased within a reasonable time after use, and that they could offer no resolution to the problems Meadowview was experiencing.

   a) Does Meadowview have any claims pursuant to the *Sale of Goods Act*?

   b) If so, what remedies are available to Meadowview? Which would be preferable, and why?

11. Harold Mertma was a wood crafter who made furniture by special order. He worked in a workshop out behind his house. Alison Snodgrass had placed an order with Harold for an oak bookshelf/entertainment unit. She wanted specially crafted hollow shelving, so that the unit would not be exceptionally heavy. Alison lived in an older home, and had some concerns that the floor might not be able to bear the weight of a solid wood unit.

   When Harold finished the unit, he had Alison come over to the shop to inspect it. She was happy with the work. The next day, Harold delivered the unit to her house, and set it up. However, after two weeks, Alison noticed the floor sagging. She called a building inspector, who confirmed that the unit was at least 50% too heavy for her floor support, and that it would cost some $10,000 to repair the damage already done. Alison called Harold and told him to take the unit back, and to provide a cheque for the $10,000 it would cost her to fix the floor.

   a) Does Alison have any legal basis for the claim she is making against Harold?

   b) What arguments does Harold have to defend Alison's claim?

   c) Who would bear responsibility for the cost of the unit if Harold's workshop burned to the ground after Alison inspected the unit, but before Harold delivered it?

Retail Sales

12. a) Is a retailer under any legal obligation to take back, or exchange, clothing which is bought but does not fit?

   b) Does it make any difference if there is a sign posted by the cash register which reads "All goods satisfactory, or money refunded"?

13. Frank Flude bought a used car from Gorjeta Used Cars. At the time of the purchase Gorjeta offered Flude a one-year warranty through a warranty company for $1,000. Flude refused.

   Two days after delivery, the car had problems and these continued for three months. Gorjeta has refused to pay for the cost of the repairs, claiming that Flude had the opportunity to buy a warranty and refused, and so Gorjeta had no responsibility to pay for the repairs.

   a) Is Gorjeta correct?

Consumer Protection

14. Tina took her car in to Alliance Auto Services for an estimate on repairing the brakes in her car. Alliance gave her a written estimate of $1,000 so she agreed and told them to do the work. When she came to pick her car up the next day Alliance gave her a bill for $1,300. Tina questioned the

price increase and they told her the job took much longer than it had anticipated and there were some other problems they discovered once they started to work.
a) What legally will Tina have to pay?
b) What steps should Alliance have taken to avoid any complaints by Tina?

15. On April 1 John agreed to purchase a new boat from Stoney Cove Marina for $25,000. He paid a $10,000 deposit and was to finance the balance through a credit program Stoney Cove offered. The contract stated that the interest on the balance would be calculated at 2% per month. The contract also stated that a $100 luxury tax would be added to the total price. The boat was to be delivered on May 1.

On May 1 Stoney Cove told John that the boat was not ready, but it would keep him updated on the delivery date. As the summer progressed the boat was still not ready and John had to lease a boat from another marina. Finally on July 25 Stoney Cove called to say the boat was ready for pick-up. John was furious and does not want the boat.
a) Under the Consumer Protection Act what could entitle John to get out of the contract?
b) What other violations of the Consumer Protection Act occurred in this transaction?

16. Which of the following contracts would have a cooling off period in Ontario and if so, how long is the cooling off period?
a) purchase of a time share condominium at a ski resort for 1 week per year
b) purchase of new computer bought at a flea market
c) 2 year lease of a new gas water heater
d) purchase of cosmetics from a seller who came to your home to make the sale
e) a contract for 3 months of yoga lessons
f) purchase of a new house that has just been built
g) a contract for a $200,000 mortgage on a condominium
h) a $300 loan for a 2 week period from a pay day loan company

Competition Act

17. Regarding the *Richard v. Time Inc.* case:
a) What actual monetary loss did Richard suffer?
b) Why did the Supreme Court of Canada say that Richard's, or any individual consumer's, personal level of sophistication was irrelevant to the test of whether a consumer would be misled?
c) Why did the Supreme Court of Canada reduce the award from $1.2 million to $15,000?
d) Do you think that Richard should have gotten the punitive damages of $15,000?
e) There is a specific section in the Competition Act (s.53) prohibiting deceptive notices of winning prizes. Why do you think that Richard did not make a complaint to the Competition Bureau rather than suing himself? Do you think this choice of a personal action rather than a complaint to the Competition Bureau influenced the amount of the award given by the Supreme Court of Canada?

18. Super Buy wants to advertise, "We will not only match but beat any advertised price by 10%"
a) What provisions of the Competition Act would be relevant?
b) What factors would be examined to see if the advertisement would violate the Act? What conclusion do you think the Bureau with draw respecting this practice?
c) If the practice did violate the Act, what remedies would be available to the Bureau?

19. Smart Apps Ltd. and Best Apps Inc. are competitors. You are a vice president in Smart Apps. One day the president comes into your office and says, "We just got a prepublication price list from Best Apps. Send those guys one of our prepublication price lists. When you raise your eyebrows in response, the president says, "Don't worry, were not going to talk to them, just exchange price lists. Nothing more, absolutely. Were just going to make sure we don't undercut each other."
a) Is there any risk in your sending the price list over to Best Apps?

20. Arkady Ltd. was a record label that produced CDs for several bands. One group in particular—the Darlings, whose last CD was entitled *The Darlings Die Live*—was very popular, and sales had been steady. Unfortunately, the group had disbanded, and there would be no future recording sessions.

Jackson, the vice-president of sales and marketing, came up with a clever marketing plan to maximize the label's income from the group's popularity. An advertising campaign was started, stating that no further copies of the group's last CD would be available or would be manufactured after June 30. CD sales picked up appreciably, and the stock was cleared out. In the meantime, Jackson had already commenced planes to reissue the CD under the new title *The Darlings Remembered* in time for December sales.

a) What is the representation? Is it true?

b) Has an offence under the *Competition Act* occurred here? If so, which one?

c) What test that would be applied to determine if Arkady Ltd. has committed the offence?

Purchase Order

ATTAR CHEMICALS INC.
Purchase Order Terms

---

1. **INCLUSIONS/DISCOUNTS.** The price shall be fixed and shall include the cost of the Goods, storage, transport and installation. Invoices shall be paid within 30 days of receipt of the Goods. Periods established relative to discounts shall be calculated as of the date of receipt of the relevant invoices. However, if the invoice is received before the Goods, the starting point of the discount period shall be the date the Goods are received.

2. **PACKAGING/SHIPPING AND SHIPPING NOTICE.** All Goods must be properly packed in boxes or otherwise prepared for shipping, so as to prevent any damage during shipping, handling and storage. The Supplier shall be liable for any damage resulting from poor packing. All packing charges shall be paid by the Supplier. Immediately when the shipment of Goods is dispatched, a copy of the shipping notice, packing slip and bill of lading shall be forwarded by Supplier to Purchaser identifying the Goods to be shipped, the Purchase Order Number, carrier, carrier number and routing. Routing shall be by the most economical and expedient route. The Purchase Order number shall appear on all shipping documents, as well as on the packaging and the delivery order. The Purchaser reserves the right to return, at the Supplier's expense, all Goods that do not bear the required inscriptions.

3. **DELIVERY.** Delivery shall be FOB Port of Departure. Delivery shall be performed on the date and according to the delivery method provided for herein. If the Supplier fails to deliver the Goods by the date specified herein, the Purchaser may claim as liquidated damages the sum of 5%, of the total amount of the Purchase Order, for each business day the delivery is delayed, notwithstanding the causes of such delay. Both Purchaser and Supplier agree that 5% of the total amount of the Purchase Order for each business day delivery is delayed is a fair and reasonable estimate of the damages that Purchaser would suffer if the Goods are so delayed. The liquidated damages shall be payable by Supplier to Purchaser as of the first day of the delay without formal notice and at the simple request of the Purchaser, or, Purchaser may at its sole discretion hold back the said amount on the balance owing under this Purchase Order. The liquidated damages are payable in addition to any other recourse the Purchaser may have with regard to the Supplier.

4. **TITLE/INFRINGEMENT.** The Supplier warrants that the delivered Goods are free and clear from all encumbrances and liens and that all Goods shall be free of any claim, whether rightful or otherwise, of any person by way of infringement of any patent, copyright, trademark or industrial design or the like, and shall indemnify, hold harmless and defend Purchaser from any and all such claims and legal proceedings arising thereon and from all expenses and costs resulting or claimed to have resulted from any and all such claims and legal proceedings.

5. **WARRANTY.** The Goods shall be of a merchantable quality and of the best grade of their respective kinds. Supplier warrants to Purchaser that the Goods shall be suitable for the service and performance intended and of the quality specified and shall conform to the specifications, drawings, or samples, and other descriptions contained under this Purchase Order. Supplier guarantees the Goods against any and all defects in workmanship and materials for a minimum of twenty-four months following acceptance of the Goods by Purchaser and if the Goods are to be operated on-site, for twenty-four months following the successful installation of the Goods.

Supplier agrees to repair or replace any and all defects in the Goods or the performance of the Goods in a good, workmanlike manner to the satisfaction of Purchaser and without cost to Purchaser, and such work relating to the

Goods shall commence no later than ten (10) days upon receipt of notice to this effect from Purchaser. The Goods are ordered by Purchaser in reliance of each and all of the warranties and guarantees specified in the Purchase Order and Performance Guarantee and implied by law or usage of trade, and unless otherwise expressly stated in the Purchase Order, these warranties and guarantees shall control. The Supplier acknowledges that the Purchaser has made known the purpose for which the Goods are being supplied and performed and that Purchaser relies upon the Supplier's skill or judgement such that the implied warranty of quality of fitness applies to the Goods.

6. **INSURANCE.** The Supplier undertakes to conform to the written directives of the Purchaser relative to the types of insurance policies required, where applicable.

7. **COMPLIANCE.** Supplier warrants that the Goods supplied hereunder shall have been produced, sold, delivered and furnished in strict compliance with all applicable laws, regulations, labour agreements, working conditions and technical codes or requirements to which the Goods are subject. Supplier shall executive and deliver such documents as may be required to effect or evidence compliance. Any and all laws and regulations required to be incorporated into agreements of this character are deemed incorporated by reference.

8. **TERMINATION OF AGREEMENT.** Either party may terminate this agreement when the other party breaches an obligation hereunder and fail to remedy such breach within 30 days of receipt of a written notice to that effect.

9. **NON-WAIVER.** Failure of the Purchaser to insist upon strict performance of any of the terms or conditions under the Purchase Order or failure or delay to exercise any rights or remedies provided hereunder shall not be deemed a waiver of any of Purchaser's rights under this Purchase Order.

10. **GOVERNING LAW.** The parties agree that this agreement shall be governed by the laws of Alberta. The parties further agree to submit to the courts of Alberta.

11. **CANCELLATION.** The Purchaser reserves the right to cancel this order or any part of it if the order is not delivered within a reasonable time period and upon such cancellation may procure substitute goods similar to those to which the order is cancelled, or complete the finished Goods by whatever method it chooses. Purchaser may then withhold further payments to Supplier and Supplier shall be liable for the difference between the cost of such substitute Goods or the cost of finishing such Goods and the price set forth in this Purchase Order for such Goods.

    In the event of rejection for any or all non-conforming Goods, the Purchaser may, at its sole option, grant additional time for Supplier to correct the non-conformance. Should Supplier fail to do so within such additional time, or should additional time not be granted, Purchaser may, at its option, either cancel the order as to the non-conforming Goods and retain the same rights with respect to substitute Goods as are set out in the preceding paragraphs and, in addition, recover the costs incurred by Purchaser in removing the non-conforming Goods and installing substitute Goods, or cause the non-conformity to be covered at the Supplier's expense.

12. **CHANGES.** Purchaser may, by written change order, make changes in, including additions to, or deletions from, the Goods. If any such changes affect the amount due or the time of performance under the Agreement, an equitable and reasonable adjustment shall be made.

13. **ENTIRE AGREEMENT.** The Purchase Order, including these Purchase Order terms and conditions, any Schedules attached hereto and any additional terms and conditions incorporated in writing and attached to the Purchase Order constitute the sole and the entire agreement between the parties. No other terms or conditions shall be binding upon the Purchaser unless accepted by it in writing. Supplier may not subcontract or assign all or any part of its obligation under the Purchase Order without Purchaser's prior written consent.

The Organization of a Business

Initial Considerations

Choosing a Name

A name is a valuable asset for a business, and choosing a creative name is often a difficult task. It is legally acceptable to use your own name, unless it has become widely associated with another business in the same industry. Doreen McDonald, for example, could not open a fast-food restaurant called McDonald's. She could, however, quite legally set up a clothing store with that name.

Once a name is found for the business, the next step is to make sure that its use will be legally permitted. There are several legal restrictions to consider. A business cannot use a name that is similar to one already in use or it could be liable for passing off or a trademark violation. It cannot use terms such as Limited, Ltd., Corp. or Inc. in the name unless it is an actual corporation.

Trade Names

Sometimes a business uses a name other than the one it first registers with the government. This is a **trade name**—a name used by a business, often in addition to the registered or incorporated name. *The Bay* is a trade name of the Hudson's Bay Company Canada, Ltd., and *Panasonic* is a trade name of Matsushita Electronic of Canada, Inc.

trade name
a name used by a business, often in addition to the registered or incorporated name

As will be discussed later in the chapter on Intellectual Property there are advantages to a trademark registration in that provincial registration. A provincial registration or an incorporation procedure may only check for, and prevent use of, similar names within the province, for example Ontario; while a trademark registration is enforced throughout Canada and may give a basis for enforcement in other countries.

Also, consideration should be given to registration with domain name agencies. These are private agencies and do not require any proof that the name sought for registration is free of conflict with the above noted government protections, even trade mark registration. So a business may find that even a name that has been registered as a trademark is being used by another person as a domain name.

Example: A woman in Alberta started a dessert business through a numbered corporation operating as "The Queen of Tarts." However a woman operating a pastry business in Ontario had registered the name as a trademark and successfully sued the Alberta corporation for infringement obtaining an order for damages and forcing it to the expense of changing the business name.

Business Alert!   Protection of Business Names   A business name can be protected by:

- Registration as a business name, sole proprietorship or partnership
- Incorporation
- Trademark
- Domain name registration

Numbered Companies   Since choosing the right name is sometimes a difficult and slow process, there is a procedure for incorporating a business without having to register a name at that time. When the incorporation is approved, the government simply assigns the next number in line to the new corporation, so that it becomes known as, for example, 76324 Canada Limited. The corporation's name could be changed later by a formal application to the government, but this would involve additional legal expense. Often, therefore, numbered companies simply use a trade name, and are described as "76324 Canada Limited, carrying on business as Confidential Management." The short forms, *COB* and *O/A*, are often used in place of *carrying on business* and *operating as*.

The Liabilities of a Business

- The source of potential claims against a business can be roughly divided into two categories, arising from contract and tort law.
- Contract—this includes money owed to suppliers, employees' wages, taxes, rent, and bank loans.
- Tort—such liability generally relates to members of the public. Some of the most common tort areas important to business are:
  a) occupier's liability (e.g., slip and fall)
  b) vicarious liability (e.g., injury done by an employee driving a company delivery van on business)
  c) products liability (e.g., selling a defective bicycle that subsequently injures a pedestrian)

Protection of Personal Assets

A serious concern that faces everyone who sets up a business is how best to protect personal assets. This is an important point to consider when deciding the form a business will take. In sole proprietorships and partnerships, the business owner's personal assets can be seized by business creditors. Only incorporation will ensure that business assets and personal assets remain separate.

The owner of a typical small business would be able to categorize assets as follows:

Personal Assets	**Business Assets**
House	Inventory
Car	Equipment
Life insurance	Delivery van
Bank account	Accounts owed by customers

There are three common ways of protecting personal assets:

- transfer to spouse
- incorporation
- insurance

Transfer a House to a Spouse   One of the common creditor protection techniques on entering a business is to put the matrimonial home in a spouse's name. If done before there is any likelihood that the person doing the transfer cannot pay creditors, this is good against the creditors. But what happens if the marriage breaks up. Has the spouse given up any claim regarding the house?

The answer may depend on a review of all marital property; however, the transferring spouse still has a claim for half of the net matrimonial property on the breakup of the marriage. So this creditor proofing scheme may not result in that spouse losing the half interest to the other spouse. A marriage contract the couple may have could also have an impact on this situation as well.

Example: Amir starts a consulting business as a financial planner and on the same day transfers his half interest in the matrimonial home to his wife making her the sole registered owner. Five years later, a client successfully obtains a judgment against Amir in negligence and seeks to set aside the transfer to the wife.On these facts, the transfer would not be set aside.

Five years later, Amir's marriage breaks down. The house is the only family asset and Amir claims a half interest. He would likely be successful. Thus he would have protected the half interest in the house from creditors, but would not have given up that value if the marriage breaks down.

Incorporation   Incorporating involves forming a separate company. Only the assets of the company are then available to creditors. However, in the case of a small business this may be of little protection, as creditors may well demand personal guarantees by the owner and spouse before granting any loan or credit.

Insurance   Insurance can cover tort liability, as well as such areas as providing income if the owner becomes sick and providing money to pay employees during the time of sickness. It cannot assist in protecting against business trade debts.

Choosing the Form of the Business

The law divides all businesses into one of four categories:

- sole proprietorship
- partnership
- limited partnership
- **corporation**—a business organization that is a separate legal entity (person) from the owners

There are other ways of carrying on business—such as franchises and joint ventures, which are also called strategic alliances—that are not separate legal forms. (A **joint venture** is an agreement between two or more independent businesses to cooperate on a particular project only.) Many people believe that the best form of business is always incorporation. This is not necessarily true, especially in the beginning stages of a business. The best form of business can be determined only after considering many factors, and obtaining the advice of a lawyer and an accountant.

Many businesses also require a municipal or professional business license. Cities also have restrictions on the type of businesses that can be carried on in different areas and are set out in zoning by-laws. You may need to seek legal help to determine if your business conforms to the local laws and you have the necessary license to operate.

Should I Incorporate?

Incorporation is not automatically the best form for a one-person business. Advice should always be sought from lawyers and accountants, as there are many factors that could influence

corporation
a business organization that is a separate legal entity (person) from the owners

joint venture
an agreement between two or more independent businesses to cooperate on a particular project only

the decision. One tax consideration is that a small business usually operates at a loss for the first year or two. If it is not incorporated, that loss can be used by the owner against personal earned income to reduce tax liability. If the business is incorporated, the loss stays with the company and can be used only against corporate income. As a business progresses and becomes more profitable, then perhaps incorporation should be considered.

■ *Critical Concepts of* Setting Up a Business

- Choose a name.
- Select the form—sole proprietorship, partnership, limited partnership, or incorporation.
- Register or incorporate.
- Obtain a municipal or professional business licence, if applicable, and see if the business complies with local zoning laws.

Sole Proprietorships

sole proprietorships
one-person businesses

Sole proprietorships, or one-person businesses, have become increasingly common today as more and more people set up "work from home" businesses. Many people believe that there are numerous legal hurdles to leap before setting up a business. In fact, you can start a one-person business or a partnership very simply. Merely choose a name and register it. If you use your own name as a business name, you do not even have to register—just start doing business.

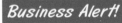

Protecting Personal Assets   In a sole proprietorship, there is no protection for the owner's personal assets. Both business and personal assets can be seized by creditors if the business owes debts, which amounts to unlimited liability.

Registration

If the sole proprietor uses a name other than a personal first and last name in the business, that name must be registered with the appropriate provincial government office. This is a very easy process that does not require the advice of a lawyer. The business owner need only visit the office, fill out a short form, and pay a small registration fee. The form is then put on public file, and anyone can search to discover the owner of a particular business. The registration must be renewed every five years.

Not registering a name means that the owner of a business may be fined. In some jurisdictions, such as Ontario and Nova Scotia, the owner cannot sue in the business's name unless it is registered. If a customer does not pay, for example, the owner of the business cannot take action to collect the debt until the business is registered.

Disadvantages of Sole Proprietorships

Though a sole proprietorship is simple, inexpensive and easy to set up, there are many problems with this form of business ownership. Entrepreneurs like the thought of being their own boss and keeping all the profits to themselves, however many businesses fail. The failure rate of businesses is high in Canada, usually 30% fail in the first year and by year 8 about 75% have failed. The main reasons for this are they lacked enough money to start and they lacked many of the necessary skills to run a business and could not or would not pay for professional advice. Few people are skilled in all the major areas of business; production, finance, marketing, human resources and IT, but they think that they can still run a successful business on their own. The failure rates prove them wrong.

The restaurant business has one of the highest failure rates, about 90%. Someone who is an excellent chef often thinks that is what it takes to run a successful restaurant. Unfortunately for success in that industry, it is not all about having good food. McDonald's is the most successful restaurant in the world. You can have great recipes; but if you know very little about accounting, costing, ordering, locating your business, marketing it, training and managing staff, then you are most likely going to fail despite your culinary talents. If you can't afford professional advice, then you should probably reconsider going into business.

The sole proprietor is very limited in how they can raise money, it is primarily through loans. Banks are often unwilling to lend, so people often turn to their families and friends and this too can cause obvious problems. The unlimited personal liability of a sole proprietorship is an obvious major drawback as all your personal assets can be taken by creditors to pay off the debts of the business. If however the business is successful, then there are tax disadvantages. The sole proprietor has to pay taxes on their profits at personal income tax rates. These rates are much higher than the tax rates for a small business that is incorporated. For many entrepreneurs a sole proprietorship is not the best form of business ownership.

Partnerships

The Formation of a Partnership

A **partnership** is the relationship between two or more persons carrying on a business with a view to profit. Normally, the advantages in sharing control of a business with others—being able to pool knowledge, experiences, and resources—far outweigh the disadvantages. Therefore, groups of people co-operating have become the method of carrying on business that tends to support the greatest growth potential. Sometimes such groups of business people will form a corporation. If they do not, then the joint business is usually run as a partnership (referred to as "firms").

partnership
the relationship between two or more persons carrying on a business with a view to profit

Small corporations are often run very much like partnerships. Thus, many of the problems encountered in maintaining co-operation among partners are also discovered among the shareholders of a corporation.

Many partnerships survive for years with few or any problems. Others run into difficulties within a very short time—choose your business partners carefully! Some of the common problem areas in partnerships have typically been:

- disagreements about how to run the business
- dishonesty by one of the partners—for example, taking partnership money secretly and leaving the country
- incompetence, such as poor performance of a contract, so that the partnership does not get paid or is sued

A partnership can be formed orally or in writing. As with any contract, it is much better to do it in writing so you have a permanent record of what you agreed to. Partnerships must register their partnership name and list the partners with a provincial business name registry office, or suffer the same penalties as a sole proprietorship.

Even if there has never been an express partnership agreement, the court can find that a partnership did exist. There are three tests that can be applied to determine if a partnership had been created. The courts will look at: 1) whether there was a joint contribution of capital to start the business 2) an intention to share profits and losses and 3) joint participation in the management of the business. If even only one of these requirements is met, it can determine that there was a partnership. This could expose parties to liabilities they had never anticipated.

Example: In *Prince Albert Co-operative Association Limited v. Rybka*, 2010 SKCA 144 (CanLII), a farmer, Paul Rybka, had been successfully sued by the Prince Albert Co-op for $53,088 for supplies he had received and not paid for. The co-op later realized that his wife, Tina Rybka, was equally involved in the farm operations and it sought a court judgment against her as a partner in the farming business. Though there was no formal partnership agreement between the spouses, they were "carrying on a business in common with a view towards profits." Their joint ownership of the land, joint bank accounts and tax returns proved they shared profits and losses and the court ruled that she was a partner and therefore also liable for the debts her "partner" had incurred.

Example: In *Brown Economic Assessments Inc. v. Harcourt Gillis*, 2004 SKCA 89 (CanLII), Cara Brown, an economic consultant did work for R. L. Stevenson. Mr. Stevenson told her he was a senior partner in a mid-sized law firm and his business card and the letters he sent listed the firm name of Stevenson, Gillis, Hjelte, Tangjerd Barrister and Solicitors. When Stevenson did not pay the consultant's bill of $23,242 she sued Stevenson and all the other partners for the money. The other lawyers all denied the existence of a partnership and any liability for Stevenson's debt. The consultant claimed that they had held out that it was a partnership and she had extended credit to Stevenson based on that relationship. The trial court and the Court of Appeal ruled that they even though they had not formed a partnership, they had held themselves out "perhaps unwittingly" to be partners, and had allowed Stevenson to so hold out. Stevenson had gone bankrupt, so the other lawyers were held jointly responsible for Stevenson's debt even though there had been no real partnership created.

■ *Business Law* Applied

❶ **Two students decided** that, as a summer job, they would run dances every Saturday night from June until September. They rented a local hall, and paid the owner a $500 deposit, each contributing $250 of this amount. The students agreed that any profits they made would be split equally between them, and that they would consult each other about all aspects of organizing the dances. The thought of partnership never crossed their minds.

   a) Would the courts find the two students to be partners?

❷ **Two Vancouver bakeries** pooled their orders of wheat from Alberta in order to take advantage of lower freight rates available when a larger volume is shipped. There was no intention of forming a partnership between the bakeries.

   a) Are the bakeries legally partners?
   b) What if both bakeries are corporations? Can they form a partnership if they want to?
   c) Does it matter that the businesses have no formal partnership agreement?

Unlimited Personal Liability

The consequences of being in a general partnership are serious. The personal assets of any general partner can be taken to pay partnership debts if the partnership assets are insufficient to cover them. A partner is personally liable for contracts related to the partnership business entered into by all other partners. A partner is also liable for torts, especially fraud, (such as stealing client's money) that another partner commits while conducting business for the partnership. Partners have **joint liability** for each other, they are each personally liable for the full amount of the debt of the partnership. So be very careful who you go into partnership with, if another partner is careless or a crook, it could cost you almost everything you own. This unlimited personal liability feature of general partnerships makes it the riskiest form of business ownership.

joint liability
a liability shared by a number of persons, each of whom is personally liable for the full amount of a debt

Example: In *McDonic Estate v. Hetherington (Litigation Guardian)*, 1997 ONCA 1019, two elderly sisters entrusted a lawyer to invest their savings in mortgages. The money was invested improperly and they sued the lawyer and the law firm for $241,755. The law firm denied any liability claiming the lawyer's investing activities were not within the ordinary course of business so they were not jointly liable. The trial court agreed but the Ontario Court of Appeal examined the details of the transactions and ruled that the law firm was also liable. The lawyer had used the firm's offices, letterhead, staff and trust accounts to handle the mortgage transactions and the firm had been involved in many other mortgage investments for other clients. The sisters were clients of the firm and had every reason to believe that the lawyer was acting within his capacity as a partner in the law firm, so the law firm was liable as well.

In Chapter 4 several professional negligence cases were outlined and the liability that followed from these cases clearly illustrates how partners are at risk for the actions of other partners in the firm. In the Castor Holdings case (*Wightman c. Widdrington (Succession de)*) a partner in a major accounting firm, Coopers & Lybrand, was found liable for negligence when the real estate investment company it had prepared the financial statements for collapsed after falsely reporting assets of $1.8 billion. The partners in the accounting firm will share the liability which may run as high as $1 billion. It was estimated that every partner in that accounting firm in Canada at the time the negligence occurred could be personally responsible for more than $4 million each. This may exceed their insurance coverage and could impact on the partners' personal assets.

In the *Strother v. 3464920 Canada Inc.* case below, a lawyer was found liable for breach of fiduciary duty and as a result the law firm he was a partner in was also found vicariously liable for his actions.

Strother v. 3464920 Canada Inc.
2007 SCC 24 (CanLII)

Robert Strother was a tax partner with the law firm Davis LLP. Strother had acted for Monarch Entertainment Corp. establishing film industry tax shelters. When Revenue Canada prohibited these tax shelters, Strother advised Monarch that these investments were no long available. But an executive of Monarch left and started his own new company, Sentinel, and then asked Strother to propose a new tax shelter scheme for Sentinel to Revenue Canada. Sentinel promised Strother part ownership and a large percentage of the profits if it was successful.

Strother submitted the new entertainment tax shelter scheme and Revenue Canada allowed it. Sentinel marketed it aggressively and Sentinel made millions. Strother had not advised Monarch of this new tax ruling. Fifteen months later Strother finally told his law firm Davis LLP that there may be a conflict of interest as he represented Monarch and Sentinel who were competitors. Davis LLP then told Strother he could not own any part of Sentinel, so Strother quit the law firm and went to work full time for Sentinel. When Monarch learned of Sentinel's tax shelters and Strother's involvement, it sued both Strother and Davis LLP for breach of fiduciary duty and breach of confidence claiming a conflict of interest.

The trial court ruled that based on a strict interpretation of the Monarch retainer agreement there was no breach of fiduciary duty and neither Strother nor Davis LLP were liable. That decision was appealed to the B.C. Court of Appeal which ruled that Strother had breached its fiduciary duty to Monarch and under the B.C. Partnership Act the law firm was liable for its partner's wrongful act. The Court of Appeal awarded Monarch all the profits that Strother had made with Sentinel (about $30 million) and Davis was also liable for the profits it had made while providing legal services for Sentinel as well. The decision was appealed to the Supreme Court of Canada.

The Court's Decision

The Supreme Court agreed that Strother had been in a conflict of interest and had breached his fiduciary duty to Monarch. He was the tax lawyer for Monarch and there was a continuing relationship of trust and confidence, and loyalty that was a fiduciary requirement. By not informing Monarch of the new tax ruling and his involvement with the competitor, Sentinel, he was clearly in a conflict of interest. The Supreme Court however reduced the amount Strother had to pay, to just the profits he earned from Sentinel during the 15 months he had acted for both companies. This is estimated to be between $1-2 million, much less than the original amount of closer to $30 million determined by the Court of Appeal.

The law firm he had worked for Davis LLP was not liable for breach of fiduciary duty as it did not know of Strother's scheme, but it was held liable under provisions in the B.C. Partnership Act making it vicariously liable for the wrongful act of one of its partners. Davis LLP was liable for the amount the court ordered Strother to pay, but the court noted Davis LLP can try to claim this money from Strother. The court noted that *"if the rogue partner cannot pay, the legislature has decided that there is no good reason why the loss or injury should be inflicted on the innocent client rather than on the partnership which put the rogue partner in a professional position to do what he or she did."*

A Partner's Responsibilities to the Partnership

Courts place strong obligations of trust on business partners, and a partner owes a **fiduciary duty** (see Chapter 4) to the other members of the partnership. One partner could not, for example, take advantage of the others by stealing a business opportunity in the same type of business in which the partnership is involved. It is up to the partnership to decide whether the opportunity is good or not. If the partnership declines to act on any business opening, an individual partner is free to take full personal advantage of it. In such circumstances, it is advisable for that partner to obtain a written release from the other partners.

Similarly, the courts would find a partner in breach of fiduciary duty if that individual failed to reveal business opportunities to the other partners. Consider a case in which the partnership is having difficulty selling a piece of real estate for $100,000, and decides to reduce the price. One partner knows that a potential buyer is in fact willing to pay the original asking price. That partner cannot keep this knowledge a secret, buy the property at the lower price, and resell it to the buyer later at the full price.

Legalese

Fiduciary   Hi-fi (high fidelity) is a precise, or faithful, reproduction of sound, and derives from *fides* (faith), the same Latin source for **fiduciary**. Fiduciary duty, then, is an obligation to show the *utmost good faith* in dealing with others. The highest standard of good faith is to be applied once a fiduciary relationship is established. The other party's interest must be put above your own. You must do unto your partner as you would have your partner do unto you. This includes the relationship between:

- business partners
- directors of a corporation and the corporation
- applicants for insurance on application forms given by the insurance company
- professional advisors, such as accountants and lawyers, and their clients

■ *Business Law* Applied

❸ **Harris and Tweed** agreed to set up an accounting firm together. Harris was introduced to Armroster at a party, and said he would be happy to do a little "moonlighting," looking after Armroster's firm's books in the evenings after normal business hours. Harris did not tell Tweed about the agreement, and kept all of the money that Armroster paid him.

Tweed later found out about the arrangement, and demanded half the fee.

a) Did Tweed have any right to a share in the fee?

A Partner's Responsibilities to Outsiders

Perhaps the greatest liability that a partner faces is being responsible for the acts of fellow partners. If one partner enters into a contract in the partnership's name, all members are individually held to that agreement, as well as the partnership itself. Partners can restrict the authority of any one of their members, but unless outsiders are made aware of that limitation, they are not bound by it.

Partners are generally regarded as having the authority to sign contracts on behalf of the partnership (apparent authority). Any private restrictions on this usual or normal authority are not binding on outsiders unless they are specifically told of the limitations. This is sometimes called the **indoor management rule**—"indoor," or private, management restrictions do not

indoor management rule
the principle that a person dealing with a corporation is entitled to assume that its internal rules have been complied with unless it is apparent that such is not the case

affect outsiders. It is the principle that a person dealing with a corporation is entitled to assume that its internal rules have been complied with unless it is apparent that such is not the case.

Limitations of a Partner's Rights

There are two limitations on a partner's right to bind the partnership to any agreement. Contracts that are made outside the normal course of business will not be binding on the partnership. For example, a partner in a clothing store orders a large supply of books on gardening—an action not in the normal course of running a clothing store. The book supplier could not enforce this contract against the partnership.

Similarly, unless specific restrictions on a partner's authority are made known to outsiders, the partnership can be held to any agreement that a partner makes on behalf of the business. If, for example, the partners in a clothing store inform the Arrow Shirt Company that no partner can place an order for an amount over $10,000, the store cannot be held liable should one partner in fact order $15,000 worth of inventory. If the shirt company had not been previously told of this policy, it could enforce the contract for $15,000.

Business Law   Applied

❹ **Singh and Ghandi** were partners in a travel agency. The firm specialized in package tours, for which customers always had to pay a deposit of 10 percent of the full cost when the tour was booked. On August 1, the travel agency had $100,000 in its bank account, all of which was owed to a tour organizer. On August 2, Singh withdrew the money and left the country. No one knows where he is now.

The travel agency's customers sued the firm for the return of their deposits.

 a) Was Ghandi liable to repay the money?

❺ **Mike Pappas and** Chris Christopolous were partners in a record shop called More Music. While Pappas was on vacation in Banff, Christopolous ordered 1,000 copies of a CD by an unknown artist he believed would soon be famous. Christopolous also felt that the business should diversify, and so ordered 100 expensive cameras.

There was a downturn in the business, and More Music was unable to pay anything on either of these two contracts.

 a) Was Pappas personally liable on the contract with the supplier of the CDs?
 b) Was Pappas personally liable on the contract with the supplier of the cameras?
 c) If Pappas and Christopolous had a written partnership agreement, specifying that all contracts must be signed by both partners, would Pappas's liability be any different?

❻ **More Music's troubles** have only just begun. The company that supplied the CDs submitted an invoice for $10,000. Full payment was requested immediately, or it would sue More Music for breach of the contract that Christopolous had signed.

After other secured debts were paid, More Music had assets of only $2,000. Pappas had personal assets consisting of:

 ■ a half-interest in More Music
 ■ a house
 ■ a car

 a) Which, if any, of Pappas's assets could the record company seize to satisfy its claims?

Partnership Agreements

When a partnership is first formed the parties should write a partnership agreement that will set out many of the key terms they had agreed upon and ways to resolve possible disputes. It is best to see a lawyer to assist you in this process. Spending a small amount of money at the planning stage could save you very high legal fees later on if you do not have a properly drafted partnership agreement, as illustrated earlier in Chapter 5 in the *Lyons v. Multari* case.

Typical clauses in a partnership agreement would deal with the following topics:

- Contribution expected from each partner, in money, as well as in work
- How profits are to be divided
- What draws are permitted against future profits
- Banking arrangements and signing authority
- How disputes will be resolved
- Expansion of the business
- Admission of new partners
- Buying out other partners
- Resignation, expulsion or death of existing partners
- Non-competition clause
- Termination of the partnership

If the parties do not have a partnership agreement, then a provincial Partnership Act will apply. These laws were written originally around 1890, and the principles that are included may not always be appropriate for 21st century businesses. A typical set of sections from a partnership act are provided below. If you read them carefully you will see that in many partnerships, these would not be the terms the parties would want imposed upon them. For example: all partners share equally in the profits, nobody can receive remuneration for working in the partnership, and no change can occur in the nature of the business unless all partners consent. Given the strict clauses in the legislation, it is very important that people entering into a partnership hire lawyers to write their own particular partnership agreement that suits their specific circumstances, rather than have this legislation dictate their relationship.

The Partnership Act

24. The interests of partners in the partnership property and their rights and duties in relation to the partnership shall be determined, subject to any agreement express or implied between the partners, by the following rules:

1. All the partners are entitled to share equally in the capital and profits of the business, and must contribute equally towards the losses, whether of capital or otherwise, sustained by the firm.
2. The firm must indemnify every partner in respect of payments made and personal liabilities incurred by him or her,
   (a) in the ordinary and proper conduct of the business of the firm; or
   (b) in or about anything necessarily done for the preservation of the business or the property of the firm.
3. A partner making, for the purpose of the partnership, any actual payment or advance beyond the amount of capital that he or she has agreed to subscribe is entitled to interest at the rate of 5 percent per annum from the date of the payment or advance.

4. A partner is not entitled, before the ascertainment of profits, to interest on the capital subscribed by the partner.

5. Every partner may take part in the management of the partnership business.

6. No partner is entitled to remuneration for acting in the partnership business.

7. No person may be introduced as a partner without the consent of all existing partners.

8. Any difference arising as to ordinary matters connected with the partnership business may be decided by a majority of the partners, but no change may be made in the nature of the partnership business without the consent of all existing partners.

9. The partnership books are to be kept at the place of business of the partnership, or the principal place, if there is more than one, and every partner may, when he or she thinks fit, have access to and inspect and copy any of them.

Business Law   Applied

❼ Simone and DiCarlo started a business together, naming it Mega Fitness Health Club. No partnership agreement was signed, and little discussion of the organizational aspects of the business took place. Simone advanced $10,000 as start-up capital, while DiCarlo put in $5,000, promising another $5,000 as soon as he could.

Simone proved to be a good salesperson, and signed a large number of patrons for yearly memberships. DiCarlo worked the same number of hours, but generated a far smaller amount of business. At the end of the first year, the business earned a profit of $100,000.

Simone claimed that, because he contributed twice as much capital and generated twice as much business, he was entitled to 75 percent of the profits. DiCarlo disagreed, and insisted the profits be evenly divided.

  a) Who was legally correct?
  b) How might Simone have safeguarded his interests?

❽ Assume the same facts as in the previous question, except that the business is a variety store. There is frequent employee absence, and Simone always has to fill in, averaging about 60 hours a week.

DiCarlo has another job and is rarely available to do extra work, averaging about 40 hours a week in the store.

At the end the year, Simone wants some salary compensation for the additional 20 hours he has worked every week. DiCarlo refuses.

  a) Is Simone entitled to the extra compensation on a merit basis?
  b) What could Simone have done to protect his interests?

❾ A real estate brokerage firm has four partners—A, B, C, and D. There is no partnership agreement of any type. Partners A, B, and C want X admitted as a new partner, but D does not.

A, B, and C call a meeting and vote in favour of X as a partner. D votes against the proposal.

  a) Is X a new partner?

Disputes in a Partnership

Partnerships are often like a marriage; they start out very optimistic and don't anticipate major disputes that may occur in the future. Fights are a major problem in partnerships. Whether it is about the division of work, taking out profits or reinvesting them in the business, expansion, admitting new partners or the death of a partner, there are most certainly going to be problems that arise. The more comprehensive and carefully worded a partnership agreement is, the easier it will be to resolve some of these issues.

Buy-Sell Clauses in a Partnership Agreement

There are many situations in which the owners of a small business might decide to end their association, including one partner's wish to leave, personality conflicts, death, retirement, or long-term disability. Under such circumstances, a buy-sell clause provides a method for determining the value of the business and each owner's share in it. The four usual methods of fixing value are by:

- expert appraisal
- a fixed-priced formula
- arbitration
- a shotgun clause

The appraisal method of evaluation is often avoided because of the potential costs involved. There are people—usually chartered accountants—who specialize in estimating the value of businesses, and their fees can be significant.

A fixed-price formula might value a partner's holding as, for example, "three times earnings." Earnings would then be defined as the average of that partner's share in the business over the past five years. The average over a five-year period is used to prevent an atypical or unusual value being caused by the partner dying in either an exceptionally good, or an unusually poor, year.

The cost of arbitration can be underestimated. Both sides in any dispute might have to retain lawyers. As well, they will have to agree to, and appoint, an arbitrator and pay that individual's fee. Arbitration will likely be held as a mini-trial, at which both sides present evidence of the value of the partnership, including evaluations by two sets of estimators.

The Shotgun Buy-Sell

The cost of a business valuation can be under estimated as well. For even a small business, it can be $40,000. If there is litigation, then there might be a need for an expert for both parties, resulting in an expense of $80,000. One method to avoid the cost of an expert is called the Shotgun Buy-Sell. The term refers to the method in bygone days that a father, whose daughter a young man got pregnant, ensured the young man did the honourable thing and married her.

This method also assumes that most business owners, like most homeowners, have a rough idea of the true value of their business. The method is that one partner must first make an offer at a specific price. The other partner has the choice to either sell at that price or to buy the offering partner's shares at that price. This forces the offering partner to offer what is believed to be the true value.

Example: Smith and Wesson is a two-person partnership worth $100,000. If Smith offers to buy Wesson's shares at $40,000, Wesson will choose instead to buy Smith's shares at that price and Smith will lose $10,000. If Smith offers to buy Wesson's shares at $60,000, Wesson will sell and Smith will pay $10,000 too much. Thus, Smith is forced to offer $50,000, the true value of a 50% interest, to get the best financial deal.

However there could be a downside to this method. If one partner, the offering partner, has the financial ability to pay for the other partner's interest, but that other partner has no ability to purchase the offering partner's interest, the offering partner can give a very low ball offer and the receiving partner would have no alternative but to accept.

Forced Buy-Sell Clauses

These clauses are worded so that when a specific event—such as the death of a partner—takes place, the partner (or the heirs) must sell that individual's shares, and the other partners must purchase them. There is no choice. The purchase price is often set out as a fixed-price formula in the partnership agreement.

Voluntary Buy-Sell Clauses

These clauses are usually of the shotgun variety, and allow a partner to end the partnership at will. One partner might simply want out of the partnership agreement.

A Typical Buy-Sell Clause

If either partner desires to sell her share in the business, she shall be at liberty to do so, and shall first offer such share to the other partner at a price to be agreed upon or fixed by arbitration, and if the other partner shall not, within seven days, accept such offer, then the selling partner shall be at liberty to sell her share to any other person or persons.

The Death of a Partner

When they first begin operations, few business people consider the potentially devastating effects that death—their own, or their partner's—can have on the firm. A deceased partner's heirs are entitled to demand payment of the full value of that individual's share of the partnership. The partnership itself dies with the partner, but in actuality the business continues—unless there is no money to pay for the claims against it. You might want to be in business with your partner, but you may not want to end up in business with your partner's spouse.

Corporations have a separate legal existence apart from their owners, and do not cease to exist when a shareholder dies. But, for small corporations with only one or a few shareholders, the situation is similar to a partnership. If a shareholder was in a key management position, the surviving owners are faced with problems such as:

- purchasing the deceased's shares (the holder's proportionate interest in the assets of a corporation) to avoid control of the corporation going to people the surviving shareholders do not want
- finding the money to pay for the shares
- establishing the least expensive, but fairest, way of determining the value of the shares

Planning by Agreement

The law stating that the partnership dissolves on death can be varied by a term in the partnership agreement. Such a clause specifically sets out that the partnership will not be dissolved on the death of one member, and determines how the deceased partner's estate will be paid.

Usually, a careful business plan involves a combination of the following factors, plus personal wills that deal specifically with the transfer of the interest in the partnership on death.

Insurance

Life insurance can be obtained for each partner, with the surviving partners the beneficiaries of the policy. In some large businesses, rules insist that not all key personnel, including partners, travel on the same aircraft, so that a situation in which all critical managers die at the same time—thus making continuation of the business impossible—never occurs.

Self-Insurance

The partnership can choose to set aside a percentage of the annual profits in order to cover buying out a deceased partner's interest or shares.

Valuation

The value of the deceased's shares or interests in the business is determined by a formula that is usually contained in a buy-sell clause in the agreement.

■ *Critical Concepts of* Partnerships

- Partnerships should have a written partnership agreement and should register their name with the provincial registry
- Even if there is no formal partnership agreement the court may determine that one has been created due to their activities
- General partners have unlimited personal liability and are jointly liable for all the partnership debts
- Be careful who you enter into a partnership with as your personal assets could be at risk
- Seek legal advice when preparing a partnership agreement as there are many potential problems and the agreement should be drafted to help minimize future disputes

■ *Business Law* Applied

⑩ **Michael Bereskin worked** loyally for a small grocery store for 20 years. The business was owned by two partners, Parr and Manza. Parr liked Bereskin and told him that, next year, he would sell him his share of the business and retire. Unfortunately, Parr died six weeks later. Manza does not want Bereskin as a partner.

a) Does Bereskin have the right to become a partner?

⑪ **Castellian and Lynkowski** are equal partners in a boat-rental business. There is a written partnership agreement containing a shotgun buy-sell clause. Castellian wants to retire, as he has become tired of the business. He believes the business is worth $50,000. Castellian is thinking of offering Lynkowski $10,000 to see if he can get Lynkowski's half-interest for a bargain price, then sell the entire business at a profit, and retire.

a) Would you advise Castellian to take this course of action?

limited partnership

a partnership in which some of the partners limit their liability to the amount of their capital contributions and are not active in conducting the business

Limited Partnership

Before the widespread use of corporations, the only way to limit liability was through use of a **limited partnership.** This is a partnership in which some of the partners limit their liability to the amount of their capital contributions and are not active in conducting the business. An investor who does not want to take part in the day-to-day running of the business can still give advice, and be at risk only for the amount of money put into the business. The personal assets of a **limited partner** (a partner in a limited partnership whose liability is limited to the amount of his or her capital contribution) cannot be seized.

There are two types of partners in a limited partnership—the general partner and the limited partner. A **general partner** is a partner in a limited partnership whose liability is not limited, and who usually runs the business. It is only the limited or silent partners who are prevented from taking part in day-to-day management.

To obtain protection as a limited partner, the business must register as a limited partnership under relevant provincial legislation. Most provinces have an act specifically called the *Limited Partnership Act*, which usually requires certain information to be given on the public registration form. This generally includes:

- the firm's name
- the name and address of each general partner
- the name and address of each limited partner
- the date the partnership commences
- the date the limited partnership is to end

Limited partners become liable as general partners if:

- the partnership is not registered as set out above
- the partnership continues beyond its expiry date without a renewal certificate being filed showing the intention to extend the limited partnership
- false or misleading statements are given on the certificate of registration
- a limited partner takes an active part in the management of the business
- a limited partner's name is used in conjunction with the firm's name, or a limited partner claims to be a general partner

Though less common than they used to be, limited partnerships are being used in some new forms of business organizations. In the world of franchising, for example, Journey's End Motel uses a limited partnership in the structure of its business organization.

Limited partnerships can be used to raise capital in place of the corporate form. The silent or limited partners have the same protection as a shareholder in a corporation in that they have no liability for the limited partnership obligations of any type. To complete the limitation of liability, the general partner is often a corporation which has no assets.

Example: A group of investors want to buy at a hotel since they form a limited partnership called the Ambassador Hotel Partnership. The general partner is 96475 Ontario Ltd. the Limited partners are 50 individual investors. An hotel guest falls from a balcony resulting in serious injuries and obtains a judgment for $2 million against the partnership, which has insurance for only $1 million.

The balance of the judgment is enforceable only against the assets of the general partner, 96475 Ontario Ltd. None of the 15 individual limited partners are liable on it.

limited partner
a partner in a limited partnership whose liability is limited to the amount of his or her capital contribution

general partner
a partner in a limited partnership whose liability is not limited, and who usually runs the business

■ *Critical Concepts of* Limited Partnerships

- In a limited partnership, only the general partner has unlimited liability for the partnership's obligations.
- The limited partners have no liability for partnership losses.
- Unlike partnerships, which may come into existence by operation of law, limited partnerships are only created when the proper form is filed with the government office.

■ *Business Law* Applied

⑫ **A creditor has** a $100,000 judgment against a certain partnership. The business is valueless. The partners have a written partnership agreement making A and B general partners, and C a limited partner whose contribution is $10,000. C has a house worth $100,000, but A and B have no personal assets.

The creditor searches, and finds no registration of the limited partnership.

a) What right has the creditor against C?
b) Is C's liability limited to $10,000 because he is a limited partner?

Limited Liability Partnerships

limited liability partnership

a partnership in which partners who are not negligent are not personally liable for losses caused by the negligence of another partner or of an employee directly supervised by another partner

Since 1998 all provinces except Prince Edward Island, Yukon and Nunavut have passed amendments to their partnership acts which permit a new type of partnership called a **limited liability partnership**—a partnership in which partners who are not negligent are not personally liable for losses caused by the negligence of another partner or of an employee directly supervised by another partner. To have this limitation, the partnership must be registered as such and the term "limited liability partnership" must be clearly shown on letterhead and signs so that clients are made aware that they are dealing with a limited liability partnership before they engage that partnership. The partnership name must contain a notice of the limitation of liability such as, "Smith and Jones, LLP."

The partnership as a business continues to be liable for the negligence of any partner or employee, and so the firm's assets remain at risk. The limitation applies to negligence only and protects the innocent partners' personal assets but not the partnership assets. Protection does not apply to partnership debts from contracts or due to fraud. So in the Strother case above, the individual partners in the law firm Davis LLP were made responsible for the fraudulent acts of the one partner.

Limited Liability Partnerships are often only permitted to be used by professionals such as law firms and accounting firms, though some provinces do allow other professions to use this form of ownership. The professional associations also require LLPs to maintain a minimum amount of liability insurance. The extent of liability protection a LLP provides varies significantly among the provinces and should be carefully examined by professionals and their clients when claims arise.

Example: Consider an accounting practice with 2 partners, Brian and Erwin. The relevant assets are:

Partnership – building $500,000 and accounts receivable $100,000
Brian – house $500,000 car $50,000
Erwin – cottage $200,000 car $30,000

Assume that Brian was negligent in giving advice to a client and caused the client losses of $1,500,000. In an ordinary partnership all of the above assets could be seized by the clients pursuant to a judgment in a lawsuit. However, in a limited liability partnership only the partnership assets and Brian's assets could be seized. Erwin's assets are protected.

■ *Critical Concepts of* LLP

- This form of partnership must be in writing and registered
- The LLP designation must be shown as part of the partnership name
- The limitation applies only to negligent acts, but not contract debts or fraud

Ending a Partnership

Most partnership agreements have terms that set out the requirements for ending the partnership. One common term is that if one partner wants out, the partnership is not dissolved, but that partner's share is purchased by the remaining partners under the conditions of a buy-sell clause.

In the absence of a partnership agreement, the association is still very easy to bring to an end. This is an advantage to a party wanting to do so, but it is a great disadvantage to partners who want to continue the business. Dissolution of a partnership means the business, including the assets, must be sold, all creditors paid, and, if there is any money left over, it must then be divided among the partners.

A partnership can be dissolved, unless the terms of the partnership agreement provide to the contrary, when:

- Any partner gives notice of intention to withdraw and dissolve the partnership.
- A partner dies, declares bankruptcy, or becomes insolvent.
- A date is specified in the partnership agreement to bring the partnership to an end.
- A court order is issued under the provincial partnership act. The court might make this order on several grounds:
  a) the business is operating continually at a loss
  b) the business is engaged in some illegal activity
  c) one partner becomes mentally incompetent, or is unwilling or unable to perform partnership responsibilities
  d) dissolution is just or equitable

Agency

Agency Relationship

Agency is another important business relationship that exists when one party represents another party in the formation of legal relations. An **agent** is a person who is authorized to represent and act on behalf of another, known as a **principal**. An agent typically sets up a contract between a principal and a third party. Agents' acts, when done within the scope of the authority they have been given, bind the principal as if they had committed those acts personally. If the agent has acted properly for a disclosed principal, and disputes arise between the principal and the third party, the agent is not liable.

agent
is a party who represents and acts on behalf of a principal

Agency Triangle

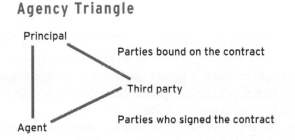

Agency Triangle

Principal

Parties bound on the contract

Third party

Parties who signed the contract

Agent

Agents can be independent contractors or employees. But not all employees are agents for their employer, as they do not all have signing authority to make contracts on behalf of their employer. Under the law of partnerships, partners are also considered to be agents for each other. Agents should be sure that when they sign contracts on behalf of the principal they sign their name "per" the principal on the documents so that it indicates they are acting as an agent and then they are not personally liable for the contracts.

Mohammed Abdi		Prestige Enterprises Ltd.
Per: _Michael Silver_		Per: _Linda Decahanas_
Michael Silver		Linda Decahanas
		Vice-President

The agency relationship is commonly seen when executives or buyers for a company negotiate and sign contracts on their behalf. The term agency is frequently used by travel agencies and real estate agencies, even though they do not have the authority to sign or bind their principals (their clients) in contracts.

■ Business Law Applied

⑱ **Maurice Sosnovich asked** his neighbour, Rod Carswell, owner of the Sun Seekers Travel Agency, to transfer $20,000 to a relative in Poland. Carswell said he would be glad to do so for a minimum fee of $100. Sosnovich handed over a cheque for $20,000, and Carswell gave him a receipt, signed:

Sun Seekers Travel Agency Inc.
Per: _Rod Carswell_
Rod Carswell
President

When the relative did not receive the money, Sosnovich asked Carswell what happened. Carswell replied that by mistake, his bookkeeper deposited the money in a general account, and used it to pay current creditors. Unfortunately, the travel agency has now gone bankrupt. Carswell owns a large home, free of any mortgage.

Sosnovich demanded the money from Carswell, who replied that he did not owe the money: the company—now bankrupt—did.

 a) Draw an agency triangle diagram and identify each party in this question on it.
 b) Is Sosnovich's contract with Carswell or with the corporation?
 c) Is Carswell personally liable?
 d) What could Sosnovich have done to ensure that Carswell would have been personally liable?

Authority

An agency relationship is usually created by actual authority where the principal expressly gives the agent the power or authority, either in writing or orally, to make contacts on their behalf. A common example of this is a power of attorney. People often give another person their power of attorney (often called a living will) to make medical and financial decisions for them when they are unable to do so themselves.

An agency can be created by apparent authority, where the principal had not given any actual authority to the agent, but the principal's conduct suggests to a third party that the agent does have the authority to act. For example third parties can assume that an employee with the title of a "buyer" for a company has the right to act as their agent and buy goods unless told otherwise.

If an agent has apparent authority but acts beyond their authority, the principal is not bound by the contract. If however when the principal finds out about this unauthorized act and decides it wants to accept the deal, then the principal can chose to ratify or accept the contract and then it will be enforceable.

Example: In *John Ziner Lumber Ltd. v. Kotov*, 2000 CanLII 16894 (ON CA), the court ruled that a home owner was liable as an undisclosed principal for lumber purchases that his agent made even though they were beyond the agent's authority. Since the home owner accepted and used the lumber in the construction of his house though the court implied that he had ratified the contracts the agent had made and was therefore liable for the cost of the lumber.

In most situations the agent clearly discloses to the third party the principal that they are acting for, though it is possible for an agent to act for an undisclosed principal. This sometimes occurs when a developer wants to buy up property but does not want the land owners to know who is behind the deal. The developer may fear that knowledge of who is buying the land may result in higher selling prices or overall resistance to the deal. If the agent acts for an undisclosed principal the agent can be personally liable on the contract. If the agent had the authority to make the contract and the third party discovers they acted as an agent, the third party can sue either the agent or the principal, but not both.

It is possible for an agent to act for more than one principal selling the same product at the same time, if there is full disclosure of the relationship and the principals agree.

Agent's Duties

Agents owe the principal a fiduciary duty. This is the highest duty of care, one of utmost good faith and requires the agent to use their skills and talents and always act in the best interests of the principal. An agent must be competent to carry out the task assigned and conduct the transaction or business to the level of any reasonable person claiming to be qualified to do that particular job. If she falls below that standard, and the principal suffers a loss, she would be liable to compensate the principal for that loss.

Example: In *Pointe of View Developments Inc. v. Cannon & McDonald Ltd.*, 2008 ABQB 713 (CanLII), a developer successfully sued its insurance agent (and the insurance companies involved), for negligence. The developer had requested 100% insurance coverage for a condominium project it was building. The agent thought he had arranged full coverage, but he had mistakenly only arranged for 80% coverage. A major fire occurred and the agent and the insurance companies were liable for damages equal to the 20% that was not covered by insurance which totaled $1,090,070 plus interest and costs.

The agent should not be in conflict of interest nor put their own self-interests or personal gains ahead of the principal's best interests. Real estate agents sometimes are in the position where they may be acting for both the buyer and the seller in a real estate deal, so that compromises their ability to act in the best interests of one party. Real estate agents also must not purchase properties from their clients knowing it is a good deal and then later resell the property for a personal profit unless full disclosure is given.

The agent must act within the scope of their authority. For example if they are hired to sign up a well-known sports personality for speaking engagements, you must do exactly that. If you enter into a contract whereby you agree the sport celebrity will endorse a certain product, you have acted beyond your authority.

The agent must follow the instructions of the principal and keep them updated and fully informed. There is a duty of full disclosure on the agent to fully disclose all information to the principal

Example: In *Volkers v. Midland Doherty Ltd.*, 1985 CanLII 415 (BC CA), an experienced investor told his stock broker (his agent) to purchase 11,000 shares in a particular stock as soon the stock market opened the next day. The broker who took the order wanted to discuss the possible risk of this transaction with another broker so the order was not put in when the market opened. Shares traded in the stock at about $6.00 per share for the first 2 hours that day, until the securities commission ordered all trading in those shares to cease. When trading resumed 2 days later, the broker made the purchase at $12.50 per share. The investor then sued the broker

Westrheim et al v. Gao et al, 2007 BCSC 274 (CanLII)

The plaintiffs put their Vancouver condominium up for sale for $529,000. A real estate agent, Diana Gao, submitted a conditional offer from one of her clients of $517,500 subject to them obtaining financing. When the client was unable to get the funds, they withdrew their offer. Gao then submitted an unconditional offer to the plaintiffs of $517,500 on behalf of her husband Norman Chan, who was also a real estate agent in the same agency. Gao informed the sellers that her husband was a real estate agent and completed the necessary disclosure document real estate agents must complete when purchasing. The form indicated that the purchaser planned to use the condo for personal or rental use. The box indicating they planned to resell it had also been checked off but when it was faxed it did not show up as being checked. The sellers specifically asked if Chan was buying it for resale purposes and they responded orally that it was being bought for rental and investment purposes only and not for resale.

The deal closed on August 31, 200 and Gao then listed the condo for sale 6 days later at $639,000. Gao and Chan then had it painted, installed hardwood floors and had a decorator "stage it" with rental furniture. About a month later Gao sold the condo for $613,000. The net profit was $61,500 after expenses.

The plaintiffs sued Gao and Chan and the agency that they worked at for breach of fiduciary duty. The sellers claimed that they had relied on the statements by Gao about the value of the condo and that Chan was not buying the condo for resale purposes. Gao and Chan denied they owed the sellers a fiduciary duty and the price increase was just typical of the Vancouver housing market.

The Court's Decision

The B.C. trial court ruled that the fiduciary duty will arise if the real estate agent provides or omits information that he/she knows will influence a seller's decision and the seller relies on that information. The sellers had placed a degree of trust in the real estate agents and relied on their statements that they had not purchased the condo for resale purposes. The court held that Gao was aware that the condo was worth more than the selling price and she presented her husband's offer immediately upon the withdrawal of her client's offer. She represented that she was not going to resell the condominium, which the plaintiffs relied on. Gao and her husband and the agency were therefore liable for breach of fiduciary duty.

The court awarded damages to the sellers in the amount of $61,500 for the profit Gao made on the resale plus $8,108 for Chan's commission in the transaction.

---

for not following his instructions to purchase as soon as the market had opened and he sought about $70,000 for the increased price he paid due to the broker's delay. The broker insisted he was acting properly and in the client's best interest in discussing the risk of the purchase with the other broker. The trial court agreed with the broker, but the B.C. Court of Appeal disagreed. The agent's duty was to follow the client's orders and when it did not make the purchase it should have advised the investor immediately so he could have taken alternative actions. The broker and his firm were liable for the client's losses.

If the agent discloses their agency role and fulfils their duties properly, if any contractual disputes arise between the principal and the third party, such as money not paid or the proper goods are not received, the agent is not personally liable. If however, the agent never disclosed to the third party that they were an agent and contractual problems arise, the third party can sue either or both the agent and the principal. If an agent makes a contract outside the scope of their authority, a disclosed principal can ratify the contract and it is enforceable. If it was an undisclosed principal, ratification is not possible.

An agent is personally liable for the torts that they commit. The principal is vicariously liable for any torts that the agent commits while acting on the principal's behalf and within the scope of the agent's authority.

Example: In *Straus Estate v. Decaire*, 2012 ONCA 918 (CanLII) the Ontario Court of Appeal upheld a trial court decision that found two mutual fund companies liable for negligence and damages totalling $254,471 for the actions of one of their agents. The agent had persuaded his clients into investing most of their life savings into shares of a risky start up technology company that the agent was not even authorized to sell. The mutual fund companies were liable for the inappropriate investments their agent had put the clients into while he was working for those companies. The court stated the mutual fund companies had placed the agent into the community to get the client's trust and confidence, but failed to give the proper supervision and governance of this agent.

In *Wilson v. Clarica Life Insurance Co.*, 2001 BCSC 1696 (CanLII) an insurance company was liable for deceit and damages of almost $200,000 when one of its agents acted fraudulently. The clients thought they had purchased an annuity from the insurance company, but the agent had the cheques made out to him personally and he stole the money.

Principal's Duties

The principal must pay the agent for the work they have done and if no fee has been stated, the court will set a reasonable amount based on similar services. The principal must assume liability for contracts that the agent has signed on their behalf. If a principal has been using an agent, but then decides it does not want to use the agent to act on their behalf any longer, the principal should inform third parties of this change. If they fail to inform the third parties, the former agent may have apparent authority and the principal could be bound by their actions.

Business Law   Applied

⑭ **Mas Kikuta,** a sales representative with Hakimoto Electronics Inc., called on Geraldine Heider, vice-president of MacroSoft Computers Inc. Two weeks before the sales call, Hakimoto had warned all its representatives that they should not accept large orders for a particular microchip, as it was proving difficult to obtain component parts from other suppliers. As a result, supplies of the microchip were very low. Normally, Hakimoto's salespeople accepted sizeable orders for this chip from their clients every week, committing the company to supply the item quickly.

Heider ordered a large quantity of the microchips for MacroSoft, stating that delivery was needed by August 1, which was two weeks away. Kikuta wrote up the order, and faxed it to his head office.

One hour after receiving Kikuta's fax, Hakimoto sent a fax to Heider at MacroSoft, cancelling the order.

  a) In what legal position was Kikuta acting?
  b) Did Kikuta have actual authority to bind Hakimoto Electronics Inc., the principal? Is the contract that was signed by Kikuta and Heider binding?
  c) Is Hakimoto's restriction on the authority of its sales representatives effective?
  d) Can Hakimoto legally cancel the contract?

⑮ **Mrs. McGregor owned** an 18-unit apartment building. She decided to winter in the Caribbean from November till May, and told the tenants that her son, Rob, would collect the rent cheques while she was away. Rob McGregor collected all the cheques for November, December, January, and February.

Tiring of her vacation, Mrs. McGregor returned in late February, and told her son not to collect the rents for March. During the morning of March 1, Rob McGregor went to the apartment building, where he collected all the rents for that month. He then went and paid a sizeable gambling debt, using the money he had collected.

Late in the afternoon of March 1, Mrs. McGregor visited the apartment block, intending to collect the rents for the month. All the tenants told her they had already paid. Mrs. McGregor demanded that they pay her again.

  a) By what type of authority did Rob McGregor collect the cheques on his mother's behalf for the first four months of her vacation? When he collected them on March 1, did he have any authority?
  b) Do the tenants have to pay a second time?

⑯ **Kamieh Nicola knew** that Cadillac Enterprises Corp., Ltd. wanted to purchase a certain type of machine for its plant. Nicola learned of a used machine, available at an exceptional price; however, another firm was ready to buy it. Nicola signed an offer to purchase the machine as agent for Cadillac Enterprises Corp., Ltd. on the spot. She then took the agreement to Cadillac, which approved the deal.

Later, Cadillac decided it did not need the machine, and negotiated out of the contract. Nicola asked for the normal finder's fee payable in these situations—10 percent of the sale price. Cadillac refused to pay her, claiming the company had not asked her to do the work, which proved of no benefit to it anyway.

a) What is the technical name for Cadillac's action in approving the agreement to purchase?
b) What legal relationship did it create between Nicola and Cadillac?
c) What legal relationship did it create between Cadillac and the owner of the machinery?
d) Does Cadillac have to pay Nicola's commission?

■ *Critical Concepts of* Agency

- An agent is hired by a principal to act on their behalf and to set up contracts between the principal and a third party.
- The agent should clearly indicate they are an agent when they sign documents and sign their name "per" the disclosed principal.
- The agent owes the principal a fiduciary duty and must act in the principal's best interests and within the scope of their authority, give full disclosure, follow instructions and keep the principal updated.
- An agent must disclose to the third party that they are an agent or else the agent is personally liable for the contract.
- If the agent acts properly for a disclosed principal, the agent is not personally liable, and the principal alone is bound in contract for the obligations and benefits created by the agent on the principal's behalf.

Franchises

What Is a Franchise?

A franchise in law is a special kind of licence, granting the right to use trademarks, trade names, and a business system for products and services.

A franchise agreement is made between the founding company—the franchisor—and the small business outlet—the franchisee. Because of the extreme difficulty in differentiating between these two terms, the founding company is usually referred to as the parent company.

There are over 1,000 franchisors in Canada and over 100,000 individual franchise units across Canada employing over 1,000,000 people. The Canadian Franchise Association website (www.cfa.ca) states that franchising accounts for one out of every five consumer dollars spent in the country on goods and services and franchising accounts for about 10 per cent of Canada's Gross Domestic Product. It is adaptable to a wide variety of companies and some of the most successful ones in Canada include; Tim Hortons, McDonald's and Canadian Tire.

Franchising has many advantages. To the founding company it offers expansion without expenditure of capital. It also offers the large multinational corporations the chance to imitate small business patterns within their large organizations. One of the current theories is that small businesses are more flexible and sensitive to customer demands. The franchise arrangement seems to combine the best of large and small business—the small-business person has access to sophisticated marketing and design that only a large corporation can afford, as well as a complete system that has been tried and proven successful. As well, the franchise arrangement provides working systems that can be inspected.

Business entrepreneurs often assume that purchasing one of these working systems means their business is more likely to succeed. While this is frequently true, franchising is a trouble-fraught area. Many small businesses are unhappy with their situation, and several large litigation matters are in progress against franchise corporations by groups of their franchisees.

The Standard Franchise Agreement

These agreements are governed by normal contract law. There are standard form contracts that contain many of the terms that appear in other standard form agreements. Some of the terms that are unique to franchise agreements are as follows.

- Initiation fee/franchise fee—an up-front payment that varies with the prestige of the franchise. The franchise fee for a McDonald's outlet, for example, can be $500,000.
- Royalties—these are usually paid monthly to the parent company, and are based on a percentage of sales or profits. Royalties can range greatly from about 1%–14% of gross sales, with the average royalty of about 4 per cent.
- Advertising fee—this is usually expressed as a flat rate, and is a contribution to advertising taken out by the parent company for the benefit of all franchises on a regional basis.
- Optional advertising fee—sometimes, the parent company undertakes localized advertising that benefits only a small number of franchisees.

Common Terms of the Standard Form Franchise Agreement

Some clauses are found in the standard form franchise agreement. The following are among the most important.

- Non-competition—the franchisee will agree not to be involved in a competitive business during the franchise agreement term, and for some time after it expires. The validity of this term depends on the reasonableness of the restrictions as to time, geographic area, and subject matter.
- Confidentiality—much of the success of the franchise organization will be internal business systems that it has developed and published in training manuals. Franchisees will have to agree not to reveal these techniques. This will extend after the franchise agreement has been terminated.
- Tied selling—the agreement may require that the franchisee purchase supplies only from the parent company or suppliers that the parent company approves. This arrangement may result in volume discounts; however, unscrupulous parent companies have been suspected of abusing the power given by this type of arrangement and receiving kickbacks. This is a reviewable transaction under the *Competition Act*.
- Exclusivity—this clause prohibits the parent company from selling the rights to another franchise within a defined area without the written consent of the franchisee.
- Right to sue—many franchise agreements contain a clause in which the franchisee acknowledges that the parent company does not intend to be bound by the franchise agreement. In this way, the parent company cannot be sued if it violates the agreement. If you see such a clause in an agreement, you should be very wary of dealing with this parent company, and investigate very thoroughly.
- The franchise agreement may have a termination date and no right for the franchisee to renew the agreement even if it is profitable and they want to continue.

Complaints by Franchisees

The most common complaint by franchisees is that they are not earning the profits that they expected. A franchise agreement is not a guarantee—success depends on many factors, and any business always has risks. It is important to investigate the parent company before signing any franchise agreement. The following complaints are not presented here as facts, but as **allegations** (statements made that have not yet been proved) commonly made by dissatisfied franchisees. The parent companies involved always deny the allegations.

allegations
statements made that have not yet been proved

- The parent company makes its money by taking initiation fees, making it impossible for the franchisee to carry on business, and then closing the franchise. The business is then resold to a new franchisee, who in turn pays a large initiation fee.

- The parent company takes out the lease on the site (head lease), and leases the site in turn to the franchisee (sublease). The parent company adds a secret amount on to the rent, above that set by the owner. For example, the rent from a plaza owner might be $5,000 a month, but the parent company charges the franchisee $6,000 per month. This increase is not disclosed to the franchisee.
- The franchisee pays rent directly to the parent company and, sometimes, the royalty payments are expressed as part of the rent. This gives the parent company exceptional power over the franchisee, because commercial lease law is very strict, with none of the protection found in a residential tenancy. Unsophisticated franchisees, relying on their experience of residential tenancy law, may not realize that being late in paying rent permits the parent company to send in a bailiff and lock out the franchisee. No notice or warning need be given.
- Volume rebates are obtained from original suppliers, but these are not passed on to the franchisees. Sometimes, the franchisees allege that the owners are receiving kickbacks from the suppliers, and are not finding the cheapest supplier of the same quality.
- The parent company inflates average sales figures during sales presentations. Sometimes, it is not revealed that it can be many years before the average is achieved.
- The franchise agreement may have a termination date and no right for the franchisee to renew the agreement even if it is profitable and they want to.

Legalese

deposit
a sum of money paid by the buyer to the seller, to be forfeited if the buyer does not perform its part of the contract

Giving a Deposit   It is always very dangerous to give money up front without concurrently obtaining something of equal value in exchange. Many franchisors (parent companies) ask a large deposit or initiation fee on the signing of the franchise agreement. A **deposit** is a sum of money paid by the buyer to the seller, to be forfeited if the buyer does not perform its part of the contract. Not infrequently franchisees have given over their life savings in such an arrangement only to find that the franchise company went bankrupt and the money was used to pay its normal business expenses. While this situation occurs more frequently with start-up franchises, it can happen even with established ones.

At a minimum, franchisees should insist that any money paid to the franchisor corporation be held in trust until the individual franchise unit is completed and turned over to the franchisee. If the franchisor agrees that the money is to be held in trust, then that money cannot be used for any other purpose. The directors of the corporation would likely be personally liable for the amount. Of course, if the directors do not have personal assets, this precaution is of no help to the franchisee.

Unfortunately, franchisees often sign 40-page franchise agreements in the excitement of a franchise trade fair. In their enthusiasm they don't consider the very real need for independent investigation of the franchise and legal and accounting advice.

Buying a Franchise

The purchase of a franchise is a contract, and so all the remedies in contract law apply. But these protections cannot be a substitute for careful business judgment based on very thorough investigation of the intended franchise purchase. Sometimes purchasers do not fully understand the risk involved and incorrectly believe that a franchise is a guarantee of profitability. If a purchaser is relying on statements made by the franchisor, those statements should be in writing, as the next case shows.

Business Alert!

Buying a Franchise   While franchising is a very common, and often successful, form of doing business, not all franchisees are happy with their parent companies. In the Ontario legislature, an MPP criticizing the lack of legislative protection for franchisees said, "Franchising is beginning to look like the Wild West of business."

447927 Ontario Inc. v. Pizza Pizza Ltd., [1987] 62 O.R. (2d) 114

This case involving Pizza Pizza provides an example of frequent complaints made by franchisees. You will have to judge whether you think the complaints are justified, or a result of unrealistic expectations. The case demonstrates that exemption clauses can be effective. While there are some bases for attacking the clauses and making them ineffective, it is not wise to allow yourself to be put in a position where you have to rely on these legal technical arguments.

Khursheed Hamidani and Mohammed Khan decided to purchase a Pizza Pizza franchise, located in a shopping centre at Jane and Alliance in Toronto. The two had seen the business advertised in the local newspaper.

There were several meetings between Hamidani, Khan, and Pizza Pizza officers about the sale of the franchise. Before signing the agreement, Hamidani and Khan retained a lawyer to negotiate on their behalf. The lawyer made several changes to the agreement. The franchise initiation fee was $30,000.

After taking possession of the business, problems began to develop, and Hamidani and Khan defaulted on the agreement. They were locked out by Pizza Pizza as a result, and the franchise was subsequently sold by the parent company to another franchisee. That franchisee was able to run the business successfully and meet average sales figures for Pizza Pizza operations.

The franchise agreement signed by Hamidani and Khan contained a standard form exemption clause.

Hamidani and Khan sued Pizza Pizza for misrepresenting the profitability of the outlet during the pre-purchase negotiations.

The Court's Decision

The court found against Hamidani and Khan on all issues. It identified four issues of fact and law to be decided.

1. Did any of the statements made in the negotiation process amount to representations in the legal sense—that is, pre-contractual statements of fact, and not of opinion?

There was a conflict in the evidence, in that Hamidani and Khan claimed they were told that the business would earn daily sales of between $4,500 and $5,000 from the outset. Pizza Pizza Ltd. said Hamidani and Khan were told that these were sales averaged over all Pizza Pizza outlets, and were only estimates for an individual unit.

The court found that Pizza Pizza's evidence was more credible, and more consistent with the written material that was also supplied to the plaintiffs before the contract was signed. The statements made by Pizza Pizza were not representations in the technical sense, but were merely estimates.

2. Was there misrepresentation in the sense of any inaccuracy?

The average figures stated for Pizza Pizza outlets were accurate, and the two franchisees did not offer any evidence to the contrary. The fact that the outlet did not achieve the average store results may have been due to the plaintiffs' lack of business skills. Very condemning evidence was the fact that the franchise was resold, and the new owners achieved the average Pizza Pizza outlet earnings.

3. Was there negligence?

There was no fault proven on the part of Pizza Pizza Ltd. in calculating the figures.

4. Was the entire agreement clause valid?

The franchise agreement contained an exemption clause stating that there was no representation or warranty, unless expressed in writing as part of the agreement. As Hamidani and Khan had retained a lawyer to negotiate the agreement for them, and changes had been made at the request of this lawyer, Hamidani and Khan were not able to establish any of the grounds holding the exemption clause to be ineffective.

Franchisees often allege that failure is not because of business factors, but because of unfair advantages taken by the parent company. It is wise to be very careful in selecting a franchise operation. Before signing any franchise agreement or handing over any money, make sure you do each of the following.

- Check with several other franchisees—not selected by the sales personnel of the parent company.
- Check with the local Chamber of Commerce, Better Business Bureau, and provincial consumer and commercial affairs department yourself.
- Retain a lawyer and an accountant early in the proceedings.
- Ask your bank manager to check into the parent company.

Provincial Franchise Legislation

Five provinces (Alberta, Ontario, Manitoba, New Brunswick and P.E.I.) have instituted special legislation to protect franchisees. Other provinces have discussed such legislation, but have not as yet enacted it.

This legislation requires a disclosure document with **material facts** by the franchisor including:

- file financial statements publicly
- give a history of any bankruptcy or criminal records of their officers and directors
- list all past and current lawsuits alleging deceptive business practices
- list all franchisees, current and past
- full franchise costs
- background information in earnings projections are given
- supply costs and supply acquisition rules
- advertising costs
- lease terms
- renewal and termination terms

The disclosure requirements are enforced strictly by the courts. The disclosure must be complete in that all information must be contained in the disclosure documents and they must be delivered before the purchaser commits to buy the franchise.

If complete and truthful disclosure is not given the contract may be **rescinded** and money refunded.

Example: In *1490664 Ontario Ltd. v Dig This Garden Retailers Ltd.*, 2005 CanLII 25181 (ONCA), a franchisee who had operated an unsuccessful franchise for 13 months, was entitled to a return of her initiation fee, set up costs and damages totalling $172,000 when the court ruled that the franchisor had not met the disclosure information of the Ontario franchise law. The disclosure information was given in bits and pieces, not one document as required, and had only complied with 70% of the disclosure requirements. She was also able under the Act to sue the two people who had negotiated the agreement for the franchisor as well, since they were shareholders, officers and directors of the company.

6792341 Canada Inc. v. Dollar It Ltd., 2009 ONCA 385 (CanLII)

In November 2007 the appellant franchisee entered into a franchise agreement to operate a Dollar It store in Ottawa. The business was unsuccessful from the very beginning and after about 6 months, the franchisee served notice on the franchisor that it wanted to rescind the franchise agreement and get a refund of its investment pursuant to s. 6 of the Ontario Arthur Wishart Act (Franchise Disclosure).

This Ontario law allows a franchisee to rescind the contract within 2 years if the franchisor had not met the disclosure requirements under the Act. The franchisee claimed that there was so little disclosure given, it was effectively no disclosure. The franchisor claimed that they had completed the franchisor's disclosure document, and though there was some information missing, the franchisee's right to rescind under the law was only for a 60 day period when information was incomplete, and that time limit had passed. The trial judge agreed that there had been some disclosure, so the 60 day limitation period applied and therefore the right to rescind the franchise agreement was denied. The franchisee appealed.

The Court's Decision

The Ontario Court of Appeal carefully examined the information that the franchisor had disclosed before the franchise contract was signed and ruled that the franchisor's disclosure was so "materially deficient in its substantive content" it did not fulfil the requirements of the Act. The court ruled there was effectively no disclosure, so the franchisee was entitled to the extraordinary right of rescission. The court noted that just giving a document that was titled a " franchise disclosure document" does not mean that it actually was one and it did not thereby automatically reduce the franchisee's rescission right to just 60 days.

The franchisor had not included many important documents that the law required. There had not been a proper Franchisor Certificate completed, financial statements were not provided, details of the exclusive territory and the proximity of other franchisees was not given, nor was the main lease for the property that franchisee had the sublease on provided. The court noted that the absence of some of these requirements on their own would justify a ruling of no disclosure and thereby entitle the franchisee to the 2 year rescission period. Since all of this informa-tion was either incomplete or missing, the franchisee succeeded in their claim for rescission and a refund of their investment plus related costs.

The Statutory Duty of Good Faith—Franchise Agreements

While in most contracts made between businesses the competition model of "every person for themselves" governs, there are some exceptions. For example, where there is a contractual relationship with an adviser such as a lawyer or an accountant, that advisor owes the client, even a business client, a fiduciary duty.

However, there are some relationships, once a contract is formed, into which the law, either by common law or statute, imposes a middle level duty of good faith. Provincial franchise laws impose a statutory duty on franchisors to act in good faith.

For example, an insurance company does not have a fiduciary duty to the insured policy holder in paying a claim, but does have a common law duty of good faith to pay out a valid claim and not, for example, to refuse to pay a valid claim, force the insured to sue and use the cost of litigation to make that insured take a lower settlement. Breach of that obligation alone would result in an award of damages relating to bad faith conduct. Franchise agreements have this duty imposed by statutes in provinces where they have been passed.

Example: It has been a common practice for franchisors, on the request to renew a franchise agreement by the franchisee, to insist that, as a condition of permitting the franchisee to continue using the franchise, that it had to give a full release to the franchisor. The Ontario Court of Appeal said that requiring a release in the context of franchise relationship is a breach of the duty of good faith implied by the relevant franchise act. (*405341 Ontario Limited v. Midas Canada Inc.*, 2010 ONCA 478).

■ *Critical Concepts of* Good Faith

- A party may act in self-interest but must have regard to the interest of the opposite party which means he must deal honestly and reasonably with the opposite party.
- Good faith is a minimal standard, in the sense that the duty to act in good faith is only breached when a party acts in bad faith. Bad faith is conduct that is contrary to community standards of honesty, reasonableness or fairness.

Salah v. Timothy's Coffees of the World Inc., 2010 ONCA 673 (CanLII)

Mr. Salah and the company that he formed were franchisees that operated a Timothy's coffee shop in the food court on the third floor of an Ottawa shopping centre. The agreement was just for a 4 year period because Timothy's only had 4 years remaining on its lease with the mall for that store location. The agreement with Salah stated that if Timothy's renewed the lease at the Bayshore Mall, then Salah would have the right to renew the franchise agreement.

When the 4 year lease at the mall expired, Timothy's signed a new lease for a new store located on the second floor of the mall. Timothy's then sold a franchise to a new franchisee for the second floor store and informed Salah that his agreement had ended. Timothy's maintained that Salah's rights to renew his franchise only extended to a store located on the third floor. Salah claimed that he had a right to a new lease term, and this right was not restricted to their third floor location, but extended to any location in the mall where Timothy's signed a lease. Timothy's asserted that Salah had no right of renewal and that the franchise agreement ended at the same time as the lease. Salah sued Timothy's for breach of contract and breach of a duty of good faith and fair dealing.

The trial court ruled that Timothy's had breached the agreement when it did not offer Salah the option to operate the store on the second floor and the franchisor was also liable for breach of its duty of good faith and fair dealing. The Court awarded Mr. Salah and his company $153,899 for past lost income, $230,358 for future lost income and $50,000 for breach of good faith and mental distress. Timothy's appealed.

The Court's Decision

The Ontario Court of Appeal agreed with the trial court's decision. It ruled that the agreement for Salah's renewal applied to any lease that Timothy's signed with the mall, not just for a store on the third floor. It noted that all the franchise agreements involved referred to the Bayshore Shopping Centre location and none limited the renewal rights to just a third floor lease. Timothy's had withheld critical information from Salah and had refused to return his phone calls and told the mall representatives to not discuss new location negotiations with Salah. Timothy's was liable for the financial losses for its breach of the franchise agreement.

Section 3 of the Ontario Act also imposes on franchisors and franchisees a duty of fair dealing and a duty to act in good faith in accordance with reasonable commercial standards. The court ruled that Timothy's had breached that duty of good faith and fair dealing by not offering the second floor location to Salah. The Act also allows for personal damage claims and the court recognized the impact it had on Salah's emotional health when it upheld the award for damages for mental distress as well.

Franchise ADR

Even with profitable franchise business concepts and best practices, there will be problems to overcome and disputes to settle. To meet the challenge of how to establish cost effective dispute resolution mechanisms to avoid both the skyrocketing costs of litigation and the damaging consequence to the franchise brand of public trials, the Canadian Franchise Association has initiated an ombudsman program. The project was spearheaded by McDonald's Canada.

In Summation

Starting a Business

Restrictions on choosing a name come from several areas of law:

- A name cannot be similar to a registered trademark, whether it deceives the public or not.
- The words *Limited, Corp.* or *Inc.* cannot be used unless the business is a corporation.

Protection of Personal Assets

- The form of a business is an important consideration to a business person from the point of view of protection of the owner's personal assets from business creditors.
- The forms of business are:
  a) sole proprietorship
  b) partnership
  c) limited partnership
  d) corporation
- Businesses must often have to obtain a license to operate and must comply with local land use zoning by-laws.

Sole Proprietorship

- This is a one-person business. There are very few legal restrictions, but if the owner's first and last name is not used, it must be registered publicly so that the public will know who is behind the business name.
- There are many disadvantages to a sole proprietorship such as; unlimited personal liability, higher tax rates on profits, lacks of skills, difficulty in raising money.

Partnership

- A partnership is an association of two or more people for business purposes, with a view to profit.
- All partnership names must be registered.
- A partnership can be intentional, but it can also be unintentional—that is, implied by the court.

- While partners can decide how various matters are to be resolved by a partnership agreement, in the absence of such a document, the *Partnership Act* will be used to settle matters which are often disputed, such as division of profits, the right to take part in management of the business, and the right to salary for work done by a partner for the partnership business.

- Partnership agreements can vary the *Partnership Act* provisions and also deal with other matters, such as specifying events when one partner can buy out another (buy-sell clauses), and setting out a means for establishing the value of each partner's share of the partnership (shotgun buy-sell clause.)

- The consequences of entering into a partnership are serious:
  a) Partners have a fiduciary duty to each other.
  b) Partners are responsible to outsiders for the acts of other partners and employees:
     i)   for contracts made within the usual course of a partnership business
     ii) for torts of partners committed in the course of the partnership business
     iii) for torts of employees by vicarious liability
  c) All partners are jointly responsible for the above liabilities.

Limited Partnerships

- To restrict the above liabilities a limited partnership can be formed.

- The limited partner will not be responsible for the liabilities of the partnership beyond the investment of capital.

- The limited partnership must be registered as a limited partnership.

- The limited partner cannot take an active part in the business.

- In Ontario it is possible to form a limited liability partnership, which permits a partner to be active in the business but restricts her liability to her own torts and those of employees she supervises directly.

Agency

- An agent is hired by a principal to act on their behalf and to set up contracts between the principal and a third party.

- The agent owes the principal a fiduciary duty and must act in the principal's best interests and within the scope of their authority, give full disclosure, follow instructions and keep the principal updated.

- An agent must disclose to the third party that they are an agent or else the agent is personally liable for the contract.

- If the agent acts properly for a disclosed principal, the agent is not personally liable, and the principal alone is bound in contract for the obligations and benefits created by the agent on the principal's behalf.

Franchises

- Franchises are not treated as a separate legal form. They are a collection of various rights that permit the use of the parent company's business advantage—brand names, logos, confidential recipes and formulas, and so on.

- Many provinces have specific laws regulating franchises and require the franchisor to issue complete disclosure document prior to a franchise agreement being signed.

- Many provincial laws also impose a duty of good faith and fair dealing on franchisors and franchisees.

Closing Questions

Partnerships

1. Kathryn Cameron, who has just inherited $1,000,000, is considering going into the travel-agency business with Amy Jones as a partner. Jones has considerable ability, especially in accounting, and will supervise all bookkeeping staff, but she owns only her car and owes $5,000 on credit cards.

The partnership will have $200,000 in a working capital as a result of a loan from the bank. It will have about $500,000 normally on deposit from customers.

a) What are the partnership's assets and liabilities? What are the partners' personal assets and liabilities?

b) What risks are associated with this business?

c) What are the risks for the partnership and for each partner?

d) What advice would you give to each partner to limit her exposure?

e) Assume that Amy cannot pay the amount owing on her credit card. Can the bank sue the partnership for this debt? Assume further that the bank eventually obtains a judgment against Amy. Is there any way that the bank can collect on that judgment against the partnership?

2. The section of the partnership act given in the text states: "... subject to any agreement express or implied between the partners..."

a) What does this phrase mean and what effect does it have?

b) What value does it reflect regarding freedom of contract versus control by legislation?

c) Will this value always work to the benefit of a weaker party? Do you know of legislation which prohibits varying its terms by contract? Does it relate to consumer situations or business situations?

3. Harris Investments Inc. specializes in land speculation, buying land for the purpose of reselling it at a profit. From time to time, Harris Investments finds itself short of cash, and enters into an arrangement with Mitsu Enterprises Ltd., whereby each corporation puts up some money to buy the land.

In one deal in which Harris Investments and Mitsu Enterprises agreed to buy a piece of land, it was Mitsu Enterprises that signed the agreement. Mitsu Enterprises began to find itself in financial difficulties, and did not close the deal. The market price of the property has dropped, and the vendor wants to sue for his lost profits. Unfortunately, Mitsu Enterprises' efforts to refinance did not work out, and it went into bankruptcy.

a) Does the vendor have any grounds for suing Harris Investments, even though it did not sign the agreement of purchase and sale?

4. Which of the following would constitute a partnership?

a) Hank and Rick pooled their money to buy a 1965 Mustang, which they intend to repair and resell.

b) John and Juan bought a cab together. John drives it during the day, while Juan drives it at night. They split the cost of maintenance.

c) Karin and Ricki both have delivery services. Whenever one of them has a delivery, she checks with the other to see if she has anything that needs delivered in that direction. The delivery charge for the item is split between them.

d) Ellis and Joe purchased an old house, which they renovated. When renovations were nearly completed, they purchased another house described as a "handyman's delight," using the first house as collateral for the purchase of the second. The first house is now on the market and renovations are underway on the second house.

5. What are a partner's obligations to:

a) the other partners?

b) persons who have made contracts with the partnership but signed by another partner?

c) persons who have a claim in negligence against the partnership for an act done by another partner?

d) persons who have claims against the partnership for an act done by employees in the course of employment?

6. Ally, who is 17, and Taiko, who is 20, decided to set up a partnership to provide costumes to local theatre groups. Ally was an excellent seamstress and would take care of that side of the operation, while Taiko would look after sales. Taiko was an excellent salesperson and, before long, the two of them were extremely busy. It became necessary to acquire two more sewing machines under a lease-to-buy arrangement over a 24-month period.

A friend of Taiko's provided a loan of $20,000 to the partnership at 10 percent interest to purchase a large quantity of material that would be used to make the costumes. Ron was recently hired as a part-time employee at a rate of $15,000 a year to help Ally with the costume creation. A partnership agreement, which requires the two partners to split any depths or profits, had been created at the time the lease and loan were taken out. Ally has now decided that she wants to leave the partnership.

a) Is Ally bound by the partnership agreement, and if not, why not?

b) Since Taiko had entered into the lease, loan, and employment contract on the understanding that these things were partnership contracts, is she in any way obligated to live up to the contracts?

7. Beverly, Jordy, and Will formed a partnership to sell articles and memorabilia related to various futuristic science-fiction movies and television shows. On a holiday to the Far East, Will attended a manufacturers' convention, where he saw excellent reproductions of a medallion worn on a very popular space TV show, and which was to be made available to the market in the next year.

On his return home, Will raved about the sights he had seen on his holiday, but said nothing about the item that he had come across. He then set up a separate proprietorship under the name Loxana Sales, and placed an order for 2,000 of the medallions, which he intended to sell at $20 each.

a) Since Will came across the medallion on a personal holiday, is he under any obligation to tell his partners about it?

b) What would be the result if Will did have a duty to his partners concerning this item?

8. You have been authorized to act as an agent on behalf of your employer in obtaining janitorial services for your small business, a retail antique shop. Are you breaching any of the duties of any agent if you do the following?

a) Hire Breeze-Pro to come in twice a week to dust and vacuum and empty trash, and to clean windows and wash floors twice a month.

b) Hire Breeze-Pro to do what is noted in a) above, for one year, in exchange for any two antiques of their choice.

c) Hire Breeze-Pro to give the carpets an odour-free treatment.

d) Hire Breeze-Pro to water the plants in your showroom.

e) Hire Breeze-Pro to do a) above. You are the owner-operator of Breeze-Pro.

f) Subscribe to a publication, *A Cleaning News@*, which lists the latest in businesses offering janitorial services in your community.

g) Hire Breeze-Pro to do what is noted in a) above. Breeze-Pro totally ruined all the carpets in your showroom in an attempt to clean them. It turns out Breeze-Pro was reported to consumer affairs six times in the last six months for shoddy work, and had its membership pulled from the Better Business Bureau.

h) Hire Breeze-Pro to do what is noted in a) above. Your friend Louis runs Breeze-Pro, and has promised to do you a favour some time if you give him the contract. Breeze-Pro's quote was only slightly above that of two other bidders.

i) Hire Breeze-Pro to do what is noted in a) above. Breeze-Pro has never cleaned an antique store before, and it damages several items in its first month on the job, causing a $5,000 loss.

9. Adam Chin met Tracy Geen, a real estate agent, while looking to purchase a house. Geen showed Chin a number of properties, and he found the home of his dreams, which, unfortunately, carried a high price. Chin had already organized a first mortgage with his bank, the Municipal Bank of Mellenville, but he would require a second mortgage to be able to purchase the house. While telling Geen of his need for a second mortgage, he also mentioned that he required fire insurance for the house once the purchase was completed. Geen, who also happened to be an *insurance agent* for Metro Life Insurance Company, offered to help Chin with his insurance needs and, for a fee, to assist him in placing a second mortgage.

Unknown to Chin, the vendor of the house had indicated to Geen that she was prepared to take back a second mortgage on a three-year term at 15 percent if it would assist in helping to sell the house. Chin left it to Geen to negotiate the terms of the second mortgage saying, "The lower the interest rate, the higher the return—nudge, nudge, wink, wink."

Geen negotiated the interest from the vendor down to 12 percent for a five-year term. The offer on the house was finalized. Geen and Chin met the day before the purchase of the house and completed the necessary insurance forms. Chin gave Geen a cheque for his first premium, and Geen put the forms and the cheque in an envelope, placed them in her briefcase and, patting it, told him he was in good hands. She would submit the insurance application to Metro Life later that day.

Six weeks later, Chin's house was destroyed by fire and the Municipal Bank of Mellenville demanded payment under the mortgage, as did the vendor as second *mortgagee* (lender). Chin contacted Metro Life, which said it had no records of Chin's application, and refused to pay either the bank or the second mortgagee. Chin then contacted Geen, who vaguely recalled her meeting with Chin. Checking her briefcase, she found the envelope containing his application forms and cheque stuck in the top corner of the lid. Geen phoned Chin, and told him the application had never been submitted. She felt just awful that all this had happened; however, he was not covered for insurance on his house.

a) Advise Chin as to the nature of his legal action, and whether it would be Metro Life or Geen that he would pursue for his remedy.

b) Has Geen met the terms of her agency relationship with Metro Life, and if not, explain what standard she has fallen short of and why?

c) Now that the parties are all talking directly to each other, the vendor/second mortgagee has found out about the second-mortgage financing arrangement between Chin and Geen. What advice would you provide her in the circumstances?

d) Other than finding a new profession, what advice would you offer Geen in order to help her arrange her future business dealings?

prospectus

a document issued to inform the public about a new issue of shares or bonds that a corporation is required to publish when inviting the public to buy its securities

10. Portia Playfair had decided to take her money out of the bank and put it in the hands of a stockbroker in order to receive a better return on it. Clever Carl Corban, her stockbroker, strongly recommended that she place it in a mutual fund, and provided her with a prospectus from the fund. (A **prospectus** is a document issued to inform the public about a new issue of shares or bonds that a corporation is required to publish when inviting the public to buy its securities.) This document specifically emphasized that there were no fees payable by the investor, either at the time of making the investment or when the money was removed from the fund. Playfair decided to go with Clever Carl's suggestion, and placed $50,000 in the mutual fund based on the prospectus and his recommendation.

A year later, Playfair wished to remove half her money from the mutual fund in order to purchase a recreational vehicle to tour the Yukon. When she asked Corban to make the arrangements, he convinced her to leave the funds in and to arrange a bank loan to make the purchase. She followed his advice. Several months later, struggling to make her monthly loan payments, Playfair read an article in the financial section of the newspaper that indicated some mutual funds paid an annual fee of anywhere from 1 to 2 percent to the broker who placed the money in the fund, for as long as the money remained there. Curious, Portia looked through the prospectus for the mutual fund and found no reference to such a fee. She then telephoned the newspaper reporter and asked if his research indicated that her particular mutual fund followed this practice. When the reporter said that it did, she contacted Corban and asked him directly if he was receiving a fee from the mutual fund for the amount and length of time her money stayed in the fund. Corban said he would have to get back to her.

a) Has Corban breached a duty and, if so, what is the nature of that duty and the breach?

b) To whom did Corban owe this duty—Playfair or the mutual fund?

c) If the duty was owed to Playfair, what would be the result of a court action for breach of that duty?

11. Alice has been hired as a sales rep to sell franchises in Ontario. She believes that there is no duty of good faith in negotiating a contract, each party is entitled get the best deal for itself. Is she correct?

12. Mustafa and Hussein are partners in a computer repair business. Mustafa's uncle asks him to repair the uncle's computer and pays $100, which Mustafa pockets. He does not tell Hussein because the deal came from his relative and not through the partnership business. Is Mustafa correct?

Corporate Law and White-Collar Crime

The Concept of a Corporation

The idea of an artificial legal personality dates back to the time of the Phoenician traders. In medieval times, artists and craftsmen would meet and discuss matters of common interest over a meal, usually dinner. The groups thus became known as *cum panis*, or "with bread." The word *company* derives from this phrase.

In England, merchants and craftsmen formed business organizations known as guilds. It was recognized as important that these organizations should carry on even after current members died, and so the sovereign would issue a royal charter, granting the guild many of the rights of an actual person. This included the power to enter into contracts, and the right to own property and to conduct lawsuits. Thus, the guild survived any change in membership, and would cease to exist only if the monarch cancelled the charter.

The world's oldest corporation is a Canadian company. The Hudson's Bay Company received its charter on May 2, 1670, from Charles II of England. The original name of the company was "The Governor and Company of Adventurers of England Trading into Hudson's Bay."

Separate Legal Person

A corporation is considered to be an artificial person, and has a separate legal existence from its owners. A **legal person** is an entity (a corporation or a human being) recognized at law as having its own legal personality. This distinction has led to the awkward use of the terms *corporate person*, and *natural person* or *individual*, to distinguish between the two. When the word *person* is used on its own, both types of persons are meant. The corporation has been called a legal fiction, as it is only a concept and has no physical existence—therefore, it never "dies."

Corporation **Corporation** derives from the Latin word *corpore*, meaning body. A corporation is a group or body of people who join together to form an organization that acts as one person. Of course, a single individual can also form a corporation.

legal person
an entity (a corporation or a human being) recognized at law as having its own legal personality

Legalese

Limited Liability

limited liability

the principle that a corporation can shield owners, directors, and managers from liability for many obligations of the corporation

The concept of a separate legal entity or person is the foundation for **limited liability**, which is the principle that a corporation can shield owners, directors, and managers from liability for many obligations of the corporation. Creditors of a corporation can seize only the corporation's assets—not the shareholders' personal assets, as in a partnership or sole proprietorship. The shareholder loses only the amount of money paid for the shares.

Salomon v. Salomon & Co. Ltd., [1897] A.C. 22 (H.L.)

Joseph Salomon had a successful shoe-manufacturing business and wanted to incorporate. He therefore formed a corporation called Salomon & Co. Ltd., and sold the shoe-manufacturing firm to it. Since the newly formed corporation had no money, Joseph Salomon personally took back a mortgage from the corporation, with the assets of the shoe-manufacturing business as security.

The new corporation continued in the old line of business and, over time, incurred debts from suppliers. Unfortunately, the business ran into many problems and became insolvent. The creditors all brought claims for unpaid accounts. Joseph Salomon was one of those creditors, and sued the corporation for payment of the mortgage. The problem with this was that there was so much owing under the mortgage, Salomon would take all of the assets of the business, leaving nothing to pay the other creditors.

The creditors cried foul, claiming that Joseph Salomon and Salomon & Co. Ltd. were really one and the same. He therefore should not be able to take money in priority over other creditors.

The Court's Decision

The court noted that, in law, a corporation is a separate legal entity from its owners. They affirmed that this concept had a real meaning, and therefore a corporation could give a mortgage to its shareholder (owner) just as if the shareholder were a stranger. Accordingly, Joseph Salomon could enforce his mortgage and take the assets of the business.

Business Alert!

Corporate Assets The Salomon case was decided at a time when the use of a corporation, and all it implied, was not widely known. Today, before offering credit, sophisticated creditors always search the assets of a corporation to determine if there are any free assets. Normally, small businesses such as Salomon have few assets. Those they do possess are usually subject to a lien from the bank. So, when a person gives credit to a corporation, that person is relying on the fact that the business is sound and able to pay its bills from its income.

Business Law Applied

❶ **Three shareholders formed** a corporation to carry on their business. To celebrate the end of their first successful year, they went on a fishing trip together, leaving the company in the control of its manager. The aircraft in which the three were travelling crashed on the way to their destination. There were no survivors.

A creditor who had not been paid by the corporation obtained a judgment against it for $10,000. On hearing of the death of all three shareholders, the creditor claimed that the corporation had ceased to exist, and sought to seize the deceased shareholders' personal assets.

a) Was the creditor correct under law?

Incorporating a Business

The process of incorporation is a simple one that involves obtaining the proper form, filling it out, filing it with the appropriate government office, and paying a filing fee. Some stationary companies carry legal forms: incorporation forms sell for about $10. The filing fee will vary but it is usually around $360.

An organization can incorporate under either federal or provincial law. If it is a large business that plans to carry on operations across Canada, you would probably incorporate under the federal law. Even if you chose to incorporate under a provincial law, you can still carry on business outside of that province and outside of Canada. However if you carry on business in another province you may have to fulfil certain registration requirements in order to operate there. The law you chose to incorporate under has more effect on the internal operations of the corporation such as rules for electing directors, shareholders meetings, declaring dividends and other matters.

The process of filling out the forms is not that difficult; however, choosing whether incorporation is the correct form of business, and the consideration of problems and dispute resolution by way of a shareholder agreement, are both matters of some complexity and require professional advice from a lawyer and an accountant.

An example of **Articles of Incorporation** (the basic document creating a corporation in most Canadian jurisdictions) for an Ontario corporation is shown in the Appendix to this chapter. This is a one-person company. The particular clauses are worded generally so that they can be used by most small businesses.

Articles of Incorporation the basic document creating a corporation in most Canadian jurisdictions

In some jurisdictions to incorporate Letters Patent or Memorandum of Association are used instead of articles of incorporation. There are some technical differences in these different forms, but for our purposes, we will assume that a corporation is incorporated under the articles of incorporation process.

Corporate Governance

The articles of incorporation and the by-laws create the internal management structure for the corporation and set the rules for how the corporation should be run. Corporate governance is the term that refers to how a corporation is internally organized and managed to meet both its internal and external responsibilities.

Due to major corporate scandals in the U.S. in the 1990's such as the failure of Enron, Tyco and WorldCom, when shareholders and creditors lost billions, the U.S. passed the Sarbanes-Oxley Act of 2002. The purpose of this law was to tighten the rules on corporate governance and the duty of accounting firms auditing public corporations. This law should give greater protection to shareholders and creditors by forcing corporations to have better accountability within the corporation, more checks and balances on decision-making and authority, more transparency, more independent directors and greater disclosure. It clearly established the auditors' duty to shareholders and the investing public to be accurate and fairly disclose information about the corporation.

Large accounting firms often provide both accounting services and consulting services to public corporations, and they were frequently in the position of potentially losing large consulting fees if the corporate executives did not like the accounting statements that the auditors had prepared. This law increased the duty on the auditors, top executives and directors to release accurate financial statements and the penalties for fraud were increased, to protect the public.

Canada tightened up some of its regulations in response to the U.S. law and the need for greater disclosure, fair and accurate financial statements and improved corporate governance.

Professional Corporations

Many professionals are not allowed to incorporate their practices due to the provincial laws governing that profession and/or the particular rules of the governing body of that profession. For example the Law Society of Alberta regulates Alberta lawyers and the College of Physician and Surgeons regulates doctors in Ontario. LLPs as discussed in the previous chapter do allow partners in some professional firms to obtain some protection from liability. But most provinces now also allow the formation of a professional corporation (PC).

Provincial laws will list what specific professions are allowed to incorporate and form a PC and it must also be permitted by the provincial governing body as well. In Ontario in 2000 the laws were changed to allow PCs by professionals such as; accountants, lawyers, doctors, dentists, pharmacists, chiropractors, social workers and psychologists. The letters PC must appear in the name. The creation of a PC either alone or with other persons in the same profession does not limit the professional's liability to their clients though. The professional is still personally liable for their misconduct, the same as if was not a PC, and they purchase malpractice insurance in case they are sued. The creation of a PC does however limit the individual's personal liability to others such as creditors including lenders, suppliers or landlords.

The main benefit of a PC however is not in reducing liability, but in tax advantages that sole proprietors and partnerships cannot claim. The professionals become shareholders in the business, but their spouses and children also can hold non-voting shares, which allows for income splitting for tax purposes. Small business tax deductions are also allowed in this form of ownership not previously permitted by professionals and there can also be significant capital gains tax advantages if they eventually sell their practice for a profit. Consultation with a lawyer skilled in this area is necessary to determine the proper structure for any professional practice.

Keeping the Protection of the Corporate Form

The limited liability of a corporation affords no protection unless it is clearly indicated on every contractual document that the document is being signed on the corporation's behalf. Merely signing an agreement could make the individual personally liable, even if the contract or promissory note states in the body of the document that the agreement is with the corporation. All documents signed on behalf of the corporation should contain a clause such as the following:

> The Systems Co., Inc.
>
> Per: _Claire La Mort_____
>
> Claire La Mort, President

You will sometimes see the phrase "authorized to bind the corporation" below the title of the corporate officer. This is required by various provincial registry acts when signing documents that relate to land. It is not necessary to use that phrase in normal business transactions.

Business Alert!

Pre-incorporation Contracts   A business might find it necessary to sign a contract before incorporation is granted by the government. In order to avoid personal liability of the individual signing such an agreement, there should be a clause immediately above the signature, expressly stating that the signer does so on behalf of a corporation and without personal liability. This is effective so long as a corporation is in fact subsequently formed.

> Claire La Mort, on behalf of a company to be incorporated, and without personal liability
>
> Dated at Vancouver this 20th day of November, 1997   _Claire La Mort_____
>
> signature

Bank of Nova Scotia v. Radocsay, [1981] 33 O.R. (2d) 785 (C.A.)

John Radocsay went into partnership with one other man, in a business called Classic TV & Sound. Five days later, Radocsay had another company incorporated, under the name Radocsay Televisions Ltd.

Two years later, Radocsay signed a demand promissory note in favour of the bank for $12,500.

The bank sued Radocsay personally when the note was not paid.

Radocsay defended saying he signed on behalf of the corporation, and that as the bank was notified of the new corporation, the bank should have realized that he was signing in this capacity.

I promise to pay on demand the sum of $12,500.

Dated: July 20, 1976

John Radocsay

J. Radocsay

The Court's Decision

The court stated that the incorporation of a firm enables a merchant to carry on that business much as before, but with the advantage of not being liable for the debts of the business if things go wrong. But the merchant must be careful that the debts are those of the corporation and not personal debts. The merchant is the one to reap the advantages of this wonderful new creation, and so is the one who must demonstrate that old contractual relationships have been severed, and new ones created.

It was the duty of the person signing the note to make certain that the note, on its face, clearly showed that it was being signed in a representative capacity, on behalf of a corporation. As the note was signed by Radocsay without anything more, Radocsay was personally liable.

Signing Corporate Documents   The case of *Bank of Nova Scotia v. Radocsay* demonstrates the need for clarity in signing a corporate document. A number of cases have found the opposite, and have held that a person signing a note on which the corporate name appears somewhere is signing as a representative of the corporation. However, you do not want to be in a position where that is left for a court to decide. The best protection you can have is to make certain all corporate documents are clearly identified as being signed on behalf of the corporation.

Business Alert!

Business Law Applied

❷ **Eleanor Marathon negotiated** a loan with a small finance company for her new business, Marathon Fashions Inc. The loan was to be used to purchase a new computer system for cash, accounting, and inventory controls. Eleanor Marathon was clear that she did not want to sign a personal guarantee for the loan, and the finance company agreed. As part of the security documentation, Commercial Finance Company asked Marathon to sign a loan repayment agreement which read in part:

In consideration for a loan by Commercial Finance Company to Marathon Fashions Inc., the undersigned hereby agrees to make the monthly instalments.

Dated at the City of Edmonton in the Province of Alberta this 26th day of September, 1999

a) In signing this loan agreement, did Marathon take on liability personally, or on behalf of the corporation?

b) What alteration should she make to the agreement to ensure that she does not assume personal liability?

Modern Creditor-Proofing Schemes

The corporate form has been used to protect individuals from liability to creditors in a number of ways. Here is one example of a creditor-proofing scheme used to protect a small-business person from liability on a lease and from trade creditors.

Two corporations are incorporated. One is the parent, in this case called a holding company ("Holdco"). It owns all the shares of a subsidiary, which is the operating company and which is named Perfect Jewelers Inc. Assume the operating company makes a profit of $10,000 in a given year. These profits from Perfect Jewelers could be used to purchase inventory and other assets. Instead, they are sent to the parent company by a way of **dividends** (sums declared by the board of directors as payable to shareholders). The dividends go tax-free from the subsidiary to the parent. The parent then lends the subsidiary the same $10,000 back. The subsidiary, in turn, gives the parent security for the loan by way of a **lien** (a claim against property) on its assets to the extent of $10,000. This security agreement will have priority over claims of creditors to the assets of Perfect Jewelers to the extent of the $10,000.

This transaction can be done any time there is profit in the operating company. After a time, all the assets of the operating company will be subject to a lien in favour of the parent. If the profits had been left in Perfect Jewelers and used to buy assets, these assets could be seized by creditors.

dividends

sums declared by the board of directors as payable to shareholders

lien

a claim against property

A Creditor-Proofing Scheme

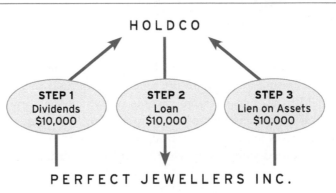

Business Alert!

Creditor-Proofing Schemes   Many people believe that if they are dealing with a corporation, they are dealing with a business of substance that can pay its debts. However, the opposite is true for many corporations, especially small companies. In the majority of cases either a creditor (such as a bank) will have liens upon all of the assets, or the owners will have a creditor-proofing scheme in place.

If you are extending credit to any business, you should, at an early stage, obtain advice from an accountant or a lawyer to understand the risks involved and what steps can be taken, if any, to reduce those risks. Learn what a bank does in similar circumstances and take the same precautions.

Piercing the Corporate Veil

Piercing the corporate veil is a remedy aimed to make shareholders personally responsible for corporate debts.

Historians and economists are usually united in giving the unique development of the corporate form by the common law as one of the major reasons for the economic success of the West. The corporate form permits innovative businesspeople to start risky businesses without losing their personal assets, creating a better environment for new business ventures.

However, that form can be abused. It is only in narrow circumstances of abuse that the protection of the corporate form will be lifted.

In the landmark case of *Salomon and Salomon*, above, while establishing a strong protective corporate form, the court also stated that the form could be abused and could be pierced. Although there is no clear principle of when the corporate form is considered abused in law, cases where that is done usually involve small corporations, that are similar to sole proprietorships or small partnerships, when assets have been removed from the corporation so it cannot pay its debts, or there has been some restructuring of the business so that the original corporation is made a shell corporation without assets. Fraudulent acts would justify piercing the corporate veil.

Example: Smith and Jones are the sole shareholders, officers and directors of Target Sport Uniforms Inc. It has been minimally profitable the last few years, but this year it became clear the business will fail. The corporation owes $50,000 to Crests R Us. The shareholders, Smith and Jones, check their business's account and see the last $50,000. They transfer the funds to themselves and walk away leaving the corporation insolvent. It is in this situation that a court will pierce the corporate veil and make shareholders Smith and Jones personally liable for the debt.

It should be noted that the court will not penetrate the corporate structure just because a situation is unfair or to achieve justice. It is only given in a situation where a wrongful act such as fraud has occurred.

Shoppers Drug Mart Inc. v. 6470360 Canada Inc. (Energyshop Consulting Inc./Powerhouse Energy Management Inc.), 2014 ONCA 85 (CanLII)

In October 2005 Shoppers Drug Mart contracted with Michael Beamish and his company Energyshop (which was not a corporation at that time) to manage and pay its utility bills on a nationwide basis. Shoppers operates over 1,000 stores across Canada. Soon after the contract was signed Beamish incorporated Powerhouse Energy to conduct the business of Energyshop. Beamish was the only shareholder, officer and director of Powerhouse. Shoppers directed utility companies to send Shoppers' utility bills to Powerhouse, which would then organize all the bills and send Shoppers an invoice for the total amount owing plus a processing fee. Shoppers then transferred money to a joint bank account in the names of Powerhouse and Beamish to pay the bills.

In 2008 Shoppers received an anonymous notice that some money it had sent for its utility invoices had been transferred to a different joint account Beamish and Powerhouse had set up and used for purposes other than paying Shoppers utility bills. Shoppers investigated and then sued Beamish and Powerhouse for $970,000 which it claimed they had wrongfully taken.

The initial court decision ruled that Powerhouse was liable for the money as it had been incorporated to carry on the business of Energyshop. It did not consider the misappropriation of the money though to be a fraud or a breach of trust, but it was a considered to be a "wrongful act" and Powerhouse had been unjustly enriched at Shoppers expense. The trial judge however refused to pierce the corporate veil though and it did not hold Beamish personally liable. The court noted that when Powerhouse was originally incorporated it was not created for an illegal or fraudulent purpose, and this was a requirement to pierce the corporate veil. Since Powerhouse was not initially set up for a wrongful purpose, the directing mind behind it, Beamish, was not held personally liable for claims against it.

Shoppers Drug Mart appealed this ruling to the Ontario Court of Appeal. It claimed that Beamish was the only controlling mind behind Powerhouse and Beamish himself had been unjustly enriched by his wrongful actions, so the corporate veil should be pierced.

The Court's Decision

The Ontario Court of Appeal clarified when the corporate veil can be pierced. It quoted an earlier decision that stated typically the corporate veil is only pierced when the company is originally incorporated for an illegal, fraudulent improper purpose. But that decision also noted that the corporate veil can also be pierced if after a corporation has already been incorporated for legitimate purposes "those in control expressly direct a wrongful thing to be done." If this occurs *"the courts will disregard the separate legal personality of a corporate entity where it is completely dominated and controlled and being used as a shield for fraudulent or improper conduct."*

Since Beamish had sole signing authority of the accounts in question and had authorized the transfer of significant amounts of money to the other bank account, Beamish had caused the wrongful act. He personally had been the one unjustly enriched. Given these facts the Court ruled it was appropriate to pierce the corporate veil and Beamish was held personally liable for the money along with Powerhouse.

The decision in the Shoppers Drug Mart case makes it quite clear that when there is only one officer, director and shareholder and there is no doubt as to who was the directing mind of a wrongful and improper act, the corporate veil can be pierced. The corporation does not have to be initially incorporated for an illegal purpose, but if a wrongful act occurs after a legitimate incorporation, the veil can be pierced so the person responsible for the misconduct cannot shield themselves from liability.

Oppression Remedy

Since the enactment of the Oppression Remedy (discussed in detail later) that remedy has also been used by creditors to pierce the corporate veil and make shareholders liable for corporate debts in similar circumstances to the common law remedy of piercing the corporate veil. It can be used when assets have been removed that makes a corporation unable to pay a known debt. That remedy is wider than the common law remedy of piercing the corporate veil in that the statute permits the court to find officers and directors liable as well.

C-L & Associates Inc. v. Airside Equipment Sales Inc. et al., 2003 MBQB 104 (CanLII)

Richard Thurston incorporated Airside Equipment Sales Inc. in May 1994 and was the sole shareholder, officer and director. Thurston also incorporated another corporation in January 2000 that operated under the name Forcefield Manufacturing Co. and he was also the sole shareholder, officer and director of it as well.

In 1997 C-L Associates sued Airside for $68,892 for sandbags that Airside had purchased from C-L for use in the Calgary flood, but it had not paid for. C-L was successful in its lawsuit, but by the time the judgment was given, Airside had almost no assets and was not an active corporate entity. Thurston was carrying on his business activities through Forcefield instead.

C-L argued that Thurston operated Airfield as a shell company and the court should pierce the corporate veil and hold Forcefield liable for the Airfield debt as well as also hold Richard Thurston personally liable for this debt.

Thurston argued that there was no transfer of assets between the two companies and they were separate legal entities, so only Airside was liable for the debt owing to C-L.

The Court's Decision

The court had no difficulty determining that the two companies were affiliated. It found that Airfield was a shell company and had very little physical assets and any income it made flowed through to Thurston by way of the payment of personal expenses such as his home mortgage. Airside had no other employees and any financial benefit Airfield derived from the transaction with C-L went directly to Thurston or his wife.

The court found it quite suspicious that Thurston started using Forcefield for its business activities once C-L began it lawsuit against Airside. Despite Thornton's argument it was for legitimate business reasons, the court believed it had been done to avoid the judgment it knew was coming in the C-L case.

The court noted that under the oppression remedy section of the Manitoba *Corporations Act* the court could make "any order it thinks fit" to compensate "an aggrieved person." It ruled that C-L was in these circumstances an aggrieved person.

The court ruled this was an appropriate situation to pierce the corporate veil and order both Thurston and Forcefield jointly and severally liable for the money Airfield owed to C-L.

Business Alert! Note that this remedy aims only to assist those creditors who are harmed by corporate manoeuvres in ways that they cannot take any steps to prevent. This is distinct from the creditors in *Salomon v. Salomon*. Those creditors could have taken steps such as: getting the principal shareholder to sign a personal guarantee, or put their own security instruments over the goods they supplied in priority to *Salomon*, to name two examples of common ways creditors protect themselves when supplying goods on credit to a corporation. The next case is an example of the application of this principle. The court refused to pierce the corporate veil or apply the oppression remedy.

Parent-Subsidiaries If the wholly owned subsidiary operates as a distinct and separate business from the parent then the parent will not be liable for the subsidiary's actions so long as it was not a shell corporation and there was no fraudulent behaviour by the parent corporation.

J.S.M. Corporation (Ontario) Ltd. v. The Brick Furniture Warehouse Ltd., 2008 ONCA 183

The Brick Corporation incorporated single-purpose corporations to hold the leases at its various store locations. One such subsidiary corporation signed a lease with the landlord J.S.M. Corp. The landlord was on notice that this corporation had no assets. The subsidiary corporation, the tenant on the lease, defaulted. The landlord sued the parent corporation and two of the remedies it sought were the common-law remedy of piercing the corporate veil and the statutory remedy of oppression.

The Court's Decision

The court held that both remedies only apply to situations in which a creditor could not protect itself from internal corporate maneuvers. In the present situation, the landlord knew that it was giving a lease to a corporation that had no assets apart from its ability to earn income at that location. The landlord could have taken steps to protect itself such as a guarantee of the lease by the parent corporation, but it had failed to get that protection in the agreement.

The court noted that the oppression remedy is not a means by which commercial contracts negotiated by sophisticated business parties will be rewritten later on when problems arise to achieve what is "just and equitable."

"The oppression remedy is not intended to give a creditor after-the-fact protection against risks that the creditor assumed when he entered into an agreement with a corporation. The position of a creditor who can, but does not, protect itself against an eventuality from which he later seeks relief under the oppression remedy, is much different than the position of a creditor who finds his interest as a creditor compromised by unlawful and internal corporate manoeuvres against which the creditor cannot effectively protect itself. In the latter case, there is much more room for relief under the oppression provisions than in the former case."

The oppression remedy was rejected in this case, however the landlord was successful against the parent corporation based on its claim in contract law and the court's interpretation of other terms.

Example: In a leading case *Transamerica Life Insurance Co. of Canada v. Canada Life Assurance Co.,* 1996 CanLII 7979 (ON SC), the court refused to pierce the veil and hold a parent company liable for the actions of its wholly-owned subsidiary. The court ruled that only if the subsidiary is completely controlled and is a mere conduit for the parent and this structure was used to commit fraud or a similar wrongful act will the corporate veil be pierced. In this case the court found the subsidiary was a distinct and separate company that carried on its own business, not just a shell. There had been allegations of fraud against the officers of the subsidiary, but there were no allegations that the officers of the parent corporation were involved in any fraudulent behaviour. For these reasons the court refused to pierce the corporate veil and hold the parent liable for the subsidiary's actions.

Looking across Canada the law on when the court will pierce the corporate veil is not always predictable. Some principles have emerged though that can help avoid the piercing. If it is a parent-subsidiary relationship the owner should make sure that the two corporations have the following: different phone/fax numbers, different offices, some different directors and officers in each company, separate director and shareholder meetings with separate minutes and the parent should not pay the subsidiaries bills. The parent can however make legitimate loans to the subsidiary and take security for the loan. The corporate veil is less likely to be pierced if the two companies do not seem to be interchangeable.

Business Alert!

Critical Concepts: Piercing the Corporate Veil

- This remedy is aimed at making shareholders responsible for debts of the corporation
- It applies when a shareholder acts fraudulently or wrongfully such as transferring money out of the corporation to him or herself leaving the corporation unable to pay its debts
- An abuse of the corporate form only occurs when the shareholders use the form to avoid liability in ways the creditor could not have taken steps to prevent
- The corporate veil is not pierced just because it is fair or equitable to do so, there must be a wrongful act such as fraud before the veil will be lifted

■ *Business Law* Applied

❸ **Larry Loophole discovered** a piece of real estate that had been a landfill site many years ago. Quite deep under the landfill was a swamp. It was otherwise an excellent site for a residential condominium tower. Larry was an experienced builder and knew that problems would not surface for at least twenty years. He incorporated a business called Value Condominiums Limited of which he was the sole shareholder and director.

Value Condominiums sold all of its units quickly, but the problem also surfaced more quickly than Larry anticipated. The purchasers want to sue Larry personally because Value Condominiums has no assets. All of the profits of Value Condominiums were paid to Larry as dividends.

a) Is the fact that all of the dividends of Value Condominiums were paid to Larry sufficient to establish personal liability on Larry? What is the name of the legal remedy that the purchasers will rely on in these circumstances?

b) It is clearly not fair that Larry be permitted to use the corporate veil to escape personal liability. Can the corporate veil be pierced on the grounds of unfairness?

c) Are there any grounds for piercing the corporate veil in the above situation? If so, what are they?

❹ **Mary Brown is a mother** trying to provide for three small children. Her husband died of cancer last year. Mary has not worked for over 10 years, but all her friends tell her she has unusual skill in designing unique candles. She borrows money to start a small candle manufacturing business in her garage. With amazing luck (she thinks), she gets an order for all that she can supply. She works vigorously for three months and ships the large order to her first customer Acme Services Inc.

When Acme doesn't pay, Mary contacts the owner Sam, who says "I'm really sorry Mary, but the company is going out of business. You'll have to sue." A lawyer Mary retains tells her he has investigated. Sam did not take any assets out for his own benefit, the business failed for normal reasons as some businesses do. It's a waste of money trying to sue a corporation that has gone out of business. She will be one of many creditors fighting over very little.

Mary loses her house because she cannot repay the loan and has to move into public housing with her children. One day when coming out of a Salvation Army Thrift store after buying her children some clothes, she sees Sam driving by in a new BMW. Outraged, she wants to sue Sam personally.

a) What is the name of the remedy at common law and the similar remedy under statutory law that might assist her?

b) Is it fair that hard working Mary loses her house while Sam gets to drive a BMW?

c) Does Mary have the necessary grounds to be successful in the remedies you named in a) above?

d) What could Mary have done to better protect herself?

Public and Private Corporations

broadly held corporations

corporations whose shares are publicly traded on the stock market and who have a wide range of shareholders

closely held corporations

corporations which do not sell shares to the public

There are two types of corporations—public and private. In some provinces, public companies are technically called offering companies, since they sell their shares to the public; they are also known as reporting companies, as they must file additional financial information to government agencies that oversee the sale of shares in the stock market. Public companies, such as International Business Machines (IBM), are also referred to as **broadly held corporations**, because they are corporations whose shares are publicly traded on the stock market and who have a wide range of shareholders; private companies are referred to as **closely held corporations** (corporations which do not sell shares to the public).

Private companies do not sell shares, and are thus known as non-offering, non-reporting, or non-distributing companies. For ease of reference, we refer to companies as either public or private.

Corporate Securities

Advantages of the corporate form of business include the flexibility in raising money, combined with possible protection of the personal assets of the owners of the business. The corporation has two unique ways to raise money—selling part of the right to share in profits (shares/stocks) or by loans (bonds). These are called corporate securities. These two forms of investment are best known in public companies, and can be seen in the financial sections of daily newspapers, where market prices are listed.

Corporations can also raise money by private arrangement with banks and other financial institutions.

Shares

Most of us think of a company shareholder as an owner, but there are important restrictions on the rights of the shareholder, who, for example, has no entitlement to the use of the assets of the company. A shareholder has a right to share in the corporation's assets on the **winding up** of the corporation (dissolving, ending a corporation) if there are any assets after all creditors are paid. A shareholder of Bell Canada cannot walk into a phone centre and take a phone, saying, "I'm an owner, I have a right to this, it's an asset of Bell Canada."

winding up
dissolving, ending a corporation

A shareholder is an investor who has a right to share in the profits of a company only if a dividend is declared. The shareholder takes a risk on whether the company will make a profit. There is no automatic right to a dividend, even if a profit is declared by the board of directors. Nor is there automatic distribution of all profits to shareholders, as some may be retained for other uses (such as new-product development). The directors face two competing interests— keeping profits for business use and expansion, and pleasing shareholders so as to maintain the company's image as an attractive investment.

There are two ways that a **share** (the holder's proportionate interest in the assets of a corporation) can give a return on the investment:

share
the holder's proportionate interest in the assets of a corporation

- capital increase—the value of the share price has increased because the worth of the company and its potential for profit have increased
- dividend—this is similar to the payment of interest on a loan. It is income to the shareholder, and is paid as a share in the profits of the company

The Pros and Cons of Issuing Shares

The advantage of raising money by issuing shares is that there is no need to make any repayment in the early years of a business. This is a distinct benefit, because a new company is unlikely to earn a profit for several years. If the money were raised by bonds, the corporation would have to make regular payments, even though it did not earn any profit.

On the other hand, shares usually contain voting rights. The more shares sold, the greater the chance of control going out of the company founders' hands. Apple Computer is an example of this. The inventors lost control of the company, were removed from the board of directors, and were fired as employees.

Types of Shares

There are generally two types of shares—common and preferred—but there are many subcategories within each. Preferred shares are usually given priority in payment of dividends and of a share in the corporation's assets if the company is wound up. **Common shares** are shares carrying no preferential right to distribution of assets on breakup, but usually carrying voting rights. All corporations have to have common shares. They do not have to have preferred shares though, and many corporations choose not have preferred shares.

Issued/Authorized Share Capital

The organizers of the corporation decide how many shares to issue, having first considered both present and future monetary needs. The **authorized share capital** is the maximum number (or value) of shares that a corporation is permitted by its charter to issue. It is difficult to change this figure once incorporation is granted, and so most companies provide for flexibility in the amount right from day one. Authorized share capital determines how many shares a corporation can issue. Issued or allotted shares are the shares the corporation actually does issue.

Voting/Non-Voting Shares

Shares can be either voting or non-voting. The holder of non-voting shares has the right to participate in corporate profitability but not control. In a family business, parents might give non-voting shares to children at any early age to provide an investment income for them. In this way, adults keep all the voting shares—and hence control of the corporation—to themselves.

A corporation might have:

Authorized share capital	1000
Issued share capital	
Common	100
Preferred	200
Total	300
Unissued share capital	700

Melnitzer, Re, 1992 CanLII 196 (ON LST)

Julius Melnitzer was a prominent lawyer in London Ontario. He was also guilty of some of the most famous financial fraud in Canadian history. He persuaded a printing company to print false stock certificates and on the basis of those he obtained a $43 million line of credit from many of Canada's largest banks. He was caught when he attempted to get a further $21 million.

Over six years Melnitzer also created false financial statements and thereby obtained fraudulent loans and lines of credit worth $18,000,000 for various corporations he controlled.

The lawyer was also guilty of individual investor fraud. He defrauded individual investors of $3,725,000 based on fictitious land deals in Singapore. The investors included his partners and friends. He also defrauded another friend and two of his companies out of $10,950,000.

On February 10, 1992, Melnitzer pleaded guilty to 43 counts of knowingly making false documents and defrauding persons by deceit, falsehood, or other fraudulent means, contrary to the *Criminal Code*. He was convicted and sentenced to nine years' imprisonment and ordered to pay $20 million in compensation to his victims. He then went before the Law Society of Upper Canada for its decision on his right to practice law.

The Court's Decision

The Law Society was appalled by the level of criminal behaviour by such a trusted and respected lawyer. Melnitzer was disbarred for life and can never practise law in Ontario again.

It should be noted that Melnitzer went to jail, but after serving two years he got day parole and then full parole a year later. Many question whether the punishment fits the crime in financial fraud cases.

Raising Money on the Stock Market

initial public offering (IPO)

when a corporation first sells it shares to the public on a stock market

Each year Canadian corporations raise billions of dollars in funding by 'going public'. The first attempt to sell shares in a company to the general public on a securities exchange [stock market] is called an **initial public offering (IPO)**. Through this process, a private company transforms into a public company. Initial public offerings are primarily used by companies to provide themselves with capital for future growth, repayment of debt, or working capital.

One advantage is that a company selling shares to the public is never required to repay the share price (the capital) back to its public investors. The initial purchasers will, if they want to get their capital back, and if there is a market for the shares, sell them to another purchaser. If they sell for a profit it is a capital gain.

Significant disadvantages of an IPO include high legal, accounting and marketing costs as well as large commission fees to the brokerage firms that sell the shares. Fees can often total 25–35% of the total money raised by the sale of the shares. The corporate information revealed in a prospectus might benefit competitors as well as suppliers and customers who negotiate prices with the corporation.

There are 2 bodies that regulate the stock market in every province that has one. One is a government body, a securities commission; the other is a private organization, the stock exchange. In Ontario, for example, there is the Ontario Securities Commission and the Toronto Stock Exchange.

Approval for an IPO is obtained by filing a prospectus with the government agency, the securities commission. A **prospectus** gives information for investors such as the company's financial statements, a description of its business, profiles of its officers and directors. Once approved by the government agency, that approval can be used to apply for a listing on the appropriate stock market.

> **prospectus**
> a document disclosing information about a corporation used to obtain approval for its initial public sale of shares

The stock exchanges in Canada are provincial which means a corporation has to obtain approval from every provincial regulator in every province in which it wants to sell its shares. There is some cooperation in a "passport" agreement in that acceptance in one province will mean acceptance in another, but not all provinces participate. The federal government tried to create one federal securities regulator to reduce the duplication, expense and reputation for nurturing stock fraud that our current system has. But in a reference question put to the Supreme Court, it struck down the proposed law as it encroached on provincial powers (see Chapter 1). The Court did not deny the need for one federal regulator, but it would require provincial agreement first and that will be very difficult to achieve. In the meantime we are left with our clumsy, expensive and ineffective regulations.

Flipping

The IPO launch is done through a stockbroker firm (called an investment bank in other countries). In addition to charges for the IPO, the brokerage firms purchase shares in the corporation before they are available to the public. The intent is to make a quick profit by selling as soon as the stock price rises. A purchase and a quick resale is called flipping.

There have been concerns raised about this tactic. In a U.S. lawsuit eToys.com alleges that Goldman Sachs and other stockbrokers obtain a sophisticated type of kickback in that they pressure corporations to undervalue their shares at the time the stockbroker firm purchases before public release. The shares quickly rise to their true value and the stockbrokers can sell and make an immediate profit. These are allegations not yet proven as the lawsuit continues. (Nocera, Joe (March 9, 2013). "Rigging the I.P.O. Game". *New York Times.*)

Bonds

Corporations can also raise money by borrowing. By issuing a document called a **bond** (a certificate of a debt owed by a corporation), the corporation acknowledges that a certain amount of money has been lent to it, and will be paid back with interest at stated times. Unlike shares, the amount due under the bonds must be paid even if the company shows no profit or no dividend is declared.

> **bond**
> a certificate of a debt owed by a corporation

Canada Savings Bonds are perhaps the best-known form of bonds. By buying them, a person is contributing to the funding of the federal government, which promises to pay a fixed rate of interest each year. Corporate bonds work in the same way.

Bonds may include more than an acknowledgment of debt; they also may include mortgage-type security. This mortgage is a charge on the corporate assets.

The advantage of issuing bonds is that they do not carry voting rights; thus, there is no danger of loss of control of the corporation. The disadvantage is that regular payment must be made. If the company is not profitable, it might not be able to meet the payments and could be put out of business by the bondholders.

Consider the following example. An investor pays $100,000 for a corporate bond that requires annual payments of $10,000 principal, plus 10 percent interest. (To simplify matters, ignore the annual reduction in principal.) Each year the corporation will be required to pay the investor $10,000 principal and $10,000 interest, for a total of $20,000. If the corporation does not make a profit, it will not be able to pay.

If shares were sold for $100,000, and the company was not profitable, no payments would have to be made to the shareholders. The advantage to a new company of selling shares is obvious. The shareholders not only participate in the profits, they also share the risk. New business ventures are not usually profitable in the first few years, and so raising money through the sale of shares relieves the burden of having to make debt payments. On the other hand, there is the risk of losing control of the corporation.

Convertible Bonds

Shares and bonds represent two extremes of the types of securities a corporation can offer when raising money from private sources. There are many combinations of shares and bonds, as varied as the ingenuity of financial experts. Some securities are convertible into another form. For example, some bonds have provisions that they can be converted to voting shares if the corporation fails to make a payment. The terms of each series of shares or bonds must be examined to see the rights associated with each.

The Structure of a Corporation

A corporation is divided generally into three areas:

board of directors

the governing body of a corporation responsible for overseeing the management of the business and selecting officers

- shareholders—the people who have power to elect members of the board of directors
- **board of directors**—the governing body of a corporation, responsible for overseeing the management of the business and selecting the officers such as the CEO, CFO and President
- officers—the executives who carry out the day-to-day management of the corporation

Corporate Structure Versus Government Structure

SHAREHOLDERS ELECT → DIRECTORS who then SELECT → OFFICERS e.g. CEO, CFO, President

Shareholders

The same sections of the corporations acts apply to shareholders' rights for both public and private companies, but different sections are usually most relevant to the different shareholders' disputes.

The main problem for shareholders in public corporations is that they have a very limited right to information and no real control or influence over how the company operates. The separation of management and ownership in a corporate structure means that the shareholder, who is really an investor and not an owner, has little to do with the running of the company.

The concerns of shareholders in private companies are similar to those encountered in partnerships, including disagreements among the owners.

Shareholders Rights to Information in a Public Corporation

Shareholders are entitled only to certain confidential information of the corporation. They do not have the right to know the daily business of the company—such as new deals in the making, or trade secrets. An investor could not, for example, buy shares in Coca-Cola Limited, and then demand to know the secret formula for the making of Coca-Cola.

Shareholders do not owe a fiduciary duty to the corporation. A shareholder can own shares in Loblaws and the Bay, and owe no duty to either. Indeed, that shareholder can start a rival retail department store in competition with both. This is one reason why shareholders have a very limited right to corporate information.

Shareholders have the right to see the financial statements such as the balance sheet and income statements, but not the day-to-day accounting books and business transactions. If a certain percentage of shareholders have serious concerns about corporate mismanagement, they can apply to the court to appoint an **inspector**. The inspector is a government appointed person who will investigate the corporation's affairs. The required percentage of shareholders varies by province, the lowest is 5 per cent in B.C., and it is often difficult to obtain the requisite number in a large public corporation.

Shareholders also have the right to know whether directors and directors have been buying or selling shares in the corporation if it is a public corporation. These key inside people must declare their transactions so that shareholders can tell whether they have been using confidential inside information to make personal profits. This use of inside information to profit on the stock market is called **insider trading** and is discussed later in this chapter.

inspector
a person appointed by the court to investigate the affairs of a corporation

insider trading
the use of a corporation's confidential information to buy or sell its securities

Business Law Applied

⑤ **Sandra Keho is** a shareholder of Estate Best Development Corporation Limited, a large public real estate development company. She learned of a rumour that this corporation may be buying a particular piece of real estate for development. Keho thought this a bad idea, and asked the president of the corporation if the rumour was true. The president refused to answer. She then asked certain directors of the corporation, but they too refused to tell her.

The annual shareholders' meeting does not take place for another nine months, and Keho considers this too long to wait to ask any questions.

a) Does Keho have the right to call a meeting of the corporation before the annual meeting?
b) Does she have a right as a shareholder to force the corporation to reveal the information that she seeks?

Control in a Public Corporation

The separation of powers and functions in a corporation is roughly similar to that of voters in a democracy. People who are familiar with small corporations where the same people are shareholders, directors, and officers might not realize that shareholders have very limited control in a public company. Although there are additional remedies for shareholders, the only real control they have over the corporation is the ability to vote out board members—just as voters have only that remedy and control over Parliament. The large public corporation functions more like a small monarchy than a democracy. Often it is senior management that controls the corporation—not the shareholders.

Shareholders have the right to receive notice and attend the corporation's annual general meeting. The shareholders can call a special meeting to discuss a particular problem if the directors refuse to. A certain percentage of shareholders is needed to call a special meeting and in a large public corporation that is usually unobtainable.

proxy form

a form a shareholder uses to delegate their voting rights to another

The control by senior management at the annual general meeting can be done by the use of a **proxy form**. Proxy means agent or delegate. Management, in co-operation with the board of directors, controls the mailing out of the notice of the shareholders' annual meeting, and the proxy forms are sent in the same package. In the accompanying correspondence, management usually suggests whom they want the shareholders to nominate for their proxies—normally management itself. By doing this, senior management is, in effect, controlling who is elected to the board of directors. Therefore, senior management significantly influences the election of the very people who set the size of management salaries.

Most shareholders are unaware of the consequences of signing the proxy form, and do so according to management's recommendation as a matter of course.

Because of this use of proxies, public corporations most often act as autonomous bodies run by management, whose acts are rubber-stamped by directors over whom shareholders have little control.

Executive Compensation

Various security commissions have passed regulations that require the compensation for top-level executives to be revealed each year. Some governments require disclosure of compensation of senior civil servants. There is no requirement that union leaders reveal their compensation and union leaders have usually refused voluntary disclosure.

In the wake of the extensive failure of the subprime mortgage market beginning in 2008 causing the risk of the failure of banks that were deemed "too big to fail", executive compensation became a headline item. While thousands of low income people were losing their homes in mortgage foreclosures, the U.S. government was giving billion-dollar bailouts to keep financial institutions alive. The executives of those institutions continued to take multimillion dollar compensation packages including one type called a "retention bonus". The executives justified these on the basis that in spite of leading their corporations to the brink of bankruptcy, they were the only ones capable of running such large organizations and so it was necessary to pay them large sums or they would quit.

That reasoning did not appeal to the average shareholder. Additionally, a number of years earlier shareholder groups had formed a "say on pay" movement unsuccessfully attempting to get executive compensation as an item on the Annual General Meeting (AGM). One of the proposed reforms is to have executive compensation tied to performance.

In response to this pressure, the U.S. government passed legislation called the Dodds-Frank Act, one purpose of which was to address the out-of-control executive compensation. The Dodds-Frank Act contained a provision recommending, on a voluntary basis, that public corporations put the item of executive compensation on the agenda for the AGM for a non-binding vote. This act has influenced many Canadian corporations. They have followed the U.S. practice of putting executive compensation on agendas at AGMs for non-binding votes.

But despite these changes the income gap continues to grow. In 2012 the average CEO at one of the 100 largest Canadian corporations made $7.96 million or 171 times what the average worker made. After working for a few hours on the first day of the year that top executive has made more than the average worker will make all year. In statistics prepared by the OECD (Organization for Economic Cooperation and Development) for 2012, the rates in other countries calculated in a somewhat similar manner are as follows ("Just the Facts: CEOs and the Rest of Us," (Nov. 21, 2013) *The Globalist*)

Boards of directors set the compensation levels, but since most directors of large companies are senior executives in their own companies, they too benefit from this industry wide practice of rewarding each other with compensation excessively out of proportion to the average worker.

Comparison of Executive Compensation
to Average Worker's Wage 2012

COUNTRY	2012 - Number of times greater Executives' Compensation is than the average workers'
U.S.A.	354
Switzerland	148
Germany	147
France	104
Spain	127
Britain	84
Japan	67

Source: "Just the Facts: CEOs and the Rest of Us," *The Globalist*, Nov. 21, 2013.

Takeover Bids

A takeover bid is an attempt by a group of investors to acquire a sufficient number of shares so that they can control the corporation and replace the board of directors with the group's own nominees. Ordinarily, obtaining approximately 10 percent of the shares of a public corporation will allow this to be done. If management becomes inefficient, and the business could be run more profitably, an outside group of investors might attempt to gain control of the corporation, replace the board of directors and, in turn, fire current management.

The rules for takeover bids require that if any investors do obtain control, they must then offer to purchase all other shareholders' shares at the same price paid to acquire control.

Shareholder Power   Businesses are often accused of putting profits above all else. Increasingly, shareholder groups are organizing to persuade the corporation's board and management to take social responsibility into account—such as refusing military contracts, showing environmental responsibility, and avoiding discriminatory hiring and promotion practices.

Shareholders in Private Corporations

Private corporations are usually run along the same lines as small partnerships, and the most common dispute is a disagreement among the owners. However, there are no rules similar to a partnership act governing disputes among shareholders. Thus, a shareholder of a private corporation may simply be squeezed out of any active part in the business, and be unable to sell the shares because there is no market for them. It is difficult to sell shares of a small corporation, since a potential investor must be interested in the specific business, and willing to co-operate with the remaining shareholders.

An attempt by one group to take unfair advantage of another single shareholder or group of shareholders in a corporation is called oppression, and special sections of the *Corporations Act* are called shareholder oppression sections.

In private corporations, the founders usually have an understanding that the shares will be split equally, that each individual will be on the board of directors and have a position as an officer of the corporation, and that all business will be done by agreement. While this happens in the early stages, problems may arise, and one group of shareholders may change this balance of power arrangement. Courts have extended the concept of oppression so that it includes inability to co-operate resulting in a deadlocked company.

The **oppression remedy**—a statutory procedure allowing individual shareholders to seek a personal remedy if they have been unfairly treated—has been called a charter of rights for shareholders because it gives the court very wide powers to remedy oppressive conduct. Both federal and provincial acts contain oppression remedies.

Shareholder Oppression

The relevant section of the federal *Corporations Act* is typical of how legislation deals with this problem across the country. In reading this section, remember that shareholder is included in the term *security holder*.

---

241 Canada Business Corporations Act, R.S.C.

---

(1) Application to Court Re Oppression.—A complainant may apply to a court for an order under this section.

(2) Grounds.—If, upon an application under subsection (1), the court is satisfied that in respect of a corporation or any of its affiliates

    a) any act or omission of the corporation or any of its affiliates effects a result,

    b) the business or affairs of the corporation or any of its affiliates are or have been carried on or conducted in a manner, or

    c) the powers of the directors of the corporation or any of its affiliates are or have been exercised in a manner, or

    d) that is oppressive and unfairly prejudicial to or that unfair disregards the interests of any security holder, creditor, director or officer, the court may make an order to rectify the matters complained of.

Remedies for Shareholder Oppression

The powers given to the court under this section are very wide, and able to be adapted to a great number of situations. The law specifically states that the court can make any order that "it thinks fit." Then it lists examples of the type of orders it can issue such as; forcing the sale of shares, closing down the company, change the articles or by-laws of the company, change the directors, awarding compensation and many others. This law has gives the court wider powers than almost any other law.

---

241 (3) Canada Business Corporations Act, R.S.C.

Section 241 (3) Powers of Court.—In connection with an application under this section the court may make any interim or final order it thinks fit including, without limiting the generality of the foregoing.

    a) an order restraining the conduct complained of;

    b) an order appointing a receiver or a receiver manager;

    c) an order to regulate a corporation's affairs by amending the articles or by-laws or creating or amending a unanimous shareholder agreement;

    d) an order directing an issue or exchange of security;

    e) an order appointing directors in place of or addition to all or any of the directors in an office;

    f) an order directing a corporation, subject to subsection 6, or any other person, to purchase securities of a security holder;

    g) an order directing a corporation, subject to subsection 6, or any other person, to pay a security holder any part of the monies paid by him for securities;

h) an order varying or setting aside a transaction or contract to which corporation is a party and compensating the corporation or any party to the transaction or contract;

i) an order requiring a corporation, within a time specified by the court, to produce to the court or an interested person financial statements in form required by section 149 or an accounting in such other form as the court may determine;

j) an order compensating an aggrieved person;

k) an order directing rectification of the registers or other records of a corporation under section 236;

l) an order liquidating and dissolving a corporation;

m) an order directing an investigation under a part XVIII to be made;

n) an order requiring the trial of any issue.

Example: Alexander Tilley started a leisure clothing company, Tilley Endurables, and was quite successful. When sales declined he brought in Dennis Hails who gave design and financial advice and invested some capital. When Tilley was unable to pay Hails for his services, he generously gave hails 50 per cent ownership of the company. Once Hails was an equal owner the men quickly became incompatible. They each tried to drive the other out of the company using many nasty tactics. Finally they both went to court seeking an order under the shareholder oppression remedy to force the other to sell them their shares. The court ruled that both men had acted badly, but since Hails had Tilley falsely arrested for weapons charges and Tilley had been the one who had started the company, Hails would be forced to sell his shares to Tilley at a fair value determined by an arbitrator. (*Tilley v. Hails*, 1992 CanLII 7563 (ON SC)

Waxman v. Waxman, 2004 CanLII 39040 (ONCA)

Isaac Waxman started a scrap metal and waste business (IWS) in Hamilton, Ontario and it became a multi-million dollar success. His two sons Morris and Chester took it over. Morris's health later deteriorated and when Morris was about to go in for open heart surgery in 1983, fearing he might die, he agreed to sign documents his brother presented to him. These contracts conveyed Morris's 50% shareholding in IWS to Chester and leased Morris's lands to IWS on a long-term discounted basis.

Morris recovered from the surgery and eventually realized what had happened. He claimed that he had been tricked into conveying his shares to Chester at a time when Morris was preoccupied with his own mortality. Morris sued Chester, IWS, Chester's sons and the lawyer and accountant involved for negligence. Five actions were tried at once.

After a very complex 200 day trial over two years, in June 2002 almost 20 years after the agreement was signed, the trial judge ruled in Morris's favour. She agreed that Chester had breached a fiduciary duty to his brother. Morris had not known what he had signed, the agreement was unconscionable and also void due to undue influence. Morris and his three sons had effectively stolen the half of the family business that belonged to

Morris and his two sons. The lawyer involved had acted for both parties and he was liable for negligence. The accountant had also been negligent, but because of the *Hercules* decision he did not owe Morris a duty of care as a shareholder.

Under the oppression remedy of the OBCA the judge ordered that Morris' shares be returned to him and that he be reinstated as a 50% owner of the company. Morris was awarded 50% of the profits that IWS had made since he signed the agreement in 1983. Chester's son who had diverted millions in profits from IWS to his own companies was ordered to repay Morris his share of this money. Punitive damages of $350,000 were also awarded.

The defendants all appealed the decision to the Ontario Court of Appeal.

The Court's Decision

The Court of Appeal confirmed the trial judge's decision. The agreement was void and the remedies the judge had awarded under the oppression remedy were appropriate under the circumstances. (Note: It has been estimated that with interest and costs, Morris was awarded a total of about $50 million)

■ *Business Law* Applied

❺ **John Cole,** a chemical engineer, devised a process for producing an industrial chemical in a completely automated plant. Because he did not have enough money to set up business himself, he took Randy Palsar and Sylvia Kim as financial backers and partners. A new corporation was formed, and all three received equal shares, and were appointed as the only members of the board of directors.

Palsar and Kim became employees of the new corporation—president and vice-president. For tax reasons, Cole became an independent consultant, holding a contract with the corporation. A term of the contract was that it could be cancelled with 60 days' notice by either side.

Bickering soon began. Palsar and Kim were on one side of the arguments; Cole was on the other. At the next shareholders' meeting, Palsar and Kim voted that Cole should not be reappointed to the board. The new board—consisting of Palsar and Kim—cancelled Cole's consulting contract, giving him 60 days' notice. The board then appointed another technical consultant to become its third member.

Cole feels that he has been squeezed out of the company that was his idea.

    a) Does Cole have any remedy? If so, what is the name of that remedy?
    b) What powers of the courts set out in section 234 (3) above might assist Cole?

❻ **Montgomery is a** shareholder in Comp-lex Realty Corporation. He is a passive investor, in that he lent $100,000 to the corporation for a specific land-development project and took back shares in return. Kitchener and Clive are the only other shareholders, and the only directors of Comp-lex. They manage the day-to-day affairs of the business.

Comp-lex purchases a piece of land from Kitchener and Clive for $100,000. Montgomery learns that the land is worth only $50,000, and wants to take some action against the corporation, as well as against Kitchener and Clive.

    a) Does Montgomery have any remedy?
    b) What items in section 234 (3) might be of assistance?

Derivative Action

As a shareholder cannot be sued for debt of the Corporation, so a shareholder cannot sue for a debt owed to the Corporation. That is the trade-off involved in the limited liability given by the corporate form. Recall that it is the Board of Directors that has the right to determine whether a corporation will sue or not. If any shareholder can sue, there could be chaos. A person could buy one share of Microsoft and then sue someone using the Microsoft name. Thus, only the Board of Directors can use the corporate name in a lawsuit. However, there is an exception when the Board of Directors is not acting in the best interests of the Corporation. That usually happens when the lawsuit would cause a financial loss to members of the Board, such as when the corporation sells a piece of land worth $500,000 to a relative of a director for $100,000. These situations could be a matter of a derivative action. The term derivative means that the right to sue derives from the Corporation.

In cases where the members of the Board of Directors have done something that gives them a benefit that causes the corporation a loss, the oppression remedy is available and is a much easier procedure because it does not require leave of the court. Consequently derivative actions are quite rare in Canada.

However, there are cases where the Board refuses to sue and the corporation may have a valid case. Perhaps the Board doesn't think it's worth the risk. An example would be the auditor's negligent situation. If the auditors were negligent and the Corporation began a project believing that it had the funds for the project when it did not because of the auditor's negligence and the Corporation lost money, the shareholders would not have a remedy against the auditors because the auditors did not owe a duty to the shareholders. However, the auditors did cause a loss to the corporation. If the Board refused to sue the auditors, a shareholder could make an application to the court for leave to use the corporate name and sue the auditors. The damage award goes to the corporation not the shareholder.

Shareholder Agreements

Although the shareholder oppression remedies set out in the acts are extensive, they still depend on obtaining a judge's opinion that there has been some oppression. Therefore, shareholders are well advised to enter into a **shareholder agreement**, an agreement between two or more shareholders, similar to a partnership agreement. A shareholder agreement is a type of ownership agreement and, coupled with an employment contract, is considered the best protection for a shareholder against the problems of dispute. The employment contract ensures that the shareholders cannot be unjustly fired from the corporation.

shareholder agreement
an agreement between two or more shareholders, similar to a partnership agreement

Shareholders' agreements usually deal with the following common areas of dispute:

- The right to sit on the board of directors
- A right that the other shareholders will not sell to outsiders without giving the right of first refusal
- The right to buy the shares of the other shareholders, or force them to buy the dissident shareholders' shares, when certain events happen
- The method of valuation for the shares, either by formula, arbitration, or a shotgun-style clause

---

■ *Critical Concept for* Shareholders

- All corporations have common shareholders who elect the directors of the corporation
- All shareholders are entitled to receive notice and attend the annual general meeting (AGM) of the corporation
- Public corporations use proxy forms to effectively control the voting at the AGMs
- All shareholders are entitled to see the financial statements of the corporation
- Shareholders can request the court appoints an inspector to investigate the affairs of the corporation or that a special meeting be held, but it rarely occurs in a large public corporation
- Shareholders can bring an oppression action if they think they are unfairly treated and the court can grant broad remedies such as; forcing the sale of shares, winding up the corporation and awarding damages
- Shareholders can bring a derivative action on behalf of the corporation against the directors and/or officers if they suspect mismanagement, though this is rarely done
- Shareholders can seek leave of the court to bring a derivative action on behalf of the corporation for any action that the corporation could bring including actions against the directors

Directors

The directors of a corporation have the duty to oversee the corporation in the sense that they set the policies and make major decisions. But the day-to-day management is carried out by the executives, such as the president and vice-president, who are called officers in corporate law. These executives may also have other titles, for example, chief executive officer (CEO) or chief operating officer (COO). The directors' functions are similar to those of Members of Parliament, and the executives' functions are similar to those of senior civil servants. The directors have the power to fire the president and other executives.

A private corporation need only have one director, but a public corporation must have at least three. In a small corporation there is often only one shareholder who is also the only director and they hold all the officer positions as well.

In a large publicly traded corporation there are one or more **inside directors**, who are full time executives who work for that particular corporation. But the majority of the directors are usually **outside directors** who are usually CEOs or senior executives from other large corporations and some are often professionals such as lawyers or accountants. A large corporation may typically have 15 directors and probably 12–14 would be outside directors. Directors for large public corporations usually meet 4–6 times a year and they are often paid between $20,000–$500,000 annually for serving as a director. Outside directors usually have very demanding full time jobs elsewhere, so when they are on the Board of Directors for another corporation, and only meet a few times a year, they can only oversee major policy issues, not control the daily operations of that corporation. In large corporations, the directors choose a management committee to make most decisions, referring only major ones to the full board.

Directors are the ones who set executive salaries and are responsible for the increasingly high incomes senior officers of larger corporations make in relation to the average worker.

inside director

acts as a director and also an officer of the corporation

outside director

acts as a director but holds no other position with the corporation

Directors' Duties

Competence and Fiduciary   Directors have the ultimate control of a corporation, but with that power comes great responsibility. Both the common law, which is developed by judges, and the statute law, which is passed by the legislatures, are increasing the obligations of directors. A well-known article on directors' responsibilities in corporate governance is entitled "Why No Sane Person Should Be a Director of a Public Corporation." While the corporate shield has been maintained to protect shareholders (investors), that shield has been removed respecting directors and officers in many areas.

Directors owe a fiduciary duty to the corporation to act honestly and in good faith and to put the corporation's interests first. They must use the care, diligence and skill that a reasonably prudent person would use in the circumstances. They must disclose any interest in any contracts made with the corporation and refrain from voting on such matters. They cannot take personal advantage of business opportunities related to the corporation.

Example: The leading Canadian case on directors' fiduciary duty is *Can. Aero v. O'Malley*, [1974] SCR 592. The president and executive vice president, who were also directors of Canaero, had been negotiating a mapping contract with the Guyana government for several years. Before it was finally approved, the two men resigned and formed their own company and won the contract. The two men had no employment agreement or non-competition clause with Canaero. The Supreme Court however ruled that these directors and senior officers owed the company a fiduciary duty to act in the best interests of the company in spite of the absence of a contract requiring this duty. They could not spend several years on the company payroll developing the project, and then just before the contract is to be signed, quit and take this opportunity for themselves. The two directors were liable to Canaero for $125,000 for the value of the contract they had taken.

■ *Critical Concepts of* Directors

- Directors are elected by common shareholders and they select the officers of the corporation and set the executives' compensation

- Public corporations have inside directors who are executives of the corporation and outside directors who are not employees of the corporation

- Directors owe the corporation a fiduciary duty of care

- Directors cannot take personal advantage of business opportunities related to the corporation

Conflict of interest and fraud were considered in the following famous criminal case. The results surprised many and illustrated that weak corporate governance rules in a corporation may permit questionable behaviour by directors and officers.

Criminal Sanctions

Directors may also have liability under the Criminal Code for fraud if they take assets from the corporation for their personal benefit. However, the criminal charge must be proved beyond a reasonable doubt, while a civil claim need only be proved on the balance of probabilities. While there might be an order for restitution, meaning payment to the victims by the convicted parties, any fines would go to the government. The government would bear the cost of the prosecution. There are very few successful criminal fraud charges against directors as the following case illustrates.

R. v. De Zen et al., 2010 ONCJ 630 (CanLII)

Vic De Zen was the founder, CEO and a director of Royal Group Technologies Limited (RGTL) a large public company that made plastic building supplies. De Zen and 5 other officers and/or directors of RGTL were charged with two counts of fraud. These executives formed a company which purchased land opposite the RGTL property for $20,213,198 and then sold it the same day to RGTL for $27,390,500, for a profit of close to $7 million. The Crown alleged the sale to the company was at an inflated price and they had defrauded the company. The second fraud charge alleged five of the defendants acquired $2 million by hiding a warrant received through the sale of a subsidiary and this money should have gone to RGTL, not to the executives.

The Court's Decision

The judge noted that the corporate governance, management structure, and disclosure practices of RGTL were greatly deficient. Vic De Zen had 80–90% of the voting shares in the company even though it had gone public and De Zen controlled what the company did. The Board of Directors was not engaged in providing sufficient oversight of management's decisions and was primarily comprised of inside directors. There were no procedures in place to identify important transactions which involved related parties and conflicts of interest.

Despite these problems, the court found that there had been complete disclosure and nothing dishonest. It ruled that De Zen had actually acquired the property 2 ½ months before it was sold to RGTL and it would not accept the Crown's valuations of the land that indicated RGTL had purchased it at an inflated price. The Court ruled that since the executives had not tried to conceal the deal, they were entitled to make a profit on the land sale. The by-laws of the corporation set $60 million as the very high threshold for a reviewable transaction and this sale was below that limit.

In the fraud allegation over the $2 million warrant, again the judge noted that the transaction had not been concealed, it was openly discussed within the company, and the men were entitled to this money as a bonus.

Despite what some thought was an obvious conflict of interest and dishonest behaviour, the judge ruled that there was no fraud and the six executives were found not guilty.

Note: A shareholder class action was launched against the company over these transactions and was settled for $5 million. This case was a bitter defeat for the RCMP IMFT team (discussed later in the chapter) which specializes in financial fraud and had worked on this case for 10 years.

■ *Business Law*   Applied

⑧ **Wilson Arnott was** one of three directors of a small manufacturing company. He had recently become friends with a vice-president from a competing firm. They often went away on weekend fishing trips, and frequently played golf together.

The other directors were unhappy about Arnott's contact with a competitor and the possibility of his leaking confidential business plans and information. Arnott maintained it was none of the company's business, since it was part of his personal life.

The other directors tried to remove Arnott from his position on the board.

    a) On what grounds could they base their action?   b) Would it be successful?

⑨ **Harold Elliot was** the director of a paint-manufacturing company, Enviro Chemicals Ltd., operating in British Columbia. The firm discovered a new process for making mercury-free paint that was a lot less harmful to the environment than competitors' products.

Enviro Chemicals Ltd. decided that it would not patent the new process, preferring to keep it confidential—as Coca-Cola does with its formula. Before Enviro went into production of its new product, Elliot and a lab employee left the company and moved to Ontario, where they set up their own paint-manufacturing firm. There was no written confidentiality clause with either Elliot or the lab worker.

Enviro Chemicals brought an action to stop Elliot and the employee from producing this new product in Ontario.

    a) Would they be successful?

    b) Elliot also contacted Enviro Chemicals' long-standing customers in Ontario and made contracts with them for the sale of other paint products. Could Enviro Chemicals stop Elliot's new company from dealing with these customers?

Statutory Liability: Wages, Taxes

Various statutes impose personal liability on directors. Directors can be personally liable if the corporation fails to remit source deductions to the government for employee income taxes, and employee contributions for Employment Insurance and Canada Pension Plan. The corporation is considered to be holding this money in trust for the government.

Directors have the defence of due diligence. This defence, in effect, puts the onus on directors to prove that they have taken precautions to ensure that the money deducted is sent to the government. This defence provides a very narrow window for a director to escape liability. It means that the directors must take action to ensure that the money reaches the government, or the directors will likely pay themselves.

Likewise, directors are personally liable under most provincial and federal corporations acts for up to 6 months wages, including vacation pay, owed to employees up to the time of the corporation's bankruptcy. All provinces except the Atlantic provinces impose such liability on directors. Directors are not liable for future wages after the date of the bankruptcy such as termination or severance pay or wrongful dismissal claims.[1]

There is at present no due diligence defence in the corporations acts respecting claims for unpaid wages. However, business lobby groups have been requesting that such a defence be added, so the corporations acts may be amended to include one.

Under the Canadian Labour Code, which applies to federally regulated corporations only, directors are liable for severance pay (future wages) as well as unpaid wages to the date of the bankruptcy.

Other statutes such as workplace safety laws, employment standards laws, environmental protection laws, consumer protection laws, and human rights legislation also have provisions that will hold directors personally liable if the corporation violates these laws. Directors sometimes are able to use a due diligence defence in these situations, but not in all cases.

---

1. *Barrette v. Caltree*, [1993] 1 S.C.R. 1027.

Example: The *Soper* case is a leading case that established the liability of directors. Soper was an experienced business man who was an outside director for about 4 months for a corporation that ran a modelling school. He knew soon after he joined the board that the corporation was facing financial difficulties. It had not remitted taxes and other employee deductions to Revenue Canada during the period he was on the board. The government claimed that since he was a director during this period he was personally liable for $13,009 for these unpaid amounts. The court ruled he had not exercised due diligence. The court adopted a subjective/objective test. The personal knowledge, skill and background of the director is first considered, but it is not enough for them to then say they did their best. An objective standard should then be applied and determine what would a reasonably prudent person have done under these conditions. Soper had not shown the skill, care and diligence expected of an experienced business person to prevent these failures to remit. He had done nothing, even though he knew the business was in financial trouble. As a knowledgeable businessman his inaction prevented him from using a due diligence defence, and he was liable for this amount. (*Soper v. The Queen*, 1997 CanLII 6352 (FCA))

The issue then arose in other cases, what if a person is a director but has no business experience at all and no involvement in the company's business. Often a family member becomes a director "on paper" of another family member's business, but has no participation in how it is run and trusts their relatives are acting properly. If the corporation does not remit money owed to the government, is this inactive inexperienced family director personally liable for these amounts? What level of due diligence must they meet or is "doing nothing" enough in these situations when they have no business experience. Cases have gone in both directions over this issue. But the *Constantin* case below indicates that if there are signs the company is in financial trouble, the inactive outside family director still has a duty to ask if these government payments have been made. If not, they will be personally liable. The onus is on the director to make sure there is no failure to remit.

Constantin v. Canada, 2013 FCA 233 (CanLII)

Chantal Constantin was the common law spouse of Denis Dubois. Dubois ran a sign installation and light servicing business and Constantin was a social worker with no business background. To protect their family assets, Dubois set up his business as a corporation and Constantin was the sole director and shareholder. Dubois ran into considerable financial difficulties and failed to remit $136,028 in GST to the government for a period of 45 months ending in August 2007.

The CRA (Canada Revenue Agency) claimed that since Constantin was a director she was personally liable for this money.

Constantin claimed that she was completely unaware of the amounts owing to the CRA. She said the company was completely controlled by her spouse and he did not keep her informed about the company's financial difficulties. She claimed it was not until September 2008 that she became aware of any financial problems with the company, so she was unable to act any earlier to prevent the failure to remit. She submitted that as an outside director she had less of a duty of diligence than her spouse.

The tax court ruled that she was aware of some financial difficulties during the 45 month period and a reasonably prudent person would have asked more specific questions. She should have inquired as to whether money had been set to the CRA and she failed to prevent the company from failing to remit the money. She appealed this decision

The Court's Decision

The Tax Appeal Court said it was sympathetic with Constantin's position, but she still lost her appeal. It ruled that the trial judge had taken into account her particular circumstances but had not erred when he concluded that Constantin was not concerned about the tax remittances and she had taken no concrete action in order to prevent the company's failure to send in the money even though she knew it was facing some financial difficulties. She had not exercised the degree of care, diligence and skill to prevent the failure that a reasonably prudent person would have exercised in comparable circumstances. She was held personally liable for the company's debt to CRA.

This emphasis on preventing a failure to remit funds to the government can also put actively involved directors in a difficult position. They may knowingly not remit government source deductions because they are using that money to keep the corporation afloat in times of financial trouble. That may be in the best interests of the corporation, but it could also expose them to personal liability since they did not prevent the failure to remit the money to the government. (see *Canada v. Buckingham* 2011 FCA 142 (CanLII). A Supreme Court decision clarifying this area of law in the future will be helpful.

Business Alert!

Directors of Insolvent Corporations   If you are a director of a company that is experiencing financial difficulty, you would be well advised to consult with a lawyer immediately. You may need to resign promptly to avoid personal liability (as described above) which will derive from activities beyond your control. Additionally, in order to prove the defence of due diligence you should leave a paper trail of your efforts to make certain the relevant funds reach the government. For example, send memos to key employees such as bookkeepers, accountants, and the like, insist that deductions be put in a separate trust account, and review cancelled cheques proving sums were remitted.

Business Law Applied

⑩ **Alice Williams was** a director of Hi-Tech Promotions Inc., a Manitoba corporation. The company was experiencing financial difficulty. Williams, a skilled business woman, recommended severe cost-cutting that would have saved to the business. Unfortunately, the other directors would not accept her advice and spent money recklessly. The company went bankrupt.

Revenue Canada made a claim against Williams for $100,000 respecting sums deducted from employees' paycheques for income tax. Williams claims that she was not negligent in acting as a director: it was the other directors who were negligent. Also, when the business was set up she had ensured that there was a system in place so that any money deducted from employees' salaries was sent immediately to the government. She had no idea that the system was not being followed. Additionally, the money was used to save the business and hence kept the employees working longer.

   a) Is the fact that she was not negligent a defence for Williams?
   b) Is the fact that the money went to try and save the business, and not to her or to any director personally, a defence?
   c) Is the fact that Williams honestly believed that the money was being sent to the government according to the system that she set up a defence?
   d) Does Williams have any defence?

Personal Liability in Tort

Directors are protected from personal liability when conducting a corporation's business properly. For example, if the corporation breaches a contract, the aggrieved party cannot sue the director who signed the contract on behalf of the corporation. Directors are protected respecting contracts that they sign on behalf of a corporation.

However, a tort is a civil wrong. If a director commits a tort, even if acting in the best interests of the company and within the scope of her authority as a director, she will be personally liable.

Example: In *WS Leasing Ltd. v. Platinum Equipment Ltd.*, 2012 BCSC 558 (CanLII) two directors of Platinum Equipment were held liable for the tort of deceit. They had fraudulently prepared false invoices and intentionally lied to a leasing company to obtain financing for containers they knew they could not obtain. The directors maintained that only Platinum was liable, but the court disagreed. The corporation was liable but the directors were also liable for the torts they committed. Platinum as well as these two directors were liable for $494,974 and the directors also were each liable for $5,000 in punitive damages for their fraudulent conduct.

The torts of most concern to directors are the economic torts. These torts include ways of doing business that are considered unfair in the sense of being beyond what is acceptable competitive behaviour such as inducing a breach of contract or inducing breach of confidentiality.

There is some protection given to directors. Directors are not liable for matters that arise from concurrent (dual or parallel) liability in tort and contract. If the matter can give rise to a contract claim, that claim must be pursued in contract, where directors have no liability, and not in tort.

The term "director's liability" is often used. But the same rules apply with respect to officers or employees of the corporation. This liability is usually only of importance if the corporation is insolvent. Since the corporation is liable for acts done by directors, officers, and employees on its behalf, full recovery can be made against it if the corporation has assets.

The case *ADGA Systems International Ltd. v. Valcom Ltd.*, below, is a decision of the Ontario Court of Appeal on directors' liability in tort. It has generated much controversy. Critics ask what is the use of having a corporation if the directors are liable in tort? Supporters of the decision reply that directors are protected from all valid business risks; it is only when a director is personally involved in committing a civil wrong (a tort) that the director is liable.

Will *ADGA Systems* become law across Canada? It may be worth noting that the law in the U.S. on directors' liability in tort has been the same as set out in the *ADGA Systems* case for over 20 years.

■ *Critical Concepts of* Director's Liability

- Directors can be personally liable for source deductions such as employees' income tax, CPP, EI and HST/GST that the corporation has not remitted
- Directors may be personally liable for up to 6 months unpaid wages and vacation pay if a corporation goes bankrupt
- Directors may be held personally liable under many other statutes such as workplace safety laws, environmental, human rights, consumer protection and human rights laws
- Directors may be personally liable for torts they commit on behalf of the corporation but not for contracts made on behalf of the corporation
- Directors may have a due diligence defence in some situations
- Directors often require the corporation to purchase directors' liability insurance and/or set up a fund in case they are held personally liable

---

ADGA Systems International Ltd. v. Valcom Ltd., [1999] 168 D.L.R. (4th) 351 (Ont. CA)

ADGA Systems was in competition with Valcom in the security-systems industry. For several years ADGA Systems held a substantial contract with Correctional Services Canada for technical support and maintenance of security systems in federal prisons. On a call for tenders on renewal of the contract, Correctional Services Canada required all tendering parties to list 25 senior technicians and their qualifications.

Valcom had no such employees but interviewed ADGA employees and used their names on the Valcom tender. Curiously the tenders of ADGA and Valcom had the same names. Valcom got the award. ADGA sued Valcom's sole director and two of its senior employees for inducing breach of contract.

The Court's Decision

The court held that officers, directors, and employees of a corporation are personally responsible for their tortious conduct even though that conduct was directed in a *bona fide* matter in the best interests of the corporation, provided that the conduct was "tortious in itself."

The phrase "tortious in itself" means that the plaintiff cannot use a concurrent liability matter to obtain liability in tort when it would be unsuccessful in contract. For example, if a corporation refuses to pay on a contract, the directors cannot be sued in court for conspiring with their own company for directing that it not pay on the contract. That issue is one of contract only.

Here the conduct was tortious in itself. Valcom had made agreements with employees at ADGA to leave the employment of that company and come to Valcom if it was successful on the bid. This is the tort of inducing breach of contract. The directors of Valcom who participated in making this arrangement with the ADGA employees were personally responsible for the loss to ADGA.

Business Alert!

Directors' Liability   If you are asked to be a director of a corporation of which you are not the controlling shareholder, you should investigate the options given below for your personal protection. In some jurisdictions there are restrictions on directors' obtaining indemnification for personal liability.

- obtain an indemnity from the corporation or its shareholders
- have the corporation take out and pay for directors' liability insurance
- have the corporation set up a trust fund for legal fees to defend actions against directors
- obtain legal advice and consider early resignation if the corporation is in financial difficulties
- perform and document due diligence respecting all government remittances and employee wages

■ *Business Law*   Applied

⑪ **Joel Shuster and** Janet Russell were directors of Lion Corp. Inc. It made a special industrial-strength tape, sold only to manufacturing companies. Shuster was lucky in the gene-pool lottery of life and had inherited considerable wealth. Russell had the more usual luck and was born and remains penniless, living largely on her credit cards.

Russell learned that Fasteners Inc., a new company, was entering into competition with Lion Corp. Russell told the only supplier of the raw film, which is needed for making tape of this particular type, that the people behind Fasteners Inc. had been involved in scams in the U.S. As a result, Fasteners Inc. could not get raw product from this crucial supplier and had to cease operation. Several months later, Fasteners Inc. learned that it was Russell's interference which prevented them from getting supplies. Assume that the acts of Russell are the tort of intentional interference with economic interests and Fasteners Inc. wants to bring an action based on that tort against as many defendants as possible.

a) Has Lion Corp. committed the tort? If so, why?
b) Fasteners Inc. wants to bring a claim against Joel Shuster because Russell has no money. Is Shuster liable? If so, on what basis?
c) Is Russell liable? Does she have a defence that she was acting only as a director of Lion Corp. Inc. and in the best interests of that company? What is the downside of suing Russell?

White-Collar Crime

Offences

White-collar crime is non-violent financial crime often committed by business professionals who usually wear suits, "white shirts" and ties. The criminals are often people who others have put their trust in, such as lawyers, investment advisors, accountants and business executives. But these trusted professionals sometimes devise illicit schemes to steal money.

White-collar crime is a problem in the business world and Canada has an international reputation of being "soft" on these types of offences. In 2012 in an international survey, 36 per cent of 100 large Canadian companies surveyed reported they had been victims of white-collar crime in the previous year. The typical offence was committed by a middle management employee with 10 years' service in the company. The most common crimes involved were theft of assets, fraud, accounting fraud and cybercrimes. Fifteen percent had been asked to pay bribes and 14 percent indicated they had lost business because they would not pay the bribe. Ten per cent had losses in excess of $5 million that year due to white-collar crimes. (McKenna, Barrie. (February 24, 2014). "White-collar crime hits more than a third of Canadian organizations." *Globe and Mail*)

Some of the most common offences involve crimes such as; fraud (stock and investor fraud such as Ponzi schemes), mortgage or insurance fraud (see Chapter 15), theft, insider trading, bribery, money laundering, identity theft, cybercrimes and intellectual property infringements. Though these crimes do not usually involve physical assaults on people, they can still have devastating impacts on individuals. If someone has lost their life savings, home, job or pension due to a corporate con artist, the stress and financial impacts have significant effects on their health and wellbeing.

The chances of being caught and convicted in Canada and ever serving significant jail time are so low, that it almost encourages dishonest individuals to commit these financial crimes. In a risk versus reward analysis, many corporate criminals believe the risk of getting caught and punished is much less than the reward they get by stealing millions from others. They may never be charged, and even if they are, they often are not convicted. Or in the rare case when they are found guilty, the actual time spent in prison is so short; it is seen as a minor inconvenience or the cost of doing business. Some fraudsters are repeat offenders who have already served some jail time for earlier frauds, but since the penalties are so minor, once released, they repeat their profitable crimes.

Example: In 1998 Ronald Weinberg and his wife had been accused of defrauding the Quebec film company, Cinar, out of $122 million. They agreed to pay a $2 million fine, but never admitted any guilt. In 2005 it was alleged he was involved with Norshield Funds which allegedly cheated 1,900 investors out of approximately $150 million and Mount Real Funds which allegedly defrauded about 1,600 clients out of $130 million. The criminal trial had still not begun by early 2014 for these charges and the complex investigation was still continuing.

Punishment and Parole

Under the *Criminal Code*, RSC 1985, C. C-46 s.380. (1) the maximum punishment for fraud is 14 years in jail. The maximum sentence is almost never given out though. Also if a person is charged with multiple offences, the jail sentences are usually served concurrently (all at the same time), unlike the U.S. where the sentences are often served consecutively (each additional jail term added on to the total). Parole eligibility often makes the actual time they are imprisoned very short.

For example it only took the U.S. 7 months to charge, try, convict and sentence Bernie Madoff to 150 years in jail for his Ponzi scheme that bilked investors out of $65 billion. In Canada it took 12 years to finally convict Garth Drabinsky in 2009 of a financial fraud involving his $500 million entertainment company Livent. Drabinsky was sentenced to 5 years for one count of fraud and 4 years for another but the time was to be served concurrently. He served only 17 months in jail, most in a minimum security prison, and then was released on day parole. Full parole was granted less than a year later.

Prior to 2011, white collar criminals in Canada, unlike most other criminals, were eligible for accelerated parole and could be out on day parole after serving only one sixth of their sentences, because they were not seen as a danger to society. In a "tough on crime" move by the government in 2011, accelerated parole was removed for white collar crimes and they now must serve one-third of their sentence before parole eligibility.

Example: Ron and Loren Koval operated the posh King Medical Centre which offered medical and wellness treatments. They were convicted in 2001 of fraud totalling $94 million after bilking two financial institutions that had provided funds for medical equipment purchases. The Koval's were supposedly then leasing this equipment to hospitals. But the Koval's never purchased the equipment and instead used the money to fund their lavish lifestyle. They left the country and after a 10 week manhunt they turned themselves in. The judge said that while they were dishonest with lenders, they had had not endangered the health of patients at their clinic. They were sentenced to 7 years in jail, but were released on day parole after only serving 14 months because of the accelerated parole provisions allowed at that time.

R. v. Drabinsky, 2011 ONCA 582 (CanLII)

Garth Drabinsky and Myron Gottlieb established Cineplex in the 1980s and expanded the movie theatre business in Canada. In 1989 they left and formed a partnership, MyGar, and developed a very successful live entertainment business of theatre and concert productions, the first ever of its kind in Canada.

In 1993 MyGar did an IPO and became a public company known as Livent. It became a major player in live theatre across North America and renovated many historic theatres to stage its productions. Livent continually expanded and needed significant infusions of cash to fund its very ambitious projects. Between 1993 and 1998 it raised over $500 million through share offerings, warrants, notes, bond, debentures and loans. In 1998, new investors, the Ovitz group, were brought in to oversee the management of Livent. What Ovitz found was fraudulent financial statements that had hidden the true disastrous financial state of Livent.

Livent's accountants admitted that the statements were false and that Drabinsky and Gottlieb had intentionally overstated the value of the business by about $6 million in the financial statements for the IPO. Drabinsky and Gottlieb had a kickback scheme where they billed MyGar for fictional services and received $8.1 million in return. With Livent they had consistently fraudulently reduced expenses to artificially increase income and knowingly issued false financial statements.

The trial judge was satisfied beyond a reasonable doubt that Drabinsky and Gottlieb initiated the fraudulent accounting system to attract further investors. They were "deceitful, they perpetrated a falsehood and reasonable people would consider them dishonest."

The trial judge sentenced Drabinsky to 7 years for the Livent fraud and 4 years for the MyGar fraud to be served concurrently and Gottlieb received 6 and 4 year sentences for the same frauds. They appealed their convictions and sentences.

The Court's Decision

The Ontario Court of Appeal upheld the convictions for fraud. It ruled that the two men clearly had knowingly issued false financial statements to attract investors to maintain Livent's survival. The court noted that Livent was not created as a scam corporation designed to rip off investors. It was a legitimate important business, and the men had made major contributions to the development of the theatre industry. But the two principals became so driven to make Livent a success, that when it was in financial difficulty, they lied to the public and hid its dismal financial reality to perpetuate their entertainment business.

The Crown however had not produced any evidence of the actual financial losses this fraud caused. Livent went bankrupt not long after the fraud was discovered. Shareholders and creditors suffered losses which were not yet quantified. The complete failure of this $500 million corporation could not be blamed entirely on the fraud. Civil cases had not yet decided the exact losses. Due to the lack of evidence on the financial impact of this fraud, the jail sentences were reduced to 5 and 4 years for Drabinsky to be served concurrently and 4 and 3 years concurrently for Gottlieb.

Note: Drabinsky only served 17 months before he was out on day parole and less than one year later he was granted full parole.

The accounting firm that audited Livent was successfully sued for negligence by the Receiver/Trustee in charge of Livent's bankruptcy and ordered to pay Livent $85 million. (see Chapter 4 *Livent Inc. v Deloitte & Touche LLP*, 2014 ONSC 2176 (CanLII)). This case may however be appealed. The Hercules case has greatly limited shareholders ability to sue auditors for negligence, but in this case it was the Receiver/Trustee that sued, not the shareholders, so perhaps it may offer a way to hold accountants liable to the corporation but that remains to be seen.

In Ontario in 2005 amendments to the *Securities Act* s. 130 and s. 130.1 include provisions that now create a statutory civil liability for misrepresentations made by experts. Both primary purchasers (those who purchase when an IPO is made) and secondary purchasers (who purchase shares later on the open market) have a cause of action against experts (such as accountants, lawyers, financial analysts, engineers and geologists) for material statements that are misrepresentations. No cases have yet been tried under these new provisions, but it was considered in the Sino Forest case where a settlement was reached. It may give some limited statutory protection to shareholders whose common law rights are so greatly restricted by the *Hercules* decision.

Sentencing

Even where there are many individual investors who are harmed by the fraud the jail time served for the offence is often quite short as the Lacroix case below illustrates. The judge clearly set out the Canadian principles on concurrent sentencing in this case and observations on parole.

R. c. Lacroix, 2009 QCCS 4519 (CanLII)

On September 21, 2009 Vincent Lacroix, the mastermind of Norbourg Trust, was about to start his second criminal trial for additional charges of fraud. Norbourg Trust had defrauded 9,200 investors of over $100 million. He had been convicted in 2006 on 51 charges and sentenced to 12 years in jail and fined $255,000. Just before this additional criminal trial was to begin, he pleaded guilty to the extra 200 counts of conspiracy to commit fraud, fraud, use of the proceeds of crime, conspiracy to make false documents, and the making of false documents. The judge commented:

"The evidence shows that the acts with which Vincent Lacroix was charged and of which he pleaded guilty led to a shortfall of close to $100 million for 9,200 investors, rocked the structure of financial markets, and caused serious moral damages to the victims of this financial scandal, which was unprecedented in the annals of Canadian legal history.

This saga also reveals the weakness of controls in this area and has led to a healthy reflection on the gravity of such crimes in our era and the urgency of improving the health of financial operations in our country."

For almost 5 years Lacroix operated a well-orchestrated scam based on creating false documents and falsifying financial statements to suggest the existence of investment funds that did not exist. This imaginary wealth allowed him to steal from the existing funds, and live an extravagant and luxurious lifestyle. Lacroix even used investors' funds to pay additional income taxes to cover his trail and not alert the tax authorities.

According to the Court's notes, the moral and financial damages sustained by the victims were unspeakable. He had jeopardized the financial security of individuals and it had devastating consequences for many people and caused his victims serious harm.

The judge then discussed the nature of the sentencing process in a fraud case. He stated the criminal justice system punishes criminals, not crimes.

"under our system, sentences may not consist of terms of imprisonment lasting several hundred years for financial crimes committed by individuals whose life expectancy does not exceed eighty years.

Furthermore, the maximum sentence decreed by Parliament in this regard has been set at fourteen years' imprisonment.

Imposing sentences that are clearly disproportionate, however well-meaning to begin with, would risk bringing the administration of justice in Canada into disrepute in the medium and long term."

He commented that a prison sentence must have a functional and practical value.

"A prison sentence of several hundred years has no practical meaning and does not meet the objectives sought. It may make some people in the general public happy, but it risks damaging the integrity of a system of justice based on moral and social values that must be preserved. The Court hopes that our legal and judicial culture never chooses to go along that route."

He did note that what comes later (parole eligibility) happens on another level. The Court pointed out that parole is the responsibility of Parliament and that it is up to politicians to answer for their acts or omissions.

The reflection of the Courts cannot and must not take into account the consequences and the terms and conditions of parole, which are not their responsibility and over which they have no control.

The Court's Decision

Lacroix was sentenced to 10 years for conspiracy and making false documents, 10 years for money laundering, 10 years for fraud and conspiracy to commit fraud and 13 years for later charges of fraud and conspiracy to commit fraud, all terms to be served concurrently.

Note: Lacroix was given this sentence on October 29, 2009 and he was out on parole on January 22, 2011 (less than 15 months later), much to the dismay of his victims. The victims were able to recover most of their losses after a class action was commenced and a fund was set up to compensate them involving Quebec's securities regulator, several other financial services firms involved with Norbourg and a major accounting firm. It is unusual for defrauded victims to recover this much of their losses.

Enforcement and Burden of Proof

IMET

White collar crimes are often offences not just under the Criminal Code but also under other laws such as provincial securities acts if stocks and bonds are involved. If the person who perpetuated the crime is a professional there are other laws governing their profession that can also apply. Canada is the only major industrialized country in the world that does not have a national securities regulator. The provincial regulators have not had much success in obtaining convictions for offences in their jurisdictions. *Forbes*, a leading American business magazine, once referred to the Vancouver stock exchange as "the scam capital of the world."

In 2003 the RCMP created the IMET (Integrated Markets Enforcement Team) to target white-collar crime. There are 10 teams working in the four largest Canadian cities. Their investigators are dedicated to the investigation and prosecution of serious capital market offences that are of national significance. Unfortunately they have only averaged about 1 conviction per year in its first 10 years of operation. The failure to get convictions in some key cases, such as the Vic De Zen/Royal Group Technologies case above and the Nortel fraud case discussed below, casts serious doubts on IMET's effectiveness.

IMET, as well as provincial enforcement agencies, face many problems. They are usually understaffed, have low budgets, and pay lower wages than the private sector, so it is hard to attract and keep good fraud investigators. There is a shortage of forensic accounting specialists in Canada, so those who practice in this field are in great demand and often do not want to work for less money for the government. The enforcement agencies are often very slow to charge individuals and the legal requirements for disclosure of documents drag proceedings on endlessly it seems. In the Nortel case there were 25 million pages of documents produced. They also lack the ability to compel evidence from third parties who do not want to testify.

Burden of Proof

One of the biggest problems in obtaining a conviction for fraud is that it is the higher criminal burden of proof (beyond reasonable doubt) must be met. In cases such as a clear Ponzi scheme it can be done. In a Ponzi scheme, a con artist promises investors great returns but he funds the early investor returns by taking money from later investors, and there are little or no legitimate revenue generating investments at all, just fraudulent statements to indicate they exist. But in grey areas dealing with interpreting financial statements and accounting misstatements, reasonable doubt is more easily established by the accused, which results in not guilty verdicts.

If these cases were tried under the easier civil law burden of proof (on the balance of probabilities) as required under regulatory provisions, not the *Criminal Code*, the conviction rate could be much better. If legislation is ever passed to create a national securities regulator then offences under that law could require the civil law burden of proof to obtain convictions for violations. Some have suggested we need to establish a regulatory tribunal that deals with these types of white-collar crimes that would use the civil law standard of proof.

Important Fraud Cases

Nortel Networks

One of the most famous cases of alleged fraud involved Nortel Networks, the once superstar of Canadian business, a company that accounted for about one third of the total value of the Toronto Stock Exchange at one time. It was a world leader in telecommunications and at its height in 2000 was valued at over $300 billion and employed over 94,000 people. In July 2000 at the height of the tech bubble, its shares traded at $124.50 each, but by October 2002 the bubble had burst and its shares traded at 67 cents. By 2009 the company had declared bankruptcy, tens of thousands of jobs were lost and thousands of pensions destroyed. There was great public outcry because so many people lost money in the crash of this company and they questioned how it could have happened. Attention then turned to the executives who ran the company and how the financial statements during Nortel's period of decline had not accurately portrayed the company's true financial situation.

In February 2003 Nortel financial statements indicated the company had returned to profitability and this triggered bonuses to 43 senior executives based on these profits totalling $70 million. But by October 2003 the company declared that it would have to restate its financial statements back to 2000 due to accounting errors. When the restated financials were released it showed there had been many questionable accounting practices and there were no profits made in 2003. Some executives repaid a total of $8.6 million in bonuses but many did not. Based on these false profit figures in 2003 the CEO Frank Dunn earned a bonus of $7.8 million, CFO Douglas Beatty received a bonus of $3 million and Controller Michael Gollogly's bonus was $2 million.

A class action lawsuit by shareholders soon sprang up in the U.S. alleging fraudulent accounting schemes by Nortel and by 2006 Nortel agreed to settle the American lawsuit for $2.5 billion. Finally in 2008 after 4 years of investigation by IMET, the RCMP laid criminal charges against the three former executives Dunn, Beatty and Gollogly. They were each charged with two counts of fraud, one for defrauding the investing public and the other for defrauding Nortel Networks. The Crown alleged that these three men deliberately misrepresented Nortel's financial results.

In a crushing defeat for IMET and the Crown, the three Nortel executives were found not guilty.

R. v. Dunn, 2013 ONSC 137 (CanLII) [The Nortel Fraud Case]

In a trial that lasted a year, the judge thoroughly weighed all the accounting evidence regarding the Nortel financial documents that had been released initially and then restated. The Crown had alleged the executives had knowingly released false information to intentionally mislead investors and to obtain executive bonuses based on false profit figures.

The trial focused on accounting practices and procedures and interpretation of accounting information. The Crown did not have any specific evidence such as emails or documents to show the men had a directive to defraud the public or the company. The evidence was primarily circumstantial accounting evidence from which the Crown alleged you could infer that the fraudulent motives existed. Much of the trial was argument concerning what were accepted accounting practices and procedures in these financial situations.

The Court's Decision

In the end the judge concluded that he was not satisfied beyond a reasonable doubt that the three accused executives had deliberately misrepresented Nortel's financial statements for the periods in question.

He concluded that the decision to restate financials due to an error, can be the same thing as saying that the decision to restate was because of a difference of opinion. The difference of opinion can occur with the benefit of hindsight and can be influenced by new information. He noted that sometimes even the accounting firm involved disagreed with itself on what should be done.

He stated that in the abstract, it was true that the fact Nortel's balance sheets were restated could be capable of supporting an inference that the original financial statements misrepresented Nortel's financial results. However based on the evidence he heard he would not draw that conclusion. He was not satisfied that the actions of these executives were outside the normal course of business.

Having regard to all the evidence, he was not satisfied beyond a reasonable doubt that Frank Dunn, Douglas Beatty and Michael Gollogly deliberately misrepresented the financial results of Nortel Networks Corporation and, therefore, they were found not guilty.

This case illustrates the difficulty of getting a conviction in cases of complex accounting fraud where there are many different accounting rules and interpretations. The accused can establish a "reasonable doubt" and then a criminal conviction is not possible.

Other famous Canadian examples of fraud include the following:

Example: Castor Holdings – (see Chapter 4 *Wightman c. Widdrington* case) The accounting firm of Coopers & Lybrand was held liable for about $1 billion for its negligently prepared financial statements for Castor Holdings. Wolfgang Stolzenberg created Castor Holdings, a private investment bank, and had 100 exclusive clients including wealthy individuals and institutional investors. For 17 years he ran a Ponzi scheme supported by misleading financial statements that indicated Castor's real estate investments were profitable. The company was once falsely valued at $1.87 billion, but soon after it went bankrupt owing investors and creditors $1.6 billion. One shareholder was able to establish he had gone over the financial statements in detail when making his investment decisions, so the accounting firm did owe him a duty of care (despite *Hercules*) and therefore the accounting firm was liable for its negligence. This is the largest liability claim ever against an accounting firm in Canada, but it was decided under the Quebec Civil Code, so it may have little impact in other jurisdictions in Canada. The RCMP conducted a 7 year investigation and has a warrant for Stolzenberg's arrest on 41 counts of and since Germany does not extradite its citizens, he may never go to jail for one of Canada's fraud and conspiracy. Stolzenberg, the master fraud artist, however moved back to Germany biggest frauds.

Example: Sino-Forest – Sino-Forest was a Chinese based forestry company that chose to raise money in Canada. It became listed on the Alberta Stock Exchange in 1994 and by 2010 it has raised over $3 billion through debt and equity financing with the help of Canadian bankers, brokers, lawyers, accountants and stock analysts. It reached its peak market capitalization in March 2011 at $6 billion. It purported to have 800,000 hectares of forest reserves in China worth $3 billion. But in June 2011 a private investment research firm, Muddy Waters, posted on-line comments that Sino-Forest may be another major case of stock fraud and questioned the asset holdings and revenue the company claimed to have. Though the company founder Allen Chan denied these accusations, less than a year later Sino-Forest had gone into bankruptcy protection. Investors have lost billions.

The OSC laid fraud charges under the Ontario *Securities Act* against Chan and 4 other Sino-Forest executives for fraudulently inflating the assets and revenues of Sino-Forest and issuing false and misleading statements. The penalties could be fines of up to $84 million. The investigation continues but is hampered due to the complexity of the deals and the difficulty in obtaining information in China. Mr. Chan lives in Hong Kong now and it remains to be seen if he will return to Canada to face the charges. No criminal fraud charges have been laid by the RCMP in this case.

In 2013 a court approved a $117 million settlement reached by Sino-Forest investors with the accounting firm of Ernst & Young for the auditor's negligence in preparing false financial statements for the company. Their claim had been based on allegations of negligence and liability under the Ontario *Securities Act* for experts' misrepresentations.

The massive Sino-Forest stock fraud, not long after the Bre-X scandal discussed below, reinforces Canada's international reputation as a haven for con artists. Twice Canada's fragmented and undermanned regulatory agencies failed to protect investors. The auditors, lawyers, underwriters, bankers and analysts missed major warning signals and the thieves made a fortune at investors' expense.

Example: YBM Magnex was incorporated in Alberta in 1994 claimed it was an international manufacturer of industrial magnets. Press releases praised its growth and it raised over $890 million and was registered on the Toronto stock exchange (TSX). A former Ontario premier was on its Board of Directors and its share price rose from 10 cents to $20.15. Its head office was in the U.S., and U.S. authorities received a tip YBM had offered to bribe accountants to certify their financial statements. An investigation began and the whole fraud began to unravel. YBM had very little legitimate business. It turned out to be a money laundering operation run by one of the most wanted mobsters involved in organized crime in Russia. Simeon Mogilevich had picked Canada to incorporate in because of the weak securities laws. The company went bankrupt and all the receiver could recover was $90 million. Investors lost millions. YBM had issued false press releases and financial statements and nobody had properly investigated the company's claims of big profits. It was all a fraud. Mogilevich remains in Russia and since there is no extradition treaty with Russia, he will probably never be convicted for his Canadian crimes. Multiple class actions arose and investors settled for $85 million. The OSC reviewed the conduct of the directors and held them liable for the costs of their investigation and limited their right to serve on other boards, but there were no serious sanctions for the directors' complete ignorance of YBM's fraudulent activities.

Example: Earl Jones was an unregistered financial advisor in Montreal who ran a Ponzi scheme for 27 years promising his clients high rates of returns. He defrauded his 158 clients of over $51.3 million while he lived a lavish lifestyle. He pleaded guilty in January, 2010 and was sentenced to 11 years for fraud. He was released after serving 4 years. A class action lawsuit against the Royal Bank was launched for its failure to take corrective action when it knew Jones was passing off his personal account as his in-trust business account. The action was settled for $17 million in 2014.

Example: Hollinger – Conrad Black and two other executives of Hollinger Inc. were convicted in 2007 in the U.S. for mail fraud and Black was also convicted of obstruction of justice. The case focused on $84 million in non-competition fees paid to these executives and companies they controlled, when Hollinger International sold some of its newspaper holdings. The U.S. prosecutors claimed the payments should have been fully disclosed and the money gone to Hollinger International, not to the executives personally. They were found not guilty on some charges, but convicted on others. Black served 37 months of a 42 month sentence in Florida prisons. In 2013 the U.S. Securities and Exchange commission settled complaints it had levied against Black over these payments and he paid the SEC $4.1 million. Even though Hollinger is a Canadian corporation it was the U.S. that initiated legal action against Black and the other Canadians involved. By mid-2014 the Ontario securities regulator had still not resolved its case against Black. In 2010 the accounting firm of KPMG LLP settled a lawsuit for negligence with Hollinger Inc. for an undisclosed sum.

A smaller fraud case, but an incredible one, is the Markarian v. CIBC Wood Gundy case below. The treatment given by a major Canadian bank to a client one of its brokers had defrauded is very shocking and resulted in the elderly client eventually being awarded the money he was defrauded of plus very large punitive damages. The fraudulent broker was never charged criminally.

Markarian c. Marchés mondiaux CIBC inc., 2006 QCCS 3314 (CanLII)

Mr. Markarian was an Armenian immigrant who came to Canada with $300 and built a successful mechanical business. About 30 years later he sold it and retired. Unfortunately soon after, he met Harry Migirdic, a broker at CIBC Wood Gundy. Migirdic had made disastrous investments for some of his other clients and was looking for a way to hide their losses. Migirdic tricked Markarian into signing what he referred to as a standard bank form, but in reality it was a guarantee. This guarantee allowed Migirdic to take money from Markarian's account to make up for losses in Migirdic other clients' accounts, people Markarian never even knew.

Migirdic repeatedly took money from Markarian's account which originally had $1.5 million until finally there was only $2.54 left. Whenever Markarian questioned the declining balance in his account, the broker told him it was all just a clerical error. Finally Migirdic confessed to CIBC about his fraudulent activities and how he had defrauded Markarian. A month later CIBC contacted Markarian and informed him he only had $2.54 in his account and demanded he pay another $1.35 million for other clients' losses because of the guarantees he had signed. This was the first time that Markarian learned that all his money was gone and the standard forms he had signed were guarantees of others losses. He couldn't believe what he was told. He had to seek medical help when given this news. Markarian claimed return of the $1.5 million taken from his account by bank employee Migirdic and then refused to pay the further $1.35 million demanded by the bank on the guarantees.

CIBC fired Migirdic soon after, but refused to reimburse Markarian. CIBC insisted that Markarian was a sophisticated business man and knew what he was signing. Markarian had to sue to recover his losses. CIBC made very low settlement offers and eventually only offered to repay the $1.5 million, but no interest and none of the almost $500,000 in legal fees Markarian had incurred. Markarian continued seeking full reimbursement plus interest and costs and moral damages and punitive damages.

The Court's Decision

The trial lasted 25 days. The judged was shocked by the reprehensible conduct of CIBC. The bank had treated an honest elderly couple with contempt, and caused them 5 years of extreme stress and anxiety in their retirement years. By refusing to reimburse Markarian when it became aware of Migirdic's fraud, CIBC was an accomplice to his illegal acts. CIBC did everything in its power to benefit directly from its broker's illegal activities. The judge awarded Markarian the $1.5 million plus his legal costs, expenses and interest and he also awarded moral damages of $100,000 and punitive damages of $1.5 million.

Note: Migirdic was never charged criminally. He made 1,400 unauthorized trades in his clients' accounts and lost about $5 million of their money, all while making large incomes for himself and CIBC. Between 1991-2000 he billed over $11 million in commissions of which he kept half and CIBC got the other half. Migirdic was fined $305,000 by the IDA (Investment Dealers Association) and banned for life from selling securities, but he never paid the fine.

Dishonest Lawyers

Lawyers who misappropriate funds from their clients also often do not face criminal penalties. In a 2014 study it was discovered that in a ten year period from 2003-2013 the Law Society of Upper Canada, which regulates the legal profession in Ontario, had 236 cases where lawyers had "misappropriated a total of $61,457,642 of clients' funds. The term misappropriated can include: stolen, defrauded, improperly diverted, overdrawn or failed to account for clients' money. In these 236 cases, criminal charges were only laid in 41 cases, and of those, it appears only 12 lawyers were given jail sentences. The lawyers were disciplined by the Law Society, receiving suspensions or permanent disbarment, but the Law Society does not report their offences to the police and most were not charged nor punished under criminal law. Often the victims don't want to have to endure lengthy criminal trials and the police departments often don't have the time or personnel to handle complex fraud investigations, so these white-collar criminals usually get off without criminal sanctions. (Wallace, Kenyon and Mendleson, Rachel and Brazao, Dale (May 5, 2014). "Broken Trust". *Toronto Star*)

Insider Trading

Individuals within a corporation may have "inside" information about the business that would significantly affect the price of its shares before members of the public learn of it. For example, if you know in advance that company X is going to take over company Y, you would want to purchase shares in company Y now, because once the take-over is announced, Y's share price will increase and then you can sell your shares in Y for a significant profit. Officers, directors and many other professionals who would be involved in the deal such as lawyers, accountants, bankers, brokers, administrative help and printers would be aware of this confidential information as preparation for the takeover bid occurs. Under securities laws and the *Criminal Code* it is illegal to trade in these shares until the takeover bid is announced to the public.

Insider trading involves buying or selling a security of a public company with knowledge of "material information" about the company that has not been publicly disclosed. Under s. 76 of the *Securities Act*, R.S.O. 1990, c. S.5 s. 76 both tipping (giving the inside information) and trading on this information are illegal. The punishments under the Ontario law include fines of up to $5 million or three times the profit made whichever is greater and up to 5 years in jail. Insider trading is also an offence under the *Criminal Code* s. 382.1 RDS, 2004, c.3,s.5. and the punishment under this statute can be up to 10 years in jail. The offender can also be ordered to repay some or all of the profits made as well as pay the costs of the investigation.

Given the potential to make considerable profits by insider trading, it is suspected that this illegal activity goes on regularly. Records consistently show high volumes of trading in shares on companies that are about to be taken over just before the deal is announced, but most people don't get charged. In Canada, we average less than 2 convictions per year for insider trading, and some high profile cases have failed to win convictions or else resulted in penalties that are so low it is seen as little more than a "slap on the wrist." In has been calculated that in the U.S. the prosecution rate for insider trading is 20 times greater than in Canada and the penalties given out are 17 times greater as well.

Example: The largest penalty ever given out in an insider trading case in Canada involved two Toronto lawyers, Stan Grmovsek and Gil Cornblum. The two men were involved in an extensive insider trading scheme over 14 years involving 46 corporate transactions that netted them almost $10 million. Cornblum worked for various Toronto and New York law firms and he would search other lawyers' offices, files and garbage in these firms to find information on potential upcoming corporate takeovers. He would then tell Grmovsek who would then make the trades. When they were caught, both men pleaded guilty. Grmovsek was the first person to be tried under the new 2004 Criminal Code section for insider trading and he received a sentence of 39 months and had to repay over $1 million to the OSC, disgorge himself of $8.5 million to the U.S. Securities and Exchange Commission and pay costs of $250,000. Cornblum committed suicide the day before the trial was to begin. Grmovsek was also convicted in the U.S. and he was permanently disbarred from practising law in Ontario. (*Law Society of Upper Canada v. Stanko Jose Grmovsek*, 2011 ONLSHP 137 (CanLII))

Bre-X Fraud and Insider Trading

The largest fraud case in Canadian history involved Bre-X Minerals Ltd. a Calgary based mining company. CEO David Walsh and the other two senior executives, geologists John Felderhof and Michael de Guzman, claimed that they had discovered the world's largest gold deposits in the Busang jungle region of Indonesia. Shares in Bre-X soared from 39 cents to prices in excess of $260 per share as press releases continually indicated ever increasing gold discoveries at the site. By 1997 Bre-X had a market capitalization of close to $6 billion. Bre-X attracted investors from around the world.

But in March 1997 Michael de Guzman supposedly committed suicide jumping from a helicopter in the Indonesian jungle (many suspect he is actually still alive). A week later rumors began that Bre-X was a fraud. Sure enough, the samples turned out to be "salted" with gold dust and were really just worthless jungle rock. In 10 months it had gone from a multi-billion dollar corporation to being almost worthless. Investors had lost billions. Some of Canada's largest pension funds lost hundreds of millions they had invested in the company.

But no fraud charges were ever laid. David Walsh died of a brain aneurysm in 1998, Michael de Guzman was supposedly dead and John Felderhof had moved to the Cayman Islands. The RCMP was too understaffed and underfunded to pursue criminal charges in the biggest fraud in Canadian history and it closed its investigation in 1999 without ever laying a charge.

Finally the Ontario Securities Commission (OSC) charged Felderhof under the Ontario *Securities Act* for insider trading and knowingly issuing false statements in press releases about the company. The penalty could have been 2 years in jail and fines and restitution orders if convicted. Felderhof had sold many of his shares in Bre-X in 1996 for $84 million many months before the fraud was disclosed in early 1997. He claimed he was not involved in the fraud and was shocked there was no gold, even though he was a geologist and he had told Walsh to purchase this property. He blamed it all on De Guzman and workers in Indonesia who he claimed had tampered with the samples. He said he was "just lucky" to have sold his shares when he did, to make the $84 million profit.

The OSC decided to pursue the case in a quasi-criminal trial in divisional court where the criminal burden of proof is required, rather than go through a tribunal hearing with the lower civil standard of proof. The trial began in 2001 but due to numerous problems it did not conclude until 2007. The OSC had to prove that Felderhof definitely knew undisclosed "material" information when he sold his shares, and that the "material" information would have had an impact on the share price.

The judge ruled that the OSC had not proved beyond reasonable doubt that Felderhof knew "material" information at the time he sold his shares. Despite the fact there were over 20 "red flags" or warnings that there may not be much gold, the court ruled the warnings were not "material" information. Since the judge had reasonable doubt the warnings were material information, then there could not be convictions for insider trading or issuing false reports. Felderhof was found not guilty on all charges. (*R. v. Felderhof*, 2007 ONCJ 345 (CanLII))

Class actions against the company were dismissed in 2014 when they gave up as there was no reasonable prospect of recovering any money. The biggest fraud in Canadian history and nobody was ever punished for it.

The case of Andrew Rankin shows how profitable insider trading can be and how even if the perpetrators are caught little is done.

R. v. Rankin, 2006 CanLII 49283 (ON SC) and R. v. Rankin, 2007 ONCA 127 (CanLII)

Andrew Rankin and Daniel Duic were close friends when they attended one of Canada's most prestigious private boys' schools. Rankin became a rising young star at RBC Dominion Securities and was promoted to Vice President of Corporate Finance only two years after being hired out of university. It was alleged that Rankin gave Duic, or allowed Duic access, to inside information on companies that were takeover targets. Duic had a key to Rankin's home and Duic was a computer expert who set up Rankin's home computer system. On 10 trades in a 14 month period Duic made a profit of $4.5 million based on the information he got from Rankin. On the last trade his broker accidentally purchased all the shares in one order and the large volume triggered suspicion at the OSC.

An investigation commenced and the OSC discovered the pattern of trading by Duic and threatened to charge him for insider trading. He admitted he had actually made $7 million on inside information he had received from Rankin. He agreed to testify against Rankin on the condition that Duic would not go to jail and he'd forfeit $2 million in profits, pay Revenue Canada $1 million owing in taxes, but be would be allowed to keep $4 million of his illegal profits.

Rankin was charged under the Ontario *Securities Act* with 10 counts of tipping and 10 counts of insider trading on $4.5 million Duic had illegally made. Rankin denied ever giving Duic any inside information at all. But Rankin was found guilty on all 10 tipping charges and was sentenced to 6 months in jail for each count, but they were to be served concurrently and he was given a permanent suspension from working in the securities industry. He was acquitted of the insider trading offences as there was no evidence Rankin had traded in the shares himself.

Rankin appealed the conviction and the appeal judge ruled that the initial court had not properly assessed Duic's credibility and had not considered each separate tipping count individually. He ordered a new trial.

The OSC then tried to appeal that decision. It argued that this case was of "extraordinary importance in securities regulation." It was the first prosecution of tipping under the *Securities Act* and it was essential for maintaining the integrity of capital markets and fostering investor confidence. It was essential in the public interest and the administration of justice that the grounds on which the appeal court judge reversed the trial judge be clarified so that future tipping prosecutions could be conducted properly.

The Court's Decision

The Ontario Court of Appeal refused to hear the appeal. It saw nothing in the appeal decision that would have a negative effect on the OSC's ability to prosecute tipping either against Rankin or others. It recognized that the OSC may have suffered negative publicity as a result of having its tipping conviction overturned, but it did not see that as creating new or additional impediments to future prosecutions. The OSC had the right to go back and have a new trial on these charges.

Note: The OSC was prepared to re-try Rankin, but in 2008 just before the new trial was to begin, a settlement was reached. Rankin admitted that because of his neglect confidential information about upcoming deals was disclosed to Duic. He maintained he didn't know Duic was trading stocks on this information. The OSC dropped the charges and Rankin agreed to a lifetime ban on acting as a director or officer of a public company and a 10-year ban on trading securities. He had to pay $250,000 in investigation costs to the commission but he did not have to serve any jail time. In 2011 Rankin tried to have the settlement overturned, but was unsuccessful. This high profile case resulted in neither man going to jail and Duic had been allowed to keep $4 million of the $7 million he made in illegal insider trading. This case made some people comment that "crime really does pay." The OSC's reputation was damaged by the mild punishments that were given out in this expensive, long 7 year ordeal.

Other White Collar Crimes

There are many other white-collar crimes that are important but cannot be discussed within the limits of this textbook. Crimes such as bribery, money laundering and cybercrimes often have great economic impact. Unfortunately however, the limited funds and staff that enforcement agencies in Canada have restrict their effectiveness at controlling these offences as well.

Example: SNC-Lavalin – SNC-Lavalin is the largest engineering and construction firm in Canada and is among the largest in the world. It does mega- construction projects in over 100 countries building water systems, bridges, dams, highways and major buildings. In 2013 the World Bank banned SNC from participating in any World Bank projects around the world for 10 years due to "consulting costs" (bribes) SNC had paid to officials in certain African and Asian countries. There were concerns about illegal payments made in 13 SNC projects in these regions. Several senior executives from SNC have been charged with fraud, corruption and money laundering in Canada and other jurisdictions due to these activities. For example in one case a SNC executive is accused of paying about $160 million in bribes in Libya to Gadhafi family members and others to win contracts for billion dollar projects there, as well as pocketing millions of dollars himself. The Chief Executive Pierre Duhaime was charged with fraud related to $22.5 million in payments made relating to the construction contract for the McGill University mega-hospital as well as other contracts SNC had procured. SNC had a code name for the bribe payments in its records, PCC or "project consultancy costs". None of the SNC cases has yet gone to trial, but it has certainly added to Canada's reputation as a haven for white-collar crime.

Critical Concepts of White-Collar Crime

- Canada has a reputation of being weak on prosecuting and convicting individuals who commit white-collar crimes such as fraud and insider trading
- Very few criminals are convicted for these crimes and even if they are convicted, the jail sentences given out are low and multiple jail sentences are served concurrently
- Criminals are usually out on parole after serving only one-third of their sentences
- Enforcement agencies are under-staffed and have limited budgets so they often cannot afford to pursue long complicated major fraud cases, and the accused often leave the country and cannot be extradited
- The criminal burden of proof is often required and in many cases this cannot be met, whereas trying these cases under the civil burden of proof may result in more convictions
- Major cases of fraud and insider trading have failed to obtain convictions or else resulted in light punishments for the guilty parties
- Other important white-collar crimes have added to Canada's undesirable reputation in this area

In Summation

Corporations

- A corporation, in law, is considered a legal person with a separate identity from its shareholders.

- The fact that a corporation has a separate legal existence is the basis of the concept of limited liability. Creditors can look only to the corporation's assets, not to the assets of the owners of the corporation.

- Corporate governance refers to the internal rules governing the management of the corporation to meet its internal and external responsibilities

- Any contracts signed clearly by an individual on behalf of the corporation and a third party are made between the third party and the corporation.

- This separate identity can be lost in certain circumstances:
  a) the corporate representative does not make the other person aware that he/she is acting in a corporate capacity
  b) the corporate veil is pierced because of agency, or because of fraud or similar conduct by a person who dominates the corporation

- An individual can sign a contract on behalf of a corporation that is not yet incorporated if the correct language is used to notify the opposite party, and the corporation is later actually formed and then adopts the contract.

Corporate Securities

- A corporation can raise money by the issuance of securities. These can have various terms but are divided generally into two types:
  a) equity—shares, stock
  b) debt—bonds

- A share is an interest in the net assets of the corporation (capital).

- A shareholder has a right to a portion of the profits of the corporation, but only if the dividend is declared by the board of directors (income).

- A bond is evidence of a loan and must be repaid with interest at fixed times.

- A corporation does an IPO (initial public offering) when it first sells its shares to the public and it issues a prospectus as part of this process

The Structure of a Corporation

A corporation provides a flexible structure for carrying on business. That structure is composed of:

- Shareholders – common shareholders elect the directors of the corporation

- Directors – select the officers of the corporation and oversee the management of the corporation

- Officers – include the CEO, CFO, President and other senior executives and they work full time for the corporation and manage the day-to-day business

Shareholders

Technically, shareholders are investors with very limited control over a corporation. In a private corporation, shareholders appear to be owners, but that is because the same person or persons are often shareholders, directors, and officers.

- While the same laws apply to all shareholders, some laws are more relevant to shareholders in public corporations and other laws are more relevant to shareholders in private corporations.

- In public corporations, the shareholders' rights that are most pertinent are:
  a) the right to certain limited information, such as the corporation's annual financial statement
  b) the right to vote and elect directors if the shares are voting shares

- In private corporations, a shareholder's usual concerns are that the other shareholders and directors may use the corporate assets for personal gain and against the interests of that shareholder.

- Corporations acts contain shareholder oppression remedies that give shareholders the right to apply to the court in situations where they have been unfairly taken advantage of by the abuse of control in the corporation.

Directors

- Directors have the power to run the company; officers carry out these policies. Directors have certain duties and liabilities.

- Directors' duties are to manage the company's affairs with due care and skill (not be negligent), and to put the company's interest above their own (fiduciary duty).

- Directors set the compensation (salary, bonuses and benefits) of the officers and there is concern that in large corporations it has become excessive in comparison to the average worker's wage

- Directors' fiduciary duties includes a duty:
  a) to disclose any personal interest in the contract made by the corporation with an outsider
  b) not to take a corporate opportunity for personal benefit
  c) not to compete with the corporation

- Directors' liability, stemming from statute law, includes personal responsibility if amounts deducted from employees' salary (e.g., income tax) or taxes collected (GST, PST) are not sent to the government. This liability is imposed on the basis of status alone. The directors need not have been negligent or even aware that the sums were not remitted.

- Directors have a defence of due diligence to the above liability.

- Directors (except in the Atlantic provinces) are liable for unpaid employee wages if the corporation goes bankrupt.

- Directors are liable for torts committed on behalf of the corporation, but only if they were personally involved in committing the tort. They are not liable on the basis of their status as directors alone.

White-Collar Crime

- White-collar crime is non-violent financial crimes committed usually by business executives and professionals and includes crimes such as fraud and insider trading

- Canada has a reputation of being weak in prosecuting these types of crimes

- The few who do get charged often are not convicted due the high criminal burden of proof required

- Those who are convicted serve multiple sentences concurrently and are out on parole after a very short period of time

- Legislative changes need to be made for a national securities regulator and more resources are needed to pursue these criminals

Closing Questions

Corporate Form

1. Jane Rowe forms a corporation called Jane Rowe Ltd. She then wants to form a partnership between herself and her company called Rowe and Partners. Can she do this?

2. Ben Lee bought a two-storey building consisting of a store on the first floor with an apartment above. An offer to lease signed "Joe's Appliances Ltd., per: Joe Smith, president" was presented to Lee.
   a) Who is liable on the lease if there is a default? This is a company: will it necessarily have enough money to pay on a judgment?
   b) What precautions should the landlord take?

3. Brown Corp. Inc. manufactures bricks. It owns all the shares in White Corp. Inc., which is the sales arm of the business. The members of the board of directors of White Corp. Inc. are all officers of Brown Corp. Inc.

   A salesmen on the staff of White Corp. Inc. negligently told Systems Inc. that a certain type of cement block was suitable for a retaining wall. It wasn't, and the wall collapsed, damaging expensive machinery. Systems Inc. learns White Corp. Inc. has no assets. Any profits are sent to Brown Corp. Inc. immediately by way of dividends.

   a) Diagram the corporate structure and the contract involved. Will Systems Inc. be successful in claiming its loss against Brown Corp. Inc.?

   b) If the statements by the sales representative of White Corp. Inc. had been fraudulent, would that make any difference?

4. Eugene Summers has just gotten a job in another city and wants to sell his home as soon as possible. He hears that the market may be going up, but he can't wait. He lists his house for $200,000 and gets a signed offer for the full asking price the very next day.

   The purchaser is 928316 Alberta Limited. The president drove up in a new Lincoln to present the offer personally. Summers was suitably impressed by the president's expensive silk suit and Rolex watch. The offer came with a $1,000 deposit; it contained a clause saying that it was subject to the purchaser being able to arrange satisfactory financing in 60 days, and that the closing date was in 90 days.

   a) Evaluate the agreement and the risks involved for Summers. Should he sign it as it is? Are there any terms that you might suggest that he put into a counter-offer?

5. a) Which of the following is/are considered person(s) in law?

   i) Wilfred Corbin

   ii) Jane Smart & Daughters, Antiques

   iii) Bill and Company

   iv) Microsoft Inc.

   b) Which of the above is termed an "individual" in law? What is another legal term for "individual" in this context?

6. Mario and Grace decided to start an amusement arcade. They each contributed $5,000 for expenses, and they rented a location and purchased five Virtual Reality Helmets (interactive technology games). The arcade has been open only for one month but is already a huge success. They have now hired a manager who would like to invest some money, and they are looking at renting the premises next door in order to expand their operation.

   Four days ago, a customer attempting to fight off his 3-D attackers lashed out with his hand and struck the person waiting next in line, knocking out one of that individual's teeth. Yesterday a young woman became so engrossed and agitated by the activity that she fainted, striking her head on the floor.

   A friend told Mario that the arcade should incorporate in order to get more investment capital and to protect Mario and Grace from any lawsuits. Grace believes they should set up a partnership instead.

   a) What issues should they consider in deciding which form of business would be appropriate for their operation, considering both benefits and liabilities? Which method of operation would you recommend?

   b) What is the nature of the business operation that they are currently running?

7. Vera Marques, a single mother with three children, signs an agreement to buy May Ling's house. Relying on this agreement, Ling purchases a new house for herself. Marques must sell her own home to complete this purchase. She sells it to Madison Construction Limited, which is a small one-man company. The sole shareholder, officer, and director is Rick Madison. The purchase agreements is signed "Madison Construction Ltd. per: Rick Madison, president."

   Marques has barely enough money to make ends meet, so she checks out Madison's record carefully and learns he has been successfully buying old homes and renovating them for resale for over 20 years.

Unfortunately, before closing the deal, Madison has a heart attack and can't arrange financing. The series of agreements falls like a chain of dominoes: Ling can't close her deal; Marques can't close her deal. Ling sues Marques for her loss of $50,000, and Marques claims against Madison Ltd. and Rick Madison personally. Assume that Madison Ltd. has no assets; however, Rick Madison does have considerable personal wealth.

a) Draw a diagram of the above contracts and then determine the liability of all concerned and indicate which party will get a judgment against another party. Who will ultimately bear the loss?

b) Are there any grounds to pierce the corporate veil and make Rick Madison personally liable to Marques? Is it fair that Marques bears the loss and that Rick Madison keeps his wealth and contributes nothing to the loss? Is fairness a grounds for penetrating the corporate veil?

c) Assume that at the time that the agreement was signed, Madison Ltd. had not actually been incorporated. Rick Madison had been carrying on business as a sole proprietor and had only recently instructed his lawyer to apply for incorporation. The incorporation of Madison Ltd. was in effect a few days after Madison signed the agreement to purchase the house from Marques as described above. Is there now any ground to obtain personal liability against Rick Madison?

d) What could Marques have done to obtain personal liability against Madison?

e) In a situation such as the above sale of a home, is there any difference in risk in selling to a small company such as Madison Ltd. and to a couple with children?

Shareholders

8. Wally and Barry are equal shareholders, officers, and directors of Walbar Ltd., which operates a pool hall. There are several pool tables in the establishment, but one table in particular is not used very often by the patrons. Wally decides to take it home and set it up in his basement. When Barry objects, Wally replies, "Look, it's my company, too; I have a right to take the pool table."

a) Is Wally correct?

9. Edmond wanted to involve his family in his corporation and decided to give 20 percent of the shares to each of his two sons, retaining 60 percent in his own name. Each son was appointed a director and vice-president, and took an active part in the business.

Edmond's oldest son, Adam, began to follow a lifestyle of which his father did not approve. There were late-night clubs and excessive drinking and gambling. When Adam married a woman who called his father "Popsy," Edmond could not stand it any longer. He promptly removed his son from the board of directors and fired him from his position as vice-president, giving him sufficient notice to meet the requirements for dismissal.

a) Does Adam have any remedies?

10. Wanson Chung gets Bill Kim to invest in his company in return for 30 percent of its shares. In 1998 Chung had signed an employment agreement with this corporation by which he became president. If his employment was terminated for any reason, he would receive a severance package valued at $1,000,000.

Kim and another shareholder, who also has 30 percent of the shares, arranged to have Chung fired. Chung claims the million-dollar golden parachute. Kim says that he didn't know of this employment agreement when he invested, and didn't even think to ask about such an arrangement.

a) Is the agreement between Chung and the corporation a valid contract?

b) Does Kim have any remedy to possibly set aside the termination provision?

11. The Pagannini Corporation has authorized capital of 600 shares, of which 500 are issued. Antonia Dvorak wishes to obtain control of the company, as she thinks it has a great unused potential. She has specific ideas of how to run it. Dvorak buys 251 of the issued shares, which gives her control of the corporation by one share.

As soon as Dvorak purchases the shares, the board of directors, which is made up of the only other three shareholders apart from Dvorak, announces a need for new capital and proposes to issue the balance of the 100 shares—giving 25 to each shareholder. The resulting share structure is as follows.

	Current	Proposed
Other Shareholders	249 plus 75	324
Antonia Dvorak	251 plus 25	276

a) What will be the result of the proposed new share issue as far as control is concerned?
b) Dvorak is a majority shareholder—does she have a remedy?

Directors

12. UCM Plastics Ltd. was given the right of first refusal for a new biodegradable-plastic technology in its experimental phase. The five-member board of directors met, and the vote was three to two against the purchase of the new technology. Subsequently, Al Manian, one of the directors who had voted against the purchase, incorporated a provincial corporation and bought the new process. Six months later, the technology was perfected, and the first year's sales totalled $6,000,000.
    a) Has Manian acted properly in this situation, or is there a remedy available for UCM Plastics Ltd.?

13. Soleil Systems Inc. was a computer-software company whose reputation depended primarily on the work of Francesco Dietmar. He was a senior officer and a director of the company, but had no written employment contract.
    Agrisif Ltd. purchased the shares of Soleil Systems Inc. and proceeded to make a number of changes in the style of management. Right from the start, Dietmar did not get along with the executives of Agrisif and, four months after the purchase, he resigned, along with several key employees. They immediately started a business in direct competition with Soleil.
    a) Are there any grounds on which Agrisif would be able to sue Dietmar?
    b) Are there any unknown elements in this situation that might change your answer to a)?

14. Which of the following, if any, owe a fiduciary duty?
    a) partner in a partnership
    b) the president of a corporation
    c) a shareholder of a corporation
    d) a director of a corporation

15. Gareth Thomas was a director of Middleton Manufacturing Inc. The company put out a call for bids from suppliers for a multimillion-dollar order of the raw materials needed for the coming year.
    Fiona Ferguson, Thomas's wife, owned and operated a small independent bookstore. Business was excellent, and she planned to expand, taking over the premises next door. A few days before the Middleton board was due to make a decision on its contract, Ferguson was contacted by George Hammond, one of the suppliers who had submitted a bid to Middleton.
    Hammond offered Ferguson a loan of $30,000 at 2 percent interest, to be repaid over 10 years. "That'll give you room for a book or two!" he said.
    a) Does this loan create any legal problems for Thomas and, if so, do they depend on whether Hammond's bid is the successful one?

16. New Inspiration Mines Inc. was in negotiations with a prospector over a possible gold claim. This claim was low on New Inspiration's priority list, and negotiations were stalled.
    Michel Lebois, a director of New Inspiration, approached the owner of the claim and bought it for his own company, Successful Mines Ltd. The claim turned out to be a good one, and Successful made a profit of $5 million.
    a) Did Lebois have any duty to New Inspiration Mines Inc.? If so, what is the technical name for this duty?
    b) What could New Inspiration do about this situation?

17. Joan Compeau, a recent graduate, has been offered a directorship on the board of directors of three corporations. Each will have business cards printed for her, saying "Joan Compeau, Director." She is elated!

a) What advice would you give Compeau?

18. David Sherman was a director of Empower Corp Inc. The president of this company, Joan Galway, induced the chief researcher officer of a competitor to join their company and bring with him vital, confidential market research. However, it was all to no avail, as Empower Corp went bankrupt with no assets.

GST, which had been collected, had not been sent to the government and employee wages had not been paid for three months. The government, employees, and the competitor have sued Sherman and Galway.

a) For which of the following, if any, is Sherman responsible, and why?

    i) unremitted GST

    ii) employee wages

    iii) damages to the competitor for inducing breach of contract

b) For which of the above, if any, is Galway responsible, and why?

19. What is the difference between the remedies of piercing the corporate veil and directors' liability in tort? Give the elements necessary to establish each remedy. Which is easier to establish?

20. Compare the results in *Salomon v. Salomon & Co. Ltd.* with the results in the *ADGA Systems International Ltd. v. Valcom Ltd.* Why was the separate identity of a corporation upheld in Salomon? Why were the directors made liable in the other case?

Multi Issue

21. Match the technical word in the first column with the closest synonym in the second column.

Franchise	Substitute
Fiduciary duty	Owner
Vicarious	Trust Relationship
Corporation	Licence
Proprietor	Person

22. As discussed in this text, what is the main purpose of:

a) The Sarbanes–Oxley Act

b) The Dodds–Frank Act

Articles of Incorporation

Appendix

10

ARTICLES OF INCORPORATION
STATUTS CONSTITUTIFS

Form 1.
Business
Corporations
Act.
1982
Formule
numero 1
Loi de 1982
sur /es
compagnies

1. The name of the corporation is:

Dénomination sociale de la compagnie:

| T | , | J | , | | M | O | R | G | A | N | I | N | C | . | | | | | | | | | | | | | | | | | | | | | | | |

2.

The address of the registered office is:

Adresse du siège social:

(Street & Number or R.R. Number & if Multi-Office Building give Room No.)
(Rue et numéro ou numéro de la R.R. et, s'il s'agit d'un édifice a bureaux, numéro du bureau)

Newmarket, Ontario

(Name of Municipality or Post Office)
(Nom de la municipalité ou du bureau de poste)

| M | 1 | H | 5 | J | 9 |

(Postal Code)
(Code postal)

Town of Newmarket

(Name of Municipality, Geographical Township)
(Nom de la municipalité, du canton)

in the
dans le/la

Regional Municipality of York

(County, District, Regional Municipality)
(Comté, district, municipalité régionale)

3. Number (or minimum and maximum number) of directors is:

Nombre (ou nombres minimal et maximal) d'administrateurs:

Minimum of One - Maximum of Ten

4. The first director(s) is/are:

Premier(s) administrateur(s):

First name, initials and surname Prenom, initiales et nom de famille	Residence address, giving street & No. or R.R. No. or municipality and postal code. Adresse personnelle, y compris la rue et le numéro, le numéro de la R.R. ou, le nom de la municipalité et le code postal	Resident Canadian State Yes or No Résident Canadien Oui/Non
Terrence J. Morgan	**1234 Main Street Newmarket, OntarioM1H 5J9**	**Yes**

421

5. Restrictions, if any, on business the corporation may carry on or on powers the corporation may exercise	Limites, s'il y a lieu, imposées aux activités commerciales ou aux pouvoirs de la compagnie.

None

6. The classes and any maximum number of shares that the corporation is authorized to issue.	Catégories et nombre maximal, s'il y a lieu, d'actions que la compagnie est autorisée a émettre:

The Corporation is authorized to issue an unlimited numher of shares of one class designated as common shares, and an unlimited number of shares of a second class designated as preference shares.

7. Rights, privileges, restrictions and conditions (if any) attaching to each class of shares and directors authority with respect to any class of shares which may be issued in series:	Droits, privilèges, restrictions et conditions, s 'il y a lieu, rattachés à chaque catégorie d'actions et pouvoirs des administrateurs relatifs à chaque catégorie d'actions qui peut être émise en serie:

1. the preference shares may be issued in one or more series;

2. the directors are authorized to fix the number of shares in and to determine the designation, rights, privileges, restrictions and conditions attaching to the shares of each series;

3. the preference shares of each series shall, with respect to priority in payment of dividends and in the return of capital in the event of liquidation, dissolution or winding up of the Corporation, be entitled to a preference over the common shares of the Corporation and over any other shares ranking junior to the preference shares;

4. the holder of each common share has the right to one vote for such common share at all meetings of shareholders other than meetings of the holders of another class of shares and to receive the remaining property of the Corporation upon dissolution.

8 The issue, transfer or ownership of shares is/is not restricted and the restrictions (if any) are as follows:	L 'émission, le transfert ou la propriété d'actions est/n 'est pas restreinte. Les restrictions, s'il y a lieu, sont les suivantes:

The right to transfer shares of the Corporation shall be restricted in that no shares shall be transferred without either:

(a) the previous consent of the directors of the Corporation expressed by a resolution passed at a meeting of the directors or by an instrument or instruments in writing signed by a majority of the directors; or

(b) the previous consent of the holders of at least 51% of the shares for the time being outstanding entitled to vote expressed by resolution passed at a meeting of the shareholders or by an instrument or instruments in writing signed by such shareholders.

9. Other provisions if any, are:	Autres despositions, s'il y a lieu:

1. that the board of directors may from time to time, in such amounts and on such terms as it deems expedient;

(a) borrow money on the credit of the Corporation;

(b) issue, reissue, sell or pledge debt obligations (including bonds, debentures, notes or other similar obligations, secured or unsecured) of the Corporation;

(c) to the extent permitted by law, give a guarantee on behalf of the Corporation to secure performance of any present or future indebtedness, liability or obligation of any person; and

(d) charge, mortgage, hypothecate, pledge or otherwise create a security interest in all or any of the currently owned or subsequently acquired real or personal, movable or immovable, property of the Corporation, including book debts, rights, powers, franchises and undertakings, to secure any debt obligations or any money borrowed or other debts or liability of the Corporation.

The board of directors may from time to time delegate such one or more of the directors and officers of the Corporation as may be designated by the board all or any of the powers conferred on the board above to such extent and in such manner as the board shall determine at the time of each such delegation;

2. that the number of shareholders of the Corporation, exclusive of persons who are in the employment of the Corporation and exclusive of persons who, having been formerly in the employment of the Corporation, were, while in the employment, and have continued after the termination of that employment to be shareholders of the Corporation, is limited to not more than fifty (50), two (2) or more persons who are the joint registered owners of one (1) or more shares being counted as one (1) shareholder; and

3. that any invitation to the public to subscribe for any shares or securities of the corporation is hereby prohibited.

Nom et adresse des fondateurs First name, initials and surname or corporate name Prénom, initiale et nom de famille ou dénomination sociale	Full residence address or address of registered office or of principal place of business giving street & No. or R.R. No., municipality and postal code Adresse personnelle au complet, adresse du siège social ou adresse de l'établissement principal, y compris la rue et le numéro, le numéro de la R.R., le nom de la municipalité et le code postal
Terrence J. Morgan	1234 Main Street Newmarket, Ontario M1B 5J9

These articles are signed in duplicate

Les présents statuts sont signés en double exemplaire.

Signatures Of incorporators
(Signature des londaleurs)

_____

TERRENCE J. MORGAN

Banking Agreements and Secured Transactions

Types of Financial Institutions

There are a number of organizations from which a business can borrow money—banks, trust companies, finance companies, leasing companies, credit unions, pay day loan companies, and so on.

In borrowing from these organizations you will likely be asked to sign various types of financial documents because the lender will want collateral or security for the loan. The type of document you sign will vary depending on the size and type of loan you have negotiated. This chapter will discuss some of the most common banking documents and security agreements that major financial institutions use on a regular basis.

The Unique Business of Banking

Banks are regulated in Canada under the federal Bank Act and each country has its own banking laws. The flaw that laid the foundation for the 2007 Global Crisis was a deregulation of banks. To understand the absolute necessity of the bailouts to save the world financial system, it is necessary to understand how banking is unlike any other business. Banks do not make most of their profits by taking in money on deposit at a low rate of interest and lending it out at a higher rate. They virtually create money out of nothing.

Historically, this process likely began when wealthy citizens did not want to keep their gold in their home for fear of a home invasion. So they gave it to groups like the Knights Templar to store and received a receipt for their gold. The owners found they could use the receipt to purchase goods, even in another city because the Knights Templar had become international bankers. So a merchant in Paris could take a receipt from the Knight's Paris branch for, say one bar of gold, and use it in Damascus to purchase a camel. That camel seller also did not want to redeem the gold, but in turn used the receipt to purchase something else. Thus, there was very little demand for return of the gold.

In practice only 10% of the gold was ever redeemed. People had confidence in the paper and preferred it. The Knights realized so long as they always had 10% gold reserves in their vault, they could issue paper receipts for ten times the amount of gold, effectively creating money out of nothing. Since only a fraction of the money was lent out, it became called the fractional reserve system. This 10% rule became the foundation for modern banking.

Eventually, over hundreds of years, people have such confidence in the paper money that governments went off the gold standard. Dollars once said: Will pay to the bearer on demand $1 in gold. Presently they simply say: Legal Tender. The entire world economic system is based solely on confidence in the monetary system. If that confidence is shaken, our entire system will collapse. Historically, the rules for a 10% fractional reserve system proved rigidly necessary. There were many bank failures and violation of this reserve was often a causal factor.

Banks also learned from experience to lend mortgage loans only to people who had a good credit record. These applicants had an employment history, income about four times the amount of the loan repayment amount, and had saved 25% of the down payment of the house to be purchased. In addition, but only after meeting the credit worthy qualification, the loan was further secured by the borrower pledging the house as security.

Banks traditionally carried a small portfolio, of about 12%, of subprime mortgages (also called high ratio mortgages). In Canada these are guaranteed by a government agency, Canadian Central Mortgage and Housing (CMHC). In the U.S. and other countries, the governments deregulated banks so the fractional reserve system was reduced to 2%, from 10%, and the limit was taken off the number of subprime mortgage loans a bank could make. Loans could be made to people without good credit and without any equity. Both changes to the regulations were enacted at the same time.

Canada did not follow this deregulation and did not suffer the large subprime mortgage failures that hit the U.S. in 2007. Canada hence then became a model for the international banking community.

Digital Currencies

Recent creations of digital currencies such as Bitcoin have created problems. Bitcoin for some has become the currency of the Internet and popular among tech enthusiasts, libertarians and risk-seeking investors because it allows people to make one-to-one transactions, buy goods and services and exchange money across borders without involving banks, credit card issuers or other third parties. Criminals like bitcoin for the same reasons. Bitcoin, unlike conventional money, is bought and sold on a peer-to-peer network independent of central control. Started in 2009, by 2013 the total worth of bitcoins created was about $7 billion. It also makes it susceptible to theft and as easily as it can be created digitally, so it seems as easily it can be stolen electronically. In 2014 Canadian bitcoin bank Flexcoin had to close down when it lost $600,000 due to a hacker attack. Lack of regulation is a factor to consider before investing in digital currencies.

Expansion of Services

The banks have moved away from their traditional roles of simply receiving deposits and making business loans, to what they call the financial supermarket, a place where all financial needs can be supplied. These include traditional banking services, investment advice, stockbroking, and insurance.

Business Alert!   Insured Deposits   All deposits with banks and trust companies that operate in Canada are insured by the Canada Deposit Insurance Corporation (CDIC). Currently, deposits are insured to a maximum of $100,000 per customer, per institution. The insurance fund is paid for by banks and trust companies, who pass on the expense to customers as a cost of doing business. If your assets total more than $100,000, it is a good idea to spread various deposits among different financial institutions, thus gaining maximum insurance protection.

Trust Companies

Trust companies, like banks, can lend money and offer mortgages. They can also take deposits from the public, and must maintain certain reserves to meet demands from customers. The big difference between banks and trust companies is that trust companies can be privately controlled—they can even be one-owner companies.

Credit Unions

Credit unions are another option for those seeking financial services. They grew out of a movement among a group of German farmers in the 1850s, who pooled financial resources to buy supplies at a lower cost. This original idea still forms the basis of the modern credit union, where persons with some common bond (usually a profession or community) pool resources to provide financial services for one other. To join a credit union you must meet certain criteria such as placing a minimum deposit and being a member of the groups the credit union was formed to serve. Credit unions operate by a board of directors chosen by the membership. Profits are shared with the members as opposed to being returned to share-holders. Credit unions offer a broad range of financial services and are closely regulated by provincial governments.

Finance Companies

There are many private institutions, such as small mortgage companies, that lend money to private individuals and businesses. These are not connected with any banks, but are brokerage types of businesses, specializing in bringing together people who have money to invest and those who are looking to borrow.

Finance companies can be very large. Some not only make consumer loans but often take over financing from other businesses. For example, if you buy a car, the dealership will arrange financing for you on the spot. However, even if the documents are drawn up in the name of the dealership, that firm will usually assign the loan to a finance company. You are then given notice to make your payments directly to the finance company.

Pay Day Loan Companies

As discussed in contract law chapter 5, pay day loans are a $2 billion industry in Canada and are made by companies that specialize in making small unsecured loans to individuals, on average a $300 loan for a 2 week period. Most provinces have enacted special legislation to regulate these financial institutions, but regrettably the laws allow them to charge interest rates much higher than the criminal annual rate of interest of 60 per cent. In Ontario for example pay day loan companies can legally charge interest rates with an effective annual rate of 546 per cent. In the U.S. many states have begun to recognize the problems this type of lending creates, so hopefully Canadian provincial lawmakers will come to a similar realization soon and provide consumers with better protection.

Borrowing from Banks

A significant source of financing for most businesses is by way of bank loans. There are several different types of loans. The bank may also ask for security, often called collateral, which pledges property which a bank can cease if the loan is not paid. The common types of security are discussed in the next chapter.

You, your spouse, your friend or relative may be asked to sign a guarantee. As demand loans and guarantees are very commonly used in business loans, they are discussed next.

Demand Loans

Business loans are often made on a demand basis, to be repaid when asked by the bank. The important question is, when the bank makes a demand, how long does the business person have to come up with the money? Does *demand* mean *demand*? One judge said that a business person has the time it takes to open a desk drawer and take out a cheque book to pay a loan when demanded. Later courts have not been quite so strict.

Example: In *Mister Broadloom Corporation (1968) Ltd. v. Bank of Montreal et al.*, 1983 CanLII 1676 (ON CA), the chain of carpet stores known as Mr. Broadloom had been a 13 year customer of BMO but the bank became concerned over the company's financial difficulties. The bank called in the two owners and requested full payment of the demand loan of $1.5 million. The owners asked how much time they had to come up with the money and were told none. 45 minutes later the business was shut down and a receiver was sent in and the business was ended. The Ontario Court of Appeal recognized that a lender has the right to protect itself, but it should have given a reasonable time for the company to obtain refinancing, which in this case the company could probably have arranged. It was clear 45 minutes was not reasonable time. BMO had acted illegally and was liable for damages for trespass and conversion and the lost profits from the destruction of the business.

But the court has to take in consideration many factors, and in the case below of Maple City Ford, a very short period of time was reasonable, considering the financial situation and the dishonesty of the debtors.

Bank of Montreal v. Maple City Ford Sales (1986) Ltd., 2004 CanLII 36048 (ON CA)

David and Paul McKeand bought Maple City Ford in Chatham, Ontario in 1986. It was a car-truck dealership that had opened in 1970. By June of 1990 they were experiencing financial difficulties and their lenders CIBC and Ford Credit were concerned. The McKeands sought refinancing from the Bank of Montreal (BMO) and got a $4.5million loan secured by a General Security Agreement in favour of BMO.

The McKeands had not fully disclosed all of their debts and previous dishonest acts to BMO when they arranged the loan. Within 3 weeks of their refinancing, they had difficulty meeting the loan requirements and had gone beyond the authorized lending limits. In April 1991 the McKeands and BMO signed a forbearance agreement, whereby the bank agreed to hold off on its rights so long as the borrowers caught up in their payments and the owners and one of their wives signed personal guarantees as well.

The McKeands did not meet the terms of the forbearance agreement and BMO discovered that the borrowers had falsified sales records, hidden sales, made false accounting entries and had not disclosed $500,000 loans to shareholders. Their dishonesty and failure to make payments caused the BMO manager to call the brothers into his office on June 19,1991 and at 2:47 p.m. BMO demanded full repayment of the $2,890,560 by 4:00 p.m. that day. At 3:36 p.m. the McKeands told BMO it intended to file for bankruptcy protection, (even though they did not have a viable practical proposal worked out). So at 7:45 p.m. that night BMO sent in a receiver from Ernst & Young who took over possession of Maple City Ford. On August 27th the assets of the dealership were sold at auction.

The two brothers sued BMO denying the validity of the forbearance agreement and claiming that the 1 hour and 13 minutes they had been given to refinance was not reasonable time.

The Court's Decision

The trial judge carefully considered the facts and noted that "A reasonable time must always be allowed but, in assessing what length of time is reasonable in a particular fact situation, various factors must be analyzed."

These factors include: the amount of the loan, risk to the creditor, relationship between the debtor and creditor, ability of the debtor to raise money in a short time period and the circumstances surrounding the demand for repayment.

She noted that case law had established that the giving of little or no time is reasonable if: there is a justifiable fear of the debtor's dishonesty, the value of the creditor's security is at risk of depreciating rapidly, and/or the giving of time would serve no useful purpose because the debtor does not have the means to satisfy the demand.

Taking all these factors into consideration, the judge ruled that there was a justifiable apprehension of dishonesty and giving additional time would not have resulted in the McKeands being able to meet the demand for the money. As a result, the time "although extremely short, was reasonable."

The decision was appealed and the Ontario Court of Appeal upheld the trial judge's ruling.

Reasonable Time

How long do you have to pay up if the bank calls a demand loan? Unfortunately, no specific period, such as 10 days or 15 days, can be given. The often-recurring word *reasonable* is the test. What is reasonable will vary with the circumstances, but in the normal case, the bank cannot demand a cheque before you leave the bank manager's office. Unless there are circumstances which justify urgency, 10 days is probably a good rule of thumb.

Lines of Credit   Businesses often negotiate operating lines of credit on a demand basis. Because of the problems of an unexpected demand, businesses are now trying to negotiate term loans. A term loan has the advantage that it cannot be called on demand, and need only be repaid by the fixed date set by the term.

Business Alert!

Bank Loans   Don't be shy negotiating about interest rates when you apply for a bank loan. Bank officers take this as a good sign. It shows that you are somewhat sophisticated in financial matters. It also is an indication that you intend to repay the loan. People who default on loans are almost never concerned with interest rates.

Business Alert!

Newspapers and a number of websites often list comparative interest rates for banks and other financial institutions. There is a difference in rates, and so shopping around can be beneficial. As a rule of thumb, 1 percent difference in interest on $100,000 results in a difference in payments of $100 per month.

Loan Guarantees

A guarantee for a loan is often called co-signing. Co-signing is one of the most frequent contracts used in credit arrangements. You will encounter co-signing arrangements both as a borrower and as a business giving credit to customers. There are two types of co-signing agreements:

- guarantee—an agreement in which the third party is usually liable only if the main debtor defaults on the loan
- **indemnity** or surety—an agreement in which the third party undertakes to be equally liable for the loan owed by the main debtor

indemnity
an agreement in which the third party undertakes to be equally liable for the loan owed by the main debtor

There are two levels of legal relationship in a guaranteed lending agreement. The first is between the lender and the borrower; the second is between the lender and the co-signer.

The Guarantee Triangle

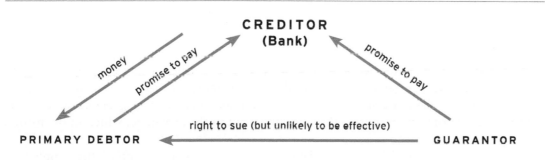

Why a Guarantee?

In business, there are three reasons a guarantee is normally required when a corporation obtains a loan:

- The corporate form implies limited liability; therefore, the owner's personal assets cannot be seized to satisfy the loan on default. The corporation might not have sufficient assets of its own.

- Even if the corporation does have assets, it may also have many other creditors. If the loan goes into default, all assets might have to be shared among creditors. The secured creditors—those who hold mortgages and other securities—will more than likely be able to seize most of the corporate assets.
- In attempting to avoid creditor lawsuits, the corporation may have tried to hide its assets through a series of complicated transactions.

If a co-signer is required to pay the loan amount, that individual can seek recovery of the sum involved from the primary debtor.

Co-signer Beware   A co-signer is required when a lender wants some reassurance that the loan will be paid and does not have full confidence in the principal borrower. This is an important consideration if you are asked to co-sign a loan. Many people agree to do so without taking into account that, if the lender does not have full confidence in the borrower, there may be good reason for this. Co-signers often do not appreciate the very real risk that they may have to pay the full amount of the loan. Such a document should be signed only after careful consideration of the consequences.

If you have signed a continuing guarantee and no longer wish to be responsible for future loans, you can likely terminate your liability for future advances, but not for current loan amounts. This is a technical question depending on the wording of the guarantee and requires legal advice.

Standard Guarantee Terms

guarantee
a conditional promise to pay only if the main debtor defaults

indemnity
a promise by a third party to be primarily liable to pay the debt

Guarantees are commonly asked as backup to the granting of credit by banks, landlords and suppliers. Often the request is made of the principal shareholder(s) of a corporation and their spouses. A **guarantee** ensures that if the principal debtor defaults on the debt then the guarantor will be called upon to pay. The promise by the guarantor, or surety as they are often called, is a secondary or conditional obligation and only arises if the main debtor first does not pay. Another document called an **indemnity** is sometimes incorrectly referred to as a guarantee, but they differ significantly. If a person signs an indemnity theirs is not a secondary obligation, they are primarily responsible for the debt just like the principal debtor, and the creditor can call on them to pay without first demanding payment from the principal debtor.

Banks often use a standard form guarantee, and its terms are so universal that bankers call them "the plane-vanilla guarantee terms." An example of a standard form Bank Guarantee Form is set out in the Appendix to this chapter. The term "Customer" is used in place of the legal term, principal debtor.

All Debts Guaranteed

The guarantee obligation is set out in the first paragraph of the form in the Appendix and is drafted in the widest possible language so that the guarantor is liable for any debts owed by the Customer to the Bank and not just the specific loan that is being guaranteed. The only limit is that the obligation is up to the amount set out in the guarantee, which in the form in the Appendix is $48,000.

Leaving out some of the technical language, the first long paragraph on the sample form says that the person who signs (the undersigned) guarantees payment of "all debts and liabilities present and future . . . arising from the dealings between the Customer and the Bank or from other dealings . . . from which the Bank may become a creditor of the Customer including . . . whether as a principal or surety."

Some of the sources of debt to the bank that the guarantor will be liable for include:

- all direct dealings between the Bank and the Customer not only the present loan but any other loans, even a mortgage loan to buy a house

- amounts owing by the Customer on credit cards even those incurred by a spouse or anyone who holds a joint credit card with the Customer
- amounts the Customer owes on any guarantees

Material Variation Clause

Many standard form guarantees have a material variation clause (Clause 8 in the form in the Appendix) which allows the Bank to make any material change or variation to the terms of the guarantee "as it may see fit" and the Bank does not have to notify or get the consent of the guarantor.

Under common law, changes could only be made with the guarantor's consent. But courts have ruled that under the principle of freedom to contract, given the business context, if the material variation clause is clear and unambiguous, this clause can be enforceable. The *RBC v. Samson Management* case below clearly illustrates this.

Royal Bank of Canada v. Samson Management & Solutions Ltd., 2013 ONCA 313 (CanLII)

Jason Brasseur owned a company, Samson Management and Solutions Ltd., and in 2005 Brasseur and his spouse Cheryl Cusack each signed personal guarantees for a $150,000 line of credit for the business given by the Royal Bank (RBC).

In 2006, RBC agreed to increase the company's operating line of credit to $250,000. Ms. Cusack and Mr. Brasseur each gave fresh personal guarantees, for $250,000, to RBC that covered Samson's present and future liabilities. These were also continuing guarantees and were not tied to any specific loan between RBC and Samson. Ms. Cusack received independent legal advice before signing the guarantees.

In 2008 RBC increased the loan to the company to $500,000 and got a new personal guarantee from Mr. Brasseur for $500,000, but did not request one from Ms. Cusack. In 2009 the loan was increased to $750,000, as was Mr. Brasseur's guarantee, but again no new guarantee was signed by his wife.

In 2011 the business failed and RBC made demands on the guarantees for $750,000 from Mr. Brasseur and $250,000 from Ms. Cusack. Ms. Cusack claimed that her guarantee should not be enforced as the indebtedness of the company had changed considerably since she signed the guarantee. The initial court decision was that since material variations to the loan agreement had been made, under common law and in equity, her guarantee should not be enforced. RBC appealed that decision.

The Court's Decision

The Court of Appeal made it clear that parties are entitled to make their own arrangements, and a guarantor's decision to contract out of the protection given by common law will usually be respected by the courts, so long as the contracting-out language is clear and unambiguous.

The court viewed the subsequent advances by RBC to the company as material alterations to the principal loan contract. However since the advances were contemplated by the parties, permitted by the clear language of the guarantee, and inherent in a continuing all accounts guarantee that contemplates increases in the size of the debt, these changes were legal and did not end the liability of the guarantor. Clause 1 of the guarantee expressly permitted RBC to change the terms of the borrowing.

So despite the material changes in the underlying loan agreements, Ms. Cusack's personal guarantee was enforceable, given the clear and unambiguous language of the guarantee and the context in which the business loan was made. RBC's claim for $250,000 from Ms. Cusack was successful, as well as the $750,000 guarantee by Mr. Brasseur.

Business Law Applied

❶ **Bernard Conway guarantees** a bank loan in the amount of $10,000 for a friend, Carl Chernos, and signs a standard form guarantee containing a continuing guarantee clause. Chernos pays the loan down to $5,000, but soon runs short of money and borrows another $5,000 so that the loan is back up to $10,000.

Some months later, the bank advances another $5,000, so that Chernos now owes a total of $15,000. Chernos goes out of business and defaults on the loans. The bank sues Bernard Conway.

a) Does Conway have to pay $5,000, $10,000, or $15,000?

b) What would the result have been at common law?

❷ Natasha Keyes was one of four shareholders of Telcorp Inc. She was asked to co-sign for Telcorp's loan of $100,000. She wasn't concerned because the bank had a lien on Telcorp's assets which were easily worth $200,000 even on a forced-sale basis.

Telcorp went belly up. Its trade creditors successfully had the lien set aside because the bank had registered it improperly. The bank now wants Keyes to pay the full $100,000. Review clauses 3 and 7 of the Bank Guarantee Form in the Appendix to answer the following questions.

a) Can Keyes successfully defend against the bank on the basis of its negligence in registering the lien?

b) What would have been the result at common law?

❸ Francisco signed a guarantee for a loan for his sister, Maria's, business for $50,000 on the bank's standard form. The business failed and the bank is suing Francisco for a debt of $10,000 that Maria's daughter incurred on a joint bank credit card with Maria. Francisco resists paying for this debt on the basis that it is not a business debt. Is he correct?

Limitation Periods

After the guarantee is signed, people tend to forget about it. But they remain in the creditor's file and may surface many years later if the principal debtor defaults. So an important question is: How long does a creditor have to sue on a guarantee?

You will recall from the chapter on the court system, that there are time limits on when a plaintiff can sue a defendant. While each province has its own limitation act, the most common time period is two years. The question in the guarantee situation is: when does the limitation period began to run? Does the time begin to run when the principal debtor defaults, which means the bank is aware of its claim, or when the bank gives written notice of a demand under the guarantee?

The standard guarantee term, (see paragraph 4 of the form in the Appendix), expressly sets out that the limitation period does not run until a formal demand has been made on the guarantor. Thus, a guarantee may have been signed ten years ago, the default over 5 years ago and the demand on the guarantor is made today, 5 years later, a total of 20 years.

Bank of Nova Scotia v. Williamson, 2009 ONCA 754 (CanLII)

In 2002 Williamson, an officer, director and shareholder of Ancon Industries Ltd., signed a guarantee for it in the standard bank guarantee form containing a clause similar to number 4 of the form in the Appendix.

In 2004 Ancon defaulted on its loan. The bank sent Williamson a letter which said, "if payment of our demand is not made as required, we will take steps to recover from you."

In 2007 Ancon's assets were sold by receivership, but there was a shortfall and the bank sent a demand for this amount to Williamson. Williamson argued that the limitation period, which was two years, began to run either when the bank became aware of its claim against him, which was when Ancon defaulted, or when it sent the first letter.

The Court's Decision

While Williamson's defenses may have been good at common-law, by the doctrine of freedom of contract, parties are free to agree to alter the law that may apply to their contract. The wording of the bank guarantee was clear. The limitation period did not begin until a demand was made. A proper demand was not made until after the receivership in 2007. The limitation period had not expired, so Williamson was found liable for the full amount.

 *Business Alert!*   Co-signer Beware   At times a person who gets no benefit from a loan, perhaps a parent or a friend, may be asked to sign a guarantee. When sued they often feel they should not

be responsible because they did not get anything. However the courts strictly enforce these guarantees.

So it is a good policy for a person asked to co-sign to consider why the bank, experienced in granting credit, does not have full confidence in the borrower. The likelihood of default may be probable.

Critical Concepts of Guarantees

- Guarantors are liable on guarantees even though they do not receive any benefit under the arrangement
- In most standard form bank guarantees, the guarantor is liable for all that is owed by the principal debtor to the bank from a wide range of sources not only the specific loan being arranged to the limit of the sum specified in the guarantee
- The standard bank guarantee term makes the limitation period run from the date of a formal demand
- A guarantor can limit the amount owing at any specific date by giving the bank written notice that he or she will not be liable for any increases after that time

■ *Business Law* Applied

❹ **Yuki Zhong guaranteed** a loan for her then husband's, Doug Liu, business by signing a guarantee in the standard form limited to $100,000. That was over 5 years ago. That marriage broke up and both have remarried. Yuki, a scrupulous saver, had saved $100,000 since leaving Doug and had totally forgotten about the guarantee.

Yesterday, she got a letter from the bank demanding payment of $140,000 on the guarantee. Doug's business had failed and he had no personal assets. Although Doug had paid off the original loan for which Yuki had signed the guarantee, the amounts claimed were the following:

- Doug's new wife's joint credit card debt—$20,000
- Doug's personal loan for a vacation to Hawaii for his honeymoon 3 years ago—$10,000
- An amount Doug owed on a guarantee he gave for his brother's business—$50,000
- The balance owed on the mortgage on a new home he had bought with his present wife—$50,000
- Legal costs in unsuccessful attempts to collect from Doug—$10,000

a) Which claims would Yuki be liable for? Refer to specific language in the guarantee form to justify your answer.
b) What is the final amount she would owe under the guarantee?
c) Assuming that the limitation period is 2 years in the relevant province, is that a defense for Yuki? Refer to a term in the guarantee to support your answer.
d) Is there anything that she could have done that might have limited her liability?

Shareholders may sign guarantees for a business, and spouses often sign guarantees for a spouse's business. When a shareholder sells a complete interest in the business, the shareholder may forget the guarantee. Also, when couples divorce, guarantees signed some years ago may be overlooked. Whether the bank will release the guarantor, will be a decision for the bank based on the individual circumstances. The bank will not give a release unless it is satisfied that it has as good or better security to replace the guarantor.

Business Alert!

However, whether the bank gives a release or not, the guarantor can give written notice to the bank that he or she will not be responsible for any amounts above the amounts now owing on the guarantee to the bank. (See paragraph 13 of the standard guarantee form in the Appendix.)

Merchants Consolidated v. Team Sports & Trophies (1984) Inc., [1995] O.J. No. 84 (O.C.J. Gen. Div.)

Peter Brill was the principal of Team Sports and an experienced businessman. He signed a guarantee for the loans to his corporation. He later sold his interest in the corporation and severed all ties with it.

The business did not fare well under new management. The bank sued Brill on the guarantee. Brill defended, saying that he believed that the guarantee would end when he left the corporation, and that he had not obtained independent legal advice before signing the guarantee.

The Court's Decision

The court found that Brill was bound to the continuing guarantee. Brill was a sophisticated businessman who was quite familiar with the company's operation and with the concept of giving a guarantee for a loan. There was no possibility of any undue influence. I.L.A. was not necessary for a knowledgeable guarantor.

Independent Legal Advice (I. L. A.)

The bank may require the guarantor to have an independent lawyer's advice on what the guarantor's obligations are under the guarantee. This process arose in the context of a wife, who was a stay-at-home wife with no business experience and who depended entirely on her husband for business advice. The banks were required in these cases to ensure the wife had her own lawyer to advise her about what she was signing.

Today there are much fewer of these traditional marriages and so there are very few cases where guarantees are set aside based on a wife's being inexperienced in business, completely dependent on her husband for advice in such matters and who did not receive ILA. The banks and other lenders now still routinely insist on any guarantor receiving ILA if they are not getting a direct benefit from the loan, as would a shareholder of a corporation guaranteeing the corporation's debts.

Enforcement Considerations

A guarantor, who is married, may be the sole owner of a house. However, in most provinces that person's spouse has a potential claim on the value of the house and must also sign on any guarantee or it does not affect that spouse's potential claim. How that amount is determined is complex so a creditor wants to avoid getting into that situation and usually demands that the spouse sign as well.

Example: Hani is the sole shareholder of Hani international Inc. He is married and is shown as the sole owner of his house on the registered deed. His wife has a potential claim for an interest in the value of the house if the parties separate under family law. Therefore a cautious lender will want the wife to sign the guarantee as well.

Additionally, the individual signing the guarantee may have no assets. As part of a creditor proofing scheme, he or she may have transferred all assets such as house and cottage, into the spouse's name. So in that case the spouse's signature would be required.

A house may be in joint tenancy. This is a type of equal ownership. For example Stephen, who is the sole shareholder, director and officer of Stephen Inc., owns a house in joint tenancy with his wife. Stephen (but not his wife) signed a personal guarantee for a loan for his Corporation on which the bank now has a judgment against him. The bank can cause the house to be sold, take the amount of Stephen's interest and pay Stephen's wife for her interest.

Defenses

A guarantee is one type of contract, so potentially all contract defenses could apply. However they are rarely successful. One of the most frequently raised defences is misrepresentation. The guarantor claims that the bank manager said something such as: This is just a formality; the corporation has sufficient assets so the bank will never need to call on the guarantee, and the like. The standard form guarantee contains an Entire Agreement clause, (see paragraph 14 of the example form in the Appendix), which is strictly enforced, so those oral statements, even if you can prove they were made, will not apply and will not relieve the guarantor from their liability under the guarantee. (*Lau v. McDonald*, 2012 BCSC 866 (CanLII)

Bank Protective Terms

As various situations arose, the court gave defenses to guarantors. For example, if a bank had security over the assets of the primary debtor and negligently forgot to register the security so that other creditors seized it, the guarantor would be given a credit for the value of that security. However, immediately after these rulings, the bank changed the terms of its standard guarantee to take away these defenses.

As one illustration, see paragraph 7 of the standard guarantee form in the Appendix, and in particular the phrase: ...and no loss of or in respect of or unenforceability of... securities which the bank may now have... whether occasioned by the fault of the bank or otherwise, shall in any way limit or less in the guarantor's liability.

These changes, which took away all defenses at common law, have been upheld by the courts on the principle of freedom of contract. This principle states that parties are free to agree, subject of course to illegality, to any terms they wish and can exclude common-law defenses.

Negotiable Instruments

Banks, trust companies, credit unions, and other financial institutions all use cheques, which are one form of **bill of exchange**, or negotiable instrument—a written order by A to B (usually a bank) to pay a specified sum of money to a named party or to the bearer of the document. A promissory note is another. There are other types of negotiable instruments, but they are less common. All negotiable instruments are governed by the *Bill of Exchanges Act*.

bill of exchange
a written order by A to B (usually a bank) to pay a specified sum of money to a named party or to the bearer of the document

Cheques

A **cheque** is a bill of exchange drawn against a bank and payable on demand. The bank holds money on deposit for the person who signs the cheque (the **drawer**, the party who draws up or signs a bill of exchange). The bank (the **drawee**, the party required to make payment on the bill of exchange) technically owes the depositor the money, and must obey the depositor's orders respecting its use. A cheque is an order to the bank to pay on demand a specific sum to a named person (the **payee**, the party named to receive payment on the bill of exchange).

The bank is given an opportunity to tell the payee whether the bank can make the payment. There are many reasons the bank will not honour a cheque—insufficient funds, a stop-payment order, a stale-dated cheque, and so on. The cheque must be presented to the bank, which must then indicate if it will pay. This process is called acceptance. Once the bank has accepted the cheque, it cannot refuse to pay. Acceptance is one form of certification.

cheque
a bill of exchange drawn against a bank and payable on demand

drawer
the party who draws up or signs a bill of exchange

drawee
the party required to make payment on the bill of exchange

payee
the party named to receive payment on the bill of exchange

Forged Cheques

The bank is liable to the customer if the bank cashes a forged cheque. However, there is a situation in which a bank will not be liable for forged cheques. The bank will not have to pay if the customer's account documents contain a limitation clause, and the forgery is reported to the bank after the time period specified in that clause.

Example: The Supreme Court in, *Arrow Transfer Company Limited v. The Royal Bank of Canada* 1972 CanLII 135 (SCC), strongly upheld the verification clause in banking agreements. This clause requires a customer to report any errors or omissions or inaccurate entries in their account to the bank within 30 days of receiving their monthly statement. In that case an accountant who had forged the signatures of the company's officers on 73 company cheques over a period of 5 years had stolen $165,109. But since none of the earlier forgeries had been discovered or reported to the bank within the 30 day time periods, the bank was only liable for the forgery reported in the last month of $9,077.

There have been a few cases where the bank has been held liable if the verification clause had been worded in a vague or ambiguous manner or the actions of the fraudster were so suspicious the bank should have detected something was wrong. But generally, the courts do not want to impose a major duty on banks to be the police force for financial transactions nor make them an insurance agent for fraud just because of their "deep pockets" (considerable wealth). Banks have now carefully drafted their financial service agreements to try to protect themselves from liability and customers are expected to read and understand these terms.

The Parties to a Cheque

A cheque is an order by the person who signs it (drawer) to the bank (drawee) to pay a named amount to a particular person (payee). Writing a cheque is sometimes called drawing a cheque. The technical names for the parties are illustrated above.

Manor Windsor v. Bank of Nova Scotia
2011 ONSC 4515 (CanLII)

Sally Styles was a bookkeeper experienced in real estate transactions and was hired to work part time for Manor Windsor Realty. Unfortunately, as if often the case, she became an addicted gambler and to support her trips to the casino, she defrauded the company of over $400,000 in a 5 year period.

The company required the signatures of both partners on each business cheque, but one of the partners was frequently away, so he left blank cheques with his signature on them in the office. Styles would then use these pre-signed cheques. In the computerized accounting system she would enter the name of a real estate broker on the cheque which the firm would often do business with, but then on the actual cheque Styles would change the name to her own name.

When the company finally discovered the fraud, it sued its bank for honouring the cheques when there was only one signature on

them. The bank's defence was that the Financial Services Agreement Manor Windsor had signed clearly stated that any errors or problems in the account, including forgery or fraud, had to be reported to the bank within 30 days. There was also a clause that required Manor Windsor to maintain a security system to control, prevent and detect fraud.

The Court's Decision

The court ruled that the Financial Services Agreement was clear and unambiguous. The real estate agency had not notified the bank of problems with the account over the past 5 years, so the bank was only liable for the last cheque Styles had written in the previous 30 days for $7,809.22. The bank was not liable for the rest of the money Styles had stolen.

Conversion Claim

Corporations that have been defrauded however may be able to recover money in a conversion claim against the bank where the fraudulent employee deposited the cheques. Suppose an employee creates a fictitious company and opens an account at bank A (the collecting bank). The employee then has signed company cheques, but made out to the false company and deposits them in bank A. When this scheme is eventually uncovered, the employer cannot usually collect any money from its own bank as it was not reported within the 30 day time period each month, but the courts may find bank A, **the collecting bank, strictly liable for conversion**. There have been a variety of cases that have dealt with this issue and they have resulted in different rulings. Sometimes the court rules that the collecting bank is liable (as in Teva below) and other cases rule they are not (as in Rouge Valley below) depending on the interpretation of The Bills of Exchange Act. This has caused considerable concern in the banking industry, and it raises issues of fairness given that the company is usually in a much better position to have detected and prevented this fraud than the collecting bank. Unless the Bills of Exchange Act is revised or the Supreme Court clarifies the issue, this confusion will probably continue.

Example: In *Rouge Valley Health System v. TD Canada Trust*, 2012 ONCA 17 (CanLII) a senior manager with signing authority wrote 78 cheques for a total of $700,000 to a fictitious company he created and deposited them in the false company's account he opened at the TD bank. When the employer discovered the fraud, it claimed TD was strictly liable for conversion for negotiating the cheques. The bank however relied on s. 20(5) of the Bills of Exchange Act that allowed the bank to avoid liability when the cheques are made out to a fictitious or non-existing person. The court agreed and held that TD was not liable for the loss of money.

But a few months later, different judges of the same court gave an opposing decision.

Example: In *Teva Canada Limited v. Bank of Montreal* 2012 ONCA (CanLII), a Teva employee set up accounts at the Bank of Nova Scotia with names similar to actual customers of Teva, but that he had fraudulently created. Then over a period of 2 years he deposited 43 cheques into these accounts thereby defrauding his employer of $4 million. The Bank of Nova Scotia had presented the cheques to Teva's bank (Bank of Montreal) and it had collected the money and credited the fraudster's Bank of Nova Scotia accounts. When Teva discovered the fraud it sued the Bank of Nova Scotia for conversion. Though the Bank of Nova Scotia claimed that this fraud had occurred because of Teva's own negligence, the court said Canadian law does not allow the bank to use a defence of negligent estoppel by the company. It is a strict liability offence under the Bills of Exchange Act, so the Bank of Nova Scotia was strictly liable for conversion and the $4 million.

Embezzlement   What's the difference between **embezzlement** and **theft**? Both terms involve stealing and are criminal offences. Embezzlement occurs when an individual has legal possession of the goods. A bank teller, for example, has legal possession of the cash in that individual's drawer, but has no right to use it personally. If the teller steals that money, it is embezzlement.

Legalese

If a customer takes the money from the teller's cash drawer, it is theft. If that individual uses force or threat in the process, then a robbery has been committed. If a weapon is used, armed robbery has taken place.

Forgery   In order to safeguard its interests against forgery, a business should take certain precautions.

Business Alert!

- Have bank reconciliations done as soon as they are received, so that notice of any discrepancies can be given within the period specified in the verification agreement (usually 30 days).
- Make sure that internal controls are in place.

■ Have employees who have access to accounting records bonded with a fidelity bond. These are issued by insurance companies, who will then repay the money should the employee steal from you.

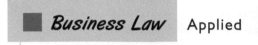

Business Law Applied

❺ **Chris Louie was** a bookkeeper for Newvest Company. He had no authorization to sign cheques for the firm. Newvest had an account agreement with the bank, containing a clause requiring notice of any discrepancies in the bank statements within 30 days, or the bank was released from liability.

Over a two-year period, Louie forged the signature of Newvest's president on 10 cheques to a phony supplier, and cashed the cheques himself. Newvest's auditor caught the last (the tenth) cheque, and the firm gave notice to the bank, within 30 days of that final cheque, that all 10 cheques were part of a fraudulent scheme.

Louie was by this time known to be a severe alcoholic, and had no ability to repay the amounts taken. The bank refused to reimburse Newvest for the 10 cheques.

a) Was the 30-day verification agreement effective for the bank?
b) Could the bank refuse reimbursement of all 10 cheques?
c) What should Newvest Company do to protect itself regarding possible forged or unauthorized cheques in the future?

Stop-Payment Orders

A cheque is an order to the bank to pay. The customer can cancel that order before the cheque is cashed—accepted—by the bank, by making a stop-payment order. If the customer issues such instructions, the bank must obey them, or must reimburse the customer if it wrongly cashes the cheque. However, the customer must have a legitimate reason for stopping payment, or the bank will not be liable for a mistaken payment.

If the customer does not have the correct information on the stop payment order, the bank's forms clearly indicate that the bank is not liable if it did not stop the payment. If a certified cheque has been written, the bank will not usually stop payment on a certified cheque as the certification indicates that the bank must honour it. If fraud or theft can be established, it may though be possible, but it is not easily done.

Other Concepts Concerning Cheques

Stale-Dating   Although in law the right to sue on a cheque extends to six years, banks as a matter of policy will not honour a cheque six months after its date.

postdated
dated later than the time when it is given to the payee

Postdated Cheques   Cheques can be signed, and dated for payment in the future. A stop-payment order can be applied to a **postdated** cheque (one which is dated later than the time when it is given to the payee), as long as the cheque is still in the hands of the payee. A stop-payment may be ineffective if the cheque has been signed over to another party— **endorsed** (signed with one's name on a negotiable instrument, e.g., on the back of a cheque).

endorsed
signed with one's name on a negotiable instrument, e.g., on the back of a cheque

At Sight/On Demand   Some bills of exchange are made payable at sight, meaning that three days' grace will be allowed to find the money to pay. On demand, however, means immediate payment is required.

The normal cheque is dated, and is payable on demand on or after that date, within a reasonable period of time. The bank must pay on the same day that a cheque is presented, provided that takes place on or after the cheque date. There is no grace period.

So, if a business gives a cheque dated January 31 to a supplier, and then calls the bank and asks that payment be held up for a day until the business gets the money to cover the cheque, the bank cannot so do. It must mark the cheque NSF (not sufficient funds) and return it on the same day.

Endorsements   Signing the back of a bill of exchange is technically an endorsement, and may mean that the person so signing has accepted liability for payment of the bill. However, signing the back of a cheque at the bank is also an acknowledgment of receipt of the money.

Restrictions on Cashing   One type of endorsement permitted in law is to put restrictions on the cashing of a cheque. A **restrictive endorsement** is an endorsement with a limitation. A common one is to specify that the cheque can be deposited only to a particular account in the name of the payee. If you are writing a cheque for a large sum it is advisable to write "for deposit only" on the reverse. This way, if it is stolen, the cheque cannot be cashed.

restrictive endorsement
an endorsement with a limitation

Bad Cheques   Knowingly writing a cheque without sufficient funds in the account can be the criminal offence of obtaining goods by false pretenses. If you write a cheque which is returned NSF, and you did so when there was no money in your account, nor the possibility of any being there by the time the cheque was likely to be presented for acceptance by the bank, the Criminal Code presumes that you intended to obtain the goods by false pretenses.

Bank Cards and Credit Cards

Consumers must be very careful with credit cards and bank cards. If a bank card with a PIN number is lost or stolen most banks will hold the customer liable for $50 of fraudulent transactions made with the card. However, if the customer wrote the PIN number on the card or used a PIN number that was too obvious, such as the year of their birth, their address, or something too simple such as 1,2,3,4—the bank card agreement clearly states that the customer is fully liable for all the fraudulent transactions made on their card. As a result consumers must make less obvious PIN numbers and protect their cards from theft or loss.

If a credit card that does not have a chip embedded in it is reported stolen or lost, the consumer is not usually liable for any fraudulent purchases made with their card. However consumers who make this claim, may have to prove on the balance of probabilities that a fraud did occur. If they cannot meet that requirement, the consumer will be liable for the charges, as illustrated in the Begum case below.

Example: In *Begum c. MBNA Canada Bank*, 2012 QCCQ 2561 (CanLII) a woman claimed that various credit cards she held with Canadian banks must have been cloned and fraudulent purchases were made with them in Bangladesh. Her father and husband made similar claims at the same time with different banks. The total for all three was about $80,000 in charges for jewellery, food and clothes purchased in Dhaka in a 3 week period. The three people had not left Canada during that time. The banks had received calls to inform the bank they were going to Dhaka and the callers were able to answer personal security questions.

The parties did not report the cards stolen and it was only later that they claimed the charges were fraudulent. The woman rarely ever used her card and it was highly unlikely her card information had been copied before the date of the questionable transactions.

The judge commented that the fact that seven frauds, involving the same three parties took place at the same time in different stores, stretched credulity. It ruled that the burden of proof was on Ms. Begum to prove that her card was lost and stolen. To meet the burden of proof, it is not sufficient for her to just claim that this was the case without giving any explanation of how the fraud took place and how the alleged fraudsters were able to obtain so much personal information about her. As a result the court did not believe the cards had been stolen and the woman was held liable for the $18,000 of charges on her card.

Letters of Credit

A letter of credit is a document in which the bank guarantees to pay a stipulated sum when a specified event takes place. When the event happens, the bank has to pay. In order to maintain the letter of credit's reliability as a business transaction, banks will make payment, and will not become involved in any disputes between the customer and the person to whom the letter was granted. Fraud, of course, is always a ground for refusal to pay. However, the banks will probably insist that the customer obtain a court order—an injunction—to stop the bank from making payment.

A letter of credit could read, for example, that the bank guarantees to pay $1 million to Photomat Corporation when the purchase of its assets by Entrepreneurial Investments Limited is completed, if Entrepreneurial Investments doesn't pay. Once the sale is completed, Photomat need only advise the bank that this has happened, and that Entrepreneurial Investments has not paid, and the bank will pay the money to Photomat. Entrepreneurial Investments cannot stop the payment by the bank for any reason short of fraud.

Letters of credit are used as a means to guarantee payment, especially in international transactions. But there can be disadvantages.

For example, a Canadian distributor makes arrangements with a Taiwanese manufacturer for the supply of kitchen utensils (knives, forks, and such). As part of the contract, the Canadian distributor agrees to post a letter of credit with a bank for $100,000 against shipment of the product. Shipments usually amount to $50,000. This arrangement means that the Taiwanese company only has to provide an invoice signed as received by the Canadian distributor to the bank and the bank has to pay the amount of the invoice to the limit of the letter of credit.

The first two shipments are satisfactory. But the third shipment worth $50,000 contains many defective items to the value of $25,000. The Taiwanese company can still obtain a full payment from the bank on the letter of credit for $50,000. While this is a breach of warranty, there is no fraud. The Canadian distributor is left with trying to negotiate a settlement or suing, probably in a Taiwanese court, for the value of the loss.

Thus, experienced Canadian business people will not easily post a letter of credit for a large amount. Additionally, they order small shipments in the beginning to be assured of quality and performance.

■ *Business Law* Applied

❻ **The Farah Company** gave a postdated cheque, no. 357, dated September 1, 1997, to a supplier for a shipment of inventory in the amount of $500. Farah did owe the money, but was short of cash, and therefore told the bank to stop payment on the cheque well before its due date. However, the cheque had been identified to the bank as no. 358, not 357, and it was paid when the supplier presented it.

a) Can a stop-payment order be put on a postdated cheque?
b) Did the bank owe a duty to the Farah Company to screen for the cheque even though the detail was inaccurate?

Promissory Notes

promissory note
a written promise to pay the amount stated on the instrument

When obtaining a loan, you will almost certainly be asked to sign a promissory note as part of the security for the transaction. A **promissory note** is, quite simply, a written promise to pay the amount stated on the instrument, and is usually required as part of a loan or purchase that is to be paid in instalments. The note might also outline the instalments and interest charges involved in the transaction.

An IOU is not a promissory note, but is only an acknowledgment of debt.

Holder in Due Course

Free transferability of negotiable instruments is what sets them apart from contracts. Because negotiable instruments are freely transferable, a **third party**—a stranger to the agreement, a person who is not one of the parties to a contract—may acquire greater rights to them than the immediate parties. This party is called a **holder in due course**: an innocent third party entitled to collect on a negotiable instrument in spite of any defences of the original parties.

An example of a holder in due course is a business which pays a roofing contractor a $500 deposit by cheque for work to be completed; that contractor signs the $500 cheque over to a building supply company as payment on a previous account. The building supplier is a third party, or holder in due course of the cheque, a negotiable instrument.

What happens if the roofing contractor does not in fact carry out its agreement with the business that paid the deposit? The business demands repayment of the $500, to which the roofing contractor replies that it no longer has the cheque, and is about to declare bankruptcy. The building supplier maintains that it received the cheque on account of a valid debt, and intends to cash it. The building supplier, as a holder in due course, can cash the cheque even though the roofing contractor defaulted on its contract with the business. The legal status of the parties is:

- the business is the drawer
- the roofing contractor is the payee
- the building supplier is the holder in due course

Great care must be used in giving cheques (especially postdated ones) and promissory notes in a business transaction as the next case brief demonstrates.

Example: In *Raymond Bibaud v Banque de Montreal*, [1975] C.A. 186 (Que.) Bibaud gave a builder a promissory note and 36 postdated cheques totalling $31,850 to build him a cottage. The builder then transferred the note and cheques to the bank for value. The builder soon went out of business and never built the cottage. Bibaud stopped payment on the cheques and the bank sued him claiming that it was a holder in due course. Bibaud claimed that the bank was not an innocent holder as it knew the builder was in financial difficulty. The court ruled that the bank did not have to do an inquiry when it obtained the note, so it was an innocent holder and Bibaud had to pay the bank. Bibaud could sue the builder to recover the money he had to pay the bank, but given that the builder had gone out of business, he would probably not get anything.

Not Negotiable   In the Bibaud case, the buyer could have safeguarded his interests by endorsing the back of the note and each cheque with restrictive words such as "not negotiable."

Business Alert!

third party

a stranger to the agreement, a person who is not one of the parties to a contract

holder in due course

an innocent third party entitled to collect on a negotiable instrument in spite of any defences of the original parties

---

■ *Critical Concepts of* Holder in Due Course

- Bills of exchange such as cheques and promissory notes are negotiable, or transferable, instruments.
- The party to whom the bill of exchange is transferred is called a holder in due course.
- A holder in due course is not affected by any defences the person who signed the bill may have against the payee, unless the holder has notice of the defences at the time the holder takes the note.

■ *Business Law* Applied

❼ **Raj Vong Associates** Inc. bought a computer system from Acu Computers Inc. at a cost of $20,000. Raj Vong did not want to get a bank loan, and so gave Acu Computers four postdated cheques for $5,000 each. Acu Computers signed these cheques over to its bank, to be applied against its loan.

There was a problem with the computer system, and Acu Computers denied liability. The bank demanded payment on the cheques from Raj Vong, who does not want to pay until the computer problem is sorted out. The bank sued on the notes.

a) What is the bank's status in relation to the cheques?

b) Can Raj Vong claim the problem with the computer as a defence to payment on the cheques?

Bank of Montreal v. Abrahams
2003 CanLII 37259 (ONCA)

The appellants were investors who in 1989 each signed a General Agreement and seven other agreements to purchase condominium units in British Columbia from Reemark. The agreements projected a transfer of title on September 30, 1990. The purchase agreement provided for payment of the purchase price by: a $1,500 deposit; a first mortgage from a financial institution for approximately 72 per cent of the price; and a promissory note in favour of Reemark for the balance.

The notes were contained in a bound volume of contract documents and, although the investors did not notice at the time they signed, the notes had a perforated (tear away) edge. After they were signed, Reemark detached the notes and assigned them to the Bank of Montreal, which had no contact with any of the defendants before the assignment. After receiving notice of the assignment of their respective notes, the investors made their payments to the bank.

In December 1991, the investors learned that the first mortgage, which was to be paid from rental income, was in default. Subsequently, the investors learned that Reemark had not transferred title to the units to them. Within a short period of time, all of the investors stopped making payments on the notes.

In May 1994, after the condominiums were sold under power of sale, the Bank of Montreal sued the investors on the notes. All parties agreed that the Bank was not, and could not have been, aware of Reemark's problems when the Bank purchased the notes and the Bank did not have any reason to believe that the investments would fail.

The trial court ruled the bank was an innocent holder in due course and the investors were found liable under their respective promissory notes. They appealed. The main issue on the appeal was whether the trial judge erred in concluding that the notes were unconditional promises to pay within the meaning of s. 176(1) of The Bills of Exchange Act.

The Court's Decision

The Ontario Court of Appeal agreed with the trial court's decision. The court ruled that the promissory notes were separate independent documents that on their face were unconditional promises to pay. They were independent from the main agreements to purchase the condos, and just because they were attached to the main contract by a perforated edge, did not mean they were conditional promises. Nothing was written on the notes to indicate there were other agreements involved.

The court noted that purpose of the Bills of Exchange Act is to facilitate business transactions and create flexible negotiable instruments and it would frustrate the purpose of the Act to hold that an apparently unconditional promissory note had to be interpreted in conjunction with a related contract on the sole ground that it was attached to the contract by a perforated edge. There was no basis to imply a term that payments on the notes were conditional upon Reemark fulfilling its obligation to transfer legal title to the condos to the investors. The bank was an innocent holder in due course and the investors were liable to the bank for the payments on the promissory notes.

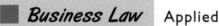

Business Law Applied

❽ **Pentagon Construction Maritime** Ltd. gave two postdated cheques for $20,000 each to Miramichi Glassworks Ltd. for installation of windows in a new building. Pentagon knew Miramichi was in financial difficulties, and made it clear to Miramichi and to its bank, the Royal Bank, that the cheques would not be honoured unless the contract was performed. Miramichi signed the cheques over to the bank to be applied against its loan.

Miramichi went into bankruptcy and did not fulfill the contract. The bank sued Pentagon on the cheques.

a) What special status could the bank rely on in bringing the lawsuit?

b) Does Pentagon have any defences?

Consumer Notes

Holder in due course status has been much abused because people today are unfamiliar with it. In consumer car sales, for example, a dealership would sometimes finance the car purchase and have the consumer sign a promissory note or give postdated cheques. The dealer would then assign those cheques to a bank or finance company. If the car broke down, the buyer still had to pay the bank in full, because it was a holder in due course.

Accordingly, the *Bills of Exchange Act* was amended to provide that, in a consumer transaction, a promissory note or bill which includes a cheque must be marked "consumer note" on its face. **Consumer notes** are promissory notes arising in a consumer credit sale. Cheques postdated more than 30 days are included as consumer bills, and must be so marked. Consumer notes are subject to the defences that could be raised by the original parties. In other words, the special status of the holder in due course does not apply to consumer notes. In the car-sale example, if the vehicle broke down, the consumer could plead that mechanical defect as a defence against payment to the bank.

If the note or bill is not stamped "consumer note" even though it is a consumer transaction, the innocent third party has holder in due course status. The person who failed to mark it will be subject to criminal prosecution, but if that individual is insolvent or has left the jurisdiction, that remedy will not help the consumer. The act also provides that failing to mark a consumer note as such will make it unenforceable by the payee. The onus, then, is on you as a consumer to make certain any such note or bill is clearly marked.

In most situations where you will be asked to sign a consumer note, you will also be asked to sign other security. The *Bills of Exchange Act* consumer note provision applies only to the promissory note or postdated cheques. For Constitutional reasons, the federal government cannot enact laws dealing with personal-property security. If, for example, a **chattel mortgage**—a mortgage of personal (chattel) property—is given at the same time, the consumer-note provision does not apply to that chattel mortgage. To cover this gap in consumer protection, many provinces have legislated requirements that all security instruments involved in consumer credit transactions be marked in the same way as consumer notes, so that a holder in due course status cannot be claimed.

Holder in Due Course Status   A business person can obtain the same protection as is afforded an ordinary consumer by endorsing any postdated cheque or promissory note on the reverse with the words "not negotiable." This prevents a holder in due course from taking the promissory note or cheque free of defences that could be raised between the primary parties.

consumer notes
promissory notes arising in a consumer credit sale

chattel mortgage
a mortgage of personal (chattel) property

Business Alert!

◼ *Business Law*   Applied

❾ **Raj Patel purchased** a used car from New Era Cars. Patel signed a promissory note and gave a chattel mortgage on the car. The note read:

September 15, 1997

The undersigned promises to pay New Era Cars Ltd. on demand the sum of thirty thousand dollars ($30,000) with interest at the rate of 10 percent per annum before and after maturity and default.

New Era assigned the note and chattel mortgage to Secure Financial Company Ltd. for value. It turned out that the car's speedometer had been turned back, and Patel wanted out of the deal, based on fraudulent misrepresentation concerning the mileage. Secure Financial Company claimed it knew nothing of the fraud, and sued on the note. New Era has gone bankrupt.

a) What type of transaction is this?
b) What special protection does the maker of a note normally have in this type of transaction? Does the above promissory note qualify for that protection?
c) Would Secure Financial Company be successful in its lawsuit?
d) What remedies does Patel have against New Era? Are they of any practical value?

Security Interests

collateral

property of the debtor that can be seized and sold by a creditor if the debt is not paid, e.g., a car may be given as collateral for a bank loan

When you borrow money from a bank, you will be asked to provide **collateral**—property of the debtor that can be seized and sold by a creditor if the debt is not paid, e.g., a car may be given as collateral for a bank loan. This collateral is called security, and because it is a type of property, it is subject to some of the laws surrounding property. Banks want collateral in order to minimize their risk of loss. The term *instrument* in this context means a formal written document.

Property Law

Property is divided into two classes in law—land, or real property, and all other property, called personal property (cars, televisions, boats, and so on).

Personal property is in turn divided into two types—tangible, or concrete, and intangible, or notional. For example, a computer is concrete property, but the right to collect money on a bill owed is notional. Notional property exists as a concept: it has no physical presence.

A business can possess all types of property, real and personal, both tangible and intangible. A small furniture manufacturing business, for example, might own the land on which the plant is built—real property—as well as tangible personal property such as machinery, tools, and inventory. It will also have **intangible property** (property that cannot be touched, such as accounts receivable) and, perhaps, a confidential formula for a special finish that makes the furniture unique.

intangible property

property that cannot be touched, such as accounts receivable

All property has two aspects that are important considerations for security purposes:

- ownership
- possession

Someone might have possession of a car but not actually own it. The vehicle could belong to a friend, or might be under lien to a bank. It is important to realize that possession of an item does not necessarily mean there is power to sell it with clear title.

Consider as an example the case of John Romanow, who purchased a clothing store from Leo Rodriguez. The store had a large inventory at the time the purchase was completed, and Romanow took possession. Shortly afterwards, the principal supplier removed most of the stock from the premises, as it had been placed on consignment and was not in fact owned by Rodriguez.

Giving Credit and Taking Security

The most important consideration in granting credit is not the asset the borrower might offer as security. The main concern is the borrower's ability to repay the sum involved in the transaction.

pledged

taken possession of by a creditor as security and held until repayment

Security is a secondary concern. If the business cannot repay the loan, the assets that have been **pledged** (that is, taken possession of by a creditor as security and held until repayment) are seized and sold, and the proceeds applied against the amount owing. There is always a risk that the assets might not realize sufficient money to cover the loan. The value of any property can change over time. Even a house—which has a fairly stable market value—can drop dramatically in its worth because of a fall in land prices. Assets other than land are also very much subject to fluctuations in value.

The forced sale of personal property often brings only 20 percent of its retail value. People mistakenly compare personal property values with land values. With land, there is only one market, but with other assets, there are two markets—retail and wholesale. The forced sale of personal property often yields about half the wholesale price, or less.

The seizure and sale of assets involves other costs. The private bailiff who carries out the seizure must be paid; should the borrower resist, then obtaining a court order will involve further expense. In addition, resale of the items is normally handled by auctioneers or other liquidators—all of whom charge a significant fee for their services.

Why Take Security?

Security on a debt offers the lender a quick remedy if the borrower defaults, without having to go to court, for **repossession** of the property (the act of taking back possession of property that has been in the possession of another). The creditor can simply employ a bailiff to seize the assets, going to the courts only if some difficulty arises. For example, if a bank holds a chattel mortgage on a car and the borrower defaults, the bailiff can seize the vehicle from the borrower's property. The car can then be resold at a reasonable commercial value without the borrower's consent. However, if the car is in a locked garage, the bailiff can enter a locked structure only with the authority of a court order. Such an order relating to secured assets can usually be obtained fairly quickly.

repossession
the act of taking back possession of property that has been in the possession of another

Creditors who have security for their loans will be repaid before any other creditors, provided that security has been registered. Suppose, for example, that a bank holds a chattel mortgage on a car belonging to a business. One of the suppliers to the business has a judgment against it for $2,000. Because the bank loan is secured by the car, the bank can seize and sell the vehicle, and thereby have first claim on the proceeds.

Car selling price at auction	$6,000		
Bank loan outstanding	$5,000	Bank loan repaid	$5,000
Supplier's account	$2,000	Supplier paid	$1,000
Total debt	$7,000	Total paid	$6,000

The bank receives $5,000; the supplier—even though a court judgment has been obtained—receives only $1,000. The two creditors do not share equally in the proceeds of sale because the bank has specific security on the car.

Types of Security Instruments

There are several types of transactions in which the creditor obtains security. Some of these deal with real estate, and are discussed in Chapter 15. The documents involved in such agreements are called security instruments. *Instrument*, used in a legal context, refers to the written form of the transaction and is a synonym for *document*. Some of the most common methods of obtaining security on personal property are outlined below.

Conditional Sales Under this arrangement, the seller retains legal ownership—title—of the property until the final payment is made, but gives possession of it to the purchaser at the start of the agreement.

Used-car sales are sometimes made under a conditional sales contract, which is then sold, or assigned, by the car dealer to a finance company, which takes over collection of the payments.

Chattel Mortgages   Similar to a land mortgage, a chattel mortgage is a lien on personal property that is pledged as security for a loan. If you buy a car by borrowing money from a bank, the bank will put a chattel mortgage on the car until the loan is paid.

There are some limitations on the use of chattel mortgages. They are only possible for tangible property of some value, which can be identified—such as a car or a manufacturing machine. They are of little value over inventory such as shoes in a shoe store. While the shoes can be identified at the time the chattel mortgage is registered, they will be constantly sold and replaced, and a new inventory will not be covered by the chattel mortgage. It is obviously not realistic to register and discharge a chattel mortgage on each pair of shoes on delivery and sale.

Although chattel mortgages are still in use, they are gradually being replaced by the general security agreement (GSA).

Legalese   Chattel   **Chattel** is the Norman French word for *cattle*. In medieval times, cattle were important personal property, and the term became associated in law with all moveable (personal) assets, as opposed to immovable assets, or real property.

Assignment of Accounts Receivable/Book Debts   A business sells goods and services, for which customers pay. Frequently, that payment is not made at the time the items actually change hands or the service is provided, but is invoiced, with payment expected within a certain time. An accounting firm, for example, might have invoices totalling $50,000 awaiting payment by clients. This amount is known as accounts receivable, or book debts.

Most such accounts will probably be paid in the weeks or months following their issue. If collection of the amounts due does seem likely, a bank will lend money on the security of the accounts receivable. The accounting firm sends out bills, and some will be paid in any given time period, so that the actual accounts owing change continually. By using them as security for a loan, the business assigns the right to collect these debts to the bank. The bank can exercise these rights if the business defaults on its loan.

Banks have policies to evaluate the accounts receivable, and will seldom, for example, give any value to accounts outstanding more than 90 days.

General Security Agreements   Chattel mortgages and conditional sales relate to tangible property. The assignment of book debts relates to intangible property. None of these security instruments has the flexibility for dealing with all the types of personal property, tangible and intangible, that a business might have. A business is usually more valuable if it can be sold on an ongoing basis—chattel mortgages and conditional sales allow only pieces of the business to be seized.

Thus, a more general security instrument has been developed, taking into account the increasing amount and value of intangible property—such as information—in the modern business. The **general security agreement** is an agreement in which all the assets of a business are pledged as collateral. The GSA has wording that allows all the personal property of a business and the business operation itself to be seized, so that the business can be run as a going concern if there is any advantage to doing so. The GSA will include the right to information in computer systems, and to computer software, as well as any confidential formulas necessary for the success of the business.

Debentures Debentures are simply another term for an instrument very similar to bonds. A **debenture** is a type of corporate bond, indicating a debt owed by a corporation. It combines security over personal and real property in one document. *Debenture* derives from the same word as *debt*, and can contain various terms. One of the most common of these is a **floating charge**—a form of mortgage on the assets of a corporation not affixed to any particular asset, but which does become affixed once a specified event takes place. A floating charge, for example, is often used with respect to inventory, which might be pledged as security for a loan—the firm can sell that inventory and replace it in the ordinary course of business. The purchaser can provide clear ownership without obtaining lien clearance. If, however, the corporation defaults on its loan payments, the security attaches to the property, and the corporation can no longer sell the inventory free and clear of the security interest. Once the security has attached, it is similar to a mortgage.

Debenture The word **debenture** comes from the Latin *debeo*, meaning debt or to owe. So, like a bond, debenture simply means money that is borrowed on a loan basis, as distinct from an equity—purchase of shares—basis.

> **general security agreement**
> an agreement in which all the assets of a business are pledged as collateral

> **debenture**
> a type of corporate bond, indicating a debt owed by a corporation

> **floating charge**
> a form of mortgage on the assets of a corporation not affixed to any particular asset, but which does become affixed once a specified event takes place

> **Legalese**

■ *Business Law* Applied

⑩ **Cristin Schmitz has** a small manufacturing business, and wants to sell three punch presses and replace them. She finds a purchaser who offers her $100,000 for the three machines. The purchase price is to be paid in instalments, with $10,000 down, and $10,000 a month for 9 months. The purchaser offers to give Schmitz postdated cheques for the payments.

   a) Do you think postdated cheques are sufficient, or is there anything else that Schmitz should do to ensure collection?

⑪ **Phoenix Technologies Inc.** makes brake systems for automotive assembly plants. It wants to borrow $100,000 to buy new equipment for expansion, and has approached Venture Capital Inc. for a loan. Venture Capital has reviewed the business plan and the history of Phoenix, and has decided it is a good investment. You are an employee of Venture Capital, and your boss asks for any comments you might have about security that Venture could take from Phoenix for the loan.

   a) Discuss the possible assets that Phoenix might have and the types of security instruments that could be employed in the lending transaction.

Leases (Financing)

Leasing is a major area in the lending industry. Such a lease is often called a financing, or equipment, lease to distinguish it from a traditional lease in which ownership is never intended to be transferred to the **lessee** (the borrower, or the tenant or person who takes possession of the leased property). The lessee usually has the option to purchase at the end of a **financing lease**, which is a security arrangement in which a third person provides credit, purchases the

> **lessee**
> the tenant or person who takes possession of the leased property

> **financing lease**
> a security arrangement in which a third person provides credit, purchases the property, and leases it to the borrower

property, and leases it to the borrower. While it is called a lease, and modelled on the rental form, it is a security instrument, and is used in place of conditional sales and chattel mortgages.

The borrower selects a piece of equipment, say a cash-register system, that it wishes to purchase for its business. It then approaches a small finance company for approval to borrow the amount necessary to purchase the equipment. Instead of having the business buy the equipment and placing a chattel mortgage on it, the finance company purchases the cash register and leases it to the business. That firm then has to pay rental—blended principal and interest payments—to repay the loan over the term of the lease. Often there is an option to buy out the equipment for a nominal value at the end of the lease.

Leasing was introduced in business financing but has recently become a consumer security technique, especially in the retail car business, where it is often advertised as "lease to own."

A lease of this nature is a loan with security. When the finance company has advanced the money, it has performed its obligations under the arrangement. There is always a term in the financing lease that expenses resulting from defects in the equipment cannot be set off against rental payments, so that the borrower's only recourse is action against the supplier. These clauses have been held by the courts to be enforceable.

One Percent Financing   Some car dealerships offer what appears to be extraordinarily low interest on leases. It's done by keeping a high sale price. If you start by telling the sales rep that you have cash or a bank loan, you can negotiate a much lower sale price. Try it! The difference in price will bring the supposedly low interest rate up to the market rate. There is no free lunch.

Defences

Leases and other security instruments are types of contracts, and so the normal contract defences apply. Some of those defences most relevant are discussed next in the context of leases. Contract defences such as these apply to all security agreements.

acceleration clause

a clause stating that if the borrower defaults on any payment, the whole of the principal sum of the debt and of accrued interest immediately falls due

There is in most leases a clause stating that if the borrower defaults on any payment, the whole of the principal sum of the debt and of accrued interest immediately falls due. Such a clause is called an **acceleration clause.**

There may also be a clause that states interest at a higher rate is charged on overdue payments. The interest default rate is often as high as 36 percent per annum. In time this interest can far exceed the purchase value of the item under lease.

Fortunately the courts have given some relief against these onerous terms. If they are out of all proportion to the real damage suffered by the leasing company, there may be penalty clauses (see Chapter 6). Recall that the leasing company must mitigate its damage. That means it must try to find another customer to take over the lease. If it does so, then the value of the new lease must be deducted from the damages resulting from the breach of the first lease. The acceleration clause often does not take into account the duty to mitigate or give credit for any mitigation.

■ *Business Law*   Applied

Ⓟ **Bennett and Jones** Ltd. wants to lease a fax machine. It selects an MBI fax machine costing $5,000. The MBI sales representative tells Bennett and Jones Ltd. about Techlease, which specializes in financing business-equipment purchases. A lease is arranged by Bennett and Jones Ltd. with Techlease. The terms are: monthly installments of $100 for 60 months; and, if any payment is missed, the entire balance of the lease becomes due, and the leasing company can repossess the fax machine on default of payment.

Bennett and Jones Ltd. makes one year of payments, then defaults. Techlease repossesses the fax machine and releases it immediately to another company on the same terms. It sues Bennett and Jones Ltd. for $4,800, or 48 payments.

 a) Does the lease agreement permit Techlease to sue for the amount claimed?
 b) Does Bennett and Jones Ltd. have a defence?
 c) What damages can Techlease validly claim?

Defective Equipment   It seems that if the equipment that is leased is defective, the lessee should be able to set off the cost of repairing the defects against the lease payment. However, this is not the case. Recall that the real nature of a lease is a loan with security. When the finance company has advanced the money, it has performed its obligations under the arrangement. There is usually a term in the financing lease stating that expenses resulting from defects from the equipment cannot be set off against the rental payments, so that the borrower's only recourse is an action against the supplier. These clauses have been held to be enforceable by the courts.

Consumer Defences

Under consumer protection legislation in most provinces, if two-thirds of the loan is paid off, then the bank cannot seize the asset simply by using a bailiff. However, the bank can sue and obtain judgment, and then seize the item to satisfy that judgment. It may take a little longer, but the same result is achieved.

In British Columbia and Alberta, if the bank repossesses the car, it cannot sue for the balance should the sale of the vehicle fail to realize sufficient money to cover the outstanding amount of the loan.

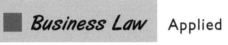 **Business Law**   Applied

⑱ **Linda Scott bought** a boat for recreational purposes, paid for in part by a bank loan of $44,000. As part of the security for the loan, the bank obtained a chattel mortgage on the vessel.

Scott made all the required payments on the loan, except the final one. The bank now wants to repossess the boat.

 a) Can the bank do so?
 b) Does it matter in which province this situation takes place?

Other Types of Securities

Consignment

Consignment is the placing of goods with a business for the purpose of sale. Goods are sometimes placed in a particular business by the manufacturer, to be sold by the business owner. The business does not buy these goods from the manufacturer, but simply stores them with instructions to sell. If the items are sold, the business keeps an agreed percentage of the selling price.

consignment
the placing of goods with a business for the purpose of sale

Whether goods on consignment are there as a security and have to be registered under the public registration system is a matter of intention between the owner and the person holding the goods for sale. (The **registration system** is a means of registering and tracking property deeds whereby the records are available to be examined.) The court will ask whether the consignment arrangement was intended to be a security arrangement, providing some security for the debtor's obligations towards the owner of the goods. Consignment can be of concern to a purchaser of the business. The business may appear to have a full inventory; however, if goods are on a true consignment basis—and therefore do not have to be registered—the purchaser may be misled as to the true size of the inventory.

registration system

a means of registering and tracking property deeds whereby the records are available to be examined

Purchase Money Security Interest

If a supplier sells and delivers a large quantity of inventory on credit one day, and the next day that business goes bankrupt, ownership of the goods has passed to the business. The trustee in bankruptcy of the business will sell that inventory and the supplier will only share with all other creditors. To protect suppliers of goods, a new security instrument called the purchase money security interest (PMSI) was devised, permitting a supplier of goods to register a lien under *Personal Property Security Act* legislation for goods supplied. If the business does not pay, or goes bankrupt, the supplier can repossess its own goods to the extent of the unpaid amount. An alternative remedy may be available under the *Bankruptcy and Insolvency Act*.

■ *Business Law* Applied

⓮ **On September 1,** Kipling Industries Inc. sells and delivers a quantity of sweatshirts on credit to Tough Sport Limited. The clothing is worth $10,000.

On September 2, Tough Sport arranges with a contractor for renovations to its premises and gives the contractor a chattel mortgage in the amount of $10,000 on the sweatshirt inventory.

On September 3, Tough Sport goes bankrupt.

   a) Can the contractor seize the sweatshirt inventory, or can Kipling Industries take it back?
   b) What could Kipling have done to protect its interests?

⓯ **Slim Fitness Inc.,** a diet business, wishes to purchase a new type of computerized body-wrap machine that is reported to help in weight loss. It arranges with Sure Leasing Inc. to obtain the money to buy the equipment. Sure Leasing Inc. buys the equipment from EMS Systems Inc., and then gives it to Slim Fitness Inc. on a financing lease.

After using the equipment for a few months, the system breaks down almost completely.

   a) Can Slim Fitness Inc. refuse to make payments on the financing lease?
   b) If not, what remedy does it have?

Personal Property Security Act

financing statement

a document setting out details of a security interest that must be filed in order to protect that interest under personal property security acts

Until recently, each type of security instrument required different technical procedures for the time and place of its registration, form of agreement, and so on. To cut through some of the red tape involved, all provinces created one set of rules governing the registration of all security transactions involving personal property. Such registration is accomplished with a document called a financing statement, and should take place as soon as possible after the transaction has been completed. A **financing statement** is a document setting out details of a security interest that must be filed in order to protect that interest under personal property security acts (often referred to as the PPSA of the particular province). This means that the lender registers notice of all liens against personal property at one place, using one procedure. As well, a purchaser has only to search for lien notices at one location. Once the lender registers their claim at the PPSA, their security interest has been **perfected** and the lender can obtain their priority ranking against other creditors. Extra care must be taken so that there are no errors in the information on the PPSA registration form because in some provinces, even a minor mistake can result in an invalid registration and the loss of the creditor's priority.

The registration concept puts the onus on the purchaser to search for liens before buying. The purchaser cannot plead ignorance as a defence—if a lien is publicly registered, it is enforceable even against innocent purchasers who were unaware of it.

■ *Critical Concepts of* Unexpected Liens

- Notice of liens can be registered in a government office, and the general public can search for evidence of a lien against any object.
- The registration of a notice of lien means it is enforceable against a stranger who purchased the object, whether the purchaser knew of the lien or not.
- Goods sold to consumers in ordinary retail sales are not subject to liens.
- Registration gives the first-registered lienholder priority over subsequently registered notices of liens.

Liens Can Be Dangerous   Liens against personal property can cause businesses two serious problems.

Business Alert!

Giving credit. When you give credit to a business, it is safest to assume that the bank and other financial institutions have liens on all of its assets. As a small business, you are concerned with the firm's ability to pay. If it should go out of business, there will very likely be little left over after the bank takes its first claim on security.

Buying. Before purchasing any item from a seller who is not selling in the ordinary course of its business, make certain that you search for liens. Because of the consumer/retail exemption for goods sold in the ordinary course of business, many people do not realize the real danger that a lien may exist on something bought outside the normal retail setting. Probably all purchases that you make as a business will be outside the retail/consumer context.

The Bank Act

The federal Bank Act has been a law long before the provinces enacted their PPSAs. The Bank Act allows banks to register their security interests when loans are made to manufacturers, wholesalers or retail purchasers or shippers of agricultural, forestry, or fishery products. The law allows the debtors to sell the goods in the course of business, but still preservers the banks' security interests. Once the PPSAs were enacted it has resulted in overlap, duplication and confusion as to what law takes priority. The law is not clear in this area and it has resulted in much litigation. To be safe, searches under both the PPSA and The Bank Act should be done by creditors or purchasers before making financial decisions.

Lien Clearance Certificate

Recognizing that many consumers are not aware of the need to search and obtain lien clearance before buying an expensive object, the Ontario government has passed laws requiring the vendor of a motor vehicle to provide a lien-clearance certificate on the private sale of a car. Purchasers of cars sold by car dealers in the ordinary course of business are not subject to liens. To date, Ontario is the only province that has this legislation in place. It also applies only to cars, and to no other objects. The Giffen case below illustrates the importance of registering your security interest at the PPSA, and how your failure to do so can result in losing your claim to the assets.

Giffen (Re), [1998] 1 SCR 91

Telecom Leasing Canada Ltd. (TLC) leased a car to the B.C. Telephone Co. (T), which in turn leased the car to one of its employees, Carol Giffen. The lease was for longer than one year so the lease was subject to the B.C. PPSA. A year after her car lease began, Giffen voluntarily declared bankruptcy.

Neither TLC nor T had registered the lease (their security interest) at the PPSA though. TLC took back the car and sold it, but Giffen's trustee in bankruptcy claimed the proceeds of the car sale for her creditors, because TLC and T's security interests in the car had not been perfected (registered at the PPSA). TLC and T claimed that since Giffen did not own the car, she only had the right to use and possess it, so the trustee in bankruptcy could not have a greater interest in the car than Giffen herself had and the trustee was not entitled to the sale proceeds.

The trial court ruled in favour of the trustee in bankruptcy, but the decision was reversed on appeal. The case then went to the Supreme Court of Canada.

The Court's Decision

The Supreme Court ruled that under s.20(b)(i) of the B.C. PPSA an unperfected (unregistered) security interest has no effect against the trustee. It is not an issue of title or ownership, but one of the priority of competing rights and interests. The trustee in bankruptcy can get a greater interest in the disputed property than the bankrupt woman actually had herself due to the provisions in the PPSA. The trustee in bankruptcy had priority over TLC and T, so the trustee was then entitled to the proceeds from the sale of the car to use to pay Giffen's creditors.

Business Law   Applied

⑯ **Franka Marques wanted** two cars for her family. She bought a van for family use and a subcompact for driving to work. The van was purchased from a used-car lot; the subcompact she acquired by private sale from an ad in the local newspaper.

It turns out there were liens registered against both vehicles by banks, who now want to repossess the cars because the original borrowers have defaulted.

   a) Is the lien registered against the van enforceable against Marques?
   b) Is the lien registered against the subcompact enforceable against Marques?

⑰ **Chester Gryski saw** a newspaper ad for the private sale of a car, and agreed to purchase the vehicle for $20,000 on August 1, from John Fairburn. Fairburn knew that he would soon be leaving the country, and borrowed $10,000 against the security of the car, giving the bank a chattel mortgage. Fairburn had no intention of repaying the loan.

At 9:30 a.m. on July 31, Fairburn obtained a lien certificate that the car was free and clear. At 10:00 a.m. the same day, the bank registered its security against the loan to Fairburn.

On August 1, Gryski met Fairburn at the Ministry of Transportation office, where Fairburn gave Gryski the lien clearance certificate and the ownership to the car in exchange for a certified cheque for $20,000.

Fairburn left the country. The bank seized the car and claimed the lien for $10,000.

   a) Did Gryski know of the lien?
   b) Does the bank have a valid lien for $10,000?

Receivers/Managers

When a business borrows money from a bank or other creditor, one of the terms may provide that on default the creditor can appoint a receiver. The **receiver** is a person appointed by a **secured creditor**—a creditor who has the right to seize and sell specific assets of a borrower to pay off a loan—to retrieve the assets to satisfy the debt. The receiver takes control of the business and/or its assets, according to the provisions of the agreement. The receiver replaces the current board of directors and has the powers of the board, which include firing all employees. In a typical case, the receiver and staff will arrive at the business premises and physically take control of the premises and all business records. If the owner resists, the receiver can make an application to the court. If the owner resists that court order, the owner may be in contempt of court.

Few business owners resist the receivership, so most proceed voluntarily and without the need of court intervention. In a receivership, the business is considered insolvent, that is, unable to pay its debts. However, a formal application in bankruptcy is not made. That expense is saved by the creditor. Receivers have to register with the Superintendent of Bankruptcy, so anyone can search at that office to see if a business is in receivership.

Frequently, the duties of receiver and manager are undertaken by one person or firm. However, the legal responsibilities of each position are distinct. A receiver/manager can be anyone. There are no requirements for specific qualifications. However, a receiver is usually a chartered accountant who is also a licensed trustee in bankruptcy. The bank has to guarantee the payment of the receiver's fees, but these are added on to the debt and eventually borne by the debtor if the debtor has sufficient assets.

A receiver:

- is an agent who takes over the assets that are subject to a general security agreement
- takes control of the assets with a view to disposing of them as quickly as possible, at a reasonable commercial value
- has no power to run the business

A manager:

- takes over the function of the board of directors, and has the power to run the company as an ongoing concern. Legally, the business is considered to have ceased operation at the time the receiver/manager is appointed, and afterwards is started afresh.
- has the power to fire all employees on one day's notice, with no compensation. This is a considerable advantage because many employees may be loyal to the business owner, and antagonistic to the manager who they feel has harmed their former employer. However, the ability of the manager to control their continuing employment helps to ensure their co-operation.
- is appointed when there is some hope of either making an agreement with the creditors to keep the business alive, or selling the business as an ongoing enterprise. Usually, a business has more value if it can be sold while it is in operation.

Types of Receivers

A receiver can be appointed by either:

- private arrangement under a general security agreement (GSA)/debenture type of security, or
- the court

A typical GSA provides for the appointment of a receiver on notice to the debtor. In this way, the bank or other creditor sends out a letter appointing a receiver, who goes directly to the business and takes over the assets. The courts do not want to become involved in this

receiver

a person appointed by a secured creditor to retrieve the assets to satisfy the debt

secured creditor

a creditor who has the right to seize and sell specific assets of a borrower to pay off a loan

part of the debt-collection process if it can be avoided, and will appoint a receiver only if the self-help remedy is ineffective. Such a situation would be if the receiver goes to the business and the owner refuses to turn over the assets.

There are provisions for the appointment of a receiver whenever the court feels it is just and convenient—such as when another remedy is found to be ineffective, and the assets are in danger of disappearing.

A receivership is an expensive proposition, and receiver's fees are quite high. If the proceeds from the sale of the assets are not enough to cover the receiver's fee, the bank has to pay the difference.

In Summation

Financial Institutions

- There are a number of lending institutions through which a business might finance its operations.

- Trust companies are also available for financing operations, and may be privately owned or controlled.

- Credit unions are another option for financial services. They are member-owned and controlled, and are non-profit.

- Finance companies, usually private institutions and pay day loan companies, are another source of financing, and may operate either by financing the transaction itself or by acting as go-betweens, connecting those with the need for capital to those with money to invest.

- Deposits with banks and trust companies are insu red under the Canada Deposit Insurance Corporation (CDIC) to a maximum of $100,000 per customer, per institution.

Guarantees

- In a guarantee a third party agrees to pay a debt if the principal debtor defaults. In an indemnity a third party agrees to pay a debt but it is not dependent upon the default of the principal debtor, the creditor can chose to go to the party that gave the indemnity first.

- Informally a guarantee is often called cosigning

- Sometimes a cosigner does not get money or any other benefit from the loan being guaranteed, but is still liable for the full amount of the guarantee

- Standard guarantee terms make the guarantor liable for all debts owed by the primary debtor to the creditor from a wide range of sources not only the specific loan that is being arranged

- The amount stated in the guarantee limits the amount of the guarantor's liability but does not limit it to the loan being arranged

- The limitation period, by the standard wording in a guarantee, begins to run from the date of the demand by the creditor to the guarantor

- A guarantor can limit liability as to the amount owing at a certain date by giving notice to the creditor that the guarantor will not be liable for any increases in the primary debtor's obligations to the creditor after that date

Demand Loans

- Financing is often done by means of a demand loan. This type of loan does not have a particular date set for its maturity. Instead, it must be repaid within a reasonable period after a demand for repayment of the loan is made by the financial institution.

Negotiable Instruments

- Although there are several types of negotiable instruments, including promissory notes and letters of credit, the cheque is the most common form used by financial institutions in their transactions.

- A customer who becomes aware of a forgery or theft involving a cheque is obligated to give notice of the situation to the financial institution. As well, a financial organization that has paid out under a forged or stolen negotiable instrument will incur obligations.

- Stale-dated cheques, postdated cheques, cheques payable on sight, and endorsements of various types all create restrictions or rights that attach to the negotiable instrument and its use.

- Other types of negotiable instruments, such as letters of credit and promissory notes, may be used depending on the nature of the financial transaction and the customer's requirements. Promissory notes and letters of credit may be transferred or negotiated between parties, and may ultimately lead to a situation in which a third party which has acquired a negotiable instrument possesses greater rights as a holder in due course than the party from which the negotiable instrument was obtained.

- To protect consumers, a negotiable instrument, such as a promissory note or cheque, that is used in a consumer transaction must be marked on its face with the words "consumer note." Negotiable instruments involved in consumer transactions are also made subject to the defences available to the original parties in the transaction. This avoids the possibility of a situation arising in which a third party becomes a holder in due course, and is able to enforce payment on the negotiable instrument when the debtor has a good defence against having to make payment under the consumer transaction.

Security Instruments

- A financing institution's decision to lend money is based on the borrower's ability to repay the loan. This decision will include a request for property, real or personal, to be given as collateral or security for repayment of the loan.

- A security interest in real property is usually created through a mortgage.

- If personal property is involved, the financial transaction is secured by what is commonly referred to as a lien.

- There are several different types of security instruments for personal property, each with distinct advantages and limitations. The various types are: conditional sale contract; chattel mortgage; assignment of accounts receivable/book debts; general security agreement (GSA); debenture; lease; consignment; and purchase money security interest (PMSI).

Liens

- The lien against personal property created by the various types of security instruments may be registered under the *Personal Property Security Act* (PPSA) registry system in almost all provinces. It may then be enforced against subsequent purchasers of that property, even if the purchaser is unaware of the lien's existence.

- The lien created by the security instrument includes the lender's right to repossess the item. This gives the lender an advantage over other general, unsecured creditors of the debtor.

- Various consumer laws protect a purchaser in a consumer transaction from the financial institution's being able to exercise its lien in particular circumstances.

- The ability to appointment a receiver/manager is a further remedy that may be available to a financial institution in a lending transaction.

Closing Questions

1. Maxine Mair sold her house for $190,000. After keeping $10,000 for living expenses, she divided the remaining $180,000 into three amounts of $60,000 which she placed in three separate accounts with the Credit Trust Company.
   a) Why has Mair deposited her money in this way?
   b) If the Credit Trust Company were to collapse and declare bankruptcy, what amount of money would she be able to claim?
   c) Would it have made any difference if Mair had made the same arrangements with a bank rather than a trust company?
   d) How could Mair have maximized protection for her money on deposit?

2. Claudette Foster runs a small promotional business that specializes in making plastic figurines of well-proportioned men and women. These are sold to health clubs as promotional items. The main assets of the business are the moulds, which Foster designed and created.

   When she receives an order from a health club, she contracts out the actual manufacture of the figurines to various plastic companies which use her moulds and then return them to her along with the completed figurines. Foster has arranged a business loan of $60,000 with Andre Fernandez.
   a) Advise Fernandez of the various types of security instruments that could be used in making his loan to Foster, and recommend which would best fit his purpose in these circumstances.
   b) Fernandez has come to you for advice. He tells you that Foster has defaulted on her loan repayments because of her poor management skills. He also tells you that the business itself would be a good one in the right hands, but Foster is making noises that if he does not drop the interest rate on the loan by half and restructure her monthly payments, she will relocate to Batavia, New York, where her cousin has a small plastics company. Restructuring the loan does not make economic sense for Fernandez. Explain to him the alternatives available in these circumstances, and what procedures would be necessary to put them in place.

3. The Konstabul and Nikakolakos families lived next door to each other in a small Canadian town; they had also lived close by in the same home town in the old country. Their friendship went back many years.

   Nikki Nikakolakos asked Kostos Konstabul to sign as a personal guarantor of a $20,000 bank loan for Nikakolakos's son, Peter. The loan was to enable Peter to buy a car, and Nikakolakos assured Konstabul that the young man had recently started a well-paying job at a factory and, playing on the Old World connection, said that she would do the same for him if he ever needed it.

   Konstabul finally agreed to go to the bank with Peter, and there he signed a guarantee containing an entire agreement clause. The loan was to be secured by a chattel mortgage registered against the car. On the day Konstabul signed the guarantee, the bank manager said, "Don't worry: the bank has a chattel mortgage on the car, which is worth far more than the loan amount."

   For several months Peter Nikakolakos made payments on the loan. However, the factory laid him off, and eventually he defaulted on the loan. The bank seized the car. Unfortunately, the vehicle had severe mechanical problems and brought only $5,000 at auction. The bank then demanded $15,000 from Konstabul, who complained that he had signed the guarantee only because the bank manager had said the car was worth more than $20,000. Konstabul asked Nikakolakos to speak to Peter and to the bank, reminding her that their families were from the same town in the old country. She replied, "Kostos, this is Canada, a new country full of opportunity; you've got to leave the Old World behind. Sorry, nothing I can do. You know what sons are like."
   a) What is the technical name in the law of contract for the defence Konstabul would raise to the bank's demand for the $15,000?
   b) Can Konstabul successfully rely on this defence? Why or why not?
   c) Does Konstabul have any remedy at law concerning Nikki Nikakolakos and/or her son Peter?

4. Andrew Brown was a director of a corporation. He signed a bank guarantee for a term loan of $100,000 on the standard Bank Guarantee Form (see Appendix). A few months later Brown resigned and left the corporation. The next month the corporation became insolvent.

The loan had been paid down to $50,000 when Brown resigned. Later it was increased to $60,000 and remained at that amount at the date of insolvency.

The bank had a lien over the assets of the corporation but failed to register it properly. If the lien had been registered properly, the bank could have realized $30,000.

The corporation had an overdraft of $20,000.

The corporation's lending by-law was invalid, and so the loan between the bank and the corporation was not enforceable.

The corporation is owed $10,000 by a customer, but the bank refuses to attempt to collect this debt even though the bank has a valid assignment of all of the corporation's accounts receivable.

The corporation owes Brown $15,000 for unpaid wages for work done for the corporation.

The corporation's credit card with the bank has an outstanding balance of $15,000, but $10,000 of this amount was used by the president for personal expenses.

a) Is Brown liable for the term loan at $50,000 or $60,000? Could Brown have done anything to limit his liability?

b) Can Brown claim a credit for $20,000 because of the bank's negligence in improperly registering the lien?

c) Can the bank claim the corporation's overdraft of $40,000 against Brown?

d) Since the original loan agreement between the primary debtor (the corporation) and the bank was unenforceable, is the guarantee of that same loan unenforceable against Brown?

e) Can Brown claim a credit for the $10,000 account receivable which the bank refused to collect?

f) Can Brown claim a credit for wages owed him by the corporation?

g) Can the bank claim the $15,000 on the corporate credit card account against Brown? Can Brown set off the $10,000 used by the president of the corporation fraudulently for personal expenses?

5. Barry and Denise Grierson have agreed to jointly and severally indemnify Frobisher Trust Company for a loan made to their small business, Barden Ltd. If Barden were to default on its payments under the loan, which of the following could the bank do?

a) Frobisher Trust Company must first attempt to collect the money from Barden Ltd. before contacting the Griersons.

b) The bank must sue both Barry and Denise Grierson for the default on the loan.

6. Loans officers normally require a shareholder as a guarantor whenever a loan is being made to a small corporation because:

a) they prefer dealing with real people rather than legal fictions

b) limited liability means that only the corporation's assets are available if the loan goes into default

c) the guarantee would allow the lending institution to step around other creditors of the corporation to obtain its money directly from the shareholder
   (More than one answer may be correct.)

7. Dominik Borgia is an accountant. When his secretary took a three-week leave of absence for an operation, Borgia called a placement agency and arranged for a temporary secretary. Part of the job of Borgia's regular secretary was to prepare cheques to pay for office expenses.

Six weeks after Borgia's regular secretary returned to work, it was discovered that the temporary secretary had forged and cashed two cheques totalling $15,000. Borgia has advised the bank that he expects it to reimburse him for the forged cheques. The bank replied it had no interest in his claim.

a) What further information would you want to know to determine whether the bank's position is a valid one?

8. Which of the following are negotiable instruments?

a) a cheque

b) a promissory note

c) a bill of sale

d) a **certified cheque** (a cheque on which a bank has indicated that it will be cashed when presented for payment)

e) an IOU

f) a bill of exchange

certified cheque
a cheque on which a bank has indicated that it will be cashed when presented for payment

9. Gabe Rufo and Muriel Napier operated a partnership that specialized in installing new drains. The firm was called Down the Tubes. Napier and her crew had completed a drain installation for an elderly gentleman, who was bedridden. When giving the customer a quote for the installation, Napier had placed a piece of paper in front of him, saying, "This is a work order—sign here." The elderly man, who was a friend of Napier's family, had misplaced his reading glasses and relied on the young woman to tell him the contents of the paper before he signed.

In reality, what he signed was a promissory note obligating him to pay $10,000 on demand. Napier later endorsed the promissory note to Quickin Finance Co. When Quickin presented the note to the old gentleman for payment, he refused to pay it, claiming he had never signed a promissory note.

a) What is the legal status of Quickin?

b) Would Quickin be successful in enforcing the note against the elderly gentleman?

c) If the promissory note had been endorsed to Rufo as an individual, instead of to Quickin, what would his status be?

d) Would the elderly gentleman have a defence to payment on the promissory note if Rufo was the person seeking to enforce it against him? If so, what is the nature of that defence?

10. Who has the responsibility for marking "consumer note" on a promissory note used in a consumer transaction?

a) the vendor

b) the purchaser

c) the bank

d) a holder in due course

e) a third party receiving the promissory note endorsed by the vendor

11. Identify the following clauses from the example Bank Guarantee Form in the Appendix.

a) entire agreement clause

b) governing law clause

c) acceleration clause

d) interest default clause

e) material variation clause

f) mailbox rule clause

12. Review the *Raymond Bibaud v. Banque de Montréal* case.

a) The case involves a buyer, a builder and a banker. What are the technical names for Bibaud, Pine Lake and the Banque de Montréal as parties to the cheques? What was he purchasing?

b) If Pine Lake had kept the postdated cheques (and not endorsed them to the bank), could Bibaud have stopped payment on them?

c) Why could the bank cash Bibaud's postdated cheques when Pine Lake had defaulted on the building contract?

d) What could Bibaud have done to better protect himself?

13. In his book *The Wealthy Barber Returns*, David Chilton warns that banks are a business and do not have their customers interests at heart but rather are motivated to make the most money from their customers. Is there a conflict of interest when banks gives advice to customers about financial planning, which stockbroker firms to use and insurance, or his opinion wrong?

14. What is the nature of each of the following types of property?

a) the name associated with a doughnut/coffee-shop franchise

b) a prize-winning show dog

c) a mobile home

d) a company's outstanding invoices to customers

e) an office building

f) a computer disk containing the original program for a highly successful word-processing program

g) an acre of undeveloped land

15. Claudia Regona bought three videos that she found in a bin of previously viewed tapes at a video store. In talking to the owner, Regona mentioned that she had always wanted to operate her own video-rental outlet. The owner said that he wanted to get out of the business, and was trying to sell off his entire stock of tapes. He offered them to Regona at a price she could not refuse. To avoid tax, she arranged to pay cash for the entire inventory.

Later that day, after renting a truck and visiting her bank to pick up the cash, Regona moved all the videos from the store to her basement. The next day, she was contacted by the Central Bank, which claimed it had a lien registered against all the videotapes owned by the video store.

a) Is the lien enforceable against the three tapes that Regona bought from the bin of previously viewed videos?

b) Is the lien enforceable against the sale by the owner of the entire inventory of the store?

c) What steps should Regona have taken to protect her interests?

16. Rod Smith lived in Vancouver, British Columbia. He borrowed $10,000 from the Bank of Victoria to purchase a car, and the bank secured the loan by a chattel mortgage on the vehicle. Several months later, Smith found a contract job in Ontario for a period of one year. Two months after relocating to Ontario, Smith defaulted on his loan payments. The Bank of Victoria repossessed the car and sold it at auction. The bank received $6,000 from the sale of the car, and is now bringing a court action against Smith in Ontario for the balance of the $10,000 loan.

a) Does Smith have a defence to the bank's court action for the balance of the outstanding loan?

17. Helen Symanski responded to a newspaper advertisement selling a 1992 Mustang. After negotiating with the owner, Symanski bought the car for an exceptionally good price, paying cash. Three days later, hearing a noise in her driveway, she looked out the window to see the car being towed away. She later discovered that a bank had a registered lien against the car.

Symanski claims she had no knowledge of the bank's lien, and was totally unaware that liens could be registered. The previous owner has already spent the money and she cannot get anything back from him. The bank claimed Symanski owed it $1,500 on the lien, as well as $250 in repossession charges—a total of $1,750.

a) Does Symanski have to pay the bank, or does her right to the car take priority over the bank's?

b) Can she successfully argue against having to pay the $250 in repossession charges?

c) If the car had been parked in Symanski's garage, what procedure would the bank have had to take in order to repossess the car?

d) Assume the same facts as above, except that the owner took out a bank loan on August 1, and signed a chattel mortgage on the Mustang for $5,000. Symanski does know that she must search for liens, and obtains a lien-clearance certificate. On August 2, she purchases the car from the owner, and transfers ownership that same day. The bank registers its chattel mortgage on August 3. Subsequently, the owner defaults on the loan. Can the bank claim a lien on the car for $5,000?

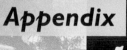

Bank Guarantee Form

GUARANTEE
to the Bank of Credit and Commerce

IN CONSIDERATION OF THE BANK OF CREDIT AND COMMERCE (herein called the "Bank")
agreeing to deal with or to continue to deal with

Joseph Fine o/a Smythe & Fine
....

(herein called the "Customer"), the undersigned and each of them, if more than one, hereby jointly and severally guarantees payment to the Bank of all debts and liabilities, present or future, direct or indirect, absolute or contingent, matured or not, at any time owing by the Customer to the Bank or remaining unpaid by the Customer to the Bank, whether arising from dealings between the Bank and the Customer or from other dealings or proceedings by which the Bank may be or become in any manner whatever a creditor of the Customer, and wherever incurred, and whether incurred by the Customer alone or with another or others and whether as principal or surety, including all interest, commissions, legal and other costs, charges and expenses (such debts and liabilities being herein called the "guaranteed liabilities"), the liability of the undersigned hereunder being limited to the sum of

Forty-Eight Thousand
Insert Limit, if any. . . . . dollars

with interest from the date of demand for payment at the rate set out in paragraph 5 hereof.

AND THE UNDERSIGNED and each of them, if more than one, hereby jointly
and severally agrees with the Bank as follows:

1. In this guarantee the word "Guarantor" shall mean the undersigned and, if there is more than one guarantor, it shall mean each of them.

2. This guarantee shall be a continuing guarantee of all the guaranteed liabilities and shall apply to and secure any ultimate balance due or remaining unpaid to the Bank; and this guarantee shall not be considered as wholly or partially satisfied by the payment or liquidation at any time of any sum of money for the time being due or remaining unpaid to the Bank.

3. The Bank shall not be bound to exhaust its recourse against the Customer or others or any securities or other guarantees it may at any time hold before being entitled to payment from the Guarantor, and the Guarantor renounces all benefits of discussion and division.

4. The Guarantor's liability to make payment under this guarantee shall arise forthwith after demand for payment has been made in writing on the undersigned or any one of them, if more than one, and such demand shall be deemed to have been effectually made when an envelope containing such demand addressed to the undersigned or such one of them at the address of the undersigned or such one of them last known to the Bank is posted, postage prepaid, in the post office; and the Guarantor's liability shall bear interest from the date of such demand at the rate set out in paragraph 5 hereof.

5. The rate of interest payable by the Guarantor from the date of a demand for payment under this guarantee shall be the Bank's prime rate applicable at the time of demand, PLUS 2% per annum.

6. Upon default in payment of any sum owing by the Customer to the Bank at any time, the Bank may treat all guaranteed liabilities as due and payable and may forthwith collect from the Guarantor the total amount hereby guaranteed and may apply the sum so collected upon the guaranteed liabilities or may place it to the credit of a special account. A written statement of a Manager or Acting Manager of a branch of the Bank at which an account of the Customer is kept or of a General Manager of the Bank at which an account of the Customer is kept or of a General Manager of the Bank as to the amount remaining unpaid to the Bank at any time by the Customer shall, if agreed to by the Customer, be conclusive evidence and shall, in any event, be prima facie evidence against the Guarantor as to the amount remaining unpaid to the Bank at such time by the Customer.

7. This guarantee shall be in addition to and not in substitution for any other guarantees or other securities which the Bank may now or hereafter hold in respect of the guaranteed liabilities and the Bank shall be under no obligation to marshal in favour of the Guarantor any other guarantees or other securities or any moneys or other assets which the Bank may be entitled to receive or may have a claim upon; and no loss of or in respect of or unenforceability of any other guarantees or other securities which the Bank may now or hereafter hold in respect of the guaranteed liabilities, whether occasioned by the fault of the Bank or otherwise, shall in any way limit or lessen the Guarantor's liability.

8. Without prejudice to or in any way limiting or lessening the Guarantor's liability and without obtaining the consent of or giving notice to the Guarantor, the Bank may discontinue, reduce, increase or otherwise vary the credit of the Customer, may grant time, renewals, extensions, indulgences, releases and discharges to and accept compositions from or otherwise deal with the Customer and others, including the Guarantor and any other guarantor as the Bank may see fit, and the Bank may take, abstain from taking or perfecting, vary, exchange, renew, discharge, give up, realize on or otherwise deal with securities and guarantees in such manner as the Bank may see fit, and the Bank may apply all moneys received from the Customer or others or from securities or guarantees upon such parts of the guaranteed liabilities as the Bank may see fit and change any such application in whole or in part from time to time.

9. Until repayment in full of all the guaranteed liabilities, all dividends, compositions, proceeds of securities, securities valued or payments received by the Bank from the Customer or others or from estates in respect of the guaranteed liabilities shall be regarded for all purposes as payments in gross without any right on the part of the Guarantor to claim the benefit thereof in reduction of the liability under this guarantee, and the Guarantor shall not claim any set-off or counterclaim against the Customer in respect of any liability of the Customer to the Guarantor, claim or prove in the bankruptcy or insolvency of the Customer in competition with the Bank or have any right to be subrogated to the Bank.

10. This guarantee shall not be discharged or otherwise affected by the death or loss of capacity of the Customer, by any change in the name of the Customer, or in the membership of the Customer, if a partnership, or in the objects, capital structure or constitution of the Customer, if a corporation, or by the sale of the Customer's business or any part thereof or by the Customer being amalgamated with a corporation, but shall, notwithstanding any such event, continue to apply to all guaranteed liabilities whether theretofore or thereafter incurred; and in the case of a change in the membership of a Customer which is a partnership or in the case of the Customer being amalgamated with a corporation, this guarantee shall apply to the liabilities of the resulting partnership or corporation, and the term "Customer" shall include each such resulting partnership and corporation.

11. All advances, renewals and credits made or granted by the Bank purportedly to or for the Customer after the death, loss of capacity, bankruptcy or insolvency of the Customer, but before the Bank has received notice thereof shall be deemed to form part of the guaranteed liabilities; and all advances, renewals and credits obtained from the Bank purportedly by or on behalf of the Customer shall be deemed to form part of the guaranteed liabilities, notwithstanding any lack or limitation of power, incapacity or disability of the Customer or of the directors, partners or agents thereof, or that the Customer may not be a legal or suable entity, or any irregularity, defect or informality in the obtaining of such advances, renewals or credits, whether or not the Bank had knowledge thereof; and any such advance, renewal or credit which may not be recoverable from the undersigned as guarantor(s) shall be recoverable from the undersigned and each of them, if more than one, jointly and severally as principal debtor(s) in respect thereof and shall be paid to the Bank on demand with interest at the rate set out in paragraph 5 hereof.

12. All debts and liabilities, present and future, of the Customer to the Guarantor are hereby assigned to the Bank and postponed to the guaranteed liabilities, and all moneys received by the Guarantor in respect thereof shall be received in trust for the Bank and forthwith upon receipt shall be paid over to the Bank, the whole without in any way lessening or limiting the liability of the Guarantor under this guarantee; and this assignment and postponement is independent of the guarantee and shall remain in full force and effect until repayment in full to the Bank of all the guaranteed liabilities, notwithstanding that the liability of the undersigned or any of them under this guarantee may have been discharged or terminated.

13. The undersigned or any of them, if more than one, or his or their executors or administrators, by giving thirty days' notice in writing to the branch of the Bank at which the main account of the Customer is kept, may terminate his or their further liability under this guarantee in respect of liabilities of the Customer incurred or arising after the expiration of such thirty days, but not in respect of any guaranteed liabilities incurred or arising before the expiration of such thirty days even though not then matured; provided that notwithstanding receipt of any such notice the Bank may fulfil any requirements of the Customer based on agreements express or implied made prior to the expiration of such thirty days and any resulting liabilities shall be covered by this guarantee; and provided further that in the event of the termination of this guarantee as to one or more of the undersigned, if more than one, it shall remain a continuing guarantee as to the other or others of the undersigned.

14. This guarantee embodies all the agreements between the parties hereto relative to the guarantee, assignment and postponement and none of the parties shall be bound by any representation or promise made by any person relative thereto which is not embodied herein; and it is specifically agreed that the Bank shall not be bound by any representation or promises made by the Customer to the Guarantor. Possession of this instrument by the Bank shall be conclusive evidence against the Guarantor that the instrument was not delivered in escrow or pursuant to any agreement that it should not be effective until any condition precedent or subsequent has been complied with and this guarantee shall be operative and binding notwithstanding the non-execution thereof by any proposed signatory.

15. This guarantee shall be governed in all respects by the laws of the Province or jurisdiction in which the Customer's main account with the Bank is kept.

16. This guarantee shall not be discharged or affected by the death or any disability of the undersigned or any of them, if more than one, and shall enure to the benefit of and be binding upon the Bank, its successors and assigns, and the Guarantor, his heirs, executors, administrators, successors and assigns.

AS WITNESS the hand and seal of the Guarantor at _____ ,

this _____ day of _____ , 20 _____.

SIGNED SEALED AND DELIVERED
   in the presence of

                                    SIGNATURE AND SEAL

| DATE RECEIVED |
| .... |
| RECORDED |
| .... |
| APPROVED |
| .... |
| E.O. AUDITOR |
| .... |

_____

N.B.–Signature of this Guarantee involves personal liability.

12

Bankruptcy

What Is Bankruptcy?

It has often been said that everybody loses when a business goes bankrupt. The owner loses the business and the investment, creditors lose money since they are not paid in full, employees lose jobs, suppliers lose a customer, and customers lose a source of supply.

A new *Bankruptcy and Insolvency Act* (BIA) was passed by the federal government in 1992 with significant changes made in 2009 to reform bankruptcy law and shift the emphasis from merely distributing a bankrupt's assets among creditors to providing possibilities for saving the business. The main purposes of the act are:

- to ensure a fair distribution of the bankrupt's assets among creditors
- to save any ongoing business where possible
- to release an honest but unfortunate debtor from debts where the burden is too great to allow a fresh start

Many famous people have taken advantage of the second chance of bankruptcy including: Abraham Lincoln, Henry Ford, Walt Disney and not least on the list, Donald Trump.

Both businesses and individuals can go bankrupt and it is a very common occurrence. Many businesses and individuals that are close to going bankrupt may try to avoid it through a proposal procedure. A **proposal** is a plan submitted to their creditors to restructure their debt. If the creditors accept the proposal, bankruptcy can be avoided. In Canada in 2013 there were 69,224 consumer bankruptcies and another 49,454 consumer proposals filed under the BIA to avoid bankruptcy, for a total of 118,678 that year, or about 325 every day. In 2013 there were 3,187 businesses that went bankrupt and another 1,094 filed proposals under the BIA to avoid bankruptcy, or close to 12 per day. In the same year another 32 larger companies that each owed more than $5 million filed an arrangement under the Company Creditors Arrangement Act (CCAA) to avoid bankruptcy (Source: Industry Canada).

There are businesses to which the BIA does not apply; banks, trust companies, insurance companies and railways. Individual farmers and fishermen cannot be forced into bankruptcy, though they can do it voluntarily.

A person is considered to be **insolvent** when they are unable to pay their debts as they become due and they owe at least $1,000, but they are not necessarily bankrupt. The typical person who goes bankrupt is a 43 year old male who owes about $60,000 not including a home mortgage and had been working in the past year. The major sources of their debts are:

proposal
a procedure where a debtor by agreement with their creditors reorganizes their debts without going bankrupt

insolvent
a party is unable to pay their debts as they become due

mortgages, credit card bills, bank loans, unpaid taxes and loans from other sources. The major causes of individual bankruptcy have been found to be: financial mismanagement, job loss or a reduction in employment income, illness and medical problems, separation or divorce, a failed business, unexpected events such as accidents or death of a family member and gambling addictions. Often it is a combination of several of these factors. The typical business that went bankrupt in 2013 owed just less than $700,000.

trustee in bankruptcy

the person who administers the property of a bankrupt for the benefit of creditors

If a person or a company goes bankrupt their assets are transferred to a **Trustee in Bankruptcy**. The trustee in bankruptcy is a highly skilled professional, and is an accountant who has been licensed by the Superintendent of Bankruptcy. The trustee will guide the debtor through the proposal or bankruptcy process, determine the debtor's liabilities and deal with the debtor's assets for the benefit of the creditors in accordance with the legal requirements. The Superintendent of Bankruptcy for Canada appoints Official Receivers for the bankruptcy districts across Canada. The trustee then deals with the appropriate local Official Receiver for the bankrupt individual or company.

How Is Bankruptcy Declared?

There are three ways in which a bankruptcy can happen:

- voluntarily
- involuntarily
- by rejection of a commercial proposal

Voluntary

No one wants to file for bankruptcy. But when situations such as extraordinary health-care costs or business setbacks occur, it can become impossible to meet heavy financial obligations. In these circumstances, both individuals and corporations can apply to the court and make a **voluntary assignment** into bankruptcy.

assignment in bankruptcy

a voluntary declaration of bankruptcy

The general test to justify voluntary bankruptcy is that is has become absolutely impossible to pay the debts owing. What a court considers impossible will vary with individual circumstances, and advice should be sought from a specialist. Many trustees in bankruptcy as well as bankruptcy lawyers offer a free initial half-hour consultation.

Involuntary

If a business's creditors have tried unsuccessfully to collect their debts by other means, they may decide to force the business into bankruptcy. This is done by way of a petition to the court. If the court agrees, it will make a **receiving order** (a court order for the transfer of debtor's assets to a trustee in bankruptcy), finding that the person is bankrupt. In order to initiate the process, a creditor must be owed a debt of more than $1,000, and the debtor must have committed an act of bankruptcy as set out in the act.

receiving order

a court order for the transfer of debtor's assets to a trustee in bankruptcy

If the business is a corporation, the corporation is declared bankrupt. If the business is not incorporated (e.g., a partnership), individual partners are petitioned personally and declared bankrupt.

The Bankruptcy and Insolvency Act   Three of the most common acts of bankruptcy are listed in this excerpt from subsection 42(1) of the act:

> a debtor commits an act of bankruptcy in each of the following cases: . . .
>
> (f) If he admits to any meeting of his creditors in any statement of his assets and liabilities that show that he is insolvent, or

presents or causes to be presented to any such meeting a written admission of his inability to pay his debts; or . . .

(h) If he gives notice to any of his creditors that he has suspended, or is about to suspend payment of his debts; or . . .

(j) If he ceases to meet his liabilities generally as they become due.

■ *Business Law*   Applied

❶ Joan Carlucci carries on business as Aquarius Electronics Company. The firm's debts are too high, and it cannot continue in business. Carlucci wants to know if the company can declare bankruptcy.

   a) Can Aquarius Electronics Company file for bankruptcy?

Proposals and Arrangements

Bankruptcy has serious legal implications. It will mark the end for a business and in a personal bankruptcy individuals may lose many of their assets and their credit rating will be negatively affected, so most debtors want to avoid bankruptcy if at all possible. When a debtor has financial problems they should try to negotiate with their creditors to come up with a workable financial solution. For many individual debtors with multiple credit card debts, consolidating their debts into one loan at a lower interest rate may sometimes be possible. If these informal attempts by the debtor on their own are unsuccessful, the debtor can have a trustee in bankruptcy work with them to file a formal legal proposal to try to avoid bankruptcy, or it if it a large corporation it can seek protection under the Companies' Creditors Arrangement Act. The rules vary depending on the debtor and the amount owed.

1) Division 1 Proposal—Commercial Proposal

A Division 1 Proposal under the BIA, often referred to as a Commercial Proposal, can be used by any commercial debtor or by any individual, usually someone who owes more than $250,000 not including a home mortgage. It usually is a plan whereby the debtor proposes to pay off a percentage of its debts over an extended period of time. Some debts such as money owed to the government and employees must be paid in full. The notice of the intention to file a proposal is given to the creditors and then the debtor has 30 days to come up with the actual proposal, though time extensions can be granted for up to 6 months. The trustee works with the debtor on how to restructure the debt. Once the proposal is completed, a meeting of the creditors occurs and they vote on the proposal. Secured and unsecured creditors vote separately and in each creditor group a majority by number and a two-thirds majority by value must agree for the proposal to be accepted. If it is accepted by the creditors, it is then submitted to the court for approval. This is not usually a problem so long as the proposal is reasonable and the unsecured creditors are receiving at least 50 per cent of what they are owed. If the creditors vote no to the proposal then the debtor automatically goes into bankruptcy.

2) Division 2 Proposal—Consumer Proposal

A Division 2 Proposal is commonly known as a Consumer Proposal as any insolvent person who owes less than $250,000, not including a home mortgage, may make this proposal to their creditors. It is a much simpler process than a Division 1 Proposal and usually does not require a meeting with the creditors unless 25 per cent of the creditors by value request it. The proposal is prepared by an Administrator, usually a trustee, who examines the debtor's finances. The Administrator then suggests restructuring and/or reduction of the debt payments (often individuals pay about 30–50% of the amount owed) over a period of 5 years or less. The Administrator provides debt counselling and files the proposal with the Official Receiver. The creditors have 45 days to decide on the proposal, or if no meeting was requested, then the proposal is deemed accepted. Court approval is not required. If the proposal is accepted the debtor makes their payments to the Administrator who then pays the creditors. While the proposal is in effect the consumer is protected against landlords terminating their lease, utility companies shutting off their services or other creditors accelerating installment payments. If a consumer proposal is rejected by creditors the debtor is not automatically bankrupt. They can amend the terms of the proposal and resubmit it or consider other alternatives including voluntary bankruptcy. The debtor must attend two mandatory financial counselling sessions and the proposal will be on their credit rating for three years after their last payment is made.

3) An Arrangement under The Companies' Creditors Arrangement Act (CCAA)

For a corporation that owes more than $5 million and wants to avoid bankruptcy, the corporation may chose not do a Division 1 Proposal under the BIA, but instead it would seek protection from its creditors and attempt to restructure its debt using the provisions of the Companies' Creditors Arrangement Act (CCAA). It is similar to what is called a Chapter 11 of the U.S. Bankruptcy Code. This federal law gives the corporation much more flexibility and time (sometimes it takes 2 years) to come up with a plan to avoid bankruptcy through a **compromise and arrangement** with the creditors. The purpose of the CCAA is to permit a corporation to restructure itself into a more efficient operation, less burdened by debt and with a good chance of recovery and a return to profitability. It may involve selling off major assets, shutting down divisions and laying off many workers if that is what it requires for survival. Some major Canadian corporations such as Air Canada, Stelco and General Motors have used CCAA protection to avoid bankruptcy. These are major companies and their collapse would have caused significant economic problems.

During the reorganization the court appoints a **monitor**, usually a large accounting firm, to supervise the process and none of the corporation's creditors, not even secured creditors, can take any action to collect the money owed to them except through this reorganization process. Special protection can be given to directors, critical suppliers and interim financers during the restructuring. Each class of creditors vote separately and within each class two–thirds of the creditors by value and a majority by number must accept for the arrangement to gain approval. The final step in the process is then court approval. If the creditors vote to reject the arrangement, bankruptcy is not automatic. Creditors however can then take action to pursue their claims, such as force the sale of secured assets, so the company often ends up in bankruptcy proceedings.

Example: In 2003 Air Canada was in a desperate financial situation. It had purchased its main rival Canadian Airlines in 2001 and was deeply in debt and was prohibited by the government from reducing its surplus staff. Then in 2001 the terrorist attacks on the World Trade Centre in New York City dramatically cut air travel around the globe and put most major airlines on the brink of financial ruin. Since Air Canada was the only national airline in Canada and serviced many unprofitable routes to unpopular areas of the country no other airlines would fly, many people and the government did not want Air Canada to collapse. Faced with debts of over $12 billion, Air Canada sought protection under the CCAA.

The restructuring process took almost 2 years to complete as various plans and refinancing schemes were considered and reworked. Eventually Air Canada terminated 6,400 workers and the remaining workers accepted almost $1 billion in pay cuts. Air Canada got a loan from General Electric for $540 million and another loan from a German bank for $850 million. A new corporation, Ace Aviation, was formed and sales of its shares raised an additional $1 billion. Through these actions, Air Canada cut its debt down to $5 billion and the company continues to operate.

Business Law   Applied

❷ **Business has gone** badly for the Wellington Corporation, and it cannot continue to pay its creditors. Prescott Manufacturers, which supplied Wellington with an essential manufacturing machine, is threatening to repossess that machine. Wellington Corporation has a very good chance of securing a large contract that will help turn its fortunes around. However, Prescott refuses to wait for payment.

   a) Can the Wellington Corporation take any steps to stop the supplier from taking its machine?
   b) If so, for how long would the delay remain in effect?

❸ **Salvadore Holdings Limited** runs a plant that is heavily dependent on electricity, and has accumulated very large arrears on its account with the hydro company. The electricity supplier has threatened to cut off Salvadore unless the full amount owing is paid immediately. To make Salvadore's life even more difficult, a supplier of leather—vital to their production—has refused to provide any further product.

   a) Is there any remedy that Salvadore Holdings can take to prevent the hydro company from cutting off the supply of electricity?
   b) Will the hydro company have to supply electricity in the future? If so, on what basis?
   c) Can Salvadore Holdings obtain an order making the leather supplier continue to supply leather?

What Happens When Bankruptcy Is Declared?

On bankruptcy, the assets of the insolvent person are transferred into the possession of the trustee in bankruptcy. Where the bankrupt is a business, the trustee will take over the business and decide whether to try to continue to run the operation for a time, or to liquidate it immediately.

The trustee will examine the affairs of the bankrupt and report to creditors on the assets and liabilities. The trustee will also determine whether there have been any illegal transfers of assets. The official receiver may also interview the bankrupt to determine whether there have any fraudulent transactions.

Creditors will file a proof of claim and, in bankruptcy of businesses, are then entitled to attend a meeting of creditors to discuss the trustee's report and decide whether any action should be taken to recover assets.

Types of Creditors

There are three categories of creditors in a bankruptcy:

- secured
- preferred
- unsecured

Secured

These are creditors who hold some form of security, such as a mortgage or general security agreement (GSA), on the assets of the bankrupt, and therefore have claim on the particular property named in that security. If the security is sold and does not cover the debt, then the secured creditor can claim before an unsecured creditor for the balance owing. If, for example, a building owned by a bankrupt business is sold for $400,000, and the bank has an outstanding mortgage of $500,000, the bank receives the $400,000, but must claim as an unsecured creditor for the additional $100,000. The bank's claim takes precedence over that of other unsecured creditors.

Preferred

The act specifically creates a class of preferred creditors who have priority over unsecured creditors. Preferred creditors include:

- funeral directors for funeral expenses relating to the bankrupt, if deceased
- trustee's and lawyer's fees incurred in carrying out the bankruptcy
- employees' wages for six months, to a limit of $2,000 per person
- municipal taxes up to 2 years
- landlord's unpaid rent for up to 3 years
- amounts owed to government agencies for taxes and worker's compensation

The trustee cannot move down the list until the preferred creditor above is fully paid.

Unsecured

unsecured creditors

creditors who have no security interest (such as a mortgage) in the bankrupt debtor's property

Unsecured creditors are creditors who have no security interest (such as a mortgage) in the bankrupt debtor's property. These are persons to whom the bankrupt owes money, but who fall outside the other two categories. The most common examples are a supplier of goods on credit who has not been paid and employees for unpaid wages in excess of $2,000.

If there is any money left after all the preferred creditors are fully paid, then the remaining money is divided among the unsecured creditors in proportion to how much each is owed. Often unsecured creditors receive between 0–50% of the money they are owed.

For example: In a bankruptcy unsecured creditors are owed a total of $300,000, unsecured creditor A is owed $150,000 (50%) and unsecured creditors B and C are each owed $75,000 (25% each). If there is $60,000 available for unsecured creditors in the bankruptcy, creditor A gets $30,000 and creditors B and C each get $15,000.

Payment of Creditors

This is a simplified version of what occurs in a bankruptcy distribution:

- The secured creditors take the assets subject to their security.
- If there is any money left over, the preferred creditors are paid in order of priority as they are listed in the act.
- If there is any money remaining after all preferred creditors are fully paid, it is divided among the unsecured creditors in proportion to how much each is owed. Unsecured creditors often receive very little of what they are owed.

■ *Business Law*   Applied

❹ **Padme Nanda is** the sole shareholder, director, and officer of Ganesh Imports Inc. The outstanding debts of the company total $200,000. Because it cannot meet its liabilities when they become due, Ganesh is declared bankrupt on August 1. At the time, the business has the following assets:

- a store valued at $100,000
- unpaid accounts from customers in the amount of $10,000
- inventory of small furniture and accessories valued at $10,000

Nanda also owns a house and a car, but he does not declare personal bankruptcy.

Scenario 1

a) Which of the above assets form part of the estate of the bankrupt company and can be sold so that the proceeds can be distributed to the creditors?

Scenario 2

One of the suppliers of Ganesh, who is owed $200,000, started a court action to reclaim that debt. Nanda also gave a personal guarantee of this debt, and has been sued in the same action. Neither Nanda nor the company has defended. On August 2, the supplier wants to obtain a default judgment against Ganesh and against Nanda personally.

b) Will the supplier succeed?

Scenario 3

The store has been sold for $100,000 and the other assets for $10,000. The following creditors prove their claims in the bankruptcy of Ganesh:

- the bank which holds a mortgage on the store: $90,000
- trustee in bankruptcy for fees: $10,000
- supplier of inventory: $20,000

c) Under which category of creditor does each of the above fall according to the *Bankruptcy and Insolvency Act?*
d) What amount will each receive on the distribution of the bankrupt corporation's estate?

Wage Claims   Under the *Bankruptcy and Insolvency Act*, the employee has a wage claim as a preferred creditor for up to six months' unpaid wages, to a limit of $2,000. This is against the corporation only. It is very unlikely that there will be sufficient assets to cover even preferred claimants' amounts.

Under the various corporations acts, the employee can make a claim against the directors personally if the business goes bankrupt. Also, many provincial governments have set up unpaid-wages funds for employees' claims, up to a limit of about $5,000 if both of the above remedies are valueless to employees.

Suppliers of Goods

A thorny problem in bankruptcy situations has been the position of a business that supplies a large quantity of **goods**—personal property consisting of tangible items that can be bought and sold—to the bankrupt and is not paid for the inventory. The trustee in bankruptcy will take this inventory, sell it, and distribute the proceeds among all the creditors. Usually the preferred creditors will take all, and the supplier will get nothing—even though it was the supplier's product that was sold.

The BIA contains provisions that give an unpaid supplier the right to the return of goods delivered in the 30 days prior to the bankruptcy. However, for many reasons, this right is generally considered to be ineffective. The provision relates only to goods supplied up to 30 days before the date of the bankruptcy, a time period unlikely to include many of the goods supplied.

A far more effective remedy for suppliers of goods on credit is the purchase money security interest (PMSI) discussed in Chapter 12. A supplier can register a PMSI in provinces that have a *Personal Property Security Act*, thus ensuring the right to take back all goods supplied but not paid for.

goods
personal property consisting of tangible items that can be bought and sold

Fraudulent Transactions in Bankruptcy

The main actions designated by the BIA as probably being undertaken in an attempt to defraud creditors are:

- gifts given to anyone by the bankrupt one year before the bankruptcy, if the trustee can prove that the now-bankrupt was insolvent at the time the gift was made. If the gift is to a relative the time extends to five years.
- payment for services or transfer of property to any related person one year before the bankruptcy. Such a transaction is a reviewable transaction.
- payment given to a creditor in preference over other creditors. A solvent business can pay creditors in any order that it wishes. However, if the business is insolvent, it must pay all creditors equally. The time limit for preferences is three months preceding the bankruptcy; however, if the payment is to a relative, the time limit is 12 months before the bankruptcy.
- payments to shareholders, either by way of dividend or repurchase of shares, made one year before the bankruptcy.
- taking any assets from the business and hiding them, or giving them to others to do so—this is a criminal offence.

The act also provides that these actions—named deceptive practices by the bankrupt during the course of the bankruptcy—are criminal offences. If fraudulent conduct occurred the trustee can void the transaction, recover the money and seek criminal penalties.

Investigation of a Bankrupt's Actions

fraudulent preference
an insolvent debtor's preferring (and paying) one creditor over another

The bankrupt's improper actions are usually divided into two categories, known as fraudulent conveyance and **fraudulent preference** (an insolvent debtor's preferring (and paying) one creditor over another). An individual facing bankruptcy might take steps to place assets out of the reach of creditors. The *Bankruptcy and Insolvency Act* contains rules that target certain transactions, automatically declaring them ineffective, or presuming them to have been made with the intention of defrauding creditors. There are usually three factors involved in deciding whether this type of transaction has taken place:

- value given or received—either too much or too little is paid for the property or services
- timing—the event took place close to the date bankruptcy was declared, when the business was insolvent
- relationship—the transaction was done with a relative or close friend, or a related corporation

arm's length
between persons who are not related or associated in any way

One of the key concepts is the non-arm's-length, or related-party, transaction. (A transaction is **arm's length** if it is between persons who are not related or associated in any way.) This is a transaction between the near-bankrupt and close friends or relatives who help the debtor to keep assets beyond the reach of creditors. Since corporations are often used today, they can be substituted for relatives. So, any corporation which is owned or controlled by a bankrupt is considered a related party.

If a person lies, hides assets, falsifies, alters or destroys records in a bankruptcy proceeding there are fines of up to $10,000 and or jail for up to 3 years possible under the BIA. Directors and officers can also be sued in a corporate bankruptcy if they did not act properly.

■ *Critical Concepts of* Bankruptcy

- Both individuals and businesses can go bankrupt either voluntarily or be forced into bankruptcy
- Both individuals and businesses may create a proposal that can restructure their debts and if the creditors accept it they can avoid bankruptcy
- A trustee in bankruptcy deals with the debtor's assets and if the assets are sold distributes the proceeds to the creditors in a specific order: secured, preferred and unsecured creditors
- If there are fraudulent conveyances or preferences given to defeat the interests of the creditors, the trustee can void the transactions and recover the money
- In a consumer bankruptcy the individual is allowed to keep certain personal assets that the trustee cannot take
- In a consumer bankruptcy certain debts are not discharged such as spousal and child support, debts due to crime and student loans less than 7 years old
- In a consumer bankruptcy the individual is discharged from their debts usually after 9 months and the bankruptcy is on their credit rating for 6 years
- In a business bankruptcy the debts are never discharged unless paid in full, so often the business owners incorporate a new corporation which is not liable for these debts

Tsymbalarou v. Gordon, 2013 ONSC 5358 (CanLII)

Natalia Tsymbalarou and the Business Development Bank of Canada brought an action against Irina Gordon based on fraudulent conveyances. The plaintiffs were seeking a court order that the transfer of two properties made by Gordon to her common law spouse and a shell numbered company that she controlled were void. The plaintiffs' claimed Gordon had transferred these properties to these non-arm's length parties before she declared bankruptcy to avoid creditors' claims.

They allege that Gordon would approach a banking institution or private lender and obtain a business loan for a non-operating business she had, based on the properties that she owned. Then Gordon would spend all that money that she was loaned on her own personal use, and sell the properties to her common law spouse or a non-operating numbered company she controlled for little or nothing. By the time the creditors would take action for their unpaid loans, the assets had been transferred out of her name. When Ms. Gordon made an assignment in bankruptcy, she showed gross assets of $2,122,800 and only $48,700 in estimated realizable value due to the large mortgages on the properties.

Both plaintiffs filed claims with the trustee in bankruptcy handling Gordon's debts. Tsymbalarou claimed she was owed $73,355 and the BDD claimed $104,402. Both plaintiffs wanted the court under the Fraudulent Conveyances Act to void the transfers Gordon had made of two specific properties. These properties would then go back into Gordon's name, so as secured creditors, or the trustee in bankruptcy, could then force the sale of the properties and recover the money for the lenders.

The Court's Decision

The court traced the activities of Gordon and found a pattern of deception. The court noted that to establish fraudulent intent it can be inferred from the surrounding suspicious circumstances known as the "badges of fraud." These badges considered include: the financial situation of the defendant, if the transaction was between relatives or associates, if the transaction would delay, defeat or hinder creditors, if the transaction substantially stripped the defendant of all of her property that would be available to creditors, if little or no consideration was given for the transfer, if the transfer was to others in trust, and the secrecy of the transaction.

The court found that Gordon had exhibited all of these badges of fraud. She had acted fraudulently with her creditors and used forgery and altered documents in her court submissions. She had a pattern of dishonesty and behaviour that had "the effect of hindering, defeating and delaying creditors and which was intended to obstruct the court of justice." The transfer of the properties was just a sham done to try to defeat the claims of creditors.

The plaintiffs had clearly established Gordon's fraudulent conveyances of the two properties. The court ordered that these conveyances were void, so Gordon was therefore the real owner of the properties and they could be sold. The plaintiffs could make their mortgage claims from the sale proceeds and the remainder would go to the trustee in bankruptcy for payment to other creditors.

The "fraudulent" conveyance in the Gordon case above, involved deceitful fraudulent behaviour by the debtor. But frequently a fraudulent conveyance is not done with criminal intent. The creditor that objects to the payment must establish that the "dominant intent" of the incorrect payment was to give a preference to one creditor.

Example: In *Logistec Stevedoring (Atlantic) Inc. v. A.C. Poirier & Associates Inc.*, 2005 NBCA 55 (CanLII), the New Brunswick Court of Appeal overruled a trial court decision that had declared a $562,574 payment to a dockside warehouse to be a fraudulent preference. Though the money had clearly favoured this one unsecured creditor, the debtor company had paid the money so that the pulp held in the warehouse could then be released and sold to generate some income, which in turn could be used to pay other secured and unsecured creditors. Paying that one particular creditor was clearly the best opportunity the company had to try and get some money to stay in business. The Appeal Court ruled that since the payment was not made with the "dominant intent" of preferring one creditor over another, the payment to the warehouse was legal and not a fraudulent preference, so the trustee could not demand repayment.

■ *Business Law* Applied

❺ Susan Suarez runs her own business, a sole proprietorship called Suzy Suarez Designs. The business is doing badly and so, on August 1, she transfers ownership of her house to her husband. On September 1 of the same year, Suarez goes into bankruptcy. The trustee in bankruptcy wants to attack the transfer of the house to the husband.

   a) Are there any special bankruptcy rules that will assist either the trustee or the business owner?

❻ John and Louise Webber were the sole shareholders of Webber Feeds Ltd. As well as being in the feed business, the company owned a few acres of vacant land. One month before Webber Feeds Ltd. went bankrupt, that land was sold for fair market value to John Wilson, Mrs. Webber's brother. At the time of the land sale, Mr. and Mrs. Webber were given an option personally to repurchase the property at the same price. They paid nothing for the option, which was to expire in five years.

One year after the bankruptcy, the land significantly increased in value, and so the Webbers exercised their option and bought the property. The trustee in bankruptcy of Webber Feeds wants to have the Webbers hand over to the trustee the money they made by purchasing the property.

   a) Are there any special bankruptcy rules that will assist the trustee?
   b) Did the option to the Webbers have any value in itself?
   c) If the corporation got fair market value at the time, was there any harm to the creditors because of the transaction?
   d) What test will the court apply to decide whether the Webbers should pay their gain to the trustee?

❼ Verne Wilkinson was the sole shareholder, officer, and director of Cleaningz Eazi Inc. when the firm declared bankruptcy. Wilkinson's aunt was a vice-president of Cleaningz Eazi, and proved a claim in the bankruptcy for unpaid wages in the amount of $5,000.

   a) In which class of creditors is a wage claimant?
   b) Are there any limits on the amount, or can the aunt claim the full $5,000?
   c) Can the aunt claim as a preferred creditor?

❽ The Phoenix Corporation operates a small manufacturing business. It was doing poorly and could not pay its creditors. The major creditor approached the owner and had him give a chattel mortgage on all of the Phoenix Corporation's machinery. The chattel mortgage was publicly registered.

One month after giving the chattel mortgage, the Phoenix Corporation went bankrupt. The trustee in bankruptcy wants to have the chattel mortgage set aside.

    a) Are there any special bankruptcy rules that will assist the trustee?
    b) Are all creditors being treated equally in this situation?

Personal Bankruptcy

In a personal bankruptcy, before the trustee sells the assets of the debtor, the individual is allowed to keep certain assets. It varies among the provinces, for example in Ontario individual debtors can keep:

- $5,650 in personal belongings (e.g. clothing, sports equipment)
- $11,300 in household goods (e.g. furniture, television, appliances)
- One motor vehicle worth up to $5,650 (e.g. car, truck)
- $11,300 worth of tools of the trade (e.g. equipment that you use to earn a living)
- Certain life insurance policies
- Money in a RRSP or RRIF (except amounts deposited within 1 year of the bankruptcy)

For many individuals, these exemptions make up most of their wealth so there are very few assets that the trustee can take to sell to get money for the creditors.

Discharge from Bankruptcy

A **discharge** is a court order whereby a person who has been declared bankrupt ceases to have the status of a bankrupt person. The debtor is given a clean slate and is freed from the obligations to pay the debts. A discharge is given to a corporation only if it is able to pay off its creditors—a very unlikely event.

    Discharges to natural persons are, however, almost automatic for first-time bankruptcies. This allows the person to begin afresh, free of past debts. In deciding whether to grant a discharge, the court will take into account the honesty of the bankrupt, particularly in revealing assets to the trustee. The court will also consider the circumstances contributing to the bankruptcy. If the court finds a bankrupt's conduct to be irresponsible, discharge will be refused.

Example: In *R. v. Messier* [1981], 36 C.B.R. (N.S.) 118 (Alta.Q.B.), a man declared bankruptcy with debts of over $326,406 and assets of only $40,500. He had spent 3 years travelling with the boxer Muhammad Ali and ran up extravagant bills at hotels, restaurants and expensive clothiers, plus debts from gambling and prostitutes. The court refused to discharge him from bankruptcy due to his reprehensible and irresponsible behaviour and lavish lifestyle, so he was still liable for his debts.

Example: In *Wehner, Re (Bankrupt)*, 2000 CanLII 19763 (SK QB) Garnet Wehner had previously declared bankruptcy. His major debt in the first bankruptcy was over $63,000 owed to Revenue Canada for unpaid taxes. When he made his second assignment in bankruptcy he owed over $156,100 in unpaid taxes. He was 43 years old, a self-employed heavy duty mechanic and had an annual income of about $91,000. The court refused to discharge his debts and told him that he should learn to organize his financial affairs and not use the bankruptcy process as a way to avoid paying taxes. He was told he could reapply for discharge after 18 months and the court would reconsider his financial situation at that time.

discharge
a court order whereby a person who has been declared bankrupt ceases to have the status of a bankrupt person

Example: In *Michael Katz (Re)*, 2013 ONSC 7426 (CanLII), the debtor had been a successful real estate developer who became a cocaine addict and then had several large business failures. He owed over $10 million and filed for personal bankruptcy. The process was delayed and after 9 years the court considered whether he should be discharged from these debts. The court noted that he still lived an extravagant life style driving expensive cars and living in wealthy neighbourhoods. He had not worked for several years and appeared to have no interest in working again. His mother owned a real estate company and was supporting him and his family and nothing was in Michael Katz's name. The court ordered Katz to pay $250,000 to the trustee before he could be discharged from his debts.

Most unsecured debts such as credit card debts, bank loans, pay day loans, lines of credit and taxes are discharged by the bankruptcy. Secured debts such as car loans and home mortgages are not discharged unless you surrendered the asset (the house or car) at the start of the bankruptcy.

There are some debts that are not discharged in a bankruptcy and the debtor is still liable to repay. In Ontario the debts not cancelled in a personal bankruptcy include:

- Student loans that exist up to 7 years after you left school
- Spousal and child support payments
- Fines (e.g. parking and speeding tickets) and most court ordered restitution payments
- Debts that arose as a result of fraud or an assault
- Income tax debts over $200,000

If the bankrupt person has complied with all the steps then for a first time bankruptcy they are automatically discharged from all their debts (except for those listed above) after nine months. If it is a person's second bankruptcy then automatic discharge takes 24 months. A first time bankruptcy stays on a person's credit rating for 6 years after the discharge is made and a second bankruptcy stays on a credit rating for 14 years after the second discharge.

If the debtor is employed during the bankruptcy period and makes over a specific net income (threshold level), the money above that threshold limit is considered to be **surplus income** and the debtor is required to pay 50% of the surplus to the trustee for distribution to the creditors. This level is set each year and is based on the size of the debtor's family. For example a single person's threshold in 2014 was $2,014/ month. For example, if that person earned $2,614 net per month, then there would be $600 surplus per month and $300 of it would have to be paid to the trustee to distribute to creditors. For a family of four in 2014 the threshold level was $3,743/month. If there is surplus income, the individual remains a bankrupt for 21 months instead of just 9 months before they are discharged from their debts.

■ *Business Law* Applied

❾ **Dylan graduated** from college 5 years ago and had a good job but he recently separated from his wife and he was injured while snowboarding and Dylan is now out of work. He owes VISA $18,000, a pay day loan company $8,000, his landlord $3,000, Rogers $1,500, unpaid income taxes of $15,000, he owes spousal support of $2,800 and he has a student loan of $22,000. He has $5,000 in a RRSP, $4,000 in government bonds and a car worth $9,000. His furniture is worth about $8,000 and his clothes and watch about $2,500. Dylan is considering his financial options.

a) What are the advantages and disadvantage of Dylan making a proposal or going bankrupt?

b) If he does go bankrupt what debts will or will not be erased due to the bankruptcy, and what assets can he keep?

c) If Dylan is able to get a job, what if any of his income would a trustee in bankruptcy be able to use to pay creditors.

Undischarged Bankrupt   Before a bankrupt is given his discharge that individual has a positive duty to advise anyone doing business with him of his status. Failure to do so means that the debt relating to that transaction is not discharged by the bankruptcy.

Business Alert!

The Toronto-Dominion Bank v. Merenick, 2007 BCSC 1261 (CanLII)

Todd Merenick was a young inexperienced financial consultant who had a short and very unsuccessful career with the Investors Group in Kelowna B.C. Shortly after he started working he received an unsolicited email from Dr. Ahmad Rehman in Nigeria who said he needed help getting $8 million in unused medical grant money out of Nigeria. Merenick was suspicious that it could be a scam, but he continued the correspondence with Rehman hoping that if he moved the money to Canada, Rehman would eventually become his client.

Eventually Rehman sent Merenick a cheque for $82,466 which he was told to deposit in Merenick's own TD bank account and then the next day Merenick was to wire the same amount to a named bank account in Hong Kong. Merenick followed the instructions and after the transfer was made to Hong Kong, TD discovered the original cheque Merenick had deposited was counterfeit and TD was unable to get the money back from the Hong Kong account.

Merenick had been another victim of the infamous Nigerian email scam. As soon as he found out, Merenick told the police, resigned his job, and admitted his liability to the TD bank for $82,466. Soon after, he declared personal bankruptcy.

The TD bank sought a court ruling that the $82,466 debt was incurred due to Merenick's fraudulent misrepresentation to the bank, and therefore the debt could not be discharged by Mereni-

ck's bankruptcy. TD claimed that his nondisclosure to the bank of the suspicious circumstances surrounding the cheque from Rehman and the wire transfer amounted to fraudulent misrepresentation by Merenick, so his debt should not be erased by bankruptcy proceedings.

Merenick claimed that he had been the victim of a fraud, but that he had not committed fraudulent misrepresentation himself. He claimed that he was obviously very negligent, but not fraudulent, so his debt to the bank could be discharged under the bankruptcy law.

The Court's Decision

The court emphasized that for the bank to prove fraudulent misrepresentation by Merenick it had to prove that his representation was false and made without belief in its truth or was recklessly indifferent to whether it was true or false and the bank had relied on the statement in turning over the money.

The judge ruled that Merenick did not owe the bank a duty to disclose the source of the cheque and to warn of its suspicious nature. Merenick had been careless and unwise, but had not acted fraudulently. He was not making any money from this deposit and transfer and he did not commit fraudulent misrepresentation. Therefore his debt to the TD bank could be discharged under his personal bankruptcy proceedings.

How Money Is Made by Going Bankrupt

People are often confused, if not annoyed to see a business person, whose business has declared bankruptcy, driving around town in an expensive car and living in a large house and very soon back in the same or very similar business to the one put into bankruptcy.

How is it done?   First recall how creditor proofing schemes are put in place to separate and protect personal assets such as cars, houses, cottages and such from creditors of the business.

Next understand the practical weaknesses of the sale of assets, or even the entire business, in a bankruptcy. Assets sold in a bankruptcy are usually at liquidation prices, which is often 10% of their value. Thus, if an owner has personal means, or can borrow funds, that owner of that bankrupt business (who knows the value of the assets) can incorporate a new corporation and then outbid any other purchaser of the assets and, in effect, repurchase his business free and clear of all debts for little over 10% of the value of the assets. The new corporation is a separate legal entity so it is not liable for the debts of the old bankrupt company, even though it may have the same owners/shareholders.

In Summation

Bankruptcy

■ Both individuals and companies can declare bankruptcy and they are very common occurrences.

■ Businesses or individuals are insolvent if there are debts greater than $1,000. However, until a receiving order is given or there is a voluntary assignment into bankruptcy, they are not bankrupt.

■ Bankruptcy may occur voluntarily if it has become impossible for the debtor to pay outstanding debts. Involuntary bankruptcy happens when the creditor can show a debt greater than $1,000 and an act of bankruptcy, or if a debtor's proposal for carrying on business is rejected by the majority of creditors.

■ Once an insolvent party files a notice of intention to make a proposal, several important factors come into effect for up to six months to provide some protection from creditors. Ultimately, the proposal must be approved by a majority of creditors in order to be put into effect.

■ A Division 1 Commercial Proposal is used by any company or an individual who owes more than $250,000 excluding a home mortgage. A Division 2 Consumer Proposal is for individuals who owe less than $250,000 and is a less formal procedure

■ Companies that owe more than $5 million can use the more flexible Companies Creditors Arrangement Act (CCAA)to try to restructure their debts and keep the company going and avoid bankruptcy if their creditors agree

When Bankruptcy Is Declared

■ The trustee in bankruptcy, under direction of the Superintendent of Bankruptcy, assumes possession of the assets or business of the debtor. An examination of the bankrupt's affairs is done by the trustee and the official receiver to determine if any dishonest transactions, such as fraudulent preference or fraudulent conveyance, have occurred. The trustee then reports to the creditors who have filed a proof of claim.

■ Suppliers of goods to a business that has since gone bankrupt are entitled to the return of any goods delivered within 30 days of the bankruptcy. The timing involved with this remedy may limit its usefulness. Suppliers may be better protected by relying on a purchase money security interest (PMSI), which can be registered under the *Personal Property Security Act* (PPSA), where available.

Creditors

■ Creditors are ranked in priority for the purposes of receiving assets or the return of the money owing.

■ Secured creditors hold a security instrument registered against a particular asset, such as a mortgage on real property.

■ The next creditors in priority are preferred creditors, who receive payment before the unsecured creditors, in an order detailed by the *Bankruptcy and Insolvency Act* (BIA). Examples are arrears for employees' wages and rent owed to a landlord. If any money remains after the first two levels of creditors are paid, it is divided among the unsecured creditors.

■ There may be alternative remedies available to employees with a claim for outstanding wages, such as a provincial fund or liability on the part of a director.

Discharge from Bankruptcy

■ Following a period of bankruptcy, the court will grant the bankrupt a discharge, and the debtor is cleared of past debts.

■ Generally, a discharge is automatic for a natural person; however, a corporation will be discharged only if it is able to pay off all of its creditors in full which rarely occurs.

■ Sometimes the owners of a bankrupt business, if they can get financing, will incorporate a new business and start again and the new business is not liable for the debts of the bankrupt company.

Closing Questions

Bankruptcy

1. a) What is the general test to justify voluntary bankruptcy?
   b) Create a fact situation which you believe would clearly illustrate that test.
   c) What is the purpose of a proposal?

2. Which of the following is (are) entitled to review the bankrupt's activities to determine the nature of any transactions which have taken place?
   a) the Superintendent of Bankruptcy
   b) the official receiver
   c) the creditors
   d) the trustee in bankruptcy

3. Laffs Ltd. operated a standup comedy night club under the name Jocularity Jane's, having obtained exclusive rights for use of the name in Canada from the highly successful Los Angeles nightclub of the same name.

   Tamara Burton was the sole shareholder of Laffs Ltd. Unfortunately, the laughs were limited and Burton soon found herself in serious financial difficulties with her employees, landlord, trade creditors, and the Los Angeles company to whom she owed licensing fees. Burton owed her 10 employees wages for two months, totalling $32,000; she owed the landlord rent arrears for one month in the amount of $1,500; the general trade creditors were owed a total of $35,000; and the **licensee** (a visitor, other than an invitee, who enters premises with the consent of the occupier) of the name was owed $2,000. Much to her creditors' unhappiness, Burton voluntarily assigned Laffs Ltd. into bankruptcy.

   > **licensee**
   > a visitor, other than an invitee, who enters premises with the consent of the occupier

   The only assets held by the corporation were the licence to operate under the name Jocularity Jane's and the balance of the five-year lease on the premises. The trustee in bankruptcy moved very quickly to sell the assets in order to recover some money for the creditors. Within a day, the trustee was approached by Biz R Corporation to purchase the licensed operating name and the balance of the lease on the premises. As no other interested party appeared to be forthcoming, a quick sale was arranged and the trade name and balance of the lease were sold for $40,000.

   Jocularity Jane's went on to become an enormous success and began to open other clubs across the country. It was not until several months later that it was discovered that the sole shareholder of Biz R Corporation was Tamara Burton. The creditors of Laffs Ltd. are outraged and have contacted the trustee in bankruptcy to see what, if anything, can be done about what they see as a gross injustice.
   a) In the bankruptcy, would the Los Angeles licenser of the name Jocularity Jane's be a secured, preferred, or unsecured creditor?
   b) Identify the classification of the various creditors, list the order in which they would be paid, and determine the total amount owed to the unsecured creditors, as well as the amount of money available to be divided among that class.
   c) Is there any legal recourse available to the creditors against Tamara Burton in these circumstances?

4. Audrey, Hank, Karin, and Mike carried on business as a partnership operating under the firm name Oceanic Importers. Time and again, their grand plans to import products for resale in Canada had stretched their budget to the breaking point, and time and again their trade creditors had agreed to a reorganization of their trade accounts in order to keep the firm afloat. When the firm's last plan to import petrified beetles to be marketed as novelty desk pets failed, the creditors had had enough.
   a) What procedures must the creditors follow in order to place the partnership in bankruptcy?

5. Terry Cavers was petitioned into bankruptcy, owing money to several creditors, including Francine Gardner, who held the first mortgage on his house. When Gardner had realized on the asset, she was still $20,000 short of the mortgage funds that had been advanced to Cavers. Gardner will rank as a preferred creditor in priority to Cavers's employees' claims for the balance of the money owed to her.
   a) With reasons, explain whether the last statement is true or false.

6. Albert Bernard Cook owns all of the shares of ABC Limited. From the Company's cash flow Cook has the Company purchase half of his shares at fair market value.

   In the next month ABC Limited's main customer switches to another supplier. Because of the loss of this customer, six months later ABC Limited declares bankruptcy.

   Which of the following describes the above purchase of the shares by ABC Limited:
   a) fraudulent preference,
   b) deceptive consumer practice,
   c) an act of anticipatory bankruptcy,
   d) fraudulent settlement.

7. Joe Gladstone from Garden Tools Inc. delivered a large quantity of garden rakes to Happy Harold's Hardware Emporium. While making his delivery, Gladstone struck up a conversation with Happy Harold and learned that Happy Harold had been humbled and might have to make some drastic financial decisions in the future. Gladstone related this information to Carole Mathews, vice-president of finance at Garden Tools Inc.
   a) If Mathews is concerned about a potential bankruptcy or insolvency on the part of Happy Harold, what measures can she take to secure Garden Tools' interest in the goods supplied? What procedures must be followed to accomplish this end?
   b) Assuming Garden Tools was owed $30,000 for the delivery of the rakes, and had received and cashed a cheque for $5,000 from Happy Harold, would it be entitled to pick up the entire delivery made to Happy Harold's in the event of his bankruptcy? Explain the reasons for your answer.

8. Which category does each creditor in the following situations occupy? Why?
   a) Carmen Richter owes the city of Vancouver $7,085 in municipal taxes.
   b) Eduardo Maindroit owes Knit Kwik Ltd. $600 for knitting needles and a correspondence course.
   c) Gary Coonves has two mortgages on his property. The first, for $100,000, is with the Bank of Central Canada; the second, for $30,000, is with Lira Trust Company.
   d) Darlene Bairn's Flower Shop owes $4,000 to her two employees for outstanding wages, and $3,000 to her landlord for rent arrears.
   e) Backstab Corp. has a number of debts. It owes:
   - $2,000 in fees to its bankruptcy lawyer and the trustee in bankruptcy
   - $4,000 in outstanding payments to Workers' Compensation
   - $1,500 in rent arrears to the landlord
   - $25,000 to Avarice Financial Corp., for a metal press bought under a conditional sale agreement and registered under the PPSA by Avarice
   - $6,000 to Ferrous Ltd., for metal supplied over the past three months
   - $2,000 to Gertrude Elsinore, mother of the company's president, Wally, for a loan made to the company when it was started last year
   - $4,000 to Tracy, Wally Elsinore's sister, for a loan she made to Wally last year when he started the company

9. In a personal bankruptcy in each of the following situations indicate what would occur if a debtor:
   a) owed Mastercard $24,000
   b) owed Revenue Canada $150,000 in back taxes
   c) owed a student loan of $47,000
   d) owed Ontario Hydro $5,300
   e) owed child support of $12,000
   f) owed a company $6,000 for breach of contract
   g) owed the government $2,000 in traffic fines
   h) owned a condo with no mortgage worth $250,000
   i) owned a car worth $17,000
   j) owned a computer and office equipment worth $8,000
   k) got a job and started earning $4,006 net per month and was single
   l) got a job and started earning $4,728 net per month and had a spouse and two children

Employment Law

What Is Employment?

The law divides persons who provide services to employers into three categories:

- employees
- **independent contractors** (people who carry on an independent business and act for a number of other persons)
- dependent contractors

independent contractors

people who carry on an independent business and act for a number of other persons

These categories are determined by legal principles. It does not matter what the parties have called the relationship, for often the relevant contract will state that the person is an independent contractor so that the employer can avoid many obligations (such as those under employment standards legislation, paying employee benefit costs such as worker's compensation and employment insurance, and withholding taxes).

The courts have affirmed an intermediate category between employee and independent contractor in view of the number of relationships in which a person is economically dependent upon another business but would not meet the strict test of being an employee. This has been called a dependent contractor (*McKee v. Reid's Heritage Homes Ltd.*, 2009 OMCA 916 CanLii).

Example: An Independent Contractor:

A golf course hires a landscaping firm to cut its lawns. The landscaping firm provides this service to a number of other businesses.

Example: A person called an independent contractor who may be an employee:

A golf course hires an individual to cut its lawns and calls him an independent contractor. He bills them monthly. However, he uses its equipment and is subject to direct supervision by one of its staff.

Example: Dependent Contractor:

A person owns all his own equipment for lawn cutting but does about 80% of his business with the golf course which creates an economic dependency on the golf course. The balance of 20% of his business is done with various customers.

To determine what categorization is appropriate, the basic question is whether the person is performing services as a person in business or on their own account. Unfortunately though, the answer to the question is often not that simple. First the courts will first look at what was the intention of the parties when the contract was formed. Then the court will do an objective two part test to determine if that intention was reality. The courts first use a **control test**. If the employer determines when, where and how the work is to be done and the person is integrated into the business organization, then the individual could be considered an employee. The court then looks at who provides the **tools** for the job. If the individual provides their own tools in the workplace, hires their own helpers, can work at other jobs and they bear the risk of profits or losses, then they could be considered to be an independent contractor.

The tax department often challenges employers when the employer classifies workers as independent contractors and as a result has not remitted deductions such as CPP and EI to the government. In some well-known cases; ballet dancers at the Royal Winnipeg Ballet were ruled to be independent contractors, Ontario youth workers employed as group home and foster care supervisors were judged to be employees, mechanics at a muffler shop were independent contractors and massage therapists working at a spa in a hotel were also independent contractors.

SB Towing Inc. v. M.N.R., 2013 TCC 358 (CanLII)

SB Towing was a towing and roadside assistance company that provided drivers assistance such as changing tires, delivering gas and boosting batteries. It operated 24 hours a day, seven days a week. The company hired tow truck drivers who signed contracts that stated they were independent contractors. The Minister of National Revenue (M.N.R.) challenged that categorization and claimed that 39 of the individual tow truck drivers were actually employees. As a result of this status change, M.N.R. claimed that SB Towing owed $50,000 in EI contributions and $90,000 in CPP contributions over a three year period for these employees.

The government showed that the towing company imposed strict performance standards on the drivers and both the company and drivers had to meet the requirements of the CAA who accounted for 90% of their business. The drivers had little flexibility in their shifts or right to reject calls, and the company had significant control over how they did their work. The company paid the drivers a 30% commission on the calls they handled or a flat fee for certain calls. The towing company also owned or leased all the tow trucks and paid for the insurance, fuel and repairs on the vehicles.

The Court's Decision

The Tax Court of Canada ruled that despite the fact that the contracts for the drivers stated they were independent contractors, they were in fact employees. The control test proved that the towing company controlled how when and where the workers did their job. Since the company provided the trucks, gas and maintenance on the vehicles it was clear the company had provided the tools the drivers used. Since the court ruled the drivers were employees SB Towing was liable for over $140,000 in past government deductions that had not been remitted.

Hiring

Labour laws, as well as federal and provincial human rights legislation and the *Charter of Rights and Freedoms*, closely control the process of advertising for and interviewing new employees. Neither the advertisement nor the interview can include questions about an applicant's race, colour, nationality, age, sex, religion, marital status, past criminal convictions that are unrelated to employment, or mental and physical disability. Labour legislation also prohibits questions about trade union membership. In Chapter 1 interview questions that would violate human rights laws were listed.

However, job applicants can be limited to those who meet the valid skill requirements—*bona fide* occupational requirements (BFORs)—for the job. These might include particular experience, or academic qualifications. For example, a company that provides security guards for residential apartments could refuse to hire someone who had been convicted of sexual assault. Equally, a school board would not hire a teacher who did not possess the appropriate professional qualifications.

The rules on testing employees for drugs and alcohol vary across Canada as this falls within provincial jurisdiction. Companies cannot do testing for drugs or alcohol as part of the screening process as it violates human rights codes. If an employer has made a conditional offer of employment though, it may be possible to test for drugs or alcohol as part of a required medical examination if the job is in a safety sensitive environment and the purpose of the testing is to reduce workplace accidents. Alberta has accepted this policy for testing, but other provinces have not.

Example: In *Alberta (Human Rights and Citizenship Commission) v. Kellogg Brown & Root (Canada) Company*, 2007 ABCA 426 (CanLII), John Chiasson was required to take a pre-employment medical and drug test as a condition of his employment for a job at Syncrude's Fort McMurray oil sands operations. He took the test and began work, but 9 days later his drug test results came back and he had tested positive for marijuana. Chiasson admitted to recreational drug use, but he was not an addict. Syncrude fired him and he challenged the termination in the Alberta Human Rights tribunal claiming he had been discriminated against. He argued that if he had been a drug addict the company would have had to accommodate his addiction, but as a recreational drug user he should receive the same protection. He said what he did on his own time was his own business. The case made its way up to the Alberta Court of Appeal which ruled that the company had the right to administer drug tests to employees who had been given a conditional job offer. The purpose of the policy was to avoid hiring drug users who may be poor employees due to increased absenteeism and the potential for on-the-job impairment and the resulting safety concerns. Because these were valid hiring objectives and safety was the major concern, its pre-employment drug testing policy was upheld and Chiasson's claim failed.

It should be noted however that random testing during an employee's employment is almost never permitted. The uncertainty around that issue was resolved by the Supreme Court decision in *Communications, Energy and Paperworkers Union of Canada, Local 30 v. Irving Pulp & Paper, Ltd.*, 2013 SCC 34 (CanLII). The court considered the impact of random drug and alcohol testing on an employee's right to dignity and privacy and balanced this right against the employer's concerns for workplace safety and discipline. Ultimately siding with the employees on this issue, the Court decided that random drug and alcohol testing of employees would not be permitted even in a dangerous work environment; unless an employer could prove that there was a general problem with alcohol or drug abuse in its workplace. Based on this decision, the vast majority of Canadian employers will not be permitted to maintain policies for random drug and alcohol testing.

Some of the information an employer cannot seek is necessary for employment records, and can be obtained after the person is hired. Labour legislation prohibits asking questions about trade union membership. Immigration laws have restrictions on the right of non-Canadians to work in the country as well.

Ontario is the only jurisdiction that prohibits requiring employees and job applicants to take lie-detector tests.

Résumés   It is easy to falsify information on a résumé. Employers usually do not have the time to check all facts thoroughly; but false statements, and even forged documents, are common, particularly with the advances in cheap printing technology. In addition to thorough checks, businesses are advised to have a term in the contract requiring that employees verify

Business Alert!

that all statements in their résumés are true. Misrepresentation of a material fact in a résumé is a ground for immediate dismissal. Credit searches, with permission of the individual, are also a way to independently check on a potential employee's past. Employers are using social networking sites such as Facebook to investigate applicants.

Clark v. Coopers &Lybrand Consulting Groups, 1999 CanLII 14878 (ON SC)

Richard Clark was hired as an IT business consultant in Ottawa by a major accounting firm on a two year contract that paid $120,000 per year plus bonuses. There was also discussion that if he performed well he would be considered for partnership. On his resume he listed he had a Honours B.Sc. (Physics), M.Sc. (Physics), and a Ph.D. (Applied Mathematics).

Clark's performance was excellent and the firm decided to verify his credentials when it was considering him for partnership. Upon investigation, the firm discovered that he had none of the degrees listed. When confronted, Clark told the firm that his PhD. was a honourary degree from the University of Illinois. When a partner offered to go to Chicago with Clark to confirm this degree, Clark refused to go. So after 23 months on the job, he was fired for these major resume lies.

Clark sued seeking 3 months' salary (notice) ($30,000) plus his bonus. The firm denied it owed him anything and it counter-claimed for $200,000 in damages it incurred for contracts it had been unable to complete after Clark was fired, the costs of moving a replacement consultant in from Toronto and damage to its reputation. Coopers & Lybrand had been put in the position that it had falsely described and in some cases certified Clark's credential to clients. Integrity was central to its relationship with clients and Clark had jeopardized their position.

The Court's Decision

The court ruled that Clark was entitled to nothing, no notice or bonus, as he would never have been hired if his resume had been truthful. His statements on his curriculum vitae were fraudulent misrepresentations made to induce the firm into hiring him.

Clark however was held liable for $47,166 in damages for his fraudulent misrepresentations for contracts the firm lost or withdrew from and for the costs of transferring his replacement from their Toronto office. Though noting that integrity and honesty are crucial in this business, the claims for damage to the firm's reputation and business loss had not been established or quantified and as such were not awarded.

The Employment Contract

An employment agreement is a specific type of contract. It can be oral or written, or both—the hiring might be done orally, and the employee told that there is an employee manual setting out many of the terms of the employment, such as benefits. The manual is not considered part of the employment contract if the employee is not told about it at the time of hiring.

Many employment contracts are oral and for an indefinite term, automatically renewed from year to year with changes in position and salary. A contract may also be for a set term, such as one year. Such contracts have become more popular recently because of economic conditions. When the term ends, the obligations of the employer cease.

Terms of an Employment Contract

Many employers use a standard form contract that can be custom tailored for a few items, such as compensation, that are unique to individual employees. Such a contract usually includes:

- a job description
- a standard period of probation
- overtime and sick-pay policies
- details about vacations, leaves of absence, and holidays
- the remuneration to be paid, including benefits and bonuses
- the notice or severance that will be given in case of layoff or dismissal

- identification of the lines of responsibility
- protection of the company's ownership of inventions or improvements to products done as part of employment
- a non-competition clause
- a trade secrets confidentiality clause
- job evaluation methods
- certification by employees of their education and qualifications

One significant term from the above list is the limit on an employee's claim for damages upon being fired. As explained later an employee may be entitled to damages relating to reasonable notice for, say, one year, but a term in the employment contract may stipulate the employee can only claim three months' damages. These claims are often enforced.

■ *Business Law*   Applied

❶ **John Harris is** HIV-positive. He applies to be a file clerk in a business. At the interview, the business owner tells him that he must undergo drug testing on the first day of his employment. Harris does not want to take the test because it will reveal his HIV-positive status.

   a) Can the employer legitimately require Harris to take the test, or does Harris have any grounds for refusing without revealing his medical condition?

❷ **Saleh Mohamed was** hired by Promoters-Canada Limited. During the interview he was told of the employee manual, and on his first day on the job he was given a copy of it. The manual states that the employer can terminate an individual's employment with four weeks' notice. Five years later, because of a downturn in the economy, Mohamed is fired, and given the four weeks' notice.

He wants longer notice, but his employer points to the manual. Mohamed says that he did not read the document when he received it, and so it is not part of his employment contract.

   a) Is Mohamed correct?

Avoidance of Restrictive Covenants

You will recall in the chapter on contracts that employment that restricted an employee's ability to earn a living after leaving an employer are often not enforced by the courts on the grounds of public policy, i.e., the public have an interest in making certain that everyone has the ability to earn a living and then not be on welfare. Courts generally do not like to enforce a restrictive covenant that is greater than 12 months for the public policy concerns discussed in Chapter 5. In many cases courts prefer a non-solicitation clause that restricts the employee's right to contact former clients other than basic contact information such as the employee's new location, rather than a total non-compete clause. Employees should carefully consider any non-competition clause in a contract they sign when offered a job.

One alternative to a restraint of trade clause, which may be enforced, is a repayment of training expenses if the employee leaves and works for a competitor.

Example: An employee who had no experience in the real estate business was hired on a three-year contract and was to be trained by the employer. A term of the contract stated that he agreed to repay a specified amount relating to training expenses if he left before the three-year period, the amount to be determined according to a formula in the employment contract. The court found that the formula was a reasonable pre-estimate of damages the employer would suffer if the employee left before the three-year period and upheld the clause (*Renaud v. Graham,* 2007 CanLii 5680 (ONSC).

Duties of Employees and Employers

An employee should perform their job duties in a competent and careful manner, follow reasonable instructions, be punctual, courteous, honest and loyal. Only senior personnel at executive levels who have the ability to make decisions fundamental to the firm owe a fiduciary duty to the employer. Those executives must act in the company's best interest and not place themselves in a position of conflict of interest between their own personal interests and the company's.

The employer should provide a safe workplace and hire competent people who can perform their work properly. The employer must pay the employee according to the terms of the contract and not violate any employment laws.

Government Regulations of Working Conditions

Both federal and provincial governments have legislation governing employee work conditions. In some provinces, there is an *Employment Standards Act*; in others, the provisions are included in a *Labour Act*. While the details vary from province to province, the legislation all deals with such areas as wages, rest periods, holidays and vacations, sick days, and maternity leaves. It is an ever-changing area of the law, and the Employment Standards Offices of the provinces will supply up-to-date information and answer any questions that you have. Here is a summary of the main issues:

Wages

- The minimum wage in most provinces is about $10–$11 an hour for people 18 or older.
- Certain jobs, such as farm workers and waiters, are exempt from minimum-wage requirements.
- There is a minimum number of hours per day an employee should be asked to work.
- After eight hours a day, or 44 hours a week, overtime—in most provinces 1.5 times the regular rate of pay—must be paid.
- Male and female employees must receive equal pay for substantially similar work.

Rest Periods

- Employees are entitled to one 30-minute rest period, without pay, for every five hours worked.
- They are entitled to a minimum weekly rest of 24 continuous hours every seven days.
- In Ontario, an employee in a retail business establishment may refuse to work on Sunday.

Holidays and Vacations

- Employees are usually entitled to 9 paid statutory holidays a year (this varies by province). If an employee works on a statutory holiday, a premium rate must be paid, or time off given instead (often 2.5 times the regular rate).
- Normally, a minimum of two weeks' vacation with pay is required, but some provinces guarantee three or four weeks after five or more years of service. Most employers simply continue to pay regular wages during employees' time off, as this usually amounts to the equivalent of vacation pay for two weeks. Vacation pay is calculated as 4 percent of the employee's usual annual earnings.

Sick Days and Leaves

- The laws governing sick days are unclear, but if most businesses in your line of work offer sick days, you must do the same.
- The minimum amount of unpaid maternity leave ranges from 17 to 18 weeks, depending on the province.
- Some provinces also guarantee additional unpaid parental leave for mothers and/or fathers, including adoptive parents often for 35 weeks which the parents can divide up between them.
- Some provinces allow emergency leave of up to 10 days off unpaid per year to deal with a family emergency (such as illness or injury to a family member) if employed by a business with approximately 50 workers or more
- Some provinces allow family leave of up to 8 weeks off unpaid to care for a dying family member

Employers who violate the provincial employment standards laws can be fined and the people responsible for the violations can even face possible jail sentences.

Example: In 2012 the sole director of six Ontario companies that failed to pay 61 employees over $142,000 in wages over a 31 month period was fined $280,000 and sentenced to 90 days in jail for violating the Employment Standards Act. The company had been issued 113 orders over this period to comply with the law, but the orders had been ignored. (*R. v. Blondin*, 2012 ONCJ 826 (CanLII))

Health, Safety and Workers' Compensation

Every province has workplace health and safety legislation. The main purposes of these laws are to provide safe working conditions by setting safety standards in areas such as protective equipment required, hazardous activities and substances and to establish programs to educate employers and workers on how to create safer workplaces.

In most provinces occupational health and safety acts require an employer to have a hazard assessment done whenever employees work alone. Appropriate steps must be taken for the employee's protection such as: a means of communication, visits by other employees and such. Garda Canada Security Corp. was found in breach of the Alberta law for failing to take steps to protect a female security guard who was raped while checking a construction site in the early hours of the morning. Garda had not done the hazard assessment.

Inspection officers can go into workplaces and levy fines and even shut down a worksite if it is considered too dangerous. In Canada there are about 1,000,000 workers who are injured at work each year and about 1,000 who die annually. Approximately 35–45% of the deaths are due to accidents and traumas while the other deaths are due to occupational diseases.

Workers who are injured on the job in Canada are generally not able to sue their employers or other employees, even if their injuries were caused by negligence or violations of the health and safety laws. They are often also prohibited from suing other employers and their employees if they caused the injury. Provinces set up their own no-fault systems and employers pay into an insurance scheme based on how dangerous their workplace is. Workers make a claim from the fund when they are injured and are paid a percentage of their regular wages. In Ontario in 2014 an injured worker was entitled to 85% of their wages up to an annual maximum of $71,485. These worker compensation schemes are complex and often criticized and many operate at a large deficit. In Ontario by 2012 the unfunded liability of its fund had grown to over $14 billion. Common criticisms are that seriously injured workers are not compensated adequately, companies are charged rates that are too high and fraudulent claims are hurting the system. All provincial governments face significant challenges to try and improve the systems that try to prevent and deal with workplace injuries.

R. v. Metron Construction Corporation, 2013 ONCA 541 (CanLII)

On Christmas Eve 2009, six men were working on a suspended work platform repairing balconies on the outside of a Toronto apartment building. At the end of the day as the men were about to descend, the platform broke and five men fell 14 floors to the ground below. Only one worker was wearing a lifeline and did not fall and was not hurt. But four workers were killed and the fifth one was seriously injured. The men ranged in age from 25-40 years old and were recent immigrants from the former Soviet Union. Toxicology tests proved some had marijuana in their systems at the time of the accident.

The company had not provided proper training or equipment and had allowed 6 workers on a platform built for two people that had only 2 lifelines.

The owner/director of the company was found guilty under the Ontario *Occupational Health and Safety Act* and fined $112,500. For the first time in Ontario, the *Criminal Code* was used to hold the company guilty of criminal negligence causing the death of the workers. The trial judge fined the company $200,000, but the Crown appealed the sentence to the Court of Appeal claiming the fine was too low and "manifestly unfit" given this terrible preventable tragedy.

The Court's Decision

After reviewing the facts and the families that were impacted, the Court of Appeal agreed that the fine was much too low.

"A sentence consisting of a fine of $200,000 fails to convey the need to deliver a message on the importance of worker safety. Indeed, some might treat such a fine as simply a cost of doing business. Workers employed by a corporation are entitled to expect higher standards of conduct than that exhibited by the respondent. Denunciation and deterrence should have received greater emphasis. They did not. The sentence was demonstrably unfit."

The Court noted that the criminal negligence of the site supervisor who died in the accident was extreme. Three times as many workers were on the platform when it collapsed as should have been and three times as many workers were there as were lifelines available, and even then, only one of the lines was properly attached.

The Court of Appeal increased the fine on the company to $750,000 to emphasize the importance of worker safety and to deter other companies from operating dangerous worksites.

Human Rights Issues

Discrimination

Human rights legislation is one of the developing areas of law (see Chapter 1). A business must take reasonable steps—short of causing the business undue hardship—to adapt any work rules that would discriminate against an employee. Courts have made it clear that employers must make reasonable efforts to **accommodate** a worker's religion or disability unless the employer can prove that it causes the employer **undue hardship**. Cases where an employer has to accommodate a person's religion or physical disability are well established (See Chapter 1). Other cases involving discrimination based on family status and mental disabilities are becoming increasingly more common.

Example: An employer was found to have discriminated against a worker based on family status when the Canada Border Services Agency told a female employee if she wanted to work regular fixed shifts so she could look after her children, instead of the usual irregular hours and shifts, she would have to switch to part time status. The court ruled that the employer could have accommodated her request without it causing undue hardship. The agency was liable for discrimination based on family status and had to pay $35,000 in damages due to lost pay and benefits. (*Canada (Attorney General) v. Johnstone*, 2014 FCA 110 (CanLII).

Example: In *Devaney v. ZRV Holdings Limited*, 2012 HRTO 1590 (CanLII) an architect who took considerable time off to care for his elderly mother was fired due to his frequent absences. He claimed discrimination based on family status. The court ruled the company had not properly accommodated his needs and it would not have caused undue hardship to have done so. He had mitigated and found a higher paying job after he was dismissed; but the tribunal awarded him $15,000 for injury to dignity, feelings and self-respect. The employer was also ordered to develop appropriate policies and training on discrimination in the workplace.

Example: In *Fair v. Hamilton-Wentworth District School Board*, 2013 HRTO 440 (CanLII) a human rights tribunal ordered a school board to pay Sharon Fair almost 9 years of back wages and then reinstate her to a new job because it had not offered her alternative employment that would have accommodated her anxiety disorder. Fair had worked as a supervisor for the removal of asbestos from board properties and developed anxiety as she feared if she made a mistake she could be held personally liable for asbestos related injuries under the *Occupational Health and Safety Act*. She was off work for 2 years suffering anxiety and post-traumatic stress. When she felt able to return to work, the board said there were no supervisory positions she could do as they all involved the risk of personal liability, so she was fired. She took her complaint to the Human Rights Tribunal and almost 9 years later the board ruled she had been discriminated against due to her disability. The board had to rehire her and owed her almost 9 years of back wages (about $419,238) plus $30,000 for damage to her dignity, feelings and self-respect. Some employers fear people will pursue wrongful dismissal claims through the human rights tribunal now because of the high damages it can award due to long delays and the reinstatement option that is not allowed in civil courts.

Harassment

Harassment can be defined as engaging in a course of vexatious comments or conduct that is known or ought reasonably to be known to be unwelcome, causes a person to be uncomfortable or interferes with employment opportunities. If the unwelcome behaviour is sexual in nature then it is sexual harassment. Sexual harassment can range from inappropriate comments due to a person's sex, requests by superiors for a date that the employee feels compelled to accept, or all the way to outright physical assault. The Robichaud case in Chapter 1 illustrates a clear example of extreme sexual harassment. A company should develop clear company policies on harassment in the workplace and provide training on this issue and have a clear complaint procedure where those who feel harassed can report their problems without fear of retribution. Punishment for offenders such as warning, suspension and even firings should be clearly set out.

Example: Robert Ranger was a homosexual prison guard who laid a complaint of harassment and discrimination related to his sexual orientation against the Ministry of Community Safety and Correctional Services. He repeatedly endured taunts, insults, simulated sex acts, offensive language and derogatory emails expressing anti-gay opinions. He claimed the employer did not prevent fellow employees and managers from discriminating against him, thereby creating a homophobic and poisoned work environment. He became depressed and suicidal and went on disability benefits for 3 years. When he was able to return to work they gave him temporary jobs, but it took 5 years before they finally found him a permanent position elsewhere. He was awarded $45,000 for the discrimination and harassment, $53,000 because it took them so long to find him a new job and he was also awarded $244,242 in lost wages for the 8 years it took before he was finally given a new permanent position. (*Ontario Public Service Employees Union (Ranger) v Ontario (Community Safety and Correctional Services)*, 2013 CanLII 50479 (ON GSB),

Example: In *Sulz v. Minister of Public Safety and Solicitor General*, 2006 BCCA 582 (CanLII) Nancy Sulz was a female RCMP officer in B.C. who was awarded $950,000 in damages for harassment that she suffered when her superiors repeatedly made negative comments and insults and questioned whether she should be an officer. The psychological impact and depression she suffered was so significant the court ruled she would never be able to hold down meaningful full time employment again.

This problem of bullying and harassment of female officers in the RCMP was not an isolated case. In 2013 about 300 female RCMP officers applied to the court to have a class action certified against the RCMP for sexual harassment. As of yet a decision on the certification has not been given.

❸ **John Goodman is** Jewish. He is an employee of a small business that has decided to stay open on Friday evenings. There are about 20 people on staff. Goodman protests, but the manager says that everyone has to work on Fridays.

a) Does Goodman have any grounds for refusing to work?
b) In what circumstances would the employer have to agree to let Goodman not work Friday evenings?

Berry's World

© 1994 by NEA, Inc.

"But enough of my little jokes. You're probably wondering why I asked you to come by my office!"

Dismissals and Resignations

In the employment relationship employers often dismiss employees, with or without a valid reason, and employees often resign for a variety of reasons as well. The court will look very carefully at the circumstances surrounding the dismissal or resignation and depending upon the facts may come to a variety of conclusions and remedies.

just cause dismissal

the employee has done something so wrong the employee can be terminated without any warning or notice

■ The court may find that the employee did something so wrong that it went to the "heart of the employment relationship." This would be a **just cause dismissal** or summary dismissal and the employer had the right to terminate the worker without any warnings or notice and the employer owed them nothing.

■ The court may find that the employee did nothing wrong and was not given adequate termination notice in which case the termination would be a **wrongful dismissal** and the employee can claim remedies such as termination notice and damages and in very limited situations even get reinstated in their previous job.

progressive discipline

steps an employer may be required to follow before terminating an employee for improper conduct

■ The court may find that the employee did do something wrong, but it was not so bad as to be a just cause and allow summary dismissal (dismissal without any advance notice). The court may rule that the employer should have de-hired the worker using **progressive discipline** (such as warnings, suspension and demotion) rather than go straight to termination. If the court rules that progressive discipline should have been used and the employer had failed to do so and had just fired the worker, this is also considered a wrongful dismissal and entitles the employee to their full remedies.

- The court may find that the employee quit because the employer made a fundamental change to the employment agreement. This fundamental change can include; a large change in duties, substantial cut in pay and/or benefits (usually 15% reduction or more in total remuneration) or there was an intolerable "poisoned" work environment. The court can rule that this was a **constructive dismissal** and the change to the job was so major it in effect forced the employee to quit. Constructive dismissal is considered a type of wrongful dismissal, and the employee can seek the appropriate remedies.

- The court may find that the employee quit, not because of any wrongful act by the employer, but the employee did not give the employer adequate notice that they were leaving. For most employees 2 weeks is adequate notice, but for highly skilled workers who are difficult to replace, two weeks may be inadequate. The employer may then sue the employee for **wrongful resignation** and if successful, the employer may be able to obtain damages for their lost profits which could be a very large amount.

constructive dismissal
a fundamental change is made to the employment agreement forcing the employee to quit and allowing them to sue for wrongful dismissal

wrongful resignation
an employee quits but failed to give the employer adequate notice

Progressive Discipline

In union contracts there are usually specific detailed steps that must be followed if a worker has failed to perform properly. Summary or immediate dismissal is often not the proper first response by the employer. The required discipline is usually progressive (often called de-hiring) and the employer would follow these steps listed below if the employee's inappropriate conduct continues:

- Oral warning
- Written warning
- Rehabilitation (e.g. if there is drug or alcohol addiction)
- Suspension
- Demotion to a lower position
- Termination

If the initial misconduct is quite bad, the first disciplinary step could be, for example, a suspension, rather than just a warning. Only if the behaviour is so serious that it has destroyed the employment relationship, can immediate termination for just cause occur without using some progressive discipline. Often though, the courts prefer that the company de-hires using these steps before the worker is fired.

In non-unionized workplaces the courts have also held that progressive discipline may be appropriate rather than terminating an employee. Many non-union employment contracts now allow the employer to use progressive discipline with their employees for improper conduct. If the court rules that progressive discipline should have been used, but the company had not done it and simply fired the worker instead, this can result in a wrongful dismissal and entitles the worker to compensation, even though they had done something wrong. Employers must be aware of the need for progressive discipline in many situations to avoid costly lawsuits.

Example: Franklin Andrews, a senior policy analyst in the federal Department of Citizenship and Immigration (CIC) with 27 years of discipline-free service, was found to have been spending 50-75% of his time at work in a 7 month period surfing the Internet viewing sports and news sites and downloading pornography. When this was discovered he was fired, but he complained that he had not been given enough work to do and that given his long work history, this behaviour did not justify termination. The adjudicator at the Canadian Public Service Labour Relations Board agreed and found that his supervisors should have regularly assessed his workload and production. She also ruled that this excessive computer use was not time theft as there was no fraudulent intent. Given his lengthy service with no previous disciplinary problems and the remorse he showed, the Board ruled that firing was inappropriate. Instead he was given a 9 month suspension without pay and then reinstated back into his position. (*Andrews v. Canada* 2011 PSLRB 100)

Business Alert!

Checklist for Termination Letter

It is best to consult a lawyer as early as possible when problems with an employee arise, and before actually dismissing that individual. The notice of dismissal should include:

- the reason for dismissal
- the termination date
- the proposed notice, or pay in lieu of notice
- details of any payout under employee benefit plans, or requirements to convert insurance coverage, such as group life insurance
- details of statutory amounts to be paid, such as severance pay, vacation pay, and wages to date, including overtime
- a request for the return of employer's property, such as computers, keys, company credit card, and confidential documents
- a time by which the employee's personal effects must be removed from the company's premises
- information about any relocation assistance, such as counselling, reference letters, or secretarial help, that the employer is willing to offer
- a release for the employee to sign

Just Cause

just cause
a valid reason for dismissing an employee without notice

If an employer has a good reason to fire an employee, this is just cause in law and the individual can be dismissed immediately without notice, and without payment of damages. Not every transgression or fault of an employee amounts to just cause. The wrongful action must be so serious that it "goes to the heart of the employment relationship" such as violating an essential condition of the employment contract, or destroying the employer's inherent faith in the employee. Some of the most common situations involving just cause are:

- theft
- dishonesty
- frequent absenteeism, not because of illness
- intoxication affecting the employee's work
- insolence and insubordination
- frequent lateness
- incompetence
- conflict of interest
- illness that prevents the employee from doing the job for which the individual was hired

Just cause can also be discovered after the dismissal has taken place.

Incompetence

On the surface, it would seem that incompetence would be the easiest basis on which to have an employee dismissed—but it is not. It is therefore important to have a term of probation to make certain that new employees are capable of performing the job for which they were hired.

Before an employee can be found incompetent, the individual must be given written warnings. It is also important that the employer not be found to have approved the conduct. Sometimes, well-meaning employers are reluctant to correct an employee, who can then claim to have been doing the job for several years without being told of incompetence.

Example: In *Radio CJVR Ltd. v. Schutte*, 2009 SKCA 92 (CanLII), Grant Schutte was hired as program and music director and morning show host at a new AM radio station. An outside consultant was brought in to regularly evaluate performance at the station. Schutte was warned that he was often late, others found him very difficult to work with, he failed to provide guidance and leadership, ignored details and would not meet with his co-host to plan the morning show. He was observed as having low energy and low effort. Management went over their expectations again and after 16 months warned him if there was no improvement he would be terminated. The situation did not change and he was terminated. He sued for wrongful dismissal. The trial court agreed with Schutte and awarded him 5 months' notice.

On appeal the Saskatchewan Court stressed the difference between incapable of doing the job and consistently failing to meet a reasonable standard of performance. An employer does not have to prove that the employee was incapable of doing the work to establish he was incompetent, it only has to prove that the employee failed to meet reasonable work requirements. The radio station had clearly set its standards and Schutte had failed to meet these requirements. He was warned there needed to be improvements within a certain time and the employee did not change. The Court of Appeal ruled that it was a just cause termination and Schutte was not entitled to compensation.

Business Law Applied

❹ **Felipe Suarez was** foreman of a meat-packing plant. One day several employees called in sick, and as a result his crew was short-staffed. Those employees who were present had to work hard to get the day's work done. At the end of the day, Suarez rewarded the workers by bringing in some beer.

The next day, the supervisor found empty beer bottles and now wants to fire Suarez for allowing employees to drink on the job.

a) Does the company have just cause for dismissing Suarez?
b) What do you think the company is legally required to do?

Dishonesty and other Misconduct

Misconduct as a basis for dismissal includes a wide range of activities such as dishonesty, cheating on expense accounts, disrespect, uncooperative attitudes, and failure to obey reasonable orders.

Courts had taken two different approaches when determining whether dishonesty or inappropriate behaviour is just cause for dismissal. The **automatic approach** held that any act of dishonesty by an employee, no matter how minor, was automatically considered just cause. The **contextual approach** however required the court to consider the nature and degree of the dishonesty with respect to the entire employment relationship and whether termination was justified.

Example: Roanna Hum was a deaf chambermaid who thought guests had already checked out and she took 7 beers she found left in the room. The guests reported the beer was missing and she was stopped on her way out and admitted her error and returned the beer. The hotel fired her for theft. The Court considered theft to be a very serious issue, but given her good 18 year work record with the hotel, it ruled that a 6 month unpaid suspension was appropriate, not termination, and she was reinstated in her job after the suspension was served. (*Delta Toronto East v. Unite Here, Local 75*, 2008 CanLII 9604 (ON LA)

In the McKinley case below the Supreme Court has made it clear that the **contextual approach** should be adopted and the actions the employer takes should be **proportional** to the nature and degree of the employee's misconduct.

McKinley v. BC Tel, 2001 SCC 38 (CanLII)

McKinley was a chartered accountant who worked for B.C. Tel for to almost 17 years. He became Controller, Treasure and Assistant Secretary to certain B.C. Tel companies. He experienced high blood pressure as a result of hypertension. By June 1994 his condition was so serious he took a leave of absence from work. After several months McKinley attempted to obtain a less stressful position with the company, but B.C. Tel refused and terminated his employment.

Initially B.C. Tel claimed that the contract had been frustrated due to McKinley's health condition, but later changed its claim to a just cause dismissal because McKinley had lied about the actual state of his health. The employer discovered a letter from McKinley's doctor that indicated if he took certain medication he could resume his previous job. McKinley however had refused to take the medicine due to its side effects, so B.C. Tel argued that by lying about his true medical condition, it had the right to fire him for his dishonesty.

The trial judge advised the jury that it could not rule it was a just cause dismissal due to dishonesty unless the conduct would undermine or seriously impair the trust and confidence the employer had placed in the employee in the circumstances of that relationship. Using this contextual approach, given the length of time he had been there and the nature of his dishonesty, the jury found it was a wrongful dismissal. He was awarded 22 months' notice, plus 4 months more for bad faith/Wallace damages plus $100,000 in aggravated damages.

B.C. Tel appealed the decision to the B.C. Court of Appeal which ruled that the trial judge should not have instructed the jury that the "degree" of dishonesty was relevant. The appeal court stated that dishonesty within the employment contract is always just cause, and the entire employment relationship did not have to be considered. It ordered a new trial. But McKinley appealed the Court of Appeal decision to the Supreme Court of Canada.

The Court's Decision

The Supreme Court of Canada agreed with the Trial decision. It rejected the absolute unqualified rule that an employer is entitled to dismiss an employee for a single act of dishonesty, however minor. This approach would result in the consequences for dishonesty being the same no matter how severe the dishonest actions were. The Court believed this could lead to unreasonable and unjust results.

The Court recognized that termination on a ground as morally disreputable as dishonesty may have overly harsh implications for the employee. For this reason the circumstances and nature of the dishonest conduct must be considered to see if termination is justified.

The court proposed the principle of **proportionality**. It stated an effective balance had to be struck between the severity of the worker's misconduct and the sanction imposed. The important role that a person's employment has on their sense of identity and self-worth was noted, and illustrates why this approach should be taken.

> "The test is whether the employee's dishonesty gave rise to a breakdown in the employment relationship...Just cause dismissal exists where the dishonesty violates an essential condition of the employment contract, breaches the faith inherent to the work relationship, or is fundamentally or directly inconsistent with the employee's obligations to the employer."

The Supreme Court emphasized that a **contextual approach** to the dishonest act should be adopted, to evaluate how the conduct impacts the employment relationship. It also suggested that an employer may be entitled to impose lesser sanctions for less serious types of misconduct in certain circumstances. This could result in unpaid suspensions, as are allowed in a unionized workplace, may be appropriate in non-union settings.

The jury award was upheld except for the aggravated damages.

The courts may consider that one act may not be serious enough for a just cause dismissal, however several acts of misconduct together may constitute a just cause. The test is whether the actions of the employee have destroyed the employment relationship.

Example: Michael Dowling had worked for the Workplace Safety Insurance Board for almost 25 years and was one of two managers in the Ottawa office. The trial court found he had committed several acts of misconduct. Dowling had secretly purchased two computers from a client at a discount for his personal use and though he had paid for them, it was against WSIB rules. He also had accepted a $1,000 bribe from a client and when questioned about it he lied. He claimed it was actually a loan and even prepared a false loan contract to try to substantiate the lie. After an investigation WSIB discovered the truth and fired him for just cause. The trial court ruled it was a wrongful dismissal, but when WSIB appealed to the Court of Appeal it ruled that the dishonest acts taken together had led to a breakdown in the employment relationship. A key part of his job required that he act with honesty, impartiality and exclusively in the Board's best interests. The trust, faith and confidence necessary for his position and the employment relationship had been destroyed by his misconduct. It was ruled a just cause dismissal. (*Dowling v. Ontario (Workplace Safety and Insurance Board)*, 2004 CanLII 43692 (ON CA)

Example: Aloysia Pinto was an investment advisor with BMO who repeatedly made unauthorized and impermissible discretionary trades with her clients' funds without their knowledge causing them considerable losses. She then made up evidence to conceal her illegal activities. BMO settled with her clients for close to $500,000 for their losses and fired Pinto. The court ruled it was a just cause dismissal given she was entrusted with investing large sums of money in an unsupervised environment and she had clearly violated the trust and performance standards required of this job.(*Pinto v. BMO Nesbitt Burns Inc.*, 2005 CanLII 18720 (ON SC)

Long Term Illness or Disability

If an employee has a permanent disability or constantly recurring illness it may entitle the employer to consider the contract **frustrated** and therefore ended. It is not a just cause dismissal, it is a frustrated contract, so the employee is not entitled to common law notice. They are however entitled to statutory termination notice and severance pay. Remember though that under human rights legislation the employer must make **all reasonable efforts to accommodate a person's disability up to the point of undue hardship**. Once the accommodation obligation has been met, it may then be possible to treat the contract as frustrated. The employer must be careful and ensure it has proper medical documentation to substantiate its claim that there is no reasonable prospect they can return to work in the reasonably foreseeable future. If they terminate the employee without adequate medical evidence, the termination will be treated as a wrongful dismissal.

Example: Frank Naccarato worked as a clerk for Costco for 17 years and then went on long term disability for 5 years due to depression. When Costco claimed the contract was frustrated and therefore ended (including his long term disability benefits), he sued for wrongful dismissal. The court ruled that Costco had not established enough medical evidence that indicated there was no reasonable likelihood that Naccarato would be unable to return to work in the foreseeable future. The only evidence was that his doctor was trying to find him a new psychiatrist. Since he was not a key employee, his absence was not causing the company an undue hardship. The employee was awarded 10 months' notice for the wrongful dismissal. (*Naccarato v. Costco*, 2010 ONSC 2651 (CanLII)

Inappropriate Computer Use

Relatively new grounds for dismissal for misconduct is the use of a company computer for downloading or distributing racist or pornographic materials. Where a company has a clear policy prohibiting employees from using company computers for such personal uses, the employee who does so can be dismissed without any need to give prior warnings to stop the misconduct (as shown in the Poliquin case below).

Poliquin v. Devon Canada Corporation, 2009 ABCA 216 (CanLII)

Claude Poliquin was a 50 year old senior production foreman at Devon Canada in an office in Northern Alberta. He had worked for the company for 26 years and supervised 20–25 men in the gas and oil divisions. He was dismissed for cause for violating the company's conflict of interest policy when on two occasions he had asked suppliers to do personal landscaping and grading at his home and he never paid for the services. He also used his work computer and internet access to view and transmit pornographic and racist emails in violation of the company's Code of Conduct. He had been warned previously for viewing pornographic material at work, but he had continued. The trial court ruled it was a just cause dismissal and he appealed.

The Court's Decision

The Alberta Court of Appeal examined the case carefully and agreed it was a just cause dismissal. Poliquin had taken a "secret benefit" when he had asked Devon suppliers to do personal landscaping and grading at his home. The court ruled this action destroyed the company's confidence in the employee as he may not be able to act in the employer's best interests in future dealings with suppliers. The court noted that these actions alone, given his senior supervisory position, were just cause for dismissal.

A company investigation found 881 pages of emails, many with related pornographic photos attached. Poliquin admitted to receiving them and he forwarded 2 of them to other employees. One email was racist and referred to non-whites as criminals and he forwarded that to 30 others including Devon employees, suppliers and business contacts. Though Poliquin admitted that the emails were inappropriate, he said it was typical of the culture in a small town in the middle of the northern Alberta oil patch.

The court did not accept this argument. The company's IT Code of Conduct clearly prohibited these types of emails. As a supervisor he had a responsibility to prevent this type of behaviour, and instead his deplorable course of conduct contributed to discrimination and harassment. He could have seriously compromised the company's reputation in the business community by sending these emails to outside contacts that clearly identified the name of the employer. The court stated that these emails, even on their own, were just cause for his dismissal.

Disrespectful Social Media Postings

Disrespectful comments in a blog about fellow employees may be grounds for dismissal. An employee wrote on her blog: "Does anyone else out there live in a world like mine with imbeciles and idiot savants (no offence to them) running the ship . . . and is anyone else's ship being sailed down the highway to hell?" An arbitration panel, upheld by the Alberta Court of Appeal held that the contempt expressed by the employee in her public blogs respecting her coworkers, management and administration of the department seriously and irreparably damaged the employment relationship justifying the termination (*Union of Provincial Employees v. Alberta* QB 2009 and ABQB 2008 [Nielsen J.]).

Cases are becoming more common where employees are fired for critical comments they post on Facebook, Twitter or You Tube about their company, supervisors or customers, and many have been upheld by the courts as just cause dismissals. Even if the employee thinks that their postings are private and done on their own time, the courts often rule that the rude, derogatory remarks are not private and are a just cause for termination. A mill worker who posted insulting and threatening Facebook comments about her supervisors was dismissed for just cause. (*Communications, Energy and Paperworkers Union of Canada, Local 64 v Corner Brook Pulp and Paper Limited*, 2013 CanLII 87573 (NL LA) — 2013-12-11)

Example: In *Lougheed Imports Ltd. (West Coast Mazda) v. United Food and Commercial Workers International Union, Local 1518*, 2010 CanLII 62482 (BC LRB), two workers at West Coast Mazda repeatedly updated hundreds of "friends" on Facebook about their workplace. One worker accused his two male supervisors of sexual acts in the washroom, called one a complete jackass and attacked the company's products and customer service, and made threatening statements. The other worker shut down his Facebook account quite quickly and apologized, but the harm had been done. The employer had been monitoring their postings. The court ruled the company had just cause to fire them for this misconduct.

Employers also often have a Code of Conduct that applies when the worker is off duty so that the employer can protect its brand or image. For example three Toronto firemen were terminated for sexist remarks on their Twitter account. One had posted "Reject a woman and she will never let you go. One of the many defects of their kind. Also weak arms." The city has as one of its core values a diverse and welcoming workplace and the tweets violated these principles.

Even a stupid act, such as when a worker made a video on his lunch hour where he nailed his genitals to a piece of wood and posted it to You Tube, was grounds for termination. It was clear in the video from his uniform what company he worked for and since it was in a safety sensitive industry, this idiotic behaviour justified the firing. (*International Union of Elevator Constructors, Local 50 v. ThyssenKrupp Elevator (Canada) Ltd.*, 2011 CanLII 46582 (OLRB)

Sexual Harassment

If an employee engages in any act that violates human rights legislation, such as making discriminatory remarks or unwelcome sexual comments, that individual can be fired. The employer is responsible under human rights legislation for the acts of the employee, and could be fined.

Employers must conduct a proper investigation of any allegation of sexual harassment. There are several cases in which employers responded to claims of sexual harassment by firing the alleged offender immediately; it was held that the employers acted too quickly, and did not investigate the incident. The alleged sexual harassment allegations were found to be untrue. More recent cases have held that the employee must be given notice of the offensive conduct and an opportunity to change.

Menagh v. Hamilton (City), 2005 CanLII 36268 (ON SC), Menagh v. Hamilton (City), 2007 ONCA 244 (CanLII)

Robert Menagh was a labour lawyer who worked for 13 years for the City of Hamilton and became the Director of Labour Relations, Employee Wellness and Health and Safety. He became romantically involved with Maureen Wilson the Mayor's chief of staff. But when she ended their relationship after several years due to their differences and his drug and alcohol use, he refused to accept it was over and began to harass her.

He stalked her at work and at home, stared at her through her office window, parked beside her car constantly, called her parents and co-workers who reported to her and made uninvited visits to her home. When his repeated attempts to reconcile were rejected, he set out to destroy her. He revealed private details about their relationship to their co-workers and lied to the mayor to try to get her fired. When she began to date another city worker he told his supervisor he felt like killing them both and then himself. He drove his speeding car at her new boyfriend almost hitting him and swore at him as he drove away.

Menagh was charged with uttering death threats, criminal harassment and dangerous driving. The charges were only dropped when he agreed to sign a peace bond and signed a letter of apology to the couple. The City then conducted an internal investigation and fired him for his sexual harassment, insubordination, abuse

of power, dishonesty and unprofessional conduct. Menagh sued for wrongful dismissal.

The trial court was appalled by his behaviour. The judge noted that Menagh was untrustworthy and disrespectful of the legal system. He had even admitted that he never meant the apology he had made to be freed from his criminal charges. He ruled that the city had just cause to terminate him and ordered Menagh to pay the city $200,000 for its costs. Menagh appealed the decision to the Ontario Court of Appeal.

The Court's Decision

The Ontario Court of Appeal was equally disgusted by Menagh's misconduct and upheld the Trial court's decision. It found Menagh's harassment, sexual harassment, retaliation, conflicts of interest, abuse of authority and insubordination were disruptive of the workplace. Given his position, as Director of Labour Relations, he was entrusted with employment relations for the City and he was breaking the rules his department had established and had a duty to uphold. His highly offensive behaviour justified his summary dismissal. The Appeal Court ordered him to pay an extra $23,344 for Hamilton's legal costs.

Conflict of Interest

If an employee is in a position of a conflict of interest with his employer it may be just cause for dismissal. A company had just cause to dismiss an employee who was "moonlighting," taking a second paying job in the same industry as his employer. This was in direct competition with his employer and since he had not obtained permission to do so, the company had a right to fire him (*Millard v. Seven Continents Enterprises Inc.* [1992] 44 C.C.E.L. 119).

A company had just cause to fire Andrew Liu, the executive assistant to the Vice President of Operations, when he repeatedly lied and told them his wife was working in an administrative role for a competitor. When the employer discovered the wife was actually a buyer for the competitor, Liu was fired. The court ruled that the seafood industry is highly competitive and supply sources are kept confidential. Liu had a potential conflict of interest and the company had just cause for his termination. (*Liu v. Tri-Star Seafood Supply Ltd.*, 2004 BCSC 912 (CanLII)

Firing: Employers   At the earliest sign of difficulties with an employee, you should seek legal advice.

Business Alert!

- If the conduct can be remedied, you should give the employee notice in writing, and start a paper trail by keeping track of all incidents by writing and filing memos.
- If you have to fire an employee, do so in a private office, and have a witness. Do not fire the individual in front of other employees, thus causing mental stress and humiliation.
- Follow up the termination interview with a letter containing the amount and terms of any severance package offered if the firing is not for cause. A release for the employee to sign should be included, with a comment that legal advice should be sought. A release signed by an employee is probably not enforceable unless that individual has obtained independent legal advice.
- If you are firing for cause, do not give a letter of reference without discussing the matter with your lawyer. It could be used by the employee to prevent you from establishing just cause.

Business Alert!

Being Fired: Employees   If you are fired, do not sign anything or agree to anything; ask for time to consult a lawyer, and do so.

Constructive Dismissal

constructive dismissal

employer conduct that amounts to a fundamental breach of the employment contract and justifies the employee quitting

Sometimes an employee is not fired, but the employer makes such a fundamental change to their job, and that forces the employee to quit. Such acts by the employer are called a **constructive dismissal**, as the employer's conduct amounts to a fundamental breach of the employment contract and justifies the employee quitting. Fundamental changes that may trigger a claim for constructive dismissal could include actions such as; a significant cut to pay and/or benefits (usually 15% or more reduction in total remuneration), significant change in job duties such as a demotion, significant change to job hours, reassignment to a new geographic location that was not part of the terms of the employment contract, or a "poisoned work environment."

poisoned work environment

an employee is subjected to serious wrongful behaviour that makes it impossible for them to continue working there

The term **"poisoned work environment"** refers to serious wrongful behaviour that is persistent or repeated and renders continued employment impossible. It usually requires a pattern of offensive behaviour over a period of time, but in some cases one single egregious incident may be so severe, it creates this toxic work environment. It is an objective test, not whether the plaintiff thinks the workplace was poisoned, but rather, would a "reasonable person" in the plaintiff's shoes come to that conclusion. The wrongful actions must be repeated persistent behaviour that torments, undermines, frustrates, frightens, provokes, intimidates or incapacitates the employee. It can consist of insulting, yelling, degrading, embarrassing, belittling, threatening, mocking or harassing comments or gestures. It is the synergy of repeated abuse that leads to the toxic work environment that forces the employee to quit. A claim of constructive dismissal is a claim of a wrongful dismissal so the same remedies will then result.

Example: A bank manager who had been abusive to the 11 employees reporting to him was reprimanded and told that he would be transferred to a new position at the same salary but with no supervisory duties. He quit and successfully sued for constructive dismissal. (*Chandran v. National Bank of Canada*, 2012 ONCA 205 (CanLII0.)

Example: A General Manager of a car dealership who had failing eyesight and diabetes was basically told to go on long term disability and his job would be waiting when he was healthy. The dealership hired a new general manager a month later. He sued for constructive dismissal and won. The court ruled that since there was little evidence of his actual medical condition presented at trial and the company had no plan for his return and it quickly hired a new general, it was a constructive dismissal. (*Irvine v. Gauthier (Jim) Chevrolet Oldsmobile Cadillac Ltd.*, 2013 MBCA 93 (CanLII)

Carscallen v. FRI Corp., 2005 CanLII 20815 (ON SC), Carscallen v. FRI Corporation, 2006 CanLII 31723 (ON CA)

Christina Carscallen, 43, had worked for FRI Corp. for 17 years and had been promoted to vice president of marketing. She earned an annual salary of $80,000 including benefits and bonuses. FRI developed software and data information for the securities industry. On one occasion she was responsible for sending a booth and materials from Toronto to Barcelona, Spain so FRI could participate in an international trade show. The booth and the materials did not arrive in time for the show as Fed Ex had encountered customs delays in France.

The hot tempered CEO, Eligio Gaudio, arrived in Barcelona and he was furious with Carscallen over the lack of a booth and materials. Several heated email exchanges occurred between the two over this problem and they accused each other of arrogance and carelessness. Soon after the Director of HR informed Carscallen that she was suspended indefinitely. A week later she was told that she was being demoted to a manager, her private office was no longer hers and she would have a cubicle in a common area and lose her right to flex hours. Carscallen left that day never to return again and she sued the company for constructive dismissal.

FRI claimed that it had just cause to dismiss her due to her poor planning for the Spanish trade show, the insubordinate emails and past misconduct. It claimed she had abandoned her position as well when she refused to return after the suspension.

The trial court ruled that though she had committed some errors at work over the years, there was not just cause to dismiss her. She had not been guilty of a flagrant dereliction of duty. Her email was out of line, but it was not atypical of the business relationship she and the CEO had developed over the years, and it did not amount to just cause. Her contract did not allow for a suspension, and since the company did not have just cause, the suspension was a constructive dismissal. The demotion to a manager, the loss of her private office and the withdrawal of her flex hour privileges was seen as punishment, rather than fair and reasonable discipline. The court saw these actions as "piling on" and showed a "thirst for blood" by management.

The Court awarded her 9 months' notice for the constructive dismissal and an additional 3 months' pay for the punitive, mean spirited and humiliating manner in which the CEO had treated her at the time of the suspension. FRI Corp. appealed the decision

The Court's Decision

The Ontario Court of Appeal agreed with the trial judge. It considered that the CEO's actions to suspend her without pay and the other sanctions were an ad hoc/knee jerk reaction done out of anger with the intention of embarrassing her. It was not reasonable discipline and there was no right to suspend her in the employment contract, so it was clearly a case of constructive dismissal.

■ *Business Law* Applied

❺ Julie Stolzak is Vice-President, Public Relations, of Magnum Computer Corp. Limited. Her annual salary is $80,000. Because of difficult times, Magnum is restructuring, and has eliminated this particular position. Stolzak has been offered the position of General Sales Manager, at an annual salary of $70,000. She would then report to the Vice-President, Sales.

a) Stolzak does not want to accept this position because she feels she would lose face in front of all the company employees. Does she have to accept the position?

b) What are her alternatives if she does not accept the new job?

Privacy Issues

Increased sensitivity to privacy rights has impacted the law of constructive dismissal as well. A court ruled in the *Colwell* case below that an employer who secretly installed a hidden camera in an employee's office, without her knowledge and without a plausible explanation or valid suspicion of wrongdoing, had constructively dismissed the employee based on a privacy violation.

Employers should consider all other less intrusive means of combatting workplace issues before secretly invading an employees' privacy. Companies however can use surveillance cameras if they do have strong suspicions of wrong doing. In *MacBurnie v. Halterm Container Terminal Limited Partnerships*, 2013 NSSC 361 (Can LII), an employer hired a private detective to video an employee who repeatedly claimed his back pain was so bad he could not get out of bed. Video evidence of him walking briskly from his home to the beer store hours after he had called in sick was considered valid and not a violation of privacy or employment rights and it substantiated the company's just cause dismissal.

Colwell v. Cornerstone Properties Inc. [2008] CanLII 66139 (ON S.C.)

A commercial manager, Ms. Colwell, learned that a hidden camera was installed in her office by her immediate boss at Cornerstone Properties Inc., ("Cornerstone"). Ms. Colwell found out about the existence of the camera when she saw the image of her office on a monitor in the presence of her immediate boss and the vice-president of Cornerstone.

Ms. Colwell confronted her immediate boss, who indicated to her that the camera had been installed approximately nine months prior to her being aware of its existence. He also indicated to her that she was not considered to be involved in any alleged thefts— either as a victim or a suspect. The camera, she was told, was to assist in detecting theft by the maintenance staff. However, even though Ms. Colwell was the person directly responsible for the maintenance staff, she was never advised of any thefts or the camera set up to capture them. The camera in her office was the only hidden camera installed in Cornerstone's office area, yet there was no plau-

sible explanation given as to why her office was thought to be most likely the subject of a theft.

The Court's Decision

The judge stated, "A secret camera installed in a trusted manager's office without her knowledge, although perhaps acceptable employer conduct in itself, coupled with a totally implausible explanation, renders the actions unacceptable." The judge found that Ms. Colwell's contract of employment contained an implied term of good faith and fair dealing, throughout the existence of the contract, which was breached by the actions of her employer. As such, the judge held that Ms. Colwell was constructively dismissed and was accordingly justified in leaving her position at Cornerstone. She was ultimately awarded seven months pay in lieu of notice (she had been employed by Cornerstone for in excess of seven years).

Wrongful Dismissal

A dismissal can be considered a wrongful dismissal if one of the following occurs:

- the employer fired the employee with no notice and it did not have a just cause to do so
- the worker had done something wrong, but the court rules that they should have received progressive discipline rather than termination, and this de-hiring was not done
- there was a constructive dismissal (the employee was justified in quitting because a fundamental change had been made to the employment contract)
- the employer terminated the employee with notice or pay in lieu of notice, but it was an inadequate amount

Example: In *Leitner v. Wyeth Canada*, 2010 ONSC 579 (CanLII) a Group Product Manager who oversaw the marketing of a drug company's top selling product was fired over 3 false expense account claims that totalled less than $500. Leitner had been with the company for over 8 years and managed a promotional budget of $19 million for its number one product. The expenses claimed were clearly false, but he said it was done accidentally and not fraudulently. The company however fired him claiming it was a just cause. The Court believed that Leitner's actions were negligent, but not fraudulent, as they were obviously wrong expense claims. The Court ruled that using a contextual approach, firing an employee with an excellent work record over less than $500 in careless expense claims was disproportionate to the offence he had committed. Therefore it was a wrongful dismissal and he was entitled to 10 months wages (about $118,300).

Notice

Statutory Termination Notice

Employment standards legislation and labour acts set out the minimum statutory notice required by law that an employer must give an employee if they are terminated without just cause. In most jurisdictions this is normally 2 weeks' notice, or pay in lieu of notice, after the first year of service, and one week per year of service after that, to a maximum of 8 weeks' notice for anyone who has worked there over 8 years. Many employers prefer to give the employee the pay and have them leave immediately, rather than have them work during the notice period. Statutory notice is the minimum notice period allowed by law.

Severance Pay

In most jurisdictions the employment standards legislation also entitles employees who work for larger companies to receive severance pay as well as statutory termination notice. In Ontario for example, a worker is entitled to severance pay as well as statutory notice if they have worked for 5 years or more at a company that has a payroll of $2.5 million or more (often about 50 employees). The employee would then receive in addition to their statutory termination notice, one week's pay per year of service to a maximum of 26 additional weeks' pay as severance pay.

Common Law Notice

Employees have another alternative when they are dismissed. Instead of claiming statutory notice and severance pay, they can claim they are entitled to reasonable notice based on common law rather than statutory law. If an employee is awarded common law notice then they cannot also receive statutory termination notice and severance pay. When a wrongful dismissal claim is heard by a court, the judge will determine what is reasonable notice based on previous cases and by examining the particular facts of that employee's employment situation.

Common law notice is greater than statutory notice and though no upper maximum limit is set, sometimes common law notice can be in excess of 24 months for employees who have been with an employer for a very long time. Statutory notice is calculated based entirely on how long the employee worked for the employer, but common law notice takes into account other factors; that is why there can be so much variation. Some older senior employees who are only there for 2 years may receive 12 months' notice, and other younger workers who have been there for 15 years may only receive 9 months.

There are four factors that the court considers when determining appropriate common law notice and they were established in the *Bardal* case below. The **Bardal factors** include: the character or type of job held, their length of service with the employer, their age, and the availability of similar employment opportunities given the employee's experience, training and qualifications.

Bardal factors
four factors the court considers when determining common law notice

Bardal v. The Globe & Mail Ltd., [1960] 24 D.L.R. (2d) 140

In 1942, Bardal was appointed advertising manager for the *Globe & Mail*. In 1959, the newspaper became dissatisfied with his efforts, and thought it could find an advertising manager who would produce better results. The position of advertising manager is one of the most important in the newspaper business, since it is the revenue generated by advertising that makes the newspaper profitable.

The president of the *Globe & Mail* informed Bardal that the newspaper wanted to get someone who could improve business in the advertising department, and asked for Bardal's resignation. When Bardal refused, he was given written notice of termination on April 24, 1959.

Bardal sought new employment immediately, and secured a position with an advertising firm on July 1, 1959, but at a lower salary. Bardal then brought an action against the *Globe & Mail* for his lost salary during the period of unemployment, and for the difference in salary between his old and new employment for the balance of the reasonable notice period.

The Court's Decision

The court stated that, although counsel for the *Globe & Mail* had cited many precedents where six months was the highest period given for reasonable notice, these did not establish that six months was, as a matter of law, the longest reasonable notice period. These cases were decided on particular facts, and different circumstances would suggest different notice periods.

The court held that what constitutes reasonable notice must be decided in each particular case, taking into consideration the type of employment, length of service of the employee, age of the employee, and the availability of similar employment given the employee's experience, training, and qualifications.

In applying this principle, the court found that Bardal had a lifetime of training and was qualified to manage the advertising department of a large metropolitan newspaper. He had been in the advertising departments of two large daily newspapers. There were few similar situations available in Canada, and so Bardal had taken employment with an advertising agency. However, that employment would be of a different character. Taking all these factors into account, the court decided that one year was reasonable notice in this case.

Bardal was entitled to the lost salary between his last day of employment and commencing new work. He was also entitled to the difference between his new and old employment for the balance of the reasonable notice period of one year.

■ *Critical Concepts of* Notice at Common Law

- An employer can fire without just cause, but must give reasonable notice or pay the equivalent in salary.
- Reasonable notice depends on age, length of service, level of position, and length of time to obtain alternative equivalent employment.

Each case is decided on its individual merits. A list of the average notice periods awarded by judges from 1995–2006 for all ages and job categories in 868 cases is listed below.

Years of Service	Average Notice Awarded (in months)	Months Per Year of Service
.6 to 2.5	3.94	2.6
2.6 to 5	5.43	1.4
6 to 10	8.56	1.1
11 to 15	11.82	0.9
16 to 20	14.48	0.8
21 to 25	15.52	0.7
26 to 30	16.72	0.6
31 to 40	21.23	0.6

Source: Barry Fisher, *"Revisiting Reasonable Notice in Wrongful Dismissal Cases,"* 2006.

Bardal Factors

Businesses often used the rule of thumb of one month for every year of service to determine notice awards. However useful this might be for settlement purposes, it is not what the courts apply, and is not supported by the above list, particularly in the earlier years.

Interpreting statistics, however, is always tricky. For example, the average notice awarded of 3.94 months for .6 to 2.5 years of service is probably affected by the fact that most employees who sue after a short period of service are older, and have left positions where they held seniority. A 45-year-old who left a previous job after 10 years, and then was fired from a new position after one year, would likely receive several months' notice. A 25-year-old, with no previous experience, would probably only get a month's notice after one year's service. This factor is not accounted for in statistics.

Considerable discussion has been given to the weight that should be given to the individual Bardal factors when determining common law notice. Courts in the past had given greater weight to the character or type of job that the employee held when determining common law notice. Courts had relied on the proposition that it would take much longer for a higher level employee to find alternative employment than a lower level unskilled worker. This resulted in people employed in professional or managerial jobs receiving much greater common law notice than unskilled workers. One 1995 case had even indicated unskilled workers should have a cap of 12 months as their maximum common law notice. But was this appropriate? Was it true that senior employees have more difficulty getting a job? Or was this a form of elitism or class prejudice that courts were perpetuating to the detriment of lower skilled workers?

In recent years however courts have rejected this assumption that junior employees have an easier time finding a new job, and some judges have questioned if this proposition was ever actually correct. Many reliable empirical studies have shown that exactly the opposite was true; highly skilled or executive employees have an easier time getting alternative employment than unskilled or junior employees. As a result, some courts have now stated that the type or character of the job the worker held should not be given greater weight than the other Bardal factors. Some have even commented that it is almost an irrelevant factor other than in the case of a small class of very senior employees. The other *Bardal* factors; their years of service, age and availability of employment opportunities should be equally considered when determining reasonable notice. Recently we are seeing common law notice awards for unskilled workers that are at the levels once only given to senior employees. The *Di Tomaso* case below illustrates the new fairness and reality that is emerging in awarding common law notice.

Example: Joe worked for a large company in Ontario for 30 years and then he was fired without just cause. Under Ontario employment standards legislation he would be entitled to 8 weeks statutory termination notice and an additional 26 weeks in severance pay, for a total of 34 weeks' pay. If however he sues the company to get common law notice instead of the statutory payments, he would be awarded a much higher amount instead. How much more he gets will depend on the type of job he had, his age, and the availability of new employment opportunities. If he is in his late 60s with little chance of a new position he could get close to 2 years notice as the Di Tomaso case would indicate. If he was a senior executive in the same circumstances it could even exceed 2 years by a few months.

Lesser Notice

Not surprisingly employers do not like having to pay large amounts for common law notice, especially now that junior level employees are being given large notice awards that previously only senior level employees obtained. But given the right of freedom to contract, the approach many companies take is to have a term into the employment contract that states upon termination the employee is entitled to a lesser amount than would be given under

Di Tomaso v. Crown Metal Packaging Canada LP, 2011 ONCA 469 (CanLII)

Antonio Di Tomaso was employed as a mechanic and press maintainer for over 33 years at Crown Metal which manufactured metal packaging. In September 9, 2009 he was given notice that his services were no longer required and his termination date was set at November 6, 2009. The company extended the termination date four more times for "temporary periods" until he was finally terminated on February 26, 2010. He was 62 when the factory was closed and his employment ended. He was given 26 weeks' severance pay in compliance with the requirements under the *Ontario Employment Standards Act (ESA)*.

Di Tomaso sued the company claiming that he had not been given adequate notice under the ESA and he sought common law damages for wrongful dismissal equivalent to 24 months' pay. The company claimed that all the extensions over the 5 month period counted as working notice and given the severance pay he received and the type of job that he held (unskilled and a lower level position), his common law notice should be capped at 12 months.

The trial judge ruled that the company could not count all the extensions of notice as effective working notice, and the law properly interpreted allows only one single period of temporary work that is not to exceed 13 weeks after the first termination notice is given. Otherwise a company could just continue to extend the notice of termination period indefinitely and a worker would have no certainty as to when their job was ending.

The trial judge also rejected the company's position that the character of the employment should be given the greatest weight in determining reasonable notice and that unskilled employees have an upper limit of 12 months. Considering Di Tomaso's age, length of service and difficulty in finding new employment the trial judge set his common law notice at 22 months. The company appealed this decision.

The Court's Decision

The Ontario Court of Appeal agreed with the initial judge's decision. It stated that the type or character of the job should not be emphasized when determining reasonable notice, and that if anything, it is today a factor of declining importance. It is particularly so if an employer attempts to use it to say that low level unskilled employees deserve less notice because they have an easier time finding alternative employment. In fact empirical studies of indisputable accuracy challenge that proposition.

The Appeal Court felt the judge had conducted an appropriately holistic review of the case and gave fair weight to all of the Bardal factors. The character of the employment was carefully considered but it was not as relevant as the other three factors. The Appeal Court confirmed that the award of 22 months' notice was appropriate in this case.

common law. It is legal to have a provision for lesser notice, so long as the lower amount is equal to or greater than what the employee would receive under statutory termination notice and severance pay requirements.

Because of this, employers should seek good legal advice when creating termination clauses in employment contracts, as it could save them considerable money in the future if the employee is terminated without cause. Employees on the other hand should also be very cautious when signing an employment contract. When you are offered a job, rarely are you contemplating termination, but the contract may be limiting what your will receive upon termination and it could end up costing you many months of salary that you would have been entitled to under common law. As with any significant contract, seeking legal advice before you agree to an employment contract is important.

Example: Karl Weselan was an independent engineer who signed an employment contract that limited his termination notice to 90 days. After more than 29 years of work associated with the company he was terminated without cause. The minimum statutory termination notice was 8 weeks so the 90 day notice requirement in the contract exceeded that minimum requirement. The 90 day notice entitled Weselan to $18,925. The court stated that he would have been entitled to 24 months' notice under common law ($151,400), but since the 90 day termination notice in the contract exceeded the statutory minimum it was enforceable. Since he had agreed to the contract and there was no fraud, misrepresentation, undue influence, duress, coercion or unconscionability, the 90 day notice was valid. (*Weselan v. Totten Sims Hubicki Associates (1997) Ltd.*, 2003 CanLII 49300 (ON SC).

The *Wright* case below clearly illustrates that if a company wants to limit termination notice, it must draft the clause very carefully. It must not violate any statutory termination requirements under any circumstances, because if there is any violation, then the clause will be unenforceable and the employee will be entitled to full common law notice.

Wright v. The Young and Rubicam Group of Companies (Wunderman), 2011 ONSC 4720 (CanLII)

John Wright was hired as the Executive Vice President and Director of Integrated Marketing for a major advertising agency at a base salary of $230,000 plus stock options, benefits and bonuses. The employment contract he signed had a termination clause that provided for specific notice payments upon termination depending on the number of years of service.

Mr. Wright's was promoted to president but after 5 years with the firm he was terminated without cause. The company paid him 13 weeks' base salary as stated in his employment contract. It also paid 13 weeks' of RRSP matching contributions, 13 weeks' of car allowance and parking payments and 13 weeks of group benefits, even though the contract stated the salary to be paid in the notice period was exclusive of all benefits.

Wright admitted that the employer had more than complied with the statutory termination notice requirements under the Employment Standards Act (ESA), which were a total of 10 weeks' pay (5 weeks termination notice plus 5 weeks' severance pay). But he claimed that the termination clause was unenforceable for two reasons: 1) the contract had not stated that all benefits were to continue during the notice period and 2) the amount of notice stated in the agreement to be paid in some situations did not meet the total ESA requirements, even though it had done so in his particular case.

The employer maintained that it had met all the ESA requirements in this particular situation so the termination clause in Wright's contract was enforceable.

The Court's Decision

The court ruled that the ESA states that the employee is entitled to all compensation during the notice period and this includes all benefits. The wording of the termination clause in Wright's contract though had only provided for base salary and had explicitly stated it excluded all benefits, so the clause violated the ESA requirements. The employer stated that it was implicit it would continue paying benefits during the notice period, and it had paid them, but the court disagreed. The actual wording of the clause excluded benefits, so it violated the ESA, and what the company had actually done did not change the wording.

The court also ruled that in some situations, such as if Wright had worked for 8.5, 9.5, 10.5 or 18.5 years, this clause would have violated the ESA requirements. In each of these hypothetical cases it would have provided .5 week's less severance pay than was required under the statute. It had not violated the ESA requirements for the 5 years that Wright had been employed there, but since it would have under these other situations, the court ruled the entire termination clause was void.

The court noted that there is no particular difficulty for an employer to draft a termination clause that would not violate ESA standards, *"so there is no compelling reason to uphold a termination clause which the draftsman may be reasonably understood to have known was not enforceable either at all or under certain circumstances."*

Wright was therefore entitled to 12 months common law notice (39 weeks longer than the contract had tried to establish in the contract). This poorly drafted clause ended up requiring the employer to pay more than $230,000 to the employee than it had anticipated, as well as considerable legal fees to fight the case. This case has made many companies review their employment contracts to ensure that no part of a termination clause violates statutory requirements under any circumstances.

Business Law Applied

➏ **LeeRoy Devon was** a 20-year employee at Forzan Electric Limited. He began as a salesperson and signed an employment contract at that time, indicating that if he was dismissed for any reason, his severance package would be based on one month per year of service, to a maximum of four months. He worked his way up to his present position as vice-president of sales in the company. When Forzan was taken over by a competitor, most of the senior executives were fired.

Devon wants the equivalent of reasonable notice in a lump-sum payment. Forzan checked its files, found the employment contract, and said it would only pay four months. Devon replied that the contract was signed 20 years ago, and he had forgotten all about it.

a) What reasonable notice would be likely in these circumstances?
b) Is the contract term to limit reasonable notice to four months enforceable?
   The CEO has become a good friend of Devon over the 20 years, and is embarrassed. He feels that he cannot face firing him in person, and wants to send Devon a letter of termination by courier to his home address.
c) Is this a wise course of action?

❼ **Dana Zubas was** vice-president of public relations for the Harris Group of companies for 10 years. Because of the need to restructure the company, this position has been eliminated. The Harris Group offers her a position as a public relations officer, at the same salary. Zubas objects, saying that the head of public relations used to report to her.

a) What is the technical name in law for the offering of the alternative position?
b) Is Zubas required to accept it?

Remedies for Wrongful Dismissal

Monetary Damages

Factors That Affect Damages

Factors that tend to increase the amount of damages the courts will award include:

- the employee was induced to move from one province to another to take the position from which the individual was subsequently fired
- the employee's health at the time of termination would make it difficult to find alternative employment
- the employee was laid off for three months before being recalled to work, then fired by the employer although the employer had intended the dismissal before the layoff
- the employee had a secure position and was enticed away from that position by the present employer
- the employee was terminated in a harsh or insensitive manner

Employees have often been given special consideration by the courts. If any employer raises defences in a court action, which the court views as without merit or done for tactical reasons to force the employee to settle, the court will increase the damage award to the employee significantly.

The court recognizes that when an employee is terminated, it has a devastating financial effect on the employee. If an employer uses the court process to increase legal costs, the employee often cannot afford the expense of litigation. To discourage employers from raising sham defences to make it difficult for employees to sue, the courts will significantly increase the award to the employee in this circumstance.

Factors that have been found to reduce the amount of damages include:

- the employee had been looking for a position prior to dismissal
- the employee was employed in the construction industry, which is highly cyclical in nature
- the position itself was insecure, and before accepting employment the employee was aware of the fact that the employer was having financial difficulties
- the employer provided job-relocation counselling
- the employee rejected the employer's offer of free placement services

Near cause—that is, poor behaviour that is just short of justification for firing—cannot be used to reduce the award of damages.

Thus in determining the size of an offer of severance pay for an employee who has been fired without just cause, poor performance, which is less than cause for dismissal, does not reduce the amount of severance pay.

a) Reasonable Notice

When courts calculate the monetary damages for wrongful dismissal, the court first determines what reasonable notice was required under the circumstances, whether it was statutory or common law notice. Then if the employer has not given that notice or pay in lieu of notice, the employee is awarded money equal to the notice that was required.

Mitigation   Like any contract situation, there is a duty on the employee to mitigate their damages. Once terminated an employee should seek new employment and be sure to keep records of all the attempts they make, such as letters to prospective employers. They are not required to accept a job that is significantly below their qualifications and experience, nor are they expected to relocate a large distance just to obtain employment. But they must show they have made reasonable efforts to obtain a reasonably similar job. If they take a lesser position they can claim for the difference in income from that position and one at their appropriate level. If their employer offers them their job back, they are expected to accept it unless the work environment is so unfavourable that the court would not expect them to return to it.

If they do not make a serious attempt to mitigate, the court can reduce the amount of damages awarded by the amount the person could have earned during the notice period. Any costs incurred in mitigation can be claimed by the employee but any money that they do earn while working in the notice period will be deducted from the total notice award.

Re-employment   Employees are not required to reveal to employers that they have found re-employment after termination. Careful employers now insist on having employees swear an affidavit that they have not found re-employment when employers are negotiating settlements with the former employees.

Business Alert!

Employers also often structure the settlement payments so that they are paid over a period of some months. The employee is required to report each month on whether that individual has found employment. Once the former employee has found re-employment, the payments either cease or are reduced significantly.

Employment Insurance   Employees who are fired without cause are entitled to collect Employment Insurance if they had worked long enough to qualify. If for example an employee is given a lump-sum settlement package of 6 months' notice from the employer, they must advise EI of this amount and then their EI benefits would begin after the 6 month period had elapsed. If a worker quits or is fired for cause they are not entitled to EI. If it is a constructive dismissal or the employer alleged just cause but there was none, EI can make inquiries to determine if the person is actually entitled to receive benefits.

Employment Insurance and Severance   If an individual collects employment insurance for some time while negotiating a severance package with a former employer, that employer must deduct the amount that has been paid from the final agreed package. If the employer does not do so, and pays it to the employee, the employer is liable and may have to pay twice—once to the employee and once to the commission. When a settlement is reached, the employer, not the employee, must reimburse the commission for the payments made. If it pays the money to the employee, the commission will collect it again from the employer.

Business Alert!

b) Bad Faith Moral Damages and Aggravated Damages

In the 1997 Supreme Court case of *Wallace v. United Grain Growers Ltd.*, [1997] 3 SCR 701, the Court awarded what have been called Wallace or bad faith or moral damages in cases of wrongful dismissal where the employer engaged in bad faith conduct or unfair dealing in the course of the dismissal. Actions such as lying, falsifying just cause, misleading acts, unduly insensitive behaviour, humiliation and embarrassment and "hardball" tactics could result in additional compensation for the employee. To compensate for this bad faith behaviour by the employer, the Court ruled that the notice period should be increased. This case resulted in an almost automatic "Wallace bump" of several months extra notice being awarded in a great many wrongful dismissal cases, even if there was little proof of the actual impact of the behaviour.

Finally in 2008 in the *Honda v. Keays* case, the Supreme Court revisited the issue of these bad faith damages and narrowed its application. It should now only be awarded if at the time of the actual dismissal the employer's conduct was unfair or in bad faith and there must be proof of actual harm. The distinction between Wallace bad faith moral damages and aggravated damages for mental anguish was removed. If the employer's conduct meets this new higher threshold and there was medical proof of its impact (such psychiatric treatment), then an additional specific amount of money can be awarded, but no longer would it be extra months of notice added on.

Employees often feel a sense of loss, humiliation and depression when they are fired even if the employer acted properly in the termination process. The courts have recognized the major impact losing a job can have on a person's self-worth. However aggravated damages for mental stress are only awarded in extreme cases and usually require a psychiatric report to substantiate the claim.

Honda Canada Inc. v. Keays, [2008] SCC 39 (CanLII)

Keays had worked 11 years for Honda, first on an assembly line and later in data entry, when, in 1997, he was diagnosed with chronic fatigue syndrome. He ceased work and received disability benefits until 1998, when Honda's insurer discontinued his benefits. Keays returned to work and was placed in a disability program that allows employees to take absences from work if they provide doctor's notes confirming that their absences are related to their disability.

Keays' employer became concerned about the frequency of his absences. Moreover, the notes Keays offered to explain his absences changed in tone, leaving the employer to believe that the doctor did not independently evaluate whether he missed work due to disability. As such, the employer asked Keays to meet Dr. Brennan, an occupational medical specialist, in order to determine how Keays' disability could be accommodated.

On the advice of his lawyer, Keays refused to meet Dr. Brennan without explanation of the purpose, methodology and parameters of the consultation. In March 28, 2000, the employer gave Keays a letter stating that it supported Keays' full return to work but that Keays' employment would be terminated if he refused to meet Dr. Brennan. When Keays remained unwilling to meet Dr. Brennan, the employer terminated Keays' employment.

Keays sued for wrongful dismissal. The trial judge found that Keays was entitled to a notice period of 15 months. He held that the employer had committed acts of discrimination, harassment and misconduct against Keays. He increased the notice period to 24 months to award additional aggravated damages (called informally: Wallace damages) because of the manner of dismissal. He also awarded punitive damages against the employer in the amount of $500,000, a costs premium, and costs on a substantial indemnity scale.

The Court of Appeal reduced the costs premium and, in a majority decision, reduced the punitive damages award to $100,000. The Court of Appeal otherwise upheld the trial judge's decision.

The Supreme Court of Canada's Decision

The Plaintiff was wrongfully dismissed and the award of damages reflecting the need for 15 months' notice should be maintained.

However, the court reversed the trial judge's finding first on facts as not supported by the evidence; Honda had not acted in bad faith in the manner of dismissing Keays.

Secondly, as a matter of law, while the court affirmed the availability of the remedy of damages that result from an employ

c) Punitive Damages

Punitive damages are only awarded when the employer's actions were intentionally wrongful and the acts are so malicious and outrageous that they deserve to be punished on their own. The *McNeil* case and the Pate Estate cases below are examples of situations where the employer's actions were so evil (false accusations of theft resulting in criminal trials) that large punitive damages were justified.

Example: In *McNeil v. Brewers Retail Inc.*, 2008 ONCA 405 (CanLII), a beer store employee was charged with theft when his employer produced video tape of him taking money out of the till. McNeil was convicted and terminated from his job. Later it was discovered that the employer had withheld the video tape that showed McNeil had put the money back in the till as he had claimed. His criminal conviction was reversed and he successfully sued the employer for malicious prosecution. He was awarded a total of $2,078,120 including $500,000 in punitive damages.

Pate Estate v. Galway-Cavendish and Harvey (Township), 2013 ONCA 669 (CanLII)

John Pate was employed as a building inspector for the Township of Galway-Cavendish and Harvey for 10 years. His supervisor claimed that they had uncovered discrepancies regarding building permit fees that Pate was responsible for but he had not remitted to the Township. Pate was never provided with the details of these allegations and was not allowed to respond to the allegations. The chief building official told Pate if he resigned he would not contact the police. Pate refused to resign so he was fired.

His boss (a former police officer) turned over some information to the police, but the police were reluctant to lay charges. Pressure was put on the force by the Township to proceed with the case, so Pate was finally charged with theft and fraud. Pate had to go through a 4 day criminal trial before being found not guilty. The Court found that the Township had uncovered evidence in the course of its own investigation that was in Pate's favour, but the Township had deliberately withheld that information from the police. If the police had received this information, it would never have proceeded with the charges.

Pate lived in a small town and the case got considerable media coverage. His reputation had been seriously damaged, and Pate was never able to get another municipal job again. The stress took a considerable toll, his marriage ended, a family business failed and Pate died in 2011.

Pate had sued for wrongful dismissal for which the Township admitted liability early on and had paid Pate 12 months in damages. He also claimed punitive damages for the false allegations and the outrageous manner in which he was treated. The trial court awarded him $25,000 in punitive damages, but he appealed this award considering it to be too low. The Court of Appeal agreed and sent it back to the trial court on that issue alone and the re-trial the punitive damages were increased to $550,000. The Township appealed this decision.

The Court's Decision

The Ontario Court of Appeal reviewed the facts of the case and the purpose of punitive damages. The first consideration is; how bad was the employer's conduct. Was it malicious and high handed? If so, the objective of punitive damages should be retribution, deterrence and denunciation. The Court looked at the blameworthiness of the defendant's conduct, the degree of vulnerability of the plaintiff and the harm done and the need for deterrence. It also noted that the financial means of the defendant is relevant, as an award of $100,000 against a middle class individual would be meaningful, but meaningless to a large multi-national company.

In Pate's case, the Court ruled that the Township's actions of pressuring the police to lay fraud charges and then intentionally withholding evidence that would have cleared Pate's name clearly demonstrated malice and justified a large award of punitive damages and also an award of damages for malicious prosecution. The judges reduced the punitive damage award, but only slightly, to $450,000.

Job Reinstatement

Most employees cannot get their job back if they are wrongfully dismissed. Monetary damages are their only remedy. Unions however have usually negotiated terms in their collective agreements that permit a labour arbitrator to reinstate a unionized worker back in their job if the arbitrator thinks it is appropriate. This right also exists for non-union employees who work in industries governed by the Canada Labour Code such as banks, airlines or railways. As a result this remedy is commonly sought in these workplaces.

Human Rights tribunals also have the authority to reinstate a worker to their job if they had been successful in their complaint of harassment or discrimination. The *Fair v. Hamilton Wentworth* case earlier in this chapter is an example of a worker who had a discrimination complaint and finally after 9 years she was reinstated to a new job with her employer as well as paid her wages for this lengthy time period when the dispute dragged on.

■ *Business Law*   Applied

❽ **Villma Mednic was** a receptionist with Geller company for approximately one year. During that time, she had made personal long-distance calls during office hours, charging them to business files. The company's auditor discovered these calls—90 in all, for a total of about $500. On discovery, Mednic repaid the money and promised not to do it again. Geller Enterprises does not want an employee who is dishonest, and would like to fire her. Mednic claims the company suffered no harm, as the money was repaid.

   a) Does the company have just cause to fire Mednic?
   b) If the company fires Mednic and is wrong, what can Mednic claim in a court proceeding?
   c) What are the relevant common law and statutory notice periods?
   d) How long do you think it would take a receptionist to find another position?
   e) If a company was found not to have just cause for her dismissal, could Mednic obtain an order that the company reinstate her?

❾ **The Vitale Group** is facing large losses and, in order to survive, must fire the regional sales manager, Mary Meccelli, who is 45 years of age. Meccelli has been with the company for 16 years, and currently earns $60,000 a year. An employment agency says that it usually takes about one year for a person in Meccelli's situation to find another position.

   a) Is firing for economic necessity just cause?
   b) What will determine the length of notice that must be given to Meccelli?
   c) What notice do you think the court would award in this case?

Wrongful Resignation

It is clear now that employers have to give employees reasonable notice if they want to terminate them when there is no just cause. Employees too often want to end their employment even though the company has done nothing wrong, and the employee is also obligated to give their employer notice. Generally though the notice the employee must give is much shorter than the time the employer is required to give. If the employee gives the employer two weeks' notice, and then the employer tells them to leave immediately, the employer still must pay the employee for the two week notice period, (provided there is no contractual term stating otherwise).

In many employment situations two weeks' notice by the employee is reasonable, as the employer can often hire and train a replacement in that amount of time. However in cases where the employee has specialized skills or talents that are not easily replaced, the courts may require that they give their employer much more notice they are resigning. If they do not give reasonable notice the courts have held that they can be liable for **wrongful resignation** and can be liable for the **lost profits of the employer**. If they are a senior employee with a fiduciary duty who leaves to start a competing business and they take confidential information from their previous employer, the resulting damage awards can be very large.

There have been several recent cases that have caused considerable discussion where the employees have been held liable for profits for many years after they have left. The damages have been in the millions and it has many questioning whether these damage awards are reasonable. Employees should have the freedom to work where they want, and the possibility of being liable for huge damage awards if they are highly skilled or in managerial positions and do not give enough notice, appears to significantly limit their freedom to switch jobs or start their own company.

wrongful resignation
an employee may be liable if they quit and did not give the employer reasonable notice they were leaving

Example: In *GasTOPS Ltd. v. Forsyth*, 2012 ONCA 134 (CanLII) four very specialized aviation maintenance software specialists gave their employer GasTOPS Ltd. two weeks' notice that they were leaving and then left to start their own company Mxi Technologies which began to compete with their former employer for lucrative aviation contracts. Soon after 15 other employees left GasTOPS to come and work for their new company. GasTOPS sued the four who had left for breach of contract due to inadequate notice of resignation, breach of fiduciary duty and breach of confidence.

Finally after 13 years and a 7 year trial with 295 days of court testimony (an Ontario record), the trial judge ruled that the four executives were liable on all the claims. The court believed that they breached the employment contract and should have given 10 months' notice that they were leaving. This is the amount of time it would have taken to recruit, hire and train replacements. They had breached their duty of confidence when they took confidential information from their former employer. They had breached their fiduciary duty by soliciting GasTOPS clients and portraying Mxi products as a "spin off" and the next iteration of GasTOPS products. The surprising part of the case though is the award of damages. Mxi and the four executives had to pay $19 million in damages, for the profits that the court estimated GasTOPS lost over a 10 year period. No other case has held former employees liable for profits over such a long period of time. Commentators question if this 10 year time period is excessive and prevents talented executives from being able to start competing businesses.

Example: A senior executive at Blackberry had a term in his employment contract that if he left he had to give the company 6 months' notice. He was given a promotion to Executive Vice President but two months later he accepted a position at Apple and gave Blackberry 2 months' notice he was leaving. Blackberry took him to court and the court declared that the 6 month notice clause was enforceable so he could be asked to help in his transition out of the company until the 6 month period had expired. Blackberry was undergoing major problems and many believe it wanted to send a message it did not want all its top personnel abandoning the sinking ship. (*BlackBerry Limited v. Marineau-Mes*, 2014 ONSC 1790)

■ *Critical Concepts of* Employees' Post-Termination Obligations

The law implies obligations on employees to their employers post-employment:

- fiduciary level employees owe a duty not to compete for a reasonable period
- all level employees owe a duty to give reasonable notice of quitting
- all level employees owe a duty not to use their former employer's confidential information

RBC Dominion Securities Inc. v. Merrill Lynch Canada Inc., [2008] SCC 54 (CanLII)

Don Delamont was the manager of the investment advisors at the Cranbrook Branch of RBC Dominion Securities ("RBC"). Cranbrook is a small city in British Columbia. RBC is the stock broker arm of the Royal Bank of Canada. Delamont was a personal friend of the manager of a competitor, the defendant Merrill Lynch Inc.

In November, 2002 Delamont left RBC to join Merrill Lynch's Cranbrook branch and took with him almost the entire Cranbrook sales team. Prior to leaving Delamont copied all RBC confidential customer information and brought it to Merrill Lynch. The RBC branch was effectively hollowed out and all but collapsed. On discovering the confidential information, Merrill Lynch returned it immediately and RBC accepted that no damage had been done resulting from this breach.

RBC sued the former employees and Merrill Lynch successfully on the basis of several economic torts, which will not be discussed here, but also sued the departing employees alleging two implied terms in the employment contract of any employee **at any level** even non-fiduciary employees:

    a) to give reasonable notice of termination
    b) not to compete during the notice period.

RBC argued that Mr. Delamont, even though he was not a fiduciary, had an implied duty of good faith to retain employees under his supervision.

The trial court awarded over $2 million in damages including $250,000 in punitive damages. As part of this award Mr. Delamont was held liable for breaching an implied duty of good faith and was held liable for the lost profits of the RBC branch for a period of 5 years totalling $1.48 million. The B. C. Court of Appeal lowered the overall award and rejected the large award made against Mr. Delamont. It stated non-fiduciary employees have a right to compete once they leave unless there is a non-competition clause, which in this case there was not. The damage award should reflect what was in the reasonable contemplation of the parties when the contract was formed, so on this basis the trial award of 5 years lost profits was inappropriate. RBC appealed to the Supreme Court.

The Supreme Court of Canada's Decision

This Court found that although contract of employment ends when either the employer or employee terminates the employment relationship, residual post-employment duties may remain. An employee terminating employment may be liable for failure to give reasonable notice in breach of these residual duties. Subject to these duties the employee is free to compete against the former employer.

The Court found that reasonable notice in this situation was 2.5 weeks. That is the time in which a replacement employee could be found. During this period of time the employee has a duty not to compete and is only liable for damages for failure to give reasonable notice. The damages relating to the failure to give reasonable notice were estimated at $40,000.00 for all employees.

The Supreme Court however also ruled that in the case of Mr. Delamont, even though he was not a fiduciary, he did owe RBC a duty of good faith. He breached this duty by recruiting other investment advisors to join him on the move to the competitor. He was held liable for 5 years of lost profits for the RBC branch, $1.48 million.

This case has caused considerable discussion. It is the first time a non-fiduciary employee has had this duty imposed on them. The investment industry is an extremely competitive industry and firms use very aggressive recruitment tactics. Often brokers give notice in terms of hours or minutes. The ruling on Mr. Delamont now imposes potentially huge financial liability on "quasi fiduciary" managers if they decide to leave, share the prospects of alternative employment with others and then go on to compete with their former firm. The dissenting judge commented that the damage award was grossly disproportionate. She stated; *"Employees are not indentured servants. In the absence of a fiduciary relationship or a non-competition clause they are legally free to leave and enter into competition with former employers, either individually or in a group."* This decision seems to contradict that position.

Business Law Applied

ⓘ **Satinder Khalsa** is the CFO of Think Prudent Mortgage Corp. Inc. ("Think Prudent"). Ami Raj is a bookkeeper in the same business. Both quit without notice.

Khalsa goes to a large bank and Raj goes to a credit union. Both of these businesses compete with Think Prudent in the mortgage lending market.

    a) Does Khalsa have any obligation not to compete with Think Prudent for a reasonable period? Give reasons.
    b) Does Raj have any obligation not to compete with Think Prudent for a reasonable period? Give reasons.

c) How could Think Prudent have prevented Raj from contacting its customers for a reasonable period?

d) Think Prudent has good reason to believe Raj took its customer list and has it hidden in his home. Is there any remedy available to Think Prudent to get the list back?

Settlement and Confidentiality

As with any civil law matter, it is often advisable that the two sides reach a settlement rather than proceed to a full trial. It can save money, time and result in a resolution that both sides have negotiated and is more acceptable to both parties. In many settlement agreements there is a confidentiality clause that states the employee cannot disclose the terms of the settlement. This clause must be taken seriously as a violation of it can result in the employee having to return some or the entire amount of the settlement. In Florida, a teenager posted on her Facebook page that her father had won his case against his former employer, and she bragged it would be paying for her trip to Europe that summer. The employer claimed this breached their confidentiality agreement and the court agreed. Her father had to repay the entire $80,000 settlement he had received.

Example: Jan Wong was well known writer who was terminated by the Globe and Mail. She sued for wrongful dismissal and after a bitter dispute; the two sides negotiated a settlement agreement which included a confidentiality clause. Ms. Wong wrote a book about the depression she suffered as a result of her termination. In the book she wrote about her legal dispute and stated that the newspaper had paid her "a big pile of money to go away." The Globe claimed that statement was a violation of the confidentiality agreement and the court agreed. Ms. Wong had to repay the entire settlement amount, which the Globe said it would donate to a mental health centre. (*Globe and Mail and CEP, Local 870M*, (2013), 233 L.A.C. (4th)

Confidential Information

Employees want to know what they can do if they go to work for someone else, or set up business on their own. Employers need to know how much of their business expertise and knowledge can be protected, so that employees cannot learn all there is to know, and then go into competition using that information.

It is sometimes difficult to draw a line between where an employer's confidential information ends and employees' general knowledge begins. Normally, the principle that separates confidential, protected information from general knowledge is that confidential information is objective—for example, formulas, processes, or market research such as consumer surveys or market analyses. However, knowledge or skill acquired by employees on the job—"know-how"—is subjective information, and is not the confidential property of the employer.

Confidential formulas and processes are obvious examples of protected information. Common disputes arise over information about customers. Employees, especially salespeople, may develop a personal relationship with a number of customers. Can the employee leave, go to work for a competitor, and call on the customers to get them to switch to the new company?

Employers argue that the customer relationship arose because of employer's expense. The employer may have spent a considerable amount of money on advertising and marketing to develop the relationship with the customer.

Under law, a former employee cannot directly contact customers from the previous employer for a reasonable time afterwards in an effort to try to get their business. What is a reasonable time will vary with each circumstance, but a rule of thumb would be about six months for most situations. Although direct solicitation is prohibited, former employees could place an advertisement in a newspaper announcing their new business. If a customer approached them as a result of the ad, the employees would be entitled to deal with the customer.

■■■ *Critical Concepts of* Trade Secrets/Confidential Information

---

confidential business information

information that provides a business advantage as a result of the fact that it is kept secret

There are three distinct areas of law that govern **confidential business information** (information that provides a business advantage as a result of the fact that it is kept secret):

- Breach of confidence—if information is given to a person in circumstances that make it clear the information is intended to remain confidential, that confidence can be enforced by court action.
- Breach of fiduciary duty—if there is a special relationship, such as employer/employee, and the employee learns of the information as a result of this relationship, then the employee is under a duty not to disclose it.
- Breach of contract—if the employee signs a term in an employee agreement (a non-competition clause), that clause is enforceable.

Labour Unions

Of the nearly 15 million people in the Canadian labour force, about 30% of the workers are in labour unions. Of the workers in unions, about 57% work for the government and 43% work in the private sector. Though the percentage of the Canadian workforce that is unionized has declined slightly, we have a much higher percentage than the U.S., where only about 12% of their workers are unionized. Studies have shown that unionized workers earn higher wages (about 7–15% higher) and they can retire about 4 years earlier than non-unionized workers.

There are both federal and provincial statutes relating to unions and collective bargaining. It is estimated that about 90 percent of labour matters fall under provincial jurisdiction. While there are provincial variations, there are many common areas, and these are discussed in this section.

In **collective bargaining**, the union is called the bargaining agent, and the employee group is the bargaining unit. The unit includes all employees of that type of business, whether they are union members or not. The contract made as the result of collective bargaining is therefore called a group, or **collective, agreement**.

collective agreement

is the contract created by collective bargaining between an employer and a labour union

Certification

Employers can recognize unions voluntarily but, if they refuse to do so, a union can apply to the provincial labour board for certification. The labour board is similar to a court, but is more informal, and is called a tribunal. It is this body that settles most collective bargaining disputes. A person need not be represented by a lawyer to appear before a labour board.

In most jurisdictions, a vote of 50 percent of the employees is sufficient for the board to certify the union as the bargaining agent. Some provinces do not require a formal vote, but will certify the union if 50 percent of employees have signed union membership cards.

The Supreme Court made it clear though that the *Charter of Rights and Freedoms* section 2.(d) on freedom of association does not grant workers the right to unionize. As outlined in Chapter 1 in the case of *Ontario (Attorney General) v. Fraser*, 2011 SCC 20, the Supreme Court upheld an Ontario law that prohibited farm workers from joining unions. The court ruled that since they were allowed to form employee associations instead, that fulfilled their freedom of association rights. The Charter does not specifically guarantee any particular form this association must take such as membership in a union.

Unfair Labour Practices

Collective bargaining laws place restrictions on both the employer and the union. The labour boards keep a close eye on the employer while a union is organizing, so that no unlawful methods are used to resist its formation. Employer activity is scrutinized during this time, and any statements made to employees are interpreted very strictly. If those statements or the employer's conduct are tainted by anti-union sentiment, the employer may end up paying large damage awards, while the union is still certified as the bargaining agent.

Collective Agreements

Collective agreements are similar to standard form employment contracts, and are negotiated by the union on behalf of all employees. They apply to all bargaining union employees, and no individual worker can make a private employment contract. A collective agreement contains the usual terms of an employment contract, including clauses that:

- set out a procedure for laying off (temporary letting-go)
- give notice periods for termination (permanent firing)
- set salary, vacation time, and fringe benefits
- provide a method for settling grievances

Types of Unions

One of the terms in the collective agreement is usually that the union is entitled to a closed shop. There are several types of closed shops.

- Closed shop—an individual must be a member of the union before being hired
- Union shop—the employer can hire anyone but once hired they must then join the union
- Rand shop, or rand formula—an individual must pay union dues, but does not necessarily have to join the union as a condition of employment

In some provinces, the rand formula is mandatory, and the employer may be required to collect dues on the union's behalf.

In the U.S. many states have passed "right to work laws". This allows workers who work in a unionized workplace to not have to join the union and they also do not have to pay union dues. This weakens the power of the unions where these laws are in place and workers' wages and benefits in states with these laws are significantly lower than in other states that have not passed this legislation. There has been talk that right to work laws may come in to Canada, but as yet no province has adopted this legislation. Canadian unions are obviously opposed to this legislation, they often refer to it as the "right to work for less" law.

Grievances

Labour laws require that all collective agreements contain a procedure for solving disputes over the interpretation of a collective agreement. Such disagreements are known as grievances. For example, an employee may have a dispute about the calculation of overtime pay, or a group of employees may object to hidden-camera surveillance, or mandatory drug testing.

The early stages of a grievance are usually dealt with by negotiation but, if this fails, the grievance goes to arbitration. The arbitrator is normally chosen by the employer and the union. In some provinces, if they cannot agree, either side can apply to the minister of labour to have an arbitrator appointed.

The Right to Strike

Legislation restricts when a union has the right to strike. A strike can be called only at the negotiation stage of a collective agreement; while the agreement is in force, there is no right to strike. There are certain procedures that must be followed before a strike; otherwise the strike is illegal.

- The parties must bargain for a specified period of time.
- The union must hold a strike vote, and give notice of a successful strike vote to the employer.
- Both sides must submit to a conciliation process, in which an outsider attempts bring the parties to agreement. The conciliator cannot force any terms on either side.
- If conciliation fails, there is a cooling-off period before the employer can lock out the employees, or the employees can strike.

Certain unionized employees who work in essential services do not have the right to strike to protect the safety and security of the public. Nurses, police and fire fighters are workers included in this group. In certain situations the government can pass legislation to force other workers back to work if they are on strike if it is having a detrimental effect on the public or industry. Airline workers, rail workers and Canada Post workers and teachers have at certain times been subject to back to work legislation when they were on strike. The Supreme Court made it clear that the *Charter* right to freedom of association does not guarantee the right to strike. (Reference Re Public Service Employee Relations Act (Alta.), [1987] 1 SCR 313)

Business Law Applied

① **A truck driver** was required to drive his vehicle on a ramp beside an open pit at a mine. There was a slight rain, and the ramp was slippery. In addition, approximately 100 metres of the protective railing at the side of the ramp was missing.

The truck driver refused to drive on the ramp as it was unsafe, and the union called a strike.

   a) Was striking the proper procedure? If not, what was?

Picketing

If the strike is legal, picketing is permitted. Picketing involves strikers' standing near the company's premises, or marching, as they display signs to dissuade people from doing business there. All such activity must be peaceful, and the information on the signs and banners the picketers carry must be accurate.

labour relations board
an administrative tribunal
regulating labour relations

If picketing goes beyond simple communication and becomes intimidation, the **labour relations board** (an administrative tribunal regulating labour relations) may restrict the number of picketers permitted near the business at any one time. The individuals on the picket line are subject to other laws, such as tort and criminal law, and cannot commit defamation or any criminal offence.

Primary/Secondary Picketing

All provinces permit employees to picket the plant or factory where they work—this is called primary picketing. However, the employer may carry on business at other locations; if they, too, are picketed, this is called secondary picketing. In most provinces, secondary picketing is not allowed. Businesses that are unrelated to the main employer cannot be picketed.

Example: In *Telus v. T.W.U.*, 2005 BCSC 1236 (CanLII) striking telecommunications workers were picketing the homes of their managers and co-workers as well as local restaurants and hotels where these managers went. The strikers were very aggressive and insulting and used intimidating behaviour. The court issued an injunction against the picketing workers to stop picketing at these locations because their conduct was both a public and private nuisance.

Example: In *Vancouver Island University v Vancouver Island University Faculty Association*, 2011 CanLII 49028 (BC LRB) a union representing vocational instructors at a B.C. University went on strike. The university leased space in a waterfront facility away from the campus so that other instructors in a different union could teach ESL courses to their international students. The striking vocational instructors then set up a picket line at the waterfront facility and the ESL instructors refused to cross the picket line. The striking union said that it had the legal right to picket as the university was conducting an "offsite work activity." The B.C. Labour Board ruled that since the ESL instructors were not doing work that the striking workers did at this temporary waterfront facility, the picketing was illegal. An injunction was issued ordering them to stop picketing.

Replacement Workers/Scabs

Everyone has the right to cross a picket line. Customers can continue to do business; suppliers can still deliver goods and services to the employer, which has the right to carry on normal business activities. If the employer can persuade other employees to cross the picket line, they must be permitted to do so.

Most controversy surrounds the crossing of picket lines by what are called replacement workers or scabs—depending on the point of view of the speaker. In most jurisdictions, employers are permitted to bring in substitute employees to help run the business during a strike. Under federal legislation, and in the provinces of B.C. and Quebec, there are statutes prohibiting the use of strike-breaking employees. Similar legislation was repealed in Ontario in 1995.

Example: The most violent union dispute in Canadian history resulted in the murder of 9 miners during a strike/lockout at the Royal Oaks gold mine in Yellowknife in 1992. Three replacement workers and six union members who had crossed the picket line to work were murdered when a bomb exploded underground. One of the striking miners, Roger Warren, pleaded guilty to nine counts of second degree murder. (see Chapter 4 the case of *Fullowka v. Pinkerton's of Canada Ltd.*, 2010 SCC 5).

Alberta (Information and Privacy Commissioner) v. United Food and Commercial Workers, Local 401, 2013 SCC 62, [2013] 3 SCR 733)

During a 305 day strike at the Palace Casino in the West Edmonton Mall, the union for the striking workers photographed and videotaped people crossing the picket line and threatened to post these images on a website. People complained that this violated their privacy rights under the Alberta privacy law PIPA (Personal Information Protection Act). The union challenged this position by claiming that its rights under the *Charter* s. 2 freedom of expression were violated by the Alberta privacy law and it should have the right to freely communicate its position.

The adjudicator ruled the Alberta privacy law prohibited this union activity and it was a legitimate protection of privacy rights. The Union appealed to the Alberta Court of Appeal and it overturned that decision in favour of the union. It ruled the Alberta law was too broad and violated the union's fundamental *Charter* rights. The Alberta Privacy Commissioner appealed the decision to the Supreme Court.

The Court's Decision

The Supreme Court agreed that the Alberta privacy law did violate the union's right to freedom of expression. The privacy law was overly broad and it imposed restrictions on the union's ability to communicate and persuade the public of its cause. This impaired its ability to use one of its most effective bargaining strategies in the course of a lawful strike. The importance of freedom of expression in the context of labour disputes was stressed.

Alberta was the only province that did not protect the rights of unions to communicate in their privacy legislation. The Court struck down the entire law Alberta privacy law and gave Alberta one year to rewrite it.

Business Law Applied

⑫ **Coal Codvill Inc.** was a distributor for the IGA food-store franchises. Its employees went on strike, and picketed the plant. One of the franchisees that Codvill supplied was Dussessoy's IGA, and Codvill's employees began to picket that location. All its signs said "Codvill—distributor to IGA—employees on strike." The picketing was peaceful, and customers were allowed freely past the picket line.

   a) Did the Codvill employees have the right to picket this site to which Codvill delivers?
   b) What could Dussessoy's IGA do about the picketing, if anything?

In Summation

Hiring

■ Whether a worker is an employee or an independent contractor is determined by a two part test of who controls how the job is done and who supplies the tools for the job.

■ The process of advertising for and interviewing potential employees is closely controlled by human rights legislation and labour laws. *Bona fide* occupational requirements may be used in selecting applicants; however, questions related to certain matters, such as race, sex, and religion, may not be asked during the interview process. Some types of information maybe obtained from the employee for employment records after being hired.

Employment

■ An employment agreement is often a standard form contract customized for the individual employee and the position being filled. Frequently, there is a reference to an employee manual stated in the employment contract. The manual details the terms of employment.

■ An employer is advised to have the employee verify the truth of statements on his or her application and résumé. Misrepresentation by the employee on these documents is a ground for immediate dismissal.

■ Employment legislation exists at both the federal and provincial levels. These statutes deal with such issues as wages, discrimination, sexual harassment, occupational health and safety, and maternity leave and workplace safety.

Firing

■ An employer can dismiss an employee for just cause (actions inconsistent with the duties of employment). Such actions would include, among others, theft, conflict of interest, or incompetence.

■ If the dismissal is not for just cause, it is a breach of the employment contract and will result in payment of damages based on a period of notice.

■ The Supreme Court ruled that employers should take a contextual approach to discipline and it should be proportional to the nature and degree of the employee's misconduct.

■ A worker may have done something wrong but the court may require that the employer use progressive discipline (such as warnings, suspension, demotion, rehabilitation) before termination. If this de-hiring was required and not done, then the termination can be a wrongful dismissal.

■ The employee may be forced to quit because of a fundamental change to their job such as a significant cut in pay and/or benefits, a demotion, relocation or a "poisoned work environment". This is a constructive dismissal and the employee can sue for wrongful dismissal.

■ Confusion exists as to what will constitute an appropriate notice period because both the common law and the statute law contain notice periods.

■ Statutory notice, set through employment standards acts and labour acts, is the minimum notice period required.

■ The common law requires reasonable notice to be given based on the circumstances of each case. It attempts to balance a number of factors, including age, length of employment, anticipated time to locate other employment, and level of position, when determining what would be reasonable notice (Bardal factors).

■ If the amount of notice required has been previously established and incorporated in the employment contract, it may be seen as enforceable if it is equal or greater than the statutory minimum notice and severance pay.

■ Damages for bad faith or mental distress arising from termination may be available to the employee if the manner in which the termination has been handled has caused extreme mental suffering.

■ Punitive damages are only awarded if the employer's actions were intentionally wrongful and the acts were so malicious and outrageous that they deserved to be punished on their own.

Mitigation

- An employee who has been terminated has a positive obligation in law to make an effort to find other employment. The employee's attempts to mitigate will be taken into consideration by the court in determining any award to be given as a result of the termination.

- If an employee's position has been so altered that the circumstances could be construed as constructive dismissal, that employee may have to accept the lesser position while looking for other employment.

- The severance package offered to a terminated employee may affect that individual's claims under such government programs as employment insurance.

Confidential Information

- Confidential business information may be protected by the employer through a court action to stop the employee from using the material after employment has been terminated.

- The employer will not be successful in preventing an employee from using the skill or knowledge acquired on the job, either to benefit another employer or for the ex-employee's own purposes.

Labour Unions

- Both federal and provincial legislation exists dealing with unions and the collective bargaining process.

- Once certified in accordance with provincial requirements, the trade union becomes the bargaining agent on behalf of the employee group.

- The collective agreement details a number of terms and conditions on behalf of all employees. These would include salary, termination, grievance procedures, and whether the union is entitled to a closed shop.

- Matters such as the right to strike or picket, and the use of replacement labour during a strike, are dealt with through legislation and not through the collective bargaining process.

Closing Questions

Hiring

1. Biosyn Ltd. had recently purchased some new technology that claimed to be able to determine, through analysis of hair and fingernail samples, whether an individual would be prone to particular diseases. The vice-president, human resources, received a copy of the internal memo circulated concerning this new technology, and thought it might be used to Biosyn's advantage in dealing with its employees. If they could require new employees to undergo the testing, then they could determine whether they were susceptible to any diseases that might involve lengthy periods off work, or that could lead to less-than-optimum performance.

    Biosyn would be able to reduce absenteeism and increase production, or at least allocate the employee to an appropriate department where the impact of the potential illness could be lessened. A further benefit would be that it would be possible to monitor changes in the body chemistry of employees who worked in departments dealing with different bacterial life forms. In this way it would be possible to see if there were any change in their health status, so that the company could take active measures to assist that employee.

    a) The vice-president, human resources, has asked you to prepare a report, giving full reasons whether or not Biosyn can require the employees to provide hair and fingernail samples for testing. She also needs to know under what circumstances the testing would have to be done.

2. Melita Andersson had been employed by Computoch Inc. for three years in the sales department. When she was hired, she signed a standard form employment contract that included a job description, as well as terms relating to vacations and so on.

Recently she was told by her vice-president that all employees in the sales department are required to sign a confidentiality agreement. This agreement includes a non-competition clause covering the possibility of the employee's leaving Computoch. When Andersson asked what would happen if she did not sign the contract, the vice-president merely laughed, pulled her finger across her throat, and pretended to throw something over her shoulder.

Before all this comes to a showdown, Andersson has decided to inform herself as to her rights, and has contacted you, knowing that you took a business law course.

a) Advise Andersson as to the nature of the issue that is being raised by Computoch's request and whether she is required to sign the agreement.

b) Would it make any difference if Computoch were requiring the same non-competition/confidentiality agreement to be signed by all its employees, and not just those in the sales department?

3. Morty Lake is a supervisor at a not-for-profit organization that advises people on occupational health matters. Lake's job is to review the case studies of the six field workers who do the interviewing and assist the clients. Because it is a not-for-profit organization, funds for leasing premises were limited, and so the organization is housed in what used to be a men-only club. Anna Lee recently joined the organization and, much to her surprise, on the first day found that, although 55 percent of the staff are women, there is only one women's washroom. This is housed in a very small trailer, attached to the far back of the building. The washroom is frequently crowded, and often it is an office joke that people need to take a number in the morning in order to ensure that they have an opportunity to use it in the course of the day.

This issue has been raised with Lake a number of times by his staff, and he has always promised to look into it. What he means by this, the staff are not sure, because the female staff have always been a little uncertain why he feels a need to close his office door whenever one of them is in discussing an issue with him. The director of the organization is usually absent from the premises, out looking for funding, and Lake is the next person in charge—consequently, the female employees have been reluctant to raise the issue of his interviewing techniques.

Today was the last straw for Anna Lee when, during an interview in Lake's office to discuss a client's file, he suggested he didn't need sugar in his coffee as there was "obviously enough sweetness present." Leaving the office as quickly as she could, she went through her employment package to see what procedures should be followed for complaining about this behaviour. The only help she found in it was a statement encouraging employees to speak up if harassed.

a) What grounds does Anna Lee have for registering a complaint, and which legislation deals with these issues?

b) With reasons, explain which of the following would be liable for the conduct complained of:
    i)   Morty Lake
    ii) the director
    iii) the not-for-profit organization

c) What steps would you suggest the employer immediately take to protect itself and ensure this type of situation does not arise again?

d) Does the not-for-profit organization have grounds for immediately terminating Lake's employment, or is there any other obligation which it must meet prior to taking that step?

4. If an employee works on a statutory holiday, can the employer require that individual to take another day off in compensation?

5. Alex Alexander was interviewed for a position with an advertising company. The interview was conducted by the vice-president, human relations, for the company, who had previously run as a candidate in a federal election. He asked Alexander if he had voted for the party currently in power (not the party with which the vice-president is affiliated). The fact that Alexander avoided answering the question was written down in the interview notes.

Later in the interview the vice-president, laughing, said to Alexander, "You seem to be an absolutely sterling, top-notch candidate: great recommendations, excellent academic background, almost too good to be true. Don't tell me you are a closet drinker." When Alexander responded with laughter as well, the vice-president wrote in his interview notes, "Did not deny potential drinking problem."

Alexander was not offered the job, and later found out from a friend who worked in the advertising firm that these notes had been made about his interview and, as a direct result, the job had gone to another candidate.

a)   Which laws deal with the types of questions asked of Alexander in the interview process?

b)   Is there any legal remedy available to Alexander as a result of this interview?

6. Waleed had been unemployed for three years. He found that most employers considered him over-qualified for the positions for which he had applied. In desperation, Waleed rewrote his résumé, deleting the reference to his university degree, and describing his working experience in much more general terms. He was recently offered a position doing shift work in the bottling department of a brewery. On his first day on the job, he was asked to sign an employment contract which required him to certify the truth of his statements concerning his education and qualifications.

Within the first week, Waleed had irritated his supervisor by making several suggestions as to how procedures could be streamlined to increase productivity, as well as pointing out a couple of occupational safety issues that needed to be dealt with. Waleed had implied that if corrective measures were not taken, he would register a complaint with the appropriate government department. His supervisor has spoken to some of Waleed's co-workers, and discovered that Waleed had let slip that he had a university degree and specialized training in time-management efficiency.

a)   Can the supervisor terminate Waleed's employment?

b)   If termination is possible, what would be the grounds, and what length of notice must be given Waleed?

c)   What defences are available to Waleed given the information you have from the fact situation above?

d)   If the company were to terminate Waleed's employment immediately, and to use him as an example to other employees by firing him in front of his co-workers, what damages would a court award in these circumstances?

7. Has an employer met his obligations related to industrial health and safety if he does so in the following manner? Explain.

- Safety glasses are made available to employees working on drill presses.
- To obtain the safety glasses, employees are required to ask for them at a specific office in another part of the building.
- In an attempt to keep overhead costs low, employees are required to sign the glasses out and return them at the end of the day.

8. Anayat Daniels wishes to hire Asja Lublin as an accountant for his business but he wants to avoid a lot of government paper work so he has her sign an employment contract which states that she is an independent contractor. It is his belief that because of this term in the contract, if he fires her he does not have to pay her severance pay. Is he correct?

Firing

9. Harvey Keach was employed as a professor of advanced mathematics. He had an unusual style, and had won awards for excellence in teaching. Roger Slown approached Keach with the idea of making videotapes of his class lessons, and then selling them as review aids to mathematics students or, alternatively, selling them to the general public, who might wish to upgrade their mathematics skills. Keach's employer became aware of the videotapes and their sales, and has called Keach in for a discussion.

a)   On what basis could Keach's employer terminate his employment?

b)   Would such a firing be with or without cause?

c)   Would Keach have any legal rights regarding his termination?

10. Four days out of five each work week, Susan Douthwaite was 10 to 15 minutes late in arriving at her office in the building where she was employed. Her supervisor has told her that this lateness is unacceptable, and Douthwaite's response was that she was always in the company parking lot on the hour, but it took 10 minutes to walk to her office.

a)   Discuss whether the company has just cause for terminating Douthwaite's employment based on her lateness.

11. Brian Dooley had been employed as an instructor at a community college for 15 years. An internal study to meet budgetary restraints indicated that instructors could be hired on contract at half the price of instructors on full-time employment. This would result in considerable savings to the college, allowing it to maintain its services to the student body.

Dooley, who is 50 years old, was approached about early retirement. The package offered was not particularly attractive, and he turned it down. The next week, Dooley received a termination notice.

a) Does Dooley's refusal to accept the early-retirement package allow his employer to terminate him with cause?

b) What other information would you require in order to be able to advise Dooley as to what would be a realistic settlement of this matter with his employer?

c) How would that information help you in arriving at your advice to Dooley?

12. Harold deSouza's employment with Arbour Inc. was terminated after 10 years. His dismissal was without cause, although there had been incidents of misconduct that could have justified terminating his employment. Arbour is currently negotiating with deSouza about the number of weeks of notice on which his severance package will be based. The company has suggested a minimum period given the background issue of misconduct, while deSouza is insisting on a much longer period of notice. DeSouza is currently looking for other employment and has requested a letter of reference.

a) What are the two sources of authority on which deSouza and Arbour are basing their negotiation for the necessary period of notice?

b) What potential problem could Arbour be creating if it were to provide the letter of reference?

c) What general principle of contract law is deSouza following in his attempt to locate other employment?

d) What are the qualifications on his obligation to accept an offer of employment elsewhere?

e) Arbour is considering referring the dispute to a tribunal for decision, and feels quite strongly about the issue of misconduct being a factor in any final resolution of the matter. What concerns should Arbour address before it makes its decision on whether to refer this matter to a tribunal?

13. Hector Berlioz was a student employed for the summer by Bob's Urban Reusable Products. When Berlioz received his first paycheque, he noticed that a sizeable amount had been deducted for union dues. He immediately called payroll to explain that an error had been made, suggesting that his paycheque had been confused with someone else's.

The payroll person replied that there was no mistake; union dues were deducted for everyone who was not management. When Berlioz persisted, complaining that he was not a union member, that no one had told him he must pay union dues (especially in this amount), that he was a summer student employee, and that this was unfair treatment, the voice from payroll said, "Quit whining, kid. Management doesn't like it either, and we have to collect the dues on behalf of the union. Take it up with them; they're your representatives."

a) What is the type of union shop operated at Bob's Urban Reusable Products?

b) In what document would Berlioz be able to find the details related to the union and its shop?

c) Does the union represent Berlioz in this situation?

d) Do you agree with the young man's assessment that this type of union shop is unfair in these circumstances?

e) Is there a *Charter of Rights* argument available to Berlioz in these circumstances? If not, should there be?

14. Match the following:

Column A	Column B
Constructive dismissal	Reduction of loss
Termination	Confidential information
Just cause	Demotion
Mitigation	Firing
Trade secret	Valid grounds for firing

Intellectual Property and Computer Law

The Information Revolution

The laws of intellectual property balance the rights of creators to have some control and financial reward to promote creativity, against the interests of the public. Because many advances in technology are based on prior innovations, the public benefits by making the breakthroughs known and used by later inventive minds. The debt to prior creative minds was perhaps expressed the best by Sir Isaac Newton (1855): "if I have seen further, it is only by standing on the shoulders of giants"—a concept traceable to ancient Greece but made famous by Newton.

The ease of copying and distribution was again accelerated with the invention of digital technology and the Internet. Now every household, and even children, can copy creative works and distribute them worldwide without paying royalties to the creators. One of the extreme examples is peer to peer sharing whereby an extremely large number of home computers can be linked, the owners can put files, for example music, that they have copied onto their computer hard drive into shared file folders which are then indexed on a central search engine. All who participate in the scheme can have access to copy music that is on any of the other participating computers throughout the world—for free.

Thus the ability to copy easily and distribute cheaply has impacted greatly both on business models and the laws of intellectual property.

Intellectual Property   **Intellectual property** is non-tangible, created by mental effort, and cannot be held in your hand. Even though intellectual property cannot be seen, it is still protected by various rights, such as copyright, patents, and trademarks.

Legalese

Intellectual Property Rights

Intellectual property covers a variety of creations and different laws apply to the different types of creative works or confidential information. The length of protection, registration requirements and remedies for illegal copying vary depending on the type of intellectual property that is considered. The main types of intellectual property rights are:

- Personality rights—protect against the unauthorized use of names and distinctive features associated with celebrities
- Copyright—protects creative works, such as a song or a book
- Trademarks—protect brand names, business names, logos, and symbols, such as the apple of Apple Computer, and the stylized M known as McDonald's "golden arches."
- Industrial design—protects a distinctive shape or design that is a pattern to be reproduced many times, such as the design on fine china
- Patents—protect inventions such as the Pentium computer chip or the electric light bulb
- Confidential information—protects trade secrets, such as the formula for Coca-Cola (which has never been patented)

Personality Rights

Celebrities, such as prominent political, sports and entertainment figures, have personality rights relating to their personas—how they are seen by the public. The tort of appropriation of personality protects a person's right to control the commercial use of their distinctive features such as name, image, voice and likeness. Unfortunately for the celebrities this right does not extend to the use of photos when they are out in public places, hence it is no protection from the paparazzi.

In British Columbia, Saskatchewan, Manitoba and Newfoundland there are statutory laws that deal with invasion of privacy and personality rights are included in these statutes. In the other provinces, only the common law right for the tort of appropriation of personality provides any protection. There are not many cases dealing with appropriation of personality in Canada. In tort law the plaintiff must prove; that their image was used for a commercial purpose without their authorization, their image was clearly identifiable to the public and captures their personality and some cases have required that there must be a suggestion that there was an endorsement of a product or service by that person.

Horton v. Tim Donut Ltd., 1997 CanLII 12372 (ON SC)

The widow of the famous hockey player Tim Horton sued the corporation that owned the Tim Hortons coffee chain, for misappropriation of her late husband's personality. Tim Horton had founded the business in 1964 but died in a car accident in 1974 and his partner took control of the business. Slides that Delores Horton claimed she had the rights to, were loaned to a famous Canadian artist, Ken Danby, to paint a portrait of the famous hockey player. The painting was then reproduced in posters and placed in Tim Hortons' stores and the posters were sold to raise money for the Tim Hortons Charitable Foundation which funds children's summer camps. Ms. Horton claimed that the corporation had unlawfully appropriated the commercial personality of her late husband by selling these posters and had infringed her copyright in the slides which were used to prepare the portrait.

The corporation brought a motion to dismiss her claim on the grounds there were no genuine issues for trial.

The Court's Decision

The court noted that this was the fourth time over the years that Tim Hortons had made commemorative posters of her husband and sold them to raise money for the children's charitable foundation. This was the first time she had objected to the activity. She had also been recently involved in other litigation against the corporation and had been unsuccessful.

One of the requirements for an action in appropriation of personality is that it is done for a commercial purpose. The court stated that the portrait had been commissioned for a charitable purpose and it was neither exploitative nor commercial, so this was a protected use. The portrait perpetuated in a dignified and creative way the memory of Tim Horton. Any commercial purpose was incidental at best. The personality of Tim Horton had not been unlawfully appropriated.

Her claim of copyright infringement also failed. The photographer who took the slides that were used to create the painting owned the copyright in the slides. The court did not accept the material Ms. Horton produced as proof that the photographer had transferred those rights to her, so that claim failed as well. The motion was granted and her claims were dismissed.

■ *Business Law*   Applied

❶ **Chrysler Canada** distributed a device called a "Spotter" which consisted of two discs inserted between 2 cardboard sheets which TV viewers could use to find the names of professional football players from the numbers on their jerseys. The central image on the Spotter showed a dramatic collision between Krouse, a Hamilton Tiger-cats defensive player, and an opposing ball carrier. Krouse sued for compensation for the commercial use of his picture.

   a) What tort would Krouse rely on?
   b) Has Krouse established all of the elements of the tort?
   c) What would Chrysler Canada's arguments be?

Copyright

What Is Copyright?

Copyright literally means the right to copy. It gives the creator of a work an exclusive right to reproduce it or authorize others to do so. In this context the creator or originator is called the author; the product is called the work. The work must be original, not a copy of another work, and it should be the result of an independent creative effort where the author or authors employed skill, experience, labour, discretion and more in its creation.

copyright
the right to prevent others from copying original works

Copyright protection applies to artistic works such as; literature, plays, music, films, paintings, photographs, drawings, maps, and pieces of artwork. Recent cases have ruled that the design and layout on a menu can be an artistic creation and has copyright protection, modules in a training program for a dental secretary and designs for a house also have copyright protection. The design for a fence is not an architectural work and has no copyright protection. Although traditionally thought of as applying to artistic endeavors, copyright protection has also been extended to computer software in Canada.

Copyright is designed to encourage production of these types of creative works by allowing the authors to keep the profits for themselves. As soon as a work is expressed in concrete form [fixed], even in electronic form, it is protected. Neither the application of the copyright symbol or registration with the government is required. For most creations, the creator has an exclusive right to use, sell, license or assign the rights to their creation for their lifetime plus 50 years.

It is the way that an idea is expressed (the **How**), not the idea itself (the **What**), that is protected. Shania Twain wrote a song, *It Only Hurts When I'm Breathing*. She can claim copyright protection as the owner of the song because she conceived of it (originator) and first wrote it on paper (fixed). However, she could not claim copyright interest over the idea of a "heartbreak" song. There were many of such written before, and there will be many written after, all different in form yet same in idea.

Example: Bisson–Dath and his wife had sent a story idea to Sony in 2002 based on Greek mythology. In 2005 Sony shipped the computer game "God of War". Bisson–Dath and his wife sued Sony for copyright infringement. The court rejected Bisson–Dath's claim. It said that the idea of a mortal human on a quest on behalf of a Greek god was in the public domain and not protected. The expression of this idea by Sony in terms of plot, character, theme and such were not similar enough to the story submitted by Bisson–Dath to be evidence of copying the expression of the idea. (*Bisson-Dath v. Sony Computer* (Copyright, D. Cal. 2010, Judge Patel No. C08-1235MHP)

In the music industry some of the leading singers and groups have been accused of illegally copying other singers' songs. The Beatles, The Rolling Stones, Madonna, The Black Eyed Peas, Rod Stewart, Oasis, Avril Lavigne, Beach Boys, Radiohead and Led Zeppelin are among the many who were successfully sued or agreed to out of court settlements when they were accused of copyright violations.

Cinar Corporation v. Robinson
2013 SCC 73

Claude Robinson spent years developing an educational children's television program, the *Adventures of Robinson Curiosity,* complete with television scripts, story boards and promotional materials. The program was inspired by the famous children's novel, Robinson Crusoe, written in 1719 by Daniel Defoe. Robinson approached Cinar Corporation, a major producer of children's entertainment about bringing his creation to market, but after several years with no success, he gave up on the project.

About eight years later Cinar ran a television series entitled Robinson Sucroe. Claude Robinson was shocked when he saw it and claimed Cinar had copied many aspects of his *Robinson Curiosity* series. He commenced legal proceedings against Cinar and three individuals responsible for the Sucroe series for infringing his copyright.

Cinar claimed that the original novel and its ideas were in the public domain so there was no copyright violation. It said the story of a man marooned on an island interacting with animals and native peoples is a generic plot and has been reproduced for centuries. Cinar claimed that if the two television creations were examined piece by piece, there were so many differences; it proves that Cinar had not substantially copied the Robinson Curiosity material.

The trial court and the Quebec Court of Appeal ruled in favour of Claude Robinson and found his ideas were not generic and had been wrongfully copied by Cinar. He was awarded significant pecuniary, non-pecuniary and punitive damages. The case was then appealed to the Supreme Court of Canada.

The Court's Decision

The Supreme Court had to determine what part of the material was in the public domain and what fell within individual copyright protection. The test to determine whether a copyright had been breached was whether Cinar had copied a substantial amount of Claude Robinson's work.

The Court stated that Cinar had not just copied an idea that was in the public domain, it had copied Robinson's "expression of the idea" and that was a copyright violation. The appearance and personality of the main character and some secondary characters was copied, as well as the graphic appearance of the village. These findings were not confined to the reproduction of an abstract idea, they focus on the detailed manner in which Robinson's ideas were expressed.

The Court stated a "qualitative and holistic approach must be adopted" when deciding whether someone's idea had been illegally copied. In order to determine whether "a substantial part of Robinson's work was copied, the features that were copied by Cinar must be considered cumulatively, in the context of Robinson's work taken as a whole." This is not done by dissecting both works and comparing the individual features and differences in isolation.

Robinson, using his skill and judgment, had created characters and settings and Cinar and the three executives involved had substantially copied Robinson's creations and violated his rights under the *Copyright Act.* The court awarded damages in excess of $4,700,000 including; compensatory damages of over $600,000, disgorgement of profits in excess of $1,700,000, non-pecuniary damages for Robinson's psychological suffering of $400,000, punitive damages of $500,000 and costs of about $1,500,000.

Copyright protection consists of three basic rights; the right to produce or reproduce a work in any material form, the right to perform the work in public and the right to publish the unpublished work. These rights also include rights to translate, adapt format, (for example, from novel to movie or vice versa), and reproduce the material by playing it over sound systems. Restaurants that play CDs are required to pay royalties to a music collective. To avoid this, some restaurants play radio stations over their sound systems. The radio stations have already paid for the right to broadcast.

The concrete expression is sometimes mistaken for the rights. When you buy software on a disc, you are paying mostly for the right to use the software on it, the cost of the disc is minimal. Bill Gates understood the difference between the product and the rights associated with it. In 1980 IBM wanted to enter the home computer market and approached Gates, president of the fledgling company, Microsoft. Gates agreed to write a better operating system for IBM, but, in what has been described as the deal of the century, negotiated to keep the rights to the software and to market it separately.

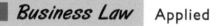

■ *Critical Concepts of* Copyright

- To qualify for copyright a work must be original and in a concrete (fixed) form
- Copyright protection consists of three basic rights: right to produce or reproduce a work in any material form, right to perform a work in public, and right to publish an unpublished work.
- Copyright covers artistic creations such as literary works, music, film, photographs, art works, drawings, maps and also computer software.
- For most creations, the *Copyright Act* gives the creator an exclusive right to use, sell, assign or license their creation for the creator's lifetime plus 50 years.

■ *Business Law* Applied

❷ **An auditor was inspecting** the inventory of a company that listed, as an asset, the rights to twenty Charlie Chaplin films. The auditor took the list, inspected the storeroom and found that in fact there were 20 canisters of film marked with these titles. To be certain, he randomly selected 3, opened them and saw that they contained the titles on the canister. He also put them on a projector provided for the purpose and verified that they were the films that they purported to be.

a) Can the auditor be sure that the company that had the 20 films in its storeroom actually owns the rights to these films?

Moral Rights

Even when an author assigns the rights of a work to someone else, the author retains the **moral rights** (the rights of an author or creator to prevent a work from being distorted or misused): these cannot be assigned. These rights mean that the work cannot be altered so that it no longer reflects the author's intentions when it was created. Moral rights, in other words, protect the author against someone destroying the integrity of a work.

moral rights
the rights of an author or creator to prevent a work from being distorted or misused

mandatory injunction
an order requiring a person to do a particular act

Snow v. Eaton Centre Ltd., [1982] 70 C.P.R. (2nd) 105

The Eaton Centre commissioned Michael Snow to create a mobile, called "Flight Stop," of Canada geese. The completed sculpture was hung in the Eaton Centre in downtown Toronto. At the beginning of the Christmas shopping season, Eaton Centre management had the 60 geese decorated, tying red ribbons around the birds' necks.

Snow took offence at this, and claimed the decorations were defacing the artistic value—destroying the integrity—of his work. Eaton Centre management refused to remove the ribbons, and so Snow sued for a mandatory injunction—a court order forcing them to do so. (A **mandatory injunction** is an order requiring a person to do a particular act.)

The Court's Decision

Although Snow had sold the copyright to the Eaton Centre, he retained the moral right over his work, since this right cannot be sold. Thus, the artist maintains a certain control over how any work is to be displayed. The purchaser cannot alter it, because it will injure the reputation of the artist and consequently that individual's ability to earn a living.

The court ordered the Eaton Centre to remove the ribbons.

What is Not Protected   The requirement of concrete form helps to differentiate between unprotected ideas and protected expression. For example, it does not protect conversations.

Example: An author interviewed Canadian pianist Glenn Gould and published a book containing the interviews after Gould's death. Gould's heirs sued the author for copyright infringement claiming he had to pay something to them to use the interviews. However, the court said that there was no copyright in conversations because they were not put in a permanent form. Rather it was the notes made by the author that satisfied the requirement of being in a permanent form. (*Glen Gould Estate v. Stoddart Publishing Co. Ltd.*, 1998 CanLII 5513 (ON CA))

Additionally, not every creative, fixed expression is subject to copyright protection. Sometimes only part of the work is. A newspaper article that reports of events is protected as to the way the article is written, but not the contents. The facts are considered to be in the public domain. Also, short expressions such as titles, slogans and utilitarian designs are not protected under copyright law, but may come under other areas of intellectual property such as trademark law.

Lucasfilm Ltd. & Ors v. Ainsworth & Or [2009] EWCA 1326

In the course of making the first Star Wars film a number of works were created. Andrew Ainsworth was asked to produce a plastic version of the Storm Troopers helmet from a two-dimensional design, which was done using sculpting techniques. Ainsworth made a mold from the sculpture to produce the number of helmets necessary for the film. He kept the mold and sold helmets made from it online. Lucasfilm's sued for breach of copyright. Ainsworth defended on the basis that the helmets he now produced were not sculptures but rather, in Canadian terms, the subject of an industrial design.

The Court's Decision

For copyright protection, which would last for the life of the artist plus 70 years under British law, the work must be a sculpture. The court said that sculpture should have its ordinary meaning, which was a single model produced by the hands of the sculptor. However this work was produced by an industrial method for making many copies of an original sculpture. The work could be within the category of the Canadian equivalent of industrial design, but that has only a 15 year limitation period in Britain, which had expired by the date of the hearing. Lucasfilm's claim was dismissed.

Comment: In contrast, in 2006 the United States District Court for the Central District of California gave a summary judgment of $20 million for Lucas finding that the helmets were a sculpture and were protected by U.S. copyright law. Ainsworth had not defended. The U.K. court said it would enforce that judgment against Ainsworth in the U. K.

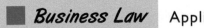

Business Law   Applied

❸ **Tom Ng just bought** a 3-D printer and saw a newspaper article about Ainsworth's win against Lucas Films in Britain. He intends to make miniature storm trooper helmets and sell them at a vendors' table at comic book conventions around British Columbia.

  a) What copyright issue does Ng face ?
  b) What legal cases would be relevant?
  c) What will the result be?

Employment   The Copyright Act (s.13 (3)) makes the employer the owner of the copyright in any work done by an employee in the course of employment. Employment contracts can also specifically deal with the ownership of works created on the job.

Corso v. NEBS Business Products Ltd.
2009 CanLII11215 (ON SC)

Mr. Corso worked for NEBS Business Products Ltd. which sold payroll services using cheques. On his own time, Corso developed software for a chequeless method for accounts payable called "eVault".

When NEBS learned of this they fired Corso and claimed ownership of the software.

Corso sued for wrongful dismissal and a declaration of ownership of the software claiming he developed it on his own time.

The Court's Decision

The court found that pursuant to Section 13(3) of the *Copyright Act* the eVault program was done while Corso was employed by NEBS. As an employee, Corso, had a good faith duty to give ideas for product improvement to his employer. His software was directly competitive to his employer's product and it did not matter that he had developed it on his own time.

As Corso breached his good faith obligation to his employer, his dismissal was justified and the copyright for eVault belonged to NEBS.

Notice and Registration

Notice   As copyright protection is automatically given the moment it is put in a tangible form of expression, it is not necessary to add the copyright notice. However doing so assists in establishing the date of ownership and assists in applications for registration, particularly under international treaties with other countries should the owner wish to apply. The notice must contain 3 elements: the owner's name, the copyright symbol or an equivalent, and the year of copyright. For example, Canadian illustrator Joel Shuster, who conceived of and drew the first image of Superman, could have put a copyright notice at a visible spot on the comics **– Joel Shuster © 1938.**

Registration   Registration for Canadian protection is done with the Canadian Intellectual Property Office (CIPO) by filling out a form and paying a small fee. The process is very simple, instructions are available online, and there is no need to retain a lawyer.

While registration assists in proving the date of creation, it is not a guarantee of ownership of the copyright in the work. Another author could prove that he or she had created the same work earlier, have the first registration set aside and obtain the copyright registration. Registration is necessary to sue for infringement.

Copyright protection can be extended to a number of other countries by further registration through treaties and organizations. Canada is a signator to a number of international intellectual property treaties: The Berne Copyright Convention, The Universal Copyright Convention, the Rome Convention; and is a member of the World Trade Organization.

Length of Copyright   Copyright protection in Canada is generally for the life of the creator plus fifty years. In the U.S. and the European Union copyright protection has been extended to life plus seventy years.

Business Law   Applied

❹ **LeeRoy Washington was** an accountant who specialized in accounting and bookkeeping for small businesses. To advertise a new idea for on-time accounting, Washington designed a new brochure. He spent several days composing the wording and deciding on the format and illustrations. Washington did not mark it "© 1995 Washington," nor did he register it. The brochure was a success.

A few months later, Washington saw a brochure put out by a rival, Joe Cordeiro. It was obviously a copy of Washington's pamphlet but had "© 1995 Cordeiro" printed on it. When confronted by Washington, Cordeiro stated that he had registered this pamphlet with the copyright office in Ottawa, and had a Certificate of Copyright. As a result, Cordeiro claimed he was the owner of the copyright in the pamphlet.

a) Who holds the copyright?

The "No Rights Reserved" Movement   Many creative people do not want the automatic copyright protection and want to give notice to others of permission to use and improve their copyrighted work. They have created a number of organizations to provide this notice, and licenses that grant permission provided there is attribution, which means recognition of the originator, and that then specify various degrees of permission from only copying to altering. The Creative Commons has a set of online license forms for public use and various designations for the type of permissions. Wikipedia is an example of an organization that uses the Creative Commons license. Another group devise the reversed copyleft symbol as a parody on the copyright symbol.

■ *Critical Concepts of* Notice and Registration

- Copyright protection is given automatically there is no need to place the copyright symbol on the work or to register it
- Registration in Canada will assist with applications for recognition in foreign countries who have signed treaties with Canada
- Registration is necessary to sue for infringement
- Copyright is determined by the first creation date not the first registration date

Legal Copying

While even one copy is a breach of an owner's copyright, there are situations in which minor copying is allowed. A teacher may wish to hand out a few pages of text to students. However, should the teacher be allowed to hand out a full chapter? The question at issue is a fair balance between the owner's rights to fair compensation for the work done and the public's right to some minimal use of the work without having to ask permission or pay.

The *Copyright Act* specifies that uses for certain purposes may be allowed. The underlying principles are: that the use is minimal and will likely not affect the market for the work. The exemptions that are most relevant to business are called Fair Dealing. The relevant section of the *Copyright Act* is:

> **29.** Fair dealing for the purpose of research, private study, education, parody or satire does not infringe copyright.

Much discussion has centred around how much teachers or researchers can copy legally. Is it fair to photocopy a sheet of extra questions to give to a class, is an entire chapter still fair dealing?

Example: The Supreme Court dealt with this issue in In *Alberta (Education) v. Canadian Copyright Licensing Agency (Access Copyright)*, 2012 SCC 37. Access Copyright represents authors and publishers of literary and artistic works. They charge a tariff with respect to the reproduction of its works for use in schools and post secondary institutions. The Copyright Board had ruled that the use by elementary and high school teachers did not constitute fair dealing and royalties had to be paid to Access Copyright. When that decision was appealed to the Supreme Court, it stressed that each situation had to be evaluated based on its purpose, character, amount, alternatives and the effect of the dealing on the work. The proportion between the excerpted copy and the entire work is also a key issue. The court gave a broad interpretation of research and private study and stressed that users rights should not be interpreted restrictively. It ruled that the teachers' use was fair dealing so the royalties were not required.

Colleges and universities students had extra costs added to their fees for an annual Access Copyright levy. Since this court decision, some colleges and universities have refused to have their students pay this annual $26 fee since their use may be covered under "fair dealing." The institutions also pay millions annually to purchase electronic databases which have much of the material so they decided this extra fee was not necessary. Access Copyright has sued York University over its decision to not pay Access Copyright fees and the legal dispute is ongoing and being carefully watched.

Example: Research—The Collective that obtains royalties on behalf of performers and song-writers (explained below) sued a number of online music providers and focused on Apple's iTunes' function which gave purchasers a thirty second sneak preview of songs before purchasing. The Collective wanted Apple to pay for that reproduction of copyrighted works. Apple contended the preview was within the research exemption of section 29 of the Copyright Act and the dealing [use] was fair in that the preview would not affect sales of copyrighted music in the marketplace. The court agreed with Apple. (*Society of Composers, Authors and Music Publishers of Canada v. Bell Canada*, 2012 SCC 36 (CanLII)).

Mash Ups.   The fair dealing section of the Copyright Act was amended to account for changing technology so that it now includes user generated content that is displayed on the website where no payment or profit is involved, the use is a fair dealing exemption (informally called the 'You Tube' clause). Thus a person can take an image and add a song, both of which may be copyrighted, and display them on a non-commercial website.

Back Ups.   Since technically any second copying of copyrighted content, even though legally obtained, is infringement, the Act specifies, for the sake of clarity, certain copying for private use such as: making backups, copying from CDs to MP3s (format shifting) and recording a TV show (timeshifting) are not infringements.

Illegal Copying.   Students are repeatedly warned not to plagiarize material in their work as it is a violation of copyright law and the educational institution's academic policy. In the case below, the professor plagiarized a former student's work and he was held liable for a copyright violation.

Example: Boudreau had completed an MBA at the University of Ottawa. One of his former teachers, Professor Lin, published a case book and included Boudreau's paper without his knowledge. The casebook had also deleted Boudreau's name and inserted Lin and another professor's names on the case. When Boudreau discovered this, he contacted the university, but it tried to brush it off as a simple mistake. Lin had also presented the paper at conferences and used it to try to gain a promotion. The court ruled it was a clear case of copyright violation and Lin and the university were together liable for damages of $7,500. (*Boudreau v. Lin* 1997 CanLII 12369 (ON SC))

Students are also warned not to make or purchase illegal photocopied versions of textbooks. Photocopy shops, often located near colleges and universities, that make a business selling illegal copies of textbooks have been found guilty of infringing the *Copyright Act*. It has been estimated that as much as 25 percent of sales are lost due to illegal copying of textbooks.

Example: Riaz Lari, who operated U-Compute near universities in Montreal, was found to have repeatedly illegally copied textbooks and ignored three separate court orders to cease and desist the practice over a 5 year period. He was found with over 2,000 copies of infringed works and had an "inventory" of 468 textbooks. He was ordered to pay $500,000 in statutory damages, $100,000 in punitive damages and $100,000 in costs. When he ignored the third court order he was sentenced to 6 months in jail, but it was a suspended sentence and instead he was allowed to do 400 hours of community service over 13 months.(*Lari v. Canadian Copyright Licensing Agency*, 2007 FCA 127 (CanLII)

❺ **Annie Leibovitz** was a famous photographer of celebrities. One of her iconic photos was a side profile of a pregnant, naked Demi Moore that was featured on the cover of Vanity Fair, its best-selling issue ever. Paramount Pictures launched an advertising campaign promoting its 3rd Naked Gun movie showing the head of Canadian actor Leslie Nielsen photoshopped onto the side profile of the body of a pregnant naked woman – not Demi Moore's.

Leibovitz sued Paramount for breach of copyright. Assume the present version of the Canadian Copyright Act applies.

a) What arguments does Leibovitz have?
b) What argument does Paramount have?
c) What would be the result?

Assignment or Licensing

The creators of works can assign or license others to copy their work. This is often necessary because authors cannot afford the cost of marketing a work. Books, for example, often contain a copyright in the name of the publisher, indicating that the author has assigned the copyright to that publisher.

Assignment involves a complete sale of the copyright, while a licence is permission to use it for a specified time. Most of us have purchased a license to use software whether we know it or not. When we buy a product such as Microsoft Office, in law we are buying a license to use that software according to the terms contained in the License Agreement. While we may also be buying a hard copy of a CD, that disc's value is very minimal. It is the content that is of value.

Example of License: The RCMP gave the Walt Disney Company (Canada) a five-year licence to market the Mountie image in making souvenirs, T-shirts, and so on, but retained the rights to that image. When the product licence expired at the end of 1999, it was not renewed; the Mounted Police Foundation now manages all product licensing.

Example: Assignments of Intellectual Property rights are contracts and enforced as such. Canadian born illustrator, Joe Shuster, co-creator of the Superman character for Action Comics (later named D. C. Comics) sold the rights to the Superman character for $130.Shuster had worked for the Toronto Star and named the fictional newspaper, where Clark Kent worked, the Daily Star (changed by D.C. to Daily Planet) and modeled Metropolis after Toronto.

Unfortunately, Schuster was a one-hit wonder and failed to earn any money later in the illustration business and ended up as a delivery driver. In 1946 he tried to sue D. C. Comics to attack the original assignment contract, but failed. D. C. Comics paid Shuster, and co-creator Siegel jointly, a voluntary payment of $96,000. By 1975 Shuster was nearly blind and confined to a nursing home. He started a publicity campaign on the internet just before the release of the first Superman movie and Warner Bros. agreed to pay him a pension of $20,000 per year plus medical benefits. Shuster died in 1992.

Business Alert!

When you post content on Tumblr, Facebook and Instagram you grant each of them a transferable, sub-licensable and royalty-free licence to use and publish your images or content world-wide. Businesses using social media in marketing will want to consider this rights transfer when posting.

Access to Copyrighted Materials

The Canadian Copyright Licensing Agency (Access Copyright) is a copyright collective for authors and publishers. It is a non-profit organization, representing thousands of authors and publishers across Canada. The purpose of Access Copyright is to collect royalties on behalf of its members when their material is photocopied or reproduced, and to make annual payments to them.

Socan   Creative people in the music world are represented by Socan, the society of composers, authors and music publishers of Canada. This body licenses the public performance of music in Canada so that all organizations using music publicly—from radio and television stations to banquet halls and bars—must pay a licence fee. The fees collected are then distributed to members.

The method of distributing the fees is based on a percentage of music sales. Thus, the most popular songs earn the highest proportion of fees for their creators.

Infringement

A single copy of a copyrighted work is a potential breach of the owner's rights called infringement. While the law protects the 'substantial work', which means it may permit copying of very minimal parts of the work beyond fair dealing, this exemption is very narrow and the test is very subjective. It is better not to risk having to rely on this limitation, but rather to consider obtaining permission before copying even a small part of the work that is not clearly within fair dealing.

The movie and music industry have a number of online antipiracy information sites that report data to show the harm to their industries and the effect on the economy. The Copyright Act has been amended to assist in making new ways of unauthorized copying an infringement. Here are just a couple of the statistics:

- Since peer-to-peer (p2p) file-sharing site Napster emerged in 1999, music sales in the U.S. have dropped 53 percent, from $14.6 billion to $7.0 billion in 2011.
- Music piracy cost the U.S. economy an estimated 71,060 jobs in both the sound recording industry and downstream retail industries. In addition, music piracy cost U.S. workers $2.7 billion in earnings.

Much discussion exists over these figures. Studies have shown that music sales have declined for other reasons, not just illegal downloading. The high price of CDs, the few number of "good" songs on a CD, peoples' desire to do different things in their spare time such as surf the Internet, play video games and social networking rather than listen to music are also factors that contributed to decreased music sales. Assuming that every person who illegally downloads a song or a movie would have actually purchased that product is also a questionable assumption, as people may not have ever purchased the product but download it only because it was free. There can be no doubt however that illegal downloading has reduced music sales overall.

Example: An Edmonton bar was ordered to pay $20,000 in statutory damages for breach of copyright for using intercepted signals to broadcast closed circuit pay-per-view Ultimate Fighting Championship (UFC) events without permission on two occasions. Though the bar claimed nominal damages were appropriate as only 15 customers were in attendance, the court gave a larger award to deter this behaviour. (*Setanta Sports Canada Limited v. 840341 Alberta Ltd. (Bres'in Taphouse)*, 2011 FC 709 (CanLII)

Example: A Montreal company decoded Polish television signals and reproduced it without authorization, edited it and sold individual episodes of news, sports and movies for a $5–$6 monthly fee. It was ordered to pay $301,350 in statutory damages (2,009 shows X $150 each) for its copyright violations. (*Telewizja Polsat S.A. v. Radiopol Inc.*, 2006 FC 584, [2007] 1 FCR 444)

Example: The Di Da Di karaoke bar in Richmond B.C. had acquired copies of seven audio-visual karaoke songs and illegally reproduced them by installing the songs on their computer system so patrons could perform them. The owners of these songs notified the bar of its copyright infringement and sent cease and desist orders for two years which the bar ignored. The federal court awarded statutory damages of $105,000 ($15,000 per song) plus $100,000 in punitive damages. (*Entral Group International Inc. v. MCUE Enterprises Corp. (Di Da Di Karaoke Company)*, 2010 FC 606 (CanLII)

Example: Madeleine Rundle was ordered to pay $60,000 in statutory damages when her language school in Ottawa gave students six different practice tests that had the actual questions that the federal government had on its language proficiency tests for bi-lingual civil service jobs. The questions were copyrighted and she had asked previous students to tell her what questions were on the tests. Rundle's students were 11 times more likely to achieve a high status score and 40 times more likely to get a perfect score than other candidates. Over 100 of her students were also required to retake the test. (*Attorney General of Canada v. Rundle*, 2014 ONSC 2136 (CanLII)

Microsoft Corporation v. 9038-3746 Quebec Inc., 2006 FC 1509 (CanLII)

Microsoft brought a civil action against a Montreal-area software distributor Inter-Plus for 25 illegal copies of Microsoft software. The company had been investigated twice before but no criminal charges had been laid. Microsoft then commenced civil proceedings against Inter-Plus and its principal, Carmelo Cerrelli, for copyright and trade-mark infringement.

Inter-Plus had not made the illegal copies, they had been imported. Cerrelli maintained that he did not know the copies were counterfeit. Inter-Plus had annual gross revenues of $3–5 million and about 60% of its sales were Microsoft products. It sold to retailers and system builders but not directly to end users.

The Court's Decision

The judge called Cerrelli a liar and believed he was caught up in a web of deceit with Inter-Plus and he had shown utter disregard for the process of the court. He had wilfully, knowingly and deliberately engaged in a course of conduct likely to infringe Microsoft's trade-marks and copyrights.

The judge awarded the maximum statutory damages of $500,000 based on $20,000 × 25 illegal copies. Noting that the defendants' conduct was "outrageous", the court awarded an additional $200,000 in punitive damages, $100,000 of which was to be paid by Cerrelli personally.

Business Law Applied

❻ Edna Morrera bought the latest version of a much-improved word-processing software program. She copied the program onto several disks for back-up. She then lent the program to her brother, who copied it onto the hard drive of his own computer, and made more copies on floppy disks. These copies he sold for $25 each to friends at school.

 a) Did Morrera's brother infringe the copyright of the software manufacturer?
 b) Did the back-up copies made by Edna Morrera constitute copyright infringement?
 c) Did lending the disks to her brother so that he could copy the program onto his hard drive constitute copyright infringement?
 d) Is Edna Morrera liable in her brother's sale of copies to his friends?

❼ Dalton Myers started a club at school called CD Swap. The idea of the club was that members would lend CDs to each other, and it was common knowledge that these CDs were frequently copied onto tape by their borrowers. Myers made no money, but simply acted as the organizer, making sure that the CDs were returned to the original owners.

 a) Did the members of the club have the right to make copies of the disks?
 b) Would the fact that Myers did not do the copying himself provide a defence to any claim of copyright infringement against him?

Music and Video Swapping   Users who upload copyrighted material on P2P servers so that other users can download the files are infringing copyright as are those who download the files. In the first lawsuit on this issue to go to court in the U.S., the record companies obtained a jury award of $1,920,000 against a woman on the basis that she uploaded 24 songs which were made available to other users to download. This award was reduced to $220,000 on appeal. (*Capitol Records, Inc. v. Thomas-Rasset*, 680 F. Supp. 2d 1045—Dist. Court, Minnesota 2010).

In the U.S. there have been about 30,000 lawsuits against individual users by music companies alleging infringement. Most settle out of court for a payment of $3,000-$5000. In those cases, "**copyright trolls**", which are bill collector style organizations employed by the copyright owners, send out letters on behalf of the music or movie makers to people who are alleged to have illegally downloaded content, threatening to sue them in court for a hefty amount but offering to settle for several thousand dollars. If even a portion of the people pay, the company profits. The most lucrative targets are those that download pornography illegally.

Canpri, an antipiracy enforcement firm, has stated that it is bringing this model to Canada. It has begun gathering evidence about Canadian users involved in copyright infringement on the Internet. Statutory damages however are limited to a maximum of $5,000 for all non-commercial copying done by one individual, whereas statutory damages in the U.S. can be up to $150,000 per illegal copy for individuals illegally copying.

Voltage Pictures LLC v. John Doe and Jane Doe, 2014 FC 161

Voltage Pictures, maker of hundreds of films including the Academy award-winning Hurt Locker, sought an order that TekSavvy, an internet service provider, disclose the names of 2,000 TekSavvy subscribers. In 2012 Voltage retained Canpri, a forensic software company, to investigate whether Voltage's movies were being copied and downloaded in Canada on P2P networks using BitTorrent. Canpri, by use of specialized software, could identify the IP addresses of users downloading Voltage films illegally but nothing further. Disclosure of the names of the people who owned those computers would be needed from the service providers, in this case TekSavvy.

TekSavvy was concerned that release of its customers' names would violate their customers' privacy rights under PIPEDA.

The Court's Decision

The evidence showed a probable case for infringement and that would ordinarily be sufficient to order the disclosure requested. However, there was also evidence of abuse of that disclosure in other countries by "copyright trolls" who then sent collection letters threatening lawsuits claiming large amounts of money, but also an offer of settlement if the individuals paid thousands of dollars. This is an effective business model if done over a large number of people, and the Court was concerned about these practices coming to Canada.

The Court stated that it would grant the order and privacy concerns and PIPEDA could not be used to shield wrongdoing. The Court however stressed that it would ensure protections are given so that it would not be support a copyright trolling business model. The Court order required Voltage to come back to court before it did anything with the information that it received from TekSavvy. Voltage would have to pay all the considerable costs that TekSavvy incurred in retrieving this information. The court would supervise the content of the letters sent out to alleged infringers to ensure they were not intimidated into making a payment without understanding their legal rights. The court also commented that it should ensure that the remedy granted is proportional to the value of the loss suffered.

Comment: Given that statutory damages for individual non-commercial copying range from $100–$5,000 in total in Canada and since the filmmaker must pay the high costs the ISP incurs retrieving the user information, it may not be worth it for copyright trolls to set up business in this country.

There had been orders made against service providers including Bell, Rogers and Cogeco earlier, but they were not acted upon. Parliament amended the Copyright Act to reduce the statutory damages payable on proof of violation of non-commercial copyright. This is viewed as a response to the abuse of copyright litigation against small users in the U.S.

Canpri uses another approach to combat piracy, file saturation. The firm uploads a harmless file to sharing websites which closely resembles the content users are seeking. There is one key difference: This particular file is completely useless.

Enablers In the last 15 years the Recording Industry Association of America, has sued Napster, Grokster, LimeWire, Megaupload, its successor Mega and some of their users, for allowing users to engage in downloading infringing content. The technical defense raised by Mega and others is that its business is analogous to that of renting storage lockers. The storage business does not inspect the contents of every box that a renter stores in a unit and hence is not responsible for the contents. In a similar way Mega does not review every part of every uploaded file in its storage system. There is a lot of non-copyright material. It would be an impossible task to examine and check out the millions of files uploaded daily for content.

While that defence may have been available in previous legislation, amendments to the Copyright Act have given authors an exclusive "making available right" to allow them to control the release of their performances and sound recordings online and stop unauthorized services that connect users wanting to share files over peer-to-peer networks.

TPMs Technological Protection Measures include technology that provides digital locks preventing individuals from undertaking a variety of actions, such as copying, printing or making alterations, or controlling viewing. Prohibitions regarding the circumvention of TPMs are provided under section 41, and the criminal remedies are provided under the section 42(3.1).

■ *Critical Concepts of* Antipiracy Measures

The Copyright Act specifies certain conduct as infringing to combat copyright piracy:
- Uploading and downloading copyright content using P2P software
- Providing of P2P software
- Unlocking TPMs (technological protection measures)

Remedies

The *Copyright Act* provides for both civil and criminal remedies for infringement. The civil remedies include those that are similar to a breach of contract: damages for actual loss; the amount of profits earned by the infringer, aggravated, punitive damages. Non-monetary remedies such as an Anton Piller order, a deliver up order and an accounting and an injunction are often given.

Proving actual damages in a copyright infringement case can be difficult, particularly where the defendant is uncooperative and claims not to have any sales records. Section 38.1 of the *Act* provides that copyright owners may elect to recover **statutory damages** instead of lost profits and damages suffered as a result of the activities of the infringers. There is no requirement for proof of loss, but if Statutory Damages are chosen, no actual loss damages can be awarded in addition. However, aggravated and punitive damages can be awarded. The amount of the Statutory Damages is in the discretion of the judge but will depend on the gravity of the infringing conduct. In commercial cases the range is between $500 and $20,000 for each work infringed.

private use infringement
illegally downloading copyrighted material for private use

Because of the *Thomas decision* (above) and the aggressive use of the court system by the music and movie industry in the U.S., the Canadian Act was amended to add a special section on Statutory Damages for non-commercial use, called **private use infringements** (e.g. illegally downloading a musical work for private use), the range of statutory damages a court may award is between $100 and $5,000 for all of the infringements alleged in the lawsuit.

Criminal penalties are also possible under the Copyright Act and include fines of up to $1 million as well as up to 5 years in jail.

Example: In 2013 in the Federal Court of Canada, Twentieth Century Fox obtained a judgment for $10 million in commercial statutory damages, and $500,000 for aggravated and punitive damages against Nicholas Hernandez (who did not defend) who up loaded all the episodes of The Simpsons and Family Guy programs to a server which permitted the public to download them for a small fee to Hernandez. (*Twentieth Century Fox Film Corporation v. Nicholas Hernandez, John Doe and Jane Doe*, Docket: T-1618-13, 3 December 2013).

Trademarks

What Is a Trademark?

Trademark Origins

Trademarks may be one or a combination of words, sounds or designs used to distinguish the goods or services of one person or organization from those of others in the marketplace. Trade-marks come to represent not only the actual goods or services, but also the reputation, of the producer. As such, trade-marks constitute valuable intellectual property.

    Sales and marketing campaigns are founded on branding. The legal protection for branding falls under the law of Trademarks. It gives exclusive rights to the owner to the use of that mark. The marking of products started with the trade guilds of the Middle Ages. A trade guild would put its mark, a symbol, on its product as a guarantee of quality. Consumers today similarly rely on a brand name as a guarantee that they are going to get what they paid for. A key point is that the mark must distinguish the goods or services from other businesses. It builds a business's identity in the marketplace

> **trademark**
> any visual characteristic of a product distinguishing it from a product made by competitors

What Can Be A Trademark

The Trade-marks Act currently allows words, names, symbols, designs, slogans, sounds and three-dimensional objects to be registered as trademarks. To keep pace with business marketing trends, the Act may soon be amended to allow for the registration of holograms, motion marks, and trademarks applied in a particular position on a three-dimensional object.

    If a logo contains a word such as the Coca-Cola logo, the word Coca-Cola would be registered in block letters as a word mark, and the unique script as a design mark.

    Slogans companies create can have trademark rights as well. Famous slogans such as; "Just do it" (Nike), "Quality is Job 1" (Ford), "You Deserve a Break Today"(McDonalds), "The Ultimate Driving Machine"(BMW), "We Try Harder"(Avis), "Snap!Crackle! Pop!" (Rice Krispies), "Don't Leave Home without it" (American Express), "A Diamond is Forever" (DeBeers), "The King of Beers" (Budweiser), "Finger Lickin" Good" (KFC), "Nothing Runs like a Deere"(John Deere), "Melts in your Mouth Not in Your Hands" (M&M candies) are all well-known trademarks owned by the companies.

    Another type of mark is known as the "distinguishing guise." A **distinguishing guise** is essentially a shaping of goods or their containers, or a mode of wrapping or packaging goods. Examples are the unique shape of the original form of the Coca-Cola bottle- modeled after the feminine form, the Perrier bottle, or the triangular shape of a Toblerone chocolate bar.

> **distinguishing guise**
> a distinctive look or shaping of goods or their containers or packaging that has trademark protection

    Pharmaceutical companies often try to establish a trademark right in the size and shape of their particular pill on the basis of distinctiveness. Most of the applications fail though as it is a high burden of proof to establish that a similar medication with the same size and shape would cause confusion since doctors and patients refer to prescription medicines by the actual name, not just "the little yellow pill". Viagra failed in its application to have its blue diamond shaped design for a pill registered as a distinctive trademark. (*Novopharm Limited v. Pfizer Products Inc.*, 2009 CanLII 82127 (CA TMOB) Courts have noted that there are only so many shapes that pills can have for digestive reasons and a company cannot have exclusive rights to those few shapes.

Example: Your business is launching a new running shoe brand called *Thunderbolt*, through a new division called *Lightspeed Creations*. The shoe will have a uniquely designed lightning bolt in a golden yellow on the side. The advertising slogan will be "Velocity Running" in a forward slanting script followed by a swoosh sound. Since they are words, you could register the product name and the slogan. The slanting script of the slogan would be a design mark. The lightning bolt could also be registered as a design, as Nike did with its check mark. The swoosh, being a sound, can be registered, as can the exact shade of golden yellow colour.

The name for the new division could not be registered as a trade mark because it is not used in association with a product or service. Only when the business name is the same name associated with the product can that name be given trademark registration. For example, if a company called the Ice Cream Company put out its product only under that name, that name could be the subject of a trademark registration.

■ *Critical Concepts*

- Trademarks today can protect many ways a business distinguishes its product and services from competitors through words, designs, sounds and combinations of them, and is a foundation for "branding"
- distinguishing guise protects the look of a product or its packaging
- the protection gives a monopoly right to the use of the mark

No Requirement to Register   There is no requirement to register a trademark for protecting its exclusive use. The tort of **passing off** was discussed in the chapter on Intentional Torts. Often called a poor man's trademark protection, a passing off claim can be made to give protection to trademarks even though they are not registered. However the protection only extends to the province in which the mark is used. The notation 'TM' can be used for unregistered trademarks.

Registration

Even though a trademark does not have to be registered as it has some protection at common law, you can register a trademark through the federal government's Canadian Intellectual Property Office (CIPO). About 45,000 trademark applications are made annually in Canada. There are reasons to register the mark:

- Trademark registration provides protection throughout Canada for 15 years, even if it is only used locally. The trademark can be renewed every 15 years after that indefinitely.
- It establishes an evidentiary advantage if the trademark registration is challenged, in that there is a record of the date of first use.
- It will assist in obtaining registration in foreign countries pursuant to treaties such as The Paris Convention for the Protection of Industrial Property.
- It is necessary to enforce the infringement remedies under the Trade-marks Act

Business Alert!   Trademark Search   Before deciding on any business or brand name or slogan, you can do an online trade mark search at the Canadian Intellectual Property office: cipo.ic.gc.ca.

Example: Linda Kearney sold her special home recipe lemon tarts at an Edmonton farmer's market. Her six-year old granddaughter suggested that she call her stall, the Queen of Tarts, a reference to Alice in Wonderland. The farmers' market sales were so successful that in 2010 Kearney Incorporated a company under that name provincially and opened a café on a main street in Edmonton using it. That same name was used by Stephanie Pick, a Toronto pastry chef beginning in 1999. For a Christmas present, Pick's father paid for the name registration as a trademark in 2006. When Pick learned of Kearny's business, she sent her a letter advising of the trademark registration and offering a license. When Kerry did not respond, Pick sued for trademark infringement. Kearney also did not respond to the lawsuit. The court awarded Pick damages of $10,000 and legal costs for infringement. (*Pick v. 1180475 Alberta Ltd. (Queen of Tarts)*, 2011 FC 1008 (CanLII)).

Notice: Canada's trademark act is completely silent on the use of notice. In other countries, the ® symbol is used, sometimes required, to signify a registered trademark. It is neither required nor prohibited in Canada. However, it is advisable to use it if there is an intention to apply for trademark registration in other countries.

Business Alert!

Requirements for Registration   Ownership. Ownership of a trademark is not determined by originator or author, but by the first to use it in Canada, or by the filing of an application to register based on a proposed use in Canada. The proposed use must be done within 3 years of the application or within 6 months of notice of successful registration.

Example: An Alberta retirement home had been using the name Masterpiece The Art of Living since 2001 but had not registered the name as a trademark. In 2006 an Ontario retirement home registered the trademark of Masterpiece Living. The Alberta company complained the names were too similar, it would cause confusion and since it had used the name first it was entitled to the trademark. The Supreme Court stressed that it is the use of a trademark and not registration that confers priority and the exclusive right to the trademark. The Alberta company was entitled to this trademark as it had used it first and the names were so similar it could cause confusion. The Ontario company's registered trademark was expunged (cancelled). (*Masterpiece Inc. v. Alavida Lifestyles Inc.*, 2011 SCC 27)

Distinctiveness   The fundamental concept underlying trademarks is that they protect the ways a business distinguishes its products from competitors. Words that are merely descriptive of the product itself cannot be part of the trademark. For example, a fruit company that specializes in the sale of apples could not obtain a trademark registration for the word "Apple" in association with the sale of fruit. However, a computer company could obtain such a registration, because that term does not describe its products but rather distinguishes its product from similar products in the marketplace.

Sometimes a descriptive work can be included with other words in the trademark. However, the use of the mark must contain a notation that the trademark does not in any way prevent the use of that descriptive word in association with other words.

Example: Apple applied to register a trademark—iPad mini. The U.S. patent office granted the application but only on the condition that Apple add this disclaimer: No claim is made to the exclusive right to use "MINI" apart from the mark as shown. (United States Patent And Trademark Office, April13, 2013, Application Serial No. 85780375).

A mark will not be distinctive if it can be confused with another trademark. So **confusion** is a basis for a competitor opposing a trademark application. But there must be true confusion. The test is would the ordinary hurried purchaser be confused, not that of a sophisticated or deliberate purchaser. Trade-mark examiners take into account various factors when determining whether trade-marks are confusing, the most critical ones are:

- whether the trademarks look or sound alike, and
- whether the trademarks are used in a similar market
- whether customers would think the products came from the same source

Montres Rolex S.A. v. Balshin et al., 31 C.P.R. (3d) 180

Technology has made copying infinitely easier. Knock-offs, or imitations, are easily found today for many products. Montres Rolex S.A., the Swiss watchmaker, marketed expensive watches through the Rolex Watch Company of Canada. Palmer imported and sold similar watches that included the crown design, and the name Rollex (itself a registered trademark) in small letters on each watch.

The imitation watches sold for $40, while the Rolex watches range from $2,500 to $10,000 and more. Palmer provided a card that included a disclaimer indicating that the Rollex was not a Swiss Rolex. This card clearly stated that it was an imitation.

Palmer argued that the buyers were not fooled—they knew they were not getting a genuine Rolex for $40. He further claimed that there was a thriving industry generally known as imitation art—even famous oil paintings are copied and sold as imitations.

The Court's Decision

The court stated that the relevant question was whether the imitation watches were so similar to the Swiss watches that they would confuse the public as to the source of the goods. A unique point of this problem was that the buyer was not fooled. The buyer bought the imitation watches because of the goodwill of the Swiss Rolex watches. The buyer wanted to give the public the impression of owning the expensive luxury watch; thus, the public was deceived by the buyer, not by the imitator/seller.

Part of the appeal of the Rolex watches was that they were known to be a high-quality timepiece. If it became widely known that very similar watches were selling for $40, the market for Swiss Rolex watches would be badly affected.

The court held that Palmer was infringing the trademark of the Rolex Watch Company of Canada and ordered him to cease marketing these watches.

Example: Veuve Clicquot, a famous expensive French champagne maker, had sold its champagnes here for over 100 years and registered its trademark in Canada in 1909. In 1995 a retail clothing chain began selling mid-priced women's clothes in six stores in Quebec and Ontario using the names Boutiques Cliquot and Cliquot. The French champagne maker sued for trademark infringement claiming the names were so similar (only a letter "c" different in the spelling) it would cause confusion and tarnish their reputation as a producer of luxury goods. The Supreme Court ruled that since they were selling very different products and no evidence had been submitted that consumers were confused, there was no trademark infringement. (*Veuve Clicquot Ponsardin v. Boutiques Cliquot Ltée*, 2006 SCC 23)

Example: Kraft had the rights to sell Toblerone chocolate bars in Canada, which is known for its sectioned peaks and triangular package. Hagemeyer began to sell a chocolate bar, Alpenhorn, that was similar in shape and packaging to the famous Toblerone bar. Kraft Canada began an action against it for passing off and violation of the Trade-marks Act. Hagemeyer maintained that the colours and writing on its package were not the same as Toblerone, so the public would not be confused. Kraft successfully argued that the public would be confused into thinking that the same company made both chocolate bars. The court ruled Kraft's test was the appropriate measurement for confusion, and the Alpenhorn was a violation of their trademark as well as passing off. A permanent injunction was issued preventing the sale of Alpenhorn and a deliver up order forcing Hagemeyer to deliver all Alpenhorn products and advertising material to Kraft and a reference was ordered to determine the damages Kraft was entitled to. (Kraft Jacobs Suchard (Schweiz) AG v. Hagemeyer Canada Inc., 1998 CanLII 14780 (ON SC)

Example: Since cowboys drink beer does a well-known Wrangler Jean trademark prevent the registration of a Wrangler brand beer? Big Rock Brewery filed for trademark registration of a new beer to be called "Wrangler". Wrangler Apparel Corp., which sells jeans under the brand name 'Wrangler' opposed the application under Section 6(2) of the Trade-marks Act claiming the public would be confused by believing that the beer was marketed by the well-known jeans company. The court disagreed and said that the hurried consumer would not be confused mainly because the markets, jeans and beer, are different. (*Wrangler Apparel Corp. and Big Rock Brewery Limited Partnership*, 2010 FC 477).

Mattel, Inc. v. 3894207 Canada Inc., [2006] 1 S.C.R. 772

Barbie's Restaurant, which operated five bar and grill restaurants in the Montréal area, applied for a trademark of the world "Barbie's" with regard to restaurant services. Mattel Inc., owner of the "Barbie" trademark for the iconic doll, opposed the registration on the basis of confusion. The restaurant responded by stating that the term "Barbie" was also widely understood to mean, barbecue, such as in the phrase, "Throw it on the barbie", so the public would not likely believe that the Mattel Corporation was the owner of these Montréal restaurants.

The Court's Decision

The court acknowledged that an important factor in determining the likelihood of confusion in the mind of the hurried customer was whether the relevant products were in the same product line. However, some brands could become so famous that their influence transcended product lines. Each of these cases had to be decided depending on the specific circumstances of the case.

Here the Court concluded that, although the Barbie doll brand was widely known, it was unlikely that a hurried customer would believe that the doll manufacturer was running these restaurants. The court rejected survey evidence by Mattel that was based on hypothetical questions. The court found the questions were not reliable as framed. Perhaps actual evidence of confusion might have been helpful. The restaurant's trademark application was approved.

Domain name registries and social media sites do not screen for ownership or unauthorized use of a trademarked name. However, The Internet Corporation for Assigned Names and Numbers (ICANN) has established a "Trademark Clearinghouse", which allows trademark rights-holders to register trademarks in order to protect rights online. Many social media sites now have a similar provision for a business to register its trademarks so that no confusing names will be allowed within their system. Once a trademark application is allowed, the mark should be registered with these organizations.

Business Alert!

Restrictions.   There are other restrictions to registration which are listed in detail on the CIPO website. They include: names and surnames, unless that name has acquired through use an additional business meaning. For example, 'John Smith' could not be trademarked but the name 'Disney' could. Deceptive descriptions such as 'sugar sweet' for candy artificially flavoured are not accepted. There is also list of prohibited marks such as those that would give the false impression the business is a government agency and the like.

■ *Business Law*   Applied

① Readi-Mix Drinks Corporation has developed a new line of tropical fruit beverages and wants to register the following as trademarks:

■ a stylized line drawing of a trader with the words "Trader John's."

- the words "Thirst Buster"
- these names for the different flavours:
- Shaka's Revenge
- King Tut's Curse
- The Grape Gretzky

a) Which of the above could be registered as trademarks?

❾ **You are an** employee in the Trademarks Registry Office and receive the following applications. Which do you think can be registered?

a) a new brand of bandages called Red Cross Bandages
b) a brand of records showing a portrait of Elvis Presley, bearing the slogan "The King's Choice"
c) the logo of a small mortgage broker which displays the Canadian coat of arms
d) a computer software shareware organization that uses the name in the following style: d'LOAD.

No guarantee of ownership   Registration is not a final guarantee of ownership by the government department. A trademark registration can be attacked by a competitor on any of the above grounds and the registration set aside or rendered ineffective at any time.

Example: The Canadian Shredded Wheat Co. Ltd. had a Canadian patent on the process for making shredded wheat. When that patent expired, it registered the words, "Shredded Wheat" as a trademark associated with breakfast cereals. The U.S. firm, Kellogg, entered the Canadian market with Kellogg's Shredded Wheat. The Canadian company brought a court application to prevent Kellogg from using that term. Kellogg's defended saying that the registration by the Registrar (a civil servant) was improper in that the words: Shredded Wheat were not terms that distinguish a product from its competitors but rather a description of the product itself. The court agreed and dismissed the Canadian businesses application. (*Canadian Shredded Wheat Co. Ltd. v. Kellogg Co. of Canada Ltd. and Bassin*, 1936 CanLII 116 (ON SC).

Example: Danish toy manufacturer Lego's patent on its plastic bricks expired in Canada in 1988. Subsequently Canadian toy manufacturer, Mega Brands, produced similar blocks with the interlocking shape and Lego sued Mega Brands for passing off. Lego claimed that it had trademark rights in the distinctive shape of its blocks. The Supreme Court rejected Lego's claim. It stated that a purely functional design may not be the basis of a trade-mark, registered or unregistered. The law of passing off and of trade-marks may not be used to create endless monopoly rights once a patent had expired. The patent protection had ended and the market for these products was now open, free and competitive. Lego's claim for passing off against Mega Brands failed. (*Kirkbi AG v. Ritvik Holdings Inc.*, 2005 SCC 65, [2005] 3 SCR 302). Lego received similar decisions in other courts around the world as well.

■ *Critical Concepts*

- Ownership of the trademark is determined by actual or proposed use not by first originator
- Descriptive words cannot be registered as a trademark
- A descriptive word describes the product that is sold by various companies, it does not differentiate for the customer which company manufactures that product or provides that service
- A purpose of trademark protection is to help a business differentiate its product from competitors, confusion is also a ground that will prevent registration of a trademark

Loss of a Trademark

If a registered trademark is not used for long periods of time it can be lost through abandonment under the Trade-marks Act. Others who want to use that mark can apply to the courts to have the existing registration expunged from the Register.

If you do not prevent others from using your trademark you can lose your rights if the registered trademark is no longer descriptive or distinguishing, and has become the **generic** name by which similar goods are known no matter who makes them. For example terms such as; zipper, bubble wrap, laundromat, aspirin, scotch tape, thermos, trampoline and escalator were all words that were once trademarked, but lost their protection as others were not stopped from using the term for similar products.

generic
a word that is in common or general use

Example: Bodum makes a specific non-electric coffee maker where the coffee grains are pressed in a glass cylinder and in 1997 it registered a trade-mark in Canada for the words French Press. Other companies made similar style coffee makers and called them a French Press as well. Twelve years later, Bodum sued the companies for trademark infringement. The court ruled that the term French Press is a generic term and the trademark should have never been registered. It ordered the trademark registration to be expunged (cancelled) and ruled there had been no infringement. (*Bodum USA, Inc. v. Meyer Housewares Canada Inc.*, 2012 FC 1450 (CanLII)

Infringement

Trademark infringement occurs when a person uses a trademark identical or confusingly similar to a trademark owned by another. The Act permits a claim for damages for actual loss, the amount of profits earned by the infringer, aggravated, punitive damages and non-monetary remedies such as an injunction and a deliver up order. If the trademark is not registered, a civil action for the tort of passing off can be taken against the illegal use. Suing for trademark infringement or passing off is how companies try to stop the sale of counterfeit goods.

Example: Advanced Systems Concepts marketed a software product by a trademarked name "Active Batch". Network Automations, which marketed a similar product, bought the search term "Active Batch" from Google and Microsoft Bing. When users searched that term, they were directed to Network Automation's website. Advanced system sued Network Automation for trademark infringement. The Court found that users searching for this software would be very sophisticated and would not be confused into thinking that they were buying an Advanced Systems product. Rather the purpose was to give consumers choice by showing comparable products. There was no infringement. (*Network Automation, Inc. v. Advanced Systems Concepts, Inc.*, 638 F.3d 1137 (9th Cir. 2011)). [Note: These are new situations. Whether Canada will follow the reasoning in this decision is still an open question.]

Example: Trans-High Corporation ran a newspaper called "High Times" which it described as dedicated to the counterculture and the medical and recreational use of marijuana movement. It received a trademark for the high times name in 1980. It sued High Times Smokeshop and Gift in Niagara Falls for trademark infringement. The smoke shop sold paraphernalia associated with the smoking of marijuana. It did not respond. The court ordered damages of $25,000 and legal costs of $30,000 to be paid by the smoke shop. It was prohibited from using the name high times. (*Trans-High Corporation v. Hightimes Smokeshop and Gifts Inc.*, 2013 FC 1190)

Louis Vuitton Malletier S.A. v. Singga Enterprises (Canada) Inc., 2011 FC 776 (CanLII)

Vancouver-based companies, Singga Enterprises Inc. and Carnation Fashion Company, along with Altec Productions of Toronto had a large scale operation selling imitation designer purses and accessories across Canada. They knowingly and wilfully manufactured, imported, advertised and sold counterfeit and infringing fashion accessories with Louis Vuitton and Burberry trademarks

from 2008-2010. Illegal copies of Coach, Guess, Prada and Chanel products were also available through these companies.

The defendants operated back alley stores and had active online sales operations as well. They would also take orders for any products the designers made and have them reproduced in China and then flown to Canada. Most products were sold for $25 per item. Louis Vuitton hired its own investigators to uncover these operations and document the violations.

Louis Vuitton and Burberry commenced an action against the defendants for trademark and copyright infringement and sought significant damages.

The Court's Decision

The judge found that the defendant's actions were clearly trademark and copyright violations. The use of the plaintiffs' trademarks would cause confusion and serious damage and irreparable harm to the reputation and goodwill generated by the superior character and quality of the genuine Louis Vuitton and Burberry products.

The defendants also attempted to deliberately conceal or cover up their wrongdoings, avoiding dealing with unknown individuals (possible investigators), obscuring domain name ownership and switching websites, and/or hiding such goods from view of the public or anyone entering their premises. "Given the egregious nature of their activities, the normal trademark and copyright profit or damages assessments would not be sufficient, and punitive and exemplary damages should be awarded."

The plaintiffs were awarded $2,400,000 in damages including $500,000 in punitive damages plus legal costs.

Comment: Louis Vuitton adopted of a "zero-tolerance" policy for counterfeit goods in 2004, which has led to more than 13,000 legal actions, 6,000 raids and about 950 arrests, according to the company's website. A crackdown against stores in Vancouver-area shopping malls led to a successful 2008 lawsuit in which Louis Vuitton won $980,000 in damages and about $50,000 for court costs.

■ *Business Law*   Applied

⑩ **BoneChill Company,** a large U.S.-based multinational marketing firm, wants to register the following trademarks in Canada, and has asked your advice on which will be permitted. What will you tell them?

   a) A brand name registered and used in the United States as a trademark, but only in the southern states. It has not been heard of outside those states. It is to be used in Canada in about two years' time.
   b) A brand name registered and used extensively in the United States as a trademark. The advertising appears in U.S. magazines that have a high circulation all over North America.
   c) A new name for a brand to be introduced into Canada in three months' time.

⑪ **New Tech Company** Limited has been operating since 1980 in Fredericton, New Brunswick, marketing alarm clocks under the brand name SureWake. On a trip to Regina, the president of New Tech sees that the Ultra Clock Company has an identical brand, using the same name and configuration. Ultra Clock operates only in Saskatchewan, and had registered the trademark one year prior to the discovery by New Tech Company. New Tech wants to attack the trademark registration.

   a) Does New Tech Company have a remedy, or is the trademark registration final?

The Social Media Factor   In the past it has been considered a necessary practice, to prevent dilution, that is weakening the distinctiveness of the trademark, to attack vigorously any business that used a similar mark. However, that practice developed before social media. Large businesses attacking small businesses may find that even though they may be winners in a court of law, they are losers in the court of public opinion.

Example: Lassonde, a company with annual revenues of $760 million, sells juices under the trade name of Oasis. It opposed the registration of Olivia's Oasis by a small beauty products company, L'Oasis d'Olivia., with annual revenues of $250,000. It also sued L'Oasis d'Olivia for trademark infringement. The trial judge dismissed Lassonde's infringement claim and awarded L'Oasis d'Olivia legal costs of $100,000 and $25,000 punitive damages for Lassonde's "untoward use of economic power."

However, the Québec Court of Appeal reversed the trial judge's findings saying that Lassonde's acts were "acceptable corporate behavior and in the legitimate interests of protecting its brand". However, the decision was reported in the newspapers and led to a social media campaign against Lassonde. It backed down and agreed to a settlement witch Olivia. (*Where's My Oasis? Canadian Juice Company Wins in Court but Loses the Social Media Battle*, April 12, 2012, Technology and Intellectual Property Bulletin, Fasken Martineau).

Ambush Marketing

Companies often pay large amounts of money to be an official sponsor of a company or organization. Ambush marketing occurs when other companies that have not paid to use the trademark market their products to look as if they are official sponsors. The COC (Canadian Olympic Committee) sued the corporation that makes the North Face line of sports clothing for trademark infringement. North Face, just prior to the Sochi Winter Olympics, sold a line of clothing called Villagewear which was red and white and had Canadian flags on it, as well as other clothing with references to Sochi. North Face had not paid to be an official Olympic sponsor. The COC claimed the clothing was in infringement of their trademark.

Dangers of Counterfeit Products

Many of the court cases involving counterfeit products are related to designer fashions and accessories such as purses and watches. Though this has significant economic impact on the creators of the original products, the health and safety of the public is not at risk with these goods. What many people are not aware of however is that there is a multi-billion dollar world-wide industry of counterfeit goods involving products such as auto and airplane parts, prescription medicines, electronic goods, toys and food. It has been estimated that counterfeit and pirated goods are a $700 billion industry world-wide and in some cases the public's health and safety are at risk. Fatal car and plane accidents have been linked to counterfeit parts, as well as deaths from counterfeit drugs that contained deadly ingredients. Organized crime is often involved and governments are ineffective so far at combatting this growing problem. (See CBC documentary Counterfeit Culture http://www.cbc.ca/player/Shows/ID/2324420977/)

Industrial Designs

What Is Industrial Design?

Industrial designs are essentially unique patterns, shapes, or ornaments that appeal to and are judged solely by the eye and distinguish a finished product. It can apply to a diverse range of goods such as a uniquely designed chair, handle, spoon, wallpaper or dish pattern, ornamentation added to a T Shirt, perfume bottle, a shape of a boat hull or computer icon. There is much room for dispute over whether a design should be subject to registration as an industrial design, or as patent, trademark, or copyright work, since designs can often be classified as any one of these. This is another example of a term having a specific technical legal meaning that is different from the way the word is used generally.

industrial design
a distinctive shape or design that is a pattern to be reproduced many times, such as the design on fine china

Companion with Other Intellectual Property

There are several criteria to consider when deciding if a particular item is an industrial design.

- An industrial design is judged solely by the eye, and is primarily ornamental—a pattern of china, or Web page design.
- A patent must be useful, and not just ornamental.
- An industrial design can also be registered as a trademark, as a distinguishing guise.
- Designs may also be copyrighted as distinguishing shapes. However, if they are used for patterns to produce articles in quantities of more than 50, the design cannot be copyrighted but must be registered under the *Industrial Design Act*.
- No principle of manufacturing or construction can be registered as an industrial design.

Registration and Protection

An industrial design must be registered with the government or there is no protection against copiers. Only the owner of the original design can register and registration must be made and completed within one year of the design's becoming known to the public. It should be marked with an encircled capital "D" and the design owner's name or an abbreviation of the name on its packaging or label. If it is registered but there is no "D" mark, an injunction can still be granted against anyone who infringes, but damages cannot be awarded. Registration entitles the owner to a 10 year exclusive right, however after the first 5 years, a fee must be paid to continue for the last 5 years or the registration expires.

Reproduced with the kind permission of the copyright owner, Royal Doulton

■ *Critical Concepts of* Industrial Design

- Industrial designs apply to original visual shapes, patterns or ornaments applied to a finished article or manufactured product
- Only the owner of the design can register and registration is required to get protection from infringers
- If registered the owner gets 10 years of protection but at the end of the first 5 years a fee must be paid to continue for the last 5 years
- The design should be marked with an encircled "D" and the owner's name to be able to sue infringers for damages and in injunction
- If it is registered but not marked, the owner can only get an injunction

Bodum USA, Inc. v. Trudeau Corporation (1889) Inc., 2012 FC 1128 (CanLII)

Bodum, a Swiss company, designed drinking glasses with a double glass wall and began to sell them in Canada in late 2003. These two layers of glass kept hot drinks hot and cold drinks colder longer. In July 2004 Bodum applied for an industrial design in Canada and in February 2006 the government registered Bodum's two industrial designs.

In 2006 Trudeau Corp., a Quebec company that made housewares, sold similar double glass wall glasses. Bodum brought an action against Trudeau claiming infringement of its industrial designs. Trudeau denied that its designs were similar and it also counterclaimed that Bodum's industrial designs were invalid and should never have been granted and should now be expunged because they were not substantially different from previous glass designs.

The Court's Decision

The court first examined whether Bodum and Trudeau's designs were similar. It stressed that it is not a test of functionality, it is purely a visual test. Though both glasses had two separate layers of glass, some of Bodum's designs were concave and convex and Trudeau's were all convex. They were not the same configurations so Trudeau had not violated Bodum's industrial design.

The court also went on to recognize that double walled glasses had been in existence long before Bodum had applied for an industrial design in 2003. Some similar glasses dated back to the 19th century. The court stressed that for an industrial design to be registered the design must be substantially different from previous art. With glasses, for the most part, over thousands of years, all shapes had already been explored in other prior designs. It agreed with Trudeau that Bodum's industrial designs were not substantially different from other glasses that had been created, so the court declared their registrations to be invalid and they were expunged from the Register.

■ *Business Law*   Applied

⑫ **Tookta Van Kunek,** an architect, devised a new construction system for building large residential subdivisions. The prefabricated components of the house were built in a factory on site. The factory itself was designed so that on completion of the houses, the factory could easily be converted to a shopping centre. Van Kunek wants to have this system registered as an industrial design.

   a) Is this system the proper subject matter for registration as an industrial design?

⑬ **Helena Theodoseos designed** a new pattern for wallpaper, to be sold throughout Canada.

   a) Is this wallpaper design the proper subject matter for registration as an industrial design?
   b) What is the length of time that Theodoseos has to complete registration of the design?
   c) How long will the protection last?
   d) Could Theodoseos also obtain copyright on this design?

Patents

The Nature of a Patent

The patent system applies to inventions, and is designed to encourage further inventions. To obtain a patent, the inventor must reveal the invention process in exchange for an exclusive right to use it for 20 years. Although the patent cannot be copied outright, it can suggest ideas for new inventions that build on the original idea. Perhaps one of the most famous patents ever granted was to two Canadians, Dr. Frederick Banting and Dr. Charles Best, in 1923 for the insulin used to treat diabetes. Other examples of patented inventions are the fax machine, which was originally patented in the late 1800s, and the telephone.

   A patent:

   ■ is a government-granted monopoly to use an invention
   ■ protects the idea itself in a working model, not the expression of the idea
   ■ comes into existence only when registered
   ■ gives protection for 20 years, but requires disclosure of the invention

After 20 years anyone can use the item patented, and the monopoly ceases. Some inventors do not wish to reveal the invention process and do not apply for patent protection. They simply keep the process a secret. The formula for blending Coca-Cola, which was invented in 1891, was never patented, and has been maintained by secrecy.

Legalese

Patent   Once a patent has been granted, the invention process is made public. The grant of a patent from the government is given in a form called **letters patent**. *Letter* is used here in an older meaning of written communication. The word **patent** is derived from a Latin word meaning *open*, *disclosed*, or *revealed*—hence, to make public.

What Can Be Patented?

Only inventions can be patented. The *Patent Act* defines an invention as: "Any new and useful art, process, machine, manufacture or composition of matter."

Farcus
© 1992 Farcus Cartoons/dist. by Universal Press Syndicate   WAISGLASS/COULTHART

"Okay, so what else does it do?"

Any new and useful improvement on a previously patented invention is also patentable, but a new patent must be sought.

In order to be patented, an invention must have three qualities:

- **ingenuity**—it must be more than just an obvious step that a person with reasonable skill would have taken
- **utility**—it must be of practical use. It must cause a change or condition in the character or condition of the physical object.
- **novelty**—it must not already be known to the public (in the public domain), although the Patent Act permits disclosure 1 year before the application for a patent.

The invention can be a product, say a wide-angle lens that can fit over an iPad camera lens; a chemical composition used to clean that lens; an apparatus, the machine used to grind the lens, and the process for making the unique lens, or an improvement on any of these.

What Cannot Be Patented?

Not all inventions can be patented. An invention that is to be patented must contain a novelty value; therefore, certain already-known inventions are not patentable. Other inventions that cannot be patented are:

- methods of medical treatment
- industrial designs, copyrighted items, and trademarks
- devices that simply change the shape of existing devices
- mathematical formulas or abstract theorems

There is much debate as to whether computer programs should be a matter of patent or copyright. Computer programs are considered similar to mathematical formulas, and currently cannot be patented. However, they are subject to copyright. Computer programs that are an integral part of a new machine (computer apparatus) may be patentable. There is considerable pressure from the electronics industry to make programs patentable, and the law in this area may change. However at present software standing alone is not patentable.

Canada (Attorney General) v. Amazon.com, Inc., 2011 FCA 328 (CanLII)

Amazon invented a method for completing an online purchase using only a single mouse click. The invention eliminates the string of transactions customers must follow to finalize a purchase. The customer's payment information is stored in a "cookie" so when they want to make a purchase they avoid the usual "check out" steps by using just "one click" and the purchase transaction is complete very quickly. Amazon had patented the method in the U.S. and other countries.

The Commissioner of Patents rejected a patent application by Amazon for its "1-Click" method in Canada. The Commissioner believed that a business method could not be patented because it was abstract like a theorem and not something that caused a change on a physical object. Amazon.com appealed.

The Court's Decision

The Federal Court of Appeal disagreed with the Commissioner saying that a business method might be patentable depending on the circumstances and referred the claim back to the Commissioner for reconsideration. The Commissioner issued a patent to Amazon for this business method. CIPO have now released a new practice notice that, if a computer is found to be an essential element of a claim, the claimed subject matter will generally be patentable.

With the development of bioengineering, a new issue has arisen as to whether life forms should be patentable. In the first case in Canada to consider this matter, Harvard University applied for a patent for a genetically engineered mouse called the Harvard Mouse. The patent was rejected because the mouse was not reliably reproducible. The issue of whether higher life forms can be patented was left open. Patents have been granted on plants and bacteria but not on higher forms of life such as animals.

Business Law Applied

⑭ **On a visit** to some Pacific Rim countries, Marlene McIvor discovered a surprisingly effective traditional herbal remedy for the common cold. Its advantage was that it came in a small sugar-coated tablet about the size of an aspirin, and would be easily saleable in the North American market, where it was hitherto unknown.

 a) Could McIvor obtain a patent for this item in Canada?

⑮ **After several years** of experimentation, Vivian Prus developed a system for home water filtration. She lived in Edmonton, Alberta, but hoped to market the system throughout North America. On a trip to New Brunswick she found a local manufacturer had been selling a similar system for about five years, but only locally.

 a) Is this water filtration system a subject for a patent?
 b) If so, who can obtain the patent—Prus or the New Brunswick manufacturer?

⑯ **Robert Roth invented** a machine that made frames for aluminum doors and windows much more cheaply than any similar machine on the market. He started his own small company, and supplied window frames locally for about five years. A friend advised him that he could sell his machine nationally to other manufacturing companies. First, however, Roth decided to apply for a patent on his machine.

 a) Would he be successful in obtaining a patent?

Applying for a Patent

Copyright exists as soon as you create an original work; patents, however, must be applied for. It is possible to apply for a patent yourself, and there are many self-help books and inventors groups that can explain the process.

patent agent

a registered agent (often an engineer) who pursues applications for patents on behalf of individual inventors

Most inventors use a **patent agent**—a registered agent (often an engineer) who pursues applications for patents on behalf of individual inventors. The government receives over 30,000 patent applications annually. An examiner at the government patent office will then check the patent application and, if it conforms with the law, the patent will be granted. A grant of patent gives the holder monopoly rights to the invention for 20 years.

Canada now uses a first-inventor-to-file registration system. If two individuals quite independently create the same invention, the first to file will be granted the sole patent rights. As with copyright, if the invention is found by the patent office examiner to have been made under the terms of an employment contract, the patent rights will belong to the employer. An inventor, therefore, must be very careful in outlining what is, and is not, the employer's in any employment contract.

The value of proper patent protection was dramatized when Kodak put a number of its patents up for auction claiming of value of $2.6B. One of the significant patents was set aside by a court challenge reducing the value of the Kodak patent collection to half a million dollars. (Patent Tossed by Judge, Wall Street Journal, May 22, 2012).

The value of patents was illustrated when the once great Canadian telecommunications company Nortel declared bankruptcy and sold its patents to several buyers including Apple, RIM, Microsoft, Sony and Ericsson for $7.7 billion, one of the largest asset sales in Canadian history. Comments have been made that if the company had understood the true value of its patents, it might have monetized them and avoided bankruptcy.

Non-Disclosure Agreement

Because obtaining a patent can be expensive, sometimes an inventor does not have the money to do so and must approach a large business to obtain funding. In order to protect the invention rights, the inventor should have the business sign a non-disclosure agreement, in which the business acknowledges that it does not already know of the invention, and agrees that it will not use the invention or disclose it to anyone else. This is some protection for the inventor in the event that the negotiations for funding fall through with this business.

Identifying Patents

If a patent is granted, anything produced under that patent must state that it is patented and the date the letters patent were granted (e.g., Patented, 2001). It is an offence under the *Patent Act* not to display this patent identification. It is also an offence under the act to use this identification if the item is not in fact produced under that patent. You will often see the words "Patent Pending" on goods. They are of no legal effect.

International Patent Protection

There is no international patent, however the Patent Cooperation Treaty assists in making foreign applications in signatory countries by having a centralized patent database search and a standardized application form. The office will give an opinion as to whether the claim is patentable in treaty countries. After that, the applicant has to make an application in every country for which patent rights are sought. The individual countries retain the right to accept or reject the application.

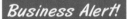

Patent Applications   The Canadian Patent Office publishes a manual of its practice and procedure, which can be obtained by contacting that office. There are branches in major cities in all provinces, and they are listed in the government section of the telephone directory. Most libraries carry self-help books on how to make your own patent application. There are also inventors groups that can assist. These are often listed in classified sections of newspapers and special interest magazines dealing with topics such as electronics.

Patent Protection vs. Copyright, Trade Secrets

Patents give the strongest form of intellectual property protection. Copyright and trade secrets only protect against copying. Independent creation is a defence against claims to copyright or trade secrets.

Example: Two independent creators of same product: John, in Ontario, designs a software program that speeds up on-time delivery for business products. He successfully registers a copyright for this software.

Mary, in British Columbia, develops, completely on her own and without any knowledge of John's product, the identical program. John cannot stop the sale of Mary's product for she did not "copy" John's work.

However, if the product had been patentable, the first inventor to register would hold the patent rights and be able to prevent the other from using the invention.

Impeachment

Registration of a patent is not a final guarantee of ownership. The registration can be impeached [set aside] at any time on the basis of improper registration. One of the requirements on application noted above is **disclosure**. The very foundation for granting patent rights involves a trade-off. The inventor gets monopoly protection for a time, but must fully disclose how the invention is made so that the society can benefit from other inventors who can use or improve the product. They must adequately disclose all the material on how the product or process is made and if full disclosure is not given, then this can be grounds for the court to declare the patent invalid. The Pfizer case below illustrates how that drug company lost its valuable Viagra patent due to its inadequate disclosure.

The other requirements of ingenuity, utility and novelty can also be used to attack the validity of a patent.

Teva Canada Ltd. v. Pfizer Canada Inc., 2012 SCC 60 (CanLII)

In 1994 Pfizer applied for a patent for its drug, Viagra, as a treatment for erectile dysfunction. It was granted the patent in 1998 and it was to expire in 2014. The application listed a number of compounds including sildenafil and indicated it as "one of the especially preferred compounds that induces penile erection in impotent males".

A competitor, Teva Canada Ltd., that wanted to make a generic version of Viagra, attacked the patent on the basis it did not meet disclosure requirements. Only sildenafil was effective, but it was not so identified. Rather it was simply included in a very long list of other, but ineffective, compounds.

The Court's Decision

The Court reaffirmed the "patent bargain". The inventor was given exclusive rights in a new and useful invention for a limited period of time in exchange for disclosure of the invention so that society can benefit from this knowledge. "The description must be such as to enable a person skilled in the art or the field of the invention to produce it using only the instructions contained in the disclosure." If there is not proper disclosure then exclusive monopoly rights will not be given by granting a patent.

Pfizer's disclosure did not indicate sildenafil was the effective compound and so it did not meet disclosure requirements. Even though Pfizer had been making significant profits on its sale of Viagra for 18 years, the Court declared the patent to be invalid.

Prior Disclosure. As noted previously, one of the central requirements of patentability is "novelty" – the invention must be new, the first of its kind in the world. A requirement of novelty is that the product must be registered within a year of any disclosure, which would enable another person to reproduce the invention, called an "enabling disclosure".

Example: A device was manufactured and rented to a third party for use in drilling an oil well in Texas more than a year before date of the Canadian patent application. This earlier use invalidated the patent, since it constituted an "enabling disclosure" of the invention more than 12 months prior to filing of the patent application. To prove when the earlier device was invented and disclosed, an expert was called in to examine the metadata for the design drawings to verify when the drawings were created. (*Wenzel Downhole Tools Ltd. v. National-Oilwell Canada Ltd.*, 2011 FC 1323 (CanLII)

Damages for Infringement

If a party is found to have infringed a patent, the damages are calculated on the basis of the inventor's lost profits, rather than an accounting of the infringer's profits. In the largest patent infringement award ever given in Canada, Merck was awarded over $119 million in damages when Apotex produced an infringing version of Merck's anti-cholesterol drug, Lovastatin. Apotex had the right to produce a non-infringing version, but instead had used a different process which was an infringement of Merck's patent. (*Merck & Co., Inc. v. Apotex Inc.*, 2013 FC 751 (CanLII)

Confidential Information in Business Deals

Confidential Information in Business Deals

The concept of Trade Secrets, a term originally developed with reference to technical information such as formulas, has been expanded in modern usage under the term Confidential Information. Often the two are used interchangeably. It may be information of any sort; an idea of a scientific nature, or of a literary nature, or a client list, as long as it gives an economic advantage to the business. Additionally, there must be some element of secrecy. It does not have to fit into any of the other categories of Intellectual Property.

Confidential information can be understood as a form of intellectual property that meets the following criteria:

- it has commercial value
- it is not in the public domain
- its secrecy has been reasonably protected
- it has been communicated to others in confidence

The recipes for Coca-Cola and Mrs. Fields Chocolate Chip Cookies are well-known examples of formulas that have been secret. The Coca-Cola Company has been successful in keeping its formula confidential since 1886.

Business Alert!

To ensure confidentiality owners of formulas often divide the formula into parts giving only one part to each of several employee blenders so that no employee ever sees the entire formula.

Unlike patents, trademarks and copyright, confidential information has the potential to last indefinitely. However, there is no ownership of confidential information once it is disclosed. There is the risk that if it is disclosed, even by accident or reverse engineering, the protection may be lost. Additionally, someone else may independently create or discover the secret and disclose the contents in, for example, a Creative Commons Licence, or register it as a patent and gain the exclusive rights.

Examples of confidential information include:

- ideas
- data
- customer and supplier lists
- recipes (such as food and chemical recipes)
- blueprints and designs
- internal business processes and methods
- financial information
- business plans

For cash strapped start-ups, the only business advantage they have may be a better way of doing something. In many cases the method cannot be patented and even if it could be, the time and expense required is outweighed by the need to immediately make money by getting their product or service to market.

For other start-ups, typically biotechnology companies, a great deal of time and money is invested in developing a particular procedure to accomplish a specific goal. Since the process itself likely cannot be copyrighted or patented, it is usually kept secret.

■ *Business Law*   Applied

⑰ **Laura Chen** has invented a solar panel for plaza parking lots so that electric cars can charge while the owners shop. It is a large umbrella like structure. With the solar panels on the top, it also provides shade for the cars underneath. The key to making it work is a special chemical formula that assists in the transformation of light into electricity. She made a working model in her father's garage and, having no money, wants to pitch the idea for funding on Dragons' Den.

a) What intellectual property issues should she consider?

Breach of Confidentiality

Breach of Confidential Information is a separate and potentially wider cause of action [remedy] from other remedies discussed earlier such as, breach of fiduciary duty in partnerships, corporations or employment relationships or by contractual terms. The test to determine whether a duty of confidence arises is whether a reasonable person, standing in the shoes of the recipient of the information, would have realized that the information was given in confidence. While fiduciary duties will not arise in arms-length transactions, obligations relating to confidentiality may. In the *Lac Minerals* case, below, the court said confidentiality could govern even comments exchanged by geologists in the field.

Thus the duty of secrecy may arise in any number of situations such as: when confidential information is exchanged in contract negotiations even when no contract is agreed upon; when an inventor seeks funding and it is refused, or when parties discuss a joint venture that never materializes (*Lac Minerals*).

Even though there may be a wide common-law protection for confidential information it is still advisable to have a Nondisclosure Agreement (NDA) so the elements of breach of confidential information do not have to be proved apart from the breach itself.

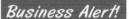
Business Alert!

A claim for breach of confidentiality requires three elements:
The information was confidential
The information must have been communicated in confidence, and
The information must have been misused by the party to whom it was communicated to the detriment of the party who confided it.

LAC Minerals Ltd. v. International Corona Resources Ltd., [1989] 61 D.L.R. (4th) 14 (S.C.C.)

Corona was in the business of exploring potential gold-mining properties in northwestern Ontario. The company decided to purchase the property next to the land on which it already held a claim. Corona entered into negotiations to purchase this adjacent property, which was referred to as the Williams property. LAC Minerals Ltd. heard about Corona's exploration plans and began discussions with the company for the purpose of forming a joint venture or partnership to develop a gold mine on the Williams property. Through information provided during the negotiations, LAC found out Corona did not yet own the Williams property. When discussions between LAC and Corona broke down, LAC purchased the Williams property itself and developed the gold mine, which yielded huge profits.

Corona brought a court action against LAC for breach of confidentiality and breach of fiduciary duty.

The Court's Decision

At the trial and Ontario Court of Appeal levels, LAC was found liable for breach of confidence and breach of fiduciary duty because the information about the Williams property was confidential. It had been revealed in confidence in the course of well-developed joint venture discussions.

The Supreme Court of Canada confirmed that a breach of confidence had clearly occurred. However, three of the five judges found the element of dependence by one party on the other required to establish a fiduciary duty was not sufficiently proven on the part of Corona.

Breach of confidence was enough to enable the Supreme Court to confirm the lower courts' decisions requiring LAC to turn the gold mine over to Corona after Corona paid LAC's development costs. It was one of the largest gold discoveries ever in Canada with deposits valued at over $1 billion.

Example: One of the most famous possible breach of confidentiality cases involved Cameron and Tyler Winklevoss and Divya Narendra, three Harvard students with a bright idea but not a lot of computer expertise. They asked a sophomore named Mark Zuckerberg to help them build a social-networking site for college students. Zuckerberg left them and started Facebook. The three other students sued Zuckerberg claiming he stole their confidential business plan and the code he developed for them. A settlement agreement was reached in February 2008, in which Zuckerman paid his former associates $65 million.

Business Alert! Some businesses combine the protections of patent and confidential information. They patent the original invention, but keep all improvements confidential.

■ *Business Law* Applied

⑱ **A night club owned by Christou** operated a My Space page. Its patrons joined as Friends. Their names were shown, but their contact information, mailing addresses, email addresses, could only be accessed by password. The Friends were given advance notice of special events and discount coupons. The club's manager, Bradley, quit and started his own nightclub down the street. He accessed the Friends' contact information using the password he had been given as manager at Christou's club and sent them announcements about his own club.

Christou wants to sue for breach of confidence. Bradley claims the names are public and he could get their contact information from other sources so they are not confidential in law.

a) Is the Friends' list confidential information?

Business Alert! Social media have become an important marketing tool for businesses. Employment contracts should specify that passwords in themselves are confidential information and cannot be used to access information on employer operated social media sites except on the employer's business.

Computer Law

Criminal Law

Misuse of confidential information through either the elimination of or interference with data carries the possibility of a criminal prosecution and a criminal record. The criminal offences most likely to arise where there has been an unauthorized or illegal taking of confidential information or a trade secret by an employee are theft, fraud, unauthorized computer use, and mischief in relation to data *(Criminal Code, R.S.C. 1985, c. C-46, s. 322, 342.1, 380,* and *430 (1.1)* respectively).

The liability extends further than just the individual who has committed the criminal act. An ex-employee's new employer may also be held liable if the knowledge or information that the new employee brings is used for the benefit of the new employer. If the new employee has a disk containing confidential marketing information, or a copy of a software program, or has knowledge that would be considered a trade secret or confidential information and that will be used for the benefit of the new employer's business—then the ex-employee may be facing possible imprisonment, and the new employer's business or corporation, as well as the officers and directors, could be fined and required to hand over any monetary gains resulting from the ex-employee's criminal act.

Theft

Theft (section 322 of the Criminal Code) is the intentional and unauthorized taking of another person's property dishonestly and with knowledge that there was no right to do so. It can take any form—from an ex-employee's removing documents, design printouts, or computer disks with information stored on them, to a stranger's entering the premises and taking a prototype. It could also involve the theft of an idea that has been written on a piece of paper—stealing an idea is not a criminal offence, but taking the paper (tangible property) is.

Theft—Canadian Criminal Code, R.S.C. 1985, c. C-46

---

s. 322. (1) Every one commits theft who fraudulently and without colour of right takes, or fraudulently and without colour of right converts to his use or to use of another person, anything whether animate or inanimate, with intent,

(a) to deprive, temporarily or absolutely, the owner of it, or a person who has a special property or interest in it, of the thing or of his property or interest in it;

(b) to pledge it or deposit it as security;

(c) to part with it under a condition with respect to its return that the person who parts with it may be unable to perform; or

(d) to deal with it in such a manner that it cannot be restored in the condition in which it was at the time it was taken or converted.

s. 334. Except where otherwise provided by law, every one who commits theft

(a) is guilty of an indictable offence and liable to imprisonment for a term not exceeding ten years, . . . where the value of what is stolen exceeds five thousand dollars,

(b) is guilty

   (i) of an indictable offence and is liable to imprisonment for a term not exceeding two years, or

   (ii) of an offence punishable on summary conviction, where the value of what is stolen does not exceed five thousand dollars.

R. v. Stewart, [1988] 1 S.C.R. 963 (S.C.C.)a

The accused, Stewart, was asked by a representative of a union seeking to form a bargaining unit in a large hotel complex employing approximately 600 people to obtain the names, addresses, and telephone numbers of the employees. The information, which was confidential, could be obtained only through the personnel files or a payroll computer printout.

Stewart contacted a security worker at the hotel and offered to pay for the information. He suggested the information be secretly copied from the confidential records without removing or otherwise affecting the records themselves. Stewart was charged with counselling a hotel employee to commit the offence of theft by stealing information which was the property of the hotel and its employees.

The Supreme Court's Decision

The court held that confidential information is not considered property under the Criminal Code and that if information of a commercial value is to be given protection through the Criminal Code, it should be left to Parliament to enact laws that did so. Confidential information is not tangible property. The accused's conviction for theft at the appeal court level was reversed.

The court went on to consider whether the confidentiality of the information could be the subject of theft. It decided that since the confidential nature of the information cannot be taken or converted in a way that would deprive the owner of the use or possession of the information, confidentiality itself cannot be the subject of theft.

Fraud

If the actual document or disk containing the information is not taken, but an unauthorized copy of it is made with the intention of using the material in a way that would or could cause a financial loss to the original owner of the property, the offence of fraud has been committed.

The criminal offence of fraud (section 380(1) of the Criminal Code) occurs when someone is defrauded of any property, money, or valuable security, by deceit, falsehood, or other fraudulent means. In essence, this means any act that would be considered dishonest by a reasonable person and that is done with the intention of causing an economic loss to the victim. That economic loss might occur through either an actual loss or merely by putting the victim's economic interests at risk.

R. v. Ram, [1987] 47 Can. Computer L.R. 109

Mr. Ram had operated a business through which, for several months in 1985, he copied without permission and sold computer software (Display Write 2) and a manual owned and copyrighted by IBM Corporation. During that same period, Ram had also copied and sold without permission computer software and a manual entitled Advanced Productivity Systems, owned and copyrighted by Arrix Logic Systems Incorporated.

The Court's Decision

The court held that the unauthorized reproduction of the software and the manuals caused a risk of economic loss to the software manufacturers. Ram was convicted on three counts of fraud involving the unauthorized reproduction of software and computer manuals. He was given a jail sentence and also put on probation for three years, during which time he was required not to take part in any business that made copies of computer software for renting or resale.

Unauthorized Use of a Computer

The unauthorized use of a computer (section 342.1 of the Criminal Code) is aimed at protecting the privacy of your computer system from people who might try to intercept your data, either directly at the source or from a remote location. The actions of hackers who enter your system and retrieve computer programs or data from your files would fall within this section of the Criminal Code.

An example of this type of activity involved a hacker who broke into a telemarketing firm's database, getting names, credit card numbers, and expiry dates. He used the credit card numbers to make purchases and generously shared some of the numbers with friends. To avoid detection, he reformatted his hard drive and reinstalled all his programs. Unfortunately, the RCMP's High Tech Crime Section recovered enough file fragments to allow the telemarketing firm to confirm that the information had been copied from its database. The hacker was outsmarted and convicted.

For the purposes of section 342.1, "computer service" includes data processing and the storage and retrieval of data, while "computer system" is defined to include a computer program. Unauthorized computer use occurs when, without authorization, a computer service is intentionally obtained, or data is intentionally retrieved. It also occurs when a function of a computer system (for example, data processing) is intentionally intercepted by a computer system being used for that purpose. Consequently, if an employee dishonestly and without authority were to use a new employer's computer system with the intention of accessing a previous employer's computer service or intercepting communications within the previous employer's computer system, then likely the offence of unauthorized use has occurred.

Mischief Related to Data

The aim of section 430 (1.1) is to control, for example, the actions of people who might access a computer system and encrypt a software program so that the owner is unable to get into the data. As another example, the records of an intensive care unit in a Los Angeles hospital were tapped into by a hacker who, with a warped sense of humour, altered the data in the computer system by doubling the dosage of medication for all the patients.

Section 430 (1.1) of the Criminal Code states:

> Every one commits mischief who willfully
>
> (a) destroys or alters data;
> (b) renders data meaningless, useless or ineffective;
> (c) obstructs, interrupts or interferes with the lawful use of data; or
> (d) obstructs, interrupts or interferes with any person in the lawful use of data or denies access to data to any person who is entitled to access thereto.

The offence of mischief in relation to data includes both data as it is usually understood as well as computer programs. Computer programs are defined to mean data that represent instructions and statements that, when executed in a computer system, cause the computer system to perform a function.

The combination of sections 342.1 (unauthorized use) and 430 (1.1) (mischief related to data) will certainly help deal with problems unique to the area of information technology, such as computer viruses, mail bombs, and time bombs. Should an unhappy employee, when creating a piece of software, deliberately implant a time bomb or virus to destroy the program after a certain period of use or if some future event occurs, such as the employee's termination, the act of implanting the virus or time bomb would fall within the offence of unauthorized use of a computer (section 342.1). If, when the time bomb goes off or the virus surfaces, data is destroyed, that act would be seen as mischief in relation to data and an offence under section 430(1.1).

■ *Critical Concepts of* Criminal Liability

Criminal responsibility for wrongful actions related to information and technology will likely fall within the following four sections of the Criminal Code, depending on the nature of the action and the item affected:

- Section 322 (theft) will assist if a disk or some tangible property is removed without authority. It is of no assistance at this point in protecting such intangible elements as confidentiality or information itself.
- Section 80 (fraud) may be available for actions that do not constitute theft but are dishonest acts done with the intention of using the commercially valuable information or technology to cause or threaten to cause the victim an economic loss.
- Section 342.1 (unauthorized use of a computer) may be available for retrieving data (a "computer service") or downloading a computer program (a "computer system") intentionally and without authorization, whether at source or remotely, which may be seen as the criminal offence of unauthorized, punishable in certain circumstances by a prison term of up to 10 years.
- Section 430 (1.1) (mischief related to data) may apply for willful destruction, interference with, or interruption of data or computer programs or access to them, which constitute the crime of mischief related to data. An action which attracts the criminal liability of section 342.1 will often entail liability under section 430 (1.1) as well.

■ *Business Law* Applied

⑲ **Using his own** disks, Jody Canard made copies of a software program used by his employer for calculating the odds for bets placed on horse races. Each night before leaving work, he would print out 10 hardcopies of the five-page manual for the program on coloured paper he had bought for that purpose. Jody would then sell the manual along with copies of the program at the racetrack.

Jody was fired when his employer learned of his activities. However, before being escorted from the building, Jody had an opportunity to access the software and change some of the data so that the odds would be miscalculated in a subtle but effective way.

a) Explain whether Jody has committed one or more of the offences of: theft; fraud; unauthorized use of a computer; mischief related to data.

Canada's Anti-Spam Legislation

Canada's Anti-Spam Legislation (CASL) is aimed at stopping unwanted bulk electronic messages commonly referred to as Junk Mail. It is estimated that about 75% of the world's email traffic is spam. The legislation regulates what it defines as all commercial electronic messages (CEM's). A CEM is a message sent by any means of telecommunication, e.g., text, sound, voice or image, to an electronic address if one of its purposes, even a minor one, is to encourage participation in a commercial activity. This definition is wider than the general understanding of spam. It may include communications across social media platforms, and would likely include emails that may not come within this definition but contain hyperlinks to commercial websites. Businesses will be responsible for the acts of any employee, subject to a due diligence defense

The take away for businesses is that they can only send out email in bulk mailings to customers who have given express consent. There are exceptions: solicitations for political contributions, charities and internal organization matters.

The enforcement will be by government agencies and there is a government website for reporting spam "fightspam.ca". In 2017 provisions will come into effect to allow private actions against spammers.

The profitability of sending junk email was illustrated in the U.S. case of Jeremy Jaynes. He was convicted under a Virginia anti-spam law of sending over 10 million unsolicited junk emails per day to @aol.com email addresses that had been stolen and given to him by a former AOL employee. He was selling useless products such as a $39.95 program on how to select penny stocks or software that promised to clean computers and also pornography. About 1 in every 30,000 people who received an email purchased and he grossed about $400,000–$750,000 per month. Jaynes conviction was overturned later as the Virginia law violated his freedom of speech rights. (*Jaynes v. Commonwealth of Virginia*, 276 Va.443, 666 S.E. ed 303(2008))

Email Mining.   There are a number of businesses that use various means to obtain (harvest) possible valid email addresses from the internet use by software called spambots, and sell the lists. The software checks (hacks into) websites or catches unencrypted emails in transmission. Then an email is automatically sent supposedly from a website recently visited (spoofing) to elicit a response, even by "remove" or "unsubscribe" to confirm that this is a valid and active email address. There is a great ingenuity and creativity involved in a number of "hooks" devised to provoke a response. Some current ones are (each of these emails contain your exact name):

- You have just received a package from FedEx but it was undeliverable. Please reply with the time and date so it can be redelivered, or open this attachment and fill in the form to give this information.
- You have purchased a warranty with a car. About a year later the warranty program sends you a notice that it wants to update your information to keep your warranty valid.
- You are given a notice that you have been sued in a local court and have twenty days to put in a defense. Details available by opening the attachment.

One of the ways that makes an email address a bit more spambot proof is to never enter the '@' or '.' on a website but rather spell them out, such as: Astonatconnectdotcom.

Business Alert!

Business Law Applied

🐝 **Lisa is a sales manager** for Canadian Girl, a clothing retailer whose target market is preteen girls. Many customers, girls and their parents, have visited its Facebook page and 'liked' certain product lines with comments that disclose their email addresses. Lisa decides to award their loyalty by sending them advance notice of a once in a lifetime opportunity to buy at special discount prices, often below cost, for one week.

a) Are there any concerns for Lisa and her employer?

In Summation

Intellectual Property

■ Your creativity, expressed through such media as drawings, a new process, a new machine, a multicoloured logo, a design, or a formula, is known as intellectual property. It is a type of non-tangible property that carries with it enforceable rights. These rights allow you to protect the ownership, use, reproduction, copying, and goodwill value of the intellectual property.

Personality Rights

■ Celebrities have the right to control the use of those elements of their personality which have become attached to their celebrity status, such as some aspect of their physical image, or their name.

Copyright

■ This area of intellectual property is governed by the federal *Copyright Act*. Copyright protects the author's creative expression but not the idea expressed. No other person may use the author's intellectual property for a period that extends to 50 years after the author's death. There are some limited exceptions to this period of time for protection.

■ Protection in Canada is automatic without any requirement to register, although registration may assist in providing evidence as to when the work was created. Protection in other countries is available through international copyright conventions.

■ The author of the work is the owner of copyright except in particular circumstances, such as when a work is created in the course of employment.

■ Copyright works can be copied without permission of the author in very limited situations called fair dealing

■ While ownership of copyright can be assigned or a licence can be given, the moral rights, aimed at protecting the integrity of the created expression, cannot be assigned.

■ Infringement of copyright occurs when someone uses, or assists in using, copyrighted material without the owner's consent. Special situations exist permitting copies to be made without consent. Copies made of short passages for use in schools or for research are examples of these exceptions. Remedies for infringement include damages, an accounting for profits made from the illegal use, an injunction, and criminal penalties under the *Copyright Act*.

■ Remedies for commercial infringement include the usual contract damages and a claim based on the profits made by the infringer.

■ There are statutory damages which do not require any proof of loss. A cap has been put on these damages for consumer violations.

Trademarks

■ A trademark is a distinctive mark or symbol that distinguishes and identifies the product or service of one party from those of another.

■ Trademarks can take many forms, from a name to a shape, and include slogans, certification marks, and distinguishing guises based on a distinctive shape.

■ Several factors are involved for protection of a trademark to be granted. Use or proposed use, along with such elements as being confused with an existing trademark, are looked for when registration is sought.

■ The registration process follows a particular procedure and, if granted, protects the trademark for 15 years, renewable indefinitely.

■ Infringement is proven by showing that the other mark is likely to cause confusion in the mind of the public as to the source of the goods.

Industrial Design

- An industrial design is aimed at protecting the shape or design pattern of an object from being reproduced. Visual appeal in a useful object such as a bottle shape is a key element in applying for protection for this type of intellectual property.

- Once granted, protection for reproduction of the item is given for up to 10 years. The word *registered*, or an abbreviation, along with the year of registration, must appear on the article reproduced from the protected design.

Patents

- A patent protects an idea for 20 years and gives its inventor a governmental monopoly on the use of the invention that embodies the idea.

- To make it through the rigours of the patent application process, an idea must first be seen as an invention. This is defined by the federal *Patent Act* as any new and useful art, process, machine, manufacture, or composition of matter. The invention must then be seen as possessing the qualities of ingenuity, utility, and novelty. A thorough examination process follows, leading, possibly, to a grant of letters patent.

- A patent application requires full disclosure of the invention and consequently ends any protection available under the area of trade secret or confidential information.

- Anything produced under the patent must bear a statement that it is patented along with the date the patent was granted, although protection begins from the date of application.

- Applying for a patent in every country in which use is anticipated is necessary as there are no international conventions for patent protection.

- The owner of a patent may be required to give a licence for the use of the invention if the patent rights are being abused through, for example, improper use.

Confidential Information

- Confidential Information involves a separate cause of action and may apply in circumstances where there is no fiduciary duty

- There are 3 elements: the information has been kept confidential, it was revealed in confidence, and it was misused in a way that harmed the party who revealed it in confidence

Computer Law

- Criminal Code provisions can apply to the use of a computer, such as, theft, fraud, unauthorized use of the computer and mischief related to data

- Any email sent by a business to anyone for a commercial purpose may be a CEM (Commercial Electronic Message) and a violation of Canada's Anti Spam Legislation (CASL)

- Employers will be liable for any violation of CASL unless they had taken reasonable steps to ensure employee compliance with that legislation

Closing Questions

The Protection of Creativity

1. Is reselling a textbook a breach of copyright?

2. Dudley Cooke enjoyed making homemade wine. In September 1994, in the course of his experimentation, he discovered a new process by which berries from a particular plant could be distilled and a rather exotic flavour obtained. He kept this process a secret, and enjoyed the curious looks and questions that were raised whenever he introduced anyone to his particular wine, which he labelled Dudley Do It Right.

   Unknown to Cooke, Jennifer Paik, another inventor, was hard at work attempting to create a new fragrance. By accident, Paik discovered the same process used by Cooke, and which could be applied to any fruit or berry to create an enhanced flavoured wine. Excited, she packed up her notes and headed off to talk to an intellectual-property lawyer, who applied for a patent on the process on her behalf. Paik's patent for the new process was granted on July 16, 1996. Two years later, when she discovered that Cooke was now marketing his wine-making process locally, she brought an application to stop him.
   a) Would Paik be able to enforce her patent against Cooke and stop him from being able to use the process that he discovered on his own and has been using since then?
   b) To what date will Paik have a monopoly over the process that she has patented?

3. Previous or proposed use is required for which of the following?
   a) patent protection
   b) copyright
   c) trademark
   d) industrial design

4. Winston Basset was an aspiring composer, and had been writing music for a couple of years. He entered a radio station's contest, submitting a tape of his music along with the entry form which stated that all entries became the property of the radio station and would not be returned. Basset was not one of the winning entries.

   Several months later, while listening to the radio, he heard his music being played as background for an advertisement for the radio station. When Basset telephoned the station manager to complain about the use of his music without his permission, the station manager replied, "You're a big boy; you knew the rules. We can do what we want with it."
   a) What would be the legal remedy that Basset would pursue, and in what area of law does that remedy lie?
   b) With reasons, explain the issues concerning the ownership of the music being used in the radio station's advertisement, and give a decision as to who would be successful if this matter went to court.

5. Tokay is an artist who often painted her own designs on T-shirts and sweatshirts that she wore. She had done a few T-shirts for friends on which she drew exotic birds with bright-coloured feathers. The body of the bird was on the front of the T-shirt, and the tail feathers extended around the body to cover a good percentage of the shirt's back. Her friends enjoyed the designs so much that she decided to begin marketing them. Tokay arranged to buy T-shirts and have the designs reproduced on them. She decided to market the shirts under the name Too-Right-Designs.
   a) What measures should Tokay take to protect her designs and business name?
   b) One day, while wandering through a mall looking for potential customers for her designer T-shirts, Tokay saw sweatshirts that had designs of exotic birds on them, almost exactly like hers. The only differences were that other colours had been used and, rather than having the tails of the birds finishing on the back, the entire bird was produced on the front of the sweatshirt. Tokay is extremely upset because she has not yet signed up any store outlets to sell her T-shirts, and with the sweatshirt already on the market she may be out of luck. Explain with reasons whether Tokay has the legal right to stop the sweatshirt company from selling its product, and in which area of law she would base her court action.

6. Walt Whitmore liked to carve figures out of wood. He worked in construction and one day, while on coffee break, he picked up some of the foam sponge insulation that was used in the new houses that were being built. He took out his pocket knife and carved a small football out of the sponge, which he and his co-workers then used to play tag ball during their breaks.

   Suddenly struck with brilliant inspiration, Whitmore realized that he had a new product on his hands, so to speak. Calling it a Squange ball, he ordered several sheets of the foam sponge insulation and began to experiment with various shapes that could be used for different types of games. He began to market these items under the name Squange and became independently wealthy in a short period of time. His old tool belt now hangs on the wall as a symbol of his retirement from the construction trade.
   a) Will Whitmore be successful in applying for a patent for his Squange ball?
   b) If he were unsuccessful in patenting the ball, what areas of intellectual property would offer Whitmore protection from competitors, and what elements of his new business should he be looking to protect?

7. Aurora and Sonia co-wrote a manual on golfing techniques. The manual was completed on April 1, 1996. Aurora was in a car accident, and died from her injuries on June 1, 1997. Sonia continued to enjoy the royalties paid on the sale of their manual until her death on January 30, 2015.
   a) If Aurora and Sonia did not register the copyright in the manual would they have protection under the *Copyright Act*?
   b) What advice would you give them if Aurora and Sonia intended to sell the manual outside Canada, particularly if they were thinking of selling it in the United States?
   c) Assuming that copyright in the golfing manual was registered on May 30, 1996, on which of the following dates does that copyright expire?
      i) April 1, 2016
      ii) May 30, 2046
      iii) June 1, 2047
      iv) January 30, 2065

8. Would the *Industrial Design Act* provide the best protection from competitors for your product if the shape in which it is designed distinguishes it from other goods in the same field?

9. Carmen was commissioned to create a mural for the lobby of an office building. The mural that she designed had a picture of a farmer's field, with three-dimensional trees emerging in the foreground from the wall. One day, while walking past the building, Carmen was surprised to see what appeared to be blinking lights hanging from the trees in her mural. When she asked the building superintendent who had hung the lights, he told her that they changed the tree decorations according to the seasons, and since this was Christmas they thought flashing coloured lights would be a great idea. He added that she wouldn't believe what they have planned for the Canada Day celebrations.
   a) Does Carmen have any right to have the lights removed from the trees and, if so, on what would she base her legal action?

10. Angela Wong had an elderly grandfather who required a walker in order to be able to move about. Noticing that he would tire quickly and require a place to sit down, Wong designed a walker that could be easily collapsed and restructured into a chair with the use of two levers. She has named her prototype stroller/chair the Supportive Stroller.

    Which of the following areas of intellectual property would protect Wong's creation, and for what period of time?
    a) industrial design
    b) trademark
    c) patent
    d) copyright
    e) trade secret

11. Lee Park bought a new dance videogame. Does he own it? Discuss the possible copyright issues of creator, marketer and end user.

12. Jane Walker, a second year college student, was walking along the street approaching a new mural painted on the outside of a building. Celine Dion happened to be walking the other way. A photographer snapped a shot of both women framing the mural for use in an "Our City" special magazine feature article. Discuss the potential IP issues.

13. Sofia realized her life dream of opening a teashop with exquisite decor and premium teas. It was a hit. One popular feature was her choice of background music from her large private collection of CD's. 'Hey I paid for them, I can play them anywhere,' she said to her friend Carl who had just taken a course in law and thought to the contrary.
    a) Who is correct and why?
    b) If Carl is right, is there an alternative that would not involve paying royalties.

14. April Ravine is a popular rock star and is also a strong supporter of Greenpeace. To get a record deal she assigned the copyright in all of her songs to First City Records Inc. Shortly afterwards, she heard a large logging company, one that she viewed as an enemy of the Canadian ecosystem, using one of her songs in its advertisements. She complained to the logging company, but it showed her that it had a proper license from First City Records for a substantial payment and had checked that it had the right to grant the license by reviewing the assignment of ownership from herself to the record company. Is there anything April can do to stop the logging company from using her song?

15. The Attar Chemical Corporation has the following, all of which it has developed in-house:
    a) a manual for operating software
    b) a website
    c) a custom software program.

    Which of the above, if any, are intellectual properties? If any are intellectual property, what type of intellectual property are they?

16. The Winklevoss brothers either didn't have a business law course or didn't listen in class.
    a) What are the statutory IP protections?
    b) Before meeting with Zuckerberg, could they have protected their idea of a social media connecting website by any of the statutory IP types?
    c) Could it have been protected as a business method like the Amazon 1-Click method?
    d) Was there anything that the brothers could have done to protect their idea on meeting with Zuckerberg?

17. In the LAC Minerals case:
    a) The plaintiff based its claim on two causes of action [remedies]. What were they?
    b) Which one was unsuccessful and why?
    c) Which one was successful and why?

18. A friend of yours who developed a unique software package has just telephoned for advice. Apparently, an unhappy employee who had been terminated on Friday, accessed the computer system over the weekend and uploaded the software onto the Internet. Calls are coming in from all over the world from people who have downloaded the program and want to obtain the next version of the software when it comes available.
    a) Advise your friend if there is anything she can do about the actions of Rex, her ex-employee.
    b) Identify and explain to her the intellectual-property law issues which have arisen now that the software is on the Internet. How does this situation affect copyright? How does it affect confidentiality?
    c) Do the implied warranties and conditions of the relevant *Sale of Goods* legislation help the people who have downloaded the software but are experiencing problems with it?
    d) Assuming clever Rex used his own phone to do the deed and it can be traced back to him, explain what criminal charges, if any, he might face.

Real Estate and Insurance Law

What is Real Estate?

Real Estate is land. It got its seemingly unrelated name in medieval times. A lawsuit claiming compensation regarding land was called a real action, hence land became known as Real Estate.

Karl Marx believed that whoever controlled the land in a country controlled its economy. The American humorist Will Rogers is famous for rephrasing Marks, and saying "Buy land, they're not making it anymore." The importance of land in the economic development of the country has long been recognized, and land law was one of the first branches of the law to develop. As a result, most of the legal terms and rules you encounter in land law today were first heard in medieval times and its quaint terminology still survives.

What Is Land?

Land includes the surface of the land, all that is under the surface (including the minerals and oil), and everything above the surface permanently fixed, such as buildings. It includes all that is attached to it—trees, fences, buildings, and so on. A deed to land might therefore describe that land in measurement terms only, making no mention of anything that is on it. However, because of the legal concept of land, all **fixtures** (objects that are permanently attached or fixed to land or to a building) automatically go with the land. So, if you lease a house and build a garage beside it, the garage is considered part of the land. The landowner automatically owns the garage.

In earlier times, it was said that land rights extended down to the core of the earth and upwards to heaven. Since the time of that rather idealistic image, the practical realities of modern living have severely restricted the use of air space. The right of aircraft to fly over land without having to pay anything to the property's owners is one example. Similarly, ownership of land does not always mean possession of mineral rights to the area. In mining areas, it is not unusual to find that the deed of land does not convey the right to mine the minerals. That right has been sold by a previous owner to a mining and exploration company. Grants of land from the Crown typically contain a clause that the mineral rights are kept by the Crown.

land
the surface of the land, all that is under the surface (including the minerals and oil), and everything above the surface permanently fixed, such as buildings

fixtures
objects that are permanently attached or fixed to land or to a building

Types of Ownership

In feudal times, it was established in England that the Crown owned all of the land, and that the nobles merely held that land for the Crown. They, in turn, were able to grant a portion of their estates to their vassals. Ownership of land then became known as an estate in land. That concept is maintained in law today. While we say that a person owns a house, in law, the Crown owns the house and that person holds the fee simple estate.

The monarch of Britain is still nominally the head of state in Canada, and so the federal government is referred to as the Crown. Thus, government-owned land is called Crown land.

■ *Critical Concepts of* States in Land

The only relevant estates today are:

- estate in fee simple
- life estate
- leasehold
- condominiums

Legalese

Tenant   The current meaning of **tenant** is someone who rents a building, apartment, or house from a landlord. The original meaning of tenant is derived from the Latin *tenure*, to hold. The tenant is one who holds land.

Fee Simple

fee simple

the highest form of ownership of land in law, allowing a person to dispose of the land during life or after death

Fee simple is the technical term for what is commonly called ownership of land. It is the highest form of ownership of land in law, allowing a person to dispose of the land during life or after death.

Life Estate

life estate

an estate in land that lasts only while the person is alive

A **life estate** is an estate in land that lasts only while the person is alive. It is created when the owner of a property in fee simple divides the ownership and use of that property. Usually used within a family arrangement, the owner in fee simple gives the fee simple interest to one person or retains it himself while giving a lifetime right to use the land to another. The person who holds the fee simple interest subject to the life estate is said to have the remainder, or reversion, interest. The existence of a life estate usually makes it impossible to sell the land, as the purchaser would be subject to the life estate as well.

Leasehold Estate

leasehold

an interest in land for a period of time created by a lease

A **leasehold** estate is commonly called a lease. It is an interest in land for a period of time created by a lease. The landlord gives the tenant a right to exclusive possession of the property for a limited time—a term. At the end of the term, the tenant's right to occupy reverts to the landlord.

The rights concerning the property are split. The tenant has the right to occupy, while the landlord has the right to enforce the terms of the lease (primarily, collect the rent) and the right to repossess the property at the end of the lease. The landlord has no right to occupy the property if it is leased out, unless specifically given that right in the terms of the lease.

Business Law   Applied

❶ Angela Bennett buys a hectare of land from the Crown and builds a house on it. She rents the house to Carol Dodd for two years. About three months into the lease, Bennett is driving by and sees that Dodd is out and has left every light on in the house.

Muttering about the waste of electricity, Bennett uses her key, goes in, and turns off all the lights. Dodd learns of this, is furious, and wants Bennett charged with trespassing. Bennett says that is nonsense; she has every right to enter the house since she is the owner.

a) What is the legal name for Angela Bennett's ownership of the land she purchases from the Crown?
b) What is the legal name for Angela Bennett's and Carol Dodd's interest in the renting of the house?
c) Does Bennett have the right to enter the house as she did?

Condominiums

Land law has not changed significantly in its basic theories since medieval times. However, one particular new concept of ownership, or estate in land, has developed in the last 40 or so years—the condominium. Shortage of land created the need for a combination of individual and shared ownership, and this is the basis of condominium properties. Condominium projects take many forms: some are apartment buildings; others are row houses; others are detached dwellings. Some office buildings, too, have become condominiums in recent years. A **condominium corporation** is a corporation allowing a way of holding property co-operatively, in which the members are the unit owners.

In condominium ownership, an individual owns one unit in a larger development, such as an apartment building, townhouse complex, or office block. As well as owning the actual unit, that person also owns a share of all of the other features necessary for the running of the project as a tenant in common. These are known as the **common elements**, the structures and areas external to a unit in a condominium, including hallways, elevators, swimming pools, and such.

condominium corporation
a corporation allowing a way of holding property co-operatively, in which the members are the unit owners

common elements
the structures and areas external to a unit in a condominium, including hallways, elevators, swimming pools, and such

Condominiums

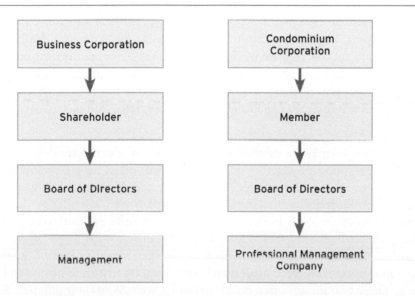

The individual owner has the right to exclusive possession of the unit owned, and a membership in the condominium corporation which has control over all of the common elements. The condominium corporation functions like a normal corporation; however, the homeowners are called *members* rather than *shareholders*. The day-to-day running of the corporation is usually looked after by a professional management company.

Disputes in Condominiums

People are often naïve when they purchase a condominium of all the rules and regulations that the condominium board can impose on the people living in the condominiums. Restrictions on pets, children, noise and many activities are commonplace and if the residents break the rules the condominium board can levy fines or even force them to sell their condo and move out. Some noise-related fines in upscale buildings can easily cost a resident $1,500 for one offence. One owner paid over $80,000 in fines until they finally sold their unit and left. Restrictions on the number, size and type of pet is common as well, if they even allow pets at all. Some of the restrictions are so unreasonable they even violate human rights legislation.

Example: In *Pantoliano v. Metropolitan Condominium Corporation No. 570*, 2011 HRTO 738 (CanLII) a woman challenged the by-laws of her condominium that stated no children in diapers (even swim diapers) were allowed in the 2 swimming pools and children under the age of 16 had very limited hours of access and had to be accompanied by an adult. Children were only allowed in the pools between 1-5 on weekdays and since most parents were working in those hours that effectively prohibited children's use Monday to Friday. On weekends they were only allowed in from 9-1 even on hot summer days. When she complained to the board she was treated with hostility, and though a vote was taken to consider changing these rules, the results were in favour of keeping the restrictions.

She then took her case to the Ontario Human Rights Commission. It ruled this was discrimination based on family status and the condominium board did not have a bona fide health reason for these restrictions. The board was told to rewrite its by-laws to comply with the law and the woman was awarded $10,000 for the injury to her dignity, feelings and self-respect. Needless to say it was a very strained environment at the condo after this court case.

Sometimes residents' behaviour is so offensive that the board can take them to court to have them forced to sell their condominium and leave the complex as illustrated in the *Korolekh* case below.

Example: In a similar case in B.C. a mother and her 20 year old son constantly harassed other condo owners. Loud noises, spitting, swearing, intimidating and abusive language and rude gestures were actions repeatedly done by the pair. They had been fined over $20,000 by the condo corporation for their actions, but they refused to pay, claiming they were illegal fines. The court recognized there was no other reasonable resolution, so it ordered them to sell their unit and move out. (*The Owners Strata Plan LMS 2768 v. Jordison*, 2012 BCSC 31 (CanLII)

Condominium boards are often controlled by a few elected residents who sometimes delight in the new found power they have. The boards often have large budgets to manage due to the high monthly maintenance fees that are levied. Unfortunately some of the people managing these million dollar budgets have little expertise or knowledge in finances. Condominium owners in the same building often have very different outlooks on money. Some want to keep the maintenance fees as low as possible, others want to put more aside for large scale repairs or renovations that will be necessary in the future. This also causes many problems. Many new condos are very small which attract young first time buyers and older people downsizing. These two groups often do not get along well given their different lifestyles, noise levels and financial and personal goals due to the significant age range.

Metropolitan Toronto Condominium Corporation No. 747 v. Korolekh, 2010 ONSC 4448 (CanLII)

Natalia Korolekh purchased a condominium in 2005 in an upscale development in the Yorkville area of Toronto. There are only 30 low rise town house units in the development of which half are on the ground floor with gardens and half on the second floor with balconies. They all share a common courtyard, which prior to Korolekh's arrival, had been a vibrant gathering place for residents. Once she arrived it became desolate and deserted in large part due to her activities.

Korolekh was repeatedly drunk and insulted her neighbours with racist and homophobic slurs. On four occasions she physically assaulted other unit owners. She owned a 150 pound Rottweiler dog that she let lunge at people she disliked. She let it run free in the courtyard and did not clean up its feces. People were intimidated by her and her dog and avoided the courtyard because of this.

Owners complained on several occasions she also damaged their property. She had destroyed an owner's plants, egged another's windows, threw gravel and garbage at another, stole one owner's hose and disturbed the cable TV connection for others. She insulted guests and relatives of other owners when they came to visit with racist rants, sexually offensive comments and repeated swearing. She also regularly played music very loudly to disturb others.

Korolekh denied these complaints stating that she was a very busy stockbroker trained in Moscow and worked very long hours doing international currency trading and had no time to commit the acts she was accused of. She says she suffered considerable stress from her high pressure job and failed infertility treatments she had undergone.

The condo corporation had warned her repeatedly that this conduct must stop and that she had to get rid of the dog, but she ignored the warnings. Finally the condominium went to court to force her to sell her unit and leave the complex.

The Court's Decision

The judge stated that ordering a forced sale of a condominium is an extreme measure that the court would not easily award. However in this case, it appeared to be the "perfect storm" and this was the only reasonable remedy to grant. Ms. Korolekh's conduct was so serious and persistent and it had such a significant impact on a small community that her removal was necessary. She appeared to be incorrigible and unmanageable, she had denied her bad behaviour and there was no realistic chance that she would alter her conduct.

The judge noted that the nine residents who submitted affidavits outlining her behaviour were vulnerable and fearful of reprisals by her. She had been warned of her misconduct but there was no sign she was willing or able to change her ways.

He noted residents in a condominium are entitled to security and quiet enjoyment of their property. People join condominium corporations voluntarily on the basis that they agree to share certain collective property and to abide by a set of rules and obligations. There is no right to continue that membership in that community once a clear intention to harm it and a persistent refusal to abide by its rules have been exhibited in the extreme ways seen in this case.

It would be unwise to try to reintegrate Ms. Korolekh into the community that fears her and that she has persistently tried to intimidate. She has irreparably broken the bond with her community and an effective order could not be made that would force these parties to now join together again.

The court ordered Korolekh to sell her unit within 90 days and to pay $35,000 of the $54,768 claimed in legal costs by the condominium corporation.

Purchasers should be very careful before they purchase a condominium and do their research. Buyers should research the contingency fund set up for future repairs and the age of the building and read the by-laws the condominium board has passed before they buy. Sometimes these restrictions are so severe the person may have preferred to not live there if they had known before they bought. As in any major purchase, buyer beware. Do your homework.

Tenancy in Common

When two or more people own property together, they are called either tenants in common or joint tenants. **Tenancy in common** is co-ownership of land whereby each owner can deal separately with his or her interest, may have unequal interest, and can sell his or her interest or dispose of it by will. This is one type of estate in fee simple.

Joint Tenancy

Joint tenants are equal owners with a unique type of relationship, known as the right of survivorship. **Joint tenancy** is shared ownership with right of survivorship. If one of the

Tenancy in common
co-ownership of land whereby each owner can deal separately with his or her interest, may have unequal interest, and can sell his or her interest or dispose of it by will

joint tenancy
shared ownership with right of survivorship

joint tenants dies, the surviving tenant automatically becomes the sole owner. The deceased's interest is considered to have died with the owner. A joint tenant cannot will an interest in the property to a third party, because at death that interest has ceased to exist. Most husbands and wives hold the matrimonial home in joint tenancy.

Joint tenants can break a joint tenancy by severing, so that it is then changed to a tenancy in common. The normal way of doing this is to transfer the interest to another person. Of course, a person cannot benefit from a wrongful act—AB could not kill CD and thereby become sole owner.

While the term *co-owners* is used, it is not a legal term. Co-owners are either joint tenants or tenants in common.

■ *Critical Concepts of* Real Estate

- Land includes all things affixed to it.
- All land is technically owned by the Crown.
- The legal term for ownership of land is an estate in fee simple.
- Sole ownership is one type of estate in fee simple.
- Joint tenancy has the right of survivorship, which means that the deceased's right ceases and the surviving joint tenant becomes the sole owner.
- Tenants in common are co-owners who can deal separately with their interest.

■ *Business Law* Applied

❷ **Adam Barnes sells** his house to Cliff Dares. Before the date of closing, Barnes removes the garage from the house and sets it up at his farm. Barnes claims he did not sell it to Dares, as it is not specified in the agreement of purchase and sale.

   a) Is Barnes correct?

❸ **Brothers Don and** Jon Davis own an apartment building in joint tenancy. The brothers are on bad terms. Don Davis dies and, in his will, leaves his interest in the apartment building to his son.

   a) Does his son own the interest in the building?
   b) If Don Davis had transferred his interest to his son before he died, would that transfer be effective?
   c) What type of ownership would the son have with his uncle?

❹ **Amy Bondi and** Calvin Donald are business associates and hold a piece of vacant land in joint tenancy. The land goes up in value. Donald experiences severe financial difficulties and murders Bondi.

   a) Does Calvin Donald becomes the sole owner of the property?

❺ **Ron Starr and** Cynthia Brookes are married, and they own two vacant lots. Lot A is owned in joint tenancy, and Lot B is held as tenants in common. In his will, Starr leaves his interest in Lot A to his son, and his interest in Lot B to his daughter.

   a) Does the son become owner of the interest in Lot A?
   b) Does the daughter become owner of the interest in Lot B?

Other Rights over Land

Other rights over land are termed interests lesser than estates. Such interests give the right to use the land for a limited purpose, but do not give exclusive possession. The most common are:

- easements
- licences

Easements

An **easement** is a right enjoyed by one landowner over the land of another for a particular purpose, such as access to water, but not for occupation of the land. The most common easement is a **right of way** (an easement that gives the holder a right to pass back and forth over the land of another in order to get to and from his or her own land). Mutual driveways are examples of easements. Each owner owns the half of the driveway on that individual's side of the property, and has an easement for the use of the other half.

There are also statutory easements for public utility and telephone companies, giving such firms the right to lay cables and enter properties for maintenance and repair.

easement
a right enjoyed by one landowner over the land of another for a particular purpose, such as access to water, but not for occupation of the land

right of way
an easement that gives the holder a right to pass back and forth over the land of another in order to get to and from his or her own land

■ *Business Law* Applied

❻ **Two neighbours,** Anthony Bello and Doug Coombes, share a mutual driveway. Over some time, they start to quarrel. Out of spite, Bello leaves a garbage can on his side of the property, blocking use of the driveway. When asked to remove it, Bello tells Coombes that the garbage can is on Bello's own land and he has a right to put it there. In retaliation, and claiming he has an easement, Coombes leaves his car parked in the driveway for long periods of time.

a) Does Bello have the right to leave the garbage can on his own side of the driveway? Does Coombes have any rights over this part of Bello's property?
b) Can Coombes park in the driveway?

Licences

Licences can apply to all property, not merely land, and are technically a matter of contract law. In the context of land law, a licence gives permission for the use of land. One of the most common is the implied licence to enter that a retailer gives the public for the purposes of shopping. That licence can be withdrawn by the retailer.

■ *Business Law* Applied

❼ **Bo's Bootery,** a retail shoe store, gives Angie Carr, a neighbourhood kid, the right to set up a table in front of the store to sell jewelery she has made. Some time later, arguments develop because the store owner believes customers are not frequenting his store because of the number and type of clients Carr is attracting. He asks her to leave, but she refuses.

a) What is the name of the right by which Carr was allowed to set up on the business property?
b) Can the store owner revoke that right?

Adverse Possession   Adverse possession is not very common any more. In some limited situations though it is still possible to acquire ownership of land by use alone and without paying for it through adverse possession, sometimes called squatters' rights. If the owner does not use the land and someone else does, the owner may lose it. Despite the fact almost all land is registered in the Land Titles system now, depending on when the adverse possession occurred, it may still be possible to claim ownership this way. Most of these claims are due to misplaced fences, driveways or even buildings that extend over a property boundary, often originally by mistake.

The party claiming another's land must hold the property in a certain way for a certain amount of time. The time is set by statutes in the various provinces and ranges from 10 to 20 years. The use must be open (so the owner can see it); exclusive (so no one else used it); adverse (meaning against the owner's interest); and continuous for the entire required time period. In Ontario if those conditions are met for at least 10 years before the land entered the Land Titles system, then the claim for adverse possession, if proven, can succeed. Claims of this nature are becoming increasing rare and as the case below illustrates, often are not worth the cost of the dispute.

Example: Frank and Dolores Lipischak are next-door neighbours to Diana DeWolf and Joe Russ in the eastern Ontario town of Lakeshore. When the Lipischaks bought their house in 1969, a wire fence separated the two properties along what they thought was the lot line. The Lipischak fence however extended onto the DeWolf property by about 3.6 inches. A bitter dispute broke out as each family claimed ownership of the 3.6 inch strip of land. DeWolf removed the chain link fence, cut the concrete sidewalk and installed a new fence in the space between the two homes.

The judge ruled the Lipischaks had established the criteria for adverse possession, so the strip of land became theirs. The trial judge was angered by DeWolf's conduct, and the arrogance of taking the law into her own hands. The Lipischaks were awarded $5,934 plus taxes for the new fence and sidewalk, $7,500 in punitive damages for DeWolf's "horrific and excessive conduct," and a further $15,000 in damages for trespass. DeWolf was also ordered to pay the plaintiff's court costs of $89,371 for an 11-day trial. DeWolf and Russ appealed, which was dismissed with appeal costs of $20,000 to the Lipischaks. The damages and costs awards against the defendants totalled $138,577, in addition to their own lawyer's bill of perhaps another $100,000 plus. (*Lipischak v. Russ*, 2011 ONCA 634 (CanLII).

After the trial, DeWolf and Russ sued the Lipischaks claiming the right to travel over the parcel of land they had lost. As well, they also sued the prior owners of their property for the cost of defending their title and for the loss resulting from the change in the property line. This only added further expenses to already very large legal costs all over 3.6 inches of land. (Bob Aaron, "Badly placed fences make angry neighbors." The Toronto Star, February 4, 2012.)

Family Law Interest   There is an important unregistered possible interest in every matrimonial or family home. The family law acts of the provinces treat family assets like the assets of a partnership. The increase in the value from the date of marriage to the date of separation of the assets is to be divided equally, with the one exception: the matrimonial or family home. The family home's full value is put into the family asset mix regardless of who paid for it or in whose name it is registered.

Example: Sam has an investment worth $100,000 on the date of marriage, which has increased in value to $110,000 on separation. The amount to be put into the family asset calculation is the increase of $10,000.

Ana owns a house in her own name, which she paid for, on the date of marriage (which remains in her name alone) worth $500,000 and is worth $600,000 on separation. The full $600,000 is put into the family assets calculation to be divided equally.

Their family assets are $610,000 and each spouse's interest is $305,000.

If the spouses want to vary this result, they can enter into a **marriage contract** specifying how the family assets will be divided on separation. Usually made before marriage, it is often called a Prenuptial Agreement. When people are considering marriage, it is often very wise to think of a marriage contract, especially if one party owns the home or considerably more assets before the marriage.

It is only a potential interest until separation occurs. Then it comes into effect, not as a direct interest in the home, but in the asset pool. The matrimonial home may be registered in the land registry office in the name of one spouse alone. To prevent that spouse from dealing with it to affect the interests of the other spouse in any way, such as selling or mortgaging it, any attempt by one spouse to deal with the matrimonial home is ineffective against the interest of the other spouse unless that spouse's written consent is obtained. That is why banks, for example, on obtaining a guarantee from one spouse for a business loan often insist that the other spouse co-sign so there can be no issue over the ability to seize the matrimonial home if there is a default on the loan. (See the *Iori v. Village Building Supplies* case below)

Virtual Real Estate   While not a legal interest (yet), gamers are selling virtual real estate at real real estate prices.

Jon Jacobs made history by selling virtual property for a reported total of $635,000. Club Neverdie is a virtual asteroid in the online game Entropia. The Entropia Universe has its own virtual economy that has a fixed exchange rate correlated to the real world. When you make 100 PED (as the Entropia currency is called) you can trade it out for $10 USD at any time, and vice versa. Using Club Neverdie as a resort destination for thousands of Entropia players, Jon Jacobs was able to make $200k a year in revenue. Selling an imaginary playland for hundreds of thousands of dollars sounds impossible, but it happened. (*Meet The Man Who Just Made A Half Million From The Sale Of Virtual Property*, Oliver Chiang, Forbes, 11/13/2010)

The law may have to develop new categories to account for the online world. In the real world, these are more likely to be classified under contractual rights. However, that remains to be seen.

Registry Acts

All provinces have a registry act specifically stating that unregistered deeds are considered completely ineffective against those that have been registered. The registry acts in most provinces resulted in the purchaser's lawyer searching back the property's title for at least 40 years to make sure the seller was the legal owner and that there were no outstanding claims on the property. This was a long slow process and was replaced with the Land Titles System that is computerized and the government guarantees the title and accuracy of the documents registered under the system. In Ontario, 99% of all land is now under the Land Titles System.

The Land Titles System

The **land titles system** is also sometimes known as the Torrens system of land registration. It is a system of land registration in which the land titles office certifies registered interests as being correct. The rules concerning the system are set out in the land titles acts of the various provinces. Generally, the system requires that the provincial government maintain a registry which records the following on a document called the Certificate of Title:

land titles system
a system of land registration in which the land titles office certifies registered interests as being correct

- the legal description of the land
- the "highest" type of interest held (for example, an estate in fee simple)
- the owner(s) of that interest
- other parties who have a lesser interest in the land, and what type of interest they claim

The key feature of the land titles system is a guarantee—what you see on the title to a piece of property is what you get (with a few notable exceptions listed below). You do not have to search back in time to figure out who owns a piece of property and who else claims an interest in it. The *Land Titles Act* guarantees that what is on the Certificate of Title is right—and if it is not, you can make a claim for compensation against a government-maintained fund (called an assurance fund).

Some other important features of the land titles system:

fraudulent transfer

a transfer of property by a debtor, usually to a related person, so that creditors cannot seize it

- If there is no registration, then there is no claim against subsequent owners. You must check to determine if there are prior interests already registered.
- The order of registration determines the order of priority. The rule is simple—interests which are registered first have first priority.
- Some provincial land titles acts do allow interests that are not registered to be valid such as; unpaid taxes and highways so appropriate inquiries must be made.
- If you acquired your interest through fraud, the Land Titles guarantee of title may not be valid.

Iori v. Village Building Supplies (1977) Ltd., 2005 CanLII 23122 (ON SC)

Giuseppina and Nicola Iori were married and lived together in their matrimonial home on Novaview Cres. in Woodbridge, Ontario. The home was registered in the wife's name, only. Her husband, Nicola, owned and operated a dry wall installation business, Blue Willow Contracting.

Blue Willow became indebted to Village Building Supplies for $100,527 on account of dry wall and other related products it had purchased. Village Building supplies registered a lien on the Iori home but it later agreed to remove the lien when it was provided with a registerable mortgage on the Novaview Cres. home for $102,000. Nicola forged Giuseppina's signature on the mortgage and it was registered against the property in favour of Village Building Supplies.

When the mortgage payments were not made, Village Building gave notice it would sell the home. Giuseppina was shocked, as she knew nothing of this mortgage and asked the court to declare the mortgage void due to fraud. The couple had separated since the mortgage was registered and she was also suffering from cancer.

The Court's Decision

It was conceded at trial that her signature on the mortgage was forged. The unchallenged evidence was that she did not sign the mortgage, that it was registered without her knowledge and consent and that she did not speak with representatives of Village Building Supplies. She certainly had never received independent legal advice either.

The judge noted that past cases where a person has forged the signature of their spouse on a mortgage on a matrimonial home the decisions have gone in both directions. Some courts have declared the mortgage void due to the fraud, but others have declared the mortgage valid due to the specific facts of the case.

In this case the court accepted that the wife was unaware of the forgery and that Village Supplies was equally innocent that the signature was a fake. The court however stressed that in a mortgage on a matrimonial home, especially where the spouse was sick, Village Supplies or its lawyer should have ensured that independent legal advice had been given to both spouses. If that precautionary step had been taken, the forgery would have been prevented.

As a result the mortgage was considered void and Village Building Supplies was unable to force the sale of the home to obtain the money it was owed.

Business Law   Applied

❽ **Jeff and Tina** were married for 12 years and had two children. When they were married Jeff owned the house and it was worth $400,000. Tina owned a condo which she sold for $300,000 and invested the money. When they divorced the house was worth $800,000 and Tina's investments were worth $400,000.

   a) How will these assets be divided?

   b) Shortly before the divorce Jeff took out a $600,000 mortgage on the house to pay off his gambling debts. Jeff has not paid the mortgage and the bank wants to sell the house to get its money. Tina never knew of the mortgage and Jeff had forged her signature on the mortgage. What would a court rule?

   c) If they had a marriage contract that stated Tina was not entitled to any interest in the house if they divorced, how would that affect the division of assets between them?

❾ **Lambert Fisk was** a farmer in southern Saskatchewan. He wished to purchase an additional quarter section of land for his operation, but had to borrow money to so do. His uncle, Filbert Fisk, agreed to lend him the money, but wanted a mortgage against the new farmland to protect himself in case Lambert could not pay him back. Lambert and Filbert signed the mortgage and Lambert because the proud owner of a new quarter section of land. Filbert did not register his mortgage at the land titles office.

Soon after purchasing the property, Lambert found that he could not make the payments and made a quick sale of the newly acquired land to his neighbour, Elmer Filkowski. Uncle Filbert is very unhappy and feels he should be able to get the farmland for himself, since he has a mortgage on it.

   a) Can Uncle Filbert enforce his mortgage against Elmer (that is, foreclose on the land to try and recover his loss)?

   b) What should Uncle Filbert have done to protect his claim against the land?

   c) What should Elmer (or his lawyer) have done prior to going through with the land sale, to find out who else had a potential claim against the property?

Commercial Leases

Commercial leasing is a complex area in which there can be many different leasing situations. This section focuses on the small retail business in the shopping centre or plaza—a relatively common situation that contains concerns beyond those of renting an isolated unit. A shopping centre tenant, for example, must consider not just the aspects of the store rented, but also those of the whole shopping centre. A tenant might rent a store on a five-year lease to start an upscale jewelry shop. What happens if the mall then rents a kiosk that sells hotdogs right in front of the door? Or what can be done if the landlord rents another jewelry store nearby? The tenant is stuck for five years unless the lease contains protective clauses.

A new trend in leasing law is adding to its complexity. Leasing law was developed in accordance with very strict and technical land law principles, and contract principles were developed quite distinctly. However, the old and very technical principles of leasing law are now being replaced with contract principles that are more in accord with the modern business environment.

Also, most conflicts between a landlord and tenant are governed by the terms of the lease—the contract—and not by the principles of leasing law. So it is often more important to understand the terms of the lease than it is to have an in-depth knowledge of general leasing law principles.

Note that residential tenancies (like the type that would cover an apartment you rented) are covered by special legislation, and the rules which apply to commercial leasing may well not apply to the residential situation. Generally, the rules concerning residential tenancies afford special protection for the tenants.

The Terms of the Lease

Permitted Use

The landlord will insist that the premises be used only for the stated purposes. Other uses might cause more wear and tear, interfere with other tenants, or even result in the cancellation of the landlord's insurance. If a store is leased as a clothing store but the owner converts it to a restaurant, for example, the landlord's fire insurance policy would likely be cancelled.

Tenants will also be concerned that the landlord obtain similar clauses from other tenants, so that a competing business cannot be set up in the same mall. An exclusive-use clause states that the tenant shall be the only business of the type in the shopping centre.

Example: A Mailboxes Etc. store in a N.S. mall had an exclusivity clause that prevented the landlord from allowing any other store to offer services that competed with its primary services which included; mailbox rentals, packaging, shipping, printing and photocopying. The landlord later rented space to a large Staples store which as part of its services offered photocopying and printing. Those services accounted for about 4 ½–5 % of Staples total sales and had a significant impact on Mailboxes Etc.'s revenue. The mailbox store successfully sued the landlord for breach of the exclusivity clause and was awarded damages of $75,000 for its lost net earnings and $50,000 for loss in business goodwill. (*Plazacorp Retail Properties Ltd. v. Mailboxes Etc.*, 2009 NSCA 40 (CanLII))

The permitted use covenant has been used as a basis to develop a new principle of law which, in certain circumstances, may give a tenant a right to enforce a covenant in a lease to which that tenant is not a party and which was made exclusively between the Landlord and another tenant.

The community of interest principle creates an exception to the otherwise very strictly applied doctrine of privity of contract. This exception will likely not be expanded. In *Spike v. Rocca Group*, next, there was a restrictive covenant in the lease between the landlord and Big John's by which its permitted use was men's haircutting only, but it started to cut women's hair. The landlord refused to enforce that covenant so one tenant, who did not have any contractual relationship with the other tenant, started an action to enforce the covenant in the lease between the landlord and the other tenant in a similar business.

Spike v. Rocca Group Ltd., [1979] 23 Nfld. & P.E.I.R. 493 (S.C.)

A new concept in leasing law is developing as a result of the modern multi-tenant situation found in shopping centres, malls, and plazas. The courts realize that what one tenant does may greatly affect another. This is called a community interest and, in some circumstances, permits tenant A to sue tenant B, based on the terms of the lease between tenant B and the landlord.

Louise Spike operated a women's hairdressing salon under the name of Plaza Beauty Parlour. She signed a lease with the Rocca Group for space in its University Plaza. That lease contained a clause that said Spike would restrict her business to the cutting of women's hair.

> 7.26 The tenant will not use or occupy the leased premises or any part thereof for any purpose other than the operation of the business of women's hairstyling under the name of Plaza Beauty Parlour.

The lease also contained an exclusive-use clause.

9.19 The landlord agrees that during the term of this lease or any renewal thereof, it will not lease any other premises in the shopping centre or in any addition built to the present shopping centre to a tenant doing women's hairstyling and/or operating a unisex beauty salon.

John Muise, who operated a men's barber shop called Big John's Place, signed a similar lease with the Rocca Group. That lease contained a clause limiting the use of the unit to men's hair cutting. Another clause guaranteed him the exclusive right to carry on the business of cutting men's hair similar to the Spike clause.

Big John's Place began to cut women's hair. Spike complained to the Rocca Group but it refused to do anything about the situation. Spike brought an action against Big John's, requesting an injunction to stop the firm from cutting women's hair. Big John's defended, claiming Spike was not a party to the lease containing the permitted use clause and therefore had no legal basis to sue.

The Court's Decision

The court held that the growing number of shopping malls across the country is creating a new body of law particular to it. Spike thus had the right to an injunction against Big John's to stop it from violating its permitted-use clause. Even though there was no privity of contract, each business had agreed not to use the premises except for specific uses. Each business received the benefit of this covenant. This is the essence of a shopping mall lease.

The mutual advantage created a community of interest between tenants of similar businesses, giving each a direct interest in the carrying out of the terms of the lease by the other. Therefore Big John's was prohibited from the business of cutting women's hair.

Example: Salmon Arm Pharmacy had a lease with the landlord of a mall containing a permitted use clause that restricted its use to a pharmacy. There was a clause by the landlord agreeing not to permit another tenant to carry on a pharmacy business. There was no such relevant restriction in the lease between the landlord and Canada Safeway Limited, a retail grocery store. Safeway opened a pharmacy within its store. Salmon Arm sued the landlord who sued Safeway claiming that the community of interest doctrine would imply a term into the Safeway lease that it would not open a pharmacy in competition with another tenant. The court rejected implying such a term and stated that the community of interest rule would only apply where there was an express covenant in the lease between the landlord and the targeted tenant. (*Salmon Arm Pharmacy Ltd. v. R.P. Johnson Construction Ltd.*, 1994 CanLII 1739 (BC CA)).

■ *Business Law* Applied

⑩ **Andrew Reich ran** a news stand and variety store at a major intersection for a number of years. A developer wanted to buy it and the surrounding properties to convert them into a shopping mall. Reich agreed to sell and took a lease for a kiosk at the entrance of the new shopping mall. He agreed as a term of the lease to limit his business to that of a news stand.

Business went well for about a year, and then it dropped off. Reich learned that a pharmacy had opened in the mall and was selling newspapers and magazines. A clause in the pharmacy's lease stated that it would only carry on the business of a pharmacy.

Reich wants to know if there is anything that can be done to stop the pharmacy from selling newspapers and magazines.

  a) What additional clause could Reich have negotiated in his lease?
  b) Does the landlord have any right to stop the pharmacy from selling newspapers? What is the technical name for that remedy?
  c) Will the wording of the permitted-use clause in the pharmacy's lease give it a possible defence?

An unexpected oversight such as that in the Salmon Arms case indicates why it is necessary to have a solicitor review a commercial lease. Solicitors review cases such as that one and so can advise tenants so their rights are protected. A solicitor for a pharmacy such as Salmon Arms might obtain a covenant from the landlord that there was a restrictive clause in all other tenants' leases and might even go further and review relevant leases to ensure the presence of such a clause.

Business Alert!

Other Exclusive Use Issues   While the courts will not expand any relief beyond privity of contract based on community of interest, there may be other bases in law for relief when permitted use is affected. The courts may well imply a term, as between landlord and aggrieved tenant, that the landlord will not lease to another tenant that will create a **nuisance** for the first tenant. What if one day a landlord leases a second floor to a Buddhist Meditation Center, and the next day, leases to a studio used by rock bands for practice sessions 24/7 in the unit directly underneath.

Also, the conduct may not be a nuisance, but may be a complete interference with the tenants use so that the tenant does not get what the tenant paid for. What if the landlord leased one unit to a day care center and the adjoining unit to a halfway house for criminals on parole, or one unit to an upscale woman's clothing boutique and the adjoining unit to a temporary employment office for unskilled workers which always had a large number of applicants hanging around its entrance.

Example: Jean Deiuliis operated a woman's hair salon in a plaza. The landlord leased an adjoining unit to a fish market. Deiuliis's business dropped significantly and one staff member quit because of the smell. The court implied a term into the lease that the landlord would not lease to a tenant whose use would create a nuisance for Deiuliis which gave her the right to claim damages against the landlord but did not permit her to terminate the lease. (*MSM Construction Ltd. et al. v. Deiuliis*, 1985 CanLII 2052 (ON SC)) confirmed by the Ontario Court of Appeal 7 O.A.C. 332

Example: Penny Powers operated a high and the woman's clothing boutique called 'Walkabout Custom Wear. At first all went well, but once the warmer weather began the store began to manifest an unpleasant odor. Clients and staff complained. The cause could not be located, but was suspected to be in the heating and air conditioning system. The judge accepted this odour existed and was substantial enough to defeat the very purpose for which the space was leased, which amounted to a fundamental breach, entitling her to terminate the lease. (*Stearman v. Powers*, 2013 BCSC 1160 (CanLII)).

Example: Where "smelly, greasy fluid" seeped onto the floor of a grocery store from a restaurant directly above it and the landlord either would not or could not eliminate the problem, the seepage was a fundamental breach allowing a grocery store tenant to terminate its lease.(*Shun Cheong Holdings B.C. Ltd. v. Gold Ocean City Supermarket Ltd.*, 2002 BCCA 451 (CanLII)).

■ *Critical Concepts of* A Tenant's Use Disturbed

A tenant may have several remedies in law if its use is affected:

- A tenant may be able to directly sue another tenant to prevent it from opening a competing business if there is an express covenant in the lease between the landlord and the offending tenant prohibiting that type of business based on community of interest.
- The community of interest principle will not be expanded to a situation where there is no express restriction on the relevant permitted use in the targeted tenant's lease.
- A term may be implied into a lease that the landlord will not lease to another tenant whose business would substantially interfere with the business of the first tenant (nuisance)
- If a premises becomes unusable for any reason, that may be a fundamental breach that could terminate the lease.

Rent

In a modern retail store lease, especially one in a shopping centre, there may be many items other than rent included in the tenant's monthly payment obligation. The most common of these include:

- percentage rent (a percentage of annual sales, and is applicable only in a retail situation)
- utility charges (water, heating, air conditioning, ventilation, and so on)
- a proportionate share of common-area costs, such as escalators, elevators, or hallways, and the cost of the housekeeping, maintenance, and repair to them
- merchants' associations dues and other advertising costs
- a proportionate share in business and realty taxes and insurance

The landlord will want all of these items to be called rent, so that it can take advantage of special leasing remedies for enforcement if a tenant fails to pay. The tenant, on the other hand, will want such costs to be called tenant's expenses.

Radius Clauses

When a tenant agrees to pay percentage rent, the landlord will insist that a radius clause be included in the lease. For example the tenant cannot open another branch within a radius of five kilometres of the shopping centre. Landlords insist on such a clause in case a tenant is able to lease other space in the neighbourhood, where a percentage rent is not demanded.

These radius clauses are covenants in restraint of trade and, like non-competition clauses, must be a reasonable restraint regarding subject matter, time, and distance.

Gross/Net Lease

Often landlords will want all expenses to be paid by the tenant. The landlord will assume certain specific financial obligations, and the tenant will pay insurance, realty taxes, and utilities. This is called a net lease.

In a gross lease, the tenant pays only regular rent, and the landlord is responsible for the other expenses. The landlord and tenant may agree to any combination of the two leases.

Repairs

Common law puts the responsibility for repairs on the tenant, except when the premises become so unusable that it amounts to eviction. Repair obligations are expressly set out in the lease, and they should be reviewed with care. The normal clause reads that the landlord will be responsible for structural repairs, and the tenant for repairs to the internal part of the premises.

The tenant will normally insist that the landlord be responsible for internal repairs caused by problems with construction, or by a catastrophe such as fire or hurricane, for which the landlord can carry insurance. Also, the tenant is exempted from having to repair deterioration caused by reasonable wear and tear.

◼ *Business Law*   Applied

⊕ **Insect Communications Inc.** has leased a retail unit in a plaza. The standard form lease contains a term: "The landlord will be responsible for structural repairs and the tenant for repairs to the interior portion of the premises."

A pipe for the air conditioning system travels from a central unit at the back of the premises through the wall to the exterior. It cracks along the whole length.

a) Who must repair the pipe?
b) How could the landlord and tenant have avoided the problem of deciding responsibility?

Repair Clauses   The drafting of repair clauses requires the advice of an experienced leasing lawyer. Do not rely on standard form agreements purchased from a stationery store. For example, are the piping and wiring that are located within the walls and floors part of the interior or the exterior of the premises? Countless court actions have been commenced on the wording of repair clauses. A careful draftsperson will refer specifically to completed, as-built, drawings of the property to remove some of the ambiguity.

A tenant should also insist on a clause stating that the landlord has insurance to cover agreed repair costs. An agreement by the landlord to repair will be of no value if the landlord cannot raise the money to do so. Discuss the repair situation with an insurance agent, to establish your position on such matters as business interruption loss or loss of profits if the repairs prevent the carrying on of business.

Breaches of the Lease—Landlord's Remedies

The emphasis in this section is on the landlord's remedies—not because the tenant's remedies are less important, but simply because they are less complicated. Also, a tenant must understand that, although traditional leasing law gives landlords special and very effective remedies, the courts restrict the landlord's use of these by demanding absolute technical compliance. The tenant must know these technicalities if it wishes to take advantage of them in defending against a landlord's actions.

Eviction

The events that permit the landlord to evict the tenant are divided into two categories:

- failure to pay rent
- breach of a condition of the lease, unrelated to rent

When a landlord evicts a tenant, this is a termination of the lease, and is called the forfeiture of the lease. Locking the tenant out by changing the locks is a common method of terminating the lease. The landlord can also apply to the court for an order ending the lease and evicting the tenant.

Failure to Pay Rent

Specific rules relate to a tenant's failure to pay rent. Under them, the landlord is given far more effective remedies than would be available in contract law. A landlord can retake possession of the premises and evict the tenant without need of a court order. For this reason, a landlord will attempt to have as many tenant expenses as possible included as rent in a lease.

By statute and the common law, the landlord can take possession of the premises, without notice to the tenant, for failure to pay rent after 15 days. (The period can be varied by the lease.) The tenant has until midnight on the day the rent is due to pay the sum owing.

■ *Critical Concepts of* Eviction for Not Paying Rent

- The landlord can evict the tenant 15 days after the rent was due.
- The tenant has until midnight on the day the rent is due to pay.
- The landlord need give no notice to the tenant before taking possession—that is, evicting the tenant.

Franchises and Rent   In franchises, the parent company often attempts to become the landlord by renting the premises and then subletting to the franchisee. The franchisee's royalty payments and other fees are described as rent in the sublease, so that the parent company can take advantage of the special lease rent-default remedies.

■ *Business Law*   Applied

⑫ **The rent is** due on the lease on the fifteenth of the month, and when it is not paid by close of business at 5:00 p.m. on that day, the landlord has the bailiff change the locks and post a notice to the tenant that it is evicted. The tenant comes in the next morning and is shocked. It has an automated computer system and by some mistake, the rent cheque was not sent to the landlord when it should have been.

   a) The tenant claims that it received no notice of the overdue rent, and so the landlord's taking possession is improper. Is that correct?
   b) Does the tenant have any defences?

Eviction for Breach of Other Terms

Terminating the lease and evicting the tenant for breaches other than those involving rent must follow strict procedures. Notice of the breach must be given to the tenant, detailing the problem and giving the tenant time to deal with the situation. The slightest mistake in following this process will be fatal to the landlord, as the courts are very ready to protect the tenant's rights. One notice of breach given by a landlord mistakenly described the lease as being dated January 11 instead of January 8. The judge declared the **re-entry**—the landlord's remedy of evicting the tenant for failure to pay rent or for breach of another major covenant—by the landlord invalid and said, "A little inaccuracy is as fatal as the greatest."

re-entry
the landlord's remedy of evicting the tenant for failure to pay rent or for breach of another major covenant

---

■ *Critical Concepts of*   Notice

- Notice of the breach must be given to the tenant.
- The notice must be accurate in every detail.
- The notice must clearly advise the tenant of the nature of the breach, e.g., that the roof is leaking and it is the tenant's responsibility to repair this.
- The tenant must be permitted a reasonable time to remedy the breach.
- If the landlord accepts rent after it first becomes aware of the breach, it cannot terminate the lease.
- Even though the landlord loses the right to terminate or evict the tenant for breach of a condition of the lease by accepting rent after notice, the landlord can apply to the court for an order remedying the situation.

■ *Business Law*   Applied

⑬ **A tenant signed** a lease that contained a clause permitting it to operate a variety store that will not sell dairy products. Because a competing variety store a short distance away began to sell dairy products, the tenant began to sell them also.

The landlord served the following notice on the tenant:

   Take notice that you are in breach of the terms of your lease and unless you remedy the breach immediately, the lease will be terminated.

The tenant ignored the notice and continued to sell dairy products. Three days later, the tenant came to the store to find it padlocked, and a notice on the door saying that the premises had been seized on behalf of the landlord.

a) Does the tenant have any grounds to attack the termination of the lease?

⑭ **A tenant agreed** by terms of the lease to repair the plumbing in the premises. A pipe began to leak; the landlord noticed this, and gave the tenant written notice on November 30 to repair the leak. The next day, December 1, the landlord came again to collect the rent which was due on the first day of every month. While taking the cheque, the landlord noticed that the leak had increased, and became worried that, as the pipe went across the ceiling, the entire ceiling could collapse unless it was repaired immediately. The tenant said that it didn't have money to do the repair, and so the next day the landlord had the tenant locked out. The landlord terminated the lease and began to do the repairs.

a) Was the landlord's re-entry proper?

Seizure of Tenant's Goods

distress

the right of the landlord to distrain (seize) a tenant's assets found on the premises and sell them to apply to arrears of rent

If the tenant has the ability to pay and the landlord wants to keep the lease alive, the landlord has the remedy of **distress**, the right of the landlord to distrain (seize) a tenant's assets found on the premises and sell them to apply to arrears of rent. Distress must be done strictly according to the proper procedure, or the landlord will be liable in damages for the improper seizure of goods.

The process is normally carried out by a licensed bailiff. If the value of the goods seized is far in excess of the rent owing, the landlord will be liable for the value of the goods seized, and for any consequent business loss. While the landlord has this very unusual remedy, the courts make certain that the landlord does not abuse its privilege. In one case, the landlord's lawyer was ordered to pay the tenant's damages after the lawyer failed to instruct the landlord's bailiff on distress procedures, and the distress was irregular.

The landlord should not need to use force because the landlord should have a key to the premises. If the tenant has changed the locks, the landlord can change the locks back, but must give the tenant a key.

The remedies of suing for rent arrears and taking goods are alternatives. If the landlord seizes the goods, it cannot sue until the goods are sold and the proceeds applied to the amount owed, and any arrears remaining become evident.

■ *Critical Concepts of* Distress

- Seizure of a tenant's goods can be done only during daylight hours, and never on Sunday.
- The landlord cannot use force to enter the premises.
- The landlord must hold the goods for five days before selling, and have them valued by two appraisers.
- The goods must be sold for the best price.
- The quantity of the goods seized must not be excessive.

Business Law   Applied

⑮ **The Thompson Corp.** is a tenant, and is in arrears for two months' rent—$2,000. It has inventory of furniture which could be sold at an auction for $2,000 if seized by the landlord. Thompson Corp. has changed the locks, and the landlord can't get in. The landlord has a locksmith change them again and puts a notice on the door to the tenant that the goods are seized. The furniture would retail for $5,000 if sold by the tenant in the normal course of business.

    a) Can the landlord seize the tenant's inventory without a court order? If so, what is the process called?
    b) Is the seizure by the landlord proper?
    c) If the seizure is not proper, what damages could the tenant claim?
    d) How could the landlord have made a proper seizure?

Distress   A common mistake landlords make is to evict a tenant for non-payment of rent by changing the locks and also seizing the tenant's goods. If the landlord evicts the tenant, the lease is terminated, and the landlord cannot seize the tenant's goods.

Business Alert!

YK Human Resources Corporation v. Dinco Holdings Inc., 2005 CanLII 45413 (ON SC)

YK Human Resources was an employment placement agency that leased a unit from Dinco Holdings. It had signed a 2 year lease and two days before the lease expired, the landlord came into the office, ordered the employees to leave and changed the locks. The landlord claimed the tenant owed two months' rent ($4,361). The tenant gave the landlord two post-dated cheques for this amount, but the landlord refused to allow the tenant back into the unit to deal with its goods until it had actually received the money. Despite repeated requests, the landlord refused to allow the tenant access to the unit which contained all its records, files, office equipment and furnishings.

The landlord then sold the goods in the unit without proper notice or an accounting of the profits. YK claimed that it was an illegal distress sale. YK claimed it had $40,000 in goods and chattels in the unit which had been illegally taken and sold, so it sued the landlord for wrongful conversion.

The Court's Decision

The judge noted that a landlord is entitled to exercise the self-help remedy of distress, but only in limited circumstances. The landlord can inventory and tag the tenant's goods and leave them in the tenant's possession or remove them and put them in storage. However, either option requires proper notice to the tenant. This includes, at a minimum, notice of the reason for the distress, the amount of outstanding arrears, an inventory of goods and the time and place of the intended sale.

In this case the tenant received no list of inventory, no appraisal and no proper information regarding the sale. The distress and disposition of the tenant's goods and chattels was wrongful and not in compliance with the *Commercial Tenancies Act*, R.S.O. 1990, c.L.7. The landlord had wrongfully disposed of the goods without accounting for the proce___ sale.

The judge also found that the value of ___ taken also vastly exceeded the arrears owing and ___

The judge set the depreciated ___ ___iture, equipment, computer, telepho___ ___at $26,500. The judge also rule___ handed and non-responsiv___ on the tenant who was u___ the defendant's unlawful co___ ___00 were also justified.

Breaches of the Lease—Tenant's Remedies

Relief from Forfeiture

Apart from defects in the strict procedure that may make actions by the landlord invalid, the tenant's main remedy is **relief from forfeiture**. The courts are very ready to order the lease reinstated upon payment of rent arrears or remedies the breach—such as repairing damage or paying the landlord's costs of doing so.

relief from forfeiture
a court will re-instate a lease if the tenant pays the rent arrears or remedies the breach of contract

Example: Gary Vannek operated a BP gas station. One of his employees, Taylor, was a bookie and used the phone for his illegal gambling and bookmaking business. Taylor was caught and convicted. The landlord served a notice that Vannek had breached a term of the lease prohibiting illegal use. Vannek asked for relief from forfeiture. The court found that an illegal activity had been carried on in breach of the term of the lease, but since Vannek was not personally involved, it granted him relief from forfeiture. (*BP Canada Limited v. Bamsa,* [1976] 14 O.R. 92d) 508)

Rights of Renewal

Commercial leases often have a clause that entitles the tenant the right to renew the lease so long as the tenant gives proper notice and they are not in default of any terms in the lease. Renewal rights are very important because if it is a profitable business, continuing operation in the same location is often vital for future success. Sometime landlords want a problem tenant to leave and do not want them to exercise the renewal option. The court may have to determine if the tenant can exercise its renewal right.

Example: A tenant had signed a 10 year lease and was required to give 180 days notice if it wanted to renew the lease for a further 5 year term. The tenant ran a bar and repeatedly had over-served customers who regularly were drunk, loud and obnoxious when they left the bar. Repeatedly they would vomit and urinate and defecate outside the bar and sometimes were in fights and nearby windows were broken. Other tenants were very angry by this situation. The tenant gave 180 days notice that it intended to renew the lease. The landlord claimed that at the time the tenant gave its renewal notice, the tenant was in breach of the lease for over-serving and allowing this offensive behaviour and this justified its right to refuse the renewal. The trial judge granted the right to renewal, because the landlord had continued to accept rent and had not taken any steps to remove the tenant for these alleged breaches. The Court of Appeal however reversed the decision. It stated that over-serving alcohol was a breach of the lease and since it occurred at the time of the renewal date, the tenant was in breach of the lease terms and had forfeited its right to renewal. (*1383421 Ontario Inc. v. OLE Miss Place Inc.*, 2003 CanLII 57436 (ON CA)

No Withholding of Rent

The tenant's agreement to pay rent is considered a term separate from any of the landlord's agreements in the lease. So, if the landlord breaches the agreement by, for example, not repairing damage to the structure, the tenant cannot withhold rent. Instead, the tenant must bring a court action for an order compelling the landlord to perform, or for damages for the cost of doing the repair by the tenant, including, for example, loss of business if that happened because of the lack of repair.

■ *Critical Concepts of* Tenant's Remedies

- If a tenant is locked out, the tenant can apply to the court to have the lease reinstated by a remedy called relief of forfeiture.
- The court will usually order the tenant to make good any loss to the landlord before reinstating the lease.
- The court is usually very ready to grant tenants relief from forfeiture.
- A tenant cannot withhold rent if the landlord fails to perform one of its agreements in the lease.

Magnum T.O. Inc. v. Highland Hotel Limited, 2009 CanLII 60778 (ON SC)

The plaintiff purchased the business known as Remington's Men of Steel for $400,000 and took over the commercial lease for this bar and club on Yonge Street in downtown Toronto in July 2007. Remington's was a gay burlesque bar in the heart of the gay community and had been there for many years. The plaintiff/tenant then invested more money in club improvements. However for the 11 month period beginning in May 2008, the tenant was repeatedly late or under paid the rent. Finally in April 2009, when $42,076 was owed, the landlord changed the locks and gave notice that the lease was terminated.

The tenant immediately applied for an order allowing it to re-enter the premises. The court required the tenant to pay all the rent owing plus 3 months of accelerated rent, which it did, and the re-entry permit was granted. The tenant then continued operations and applied to the court for a relief of forfeiture to prevent the termination of the lease.

The landlord claimed it was entitled to terminate the lease due to the previous rent arrears and that there was also improper conduct and criminal activities going on at the club which also justified forfeiture of the lease.

The owner of Remington's presented evidence that during that 11 month period, he was not aware the rent had not been paid. His business manager at the time was a very troubled person who suffered from AIDS, alcohol and drug abuse problems and finally committed suicide. The business manager had not told the owner of the rent problems and in fact the owner claimed that the manager had been stealing money from the business during this period.

The owner claimed that he didn't learn of the unpaid rent until he was locked out of the club and received the notice of forfeiture. The owner claimed that he was entitled to relief of forfeiture since he paid the arrears and the 3 months accelerated

rent to get the re-entry permit. He had not been in default since the re-entry and he had also invested another $136,735 in club improvements since that time.

The plaintiff claimed that continuing his business in this location is vital to its success as it is in the heart of the gay community. Given the significant investment he has made in the business and the key location of the club, forfeiture of the lease would destroy his business. He denied that any immoral and criminal activities went on at his club. The landlord, who is also in the adult entertainment industry, knew what type of business Remington's was when the lease was signed. The club has not been charged by the police with any crimes and it operates within the terms of its business license.

The Court's Decision

The judge noted that termination of a lease can be a very serious event with possibly devastating consequences, and would be so in this case. The court accepted that the plaintiff had been in arrears due to the mismanagement by the business manager and when the owner became aware of the situation, the rent was immediately paid and no further rent payments have been in default.

The landlord had failed to produce evidence of improper conduct or illegal activities at the club, so those grounds for forfeiture were dismissed.

Given that the tenant had invested over $750,000 in the club and the fact it had not defaulted since the arrears were paid, the court granted the relief from forfeiture. The lease and its full renewal rights would continue so long as the tenant continued to make all its payments on time and did not break any other conditions of the lease.

Termination of Lease by the Tenant

If a statute or a lease provides that a tenant must give notice to end a lease, that notice must be given in clear days. For example, if a tenant could terminate a lease on two months' notice and rent was to be paid on the first of the month, the notice must be given on the 31st of the preceding month and not on the first. There must be a full—clear—month's notice. If notice is given on the first, there is not a complete month.

Business Law Applied

⑯ **A tenant rented** a building and saw a crack in the plaster ceiling. The landlord promised to repair it, but was slow getting around to it. After the tenant began business, a piece of plaster fell and hit a customer. The customer successfully sued the tenant for $6,000 in Ontario small claims court, and the landlord refused to reimburse the tenant for this amount.

When the next rental amount of $1,000 was due, the tenant refused to pay, saying that this amount would be offset against the $6,000 the landlord owed. The rent was due on the first of the month. On the 20th of the month, the tenant came to work to find the locks changed by a bailiff, and a notice that the landlord had seized the property and terminated the lease.

a) Is the termination of the lease by the landlord proper?
b) Can the tenant deduct the $6,000 from the rent?
c) Does the tenant have any remedy? If the tenant succeeds in getting the lease reinstated, what amounts will the tenant likely have to pay the landlord in addition to the rent?

Mortgages

The Mortgage Transaction

mortgage transaction
the Bank gives a loan; the borrower puts up their house as security

While under the Land Titles system, a mortgage is called a charge, the term mortgage is so well-established in common use, that this text will use the term mortgage. People talk of going to a bank to get a mortgage; however, that is incorrect. The correct understanding is fundamental to understanding the relevant law. There is a two-step transaction involved. The customer seeks a loan from a lender (here referred to as the Bank for simplification). The Bank agrees to provide the money and the customers agree to repay. This agreement to repay in mortgage jargon is called the customers' **covenant**. This is one related but separate transaction. The customers then pledge their house as security for repayment of the loan, a separate transaction.

covenant
a promise

Banks have a standard for lending which typically involves first determining an applicant's creditworthiness (the value of the covenant) and only then, if there is sufficient equity in the house so that the security is meaningful. Creditworthiness is determined by a number of criteria such as: having a present income equal to 3 or 4 times the mortgage installment payment, a current job and good employment history, good credit history and a minimum of 20% of the down payment. High ratio mortgages are given with less than 20% down payment, but when this is done extensively and real estate prices fall, it can lead to a financial crisis as occurred in 2007. Home owners with little invested in the property will just walk away and the lender has little hope of recovering their losses.

Mortgagee   The lender is the **mortgagee** (a lender who takes a mortgage as security for a loan); the borrower is the **mortgagor** (a borrower who gives an interest in land as security for a debt). To simplify matters, we refer to the mortgagee as the lender throughout this text and the borrower is also referred to as the owner of the property.

Legalese

mortgagee
a lender who takes a mortgage as security for a loan

mortgagor
a borrower who gives an interest in land as security for a debt

Multiple Mortgages

It is common to hear of first, second, third and sometimes further mortgages on the one property. Remember that the date of registration, not when it is signed, determines the priority of the interest in the land. If any one of the mortgagees (lenders) is not paid they can force the sale of the property. However the sale proceeds must first go to pay off the first mortgagee in full and if there is any money left then it goes to pay the second mortgagee and if they are paid in full then money can be used to pay the third mortgagee etc.

For example, a house has been sold for $200,000 after default of the registered mortgages:

First mortgage	$150,000
Second mortgage	$100,000
Third mortgage	$ 25,000
Total mortgages	$275,000

The distribution of the proceeds of sale would be as follows:

First lender receives	$150,000
Second lender receives	$ 50,000
Third lender receives	Nil

In order to protect their interests, holders of other mortgages may have to pay the first mortgage and keep it in good standing until the property has sold. They might also have to take over the sale of the property, because if the first lender conducts the sale, it will be done so as to cover the first mortgage amount. Although the first lender is obliged to obtain a fair market value for the property, it is difficult to prove any fault if the house is sold for between 10 to 20 percent less than that amount. In addition, forced sales almost always bring a lower price. Thus, in order to obtain the best price, the second lender will probably be forced to take over the expenses and time involved in conducting the sale.

Lender's Remedies

The mortgage loan is a contract and involves obligations on all sides. The lender advances the money at the beginning of the contract. The borrower must conform to the agreement as well. The main default is, of course, failure to make the monthly payments.

The lender has several remedies if the borrower defaults:

- Sue on the promise to pay for the outstanding amount. There is usually an acceleration clause in the mortgage document, stating that on any default the full amount of the mortgage becomes due.
- Sue the previous owner on the covenant. If a house is sold and the mortgage is taken over by the new owner, the previous owner is still obligated on the loan covenant. To protect against this, the seller may require the purchaser to arrange a new mortgage and discharge the current one. This law varies among the provinces—in some, the lender is not permitted to sue the previous owner.
- Sell the property under court supervision (judicial sale). If the sale realizes more than the amount owed, the difference must be paid to the owner.
- **Foreclose.** This is a court proceeding. The lender will ask the court for an order foreclosing the interest in the property (equity of redemption) so that the lender becomes the owner of it. The lender can sell it and apply the sale proceeds against the loan. Even if the property exceeds the value of the loan, the lender can keep the excess amount.
- Sell privately (often called **power of sale**). A standard form mortgage agreement usually contains terms allowing the lender to sell privately. The private sale is regulated by legislation. There is a notice requirement, usually one month or a little longer. On the sale, the lender must attempt to obtain fair market value, and any amount over the loan amount must be paid to the owner.
- Take possession. The lender can obtain possession of the property by court order and have the owner evicted.

Power of Sale

Power of sale is a right of the mortgagee to sell mortgaged land by the terms of the mortgage or by statute upon default. If the lender opts to use the private power of sale, there are no grounds for any extensions. The borrower must be given notice—usually 30 days or a little longer. If the borrower refuses to vacate the property, the lender must obtain a court order for possession. This can add a short time on to the borrower's ability to stay on the property, but from the time of service of the notice of intent to exercise the power of sale, it will be a matter of only a few months before the lender can have the borrower evicted.

power of sale
a right of the mortgagee to sell mortgaged land by the terms of the mortgage or by statute upon default

Foreclosure   In everyday language, remedies to do with mortgages are often referred to as **foreclosure**. Technically, *foreclosure* refers to closing out the legal interest of the owner. This means that the lender has the common law title (fee simple) and therefore can sell the property as sole owner. The judicial and private sale remedies are often called foreclosure, but this is technically inaccurate.

■ *Critical Concepts of* Lender's Remedies

On default, the lender can take the following actions to enforce the mortgage loan transaction:

- suing for the loan amount
- foreclosing, to extinguish the owner's rights and become sole owner of the property
- judicial sale—sale of the property under court supervision
- power of sale—private sale by the lender
- possession—evict the owner by court order, and take possession of the property

Provincial Differences

foreclosure

an order by a court ending the mortgagor's right to redeem within a fixed time

Three provinces, Alberta, British Columbia, and Saskatchewan, provide rules that prevent the lender from taking the property and suing for any balance still owing on the personal covenant. This is done by restricting the lender's right to **foreclosure**—an order by a court ending the mortgagor's right to redeem within a fixed time—but also requiring a judicially supervised sale. In Saskatchewan and Alberta this applies only to residential mortgages.

In all other provinces, the lender can seize the property and sue on the covenant by choosing to exercise the right to a private sale (power of sale). In Nova Scotia, the technical action is called foreclosure, but a personal action for debt on the covenant is permitted. The restriction on the right to take the property and not sue for debt on the covenant is a fair rule. However, in practice, it is of little effect, for if a mortgage is in default the borrower usually has no other assets anyway. The sale of the property usually does not exceed the mortgage debt—if it did, the borrower would be able to sell it and pay off the loan, or even refinance the mortgage loan transaction.

Borrower's Remedies

The Power of Sale

The Power of Sale procedure, which is a self-help remedy, combined with a lawsuit for possession to evict the mortgagors involves the fewest procedural hurdles and is the preferred method by many mortgagees. The lawsuit often only claims a right to possession but not a claim for judgment on the amount owing. The order for possession can be easily obtained by default, which means basically filing the papers with the court office. However, obtaining a judgment for the amount owing involves additional procedures, expenses and delays. If debtors are losing their home, it is highly unlikely if they have any other assets. So obtaining a judgment for the amount owing would not be collectible and therefore not worth the expense and delay.

Dispute Amount Claimed: There is nothing that the mortgagors (borrowers) can do to defend or delay against a Power of Sale proceeding if they in fact owe the amount claimed. However, if the amount owing under the mortgage is not properly calculated or involves amounts improperly included, the mortgagors can file a defense in the action for possession asking for a hearing, called an accounting, in which the mortgagee has to justify the charges. This is not a defense to possession. This hearing for an accounting will likely take place after the house has been sold.

Dispute Mortgagee Legal Costs: There are unscrupulous mortgagees who realize that many mortgagors are not sophisticated enough to be able to understand how to calculate the valid charges under a mortgage and so add significant improper amounts to the legal costs. There is an inexpensive way for the mortgagors to have an independent review of these costs by a judicial officer experienced in the matters. These are often done by assessment officers who have experience in reviewing lawyers' accounts. See, for example, section 45 of the Ontario *Mortgages Act*.[1] The mortgagors do not need a lawyer, the assessment officer will assist them and protect their interests.

Business Alert: Sale by Mortgagor

Although it is a difficult emotional decision, especially when a family home is involved, if the mortgagors cannot make the mortgage payments, it is far better for them, at an early stage, to put their house up for sale. If they approach the mortgagee (lender), the mortgagee will likely give them a few months to sell and postpone any collection procedure. Also, the homeowners are much more likely to get a far better price for the house. If the mortgagee takes possession, all potential buyers will note that it is a mortgage sale and will only offer fire sale prices. The house will be vacant and will not show well. The mortgagee will not be concerned to get top dollar but just enough to cover its debt and all the costs of disposition such as legal fees and real estate commissions.

Foreclosure

Because foreclosure is such a drastic remedy in that it cancels the mortgagors' ownership (equity) in their home, the courts developed procedural protections for the mortgagors. The mortgagors can asked for a period to redeem, which is set by statute, and which runs from 3 to 6 months. They can also ask to have the matter converted to a sale, after which, like with a Power of Sale proceeding, the mortgagors get any excess of the sale price over the mortgage debt.

Mortgage Fraud

Mortgage fraud is a serious and growing problem in Canada. In 2011 it was estimated that mortgage fraud in Canada totalled $400 million, about 33% of the total financial fraud that year. But by 2012 mortgage fraud was estimated at $600 million, 66% of the total financial fraud in the country. Much of it is due to the ease by which people can obtain fraudulent documents to substantiate a fraudulent mortgage application. Many websites offer false pay stubs, employment letters and T4 slips. Lenders need to be much more careful and do better investigations when lending to prevent this very serious crime. The Land Titles system, designed to save disputes over interests in land, has created a new opportunity for scammers.

Types of Mortgage Fraud

Identity Theft

An issue that is central to one type of mortgage fraud involves identity theft. The complicating factor is that the Land Title system states that the registered owner is in fact the true owner and any person, such as a purchaser or mortgagee, can rely on that representation. So the question

---

1. (4) A mortgagee's costs of and incidental to the exercise of a power of sale, whether under this Part or otherwise, may, without an order, be assessed by an assessment officer at the instance of any person interested. *R.S.O. 1990, c. M.40, s. 43 (4), 1993, c. 27, Sched.*

Karen Beattie, "Finding Mortgage Fraud", Current Mortgage Trends, Sept. 24, 2013. http://www.canadianmortgagetrends. com/canadian_mortgage_trends/2013/09/fighting-mortgage-fraud.html

becomes, if a person applies for a mortgage, gives the mortgagee sufficient proof of identity, which is the same name as on the registered title document, but that person is impersonating the true owner with false ID, and the mortgagee relies on the guarantee by the Land Titles Act, who wins: the true owner or the mortgagee?

Legislation was finally passed in Ontario that protected innocent home owners who were the victims of mortgage fraud. Previously they had been forced from their homes when a fraudulent sale and mortgage had been registered against their property, and left to claim money from the Land Titles assurance fund. They got money eventually from the fund for the value of their loss, but they had lost their home in the process. Now they are entitled to stay in their homes when this fraud has been committed. The lenders who usually had contact with the fraudsters could have prevented the fraud more easily than an innocent home owner who had no idea any documents were being registered against their property.

It is also worth noting, when reading the next case, that it is unlikely in Land Titles issues that either of the innocent parties will ultimately bear the loss. The Land Titles office has an Assurance Fund that will cover the claims of persons harmed by that office's guarantee of title. It is also likely that a purchaser or mortgagee would have taken out title insurance at the time of the transaction. So it would be one or the other of these two funds that would ultimately pay. The Land Titles Assurance Fund is financed by the user fees on registration of documents. Title insurance premiums are paid by persons such as purchasers and mortgagees. The

Lawrence v. Maple Trust Company, 2007 ONCA 74 (CanLII)

Susan Lawrence owned a house in Toronto. An imposter posing as Susan brought a phony agreement to sell her house to a fellow scammer, Thomas Wright, to a lawyer to act on her behalf. Wright then applied to Maple Trust Company for a mortgage of $291,000 to purchase the property and pay off an existing mortgage to the TD bank. The fake sale agreement and new mortgage were registered against the property and Wright obtained the money from Maple Trust. Two months later the real Susan Lawrence went to sell her house and found out about the fraudulent transfer and mortgage and told Maple Trust of the scam. Maple Trust had not been receiving mortgage payments from Wright and it started a lawsuit for possession of her property claiming that since Wright was the registered owner of the property on the Land Titles registry, Maple Trust's mortgage was valid and it had the right to sell the house.

The trial judge held in favor of Maple Trust saying that the registration showed Wright as owner and the lender could rely on it. Ms. Lawrence could make a claim against the Land Titles Assurance Fund for her losses. Ms. Lawrence did not want to be forced out of her home so she appealed.

The Court's Decision

The Court acknowledged that under common law Maple Trust's mortgage was void because it took from Wright who could not give what he did not have.

However, there was a concern that the main provision of the Ontario Land Titles Act [s. 78 (4)] provided that registration was effective proof of title. Another section, s.155, stated that subject to the Act, a fraudulent document remained fraudulent.

However, if a fraudulent document remained fraudulent without limitation, then if a fraudulent document had been registered 40 years ago, it might defeat the whole chain of ownership after that, and completely defeat the purpose of the Land Titles system. So how are the two principles to be resolved?

The Court decided that registration of a fraudulent document would not be effective in the sense that it was a guarantee of ownership to the fraudster. Registration would only be a guarantee of title to a bona fide purchaser for value without notice who bought from the fraudster. As a result, Wright did not have good title and could not put a mortgage on the property. The Court commented that the lender is in a better position to take precautions to prevent the fraud than the home owner who had no contact at all with Wright.

The Maple Trust mortgage was void due to fraud and Susan Lawrence kept her property.

point is: it is not a victimless fraud. User fees and insurance premiums go up to cover the costs of fraud.

Note: According to counsel for Maple Trust, it had taken out Title Insurance and made a successful claim against that company and so did not claim against the assurance fund.

The Texas Two-Step

This scheme was popularized in the great state for which it is named during the Savings and Loan crisis in the US in the late 1980s. There the technique was used to strip money out of the Savings and Loans companies, but it can be applied to a single mortgage application process. It involves a flip, which refers to quick transfers of ownership and is often combined with a Ponzi scheme to delay detection of the fraud.

Example: A scammer finds a piece of junk property in an otherwise respectable area. It may, for example, contain a dilapidated building; the cost of tearing down the building might nullify the value of the robbery. He buys it for $10,000 through one of his corporations and in a short time sells it (flips) it to another of his corporations for a supposed $100,000 sale price, then a little later to another of his corporations showing a sale price of $500,000. Recall that corporate searches do not reveal shareholders, so the corporations will be made to appear as if owned by strangers. The transactions now give the impression of actual market sales supporting a value of $500,000. He needs the assistance of a fraudulent appraiser and a corrupt mortgage manager at a lending institution. He then gets an 80% mortgage on the property of $400,000 from a lender.

He then puts $300,000 in a foreign bank account and uses the $100,000 to make some monthly mortgage payments. This builds up his credit rating to even get further fraudulent mortgages. Once the money runs out he leaves the area and does the same thing elsewhere. After the initial purchase price, and payments to those who assisted in the fraud, he probably makes a profit in excess of $250,000.

The Oklahoma Flip

This form of fraud is mostly practiced on recent immigrants by real estate and mortgage brokers from their own community, trusted because they are countrymen. The mortgage brokers involved are called remote mortgage brokers in that they do not work in an office but meet with potential clients in their homes or donut shops. They are paid by mortgage lenders, such as banks, a finder's fee for bringing the business to the mortgage lender.

The ideal victim is one who has recently arrived from a country where they had lived with multiple families in a crowded apartment, have experienced a rapid increase in their standard of living and cannot evaluate when something is too good to be true.

A house that is valued at below the neighbourhood average is located and bought. Then the house is "sold" on paper and the title is transferred quickly numerous times with the value on paper going up on each transfer. Once it reaches a high level, a straw buyer (victim) is found and convinced to apply for a mortgage to "buy" the home at the inflated price. The straw buyers are promised a cash payment of a few thousand dollars for simply applying for the mortgage. They are told that the mortgage is transferrable and would be transferred out of their name soon after the mortgage was obtained.

The mortgages however were not transferred and the straw buyers were left with a mortgage on land they did not even own. Many of the straw buyers were sued and owed substantial judgment amounts.

The fraudulent real estate agent and the mortgage broker on a $600,000 flip could make profits such as: real estate agent $36,000 (6%commission) and the mortgage broker $6,000

(1% commission) all for just a few hours work. The straw buyers went through a financial and legal nightmare because of this fraud.

Example: In December 7, 2012, Josip Seremet pled guilty and was sentenced to 4 years in jail for having committed 22 counts of fraud against 11 financial institutions in an Oklahoma Flip. The total sum of monies advanced as a result of the mortgage fraud scheme in which Mr. Seremet was a party was in the sum of $3,653,122. The actual loss to the financial institutions was $515,617. There was no evidence at his criminal trial as to the actual losses to the individual straw buyers who were also victims of the scheme but the court noted it was a significant amount. (*R. v. Seremet*, 2013 ABQB 291 (CanLII)

Insurance

insurance policy

the written evidence of the terms of a contract of insurance

premium

the price paid by the insured to purchase insurance coverage

Insurance is a contract that shifts a potential loss from the person who purchases the policy (the insured) to the company (the insurer) that gives the **insurance policy** (the written evidence of the terms of a contract of insurance). The insured pays a **premium** (the price paid by the insured to purchase insurance coverage) for the insurance policy. If you buy a car, you are legally required to carry insurance. If you accidentally knock down a pedestrian who breaks an arm, the pedestrian has a claim against you, which is paid for by the insurance company. The risk of paying for the accident has been shifted to the insurance company.

Because businesses face significant risks, failure to insure adequately for those risks could result in bankruptcy. Thus, insurance is an important part of business planning

How Does Insurance Work?

insurable interest

an interest which gives a person a financial benefit from the continued existence of the property or life insured, or which would make the person suffer financial detriment from the loss or destruction of that property or life

An insurance contract is based on the concept of **insurable interest**, which is an interest which gives a person a financial benefit from the continued existence of the property or life insured, or which would make the person suffer financial detriment from the loss or destruction of that property or life. An insured business owns its building and thus has a financial benefit from its continued existence, or it will suffer a financial loss if the building is destroyed.

To continue the example, the insured is the owner of the building and so the risk of a real financial loss is transferred to the insurance company. Because of the insurable-interest rule, a person cannot insure another person's building for fire loss on the speculation that it might burn down. If this could be done, arson might be encouraged. Also, a person cannot insure another person's life without the express consent of that person. If a person could insure another person's life without consent, murder might be encouraged.

People other than the "owner" may have an insurable interest. The mortgagee of a property may be entitled by the terms of its mortgage to have the building insured and be a named beneficiary on the policy. Mortgage companies usually require a copy of the policy with such a clause before releasing the mortgage funds. A tenant may have an arrangement with a landlord for the provision of insurance on the building (a commercial tenant still has to pay rent to the end of the lease even if the building is destroyed). In this case, the tenant should check to see that its name is on the policy as a beneficiary.

An **insurance agent** works for one insurance company and is their sales representative. An **insurance broker** is an independent business that arranges insurance coverage for its clients and deals with many different insurance companies and tries to find the best insurance coverage at the right price for its clients. When purchasing insurance it is very wise to shop around and often to use a broker who can help you with your insurance needs. Agents and brokers are not the same.

■ *Business Law*   Applied

⑰ **Arjun Patel bought** a car from Infallible Autos Inc. the purchase price of which was to be paid in installments. Because Patel was young and did not have a credit history, the dealership required a co-signer, Vish Aggarwal. The dealership had the provincial government ownership permit put in Aggarwal's name. Patel thought nothing of it.

Patel insured his new car with All Safe Insurance Company. When it was stolen six months later, Patel made a claim. The insurance company refused to pay saying Patel was not the owner of the car.

Was the insurance company correct on these grounds for refusing to pay for the claim?

Types of Insurance

Personal

There are personal risks of loss of income because of untimely death, physical disability, old age, and unemployment.

If you are a sole proprietor of a business, you will want to plan for circumstances in which you cannot work for a period of time because of illness or accident. If you are a partner or a shareholder in a business, one of the group may become incapacitated. There may be a need to fund a temporary replacement. If a partner or shareholder dies, money may be needed to buy out the interest of that person's estate. Life insurance and sickness and accident (also called disability) insurance can provide for those needs.

There are a number of types of life insurance, which go by names such as indemnity, double indemnity, whole life, term, and such. Some of these contain a savings component as well as pure insurance. Personal insurance without any savings component is called **term insurance.** Term insurance premiums are usually the lowest because there is no savings component. Thus, it is often the preferred type of life insurance for business needs.

term insurance
personal insurance without any savings component

With key person insurance, the loss of very important executives is insured so that if they die, the insurance covers the cost of finding and training a replacement. For this reason a business has an insurable interest in the lives of its executives. The death benefit is paid to the business.

Many companies have requirements that their key executives cannot fly on the same plane, ride in the same car, or even ride in the same elevators to prevent a serious loss of leadership to the company.

Many companies also purchase **kidnap and ransom insurance** for their executives. It is estimated that over 15,000 kidnappings at least occur each year and over $500 million is paid annually in ransom. It is a very common occurrence in Latin America, but many kidnappings also happen in the U.S. Companies will take out the insurance to protect their executives and the company from these threats.

Property

A large part of a business's wealth is often in the form of some kind of property: buildings, equipment, commercial vehicles, raw materials, inventory, field crops, and livestock, to name a few examples. Fire may destroy a building, thieves may steal inventory or equipment, and soil may give away and cause the side of a building to collapse.

The most common type of property insurance for a business today is called comprehensive general liability insurance. There are separate policies for perils such as fire, theft, flood, and such. But with business insurance the more general practice is to take out comprehensive general liability insurance rather than insuring for specific perils.

Vehicle insurance is mandatory in all provinces for public liability insurance. If a business's truck runs into a car, for example, the injuries suffered by the occupant and the car are covered by public liability insurance. Comprehensive insurance covers the cost of repair or damage to the business's truck.

Computer Theft   According to the Insurance Bureau of Canada, the most common objects stolen are computers. Low buildings with an easy access from the ground are particularly vulnerable. Like lightning, thieves often strike in the same place. It frequently happens that stolen computers are replaced only to be stolen a second time. The thieves know that they are getting new computers this time.

It is a good practice to review computer-theft prevention practices with your broker and the local police department. Most police departments have a computer-theft prevention program, which includes placing serial numbers in hidden places so that the ownership of the computer can be traced, and the police have the necessary elements to prove theft at trial.

Operation of a Business

Additionally, damage to physical property may have an effect on the operation of the business, and create a greater loss than the loss of the property. Assume your business manufactures parts for the car industry and your business's building is completely destroyed by fire. It takes one year to rebuild the plant and start production. There is no income during this time, but you still have to pay realty taxes, mortgage and loan payments, and such. It may take months to regain your customer base and your normal profit level. Business-interruption insurance can provide coverage for these risks.

Business-interruption insurance   insures part of the loss of profit caused by specified peril such as accident fire and flood. It also covers expenses necessarily made to continue the business and expenses made to reduce loss, such as moving to a new premise. However, business-interruption loss is calculated according to a formula set out in the policy. It is not the same as loss of profit, as normally calculated on an income statement by accounting principles. Therefore, it is critical to have your agent or broker do a rough calculation to show you the difference between business-interruption coverage and loss of profit for your business.

Fidelity insurance or a **fidelity bond**   is insurance against loss caused by fraud, theft or embezzlement committed by employees of the insured.

Credit insurance   is available to protect against bad-debt losses from customers who do not pay. The premium depends on the insurance company's assessment of the collectibility of the debts (accounts receivable). Good credit-granting practices, such as those employed by banks and large companies, are essential to obtain the best premiums.

Employee benefits are frequently in the form of medical and dental plans covered by insurance. Plans of this type may have a premium shared by the employer and the employee. They usually cover members of the employee's family.

Disaster Recovery   The possibility of a complete disaster to a business either by data loss because of hackers or by acts of terrorism has become a prime concern for modern businesses. Thus, any plans for business-interruption insurance now often include a scenario for a situation where the business has to be rebuilt from scratch.

Public Liability   Businesses are exposed to many legal responsibilities or liabilities to the public, from slip and fall claims to claims for personal injury resulting from employee vehicle accidents. Recall that employers are responsible by the doctrine of vicarious liability for torts committed by employees.

Additionally, businesses are held to strict standards of product safety under the law of torts, and so they usually obtain product-liability insurance to cover claims by members of the public who are injured by their product.

Professional liability insurance, also called **errors and omissions insurance** (E & O), is insurance to protect professionals in the event that their own negligence causes injury to others. For example, if an engineer makes a mistake on the design of the condominium structure so that it is unsafe and has to be repaired, a claim by the owner for a loss because of this mistake would be covered by an engineer's professional negligence policy. Directors of companies also may obtain coverage for claims against them for acts done in their role as directors by shareholders or creditors. Such coverage is recommended because it fully protects directors by providing insurance (including litigation costs), and makes them more willing to remain with a company in difficult times.

Coverage

Applying for Insurance

When applying for insurance there is a common law duty on the applicant to act in **utmost good faith** (a duty owed when a special measure of trust is placed in one party by the other). That means that the applicant must reveal, whether specifically asked or not, any important matters that might affect the assessment of the risk. The clearest example is with life insurance. If the insured has a serious illness such as cancer, the insured must reveal that. Failure to reveal information that would materially affect the risk means that the insurance company can refuse to pay a claim made on the policy. Traditionally this duty has been strictly enforced and if there is a failure to disclose a material fact, the policy is ineffective for any claims. Where an insured failed to disclose a previous fire, a claim for stolen goods was denied.

That strict interpretation has been modified slightly in more recent times. In one case, a business said that it had a night watchman but it did not. A claim for theft that occurred in the afternoon was upheld by the court. The insurance company had to pay.[2]

Insurance companies refer to the causes of losses such as fire, flood, and tornado as perils. The situations which increase the likelihood of perils occurring are called hazards. If a building is situated by a river, it usually has a greater likelihood of flood. If that building is on a hill by the river, that hazard is less. Risk management can be seen as attempts to reduce hazards. Of course, a building worth $10,000 next to the river may be a lesser risk in total value to the insurance company than a building on a hill that is worth $1 million.

Example: A woman had told an insurance company that she had never had her home insurance cancelled or declined, even though she had twice had it cancelled for failing to make payments with another insurer. When she had a house fire, her new insurer was able to deny coverage because her policy was void due to her misrepresentation. If she had told the truth it may have charged her a higher rate or declined coverage. (*Lyons v. Gore Mutual Insurance Co.*, 2000 CanLII 22717 (ON SC)

Similarly a firm of mortgage brokers when it applied for professional liability insurance had falsely stated that it had not had any previous claims for negligence or fraud. When it was later sued for fraud, previous claims were uncovered and the insurance coverage was void due the brokers' material misrepresentations. (*Lavoie v. T.A. McGill Mortgage Services Inc.*, 2014 ONCA 257 (CanLII).

Example: But the court can rule differently if it thinks that the breach was not material. In *Kozel v. The Personal Insurance Company*, 2014 ONCA 130 (CanLII) a 77 year old woman had forgotten to renew her driver's license in Ontario. She was driving in Florida and injured a

errors and omissions insurance
insurance to protect professionals in the event that their own negligence causes injury to others

utmost good faith
a duty owed when a special measure of trust is placed in one party by the other

---

2. *Case Existological Laboratories Ltd. v. Century Insurance Company* (1982), 133 D.L.R. (3d) 727.

motorcyclist. Her insurance company denied her coverage because the policy required that she had a valid driver's license. The court ruled that her breach had not affected her ability to drive safely or the amount she paid for insurance. Using a proportionality analysis, if she was denied coverage it would create a great disparity. She would lose up to $1 million in coverage and the insurer would not have suffered any losses. The Court ruled the breach was not significant and the driver was entitled to insurance coverage under her policy.

■ *Critical Concepts of* Insurance Policies

- An insurance policy is a contract and all rules of contract law apply to it.
- An applicant for insurance owes a duty of utmost good faith to reveal to the insurer any material facts that might affect the assessment of the risk, whether asked or not.

■ *Business Law* Applied

℗ **Slippery Sam is** the president of Smooth Sales and Distributors Inc. About 10 years ago, one of the cans of grease, the contents of which are essential to Sam's method of operation, spilled and there was a small fire. Sam did not claim that fire on the current insurance policy because the damage was slight and he did not want the premiums to go up.

When applying for new all-risks coverage, Sam notices that the broker, who is filling out the application form, forgets to ask about previous fires. The broker also forgets to have Sam sign the application. Sam decides to say nothing about the fire.

Because of an unusually heavy rain, the storage area floods, damaging the Smooth Sales inventory. It makes a claim on its policy. During the investigation, the insurance company's adjuster notices signs of a fire, searches the record of the local fire department, and discovers a record about the undisclosed fire. On this basis the insurance company declines coverage.

Sam claims that he should be paid based on three factors:

- he was not asked about previous fires
- he did not sign the application form
- the non-disclosure was with respect to fire but the loss was caused by water damage

a) Discuss whether any of Sam's grounds will be successful in countering the insurance company's claim of non-disclosure.

Obtaining Adequate Coverage

The policies that you are most likely to come across are: homeowner, automobile, and for businesses – the Commercial General Liability policy (CGL). The CGL covers not only claims for losses (indemnity) but also the cost of litigation, called the duty to defend. Given the high frequency of litigation and its high cost, this provision may be the most important one in the policy. Businesses are being subjected to unfounded claims, by individual and class actions, which appear to be calculated to force a settlement on the business in preference to its incurring very high legal costs and adverse publicity (sometimes called "Greenmail" by reference to the color of the US dollar bill).

To make certain that your policy contains adequate coverage for your needs, you need to review the coverage in detail with an independent broker. Where there are many risks, it is a good idea to have the broker attend at your business.

Each insurance company has standard clauses that are prepared in advance. A broker will assemble a number of these clauses into one document, which results in a policy. If some additional coverage above that company's standard clause is required, that coverage is done by a clause called a **rider** (an additional clause to a standard policy of insurance). If there is a later change in the coverage, this clause is called an **endorsement** (a clause which changes the terms of an insurance policy).

rider
an additional clause to a standard policy of insurance

endorsement
a clause which changes the terms of an insurance policy

The standard wording of insurance coverage clauses may not always meet a business's individual needs. For example, computer software companies cannot rely on standard product-liability insurance. This coverage insures for property damage or personal injury. If a pop bottle explodes in a consumer's car and damages the upholstery (property damage) and cuts the consumer's face (personal injury), this damage is covered under the standard product-liability clause.

However, the damage done by software will more likely be to data loss or loss of profits because of downtime. This type of risk is more similar to professional liability (also called errors and omissions) insurance. So, a software company will have to make certain that its new and unique risks are covered. It cannot rely on standard clauses.

As noted above, there are individual policies for specified risks such as fire, theft, and the like. There is also an all-risk policy, which is called comprehensive general liability insurance. The premiums may be higher, but the general coverage is usually recommended. However, the term *all-risk* is misleading, for there are exceptions to this coverage. One common exception is that machinery is covered for external damage such as fire, but not for design defects. Other common exclusions are normal wear and tear, war, or intentionally caused damage. (See Appendix to this chapter for an example of an All Risks Policy and exclusions.)

Interpretation of Coverage Terms

Insurance policies are contracts; so the general rules of contract interpretation of standard form contracts apply. The courts first look at the language of the policy to determine the intention of the parties. If the provisions are ambiguous, the words will be given a meaning, which if reasonable, favours the insured. This is considered fair because the language used was chosen by the insurer.

Coverage issues are a frequent subject of litigation. Coverage provisions will be interpreted broadly and exclusions narrowly.

Example: A pickle producing plant was without power for 27 hours during a province-wide blackout. It suffered over $160,000 in losses due to spoilage and clean-up costs. The insurer denied coverage as the exclusion clause denied coverage caused by "mechanical or electrical breakdown or derangement." The Court ruled that there was no mechanical breakdown with the equipment at the plant, the equipment didn't work because there was no electricity available. The insurer had to pay the company's claim. (*Caneast Foods Limited v. Lombard General Insurance Company of Canada,* 2008 ONCA 368 (CanLII)

The typical car insurance policy covers injury caused by the "use or operation" of a vehicle. There have been a number of unusual claims under this wording:

- A car jack victim was covered for her injuries,
- A deer hunter who drove to this site and was wounded by a fellow hunter was not.

Example: Drive-by Shooting—A woman walking into a donut shop was hit by a wild bullet in a drive-by shooting which made her a paraplegic. She sued arguing that the shooter did not leave the car as in the deer hunter case. However, the court rejected her claim for coverage stating that the injury was not caused by the driving (use of the vehicle) but by the shooting. (*Russo v. John Doe,* 2009 ONCA 305 (CanLII)

Also the meaning of "Accident" has been interpreted. Risky activities are not an accident.

Canadian National Railway Co. v. Royal and Sun Alliance Insurance Co. of Canada, 2008 SCC 66, [2008] 3 SCR 453

In the early 1990s, CNR established an elaborate and sophisticated process to design and construct the largest customized tunnel boring machine ("TBM") of its kind in the world for use in the construction of a tunnel under a river linking Ontario and Michigan. CNR had insured the project under a builders' all-risk policy covering all risks of direct physical loss or damage to all real and personal property including but not limited to the TBM, plus any consequent economic loss caused by delay in the opening of the tunnel. Losses due to faulty or improper design were excluded.

CNR engineers anticipated that it would have to withstand 6,000 metric tonnes of pressure from the weight of the water and soil above it. The machine was designed to withstand those pressures according to the "state of the art" technology at this time.

The machine however failed to perform as required and dirt entered the internal components of the TBM. Repairs had to be made and the project was delayed a total of 229 days. CNR lost more than $20 million as a result of repair costs and delays on the project. CNR claimed its loss under its all-risks policy. The insurers denied coverage because the exclusion clause denied claims due to "faulty or improper design."

The trial court held the insurers liable as the design of the TBM was state of the art at the time, so it was not faulty or improper. The Court of Appeal overturned the decision finding the exclusion clause required the design to succeed in withstanding all foreseeable risks, and it had not, so the insurance coverage was denied. CNR appealed to the Supreme Court.

The Court's Decision

The Supreme Court in a 4-3 decision ruled that CNR was entitled to insurance coverage and the exclusion clause did not apply in this situation. The losses were not caused by faulty or improper design. The tunnel boring machine had been designed to state of the art specifications at the time it was made. The failure to address a risk that only became known with the help of hindsight did not render the design faulty. The damages caused by the design failure were, therefore, properly covered by the insurance policy.

The design is not considered faulty just because it failed to work for its intended purpose or because it failed to withstand all foreseeable risks. A design is only faulty if it did not meet the standard set by the state of the art at the time it was used.

Example: Contraction of Herpes—An insured man under a group accident policy contracted herpes through unprotected sex. It caused a rare complication which paralyzed him from the waist down. He made a claim on the basis that his contraction of herpes was an accident.

The court found that this contraction of disease was a natural process and not an accident. Such a claim might have been covered under a health policy but not under an accident policy (*Co-Operators Life Insurance v. Gibbens*, 2009 SCC 59).

Business Alert!

Paper Trail   When discussing coverage with an insurance agent or broker, obtain and keep copies of all forms that you fill out. Especially ask for copies of the agent's or broker's worksheets, which will detail in handwriting the scope and the amount of coverage discussed.

If the insurance company denies a claim as being outside the coverage, the documentation will be essential in order for your lawyer to determine if there is a valid claim against the insurance company on the basis that the loss is indeed covered, or against the agent or broker for failing to advise you on adequate coverage

Deductible

deductible
a fixed amount of loss that the insured is required to bear

Insurance policies have a deductible, an amount that is deducted first (and the insured party will not receive) before the insurance company makes any payments. Insurance companies have the deductible to prevent them from having to process small claims which have administrative costs far in excess of the value of the claim. The size of the deductible may also affect the size of the premium; the larger the deductible, usually the lower the premium.

Exclusion Clauses

When purchasing insurance you must be very careful to determine what coverage you actually have. An "all risk" policy does not cover "all risks" that can occur and exclusion clauses can significantly reduce coverage. Exclusion clauses may be more important to defining the scope of coverage than the actual coverage clauses. Review the example insurance policy in the Appendix to this chapter. Note the very short coverage clauses for property and perils and the very lengthy Property Excluded and Perils Excluded clauses. Since insurance contracts are standard form agreements, if there is any ambiguity in the terms, it should be interpreted in favour of the insured person not the insurance company that wrote the agreement.

The examples given below are standard exclusion clauses; however, coverage for many these types of situations may be negotiable.

Some common exclusion clauses:

- **Exclusion for pollution**—this excludes loss because a business pollutes its own land or adjoining land and is sued by governments or neighbors for damage or cleanup costs.
- **Criminal acts**—as insurance is based primarily on accidental (unintentional), intentional acts, such as criminal acts, are usually excluded. Some criminal activity can never be covered by a common-law principle that insurance should not be allowed to make crime pay. If there is an insurance policy on the life of one spouse naming the other spouse as beneficiary, and the beneficiary spouse murders the insured spouse, the murderer cannot collect on the policy, even though some people have tried.

Example: An insurance company successfully denied coverage of a residential house that burned down due to a short in the electrical system. The clause in the policy excluded coverage if the premises constructed were used for a criminal activity. The insured "found" some marijuana plants growing wild and brought them to her basement to dry, planning to sell them (trafficking). The street value was estimated at $20,000. The cause of the fire was not related to the plants, however the court applied the exclusion clause literally and upheld the denial of coverage. (*Promutuel Bagot c. Lévesque* (published at EYB 2011-184931 (C.A.))

Comment: This case maybe fact specific. Exclusionary clauses relating to criminal activity may be interpreted more favorably to the insurer then exclusionary clauses in other situations. But to be safe, don't sell marijuana from your parents' basement or garage. Their insurance policy may not be enforceable.

- **Vacancy**—property policies often exclude coverage if a building is vacant for more than 30 days. There is a very significant difference in the risk relating to an occupied building and a vacant building.

Example: The Wu's purchased a house to rent out as an investment and insured it with a standard fire insurance policy which contained the usual exclusion clause that the policy would not cover the house if it remained vacant for longer than 30 days and notice must be given of any material change of risk.

The first tenants were so unclean that neighbors complained of a rat infestation and the city gave notice to the Wu's to clean it up. The tenants vacated in August, the Wu's worked diligently for 6 weeks to put the house in rentable shape and managed to get a new tenant for November 1. Unfortunately, in mid-October, the house was damaged by fire to the extent of $130,000. The insurance company denied the claim based on the 30 day vacancy exclusion and the material change in the rest. Even though the Wu's had attended every day to inspect the property, they did not stay overnight so the court held that it was vacant and the exclusion clause and the notice of change of risk clause both applied to defeat the Wu's claim. (*Wu v. Gore Mutual Insurance Company*, 2009 CanLII 68220 (ON SC))

Exclusion clauses that effectively nullify the coverage may however not be enforceable.

Example: Homeowners bought property insurance for their house. The policy contained an exclusion clause for "settling, expansion, moving, bulging, buckling, of any insured property" and also excluded coverage of damage to outdoor swimming pools. The homeowners purchased an endorsement for coverage of their outdoor swimming pool. The endorsement stated that all other terms of the policy applied. When the swimming pool buckled because of movement in the soil, the insurance company denied coverage relying on its exclusion clause. However, the court held that the exclusion clause effectively nullified coverage and was not enforceable, so the insurer had to pay the claim . (*Cabell v. The Personal Insurance Company*, 2011 ONCA 105 (CanLII)

Making a Claim

Terms of an insurance policy usually require immediate notice of any possible claims, but in any event it will always include a very short time period for giving notice. Additionally, there is usually a limitation time for starting an action. The limitation for commencing an action on contract in law is two years; however, by the terms of the standard insurance policy that period is shortened to ranges as short as 60 days to one year. Thus, it is important to notify the company immediately by phone and to confirm this in writing so that there is evidence of the notification.

Double Recovery of Damages

If you take out insurance and you are injured or your property is damaged and the insurance company pays out, do you have to deduct that amount from any claim for damages in a lawsuit? In other words can there be double recovery: you get paid by the insurer and by the defendants in the lawsuit.

The answer is generally: Yes, there can be double recovery. The justification being that you pay the premiums and so suffered a detriment. The defendant should not be entitled to the benefit of your expense. This right to double recovery is called the "private insurance exception".

Example: The case of *Krawchuk v. Scherbak* 2011 ONCA 352 (CanLII),as discussed in Chapter 7, is an example of this situation. Soon after Krawchuk purchased a house she discovered major structural problems the vendor had not disclosed on the SPIS (seller's property information sheet). The purchaser incurred repair costs of $110,742 and recovered $105,742 from the title insurance she had taken out. But she was also awarded $110,742 in a negligence claim against the vendors and the real estate agent and agency involved. The court recognized her right to double recovery. The defendants were not entitled to escape liability because she had the wisdom and forethought to purchase title insurance.

Bad Faith Denial of Claims

As the insured has a duty of good faith in disclosing all relevant matters to the insurance company in the application, the company has a duty of good faith in paying a valid claim. Breach of that duty may attract a serious amount of punitive damages.

The facts of the following case, *Whitten v. Pilot*, were extreme. Not every refusal to pay would result in a breach of a good-faith duty. Sometimes a company may have a valid reason for denying a claim even if ultimately that reason is proved wrong. The next few years will undoubtedly see cases which provide guidelines as to when an insurance company's conduct breaches the good-faith requirement.

Whitten v. Pilot Insurance Company, [2002] S.C.R. 1

Mrs. Whitten had insured her house for fire. She discovered a fire in the house just after midnight in January. She, her husband, and their two daughters fled from the house wearing only night-clothes into the –18 degree Celsius weather. Mr. Whitten gave his slippers to one of the daughters to go for help, and suffered severe frostbite to his feet. The fire totally destroyed their home and all contents.

The insurance company made a $5,000 expense payment and paid a few months rental, and then cut the Whittens off completely from any payments. The insurance company took the position that the Whittens set fire to their own house, even though the local fire chief and the company's own expert said that was unlikely. At trial a jury awarded $1 million in punitive damages against the insurance company for bad faith. The court of appeal reduced that to $100,000. Mrs. Whitten appealed to the Supreme Court of Canada and asked that the trial award be reinstated.

The Court's Decision

The insurance company's conduct was exceptionally reprehensible. It was intended to force the insured to make an unfair settlement. Insurance contracts are purchased for peace of mind. The more devastating the loss, the more the insured will be at the financial mercy of the insurer and the more difficult it will be for the insured to challenge a wrongful refusal to pay.

The obligation of good faith means that the insured's peace of mind should have been the company's objective and her vulnerability should not have been exploited by a negotiating strategy.

An award of punitive damages in contract cases are rare. Here, in addition to the contractual obligations to pay the claim, the insurance company was under a distinct and separate obligation to deal with its policyholders in good faith. This distinct obligation could support a claim for damages for bad faith.

The jury intended to send a powerful message criticizing the company's behaviour. While the amount was much higher than any previous award in this country, it was, in these circumstances, within rational limits. The trial judgment of $1 million was restored.

Notice   It is a very good practice to give the insurance company notice of any potential claim. For example, a business has a public liability policy covering slip and a customer does slip, does not appear to be injured, and leaves without a comment. The insurance company should be notified because the next time the business hears from that customer may be a lawsuit served six months later. The insurance company may raise the lack of notice as a defence against the claim on the policy by the business.

Business Alert!

Insurance Fraud

Fraudulent claims against insurance policies are frequent and are the cause of high insurance premiums. The Insurance Bureau of Canada estimates that insurance fraud costs Canadian insurers, policy holders and Canadians over $1 billion annually about 15 per cent of premiums go to covering fraudulent claims. Fraud can occur in all types of insurance and are often perpetrated by organized groups using carefully crafted schemes. Here are a couple of the usual car accident techniques:

- **The Rear-and Collision**—The scammer first disables the brake lights on his car, loads it with passengers, usually from his community, then when driving along the road at a good speed slams on his brakes claiming, for example, a cat, ran across his path. A following car cannot stop and rear-ends the car. All the passengers claim whiplash, which is an injury that does actually occur without any objective evidence such as bruises or internal injuries that would show up on any medical instrument. They then claim they go to rehabilitation clinics for treatment, though the scammers run dishonest rehabilitation clinics that falsely bill insurance companies for treatments that were never given to people who were never injured.

In one scam 44 people were paid $100 to ride a public transit bus and then the fraudsters gently hit the back of the bus with a rental truck. The 44 people all complained of neck and back injuries and were then going to claim regular treatments at rehabilitation centres they would never receive. The transit authority and the police suspected fraud and some passengers finally confessed. Three men were convicted in that scam.

■ **The Helpful Wave**—The scammer, who has the right-of-way and is stopped, acts the polite Canadian, waves for the other driver to proceed, then plows into him denying that he made the wave. The scammer's car will also be loaded with passengers who claim they suffered whiplash.

Example: In Project Whiplash the Ontario government, police, insurance companies and the Insurance Bureau of Canada began an investigation into staged accidents and false insurance claims. It is estimated there is over $600 million of this type of fraud every year in Canada. There were 37 people arrested in one raid under this project. In early 2014 three rehabilitation centres were given fines ranging from $75,000–$200,000 and one had to pay restitution of $120,000. The principals of these centres were fined $5,000–$10,000 each. In a similar scam a man was sentenced to 3.5 years in jail and ordered to repay $375,000.

The most serious claims, however, involve arson. The difficulty for the investigator is that the fire set by the criminal destroys the evidence of the crime. Some arsonists do get caught, and sometimes by their own villainy.

Example: In what was one of the biggest fires in Toronto's history, Woodbine Building Supply was destroyed on Christmas Eve in 2001. Toronto Fire Services required more than 170 firefighters and 40 vehicles to bring the six-alarm blaze under control. The building was fewer than 50 metres from residences in the neighbourhood and more than 50 families had to evacuate their homes on Christmas eve. Residents were temporarily housed in TTC buses, being allowed to return to their homes around 7 a.m. on Christmas morning.

One of the hired arsonists, Sam Paskalis, severely burned and disfigured, remained in a coma for several months. Two weeks after the fire, investigators sifting through the rubble found the charred corpse of the other arsonist, Anthony Jarcevic. Both arsonists, being inexperienced, got caught in their own fire.

John Mango, co-owner of the store, was convicted of manslaughter and arson. The Crown Attorney alleged Mango wanted to destroy the failing business to collect a fraudulent insurance claim and clear the site for construction of a family initiated condominium development. Construction of the condominium building got underway as of 2013.("Toronto Businessman jailed for Fatal Fire". Toronto Sun. 2011-09-23.)

In Summation

Land

■ Real property includes the land and all items attached to it.

Interests in Land

■ There are various types of estates in land. A fee simple estate is the broadest form of ownership; a life estate allows one party lifetime use of the land; a leasehold estate gives the tenant the right to possession for a fixed period of time; and condominium is a combination of private ownership along with a share of a corporation that allows access to areas used in common with other individual owners.

■ Condominium boards set many by-laws, rules and regulations and tenants who break the rules can be fined or even forced to sell their condominium if they do not obey these rules. Read the rules before you purchase a condo.

Title/Ownership

■ Ownership of land by an individual is held in fee simple. If more than one person is holding title to the land, it is held in fee simple either as tenants in common or as joint tenants.

■ Joint tenancy carries the right to survivorship, and is often used between spouses.

Other Rights over Land

■ An easement allows one property owner the right to use the land of another for a particular purpose. Access to a beach by crossing the land of another is an example of an easement.

■ The exercise of an easement over another's land without consent for a period of time may give rise to a prescriptive easement.

■ Ownership of land by occupation under specific conditions for a period of time without permission of the owner may give rise to a claim of ownership based on adverse possession.

■ Family law can have a significant impact on ownership of the matrimonial home regardless of who paid for it or whose name it is registered in. A marriage contract may be advisable in some situations to change the division of this property.

Land Registration

■ Most registration of documents indicating an interest in the land is done under the Land Titles system.

■ Registration of the document provides public notice of the interest in the land, as well as establishing priorities among interest holders. It also allows a search to be done to establish outstanding interests in, and ownership of, land before it is purchased.

Commercial Leases

■ Commercial leases are a complex area in which contract principles are playing a greater role.

■ Negotiations usually conclude with the parties signing an offer to lease that sets out a number of terms and conditions to be incorporated into the lease itself. These terms will be included along with a number of other basic terms relating to the use of the premises.

■ The lease terms to be negotiated by the parties will cover whatever issues are of importance to them for the operation of the business. Some terms of particular concern are: permitted use, exclusivity, disturbing uses, and radius clauses.

■ The rental payment may include a number of other charges to be paid by the tenant, such as insurance or water, and should be made clear by the parties in the lease.

Breach of the Lease—Landlord

■ In the event the lease is breached, the landlord must comply exactly with the technicalities required to exercise the remedies available, or the remedy will not be upheld by the court.

■ Eviction is possible for failure to pay rent, and for breach of some other conditions of the lease.

■ The form, content, and notice period required by statute and common law in order for a landlord to exercise its rights must be followed to the last detail.

■ The right to seize the tenant's goods (distress) and sell them for rent arrears must be done under set circumstances and according to the proper procedures, or the landlord may become liable for damages.

■ Distress and lease termination are alternative remedies.

Breach of the Lease—Tenant

- The tenant can ensure that the landlord follows the terms and conditions of the lease by using such remedies as an action for trespass or a court order to compel performance. The tenant may not withhold rent.

- The tenant's main remedy is relief from forfeiture and having the lease terminated, and the courts are often ready to have the lease reinstated upon the tenant bringing the outstanding issue, whether it be arrears of rent or performance of some condition under the lease, into good standing.

- Termination of the lease by the tenant must be done in strict accordance with the lease or the governing statute.

Mortgages

- A mortgage, or charge of land, acts as security for the loan of money by a lender to the owner of the property. It must be registered against the property to be effective in protecting the interest of the lender. There will often be more than one loan secured against the value of the property. These mortgages or charges will rank in priority according to their date of registration.

- Mortgage fraud is a serious problem in Canada and various types of mortgage fraud exist. Title insurance and the land titles assurance funds can protect the victims.

Default of a Mortgage

- In the event the borrower defaults in making regular payments or breaches some other condition of the loan, the lender has several remedies available. The lender may sue on the loan, may exercise rights under the mortgage to take over ownership of the land (foreclosure), or may decide to sell the property to recover the debt owed (power of sale).

- The borrower has the opportunity to ask for a redemption period in which to pay off the debt, or for a judicial sale if foreclosure has been exercised. There are usually practical solutions available as well that can be used prior to the lender exercising rights under the mortgage.

Insurance

- Insurance can classified into three types according to risks:
    a) personal: untimely death, sickness, disability
    b) property: buildings, equipment, commercial vehicles, inventory, livestock
    c) liability to others: occupier's liability, vicarious liability for employees, negligence, product liability

- Insurance is a method of sharing the losses of the few individuals in a group who suffer the loss among the members of the group who do not.

- When applying for insurance, whether specifically asked or not, there is a duty of good faith on the applicant to volunteer any fact that might influence the insurance company in setting the premium or determining whether to accept or reject the risk.

- Coverage clauses must be reviewed to see what is specifically included or excluded. "All risks" does not literally mean all risks.

- There is a rule of interpretation which assists the insured: coverage is to be construed widely and exclusions are to be construed narrowly.

- In determining whether the claim should be paid, and if so in what amount, an insurance company will look at:
    a) what is covered by the policy? (a building, a machine)
    b) what perils are covered? (fire, flood)
    c) are there extensions of coverage? (riders, endorsements)
    d) are there exclusions, deductibles?
    e) are there conditions? (notice of changing risk, timing of notice of loss)

- An insurance company has a duty of utmost good faith in paying a valid claim.

- Insurance fraud is a significant problem and costs insurance companies and their clients millions each year

Closing Questions

General Concepts

1. Would a central air conditioning unit attached to the side of a house be considered real property or personal property? Explain the reasons for your answer.

2. Samson Mephisto's house was for sale. He was an avid gardener and had collected unique plants from a number of different sources which he had planted in his garden. Delia Jones submitted an offer to purchase the house.

   The transaction was completed, and Jones took possession, anticipating the joy of giving her first garden party. She was horrified when she walked out into the garden to discover that all that remained was a couple of small trees. The rest of the garden was a series of deep holes where all the shrubs and plants had been dug out.
   a) What are Delia Jones's rights in this case of the missing plants?

3. Which of the following is correct? The purpose of registering documents of ownership for property is:
   a) giving public notice
   b) generating money for the government
   c) protecting the document from theft or fire
   d) saving on sheepskin

4. a) What is an express term and what is an implied term in a lease?
   b) When will the court allow tenant A to sue tenant B based on a lease to which Tenant A is not a party?
   c) Name 3 possible grounds discussed in the text that are available to a tenant whose use of the leased space is being affected.

5. Nora Mogambo had a beautiful piece of lakefront property in Slime Lake, Alberta. She wished to sell it and use the proceeds to travel. Not too long after putting the property up for sale, Nora agreed to sell to Alex Fontana for $150,000. Alex did a search on the property at the Land Titles office and found nothing registered as an interest against the title.

   A few days before closing, Corey Kazima called up Alex and said, "You realize, of course, that I have a lease on this property for the next seven years." Sure enough, when Alex went out to a remote corner of the property, he found that Corey was living in a cabin.
   a) Is Alex stuck with Corey as a tenant? Why or why not?
   b) Would it make any difference to your answer above if Corey's lease were for 12 months?

Commercial Leases

6. Linda Chierne operated a pet shop under the name Urban Pets, in the Runnymede Shopping Centre. She specialized in the sale of cats and small dogs, such as toy poodles, cairn terriers, Scotties, and chihuahuas. Her lease contained a clause restricting her business to the carrying on of a pet shop, and the sale of small dogs and cats.

   Several months after opening her shop, another pet shop opened in the same shopping centre under the name Exotic Pets and Fish. It was run by Gregory Pushkin, known as Push to his friends. Push specialized in the sale of such exotic pets as iguanas, snakes, and saltwater marine fish. He had a clause in his lease restricting his business to the carrying on of a pet shop, and the sale of exotic pets and fish.

   After a few months, Push decided to begin selling Shar-Pei dogs (Chinese wrinkle dogs), and basenjis (barkless dogs). When Chierne complained to Covert Ltd., the firm that managed the shopping centre, it wanted nothing to do with the problem. She next approached Push, and he responded, "People want real dogs, not those rats with hair you sell. What'cha gonna do about it? Want to borrow a cup of real kibble?" She left in a furious temper, determined to bite back.
   a) Who can Chierne bring action against in these circumstances?
   b) What remedy would she be asking for?

    c) What measures could Chierne have taken to avoid this situation?

    d) What is a Shar-Pei, and is it exotic?

7. You are interested in leasing a main floor location in a shopping plaza for the purposes of operating a book and art shop, where customers can buy coffee to drink while browsing.

    a) What particular terms and conditions would you want to include in your negotiations with the landlord?

    b) As a landlord, you think this operation might be very successful and you would like a percentage of the gross income. What clause would you want included in the lease?

8. Which of the following best describes distress?

    a) a remedy for the tenant

    b) another expression for being upset

    c) a remedy enabling the landlord to end the lease

    d) a remedy enabling the landlord to get money for rent arrears

    e) something educators practice on their students

Mortgages

9. Helmut and Luzinda Schwartz bought a 10-hectare piece of undeveloped real estate for $130,000. They took out a first mortgage of $100,000 when it was bought, and later decided to build a house on the land. Once their plans for the house were drawn up, a real estate appraiser gave them an estimate that the property, when all was completed according to the plan, would be valued at $350,000.

    With their plans and appraisal in hand, the Schwarztes approached a wealthy friend of theirs, Aaron Ritche, about financing for the house construction. Ritche, who made his money in the stock market, was not very knowledgeable about real estate financing. Nevertheless, he agreed to lend the Schwartzes $150,000, secured by a promissory note from both of them, with a collateral mortgage registered on the property. Ritche figured the promissory note would allow him to get his money back faster if he needed it.

    The Schwarztes began work on construction of their house but it was not long before things went terribly wrong. The contractor they hired to build the foundation was inexperienced. Originally the foundation was to be finished in September, but it was not completed until December that year. The carpenters and bricklayers who had been scheduled to begin work in September were required to look for other contracts as a result, and then were not available in December when the foundations were finished. Because of poor workmanship and exposure to winter conditions, the basement walls cracked and collapsed over January and February, so that the entire foundation had to be rebuilt in the spring. Helmut and Luzinda Schwartz ended up in a long court battle with the contractor over the bill for the foundation work, as well as with the carpenters and bricklayers who had lost money because of the delays.

    By this time, the Schwarztes were short of money again and the house was only three-quarters finished. The real estate market in the area had gone flat, and a recent appraisal put the value of the land and house at $240,000. However, the appraisal noted that it was anticipated land values in the area would rise again in one year once a new car-manufacturing plant was completed and operating in the area. The estimated value in those circumstances would be $280,000.

    The Schwarztes lost their court case with the builder, and are unable to pay the money the court awarded him. They are considering personal bankruptcy proceedings.

    Aaron Ritche has been told all this by Helmut and Luzinda, who are no longer close personal friends, and has come to you for advice on where he stands in all this financial mess, and what his options are to protect his interests.

    a) Advise Ritche with full reasons as to what actions he might take under the promissory note and the collateral mortgage. Include in your discussion the effect, if any, a bankruptcy would have on your advice. Complete your advice by suggesting a course of action for Ritche to take, and why you recommend it.

10. Mario Montell entered into a mortgage for $100,000 with the Canadian Commercial Bank. He then took out another mortgage with Cross Town Credit Union for $55,000. Unknown to the other two lenders, Montell also had taken out a third mortgage with Kiva Sivananda for $30,000.

All three lenders registered their mortgages at various times in the following order—Cross Town Credit Union, Canadian Commercial Bank, and Kiva Sivananda.

Montell has defaulted on his payments on the mortgages, and all three lenders have recently become aware of one another. Cross Town Credit Union has indicated that it intends to proceed by power of sale, and hopes to do a quick sale for approximately $150,000. Canadian Commercial Bank had recently done an appraisal on the property, and estimated that even under power of sale it should go for $175,000.

a) List the lenders in order of priority.

b) What is the nature of the interest that Montell transferred to the Canadian Commercial Bank, Cross Town Credit Union, and Kiva Sivananda?

c) If Cross Town Credit Union proceeds under power of sale, what would be the financial results for Canadian Commercial Bank and Kiva Sivananda?

d) If you were advising the Canadian Commercial Bank, what actions would you suggest it take once it receives notice from Cross Town Credit Union of the intention to proceed by power of sale?

e) What remedies, if any, does Kiva Sivananda have if Cross Town Credit Union proceeds by power of sale?

f) Would your answer to e) be different if this situation took place in Alberta?

11. Ashley Marchbanks and Joe Magee were partners and decided to purchase an office building at a busy downtown intersection. In order to complete the purchase the partnership took out a first mortgage against the property in the amount of $250,000. Several months later, Magee left the partnership because he was tired of dealing with the problems associated with being a landlord.

Two years later, Magee received a letter from the bank that held the mortgage. In it, the bank indicated that the mortgage was in default, and the bank would be looking to Magee for any funds owing if the sale of the property was not sufficient to meet the balance due on the mortgage.

a) With reasons, advise Magee whether he is liable for the balance due under the mortgage with the bank.

b) What steps, if any, should Magee have taken in these circumstances?

12. On Saturday night Maxwell Grant just happened to be driving by the house on which he held the first mortgage. He noticed that a rather large and noisy party was taking place on the premises. Several windows appeared to be broken, the lawn was full of tall weeds, and the cavestroughs were hanging off the house. On Sunday, he returned to talk with the neighbours about the party, and discovered that over the past few months the neighbours had became more and more upset because the owners have been letting the house fall apart. The neighbours are also concerned that the property values in the area will drop if the house is allowed to get any worse.

a) As lender on the mortgage, what action should Grant be taking at this time to protect his investment?

13. Which of the following covenants would you not expect to find in a mortgage document?

a) payment of property taxes

b) maintaining the property in good condition

c) obtaining the consent of the mortgagee prior to the sale of the property

d) maintaining fire insurance

e) obtaining the consent of the mortgagee to negotiate a new mortgage on the property

14. Mortgagees can have an appraisal of the property done according to two common ways: with or without an interior inspection. In the *Lawrence v. Maple Trust* case the mortgagee used a "drive-by" appraisal meaning without an interior inspection. A drive-by appraisal typically costs $250 and one involving an interior inspection costs about $100 to $150 more.

a) If you are an employee of a mortgage company, from a risk management point which type of appraisal would you recommend and why? Is there anything short of an interior inspection that might better protect the mortgagee?

b) If you were an employee of a title insurance company or a civil servant in the Land Titles Assurance Fund, what provisions might you recommend that they put in their policies.

c) One of the policy reasons that supports the court's decision in *Lawrence v. Maple Trust* is that the mortgagee is in a position to do something to protect itself. Do you agree?

15. a) How does insurance shift the risk of loss and then spread that risk?

b) What is the difference between an insurance agent and an insurance broker? Which owes a duty to whom?

c) What is an insurable interest?

16. Which of the following are valid insurance contracts according to the principle of insurable interest?

a) a fan wants to insure the life of Céline Dion

b) a mortgagee wants to insure a building on which it has a mortgage

c) a partner wants to insure her business partner's life

d) a business involved in a lengthy trial wants to insure the life of the judge

17. Match each term in Column A with its related term in Column B:

Column A	**Column B**
deductible	risk transfer
risk	consideration
liability	extent of protection
insurance	prevention
premium	risk retention
coverage	obligation
risk management	chance of loss

18. a) What is meant by utmost good faith?

b) How is it relevant to a person applying for an insurance policy?

c) How is it relevant to an insurance company?

19. Match the following terms:

Column A	**Column B**
An insurance broker puts an ad in a paper indicating he has the best rates	offer
A customer sends an application to an insurance company	insurable interest
After an insurance company issues a policy, the insured pays the premiums	acceptance
The mortgagee's interest is shown on an insurance policy	invitation to treat

20. Amit took out a commercial risks insurance policy which had expressed coverage for libel and slander. It had an exclusion clause stating there was no coverage for defamation that was communicated to a third-party.

    Amit had a serious argument with an employee, fired him and told the story on the company's website blog. The employee sued for libel and Amit filed a claim for coverage with his insurance company. The company denied coverage relying on the exclusion clause.

a) Does Amit have a good case to enforce coverage against the insurance company?

Comprehensive Condominium All Risks Policy

THIS SECTION INSURES FOR THE COVERAGE AND TO THE EXTENT SPECIFIED IN PART ii OF THE DECLARATIONS SUBJECT TO ALL PROVISIONS OF THIS SECTION APPLICABLE TO THE COVERAGES AND IS ALSO SUBJECT TO THE GENERAL CONDITONS SECTION OF THIS POLICY.

PROPERTY COVERED

On all property of every kind and description, including but not so as to limit the generality of the foregoing, the units and the common elements, all buildings and structures together with their additions extensions and attachments, and all equipment, furniture, fixtures, material and supplies and generally everything of an insurable nature whether specifically mentioned herein or not: the property of the insured or for which they are legally liable or for which they may be responsible and/or in which they have an insurable interest.

"COVERAGE AWAY FROM PREMISES"

This policy covers property as described herein normally kept at the premises insured, while temporarily removed from said premises but only within the territorial limits of Canada and the Continental United States (excluding Alaska). The insurers liability hereunder shall not exceed $150,000 any on occurrence.

PROPERTY EXCLUDED

This policy does not insure:

(a) Sewers, drains, watermains, gas and other utility lines located beyond the boundary of the premises:

(b) Electrical appliances or devices of any kind (including wiring) when loss or damage is due to electrical currents artificially generated, unless fire or explosion ensues.

(c) Street clocks, electrical signs, mechanical signs, vitrolite or terrazzo floor or wall tile or similar materials, unless loss or damage is caused directly by fire, windstorm, hail, lightning, explosion, riot, impact by aircraft or vehicle, smoke (meaning smoke due to sudden unusual and faulty operation of any stationary boiler or furnace or apparatus used solely or partly for heating the premises insured or for warming water), sprinkler leakage, malicious damage, vandalism or theft including attempt thereat:

(d) Pressure vessels over 24 inches in diameter and boilers (including all piping and apparatus attached thereto): if loss or damage is caused by or resulting from explosion, rupture, bursting, cracking, burning out or bulging of such boilers or pressure vessels or piping or apparatus attached thereto, while connected ready for use;

(e) Personal property belonging to the owners of individual Condominium Units;

(f) Animals, fish, birds, growing plants (except those which are used for decorative purposes within buildings), automobiles (unlicensed automobiles or tractors excepted) motor trucks, motor cycles, aircraft, watercraft or other conveyances, money, notes, securities, stamps, accounts, bills, deeds, evidences of debt, letters of credit, passports, documents, railroad or other tickets;

(g) Furs, jewels, jewellery, watches, pearls, precious and semi-precious stones, gold, silver, platinum, other precious metals and alloys.

(h) Improvements and betterments to individual Condominium Units made or acquired by the Owners of such Units.

PERILS INSURED

This Policy insures against ALL RISKS of direct physical loss or damage except as herein provided.

PERILS EXCLUDED

This Policy does not insure against:

(a) Loss or damage caused by or resulting from earthquake (unless such coverage is specifically endorsed hereon), except that the insurer shall be liable for damage caused by ensuing fire, explosion, smoke or sprinkler leakage not excluded elsewhere by this Policy;

(b) Loss or damage by flood, whether or not caused by water inundating or flooding land as the result of waves, tide or tidal wave, or the rising of or the breaking of boundaries of natural or man-made lakes, reservoirs, rivers, or other bodies of water, the accumulation on land of water immediately derived from natural sources: all whether driven by wind or not; or whether caused by or attributable to earthquake, except that the insurer shall be liable for ensuing fire, explosion, sprinkler leakage or smoke (meaning smoke due to a sudden unusual and faulty operation of any stationary boiler or furnace or its apparatus used solely or partly for heating the premises insured or for warming water) not excluded elsewhere by this Policy;

(c) Loss or damage caused by seepage, leakage or influx of water derived from natural sources through basement walls, foundations, basement floors, sidewalks or sidewalk lights, or the backing up of sewers and drains unless caused by or resulting from a peril not excluded elsewhere by the Policy;

(d) Loss or damage caused by settling, expansion, contraction, moving, shifting or cracking, unless caused by or resulting from a peril not excluded elsewhere by the Policy;

(e) Loss or damage caused by or resulting from explosion, rupture or bursting of pressure vessels over 24 inches in diameter, or boilers including all piping and apparatus attached to such pressure vessels or boilers, unless fire ensues and then only for the loss or damage caused by such ensuing fire;

(f) Loss or damaged caused by or resulting from dampness of atmosphere, dryness of atmosphere, changes of temperature, freezing, other than freezing of fire protection system or plumbing or air conditioning, heating, shrinkage, evaporation, loss of weight, leakage of contents, exposure to light, contamination, pollution, change in colour or texture or finish, rust or corrosion, marring, scratching or crushing, but this exclusion does not apply to loss or damage caused directly by fire, lightning, smoke, windstorm, hail, explosion, strike, riot, impact by vehicle or aircraft, leakage from fire protection equipment, rupture of pipes or breakage of apparatus not excluded under paragraph (a) hereof, vandalism or malicious acts, theft or attempt thereat. Damage to pipes caused by freezing is insured provided such pipes are not excluded in paragraph (a) hereof.

(g) Loss or damage caused by or resulting from rodents, vermin or insects;

(h) Loss or damage caused by or resulting from delay, loss of use or occupancy;

(i) Mechanical or electrical breakdown, latent defect or faulty material or workmanship, inherent vice, gradual deterioration, wear and tear;

(j) Loss or damage attributable to radiation of, or contamination by, any radioactive, lissionable or fusionable materials, whether or not consequent upon loss or damage otherwise insured hereunder;

(k) any mysterious disappearances; any loss or shortage disclosed on taking inventory;

(l) Loss or damaged resulting from misappropriation, secretion, conversion, infidelity or any dishonest act on the part of the insured or other party of interest, his or their employees or agents or any person or persons whom the property may be entrusted (bailees for hire excepted);

(m) Loss or damage to goods occasioned by or happening through their undergoing any process involving the application of heat;

(n) Loss or damage caused by war, invasion, act of foreign enemy, hostilities (whether declared or not), civil war, rebellion, revolution, insurrection or military power, and loss or damage caused by contamination by radioactive material directly or indirectly resulting from an insured peril under this Policy.

Copyright Acknowledgments

Glossary

absolute privilege complete immunity from liability for defamation, whereby the defamatory statement cannot be the grounds for a lawsuit

acceleration clause a clause stating that if the borrower defaults on any payment, the whole of the principal sum of the debt and of accrued interest immediately falls due

acceptance an unqualified and unconditional agreement to the terms of the offer

accounts receivable (book debts) amounts owed to a person which can be sold, usually at a discount, or pledged as security for a loan

act of God the violence of nature

ADR (alternative dispute resolution) private procedures, such as mediation or arbitration, to resolve disputes, replacing or supplementing the traditional court process

adverse possession the exclusive possession of land by someone who openly uses for a long period like an owner, but without the permission of the owner

age of majority the age at which a person is recognized as an adult according to the law of his or her province

agency the relationship that exists when one party represents another party in the formation of legal relations

agent a person who is authorized to act on behalf of another

aggravated damages compensation for injuries such as distress and humiliation caused by the defendant's reprehensible conduct

allegations statements made that have not yet been proved

annual general meeting (AGM) the general meeting of shareholders of a corporation that is required by law to be held each year to transact certain specified business, including election of directors

Anton Piller order an order that the defendant must permit its premises to be searched without informing the defendant, made without notice to the defendant if giving notice would defeat the plaintiff's ability to obtain the remedy

apparent authority a situation in which there is no actual authority but the conduct of the principal suggests to a third party that the agent does have authority to act

appeal a request that a higher court review a decision made by a lower court

arbitration a form of alternative dispute resolution in which the parties agree to refer the dispute to an arbitrator, who decides the matter

arm's length between persons who are not related or associated in any way

articles of incorporation the basic document creating a corporation in most Canadian jurisdictions

assault the threat to do harm to a person

assignee the third party to whom rights under a contract have been assigned

assignment a transfer by a party of its contract rights to a third party

assignment in bankruptcy a voluntary declaration of bankruptcy

assignor the party that assigns its rights under a contract to a third party

attorney a lawyer in the United States

auditors outside accountants ("watchdogs" over accountants) who review financial statements for a company according to accepted auditing principles to determine whether the statements are properly done

authorized share capital the maximum number (or value) of shares that a corporation is permitted by its charter to issue

bailment transfer of possession of personal property without transfer of ownership

bait and switch advertising advertising a product at a bargain price but not having a supply in reasonable quantities

bankrupt declared insolvent by the court, incapable of paying debts

barrister lawyers who represent clients in court; compare with solicitor

battery physical contact with a person without consent

beneficiary the person who enforces the contract against the insurance company and receives the benefits

bid-rigging agreeing in advance what bids will be submitted

bill of exchange a written order by A to B (usually a bank) to pay a specified sum of money to a named party or to the bearer of the document

bill of lading a receipt signed by a carrier or transportation company acknowledging that certain goods have been given to it for shipment

board of directors the governing body of a corporation, responsible for the management of its business and affairs

bona fide **occupational requirement (BFOR)** a genuine requirement for a job, such as the need to wear a hard hat when working on a construction site; a BFOR is a defence that excuses discrimination on a prohibited ground when it is done in good faith and for a legitimate business reason

bond a certificate of a debt owed by a corporation

breach failure to live up to the terms of a contract

brief a summary of a case (for use at trial) including evidence and law, or a summary of a court decision such as those used in this text

broadly held corporations corporations whose shares are publicly traded on the stock market

burden of proof the requirement that a party who claims a fact to be true must lead evidence to establish it in a court proceeding

capacity the legal capability of entering into an agreement; some individuals, such as minors, and mentally incompetent or intoxicated persons, are not seen in law as having the capacity to enter into a contract

causation one of the elements of negligence, relating to whether the action produced the damage or injury

caveat emptor let the buyer beware

certified cheque a cheque on which a bank has indicated that it will be cashed when presented for payment

chattel mortgage a mortgage of personal (chattel) property

cheque a bill of exchange drawn against a bank and payable on demand

C.I.F. cost, insurance, and freight, a designation for goods, making the seller responsible for arranging the insurance (in the buyer's name) and the shipping charges, with the goods remaining at the seller's risk until delivery to the purchaser

civil law the law in a common law system which applies to private rights, such as contracts

claim a written statement or basic summary of a plaintiff's allegations against a defendant in a lawsuit

class action an action in which one individual represents a group and the judgment decides the matter for all members of the class at once

click-wrap rule contract terms which are accepted when the user clicks an appropriate icon on a website document

closely held corporations corporations which do not sell shares to the public

closing date the date for completing a sale of property

COD cash on delivery, a contractual term requiring the purchaser to pay the shipper cash on delivery of goods

collateral agreement a separate, side agreement between the parties made at the same time as, but not included in, the written contract

collateral property of the debtor that can be sold by a creditor if the debt is not paid, e.g., a car may be given as collateral for a bank loan

collective bargaining negotiation between an employer and the union bargaining agent for its employees, in order to establish conditions of employment

common elements the structures and areas external to a unit in a condominium, including hallways, elevators, and swimming pools

common law rules that are pronounced in judgments

common shares shares carrying no preferential right to distribution of assets on breakup, but usually carrying voting rights

compulsory licensing granting a licence to a person to use a patent without the consent of the owner of the patent

conditions major, essential terms which, if breached, give the innocent party the right to terminate the contract and claim damages

condominium corporation a corporation allowing a way of holding property co-operatively, in which the members are the unit owners

confidential business information information that provides a business advantage as a result of the fact that it is kept secret

confidentiality the obligation not to disclose any information without consent

consideration the price paid for a promise, something of value promised or paid that is taken to indicate that the person has considered the agreement and consents to be bound by it

consignment the placing of goods with a business for the purpose of sale

constructive dismissal employer conduct that amounts to a fundamental breach of the employment contract and justifies the employee quitting

consumer notes promissory notes arising in a consumer credit sale

contract an agreement that is enforceable in a court of law

contributory negligence negligence by an injured party that helps to cause or increase (contribute) to his or her own loss or injury

conversion unauthorized use of the goods of another

cooling-off period a specified time after a contract is made during which a buyer may terminate the contract by giving written notice to the seller

copyright the right to prevent others from copying original works

corporation a business organization that is a separate legal entity (person) from the owners

costs legal expenses that a judge orders the loser to pay the winner

counsel a lawyer, usually a barrister

counterclaim a claim by the defendant against the plaintiff arising from the same facts as the original action by the plaintiff, and to be tried at the same time as that action

counter-offer the rejection of one offer and the proposal of a new one

covenants terms of agreement

crumbling skull plaintiff rule the principle that a defendant may be responsible for increasing a pre-existing weakness

cybersquatting the registration of a domain name containing a business name of another person, with the intention of selling the domain name to that business

damages monetary compensation in a lawsuit for the loss suffered by the aggrieved party

debenture a type of a corporate bond, indicating a debt owed by a corporation

deceit fraud, deliberately misleading another and causing injury

deductible a fixed amount of loss that the insured is required to bear

deed any document (not only a deed to land) under seal, which today is usually a small red paper wafer

defamation making an untrue statement that causes injury to the reputation of an individual or business, including both libel and slander

defendant the party being sued

deposit a sum of money paid by the buyer to the seller, to be forfeited if the buyer does not perform its part of the contract

discharge a court order whereby a person who has been declared bankrupt ceases to have the status of a bankrupt person

discharge of contract occurs when all the parties have done exactly what they were required to do under the terms of the agreement: the promises have been completed and the parties have no further obligations to each other

discovery of documents   making each side's relevant documents in a litigation available to the other side

discrimination   the act of treating someone differently on grounds that are prohibited by human rights legislation

distinguishing guise   the distinctive shape of goods or their containers, or a distinctive way of wrapping or packaging, necessary to establish grounds for trademark

distress   the right of the landlord to distrain (seize) a tenant's assets found on the premises and sell them to apply to arrears of rent

dividends   sums declared by the board of directors as payable to shareholders

domain name   the address of a website

dominant position   the offence of taking unfair advantage of a monopoly or dominant position in the marketplace

double ticketing   the offence of failing to sell at the lowest of the two or more prices appearing on a product

down payment   a sum of money paid by the buyer as an initial part of the purchase price, and not completely forfeited if the contract is breached

drawee   the party required to make payment on the bill of exchange

drawer   the party who draws up or signs a bill of exchange

due diligence   a defence to certain charges, by doing everything reasonable to prevent the problem leading to legal liability

duress   actual, or threatened, violence, or unreasonable coercion used to force agreement

duty of care   an obligation (in torts) to take care not to injure another

easement   a right enjoyed by one landowner over the land of another for a particular purpose, such as access to water, but not for occupation of the land

e-commerce   doing business on the Internet

encrypt   make data on the Internet unreadable without the key for privacy and security

endorsed   signed with one's name on a negotiable instrument, e.g., on the back of a cheque

endorsement   a clause which changes the terms of an insurance policy

entire agreement clause   a term in a contract in which the parties agree that their contract is complete as written

equitable assignment   an assignment, other than a statutory assignment, which does not require that the assignment be absolute, unconditional, in writing, or that notice, written or oral, be given by the assignor

equity   rules of law developed by the courts of equity to relieve the harshness of the common law

equity of redemption   the right of the mortgagor to redeem the title to the mortgaged land on payment of the debt in full

errors and omissions insurance   insurance to protect professionals in the event that their own negligence causes injury to others

estopped   stopped or prevented

examination for discovery   processes allowing each party to examine the other party orally on all issues in the lawsuit, and to have the testimony recorded by a reporter

exclusive dealing   the supplier requiring that the retailer use only, or primarily, its particular products in the retail outlet

executed contract   a contract in which both parties have performed their obligations

executors   the personal representatives of a deceased person named in his or her will

executory contract   a contract in which an agreement has been made but there has been no performance

exemption clauses (disclaimers)   clauses in a contract that limit or completely eliminate the damages or other relief that the court would normally award against a party who has breached a contract

expectation damages   an amount awarded for breach of contract based on the expected results if the contract had been properly performed

express terms   actual stated terms, written or oral

factor   the business of buying accounts receivable, usually at a discount, and then collecting directly from the customer

fair comment   a defence to an action for defamation in which the harmful statements were made about public figures

false arrest   causing a person to be arrested without reasonable cause

false imprisonment   unlawfully restraining or confining another person

fee simple   the highest form of ownership of land in law, allowing a person to dispose of the land during life or after death

fidelity bond   insurance against loss caused by fraud, theft, or embezzlement committed by employees of the insured

fiduciary duty   a duty of good faith imposed on a person who stands in a relation of trust to another

financial statements   annual accounting statements that normally consist of a balance sheet and income statements

financing lease   a security arrangement in which a third person provides credit, purchases the property, and leases it to the borrower

financing statement   a document setting out details of a security interest that must be filed in order to protect that interest under personal property security acts

fixtures   objects that are permanently attached or fixed to land or to a building

floating charge   a form of mortgage on the assets of a corporation not affixed to any particular asset, but which does become affixed once a specified event takes place

F.O.B.   free on board, a designation for goods when the seller must arrange and pay for transportation to the shipper, and the goods remain at the seller's risk until delivery

foreclosure   an order by a court ending the mortgagor's right to redeem within a fixed time

forfeiture   loss of money, such as a deposit, or of a right because of a breach of contract

franchise agreement   an agreement under which a franchisor (the founding company) grants to the franchisee (the small-business outlet) the right to market the franchisor's products

fraudulent misrepresentation   an incorrect statement made knowingly with the intention of causing injury to another

fraudulent preference   an insolvent debtor's preferring (and paying) one creditor over another

fraudulent transfer   a transfer of property by a debtor, usually to a related person, so that creditors cannot seize it

frustration   an outside event that makes the performance of the contract impossible, and excuses a party from performance

fundamental breach   a breach of the whole contract or of an essential term that is so serious that it means that the contract is not fulfilled in a fundamental manner, and the defaulting party cannot rely on an escape clause to avoid liability

gage   a pledge

general meeting of shareholders   a formal meeting of shareholders at which they are able to vote on matters concerning the corporation

general partner   a partner in a limited partnership whose liability is not limited, and who usually runs the business

general security agreement   an agreement in which all the assets of a business are pledged as collateral

goods   personal property consisting of tangible items that can be bought and sold

goodwill   the value of the good name, reputation, and connection of a business

gratuitous promise   a promise for which no consideration is given

guarantee   a collateral promise by one person to pay the debt if the primary debtor defaults

guarantor   a co-signor, a person who signs a guarantee

hearsay   evidence by a witness who simply repeats a statement by another person who will not testify at the trial

holder in due course   an innocent third party entitled to collect on a negotiable instrument in spite of any defences of the original parties

illegal contracts   contracts which cannot be enforced because they are contrary to legislation or public policy

immediate parties   the parties who have had direct dealings with each other

implied terms   terms which are added to a contact by statutes, by custom and usage of a particular business, or by the courts, based on what they think is necessary to meet the fair and reasonable expectations of the parties (the "officious bystander" test)

implied term of fitness   a term implied into the contract that the goods are of a type that is suitable for any special purpose for which they are bought

Incoterms   a set of standard contractual terms commonly used in purchase orders, and adopted by the International Chamber of Commerce

indemnity   an agreement in which the third party undertakes to be equally liable for the loan owed by the main debtor

independent contractors   people who carry on an independent business and act for a number of other persons

indoor management rule   the principle that a person dealing with a corporation is entitled to assume that its internal rules have been complied with unless it is apparent that such is not the case

inducing breach of contract   intentionally causing one person to breach his contract with another, e.g., persuading a key employee of a competitor to leave that company to join yours

industrial design   a distinctive shape or design that is a pattern to be reproduced many times, such as the design on fine china

injunction   an order instructing one party to halt a particular process or action

injurious falsehood   a false statement about goods or services that is harmful to the reputation of those goods or services

innkeeper   a person who maintains a business offering lodging to the public

innuendo   a statement that implies something derogatory about another individual without directly saying it

insider trading   the use of a corporation's confidential information to buy or sell its securities

insolvency   the inability of a business to pay debts as they come due

insolvent person   a person who is unable to meet, or has ceased to pay, his or her debts as they become due, but has not been declared bankrupt by court order

inspector   a person appointed by the court to investigate the affairs of a corporation

insurable interest   an interest which gives a person a financial benefit from the continued existence of the property or life insured, or which would make the person suffer financial detriment from the loss or destruction of that property or life

insurance adjuster   a person who handles and investigates a claim of property losses

insurance agent   an agent or employee of the insurance company

insurance broker   an independent business which arranges insurance coverage for its clients and deals with several insurance companies

insurance policy   the written evidence of the terms of a contract of insurance

insured   the one who buys insurance coverage

intangible property   that cannot be touched, such as accounts receivable

intellectual property   personal property in the form of ideas and creative work, created by the intellect

intentional torts   harmful acts that are committed on purpose and for which the law provides a remedy

interlocutory injunction   a temporary injunction which lasts only until trial

invitation to treat   the technical legal term for the invitation to engage in the bargaining process

impeachment   an action challenging the validity of a patent

joint liability   a liability shared by a number of persons, each of whom is personally liable for the full amount of a debt

joint tenancy   shared ownership with right of survivorship

joint venture   an agreement between two or more independent businesses to cooperate on a particular project only

judgment debtor   a party who has been ordered by the court to pay a sum of money

jurisdiction   the province, state, or country whose laws apply to a particular matter

just cause   a valid reason for dismissing an employee without notice

labour relations board   an administrative tribunal regulating labour relations

land   the surface of the land, all that is under the surface (including the minerals and oil), and everything above the surface permanently fixed, such as buildings

land titles system   a system of land registration in which the land titles office certifies registered interests as being correct

lease   a contractual arrangement where the owner of property (the landlord) allows another person (the tenant) to have possession and use of the property for a certain period in return for the payment of rent

leasehold   an interest in land for a period of time created by a lease

legal person   an entity (a corporation or a human being) recognized at law as having its own legal personality

lessee   the tenant or person who takes possession of the leased property

letter of credit   a written promise by one person's bank to pay another person when specified conditions are met

letters patent   a document incorporating a corporation, issued by the appropriate authority, and constituting the charter of the corporation

libel defamation in which the harmful statement is written or broadcast

licensee a visitor, other than an invitee, who enters premises with the consent of the occupier

lien a claim against property

life estate an estate in land that lasts only while the person is alive

limitation periods rules requiring that a lawsuit be started within a specified time after the offending conduct takes place

limited liability the principle that a corporation can shield owners, directors, and managers from liability for many obligations of the corporation

limited liability partnership a partnership in which partners who are not negligent are not personally liable for losses caused by the negligence of another partner or of an employee directly supervised by another partner

limited partner a partner in a limited partnership whose liability is limited to the amount of his or her capital contribution

limited partnership a partnership in which some of the partners limit their liability to the amount of their capital contributions and are not active in conducting the business

liquidated damages the amount of damages (in cash, or liquid, form) to be paid should the agreement be breached

litigation a court action when one person sues another

maker the party who signs and delivers a promissory note

malicious prosecution causing a person to be prosecuted for a crime without an honest belief that the crime had been committed

mandatory injunction an order requiring a person to do a particular act

mediation a form of alternative dispute resolution in which a neutral third party assists the parties to reach a settlement

memorandum of association a document setting out the essential terms of an agreement to form a corporation

mens rea a guilty mind

minor (infant) a person who has not attained the age of majority according to the law of his or her province, and therefore is not legally an adult

mitigation acts by the plaintiff to reduce loss caused by the defendant

moral rights the rights of an author or creator to prevent a work from being distorted or misused

mort passive or dead

mortgage the title of property that is held by the lender as security

mortgagee a lender who takes a mortgage as security for a loan

mortgagor a borrower who gives an interest in land as security for a debt

necessities (necessaries) the basic goods and services required to function in society

negligence an act or omission that carelessly causes injury to the person or property of another

negligent misrepresentation an incorrect statement made without due care for its accuracy

negotiation direct communication between the parties to agree on a contract, or efforts to resolve disputes without third-party intervention

non est factum ("it is not my doing"), a plea that a person didn't know what he or she was signing

notary public a person (usually but not necessarily a lawyer) authorized to take sworn testimony such as an affidavit

novation the process of substituting a new contract for an old one

nuisance an activity that substantially interferes with the enjoyment of the land of others in the vicinity

occupier any person with a legal right to occupy premises

offer a promise made by one party that contains all necessary terms so that the other party need only say "I accept" and a contract is formed

offeree the person who receives the offer

offeror the person who makes an offer

official receiver a government-appointed administrator responsible for the supervision of bankruptcy proceedings

open mortgages mortgages permitting repayment of the debt at any time without notice or bonus

oppression remedy a statutory procedure allowing individual shareholders to seek a personal remedy if they have been unfairly treated

option a new and separate contract to keep an offer open for a specified time in return for a sum of money

parol evidence rule the rule that a court will not ask the parties to a contract for their testimony as to the meaning of any term

partnership the relationship between two or more persons carrying on a business with a view to profit

partnership agreement an agreement between persons which creates a partnership and sets out its terms

passing off misrepresenting goods, services, or a business in order to deceive the public into believing that they are another's goods, services, or business

past consideration the consideration has already been given

patent agent a registered agent (often an engineer) who pursues applications for patents on behalf of individual inventors

payee the party named to receive payment on the bill of exchange

penalty clause terms specifying an exorbitant amount for breach of contract, intended to force a party to perform

pleadings the documents used in a court action, including the statement of claim, the statement of defence, and any counterclaim

pledged taken possession of by a creditor as security and held until repayment

postdated dated later than the time when it is given to the payee

power of attorney a type of agency agreement authorizing the agent to sign documents on behalf of the principal

power of sale a right of the mortgagee to sell mortgaged land by the terms of the mortgage or by statute upon default

precedent the principle in the common law system which requires judges to follow a decision made in a higher court in the same jurisdiction

premium the price paid by the insured to purchase insurance coverage

principal the person on whose behalf the agent acts

priority right to be repaid out of the debtor's property ahead of other claimants

privity of contract the principle in law that since a contract is created by two or more people exchanging promises, it is generally only those individuals who are direct parties to the agreement who are subject to its obligations and entitled to its benefits

promissory estoppel a remedy against a person who made a promise without giving any consideration for it, often used when a creditor waives strict compliance with payment dates and then notifies the debtor in default for not making timely payments

promissory note a written promise to pay the amount stated on the instrument

prospectus   a document issued to inform the public about a new issue of shares or bonds that a corporation is required to publish when inviting the public to buy its securities

punitive damages (exemplary damages)   compensation for damages beyond the plaintiff's actual losses, awarded to punish the wrongdoer

qualified privilege   immunity from liability for defamation when the statement is made in good faith to a person or body which has authority over the person defamed

quantum meruit   "as much as is merited," the amount a person deserves to be paid for goods or services provided to another person requesting them, even if some of the elements of a contract are missing

real property   land, buildings, and fixtures; land and anything attached to it

reasonable foreseeability   the test of what a person could have anticipated would be the consequences of his or her action

reasonable notice   notice calculated on the basis of level of position and length of employment

reasonable person test   a test or standard based on what a reasonable person would have done in similar circumstances

rebutted   proven to be false

receiver   a person appointed by a secured creditor to retrieve the assets to satisfy the debt

receiving order   a court order for the transfer of debtor's assets to a trustee in bankruptcy

rectification   a court order which corrects a written document to reflect accurately the contract made by the parties

re-entry   the landlord's remedy of evicting the tenant for failure to pay rent or for breach of another major covenant

registration system   a means of registering and tracking property deeds whereby the records are available to be examined

rejection   the refusal to accept the offer

release   a written or oral statement freeing another party from an existing duty

remoteness of damages   the principle of whether the damages are too far removed from the original negligent act

repossession   the act of taking back possession of property that has been in the possession of another

repudiation   an indication by a party that he or she will not go through with the agreement as promised

retail price maintenance   the attempt by a supplier of goods to control their resale price

res ipsa loquitur   the facts speak for themselves

rescission   the cancelling of the contract, with both parties put back into their original positions

respondent   the party who defends on an appeal

revocation   withdrawal of an offer before acceptance, and communicating the withdrawal to the offeree

restrictive endorsement   an endorsement with a limitation

rider   an additional clause to a standard policy of insurance

right of way   an easement that gives the holder a right to pass back and forth over the land of another in order to get to and from his or her own land

risk   the possibility of loss

rule of law   established legal principles that treat all persons equally and that government itself obeys

secured creditor   a creditor who has the right to seize and sell specific assets of a borrower to pay off a loan

self-defence   a response to an assault or battery with as much force as is reasonable in the circumstances

share   the holder's proportionate interest in the assets of a corporation

shareholder agreement   an agreement between two or more shareholders, similar to a partnership agreement

shrink-wrap rule   contract terms relating to a shrink-wrapped product, often including a limitation-of-liability clause which limits or excludes the manufacturer's liability for damages that may occur from the use of the product

slander   defamation in which the harmful statement is spoken

sole proprietorships   one-person businesses

solicitor   lawyers who deal with commercial and other legal matters that do not involve going to court; compare with barrister

special damages   damages to compensate for expenses and quantifiable losses, e.g., hospital bills

special meeting   any meeting of shareholders other than the annual general meeting

specific performance   an order requiring the defendant to undertake a specified task, usually to complete a transaction

standard form contract   an offer presented in a printed document, the terms of which are the same for all customers, and which becomes a contract when signed (accepted) by the customer

stare decisis   the principle by which judges are required to follow the decision made in a similar case by an equal or higher court

statement of claim   the document which often starts a lawsuit, setting out briefly the nature of the complaint and the facts alleged as the basis of the action

statement of defence   the response to a statement of claim by the defendant

statutes   summarized or codified short-code formats of common law, comprising acts or legislation passed by Parliament

statutory assignment   an assignment that complies with statutory provisions enabling the assignee to sue the debtor without joining the assignor to the action

stop payment   an instruction from the drawer of a cheque to the bank not to pay the cheque

stoppage in transit   reclaiming possession from the carrier of the goods while in transit, in order to stop delivery to the buyer, if the seller discovers that the buyer is insolvent

strict liability offences   offences in which responsibility is imposed even when there was no intention to do the act, unless the defendant can show that he or she took reasonable care (due diligence)

subrogation   the right of an insurer who has paid a claim to "step into the shoes" of the insured and sue the person responsible for the loss

subsidiary corporation   a separate corporation owned or controlled by a parent corporation

systemic discrimination   discrimination that is the consequence of a policy, whether the effect of discrimination was intended or not; for example, a policy that a police officer be 6 feet tall would discriminate on gender and race

telemarketing   the use of the telephone to sell products

tenancy in common   co-ownership of land whereby each owner can deal separately with his or her interest, may have unequal interest, and can sell his or her interest or dispose of it by will

term insurance   personal insurance without any savings component

thin skull plaintiff rule   the principle that a defendant is liable for the full extent of a plaintiff's loss even where a prior weakness makes the harm more serious than it otherwise might be

third party   a stranger to the agreement, a person who is not one of the parties to a contract

title   a legal concept roughly equivalent to ownership

title search   an investigation of the registered ownership of land

tort   a wrongful act done intentionally or unintentionally to the person or property of another for which the law gives a remedy

trade name   a name used by a business, often in addition to the registered or incorporated name

trademark   any visual characteristic of a product distinguishing it from a product made by competitors

transfer   the equivalent (under the land titles system) of a deed transferring ownership, not made under seal

trespass   the entry onto the property of another without the owner's permission, or some lawful right, to do so

trespasser   one who enters without consent or lawful right on the lands of another, or who, having entered lawfully, refuses to leave when ordered to do so by the owner

trustee in bankruptcy   the person appointed to administer the property of a bankrupt for the benefit of creditors

ultra vires beyond the powers of

unascertained goods   goods that have not been set aside (identified and separated from a group) and agreed upon as the subject of a sale

undisclosed principal   an agent who does not reveal either the identity of the principal or the fact that he or she is working for the principal

undue influence   the misuse of influence and the domination of one party over the mind of another to such a degree as to deprive the latter of the will to make an independent decision

unsecured creditors   creditors who have no security interest (such as a mortgage) in the bankrupt debtor's property

utmost good faith   a duty owed when a special measure of trust is placed in one party by the other

vicarious liability   the responsibility of an employer to compensate for harm caused by employees in the normal course of their employment

void   never formed in law

waiver   an agreement not to proceed with the performance of a contract or some term of it

warranties   minor terms which, if breached, permit only a claim for damages but not the refusal to complete the contract

winding up   dissolving, ending a corporation

workers' compensation   a scheme in which employers contribute to a fund used to compensate workers injured in on-the-job accidents, in place of their right to sue in torts